Genealogies of
PENNSYLVANIA FAMILIES

From The Pennsylvania Magazine
of History and Biography

Genealogies of
PENNSYLVANIA FAMILIES

From The Pennsylvania Magazine
of History and Biography

OLATHE PUBLIC LIBRARY
OLATHE, KANSAS 66061

With an Introduction by
MILTON RUBINCAM

Baltimore
GENEALOGICAL PUBLISHING CO., INC.
1981

Excerpted and reprinted from *The Pennsylvania
Magazine of History and Biography* (with added Publisher's Note,
Table of Contents, Introduction, Index, and
textual notes) by Genealogical Publishing Co., Inc.
Baltimore, 1981. Copyright © 1981, Genealogical
Publishing Co., Inc. All rights reserved.
Library of Congress Catalogue Card Number 81-80330
International Standard Book Number 0-8063-0935-0
Made in the United States of America.

Note to the Reader

THIS VOLUME is composed of articles excerpted from *The Pennsylvania Magazine of History and Biography*. It contains all but one of the family history articles published in the *Magazine* up to 1935, when genealogical contributions were discontinued. The omitted article—"The Descendants of Jöran Kyn, the Founder of Upland," by Gregory Keen—totalled 250 pages and was thought to be too extensive for inclusion in a volume already exceeding 900 pages. We have also omitted a few articles which are rather more historical or biographical in nature than genealogical. At the same time, to broaden the genealogical basis of the work, we have included every Bible record and genealogical fragment known to have been published in the *Magazine* (see the Appendix).

This space affords us an opportunity to thank the various persons who cooperated or assisted in the production of this book, and therefore to all who were involved we offer our warmest thanks. We wish, in particular, to express our gratitude to James E. Mooney, Director of The Historical Society of Pennsylvania, for granting us permission to reproduce articles from the *Magazine;* to Milton Rubincam, Fellow of The American Society of Genealogists, for furnishing an informative Introduction; to Robert and Catherine Barnes for preparing the Index; and to Edgar Heyl for collecting and arranging the articles.

Genealogical Publishing Company

Contents

Introduction

Atkinson Families of Bucks County, Pennsylvania, by Oliver Hough, from Vol. XXX (1906), 57-59, 220-237, 332-347, 479-502; Vol. XXXI (1907), 120, 157-175, 429-446 1

Bedant-Robbins-Lake Bible Records, copied by Sarah A. Risley, from Vol. XXXVII (1913), 253-256 120

Bennett-Shockley Genealogical Notes, from Vol. XXXIII (1909), 377-379 124

William Biles, by Miles White, Jr., from Vol. XXVI (1902), 58-70, 192-206, 348-359 126

Boone Genealogy, from Vol. XXI (1897), 112-116 166

Carpenter Genealogical Notes, from Vol. XXXI (1907), 371-372 171

Chandler Genealogy, by Gilbert Cope, from Vol. IX (1885), 234-236 172

Genealogical Notes of the Chapman Family of Bucks County, Pennsylvania, from Vol. XXVII (1903), 112-115 174

Claypoole Genealogy, by J. Rutgers LeRoy, from Vol. XIV (1890), 86-88 177

Three Generations of the Clymer Family, from Vol. IX (1885), 353-355 180

Captain William Crispin, by M. Jackson Crispin, from Vol. LIII (1929), 97-131, 193-202, 289-321 183

Jacob Dubs, of Milford, by Joseph Henry Dubbs, from Vol. XVIII (1894), 367-376 273

Pedigree of Rowland Ellis, of Bryn-Mawr, From His Own Manuscript, 1697, by Thomas Allen Glenn, from Vol. XIV (1890), 199-200 283

Parentage of Major John Fenwick, Founder of Salem, New Jersey, by Edwin Jaquett Sellers, from Vol. XLIX (1925), 151-162, 256-260; Vol. L (1926), 267-272 285

Captain Gerlach Paul Flick, Pennsylvania Pioneer, by Alexander C. Flick, from Vol. LIII (1929), 230-268 308

The Foulke Family of Gwynedd, Pa., by Howard M. Jenkins, from Vol. XII (1888), 369-370 347

Old Records of the Foulke, Skirm, Taylor, Coalman, Woolley, and Gaskill Families, from Vol. XI (1887), 207-212 349

The Franks Family, by Charles Henry Hart, from Vol. XXXIV (1910), 253-255 354

Delaware Bible Records [Futcher], by C. H. B. Turner, from Vol. XXIX (1905), 467-469 357

Record of the Descendants of James and Phebe Gillingham, from Vol. XXIV (1900), 224-229 360

The Gilpin Ancestry, by Alfred Rudulph Justice, from Vol. L (1926), 97-116 366

Genealogical Notes Regarding the Family of Glen, or Glenn, by Thomas Allen Glenn, from Vol. XXXVI (1912), 480-499 387

Graham Family Records, from Vol. XLII (1918), 184-186 407

Records of the Hall Family of Bristol, Pennsylvania, from Vol. XI (1887), 309-317 409

Hall-Brading-Carmicke, from Vol. XVII (1893), 113-114 418

Genealogical Sketch of General W. S. Hancock, by Howard M. Jenkins, from Vol. X (1886), 100-106 419

English Ancestry of Samuel Hedge, Son-In-Law of Major John Fenwick of Salem Colony, New Jersey, by A. H. Hord, from Vol. LVI (1932), 270-274 426

Records of the Hill Family of Massachusetts, by Charles Austin Robinson, from Vol. XI (1887), 497-499 431

Hill Records, from Vol. XXXI (1907), 374 433

The Descendants of Sarah Holme, Daughter of Thomas Holme, by Richmond C. Holcomb, from Vol. XLIV (1920), 158-169 434

Hudson Family Records, by Howard Williams Lloyd, from Vol. XVI (1892), 108-110 447

Husband-Price-Haines Families, by Thomas Maxwell Potts, from Vol. X (1886), 119-121 449

Hutton, Plumsted and Devereux Families, by Gregory B. Keen, from Vol. XLIII (1919), 257-261 452

The Jones Family of Bethlehem Township, by J. H. Dubbs, from Vol. IV (1880), 209-217 457

Genealogical Records of the Jones Family of Wales and Pennsylvania, by Lewis Jones Levick, from Vol. XXX (1906), 366-371 466

The Wife and Children of Sir William Keith, by Charles P. Keith, from Vol. LVI (1932), 1-8 472

Ancestry and Children of Isaac Lea, from Vol. LII (1928), 90-92 481

Some of the Descendants of Evan Robert Lewis of Fron Gôch, Wales, from Vol. XXIV (1900), 203-206 483

Genealogical Records [Manlove, Master, Mason, Bibbe, Broxson, Kellam, Burroughs, Polk, Shaw, Chipman, and Brown], by C. H. B. Turner, from Vol. XXXI (1907), 251-253 487

Genealogical Records of the Marshall Family of Lewes, Delaware, 1737-1839, by C. H. B. Turner, from Vol. XXIX (1905), 331-333 490

Delaware Bible Records [Marshall], from Vol. XXX (1906), 245-246 493

Sketch of Colonel Ephraim Martin of the New Jersey Continental Line, from Vol. XXXIV (1910), 480-483 494

Some Additional Information Concerning Ephraim Martin, Esquire, Colonel of the Fourth New Jersey Regiment of the Continental Line, by Edmund J. James, from Vol. XXXVI (1912), 143-161 498

James Miles and Some of His Descendants, by Thomas Allen Glenn, from Vol. XXXVII (1913), 240-247 517

Morton of Calcon Hook, by Thomas Allen Glenn, from Vol. XXXVI (1912), 362-366 525

Owen of Merion, by Thomas Allen Glenn, from Vol. XIII (1889), 168-183 530

Genealogical Gleanings, Contributory to a History of the Family of Penn, by J. Henry Lea, from Vol. XIV (1890), 50-63, 160-181, 281-296; Vol. XVI (1892), 330-342; Vol. XVII (1893), 55-75 546

Family Records Contained in the Bible of Jonathan Platts, from Vol. XXIX (1905), 115-117 632

Porter Families of Chester County and York County, Pennsylvania, by Porter Farquharson Cope, from Vol. XXVI (1902), 156-158 634

A Sketch of Some of the Descendants of Owen Richards, Who Emigrated to Pennsylvania Previous to 1718, by Louis Richards, from Vol. VI (1882), 69-85 637

A Record of the Richards Family From an Old Welsh Bible, by Howard Williams Lloyd, from Vol. XXII (1898), 254-255 .. 655

Rohrer Records, from Vol. XXXIV (1910), 484-486 657

Descendants of John Rush, from Vol. XVII (1893), 325-335 .. 660

Genealogical Records Copied From the Bible of Thomas Say, from Vol. XXIX (1905), 216-223 671
Descendants of Dr. William Shippen, by Chas. R. Hildeburn, from Vol. I (1877), 109-111 679
The English Ancestors of the Shippen Family and Edward Shippen, of Philadelphia, by Thomas Willing Balch, from Vol. XXVIII (1904), 385-402 682
Notes on the Steelman Family of Cinnaminson Township in Burlington County and Greenwich Township in Gloucester County, New Jersey, by Arthur Adams, from Vol. XXXVI (1912), 464-472 702
Records From the Taylor Family Bible, from Vol. XVI (1892), 121-125 711
Catharine Tennent, by A. D. S., from Vol. VII (1883), 113-115 ... 715
The Washington Pedigree: Corrigenda and Addenda, by Charles H. Browning, from Vol. XLV (1921), 320-363 718
The Washington Pedigree, by G. Andrews Moriarty, Jr., from Vol. XLVII (1923), 58-66 762
The Wharton Family, by Anne H. Wharton, from Vol. I (1877), 324-329, 455-459; Vol. II (1878), 50-57, 211-218 771
The Williams Family, from Vol. X (1886), 107-114 798
Genealogical Gleanings of the Wilson, or Willsons, of Ulster, by Thomas Allen Glenn, from Vol. XXXVIII (1914), 346-354; Vol. XL (1916), 351-357 806
Wiltbank Family Record, from Vol. XXIX (1905), 339-342 ... 822
Notes on the Woods Family of Bedford, Pennsylvania, by Joseph L. Delafield, from Vol. XXXII (1908), 335-344 826
Zane Family, from Vol. XII (1888), 123-125 835

Appendix

Achey-Stiegel Genealogical Notes, by Luther R. Kelker, from Vol. XXIV (1900), 393 839
James Anderson of York County, Penna., from Vol. XXXI (1907), 507 839
York County, Penna., Genealogical Notes, 1780 [Anderson, Binkele], from Vol. XXXI (1907), 243 840
Record of the Anthony Family of Philadelphia, from Vol. XXX (1906), 109 840
Bartow Genealogy, by B., from Vol. XIV (1890), 214 841
Bartow, from Vol. XXII (1898), 125 841
Battle-Price, from Vol. XXX (1906), 246-247 842

Records on the Back of the Marriage Certificate of William Blackfan, Jr. and Esther Dawson, from Vol. XXVII (1903), 112 843
Buck Family Record, from Vol. XII (1888), 496 843
Carter-Sutton-Morris-Hill-Ridgway, from Vol. XVI (1892), 248-249 844
The Chevalier Family of Philadelphia, by C. R. H., from Vol. VII (1883), 483-484 845
Clowes Family Record, from Vol. XXIX (1905), 489-493 845
Clowes-Clark Genealogical Records, by C. H. B. Turner, from Vol. XXXII (1908), 252-253 850
Coate[s], Leeds, and Steelman Family Record, from Vol. XIV (1890), 325-326 851
The Family Record of Hercules and Sarah Cooke, from Vol. XXIII (1899), 125 852
Corell, from Vol. XXI (1897), 500 853
Dillwyn Genealogical Notes, from Vol. XXVIII (1904), 248-249 .. 853
Dodd-Holland, and other family records, by C. H. B. Turner, from Vol. XXXV (1911), 380-381 855
Drinker Genealogical Notes, from Vol. XXII (1898), 373-374 856
Duer Family Bible Records, by James B. Laux, from Vol. XXXIX (1915), 218-219 857
Dungan Genealogical Notes, from Vol. XXIV (1900), 118 858
Dunton Genealogical Notes, from Vol. XXIV (1900), 116-117 858
Bible Records of Col. William Edmonds of Fauquier Co., Virginia, by Emma B. Belt, from Vol. XXXIII (1909), 253-255 859
Emlen Family: Entries Regarding Corrected, by P. S. P. Conner, from Vol. XXIX (1905), 504 860
The Fischel Family of York County, Pennsylvania, and North Carolina, from Vol. XXXI (1907), 508 861
Fishels Buried at the Roth Church, by Frank L. Crone, from Vol. XLIV (1920), 287-288 861
Family Records of Thomas Franklin, Jr., from Vol. XXI (1897), 129-130 863
Gardner Bible Records, by Mrs. A. W. Hand, from Vol. XXXVIII (1914), 253-254 864
Gerhard Genealogical Notes, from Vol. XXIV (1900), 117-118 ... 864
Gray-Emerson-Draper-Fowler Genealogical Records, by C. H. B. Turner, from Vol. XXXII (1908), 253-254 865
Guest-Morris-Powell, by A. S. M., from Vol. VII (1883), 495 867
Family of William Guest, of West Jersey, from Vol. XII (1888), 496-497 868
Captain John Hewson, by R. Ball Dodson, from Vol. XXXVII (1913), 118-119 868
Hinchman-Harrison-Blackwell-Benezet, by Thomas Maxwell Potts, from Vol. XII (1888), 497 869
Hoeffner-Sürer Notes, from Vol. XXXIII (1909), 380 870
Hunsicker, by T. S., from Vol. XVI (1892), 247-248 870

Hynes Family Data, by James B. Laux, from Vol. XXXVII (1913), 118 871
Some Genealogical Notes of the Ireland Family of New Jersey, from Vol. XXV (1901), 417-418 871
Kean-Macomb Family Record, from Vol. XX (1896), 276 872
King Family Records, from Vol. XLIII (1919), 277-278 873
Lake-Leak-Heath, from Vol. XXXI (1907), 118 874
Leoser Genealogical Records, by James B. Laux, from Vol. XLII (1918), 183-184 874
Loxley Family Records, from Vol. XXIII (1899), 265-266 875
Lucken-Luken Family Records, by Miss Annie M. Daniels, from Vol. XXIII (1899), 270-271 876
Lucken Genealogy, by Theodore Cooper, from Vol. XXIII (1899), 408 877
Lynn-Marshall, from Vol. XVII (1893), 376-377 878
McCulloch-Roach, from Vol. XXII (1898), 245-246 879
Mason, by Frank D. Green, from Vol. XXII (1898), 373 879
"Account of the Offspring of William Maul and Bethiah Guthrie, Ancestors of the Logan Family," from Vol. XXVI (1902), 479-480 880
Meade Family, by Mrs. Ellis, from Vol. XXIV (1900), 242-243 ... 881
Miller Records, from Vol. XXXVII (1913), 382 882
Morris-Walton, by T. S., from Vol. XXI (1897), 500 882
Norman Family Genealogical Notes, by C. H. B. Turner, from Vol. XXXI (1907), 500-501 883
Record of the Ormsby Family, by G. P. P., from Vol. XXIV (1900), 119 884
Osborn-Renaudet-Chevalier Genealogical Records, from Vol. XXXII (1908), 120-122 884
Paynter-Jacobs-Truxton-Green-Thompson Notes, by C. H. B. Turner, from Vol. XXXI (1907), 374 886
John Benedict Peter, from Vol. XXXI (1907), 125 886
Pierson Family, by James B. Laux, from Vol. XXXVIII (1914), 252 886
Powell, by P. S. P. Conner, from Vol. XXI (1897), 121 887
Price-Shute-Courtney-Cooper-Rudolph Genealogical Notes, from Vol. XXIV (1900), 118-119 888
Notes on the Prichett or Prickett Family of New Jersey, from Vol. XVIII (1894), 512-513 888
Family Records Extracted From the Bible of Anna Raguet, Newtown, Penna., by Mrs. Israel H. Johnson, from Vol. XXXI (1907), 503-504 889
Genealogical Notes of the Family of Zachariah Rice, by J. M. Hartman, from Vol. XXIV (1900), 524-525 891
Ridgway, by Barclay White, from Vol. XVII (1893), 516-517 892
Genealogical Notes of the Rose Family of Ireland and America, from Vol. XXVIII (1904), 102-104 892
Rothrock, from Vol. XXI (1897), 498-499 894

Scudder, Anderson, and Wikoff Family Records, from Vol. XV (1891), 243-244 ... 895
Copy of Family Records in the Selden Bible, by Mrs. Harry Rogers, from Vol. XXVII (1903), 111 ... 896
Sitgreaves, by L. A. S., from Vol. XIII (1889), 254-255 ... 897
Genealogical Notes of General Walter Stewart and His Children, by Miss Mary Trumbull Morse, from Vol. XXII (1898), 381-382 ... 898
James Stratton, from Vol. XIV (1890), 212 ... 899
John Walker, by C. H. Browning, from Vol. XXVIII (1904), 118-119 ... 899
Data From the West Family Bible, from Vol. XXXII (1908), 118-119 ... 901
Ancestry of Benjamin West, by Albert Cook Myers, from Vol. XXXII (1908), 508 ... 902
Wright-Batten, by W. M. Mervine, from Vol. XXX (1906), 379 ... 903

Index ... 905

Introduction

THE PENNSYLVANIA MAGAZINE OF HISTORY AND BIOGRAPHY (generally abbreviated to *PMHB*) was founded in 1877 by The Historical Society of Pennsylvania in Philadelphia. In the 104 years that have passed it has been a gold mine of information relating to the history and biography of the Keystone State and neighboring areas. From its very first issue until about 1934, when its editors seemingly lost interest in the subject, *PMHB* contained voluminous articles on compiled family histories, Bible records, censuses, passenger lists, etc. (For a consolidation of articles on the last-named subject see *Emigrants to Pennsylvania,* Baltimore, 1975.)

The Genealogical Publishing Company has performed the same service for Pennsylvania genealogists that it performed for Maryland and Virginia genealogists when it went through the *Maryland Historical Magazine* and *The Virginia Magazine of History and Biography* and extracted all family articles and republished them under the titles *Maryland Genealogies* (2 vols., 1980) and *Genealogies of Virginia Families* (5 vols., 1981). It has culled all family history articles and Bible records from the first fifty-six volumes of *PMHB* and has issued them herein as a collective work on families of the Commonwealth and certain other states.

Some of the authors represented in *Genealogies of Pennsylvania Families* were among the most distinguished family researchers of the state. Gilbert Cope (1840-1928) was the dean of Pennsylvania genealogists. He is remembered chiefly for two works, *History of Chester County, Pennsylvania* (in collaboration with J. Smith Futhey, 1881) and *Historic Homes and Institutions and Genealogical and Personal Memoirs of Chester and Delaware Counties, Pennsylvania* (with Henry J. Ashmead, 2 vols., 1904). He was the author of a dozen or more family histories, all of which bear the stamp of painstaking and conscientious effort in ascertaining the facts based upon documentary evidence. He was a great Quaker authority, and early in this century he went to England to make digests of all of the registers of births, marriages, and deaths (from the earliest records to 1725) preserved in the Archives of the

Society of Friends. His digests, in many volumes, are in the collections of The Genealogical Society of Pennsylvania, which also houses ninety volumes of his professional work as a genealogist. The Manuscripts Department of The Historical Society of Pennsylvania possesses his vast collection of records relating to southeastern Pennsylvania and nearby New Jersey.

Thomas Allen Glenn is noted as an authority on Welsh genealogy. His two standard works, *Merion in the Welsh Tract* . . . (1896) and *Welsh Founders of Pennsylvania* (2 vols., 1911-13), were both reprinted by the Genealogical Publishing Company in 1970. He was the author of numerous genealogies and of the book *Some Colonial Mansions and Those Who Lived in Them, with Genealogies of the Various Families Mentioned* (1898). He knew the Welsh language and conducted many investigations in Wales and England. His works show a devotion to scientific genealogical research, judging from his careful source citations.

In addition to Glenn, other genealogists of Welsh families are represented in this volume. Howard Malcolm Jenkins (1841-1902) was the author of *Historical Collections Relating to Gwynedd . . . Settled, 1698, by Immigrants From Wales* (1897), and "The Early Welsh Quakers and Their Emigration to Pennsylvania" (*PMHB*, Vol. VIII, 1884). He is also noted as the author of *The Family of William Penn, Founder of Pennsylvania, Ancestry and Descendants* (1899) and *Pennsylvania, Colonial and Federal* (3 vols., 1903). Howard Williams Lloyd, whose "Hudson Family Records" appears in this volume, was an avid collector of data on his Welsh and English families. His papers were assembled by Thomas Allen Glenn, according to families, and published under the title *Lloyd Manuscripts* (1912). Charles Henry Browning, whose extensive corrections and additions to the Washington pedigree are given in this work, wrote the scholarly *Welsh Settlement of Pennsylvania* (1912, reprinted by GPC, 1967), but he is chiefly remembered as the compiler of royal and Magna Charta lineages that have come under fire because of their inaccuracy. His honesty was such that in later editions he corrected errors found in earlier editions, but even so the later editions must be treated with caution.

Oher authors in this collection deserve comment. Gregory B. Keen, LL.D. (1844-1930), was an Episcopalian clergyman who was converted to Catholicism. He was a great authority on the Swedish settlements on the Delaware and contributed an excellent chapter on New Sweden to Justin Winsor's *Narrative and Critical History of America,* Vol. 4 (1884). He was Librarian of The Historical Society of Pennsylvania and President of The Swedish Colonial Society. Charles Penrose Keith, Litt.D. (1854-1939), wrote much about Pennsylvania's colonial governor, Sir William Keith, Bart., to whom he was not related. Among his books were *The Provincial Councillors of Pennsylvania Who Held Office Between 1733 and 1776* (1883) and *Chronicles of Pennsylvania from the English Revolution to the Peace of Aix-la-Chapelle, 1688-1748* (2 vols., 1917). Edwin Jaquett Sellers (1865-1946) was a descendant of Jean-Paul Jaquet, director (governor) of the Dutch colony on the Delaware, and wrote genealogies of the Van Culemberg, Jaudon, de Carpentier, Draper, Wayne, Pfeiffer, Jaquett, Sellers, and other Pennsylvania and/or Delaware families. Thomas Willing Balch, LL.B., L.H.D. (died 1927), an attorney, wrote learned works on international law and histories of the Balch, Brooke, Shippen and other families of Pennsylvania. The Rev. Joseph H. Dubbs, D.D. (1838-1910), was an eminent theologian and church historian, who wrote a history of Franklin and Marshall College (1903) and, for the Pennsylvania German Society, a history of the Reformed Church in Pennsylvania. Oliver Hough, whose Atkinson paper is the lead article in this collection, is described in Hampton L. Carson's *A History of The Historical Society of Pennsylvania* (1940), Vol. II, p. 100, as "a diligent investigator, and a strange recluse in an ancient mansion in Newtown, Bucks County, Penna." He was the author of scholarly, well-documented articles in *PMHB* relating to colonial celebrities. Anne Hollingsworth Wharton (1845-1928), one of the few women among our contributors, belonged to one of the Commonwealth's most distinguished families and wrote books on the social history of the colonial period.

Much could be said of some of the other Pennsylvanians who contributed to this volume, but note should be taken of three authors who did not specialize in Pennsylvania records: Dr. Arthur Adams, FASG (1881-1960), co-founder and first President of The American Society of Genealogists, whose fields of inquiry were New Jersey, New England, and old England; Alexander C. Flick (1872-1942), a prolific writer on church and world history, and on New York State history; and G(eorge) Andrews Moriarty, Jr.,

FASG (1883-1968), a specialist on the genealogy of New England and of medieval England, who had interests also in Lower Norfolk County, Virginia.

It is good to have these articles collected in a single work. Until now they have been "buried" and well-nigh forgotten. The publication of *Genealogies of Pennsylvania Families* is a fitting tribute to family historians of the late nineteenth and early twentieth centuries who based their work on documentary evidence.

Milton Rubincam
CG, FASG, FNGS, FGSP, FTSGS

Genealogies of
PENNSYLVANIA FAMILIES

From The Pennsylvania Magazine
of History and Biography

ATKINSON FAMILIES OF BUCKS COUNTY, PENNSYLVANIA.

BY OLIVER HOUGH.

[There were two distinct families of the name of Atkinson, both of considerable note in the annals of Bucks County, but not related to each other in any degree known to their founders; (though it is possible they may have had a common origin many generations back in England). One descended from Thomas Atkinson, a minister of the Society of Friends, who came from Yorkshire, in 1681; and the other from the brothers Christopher and John Atkinson, of Lancashire, who sailed for Pennsylvania in 1699, both dying during the voyage, but whose surviving children (and the wife of Christopher) arrived in the province and settled in Bucks County. As many erroneous statements have been written and printed concerning these families, some writers confusing the two where Christian names were alike, this sketch is designed to give an accurate account of several of the earlier generations of each, and call attention to and correct such errors as have found their way into print or into manuscripts deposited in public places.

In 1890, Mr. John B. Atkinson, of Earlington, Kentucky, published a small book, entitled *The Atkinsons of New Jersey*. This was primarily a sketch of his own family, descended from William Atkinson, who settled in or near Burlington, West New Jersey, about 1683, and married March 9, 1686, Elizabeth, daughter of Thomas Curtis; and the genealogy of this line is given quite correctly.

But the book also contains more or less brief accounts of other Atkinsons early settled in West Jersey, and the Bucks County, Pennsylvania, Atkinsons as well; and in these accounts, Mr. Atkinson having evidently made little or no personal investigation into their subjects, tradition, and in at least one instance, imagination, have apparently been drawn on. (In justice to Mr. J. B. A., it should be mentioned that his sketches of the Atkinsons not of his own family, were largely made up from some notes hurriedly put together by the late Judge Clement, usually a very careful genealogist, but who, in this instance, accepted a good deal of hearsay information, not having time to properly verify the same). These accounts are biographical, not genealogical, (with one exception, noted below). Their subjects are, (the sequence below is not that of the book):

(A). James and Thomas Atkinson, from Belfast (though said to have been Scotchmen), in ship Antelope, 1681. They are not stated to have been brothers, but that is the inference. Both eventually settled in West Jersey, and James married the widow of Mark Newby, in 1684. J. B. A. gives a fanciful word-picture of their landing and immediately subsequent actions, and attributes to them personal characteristics he could hardly have had any means of knowing. (This is mentioned with all respect to Mr. Atkinson, and only as a necessary step in the correction of error, since it parallels a similar treatment of the progenitors of one of the Bucks County families in his book.)

(B). *Christopher* and *John Atkinson*, founders of one of the Bucks County families; this account is almost totally incorrect; it will be taken up in detail under the proper head below.

(C). Several William and Thomas Atkinsons, of West Jersey, not identified with any of the foregoing; Timothy Atkinson, who settled in Maryland; and a number of other early Atkinsons not known to be related to any of those above. None of these is treated of at any length.

(D). *Samuel Atkinson*, of Chester Township, Burlington County, West Jersey. He was son of *Thomas*, of Bucks County, Penna., though J. B. A. fails to so identify him. This is the one exception mentioned above in which some genealogy is given, (two generations); the said genealogy, as well as the speculations regarding Samuel's parentage, containing some mistakes, which will be corrected under the caption "Samuel Atkinson," in the Thomas Atkinson line, below.

In the book *Isaac and Rachel Collins*, (Phila. 1893), Appendix, pages 149–150, there are some radical errors in the issue of Samuel Atkinson (son of Thomas), as well as in the genealogical sketch of the Stacy family, into which he married; these will be noted below.

In the MSS. Collections of Isaac C. Martindale, in the library of The Historical Society of Pennsylvania, vol. 6, the two Bucks County families are greatly confused, and some wrong dates given; these will be noted and corrected in the proper places.

THE PENNA. MAG. HIST. & BIOG., vol. XI, pp. 309–317, has *Records of the Hall Family, of Bristol, Pennsylvania*, copied from the bible originally belonging to John Hall, whose third wife, Hannah, was granddaughter of Thomas Atkinson, the minister. Notes to this record have some errors regarding both Thomas Atkinson and his son William, which will be corrected in their individual sketches; also in the related Radcliffe family, for which see Note E hereafter; and on page 315 occurs the error that Christopher Atkinson settled in Bucks County.]

PART I.

The Thomas Atkinson Family.

I. JOHN ATKINSON, (the father of Thomas), by the statement of his daughter-in-law,[1] was of Thrush-Cross, in Yorkshire, England. The identification of this place was somewhat difficult, but it is now known to be a township at present called Thruscross (and sometimes Thurcross), containing a small village of the same name. Samuel Lewis's *Topographical Dictionary of England*, 3rd edition, (London, 1838), thus describes it:

"THURCROSS, a chapelry, in the parish of FEWSTON, Lower Division of the wapentake of CLARO, West Riding of the county of YORK, 9 miles (w. by s.) from Ripley, containing 601 inhabitants."

The 5th edition of Lewis, (London, 1845), gives the name as Thruscross,[2] and describes it:

" THRUSCROSS, or WEST-END, a chapelry, in the parish of FEWSTON, union of PATELEY-BRIDGE, Lower division of the wapentake of CLARO, W. riding of YORK, 10 miles (N. N. W.) from Otley; containing 576 inhabitants. The chapelry comprises the hamlets of Bramley-Head, West-End, Low-Green, Thruscross-Green, and Rockingstone-Hall, and contains about 6340 acres."

The same edition of Lewis, article " Fewston" (parish), states that the parish contains the townships of Blubberhouses, Clifton with Norwood, Fewston, Thurcross and

[1] Jane Atkinson, in her *Testimony* concerning her late husband (1687), published in *A Collection of Memorials*, etc. (Phila., 1787), page 10, and in *The Friend* (Phila., 1854), vol. XXVII, p. 172. These are mentioned more fully in the text further on.

[2] Though the map of Yorkshire accompanying this edition has it Thurcross, being doubtless printed from the same plates as that in the 3rd edition. Also under article "Fewston," in same edition (quoted in text below), it is spelled Thurcross.

Great Timble; that the parish church was St. Lawrence's;[1] and that there was a chapel of ease at Thurcross.

In a gazetteer of Yorkshire, by Edward Baines,[2] published in 1822, Thurcross is given as a township in the parish of Fewston, wapentake of Claro, and liberty of Knaresborough, 5 miles south of Pateleybridge.[3]

From the above it would appear that the township, the civil division of the parish, was identical with the ecclesiastical chapelry; a parish being always a civil, as well as an ecclesiastical, unit of division.[4] This locality was all, in former times, within the Forest of Knaresborough.[5]

---

[1] The 3rd edition says that the parish church was St. Mary Magdalene's, so the name must have been changed between 1838 and 1845. The earlier one was probably the name in John Atkinson's time. The 3rd edition also mentions the chapel at Thurcross.

[2] *History, Directory and Gazetteer of the County of York;* volume 1, West Riding; by Edward Baines; Leeds, 1822. This is practically a gazetteer only, and must not be confused with the four volume history, *Yorkshire, Past and Present,* by Thomas Baines, (no date, about 1870).

[3] In vol. 14, Yorkshire Arch. & Top. Journal, there is mention of a Thurcroft in Yorkshire, probably in Claro wapentake, which about 1750, was the seat of William Beckwith; this might be our Thurcross, or perhaps only the name of Beckwith's estate. In some of the church registers, etc., of the shire, occasionally occurs the family name of Thriscross, sometimes Thurscrosse; this family no doubt in early times owned land in the township, taking their surname from the place.

[4] For some explanation of these names for divisions and subdivisions of English counties, see the description of Knaresborough, below. Those of Yorkshire are especially difficult of understanding to the uninitiated.

[5] From Thomas Allen's *History of Yorkshire*, (London, 1831), vol. III, p. 396, we glean the following: The forest of Knaresborough extends from East to West, upwards of 20 miles, and in some places is 8 miles in breadth. By the general survey completed in 1086, we find there were then only 4 townships in the forest, viz., Birstwith, Fewston, Beckwith and Rosset. In 1368 there appear to have been 3 principal towns [townships] and 16 hamlets :

1. Thruscross, with its seven hamlets, Hill, Bramley, Padside, Thornthwaite, Menwith, Holme, and Darley;
2. Clint, with its five hamlets, Birstwith, Fellescliffe, Fearnhill, Hampsthwaite, and Rowden;

The village of Thruscross is about 13 miles west from the town of Knaresborough; within about 20 miles around it are the other well-known towns of Ripon, Ripley, Otley, Keighley, Skipton, Settle, Masham and Aldborough, from several of which Friends came to Pennsylvania.

While John Atkinson might have lived in any part of the township, his residence was most likely in the hamlet or village of the same name, called in one place above Thruscross–Green; for had he lived in some other part, his daughter-in-law would probably have used the name of the nearest hamlet, rather than that of the township. This place we must take to be his residence during the time (or most of it) within his daughter-in-law's knowledge, say from her marriage, 1678, till her *Testimony* was written, 1687; but from the fact that his son was born at Newby, he must have lived some time at that place; whether this residence was only temporary, or whether John Atkinson himself was born there, we have no evidence now at hand; the latter supposition seems the most plausible. However, from a date given in Besse's *Sufferings* (see below), he appears to have moved to Thruscross or its vicinity when this son was quite a young child, before 1659; and no doubt continued there till his death.

From our present scanty means of judging, he was seem-

3. Killinghall, with its four hamlets, Beckwith, Rosset, Bilton, and Harrogate.

The names of the townships of 1086 have become those of hamlets in 1368, except Fewston, which disappears; but Fewston as both township and parish appears again later. Baines's *Yorkshire Past and Present*, vol. II, p. 609, says that the Forest was formerly divided into 11 constabularies, of which Thruscross was one. In a list of assessments for 1584, we find Thurscrosse (another spelling), in "Libertat' de Knaresburge," assessed at four shillings. (J. Horsfall Turner's *Yorkshire Notes and Queries*, vol. i, p. 147, year 1888.)

Rev. Francis Hutchinson, D.D., in his *Historical Essay on Witchcraft*, (London, 1718), p. 35, mentions a prosecution in 1622, by "*Edward Fairfax* of *Fuyston*" [Fewston] "in the Forest of *Knasborough*, Esq." This brings us down to about John Atkinson's time.

ingly in fairly comfortable circumstances. A recent writer[1] emphasizes the point that most of the early converts to Quakerism were persons of consideration in their localities, those in the country districts belonging largely to the landholding or " squire" class ; the arrangements of the meetings being " only adapted for those having their time at their own command." Our increasing knowledge of those English Quakers who came early to Pennsylvania strongly corroborates this. While in the absence of any record to such effect, the presumption is against his being a squire himself, he may have been a smaller landowner, or a yeoman a generation or two from gentle blood ; though his name does not appear on any of the printed pedigrees of the gentle families of Yorkshire.[2]

[1] C. D. Sturge, in *Journal of Friends' Historical Society*, vol. i, p. 90, (London, 1904).

[2] If he were grandson, or even son, of a younger son, his name would be unlikely to so appear. The pedigrees of Yorkshire Atkinsons to be found in print are, however, very few ; those known to the writer are only four : Atkinson of Skelton (Bulmer wapentake, North Riding), in Dugdale's *Visitation of Yorkshire*, 1665–66, Surtees Society's vol. 36, (1859) p. 364 ; Atkinson of Leeds, in Ralph Thoresby's *Ducatus Leodiensis*, 1st ed. (Lond, 1715), p. 80, 2nd ed. (Leeds, 1816), p. 76 ; Atkinson of Little Cattall, in St. George's Visitation of 1612, (published by Joseph Foster, Lond. 1875), p. 489 ; and the family descended from Myles Atkinson, buried 1637/8, in J. Horsfall Turner's *Yorkshire County Magazine*, vol. III (1893), pp. 180–182. Little Cattall, the seat of one of these families, was in the wapentake of Claro, in which John Atkinson lived, but the pedigree ends too early for him, even if he belonged to that family. Joseph Foster's *Yorkshire Pedigrees* has the names of a number of Atkinson's intermarried with other families, though no Atkinson pedigree ; from this and many other references we find that there were quite a fair number of Atkinsons among Yorkshire gentry, whose pedigrees have not been published, one of which might have included John Atkinson. There was a gentle family of Atkinsons at Hatfield-Woodhouse, in township and parish of Hatfield, wapentake of Strafforth & Tickhill, whose heads were, about 1700, Richard, Sr., and his son Robert ; no pedigree of this is known. In the same wapentake was Wentworth-Woodhouse, the seat of Sir William Wentworth, and his son the celebrated Sir Thomas Wentworth, 1st Earl of Strafford ; Sir William's wife was Anne Atkinson, but she was not of a Yorkshire family, being daughter of Robert Atkinson of Stowell, Co. Gloucester.

John Atkinson was among the earliest converts to the Society of Friends in Yorkshire; his daughter-in-law[1] calls him "an honest Friend." The following extract from Besse's *Sufferings of Friends*, is presumed to refer to him, though there were other Friends of the same name in the vicinity: Vol. II, p. 97, Year 1659. "In the same Month of November, John Atkinson, of Finston, was summoned to appear at a Manour-Court, at the Suit of Several Impropriators, for Tithe: Accordingly he appeared personally, yet his Appearance was not accepted, but he was fined, and had his Goods taken away to the Value of 4 l. About the same time, Agnes Atkinson, as she was passing about her Business through a Grave-yard, was met by a Priest, who without Regard either to Law or Equity, under Pretence of Tithes due to him took from her six Yards of Cloth by Force, and kept·it."

Agnes may have been John's wife, of whose name we have no other record. The name Finston is probably a slip of the pen (or type) for Fewston (spelled *Fiuston;* compare *Fuyston* above); no such place as Finston having been found. Besse, in volume II, chapter on Yorkshire, mentions a number of Atkinsons, among them a John several times, but it is doubtful if any of these were our subject or his relatives.[2]

[1] In her *Testimony;* see previous footnote.
[2] Page 101. Among the names of 229 persons imprisoned in the West Riding in 11th and 12th months, 1660, for refusing to take oaths, were those of Edward, George, John and Robert Atkinson. Page 110. Among 20 committed to York Castle in 1664, was Edward Atkinson ; these were taken from a meeting at Thomas Taylor's in Sedbergh. In the same year, among those fined for not contributing to the charges of the county militia, were : John Atkinson, 6 s., and Edward Atkinson, of Bradley, £2. In 1665, Robert Atkinson suffered distress of tithes, £10. Page 120. In the year 1668, Edward Atkinson of Sedbergh, had goods worth about £1, 1 s. taken for "steeple-house-rates." The places mentioned, though all in the West Riding, were a considerable distance apart, so even those of the same name may not have been the same persons. Sedbergh is 40 miles northwest from Thruscross; Bradley (or Bradleys Both) is 12 miles southwest from Thruscross.

Some years later, when the persecutions died down and meetings were regularly established, John Atkinson belonged to the Knaresborough Monthly Meeting. The meeting house was in the town of that name, which Lewis (3rd ed.) describes:

"KNARESBOROUGH, a borough, market-town, and parish, partly within the liberty of St. Peter's, East Riding, and partly in the Lower Division of the wapentake of Claro, West Riding." Allen's *History of Yorkshire* says: "The parish and borough town of Knaresborough is situate in the liberties of St. Peter, York and Knaresborough." Baines's gazetteer says the town is in the parish of Knaresborough, wapentake of Claro, and liberty of Knaresborough and St. Peter's in the West Riding. The town which is 18 miles west from the city of York, is situated on the northeast bank of the river Nidd. Knaresborough Forest (mentioned above as including Thruscross), is to the southwest, across the river.

A word as to Yorkshire topography, (to use the English term), may not be amiss, as well as some explanation of the designations of its subdivisions. In England the counties are divided primarily into *hundreds*; in the northern counties, once occupied by the Danes, their term *wapentake* (originally a division for military purposes) survives, and is used instead of *hundred*. Yorkshire, the largest county in England, has first three grand divisions called *ridings* (North Riding, East Riding and West Riding), which in turn are divided into wapentakes. The latter are then subdivided into *parishes*, originally ecclesiastical divisions, but soon falling into place in the civil scheme; parishes however, probably on account of this origin, did not always fall within hundred bounds, some overlapping from one hundred into another. Large wapentakes were sometimes split into divisions, (as that of Claro mentioned above, into the Upper and Lower Divisions); this did not interfere with the parishes, each division containing certain parishes. The parishes were composed of groups of *townships*, which consisted of a small town or village with the surrounding land, including other smaller villages or hamlets contained therein.[1] Besides this com-

---

[1] In Pennsylvania and other American States, the *township* is the primary subdivision of the county, with well defined boundaries, and not dependent for its existence on the villages within it, being in fact identical with the English *hundred*. In some states, for instance

paratively simple system of division, there were others more complicated. *Liberties* are tracts of land either excluded from parishes or superimposed upon them, and whose limits were frequently uncertain ;[1] they are districts "within which certain privileges are granted, or whose inhabitants have special rights or immunities;" each liberty had its special court, and in this was independent of the parish government, which came under the manor court. The *unions*, (Lewis's 5th edition mentions Thruscross as in the "union of Pateleybridge"), are amalgamations of parishes for administrative purposes ; they were formed early in the 19th century, long after John Atkinson's time.

Some facts concerning Knaresborough may serve to elucidate the above explanations, as well as to present something of its history: The name Knaresborough has covered a (1) manor, (2) honour, (3) castle, (4) forest, (5) parish, (6) liberty, and (7) borough-town. (An *honour* is composed of several manors, or a principal manor exercising jurisdiction over subordinate manors, the honour-court supplanting the several manor-courts. Wills were formerly filed in the honour-courts. The *Yorkshire Archæological & Topographical Journal*, vol. 10, p. 444, states that the wills in the Honour Court of Knaresborough, from 1640 to 1858, have been transferred to the Wakefield District of Her Majesty's Court of Probate). From Allen's History (vol. III, p. 395 et seq.) and

---

Delaware, the counties are divided into *hundreds* as in England, and the term *township* not used. In this country we have nothing to correspond with the English township idea. *Parishes* have no status in the civil scheme here; where they exist they are the private limits of jurisdiction of the several churches. But in some states, formerly French territory, as Louisiana, *parishes* take the place of *counties*.

[1] See Lewis's description ot Knaresborough, above, which was partly in the liberty of St. Peter's, East Riding, and partly in the wapentake of Claro, West Riding ; and compare Allen, who places the town in three separate liberties, those of St. Peter, York and Knaresborough. Pepys's Diary (April 7, 1669), mentions a case at law as to "whether the Temple be within the liberty of the City or no" (London); inferring uncertainty as to limits.

The term *liberty* is familiar to students of early Philadelphia local history, as applied to lands ("the liberty lands" or "liberties of Philadelphia") laid out immediately surrounding the city proper, but not included in it, nor in the townships composing the rest of the county. The liberties in Yorkshire were somewhat, but not altogether the same, for we have not only the liberty of Knaresborough, a town, and that ot York, a city, but the liberty of St. Peter's, a church, and the "Forest liberty."

other sources we learn that at the period of the Conquest Knaresborough was a complete Saxon manor, viz., one township presiding over 10 others; it comprised the town of that name and ten surrounding villages, and was a crown demesne. It was given to Serlo de Burgh, Baron of Tonsburgh (in Normandy), who was succeeded by his brother John, whose son lost it; after which the lordship changed hands many times. Serlo built the castle, which was the residence of the lords of the manor. The manor remained in existence until the Civil War, during which the castle was rendered untenable by order of the Parliament in 1648.

The honour of Knaresborough comprised the borough, the Forest (in which Thruscross was situated) and the Forest liberty. About the time of King John the Forest belonged to the De Sturteville family; (it was then technically not a "forest," but a "chase;" a "forest" must belong to king or sovereign alone; if it fall into the hands of a subject it becomes a "chase.")[1]

The date of John Atkinson's death is not known. He had at least two children:—

  2. THOMAS ATKINSON, b.   d. 8. 31. 1687.
    Founder of the Bucks County family.
  3. JOHN ATKINSON, b.   d. 3. 2. 1688.

Went to Pennsylvania with his brother Thomas, who left him by will 100 acres of land in Bristol township, Bucks County, but as John died without issue (and apparently unmarried) within a year thereafter, the land reverted to Thomas's children. John's death is on the Middletown Monthly Meeting register.

 2. THOMAS ATKINSON, son of John Atkinson, was born at Newby, in Yorkshire, before 1660. In 1838 there were five townships called "Newby" in Yorkshire,[2] (not counting one called "Newby-Wisk," in the North Riding), which all seem to have borne the name from a much earlier period. Three of these, being in the North Riding, may be left out of consideration. The other two are in the West Riding:

 (a). Newby, a joint township with Clapham, in parish of

---

[1] See also description of the manor and forest of Knaresborough in 1608, vol. I, p. 233, *Yorkshire Notes & Queries*, J. Horsfall Turner, 1888.

[2] See Lewis's *Topographical Dictionary*, 3rd edition.

Clapham, Western Division of the wapentake of Staincliffe & Ewcross, 7¼ miles (N. W.) from Settle. This Newby-cum-Clapham was 28½ miles W. by N. from Thruscross and over 40 miles from Knaresborough. It is unlikely that this was the one in which Thomas Atkinson was born.

(b). Newby, a joint township with Mulwith, in that part of the parish of Ripon which is in the liberty of Ripon, Lower Division of the wapentake of Claro; on the river Ure; 3¼ miles (S. E.) from Ripon. This one was 14 miles E.N.E. from Thruscross and about 7¼ miles N. from Knaresborough. Being thus the nearest to both these places, it was almost certainly that one mentioned as Thomas Atkinson's birthplace. It was besides the best known, and was generally called simply "Newby."[1]

Thomas Atkinson must have removed with his parents from Newby to Thruscross when quite a child; by the time of his marriage (1678) he had moved again to Sandwick or Sandwith, in Addingham parish, and was there in 1679, the last we hear of him till his coming to America.[2] This place has not been identified; it was doubtless the name of a hamlet, not of the importance of a township. Lewis (3rd ed., 1838), says of the parish, (the name of the church in parenthesis):

"ADDINGHAM (*St. Peter*), a parish, partly in the

[1] It was not from any large population that it was better known, for Lewis in 1838 speaks of it as "containing with Mulwith, 39 inhabitants," while Allen, seven years earlier, says: "*Newby with Mulwith* has fifty-two inhabitants;" (perhaps there were still more earlier, in Thomas Atkinson's time). But its principal claim to notice was that it contained Newby Hall, built by Sir Edward Blacket, about 1705, long after Thomas Atkinson had left there. For description and engraving of Newby Hall (in 1831, then the seat of Lord Grantham), see Allen, vol. III, p. 376.

[2] A note to *Records of the Hall Family, of Bristol, Pennsylvania*, PENNA. MAG. HIST. AND BIOG., XI, 316, speaks of "Thomas Atkinson of Newby, County York, England;" as we have seen, he was born there, but had moved away long before going to Pennsylvania. I have repeated this inaccuracy in a footnote to *Richard Hough, Provincial Councillor, ibid.* XVIII, 33, stating, even more inaccurately, that he came "to Pennsylvania from Newby." O. H.

Eastern Division of the wapentake of STAINCLIFFE and EW-
CROSS, and partly in the Upper Division of the wapentake
of CLARO, West Riding of the County of YORK, containing
2251 inhabitants," . . . "6 miles (E. by S.) from Skipton." Lewis mentions a place of worship of the Society of
Friends in the vicinity, but does not name it; no doubt
Beamsley Meeting House, in the township of the same name,
which possibly also included Sandwick or Sandwith, as
Thomas Atkinson attended Beamsley Meeting. Lewis (3rd
ed) has:

"BEAMSLEY, a township, partly in that portion of
the parish of ADDINGHAM, but chiefly in that portion of
the parish of SKIPTON, which are in the Upper Division
of the wapentake of CLARO, West Riding of the county
of YORK, $6\frac{1}{2}$ miles (E. by N.) from Skipton."

Thomas Atkinson joined the Society of Friends when
quite young, probably at the same time as his father, and
was an accepted minister of that body before his marriage
in 1678, at what must have still been an early age.[1] Of
the details of his ministry we have no record.[2] Sandwick
or Sandwith (whatever or wherever it exactly was,) was
within the compass of Knaresborough Monthly Meeting, in
whose register the entries of Thomas Atkinson's marriage,
etc., were made.

In 1681, Thomas Atkinson obtained a certificate from
Beamsley Meeting[3] for himself and family, and they

[1] Most of the personal data here and later are from Jane Atkinson's *Testimony*; see previous footnote.

[2] Although the gospel labors and sufferings of a Thomas Atkinson
are mentioned a number of times in Friends' writings, all so far published
appear to relate to a contemporary, but much older man, Thomas
Atkinson, of Lancashire, also presumably a minister. See Note A.

[3] Jane's *Testimony* says the Monthly Meeting, but *The Friend* sketch
of Jane herself says Beamsley, which as stated above, was the particular
meeting to which Thomas Atkinson belonged, and one of those constituting Knaresborough Monthly Meeting. At this time Friends sometimes obtained certificates from their particular meetings, or meetings
for worship; the practice later was for the monthly meeting only to issue
them.

At a County Court held 1 mo. 18, 1695/6: "Adress being made to this Court by Phinehas Pemberton on behalf and at the request of Jane formerly the wife of Thomas Atkinson but now wife of William Biles requesting the approbation of this Court for the disposing of 300 Acre of land given to her by her husband Thomas Atkinson by will during her natural life and after her decease to his three sons Isaac, William, and Samuel. William Biles declared he quit his claim and interest in right of his wife."[1]

In pursuance of the above William and Jane Biles made a deed[2] to George Biles (son of William) 4 mo. 10, 1696, for this 300 acres, "in New Bristol township, taken up by Thomas Atkinson, but never paid for by him." On the same day William Biles gave his bond, to Phineas Pemberton and Richard Hough in trust to secure the money to the children, and the deed was acknowledged before the court.[3] As these sons came of age they executed releases for this land, Isaac's being 4 mo. 11, 1700, William's 4 mo. 9, 1702, and Samuel's March 9, 1707/8;[4] Isaac's and William's were to George Biles, and Samuel's to William Paxson; (G. Biles had sold to Solomon Warder, and Willoughby Warder to William Biles, Sr., who sold to Paxson.)

At the session of the Board of Property, 12 mo. 23, 1701,[5] George Biles produced this deed of 4 mo. 10, 1696, for 300 acres of land in "New Bristol township, Bucks County," bounded west by John Rowland, north by William Dungan, east by Randal Blackshaw, and south by Charles Brigham, sold by William Biles and wife Jane, relict of Thomas Atkinson; also Isaac Atkinson's release; and requested a resurvey to make title to Solomon Warder to whom he had sold it. The board ordered him a warrant, and a patent to be issued on the return, Biles paying for "overplus," and the alienation from the Proprietary being further inspected.

Thomas Atkinson, in his will, empowered his executrix to sell "that one hundred ackers of land wch I bought of Joseph English." As no deed to Atkinson, nor from his executrix, has been found for this, it is impossible to exactly locate it.

He also bought from the Proprietary a tract in Northampton township, laid out for 500 acres. The date of this purchase is unknown, as the patent has not been found on record, but the deed for its sale says

[1] From Court docket in Quarter Sessions Office, Doylestown.
[2] Bucks County Deed Book 2, p. 81.
[3] Court Docket and Deed Book 2, p. 82.
[4] Bucks County Deed Book 3, pages 20, 104 and 404 respectively. Samuel's was not dated, but was acknowledged on the date given above.
[5] Minute Book G, Board of Property; Penna. Arch., 2 ser., XIX, 277.

the warrant was dated 6 mo. 25, 1684, and that it was laid out by the Surveyor General's order, 8 mo. 20, 1684. It is shown on Holme's Map in Atkinson's name, triangular in shape, bounded southwest by Job Howell's and Arthur Cook's land, northwest by a tract unnamed, and east by a road.

Davis says, (1st ed., p. 355): "Thomas Atkinson owned five hundred acres north of the road leading from Addisville to Newtown, reaching six hundred perches northeast of that village" [i. e. Addisville]. "Adjoining this tract on the north was John Holme, seven hundred acres, which he conveyed to Jeremiah Dungan in 1716."

He sold it to Joseph Kirkbride by deed[1] of 8 mo. 12, 1687, which was acknowledged in the County Court 10 mo. 4, by Robert Dove, attorney for Thomas Atkinson, (who was then deceased).

In a list called "Old Rights" among the papers in the Land Office of Pennsylvania,[2] occur the following:

18. Thomas Atkinson, warrant for 500 acres, dated 5. 26. 1684.
19. " " " " 40 " " 8. 28. 1684.

The first is no doubt for the Northampton tract, the figures here for month and day being only a transposition of those in the deed (5. *26—6. 25*). The second may be for some allowance, but just what or where is uncertain, as he is not known to have had any tract that size.

In Bucks County Thomas Atkinson joined Neshamina (afterwards Middletown[3]) Monthly Meeting, on the minutes of which body his name first appears at the meeting held at Nicholas Waln's 7 mo. 2, 1684, when he and Nicholas Waln were appointed to attend the Yearly Meeting. He was appointed on committees of Neshamina Mo. Mtg. on 5 mo. 4, 8 mo. 1, and 11 mo. 7, 1685, and 1 mo. 4, 1686 [1685/6] after which he transferred his attendance to Falls, and was on committees of that meeting 12 mo. 2, 1686 [Feb. 1687, N. S.] and 4 mo. 7, 1687. At this time Friends sometimes transferred this way without certificates when the meetings were about equally near their homes, though the meeting losing the member generally protested.

[1] Bucks County Deed Book 1, p. 132; recorded 10 mo. 15, 1687.
[2] Penna. Arch., 3 ser., III, 54.
[3] Neshamina Monthly Meeting was first called Middletown on the minutes of 3 mo. 2, 1700. Ezra Michener, in his *Retrospect of Early Quakerism*, (Phila., 1860), p. 77, says it was first so called in 1706, evidently a slip of the pen or misreading of the manuscript.

removed to West Jersey, in America, persumably on the
"Yorkshire purchase" on the upper side of Burlington.
Their stay here was only temporary, for in 1682 they were
living in Bucks County, in the Province of Pennsylvania,
where Thomas bought a plantation in what was afterwards
Bristol township.[1]

In the formation of social lines in this new settlement,
the Atkinsons naturally gravitated into that class of families
which took the lead in the social and political life of the
county, and,—most of these being Friends,—in meeting
affairs also; this is a strong indication that they were of no
mean extraction abroad, for many of these families had
solid claims to gentle lineage in England. That his position as a minister of the Society of Friends would have
given his family this standing without other qualification,
can hardly hold here, for no mention of him as a minister
appears on the meeting minutes, and it is likely that ill-
health prevented any activity in the ministry, after his
arrival in America; and besides there are sufficient instances
of persons of obscure origin becoming very worthy in the
ministry, but receiving no social recognition. Nor was it
wealth that gave Thomas Atkinson a high place among his
fellows, for his worldly fortunes were not prosperous, partly
because of his poor health after coming here, and partly
owing to his temperament being more that of the religious
enthusiast than of the business man. He was, indeed, a
considerable landowner, but the inventory of his estate[2]
shows that he had been unable to pay for all of it before his
death; and at the Falls monthly meeting of 5 mo. 4, 1683,

[1] A note to *Records of the Hall Family*, PENNA. MAG., XI, 316, states
that he settled in Northampton township; it is true he bought land in
that township also, but the land on which he resided was in Bristol
township. I have copied this error, in footnote to "Richard Hough,"
PENNA. MAG., XVIII, 33, O. H.* The account of Thomas Atkinson's
residences, location of his lands, list of children, etc., on the 54th
page (front and back), vol. 6, of Martindale's MSS (at Hist. Soc. of Pa.)
is so totally erroneous, that it is useless to mention errors in detail.

[2] Filed with his will, see below.

*A political biography, not used in this book.

" William Biles reported that Thomas Atkinson of Neshamine[1] is in want as to his outward concerns, and he and some others hath took his condition into their consideration and have bought him a cow and a calf—the price is five pounds and do desire this meetings assistance toward the payment of the said cow and calf; " on 8 mo. 3 some subscriptions for this purpose were reported.[2] Again, shortly before his death, Thomas Atkinson himself told the same meeting, 7 mo. 27, 1687 that he and his family were very weak, and could thresh no corn, nor had any hay for his cattle, and desired some assistance from Friends.

Thomas Atkinson bought, presumably from the Proprietary and soon after his arrival, three hundred acres of land, but as no patent, warrant nor deed for the same has been found the date and seller's name are not known. This was laid out in what became Bristol township, and was the plantation on which he resided. It is shown on Holme's map in Atkinson's name, but without exact boundary lines. In his will, he left 100 acres of this to his brother, John Atkinson, to revert to Thomas's sons, if John died without issue, which is what happened; and the balance of the tract to his wife, Jane, for life, and then to his three sons, Isaac, William and Samuel Atkinson.

At the Falls monthly meeting 9 mo. 8, 1693, "Jane the wife of William Biles proposed the sale of the Plantation she formerly lived upon . . . and upon a due consideration of the matter it was by this meeting thought most profitable for the children of Thomas Atkinson that it be sold for a valuable consideration and the money its sold for be secured at interest to be paid them with the profits arising by the said interest as they come of age."

[1] The region in early times called Neshamina, on both sides of the creek of that name, (now spelled Neshaminy), included lands afterwards erected into Middletown township, and parts of the adjoining townships of Bristol, Bensalem and Northampton.

[2] This and other quotations from and references to the various meeting minutes, are from the minute books in possession of the clerks or other custodians of the Society of Friends. The Falls minute books are at the Friends' Library, (Orthodox), 142 No. 16th St. (16th & Race), Philadelphia; they are, men's minutes, books A to E, 1683–1827; women's, three books, 1682/3–1852; some of these are copies, the originals being in the Newtown bank. The Middletown minute books are kept in the meeting house at Langhorne.

He was a member of the Grand Jury on 4 mo. 1, 1685, but held no public office. We have no specimen of his signature; his will and the deed to Kirkbride, of 8 mo. 12, 1687, were signed with his first initial only, T, he being then very ill.

Thomas Atkinson died 8 mo. 31st, 1687,[1] at his residence in Bristol township, and was most likely buried on his own plantation, though possibly in the ground on Slate Pit Hill belonging to Falls Mtg.; Middletown Meeting had no burial ground so early. The Philadelphia Yearly Meeting published a memorial of him, consisting of his wife's testimony concerning him, in a book entitled *A Collection of Memorials concerning Divers deceased Ministers and others*, etc. (Phila. 1787), page 10:

Jane Atkinson's *Testimony concerning her late husband* THOMAS ATKINSON.

He was born at Newby in the County of York, being the son of John Atkinson, of Thrush-Cross, was convinced of the truth and had received a gift of the ministry before I knew him. We were joined in marriage in the year 1678, and lived together in love and unity. He was a zealous man for the truth, and according to the gift which he had received, bore a faithful testimony unto it, of which many were witnesses in that country from whence we came. In 1682 we came into this country, with one consent, and in the unity of our dear friends and brethren, who gave a good testimony for us, by a certificate from their monthly meeting; and my soul hath good cause to bless the Lord, and to prize his mercies, whose presence was with us by sea and land. Since we came into this part of the world, he retained his love and zeal for God and his truth, his treasure not being in this world, and as it often opened in

---

[1] So stated in Jane's *Testimony*, and in the probate of his will and in the inventory; Middletown Mo. Mtg. register has 9 mo. 1, but the meeting records have in other places been found a day late. The note to *Records of the Hall Family*, quoted above, PENNA. MAG., XI, 316, has October 1682, the last figure of the year being a typographical error.

his heart, did exhort others to stand loose from things which are here below, and diligently seek after those things that are above. He was a tender husband, ready to encourage and strengthen me in that which is good. About the latter end of the fifth month 1687, he was taken with the ague and fever, which much weakened his body, in which he continued a considerable time; being well content with the dealings of the Lord: His heart was often opened in prayer and supplication unto his God, to preserve him in patience unto the end of his days, and that none of us might think hard of any of those exercises that he is pleased to try us withal. At times he would look upon me and say, *my dear wife, the Lord preserve thee and take care of thee, for I must leave thee and go to my rest;* with many more sweet and heavenly expressions and exhortations, in the time of his great weakness, which continued until the 31st of the eighth month, when he once more exhorted me to be content, and that I would desire his brother (who was then absent) to be content also; After which he passed away as one falling into a quiet sleep. And as the Lord hath hitherto been my strength and my stay in the time of my great distress, so the desire of my heart is, that I, with my brethren and sisters, who yet remain behind, may also finish our course in faithfulness, that in the end we may receive the same reward with the righteous that are gone before.

JANE ATKINSON."

An account of him prepared by Nathan Kite, in *The Friend*, vol. XXVII, p. 172, (Phila. 1854), includes the above *Testimony*, worded slightly differently in some parts, making it a little longer, but substantially the same; one additional particular being an account of her own illness before her husband's, (contained more fully in memorial of her to be given below). It is in this version that Jane speaks of her father-in-law, John Atkinson, as "an honest friend." There is an introductory paragraph which speaks of their being in

New Jersey in 1681, while Jane says they came to this country in 1682, though she may have meant Pennsylvania only.

In his will[1], dated 8 mo. 10, 1687, proved 3 mo. 21, 1688, Thomas Atkinson appointed his wife, Jane, executrix, and for the better payment of his debts empowered her to sell the 100 acres that he had bought of Joseph English. To his brother, John Atkinson, he left 100 acres of that "tract on which I now dwell," the same to return to Thomas's children, if John died without issue, (which he did). To his wife, Jane, he left the remainder of his real and personal estate during her life, and afterwards the remaining part of his home plantation (100 acres of which was given to brother John) to his three sons Isaac, William and Samuel. The inventory, dated 12 mo. 11, 1687, mentions the 100 acres which Jane was to sell, and among the debts in Jane's account, dated 2 mo. 10, 1689, are £12 owing to the Governor for land, and £14, 14s. 11d. to Joseph English; the inventory and account are filed with the will.

Thomas Atkinson married 4 mo. 4, 1678 (O. S.) under care of Knaresborough Monthly Meeting, in Yorkshire, Jane Bond[2]. Neither her parentage nor previous residence are known to the writer.

Jean Atkinson That she was unusually well educated for a woman of her time is proved by some writings she has left, such as her *Testimony* concerning her husband, as well as the cultivated style of her signature.[3] She was

[1] Bucks County Will Book A1, p. 50; registered 5 mo. 5, 1688.

[2] The meeting register is somewhat illegible at this point; some copyists have rendered this name *Boid*, and one *Bord*, but as these names are unknown in the locality, while that of *Bond* occurs frequently, the preference is for the latter. Miles White, Jr., in *William Biles*, PENNA. MAG., XXVI., 353 n, has *Boid*. The marriage record gives Thomas's residence as *Sandwick*, while that of the birth of his son Isaac, has it *Sandwith*.

[3] The signature herewith produced is from her bond as executrix, filed with her husband's will.

a minister of the Society of Friends, and "is said to have had an eminent public testimony."[1] On coming to Bucks County, she first attended Neshamina (Middletown) Monthly Meeting; on 10 mo. 3, 1684, she and Mary Hayhurst were appointed to inquire into the " clearness " of Joan Comly, whose marriage was proposed with Joseph English; she served on a similar committee 12 mo. 3, 1685. After that she attended Falls Monthly Meeting and was on committees there 6 mo. 4, and 8 mo. 6, 1686, 5 mo. 6, and 10 mo. 7, 1687, (and numerous others after her second marriage). She attended Middletown Monthly Meeting again, but not as a member, 11 mo. 5, 1687, and offered to accept the meeting's order in settlement of a difference that had been pending between her husband, lately deceased, and Thomas Stackhouse, Jr.; the meeting ordered her to pay Stackhouse 30 shillings. Falls made her a representative to the Yearly Meeting 7 mo. 1, 1686 and 6 mo. 15, 1688.

" In 1687 she was taken very ill, and both she and her husband thought she would die. After a time he told her he believed she would be raised up again and that he should be taken instead. This proved to be true, for that very day he became unwell, and, after lingering for eight or nine weeks, died; while she, by whom much labor in the militant church was yet to be performed, grew stronger and stronger. " (White's *William Biles*, condensed from *The Friend's* account of her.)

Thomas and Jane Atkinson had issue:

4. ISAAC ATKINSON, b. 1.2. 1678/9, d. 11.3. 1720/1. Mar. 4. 23. 1708, Sarah Hough.

5. WILLIAM ATKINSON, b. ——.——. 1681, d. 8.29. 1749. Mar. 1st, 2.6. 1704, Mary Hough. 2nd, 4.5. 1722, Margaret Baker.

6. SAMUEL ATKINSON, b. 5.17. 1685 O. S., d. 2.21. 1775, N. S. Mar. 7. 12. 1714, Ruth (Stacy) Beakes.

Jane Atkinson, widow of Thomas, married, second, 10

---

[1] White's *William Biles*, PENNA. MAG., XXVI, 353.

mo. 11, 1688, William Biles, of Falls township; [1]they were married at the latter's house. They had no issue. William Biles was one of the most noted men in the Province of Pennsylvania, a minister of the Society of Friends, and a large landowner in Bucks County. He was a Provincial Councillor, and many years a member of the Assembly, and a Justice of the Bucks County Court. For an extended sketch of his life, see *William Biles*, by Miles White, Jr., PENNA. MAG. HIST. & BIOG., vol. XXVI, pp. 58–70, 192–206, 348–359. His children, by his first wife, intermarried with the Beakes, Langhorne, Hughes, Blackshaw, Yardley and Janney families, all prominent in Bucks County, and the distinguished Lambert family of New Jersey, and with their connections, constituted a large part of the old Colonial office-holding aristocracy of the county.

After her second marriage, Jane moved, with her children, to her new husband's plantation in Falls township, more directly within the compass of Falls Mo. Mtg., and continued her activity in the affairs of that body.

An account of her life is given in *The Friend*, vol. XXVIII (Phila. 1855), pp. 93, 102. By it she appears to have been an acknowledged minister before they removed to New Jersey (which this account says was in 1682), and it tells some of the particulars given above and below. When she married William Biles, "in her he had a faithful helpmeet, and one well calculated to assist him in his journey heavenward." (White's *William Biles*.) At this time she began to travel in the ministry of the Gospel, and her husband generally accompanied her. In 1st mo., 1689, with the unity of Falls Monthly Meeting and the approbation ot the General Meeting of Ministers, she visited Friends in East Jersey and on Long Island.

" When George Keith began his quarrel with Friends in Philadelphia, he worked insidiously amongst country Friends, who had not an opportunity of immediately testing

---

[1] Register of Middletown Mo. Mtg.

the truth of his assertions, and in some instances got up a prejudice against the friends of truth and sound doctrine in those who were themselves sound in the faith." "So it was with Jane Biles. She thought for a *short* time that George Keith was a sound Friend and an injured man." "She was not long suffered to remain in that delusion. She took to the Select Yearly Meeting, held in the First month, 1693, a testimony against George Keith, which ' was read and approved.' " (*The Friend.*)

On 5 mo. 1st, 1696, she and her husband proposed to Falls Monthly Meeting to visit Friends in New England; they were granted a certificate and visited those Friends to their satisfaction. William and Jane Biles were appointed on a committee, 9 mo. 3, 1697, to draw up a Testimony "concerning Thomas Janney's labors and service amongst us in the Truth."

At a General Meeting ot Ministers in 10 mo. 1699, Jane Biles laid before it a concern that had long rested on her mind to pay a religious visit to England. William Biles opposed her going she being " but weakly in body," but in 7 mo. 1700 the meeting gave its consent, not considering his opposition an obstacle.[1] On 11 mo. 5, 1700 she proposed the same to Falls Monthly Meeting, her husband consenting and offering to go with her; Falls issued certificates for both 1 mo. 5, 1701 [1700/1]. They sailed early in 1701 and went to both England and Ireland. " They returned towards the close of 1702, having been absent from America something under two years. In giving an account of their labors to their Friends at home, they expressed the satisfaction they had had in the performance of their duty in England and Ireland."

" Jane appears to have been strengthened in her bodily health, so as to perform the service assigned her abroad, and after her return, we have evidence that she was for several years able to attend to her religious duties. She frequented

---

[1] See also White's *William Biles*, p. 353.

her own Yearly Meeting, and we find her at the Yearly Meetings for worship, which were held at divers places. Her concern for the promotion of the cause of Truth, led her to open in the Select Yearly Meeting, in First Month, 1706, the case of a venerable Friend who had gone to a marriage consummated at the house of one who had separated from Friends." After hearing the Friend him-himself in reply to Jane's charge, the meeting decided that he " was condemned therein, and that he was mistaken in the motion that led him thereto."

" The last service I find Jane Biles engaged in, was in the year 1706, but doubtless she continued faithfully labouring as long as strength and health were afforded." (*The Friend.*)

The minutes of Falls Monthly Meeting of 11 mo. 4, 1709 record : " Our dear friend Jane Biles is deceased." She was buried 10 mo. 21, 1709. William Biles died in 1710, and was buried 3 mo. 19.

(To be continued.)

ATKINSON FAMILIES OF BUCKS COUNTY, PENNSYLVANIA.

BY OLIVER HOUGH.

4. ISAAC ATKINSON, born at Sandwith, parish of Addingham, West Riding of Yorkshire, England, 1 mo. [March] 2, 1678/9,[1] died in Bristol township, Bucks County, Pennsylvania, 11 mo. [Jan.] 3, 1720/1,[2] son of Thomas and Jane Atkinson, came to America with his parents when about a year old, and after the brief sojourn in West Jersey, lived first with them in Bristol township, and after 1688, with his mother on her second husband's plantation in Falls township, until his majority. He belonged to Falls Monthly Meeting of the Society of Friends, having been brought up within its fold from early infancy, but it is uncertain if he continued a member after 1713.

On 4 mo. 11, 1700, being then of age, he executed a release[3] to George Biles, for his interest in his father's land, which his mother had sold to Biles 4 mo. 10, 1696.

He bought of John Guy, 10 mo. 9, 1700,[4] 200 acres in Falls township, next below the plantation of his step-father, William Biles, on the Delaware River. This had been originally part of Samuel Darke's tract, shown on Holme's Map in the latter's name. 10 mo. 9, 1702, he sold this to Jonathan Taylor.[5]

Isaac Atkinson afterwards bought three separate "parcels of land" (two of them contiguous however), in Bristol township. They were all within a tract shown on Holme's Map, adjoining the lower side of

---

[1] Knaresborough Monthly Meeting register has 1 mo. 2, 1679, meaning March 2, 1678/9, O. S. Although the year did not officially begin until March 25, people frequently began dating the new year on March 1.
[2] Register of Falls Mo. Mtg.
[3] Bucks County Deed Book 3, p. 20.
[4] Bucks County Deed Book 3, p. 32.
[5] Bucks County Deed Book 4, p. 207.

Pennsbury on the Delaware River, inscribed with six names in the following order:

    William Dungan.   John Tully.
    Mordecai Bowden.   Thos. Dungan.
    Clement Dungan.   Rich. Lundy.

Some of these persons never owned any of this land, either because the rights intended to be located here when the map was made, were afterwards laid out elsewhere, or because they sold their warrants before the patents were made out, and the latter issued to the purchasers. But the three Dungans all owned here. The jury of 1692 made the line between this tract and Pennsbury the boundary between Bristol and Falls townships, as it remains to this day, Pennsbury being in Falls and these lands in Bristol. The individual boundary lines of the several owners ran back from the river parallel to the Pennsbury line. (The lots appear to have been too narrow on the scale of the map for each name to appear on a lot, hence the above arrangement.)

    The first next the Manor was 400 acres patented to John Sirket 7 mo. 3, 1701, together with 90 acres of the back part of the tract below,[1] and 46 acres 35 perches additional, probably "overplus."

    The next was William Dungan's, patented to him 11 mo. 7, 1692, as 200 acres.

    Next John Green, 200 acres, patented 1684.

    Next Thomas Dungan, 200 acres, patented 8 mo. 1, 1692.

    Next Clement Dungan, 200 acres, patented 11 mo. 7, 1692.

John Sirket sold his holding 7 mo. 8, 1703, to William Atkinson, who sometime thereafter[2] sold one half of it to his brother Isaac. Sirket's sale was of 536 acres 35 perches (including the back part of Wm. Dungan's original patent), and it seems to have been William Atkinson's intention to sell Isaac an exact half (268 acres 17 perches) reserving

---

[1] Wm. Dungan, whose patent was nine years earlier than Sirket's, appears to have sold 90 acres to the latter before his (Sirket's) patent was issued, though no record of the sale has been found. The only record of Dungan's disposal of any of it is his bequest of the river front half, 100 acres, to his son William (1711); no doubt Sirket really got 100 acres, which accounts for his "overplus" on later survey.

[2] The date is uncertain, as no deed has been found for this sale, but it was between 1703 and 1710; for by deed of March 26, of the latter year, William Atkinson sold John Smith the other half (Deed Book 4, p. 288), and in this deed mention is made of 6 acres 96 perches already sold to Isaac Atkinson, and the bounds given show Isaac to have owned the other portion. For authorities for other deeds and facts mentioned in above paragraph, see under William Atkinson.

25

an exact half (268 acres and 18 perches,) to himself (which he afterwards sold to John Smith); but Isaac's purchase included a curious wedge-shaped lot of 6 acres 96 perches of meadow right in the heart of the other half and not within 70 perches of the rest of his land; that this was intended to be a fraction of Isaac's half and not of the other, is shown by Smith's deed which states that "The sd lands within ye first mentioned bounds (hereby granted to ye sd John Smith) contains besides ye six acres and ninety-six perches herein excepted, 268 acres and 18 perches, being ye moiety or one-half part," etc. Isaac, however, must have got that much above his half, for when his tract (though no longer his) was sold by the Sheriff in 1727, it contained the full 268 acres 17 perches in the main lot and the 6 acres 96 perches besides.

Isaac's purchase (excluding the small lot) was the river front half of Sirket's plantation, running along the Pennsbury (now the Falls) line. Common Creek, (not shown on Holme's map) flowed from Pennsbury quite across Isaac Atkinson's land, and emptied into the Delaware on the line between him and Dungan, forming their boundary for a few perches from the mouth. This land corresponds to the spot on Holme's Map on which the name of John Tully appears, and while it is easily seen that the six names in one plot, of which his is one, only indicate ownership within those limits and not more exact locations, this has led to some confusion, from the fact that the modern village of Tullytown lies mainly just across the border of and partly extends into this land; Oxford Street of the village, running back from above mentioned creek, being the township line. Davis, in his *History of Bucks County*, (1st ed., p. 115) says that Tullytown " was called after a man named Tully, who owned land there;" and in a footnote: "John Tully was an original settler in Bristol township on the line of Falls." But Tullytown is on the Falls side of the line, while this tract, even if Tully ever owned it, which is doubtful, was on the Bristol side. Again, Tullytown was laid out by Thomas Riche about 1800, and long called Riche-Town. Which puts a gap of nearly 200 years between the John Tully of Holme's Map (who did *not* own its site) and the Tullytown of the 19th century.

Isaac Atkinson no doubt disposed of this plantation before removing from Bucks County in 1713, for when John Smith sold Robert Smith the adjoining land in that year, the land on this side was said to be "John Lanning's formerly Isaac Atkinson's." But no deed from Atkinson has been found. On April 12, 1727, Sheriff Timothy Smith sold the two lots 268 acres 17 perches and 6 acres 96 perches as the property of John Maddox.[1]

---

[1] This deed is not recorded, but is recited in deed of John Martin to Timothy Titus, Aug. 20, 1792, Bucks Co. Deed Book 27, p. 245.

On June 10, 1708,[1] Isaac Atkinson bought of Esther Willson, relict of Richard, two tracts in Bristol township, on the Delaware River, one of 100 acres and one of 50 acres. These were adjoining and both within the six-named tract on Holme's Map. The 100 acres was the river front half of Thomas Dungan's original patent of 200 acres. It passed from him to Thomas Dungan Jr., to John Scott, to Tobias Dymock and Sarah, his wife. The other was a quarter of Clement Dungan's patent, taking in half the river front; from him to his brother-in-law, Edward Doyle, and from the latter's widow to Tobias and Sarah Dymock. After her husband's death Sarah Dymock sold both to Richard Willson, whose widow sold to Isaac Atkinson. The latter (and wife) sold them March 18, 1709 [1708/9],[2] to Willoughby Warder and Sarah his wife.[3]

Isaac Atkinson no doubt moved in 1700 from his stepfather's plantation[4] to that he bought of John Guy in Falls township. After selling that, he lived in Bristol township on the land he bought there from his brother, until 1713, when he moved to the upper part of Burlington County, West New Jersey. On 1 mo. 4, 1712/3, he requested Falls Monthly Meeting for a certificate to Chesterfield Mo. Mtg. in that county, his wife, Sarah, asking one from the women's side the same day; hers was signed a year later, 1 mo. 7, 1713/4, and his doubtless then or previously, though not on the minutes; they must have then already moved. Just where they located is uncertain; possibly in or near Trenton, which was within the compass of Chesterfield Monthly Meeting, and then in Burlington County, though now in Mercer.

[1] Bucks Co. Deed Book 4, p. 9.
[2] Bucks Co. Deed Book 4, p. 125.
[3] I take this occasion to acknowledge the valuable assistance of Mr. Warren S. Ely, of Doylestown, in searching the Bucks County deed records, enabling me to locate exactly lands once owned by Isaac Atkinson and his brother William; as well as for other help in the preparation of this article. O. H.
[4] It appears that William Biles conveyed his plantation in Falls to his son William in 1698, and removed to one he bought of Henry Baker, either within the Manor of Pennsbury, or adjoining it on the Bristol side; see White's *William Biles*, PENNA. MAG. XXVI, pp. 65, 203 and 354. Isaac most likely lived on the Guy place some time before he was of an age to have the deed made to him.

They stayed about two years, Sarah bringing a certificate back to Falls, 8 mo. 5, 1715.[1] After returning to Bucks Co. they lived again in Bristol township, but not on any of the land mentioned above, as Isaac had disposed of it all before leaving. His brother William, now living in Bristol borough, had bought a plantation in the township in 1717, (on the river, part of the Christopher Taylor tract of Holme's Map; see account under William). It is quite likely that Isaac lived here as manager for his brother, perhaps with a joint interest, for his inventory mentions "corn in the ground," wheat and barley, cows, calves and shoats.

In some deeds Isaac Atkinson is styled "cordwainer." Miss Anne Hollingsworth Wharton, in *Colonial Days and Dames*, remarks (p. 21): "Men who came from families of good position on the other side of the water felt it no dishonor to put their hands to any honest toil that had for its object the work of home-making and nation-building. Hence among the first settlers of Pennsylvania we find many good English names connected with the trades of tailor, hatter, carpenter and the like." But though the inventory of Isaac Atkinson's estate mentions shoemaker's tools, it also indicates that he was engaged in agriculture, and we have seen above that he was, at least temporarily, a landowner; therefore it would appear that, following the custom of his class, he had the shoemaking carried on by servants, and only assumed the style "cordwainer" to conform to Quaker ideas; it is no indication of his station in life.

By his will,[2] dated Dec. 23, 1720, proved Dec. 5, 1721, which states that he was "of the County of Bucks," (but gives no township), he left £20

[1] None for her husband is mentioned in the minutes, but he evidently came too; his name does not appear on the Falls minutes after 4 mo. 3, 1713, when he "gave a paper of condemnation which was read and accepted." Chesterfield Monthly Meeting minutes have no mention of them.

[2] Bucks Co. Will Book 1, p. 59. The inventory was made 11 mo. (Jan.) 30, 1720/1.

each to his three children, John, Jane and Thomas when they came of age; his wife to have the use of the money without interest until the payment, if she remained his widow. No land is mentioned. Residue to his wife Sarah, who was made executrix, with his "loving and trusty friend" Samuel Baker to assist her. The signature to this will (reproduced here) is of a good fashion for that period.

Isaac Atkinson married 4 mo. [June] 23, 1708, at Falls Meeting,[1] Sarah Hough, (b. 4 mo. 7, 1690), daughter of Richard and Margery (Clows) Hough, of Makefield township. For account of Richard Hough, who was a Provincial Councillor, Justice of the County Court, etc., and his wife, and their connections, see PENNA. MAG. vol. XVIII, pp. 20-34, and also Note B. following this article.

Sarah Atkinson was for some years active in religious affairs, and was appointed on committees of Falls Monthly Meeting 12 mo. 3, 1719, 3 mo. 4, 1720 and 3 mo. 3, 1721, but in the latter year some violation of discipline caused her disownment, and a "testimony of disunion" against her was issued 11 mo. 3, 1721, (1721/2, exactly a year after her husband's death).

Isaac and Sarah (Hough) Atkinson had issue:

   7. JANE ATKINSON, b. 6. 6. 1709,[2] d. —— .
      Mar. 8 . — . 1728, John Wilson.
   8. JOHN ATKINSON, b. —— , d —— .
      (? Mar. 1735, Margaret Yates ?)
   9. THOMAS ATKINSON, b. —— , d. —— .

Sarah (Hough) Atkinson married, second, in 1724, Leonard Shallcross, of Falls township. They were not married under care of Friends as she was no longer a member; on 6 mo. 5, 1724, Leonard Shallcross brought to the monthly meeting "a paper of condemnation for his marriage out of the unity of Friends." He had previously been in good standing and served on a committee of Falls Monthly Meeting, 10 mo. 5, 1722.

[1] Register of Falls Mo. Mtg.
[2] Register of Falls Mo. Mtg.

Leonard Shallcross had first married 11 mo., 1702, Ann Ellet, daughter of William, and had six children; he had none by Sarah, who survived him, and was mentioned in his will, 1729/30. (See Note C. hereafter.)

5. WILLIAM ATKINSON, born 1681, died in Bristol, Pa., 8 mo. [Oct.] 29, 1749,[1] son of Thomas and Jane Atkinson. He was most likely born while his parents were in Burlington County, West Jersey, then living with them on his father's plantation in Bristol township, Bucks County, until his mother's second marriage (1688), then with her on his step-father's plantation on the Delaware River in Falls, then from about 1698 on William Biles's new home at the northwestern end of Pennsbury, until his marriage,[2] when he moved to his own plantation in Bristol township (bought 1703, see below); he lived there until about 1711, when he moved into the town of Bristol, where he resided the rest of his life.

Shortly after coming of age he executed a release[3] to George Biles, dated 4 mo. 9, 1702, for his interest in his father's land bought by Biles.

On 7 mo. 8, 1703, William Atkinson bought[4] of John Sirket 536 acres, 35 perches in Bristol township, on the Delaware River, and adjoining Pennsbury; it was the upper section of the tract shown on Holme's Map in the names of William Dungan, John Tully, Mordecai Bowden, Thomas Dungan, Clement Dungan and Richard Lundy, but some of whom were not owners, as Sirket bought 400 acres direct from the Proprietary, and had an original patent (though including part of William Dungan's former patent); this has been explained at length under Isaac Atkinson. It ran back from the river the whole length of the Pennsbury line, now the boundary between Falls and Bristol townships. William sold the front half of this, 268 acres, 17 perches, to his brother Isaac;[5] also a lot of meadow land, 6 acres, 96 perches, about

[1] Register of Falls Mo. Mtg.
[2] His marriage record on Falls register calls him of Falls tp.
[3] Bucks Co. Deed Book 3, p. 104.
[4] Bucks Co. Deed Book 3, p. 119.
[5] Date not known, as deed is not on record, but deeds to adjoining lands show it to have been before 1710, and it was probably very soon after William's purchase, say, 1703 or 1704.

the centre of the half William retained, supposed to be included in the above amount, but since shown to have been so much in excess. William held the other half until March 26, 1710, when he sold it to John Smith.[1]

March 25, 1712, he bought of John Borradaile,[2] of Burlington, a lot on the north side of Mill Street in Bristol borough; this was no doubt where he resided the rest of his life; after his death, his executors sold it to his son William,[3] in 1758.

On June 17, 1713, he bought of John Hall,[4] of Bristol (afterwards his son-in-law), 4 acres in Bristol township, part of 116 acres patented to Hall by the Commissioners of Property the same year; and sold it to Benjamin Harris,[5] July 24, 1714.

In 1717, William Atkinson bought of Thomas Rogers, Jr., a piece of land of perhaps 55 acres on the Delaware River, in Bristol township, part of the tract shown on Holme's Map as Christopher Taylor's, between William Haige and Francis Richardson, containing something less than half of Taylor's water front. The exact date and amount are uncertain, as no deed is recorded for the Atkinson purchase. He died seized of it, and his executors sold[6] John De Normandie 48 acres, 65 perches as "part of a larger tract which was conveyed to sd William Atkinson by Thomas Rogers Junr. the seventh day of Anno Domj. 1717;" which is all we know of its purchase by William Atkinson. C. Taylor's heirs had sold his whole tract to John Rowland, who sold it off in several lots, all accounted for but 6 acres 95 perches in a triangle adjoining the back of the 48 acres 65 perches sold by Atkinson's executors, which makes it appear as if that was the balance of the larger tract which he bought, making it 55 acres, but we find no record of the disposal of this portion, either by him or his executors.

He obtained 9 acres in Bristol township by failure of Nathan Watson to pay off a mortgage made July 10, 1744,[7] but as no further record of it as Atkinson's appears, perhaps Watson afterwards redeemed it.

William Atkinson was much occupied with political affairs, and held a number of important public offices; by birth, by the marriages of his mother (to William Biles) and brothers, and his own, he was strongly affiliated with the

[1] Bucks Co. Deed Book 4, p. 288.
[2] Bucks Co. Deed Book 4, p. 194.
[3] Bucks Co. Deed Book 10, p. 55.
[4] Bucks Co. Deed Book 4, p. 295.
[5] Bucks Co. Deed Book 5, p. 49.
[6] Bucks Co. Deed Book 64, p. 272.
[7] Bucks Co. Deed Book 7, p. 139.

group of families that dominated the local government of Colonial Bucks County.

He was Coroner of Bucks County for nine terms (of one year each) in 1721, 1731-35, 1737, 1739 and 1740 [1]; and a County Commissioner in 1722.

He was eleven years, from 1738 till his death in 1749, Collector of Excise, a position corresponding to the present Federal office of Collector of Internal Revenue for a District. In this office he was succeeded by his son-in-law, John Hall.

He served two terms as a Common Councilman in Bristol, 1745 and 1746 (and possibly more, as some of the lists about his time are missing.[2]

In his commissions as Coroner, William Atkinson is styled "gentleman," and some deeds call him "taylor." The first correctly indicates his rank, in a period when the term was strictly limited to that sense. The other can be accounted for by the custom of Friends' families of whatever rank, having their children taught trades, who in after life, though not following them, used such designations in accordance with Quaker precepts against ostentation. Many gentlemen also had some business carried on by "servants" (and sometimes by slaves, but William Atkinson does not appear to have been a slave owner), and if they were of the Society of Friends, designated themselves by it for the same reason. But William Atkinson's time was devoted to his landed interests, politics and particularly meeting affairs, and there was no more eminent man in Bristol, during his lifetime than he; not even excepting Thomas Brock and Anthony Burton, its founders. His family and connections were the leaders in the social life of the town, the connections, including the Radcliffes, from

---

[1] Three of his commissions as Coroner, dated Oct. 3, 1733, Oct. 4, 1734 and Oct. 4, 1737, respectively, have been published in Penna. Arch., 3 ser., vol. viii, pp. 8, 30 and 59.

[2] A note to *Records of the Hall Family*, PENNA. MAG., xi, 316, gives him only one term.

whom Radcliffe Street (then as now, the fashionable residence street) took its name, and the Burtons (the founder's family above mentioned);[1] and after his death, the foremost citizen of Bristol was, without question, his son-ln-law, John Hall.

William Atkinson's concern in Friends' meeting matters began very early in life. He belonged to Falls Monthly Meeting and soon after reaching his majority was appointed Clerk to that body, a position he held until his death forty-seven years later. The term " clerk " (of the meeting) does not occur in his first appointment, but gradually came into use, and he is so called later. The first minute in relation thereto, 4 mo. 3, 1702, reads: " William Atkinson engaged to record the minutes of the Monthly meeting." And again, 7 mo. 2, 1702: " It was ordered that William Atkinson should be paid 16s. 8d. for writing.—This meeting orders William Atkinson to take the book for births, burials, and marriage certificates into his custody, and record the same as they come to his hand."[2] He kept the records of the women's side of the meeting, as well as the men's; their minute of 12 mo. 2, 1703 being: " Agreed that Jane Biles take care to get her son William Atkinson to record all ye minutes of ye meeting from ye beginning

[1] The Burtons were connected through his first wife, Mary Hough, whose niece, also Mary Hough, married Anthony Burton, Jr., son of Anthony mentioned above. The Radcliffe connection was one of several links : William Atkinson's second wife, Margaret Baker, was daughter of Henry Baker, by his second wife, Mary, widow of James Radcliffe ; the latter was mother of Edward Radcliffe, who married his step-sister, Phebe Baker, daughter of Henry, by his first wife, Margaret Hardman ; Mrs. Atkinson was thus half-sister to both Edward Radcliffe and his wife. (See *Henry Baker and Some of His Descendants*, by Miles White, Jr., Publications Southern Hist. Assn., vol. 5, pp. 388-400, 477-496.) Again Rebecca Radcliffe, sister of Edward, was first wife of John Hall, whose third wife was William Atkinson's daughter, Hannah.

[2] The book for recording certificates of removal presented to Falls Mo. Mtg. appears at that time to have been outside the clerk's province. It was kept by Richard Hough from 12 mo. 6, 1683 until the meeting of 2 mo. 4, 1704, when he turned it over to Joseph Kirkbride.

unto ye day into ye bound book that was bought for that purpose." "Margery Hough and Jane Biles appointed on a Committee to review all ye writings before they be transcribed." At the women's meeting 1 mo. 5, 1707[1]: "The Friends appointed to examine ye book wch is in William Atkinson's hand—give an account they find ye book well and truely recorded." Similar directions for reviewing and recording re-occur a number of times, on both men's and women's minutes; William Atkinson was sometimes on the reviewing committee himself.[2]

The men's minutes have, 9 mo. 2, 1749: "William Atkinson the late clerk of this meeting being deceased William Buckley is therefore desired to undertake that service as also to get the several books and papers belonging to this meeting from the Executors of the said William Atkinson into his care."

William Atkinson was also Clerk to Bucks Quarterly Meeting; the first mention of this in Falls records is in the women's minutes, 1 mo. 3, 1707/8:

"The Quarterly Meeting book that was in William Atkinson's hand is recorded to the satisfaction of Friends." Accounts of payments to him for recording the Quarterly minutes, appear thereafter from time to time in Falls books. The *Friends' Intelligencer* of 2 mo. 13, 1886 (no. 7 of vol. XLIII, p. 108) has:

---

[1] These dates are all Old Style; this is really March 5, 1706/7; this is a case (such as referred to in a previous footnote, p. 220) of dating the new year in advance of its official beginning (March 25); the preceding minute being correctly dated 12 mo. [Feb.] 5, 1706. Such cases occur frequently in the Falls minutes and are a cause of some confusion.

[2] He was on this committee 1 mo. 4, 1718/9, 7 mo. 3, 1729 and 3 mo. 2, 1739. An entry 4 mo. 1, 1715, is: "William Atkinson having recorded the Minutes, brought them to this meeting." There are other entries to this effect, and ordering his charges paid, or stating amounts that had been paid him. On 1 mo. 5, 1735 [1734/5] he was ordered to get a new minute book, and on 3 mo. 7, it was reported he had done so.

"OLD COPIES OF THE DISCIPLINE.

Editors Intelligencer and Journal:

In 'Letters by the Way,' in the last issue of the paper, P. E. Gibbons mentions 'the first edition of the Discipline, issued in or about 1793.' I have a manuscript edition of the Discipline adopted by Philadelphia Yearly Meeting in 1719. It is in the handwriting of William Atkinson.

R. W.

Doylestown, Pa."

Falls minutes (men's) have in regard to this, 5 mo. 6, 1720: " * * * the Quarterly Meeting ordered he " [William Atkinson] " should have 15s. paid him for transcribing the revisal of the Book of Discipline, so much being our proportion which is ordered paid."

The minutes of Bucks Quarterly Meeting (now deposited in the Newtown Bank) show him to have been appointed clerk to that meeting some years before the first mention above. At a Quarterly Meeting held at Falls, 3 mo. 28, 1702: " William Atkinson having entered ye minits of ye q^{tr} meeting y^t. was Left unentered by Phinehas Pemberton it is thought fit by this meeting yt he Enter ye Births Burials & Marriage Certificat's y^t still remaines unentered in ye quarter meeting Book & y^t friends satisfie him for his Care therein." At a Quarterly Meeting held at Neshaminy 6 mo. 27, 1702: " The fr^{ds} Concerned to Collect ye acc^{tt} of w^t publick fr^{ds} have died belonging To This meeting have Brought ye s^d acc^{tt} into This meeting Therefore it is ordered y^t both meeting Lists be Joyned in one & y^t Willm Atkinson trancescribe Them against ye yearly meeting.

William Atkinson haveing given ye meeting an acc^{tt} y^t all ye Births and Burials are Recorded to this Time * * *."

At a Quarterly Meeting held at Wrightstown 12 mo. 27, 1745 [Feb. 1746] : " This meeting appoints Joseph White, Robert Collison, Joseph Chapman, Samuel Eastburn & Wm. Atkinson to view the Minuits of this Meeting Unrecorded, and when done William Atkinson is Appointed to record them." But he did not record this minute, as it is in a new hand, and was probably entered by the next clerk, after William's death. At a Quarterly Meeting held at Middletown,

9 mo. 30, 1749: " Joseph White is desired to act as Clerk to this Meeting in room of William Atkinson Deceased."

William Atkinson was appointed an Elder of Falls Monthly Meeting 11 mo. 4, 1726, and at his death had acted in that capacity nearly twenty-three years.[1] The above date of appointment is given in the list of Elders in the minutes for 3 mo. 28, 1746, of the Meeting of Ministers and Elders (of Bucks Quarter) (with the other Q. M. records in Newtown Bank), as well as in those of Falls Monthly Meeting. He appears not to have been clerk to the Ministers and Elders meeting.

He was a representative of Falls Monthly in the Quarterly Meeting at least twenty-one times; these were:

[dates of appointment, not of holding the Q. M.] 3 mo. 2, 1711; 3 mo. 5, 1714; 3 mo. 4, 1720; 9 mo. 6, 1723; 3 mo. 6, 1724; 9 mo. 3, 1725; 9 mo. 2, 1726; 6 mo. 5, and 12 mo. 3, 1730; 9 mo. 3, 1731; 6 mo. 6, 1735; 3 mo. 6, and 9 mo. 4, 1741; 3 mo. 5, and 12 mo. 3, 1742; 3 mo. 2, and 12 mo. 6, 1744; 3 mo. 1, 1745; 9 mo. 5, 1746; 12 mo. 1, 1748; 3 mo. 3, 1749.

He served on many special committees of the monthly meeting (over eighty of them, so only the most important can be mentioned here, besides some under appropriate heads elsewhere):

> Appointed 1 mo. 5, 1711/2 on committee to settle Treasurer's accounts.
>
> 2 mo. 2, 1712, to collect subscriptions from Bristol.
>
> 8 mo. 5, 1720, to collect subscriptions from Bristol meeting to assist in rebuilding Chester Meeting House, Burlington County, destroyed by fire.
>
> 4 mo. 5, 1723, to receive subscriptions to aid Shrewsbury Friends in building their Meeting House.

William Atkinson was an original member of Bristol particular meeting on its establishment in 1710. Previously the Bristol Friends had attended Falls particular meeting

---

[1] The note to *Records of the Hall Family*, mentioned above, PENNA. MAG., XI, 316, says erroneously thirty-three years.

(William had naturally done so in early life when living in Falls township); though from about 1704 they had had occasional meetings at Bristol. Samuel Smith, historian of early New Jersey and vicinity says: "Meetings for worship at Bristol were sometimes held at Friends houses till 1710 when a meeting-house was built, and a meeting settled therein." It was one of the constituent members of Falls Monthly Meeting.[1]

He was made an overseer for Bristol Meeting at the monthly meeting of 8 mo. 3, 1711, and was released from that position, 11 mo. 7, 1713.

On 2 mo. 1, and 7 mo. 2, 1713 he was on committees for accounts of Bristol meeting house. Middletown Monthly Meeting, 10 mo. 6, 1722, ordered a subscription for Friends who lost by fire at Bristol, the amount collected to be paid to George Clough and William Atkinson.

William Atkinson was one of the Trustees for lands belonging to Falls Monthly Meeting.

John Rowland, by deed[2] of 1 mo. 8, 1703/4, conveyed to Edmond Lovett, William Atkinson and Nehemiah Blackshaw, trustees, a lot 5 x 5 perches, near the house of Thomas Watson, the elder, laid out for a burying ground. At the monthly meeting 11 mo. 1, 1745/6, it was agreed that, as William Atkinson was the only surviving trustee, the deed should be renewed to others then selected. Accordingly the said survivor by deed[3] of Feb. 1, 1745/6, conveyed the said 5 perches square, in Falls township, to Thomas Watson, Joseph Wharton, Edmond Lovett and Joseph Atkinson, the persons chosen; and reported his action to the meeting 4 mo. 4, 1746.

On Feb. 1, 1706, Joshua Hoopes, survivor of former trustees, conveyed[4] to the new ones, Joseph Kirkbride, Thomas Watson (tanner), Abel Janney, Samuel Baker, Edward Lucas and William Atkinson the burying ground of 72 sq. perches, which Thomas Janney had donated the meeting, and conveyed to the former trustees, 4 mo. 4, 1690; this was

[1] In 1788 it was transferred to Middletown Monthly Meeting, where it now belongs.
[2] Bucks Co. Deed Book 3, p, 157.
[3] Not on record, but fact recited in deed of these new trustees to their successors, 9 mo. 15, 1773, Bucks Co. Deed Book 17, p. 213.
[4] Bucks Co. Deed Book 10, p. 175; it was not recorded until 1760.

the one on Slate-pit Hill, on the road below Yardley in (now Lower) Makefield township. And 10 mo. 10, 1721, Daniel Burgess (devisee of Samuel Burgess) conveyed six acres to the same;[1] it having been discovered that the six acres donated Falls Meeting by Samuel Burgess and conveyed by him to its trustees, 4 mo. 4, 1690, had been laid out in another place. On 12 mo. 7, 1774, Joseph Atkinson, as son and heir of William, last surviving trustee, conveyed these two lots[2] to new trustees; it was stated that at that time the Janney gift was walled in.

At the monthly meeting 5 mo. 7, 1714, the bequest of John Sirket for keeping the grave yard at Falls Meeting House in repair, was placed in care of William Atkinson.

He was appointed a trustee for the Bristol burying yard, by Falls Monthly Meeting, 12 mo. 7, 1710. On June 12, 1711, Samuel Carpenter conveyed[3] to Joseph Kirkbride, Thomas Stevenson, William Croasdale, George Clough, Samuel Burgess and William Atkinson, for use of Bristol Meeting, two lots in that borough, one of 4 acres, and one of 19 perches, the latter at the corner of Market and Wood streets. May 18, 1738, William Atkinson, as survivor of the above, conveyed[4] these two lots to the new trustees, Joseph Kirkbride, William Blakey, Samuel Bunting, John Hutchinson, Jr., Thomas Marriott, Jr., and Joseph Atkinson.

It will be noticed that in two of these trusteeships William Atkinson was succeeded by his son Joseph.

On 1 mo. 6, 1727/8, William Atkinson acquainted the monthly meeting of his intention of going on a voyage to sea, and requested a certificate. This was to Barbadoes; he was gone about seven months; on his return he presented to Falls, 9 mo. 6, 1728, a certificate from Friends at Barbadoes.

William Atkinson in his will[5] dated Sept. 22, 1749, proved Nov 30, 1710, speaks of himself as of the "Burrough of Bristol" and "ffar advanced in years." He left his daughter Rachel Atkinson furniture and money, and his daughter Mary Banckson and son Samuel Atkinson each a

---

[1] Fact recited in deed to their successors, 12 mo. 7, 1744, Bucks Co. Deed Book 17, p. 205.
[2] Bucks Co. Deed Book 17, p. 205.
[3] Bucks Co. Deed Book 4, p. 166.
[4] Bucks Co, Deed Book 10, p. 181.
[5] Bucks Co. Will Book 2, p. 168.

small sum, and directed the residue to be equally divided between all his children, " as well them above named as the rest." He also mentioned his son-in-law John Hall, and " cousin " Samuel Bunting (a nephew of his second wife). The executors named were his son Joseph and daughter Rachel. He gave them power to sell all real estate, but did not specify what he possessed; the inventory made Nov. 18, 1749, mentioned some woodland and a house and lot, but not their extent nor location; the house and lot were, of course, his residence on Mill Street, Bristol, which the executors sold in 1758 to William Atkinson, Jr.

William Atkinson married, first, 2 mo. [April] 6, 1704, at Falls meeting,[1] Mary Hough, (b. 6 mo. 1, 1685, d. 9. mo. 11, 1720,)[1] daughter of Richard and Margery (Clows) Hough, of Makefield township, and sister to his brother Isaac's wife. For account of Richard Hough, Provincial Councillor, etc., and Margery Clows, his wife, see PENNA. MAG., Vol. XVIII, pp. 20-34; also Note B. appended to this article.

Mary (Hough) Atkinson was active on the women's side of Falls Monthly Meeting; her particular meeting being Falls before marriage and Bristol after. She was chosen a representative to the Quarterly Meeting 3 mo. 6, 1719; and was named on committees of the monthly meeting 12 mo. 7, 1710/1; 3 mo. 4, and 10 mo. 7, 1715; 3 mo. 2, 1716; 2 mo. 1, 1719; and 5 mo. 6, 1720. She was appointed an overseer (presumably for Bristol meeting) 4 mo. 1, 1720; on 3 mo. 3, 1721 the minutes say: " By reason of the death of our ffriend Mary Atkinson, Jane Chadwick is appointed to be an overseer in her stead."

In a letter in possession of the writer, dated 3 mo. 13, 1721, from William Atkinson to Phebe Radcliffe in Bristol he says in part: " for all my private Retirements and Meditations are intermixed with a Natural Sorrow, for Loss of so many of my most near ffriends, ffirst my Dear Sister (in the nearest Relation) M : W : then of my Dear Brother : W.

---
[1] Register of Falls Mo. Mtg.

B: and then of my near Dear true Companion and Bosome ffriend, (which is most Direfull to Bear) then of my poor Brother Isaac and mother all which have so succeeded one another, that ever Since that day that I came to Neshaminy quarter meeting when M : W : Lay dying I have waded deep through unexpressable Sorrow * * *" The "Dear true Companion," etc., meant his wife; M. W. and W. B. must have been sister and brother in the religious sense only, as none of his own, nor his wife's, nor his stepfather's family, corresponding to these initials, died at this time; the mother was doubtless his mother-in-law Margery Hough, whose death followed Isaac Atkinson's as the letter states. The Phebe Radcliffe to whom the letter was written was daughter of Henry Baker & widow of Edward Radcliffe; she will be written of in Notes D and E.

William and Mary (Hough) Atkinson had issue:

(Births from register of Falls Mo. Mtg.)
10. SARAH ATKINSON, b. 1. 10, 1704/5, d. 10. — , 1706.[1]
11. HANNAH ATKINSON, b. 11. 25. 1706/7, d. 12. 9. 1760.[2]
    Mar. May — , 1734, John Hall.
12. WILLIAM ATKINSON (JR.), b. 9. 18. 1709, d. 1794.
    Mar. Sept. 24, 1734, Sarah Pawley.
13. MARY ATKINSON, b. 7, 19. 1713, d. ——.
    Mar. July 9, 1745, Daniel Bankson.
14. JOSEPH ATKINSON, b. 10. 5. 1716, d. ——.
    Mar. 1st, Dec. 8, 1743, Jennet Cowgill.
        2nd, April 13, 1762, Sarah Silver.
15. SARAH ATKINSON, b. 9. 4. 1719, d. 2. 7. 1726.[1]

William Atkinson married, second, 4 mo. [June] 5, 1722, at Bristol meeting,[3] Margaret Baker, (b. 6 mo. 2, 1693, d. 6 mo. 20, 1748),[4] daughter of Henry and Mary

[1] Register of Falls Mo. Mtg.
[2] Hall Family Bible, the entries in which were printed, with notes, as *Records of the Hall Family, of Bristol, Pennsylvania,* in PENNA. MAG., XI, 309–317.
[3] Register of Falls Mo. Mtg.
[4] So in Register of Falls Mo. Mtg.; in White's *Henry Baker,* and *Records of the Hall Family,* her death is given Dec.——, 1748.

Baker, of Makefield township;[1] at this date Henry Baker was deceased, and his widow, with her daughter Margaret, was living in Bristol borough. For an account of Henry Baker, one of the leading men of early Bucks County, see sketch of him by Miles White, Jr., in *Publications of Southern History Ass'n*, vol 5, pp. 388-400, 477-496; also Note D. following this article. Margaret Atkinson's mother, before marrying Henry Baker, was widow of James Radcliffe, an eminent minister of the Society of Friends; the Radcliffe family was connected with the Atkinsons in other ways also; see Note E.

Margaret (Baker) Atkinson served frequently on committees of Falls Monthly Meeting, viz.: 6 mo. 7, 1723; 2 mo. 7, 1724; 8 mo. 2, and 9 mo. 6, 1728; 9 mo. 5, 1729; 1 mo. 3, 1735/6; 8 mo. 5, and 9 mo. 2, 1743; 5 mo. 2, 1746; 4 mo. 3, and 5 mo. 1, 1747.

William and Margaret (Baker) Atkinson had issue:

    (Births from register of Falls Mo. Mtg.)
  16. RACHEL ATKINSON, b. 3. 23. 1723, d. 5. 8. 1803.[3]
    Mar. 10. 18. 1750, Thomas Stapler.
  17. REBECCA ATKINSON, b. 5. 26. 1725, d. 8. 8. 1731.[2]
  18. SAMUEL ATKINSON, b. 5. 12. 1729, d. ——.
  19. ISAAC ATKINSON, b. 5. 12. 1729, d. 7. 16. 1747.[3]
  20. THOMAS ATKINSON, b. 11. 19. 1732, d. 5. 7. 1734.[3]

In Martindale's MSS., vol 6, on the 32nd page Rachel's birth is given as 3. 27; on the 56th page her birth is given as 3. 21, her death as 5. 9, and Thomas's birth as 11. 9; as these MSS. have frequently been found inaccurate, we give the preference to the meeting register dates, as copied above. The mistakes on the 56th page as to Rachel's birth & death are repeated on the 61st page.

---

[1] In Isaac C. Martindale's genealogical MSS. in possession of The Historical Society of Pennsylvania, vol. 6 (not paged), on the 32nd page, Margaret Baker's husband is given as William Atkinson, of Middletown, son of John; this William was of the other (Christopher and John) Atkinson family, and the true facts as to him will be found in Part II of this article. The children named by Martindale on that page are actually Margaret's children as given above. On the 56th page her husband is correctly called William Atkinson of Bristol, son of Thomas, and the same list of children reappears.

[2] Register Falls Mo. Mtg.

[3] Martindale's MSS., just mentioned.

(To be continued)

ATKINSON FAMILIES OF BUCKS COUNTY, PENNSYLVANIA.

BY OLIVER HOUGH.

[*Addenda relating to 4. Isaac Atkinson.* On 11 mo. 24, 1712, [Jan., 1713, N. S.) Isaac Atkinson, of Bucks County, Pennsylvania, purchased 160 acres in Nottingham Township, Burlington County, West Jersey, from John Rogers, of that place, (W. J. Deeds, liber P, folio 100). This was about a month before he requested a certificate of removal from Falls Mo. Mtg. to Chesterfield Mo. Mtg. and confirms the supposition advanced on page 223 that he lived near what is now Trenton, for its site was within that township. This Nottingham Township was afterwards subdivided, none of the resulting parts retaining the name; its original area is now all within Mercer County. On April 16, 1715, Isaac Atkinson, being then of Nottingham Township, re-sold this 160 acres to John Rogers, (W. J. Deeds, liber N, folio 301). Their return to Bucks County must have been between this date and October of the same year, when Sarah presented her certificate to Falls Mo. Mtg.

Corrections to page 237. Footnotes 2 and 3 are there transposed; the dates of the deaths of William and Margaret's children, Rachel, Isaac and Thomas, should be referred to Falls Mo. Mtg. register, and Rebecca's to Martindale's MSS; not *vice versa* as it there appears.

On same page line 14, for 1725.]

6. SAMUEL ATKINSON, born July 17, 1685,[1] in Bristol Township, Bucks County, Pennsylvania, died Feb. 21, 1775,[2] in Chester Township, Burlington County, New Jersey, youngest son of Thomas and Jane Atkinson.[3] He was born on his father's plantation and lived there till about three years old, spending the rest of his minority on one or

[1] Middletown Mo. Mtg. register.

[2] Obituary notice in *Pennsylvania Gazette*.

[3] For much information concerning Samuel Atkinson and his descendants, and references for original sources of the same, I take this opportunity of acknowledging my indebtedness to Miss Helen Kirkbride Morton, of Philadelphia, and Dr. W. S. Long, of Haddonfield, N. J.

other of the plantations of his step-father, William Biles, in Falls Township, first that on the Delaware River and then that which William Penn complained encroached on his Manor of Pennsbury. After coming of age he continued in the same township until his removal to West Jersey, in 1714, in which year he is still spoken of as " of Falls Township," and he no doubt lived with some of his Biles relatives on the same land, as he had none of his own in Bucks County. On 6 mo. 4, 1714, he requested a certificate of removal from Falls Monthly Meeting, and the next day declared his intentions of marriage with Ruth Beakes at Chesterfield Monthly Meeting in West Jersey, to which she belonged. He may have stayed temporarily with his brother Isaac, then living in Nottingham Township, near Ruth's home, but after their marriage the following month, he took up his abode on his wife's property in Nottingham Township, she being a lady of large landed estate.

On 9 mo. 5, 1719, Samuel Atkinson having already removed with his family within the bounds of " New Town " (Newton) Meeting, requested a certificate from Chesterfield Monthly Meeting, which was issued 10 mo. 3. Newton Meeting a constituent of Gloucester Mo. Mtg. (now Haddonfield Mo. Mtg.) was held at Newton in Gloucester County, but included within its compass Chester Township, Burlington County, and it was in the latter township that Samuel Atkinson had located. He presented his certificate to Newton Mo. Mtg. 1 mo. 14, 1719/20.

He had purchased land in (as well as removed to) Chester Township before applying to Chesterfield for the certificate, as will be seen in the account below. (Chesterfield and Chester should not be confused; the two townships were on opposite sides of Burlington County, and there was a Friends meeting in each, the former being also a monthly meeting. Samuel never lived in *Chesterfield* Township, but in *Nottingham* Township, within the compass of *Chesterfield* Monthly Meeting, and from *Nottingham* Township removed to *Chester* Township, within the compass of *Newton* or

Gloucester Monthly Meeting.) The following accounts of Samuel Atkinson's lands are restricted to those in his own right, and such of his wife's as they had made their home; to include all of hers it would be necessary to give a history of the great landed property of her father, Mahlon Stacy, one of the principal proprietors of the Province of West Jersey, and her brother, Mahlon Stacy, Jr.

In 1707/8 he released[1] to William Paxson, all his interest in his father's land which his mother had sold to George Biles, and Paxson afterwards purchased.

By deed[2] of March 13, 1718/9, Samuel Atkinson and Ruth his wife, released to William Trent, of Philadelphia, two tracts in Nottingham Township; one of 100 acres, which William Emley by will April 21, 1704 (it then adjoining Mahlon Stacy's land) gave his daughter Mary wife of John Heywood, who sold Nov. 26 & 27, 1707, to William Beakes, who by will March 24, 1710, devised it to his son Edmund Beakes (it being the plantation William Beakes then dwelt on), who sold it Nov. 2 & 3, 1713 to his step-mother, Ruth Beakes (afterwards Samuel Atkinson's wife); the other also of 100 acres adjoining the north side of the above plantation, originally belonging to Mahlon Stacy, Senior, who on Jan. 28 & 29, 1677 conveyed to Thomas Lambert, Senior, 1/12 part of 1/100 part of West Jersey, whose son and heir Thomas Lambert on July 19 & 20, 1714, confirmed the 100 acres to the same Ruth Beakes, (now Atkinson). These adjoining lands forming one plantation were the residence of Samuel and Ruth until their removal to Chester Township.

On Sept. 20, 1719, Samuel Atkinson, "late of Nottingham Township," bought of Thomas Adams, of Chester Township, 238 acres in the latter township (Adams' late dwelling place), also a meadow of 12 acres in Evesham Township, adjoining Thomas Hooten's dwelling.[3] (Evesham and Chester then adjoined, the modern township of Mt. Laurel, which now separates them, having been laid off from the former

---

[1] Bucks Co. Deed Book 3, p. 404; deed not fully dated; it was acknowledged March 9, 1707, [1707/8].

[2] West Jersey Deeds, liber DD, folio 379. Samuel and Ruth's residence is given as Burlington County, no township stated. William Trent was the founder of Trenton, which stood on land originally belonging to Ruth's father, Mahlon Stacy.

[3] W. J. Deeds, liber HH, folio 225. In another deed this is stated to have been 237½ acres.

in 1872; the meadow was most likely in the part now Mt. Laurel Township.)

On Dec. 4, 1722, Samuel Atkinson, then of Chester Township, bought of Robert and Benjamin Field, of Mansfield Township, 200 acres in Chester Twp. adjoining the above, part of 800 acres acquired by the Field's father, also Benjamin.[1]

He had thus a plantation (not counting the meadow in Evesham) of 438 acres. By deed of Dec. 19, 1764, he conveyed to his son Samuel Atkinson, Junior, the greater part of this, 371 acres.[2] Of the 67 acres remaining no record has been found of its disposal; it is most likely he retained it to live on himself, and that it formed part of his residuary estate left to his two daughters, though it is not mentioned in the inventory, nor specifically in his will.

June 2, 1763, Samuel Atkinson, Edward Hollinshead, Samuel Stokes and Benjamin Hollinshead, signed an agreement, fixing lines and corners of their lands, which had become uncertain.[3]

On April 27, 1765, Samuel Atkinson joined Silas Crispin and others, all of Burlington County, in a quit claim to Thomas Wetherill, of Burlington City, to certain lands at Little Egg Harbor, in settlement of disputed lands.[4] What Samuel Atkinson's personal interest was in these lands, is unknown to the writer.

The Atkinsons of New Jersey, (p. 29), says he settled in Chester Township before 1719, when he bought "a large tract of land of Thomas Adams, adjoining his own, and where he then lived." But we have seen above that the purchase from Adams was the first he made here, and that it was the purchase from the Fields that adjoined the land already his. The sale of Ruth's Nottingham plantation in March, 1718/9, and the meeting's certificate, prove that it was within the year 1719 that they moved, some time before November. The book quoted gives quite a good account of Samuel Atkinson, having a few small errors like the one just mentioned, but it fails to identify him as the

---

[1] W. J. Deeds, liber HH, folio 220.
[2] W. J. Deeds, liber U, folio 528. Matlack MS, p. 929, has a note that Samuel Atkinson sold 66 acres to Nehemiah Haines, but gives no date nor reference to record. This would account for all but the 12 acres of meadow in Evesham.
[3] W. J. Deeds, liber U, folio 110.
[4] W. J. Deeds, liber W, folio 266.

son of Thomas of Bucks County, and has some very wild speculations as to his parentage. It cites the statement in his will (see below) of his father being entitled to a lot in Philadelphia, because he "came to Philadelphia with William Penn, and rendered him some service," and then deduces from accounts quoted by Thomas Shourds in his *History of Fenwick's Colony*, that these services were the furnishing beef and pork to the Proprietary by one James Atkinson, presumably a butcher, and that therefore James was the father of Samuel, confirmed by the name J. Atkinson being found on a plan of the Province (outside the city). But Samuel himself gives the true reason in his will, that is, that it was in right of his father's purchase of 500 acres, and that he saw his father's name on a plan of the city (probably Holme's "Portraiture") not a map of the Province at large. And it is likely that the James Atkinson mentioned in the beef and pork accounts was not really a butcher, but the large landowner of that name both in Pennsylvania and New Jersey, who married the widow of Mark Newbie.

But to quote the authenticated parts of this account: "This tract" [the Adams purchase] "is at the easterly end of Moorestown (then Rodmantown), and lies on both sides of the King's Road, extending from Salem to Burlington, as laid out in 1681." "His dwelling was a stately mansion for the day in which it was built, for Samuel was a man of considerable estate, and his good wife, Ruth, a daughter of Mahlon Stacy, had brought him a large fortune." "He was a man of influence in his neighborhood, as well in the meeting, of which he was a consistent member, as in the political movements of the times then agitating the Colony."

There had been a dwelling already on the Adams tract, but Samuel Atkinson either remodelled it on an extensive scale, or built another. At the time the above was written (1890) part of it was still standing, but no longer in possession of a descendant. The same account says that Stacy Atkinson, who died about 1780, grandson of Samuel, was the last of the name owning any of the ancestral acres. The house is now about one mile from Stanwick Station on the Camden & Burlington Co. R. R.

Samuel Atkinson did indeed live in lordly style on his fine plantation, and with the really "large fortune" of his wife they were without doubt wealthy beyond any in the township, the Rodmans and Adamses perhaps excepted.[1] Ruth's inheritance from her father, while large, was even more extensive from her brother, Mahlon Stacy, Jr., who died intestate and childless. Samuel joined Ruth and the other heirs of her brother in many sales of his property, but these have not been included in account of his land transactions above, for reasons there stated, and especially as they did not keep any of the land. *The Atkinsons of New Jersey* states that Mahlon Stacy, Jr., lived the latter part of his life with Samuel and Ruth " on the old homestead," presumably the Stacy homestead, but they had removed from any Stacy property long before his death (1744), and a deed from his sister Mary Pownall to her nephew Thomas Atkinson,[2] states that her brother Mahlon had lived just before his death at Bridgeton, (now Mt. Holly).

On Samuel Atkinson's plantation was a family burying ground, where he and his wife are buried, and some of their descendants; a separate lot adjoined it for the burial of slaves.[3] He owned a considerable number of slaves, as did most Quaker gentlemen in New Jersey in his day. This family graveyard has shared the fate of many other such after the surrounding land has been alienated from the family; it is in a state of great neglect.

[1] Drs. John and Thomas Rodman, originally from Long Island, and ancestors of the Bucks County family of that name. The Adamses were descended from Major John Fenwick, once Proprietor of Fenwick's Colony.

[2] May 31, 1742, W. J. Deeds, liber C.F., folio 174. This Thomas Atkinson was son of Samuel and Ruth.

[3] Woodward & Hageman's *History of Burlington County*, (Phila., 1883), p. 263; *The Atkinsons of New Jersey*, p. 32.

Samuel Atkinson's name appears on the list of freeholders in Chester Township, returned by Thomas Hunloke, Sheriff of Burlington County, April 15, 1745.[1] This does not mean the office of Chosen Freeholder, a township official, usually abbreviated to Freeholder, an office he at one time held, but this list simply shows the owners of land there at that time. Samuel, like his brother William, was active in politics, but while his influence was great in the political affairs of his township and county, the offices he held, though numerous, were only minor ones. Nevertheless, in his day politics was the gentleman's vocation, and the small local positions were frequently filled by men of the highest standing, as they are in England still. After the Revolution many of these offices came to be considered too trivial for men of means or position, and so it has continued, until the present generation has no true conception of the idea of their ancestors in accepting them. Samuel Atkinson was Freeholder of Chester Township 1725, 1726, 1727 and 1728; Overseer of the Poor, 1726, 1727, 1728 and 1729; Assessor, 1722, 1723, 1724, 1735, 1736, 1737 and 1754; Collector (of taxes), 1734; Surveyor of Roads (the modern supervisor [2]) 1738 to 1746, inclusive; Surveyor for Chester Township, elected 1 mo. 7, 1747.[3]

Samuel Atkinson was a birthright member of the Society

[1] PENNA MAG., xxix, 425.

[2] This position recalls the fact that in a few localities there has been an awakening very recently from the state of affairs mentioned above, and that in a few places (notably some townships near Philadelphia) men of great wealth and high social position are, to the benefit of their townships and boroughs, taking such offices as road supervisors, etc.

[3] The above list has been compiled from the Court Book of Records, Burlington County, p. 206 ; the First Minute Book of Chester Township, commenced 1693 ; and the Matlack MS, in possession of The Historical Society of Pennsylvania, pp. 177, 273, 320, 322. A Samuel Atkinson was Freeholder in 1774 and 1775, who was no doubt the son of this Samuel, as the latter was then nearly 90 years old, and died in the latter year. A Samuel Atkinson was Constable in 1772, who may have been neither, certainly not the father.

of Friends, and grew up under the care of Falls Monthly
Meeting (in Bucks Quarter), attending Falls particular
meeting. In 1714 he changed his membership to Chesterfield Monthly Meeting (in Burlington Quarter), and the
particular meeting of the same name, there being none
nearer to Trenton while he lived there. In 1719 he changed
again to Gloucester Monthly Meeting (then in Salem
Quarter), and his particular meeting was at first Newton,
but within a year after his settlement there, a meeting had
been established at Chester, and attached to Gloucester
Monthly. Mitchener's *Early Quakerism*, p. 123, has this:
"Samuel Smith says, the meeting-house at Chester was
built and the meeting settled there in 1721. But the Chesterfield records mention assisting Chester Friends to rebuild
their meeting-house, which had been burned in that year.
The meeting had probably existed prior to that date." The
fire was really the year before; compare the minute of
Falls Monthly Meeting (p. 232 above) when William Atkinson, brother of Samuel, was appointed 8 mo. 5, 1720,
on a "committee to collect subscriptions from Bristol meeting to assist in rebuilding Chester Meeting House, Burlington County, destroyed by fire." So there must have been
a meeting at Chester very shortly after Samuel's arrival,
and the first meeting-house burned when quite new, perhaps while unfinished. While he first attended Newton
meeting, he no doubt at once commenced to help organize
one at Chester, the advent of his family probably being the
cause of establishing the new congregation. Newton
meeting has since been "laid down " and Chester meeting
is now called Moorestown meeting, but not till after Samuel
Atkinson's death. Before 1760 Gloucester Mo. Mtg. had
come to be called Haddonfield Mo. Mtg., and in that year
Evesham Mo. Mtg. was divided from it, including Evesham
and Chester particular meetings; so after that date Samuel's
membership was in the new monthly meeting of Evesham,
provided he continued a Friend till then, which is doubtful
as we shall see below, (though he was buried in the
Friends' burying ground at Moorestown).

Samuel Atkinson took no active part in the affairs of Chesterfield Mo. Mtg. while a member there, the only mention of him in its minutes being the declaration of his intention of marriage, and the request for and granting of his certificate to "New Town Meeting in Glocester County."

But in Haddonfield (early Gloucester) Mo. Mtg. he served on committees 9 mo. 14, 1720; 6 mo. 13, 1722; 6 mo. 12, 1723; 8 mo. 12, 1730; and 8 mo. 13, 1740. He was made an Overseer of Chester Meeting 1 mo. 12, 1721 [1720/$_1$?] and released from that position at his own request 4 mo. 13, 1726; and a representative to the (Salem) Quarterly Meeting, 6 mo. 12, 1723 and 1 mo. 9, 1729 [1728/$_9$?].

On 8 mo. 12, 1730, he requested a certificate for Stacy Beakes (his step-son) to Falls Mo. Mtg., and on 2 mo. 9, 1739, one for his son Thomas Atkinson to Burlington Mo. Mtg. On 6 mo. 11, 1759, "Samuel Atkinson disunited as a member of this meeting," but whether it was our subject or not is uncertain; there were other Samuel Atkinsons within the compass of Haddonfield Mo. Mtg., besides his son, who is mentioned however as "Samuel Atkinson, Junr." But as he was buried in the Friends' graveyard it is likely this minute refers to another.[1]

Samuel Atkinson died in Chester Township, Burlington County, New Jersey, Feb. 21, 1775, aged nearly 90 years. The following obituary notice of him appeared in the *Pennsylvania Gazette* of March 1, 1775:[2]

"On Tuesday morning, the 21ˢᵗ. ult, departed this life, in Burlington County, New-Jersey, SAMUEL ATKINSON, in the 90ᵗʰ year of his

---

[1] His name certainly does not occur again in the minutes of Haddonfield Mo. Mtg. but this proves nothing, as shortly after this date Evesham Mo. Mtg. was established, to which his membership if he still retained it, would have been transferred; and the writer has not examined the minutes of that meeting. The above statements are from the several meeting records in custody of their appropriate officials.

[2] In *Index to Obituary Notices Published in the Pennsylvania Gazette*, PENNA. MAG., x, 334, the date of this paper is incorrectly given as Feb. 24.

age, and on the Thursday following his remains were deposited in Friends burying-ground at Moores-Town. In every period and station in life, he supported the character of an *honest man,* which secured him the esteem of those who were acquainted with his virtues.—With a tender and benevolent heart, he possessed extensive knowledge and good abilities, which he always cheerfully exerted for the benefit of his fellow-creatures. He endured all the infirmities of old age with christian fortitude and resignation, leaving this world with a well-grounded hope of unfading joys, in a kingdom '*not made with hands, eternal in the Heavens.*'"

His will[1] was dated 4 mo. 13, 1769, and proved at Burlington, April 13, 1775, and the inventory dated 3 mo. 27, 1775. He left his son Thomas five shillings, " having heretofore paid for him more than I could afford." To his son Samuel five shillings, "I having done sufficiently for him already." Also to son Samuel mulatto man Adam. To daughter Rebecca mulatto boy Lott. To daughter Ruth two mulatto boys Noah and Andrew. To son Thomas's two sons William and John mulatto boy Uz. "Whereas Governor William Penn deceased (as I have been very well informed) did promise my deceased Father if he would take up five hundred acres of land within his province he would give him a lott in Philadelphia together with liberty land, and my Father did take up five hundred acres as by the Survey on record may appear and dyed soon after; and the proprietor did honestly and justly lay out a lott accordingly, which I have seen in a plan or map of the City with my Father's name thereon, which said lott and liberty lands which belongeth or appertains to me I give and devise unto my two above said Daughters their heirs and assigns forever to be equally divided between them." (Whether the daughters ever obtained possession of these lots is questionable). He appointed his sons-in-law, Joshua Bispham and Thomas Say, executors. He directed that the persons to whom his slaves were left should teach them to read the holy Scriptures; and that when the slaves reached the age of thirty-five they were to be freed, if they behaved

[1] N. J. Wills, liber 17, folio 153. Burlington files 1773-1777.

well, otherwise to remain in servitude for life. All his residuary estate to be equally divided between his two daughters.

Samuel Atkinson married 7 mo. 12, 1714, at the house of Mahlon Stacy (the bride's brother) under care of Chesterfield Monthly Meeting,[1] Ruth (Stacy) Beakes, (born 1 mo. 30, 1680,[2] died 6 mo 9, 1755,[3] daughter of Mahlon and Rebecca (Ely) Stacy, of "Ballifield," Nottington Township, Burlington County, West Jersey, and widow of William Beakes, also of Nottingham Township. Mahlon Stacy, her father, one of the Lords Proprietors of the Province of West Jersey, (owning one quarter of a tenth), was one of the greatest men of that Province, and through his daughters was ancestor of many of the leading families of Bucks County, Pennsylvania, as Pownall, Kirkbride, Janney, Beakes, etc., as well as of New Jersey. He was of the landed gentry in England, being a Stacy of Ballifield, in Yorkshire, whose pedigree is given in Rev. Joseph Hunter's *History of Hallamshire.* [For further particulars of the Stacy family see Note F.] William Beakes, Ruth Stacy's first husband, was of a Bucks County family quite distinguished in early times; see Note G.

In Woodward & Hageman's History of Burlington & Mercer Counties, facing page 664 is a map of "The Site of Trenton in 1714, copied from Basse's Book of Surveys by

---

[1] List of marriages in Chesterfield Mo. Mtg. published in PENNA. MAG., ix, 349. It ¦has been claimed that in this list sometimes the date of the second declaration has been taken as the date of marriage; but the minutes of the Mo. Mtg. show that the second declaration in this case was 7 mo. 2, so the 12th is no doubt the date of marriage.

[2] Chesterfield Mo. Mtg. register; Burlington Mo. Mtg. gives 7 mo., but Chesterfield is taken to be correct.

[3] Matlack MS. p. 907. In list of burials in Friends Graveyard at Chester Meeting, Moorestown, p. 232, Matlack MS., hers is recorded as 6 mo. 10, 1754, but evidently should be the next year. Matlack's lists of burials, officials, etc. are generally correct, as taken from official lists; some of his biographical data, however, being from hearsay, are frequently wide of the mark.

Chas. R. Hutchinson." This shows Mahlon Stacy's plantation of 800 acres, on the Delaware River and both sides of Assunpink Creek; this is all now within the city of Trenton. Mahlon Stacy called it "Ballifield" from his ancestral home in England. Adjoining this tract on the south, is shown "Ruth Beaks Plantation," also with a frontage on the Delaware, near the bank of which is indicated "R. Beakes House." This is where Samuel and Ruth dwelt after their marriage; it was the 100 acres bought from her step-son, Edmund Beakes, mentioned above. Ruth also inherited large quantities of land from her father and brother, an account of which more properly belongs to a history of the Stacy family; and as such a work is now in preparation, the reader is referred to it for further particulars. [See Note F.]

Samuel and Ruth (Stacy-Beakes) Atkinson had issue, (no meeting records of their births have been found, so their relative ages are uncertain, though Thomas was eldest son; also there may have been others who died young):

21. THOMAS ATKINSON, b.
    Mar. ——, Susannah Shinn.
22. SAMUEL ATKINSON, b. ——, d. Oct. —, 1781.[1]
    Mar. ——, Ann Coate.
23. REBECCA ATKINSON, b. ——, d. ——.
    Mar. 1st, 1 mo. 12, 1739, Thomas Budd, Jr.
         2nd, 10 mo. 3, 1753, Thomas Say, M. D.[2]
24, RUTH ATKINSON, b. ——, d. ——.
    Mar. Feb. —, 1743, Joshua Bispham.[3]

The Atkinsons of New Jersey, p. 32, gives two more children, John and William, but these are shown by Samuel's will to have been grandchildren, sons of Thomas. It also gives Rebecca's first husband as Joshua Wright instead of Thomas Budd, Jr.; it was really her aunt Rebecca Stacy who married Joshua Wright. In *Isaac & Rachel Collins*,

---

[1] Evidence of his will.

[2] See *Life and Writings of Thomas Say*, edited by his son, Phila. 1796. He had been married before.

[3] She was his second wife. See *Memoranda Concerning the Family of Bispham*, by William Bispham, N. Y. 1890.

Appendix, p. 150, Samuel and Ruth are given twelve children; the list seems to be composed of a mixture of the children of Samuel and Ruth, and those of their son Samuel, Jr., with some added not known to belong to either. This book also makes Thomas Budd marry Rebecca (Stacy) Wright, instead of her niece Rebecca Atkinson, as he really did. It has some other errors to be noted in Note F.

12. **William Atkinson, Jr.**, born 9 mo. 18, 1709,[1] in Bristol Township, Bucks County, died 1794 in the City of Philadelphia, son of William and Mary (Hough) Atkinson, lived in early life in the Borough of Bristol, but about 1730 (in which year he came of age) removed to the City of Philadelphia, where he in time established himself as a shipbuilder, thus becoming a pioneer in one of Philadelphia's most famous industries. He purchased several pieces of real estate in the city.

By deed of release[2] dated March 4, 1730, William Atkinson, then of the city of Philadelphia, bought of Philip Syng and Elizabeth his wife, a lot on the south side of Gilbert's Alley, 15 feet wide and 51 feet deep, part of a larger lot which Syng had bought of the executors of Arthur Wells. He disposed of this by his will.

By deed[3] of Nov. 8, 1751, he bought of the heirs of Samuel Fisher, deceased, a house and lot on the west side of Delaware Front Street, 20 ft. 4 in wide and 35 ft. 3½ in deep, part of a larger lot originally granted to Richard Bull; this was bounded on the north partly by his lot already mentioned. He disposed of this also by will.

By deed[4] of April 17, 1752 he bought of John Dumer & Elizabeth his wife a lot (including a dwelling house and other buildings) on the north side of Sassafras Street, 33 feet wide and 51 feet deep, part of a larger lot inherited by said Elizabeth Dumer, from her father, John Furnis. This was not mentioned specifically in his will, but was probably included in his residuary estate, as no record of his previous disposal of it has been found.

On Feb. 18, 1758, he bought[5] of his father's executors, Joseph Atkinson and Rachel Stapler (with her husband Thomas Stapler), the lot in Bristol Borough that his father had purchased from John Borrodaile in 1712. He probably re-conveyed this to his brother Joseph.

[1] Register of Falls Mo. Mtg.
[2] Phila. Deed Book H3, page 357.
[3] " " " " D59, " 400.
[4] " " " " H3, " 337.
[5] Bucks Co. Deed Book 10, p. 55.

The lot on Gilbert's Alley had no house on it at the time he bought it, but he soon erected a brick dwelling which he made his residence the rest of his life. This alley, afterwards called Elfreth's Alley, (from Jeremiah Elfreth who bought the southwest corner of Front Street and the alley), and sometimes Preston's Alley, ran from Front to Second Streets, between and parallel to Mulberry (Arch) and Sassafras (Race) Streets; it is now part of Cherry Street. These small streets or alleys, off Front Street, now entirely given over to warehouses or the poorest class of dwellings, were then all occupied by families in very good circumstances, and with Front Street itself, up to the end of the 18th century, constituted the most exclusive residential locality in the city. William Atkinson was living here when Daniel Stanton and John Pemberton made their visitation to Friends' families in the city, 1757 to 1760;[1] as his son-in-law, Israel Cassell's, name also occurs on their list as living in the same street, he no doubt lived with William Atkinson.

The house on the west side of Front Street (the back of which lot adjoined the back of his home lot), was also, of course, between the present Arch and Race Streets; that and the house on the north side of Sassafras (Race) Street, he apparently purchased for investment only.

By his will[2] dated May 31, 1788, proved Sept. 15, 1794, he left his house and lot on Elfreth's Alley, and the house and lot on Front street, partly adjoining the same, to his grandchildren (the children of his deceased daughter Rebecca Cassell), Sarah, wife of Peter Letelier, Mary, wife of Josiah Paul, Elizabeth, wife of Jeremiah Smith, Lydia Cassell, Arnold Cassell and Rebecca Cassell; and to them also he left all residue of his estate, not specified; James Hartley, of the City of Philadelphia, merchant, was made sole executor.

All his children except Rebecca seem to have died before

[1] See their list of Friends' families visited in PENNA. MAG., vol. xvi.
[2] Phila. Will Book x, p. 112.

him unmarried, or at least without issue. These grandchildren, and their father Israel Cassell, lived with him, the elder ones until marriage, the younger until his death.

William Atkinson, Jr. married 7 mo. 24, 1734, at Phila. Meeting,[1] Sarah Pawley, daughter of George and Mary (Janney) Pawley, of the City of Philadelphia.[2] Mary (Janney) Pawley the mother of Sarah, was Sister of Randle Janney, a wealthy citizen of Philadelphia, connected by his marriage with Frances Righton, of a distinguished Barbadoes family, with many prominent Philadelphia families such as Biddle and Masters (the latter being allied with the Penns); Randle was also a large landholder in Cecil County, Maryland. Another brother, Thomas Janney, was ancestor of a well-known family in Cecil County, and the widow of his son Isaac married Benjamin Hough, nephew of Mary Hough, mother of William Atkinson, Jr. Their father, William Janney, of the parish of Mobberley, Cheshire, England, (whose wife was Deborah Webb, of Inkstrey, Staffordshire), was a first-cousin, of Thomas Janney, Provincial Councillor of Pennsylvania.[3] William and Sarah (Pawley) Atkinson had issue:

(Births from Falls Mo. Mtg. register).

25. MARY ATKINSON, b. 10.1. 1735, d. before 1788, probably unm.
26. REBECCA ATKINSON, b. 6.16. 1737, d. before 1788.
    Mar. 5 mo. 25, 1756, Israel Cassell.[4]

---

[1] Register of Phila. Mo. Mtg.

[2] The Phila. Mo. Mtg. register has: Mary Pawley died 2 mo. 7, 1718, wife of George; George Pawley buried 10 mo. 1, 1721, "not a Friend."

[3] For further particulars see *The Quaker Janneys of Cheshire*, by Miles White, Jr., in *Publications of the Southern History Association*, vol. viii.

[4] Son of Arnold and Lydia (Fordham) Cassell; Lydia being daughter of Benjamin Fordham, of Annapolis, Md. Arnold Cassell was son of Arnold and Susanna (de la Plaine) Cassell, and grandson of Johannes Cassell, one of the leading men in early Germantown, and one of the councilmen (called "committeemen") named in the borough charter,

27. JOSEPH ATKINSON, b. 5.5. 1739, d. 7.13.1747.[1]

28. WILLIAM ATKINSON, b, 3.16. 1741/2, d. before 1788, probably unm.

In some copies of the Falls register in the Hist. Soc. of Penna. library, Rebecca's birth has been miscopied 1734, and in one of them she has been placed at the head of the list on this account, but in the original she appears in the second place where she belongs.

May 31, 1691. His son Arnold married 9 mo. 2, 1693, Susanna de la Plaine, of a noble Huguenot family settled in New York, whose mother was Susanna Cresson, of a similar family, then of New York, now mostly transplanted into Philadelphia; one of their daughters, Veronica, married Isaac Warner, son of John, and grandson of William Warner (I) of Blockley.

[1] Falls Mo. Mtg. register.

(To be continued.)

ATKINSON FAMILIES OF BUCKS COUNTY, PENNSYLVANIA.

BY OLIVER HOUGH.

14. JOSEPH ATKINSON, son of William and Mary (Hough) Atkinson, was born 10 mo. 5, 1716, in the town of Bristol, Bucks County, lived there all his life, and died there in the early part of 1781. He succeeded his father as one of Bristol's leading citizens; besides his activity in public and meeting affairs, he conducted a cooperage business, which in Bristol, as in Philadelphia, has always been a business esteemed fit for well-born men to engage in, and one which has founded the fortunes of many prominent families in both cities. Joseph Atkinson became quite wealthy by it, and purchased considerable real estate in the town.

By deed[1] of Oct. 13, 1747, Joseph Atkinson bought of Samuel Carey of Newtown, and Sarah his wife, a house and lot in Bristol borough (size not mentioned) which had been sold by John Hall and Hannah his wife to Samson Carey and left by him to Samuel Carey.

On 2 mo. (April) 27, 1749, he bought[2] of the executors of Benjamin Harris, the 4 acres in Bristol Township, that his father, William Atkinson, had sold Harris, July 24, 1714. This Joseph sold[3] to John Baldwin on Feb. 6, 1755.

By deed[4] of July 13, 1749, Adam Harker of Middletown Township sold Joseph Atkinson, two lots in Bristol borough, one of 10 acres on Mill Street, the other of 4 acres adjoining, both on the road from Otter's Bridge to Bristol.

As one of his father's executors, Joseph Atkinson joined the other,

---

[1] Bucks Co. Deed Book 10, page 87.
[2] Bucks Co. Deed Book 9, page 276. This deed is not dated, but the receipt is dated as above.
[3] Bucks County Deed Book 9, page 277.
[4] Bucks County Deed Book 10, page 89.

sister Rachel, and her husband Thomas Stapler, in selling[1] their brother William Atkinson, Jr., Feb. 18, 1758, the lot on the north side of Mill Street, Bristol, that their father had bought from John Borradailein 1712.

On August 17, 1759, Anthony Wilson, of Middletown Township, sold[2] Joseph Atkinson a lot wide on south side of Radcliffe Street, Bristol, going back 48 feet to low water mark in the Delaware River, next to Anthony Burton's lot.

On March 26, 1762, the same Anthony Wilson (then of Bristol borough), and Anne his wife, sold[3] Joseph Atkinson two lots in Bristol borough, devised to said Anne by her father, Henry Nelson of Middletown. One of these was the last mentioned.

Joseph Atkinson was elected a Common Councilman of Bristol in 1749 and served until 1755, in which year he was made Second Burgess, which position he held for three years 1755, 1756 and 1757; at the expiration of this time, in 1758, he resumed his place as a Councilman, holding office until 1775, when the Revolution upset the old corporation. He was in office continuously 27 years.

In the affairs of Falls Monthly Meeting he was quite as prominent as his father, his particular meeting being likewise that of Bristol. During Joseph's time it became customary to send regular representatives from the particular to the monthly meeting, though of course, all members were privileged to attend the latter, as before. He first appeared as representative from Bristol Meeting at the Falls Monthly Meeting of 4 mo. 7, 1756, and very frequently afterwards. He was appointed an overseer for Bristol Meeting 1 mo. 7, 1755/6.

Between 1746 and 1766 he served on about 40 committees of Falls Monthly Meeting, and doubtless on a proportionate number during the rest of his life, (the minutes not having been examined on this point after the latter year). Some of these and similar services were:

At a monthly meeting held 11 mo. 1, 1745/6. William Atkinson being the only surviving trustee of the grave ground, it was agreed

---

[1] Bucks Co. Deed Book 10, page 55.
[2] Bucks Co. Deed Book 10, page 202.
[3] Bucks Co. Deed Book 11, page 148.

that the deed be renewed again and placed in trust to Joseph Atkinson and others ; see deed below.

2 mo. 2, 1746. Joseph Atkinson appointed one of the trustees for the bequest of John Large.

9 mo. 1, 1756. The subscriptions of Friends of Makefield toward repairs of Bristol Meeting House put in care of Joseph Atkinson.

3 mo. 7, 1764. Rules of Discipline loaned to Joseph Atkinson for one month.

12 mo. 5, 1764. Joseph Atkinson one of a committee on the proposal to build an addition to the Meeting House.

Besides the trusteeships by appointment of the monthly meeting he was custodian of other money for Friends : John Harker of Moreland Township, Philadelphia County, by will (dated March 7, 1755, proved May 5, 1755)[1] left a sum of money to Thomas Stapler and Joseph Atkinson, of Bristol, Bucks County, in trust for the "Quaker Meeting Houses" at Bristol and "Bybary."

As trustee of real estate of Falls Monthly Meeting he took part in the following transfers :

On May 18, 1738, Joseph Kirkbride, William Blakey, Samuel Bunting, John Hutchinson, Jr., Thomas Marriott, Jr., and Joseph Atkinson, were trustees to whom William Atkinson, survivor of former trustees, conveyed[2] two lots in Bristol borough, one of 4 acres and one of 19 perches at the corner of Market and Wood Streets. By deed[3] of 12 mo. 7, 1774, Joseph Atkinson, sole survivor of the above, conveyed the same premises to Phineas Buckley, Richard Hartshorne, William Bidgood, Jr., James Moon, Jr., John Hutchinson and Joseph Balderston, the new trustees. This was Samuel Carpenter's gift.

On Feb. 1, 1745, (by virtue of the meeting's order quoted above) William Atkinson, survivor of former trustees, conveyed[4] a tract 5 perches square in Falls Township, (John Rowland's gift) to the new trustees Thomas Watson, Joseph Wharton, Edmund Lovett and Joseph Atkinson. By deed[5] of 9 mo. 15, 1773, Thomas Watson being deceased, the three last-mentioned, as survivors, conveyed this lot to

---

[1] Phila. Co. Will Book K, page 292.
[2] Bucks Co. Deed Book 10, page 181 ; recorded 1760.
[3] Bucks Co. Deed Book 17, page 203.
[4] Deed not found on record, but fact recited in deed of 9 mo. 15, 1773, Bucks Co. Deed Book 17, page 213.
[5] Bucks Co. Deed Book 17, page 213.

Mark Watson, Edward Bayley, Jr., Samuel Brown, John Brown, Jr., and Moses Moon.

Joseph's transfer, 12 mo. 7, 1774, as son and heir of William Atkinson, last surviving trustee, of the Janney and Burgess gifts, to new trustees has been mentioned under William Atkinson.

Joseph Atkinson was chosen as a representative from Falls Monthly to Buck's Quarterly Meeting, 3 mo. 7, 1746; 9 mo. 6, 1751, O. S.; 2 mo. 5, 1752, N. S.; and from that time, on an average of at least one quarterly meeting a year, until his death.

By his will,[1] dated 11 mo. 6, 1780, proved May 4, 1781, he left one-third of his estate to his wife Sarah, and the remainder to his children Mary, Elizabeth, Anne, Joseph, Archibald, James and Abigail.

Joseph Atkinson married first, 10 mo. [Dec.] 8, 1743, at Burlington Meeting,[2] Jennet Cowgill, of the City of Burlington, daughter of Edmund Cowgill, then deceased. Joseph had asked Falls Mo. Mtg. 6 mo. 3, 1743, for a certificate to Burlington Mo. Mtg. to accomplish this marriage; it was granted 7 mo. 3.

There were a number of early settlers named Cowgill in Burlington County and Bucks County whose relationship has not been definitely settled. Ellen Cowgill, widow, and "family" (names not given in record), arrived in the "Welcome" with William Penn, and settled in Bucks County. Ralph Cowgill arrived in the "Friends Adventure," 7 mo. 28, 1682 and settled in Bucks County; later he married, first, Sarah, daughter of Randall Blackshaw, of Bucks County, and second, Sarah Pancoast of the town of Burlington; after which he moved to Burlington County. Jane Cowgill, of Neshamina, Bucks County, married 8 mo. 25, 1685, at the house of Nicholas Waln,[3] Stephen Sands, of the same place; among the witnesses was John Cowgill.

[1] Bucks Co. Will Book 4, page 112,
[2] Register of Burlington Mo. Mtg.
[3] Register of Middletown Mo. Mtg.

Jennett Cowgill, married 12 mo. 2, 1687, at Burlington Meeting House,[1] Bernard Lane, both of Burlington; John and Ralph Cowgill, Stephen and Jane Sands among the witnesses. John Cowgill married first 8 mo. 19, 1693, at Neshamina Meeting,[2] Bridget, daughter of Thomas and Agnes (Hathornthwaite) Croasdale, of Neshamina, also "Welcome" passengers; second, 1703, Rachel, widow of Job Bunting, and daughter of Henry Baker; see note D. Edmund Cowgill, of Newtown Township, Bucks County, married 3 mo. 29, 1702, at Middletown Meeting,[3] Catharine Blaker, of said county; (they had a son, Edmund, b. 1. 10. 1702/3, d. 1. 22. 1702/3)[3]; Catharine died 2 mo. 2, 1703[3] and Edmund then moved to Burlington, where, in 1707, he married Ann Osborne[4]; Jennet, wife of Joseph Atkinson was no doubt daughter by this second marriage. As the dates of the marriages of Jane, Jennet, John and Edmund above show they must have been born abroad, they were most likely the children of Ellen Cowgill, widow, of the "Welcome," whose family is stated to have accompanied her, but whose names are not given in the record of arrival. Ralph was probably an older son. This is borne out to some extent by their signing each other's marriage certificates, as mentioned, and it has been proven that Ralph was brother to Jennet Lane, so similar relationship of the rest is reasonably certain.

At Falls Monthly Meeting 3 mo. 2, 1744, a certificate for Jennet Atkinson from Burlington Monthly Meeting, was read and received. She was appointed on committees of Falls, 3 mo. 7, 1746; 8 mo. 5, and 9 mo. 2, 1748; 7 mo. 4, 1751; and 8 mo. 7, 1754. She was appointed an overseer for Bristol Meeting 11 mo. 7, 1753; and on 1 mo. 2, 1760 Ruth Buckley and Sarah Large were appointed overseers in room of Jennet Atkinson, deceased, and Rachel

---

[1] Register of Burlington Mo. Mtg.
[2] Register of Middletown Mo. Mtg.
[3] Register of Middletown Mo. Mtg.
[4] Proposed intentions 8 mo. 6, 1707; minutes of Burlington Mo. Mtg.

Stapler, removed. The latter was Joseph Atkinson's sister Rachel, who had married Thomas Stapler.

Joseph Atkinson married second, April 13, 1762, Sarah Silver[1]; though of a Burlington County family she appeared with Joseph at Falls Monthly Meeting and declared intentions of marriage 3 mo. 3 and 4 mo. 7, 1762. The names of her parents are unknown to the present writer[2]; some of her near relatives moved to Harford County, Maryland, where the family has long been prominent. Sarah Atkinson was appointed on committees of Falls Monthly Meeting 10 mo. 5, and 11 mo. 2, 1768; 4 mo. 6, 5 mo. 4 and 11 mo. 2, 1774.

Joseph Atkinson had issue, (the first three by first wife, and the rest by second):

29. MARY ATKINSON, b. ———. Mar. ——— Watson, before 1787.

30. ELIZABETH ATKINSON, b. ———. Unmar. 1787.

31. ANNE ATKINSON, b. ———. Mar. ——— Shaw, before 1787.

Elizabeth and Anne applied to Falls Mo. Mtg. 5 mo. 1, 1771, for a certificate to Burlington Mo. Mtg. which was granted 8 mo. 7.

32. JOSEPH ATKINSON, b. ———

Mar. 5 mo. 22, 1788, at Plumstead Meeting, Rachel Child,[3] daughter of Isaac, of Abington Township, Montgomery County. Isaac Child, a minister of Friends, was son of Cephas and Mary (*Atkinson*) Child; the latter was of the Christopher and John Atkinson family, which see.

33. ARCHIBALD ATKINSON, b. ———

A Revolutionary Soldier.

---

[1] Minutes of Falls Mo. Mtg. 5 mo. 5, 1762, when the marriage was reported as accomplished on the 13th of the last month.

[2] She was perhaps a cousin of Joseph's first wife Jennet Cowgill. At Chesterfield Mo. Mtg. (Burlington County) 2 mo. 7, 1720, Archibald Silver and Mary Cowgill, daughter of Ralph and Susan, declared intentions of marriage; these were probably Sarah's parents, as she had a son Archibald.

[3] Register of Buckingham Mo. Mtg.

34. JAMES ATKINSON, b. ———
35. ABIGAIL ATKINSON, b. ———

Miscellaneous Notes. Page 68. It was hoped that before these notes went to press, the discovery of Thomas Atkinson's certificate, or at least a record of it on the books of one of the meetings he belonged to in America, would settle the question as to whether it had been issued by Beamsley particular, or Knaresborough Monthly Meeting; but a thorough search of the records of Burlington, Haddonfield (formerly Gloucester), Middletown and Falls Monthly Meetings, as well as those of Bucks Quarter, has failed to disclose it.

Pages 72 and 76. Some explanation of Thomas and Jane Atkinson's change of membership without certificate from Neshamina to Falls Mo. Mtg. in 1686 is found in the minutes of Bucks Quarterly Meeting, 3 mo. 5, 1686: "It being demanded what monthly meeting the middle lot should belong to Edmund Lovet and Thomas Adkinson two members of the said meeting—— Reported that they Enclined to Joyne to the monthly meeting at the falls to wch this meeting assented and it was accordingly agreed that they shold appertaine and joyne with the said meeting at the falls." The "middle lots," among which Thomas Atkinson's plantation was situated, were those between the lots fronting on the Delaware River in Falls and Bristol, and the lots fronting on Neshaminy Creek in Middletown and Bristol, and included lands in all three townships.

NOTE A.

Thomas Atkinson, of the parish of Cartmel, County Lancaster, England, was born, according to statements in his own writings, in 1604; he was therefore much older than the Thomas Atkinson who went from Yorkshire to America, but he lived until after the latter had emigrated, so there is some danger of his being mistaken for the latter, especially as his gospel labors often extended into Yorkshire and Westmoreland, which adjoined his own county. For instance, among epistles recorded in London Yearly Meeting, are some signed by Thomas Atkinson (and others): one from a meeting of Friends of the northern counties held at Scalehouse, 4 mo. 5, 1658; one from a meeting at Skipton, 4 mo. 29, 1658; and one from a meeting at Kendal (Westmoreland) 1 mo. 9, 1661. This Thomas Atkinson, of Lancashire, became quite prominent among Friends and is supposed to have been a minister of their Society, though the writer has seen no actual statement to that effect.

Besse's *Sufferings of Friends* relates several instances of his persecution: Lancashire, 1659. Thomas Atkinson suffered imprisonment for tithes, 5 months. In the same year, "From *John Barrow, Thomas Atkinson, James Taylor,* and *Richard Fell,* Goods were taken by Distresses for Tithes to the Value of 27 *l.* 13 *s.* 2 *d.*" 1668. Thomas Atkinson and others had cattle and sheep taken from them by distress for tithes. 1672. Thomas Atkinson and others suffered by distress of cattle and goods. 1678. Thomas Atkinson lost cattle and goods to the value of £4. Other instances are told in his own writings (see below). *First Publishers of Truth,* (supplement to the *Journal of Friends' Historical Society*) p. 42, has : "And in the year 1674, the sd John Wilkinson, John Burnyeat, John Grave, John Tiffin, Tho Carleton & Tho: Atkinson all had meets at the sd John Nicholson's house ; " this was at Crosfield, a branch of Pardshaw meeting in Cumberland. All such references in Friends' publications seem to refer to the Lancashire Friend, and not to the Yorkshire-Pennsylvania Thomas Atkinson.

He was author of two works mentioned in Joseph Smith's *Catalogue of Friends' Books:*

—The Christian's Testimony against Tythes, In an Account of the great Spoil and Rapine committed by the Bishop of Chester's Tythe-Farmer, at Cartmell, in Lancashire, upon the people there called Quakers, in the years 1677 and 1678. 4 to. Printed in the year 1678.

—An Exhortation to all People. 4 to. No printer's name or place. [1684.] "Writ in the 8th month, in the Year of Christ, 1684. And in the 80th year of my Age. T. Atkinson." A postscript is addressed to "Edward Wilson, *who art a Justice of Peace, within* Westmoreland."

The Christian's Testimony tells that Thomas Preston (the younger), the Bishop of Chester's Tythe-Farmer for the parish of Cartmel, came to a meeting at Height in that parish, 8 mo. 7, 1677, as it was breaking up and called out: "*And where is that* Tho. Atkinson *that old Rogue of all Rogues ?* This and such like was the Language he then used against an ancient grave Person of Seventy three Years of Age." Thomas Atkinson himself figures in other episodes in this book, to which the reader is referred for a full account.

Although apparently no relation to the Yorkshire Thomas Atkinson, it seems very likely that the Lancashire Thomas Atkinson was related to Christopher and John the founders of the other Bucks County Atkinson family, for they lived not far apart in the same county and had a common religion, which was not that of the majority of their neighbors. The parish of Cartmel, in which Thomas Atkinson resided, is thus described in Lewis's *Topographical Dictionary* (5th ed): "CARTMEL (ST MARY), a parish, in the union of ULVERSTONE, hundred of LONSDALE, north of the sands, N. Division of the county palatine of LANCASTER ; containing 4924 inhabitants. The town of

Cartmel stands in the townships of Lower Allithwaite and Upper Holker, 14 miles (N. W. by N.) from Lancaster. The parish is bounded on the south by the bay of Morecambe, into which it extends for a considerable distance, where at low water there is a passage over the sands to Bolton : the longer course over these sands is nine miles; the shorter, over that part called the Leven sands, is four miles." Morecambe Bay divides Lancashire into two entirely unconnected parts, the head of the bay running into the County of Westmoreland. Scotforth, in Lancaster parish, where Christopher and John Atkinson lived, though "south of the sands," i. e. across the bay from Cartmel, was still in the same hundred of Lonsdale, and as the described distances indicate, not so far away but that intercourse between the two places was easy and frequent. Also, Christopher Atkinson's wife, Margaret Fell, lived in Cartmel before marriage, and her father, Christopher Fell, is mentioned in *The Christian's Testimony against Tythes.*

NOTE B.

As a sketch of Richard Hough's life has already been published in this magazine (XVIII, 20–34), it will be necessary to give here only some additional matter and a few corrections. In the list of years he was a Member of Assembly on page 24 of that sketch, the year 1699 was omitted, but it is included further on (p. 26) in the detailed account of his participation in the proceedings of that body.

The statement made on page 23 of the same article, viz.: "Before the Falls Meeting-House, the first in the county, was built, in 1690, his house was one of the meeting places," needs some explanation and may be somewhat expanded : Falls was not the first meeting house in the county, for that at Middletown had been built as early as 4 mo. 7, 1688, on which date a monthly meeting was held there. Falls meeting house was begun in 1689, but as will be seen in some minutes quoted below, was still unfinished in 9 mo. 1691, and some interior work was still to be done as late as 9 mo. 1693, which accounts for meetings being held at private houses as late as the winter of 1694. The minutes of Falls Monthly Meeting (either men's or women's), mention 43 monthly meetings held at Richard Hough's house between (and including) that of 1 mo. 4, 1684/5, and that of 11 mo. 2, 1694 ; perhaps there were some others, when the minutes are silent as to the place of holding. As to the Bucks Quarterly Meeting being held there, we find in Michener's *Early Quakerism*, (p. 75) : "Although the meeting houses at the Falls and at Neshaminy (Middletown) had both been built for several years, yet the Quarterly Meeting continued to be held at the houses of William Biles, Nicholas Waln, Richard Hough, Joshua Hoopes, and others, up to the year 1696." The minutes of Bucks

Quarter mention that the meeting was held at Richard Hough's 6 mo. 5, 1685; 3 mo. 5, 1686; 6 mo. 15, 1688; and 9 mo. 20, 1689.[1]

It is to be presumed that Richard Hough was a representative to the Quarterly Meeting (from Falls Mo. Mtg.) whenever the same was held at his house; the other meetings at which the minutes note his presence were the six dates given below when he was sent to the Yearly Meeting; Falls Monthly minutes only mention his appointment as a representative to the Quarterly 12 mo. 3, 1702, and 12 mo. 7, 1704; no doubt he was one oftener.

In early times each monthly meeting sent a representative to the Yearly Meeting, but when the quarterly meetings became fully organized, they alone sent such delegates. Richard Hough was appointed representative to the Yearly Meeting by Falls Monthly, 7 mo. 1, 1686; and by Bucks Quarter, 6 mo. 25, 1698; 6 mo. 31, 1699 (on which occasion he was chosen to take Quarterly's collections to the Yearly); 6 mo. 10, 1701; 6 mo. 27, 1702; 6 mo. 26, 1703; and 6 mo. 31, 1704.

He was made an overseer of Falls Meeting 2 mo. 2, 1701. On 2 mo. 2, 1690, he was made a trustee for the meeting house and graveyard, and on 9 mo. 8, 1693, it was agreed that the deeds for both be given into his sole custody. On 5 mo. 4, 1705, Hough being deceased these were delivered to Joseph Kirkbride. Between 11 mo. 2, 1683, and 7 mo. 6, 1704, he served on over sixty committees of Falls Monthly Meeting, besides a number of special appointments; some of the important ones were (the dates being those of appointment):

12 mo. 6, 1683. "This meeting doth order that Richard Hough doth keep the Book for Records and record therein all foreign certificates."

1 mo. 7, 1687/8. "Ordered that Richard Hough for the burying place on the hill and that end of the meeting take care to give an account of all Births and Burials." He kept this book until his death. At the meeting of 2 mo. 4, 1705, it was delivered to Joseph Kirkbride. Through a copyist's error transcribing the date, the footnote on page 229 of the present article, makes Richard turn over the book himself, 2 mo. 4, 1704, but in reality it was delivered to Kirkbride a year later, after Hough's death. He was on committees for fencing the burying place on Slate-pit Hill, 1 mo. 3, 1685/6, 7 mo. 6, 1688, and 11 mo. 3, 1693.

On 2 mo. 3, 1689, he was on the committee to select a site for Falls Meeting House, and thereafter served on many committees and special

---

[1] Before 6 mo. 4, 1686, the quarterly meeting was held the same day as that month's monthly meeting; at a combined meeting held that day at William Biles's, it was decided, (it being found inconvenient to transact quarterly and monthly meeting business the same day), in future to hold the quarterly meeting separately on the Fourth-day of the third week in the month.

assignments in relation to its building ; one of the latter being 9 mo. 4, 1691, to speak to the carpenter to get it completed, showing it was then still unfinished (see above). And 6 mo. 2, 1699, he was appointed one of a committee to have an addition built.

4 mo. 3, 1702. On committee to collect an account of all public Friends belonging to Falls Mo. Mtg., that had died since its beginning, to send to Friends in England, to be recorded there.

Margery (Clows) Hough, wife of Richard, was also active in the monthly meeting. She was appointed representative to the Quarterly Meeting 6 mo. 6, 1707 ; 6 mo. 2, 1710 ; and 9 mo. 3, 1713. She was made an overseer of Falls Meeting 7 mo. 4, 1695, and apparently relieved later, for she was again chosen 9 mo. 2, 1720, holding the position at her death ; on 12 mo. 1, 1720, Mary Burroughs was appointed in place of Margery Hough, deceased. She served on 47 committees of the monthly meeting between 7 mo. 6, 1689, and 2 mo. 1, 1719.

Richard and Margery (Clows) Hough had issue (the footnote on page 33 of article *Richard Hough* PENNA. MAG., XVIII, as to births of four of these children, should read Middletown *Monthly* Meeting, not *Quarterly*) :

MARY, married WILLIAM ATKINSON ; see text.

Richard, married, first, 1711/2, *Hester (Baker-Yardley) Browne*, daughter of *Henry Baker* ; see note D ; second, 7 mo. 27, 1717, Deborah Gumley, of Philadelphia, widow of John Gumley, of New Castle County. Richard Hough was a Justice of the Bucks County Court.

SARAH, married ISAAC ATKINSON ; see text.

John, born 7 mo. 18, 1693 ; married 1718, Elizabeth, daughter of Philip and Julianna Taylor, of Oxford Township, Philadelphia. John Hough was a Justice of the Bucks County Court.

Joseph, born 8 mo. 17, 1695, died May 10, 1773 ; married Elizabeth, daughter of Nathaniel and Elizabeth (Dungan) West, and granddaughter of Rev. Thomas Dungan. Joseph and Elizabeth Hough had nine children, of whom their daughter *Sarah*, married *James Radcliffe*, son of *Edward* and *Phebe (Baker) Radcliffe*. Joseph Hough, son of Joseph and Elizabeth, married Mary Tompkins, and their son *Joseph* married *Rebecca Radcliffe*, daughter of John and Rebecca (West) Radcliffe, and granddaughter of *Edward* and *Phebe*. See Notes D and E.

NOTE C.

Leonard Shallcross, by will[1] dated Feb. 28, 1729/30, proved Nov. 16, 1730, left his house and plantation to his son Leonard ; £10 each

---

[1] Bucks Co. Will Book 1, p. 134.

to his sons William and Joseph; £20 each to his daughters Rebecca and Rachel; and one shilling to his son John; and made his wife Sarah sole executrix. No deed has been found on record to show his purchase of the land mentioned, nor how many acres there were, but a mortgage[1] from John Fisher to Samuel Baker, 9 mo. 8, 1713, secured on land in Makefield Township, mentions Leonard Shallcross's land adjoining, and a deed for the Fisher tract in 1722 shows Shallcross still owned the same place.

Very little is known of Leonard Shallcross, especially his early life and birthplace. John Shallcross, Esq., of Frankford, Philadelphia, wrote an account of the family many years ago, from which Rev. S. F. Hotchkin, in his *Bristol Pike*, (Phila., 1893), drew the following (p. 40): "In 1704, John, Leonard and Joseph, brothers, came to America from Derbyshire, England, and settled in Oxford township. The old homestead, a stone dwelling house, was located upon the southeast side of the Bustleton Turnpike Road about two miles above Frankford. The house is still standing, and is occupied by a descendant of the family. In 1708, John Shallcross, the oldest of the the brothers, purchased from Mary Fletcher two tracts of land, containing together about 377 acres, extending from the Bustleton to the Bristol Road. These tracts were divided into several farms, many of which are still occupied by different branches of the family. Joseph, one of the brothers, removed to Chester County and leaves descendants, some of whom are still residing in Delaware and Chester Counties." But there is a complete absence of any contemporary account of their arrival, whence they came, how they came, or any details of their settlement, until John bought the land in Oxford in 1708. And there is at least some ground for question whether the Joseph who went to Chester County was a brother or nephew of John and Leonard. As to their coming from Derbyshire, there can be little doubt that they were younger sons (or sons of a younger son) of the gentle family of Shallcross of Shallcross, in that part of Derbyshire called 'The Peak,' made familiar to the general reader by Sir Walter Scott's novel, *Peveril of the Peak*. In this family, which held the lordship of Shallcross almost, if not quite, as far back as the Conquest, the given name Leonard was a favorite; one of its bearers was head of the family at the time of the Spanish Armada.

John Shallcross married 3 mo. 29, 1710, Hannah Fletcher.[2] In his will[3] dated 6 mo. 13, 1754, proved Sept. 11, 1758, he mentioned his nephews and nieces, Leonard, Joseph, William, Ann, Ruth, Rebecca and Rachel Shallcross, brother-in-law Edward Brooks, sister-in-law

---

[1] Bucks Co. Deed Book 4, p. 200.
[2] Register of Abington Mo. Mtg.
[3] Phila. Co. Will Book L, p. 165.

Catharine Wilmarton, widow of Paul, and kinswoman Hannah Robison; executors, wife Hannah and nephew Leonard Shallcross. The Shallcross nephews and nieces were children of his brother Leonard, except Ann and Ruth, who were wives of nephews. He left his real estate (or part of it) in Oxford Township to the nephew Leonard, who was already living there before his uncle's death. Hannah Shallcross, widow of John, by will [1] dated 10 mo. 25, 1758, proved Sept. 5, 1759, left her property to John, Hannah, Mary, Elizabeth, Paul and Rebecca, children of her kinsman John Wilmartin; Elizabeth, Mary and Edward, children of her cousin Hannah Robison, (daughter of Edward Brooks); and Mary, wife of Joseph Shallcross; she made her cousin Hannah Robison, executrix.

NOTE D.

As the account of Henry Baker mentioned in the text has already appeared in print, space here will only permit a few additions and corrections to that sketch, and a recapitulation of Henry Baker's children, with some second marriages of theirs omitted by Mr. White. In the abstract of his will given there a legacy is mentioned to *Samuel* Canby; this should be cousin *Sarah* Canby, £ 5, "which I lent her mother."

Henry Baker's residence and principal tract in Bucks Co. was about 500 acres on the Delaware River, next below Richard Hough's in Makefield (now Upper Makefield) Township. In an account of Falls Meeting and places within its compass in early times, written about 1855 by Wm. J. Buck and E. D. Buckman, contained in a MS. book called *Friends' Monthly Meeting Records, Bucks County*, now in possession of the Historical Society of Pennsylvania, it is stated that Henry Baker's was the first plantation below the present Taylorsville, and that the old mansion was still standing, the land being then owned by Mahlon K. Taylor. But in a later passage the authors said they believed the Baker mansion had stood on the site of the new house built by Janney Dawes on the Taylorsville lane, at the canal bridge. Baker also owned land in Wrightstown, Newtown and Falls Townships, and was one of the original lot holders in the borough of Bristol. The Upper Makefield and Wrightstown tracts are shown on Holme's Map; the others he bought at a later date.

Henry Baker was foreman of the first grand jury of Bucks County in 1685, and a member of the commission appointed September, 1692, to divide the county into townships. He was made a Justice of the Bucks County Court, by order of the Provincial Council of 11 mo. 2, 1689/90. He was also a Member of the Provincial Assembly in 1685, 1687, 1688,

---

[1] Phila. Co. Will Book L, p. 312.

1690 and 1698. He belonged first to Neshamina (Middletown) and afterwards to Falls Monthly Meeting, and took a very prominent part in their affairs, meetings being sometimes held at his house before the meeting houses were built; he was also a representative in the Quarterly and Yearly Meetings.

Henry Baker had issue by his first wife, Margaret Hardman:

(1). *Rachel*, born in Lancashire, 2 mo. 23, 1669; married first, 4 mo. 27, 1689, at her father's house, Job Bunting of West New Jersey; they were ancestors of the Bucks County branch of the Bunting family. Mr. White's article calls him "Robert," following the Historical Society of Pennsylvania's copy of Middletown Mo. Mtg. register, where the copyist's mistake makes it so; *Penna. Arch.*, 2 ser., vol. IX, pp. 219 & 220, has the same error. Rachel married second, in 1703, John Cowgill, of Middletown Township; see remarks on Cowgill family under 14. JOSEPH ATKINSON. Mr. White's sketch does not mention this second marriage.

(2). *Nathan*, born in Lancashire, 10 mo. 21, 1670; died there 5 mo. 27, 1680, buried 5 mo. 28.

(3). *Sarah*, born in Lancashire, 8 mo. 18, 1672; died in Penna., 2 mo.—, 1715, buried 2 mo. 29. She married first, 8 mo. 13, 1692, Stephen Wilson, of Bucks Co.; their son *John Wilson*, married, 1728, JANE ATKINSON (No. 7 in text), daughter of *Isaac*, (No. 4) and *Sarah* (*Hough*) Atkinson. Sarah (Baker) Wilson married second, 8 mo. 19, 1708, Isaac Milnor, of Bucks Co. She was a minister of Friends and an account of her is given in *The Friend* (Phila.), vol. XXVIII, p. 197.

(4). *Rebecca*, born in Lancashire, 6 mo. 24, 1674, married 1695, John Wilsford, of West New Jersey.

(5). *Samuel*, born in Lancashire, 8 mo. 1, 1676; married in Bucks Co. 9 mo. 4, 1703, Rachel, daughter of Willoughby Warder, of said county. He inherited most of his father's land, including the home plantation on the Delaware River, and made additional purchases. He was a Justice of the Bucks County Court, being first commissioned March 6, 1708; Member of Assembly, 1710 and 1711; and a County Commissioner in 1722. Like his father, he was active in the affairs of Falls Monthly Meeting.

(6). *Phebe*, born in Lancashire, 5 mo. 26, 1678; married first, in Bucks Co., 6 mo. 18, 1703, her step-brother, *Edward Radcliffe*, son of *James* and *Mary*, the latter having married Henry Baker after James Radcliffe's death. It was this Phebe Radcliffe to whom William Atkinson wrote the letter of 1721, quoted from in account of him above. See Note E, where her own and her descendants' connections with the Atkinson, Hough, and other families mentioned in this article, will appear more at length. Phebe married second, in 1722, William Stockdale; he was related by marriage to the other (Christopher and John)

Atkinson family, and some account of him will be given in Part II. Phebe's second marriage is not noted in Mr. White's *Henry Baker*.

(7). *Hester*, born in Lancashire, 6 mo. 28, 1680 ; married first, 1700, Thomas Yardley, son of William and Jane (Heath) Yardley, of Bucks Co. ; second, 1704, William Browne, son of James and Honour Browne, of Chichester, Chester Co. ; third, 1711/2, *Richard Hough*, son of *Richard* and *Margery* (*Clows*) *Hough ;* see Note B.

(8). *Nathan*, born in Lancashire, 1 mo. 8, 1684 (1684/5 ?); married in Penna., May 15, 1705, Sarah, daughter of Jeremiah Collett, of Chester Co. ; they lived in Chester County, and afterwards removed to Maryland.

(9). *Henry*, born in Bucks Co., 12 mo. 12, 1685, died there 12 mo. 16, 1685.

Margaret (Hardman) Baker, first wife of Henry, died in 1688, and was buried 6 mo. 5. He married second, 8 mo. 13, 1692, under care of Middletown Mo. Mtg., *Mary* (*Rawsthorne*) *Radcliffe*, widow of *James Radcliffe*, of Bucks Co. ; see Note E. They had issue :

(10). MARGARET, born in Bucks County, 6 Mo. 4, 1693, died there 6 mo. 20, 1748 ; married 4 mo. 5, 1722, WILLIAM ATKINSON (No. 5), son of *Thomas* and *Jane*.

NOTE E.

A note to *Records of the Hall Family*, PENN. MAG., XI, 315, says : "James Radcliffe, of Chapel Hill, in Rosendale, County Lancaster, England, (probably brother to John Radcliffe, born in 1657, son of Richard and Alice Radcliffe, of Rosendale), married June 1, 1673, the widow Mary Rawthorpe at her own house in Olden ;" etc. From some authorities quoted below it will be seen that James Radcliffe's father was probably *James* not *Richard*, his mother being Alice as stated ; also that the widow Mary *Rawthorpe* should be *Rawsthorne*, and that *Olden* should be *Holden*.

Rossendale (not *Rosendale*) is the territory which formerly comprised the Forest of Rossendale (and sometimes is still so called, although disforested in the reign of Henry VIII). It includes a number of townships, and is within the parish of Whalley, Blackburn Hundred, Lancashire. Thomas Newbigging in his *History of Rossendale* (2nd ed., Rawtenstall, 1893, p. 32) says : "We must view Rossendale as constituting a portion of the Hundred of Blackburn, or Honour of Clitheroe, parcel of the Duchy of Lancaster." Again: "Previous to and at the time of the Norman Conquest, (A. D. 1066), the four forests Pendle, Trawden, Rossendale, and Accrington were embraced in the general name of the 'Forest of Blackburnshire.'" "The forests at that time were not comprised within the limits of any township or other subdivision of property or estate." The *History of the County Palatine and Duchy of*

Lancaster, by Edward Baines, Esq., M. P., (London, 1836), vol. III, p. 274, has: "The chase[1] of Rossendale, including Brandwood, Chope and Lench, originally members of it, contains not less than 25 square miles, or 15,360 statute acres." "In 4 Edw. II it was divided into eleven vaccaries, or cow-pastures." "In 22 Henry VII the number of vaccaries, now called booths, had increased to nineteen." "These booths were the foundations of townships."

The name of Radcliffe has been connected with this region from very early times. In 17 Edw. III (1343) Richard de Radeclyve [Radcliffe,] Master Forester, had a suit with the Abbot and Convent of Whalley, in which it was shown that Thomas, Earl of Lancaster had granted the office of Forester to Richard Mereclesdene, [Marsden,] who in the reign of Edward III had granted his estate in the office to Richard de Radeclyve, whose right was confirmed by Queen Isabella, to whom her son, King Edward III, had granted the forest for life. The "Compotus of Blackburnshire," by Thomas, Lord Stanley, Master Forester and Chief Steward, [Book] A. Edward IV., (4 to, in the office of the Duchy of Lancaster), shows that Jacobo Radcliff de Radcliff paid a rent of £8,10s. for his holding, the Park of Musbury. Chapel Hill, the residence of James Radcliffe before his removal to Pennsylvania, was near to, if not adjoining, the Park of Musbury, and the records of his arrival in the said province state that he came from "Mousebury" or "Musberry." The recurrence of the names Richard and James (Jacobo) in his family strengthens the presumption that he was descended from the Radcliffes who held the Park of Musbury in the time of Edward IV. That no such line of descent has been yet established is most likely due to a lack of any genealogical investigation into the matter, and a careful search of records would very probably show the supposed connection to be a fact.

Chapel Hill, besides being the name of a real hill, was also the name given the freehold tract of land and dwelling, situated on the same, owned by James Radcliffe, and presumably by some generations of his family before him. For a description of this Radcliffe property, as

---

[1] The difference between a forest and a chase has been explained above in the account of the Forest of Knaresborough. Newbigging also says: "A Forest differs from a Chase in three things—in its Laws, its Officers, and in its particular Courts. The king appropriated the Forests for his own special use and pleasure. With Chases and Parks it was otherwise ; these could be constructed under a license, and owned and held by any subject." "The Forests of Lancaster, in which was included the Forest of Rossendale, were * * * exceptions ; for before they became the property of the Crown, they were under the Forest Laws."

well as some mention of the family, we quote from *Rambles Round Rossendale*, by J. Marshall Mather, (1st series, 1888, pub. by J. J. Riley, *Rossendale Free Press* Office, Rawtenstall, and *News* Office, Darwen), pp. 55 et seq. : "Chapel Hill is rightly named, its ecclesiastical associations reaching back to ante-reformation times. It was originally a retreat for a brotherhood of Roman Catholic recluses, who built and inhabited the old farmstead now adjoining the burial ground; and the remains of a piscina, recessed within the crumbling walls a little above the porch, are still to be seen. It is generally supposed that the name 'Chapel Hill' was derived from its associations with the Friends' Meeting House; but this is not so, for amongst the earliest recorded births are those of younger children of James and Alice Radcliff, of 'Chapel Hill.' This at once proves the name as associated with the farmstead prior to the advent of Quakerism." "Quakerism was introduced into Rossendale by William Dewsbury and Thomas Stubbs, about the year 1653." "The first to embrace the message of Dewsbury and Stubbs were Susan Heyworth, widow, and Mary Birtwistle, widow. Following these we find among the earlier names—Henry Birtwistle, Widow Rawsthorne, of Olden (Holden), Jas. Rishton, senr., and Alice Ratcliffe—whose son and daughter, James and Alice Ratcliffe, became prominent members of the sect, Alice being given to much hospitality and entertaining of Friends at her home at Chapel Hill, and her brother James granting the present square of ground on trust to the Society." This ground was that on which the Friends located their meeting-house and burying ground about 1663; an account of these is given by Newbigging, page 220, to which the reader is referred as it is somewhat beyond the scope of this sketch. Quoting again from Mather: "It is also worthy of record that in 1684, James Radcliffe, Henry Crook, Henry Hargreaves, Nicholas Rawsthorne, John Rawsthorne, John Hargreaves, Abraham Heyworth, Richard Mather, William Jackson, and Alice Hargreaves, all of Rossendale Meeting House, were committed prisoners by order of the Quarter Sessions, at Manchester, upon an indictment for being at two peaceable meetings in Musbury and Haslingden."

Besse, in *Sufferings of Friends*, vol. 1, chapter on Lancashire, notices the last-mentioned incident, as well as some previous similar ones: Feb. 17, 1660. Richard, James and Isabel Radcliffe, Mary and Alice Roysteron [no doubt Rawsthorne] were among those apprehended at a meeting at Haslenden, "and kept with a Guard all Night." On the 31st of July, 1670, some Friends met at John Ashton's house were taken without a warrant and kept in the Court house all night and next day taken before Lawrence Rawthorn of Newhall, J. P., and sent to the House of Correction in Manchester; James Radcliffe was one of them. (The Rawsthorne family appears to have been divided on the subject of religion). On January 19, 1684 [1684/5] James Radcliffe and others, [their names are given above in quotation from Mather, this being the same incident], were in prison for meeting; a few days after, they were indicted at Manchester sessions and recommitted to prison. P. 329. 1684. "Some time before this" [last incident, Jan. 19, 1684/5] "two bold Informers came to the House of *Abraham Hayworth* of *Rosindale*, when the Meeting there was breaking up : They went and made Information that *James Ratcliff* preached there, who was not at that Meeting ; however the Justices upon this Evidence fined him 20*l*. for which the Officers broke open five Doors, and took away twelve Kine and an Horse worth 39*l*." Alice Radcliffe had bedding, pewter, etc. taken, worth 15s.

James Radcliffe, born about 1645,[1] was no doubt the son of the James and Alice Radcliffe, the record of whose younger children's births is mentioned by Mather, as above. He became a minister of the Society of Friends. He married June 1, 1673, at the bride's own house in Holden, Mary Rawsthorne, who was that Widow Rawsthorne, of Holden, mentioned by Mather as one of the earliest converts to Quakerism in Rossendale. The Rawsthornes were a prominent, perhaps the most prominent, gentle family in Rossendale. One of them was Edward Rawsthorne of Newhall, one of the six captains who assisted the Countess of Derby in the defense of Lathom House in 1643, and was afterwards made Colonel of infantry by Prince Rupert, dying about 1646. This Edward's mother was daughter of Robert Holden of Holden, which may account for Widow Rawsthorne having property in Holden ; though we do not know at present which of the Rawsthornes was Mary's first husband, nor her maiden name. *Foster's Lancashire Pedigrees* includes one of this family under the name of "Rosthorne, of Penwortham and Hutton," but as it is very incomplete it does not help us on this point. Several of the family joined the Society of Friends.

In 1685, James and Mary Radcliffe, with their four children, removed to Pennsylvania. The *List of Arrivals* kept in that province recorded them as "James Ratclife, Mary Ratclife, Richard Ratclife, Edward Ratclife, Rebecca Ratclife, Rachel Ratclife, free persons from Mousebury in Lancashire." A note in the Historical Society of Pennsylvania's copy of Middletown Monthly Meeting register, apparently taken from the certificate record book, says : "James Radcliffe, of Musberry, in Rosendale, county Lancaster, brought a certificate dated 4 m 18th 1685." Both these names mean the Park of Musbury mentioned above.

---

[1] His widow's account of him says he was imprisoned when about fifteen years old, which was doubtless the occasion in 1660 mentioned by Besse ; which gives us the above date.

They went first to Middletown Township,[1] Bucks County, but very soon removed to Wrightstown (not then organized as a township), where James Radcliffe bought 200 acres of land from James Harrison (though his deed[2] was not made until 12 mo. 10, 1689, and then from Phineas Pemberton, as husband of Phebe, only daughter and heiress of Harrison). This is shown on Holme's Map, on the Neshaminy, between James Harrison's and Herbert Springett's lands. The Minutes of the Board of Property, session 6 mo. 13, 1712, state that a resurvey showed this tract to be 355 acres. Samuel Smith, the historian, writing of Wrightstown Meeting says: "In the year 1686, James Radcliff, a noted public Friend, removed to settle at Wrightstown, near John Chapman's. For the care of these two families, a meeting was held sometimes at their houses, which continued for the most part till about 1690." This statement has been quoted in Michener's *Early Quakerism* (p. 80), and repeated in Davis's *History of Bucks County*, (1st ed., p. 255), and is doubtless correct. Wrightstown Meeting, thus established, was one of the constituents of Middletown Monthly Meeting, to which the Radcliffe's already belonged. James Radcliffe was appointed on committees of Middletown Mo. Mtg. 12 mo. 2, 1687; 1 mo. 1, 1688 [1687/8]; 6 mo. 2, 1688, (two); 11 mo. 2, and 12 mo. 6, 1689.

He died 1 mo. [March] 29, 1690. His widow's "Testimony" concerning him was published by the Yearly Meeting in *A Collection of Memorials*, (Phila., 1787), p. 13. A sketch of his life has also been published in *The Friend*, vol. 27, (Phila., 1854), p. 213. After his death his widow married for her third husband, Henry Baker, as stated in Note D. After Baker's death, about 1701, she seems to have lived awhile in Middletown Township, with her son Edward and daughters Rachel and Rebecca Radcliffe and Margaret Baker, as that is given as Rachel's residence at the time of her marriage, 10 mo. 17, 1702. Very shortly after this she took her two remaining daughters into the town of Bristol to live, and stayed there until her death 3 mo. 13, 1715. On 12 mo. 15, 1704, she joined with her four Radcliffe children in the sale[3] of James Radcliffe's Wrightstown land. James and Mary Radcliffe had issue (all born in England, but births recorded on the Middletown Mo. Mtg. register):

Richard, born 4 mo. [June] 8, 1675; married 1 mo. [March] 31, 1709, in the town of Bristol,[4] Martha Stapler, daughter of Stephen, of

---

[1] Davis's *History of Bucks County*, 1st ed., p. 163, mentions James and Mary Radcliffe and four children as among the early settlers in Middletown Township.

[2] Bucks Co. Deed Book 1, p. 334.

[3] Bucks Co. Deed Book 3, p. 411.

[4] Register of Falls Mo. Mtg.

Philadelphia. They lived in Falls Township. At the session of the Board of Property, 8 mo. 7, 1713, he was granted a lease for 11 years, on about 100 acres in Pennsbury Manor, between Bridge Creek and George Heathcott's. Richard and Martha are not known to have had any children.

Edward, born 8 mo. [Oct.] 14, 1678, died 8 mo. 27, 1714; married 6 mo. 18, 1703, at Fall's Meeting House,[1] *Phebe Baker,* (his step-sister), daughter of Henry and Margaret (Hardman) Baker; see Note D. He had just previously moved from Middletown to Bristol Township and continued all his life. On 10 mo. 18, 1707, he bought[2] of John Cowgill, of Trevose, in Bensalem Township, and Rachel his wife, 200 acres of land in Bristol Tp., 100 of which had been patented to Thomas Dungan, Sr., Oct. 1, 1692, and the other 100 to Clement Dungan, Jan. 7, 1692; these had been sold by Clement, Thomas, Jr., Jeremiah and John Dungan, to Walter Pumphrey, 2 mo. 2, 1698, and by the latter to Job Bunting, 5 mo. 16, 1702; both these tracts have been described under 4. ISAAC ATKINSON above, who owned other portions of the tracts of which these were originally part. *Rachel Cowgill* who was the real seller, as relict and sole executrix of her former husband, Job Bunting, was daughter of *Henry Baker,* and sister-in-law of Edward Radcliffe; her marriages have been mentioned in Note D. Edward and Phebe had two sons: James, who married *Sarah Hough,* daughter of Joseph, and granddaughter of *Richard Hough*; and John, who married Rebecca West, and had among other children, *Rebecca,* who married *Joseph Hough,* son of Joseph, of Joseph, of *Richard*; see Note B.

Rachel, born 2 mo. [April] 16, 1682; married 10 mo. 17, 1702, at Middletown Meeting,[3] William Hayhurst. She was then living in Middletown Township. William was buried 6 mo. 2, 1713, and Rachel 2 mo. 4, 1715.

Rebecca, born 11 mo. [Jan.] 11, 1684/5, died 8 mo. 11, 1714; married 4 mo. 21, 1708, in the town of Bristol,[4] *John Hall,* of that town. Their issue is given in *Records of the Hall Family, of Bristol, Pennsylvania,* PENNA. MAG., XI, 309. John Hall married second, Sarah Baldwin, and third, HANNAH ATKINSON, (No. 11), daughter of *William* (No. 5) and *Mary (Hough) Atkinson.*

NOTE F.

The Stacy family history mentioned in the text is being prepared, under the title *An Historical Narrative and Genealogy of the Ely, Stacy*

---

[1] Register of Falls Mo. Mtg.
[2] Bucks Co. Deed Book 3, p. 406.
[3] Register of Middletown Mo. Mtg.
[4] Register of Falls Mo. Mtg.

and Revell Families, Who Founded Trenton, Province of West Jersey, 1678–1683, by Warren S. Ely, Doylestown, Pa., W. S. Long, M. D., Haddonfield, N. J. and D. B. Ely, Montclair, N. J.

In *Isaac and Rachel Collins*, (Phila., 1893), Appendix, p. 149, a short genealogy of the early generations of the Stacy family is given, the arrangement of which is rather confusing without close study, and in one instance is absolutely incorrect. It begins:

"I.—MAHLON STACY came from England in 1678, and left one son, named Mahlon, who married Sarah Bainbridge.

Issue:

II.—1. Mary Stacy married Reuben Pounal.
II.—2. Sarah Stacy married Joseph Kirkbride."
Etc., etc.

It would at first glance appear that Mary, Sarah, and the other children that follow were issue of Mahlon Stacy, Jr., (who had no children); but the roman numerals indicate correctly they were children of the elder Mahlon. But the third daughter, "II.—3. Rebecca Stacy married Joshua Wright," appears again (p. 150) as "II.—6. Rebecca married Thomas Budd." This is an error; Rebecca (Stacy) Wright married second, Thomas Potts, which marriage is not mentioned; it was her niece Rebecca Atkinson, (III.—5. in the table) who married Thomas Budd. (See list of children of Samuel and Ruth Atkinson in the text above.)

A presumably correct list of Mahlon Stacy's children, with years of their births, is given in some "Stacye Notes," in *The Literary Era*, vol. V, (Phila., 1898), p. 59; the name of the contributor of these notes does not appear, but it was doubtless Thomas Allen Glenn, the editor of the genealogical department of the magazine, who to the present writer's own knowledge, made some researches in England on the Stacy family. These "Stacye Notes" do not give all the marriages of the children; those below have been supplied from authentic sources. This list agrees with that in register of Chesterfield Mo. Mtg. from which the dates of birth below, are taken, except that in the "Stacye Notes" Sarah's birth is given as 1676.

Issue of Mahlon and Rebecca (Ely) Stacy:

1. *John*, b. 9.30. 1671, at Dore-House, Hansworth, Yorkshire, died prior to his father.
2. *Elizabeth*, b. 8.17. 1673, married Abel Janney.
3. *Sarah*, b. 7.4. 1675, married Joseph Kirkbride.
4. *Mary*, b. 4.12. 1677, married Reuben Pownall.
5. RUTH, b. 1.30. 1680, married first, *William Beakes*, see Note G.; second, SAMUEL ATKINSON, (No. 6).
6. *Rebecca*, b. 7.30. 1682, died in infancy.

7. *Rebecca*, b. 4.8. 1684, married first, Joshua Wright; second, Thomas Potts.
8. *Mahlon*, b. 2.7. 1686, married Sarah Bainbridge; died s. p.
The discrepancy in the date of Ruth's birth, between the Chesterfield and Burlington Mo. Mtg. registers, (mentioned in footnote, p. 342), can be accounted for on the supposition that the latter ignored the first Rebecca altogether, but used the month of her birth for her elder sister, Ruth.

NOTE G.[1]

William Beakes, of the parish of Backwell, County Somerset, England, married 3 mo. 12, 1661, at North Somerset Mtg., Mary Wall (or Waln) of Olverstone. (Register of No. Somerset Mo. Mtg.) William was perhaps son of Edmund Beakes, of Portshead in the northern part of Somersetshire, one of the earliest converts to Quakerism in that region, the births (but not William's), marriages and burials of several of whose children appear on the register of North Somerset Monthly Meeting.

William and Mary Beakes, with their son Abraham came to Pennsylvania in the "Bristol Merchant," arriving in the Delaware River, in 12 mo. 1682. Their sons Stephen, Samuel and William also came over, and probably at the same time, but being of age were not included with their parents in the List of Arrivals. William Beakes had by deeds of lease and release, July 26 & 27, 1681, purchased from Wm. Penn 1000 acres of land in Pennsylvania. This land, or part of it, was laid out to him in Bucks County ; Holme's Map shows two tracts on the Delaware River, in that part originally considered to be in Falls Township, but after the official division of 1692 in Makefield. A 300 acre plantation "near the Falls," one of the above, was patented to his heirs and executors, by the Commissioners of Property, 11 mo. 9, 1688. In right of his 1000 acres purchase, he had two lots in the city of Philadelphia, one on Delaware Front St., 20 feet wide, going back 396 ft. to 2nd St., and one on High (Market) St., 26 ft. front and 306 feet deep; the warrant for these was dated 5 mo. 22, 1684; surveyed 9 mo. 1, 1691; return 9 mo. 5 & 10, 1692;[2] they may be seen on Holme's "Portraiture" of the city.

William Beakes was a Member of Assembly of the Province of Pennsylvania, 1684 and 1685; and a Justice of the Bucks County Court, commissioned April 6, 1685. He died 7 mo. 14, 1687, intestate, and

---

[1] For much of the material in this note, especially the English records, I am indebted to Mr. Warren S. Ely, of Doylestown, Pa., a descendant of the first William Beakes.—O. H.

[2] Phila. Exemplification Records, Book 7, page 129.

letters of administration were granted his widow, Mary Beakes, 9 mo. 5, 1687.[1] She died 11 mo. 4, 1696, [Jan. 1695/6].[2] They had issue ; (births of Stephen and Samuel from register of No. Somerset Mo. Mtg.) :

William, b. ———; see below.

Stephen, b. 2 mo. 28, 1665 ; married 8 mo. 31, 1688, Elizabeth, daughter of William Biles. Stephen Beakes was a Member of Assembly, 1697. He bought 203 acres of Lionel Britton,[3] 8 mo. 10, 1688 ; shown on Holme's Map in Britton's name. He made a deed of trust[4] of his property to Samuel Beakes and Phineas Pemberton, for his own use during life and after his decease to the use of his wife Elizabeth, until his son John attained the age of 21 years. After Stephen's death his widow married Matthew Hughes.

Samuel, b. 1 mo. 14, 1666/7 ; married (circ.1694?) Joanna Biles, sister of his brother Stephen's wife. For account of the Biles family, see *William Biles*, by Miles White, Jr., PENNA. MAG,, XXVI, 58–70, 192–206, 348–359. Samuel Beakes was a Member of Assembly, 1705 (*vice* Peter Worrall, dec'd), 1707, 1708, 1709 and 1716/7 (*vice* Thomas Stackhouse, elected 1716, but refused to serve). He was Sheriff of Bucks County 1695–1701. He bought 120 acres of Richard Ridgway,[5] 4 mo. 8, 1691 ; shown on Holme's Map in Ridgway's name.

Abraham, b.———; married Margaret Hoopes, daughter of Joshua and Isabel, of Makefield Township. Joshua Hoopes was one of the leading men in early Bucks County, being a member of Assembly in 1686, '88, '92, '95, '96, '97, 1700, '01, '03, '05, '08, '09, and 1711, but later he moved to Chester County, with which county his descendants have been prominently identified. Abraham Beakes and wife accompanied her family to Chester County, Abraham dying there in 1703, and his widow afterwards marrying John Todhunter.

William Beakes (II), son of William and Mary (Waln) Beakes, was High Sheriff of Bucks County in 1689. He obtained from the other heirs of his father, viz: Mary, widow and administratrix, and Stephen, Samuel and Abraham, sons of William Beakes, deceased, the 300 acre plantation, which the Commissioners of Property had in 1688 patented

---

[1] Bucks Co. Adm'n Book A, vol. 7, p. 33.

[2] Middletown Mo. Mtg. register has the date 11 mo. 4, 1696, which would ordinarily mean January, 1696/7, but the probate of her will shows that in this instance the new year has been used, and that it should be 1695/6. Her will was dated 12 mo. 5, 1694/5 and proved 12 mo. 28, 1695/6.

[3] Bucks Co. Deed Book 1, p. 197.

[4] Bucks Co. Deed Book 3, p. 64.

[5] Bucks Co. Deed Book 1, p. 361.

to them all.[1] On 12 mo. 18, 1689, William Beakes (II) made a deed of trust [2] to John Worrilow of Chester and Walter Worrilow of Philadelphia, for this plantation, "in consideration of a marriage shortly (by God's permission) to be held and solemnized between the said William Beakes and Elizabeth Worrilow daughter of Thomas Worrilow of the County of Chester in this Province and for the future good and advancement of ye sd Elizabeth." William and Elizabeth sold this March 20, 1694, to John Snowden.

William Beakes married first, about 1690, Elizabeth Worrilow, daughter of Thomas, of Chester Co. They lived until about 1694 on the 300 acre plantation in Falls (or Makefield) Township, already mentioned, after which they moved to Burlington County, West Jersey. They had probably already moved when they made the deed to Snowden, as two of the witnesses were Burlington County men, Thomas Lambert and William Emley. On Nov. 26 & 27, 1707, Beakes purchased from William Emley, 100 acres in Nottingham Township, adjoining Mahlon Stacy's land; he lived here the rest of his life, his first wife Elizabeth dying here. By his will March 24, 1710, he devised it to his son Edmund. William and Elizabeth (Worrilow) Beakes had issue; (births from register of Middletown Mo. Mtg.):

William, born 8 mo. 3, 1691, died young.

Edmund, born 8 mo. 3, 1692. Inherited his father's plantation of 100 acres in Nottingham Township, and sold it Nov. 2 & 3, 1713, to his step-mother, Ruth Beakes, as stated under 6. SAMUEL ATKINSON above.

Walter, born 11 mo. 25, 1693/4, died 12 mo. 8, 1702, (register Falls Mo. Mtg.).

William Beakes married second, *Ruth Stacy*, daughter of Mahlon and Rebecca (Ely) Stacy; see note F. They had issue:

Sarah, married 8 mo. 29, 1730, Thomas Potts, Jr., of Mansfield Tp., Burlington Co., son by the first wife, of that Thomas Potts, whose second wife was Rebecca (Stacy) Wright, sister to Sarah's mother; see Note F. Their son, Stacy Potts, was sometime Mayor of Trenton.

Stacy, removed to Bucks County, Pa.; on 8 mo. 12, 1730 his step-father, SAMUEL ATKINSON requested a certificate for him from Haddonfield (Gloucester) Mo. Mtg. to Falls Mo. Mtg. He lived in Makefield Township, and married 2 mo. 19, 1733, at Falls Mtg., Mary Bickerdike, of Falls Tp.

Nathan.

After William Beakes's death, his widow *Ruth*, married 7 mo. 12, 1714, SAMUEL ATKINSON (No. 6), son of *Thomas* and *Jane*.

(To be continued.)

---

[1] Bucks Co. Deed Books 2, pp. 35 and 40.
[2] Bucks Co. Deed Books 1, p. 312, and 2, p. 38.

SHALLCROSS.—In Note C, to my article, "Atkinson Families of Bucks County, Pennsylvania," in THE PENNSYLVANIA MAGAZINE, Vol. XXX, on page 489, occurs the statement that "John Shallcross married Third month 29, 1710, Hannah Fletcher," and a foot-note refers for authority to "Register of Abington Mo. Mtg." The day in this date is an error, and the authority is not the *register* but the *minutes* of Abington Monthly Meeting. I fell into this error by following the copy of some previous abstract (I do not know by whom), which carelessly took the date of the monthly meeting at which the marriage was reported for the date on which the marriage actually took place. After my article was printed it occurred to me to look at the Genealogical Society's abstract of the Abington minutes, when I found this entry to read as follows: "Monthly Meeting held 3mo. 29, 1710: Whereas John Shorecross & Hannah Fletcher having declared their Intentions of Marriage, with each other before two mo : Meetings, Enquiry being made by persons appointed & found clear from all others on ye account of Marriage, did accomplish their marriage in ye Unity of Friends as is signified by their Marriage Certificate." From which it is evident that the marriage had taken place *before* the 29th.

I wish to call attention to the fact that this particular kind of error (*i.e.*, the mistaking the date of declaration of intention or the date of the meeting at which it was reported for the date of the marriage itself) is entirely too frequently encountered in the work of genealogists who have to do with Friends' records, and while I acknowledge my own want of care in not verifying my data before going to press, my error originated in the carelessness of my predecessor in this field, on whose accuracy I had good reason to rely. Where dates of marriage come from the *registers* the date is, of course, the exact date of marriage, but where they are from the *minutes* the exact date is seldom given, but only the dates of monthly meetings at which declarations of intention were made, or at which the committees appointed to oversee the marriages report the same as having been "orderly accomplished." Most investigators in the past appear to have taken either of these dates (and especially the latter) as the actual date of the marriage, with the result that many MS. and printed abstracts of meeting records, and works compiled from them, on the shelves of various historical and similar societies contain a great mass of errors.

In a few instances the committee reporting the marriage to the monthly meeting give the date on which it occurred, as the following: "Middletown (Bucks Co.) Monthly Meeting held 4mo. 4, 1724: Unto this meeting the ffriends appointed to see Thomas Lloyd and Mary Harker's Marriage Decently accomplished Reporte they were Married on the 14th day of last Month," etc. But such instances are rare, the committee generally reporting the event without specifying the date.

OLIVER HOUGH.

ATKINSON FAMILIES OF BUCKS COUNTY, PENNSYLVANIA.[1]

BY OLIVER HOUGH.

PART II.

THE CHRISTOPHER AND JOHN ATKINSON FAMILY.

[For much of the following, concerning Christopher and John Atkinson themselves, and their father, William Atkinson, I am indebted to Charles Francis Jenkins, Esq., one of their descendants, who very generously put at my disposal material he had collected and arranged; the following extract of his letter to me under date of 9 mo. 29, 1904, on this subject, will explain itself: "I have your letter of September 28th, and will be entirely willing to let you have all my Atkinson matter, which along the lines of John and Christopher is almost complete. I had intended publishing it in book form, but seemed never to find time to get it arranged. If you care to have the material and increase it with your investigation, I have no objections and will be glad to let you have it. It is practically ready to put in the printer's hands." I shall quote frequently below from Mr. Jenkins' manuscript. O. H.]

1. WILLIAM ATKINSON, SENIOR, father of *Christopher* and *John.* Mr. Jenkins begins: "Among the group of listeners to the words of an early Quaker preacher one First day in 1660 was William Atkinson of Scotford. Swarthmore Hall the home of Margaret Fell and of Geo. Fox where this unlawful 'conventicle' was being held is sixteen miles or more from the old town of Lancaster, the county seat of Lancashire. The distance is much less when the tide of the

---

[1] *Correction to Part I.* On page 482, (vol. xxx), fifth line from bottom, *Sarah* Pancoast, second wife of Ralph Cowgill, should be *Susannah.* Register Burlington Mo. Mtg.

shallow bay is out for then the road stretches across the shining sands with a gently winding course avoiding here and there the deeper depressions which the retreating tide has turned into shallow pools. A few hours later the rushing waters have covered the road and greatly lengthened the path of the traveler from Lancaster to Swarthmore."

On this particular day [1] we know the names of many who were gathered in this earnest company for before they had dispersed they were arrested and carried off to Lancaster castle for ' unlawful conventicle.' Let us hope the tide was out and that the little band of prisoners was able to take the shorter road across the hard and level sands.

How long William Atkinson was confined within the high wall of Lancaster castle Besse's *Sufferings of Friends* does not say. This gray pile was once the stronghold of John of Gaunt whose storm-worn effigy still sits grimly over the entrance way." Besides this imprisonment Besse mentions that in 1685 William Atkinson and Nathan Kennedy "for nine weeks absence from the national worship," had goods taken from them to the value of £3,5s.,6d.

Mr. Jenkins continues with a description of the village where William Atkinson lived, called indiscriminately Scotford or Scotforth, but which he says was no doubt anciently Scotford, i. e. the Scot's ford for it is on the high road to Scotland : " Scotforth, the home of William Atkinson is a little cross roads village nearly two miles south of the city of Lancaster, on the high road connecting the northwest of England with the south. The houses are low and small, built of dark gray stone and mostly lacking the setting of flowers and climbing vines and roses which make attractive even the humblest cottage in many parts of rural England. To the east of the village are the rising lands and hills and from the hillside nearby the gray roofs of the hamlet seem to nestle down among the green trees in the valley, while at one side runs a little stream winding its way across the intervening flats and at low tide across the sands to mingle

[1] The day was Jan. 24, 1660/1. (Besse.)

with the waters of Morecambe Bay. To the north the tall, smoking chimney stacks on the outskirts of Lancaster pierce the horizon."

This, of course, is a modern description, and was written by Mr. Jenkins from personal observation, he having made a trip to Scotforth a few years ago when he was collecting his Atkinson notes. Samuel Lewis's *Typographical Dictionary of England*, (3 ed., Lond. 1838) describes it:

" SCOTFORTH, a township, in that part of the parish of LANCASTER which is in the hundred of LONSDALE, south of the sands, county palatine of LANCASTER, 1½ mile (s.) from Lancaster, containing 557 inhabitants." As to the parish Lewis says :

" LANCASTER (*ST. MARY*), a parish, comprising the borough, port and market town of Lancaster, having separate jurisdiction, and several chapelries and townships, partly in the hundred of LONSDALE, south of the sands, and partly in the hundred of AMOUNDERNESS, county palatine of LANCASTER." The *History of the County Palatine and Duchy of Lancaster*, by Edward Baines, Esq., M. P. (London, 1836), says, (vol. iv, p. 474) : " The hundred of Lonsdale is formed into two districts, called North and South Lonsdale, the vast expanse of sands, constituting the upper portion of the bay of Morecambe, forming the broad boundary line between the two, and imparting to each the appellation of Lonsdale North of the Sands, and Lonsdale South of the Sands. This hundred is comprehended in twenty-one parishes ; of which nine are to the north of the Sands, in the district called Furness, and twelve to the south of the Sands." As we see by Lewis's description above, Lancaster parish is not all in one hundred, (although that part we are concerned with is all in Lonsdale Hundred), nor is it even all contiguous territory. Baines says of it (iv, 482) : " The parish of Lancaster comprises so many detached and distant parts, that it is not possible to describe its boundaries." . . . . " The length of the chief trunk of the parish, if it may be so called, is upwards of ten miles, from north ot south, and the breadth about nine, from west to east. The next considerable portion, consisting of Stalmine with Stainall, and Preesall with Hackensall, in the hundred of Amounderness, is about four miles by one and a half, and in some places two miles. The total number of statute acres in the parish appears to be about 68,084."

Of William Atkinson's station in life it may be said that he was of the upper yeoman class, for he was a freehold landowner, though on too small a scale for him to have claimed gentility; and while we have no knowledge at all of his ancestors, it is safe to assume that their station was the same, for at that time families in this position almost invariable remained in the same state generation after generation. Besides in William's time there were many Atkinsons in exactly similar station in the Hundred of Lonsdale, both in Lancaster parish, and in the neighboring one (that is across Morecambe Bay) of Cartmel. We have given an account of one of these, Thomas Atkinson, the preacher, in Note A, to Part I; in his book there mentioned, *The Christian's Testimony against Tythes*, he speaks of a number of such Atkinsons in Cartmel; while Besse's *Sufferings of Friends*, in the chapter on Lancashire, mentions various others.[1] William Atkinson's freehold landownership is shown by the will of his son William, as will be seen later, as well as by his own, which, Mr. Jenkins says, "you will find in the records of the Archdeanery of Richmond, deposited at Somerset House, London. The inventory of the estate was taken

[1] "There was in Scotforth about this time a Robert Atkinson, who may have been a brother of the elder William Atkinson. His will was dated June 28, 1668. His property was valued at £117, consisting mainly of amounts due him from his neighbors. Included among these was £3.12s. due him by William Atkinson, which Robert in his will gave to William. The will also mentions Ann Sasson a 'sister,' also his nephew Sasson. On February 17, 1660 Robert Atkinson was arrested, with twenty-four others, at the house of John Hartley at Trawden 'where they had assembled to worship God, by the High Constable and soldiers, and for refusing to take the oaths committed to Lancaster gaol, where they lay above five weeks.' *Besse's Sufferings*." (Jenkins.) The date was Feb. 10, 1660/1. He was again imprisoned in October. 1687. (Besse.)

Sept. 17, 1679," but he gives no further particulars except to say: "His modest estate amounted to but £68 and included a drove of thirty two sheep." Of course, it is needless to remark that this amount, (and those named in the footnote also), had a value then of many times the same sum now.

William Atkinson's wife was named Ann, but her family name is unknown, as the meeting records do not go back to the time of their marriage;[1] it was perhaps Holme, as her son William, in his will mentions his "uncle Thomas Holme," but Holme might have been an uncle by marriage. William Atkinson died in 1679, and was buried 10 mo. [Dec.] 10, of that year, in Lancaster meeting house yard. William and Ann Atkinson had issue:

2. WILLIAM ATKINSON, JUNIOR, of Scotford, eldest son, b. ——, d. unmarried, 1679/80 and was buried 11 mo. [Jan.] 14, in Lancaster meeting house yard.[2] Mr. Jenkins says: "Within a few weeks after the death of William Atkinson his oldest son William to whom he had left the disposition of his estate died also. William Atkinson, the younger, directed in his will that his body should be buried in Friends' burying place belonging to Lancaster meeting and he further gave ten pounds to 'such poor people as are in scorne called Quakers.' The little holdings in Scotford which had come to him from his father were all given to his brother Christopher, the next oldest son. He describes the property as 'those severall p'cells lying and being within the libertyis of Scotford and knowne by the names of Heron's Shreason, Cookstooll, Steell End and Great Acre all contayning by Estimacon six Acres and a halfe' and also the half of one acre 'on the backside of the same' which belonged to Christopher Atkinson but which was evidently not entirely paid for. The house where William lived, which was called Beckside, also in Scotford, was given to his brother John. After making provision for his mother, Ann, and numerous small legacies to relatives[3] and friends and after giving 'twoe of my best sheepe' to 'little John Padgett (sonne of Francis Padgett),' he appointed his brother John his executor." This

---

[1] "An Anne Atkinson of Scotforth (probably widow of William) married 6 mo. 23, 1681 at Lancaster meeting house John Townson of Radcliffe. *Lancaster Monthly Meeting records.*" (Jenkins.)

[2] Register Lancaster Mo. Mtg.

[3] "The other relatives not already named were, 'My uncle Thomas Holme' and five [ten] shilling apiece to 'All my uncles and aunts.'" (Jenkins.)

will was dated Dec. 22, 1679 and proved Feb. 11, 1679, (1679/80), in the Archdeanery of Richmond.
3. CHRISTOPHER ATKINSON, b. —— , d. July —, 1699. Mar. 8 mo. 8, 1679, Margaret Fell.
4. JOHN ATKINSON, b. —— , d. 1699. Mar. 2 mo. 8, 1686, Susannah Hynde.

3. CHRISTOPHER ATKINSON, son of William and Ann, was born no doubt at Scotford, and probably about 1657, but no record of his birth has been found. He lived in Scotford until 1699, in which year, shortly after the middle of May, he, with his wife and children, accompanied by his brother John and family, and some sisters-in-law of John's, embarked on the ship *Britannia*, from Liverpool, for Pennsylvania. There was much sickness on this ship, and in the month of July Christopher Atkinson died. Mr. Jenkins says of this voyage: "The 'Brittania' reached Philadelphia the 24th of Sixth Month (August) 1699, and immediately the Friends of Philadelphia and of the nearby meetings addressed themselves to the nursing of the sick and the care and oversight of the widows and orphans. In many families the sorrowful voyage is still traditionally remembered, and the 'Brittania' is recalled as 'The Sick Ship.' One-fifth of those who had so hopefully set out for the new world had found a grave in the ocean's deep. It would be difficult to fully realize the state of mind of the Widow Margaret, landing in a strange land with so many dependent on her and having undergone so many and so severe trials. Her sorrows however were not yet at an end, for during her stay in Philadelphia, her only son, William, together with Thomas Procter, a servant, was drowned."

Christopher Atkinson was a member of the Society of Friends[1] and had obtained a certificate of removal for himself and family dated 2 mo [April] 3, 1699, from Lancaster Monthly Meeting addressed to Friends in Pennsylvania;[2] this, his widow, Margaret Atkinson, presented to

[1] See Note A for another Christopher Atkinson, a member of the Society of Friends.
[2] See footnote under John Atkinson, below.

Neshamina (afterwards Middletown) Monthly Meeting in Bucks County, Pennsylvania, on 9 mo. [Nov.] 2, 1699. On that date Margaret Atkinson presented three certificates to that meeting, one as above, one for the children of her husband's brother John, (both he and his wife having also died on the voyage), and the third possibly for John Atkinson's sisters-in-law Mary and Alice Hynde though the minutes of the meeting do not specify as to that.

Christopher Atkinson made his will on board the *Britannia;* it was dated July 1, 1699, and proved Sept. 6, 1699, after the vessel's arrival in Philadelphia;[1] in it he described himself as "late of Scotforth in County of Lancashire, husbandman." He left half of his 1000 acres of land to his only son, William, and the remaining 500 to his wife, Margaret, to enable her to bring up their other children, Hannah, Margaret, Isabel and "ye child unborn." He also left her £40 in money, twenty to be paid out of his effects on board the *Britannia,* and twenty out of property, which, he says, "I left in England." All residue of his personal estate in England or elsewhere to be equally divided between his wife and children, William, Margaret, Hannah, Isabel and child unborn. His wife Margaret was made sole executrix. The inventory made in September estimated his personal estate at £209, a considerable sum as estates went in Pennsylvania before 1700. The will shows which of their children were living and accompanied them on the voyage. Besides those named in the will they had three others, Alice, Deborah and Joseph; we have a record of Deborah's death in Lancashire in 1690, long before they started; if Alice and Joseph lived to embark with their parents, they must have both died very early on the voyage, before July 1, the date of the will, but no doubt both had died before 1699. Of the children mentioned in the will, William and Hannah both died in 1699, the former in September and the latter in October, while "ye child unborn" either

---

[1] Phila. Co. Will Book A, p. 472.

remained unborn or died in infancy, as it does not appear in the settlement of the estate.

By deeds of lease and release dated March 17 & 18, 1698, (1698/9?)[1] William Penn conveyed to Christopher and John Atkinson, of Scotforth, Co. Lancaster, England, 1500 acres, "clear of Indian encumbrances," between the Rivers Susquehanna and Delaware, in the Province of Pennsylvania. Of this 1000 acres was Christopher's and 500 John's. After Christopher's death and his widow's arrival in Pennsylvania, she proceeded to have her husband's land laid out, and obtained a warrant dated 3 mo. 17, 1700, for the 1000 acres to be surveyed in Buckingham Township, Bucks County. In the *List of "Old Rights,"* in Penna. Arch. 3 ser., vol. III, page 54, under Bucks County, occurs: 20. Margaret Atkinson, return for 500 acres, dated 7 mo. 6, 1700.

On 4 mo. 8, 1702,[2] Margaret Atkinson, of "Bellemont," in Bensalem Township widow, relict and executrix of Christopher Atkinson, sold Joseph Gilbert, of "Weskickels," also in Bensalem Township, 500 acres, 73 perches in Buckingham Township, part of 1500 acres granted to Christopher Atkinson,[3] by William Penn, by deeds of lease and release, dated March 17 & 18, 1698, and laid out to Margaret Atkinson by warrant of 3 mo. 17, 1700. At the session of the Board of Property[4] held 2 mo. 3, 1704, it was stated that the Proprietary by warrant dated 3 mo. 17, [1700], had granted Margaret Atkinson in right of her late husband Christopher Atkinson 500 acres which were surveyed 6 mo. 23 following, and that Margaret as executrix of her husband, by deed of 4 mo. 8, 1702, had granted the same to Joseph Gilbert, of Bensalem, who requested a patent. The patent was ordered for him with special restriction to be in right only of Christopher and John Atkinson of 1500 acres, reference being made to the patent to William Atkinson [John's son] dated 8 mo. 12, 1702. Joseph Gilbert, by his will dated April 15, 1707, devised his whole estate after his wife's death, half to his son Thomas, and half to his daughters Sarah and Mary. And by deed[5] of Nov. 22, 1715, Margaret Hillborn, of Newtown, widow, and Isabel Atkinson, of Newtown, spinster, daughters and co-heiresses of Christopher Atkinson, confirmed the said 500 acres, 73 perches to Thomas Gilbert, Sarah Stackhouse, (wife of Benjamin), and Mary Gilbert. This tract is shown on Cutler's survey (1703) map of Buckingham Township,[6] under the name of "Margaret Atkinson now Jos. Gilbert."

By deed[7] of 1 mo. 8, 1702/3, Margaret Atkinson, then of "Bellemont," sold the other 500 acres of her husband's land to William Cooper, of Buckingham Township. The deed states that it was in right

---

[1] Phila. Co. Deed Book F vol. 6, p. 127.
[2] Bucks Co. Deed Book 3, p. 82.
[3] This should have read "part of 1000 acres, Christopher Atkinson's share in 1500 acres granted to Christopher and John Atkinson," etc.
[4] Penna. Arch., 2 ser., XIX, 422.
[5] Phila. Co. Deed Book G 9, p. 91.
[6] Reprinted in Davis's *History of Bucks Co.*, 1st ed., p. 267.
[7] Bucks Co. Deed Book 8, p. 200.

of Christopher and John Atkinson, purchasers from William Penn, that Christopher had left his wife Margaret 500 acres by will dated July 1, 1699, and that it was laid to the said Cooper 6 mo. 25, 1700, under warrant of 3 mo. 17, 1700 ; (Margaret Atkinson must therefore have sold Cooper the warrant before this deed was made ; a not unusual procedure). This tract is shown on the Cutler survey map of 1708 above mentioned, in Buckingham Township, in the name of "Wm. Couper." William Cooper by will[1] dated 11 mo. 30, 1709. [Jan. 30, 1709/10], proved Feb. 17, 1709/10, left the greater part of this in a somewhat indefinite manner to his son Joseph (who died 7 mo. 14, 1712), and directed some to be sold. Part of it seems to have come back in some manner to the heirs of Christopher Atkinson, for on Sept. 27, 1739, Samuel Hillborn, (son of Margaret, daughter of Christopher Atkinson), and Abigail his wife, conveyed 150 acres of the same tract to David Dawes.[2]

Christopher Atkinson married[3] 8 mo. [Oct.] 8, 1679, at Height, in the parish of Cartmel, Lancashire, Margaret Fell, daughter of Christopher Fell, of Newton in Cartmel.[4] Her father was a member of the Society of Friends, who suffered persecution for his religion, as mentioned in Thomas Atkinson's *The Christian's Testimony against Tythes*. Christopher Fell, of Tarnegreen, died 12 mo. 2, 1705, [Feb. 2, 1705/6], and was buried 12 mo. 6 at Height.[5] Though we have not been able to exactly locate Tarnegreen, it was surely in the same locality as Height and Newton, perhaps the name of a small estate, and there can be little doubt that this Christopher Fell was father of Margaret (Fell) Atkinson. Newton and Height were in the Township of Upper Allithwaite; Baines (*History of the County Palatine and Duchy of Lancaster*, 1836, iv, 785) says: "At a place called Height, above the village of Newton, is a Friend's meeting-house, coeval with the establishment of that body in North Lonsdale." Neither of these places is of sufficient importance to be described in Lewis's *Typographical Dictionary*.

[1] Phila. Co. Will Book C, p. 195.
[2] Recited in deed of 1 mo. 25, 1742, Dawes to Kinsey, Bucks Co. Deed Book 27, p. 296.
[3] Register of Lancaster Mo. Mtg.
[4] For some account of the parish of Cartmel, see Note A to Part I.
[5] Register of Lancaster Mo. Mtg.

Christopher and Margaret (Fell) Atkinson had issue, all born in Lancashire, and probably all at Scotford, (births of 5, 7, 8 and 9 from register of Lancaster Mo. Mtg.):

5. ALICE ATKINSON, b. 4 mo. 28, 1680; probably died young, before her parents started for America, as she is not mentioned in her father's will, July 1, 1699.

6. DEBORAH ATKINSON, b. ———, d. 1690, bur. 9 mo. 24.[1]

7. HANNAH ATKINSON, b. 8 mo. 1, 1685, d. 8 mo, 9, 1699,[2] She survived the voyage which proved fatal to so many of her relatives, only to die shortly after her arrival in Philadelphia, or just after reaching Bucks County.

8. JOSEPH ATKINSON, b. 12 mo. 22, 1687, died young, before his parents embarked for Pennsylvania.

9. MARGARET ATKINSON, b. 5 mo. 7, 1691, d———. She accompanied her parents to Pennsylvania, living there with her mother, first at "Bellemont," in Bensalem Township, Bucks County, and afterwards in Newtown, until her marriage. She and her sister Isabel were the final surviving co-heiresses to their father's estate; their deed of confirmation of the sale of the 500 acres, 73 perches to the Gilbert heirs, on Nov. 22, 1715, has been mentioned above.

She married[3] first, 9 mo. 8, 1711, at the house of Stephen Twining, in Newtown Township, Samuel Hillborn, son of Thomas and Elizabeth Hillborn, of Newtown Township. They had only one child, a son, Samuel Hillborn, (born 6 mo. 13, 1714)[3] who married in 1736, Abigail Twining, daughter of Stephen and Margaret (Mitchell) Twining, of Newtown Township, and granddaughter of the Stephen Twining, at whose house her husband's parents were married. Samuel Hillborn, Sr. died in 1714 and was buried 10 mo. 15[3]. "The death of Margaret Hillborn's husband about this time and the fact that her sister-in-law, Elizabeth Hillborn, had married another Aston settler, Abraham Darlinton, no doubt induced her to follow her sister Isabel to Chester County. In the fall of 1717 Margaret Hillborn, Isabel Carter and Elizabeth Darlington applied for certificates of membership from Middletown Meeting. A committee of the meeting was appointed to assist Margaret in settling her affairs " (Jenkins.)

Margaret (Atkinson) Hillborn, then of Aston Township, Chester (now Delaware) County, married second, 2 mo. 10, 1718, at Gwynedd Meeting-house,[4] John Jones, a widower, of Gwynedd Township, Philadelphia (now Montgomery) County. At the Gwynedd Monthly Meeting held 12 mo. 25, 1717, [Feb. 25, 1717/8], John Jones requested a certificate to Chester [Mo. Mtg.] in order to marry Margaret Hillborn; this was signed for him 1 mo. [March] 25, 1718. At the women's meeting held 4 mo. 24, 1718, "Margaret Jones having Produced a

---

[1] Register of Lancaster Mo. Mtg.

[2] Register of Middletown Mo. Mtg.

[3] Register of Middletown Mo. Mtg,

[4] Register of Chester Mo. Mtg.; there is no record of this marriage in the register of Gwynedd Mo. Mtg., though it took place at one of the latter's constituent meetings.

Certificate from Province[1] Monthly Meeting relating to her Life and conversation which was Read att this Meeting approved of and order⁴ to be recorded." (Minutes of Gwynedd Mo. Mtg.)

10. WILLIAM ATKINSON, b. ———, d. 7 mo. [Sept.]—, 1699, buried 7 mo. 80.[2] He was drowned in Philadelphia, about a month after his arrival there; Thomas Procter, a servant, being drowned at the same time. The 500 acres his father had left him, being not then laid out, was inherited by his mother and sisters.

11. ISABEL ATKINSON, b. ———, d. Co-heiress, with her sister Margaret, to her father's estate. Probably born about 1695.[3] Accompanied her parents on the voyage to Pennsylvania, and on arriving there lived with her mother at "Bellemont" and in Newtown, Bucks Co., until her marriage. She married 8 mo. [May] —, 1716,[4] John Carter, of Aston Township, Chester (now Delaware) County, son of Robert and Lydia (Walley) Carter, and grandson of Edward Carter, formerly of Aston, in the parish of Bampton, Oxfordshire, England, who had settled in Aston Township, Chester County, Pennsylvania. Isabel had a certificate from Middletown Mo. Mtg., which she presented to Chester Mo. Mtg., 10 mo. 30, 1717. John Carter died in June, 1760. His father Robert Carter, was a member of the Pennsylvania Assembly 1698, 1699 and 1703, and his grandfather, Edward Carter, 1688. John and Isabel had 6 or 7 children.

The *Britannia* arrived in Philadelphia in August, 1699, and after staying a little over a month in that city, Margaret Atkinson, early in October, took her surviving children, Margaret and Isabel, and perhaps Hannah, (who died Oct.

[1] Providence, one of the particular meetings constituting Chester Mo. Mtg., and which name was sometimes applied to the monthly meeting.

[2] "Records of Philadelphia Monthly Meeting." (Jenkins.)

[3] In view of the fact that she married a Chester Countian in 1716, it is quite a coincidence that an Isabel Atkinson, 21 years old, was baptized Dec. 23, 1716, at Holy Trinity (Old Swedes') Church, in New Castle County, now in the city of Wilminington, Delaware. (*The Records of Holy Trinity (Old Swedes) Church, Wilmington, Delaware*, p. 234; published by the Historical Society of Delaware, Wilm., 1890.) This could hardly be Isabel daughter of Christopher, though the age fits very well, for she had been married the previous May, and in the following year obtained a certificate of membership with Friends from Middletown Monthly Meeting, in Bucks Co. There was, moreover, an Atkinson family in New Castle Co., of which Sampson Atkinson died interstate and letters of administration were granted Ann Atkinson, widow, at Philadelphia, May 6, 1703; also Sarah Atkinson and John Butcher were married Aug. 15, 1722, at Swedes' Ch., Wilmington. (*Records*, as above, p. 270.)

[4] They "passed second meeting" 3 mo. 3, 1716, and on 4 mo. 7, the marriage was reported as having been "orderly accomplished." (Minutes of Middletown Mo. Mtg.)

9, either in Philadelphia or just after their arrival in Bucks County), to Bucks County, and took up her residence on the plantation called "Bellemont" in Bensalem Township. Mr. Jenkins says: "Belmont was the name of a ridge crossing the northern corner of Bensalem township and running down the Neshaminy. It was also given in later years, perhaps even at that date, to a portion of the large estate of 1250 acres covering the northern portion of the township originally belonging to Joseph Growdon." A large part of the Growdon estate as well as that of John Tatham adjoining it, was, about the time Margaret Atkinson settled there, in possession of Thomas Revell, of West Jersey, either as owner himself or as attorney for others. On Jan. 20, 1701/2, Revell sold 1000 acres, and on March 16, 1702/3, 2500 acres, on the south and southwest banks of the Neshaminy, to Thomas Stevenson, Jr., of Long Island. "Bellemont" was included in one, or perhaps partly in each, of these tracts. As Margaret made no purchase of land here, she doubtless rented the plantation, or the house alone, from Revell. Thomas Stackhouse, Sr., a childless widower, who had a plantation on the other side of, and further up Neshaminy Creek, came to board with her. The minutes of Middletown Monthly Meeting in 1701 mention his living at "Widow Atkinson's," and on 3 mo. 1 of that year he appeared and "condemned his actions contrary to truth," beginning as follows: "Whereas there hath been some concern between Margaret Atkinson and I relating to marriage & some reports have passed of my behavior towards her whereby truth might suffer," etc. These reports appear to have been without proper justification and the circumstance is only introduced here on account of its bearing on Margaret's residence. The judgment of the meeting was that he should not "make her house his place of abode to be at constantly;" but on 9 mo. 6, 1701, it was reported to the meeting that he was still living there. They finally declared their intentions of marriage to the meeting 12 mo. [Feb.] 4, 1702/3, committees were appointed to see that they were "clear" and to secure her children's estate, and they were married in March, 1702/3.¹ They had no issue. For some account of Thomas Stackhouse, Sr., see Note B.

After Thomas Stackhouse's death Margaret married third, March, 1708/9, John Frost, a prominent man of Newtown. They "passed meeting" the second time March, 3, 1708/9, and were married within themonth.¹ John Frost was a member of the Provincial Assembly in 1712 and 1715. He was one of three trustees to whom the "Newtown Common" was patented August 16, 1716, for the use of the inhabitants of the township. Frost Lane, the upper or northeast boundary of the borough of Newtown, was named for him. Margaret Frost (previously wife of Christopher Atkinson), died in 1714, O. S., and was buried 1 mo. 19, [March, 1715, N. S.]² John Frost died in 1716, and was buried 8 mo. [Oct.] 25, "in Friends' ground at Chester."² He was probably on a visit to his stepdaughter, Isabel Carter, at the time, or perhaps had gone to live with her after his wife's death, though in his will made five days before his death he gives his residence as Newtown. By this will,³ dated 8 mo. 20, 1716, proved Nov. 16, 1716, he left legacies to his "daughters-in-law" (stepdaughters) Margaret Hillborn and Isabel Carter, and directed that if Isabel should die without issue, her share should go to Margaret's son Samuel Hillborn, when he reached the age of 21 years, naming Thomas Hillborn and John Stackhouse trustees for him in the meanwhile. (Isabel, however, did have issue.) He also made bequests to his brothers Joseph, Edmund, Samuel, Isaac and Thomas Frost, and to his sister Elizabeth Francis; these brothers and sister probably did not live in Pennsylvania. To John Carter he left his servant man, John Jones. John Wildman was named as executor.

¹ Minutes of Middletown Mo. Mtg.
² Register of Middletown Mo. Mtg.
³ Bucks Co. Will Book 1, p. 31.

In the introduction to this article, (vol. xxx, p. 58), attention was called to the entirely imaginary description of the landing of some early immigrants given in *The Atkinsons* of *New Jersey*, and the similar account of the landing of the progenitors of one of the Bucks County Atkinson families. The latter is as follows:

"**John and Christopher Atkinson.**

On the 3rd day of Second month (April), 1699, there also landed at the same wharf[1] in Philadelphia two other men, of middle age, and the heads of families. They came from the agricultural districts of Lancashire, one of the northern counties of England, and bringing with them all their worldly goods. They were Friends, as shown by their apparel and manner of speech, and were met by some of their relatives on the shore, who had preceded them to this wilderness country." . . . . . "These men were John and Christopher Atkinson, who had landed with their wives and children, seeking a home either in Pennsylvania or New Jersey. Letters sent them from those already here, encouraged their removal, giving florid accounts of the climate, the fertility of the soil, and, above all, the liberality of the government, and tempted them to leave the old hearthstones in their native land." There is more in the same strain.

It is needless to remark that this is almost totally erroneous, except the facts that they had lived in Lancashire and were Friends. The two men and the wife of John never landed at all, for as we have seen above, they all died on the voyage. The *Britannia* arrived in Philadelphia 6 mo. 24, 1699, the date of their landing here given, 2 mo. 3, 1699, being that on which their certificates were signed at Lancaster Monthly Meeting, over a month before their embarkation.

4. JOHN ATKINSON, son of William and Ann, of Scotford,

[1] At the mouth of Dock Creek, Philadelphia.

Lancashire, was born about 1660 He was no doubt born at Scotford, and certainly lived there until 1699. He was executor of his brother William, who died in 1679/80; in papers connected with the executorship he is styled "carpenter," but as already explained, among Quakers these terms were no indication of social status, and in his marriage certificate he is styled " husbandman," a more appropriate designation for the son of a freehold landowner, following in his father's footsteps, and a very non-committal Biblical term besides, carrying no suggestion of rank, either high or low.

In the latter half of May, 1699, John Atkinson, with his wife and three children, his wife's sisters Mary and Alice Hynde, and perhaps another, Lydia Hynde, and his own brother, Christopher Atkinson, and family, set sail on the ship *Britannia* from Liverpool, for Philadelphia. He had obtained a certificate from the Lancaster Monthly Meeting of the Society of Friends, addressed to Friends in Pennsylvania, for himself and family.[1] We have already told in the account of John's brother Christopher how sickness, (it seems to have been smallpox), made such terrible havoc among the *Britannia's* passengers. Both John Atkinson and his wife succumbed to it; the exact date of their deaths was not recorded, but they occurred sometime between the middle of May and the 24th of August, probably in July 1699. Neither had made a will, so after the arrival of the *Britannia* in Philadelphia, joint letters of administration on

[1] His brother Christopher's was almost exactly similar, and with two exceptions (and perhaps these are copyist's errors) the names signed to it are the same. John's reads:
DEAR FRIENDS:
The bearer hereof, Jno. Atkinson, having had Inclinations for severall years to remove himself family to Pensylvania, and now having an opportunity, did at our last Moth. Meeting desire a certificate from us to you of his conversation and affairs here when he left us. In order to which wee did appoint some friends to make Inquire into his affairs, who at this Meeting do give us an account yt they find he has settled his affairs to ye satisfaction of his neighbors (or who he was concerned with), and also wee do hereby let you know yt as to his and wife's conversation amongst us have been as becometh truth wch they have made profession of from their youth, and have educated their children therein. Wee have nothing to certifie you of but well, so do recomend them to

both their estates were granted, Sept. 6, 1699, to Mary and Alice Hynde,[1] sisters of the wife.

John Atkinson had a right of 500 acres in the 1500 acres which he and Christopher purchased of William Penn, March 17 & 18, 1698. Mary and Alice Hynde, as administratrixes of his estate, obtained a warrant for this, 7 mo. 12, 1700. At the session of the Board of Property[2] held 4 mo. [June] 15 & 16, 1702, it was stated that the Proprietary by Lease and Release dated March 17 & 18, 1698, granted Christopher and John Atkinson 1500 acres, who coming over to this province on the ship Britannia from Liverpool, both died, and John's wife also, the said John leaving issue, William, Mary and John; and that the Proprietary by warrant dated 7 mo. 12, 1700, granted Mary and Alice Hind, sisters to said John's wife, and administrators on his estate, to take up 500 acres which were laid out in the country of Bucks, and returned by Edward Penington, (Surveyor-General) 4 mo. 24, 1701. The said Mary and Alice requested a patent to the children for the said land, which was granted. This tract was laid out in Buckinham Township, and appears on the map[3] of Cutler's survey of 1703, in the names of "Mary and Alice Hinde."

---

you for your advice and assistance in what may be necessary for their settlement amongst you. With our salutation in dear love to you wee rest your friends and bretheren.

From our Month Meeting at Lancaster ye 3 : of ye 2 : month* 1699. To our friends in ye province of Pennsylvania, these,

Signed by

Tho. Dockery,	Deborah Lawson,	Mary Waithman,
Tho. Green,	Elizabeth Patchet,	Elizabeth Jenconson,
Robt. Hubershe,	Elizabeth Green,	Agnes Wilde,
Tho. Wither,	Elizabeth Baynes,	Elizabeth Goucon,
Robt. Mayer,	Ellin Coward,	Ellin Godsalm,
Willm. Wylde,	Margret Wither,	Mary Hubershe,
Tho. Dillworth,	Agnes Tomlinson,	Margret Cornthwait.
Willm. Stout,	Jannet Backhouse,	Martha Hodgson.
Willm. Skirrow,		

*April O. S.

[1] Phila. Co. Adm'n Book A, p. 286.

[2] Penna. Arch., 2 ser., XIX, 320.

[3] Some of the maps of the Cutler survey of 1703, are now (1907) in possession of the Bucks County Historical Society, being part of the collections of Dr. John Watson, (author of a history of Buckingham and Solebury Townships), a descendant of John Watson, an early Surveyor-General. These are probably copies made for his own use by Surveyor-General Watson, the originals no doubt being in the Surveyor-General's office, (now part of the Interior Department at Harrisburg). It is certain the latter office had the Cutler maps, whether originals or copies, for Robert Smith, of Bucks County, obtained a certified copy of that of Buckingham and Solebury, from the Surveyor-General's office April 30, 1794. Gen. Davis, in the first edition of his *History of Bucks County*, page 267, reprints a map of these townships, probably from the Smith copy.

By deed¹ of April 1, 1713, William Atkinson, of Warminster Township, his sister Mary Atkinson and brother John Atkinson, heirs to their father, sold the above tract to Christopher Topham. The deed stated that the amount for this land issued to Mary and Alice Hynde was dated March 13, 1700, which do not agree with the statement before the Board of Property, but the land was the same.

At the same time that Margaret Atkinson, widow of Christopher, presented her husband's certificate to Neshamina (Middletown) Monthly Meeting, she presented his brother John's, 9 mo. [Nov.] 2, 1699; this, of course, included the three children. On the same date the meeting passed the following resolution: " It is agreed & concluded upon by this meeting that the meeting take care of all friends children that are left as orphans & unsettled, to inspect & see that all such be taken care of & settled in the best & sutablest maner according to their capacity."² Mary and Alice Hynde had brought their sister's children to Bucks County to live, somewhere within the compass of Middletown Monthly Meeting; it is possible that they lived first with Margaret Atkinson at " Bellemont." They continued the care of them under the supervision of the meeting, according to the above resolution, until Alice Hynde married William Stockdale in 1703, when the three children went with her to live on her husband's plantation, in Warminster Township. At the meeting held 1 mo. 6, 1700/1, a request was sent to Mary & Alice Hynde to come to the next monthly meeting and give an account of the children's estate in their possession. They appeared then (2 mo. 3, 1701) and at subsequent meetings, and at that of 4 mo. 5, 1701, the meeting finally adjusted their accounts, settling the allowance for the children's keep, etc. At this last meeting some books sent by the Quarterly Meeting were distributed, Mary Hynde getting two, a very desirable acquisition in those days when reading matter was scarce

¹ Phila. Co. Deed Book F 6, p. 154.
² This and the following abstracts from the procedings of Middletown Mo. Mtg. are from the official minutes thereof.

in the colony. At the meeting of 7 mo. 6, 1705, William Stockdale was desired to bring the two younger children, Mary and John, with him to the next monthly meeting, which he did and arrangements were made with him for their care.

John Atkinson married 2 mo. 8, 1686, at Lancaster Mtg.,[1] Susannah Hynde, daughter of Richard Hynde of Scotforth, Lancashire. Richard Hynde of Oreangle or Oveangle (a place not identified), Lancaster, died 9 mo. 24, 1693, buried 9 mo. 25;[2] though his residence is not given as Scotforth, he was doubtless Susannah's father, Lancaster being only a short distance away. Mary Hynde, widow, of Lancaster, most likely Susannah's mother, died 3 mo. 26, 1695, buried 3 mo. 27 at Lancaster[3] (meeting house yard).

Of other members of Susannah's family circle the Roger Hynde who signed her marriage certificate (see footnote) was probably a brother or uncle, most likely the latter. The first Richard Hynde on that document was without doubt her father. The second Richard Hynde probably a brother, and the Elizabeth Hynde following, his wife. John Hynde was doubtless a brother; John Hynde, son of Richard, of Lancaster, died 1689, and was buried 2 mo. 26.[4] Lydia Hynde seems to have been a sister; she started for

[1] Register of Lancaster, Mo. Mtg. Mr. Jenkins gives the text of the certificate: "John Atkinson of Scotford in ye county of Lancaster, Husbandman, and Susannah Hynde daughter of Richard Hynde of Scotford aforesaid did take each other in marriage ye eighth day of ye Second month 1686 in a public assembly of the people of God called Quakers mett together for yt purpose in ye public meeting house at Lancaster ye party's and themselves publishing their names before these witnesses. Roger Hynde, Alice Thornton, Henry Bishersle, Richard Hynde, Tho. Tomlinson, John Ecroyd, Ann Tomlinson, Robert Mayor, Christopher Atkinson, Wm. Gunson, Wm. Wylde, An. Wylde, Thomas Dottery, John Tomlinson, Timothy Taylor, Thomas Skirrow, Margt. Hodshan, Henry Coward, Richard Hynde, Elizabth Hynde, Ann Gunson, Eliz. Midlton, ffrancis Walling, Tho. Davison, Thomas Hadson, Ellon Coward, Lydia Padgot, John Hynde, Isabel Coward, Lydia Hynde, Sarah Davison, Isabel Taylor." This certificate was copied from the original record book in Somerset House, London.

[2] Register of Lancaster Mo. Mtg.   [3] Ibid.   [4] Ibid.

Pennsylvania [1] with her sister and family in the *Britannia* but as she is not heard of again, no doubt she died on that ill-fated ship. Though they did not sign the marriage certificate, (being perhaps too young), Susannah positively had two other sisters, Mary and Alice Hynde, who accompanied her on the voyage to Pennsylvania, and took care of her orphan children after their arrival in that province. Mary Hynde married Thomas Parsons, 4 mo. 1704, he bringing a certificate from Abington Mo. Mtg.; they passed their second meeting at Middletown 4 mo. 1, 1704, and at the meeting of 5 mo. 6, the overseeing committee reported it had been accomplished. Alice Hynde married 2 mo. [April], 1703, (they passed second meeting at Middletown 2 mo. 1), William Stockdale; for account of him see Note C. Several persons named Hinde, [Hynde] among them a Richard, are mentioned in the Lancashire chapter of Besse's *Sufferings of Friends*.

John and Susanna (Hynde) Atkinson had issue, all born at Scotforth, Lancashire; (births from register of Lancaster Mo. Mtg.):

12. WILLIAM ATKINTON, b. 1 mo. 31, 1687, d. — 1755.
    Mar. 1st, June ——, 1716, Phoebe Taylor.
    2nd, Sept. 22, 1728, Mary Hugh.
    3rd, August —— 1730, Lowry Evans.
13. MARY ATKINSON, b. 7 mo. 25, 1689, d.
    Mar. 2 mo. 12, 1716, Cephas Child.
14. JOHN ATKINSON, b. 8 mo. 25, 1692, d. 9 mo. 6, 1694, buried 9 mo. 7, at Lancaster Friends' burying ground.[2]
15. JOHN ATKINSON, b. 9 mo. 25, 1695, d. Jan. ——, 1752.
    Mar. 8 mo. 30, 1717, Mary Smith.

[1] Her name was either included in the certificate with Mary and Alice, or else she had one of the same date. Mr. Jenkins quotes from the minutes of Lancaster Mo. Mtg. of 1 mo. 6, 1698/9: "Its ordered at this meeting that certificates be drawn for Christopher Atkinson, John Atkinson, Thomas Laynfall, Thomas Willson and their families and for Elizabeth Tomlinson, Mary Hynd, Alice Hynd and Lydia Hynd and Jane Cotton in order to their transportation to Pennsylvania to certifie friends there of their Departure from us in Unity with us and of their clearness from Debt," etc. While each man had a separate certificate, there is reason to suppose Mary & Alice and perhaps Lydia Hynde had one between them, or perhaps all five of these women, in which case Elizabeth and Jane were most likely sisters of the others.

[2] Register of Lancaster Mo. Mtg.

(To be continued.)

A MODERN VIEW OF SCOTFORD.

Drawn in 1897 by Sara Atkinson (now Mrs. Engle). The village appeared to have altered little since Christopher and John Atkinson left it nearly 200 years before.

ATKINSON FAMILIES OF BUCKS COUNTY, PENNSYLVANIA.

BY OLIVER HOUGH.

12. WILLIAM ATKINSON, born 1 mo. [March] 31, 1687,[1] at Scotforth, Lancashire, England, died 1754,[2] in Upper Dublin Township, Philadelphia County, Pennsylvania, eldest son of John and Susanna (Hynde) Atkinson, came to Pennsylvania with his parents in the ship *Britannia* in 1699. Their parents having died on the voyage, William and his brother and sister, were taken by their aunts, Alice and Mary Hynde, to live with them in Bucks County, somewhere within the compass of Middletown Monthly Meeting, which (as stated above in the account of their father) took the supervision of

[1] Register of Lancaster Mo. Mtg.
[2] His will proved Jan. 1, 1755.

their rearing and education. Just where they first lived is uncertain, though probably not in Buckingham, where their father's land was laid out in 1700 or 1701. In 1703, Alice Hynde married William Stockdale, and took the three children to live on his plantation in Warminster Township. The latter, under the Meeting, acted as their guardian. At the Middletown Monthly Meeting held 3 mo. 6, 1708, William Atkinson, being of age, requested his share of his patrimony, and his uncle [by marriage], William Stockdale, informed the meeting that the money was ready. On 4 mo. 3, 1708, John Cutler and William Hayhurst, who had been appointed to settle the accounts between William Stockdale and William Atkinson, reported themselves well satisfied. Within a few months of coming of age William Atkinson removed to a plantation he had just bought (see below), adjoining Stockdale's in Warminster Township. He stayed here until 1727, when he removed to Upper Dublin Township, Philadelphia (now Montgomery) County. According to Mr. Jenkins he bought 198 acres in the northeast end of the township, but as the deed or deeds are not just now available, and apparently not of record, it is uncertain if he bought it all at once. He probably purchased several separate adjoining tracts at different periods, for in a list of landholders in Philadelphia County for 1734, made "according to the uncirtaine Returns of the Constables,"[1] he is assessed in Upper Dublin for 50 acres only. It is more probable that he did not own as much as 198 acres, but that his son-in-law, William Walton, having acquired William Atkinson's plantation, made it up to that amount by later purchases; (see footnote below).

On 2 mo. 6, 1727, he being then recently removed, Middletown Mo. Mtg. granted him a certificate which he presented to Abington Mo. Mtg. 8 mo. 30, 1727. On 5 mo. 30, 1739, William Atkinson was appointed a representative from Abington Mo. Mtg. to the Quarterly Mtg. (also named

[1] Publications of the Genealogical Society of Penna., vol. 1, p. 169.

Abington). This seems to have been his sole official service in the meeting.

As mentioned in sketch of his father above, William Atkinson, then of Warminster Tp., joined his sister Mary and brother John, in a deed [1] April 1, 1713, to Christopher Topham, for their father's 500 acres laid out in Buckingham Tp., Bucks Co.

By deed [2] of 4 mo. 15, 1708, he bought of John Swift, of Southampton Tp., 170 acres in Warminster Tp., Bucks Co., adjoining William Stockdale, William Bayley, Peter Chamberlain, John Rush and James Bond; this was part of 500 acres sold by William Penn to William Bingley and conveyed by him to Swift in 1699. On Jan. 22, 1731/2, William Atkinson, then of Upper Dublin Tp., Phila. Co., and "Lora" his wife, sold this to Anthony Skout [3].

As above stated the deed or deeds for the 198 acres in Upper Dublin have not been found on record. The Jenkins MS. continues the history of this tract, which as it also tells something of William Atkinson's descendants (not otherwise within the scope of this article) is quoted as follows: "William Atkinson sold his farm in [4]   to his son-in-law

[1] Phila. Co. Deed Book F 6, p. 154. In the mention of this deed above, under 4. JOHN ATKINSON, page 173, line 4, *amount* should read *warrant*.

[2] Bucks Co. Deed Book 4, p. 7; recorded Oct. 16, 1708.

[3] Bucks Co. Deed Book 18 (old book F vol. 3), p. 555.

[4] This date could not be determined. The Philadelphia County deed book index mentions a deed from William Atkinson to William Walton as being recorded in Book D 14, page 284, and as having been copied thereinto from the older Book A vol. 8, but it is not in Book D 14 at all. The A and B series of Phila. Co. deed books were, many years ago, taken by the Provincial Land Office, as they contained the original patents for all the counties, and partial abstracts of them were retained by Philadelphia County as part of the series called Exemplification Records. But these abstracts were of patents only (with some letters of attorney and commissions), it being apparently the intention to copy the ordinary deeds into the current deed books; which, however, was not systematically carried out, so that many of them are no longer of record in this county. The original books, now in Harrisburg, are said to be too dilapidated for general use.

The present owner of the Cherry Lane place has a deed showing that William Walton added at least 78 acres 40 perches to what his father-in-law conveyed him, for he purchased that amount from Richard McCurdy, May 27, 1760. Indeed Walton probably added all there was of the plantation beyond the 50 acres William Atkinson was assessed for on the tax-roll mentioned.

William Walton, but probably continued to live there until his death, which was prior to Jany. 1, 1755. It will be observed that he left no sons, so that with his death another line of the Atkinson name became extinct. It was only through John Atkinson, the youngest brother, that the name of the Scotforth immigrants was perpetuated in Pennsylvania.

William and Phebe (Atkinson) Walton lived at Cherry Lane (the name is of recent origin) the remainder of their lives. They were the parents of nine children, only three of whom, Hannah b. 10, 21, 1745, and Phebe and John, who were much younger, survived. William Walton died in 4th month 1770 leaving the homestead to his only son John, and an adjoining farm to the west which he had bought, to Hannah, while Phebe had a tract of 50 acres off the south corner which had also been added to the original purchase. The son John died unmarried so that a new division was made of the original tract of 198 acres, Phebe getting 78 acres including the homestead.

Hannah Walton married John Cleaver in 1785. He died in 1804 and she in 1807, leaving no issue and the whole estate then passed to the surviving sister Phebe.

Phebe Walton had married 6th mo. 1, 1781, James Shoemaker, the son of Isaac and Hannah Shoemaker, of Upper Dublin. It was not many years after their marriage, that finding the home too small, the east end, an addition larger than the original house, was built. Its date stone bears the inscription:" [blank in MS.[1]] "Nearly the whole west wall was taken up by the massive chimney within the ample space of which a row of modern closets has been built. In 1814, Phebe Shoemaker, then a widow, added the western end. The middle house, with its ceiling but a few inches above the head of a medium sized man and its doorways troublesome for one above average height, betokens its age in its construction and arrangement. Without doubt it was the first stone house built on the property and from the fact that in the seven years that William Atkinson owned the farm it increased in value from £170 to £600, it seems likely that he built it. The next year after making the first addition James Shoemaker built the barn which bears the date of 1794.

James Shoemaker died   , his widow surviving him   years. In 1814 Phebe Shoemaker gave to the Society of Friends ground for the Upper Dublin Meeting House which stands on the Jarrettown road on the western boundary of the farm. The meeting house was erected in that year. On her death the farm was divided among her four children, John, Hannah, Jesse and Jonathan. Jonathan Shoemaker's share was 78 acres including the homestead. He held it until

[1] It was some arrangement of the letters J, P, S, and date 1793.

1849 when it was bought by Thomas Atkinson of Bucks County, a descendant of John Atkinson, the younger brother of William."

The Cherry Lane property is on the Limekiln Pike, about ¼ mile from the present village of Three Tuns, or about half way between Three Tuns and Jarrettown.

By his will,[1] dated 8 mo. 15, 1754, proved Jan. 1, 1755, William Atkinson, of "uper Dubling" bequeathed £200 to each of his daughters, Susanna wife of Samuel Davis, Phebe wife of William Walton, and Hannah wife of Ellis Hughs, and the residue of his estate equally between them; to his son-in-law Ellis Ellis he left five shillings, he having already received his share. The executors were Samuel David, and Ellis Hughs. He did not bequeath any land.

William Atkinson married first, about June, 1716, Phebe Taylor, daughter of Richard Taylor, of Cheltenham Township, Philadelphia County. At Middletown Mo. Mtg. held 3 mo. 3, 1716, William Atkinson declared his intention of marriage with Phebe Taylor, a member of Abington Mo. Mtg.; but for some unknown reason the marriage was not performed under the care of the meeting and on 5 mo. 5, the overseers reported that William Atkinson and Phebe Taylor had been married contrary to the order of Friends; on 10 mo. 6, 1716, he presented the meeting a written satisfaction for the manner of his marriage and was retained in membership.[2]

Her father, Richard Taylor was a considerable landowner in Cheltenham and nearby townships; having purchased in 1795 from Thomas Fairman 300 acres; in 1697 from Silas Crispin, 519 acres (Lower Dublin); in 1698 from Edward Shippen and wife Rebecca, executors of her former husband Francis Richardson, 200 acres, (in or near Cheltenham); and in 1713 from Robert and Richard Whitton, 250 acres, (Upper Dublin).

Afterwards Taylor lived in the city of Phila. His will[3]

[1] Phila. Co. Will Book K, p. 240.
[2] Minutes of Middletown Mo. Mtg.
[3] Phila. Co. Will Book E, p. 199.

signed Oct. 21, 1732, proved Dec. 12, 1732, mentioned his wife (name not given) and children Martha and Mary; sons-in-law Wm. Morgan, John Riale, of New Britain, Bucks Co., (husb. of Martha) & Wm. Adkinson; grandchildren Hannah Morgan, Susanna, Pheby, Mary & Hannah Adkinson; friend Humphrey Murray; John Riale was made executor.

William and Phebe (Taylor) Atkinson had issue, (and perhaps others who died young, unmarried, as there seems to have been no record made in any meeting of their births, and this list is made up from their father's will and the marriage register of Abington Mo. Mtg.):

16. SUSANNA ATKINSON, b. ——.
    Mar. 1st, ——, 1743, Thomas Hughs.
    2d, ——, ——, Samuel Davis.
17. PHEBE ATKINSON, b. 9 mo. 10, 1720, (Jenkins MS.).
    Mar. ——, 1741, William Walton.
18. MARY ATKINSON, b. ——, d. before 1754.
    Mar. ——, 1746, Ellis Ellis, of Gwynedd.
19. HANNAH ATKINSON, b. ——.
    Mar. ——, 1745, Ellis Hughs.

William Atkinson married second, Sept. 26, 1728, at Christ Church, Philadelphia, Mary Hugh.[1] No particulars of her family connection are at hand; she may have been either spinster or widow. The name was often written Hughes or Hughs, but whether she was a relative of the brothers Thomas and Ellis Hughs, (sons of Rowland Hugh) who married her step-daughters, Susanna and Hannah, is now unknown. As they were not married under care of Friends, William Atkinson sent to Abington Mo. Mtg. 5 mo. 28, 1729, a paper signifying his sorrow at offending Friends by his marriage, and on 7 mo. 29 appeared personally and made acknowledgement for marrying out of unity.

He married third, in August, 1730, Lowry Evans. They "passed second meeting" on 5 mo. 27, 1730, and the marriage was reported as accomplished to the Abington Mo.

[1] Register of Christ Church, Phila.

Mtg. held 6 mo. 31.[1] They had no issue. It has not been ascertained to which of the numerous Evans families living within the compass of Abington Mo. Mtg. she belonged.

On the 32nd page of volume 6 of the Martindale MSS in the Historical Society of Pennsylvania, this William Atkinson, born 1687, son of John, is said to be of Middletown, instead of, as he was, of Warminster, and is made to marry Margaret, daughter of Henry Baker, and to die 7 mo, 29, 1749; this marriage and date of death are those of 5. William Atkinson, of Bristol, son of Thomas, of the other family, and the children given on this 32nd page (Martindale), are really those of William, of Bristol, and Margaret (Baker) as noted in Part I of this article.

15. JOHN ATKINSON, born 9 mo. [Nov.] 25, 1695,[2] at Scotforth, in Lancashire, came to Pennsylvania in 1699 with his parents, John and Susanna (Hynde) Atkinson, and died in Bucks Co., early in January, 1751/2.[3] His parents having died on the voyage, John, with his brother and sister, was taken by his aunts Mary and Alice Hynde to Bucks County, where, after Alice's marriage in 1703, to William Stockdale, they lived on the latter's plantation in Warminister Township. Middletown Mo. Mtg., which exercised a care over orphaned children of Friends within its compass, supervised the rearing and education of John Atkinson, conducted by his aunts and William Stockdale. At the meeting held 8 mo, 4, 1705, four Friends were appointed to attend to John Atkinson's education, etc., and on 4 mo. 6, 1706 they reported that they had agreed with William Stockdale that he was to take care of John until he was 14 years old. After reaching that age, in 1710 he went to live with his brother William, whose plantation adjoined Stockdale's in Warminster. On 11 mo. 3, 1716, John Stackhouse and John Cutler reported to the meeting that they had seen the accounts settled between William

[1] Minutes of Abington Mo. Mtg.
[2] Register of Lancaster Mo. Mtg.
[3] Probate of his will.

Stockdale and John Atkinson, and that John had received his portion, he being of age. At the time of his marriage, in 1717, he was living temporarily in Newtown Township. The following year, having bought land in the former Manor of Highlands, (see below), he removed to that place, which continued to be his home the rest of his life. These lands within the Manor, which about 1700 had been purchased by the "London Company," and by it sold to settlers, were at that time popularly, though not officially, considered to be part of Wrightstown Township, and the register of Wrightstown Mo. Mtg. in recording the births of John Atkinson's children, designates him as of Wrightstown; but after 1737 they were known to be part of Upper Makefield Township,[1] which he gives as his residence in his will, 1751.[2]

In 1713, though still a minor, he joined his brother and sister in the deed to Christopher Topham, already mentioned twice above.

On Feb. 20, 1718, he bought[3] from Tobias Collett, Daniel Quare and Henry Goldney, of London, (known as "Goldney and Company" or "The London Company"), 200 acres of their tract in the Manor of Highlands. Mr. Jenkins writes of this place as follows : "In 1718 John and Mary Atkinson settled in what is now the extreme northern corner of Upper Makefield township, then called the Manor of Highlands. The farm of 200 acres which John bought of the London company for £50 adjoined on the east the Windy Bush farm where lived his brother-in-law, William Smith. Tradition says that the whole country around was a wilderness and that there were but two white families in the neighborhood, but many Indians. The farm was a parallelogram having 134 rods along what is now the line of Buckingham township, and 240 rods along what is now the public road leading to Buckmanville. The latter village now occupies a portion of the southeast corner of the farm.

Here John Atkinson built his house and barn, planted out an orchard, of which one lone pear tree is still standing." ("Aunt Polly, who was 87

[1] See Davis's *History of Bucks County*, (1st ed., 1876), pages 473–474.

[2] The Martindale MS, vol. 6, 34th page, erroneously styles him "of Middletown" instead of Makefield; the rest of the page is correct, except a slight error in the date of his son Ezekiel's birth, which will be mentioned below.

[3] Phila. Co. Deed Book H 14, p. 382.

years old when she died in 1886, was frequently told when she was a girl going to school that the pear tree was one hundred years old.") "From the site where the original home stood one looks across the intervening farms to the wooded Jericho Hills, while away to the north-east is the sugar loaf Bowman's hill; from the hill top back of the house the eye reaches across to Buckingham mountain. A little water course, now dry except in rainy times ran near the house to the east, while the spring near which our ancestors always sought to build was a hundred yards away."

"Just when the original house that John Atkinson had built was torn down is not known, but William Atkinson, John's son, built the present building using the old stones and axe hewn beams in its construction. The new house was placed nearer the spring and William is said to have planted the buttonwood tree at the corner of the house, which now, 1901, is one of the giants of its race. In the basement kitchen are to be seen the blackened joists, taken from the original John Atkinson's house. Where the latter was built is still to be seen a depression in the ground, now choked with weeds and brambles.

The portion of the farm which fell to William's share has remained in the Atkinson family to this day, the generations being 1st John; 2nd William; 3rd John; 4th John; 5th John L. and since his death, his widow."[1]

John Atkinson, by his will,[2] dated 10 mo. 10, 1751, proved January 15, 1752, bequeathed 120 acres of his plantation, including the dwelling-house and barn, to his son William, and the remaining 80 acres to his son Thomas. To William was also given "my black mare Saddle and Bridle and also my great Bible." To the daughter, Mary, the "best bed and furniture thereunto belonging one new chest of drawers, all my Pewter and also my Roan Horse." To son Ezekiel £12 and a loom. The remainder of the personal estate was to be divided between Mary, Christopher and Cephas, and to Cephas was also given "one Bay Horse Colt now in possession of my brother William." The sons William and Thomas were appointed executors. In this will he styled himself "weaver," and a note to the will mentioned "looms and gears" which his sons Christopher and

---

[1] In 1887 over two-thirds of John Atkinson's original 200 acres were still in possession of his descendants.
[2] Bucks Co. Will Book 2, p. 241.

Cephas were to have, besides the loom left to Ezekiel; he also mentioned an apprentice who was to finish his term with Cephas; so it would appear that John Atkinson and sons carried on this industry as extensively as the primitive condition of all manufacturing at this period in Pennsylvania permitted.

John Atkinson married 8 mo. 30, 1717, at the house of Stephen Twining, in Newtown Township, Mary Smith, (b. 2 mo. 9, 1696, d.   ), daughter of William and Mary (Croasdale) Smith, of Wrightstown Township. Both the Smith and Croasdale families were among the earliest settlers in the vicinity, where their descendants were large landowners, and occupied prominent positions among the county families, but lack of space forbids any detailed account of them here.

John and Mary (Smith) Atkinson had issue; (births from register of Wrightstown Mo. Mtg.[2]):

20. JOHN ATKINSON, b. 6 mo. 18, 1718, died young.
21. WILLIAM ATKINSON, b. 2 mo. 17, 1721, d. ——, 1800.[3] Mar. 7 mo. 1, 1742, Mary Tomlinson.
22. THOMAS ATKINSON, b. 3 mo. 5, 1722, d, ——, 1760. Mar. 8 mo. 18, 1744, Mary Wildman.
23. CHRISTOPHER ATKINSON, b. 12 mo. 18, 1723/4, d. ——, 1795.[1b] Mar. 6 mo. 15, 1763, Lydia Canby.
24. MARY ATKINSON, b. 8 mo. 20, 1725, d. 3 mo. 22, 1789.[4] Mar. ——, John Stockdale.
25. EZEKIEL ATKINSON, b. 10 mo. 10, 1728. Mar. ——, Rachel Gilbert.
26. CEPHAS ATKINSON, b. 5 mo. 7, 1730. Mar. ——, Hannah Naylor.
27. ELIZABETH ATKINSON, b. 4 mo. 12, 1732, died young.

[1] Register of Middletown Mo. Mtg.
[2] The copy of the Wrightstown register in the Historical Society of Pennsylvania's library omits Cephas and makes Ezekiel born 5 mo. 7, 1730; but Mr. Jenkins's MS, presumably taken from the original, gives their births as in the text. The Martindale MS, while giving Ezekiel's year as 1728, gives him the same month and day as Cephas, 5 mo. 7.
[3] Martindale MS.
[4] Register of Wrightstown Mo. Mtg.

NOTE A.

There was a Christopher Atkinson, of Kendal, County Westmoreland, more prominent among Friends than Christopher, of Scotforth, and who flourished at a somewhat earlier period. Joseph Smith, in his *Catalogue of Friends' Books*, gives him as author of five pamphlets, three of them in co-laboration with others, all published between 1653 and 1655. Smith indicates him as one who had left Friends and was not known to have returned. These pamphlets were:

—The Standard of the Lord Lifted up Against the Kingdom of Satan, or, An Answer to A BOOK Entituled, "The Quakers Shaken," Written by one *John Gilpin*, with the help of the Priest of *Kendal*: . . . By *Christopher Atkinson*, a friend to the Kingdom of Jesus Christ. London, 1653.

—The Sword of the Lord DRAWN, and furbished against the man of Sin: . . . By one whose Name in the flesh is Christopher Atkinson, who am one that the world doth scornfully call a Quaker. London, 1654.

—David's Enemies discovered. . . . by us who suffer for the Truth, whose names according to the flesh are Christopher Atkinson, George Whitehead. London, 1655.

—The Testimony of the everlasting Gospel witnessed through sufferings, by Christopher Atkinson, Richard Hubberthorne, and James Lancaster. No printer's name, nor date. The part written by Atkinson is entitled: "An Epistle written in the bonds of the Gospel, to be published abroad amongst the inhabitants of England, Rulers, Magistrates and People." Dated "From the Gaol of Norwich, 13th of 10th mo. [1654]."

—ISHMAEL, and his MOTHER, cast out into the WILDERNESS, amongst the Wild Beasts of the same nature: . . . Given forth from the Spirit of the Lord in us that do suffer in Gaol of Norwich for the truth's sake. . . . Whose names in the flesh is, Christopher Atkinson, George Whitehead, James Lancaster, Thomas Simonds. London, 1655.

First Publishers of Truth, (supplement to the *Journal of the Friends' Historical Society*), page 306, in the account of Friends' beginnings at Bolland, a branch of Settle Mo. Mtg. in Yorkshire, says: "In ye year 1653, about ye 6th mo., there came two friends out of ye North, whose names were Thomas Vears and Christopher Atkinson, to a Little Town called Newton, not far from Slaidburne in Bolland, on a 7th Day at night, & was Received by James Bond, a Poor Man, & had a meeting in ye Day following, where severall People were convinced; and ye 2d Day of ye weeke had another meeting, att Cutbert Hayhurst, in Essington, where they were well received."

On page 260 of the same work, under the heading of his own meeting,

Kendal, is an account of him as follows: "Christopher Atkinson, of Kendall, was opened in a liveing Testemony, and laboured zeallously for a time in the service of truth, and suffered Imprisonmt Chearfully for the same in Kendall, and allso travelled into the south & east of England, and for a time had a service in many places. But in process of time, for want of watchfullness, run out into things Inconsistant with the proffession of truth, and persisting therein was denyed of ffriends. Let this and the like runing out be a Caution to all to keepe in Humillety & watchfullness, under ye Conduct of Gods power, that keeps stable & out of all Satans Temptations."

[Some account of C. A. also appears in "Life and Correspondence of William and Alice Ellis of Airton," by James Backhouse, pp. 315–316.]

NOTE B.

Thomas Stackhouse, Senior, of Bolland, in Yorkshire, was one of those who accompanied William Penn, in the ship *Welcome*, on his first voyage to his Province of Pennsylvania, arriving at New Castle, 10 mo. 27, 1682. Bolland Particular Meeting, to which he belonged, was a constituent of Settle Monthly Meeting, of the Society of Friends, in Yorkshire. A number of members of this monthly meeting obtained a certificate therefrom dated 4 mo. 7, 1682, in order to move to Pennsylvania, which they did on the *Welcome*. "The Settle Certificate" (as this document is familiarly known among Pennsylvania genealogists, by whom it is generally considered to be the most important single certificate issued by any English meeting in connection with the settlement of Pennsylvania) was granted to the following—most or all of them related by blood or marriage: Cuthbert Hayhurst, wife and family; Nicholas Waln, wife and three children; Thomas Wigglesworth and wife Alice; Thomas Walmsley and wife Elizabeth; Thomas Croasdale, wife Agnes and six children; Thomas Stackhouse and wife; Ellin Cowgill (widow), and children; and William Hayhurst. No names of wives, other than the three named, and no names at all of children, are mentioned, nor the number of children other than Waln's and Croasdale's. These families all settled in Buck county.

Thomas Stackhouse had married in the same year, 1682, and probably in the same (4th) month, Margery Hayhurst, their declarations of intention having been made to Settle Mo. Mtg. in 2nd and 3rd months. She was undoubtedly a sister to Cuthbert Hayhurst whose name heads the certificate. Alice, wife of Thomas Wigglesworth, also in the certificate, was another sister; her marriage 7 mo. 2, 1665, is on the register of Settle Mo. Mtg. These were children of Cuthbert (the elder) and Alice Hayhurst, of Essington, Yorkshire. Nicholas Waln was a nephew of Cuthbert Hayhurst's wife, who was Mary Rudd, her sister Jane being

Waln's mother. Cuthbert Hayhurst had a brother William who married his wife's sister, Dorothy Rudd, who died in 1676. This was doubtless the William Hayhurst of the certificate. The relationship, if any, of the Walmsleys and Croasdales (Agnes Croasdale's maiden name being Hathornthwaite, and Elizabeth Walmsley's unknown to the writer) is not so clear, but Ellen (or Ellin) Cowgill's probable relationship will be spoken of below. Margery (Hayhurst) Stackhouse died without issue 11 mo. 5, 1682, [Feb., 1682/3],[1] and was one of the first persons buried in the graveyard of Middletown (then Neshamina) meeting-house.

Thomas Stackhouse on arriving in the Province went to Bucks County and took up a tract of 312 acres in Middletown Township, on Neshaminy Creek, running back to about where Langhorne now is. This is shown on Holme's Map in the name of "Thomas Stackhouse Sr." Here he lived a number of years, but having no wife nor children, (though his nephew John is presumed to have lived with him), and getting well on to 65 years old, he no doubt felt the need of a woman's care, and so, about 1701 went to board with Margaret (Fell) Atkinson, at "Bellemont," as mentioned in the text above; (where their marriage in 1702/3 and her subsequent marriage to John Frost, are fully covered).

Thomas Stackhouse, Sr., had no issue by either wife. He died in 1706, in his 71st year. His will[2] mentioned his wife Margaret, brother John, sisters Jennet and Ellin, nephews Thomas and John, but no children. The nephew John inherited the 312 acre plantation in Middletown. The brother John appears not to have come to America, and whether the sister Jennet did is uncertain, but the sister Ellin was probably the Ellin Cowgill, widow, included in the same certificate from Settle Mo. Mtg. with Thomas Stackhouse and wife; the fact that Ellin Cowgill had a daughter Jennet (no doubt named for her sister) strengthens this theory. (See remarks on Cowgill family in Part I. under 14. JOSEPH ATKINSON, who married another Jennet Cowgill, granddaughter of this Ellen.)

Thomas Stackhouse Senior's brother John is supposed to have been the father of the two nephew's mentioned in the former's will:

Thomas Stackhouse, Jr., came to Pennsylvania as early as 1682 probably with his uncle. He obtained 507 acres of land in Middletown Township (marked "Thomas Stackhouse" on Holme's Map) and lived there all his life. He represented Bucks County in the Provincial Assembly in 1711, 1713 and 1715, and was elected for 1716 but declined to serve. He married first Grace Heaton, second Ann widow of Edward Mayos, and third Dorothy widow of Zebulon Heston.

[1] Register of Middletown Mo. Mtg.
[2] Phila. Co. Will Book C, p. 40.

John Stackhouse, Jr. was in Pennsylvania by 1685 in which year his name is signed to a paper, and probably he came with his uncle in 1682. He was a minister of the Society of Friends. John Fothergill in his *Journal* mentions lodging 12 mo. 23, 1721, at the house of J. Stackhouse, near Neshaminy; this was the 312 acres he had inherited from his uncle. He married Elizabeth Pearson. From these two nephews of Thomas Stackhouse, Sr. descended the well-known Bucks County family of that name, branches of which are now found in Philadelphia, Chester and Delaware Counties, Pennsylvania, Burlington, Camden and Gloucester Counties, New Jersey, and in Maryland.

Note C.

Shortly after the year 1700 there were two William Stockdales in Bucks County, and sometime before that there was another in New Castle County, but who died in Philadelphia. What relation, if any, these three men were to one another, is very uncertain at present. Of the one who was connected by marriage with both the Bucks County Atkinson families we have the following particulars:

The first mention of him found so far appears to be his declaration of intention of marriage with Alice Hynde in 1702/3. The reports to the meeting for a number of years thereafter, as to his care for and accounts with the Atkinson children have been noticed in the text.

By deed[1] of 3 mo. 18, 1707, William Stockdale bought from John Swift, of Southampton Township, 151 acres in Warminster Township, bounded by Abel Noble (on several sides) and by John Rush, part of 500 acres which William Penn by deeds of lease and release dated Sept. 6 & 7, 1681, had conveyed to William Bingley. Stockdale had probably resided on and rented this place from Swift for a number of years before he bought it, as the deed designates him as of Warminster.

By deed dated March 6, 1723, William Stockdale bought[2] from Thomas Chalkley and Martha his wife, 250 acres in Warminster Township, part of 500 acres originally granted to John Jones of London and laid out to his agents or attorneys in 1684. This was on the southwest branch of Neshaminy Creek. On August 16, 1734, William Stockdale and Phebe his wife conveyed[3] 97¾ acres of this (on the branch and adjoining Samuel Gilbert's land) to her sons James and John Radcliffe, of Warminster Tp. The balance, 152¼ acres, William Stockdale by will, May 17, 1738, left to his wife for life and then to his brother Ralph

[1] Bucks Co. Deed Book 3, p. 323.

[2] Deed apparently not on record in Bucks County, but fact recited in deeds recorded in Bucks Co. Deed Books 11, p. 72; 20, p. 39; and 28, p. 410.

[3] Bucks Co. Deed Book 20, p. 39.

Stockdale's son and the children of his sisters Isabel and Ann;[1] on March 7, 1744, these heirs, Thomas Beatham; of Settle, William Stockdale of "Suazom" or "Suazan," and Ralph Dinsdale, of Camm's Houses, all in Yorkshire, England, sold[2] this 152¼ acres to Charles Beatty, of Warminster Township.

William Stockdale's will[3] dated May 17, 1738, proved Oct. 30, 1738, gave to his wife Phebe Stockdale the best bed and all furniture thereunto belonging. She was to have the whole benefit of his land and plantation where he then lived, during her life, and after her death it was to go to the testator's brother Ralph Stockdale's son, and testator's sisters Isabel's and Amy's children, to be equally divided between them. To his "cousins" William Atkinson, John Atkinson and Mary Child, and to his "brother" William Atkinson, £5 each. The residue of his estate to his wife Phebe, she, with his "brother" William Atkinson, being appointed executors. His connection with the two separate Atkinson families is well exemplified by the will: the "cousins" William, John and Mary being nephews and niece of his first wife Alice Hynde, and belonging to the CHRISTOPHER AND JOHN ATKINSON FAMILY; while the "brother" William Atkinson, was the brother-in-law to his second wife Phebe (Baker) Radcliffe, and was of the THOMAS ATKINSON FAMILY.

William Stockdale married first, in 1703, as stated above, Alice Hynde. Middletown Mo. Mtg. register records the death (though not the birth) of one, and probably their only, child:

ISABEL STOCKDALE, b. ——, d. 11 mo. 22, 1720.

Alice (Hynde) Stockdale had died before her daughter, in the same year, 1720, and was buried 10 mo. 20.[4] If she had any other children they must also have died young, or at least without issue, as William Stockdale's will gives evidence of his leaving no direct heirs.

He married second, in 1722, Phebe (Baker) Radcliffe, daughter of Henry Baker, and widow of Edward Radcliffe; see Notes D and E to Part I. William Stockdale at Middletown Mo. Mtg. held 5 mo. 5, 1722, declared his intention of marriage with Phebe Radcliffe, a member of Falls Mo. Mtg., and a certificate was granted him for that purpose 6 mo. 2. On 8 mo. 3, 1728, Middletown Mo. Mtg. gave William Stockdale "and family" a certificate to Abington Mo. Mtg.; he and his wife

[1] Called "Ann" in the deed record, but "Amy" in his will.
[2] Deed recorded May 3, 1796 in Bucks Co. Deed Book 28, p. 410; it had previously been recorded July 11, 1763 in Book 11, p. 72; this first record omitting "County of York" in the heirs' residence, and having some names misspelt.
[3] Bucks Co. Will Book 1, p. 257.
[4] Register of Middletown Mo. Mtg.

Phebe (who was all the "family") presented it there 8 mo. 28. This does not mean a change of residence, but only a transfer of membership for convenience of attending meeting; Horsham, the particular meeting belonging to Abington Mo. Mtg., to which they attached themselves, being readier of access to their Warminster home.

Phebe Stockdale died only a few months after her husband. By her will,[1] dated Dec. 27, 1738, she left £10 to Horsham Meeting for fires in and sweeping out the meeting house, the money to be put at interest and Friends appointed by the meeting to see it employed as directed. To her sister Margaret Atkinson, her side saddle; to son James Radcliffe, a riding horse; and to son John Radcliffe, a mare and colt. Residue to sons James and John Radcliffe, who with her brother-in-law William Atkinson, were named as executors. By a codicil of the same date she divided wearing apparel between her cousin Rebecca Smith and sister Margaret Atkinson, and gave her brother-in-law, William Atkinson, her deceased husband's best riding saddle. The whole was probated Jan. 24, 1738/9.

A William Stockdale was a Member of Assembly from Bucks County in 1713, 1714, 1717 and 1719, but it is uncertain whether this was the above-mentioned or the following.

The other William Stockdale, contemporary in Bucks County with the husband of Alice Hynde, first appears in Middletown Township as a party to a deed[2] of the date of Sept. 11, 1711, by which he bought of Joseph Wildman 60 acres in Middletown Tp., bounded by Thomas Musgrove's, Thomas Constable's, John Croasdale's and other of Joseph Wildman's lands. Either just before or just after this (on Feb. 12, 171-) he bought from Henry Nelson (deed not found on record) 90 acres adjoining and on Neshaminy Creek. On March 6, 1713, William Stockdale and Dorothy his wife sold[3] the whole 150 acres to Thomas Stackhouse, Jr. In this last deed his residence is given as Southampton.

At the date of his will,[4] 3 mo. [May] 12, 1727, he was of Northampton Township. He made his wife Dorothy sole executrix with full power to dispose of all his goods, lands, etc., as she saw fit, but with the advice of the monthly meeting. There were no specific bequests; it was probated Jan. 30, 1732/3. At Middletown Mo, Mtg. 1 mo. 7, 1733/4, William Stockdale, lately deceased, having left all disposing of his effects to his wife, she requested assistance from the meeting in doing the same.

This William Stockdale married first, Grace ———; they had one

[1] Bucks Co. Will Book 1, p. 259.
[2] Bucks Co. Deed Book 4, p. 168.
[3] Bucks Co. Deed Book 5, p. 34.
[4] Bucks Co. Will Book 1, p. 181.

child, whose death, but not her birth, is on the register of Middletown Mo. Mtg.:

GRACE STOCKDALE, b. ——, d. 5 mo. 27, 1722.

He married second, in 1710, Dorothy Iden. He declared his intentions to Middletown Mo. Mtg. 2 mo. 6, and she being a member of Falls Mo. Mtg. he was given a certificate thereto 4 mo. 1. They had certainly the following three children, (births from register Middletown Mo. Mtg):

ROBERT STOCKDALE, born 6 mo. 8, 1711. The will of Robert Stockdale, of Northhampton,[1] dated Jan. 24, 1769, proved Aug. 10, 1772, mentioned his wife Mary, son Robert (who was to have the plantation when 21 years old), sons William, George and David, and "little daughter" Mercy; and made his wife and John Plumly executors.

ELIZABETH STOCKDALE, born 8 mo. 14, 1713, died 6 mo. 28, 1721.[2]

MARY STOCKDALE, born 7 mo. 1, 1716.

William and Dorothy (Iden) Stockdale are supposed to have been also the parents of these:

HANNAH STOCKDALE, of Falls Township, married 9 mo. 19, 1740, at Falls Mtg., Samuel Bunting, of Bristol Township, son of Samuel and Priscilla (Burgess) Bunting.

WILLIAM STOCKDALE, of Middletown Township, married 2 mo. 17, 1746, at Middletown Mtg., Sarah Field, daughter of Benjamin and Sarah, of Middletown Tp. On May 19, 1749, he bought ½ acre, and on May 16, 1750, one acre adjoining, in Middletown Tp.;[3] his executors (widow Sarah and brother John) sold[4] these 1½ acres Jan. 19, 1757. The last deed calls him "late of Wrightstown," but his will has him "of Buckingham." This will[5] dated Jan. 29, 1755, directs his executors to sell his house and lot in Middletown Tp. (the 1½ acres above); leaves one-third of his estate, real and personal, to his wife, and the other two-thirds to his three children, Hannah, William and Thomas; and appoints his wife and his brother, John Stockdale, executors. It was probated July 26, 1755, and letters were granted to Sarah Stockdale and John Stockdale, the executors named.

JOHN STOCKDALE, mentioned in will of his brother, William, 1755. This was probably the John Stockdale who married 24. MARY ATKINSON, daughter of John and Mary (Smith) Atkinson.

Dorothy (Iden) Stockdale, married second, in 5th or 6th month, 1734, Daniel Burgess, widower, of Falls Township.

[1] Bucks Co. Will Book 3, p. 207.
[2] Register of Middletown Mo. Mtg.
[3] Bucks Co. Deed Book 16, pp. 348 and 350.
[4] Bucks Co. Deed Book 16, p. 351.
[5] Bucks Co. Will Book 2, p. 283.

The third William Stockdale mentioned at the beginning of this note, was of somewhat earlier date than either of the above, and not, so far as known, ever a resident of Bucks County. He was an eminent minister of the Society of Friends, came to Pennsylvania from Ireland in 1684/5, and lived in New Castle County (now in Delaware), where he was a Justice of the County Court. In 1689 he became a Provincial Councillor, after which date he appears to have lived in Philadelphia, where he died in 7 mo. 1693. He was a member of Newark Mo. Mtg., the register of which records the deaths of his daughter Ruth 6 mo. 30, 1687 and wife Jane 7 mo. 8, 1688. He married again in 1689, Hannah Druett. No other particulars of his family appear there, nor is there any will or administration of his on record in Philadelphia, where he died. An extended account of him is given in Albert Cook Myers's *Immigration of the Irish Quakers into Pennsylvania* (Swarthmore, 1902), pp. 267–271. As he came from Ireland it is unlikely that he was any near relative of the William Stockdale who married Alice Hynde, for the latter's relatives, as shown by the deed from his heirs, March 7, 1744, lived in England. But he might have been father of the William Stockdale who married Grace ―――― and Dorothy Iden, though our lack of knowledge of any children, (except Ruth) leaves this an open question.

BEDANT-ROBBINS-LAKE BIBLE RECORDS.

Copied by SARAH A. RISLEY and Contributed by ARTHUR ADAMS.

These records were copied February 25, 1913, by Miss Sarah A. Risley from Bible records in the possession of Mr. David R. Lake, formerly of Port Norris, Cumberland County, now of Pleasantville, Atlantic County, New Jersey. Some of the records are on leaves still in place in the old Bible described below; others are on loose leaves laid therein. These loose leaves, or some of them, may have been taken from other Bibles.

The old Bible was printed by Adrian Watkins, his Majesty's Printer, and is dated at Edinburgh in 1756. The fly-leaf bears the name of John Bedant, with the date of his birth. In many instances the ink has so faded that names and dates are almost or altogether undecipherable. It will be observed that in a few cases the names of individuals are repeated with variations of dates. Probably at the time the copy was made the original was already illegible; now it is difficult or impossible sometimes to decide which is the correct date.

The records are, some of them, of so ancient a date, and the names so familiar in Cumberland County, that they should be made accessible to all who may be interested.

John Bedant was Born the 1 of March 1684

Abigil Bedant wife of John Bedant was Born March the 6, 1697

John Robbens was Born March the 29 in the year of our Lord 1719

Mary Robbens the wife of John Robens was born in the year of our Lord September 4, 1720

Mary Robbens the Daughter of John Robbens was born March the 18 Day 1752

John Robbens the Son of John Robens was born apReal 30 Day 1754

(John Bedant Robbens

Ruth Robbens was born august the 17 Day 1756
Rachel Robbens was born febuary the 3 Day 1760
Silvea hand was born December 28 Day 1767
Gabriel Gleen was born Febuary the Last Day 1753.
John Robens his book God giv him grace therein to reed look not in to look but understand that learning is beter hous or land

        John Robens
        Mary Soudars
        Ruth Dalles
        Rachel Robens

Ruth Dalles was Born august the 17 day in the year of our Lord 1756,

Mary Dalles the dater of Ruth Dalles was Born the 2 day of October in the year of our Lord 177(– (4)

Ruth is my name and Dalles coms by nater heven is my dwelling place and god is my creator when I am ded and laid in grave and all my bons are roten when this you see remember when others are forgotten
      Ruth Dalles her hand and pen

Rubin peper was Borne July the 15 day 1802
Elizabeth Lake was born febuary the 15 day 1805
Rebecca Lake was born the 14 Day of May 1808
Beaston Lake was born September the 9th, 18010
Robert Lake was born apriel 4d 1789
Henrey Hall was Born november the 17 D 1813
Robert Lake was born August the 13 d 1817
Daniel Lake was born October the 29, 1819
Charles D. Lake was Born March the 4 D 1821
John R Lake was Born May the 26 D 1823
Caroline Lake was Born febuary 27 D1825
Samuel Lake September 29th Day 1827
Daniel Lake Decesed January the 26, 1838, aged 18 yers 2 munts 28 Days

Mary L. Garrison was born December the 18 day in the year 1848

Mary L. Garrison Decesed July 12 day, 1851, aged 2 years, six munts and 24 days

Robert Lake was born october 14d 1777; Deceased September 24, 1840, aged 62, 11 months 10 days

Henrey Hall was born March 14, 1783; Deceased December the 8, 1814

The children of Mary Hall and Henrey Hall, her husband, were born as follows:

William Hall was born february the 24, 1812 and deceased february 17, 1813

Henry Hall was born November 17, 1813; deceased January the 12, 1837, aged 23 yers 1 munth 12 Dayes

In Memory of John Robbens who Departed this Life November the 28, 1780

Mary Wescoat the wife of John Robbens while both alive Departed this Life June the 9, 1795

In memary of Rachel Ledew the Daughter of John Robbins Deseat who Departed this life September the 23, 1798

In memary of Gabriel glan who Departed this life August the 22, 1798

In memary of Mary Soudars the daughter of John Robbins Deseased who Departed this Life August —25—1800

Temperance Robbins the Daughter of John and Temperance Robbins Departed this Life September the 5, 1808

In memory of Eleazer Robbins, the son of John Robbins and Temperance Robbins who departed this Life October the 2, 1801 (?) age 6 years—5

In memary of Mary Soudars, Daughter of John Robbins who Departed this Life august 25, 1800

In memory of Temperance Lon   of the Reverant David Sheppard (?) who departed this Life July 28, 17—(probably 1798 or 1799)

In memary of Mary Vanaman, Daughter of David Sheppard (?) Departed this Life January the 15, 1800 (?)

John Robbins was Born Apriel the 30, 1754, changed to 1762

Temperance Robbins the wife of John Robbins was Born March the 17, 1762 changed to 1754

Their children as follows:

John Robbins the son of John and Temprance Robbins was Born September the 3, 1780

Richard Robbins, the son of John Robbins and Temprence his wife was Born January the 2—1783

Sarah Robbins was born April the 9—1785

David Robbins was born August the 2—1787

Mary Robbins was Born Apriel the 4,—1789

Levi Robbins was Born May 5, 1791

Lidya Robbins was Born March 23,—1793

Elezar and Temprance Robbins was Born Apriel the 12—179–

Another place

John Robbins was born Apriel 30, 1755

Temprence, wife of John Robbins, was born March 17, 1762

John Robbins was born September 3, 1782

Richard Robbins was Born January 2—1784

Sarah Robbins was born Apriel 9—1786

David Robbins was Born August 2, 178–

Mary Robbins was Born Apriel 4, 1790

Levi Robbins was Born M

Liada Robbins was Born

Temprance Robbins was Born   (torn off)

Other side of sheet

John Robbins was born April 30, 1755

Temprance, wife, was born March the 17, 1762

John, son of John and Temprance, was born September the 3, 1781

"   "   "   January
Daughter of   "   6–1785
Son of   "   August the 2, 1787 (1787)

Molly Robbins Daughter of John and Temprance Robbins was Born April the 4, 1789

BENNETT-SHOCKLEY GENEALOGICAL NOTES.—Records copied from Family Bible in possession of Mrs. Shockley, Milford, Del.—
Harriot Bennett daughter of John Bennett and of Elizabeth his wife was born the 16th. day of March in the year of our Lord 1816.

John Bennett son of Nehemiah Bennett and Hester his wife was born Sept. 10th day in the year of our Lord 1785.

Elizabeth R. Bennett daughter of Geo. Rickards and Patience his wife was born Dec. 15th. day in the year of our Lord 1795.

John Bennett and Elizabeth R. Bennett were married Jan. 18th. day in the year of our Lord 1815.

Nehemiah Bennett son of John Bennett and Elizabeth his wife was born Jan. 31st. 1819 about the break of day Sunday morning.

Nehemiah Bennett born the 15th. day of April in the year of our Lord 1758.

Hester Bennett born the 31st. day of Dec. in the year of our Lord 1761.

Abigail Bennett born the 12th. [?] day of Nov. in the year of our Lord 1780 the daughter of Nehemiah Bennett and Hester.

Aaron Bennett the son of Nehemiah Bennett and Hester born the 11th. day of Dec. in the year of our Lord 1782.

Patience Bennett the daughter of Nehemiah Bennett and Hester born the 6th. day of May in the year of our Lord 1788.

Hester Bennett the daughter of Nehemiah Bennett and Hester born the 22nd. day of Feb. in the year of our Lord 1790.

Elizabeth Bennett daughter of Nehemiah Bennett and Hester his wife was born in the year of our Lord July 6th 1796.

Elizabeth the wife of Jno. Bennett departed this life Nov. the 23rd day in the year of our Lord 1819 Tuesday about 5 oclock in the morning aged 23 years 11 months and eight days.

Nehemiah son of John Bennett and Elizabeth his wife departed this life Aug. the 12th. 1820 at three oclock in the morning aged 18 months and 12 days.

Arcady S. Robinson daughter of John Robinson and Sarah his wife was born 30th. of Nov. in the year of our Lord A.D. 1804.

John Bennett and Arcady S. Robinson were married 5th of Sept. 1821 about 5 oclock P.M. Wednesday.

Joseph Smith Bennett son of John Bennett and Arcady his wife was born the 10th. of Oct. A.D. 1822 Thursday about 1 oclock P.M.

Elizabeth Rickards Bennett daughter of John Bennett and Arcady his wife was born 1st. of Feb. A.D. 1824 about 2 oclock P.M. on Sunday.

Sarah Bell Bennett daughter of John Bennett and Arcady his wife was born the 6th. of Aug. A.D. 1825 about 3 oclock P.M. on Saturday.

Hester Bennett the wife of Nehemiah Bennett decd. departed this life Feb. 11th. in the year of our Lord 1845 about 6 A.M. aged 85 yrs 1 month and 10 days.

William Shockley and Elizabeth Bennett were married Oct. the 11th. day in the year of our Lord. 1826.

William Shockley son of Wm Shockley and Elizabeth his wife was born Sept. the 10th. in the year of our Lord, 1827.

Elizabeth B. Shockley daughter of William Shockley and Elizabeth his wife was born May the 24th. day in the year of our Lord 1829.

The following records are in the back of the book:

William Lofland was born Feb. 13th. in the year of our Lord 1771 his hand and pen witnessing.

[The above was the only entry on its page.]

Entries of the Shockley Family.

William Shockley son of William Shockley and Elizabeth his wife was born in the year of our Lord 1806, Sept. the 17th day.

Elizabeth Bennett daughter of Nehemiah Bennett and Hester his wife was born July the 6th. day 1796.

William Shockley departed this life at 10 min. after 2 oclock P.M. on Wednesday Dec. the 30th. in the year of our Lord 1863 aged 57 yrs. 3 months and 13 days.

Elizabeth Shockley relict of Wm. Shockley decd. departed this life at 15 min. after 2 oclock A.M. on Wed. May 19th. in the year of our Lord 1869 aged 72 years 10 months and 13 days.

Elizabeth B. Shockley daughter of Wm. Shockley and Elizabeth his wife departed this life Dec. the 30th day in the year of our Lord 1833 aged four years seven months and five days.

WILLIAM BILES.

BY MILES WHITE, JR., BALTIMORE, MD.

At what time the Biles family first settled in Dorsetshire, and whence they originally came, is uncertain. The earliest recorded will of any of the name, in either the Consistory Court or the Archdeaconry Court at Blandford, is that of Dorothy Biles, of Dorchester, in 1693.[1] The wills of Josiah Byles, of Dorchester, in 1707, and of four others who resided at Woodland, Holwell, Weymouth, and Shilling Okeford, are all that appear of record prior to 1710, which would seem to indicate that the family had not then been long resident there.

The Register of the Parish of St. John the Baptist, of Devizes, Wilts, shows that 12 Nov., 1593, Josias Byle married Anne Lye;[2] and *Alumni Oxonienses 1500–1714* contains the names of two Byles, as follows:

" Byle, William, ' serviens' of Cornwall, Exeter Coll., matric. 26 Oct., 1660, B.A. 1664, M.A. 1667.

" Byles, John, *s.* Daniel of Dorchester, Dorset, p.p. Exeter Coll., matric. 20 Nov., 1685; aged 16, B.A. 1689."

The latter was probably related to the subject of this sketch, who, however, always spelt his name " Biles," though in contemporary records it was frequently spelt " Byles." [3]

---

[1] *Index Library, British Record Society.*

[2] *N. Eng. Hist. and Gen. Reg.*, vol. li. p. 186.

[3] A writer in the *N. Eng. Hist. and Gen. Reg.* (vol. vii. p. 300) has said that "'this name has undergone more varieties of spelling than one would suppose possible in so short a syllable. Farmer spells it ' Byles,' ' Byley' and ' Bylie.' In the *H. and G. Reg.* for 1849, p. 55, it is spelt ' Byly.' Mr. Stone in his History of Beverly spells it ' Byles.'"

In the *Visitation of Cornwwall, 1620* (Harleian Soc. Pub., vol. ix.), the name appears as Bill, Byll, Beyle, Byle, Bile, Beele, Beile, Beill, Beale, Biell, Biele, and Debyll, and it is stated that there are numerous entries of the name of Beele in the Registers of the Parish of St. Ewe, and that Roger Beyle and Walter Byle were both members of Parlia-

The names of the parents of William, Charles, and Thomas Biles do not appear in any account of the first ment in the time of Edward III., and that William Biell was an Alderman of the Towne and Borroughe of Saltashe in co. Cornwall in 1620.

The Hertfordshire family of Bill was a prominent one there from about 1400. (*Notes and Queries*, 1st ser., vols. vii. p. 286, x. p. 530, xi. p. 49 ; *Dict. Nat. Biog.*, vol. v. p. 29.) Of this family was Rev. Wm. Bill, Master of St. John's College, Cambridge, 1546, Master of Trinity College, 1551, one of Committee to prepare form of Prayer Book, 1559, first Dean of Westminster Abbey, 1560, and Lord Almoner to Queen Elizabeth. A branch of this family settled in Staffordshire and their descendants now live at Farley Hall.

There were several early settlers of New England who were named Bill, Bills or Billes, Byles and Byley (Savage's *Geneal. Dict.*, vol. i. pp. 177, 179, 326) ; of these Josiah Byles, the father of the noted preacher Rev. Mather Byles, came from Winchester, co. Hants, prior to 1695. Henry Byley came, in 1638, in the "Bevis" of Southampton, from Salisbury, where the name of the family is found in Registers of St. Edmunds Parish between 1,582 and 1636 (*N. Eng. Hist. and Gen. Reg.*, vol. li. pp. 181–8) as Bile, Biley, Byle, Byley, and Bylie ; and his grandfather describes himself in his will dated 18 Oct., 1633, proved 23 June, 1634, as Henry Biley the elder, of New Sarum, Wilts (Ibid., vol. lii. p. 44).

There was also a Thomas Bills, of Barnstable, Mass. (probably the son of William, who settled at Barnstable in 1640, and who may have been the Willen Bill of Great Torrington in Devonshire (Ibid., vol. xiv. p. 341), who at the age of 28 took oath of allegiance at Dartmouth, 20 Feby., 1634), who 1st married 3 Oct., 1672, Ann, dau. of Wm. Twining, by whom he had two daus. Ann and Elizabeth, mentioned in will of Wm. Twining (Phila. Wills, *Liber* B, *fol.* 402) ; and 2dly married 2 May, 1676, Joanna Twining (said by Savage to be niece of above Wm. Twining and by Twining Genealogy to have been his dau.), by whom he had three sons and three daus. ; most of whom were born at Eastham, Mass. (*N. Eng. Hist. and Gen. Reg.*, vol. vi. p. 43), where he removed from Barnstable, and where he was living in 1695. Wm. Twining removed from Mass., and settled in Bucks Co., Penna., and Thomas Bills and family settled in New Jersey, and were members of Shrewsbury Mo. Mtg of Friends, the Register of which shows the dates of death of Thomas and Joanna to have been respectively 2nd mo. 2, 1721, and 4th mo. 4, 1723.

Some of the above-mentioned persons may have been of the same family as the subject of this sketch, but no proof thereof has been obtained.

named, and it is not certain whether there were other children or not, and very little is known of their early life and occupations.

When William Biles became a Friend, and whom and when he married, may possibly be shown by the Minutes of Friends' Meeting in Dorsetshire; but the Register does not contain this information, nor does it make mention of any of his brothers or their families. It does, however, show the names and dates of birth of five of his children.

Pemberton's List of Arrivals [1] states that "William Biles, of Dorchester, in the County of Dorset, vile monger, and Johannah, his wife, arrived in Delaware river, in the 'Elizabeth & Sarah' of Waymouth, the 4th of the 4th M° 1679.[2] *Children.* William, George, John, Elizabeth, Johanah, Rebecca and Mary Biles. *Servants.* Edward Hancock, to serve 8 years: loose the last of the 3^{d} M° 1687. To have 50 acres of land. Elizabeth Petty, to serve 7 years: loose the last of the 3^{d} M° 1686. To have 50 acres of land.

" Charles Biles, of the town and County above. Arrived in the ship aforesaid, the time aforesaid."

Pemberton is in error as to Rebecca and Mary Biles having come, with their parents, from England. His List was not made until 1684,[3] and he evidently recorded all seven of William Biles's children, who were living at that time, instead of the five who actually came with him.

Whether Charles Biles brought with him a wife is unknown; no record of his marriage or death has been found, and as no wife or children are recorded in the List, it is quite probable that he married in America. He was a

[1] PA. MAG. HIST. AND BIOG., vol. ix. p. 225; Battle's *Bucks Co.*, p. 677.

[2] One recent account states that they "landed in New Castle County, Delaware, April 4 [sic] 1679." I have been unable to find any corroboration of this statement, and believe it erroneous, and that they landed in New Jersey. See Smith's *Hist. N. J.*, p. 109; also *Hist. Delaware Co., Pa.*, p. 447.

[3] PA. MAG. HIST. AND BIOG., vol. ix. p. 223; *Publications* So. Hist. Assoc., vol. v. p. 391.

brother of William, and appears to have always resided in New Jersey. He died and his widow remarried prior to March 9, 1697/8, as shown by a deed, dated that day,[1] but signed June 8, 1698, between Joseph Wood, of Bucks Co., Penna., yeoman, and Sarah, late widow of Charles Biles, of Maidenhead, Burlington Co., West Jersey, deceased, and Alexander Biles, second son of said Charles Biles and Sarah Biles, now Sarah Brearly, in which mention is also made of "ye two daughters of Charles Biles," names not given.

Charles Biles also had a son John, for the will of John Biles, of Maidenhead, Hunterdon Co., yeoman, dated May 29, 1740, was probated July 22, 1740.[2] In it mention is made of his wife Elizabeth, daughter Sarah, two sons John and Charles, and the Executors were "my wife and my brother Alexander Biles."

Charles Biles in 1694, in a deed, describes himself as " of Maidenhead, Province West New Jersey, yeoman," and 10th mo. 13, 1695,[3] he purchased of John English, of Burlington Co., 200 acres "above ye ffalls of the Delaware."[4]

Proud mentions William Biles as among those of the Society of Friends who arrived in the Province of New Jersey before the grant of Pennsylvania to William Penn, and who appear to be mentioned as active and useful, not only in their own religious society, but most of them also in a civil capacity in and about Burlington.[5]

How long William Biles tarried in New Jersey is not certain. The biographical sketch of him in *The Friend*[6] says he " appears to have resided a time at Burlington," and in the *History of Burlington and Mercer Counties*[7] it is stated that he settled *at* Burlington; while W. J. Buck, in his *History of Bucks County*,[8] says he settled in Bucks County in

[1] W. J. Deeds, *Liber* B, *fol.* 658.
[2] W. J. Wills, *Liber* 4, *fol.* 247.
[3] All dates in this article are Old Style.
[4] N. J. Deeds, *Liber* B, *fol.* 593.
[5] *Hist. Penna.*, vol. i. p. 159 n.
[6] Vol. xxviii. p. 102.
[7] P. 113; see also Raum's *Hist. N. J.*, vol. i. p. 106. [8] P. 20.

1679. He seems to have held large tracts of land in New Jersey, which, however, all seem to have been purchased after he settled in Bucks County, Pa.

The first purchase appears to have been that tract described in a deed [1] from Thomas Green, of Maidenhead, Burlington Co., West New Jersey, yeoman, to William Biles, of County of Bucks, province of Penna., Merchant, dated 10 day of ye month called Aprill, 1696, and acknowledged the 3d of ye first month, 1697, before Mahlon Stacy, Justice, as 300 acres, being part of 400 acres, lying above ye ffalls within ye territories of Maidenhead. Consideration £55.

In other deeds he is described as "William Biles of Bucks County, Gent," "William Byles of Bucks County, yeoman," and "William Biles of Bucks County, Merchant." His purchases were located principally in Burlington and Salem Counties,[2] and also included "$\frac{1}{30}$ part of a share of land in West New Jersey, America," and "$\frac{1}{15}$ of $\frac{1}{100}$ of a whole propriety in West Jersey." In 1702 he was appointed by William Crouch, of London, Upholsterer, and James Wass, of London, Chirurgeon, as their attorney,[3] and as such conveyed various tracts of land to John Bryarly and John Swift, of New Jersey, and to John Hough, of Bucks Co., Pa.

In 1704 Joseph Wass, of London, sailed for America, and James Wass, Sr., Chyrurgion, appointed William Biles and Edward Shippen, of Pa., Merchants, Joseph Wass, now on a voyage to Pa., and Joshua Barkstead, late of London, now of W. N. J. his attys,[4] and they in 1705 conveyed to Robt. Ayers, of Rhode Island, 2200 acres in Salem Co. and to Thomas Stanford 300 acres called Quiahocking Islands.

September 15 and 16, 1707, James Wass sold to William Biles all his several tracts of land in or near Quahoking, Cohanzie and Morris River in W. N. J.[5] and William Biles, in 1709 (after he had made his will in which he bequeathed these tracts), conveyed to Joseph Kirkbride, of Bucks Co., Pa., and Thomas Lambert, of Burlington Co., W. N. J., parts of two tracts, one called Quohokin containing 4500 acres and the other being 10,000 acres in Salem Co., bordering on Morris River and Delaware Bay.

Through his large landed interest he became a member of the "Council of Proprietors of Western Division of New

[1] N. J. Deeds, *Liber* B, *fol.* 630.

[2] N. J. Deeds, *Liber* B, *fol.* 741; AAA, *fol.* 132, 133, 134, 139, 140, 141, 142, 220, 252; BB, *fol.* 275, 309, 310.

[3] Ibid., AAA, *fol.* 89, 148, 149, 151, 153, 154.

[4] Ibid., AAA, *fol.* 115, 184, 203.

Ibid., BBB, *fol.* 345 and 347; AAA, *fol.* 412 and 413.

Jersey," and when that body, 14 November, 1706, received in Council from the Gov. Lord Cornbury a Prohibition to granting any warrants for laying out lands &c., and a Petition from Proprietors and Purchasers of West Jersey, to Lord Cornbury, was drawn up, asking for the removal of the prohibition, we find William Biles [1] among the signers.

In 1680 the first regular correspondence between the Friends in America and London Yearly Meeting was begun by an epistle from the Monthly Meeting at Burlington,[2] in which it was particularly urged that, in order to prevent impostors and designing persons from coming among them, no Friends should remove to them without certificates from the Society where they had previously lived. This epistle was signed by those present at the meeting, and afterwards by William Biles [3] and some others who were not present.

The birth of William Biles's daughter Rebeckah in 1680 is entered in the Records of Burlington Monthly Meeting, and he was doubtless then a member of that meeting, on whichever side of the Delaware River he then resided. For although in Bucks County " the Quakers had a regular and established meeting, for religious worship, before the country bore the name of Pennsylvania," [4] which meeting was held at the houses of William Yardley, William Biles,[5] and others, yet there was no monthly meeting until 1683, when the first one was set up at the house of William Biles, and continued to be held at houses of Friends till 1690, when the first Falls Meeting-House was built near Fallsington, which was the first building for worship erected in the county.[6]

It was probably on the door of William Biles's house that Phineas Pemberton, in 1683, placed a notice of the estab-

[1] *N. J. Archives*, 1st ser., vol. iii. p. 165.
[2] Proud's *Hist. Penna.*, vol. i. p. 159.
[3] Smith's *Hist. Penna.* in Hazard's *Register*, vol. vi. p. 182; *The Friend*, vol. xviii. p. 407.
[4] Proud's *Hist. Penna.*, vol. i. p. 217 n.
[5] Smith's *Hist. Penna.* in Hazard's *Register*, vol. vii. p. 116; *Friends' Miscellany*, vol. vii. p. 29.
[6] Buck's *Bucks Co., Penna.*, p. 81.

lishment of the weekly post in response to the request ot the Governor,[1] "carefully to publish" this information "on the *meeting house door*, and other public places."

In 1679 Jasper Dankers made a copy of a map of the Delaware River from Burlington to Trenton, which has been supposed to have been made by some English surveyors. On this map [2] William Biles is shown to have 309 acres on the west side of the Delaware River, and the road from Burlington to "ye ffalls" passed through it. Holme's Map of Bucks Co., Pa., begun in 1681, shows that he owned two tracts of land fronting on the Delaware River, and that William and Charles Biles owned together another tract some little distance back from the river.[3]

Davis, in his *History of Bucks County*, says [4] that "in the summer and fall of 1679 and spring of 1680 several English settlers took up land on the river bank just below the falls. . . . William Biles, three hundred and nine acres. . . . He was a man of talent and influence and a leader;" and in another place he says,[5] "Of the original settlers in Falls, several of them were there before the country came into Penn's possession. They purchased the land of Sir Edmund Andros, who represented the Duke of York, and were settled along the Delaware from the falls down; among whom were William Biles [and others], whose lands bordered on the river. These grants were made in 1678 or 1679, that of Biles embraced 327 acres, for which Penn's

[1] *Friends' Miscellany*, vol. vii. pp. 28 and 29.
[2] *Burlington and Mercer Cos.*, p. 56.
[3] This last-mentioned tract contained 472 acres, and was granted by warrant dated 2nd mo. 13, 1683, laid out by Surveyor 4th mo. 13, 1683, and confirmed by Letters Patent from William Penn dated 5th mo. 29, 1684. William and Charles Biles divided this tract 8th mo. 14, 1686 (Bucks Co. Deeds, *Liber* 1, *fol.* 102 and 105), and Charles sold his equal half, containing 236 acres, to Abel Janney 7th mo. 12, 1694, and William sold his moiety of 236 acres to John Cuff or Luff 8th mo. 18, 1686.
[4] P. 35.
[5] Pp. 103 and 104; see also Buck's *Bucks Co., Penna.*, p. 80; Hazard's *Annals of Penna.*, p. 468.

warrant is dated 9th, 8th month, 1684, surveyed 23d, same month, and patented 31st, 11th month."

These two accounts probably refer to the same tract, as the below mentioned deeds (which I am informed by Mr. W. S. Ely, who made the examination for me, are all under which William Biles obtained possession, so far as the records show) do not convey two tracts of this size and description. There are two patents recorded from Penn to William Biles, one [1] dated 1st mo. 31, 1684, for 306 acres, for which warrant had been issued by Sir Edmund Andros in 1679 and from Penn 3rd mo. 9, 1684 ; the other [2] for 173 acres, dated 5th mo. 31, 1684, containing the same recital. This last tract of 173 acres William conveyed 2nd mo. 14, 1693, to Samuel Beakes,[3] and the former he deeded 4th mo. 14, 1698, to his son William Biles, Jr., cooper, as the "Farm and Tract in Falls Township whereon I live, containing 309 acres."

3rd mo. 16, 1701, William Biles conveyed to William White [4] 100 acres which had been patented to Philip Conway 5th mo. 15, 1684, and by him conveyed, by endorsement thereon, to Thomas Biles, brother of William, "and said William purchasing same had it confirmed by patent from Penn dated March 11th, 1692," but no such patent appears of record in Bucks County. Ann Milcombe conveyed 8th mo. 6, 1685, to William Biles 200 acres patented to her in 1684, which he, 5th mo. 5, 1688, deeded to Joseph English ; and said English, 10th mo. 10, 1688, conveyed to Biles 102 acres patented to English in 1687.[5] Henry Baker, 7th mo. 1, 1698, conveyed to Biles two tracts of 100 acres and 190 acres,[6] which William conveyed to his son John 3rd mo. 24, 1707, as 300 acres. In 1705 there appears also to have been issued a patent to William Biles [7] for 472 acres in two tracts, one of 343 acres for 300 made up of Rowland's and Bennett's entries, and the other 129 acres for 100 of Harrison's ; and these two tracts correspond in size to those shown on Cutler's map of 1703, as then belonging to William Biles, situated very near the northwestern corner of the Manor of Pennsbury, on the Bristol Township line, and it was probably to this tract, or the Atkinson one mentioned below, that William Penn referred in his letter of 7th mo. 30, 1705, to Governor Evans.

[1] Bucks Co. Deeds, *Liber* 11, *fol.* 467.
[2] Ibid., *Liber* 2, *fol.* 60.
[3] Ibid., *Liber* 2, *fol.* 61 ; *Liber* 5, *fol.* 208.
[4] Ibid., *Liber* 3, *fol.* 38.
[5] Ibid., *Liber* 1, *fol.* 9, 182, 196.
[6] Ibid., *Liber* 2, *fol.* 205 ; *Liber* 5, *fol.* 133 ; *Pa. Arch.*, 2d ser., vol. xix. p. 423.
[7] Ibid., p. 473.

A tract of 300 acres which Thomas Atkinson took up but did not pay for was, after the marriage of William Biles to his widow, released by her three sons Isaac, William, and Samuel, as they severally became of age, to George Biles for a consideration,[1] and from him it passed through Solomon Warder to William Biles, Sr., and from him in 1707 to William Paxson.

Davis tells us that[2] "Biles's island, in the Delaware, a mile below the falls, and containing 300 acres, was sold to William Biles about 1680 by Orecton, Nannacus, Nenemblahocking, and Patelana, free native Indians, in consideration of £10, but was not actually conveyed by deed. The 19th of March, 1729, Lappewins and Captain Cumbansh, two Indian 'Sackemen,' and heirs and successors of the Indians above named, confirmed the said island to William Biles, Jr.,[3] son of William Biles, the elder, now deceased, in consideration of seven pounds in Indian goods. The deed contained a warranty against the grantors, their heirs, and all other Indians."

Davis furthermore states that[4] "Biles became a large land owner. He sold 5000 acres in this county near Neshaminy to William Lawrence [and others], but the purchasers could find only 2000 acres. In 1718 James Logan issued an order to survey 3000 additional acres, not already settled or surveyed." The Land Records show that William Biles, as attorney in fact for Thomas Hudson, conveyed several thousand acres in Bucks County to various individuals; and that these 5000 did not belong to him individually is shown by the Minutes of the Board of Property of the Province of Pennsylvania,[5] which state that William Lawrence and others "purchased of William Biles late of sd. County 5000 acres of Land in the sd. County belonging to one Thomas Hudson whose Atty he then was," etc., and that "The whole 5000 acres was formerly surveyed and sold to the above Persons of Long Island by William Biles, under certain Bounds, but the greater part being under an earlier survey to Dennis Rochford, is taken by his assignees."

Proud also states that[6] William Biles was a preacher among the Quakers, among the first settlers there, where he appears to have taken up land, under Governor Andros, of New York, prior to William Penn's grant of the Province. He is said to have been a very useful person both in

[1] Bucks Co. Deeds, *Liber* 3, *fol.* 86, 167.
[2] *Hist. Bucks Co.*, p. 117.
[3] Bucks Co. Deeds, *Liber* 26, *fol.* 380.
[4] *Hist. Bucks Co.*, p. 104.
[5] *Pa. Arch.*, 2d ser., vol. xix. pp. 682, 693, 697.
[6] *Hist. Penna.*, vol. i. p. 237 n.

the civil and religious line, being often in the Council and Assembly.[1]

In fact, he was an office-holder before the Province passed from under the Duke of York to William Penn, for he held office under the Pro-Provincial Government.[2] It has been said that in 1680 "the only European settlements comprised within its [Pennsylvania's] limits were included in Upland county, and were subject to the jurisdiction of Upland Court;"[3] and the records of that Court show that October 13, 1680, land was laid out by order of this Court "on ye west syde of delow^r Riv^r and on ye South East syde of hataorackan Creeke,"[4] which was about Pennsbury Manor in Bucks County.

Though no record of the appointment of officers nor the establishment of such a Court has been found (the Minutes of the Governor and Council of New York, 1678–1683, not being in existence, so far as known), yet Colonial documents still preserved at Albany show clearly that there was in 1680 a Court at Crewcorne, or Creekehorne, and that William Biles was a member thereof.

No mention of this Court has been found elsewhere than in published records of the State of New York, and no historians of Pennsylvania or of Bucks County allude to it.

In reply to inquiries, Dr. William H. Egle writes me that "Crookhorne in Falls Township, Bucks county, was the first seat of justice of the county," and General W. W. H. Davis writes, "Crewcorne was on the Penna. side of the Delaware at Trenton Falls. It had no surveyed bounds, but a frontier settlement and local court was held there. The Upland Court had jurisdiction in Bucks to the falls. The Court at Manhattan had jurisdiction in Bucks in the

---

[1] Vide *Pa. Arch.*, 2d ser., vol. ix. pp. 623, 752–754; *Duke of York's Laws*, pp. 485, 507, 523, 536, 552, 559, 565, 576, 577.

[2] *Pa. Arch.*, 2d ser., vol. ix. p. 616.

[3] Smith's *Hist. Delaware Co., Pa.*, p. 125; *Mem. Pa. Hist. Soc.*, vol. vii. p. 81.

[4] Ibid., vol. vii. pp. 185, 203.

matter of Probate of Wills. My second edition of History of Bucks Co. will have new matter about Crewcorne."

The "new town of Crewcorne" at the Falls must have been the first settlement of what is now Morrisville. "Gilbert Wheeler called his house 'Crookhorn,' a name long forgotten," says Davis,[1] and John Wood, whose plantation included the present site of Morrisville, described himself in his will, 1692, as "John Wood of Crookhorn in the County of Bucks."

In *N. Y. Colonial Documents*[2] is a Petition of "Inhabitants of the new town, near the falls of the Delaware, called Crewcorne, against the sale of liquor to the Indians," dated "April y⁰ 12th 1680" and addressed "To y⁰ Worthy Governor of New Yorke," and stating that Gilbert Wheeler's and Peter Aldrixman's houses and another one had been "broake open by Indians." This petition was signed by ten persons, and the first name is "Wilh. Biles." He probably delivered it in person, for we find, under the heading [3] "Memorandum of papers delivered to Wm. Biles, a member of the new court at the falls of the Delaware," the following:

"Wm Biles one of there new made Cort there & this day sworne under the penalty of perjury. Apr. 21–1680.

"1. His Commission.

"2. A Warrt to summon Gilb. Wheeler & P. Abr. to appeare here for selling drincks to ye Indyans.

"3. An abstract about ye Records.

"4. An order to Dan: Willet to returne Power of Magistrate.

"5. An order to have a returne about Rolf. Hoskin, drowned by Burlington."

The matter was later presented to the Council, as appears from the following entry: [4]

[1] *Hist. Bucks Co.*, p. 104.
[2] Vol. xii. pp. 645, 646.
[3] Ibid., p. 646; *Calendar N. Y. Hist. Mss.*, pt. ii. p. 87.
[4] *N. Y. Col. Doc.*, vol. xii. p. 650.

"Sundry entries respecting Upland, New Castle and Burlington.
"At a Councell &c May 21. 1680.
"Pres^t the Go : & Councell.
"A peticon from the Inhabitants at the Falls about abuse of drunken Indyans &c.
"Peter Alricks house at his Island near ye Falls & Gilbert Wheeler house broken open.
"A returne from the Commission^{rs} of Burlington at Delaware of 8 men for magistrates according to order.
"A returne from the Const. of Creekehorne at the Falls, of the names of 4 for magistrates according to order likewise," etc.

The liquor question did not rest here, however, for there is preserved the " Complaint of sundry inhabitants of Crewcorne, on the Delaware, against Gilbert Wheeler for selling rum to the Indians," dated " Crewcorne Sep. ye 13th 1680,"[1] addressed " To ye Honorable Governor of N. Yorke," in which, after detailing the great fear and damage they are subjected to, they request that selling the Indians " strong Liquors may be wholly suppressed amongst us by virtue of a Warrant from yor Honor to make distress upon proof given to ye Elected Commissioner for ye time to Come for breach of that Abreviate of ye Law which Will. Biles brought us; wch when we made our Complaint to him he told us his order w^s nothing worth, wch we accounted w^s sufficient but by his words we perseave that he intends to sell Rum himself; so hoping yor Honor in charity will help us we remain," etc.

The Minutes of Falls Monthly Meeting hereafter referred to show the accuracy of the surmise of his neighbors as to William Biles's intention to sell rum to the Indians, and the records of Upland Court show that Gilbert Wheeler's actions were not permitted to go unpunished.

The last actual session of the Upland Court under the Duke of York was held at Kingsesse 14th June, 1681, and William Biles was present and appeared in various rôles.[2]

[1] *N. Y. Col. Doc.*, pp. 658, 659.
[2] *Mem. Pa. Hist. Soc.*, vol. vii. pp. 189, 190, 194; Davis's *Hist. Bucks Co.*, p. 40; *Hist. Chester Co., Pa.*, pp. 18, 363; PA. MAG. HIST. AND BIOG., vol. iii. p. 263.

He informed the Court that Robert Michill, next heir of Robert Hoskins, deceased, was living in England, and desired him to take care of the estate of the deceased in this country. He was one of the jurors in the case of Lasse Dalboo against Swen Lom. As " Constable att ye faals" he gave information against " Gilbert wheeler att ye s^d faals, for selling of strong Licquors by retayle to ye Indians Contrary to ye Lawe & ye forwarning of ye s^d Constable," and Wheeler was fined four pounds and costs. The last act of the judges, before adjourning " till ye 2^d Teusday [13th] of ye month of Septemb^r next," was to appoint " William Boyles to bee surv^r & overseer of ye highwayes from the faales to Poetquessink Creek; hee to take care that ye s^d highwayes be made good & passable, wth bridges over all myry & dirty places."

Before the time adjourned to had arrived, notice was received[1] from " Commander and Councill," dated New York, 21st June, 1681, that William Penn had obtained Letters Patents to the Province, and the Duke of York's authority had ceased; " the old Court closed its session the 13th of September and the new Court opened the next day [?]. Among the business transacted was the appointment of William Biles and Robert Lucas, who lived at the falls, justices of the peace,[2] and pounds, shillings and pence were declared to be the currency of the country." The first entry in the Records of Chester County Court shows that it was held at Upland September 13, 1681, and that Mr. William Byles was one of the justices present.[3]

[1] *Mem. Pa. Hist. Soc.*, vol. vii. pp. 195, 196.
[2] Davis's *Hist. Bucks Co.*, p. 55; *Pa. Arch.*, 2d ser., vol. ix. p. 617.
[3] *Hist. Chester Co., Pa.*, p. 18; Hazard's *Annals of Penna.*, p. 525.

(To be continued.)

WILLIAM BILES.

BY MILES WHITE, JR., BALTIMORE, MD.

William Biles, at different times, was a witness to many wills, deeds, etc., and the fac-simile of his signature, given herein, is taken from the will of Jacob Janney, of Bucks County, dated 8th mo. 2, 1708, and still preserved in the office of the Register of Wills at Philadelphia.

An election was ordered for February 20, 1682, for members of Council and Assembly, to be holden at Philadelphia March 10 following, when William Biles, Christopher Taylor, and James Harrison were elected to the Council from Bucks County.[1]

The first session of this first Council was held in Philadelphia 1st mo. 10, 1682/3, and was presided over by William Penn in person;[2] William Biles was present, and seems to have been regular in his attendance during its sessions and to have taken an important part in framing the laws; on the 16th, 21st, and 26th insts. he was appointed on committees to which were referred the preparation of various bills for the Council,[3] and on 7th mo. 8, 1683, he and three others were appointed "to bring in a Bill concerning horses goeing out and comeing into this Province." He was also present (2d mo. 2, 1683) when the Great Charter was read and thankfully received, and was one of those who signed it.[4]

We find that, according to the entry in the original

[1] Davis's *Hist. Bucks Co.*, p. 65.

[2] *Colonial Records*, vol. i. p. 1; Proud's *Hist. Penna.*, vol i. p. 235; *Delaware Register*, vol. i. p. 331.

[3] *Colonial Records*, vol i. pp. 6, 8, 11, 24.

[4] Ibid., pp. xl, 16; Proud's *Hist. Penna.*, vol. i. p. 239; vol. ii. Appendix, p. 28; Davis's *Hist. Bucks Co.*, p. 65.

records of Bucks County of 1684,[1] showing ear-marks or brands, that William Biles, William Biles, Jr., and Charles Biles were then owners of cattle.

On May 22, 1684, the Provincial Council appointed[2] " One Inferior receiver in Every County, who shall receive directions from ye Deputy Treasurer, who shall receive Instructions from ye Govr and Councill; who Shall not be allowed above 20 lb. p. year;" among whom was "Wm. Biles, for Bucks;" and on February 11, 1685, William Biles and others were appointed to lay out a road in Bucks County.[3] The Council (2d mo. 6, 1685) " Ordered that a Comission be drawne for James Harrison, Tho: Janney, Wm. Yardley, Wm. Biles, Wm. Beaks, John Ottor, Edm^d Bennet & Jno. Swift, to be Justices of the Peace for ye County of Bucks, the year Ensueing."[4] Until the Revolution, justices of the peace were judges in the County Courts in Pennsylvania.

The Council[5] (10th mo. 1, 1685), having been requested that a " Speciall Comission be granted for ye Tryall of David Davis the next Court, who is a Prisoner in ye County of Bucks, on suspition of killing his servant," unanimously agreed " that a Comission be Expeditiously prepared for ye authorising & Impowring of James Harrison, Arthur Cook, Tho. Janney, Wm. Yardley, Wm. Biles, to be special Comiss^{rs} to hear and Determine all heinous and Enormous Crimes that shall be brought before them in ye County of Bucks, in a Court there to begin on ye 10th Ins^t, by them to be held."

The first session of the Assembly to which William Biles was elected was that of 1686, beginning 3d mo. 10 at Philadelphia, and on 3d mo. 11 he and Cornelius Empson were fined twelve pence each for being absent the previous day;[6]

---

[1] *Colonial Records*, p. 77.
[2] Ibid., vol. i. p. 57; Battle's *Bucks Co.*, p. 194.
[3] Ibid., p. 184. [4] Ibid., vol. i. p. 76.
[5] Ibid., p. 114; Battle's *Bucks Co.*, p. 246.
[6] *Votes of Assembly*, vol. i. pt. 1, p. 37.

and William Yardley and he were appointed a committee to acquaint the Council that the Assembly desired to meet the President and Council in a full body. He was a member of the Council and Assembly for so many years that an enumeration of all the committees on which he served would occupy too much space, and mention of only some of the more important ones must suffice. He was frequently appointed to acquaint the Council of the acts or desires of the Assembly, and was often a member of the Committee on "Aggrievances," through the medium of which much of the ordinary business of the Assembly was first brought before the House.

In 1687 the tax levied was given to William Biles to collect;[1] and in this year we are informed[2] that " Wm. Biles, the only merchant along the Delaware who imported and sold Rum, a leading Friend, and several times elected to the Assembly, was called to account for selling rum to the Indians, and Thomas Janney and William Yardley were appointed to wait on him." He said to them[3] that it was " not against the Law neither doth he know that it is any evil to do so, but however, if Friends desire him not to do it, he will for the future forbear it;" which caused a writer in the *Friends' Intelligencer* to say, " It was a remarkable act of a Christian man that he should discontinue to sell rum to the Indians, on account of the desire of his brethren, when it was neither a violation of law nor the Discipline."

In 1689 he served his second term in the Assembly, and was present at the opening session, 3d mo. 10; and he and Joseph Fisher were requested to find out whether the Governor and Council could listen to some proposals from the Assembly.[4] He was appointed also on the Committee on "Aggrievances."

[1] Battle's *Bucks Co.*, p. 189.
[2] Davis's *Hist. Bucks Co.*, p. 835.
[3] MS. Minutes Falls Monthly Meeting; *Friends' Intelligencer*, vol. lvi. p. 489.
[4] *Votes of Assembly*, vol. i. pt. 1, p. 48.

On 11th mo. 2, 1689/90, the Council[1] ordered that "Commissions of ye Peace be made for all ye Counties, and these persons ffollowing to be Inserted, (viz) Bucks Co. Arth. Cook, Jos. Growdon, Wm. Yardly, Tho. Janney, Wm. Byles, Nich. Newlin, Jo^n Brock, Hen. Baker."

In March, 1690, the grand jury thought it necessary that the county be divided into townships, and the court, at its next session, ordered Henry Baker and eleven others, including William Biles, to meet together at the court-house the day before the next court and perform this service; for some reason this order was not obeyed, and at the September term, 1692, the court again took up the matter and appointed a jury, on which were Arthur Cook[2] and twelve others, including William Biles (nine members of the former jury being reappointed), and ordered them " or the greater number of them to meet together at the meeting-house at Neshaminah the 27th day of this instant, and divide this county into townships," which they accordingly did.

Only fragments of the minutes of Councils for 1692 and 1693 (prior to April 26, when Governor Fletcher arrived) remain; and though William Biles was a member[3] for these sessions, it is not known whether or not he took an active part in the proceedings.

The Council of 1693[4] " came on the scene in the midst of very unsettled times; the dissensions of the past two years were still rampant, while hardly had the Council begun its administration when it was deposed by the arrival of Governor Fletcher, with his commission from the Crown, to assume Penn's government, and was supplanted by a new Council appointed by him," and William Biles, who had

[1] *Colonial Records*, vol. i. p. 278; Buck's *Bucks Co., Pa.*, p. 23.

[2] *Publications* So. Hist. Assoc., vol. v. pp. 393, 394; Battle's *Bucks Co.*, p. 190; Davis's *Hist. Bucks Co.*, p. 101; PA. MAG. HIST. AND BIOG., vol. xviii. p. 24.*

[3] *Charter to William Penn* and *Duke of York's Laws*, p. 537; PA. MAG. HIST. AND BIOG., vol. xi. pp. 151–159.

[4] Ibid., vol. xviii. p. 25.

*This last article, a political biography, has not been used in this book.

been elected for the years 1692, 1693, and 1694, went out of the Council.

In 1694 William Biles was again in the Assembly which met 2d mo. 10, 1694, at Philadelphia, and served on the Committee on "Aggrievances,"[1] and on 4th mo. 9 he and three others were ordered to attend the Governor and Council, with the Remonstrance drawn in answer to the Queen's letter and Governor's speech, and to inquire what had been done concerning the bills sent up.

In 1695 Joseph Growden, Phineas Pemberton, and William Biles were elected from Bucks County to the Council which met on April 20,[2] and on the 22d the return of the Sheriff of Bucks County of representatives in Council was read and rejected, "becaus it did not mention the day of their election, nor the rexive years for which the members were to serve;"[3] and on the 24th it was "Ordered, that new writts be issued for their election of representatives upon ye 8th of May next," when William Biles was elected for one year. On May 28 he and one member from each of the other counties "were appointed to Consider of a new frame & modell of governm^t & to make report to the Governo^r & Councill this afternoon." They reported,—

"That they had made some attempts, but Could not agree upon a new frame," and Governor Markham appointed the same committee to meet with him about it. The next day they reported[4] "That nothing could be agreed upon in ord^r to a new modell of governm^t notwithstanding all ye pains & time spent about ye same." The Governor addressed the Council, and upbraided them for taking up much time in endeavoring to lay aside the Charter, which had previously been thankfully accepted, and endeavoring unsuccessfully to make a more easy frame of government; and since the object of their meeting was to advise with him in matters relating to the government, he informed them that the Queen, upon the 21st of August, 1694, had signified, "That a Quota not exceeding eighty men, with their officers, or the value of the chairges

[1] *Votes of Assembly*, vol. i. pt. 1, p. 88.
[2] Battle's *Bucks Co.*, p. 200.
[3] *Colonial Records*, vol. i. pp. 447, 448.
[4] Ibid., pp. 450, 451.

of maintaining y⁶ same, be the measure of the assistance to be given by y⁶ sd province of pennsilvania & Countrie of Newcastle for y⁶ defence & securitie of the province of New-York," etc.

This question occupied the attention of the Legislature for more than one session, for in 1696 ¹ we again find William Biles a member of the Assembly which met 8th mo. 26 at Philadelphia, and on the 30th he was appointed on a committee to consider a way to answer the Queen's letter and preserve the people's privileges.² On the 31st they reported that they had an expedient ready to answer the Queen's letter, but that they recommended before this was put into effect the provisions of the old Charter (that before Governor Fletcher's time) in regard to election of Councillors and Assemblymen should be put in force.

William Biles was returned, as elected, to the Council that met in Philadelphia May 10, 1698, and took his seat on the 11th inst.; ³ and likewise to the Council that met May 10, 1699,⁴ on which date he " did subscribe the declaraon of fidelity, the profession of the Christian belief, & the test."

The Council which met March 30, 1700, received on April 1 the return of the Sheriff of Bucks County of representatives in Council, from which it appears that William Biles was elected for two years,⁵ and appeared and took his seat; and on April 10, the question of laws for securing the people's property in Overplus Lands being debated and left to the consideration of the Governor and Council, " y⁶ prov. Gov. appointed John Simcoke, Joseph Growdon and Wm. Biles ⁶ to meet him att night to consider yrof, & as neer as might be, to adjust y⁶ rates of overplus Lands, according to their neerness to or remoteness from y⁶ town of philadelphia."

On June 7, 1700, the opposition between the members of

---

[1] *Colonial Records*, p. 468.
[2] *Votes of Assembly*, vol. i. pt. 1, p. 94.
[3] *Colonial Records*, vol. i. p. 515.
[4] Ibid., p. 536.   [5] Ibid., p. 568.   [6] Ibid., p. 573.

the upper and lower counties about the number of members and representatives, charges, etc., prevented an agreement about the proposed new Charter,[1] and it having been voted that they would not be governed by the old Charter, but that Penn should resume government under letters patent of King Charles II., the Speaker, in behalf of the representatives in Assembly, William Biles and John Hill, in behalf of those in Council, for the Province and territories respectively, by the unanimous consent of all members present of both Council and Assembly, took the Charter and delivered it up to the Proprietary and Governor.

On October 24, at a Council held at New Castle, the Proprietary "sent for ph. pemberton, Wm. Biles & Jn° Blunston,[2] who having been qualified to be of ye Council, took yr places att ye board."

As William Biles went to England in 1701, he was absent from the meetings of Council that year.

Not only was he a member of the Council for the years 1698–1701, as above stated, but he was also during the years 1699–1701 a Puisne Judge, or one of the Justices of the highest court in the Province.[3] Prior to 1790 the Court of Oyer and Terminer, for trial of higher crimes and appeal, was held by the Justices of the Provincial or Supreme Court, who made a circuit of the counties at stated times, and we find that on April 18, 1699, Edward Shippen, Cornelius Empson, and William Biles held court at Chester.

In 1700 Phineas Pemberton, William Biles, and Richard Hough were appointed Judges of a Court of Inquiry "For the compleat Settling and Establishing of Affairs of Property in this the County of Bucks." That the powers of this Court were very extensive is shown by their commission signed by William Penn 10th mo. 18, 1700, which is given in full in Buck's *History of Bucks County*.[4]

During the early days of the Province there were no

---

[1] *Colonial Records*, p. 588.   [2] Ibid., p. 592.
[3] *Pa. Arch.*, 2d ser., vol. ix. p. 630 ; *Hist. Chester Co., Pa.*, p. 370.
[4] P. 23 ; see Battle's *Bucks Co.*, p. 366.

lawyers there, but William Biles and others appeared for their neighbors and friends, and were called attorneys. It also appears that in December, 1702, the court adjourned to William Biles's house;[1] this was soon after his return from England.

At the Assembly begun at Philadelphia on October 15, 1703, William Biles was present and signed the declaration and test,[2] and on August 21, 1704, he informed the House,[3] " that *Nathaniel Puckle* had a Letter from the *Proprietary* to be communicated to several Persons here, encouraging them to *insist* upon the Privileges of their Charter and Laws, and not tamely give them up; and instanced what Advantage it has been to the People of *Rhode-Island, Connecticut*, and other Proprietary Governments, to assert their Rights," etc.

James Logan, writing to Penn 9th mo. 22, 1704, says,[4] " That ridiculous old man, W. Biles, frequently affirms they will never grant one penny on any account till they have all their privileges explained and confirmed."

In 1704 the animosity between the Proprietary's adherents and his opponents, which had long been an undercurrent in politics, broke forth with great violence, and the country became distinctly divided into two political parties, the Proprietary or Aristocratic and the Popular or Democratic, the former under the leadership of Logan and the latter under that of David Lloyd. William Biles belonged to the latter, while some of his neighbors and personal friends belonged to the former, and were his bitter political enemies.

Logan spoke in such strongly adverse terms of the prominent members of the Popular party that the editor of the *Penn-Logan Correspondence* felt called upon several times to make excuses for him, and to say,[5] " such was the Secretary's

[1] Battle's *Bucks Co.*, pp. 250, 205.
[2] Proud's *Hist. Penna.*, vol. i. p. 455 n.
[3] *Historical Review of Const. and Govt. of Penna.*, p. 65 n.
[4] *Penn-Logan Corresp.*, vol. i. p. 344.
[5] Ibid., vol. ii. p. 34.

zeal for the Proprietary interests that he was not inclined to regard with favor those who were arrayed against them." In his letters to Penn he says,[1]—

"This people think privileges their due, and all that can be grasped to be their native right. . . . They think it their business to secure themselves against a queen's government;" and again,[2] "The generality, however, are honestly and well inclined, and out of assembly are very good men; but when got together, I know not how they are infatuated and led by smooth stories."

The fact that Logan spoke in harsh terms of the public acts of Biles and others does not seem to have affected his regard for and intercourse with them personally; for, after the Evans affair had occurred, we find him writing to William Biles under date of 8th mo. 11, 1708,[3] beginning the letter, "Loving Friend," and closing it, "I am thy well-wishing friend." This letter was partly in regard to a claim of certain persons to Biles's Island, and Logan states, "I will spare no pains nor cost to convince these persons, whoever they are, that they have been in the wrong," etc.

William Biles was Treasurer of Bucks County in 1704,[4] and also collector of money granted the Proprietary by the Legislature; and on March 28[5] he and the other collectors of this fund were summoned to attend the Council, and " to answer for their neglect in Collecting ye sd Tax within their several Districts." He was also a member of the Assembly which met at Philadelphia October 14, 1704, and was one of the committee[6] to which the bill for " the Affirmations to pass in Lieu of Oaths," etc., was committed, 8th mo. 26, and 9th mo. 14 on the committee to prepare the *Votes of Assembly* for publication, and on adjournment of the Assembly (3d mo. 23, 1705) was sued by Governor Evans in an action of £2000 pounds, as related by Logan,[7] "for saying these words on the 11th-month last; '*He is but a*

---

[1] *Penn-Logan Corresp.*, vol. i. p. 299.
[2] Ibid., vol. i. p. 323.
[3] Ibid., vol. ii. p. 299.
[4] *Pa. Arch.*, 2d ser., vol. ix. pp. 744, 743.
[5] *Colonial Records*, vol. ii. p. 124.
[6] *Votes of Assembly*, vol. i. pt. 2, p. 22.
[7] *Penn-Logan Corresp.*, vol. ii. p. 33.

boy; he is not fit to be our Governour. We'll kick him out; we'll kick him out.' And at the ensuing Court, himself not appearing, and David Lloyd, his attorney, demurring upon a plea of privilege as an Assemblyman, which was overruled, he was ordered to plead over and come to an issuable plea; but this he refused, and therefore judgment went against him yesterday. A jury of inquiry sat upon the damages, and found £300 to the Governour."[1]

William Biles wrote a letter to Governor Evans, the original of which is now in the library of the Historical Society of Pennsylvania. It has never been published, and is as follows:

[3d mo. 1705.]

"To John Evans Esqr Liftenant Goven^r of the provience of pensilvania.

"the pettition of Wm Biles of ye County of bucks In all humble manner sheweth

"that thou was pleased to comence an action against me upon Supposesion that I had spoken sum scandelous words of thee but thorough the Inadvertansy or desine of the shreife hee Sumoned me upon the day that I was actually conserned In the servis of the assembley of this provience which ocationed me to plead or Insist upon my priviledge as I was and am a member of that assembley and for that and no other Reason I declined Answering thy declaration and making further defense to thy suit and had it not been for yt I doubt not but I would have prodused such proofe as might have Invalidated that single evidence given against me or at Least Rendered It In Efectuall to maintaine thy—declaration and for my owne part I can singly say that I do not Remember that I ever spoke those words as A Leaged In yt declaration but In Regard thou hast given unto such Information and conserned so much displeasure against me and although thou hast given mee sum discouragement to make any further Application to thee upon that account never the Less I hope thou will not be offended at these few Leines whear by I do signifie unto thee as before I have done that I am

---

[1] The editor of *Penn-Logan Correspondence* (vol. ii. p. 131) remarks that "The plain import of the words was that Evans was a boy, and deserved to be turned out; the correctness of which was shown in the fact that suit was brought in a spirit of boyish petulance, and with the hope that some money might be made out of it. His course (as shown in Logan's letter of 4th mo. 12, 1706) fully establishes the truth of Biles's statement, and much more."

hearttily sorrey for any words by me spoaken at any time conserning thee which hath given thee any Just ocation of ofence neither did I ever act any thing against thee to thy hurt therefore I desiar that thou would be pleased to pas by yt which cannot be recaled and for the future I do Intend to be carfull of ofending thee

"WM BILES."

As this affair has caused William Biles more notoriety than any other event, it will probably be of interest to note some of the actions taken by the Assembly and Council in regard thereto, as it occupied the attention of both Houses on several days, and the *Votes of Assembly* and *Colonial Records* contain the proceedings in full.[1] Before doing this, however, it will be well to make some investigation as to Governor Evans.

John Evans, who succeeded Hamilton as Deputy Governor in 1704, was at the time of his appointment only twenty-six years of age, was an officer of the Queen's household, and in consequence of his previous surroundings had little sympathy with the life and character of Pennsylvania Friends.[2] With his first interview with the Assembly began a quarrel which, owing to his want of tact and his disorderly life, eventually enabled the faction of David Lloyd to thwart all his projects.[3]

Benjamin Franklin says of him,[4]—

"So unpopular was he, that an unanimous Vote of Thanks to the Proprietary was passed on his being removed, almost before his Face, for he was still a Resident amongst them."

Rev. Edward D. Neill concludes his narrative of Evans's chastisement by a countryman, whom he had ordered to turn his loaded wagon out of the road so that he, who was on foot, might pass, with the statement that "At length the

[1] *Votes of Assembly*, vol. i. pt. 2, pp. 43–48; *Colonial Records*, vol. ii. pp. 205–209.
[2] Armor's *Lives of the Governors of Penna.*, pp. 118–121; Egle's *History of Penna.*, p. 61.
[3] Keith's *Lives of Provincial Councillors*, p. 7.
[4] *Historical Review of Const. and Govt. of Penna.*, p. 71.

waggoner discovered that every governor was not a gentleman, and that he had assaulted Governor Evans;"[1] and adds, "the private life of Evans was as censurable as his public conduct."

William Penn wrote to Governor Evans 7th mo. 30, 1705,[2]—

"*Much is said of the Lewdnes of Pennsylvania.* I beg of thee to have regard to my Character and give not that advantage against me either with God or good or bad men whose ill use of it I most fear, on a publick acct. I have just now Rec'd thine of 5th 5 mo (July) and am very Sorry that wicked man D. L. could blow up any of his Mermidons to such a pitch of brutishness as thy Acct. of William Biles relates that is a meer vox et praeterea nihil, a Coxcomb, and a Prag-matick in graine. That fellow's plantation is a Robbery upon Pennsbury,[3] and if there be a grant, was not a purchase from me, nor any Towed Land writs, for it was surveyed long before and done in my absence, formerly, and Judge Mompresson can tell if I may not be deceived, in my Grant as well as the Crown, be it King or Queen,—Since, if confirmed, it was upon Surprize, and rattle an Inquisition about his eares, if not a prosecution. And know that when the time is expired of Session he may be taken to task, Since the Service he may pretend he was to attend is over. And first complain to the Friends, and if they wont or cant bow him to make Satisfaction, take it by Law thy Selfe. Pray mind what I say, be Secret, which is discreet, and fall on him or any other such unruly People at once, and make Some one Example to terrifie the rest. Thou hast not only my leave, but liking and encouragement whether called Quakers or others.''

Governor Evans's subsequent action in regard to William Biles is thus shown to have been fully approved by Penn, who perhaps was aware that in 1629, having " obtained the opinion of the judges that privilege of parliament did not protect a member from prosecution after the close of the session for offences committed during it," the Attorney-

[1] *N. Eng. Hist. and Gen. Register,* vol. xxvi. pp. 423, 424.
[2] Ibid., p. 427.
[3] The plantation referred to must have been the one near the northwestern boundary of the manor, for which patent was issued in 1705, as per minutes of the Board of Property, *Pa. Arch.,* 2d ser., vol. xix. p. 473.

General, Sir Robert Heath,[1] instituted proceedings against Holles, Eliot, Selden, and other members, and obtained judgment against them of imprisonment during the King's pleasure.

Penn's description of William Biles is not upheld by later historians, whose estimates are condensed in Dr. George Smith's statement,[2] that "He was a man of ability and the strictest integrity." Logan, sharing Penn's animosity, said of him,[3] "he very much influences that debauched County of Bucks, in which there is now scarce any one man of worth left."

However, we find that on 4th mo. 12, 1705, William Biles complained to the Assembly "against the Justices and Sheriff of the County of *Philadelphia*, for a Breach of Priviledge," and it was ordered to be considered the next week. On the 19th the House decided [4] "That it is a Breach of Priviledge of this House, that any Member duly elected to serve in Assembly, shall, without the Leave of the House, be summoned or drawn, or in any wise compelled, during the Session or Continuance of Assembly, to appear at any inferior Court in this Province, upon any Pleas or Complaints, excepting for Treason, Felony, or Breach of the Peace," and in the afternoon, upon further consideration and debate, it was decided that the Sheriff who summoned William Biles to answer the action against him, and the four Justices of the Court who denied him "his Priviledge by over-ruling his Plea in that Behalf, have committed a manifest Breach of Priviledge against this House."

On the 20th a message from the Governor to the House of Representatives was drawn up, read in the Council,[5] and approved of, in which he stated that William Biles had used the most scandalous and seditious expressions against him,

---

[1] *Dict. of Nat. Biog.*, vol. xxv. p. 347.
[2] *Hist. Delaware Co., Pa.*, p. 447.
[3] *Penn-Logan Corresp.*, vol. ii. p. 34.
[4] *Votes of Assembly*, vol. i. pt. 2, p. 43.
[5] *Colonial Records*, vol. ii. p. 205.

and he demanded that they expel Biles from the House and advise him of their action without delay. This message was read in the House that day and ordered to be read again the next day. On the 21st, after it had been again read and William Biles had withdrawn, and the matter had been debated, the minutes state that, "The Question being put, that the said *William Biles* be expelled this House, according to the Governor's Request? *It passed in* the Negative.

"*Ordered.* That an Address to the Governor be drawn concerning the said *William Biles*, which shall comprize the Opinion and Resolves of this House relating to the Premises."

On the 22d the Address, which had been prepared, was read before the House, agreed to, and ordered to be signed by the Speaker and presented to the Governor, who on the 23d laid it before the Council. In it the House stated that, while not justifying such words as were alleged to have been spoken, nevertheless, the manner of proceedings against William Biles was very offensive to the House, and that the Sheriff who served the writ and the Justices who heard the case committed a manifest breach of privilege against the House; and as they were tender of the privileges of the House, so they would gladly show their resentment of all indignities offered to the Governor; but they found no sufficient ground for expelling William Biles from the House, and requested that he be given an opportunity to call and vindicate himself, so far as he can.

The minutes of Council show that it was the unanimous opinion of the Board that it was useless to spend longer time conferring with the then present House, and was most advisable to end further debates by dismissing them. Accordingly the Governor requested the attendance of the Speaker with the whole House, made them a sharp speech, refused to let the Speaker be heard in vindication of the House, and dismissed them.

James Logan, in a long letter to William Penn,[1] stated substantially that—

[1] *Penn-Logan Corresp.*, vol. ii. pp. 131–133.

"The Yearly Meeting sent for Biles to town, and condemned him for it, and made some intercession in his behalf, stating it would be generous in the Governour to forgive him all; the Assembly also in 12th mo. interceded for him and the Governour assured Edward Shippen and the other messengers from the House that he never designed to injure W. Biles, and gave them his word that if ever he found cause to give him any further trouble he would first acquaint them therewith. In 1st mo. William Biles relying upon the assurances of Edward Shippen and others concluded he might safely venture to town. He met the Governour, shook hands with him, and all seemed well; yet the Govr. went to Robt. Ashton's and caused a writ to be drawn which he had signed and at the same time wrote a letter to Edward Shippen and the others which he took care should not be delivered until after the Sheriff had arrested Wm. Biles. These members of Assembly hurried to the Governour, with great concern, but could not move him, nor could I though I pleaded with him for nearly an hour, telling him that the Government would greatly suffer by such dishonorable proceedings. I laboured to get others to speak to him on the subject, and prevailed on the Sheriff to keep his prisoner at the public house where he had taken him, until it was evident that all intercession was in vain, when he was committed. Divers Friends were much concerned and the women took very good care of William in prison. When I came home I wrote a long remonstrative letter to the Governour, which I delivered the next day and for about an hour endeavored by the most pressing and cogent arguments to dissuade him from his course. William was kept a close prisoner for about a month, until the Governour saw he could never get any money by it, but lost his own interest with the Country and his Friends. 'Twas this, however, that first caused people to look about them. But however this ended, the disgust at one time was high."

Another writer upon the subject says,[1]—

"but finally finding the whole community incensed against him for the course he was pursuing, he released his prisoner without the fine. William was satisfied that he had allowed the warmth of his feelings to get the better of his judgment when he had spoken the honest convictions of his mind, relative to the weak-minded, quarrelsome Governor, and he hesitated not to condemn his so speaking. It does not appear but that he was as useful in religious as well as civil concerns afterwards, as he had been before this affair took place."

[1] *The Friend*, vol. xxviii. p. 109.

(To be continued.)

WILLIAM BILES.

BY MILES WHITE, JR., BALTIMORE, MD.

William Biles was a member of the Assembly which began its session at Philadelphia October 14, 1707,[1] and he and John Bethell were sent with a message to the Governor (Evans), to find out when the Assembly should meet him. They waited on him, and he made an address, the beginning of which was to the effect that he noticed that most of the members were the same as those of last year, who had lost so much time and fallen into unnecessary disputes. However, he addressed them as a new body and hoped that they would begin afresh. He made no allusion to his personal affair with William Biles in the Assembly of 1704, though this was the first time that Biles had been in the Assembly since.

The Assembly which met in Philadelphia October 14, 1708, Charles Gookin being Lieutenant-Governor, was the last one of which William Biles was a member, and on 2d mo. 13, 1709, he was on a committee to draw up an answer to the Governor's speech.

William Penn made several treaties with the Indians, the last of which was in 1686, though the place where it was held is not mentioned anywhere. After Penn's death a document was found among his papers in England, which was endorsed "Copy of the last Indian Purchase." Davis[2] says,—

"there was never any attempt to prove the deed by calling the persons who witnessed it; and the only personal evidence is that of William Biles and Joseph Wood, who declared they remembered a treaty being held, but did not know that a deed had been executed."

[1] *Votes of Assembly*, vol. ii. p. 1.
[2] *Hist. Bucks Co.*, p. 490.

William Biles's active participation in civil affairs was not greater than in religious ones. As has previously been stated, meetings for worship had been held at his house before the arrival of Penn, and the first meeting for discipline, which was the germ of Falls Meeting, took place there on 3d mo. 2, 1683,[1] as also the first Quarterly Meeting, which was held 3d mo. 7, 1684.

Charles W. Smith, in his *History of the Early Settlement of Wrightstown*,[2] gives a copy of the opening minute of the first Monthly Meeting. It was as follows:

"Men's Monthly Meeting held near the Falls of Delaware in the County of Bucks in the Province of Pennsylvania.

"At a meeting at William Biles House the 2nd day of the 3^d mo. 1683, then held to wait upon the Lord for his wisdom, to hear what should be offered in order to inspect the affairs of the church, that all things might be kept sweet and savoury therein, to the Lord, and by our care over the church, helpful in the works of God"—"and we whose names are as follows, being present, thought it fit & necessary that a Monthly Meeting should be set up, both of men and women for that purpose, and that this meeting be the first of mens meetings after our arrival in these parts."

The friends present were William Yardley, James Harrison, Phineas Pemberton, William Biles, William Dark, Lyonell Brittaine, and William Beaks. All of William Biles's services in behalf of the meeting's interests are of course not known, but the minutes record, among others, the following:[3]

On 1st mo. 4, 1685, the matter of difference so long depending between William Yardley and Eleanor Pownall was brought before the Mo. Mtg., and Henry Baker and William Biles were appointed to settle same, and on 4th mo. 3, they reported that the dividing line should be run according as surveyor first laid it out by Governor's order. 6th mo. 5, 1685, Thomas Janney, William Biles, Henry Baker and Richard

---

[1] Davis's *Hist. Bucks Co.*, p. 105 ; MS. Minutes Falls Monthly Meeting and Bucks Quarterly Meeting.

[2] P. 21 ; see also *Hist. Sketches relating to Early Settlement of Friends at Falls*, p. 30.

[3] MS. Minutes Falls Monthly Meeting and Bucks Quarterly Meeting.

Hough were appointed by the Qtly. Mtg. to adjust the difference between Jno. Brooks and Lydia Wharmby, and on 6th mo. 17, 1687, William Biles was dealt with for selling liquor to Indians.

In 1690 the first meeting-house was built near Fallsington, and was deeded to Thomas Janney, William Biles, Richard Hough, and Joshua Hoopes, in trust for the meeting. On 11th mo. 6, 1691, certain Friends, including William Biles, agreed to take the meeting's share of all books that shall be printed in the unity of Friends and by their approbation. On 12th mo. 1, 1692, William Biles took upon him to pay the balance of carpenters' account for the meeting-house. On 5th mo. 1, 1696, William Biles and wife proposed to visit Friends in New England, and were given a Certificate. On 9th mo. 3, 1697, it was "agreed that a Testimony be drawn concerning Thomas Janney's labors and service amongst us in the Truth," and Joseph Kirkbride, William Biles, Phineas Pemberton, Richard Hough, Jane Biles, and Margery Hough were appointed to prepare the same. In 1699 it was decided to enlarge the meeting-house, and William Biles, Richard Hough, and Joshua Hoopes were appointed to make the agreement with workmen. On 7th mo. 4, 1700, Joshua Hoopes and his wife Eleanor, who had had some differences, were present, but did not agree in their accounts, and Richard Hough, William Duncan, and William Biles were appointed to hear them together and give an account to the meeting. On 8th mo. 2 they reported that Elinor did not sustain her position, and a paper of Condemnation which Joshua had formerly brought in against his wife was read and approved by the meeting. On 11th mo. 5 Jane Biles proposed to go to visit Friends in some parts of Europe, and William said he formerly had opposed it, but now gave his consent and would go with her, and on 1st mo. 5, 1701, certificates for both were read and signed. On 7th mo. 6, 1704, William Biles, Joseph Kirkbride, Richard Hough, and Jacob Janney were appointed to assist Elizabeth Brock to settle her deceased husband's estate. On 11th mo. 4, 1709, William Biles was reported as being very weak, and unfit to take care of the meeting's accounts, and on 5th mo. 5, 1710, he was reported as being dead, and a committee was appointed to call on his son William for the meeting's books and papers.

George Keith caused much trouble and dissension among the members of the Society of Friends, and finally was disowned by the meetings. On 4th mo. 17, 1692, William Biles, William Yardley, and others wrote a letter to London Friends about the difficulties and divisions occasioned by Keith's separation.[1]

[1] Evans's *Exposition*, etc., p. 218.

On 4th mo. 20, 1692, the Meeting of Public Friends, in Philadelphia, gave forth its Testimony [1] of Denial against him, and among the signers was William Biles; [2] and the Yearly Meeting held at Burlington 7th mo. 7, 1692, sent out its Testimony signed by over two hundred members, including William Biles.

On account of the misrepresentations made by Keith in regard to the teachings of the Society, it was deemed wise to state clearly what these really were, and this was accordingly done; and in 1695 T. Sowle published, in London, a pamphlet entitled *Our Antient Testimony renewed concerning our Lord and Saviour Jesus Christ, the Holy Scriptures and the Resurrection, given forth by a Meeting of Public Friends and Others, at Philadelphia in Pennsylvania;* and this was also published in 1696 as an Appendix to the English translation of *The General History of the Quakers,* by Gerard Croesse. Among the thirty-nine signers of this statement were Griffith Owen, William Biles, Richard Gove, and Thomas Janney.

William Biles seems always to have been a clear-headed advocate of the principles of Quakerism, and it has been said that [3]

"There appears to be good evidence in the testimonies of various kinds left concerning this Friend, that he was one qualified by the Great Minister of Ministers, to labour in his cause, and that his Gospel labours were blessed to the good of the church. How much more useful in the Lord's hand, he and many of his fellow-ministers would have been, if they had refused all public offices, we cannot tell."

William and Johannah Biles had eight children, five of whom were born in England and three in America. The dates of birth of the former are taken from Friends' Records at Devonshire House, London, where the name is spelled "Byles," and of the latter from Records of Middletown

---

[1] *The Friend*, vol. xix. p. 86 ; Proud's *Hist. Penna.*, vol. i. pp. 365, 368 ; Hazard's *Register Pa.*, vol. vi. pp. 279, 280.

[2] Ibid., pp. 301, 302 ; *The Friend*, vol. xix. p. 109.

[3] *The Friend*, vol. xxviii. p. 109.

Quarterly Meeting, Pennsylvania, where the name is spelled "Biles." Many of the certificates of early marriages in Pennsylvania were not recorded, and this is the case with those of most of these children. From the minutes, which show when six of them received permission to marry, and from their father's will, it appears that they married as stated below.

CHILDREN.[1]

1. *Elizabeth*, b. 4th mo. 3, 1670 ; m., 1st, at house of William Biles, 8th mo. 31, 1688, Stephen Beaks, and had five children. She m., 2d, Matthew Hughes.

II. 2. *William*, b. 11th mo. 12, 1671 ; m., at Middletown Meeting, 11th mo., 1695, Sarah Langhorne, daughter of Thomas and Grace Langhorne, and had nine children.

3. *George*, b. 7th mo. 4, 1673 ; bur. 12th mo. 27, 1708/9 ; m., 1697, Martha Blackshaw, who d. 1720. They had six children. She m., 2d, 1713, Joseph Waite, of Philadelphia, who d. before her, in 1720.

4. *Joanah*,[2] b. 1st mo. 1, 1675 ; m., 1695, Samuel Beaks, and had six children.

5. *John*, b. 1st mo. 31, 1678 ; m., at Chesterfield Monthly Meeting, New Jersey, 1707, Mary Lambert, b. 2d mo. 2, 1681, daughter of Thomas and Elizabeth Lambert, and had five children.

6. *Rebeckah*, b. 10th mo. 27, 1680 ;[3] m., at Falls Meeting, 6th mo. 18, 1703, Joseph Janney, b. 1st mo. 26, 1675/6 ; d. about 1728 ; son of Thomas and Margery (Heath) Janney, and had six children, five of whom moved to Loudoun County, Virginia.

7. *Mary*, b. 11th mo. 1, 1682 ; m. —— Robbins, and had one child.

8. *Ann*, b. 4th mo. 13, 1685 ; m., 12th mo., 1706/7, Thomas Yardley, who came to America, in 1704, from Rushton Spencer, County Stafford. They had ten children. For account of them, see the *Yardley Genealogy*.

From Phineas Pemberton's letters[4] we learn that in 3d mo., 1687, a great land flood and freshet at the Falls occa-

---

[1] The number of children that each of William Biles's children is stated in this list to have had is the number whose names have been ascertained. Each of his children may have had more than herein mentioned.

[2] So spelled in English Records ; in American it is Johannah.

[3] Burlington Monthly Meeting gives her birth as 11th mo. 27.

[4] Buck's *Bucks Co., Pa.*, p. 23 ; *Hist. Sketches relating to Early Settlement of Friends at Falls*, p. 55.

sioned much sickness. Whether this was the cause of the death of William Biles's wife cannot now be stated, but she died that year and was buried 7th mo. 4.

On 10th mo. 11, 1688, he married, at his own house, Jane Atkinson,[1] widow of Thomas Atkinson, and it has been said that

"in her he had a faithful helpmeet, and one well calculated to assist him on his journey heavenward." She was a minister, and is said to have had an eminent public testimony, and is shown by the Minutes of Falls Monthly Meeting to have been useful in meetings for discipline, and to have served on numerous committees. They appear to have often travelled in the ministry of the Gospel. In 1st mo., 1689, she visited Friends in East Jersey and on Long Island, and in the summer of 1696, accompanied by her husband, she visited the meetings of Friends in New England, to their satisfaction. A concern for a long time rested on her mind to pay a religious visit to the land of her birth, but her husband discouraged it as far as he could. In 10th mo., 1699, she laid the matter before the General Meeting of Ministers, and towards the close of that year William Biles, writing to William Ellis, who had just returned from a religious visit to Friends in America, said, "My wife talks of coming to you, but how it may be upon that account I shall at present leave to the ordering hand of the Lord; the voyage is great, and she but weakly in body." When the meeting finally gave her liberty to go, "not being satisfied with the opposition her husband made," he decided to go with her, and in the early part of 1701 they both went to England and Ireland and returned towards the close of 1702, and the visit seems to have been well accepted there.

Quite a lengthy sketch of her life and labors was published in *The Friend*,[2] from which it appears that she resided in Yorkshire, and in 1678 married Thomas Atkinson, a minister in the Society of Friends; that in 1682 they removed to New Jersey, and brought a recommendation from Beamsley Meeting in Yorkshire. In 1687 she was taken very ill, and both she and her husband thought she would die. After a time he told her he believed she would be raised up again and that he should be taken instead. This proved to be true, for that very day he became unwell, and, after lingering for eight or nine weeks, died; while she, by

[1] Yorkshire Friends' Records at Devonshire House, London, show the marriage of "Thomas Adkinson of Sandwich, Adingham psh., Yorkshire, to Jane Boid, 4th mo. 4, 1678, at Knaresborough Meeting." No residence or parentage of Jane Boid being given.

[2] Vol. xxviii. pp. 93, 102.

whom much labor in the militant church was yet to be performed, grew stronger and stronger.

Her testimony in regard to her husband, Thomas Atkinson, has been published in *The Friend*.[1] She died in 1709, and was buried 10th mo. 21, leaving three children by her first husband and none by her second. William Biles did not long survive his wife, but died in 1710, and his burial took place 3d mo. 19.

His will appears not to have been recorded, but an abstract of it was published in PENNA. MAG. HIST. AND BIOG.[2] It was dated January 5, 1709, and contained the following bequests:

"To my son John Biles, 300 acres of land.

"To my daughter Elizabeth Hewes, wife of Matthew Hewes, the sum of twenty shillings.

"To my three grandchildren, John, Mary, and Grace Beakes, the sum of fifty pounds, to be equally divided between them.

"To my daughter, Johannah Beakes, the wife of Samuel Beakes, the sum of twenty shillings.

"To my daughter, Rebeckah Janney, the wife of Joseph Janney, the sum of one hundred and forty pounds.

"To their two daughters, Martha and Ann Janney, the sum of ten pounds, to be equally divided between them.

"To my daughter, Ann, the wife of Thomas Yardley, the sum of one hundred and fifty pounds.

"To my daughter-in-law, Martha Biles, the sum of five pounds.

"To my three grandchildren, Johannah, Phebe, and Sarah Biles, the daughters of my children George and Martha Biles, the sum of fifteen pounds, to be equally divided between them.

"To my three granddaughters, Ann, Grace, and Sarah Biles, the daughters of my son and daughter, William and Sarah Biles, the sum of fifteen pounds, to be equally divided between them.

"To my sister-in-law, Mary Biles, the widow of my brother, Thomas Biles, of Dorchester, in the county of Dorset, in old England, eight pounds.

"To my grandson, William Robbins, the son of my daughter, Mary Robbins, the plantation where I last lived, lying betwixt the land of Anthony Burton, and the land of my son John Biles. It being part of

---

[1] Vol. xxvii. p. 172.
[2] Vol. xv. p. 503.

the same land I purchased from Henry Barkar [Baker?] by estimation, about 200 acres.

"To my grandchildren, Johannah and Rebeckah Beakes, the daughters of my son and daughter, Samuel and Johannah Beakes, the sum of twenty-four pounds.

"To my son William Biles, all the rest, residue of my lands in West Jersey, etc.

"Signed, published, and declared this fifth day of the Eleventh month called January, 1709, in the presence of us,

"JER. LANGHORN,
"JOS. KIRKBRIDE,
"ROBERT SOTCHER."

It may be of interest to add, that upon William Biles's plantation, near Penn's Manor, there now stands a large brick dwelling of ancient date,[1] which has been represented by tradition and from the initials inscribed upon it as the homestead of William Biles, Sr., who is said to have built it of bricks brought from England.[2]

There is also a tradition that the Bible William Biles brought to America had belonged to John Waite, and had the latter's name in it, with the statement that he bought it in 1633. It has been surmised by some that this John Waite was the father of either William Biles's mother or wife.

The children of William Biles do not seem to have occupied so prominent a place in the meeting as their father did, Johannah, William, and Ann having been dealt with by Falls Monthly Meeting, though they all retained their membership.

II. William seems to have been the most prominent of the sons in civil life, and he occupied many public posi-

[1] *Hist. Sketches relating to Early Settlement of Friends at Falls*, p. 26; Davis's *Hist. Bucks Co.*, p. 105 n.

[2] Some few Colonial houses were built of "bricks brought from England," but most of such brick houses were built of bricks made near the spot. In those days bricks of two shapes or sizes were used, one called "Dutch bricks" and the other "English bricks." From "English bricks" to "bricks brought from England" was an easy step for tradition to take.

tions.[1] He was Sheriff of Bucks County 1704–1707; Coroner October 3, 1717; Justice of the Peace September 6, 1718; January 4, 1722; May 12, 1725; September 14, 1725; September 13, 1726; September 10, 1727; November 22, 1738; member of Assembly 1710, 1711, 1718–1725, 1732, 1735–1737; and Speaker of Assembly 1724–1725, having been so elected October 14, 1724.[2]

In 1721 he and five others were appointed by the court as viewers for a road from "Yardley's Ferry to the Cross Roads near Neshaminy meeting-house,"[3] and in 1724 he was on the committee to build a new court-house and prison at Newtown, the new county-seat of Bucks County.[4] He was admitted to the Bar in New Jersey December 5, 1721,[5] was a member of the "Council of Proprietors of West Jersey," and as such was one of the signers of the paper sent by that body to Governor William Burnet, against repealing an act for ascertaining the line between the eastern and western divisions of New Jersey.[6]

He was a large land-owner, both in Bucks County, Pennsylvania, and in New Jersey, having inherited some tracts from his father and bought others; among the latter was a half interest in 4000 acres in Evesham, Burlington County, which he bought of John Borradail in 1717, and sold in 1726 to Thomas Marks for £284,[7] in which deed he is styled "William Biles of Bucks County, Penna., Esqr."

In his will, made in 1737, he left certain lands on "Morris" River to his children, but they did not inherit them, for he (and various members of the Lambert family), January 15, 1738/9,[8] released for £1500 to Abraham Bennet

[1] *Pa. Arch.*, 2d. ser., vol. ix. pp. 742–759.
[2] *Votes of Assembly*, vol. ii. p. 403.
[3] PENNA. MAG. HIST. AND BIOG., vol. vii. p. 72.
[4] Ibid., p. 73; *Votes of Assembly*, vol. ii. p. 238; *Colonial Records*, vol. iii. p. 255.
[5] Snell's *Hist. Hunterdon Co., N. J.*, p. 206.
[6] Smith's *Hist. N. J.*, Reprint 1890, pp. 551–554.
[7] W. J. Deeds, *Liber* D, *fol.* 163.
[8] Ibid., *Liber* E F, *fol.* 108.

and others 10,000 acres, being part of several properties situate in Quohocking, Cohansie, and Maurice River, West New Jersey, which James Wass had released in 1707 to William Biles, his father.

The wife of William Biles, Jr., was Sarah Langhorne,[1] sister of Jeremiah Langhorne, who was Chief-Justice of Pennsylvania, Speaker of Assembly, member of the same for many years, and also filled other offices. Indeed, most of those connected with the Biles family seem to have been office-holders. Thomas Biles was Sheriff 1726–27; Langhorne Biles, Justice of the Peace 1749 and 1752; and other connections of the family for years served as Justices, and in the Assembly.

The will of William Biles, of Falls Township, was dated December 3, 1737, and proved September 27, 1739. It is recorded in *Liber* I, *fol.* 267,[2] and in it mention is made of his wife Sarah; his sons William, Charles, and Langhorne; his daughters Sarah and Elizabeth Biles, Ann Pennington, and Hannah Janney; his grandchildren William, Jeremiah, and John Beatts, [Bates], Edward, Mary, and Sarah Pennington, Thomas and Margaret Biles; to all of whom he left land, mostly in West Jersey, on "Morris" River, and to most of them some negroes. By a codicil he left the Island to his son William, who also received the home plantation after his mother's death.

The following is a list of his children and the persons they married:

CHILDREN (ORDER OF BIRTH UNCERTAIN).

1. *Thomas*, b. 6th mo. 30, 1696; d. 1743; m., 12th mo. 1729, Elizabeth Lambert, daughter of Thomas, of New Jersey. She returned to Chesterfield Meeting 11th mo., 1763. Her will proved 1771 (N. J. Wills, *Liber* 15, *fol.* 474).

2. *William*, d. 1775; m., 1st, 3d mo., 1725, Ann Stevenson,[3] b.

[1] For account of Langhorne family, see PENNA. MAG. HIST. AND BIOG., vol. vii. pp. 67–87.
[2] Ibid., vol. xv. p. 382.
[3] See *Our Family Ancestors*, p. 300.

12th mo. 6, 1704; *d.* 3d mo. 8, 1734; daughter of Thomas and Sarah (Jennings) Stevenson; *m.*, 2d, Jane ——; *d.* 1777. William and his two sons, Thomas and William, were disowned by Falls Meeting, 6th mo., 1756, for joining a military association; his will is recorded in Bucks Co., *Liber* 3, *fol.* 385.

3. *Charles, m.*, 1729, Ann Mary Baker, *b.* 4th mo. 16, 1704, daughter of Samuel and Rachel (Warder) Baker, for account of whom see *Publications* So. Hist. Assoc., vol. v. p. 480. In 1732 Charles and his wife removed from Falls to Buckingham Meeting.

4. *Langhorne, m.*, 1749, Hannah Kirkbride, *b.* 9th mo. 23, 1726, daughter of Joseph, Jr., and Sarah (Fletcher) Kirkbride. Langhorne was disowned by Falls Meeting, 1748, for joining a military association; upon his marriage, his wife was taken under dealings, and in 1756 disowned therefor.

5. *Ann, b.* 12th mo. 4, 1702/3; *bur.* 12th mo. 22, 1748/9; *m.* 10th mo., 1725, Isaac Pennington, *b.* 1700, son of Edward and Sarah (Jennings) Pennington.

6. *Grace, d.* before 1737; *m.* —— Bates, who was twice married. The will of her daughter Sarah Bates, dated 1760 (Bucks Co. Wills, *Liber* 3, *fol.* 21), mentions sister Hannah, wife of Saml. Yeardley; aunt Hannah Janney; cousin Charles Janney; cousin Bettie Janney, daughter of Abel Janney; niece Sarah Bates, daughter of brother John; cousins Ann and Elizabeth Janney; brother John Bates and half-brother Job Bates.

7. *Sarah, d. s. p.* 1781; *m.*, 1740, Lawrence Growden, who was twice married. Her will is recorded in Bucks Co., *Liber* 4, *fol.* 336.

8. *Elizabeth, m.*, 1740, Abel Janney. The marriage license, issued in New Jersey June 5, 1740, describes them as Abel Janney, of Maidenhead, New Jersey, and Elizabeth Biles, of Bucks County, Pennsylvania. It is not certain whether Abel was the son of Thomas and Rachel (Pownall) Janney or of Abel and Elizabeth (Stacy) Janney, though probably the former, whose wife was named Elizabeth, and joined Middletown Monthly Meeting in 1745; she and her husband moved to Virginia in 1746 and returned to Pennsylvania in 1748, he dying that year (see *Publications* So. Hist. Assoc. vol. v. p. 481). The latter Abel married out of meeting, prior to 1742, and that year was in Virginia, whence he returned in 1745, and in 1752 and 1753 kept a tavern in Ridley Township, Chester County, Pennsylvania. He married a second time in 1755. Whether Elizabeth (Biles) Janney had other children than a daughter Betty is not known. Records of Race Street Meeting, Philadelphia, show the burials in 1758 and 1759 of four children of Abel Janney, but do not give their mother's name.

9. *Hannah, m.*, at Falls Meeting, 3d mo., 1735, Thomas Janney, son of Abel and Elizabeth (Stacy) Janney. One of their sons, Thomas, was a Lieutenant in the Falls Company Bucks County Associators in 1775, (*Pa. Arch.*, 2d ser., vol. xiv. p. 151), and later an officer in the Revolutionary army (Ibid., vol. x. pp. 153, 449; PENNA. MAG. HIST. AND BIOG., vol. vii. p. 167).

BOONE GENEALOGY.

[Our Genealogy, etc., Wrote in 1788, March 21.]

Our Genealogy, or Pedigree; traced as far back as had come to the Knowledge of John Boone [the Son of George & Mary Boone]: Wrote by James Boone [Grandson of the Said George and Mary Boone].—

GEORGE BOONE, I. (that is the first that we have heard of) was born in England.

GEORGE BOONE, II. [Son of George Boone the first] was born in or near the City of Exeter in Devonshire; being a blacksmith; his Wife's Maiden Name was Sarah Uppey. He died aged 60; and she died aged 80 Years, and never had an aching Bone, or decay'd Tooth.

GEORGE BOONE, III. [Son of George & Sarah Boone] was born at Stoak (a Village near the City of Exeter) in A. D. 1666, being a Weaver; his Wife's Maiden Name was Mary Maugridge, who was born in Bradninch (eight Miles from the City of Exeter) in the Year 1669, being a Daughter of John Maugridge and Mary his Wife, whose maiden name was Milton. They (the said George & Mary Boone) had nine Children that lived to be Men and Women: namely, George, Sarah, Squire, Mary, John, Joseph, Benjamin, James, and Samuel, having each of them several Children, excepting John, who was never married. The said George and Mary Boone with their Family, came from the Town of Bradninch in Devonshire, Old-England (which is a Town at 8 Miles Distance from the City of Exeter, and 177 measured Miles Westward from London); they left Bradninch the 17 Aug. 1717, and went to Bristol where they took Shipping, and arrived at Philadelphia in 1717, (September 29, Old-Stile, or October 10th New-Stile); three of their Children, to wit, George, Sarah, and Squire, they sent in a few Years before. From Philadelphia they went to Abington, and staid a few Months there; thence to North-Wales, and liv'd about 2 Years there; thence to Oley in the same County of Philadelphia, where Sarah (being married) had moved to some Time before. This last Place of their Residence, (since the Divisions made in the Township of Oley and County of Philadelphia) is called the Township of Exeter in the County of Berks: It was called Exeter, because they came from a Place near the City of Exeter. And,

He the said George Boone the Third, died on the Sixth Day of the Week, near 8 o'Clock in the Morning, on the 27th of July, 1744, aged 78 Years; and Mary his Wife died on the 2d Day of the Week, on the 2d of February 1740-1, aged 72 Years; and were decently interred in

Friends Burying-Ground, in the said Township of Exeter. When he died, he left 8 Children, 52 Grand-Children, and 10 Great-Grand-Children, living; in all 70, being as many Persons as the House of Jacob which came into Egypt.

GEORGE BOONE, IV. [the eldest child of George & Mary Boone] was born in the Town of Bradninch aforesaid, on the 13th of July, 1690, about ½ H. past 5 in the Afternoon; and died in Exeter Township aforesaid, on the 20 November 1753, in the 64th Year of his Age. He taught School for several Years near Philadelphia; was a good Mathematician, and taught the several Branches of English Learning; and was a Magistrate for several Years. His Wife's maiden Name was Deborah Howell. ——She died in 1759, January 26.

GEORGE BOONE V. [the eldest Son of George & Deborah Boone] was never married, and died in Exeter Township aforesaid, aged about 24 Years.

Sarah Boone [Daughter of George & Mary Boone] was born on the Fifth Day of the Week, about ½ H. past 11 in the Forenoon, on the 18th of February 1691–2.

Squire Boone [Son of George and Mary Boone] was born on the Fourth Day of the Week, between 11 & 12 in the Forenoon, on the 25 November, 1696.

Mary Boone [Daughter of George & Mary Boone] was born Sept. 23, A. D. 1699: She was the Wife of John Webb, and departed this Life on the 16th of January, 1774, in the 75th Year of her Age; her Husband died in the same Year, October 18th, in the 80th Year of his Age.

Joseph Boone [Son of George & Mary Boone] was born between 4 & 5 in the Afternoon, on the 5th of April, 1704; and he departed this Life on the 30 January, 1776, in the 72d Year of his Age. His Wife Catherine Boone died on the 31st of January, 1778, and was interred at Exeter the next Day exactly 2 Years after the Burial of her Husband.

Benjamin Boone [Son of George & Mary Boone] was born on the 16th of July, 1706; and he died on the 14th of October, 1762, in the 57th Year of his Age. Susanna Boone [his Widow] died on the 5 Nov. 1784, in the 76th Year of her Age.

Samuel Boone [the youngest Son of George & Mary Boone] departed this Life on the 6th of August, 1745, and was buried at Exeter the next Day; aged about 54 Years.

James Boone [the sixth Son of George & Mary Boone] was born in the Town of Bradninch, in Devonshire, in Old-England, about ½ Hour past 2 in the Morning, on the 7th of July (Old-Stile), or the 18th of July (New-Stile), Anno Domini 1709. And in 1735 May 15, (O. S.) he married Mary Foulke by whom he had fourteen Children, and nine of them lived to be Men & Women, namely, Anne, Mary, Martha, James, John, Judah, Joshua, Rachel, & Moses. The said James Boone, senior, and Mary, his Wife, lived together 20 Years 8 Months & 25 Days; and she departed this Life on the 6th Day of the Week, at 20 Minutes past one o'Clock in the Afternoon, on the 20th Day of February 1756, aged 41 years & 11 Weeks, and was decently interred in Friends Burying-Ground at Exeter on the First Day of the next Week. And in 1757 October 20, he married Anne Griffith, being just 20 months after the Decease of his former Wife.——And here, for the Satisfaction of the Curious, I shall insert a few Chronological Remarks, viz.—

1. The said Mary Boone deceased in 1756 Feb. 20, at 20 Minutes past one in the Afternoon, which wanted but two Minutes and sixteen Seconds of 20 o'Clock according to the Italian Manner of Reckoning (for the Italians, Jews, and some others, always begin their Day at Sun-set); which was the 20th Day of the Jewish Month Adar, when the Moon was 20 Days old, and 4 Weeks before the Vernal Equinox.——

2. The said *James Boone*, senior, married Anne Griffith in 1757, October 20, at 20 Minutes past one in the Afternoon; that is, he was married to his second (or last) Wife exactly 20 Months after the Decease of his first, and 4 Weeks after the Autumnal Equinox.

James Boone, senior, departed this Life on the 1st Day of September, A. D. 1785, on the Fifth Day of the Week, at ten Minutes after nine o'Clock at Night, in the 77th Year of his Age; and was decently interred in Friends Burying-Ground at Exeter on the Seventh Day of the same Week. He (with his Parents, &c) left Great-Britain in the 9th Year of his Age, and lived almost 68 Years in Pennsylvania.—N.B. When he was born, it was between 9 & 10 at Night here in Pennsylvania (allowing for the Difference of Longitude); and he died between 9 & 10 at Night.

John Boone, senior, [the third Son of George & Mary Boone] was born in the Town of Bradninch, in Devonshire, in Old-England, on the Seventh day of the Week, about 10 or 11 o'Clock in the Forenoon, on the 3 January 1701–2, Old-Stile; or A. D. 1702 January 14, New-Stile. And he departed this Life on the 10th Day of October 1785, on the Second Day of the Week; sixteen Minutes after Midnight, in the 84th Year of his Age, (being the oldest of our Name & Family that we have heard of); and was decently interred in Friends Burying-Ground at Exeter the next Day. He (with his Parents, &c) left Great-Britain in the 16th Year of his Age, and lived exactly 68 years here (in North-America) from the day he landed at Philadelphia. He lived only 5 Weeks and 4 Days after the Decease of his Brother James.—N.B. All our Relations of the Name of Boone, who were living after 1785 October 10, are American-born, as far as we know.

Now I shall conclude this Paper, after I have set down the Time and Place of my own Nativity; viz.—

I *James Boone* [the eldest Son of James Boone, senior, & Mary his Wife] was born in the Township of Exeter aforesaid, on the Fifth Day of the Week, about five o'Clock in the Morning, on the 26th Day of January 1743–4, Old-Stile, or A. D. 1744 February 6, New-Stile.—The Geographical Situation of the Place of my birth, is nearly as follows; viz.—

                                                              Deg. Min.
Latitude . . . . 40 : 22 North.
Longitude from London . . . . 75 : 43½ West.

So that, the Meridian passing through said Place, is 5 Hours 2 Minutes & 54 Seconds West from the Meridian of London: or nearly so, if otherwise.

James Boone, senior [Son of George & Mary Boone] was born in the Town of Bradninch (eight Miles from the City of Exeter) in Devonshire, in Old-England, about ½ Hour past 2 in the Morning there, A. D. 1709 July 18 (N. S.). And he departed this Life A. D. 1785 September 1, at
H. M.
9 : 10 at Night, in the 77th Year of his Age.

Mary Foulke, [Daughter of Hugh & Anne Foulke] was born at North-Wales in Philadelphia County, A. D. 1714 December 5, (N. S.) James Boone, senior, & Mary Foulke were married, A. D. 1735 May 26 (N. S.),
                      Y. M. D.
and lived together 20 : 8 : 25 : She departed this Life, A. D. 1756 Feb.
H. M.
20, at 1 : 20 in the Afternoon, in the 42d Year of her Age.

The Times of the Births of the Children of the said James Boone, senior, and Mary (his first Wife), set down according to the New-Stile. The Place of their Births is Exeter Township, Berks County, in Pennsylvania.

	New Stile.
Anne Boone was born about 5 in the Afternoon . .	1737 Apr. 14.
Mary Boone was born about 1 in the Morning . .	1739 Jan. 28.
Martha Boone was born about 5 in the Afternoon .	1742 July 1.
James Boone, junior, was born about 5 in the Morning	1744 Feb. 6.
John Boone, junior, was born about 2 in the Morning	1745 Nov. 21.
Deceased at 10 o'Clock at Night, in the 28th Year of his Age	1773 Mar. 29.
Judah Boone was born about 3 in the Morning .	1746 Dec. 19.
Dinah Boone was born	1748 Mar. 19.
Deceased	
Joshua Boone was born about 4 in the Morning .	1749 Apr. 4.
Rachel Boone was born about 3 in the Afternoon .	1750 Apr. 2.
Moses Boone was born about 3 in the Morning .	1751 Aug. 3.
Hannah Boone was born	1752 June 14.
Deceased	1752 Aug. 15.
Nathaniel Boone was born, and died, in the Year 1753; being 5 Weeks old at his Decease.	

James Boone, senior, and Anne Griffith were married A. D. 1757 Oct. 20, being just 20 Months after the Decease of his former Wife. She the said Anne Griffith was born A. D. 1713 January 29th, New-Stile.

John Boone, junior, [Son of James Boone, Senior, and Mary his Wife] when he died left three Children, the Times of whose Births were as hereunder mentioned ; viz.—

1. *Hannah Boone*, was born on the 6th Day of the Week, about 4 o'Clock in the Afternoon . 1765 November 1.
2. *James Boone*, III. was born on the 7th Day of the Week, 15 Minutes after Noon . . . 1769 January 21.
3. *Susanna Boone*, was born on the 4th Day of the Week, 45 Minutes past 10 o'Clock at Night . 1771 May 1.

John Boone, senior [Son of George & Mary Boone, and Brother of the said James Boone, senior] was born in the Town of Bradninch, in Devonshire, in Old-England, on the Seventh Day of the Week, about 11 in the Morning; A. D. 1702 January 14th, New-Style. And he the said John Boone, senior, departed this Life (in the Township of Exeter) on the 2d Day of the Week, 16 Minutes after Midnight, on the 10 October 1785, in the 84th Year of his Age ; He left Old-England in the 16th Year of his Age, and he (with his Parents, &c.) arrived at Philadelphia in 1717 October 10th, New-Stile, and lived here [in North-America] exactly 68 Years; he died within 5 Weeks & 4 Days after the Decease of his Brother James.

Judah Boone [Son of James Boone, senior, and Mary his Wife] departed this Life on the 15th Day of May, A. D. 1787, on the third Day of the Week, at fifteen Minutes after Midnight, aged 40 Years 4 Months 3 Weeks & 5 Days, that is, he was in the 41st Year of his Age ; and was interred in the Friends Burying Ground at Exeter on the fourth Day of the same Week.

CARPENTER GENEOLOGICAL NOTES.—Copied from a Bible in the possession of Mrs. James Rowland, Lewes, Del.

Marriages.

Thos H. Carpenter.
Margaret M. Staton. } March 4th. 1826 Phila.

Thos. H. Carpenter.
Catharine F. Marshal. } Sept. 3rd. 1850 Lewes.

Births.

Thos. Howard Carpenter son of Jos. and Mary Carpenter, Born March 28th. 1804. Lewes.

Margaret M. Staton daughter of Warrington and Hester Staton, Born Accomac Co, Va., April 12th. 1806.

Mary Quinn daughter of Thos. H. and Margaret Carpenter born April 7 1827 Phila.,

Thos. Howard son of Thos. H, and Margaret Carpenter, Born Dec. 10, 1829 Phila.,

Jas. Henry son of Thos. H, and Margaret Carpenter, Born Oct. 9, 1838 Lewes.

John Dorman, son of Samuel Dorman and Elizabeth Staton, Born June 24, 1818 Baltimore.

Louis Marshall Carpenter son of Thos. H, and Catharine F. Carpenter was born St. Louis Mo., Oct. 5, 1859.

Mary Quinn Carpenter daughter of Thos. H. and Catherine F. Carpenter was born Aug. 26, 1861.

Annie Eliza Carpenter daughter of Thos. H. and Catherine F. Carpenter was born St. Louis, Mo., Sept. 24, 1863.

Thomas H. Carpenter son of Thomas H. and Catharine F. Carpenter was born St. Louis Mo., Aug., 19, 1866.

James Carpenter was born May. 15, 1775.

Mary Dean was born Jan 16, 1781.

Comfort H, Married a Brown, Phila., daughter of Jas. and Mary Carpenter was born June 12, 1799.

Nancy daughter of Jas. and Mary Carpenter was born Jan. 28, 1801. Died March 24, 1808. Age 7 years 1 mo: 26 days.

Elizabeth daughter of Jas. and Mary Carpenter was born Nov. 13, 1802.

Thos. H. son of Jas. and Mary Carpenter was born March 28, 1804.

Robert Howard son of Jas and Mary Carpenter was born April 18, 1806. Died Sept. 14, 1808. Age 2 years 5 mo; 16 da:

Mary Rodgers daughter of Jas. and Mary Carpenter was born Feb. 13, 1808. Died Dec. 24, 1842. Age 34 years 10 mo; 11 da:

John Dean son of Jas and Mary Carpenter was born April 13, 1810. Lived in Phila. Died Age 49 years 4 mo; 18 da:

Jane daughter of Jas. and Mary Carpenter was born July 8, 1812. Died Age 34 years, 11 mo; 17 da:

Lydia daughter of Jas. and Mary Carpenter was born June 28, 1815. Married a Conwell.
Elizabeth daughter of Jas and Mary Carpenter was born Jan 24, 1818.
James son of Jas. and Mary Carpenter was born Aug 15, 1820. Died Feb. 25, 1842. Age 21 years 6 mo ; 10 da ; Pilot.
Margaret daughter of Jas. and Mary Carpenter was born April 2, 1822. married H. Long.
Benjamin son of Jas. and Mary Carpenter was born Sept. 22, 1825. Emigrated to South married and supposed killed on Rail Road.

Marriages.

Jas. Carpenter and Mary Dean were married Feb. 15, 1798.

Deaths.

Nancy daughter of Jas. and Mary died March 24, 1808. Age 7 years 1 mo ; 26 da ;
Robt Howard son of Jas. and Mary died Sept. 14, 1808. Age 2 yrs. 5 mo. 16 da ;
Jas. son of Jas. and Mary died Feb. 25, 1842 Age 21 yrs 6 mo 10 da ; (Pilot)
Mary Rodgers daughter of Jas. and Mary died Dec. 24, 1842. Age 34 yrs 10 mo 11 da.
Jane Sweeney daughter Jas and Mary Sweeney departed June 25, 1847. Age 34 yrs 11 mo 18 da.
Thos H. son of Jas and Mary departed May, 20, 1858. Age 54 yrs 1 mo 32 da.
Mary wife of Jas Carpenter departed July 3, 1858. Age 77 yrs. 5 mo 17 da.
Jno Dean son of Jas. and Mary Carpenter died Sept. 1, 1859. Age 49 yrs 4 mo, 18 da. Lived in Phila.
Lydia Coverdale daughter of Jas. and Mary Carpenter died Dec. 15, 1859. Age 44 yrs 5 mo, 17 da ;
Jas. Carpenter departed Jan. 7, 1861. Age 85 yrs 7 mo 22 da.
James H. Carpenter son of Thos H. and Margaret Carpenter died at Corning Arkansas Nov. 13, 1877.
Mary Q. Marshall wife of J. A. Marshall daughter of T. H. and Margaret Carpenter died Jan. 16, 1886 Lewes Del.
Catharine F. Carpenter wife of Tho H. Carpenter and daughter of D. J. and Eliza A Marshall died June 29, 1869. Age 33 yrs, 6 mo 3 da.

C. H. B. TURNER.

CHANDLER GENEALOGY.*—On p. 418, Vol. IV., of the PENNSYLVANIA MAGAZINE OF HISTORY AND BIOGRAPHY, mention is made of the widow of George Chandler. There are reasons for supposing that George Chandler came from the neighborhood of Marlborough in Wiltshire, England, but it appears that he never reached the shores of America, and there is a tradition that his death was occasioned by smallpox.

The following is " A True Inventory of the goods and Chattells of George Chandler who Deceased the xiii Day of December 1687, in his passage

---

*An extensive Chandler genealogy with some material by Cope, *A Record of the Descendants of George and Jane Chandler* . . . was published in 1937.

to pensilvania; Taken & Apprized by us Whose Names are heer underwritten The xth Day of the Seaventh mo' 1688.

	℔	s	d
first His wearing Apparrell,	iii	00	00
℔t one fether bed & two bolsters, 2 blankots 1 Coverled, 1 pare of Sheets,	iiii	00	00
℔t in other beds & Bedding,	vi	00	00
℔t in pewter,	oi	xi	00
℔t in Brass,	iii	x	iii
℔t in tools & other Ironware,	oi	x	00
pt in nayles, Saws, Aug'rs, Chessells, Gouges, wedges, Locks, Keys, Riphooks & all other Iron Lumber,	ii	ix	ix
pt 2 gunns & powder & shot & powder Horne,	oi	xii	00
pt 2 Chests & five Boxes and 2 bedsteds,	oi	xi	00
pt in Sacks,	00	x	00
pt one Barrell, 1 pare of Bellows, 4 Kevers, 1 Doe trough, 2 pailes, 10 botles, & all other Lumber,	oi	00	00
pt one Sow & 9 piggs,	ii	00	00
pt 4 yards & halfe of Sarge at 4 s per yard,	00	xviii	00
pt in whitles & Childbed Linnen,	00	xviii	00
pt 1 Ell of holland or Scotch Cloth, thred, pins & tapes,	00	v	00
pt one Coverled yt paid toward the byeing of one Horse,	oi	iiii	00
pt paid towards one Hundred Acres of Land,	viii	x	00
in the whole	xl	viii	00
Debts.			
paid A Debt to John Chandler,	xxvii	00	00
To William Hues,	00	xii	00
To philip Rummin fors shooes,	00	x	00
To William Hawks for worke & provission,	00	xv	00
To Fra'cis Chadsey,	00	ov	00
To meat,	00	iii	00
To William Clowd,	oi	ii	00
The whole	xxx	vii	00

JOHN CHANLOR.
THOMAS RAUELLSION.
GEORGE STRODE."
[Indorsed, "no adm'ra'n granted hereon — hee dyed Intestate."]

He left a widow, Jane, and seven children,—Jane, George, Swithin (born 6mo. 24th, 1674), William, Thomas, Charity, and Ann. John Chandler, a brother to the elder George, emigrated from England the same year, 1687, and settled in Chichester township, (now) Delaware County, Pa., but does not appear to have left any family,—George's children receiving nearly all of his estate. He died about 1703. A Jacob Chandler settled in Chichester township as early as 1685, but whether related to the others has not been ascertained. Whether the widow Chandler landed at Chester or Philadelphia is uncertain, but if at the latter she did not long remain there, for we find that in the 1st month (March), 1687-8 she and her brother-in-law, John Chandler, were purchasing land in Chichester, and also that in the 7th month (September), 1688, she was the wife of William Hawkes of that township. Her second husband died about the year 1694, and in 1695 we find her the wife of

James Bayliss, who probably died in Philadelphia about 1716, leaving her a widow for the third time.

Jane Chandler, Jr., married Robert Jefferis, of Chichester, and afterward of East Bradford, Chester County. George, Jr., married Ruth Bezer and remained in Chichester, where he died in 1714. Swithin married Ann —— and settled in Birmingham township on the Brandywine, but subsequently removed to Christiana Hundred, Delaware. William married Ann Bowater (?) and after some years settled in Londongrove township, where he died in 1746. Thomas married Mary —— and settled on the Brandywine in Birmingham. He left no children, but made his nephew Thomas, son of William, his principal heir. Charity probably died young. Ann married first Samuel Robbins, and second George Jones. She died in Philadelphia.

As far as has been ascertained the following are the names of the

CHILDREN OF

JANE.	GEORGE.	SWITHIN.				WILLIAM.			
Patience.	George.	Jacob,	2	9,	1705.	Jane,	3	1,	1713.
Charity.	Ruth.	Charity,	1	20,	1707.	Lydia,	8	2,	1714.
William.	John.	Ann,	2	1,	1709.	Samuel,	3	17,	1716.
James.	Isaac.	Jane,	3	11,	1711.	William,	2	20,	1718.
Robert.	Rachel (?).	Sarah,	3	20,	1713.	John,	1	20,	1719–20.
George.	Susanna (?).	Swithin,	10	1,	1715.	Ann,	12	27,	1721.
Jane.	& others (?).	Thomas,	10	3,	1718.	Thomas,	6	11	1724.
Anne.		Margaret,	5	6,	1721.	Moses.			
Mary.		Mary,	5	18,	1723.	Mary.			
Benjamin.		Phebe,	3	31,	1726.				
Thomas.		Betty	1	25,	1729.	OF ANN.			
John.		Hannah	4	4,	1732.	Sarah & others (?).			

Any person having records of births, deaths, marriages, or other interesting information of the Chandler family or their descendants of other names, will confer a favor by forwarding them to

GILBERT COPE,
5 26, 1870. West Chester, Penna.

GENEALOGICAL NOTES OF THE CHAPMAN FAMILY OF BUCKS COUNTY, PENNSYLVANIA.—Copied from the original manuscript, part of which is in a dilapidated condition.

" . . . salary for a clarks wages being but three Pence   the Value of three Shillings and fore Pence.

"And in the Year 1670—Upon the 15 Day of the 7th the Constable went with a warrant from a certain Justes upon an Information Given by one Lober Wood and Ralph Smith wait that philip Scarth did teach or Preach at a Seditious meeting who Spake only to one of the Informers the Constable I Say went and laid Four Pounds of the abovesaid Scarths fine upon S^d John Chapman besides five Shillings for his one fine as they Called it: and for the S^d fines the Constable took from him 5 Kine which Cost him about three month before 10£ and praised them 14£. 10S. and sold them at the same rate Likewise in the same year the Constable went with a worrant upon an Information that [   ] Sedious meting as it was Called For which they fined him ten Shillings and took from him for that 10S. Goods to the value of 1£ 8S.

"On the Longest Day in the year 1684 John Chapman with all his family set out from Stanhah (?) in yorkshire in order to Come to Amarica.

"They took Ship at New Castle upon the river tine and Came by way of Scotland and on the 12th Day of ye 7 moth in the aboves^d year they had a mighty Storm which blew so tempestously that in short it first Carried away their [   ] afterwards their [   ] flag Stafs and all by the board before the sailers were able to Git them Cut. It likewise took their awning above the Quarter Deck and left not as much as a Yard of rope above their heads. All which was done in the Space of half an hour and they lay thus distressed by a pitfull wreck all that night (they having lost their masts about 12 °Clock in the Day) and [two] Days after at the mercy of the Seas. the waves being montanious high occasioned by the Great storm of wind. thus they Lay I say with out hopes of recovery, being then about 200 Leagues from the Land of America but through Gods mercy they Got in Sight of the Capes of virginia within [   ] Days after or thereabouts by reason of a fair wind [   ] a pasage of about Nine Weeks from Aberdeen to ye Capes of virginia.

"They thus being arrived in America Came and Settled in Wright's town about the 10 mo. Ano Domine 1684.

"John Chapman of Stanhaw (?) Dyed in Wright Town about the 5th month A.D. 1694, and was buried in the Same Township in the old Grave Yard or burying Ground on the west side of the Park.

"Likewise Jane Chapman his wife Dyed and was buried by him about the 9th Month A.D. [1699]."

An Epitaph on Jno Chapman.

Behold John Chapman
That Christian man
Who first began
To settle in this Town
From Worldly Cares
And doubtfull fears
And Satans Snares
Is here laid down
His Soul doth rise
Above the Skies
In paradice
There to ware a Lasting Crown.

Joseph Chapman was maried to Mary Worth Daughter of Joseph and Mary worth on the 19th of 9th month A.D. 1715 at Stony Brook [. . .   ] A.D. 1695^6 in Piscatuway.

They buried one Child at Stony Brook on ye 2^d Day of the 5th month 1717. Sarah the Daughter of Joseph and mary Chapman was born the 8th Day of ye 1 month about 11 at night in Wright's Town A.D. 1718^9. Ann the Daughter of Joseph and Mary Chapman was born at wright town on the 29th Day of ye 2 month about 10 at night AD 1721.

Joseph the son of Joseph and mary Chapman was born at Wrightown on the 13th Day of ye 11 m^o after [   ] in the afternoon A.D. 1723^4.

Isaac Chapman the Son of Joseph and mary Chapman was born the 17th Day of y^e [4th mo., 1725].

Benjamin the Son of Joseph and Mary Chapman was born ye 22^d Day of ye 5th month A.D. 1727.

Mary the Wife of Joseph Chapman Dyed ye 24th of the 5th month 1727 and was buried in wright Town meeting hous Grave Yard on the 26th of ye same month.

Benjaman the Son of Joseph and Mary Chapman dyed ye 6th of y^e [   ] month A.D. 1727 and was buried by his Mother.

Joseph Chapman was married unto Mary Wilkinson Daughter of John and mary Wilkinson on the 6th Day of ye 6th month A.D. 1730.

Which S^d Mary wilkinson was born in hantoron in west New Jersey on the 17th of ye 7 m^o 1708.

Joseph the Son of Joseph and Mary Chapman was born ye 18th Day of ye 6th month A.D. 1731.

Mary the Daughter of Joseph and mary Chapman was born on the 25th Day of ye 2^d month at 6 ^{o}Clock in the morning A.D. 1733.

Jane Chapman the Daughter of Joseph and mary Chapman was Born the 12th Day of ye 9th month A.D. 1736.

Margaret Chapman the Daughter of Joseph and Mary Chapman was born on the 2^d Day of the 5th month about 5 in the morning Anno Domini 1739.

Joseph Chapman the Son of Joseph and Mary Chapman dyed was Buried on the 27th of ye 11 month 1731^2.

mary Chapman second wife of Joseph Chapman dyed on ye 25th of ye 7th month at 3 in morning and was buried in wright Town by his former wife A.D. 17[   ].

Joseph Son of John and Jane Chapman the first Settlers of Wright Town dyed on ye 5th Day of the 2^d month new stild and was buried Between his wives on the 17th Day of ye S^d month A.D. 175[   ].

Abraham Chapman Son of John and Jane Chapman dyed on the 12th Day of the 2^d month and was Buried on the 14th Day of S^d month A.D. 1755.

John Chapman the Son of John and Jane Chapman dyed on the 9th Day of the 4th month And was buried in wrghtown meeting house Grave Yard on the [   ] Day of ye s^d Month 1743.

Mara Chapman the Daughter of John and Jane Chapman was married unto John Croasdel by whome she had Chidren and her said husband died.

Mara Chapman was maried ye second time unto John Wildman by whome she had Children and She died.

Jane Chapman the Daughter of John and Jane Chapman died. Joseph

Chapman was took sick on ye 8th of the 3 month 1752 and Departed this Life ye 15th of the same month being 67 Years and 3 Days old.

Isaac Chapman Came to Shammony hollow to Live on the 10th of the 1th month 1753, and died at the same place about the 29 Day of the 9 monnth 1775 aged 46 years.

CLAYPOOLE GENEALOGY.—We are indebted to Mr. J. Rutgers Le Roy, Paris, France, for the following genealogical notes relating to James Claypoole, the emigrant, and his son Joseph.

Memorandum that I James Claypoole and Helen Mercer were Joyned in Marage the 12 day 12 month 16$\frac{57}{58}$ at Bremen in Germany by Conradus Lelius a Calvin Minister.

1. The 15th day of 9 month 1658 my sonne John was borne at London in Nicholas Lane between 2 & 3 of y^e Clock in y^e Morning.
2. My Daughter Mary was borne the 14th day 8 Month 1660 near 8 of y^e Clock at night in Minsing lane in London.
3. My Daughter Helen was borne ye 6 day 9 Month 1662 about 9 of ye Clock in the Evening in Scots yard near London stone.
4. My sonne James was borne ye 12th day 6 Month 1664 about 8 of ye Clock in ye morning in Scots yard near London stone.
5. My Daughter Prissilla was borne the 25th of ye 2 Month 1666 at ¾ past 4 in the Morning in Scots yard as above
6. My Sonne Nathaniel was borne the 23^d Day 7 Month 1668 at 2 of ye Clock in ye afternoon at the Signe of the Still upon Horsly Downe in Southwark
7. My Sonne Josiah was borne y^e 9th day of 9 Month 1669 about half an hour past 9 at night in Scots yard as above.

My sonne Josiah departed this life the 2^d day 3^d Month 1670 about 7th hour at night at Kingston upon Thames & was there buried in our friends burying place.

8. My sonne Samuel was borne y^e 19th 1 Month 16$\frac{70}{71}$ about ¾ past 2^d hour in y^e Morning in Scots yard as above.
9. My second sonne Nathaniel was borne y^e 4th day 8 Month 1672 about ¾ past 6° hour in y^e Evening in Scots yard as above.
10. My sonne Georg was borne y^e 14th day 11 Month 1674 about ye 9th hour in the Evening in Scots yard as above.
11. About the End of the year 1673 my Wife was Delivered of a sonne that Dyed in the birth & was not named.
12. My sonne Joseph was borne ye 29th day 1st month 1676 at ¾ past one of ye Clock in ye Morning in Scots yard.

My sonne Joseph Departed this lyfe the 30th 6 Month 1676 about 3 in ye afternoon at Lambeth & was buryed in friends burying place by Moorfields.

13. My second sonne Joseph was borne the 14th day 5 Mo 1677 at ¾ past 8th hour at night in Scots yard as above.
14. My Daughter Elizabeth was borne the 25th day 5 Month 1678 at halfe an hour past 6 in the Morning in Scots yard.

My Daughter Elizabeth departed this life the 31th 5 Month 1678 about the 9th hour at night & was buryed in friends burying place by Moorfields.

My Sonne Samuel departed this life the 11th 1 month 16$\frac{80}{81}$ about 10th hour at night at Edmendton & was buryed y^e 13th at friends burying place by Moorfields.

My Deare father James Claypoole Departed this Life the 6 6 mo 1687 and was buried in friends burying place at philadelphia 7 6 mo.

My dear Mother Helena Claypoole departed this Life the 19 6 mo 1688 and was buryed in friends burying place at Philadelphia 20 6 mo 1688.

My Uncle Norton Claypoole departed this Life in July 1688 at the Whorekill in Lewistown.

My Sister Helen Bethell departed this Life ye 9 5 mo 1691 at Jemaca and their both her Children dyed.

My Sister Priscilla Crapp departed this Life the 16 10 mo 1698 and was buryed in friends burying place at Philadelphia 20 10 mo 1698.

Brother John Claypoole Departed this Life ye 8 9 mo 1700 and was buried in friend burying place in Philadel.

Brother Georges Wife Mary departed this Life in ye 2 mo 1702 and was buryed in friends buryind place in philadelphia.

We set Saile from gravesend the 25 5 mo 1683 and Arrived at philadelphia in pensylvania 8 8 mo 1683. we came in the ship called the Concord Captain Jeffrys Commder burthen 550 tuhn.

Memorandom that Francis Cooke and Mary Claypoole was Joyned in Marrage in the 8 mo 1687 In Philadelphia.

This May Certify Whome it May Concern that I, Joseph Claypoole & Rebecca Jennings Ware Married according to the Manor & forme of ye Church of England Prayer Book July ye 20^{dy} 1703 By Mr. Edward Maston Minister of Charles towne in South Carrolinah.

Philadelphia March ye 30dy 1704, on thursday at 6 in ye Morning Was Borne Mary my first dafter in ye house of Mary Cook My Eldest sister Living in ye high streat & dyed aged 6 yeres & 8 Months.

Philadelphia March ye 5dy 1705 James my first Son was Borne on thursday a boute two in ye Morning at my house in Wallnut Street— dyed aged 14 yers & 5 month

Philadelphia december ye 14^{dy} 1706: George My second Son was borne on Saterday aboute Nine in ye Morning at My hous in Wallnut street.

Munday Philadelphia October ye 24 dy 1709, Joseph my third Son Was borne a boute three in ye afternune at My house in Wallnut Street.

Philadelphia November ye 26 d^y 1711. Rebecca My Second Dafter Was Borne on Munday a Boute three quarters Past twelve in ye Morning at My house in Wallnut Streate

Philadelphia May ye 11 d^y 1714, Jehu My [torn] Son Was Borne on tusday a bout teen a Clock in ye Morning at My house in Wallnut Street.

Philadelphia November ye 19^{dy} 1715 Josiah My fifth Son Was Born on Saterday a bout Nine in ye Morning at My house in Wallnut Street Dyed in Nine Months.

This is to Certify whom it may Concern that Mr Joseph Claypole, & Mes Rebecca Jennings were Marry'd according to the Common prayer Book of ye Church of England July ye 20th 1703 by
                Edward Marston
                Minister de Charles Town

Philad'lphia December ye 21 dy 1710, On thursday A bout Nine in ye Morning Mary My first Dafter Died & was Buried in Christs Curch yard aged six years & Eight Months.—

Piladelphia November ye 30 dy 1715, On Wensday a boute a quarter Past twelve in ye afternune, My Most Dere & well Beloved wife Rebecca Claypoole Died at my house in Wallnut Streete & was Buried in ye ould Bering Ground By My Relations & on Saturday December ye 17 dy 1715 I had My Dafter Mary Removed from ye Church yard & Laid in My Wifes Grave with her.

Philadelphia March ye 30dy 1704, on thursday about 6 of ye Morning Was Borne Mary my first Dafter in ye house of Mary Cook my Eldest Sister Liveing in ye high Street.

Philadelphia March ye 1 dy 1705, James my first Son was Borne one thursday about two in ye Morning at my hous in Wallnut Street.

Philadelphia December ye 14 dy 1706, George my Second Sun Was borne on Saterday a bout nine in ye Morning at My house in Wallnut Street.

Philadelph October ye 24 dy 1709, Joseph My third Sun Was borne a boute three in ye afternune on Munday at my house in Wallnut street.

Philadelphia November ye 26 dy 1711, Rebecca My Second Dafter was Borne on Munday a Boute three quarters Past twelve in ye Morning at my house in Wallnut Streete.

Philadelphia May ye 11dy 1714 Jehu my forth Son was Borne on tuesday about ten or Eleven a Clock in the Morning at My house in Wallnut Street.

Philadelphia November ye 19 dy 1715 Josiah my fifth Sun was Borne on Saterday aboute Nine in ye Morning at my hous in Wallnut Streete.

THREE GENERATIONS OF THE CLYMER FAMILY.

Christopher Clymer, of Bristol, England, and his wife Catherine (who was living July 8, 1734), had, besides other children, two sons who came to America.

1. Richard Clymer,   m. Elizabeth ——
   William Clymer, whose will, naming his wife Margaret and his friend Chas. Willing executrix & executor, devises his property to his nephew William, son of his late brother Richard Clymer, dec^d., and to Daniel, son of the said William Clymer; to George, son of his late nephew Christopher Clymer, and to William, son of William Clymer of Bristol, Eng., was proven Philad^a., April 29, 1751. He was buried in Christ Ch. Ground, April 26, 1751, and his widow in the same place, March 29, 1781.

1. Richard Clymer, son of Christopher and Catherine Clymer, came to America with his wife Elizabeth prior to July 30, 1710. He was admitted a freeman of Philadelphia May 27, 1717, and then followed the trade of Blockmaker; this occupation he gradually expanded into a general shipping business, and in the course of years acquired a considerable fortune. His wife died in 1733, and was buried in Christ Church Ground, July 4th of that year. He was buried in the same place, August 17, 1734, and his will was proved two days later.
Issue:

   2. John, bapt. July 30, 1710, aged 6 days, bn. Aug.   1710.
   3. Christopher, bapt. Aug. 14, 1711, aged 3 days, m. Deborah Fitzabeth.
   4. Sarah, bapt. Sept. 30, 1713, aged 1 month, bn. May 19, 1714.
   5. William, m. Ann Judith Roberdeau.

3. Christopher Clymer^2 (Rich^{d1}), b. Phila., Aug. 11, 1711, m. Philada. Deborah, dau. of George Fitzwater. She was

buried in Frds. Grd., May 6, 1740. He was buried in Christ Church Ground, July 27, 1746.
Issue, two children.

    6. Elizabeth, buried Feb. 16, 1739–40, in Friends' Grd.
    7. George Clymer, b.   1739, m. Eliz. Meredith.

    5. William Clymer² (Ric^{d1}) b.   m. Philada. Christ Ch., Jan. 19, 1741/2, Ann Judith, 2nd dau. of Isaac Roberdeau, by his wife Mary Cunyngham, b. St. Christopher's, W. I., in 1725 or 6, and d. Morgantown, Berks Co., Penn^a., 1782. In 1745 commanded a Privateer, *N. Y. Post Boy*, *April* 1, 1745. He was lost at sea. For the descendants of Daniel Cunyngham Clymer, see the Roberdeau Family, by Roberdeau Buchanan.
Issue:

    8. Richard, bapt. Jan. 8, 1743/4, aged 7 weeks, bn. Aug. 10, 1744.
    9. Daniel Cunyngham, bn. April 6, 1748, bapt. July 2, 1748, m. Mary Weidner.

    7. George Clymer³ (Chris.², Rich^{d1}) SIGNER OF THE DECLARATION OF INDEPENDENCE, b. Philada.,   1739, m. Philada. Christ Ch., March 18, 1765, Elizabeth, dau. of Reese Meredith, who d. Northumberland, Pa., Feb., 1815. He d. Morrisville, Bucks Co., Jan. 23.
Issue:

    10. William Coleman Clymer.
    11. Julian Clymer.
    12. Henry, b. July 31, 1767, m. Mary Willing.
    13. Meredith Clymer was a memb. City Troop, and Nov. 18, 1794, on the Campaign against the Whiskey Insurgents.
    14. Elizabeth.
    15. Margaret, m. George McCall.
    16. Ann, m. 1807, Charles Lewis. Died at Trenton, Aug., 1810.
    17. George Clymer, m. Maria O'Brien.

    9. Daniel Cunyngham Clymer³ (W^{m2}, Rich^{d1}) b. Philada., April 6, 1748, m.   Mary, dau. of Peter and

Susan Weidner, of Berks Co., who d. Dec. 5, 1802, in her 40th year. He d. Reading, Jan. 25, 1810.

18. Anne, b. Reading, 1782, d. unm. Morgantown, Aug., 1852.
19. William, b. March 28, 1788, m. Susan Rightmeyer.
20. Edward Tilghman, b. Aug. 14, 1790, m. Maria C. Heister.

[Reproduced in black and white in the interest of economy.]

CAPTAIN WILLIAM CRISPIN

By M. JACKSON CRISPIN,
of New York City.

 Captain,[1] Rear-Admiral,[2] and Colonel[3] William Crispin (1627–1681/2), ancestor of the Crispins in America, who first served in the Navy of the English Commonwealth, and afterwards in the Royal Navy, was born in Kingston-on-Hull, County York, England, and was baptized there October 3rd, 1627. He had a very distinguished career, taking part in many battles and

---

Abbreviations: P. R. O.=British Public Record Office, in Chancery Lane, London.

c.=*circa* (about).

MS.=Manuscript.

[1] Thirty years ago, in 1898, in the *Pennsylvania Magazine*, Vol XXII., pages 34–56, my kinsman, Oliver Hough, gave an account of our ancestor William Crispin. So much new information has now been gathered, that this fresh presentation is published. The entire pedigree herewith given has been proven and enrolled at the College of Arms, London. It has been reviewed by Richard Holworthy, of Holworthy and Shilton, genealogists, of London, England, and the whole of this article has been critically examined by Albert Cook Myers, the historian, of Philadelphia, Secretary-Director of The Pennsylvania State Historical Commission, 1923–1927, and the recognized authority on the life and works of William Penn and the Penn family.

[2] Granville Penn, *Memorials of Sir William Penn*, II. (London, 1833) 108.

[3] *Calendar of State Papers, Colonial, 1574–1660* (London, 1860) 437.

minor engagements, while in command of a squadron in the English Channel, as well as under command of Admiral Sir William Penn (1624–1670), his uncle by marriage. As Captain of one of the ships which defeated the Dutch in the war of 1653, he was presented with a gold medal[4] by the English Parliament. He took a prominent part in the West Indian Expedition in 1655, serving as Rear-Admiral of the Fleet, and was appointed a Commissioner for the supplying of the Naval forces in Jamaica. Under King Charles II., he held various offices of trust in Kinsale, County Cork, Ireland, where he lived until he sailed for Pennsylvania, as head of the Commission "For the Settling of the Colony," and was also appointed Chief Justice, Assistant to the Governor, and Surveyor General of the Province by his cousin, William Penn, the Founder. Owing, however, to the rigour of his service to the State, his health, it would seem, had become impaired, since he died on the voyage to Pennsylvania in 1681–2.[5]

The Crispins are an ancient and honorable family in Great Britain, tracing descent from the great Norman Dukes. Of this family was Count Gilbert Crispin[6] (1000–1066),[7] of Brionne, Baron of Tillieres, first

---

[4] House of Commons Journal; William Laird Clowes, *Royal Navy* (London, 1898), 102.

[5] There is a tradition in the family that he was at one time a member of Cromwell's Trained Band and afterwards Captain of the Guard, but recent exhaustive researches show that he was at sea during the whole of the Civil War, therefore this statement may be discredited so far as he is concerned, though possibly it may relate to some other member of his family.

[6] Benedictine Monks of the Congregation of St. Maure, *Literary History of France*, Vol. 12 (Paris, 1763) 192; P. Anselm, *Genealogical and Chronological History of the Royal House of France*, Vol. 16 (Paris, 1730) 632. There has been much controversy about his identity among historians since the sixteenth century, which will be dealt with in another article.

[7] It is a well-known historical fact that Gilbert Crispin was created Baron of Tillieres about 1030 by Duke Robert II. (The Magnificent) and that he defended that castle against Henry I., King of France, about 1042.—Freeman, Anselme, Planchet and others.

cousin (by blood) of Duke Robert II. (The Magnificent), the father of William the Conqueror. Count Gilbert Crispin was the father of the three celebrated brothers: William Crispin I.[8] (1020–1074),[9] Count of Vexin,[10] Baron of Neaufles, Livarot, Blangy[11] and Lord of Pacy;[12] Gilbert Crispin, Baron of Tillieres; and Milo Crispin,[13] Lord of Wallingford (after the Conquest), all of whom accompanied William the Conqueror to England, with a large retinue of knights, and fought with much distinction in the Battle of Hastings. The eminent prelate, Gilbert Crispin,[14] Abbot of West Monastery (Westminster Abbey), from 1085 to 1117, whose tomb may still be seen in the cloister of the Abbey, was a son of William Crispin I., Count of Vexin. The descendants of William Crispin I. were related by blood to Henry Plantagenet, Count of Anjou, who be-

---

[8] William Crispin I. has been called Baron of Bec by Grimaldi and other historians, but this is an error, as this barony was not acquired by the Crispin family until 1250. The then William Crispin, head of the house, was called "the young." He was Marshal of France and Baron of Neaufles, Blangy, Estrepagny and Dangu. He acquired through his marriage to the heiress, Lady Jeanne de Mortemer, the Barony of Bec and Varengebec, which was almost as large in extent as the domains of the King of France.—A. Lechevalier, *Historical Notice of the Barons and Barony of Bec called Bec Crispin* (Paris, 1898) 22.

[9] J. Armitage Robinson, *Gilbert Crispin, Abbot of Westminster* (London, 1911) 15; also Nomina Monachorum from Necrology of Beaumont-le-Roger.—Nat. Lib. Paris (Lat. 13905).

[10] J. J. Vernier, *Charters of l'Abbaye de Jumieges* (Paris, 1916) 68–69. (Charter dated 1045–1048). Charter signed William Count of Vilcasini (Vexin).—Thomas Stapleton, *Rotuli Scaccarii Normanniae*, I. (London, 1844) 122; Stevens, *Dictionary of National Biography*, Vol. 13 (London, 1888) 100–101.

[11] LeChanoine Poree, *History of the Abbey of Bec* (Evreaux, 1901) Vol. I., page 178, Vol. II., pages 97 and 120.

[12] From the manuscript notes of Paul Gentil, Tillieres-sur-Avre, taken from the archives of the Tillieres family.

[13] Dugdale's Baronage of England; Domesday Book; Rev. H. A. Napier, *Historical Notes of the Parishes of Swyncombe and Ewelme*, I. (Oxford, 1858) 2.

[14] J. Armitage Robinson (Dean of Wells), *Gilbert Crispin, Abbot of Westminster* (London, 1911).

came Henry II., King of England.[15] It is proposed to publish at a later date an article concerning the family in Normandy and England.

The immediate family of Captain William Crispin lived at Kingston-on-Hull, Yorkshire, the three generations preceding him, having been men of substantial means, owning and commanding their own ships.

Full biographical accounts of his father, William Crispin (1602–1645), his grandfather, also named William Crispin (1573–1636), his great-grandfather John Crispin (d. 1591) and other members of the family were printed in the issue of March, 1928, of *Publications of The Genealogical Society of Pennsylvania,* Vol. X, No. 2, pages 105–122, under the title of "Crispins of Kingston-on-Hull,"[16] by M. Jackson Crispin.

At the outbreak of the Civil War in 1642, Captain Crispin's father, William Crispin, threw in his lot with the Parliamentary Party, and having had a wide experience in command of various merchant ships, including the "Adventure," in 1634. He was Master of the "Fellowship" of 28 guns, commanded by Captain, afterwards Admiral Sir William Penn, when she sailed on her second voyage from Deptford, in the Thames, on October 12th, 1644. He did not long survive, however, as will be seen from the following entries in Penn's manuscript Journal,[17] in 1645, which state that

---

[15] J. A. Giles, translation of *Beati Lanfranci, Miraculum quo beata Maria Subvenit Willelmo Crispino Seniori, ubide Nobili Crispinorum genere agitur* I. (Paris, 1844) 348.

[16] The pedigree of the "Crispins-on-Hull," which this article gives in detail, was reviewed and approved by A. T. Butler, Portcullis, College of Arms, London, in a letter to the writer of that article, dated 18th July, 1927.

[17] Information supplied by Albert Cook Myers from his William Penn Collection.

Reproduction of Entries from the Original Manuscript Journal of the "King and Parliament" Warship "Fellowship," commanded by Captain, afterwards Admiral Sir William Penn, recording the Death of Captain William Penn's Father, William Crispin, (1602–1645), Master of the Ship, who died on Board, at Carrickfergus, Northeast Coast of Ireland, April 8th, 1645, and was buried there in the Chancel of the Church.

he died on board his ship at Carrickfergus, on the coast of County Antrim, northeast Ireland:

April 1645,
"7th. Mundaye ABout 4 a C^1 in the morningh wee wayed with the wynd at the W. N. W. a hard gayle & turned up into the roade off Carickffergus & Came to an Ancker about 12 a Clock at noone, the Castel bore off vs N. W. halff northerley in 6½ ffadem waeter halff Cannel over

8th. Aprill ABout 3 a Clocke in the morningh our m^r. William Crispin departed out off this World.
& then the mounye was Carried aschoare

9th: Wednesdaye ABout 2 a Clocke in the afternoone, wee Carried our m^r ashoare & gave him 10 peeces off ordinance, & wee buried him in the Chansel in the Church off Carickffergus" [18]

A memorial window portraying St. Andrew, sailor and Apostle, has been dedicated to Captain Crispin's father in the Church at Carrickfergus. The bronze tablet beneath this window bears only his arms and parts of the exact wording of the entry concerning his death above referred to, as recorded in Admiral Penn's Journal.

In one of his letters, written in 1652, Captain Crispin states that he had been in the service of the state for ten years; thus he joined the navy in 1642, at the early age of 15. Presumably he made his first voyage with his father and was on the "Fellowship" man-of-war under Sir William Penn. It would appear more than probable that on the death of his father, Penn took an interest in the son of his old master and that this was the beginning of that great bond of friendship and esteem which afterwards existed between Admiral Sir William Penn and Captain William Crispin, for they are always found together, both on land and sea, and it was undoubtedly this association which led to the alliance of the Penn and Crispin families. In the Naval engagements in which Admiral Penn figured we find Captain Crispin until he was promoted to a separate command. On land, too, when Penn became Gov-

---

[18] Carrickfergus, County Antrim, Ireland.

ernor-General of the town and fortress of Kinsale, there also we find Captain Crispin, holding various offices of trust.

The first actual record we have of Captain Crispin at sea, was his appointment as purser of the "Truelove" frigate, on April 3rd, 1649,—"forasmuch as William Crispin hath been recommended for a faithful able man to mannage such an employment!" The warrant was signed by Admirals Deane and Blake. In early days every officer had to serve six or seven years as a seaman before he could get his commission, thus the dates would fit in exactly with the statement made by him in the letter referred to above. The "Truelove" was discharged on August 30th in the following year, when there was an amount of £2.5.7 due to him. Strangely enough just 20 years before, his father, William Crispin, made several voyages in the "Truelove" of Hull.

On August 6th, in the same year, the Admiralty Commissioners wrote to Colonel Deane that six new frigates were to be supplied with officers, and sent the petition and certificates of William Crispin for a purser's place in one of them. They instructed Deane, if he found the papers correct, to return Crispin as fit to be employed, which he apparently did, for in November, 1650, Crispin is recorded as Purser of the "Centurian," commanded by Penn, operating in the Irish Channel. On this ship he remained until he was discharged on the 19th of June, 1652.

It was in this year, 1652, in the midst of the conflict with the Dutch, that Crispin as a young naval purser, at the age of 25, entered the married state and thus allied himself with the family of Penn. His bride was Rebecca Bradshaw, the daughter of Ralph Bradshaw, by his wife Rachel Penn, sister of Admiral Sir William Penn, and daughter of Captain Giles Penn, who was grandfather of William Penn, the Founder of Pennsylvania. The wedding ceremony took place in that quaint old London Church of St. Dunstan's, Stepney, in the County of Middlesex, on September 28th, 1652, as appears by the published registers of the parish,[19] as well as by Sir William Dugdale's Visitation of Lancashire in 1664–5.[20] The groom is described as "of the Tower liberty, mariner." On this same Tower Hill, London, within sight of the River Thames, Admiral Penn, with his son William Penn, aged 8, and others of his family, then were living, and it may have been that the Admiral's niece, Rebecca Bradshaw, met William Crispin while on a visit to her uncle, and that her courtship and marriage occurred while there.

In this part of London was spent the early married life of Crispin and his wife, their oldest child, William Crispin, being baptized June 24th, 1653, in the near by Church of St. Olave, Hart Street,[21] the place of worship, a little later, not only of Samuel Pepys, the diarist, but also of Sir William and Lady Penn with their children. From his abode near the historic old Tower of London, in this center of the maritime affairs of the period, Crispin went forth on his voyages, his first-born, it would seem, having come into the world when the father was far out at sea in the height of the Dutch engagements.

In the State Papers of the Public Record Office in London there is a letter written by William Crispin, when Purser of the "Fairfax," to J. Turner, November 22nd, 1652, saying that he had mustered Captain

---

[19] Vol. II. (Canterbury, 1899) 83.

[20] There appears in *The Bristol Pike*, by the Reverend S. F. Hotchkiss, M.A., in *Colonial and Revolutionary Families*, by John W. Jordan (in the sketch of *Captain William Crispin*, by Oliver Hough), in *Captain William Crispin and the Crispin Family*, by William Frost Crispin, and in the writings of others, the statement that Captain William Crispin was first married to Anne Jasper, the sister-in-law of Admiral Sir William Penn. This error can be traced to the statement, written in 1792, by William Crispin, of Philadelphia, a great grandson of Captain William Crispin. How he made this mistake is not known.

[21] *Registers, 1563–1700* (London, 1916) 60.

Lawson's men on the "Fairfax" and found more landsmen and boys than upon any of the State's ships for the last ten years; that he discharged 18, signing their tickets, and sent down 180 men to the "Fairfax" lying off the Hope in the Thames, that when they arrived and saw the landsmen, 100 would not go, but went to other ships. This letter shows that the Admiralty were preparing for the approaching conflict with the Dutch.

There were few regular naval vessels or officers at this period, and in times of war merchant ships were pressed into the service. As, however, every merchantman was to all intents and purposes a war-ship, ready at all times to defend herself against foreign privateers or pirates, little alteration was necessary, while the commanders of these ships were either appointed captains or acted as masters, and usually sailed with merely an addition to the ordinary personnel.

A fleet was sent by Cromwell against the Dutch in May 1653, commanded by Colonel George Monk and Colonel Richard Deane. This naval force was made up of three squadrons. Colonels Monk and Deane had direct command of the first or red squadron, consisting of 38 ships. Vice-admiral Penn commanded the second or white squadron of 33 ships, in which Captain William Crispin commanded the "Assistance," 180 men and 40 guns. Rear-Admiral John Lawson commanded the third or blue squadron of 34 ships. This fleet, after two previous pitched battles, captured and destroyed, on July 29th and 30th, 1653, between twenty and thirty Dutch ships of war, and captured 1350 prisoners, driving the Dutch to their own harbours. This was a very sanguinary battle. The total Dutch losses in killed, wounded and captured were about 6000 men, including the great Admiral Van Tromp, their commander, two Vice-Admirals and three Rear-Admirals.[22]

---

[22] Granville Penn, *Memorials of Sir William Penn*, I. (London, 1833) 507, citing "Colliber."

Captain Crispin was awarded a gold medal for his services in this battle by the English Parliament, by an order dated August 8th, 1653.[23] After this engagement the "Assistance" spent the remainder of the year cruising and conveying merchantmen, and preying on the Dutch commerce, as is shown by a considerable number of letters in the State Papers, from which it is evident that he was in command of a squadron operating at that time in the English and Irish Channels.

In the British Public Record Office[24] in Chancery Lane, London, is the following holograph letter (here reproduced) of Captain William Crispin to the Secretary of the Admiralty, written on board the war vessel "Assistance," 7 mo. [September] 12th, 1653:

S^r:

I re^{cd}: yours of ye 6th Instant (but it was 3 dayes in coming downe) I thanke you for y^t faviour in Affourding me y^t Intelligence, pray Let me request you to doe me ye Like ffaviour, when anything comes to you, w^{ch}: by ye knowledge of I may be further Inabled to prosecute my duty to The Publique Service, pray Let this Inclosed be put vp in your next to ye Gen^{lls}:, I had not burthened you therewth: had I any other Conveniencie, Sir you will herein very much ffurther Ingadge him y^t is:

      Sir yours very dissirvous to
        Serve you
         W^m: Crispin

ffrom Aboard ye Assistance y^e
12th of ye 7th m̃o: 1653:

Addressed in the same hand:
 ffor my honord: ffriend Robt:
 Blackborne Esqr: Secretary
 to ye Right Hono^{ble}: ye Com^{rs}: for the
  Admiralty & navey These
     ℘: sent
 Whithall

*Wax seal impressed with his crest,
a demi griffin erased, with wings addorsed.
Letter endorsed in a contemporary hand:*
 12 7^{ber} 1653
  Capt: Crispin to M^r
   Blackborne.

---

[23] House of Commons Journal.
[24] State Papers Domestic, Supplementary, Vol. 115, ff. 69, 70.

Letter of Captain William Crispin to the Secretary of the Admiralty, written on the "Assistance, September 12th, 1653.

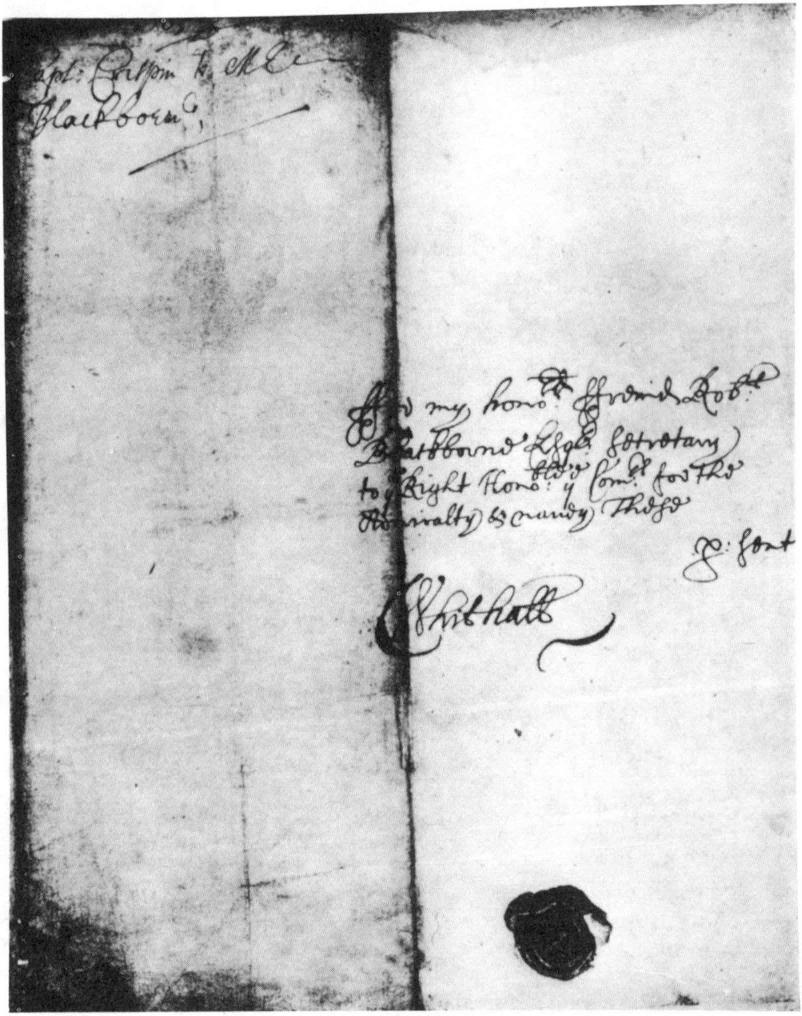

Address of Captain William Crispin's Holograph Letter of September 12th, 1653, with Wax Seal impressed with his Crest, a Demi Griffin erased, with Wings addorsed.

Seal Natural Size.

Among the ships in the squadron under his command were the "Warwick," Captain Godfrey; the "President," Captain Sparling; the "Nonsuch," Captain Penrose; the "Nightingale," Captain Humphreys; the "Hector," the "Sapphire," the "Pearl" and the "Hopewell."

A letter written by William Crispin on board the "Assistance," at Falmouth, October 22nd, 1653, to Robert Blackborne, Secretary of the Commissioners of the Admiralty, reads:

Honrd Si^r

The 10th Instant I being open of Plymouth Sound Capt Hattsell sent his whery of desiring to speake wth mee he Informed mee y^t itt was ye Gennr^{lls} pleasure y^t I should wash and tallow & victuall for 5 Months severall Command^{rs} then att Plymouth had order to give mee advice thereof also Accordingly, I made use of ye Present Spring & gott ye s^d worke finished by ye 18 Instant and then sett sayle desired in an order from Capt Hattswele to ply E^{t}ward betwene Portland & the Ile of Wight to meet ye Speaker Capt Hattswell suposing y^t Capt Saunders in ye Ruby had receaved orders to succeede mee in this Station when I came to see ye weather proved very foule and blew hard all Easterly so ye 19th I putt into Falmouth where I meet ye Warrwicke & Hopewell they both havinge men for mee ye Warrwicke havinge aboard some of them a Month butt could nott be drawne to mee to make delivery of them ye 21 ye Ruby came in by Reason of foule weather having noe Provision left upon ye sight of his orders from ye Genn^{ll} I find y^t his station is betwene Portland & ye Gasquetts & nott further westward and nott one ship under my Comand mentioned in his list. Capt Saunders informes me y^t very lately one of o^r shipps was in sight with Capt Beach. Capt Saunde^{rs} was also 3 or 4 dayes past very neere a hollands frg^{tt} of 32 guns who all 3 as he sayth are about ye Lands and so by permission I Intend to ply y^t way forthwith & nott to leave this station until I have a punctuall order to the contrary I have sent to Plymouth for ye Saphire who I hope is Ready to sayle ye Pearle is now about Silly ye Hector & President I ordered severall dayes past to ply of ye Lands end, but att present I doe nott heare they are there ye Warrwicke wants a new maynmast as the Capt sayeth wants victualls & is foule I purpose to send hir for Portsmouth ye Hopewell wants victualls they two & ye Ruby I am forced to suply from aboard this frg^{tt} Si^r pray endeavo^r y^t ye State may not be so abused by Capt Mills impresing men as now they are his order is, to press seamen but of about 40 men wch I have Receavd from him there is nott 4 seamen or men y^t were at sea they are all Plowmen thachers & Hedgers and taken from ye sd Callings to ye greate prejudice of the Country as ye Justices of Peace doth testifie those that are seamen y^t he meets with he sufers to be cleared upon feeing of ye Counstables. S^r if there be any thing worthy heerin of ye Com^a Knowledge pray acquaint them with itt. Si^r I Receaved in ye Downes ye Com^a Letter about sending of Capt Humphreis or Capt Sparlinge for Ierland and accordingly I did give Capt Humphreis ye instructions ye first of this Month and have in severall Letters given ye Rg^{tt} Honble ye Com^a & Genners¹¹ an Accompt thereof I Remaine

       S^r
    You^r very Humble servant in y^e
      Bonds of Love
        Wm Crispin

Falmouth
From Aboard ye Assistance
Frgg^{tt} ye 22 of October
1653.
  Addressed:
    To his Honnr'd Freind
    Robart Blackburne Esq.
    Secretary to ye Rg^{tt} Honble
    ye Com^{rs} for ye Admiraltye
    & Navy
      These
      present
        Whitehall
    Endorsed
    22^d October 1653.
    Capt Crispin to Mr Blackborn
    from aboard ye Assistance att
      Falmouth
Seal gone[25]

Joseph Godolphin and other Judges of the Court of Admiralty write to the Council of State for Foreign Affairs on December 13th, 1653, as follows:

R^t Honoble

In obedience to yor Ord^r of ye 8th of Decemb inst^t, for stating ye matt^r of Fact in ye Case of three small French fishing vessells, taken by the Assistance Frigat, upon the Petition of Mr Samll Terick & orther English m^rchants trading to France.

As to twoe of ye said Shipps, viz: the St Andrew of Homflare, and the St Lewis of the same Wee find ye St. Andrew is of one hundred Tunn Burthen, seaven Gunns, bound upon a trading voyage to NewfoundLand; & returning laden with Fish and Oyle, shott five or six Gunns ag^t the Assistance Frigatt, who took ye said Shipp before shee yeilded, which is with ye Lading wholly french.

---

[25] State Papers Domestic, Interregnum, Vol. 60. f. 63, in P. R. O.

The St Lewis is French both Shipp & lading, of seaven score tuñ Burthen, nine Gunns, & severall Murther's & was upon a fishing voyage to Cannady, & returned laden with about Eight hundrd̃ weight of Beav^r Skynns, & Coates, besides Fish and Oyle, Sounds, and Toungs: That meeting ye Assistance Frigot, they fought hir about an houre, and had one man killed, & six wounded, before taken.

All which appeares upon Examination of ye Masters and Companye of ye said twoe French Vessells, which are not yet condemned, but ready for sentence.

Wee have Enquired of ye Proctor & Offic^{rs} of ye Comwealth as to ye third Shipp, which appeares both Shipp and Goods to be French, & as such to be condemned already by the name of ye Nostre Dame of Houfleure to ye Comwealth.

Which is ye whole matt^r of Fact appearing to us. All which wee humbly submitt to yor Hon^{rs} wisdome being

     R^t Honble
  Your Hon^{rs} humble servants
    Jo: Godolphin
    Willm̃ Clerk
    C. G. Cock.

Drs Coms [26]
 December^r 13° 1653
  Addressed:
  For ye Rt Honble y^e
   Comĩttee of ye Councell
   of State for foreigne
    Affaires
     These
   Endorsed:
  13 Dec. 1653
  Judges of the Adm^{tie} ther
  report concerning the 3
  vessells of Houflure [27]

Captain William Crispin on board the "Assistance" in Plymouth Sound, on December 20th, 1653, writes:

Right Honble

The 9 Instant I mett with Capt. Martin in ye Bristoll of ye Lizard, he being ordered by ye Rg^{tt} Honble Generall Monck, to Command ye w^t squadron, by whome I was sent to Plymouth ye same day, with some hamburgers, & sweads shipps, I also then rec̃ an order from

---

[26] *i.e.*, Doctors' Commons.
[27] State Papers Domestic, Supplementary, Vol. 101. f. 7, in P. R. O.

him, to ply over for Ushant, to Cruce to & fro for 7 or 8 dayes as neere Brest, as wth Conveniencye I might, and to take wth mee ye Nonsuch, then att Plymouth, ye 10 Instant I sayled from Plymouth and stood over for ye Fourne Rockke, the Nonsuch came thither to mee ye 12 Foll, ye 14 we both sayled within Ushant, and went into Conquett Roade, where wee Ankered a whille, then plyed in to ye mouth of Brest river, and y^t eveninge we ankored in Cammaritt bay, hopeing in one of ye s^d places to have found some of ye Brest Men or Warr, butt Providence did nott so order itt, in Cammaritt bay sid a Flyboate of 8 guns with 5 or 6 other small french vessells, who all ran ashore where (night cominge on) we could nott well get them off, the next morninge by ye Advice of Capt Penrose, wee sayled thence, and ankored in Conquett road, neere ye s^d towne, I Caused o^r boates to fetch off two vessells being burtons one laden wth wine from Nants, ye other light, there being in ye same place neere 30 sayle more, two of which I thought to be men of Warr (they rowing in with oares) the Contrary I know nott, they with ye rest hauled close under ye houses, wch were lined with whatt Musquetteers ye Country sould affourd, wth which (itt being also ½ ebb) they beate o^r boates off, butt through mercye to us without loss, the Nonsuch boate goinge in with a small gun, o^{rs} also returned with them, and attempted to sett ye the (sic) s^d vessells a fier, but could nott, to make way for o^r boates I was drawne to fier out of o^r Frig^{tt}, into ye s^d towne, & Vessells, about 230 greate shott, which did ye enemy to o^r sight much spoyle, they havinge only one gunn which they kept plyinge all ye tyme att o^r Frigatt, till wee beate them from itt, the same afternoon spyinge a ship plyinge in towards Brest, I sent the Nonsuch after her who y^t eveninge took her, she beinge a greate Hollands Fly boate of 8 guns Laden with wine from Nants, ye next daye ye wind veered westerly, we plyed off to Sea, ye 18 I mett Capt Martin of Silly, and wth him ye Portland, he tould mee y^t I with the Nonsuch must returne for ye other 7 or 8 dayes from whence wee Came, I then acquainted him with my Condition, o^r Frig^{tt} being every where defective and quite worne out for want of good repayre, hee tould mee ye next morninge he would order a Surveigh upon her, butt att Midnight Foll wee had a very sore Storme att S^o. S^o. W^t which continued, with much violence 28 howers, in which tyme all o^r sayles att ye yard blew away, and the ship provinge very Leake, I was forced to spoone afore itt till we were to ye E^{t}ward of Torbay there meetinge ye wind all Northerly, I plyed away for Plymouth to speake wth Capt Hattsell and to fitt o^r ship to ply for Portsmouth, unto which place I must Imediately repayre, because I cannott be fitted & supplyed heere att this place, o^r wants being so greate, I am just now come to an ankor heere, and att present humbly Crave leave to subscribe

Rg^{tt} Honble
You^r Realy Devoted servant
Wm Crispin

Plymouth sound
Assistance Frig^{tt} ye 20
of ye 10 month 1653.
    Addressed:
      For the spe'iall service of ye State
      To the Rig^{tt} Honble ye Comm^{rs}
      for the Admiralty & Navy
      Humbly present Thess
                    Whitehall.
Plymouth sound
From aboard ye Assistance Frg^{tt}
ye 20th of December 1653
att 11 att night   Wm Crispin.
    Endorsed:
      20 Decemb: 1653
      C. Crispin
Seal broken in half. Three lions rampant.[28]

Whitelock in his *"Memorials,"* page 578, gives the date of this action as December 28th, 1653, whereas according to the above letter, which is dated 20 December, it must have taken place on the 15th of that month.

There was much dissatisfaction among the seamen in the Fleet, and they drew up and signed a petition which they intended to present to the Lord Protector, against the system of the press gang[29] and other grievances, by which the men complained they were confined on ships under a degree of thraldom and bondage to the utter ruin of their families, and that their pay was sometimes detained for as much as 20 months. They prayed for a relief of those grievances, also that they might reap some of the fruits of their bloodshed and hardships, and have the same freedom and liberty to serve as the Dutch seamen "against whom they have been such instruments in the Lord's hand for the good of the country." Admiral Penn on receiving this petition immediately called a council of war to decide whether it was lawful for the seamen to tender their

---

[28] State Papers Domestic, Supplementary, Vol. 115, No. 298, in P. R. O.

[29] A body of men under a captain, who had authority to "press" or compel the service of the subject for the defence of the realm; in other words, enforced service.

grievances by way of petition. The council met on board the "Swiftsure" on October 17th, 1654, and decided in general favour of the men. The following officers were the members of the Council:—Vice-Admiral John Lawson, Rear-Admiral Dakins, Captains William Crispin, Jonas Poole, Benjamin Blake, John Lambert, Leon Harris, Richard Lions, Edward Morcock, John White, Richard Hodges, William Hannum, Clark, William Vessey, Henry Fen, Robert Story, Hawkes, Lightfoote, and Hubert, Lieutenants Haward, Pride, Trafford, Hall and Wilkinson, and Mr. John Bear, Master of the "Falmouth."[30]

Cromwell in 1654 sent a secret expedition of thirty-eight ships under Admiral Penn to the West Indies, England then being at peace with Spain. Vice-Admiral Goodson and Rear-Admiral Dakins accompanied the fleet and General Venables was placed in command of the soldiers.

The "Laurel," commanded by Captain Crispin, was in Penn's squadron and carried 160 seamen, 30 soldiers and 40 guns. Fifteen ships, some from each squadron, sailed under Rear-Admiral Dakins from Spithead, on Wednesday, December 20th, 1654. The "Laurel" was one of them, as we learn from a letter given below, written by Captain William Crispin, on December 26th, 1654, off the Lizard, to the Commissioners of the Admiralty, which he must have considered of great importance, for he wrote, as will be noted under the address,—

"hast hast post hast
wth spead."

"Right Hono^{ble}

I being ordered by Reare Admirall Dackines, to Lay out to speeke wth any shipp or Vessell, homeward bound, & when any opertunity p: sented to give your Hono^{rs} an account of our Condition, Blessed be God ye Major Gen^{ll}, & all The rest Aboard This Squadron are well, we want only ye Indian who was not in our Company since we

---

[30] Clarendon State Papers, Vol. 49, f. 84, Bodleian Library, Oxford.

came to sea, The wind held Faire wth us till yesterday morning, we have it now at SSW, being in ye Latitude of 46 deg: & 50 Min: having nothing Further y^{ts} worthey your Hono^{rs} Cognicence I humbly crave leave to subscribe my selfe
Right Hono^{ble}
Your Very humble
serv^t
Wm Crispin

Lawrell Frig^{tt} ye 26th xber
at 2 in ye Afternowne, being 117 Leagues
WSW of ye Lizard 1654.
Addressed:
For ye spetiall service of ye State
  To ye Right Hono^{ble} ye Com^{rs} For
    The Admiralty & Navey
      These p: sent
        Att Whitehall
Notes on the outside
Lawrell Frig^{tt}. ye 26th xber
  at see
    Wm Crispin
hast hast post hast
  wth spead
Gent^n If This come to your hand pray cause it to be Fourthwth Conveyed into any of ye Post masters hands, to be hasted up accordingly
Wm Crispin

To any of ye Comand^{ers} of ye Comonwealthes shipps in ye Channell p:sent These
p Cadwallader Cripps
M^r of the Shipp
Marey

Rec at Sittingbourn past 4 [?8]
Rochester past 11 at night
Receaved att Canterbury
past 4 in the afternone
Seal in two halves:
On a shield, three lions rampant.[81]

On December 26th the remainder of the fleet sailed, arriving in the Barbadoes on January 29th, 1655, where they planned their campaign. It was decided to capture Hispaniola. Accordingly, the fleet sailed on March 31st, 1655, and arrived in sight of St. Domingo on April 13th, where soldiers were landed the same day. Captain Crispin remained outside, sailing along the shore for observation. On April 24th the "Journal of the

---

[81] State Papers Domestic, Interregnum, Vol. 91. f. 135, in P. R. O.

Expedition" says "Letter at 11 o'clock at night came from General Venables and the Rear Admiral on shore" (the latter in command of a party of sailors on land service). The General said that Captain Crispin had discovered a landing place to the northward of Fort Jeronimo in a little sandy bay, and that the army would march there that evening or the next morning. After fighting for several days with no results, they re-embarked and sailed on Friday, May 4th, for the Island of Jamaica, which they decided to attempt to take, and arrived in the harbour there on May 10th, excepting Captain Crispin's ship which continued to reconnoitre outside.

An attack was immediately made and the Spanish surrendered on May 17th, having offered little resistance. In this attack it has been said by Captain William Crispin's great-grandson, that he fired the first and third shots which felled the flagstaff and that the Spaniards thereupon surrendered.

It was decided shortly afterwards, on account of the scarcity of provisions, that part of the fleet should return to England, 15 ships remain in Jamaica and three go to New England for supplies. Captain Crispin remained with the "Laurel," although he desired to return.

Admiral Penn and General Venables sailed for home on Monday, June 25th, with the ships selected to leave, having placed Vice-Admiral Goodson in command, who then became Admiral. Rear-Admiral Dakins thus became Vice-Admiral, and Captain Crispin, Rear-Admiral. Granville Penn in his *Memorials of Sir William Penn* at this point says, "Some of the captains expressed their desire to go home, notwithstanding their vessels remained, *viz.*, Rear-Admiral Captain Crispin (of the Laurel), Captain Newberry and Captain Story."[32]

---

[32] Vol. II. (London, 1833) 108.

On June 9th, 1655, Generals Penn and Venables and Captain Gregory Butler on board the "Swiftsure" before their departure for England issued instructions appointing Captain William Crispin, Robert Wadeson and Thomas Broughton, to take charge of supplying the English forces in the Island and they were called by the home authorities "Commissioners for Supplying Jamaica," or "Commissioners in New England appointed to provide provisions for the ships in Jamaica." Of these, Wadeson was the Treasurer of the English Navy, and Broughton was a merchant, living in Boston, Massachusetts, of which city he was a prominent and influential citizen. In 1652 Broughton received the right to make a wharf on his ground by the waterside at Center Haven, near the Ferry which operated from Boston to Charlestown and close to the site of the present Copps Hill Burial Ground. He was a Selectman of Boston, 1658–1660. James Oliver was named to serve on the Commission in case Broughton was deceased or otherwise absent. He was the son of Elder Thomas Oliver, several times a selectman, and also an influential citizen of Boston. He was Captain of one of the eight companies from that city which served in King Phillip's War.[33]

Captain Crispin and Wadeson were ordered to take three ships to New England, supply them with victuals and provisions for the forces in Jamaica for six months at a cost of £10,000 and convey them back to Jamaica with all possible speed. They left the West Indies with the "Falcon" Flyboat, "Adam and Eve" and the "Golden Falcon," which boats were compelled to sep-

---

[33] James Savage, *Genealogical Dictionary*, I. (Boston, Mass., 1860) 263; Charles Henry Pope, *Pioneers of Massachusetts*, (Boston, 1900) 71; *New England Historical Genealogical Register*, XXXVII., 298; Justin Winsor, *Memorial History of Boston* (Boston, Mass., 1881) Vol. I. 562, Vol. II., pages VII.–VIII.; *Boston Town Records, 1634–1661* (Boston, 1877) 112, 119; Nathaniel B. Shurtleff, *Top. Des. Boston* (Boston, 1871). Some of the references about Broughton and Oliver have been received from the author's kinsman, Thomas Butler, of Philadelphia.

arate at sea, as they had a very rough voyage. The captain of the "Adam and Eve" having died on the way to Boston was buried at sea; the ships arrived in a badly battered condition requiring considerable repairs. The three Commissioners immediately made a report to the Commissioners of the Admiralty in London citing the above facts, also stating that they thought the boats would be repaired and provisioned for the voyage to Jamaica in about five or six weeks. This report was signed in Boston, on August 29th, 1655, by all the Commissioners. Captain Crispin returned to England early in 1656, in the "John" frigate, commanded by Captain John Leverett. That Captain Crispin held the rank and title of Colonel while in the West Indies is borne out by the Orders of the Council of State, dated February 13th, 1656, which report refers to the accounts of *Colonel* Crispin and others, employed by Generals Penn and Venables, to purchase provisions in New England for the forces at Jamaica.[34]

Crispin was in London on April 24th, 1656, on which day he wrote to the Commissioners of the Admiralty the following holograph letter (here reproduced), which is in the British Public Record Office,[35] in London:

Right Hono^{ble}:
I have Considered ye matter, Vpon w^{ch}: you were pleased to send for, & so strictly Examine me ye other day, About Jamaica Hides, what I then tould you was True, but having since spocken wth: Gen^{ll}: Penn, I am by his direction put into A better Cappassity to answer to your Examination About it, Viz^t: ye said hides (being About Seaven Hundreed) were delivered by Cap^{tn}: Hodges to be disposed of by me, for Gen^{ll}: Penns Use, Vnto whom since my return I have given an accompt Thereof, who ordered me to Let you know so much, & y^t if you dissird A further Accompt of y^t Parsell (before mentioned) he is readey to give it when you please, so having nothing further to trouble your hono^{rs}: wth: I remaine,
Right Hono^{ble}:
Your humble Servt:
W^m: Crispin

[34] *Calendar of State Papers, Colonial, 1574–1660.* (Lond., 1860) 437.
[35] State Papers Domestic, Interregnum, Vol. 139, f. 57.

Holograph Letter of Captain William Crispin to the Commissioners of the Admiralty, dated London, April 24th, 1656.

Address of Captain William Crispin's Holograph Letter of April 24th, 1656, with Wax Seal impressed with his Arms, on a Shield Three Lions rampant.

Seal Natural Size.

London y⁰ 24th Aprill
Wax seal bearing his arms on a shield, three lions rampant.
Addressed in the same hand:
  To yᵉ Right Honoᵇˡᵉ: Coll: Clarke
  & Mʳ: Hopkines Two of yᵉ Comissionʳˢ.
  of yᵉ Admiralty & Navy or either
  of them These
      ℔ :sent
  att Whitehall
Endorsed in a contemporary hand:
  24 Aprill 1656
  Captaine Crispin touching
    Jamaica hides.

The Commissioners of the Admiralty, May 21st, 1656, had reported that in December 1654, when General Penn went to the West Indies, there went also the "Catherine," a serviceable Dutch vessel which carried 240 soldiers and 30 guns. She was never mentioned in any of the lists and never returned. They report that she was employed on a private commission by special order of His Highness, the Lord Protector and the Council, that she had a considerable quantity of hides taken from Jamaica to New England and there disposed of by Captain Crispin. It appears from the letter of Captain Crispin to the Admiralty, above reproduced, that he had been closely examined concerning this matter, and that he had afterwards had an interview with Penn, who ordered him to inform the Commissioners that if they desired further information he, Penn, was ready to give it, when they pleased.

Oliver Cromwell had instructed General Venables and Captain Gregory Butler (one of Cromwell's special commissioners in Jamaica) to deliver this ship to Admiral Penn, which they did by special order dated December 14th, 1654.[36]

Meanwhile Penn and Venables arrived at Spithead on August 31st, 1655, and were immediately sent to the Tower, the reason being given that they had disobeyed

---

[36] Granville Penn, *Memorials of Sir William Penn*, Vol. II. (Lond., 1833) 29–30.

orders by returning to England. The real cause of their imprisonment was that Cromwell knew they both favored the exiled Charles, then residing on the continent, he having intercepted a letter written to Charles by Penn promising support. Penn was soon released, however, but was dismissed from service and retired to his estates in Ireland.

Many of the most prominent men in the Navy about this time were becoming very much dissatisfied with Cromwell for placing the authority of the army over the navy. Cromwell had hardly a friend among the sea commanders, except his land admirals, and of these last scarcely any were cordially attached to him. Principles and sentiments which had never been extinguished, but had remained inactive only through restraint, in the hearts of the seamen, began to ferment. Both officers and men (together with a large portion of the nation) had their eyes silently turned towards their exiled prince.

They had done most of the fighting for a number of years past with the foreign foes of England, and they had subdued and conquered much territory, and felt they had not received proper recognition for their services, being either dismissed or superseded by Cromwell's army officers. Most of these naval officers had been at sea, fighting the enemies of the whole English people, many of whom were royalists at heart and were lukewarm in their devotion to Cromwell and his party; Penn and Crispin belonged to this group, and when the naval party began to plan for the Restoration, they were among its leaders; this movement was afterwards consummated by General Monk. The leaders of the West Indies Expedition and their subordinates were in favour of the King, especially as they had not been in sympathy with this expedition, and when Spain declared war against England, on this account, a number of officers resigned from the service. Captain Crispin was probably one of these, and they with the officers whom Cromwell had dismissed as well as their friends in the service, formed the naval party which was active in the Restoration.

The Fifth Monarchy[37] men in 1656 held meetings and began to prepare for a revolt. The naval party and Royalists hearing of it, attempted to turn it to their benefit. An agreement was reached in March, 1657, and an uprising against Cromwell decided upon. The men "behind the curtain" on behalf of the Naval party, says Secretary Thurloe in his report, were "Vice-Admiral Lawson, Colonel Okey, Captain Crispin, Captain Lyons, Captain Dakins (Rear-Admiral of the West Indies Expedition) and some others." This scheme was doomed to failure, as it was discovered and frustrated, but the naval party continued secret activities in conjunction with other royalists. Nothing further is heard of Captain Crispin in reference to this matter. However, as Penn had lost all of his influence the chances of Captain Crispin obtaining a command at sea were very remote, so he acquired and took command of the "Boston Merchant," on a trading expedition from London to America, in July, 1656, but met with very stormy weather and was wrecked on the coast of Ireland.[38] It is not known whether he followed Penn to Ireland immediately after this unfortunate occurrence, or whether he remained in England working with others of the naval party, who were undoubtedly in

---

[37] Fifth Monarchy Men, the name of a Puritan sect in England, which for a time supported the Government of Oliver Cromwell in the belief that it was a preparation for the "Fifth Monarchy," that is for the monarchy which should succeed the Assyrian, the Persian, the Greek and the Roman, and during which Christ should reign on earth with His saints for a thousand years. These sectaries aimed at bringing about the entire abolition of the existing laws and institutions, and the substitution of a simpler code based upon the law of Moses. Disappointed at the delay in the fulfilment of their hopes, they soon began to agitate against the government and to vilify Cromwell.

[38] Chancery Decrees and Orders, in P. R. O.

constant communication with Penn. Nevertheless, he was in Ireland soon after the Restoration, for the *Council Book of the Corporation of Kinsale, 1652–1800*,[39] refers to the reading at the meeting on July 18th, 1662, of a letter of protection from arrest granted to William Crispin by Thomas Amory, dated June 20th, 1662.

Admiral William Penn took a very important part in the final events of the Restoration in 1660, for which he was knighted and made Commissioner of the Admiralty and Governor of the Town and Fortress of Kinsale. He was likewise Victualer for the Royal Navy. In April, 1665, Captain Crispin appears as Deputy Victualer at Kinsale.[40] He was also active in the management of other public affairs in and about the Fort and Town, which is made evident by many letters written by him to the Commissioners of the Admiralty, beginning with one, dated Kinsale, February 25th, 1664,[41] and ending with one for the year 1669.

Most of these letters refer to accounts for funds due to him and others for repairs to ships and matters of this kind, which came under his jurisdiction, but the government of Charles II. paid scant attention to requests for money.

Captain Crispin's first wife Rebecca, *née* Bradshaw, may have died at Kinsale in the early 1660's.[42] At any rate, in 1665, he was married a second time to Jane Chudleigh. Her father was Captain John Chudleigh (died 1653),[43] of Kinsale, who is mentioned as early as 1647 as engaged in naval shipbuilding in Ireland.[44] He was descended from the Chudleighs of the ancient

---

[39] By Richard Caulfield, 1879.
[40] *Cal. State Papers Domestic, 1666–1667* (Lond., 1864) 441.
[41] State Papers, Domestic, Supplementary, Bundle 136, in P. R. O.
[42] Ralph Bradshaw, her father, in his will, dated 1667, refers to her as deceased.
[43] Will of John Chudleigh, of Kinsdale, probated 1653.—*Indexes to Irish Wills*, Vol. II. Cork and Ross, Cloyne (London, 1910) 21.
[44] MS. Admiralty Account Generals Bill Books, Vol. 5:176, in P. R. O.

landed gentry of Devonshire, in England, as reported in the heraldic visitations of that county,[45] as represented by a baronetcy, 1622–1645,[46] and as entered in the matriculate registers of Oxford and Cambridge Universities. Beginning with Captain Chudleigh, the Chudleighs for a century and a half, according to the chief annalist of Kinsale, were one of the prominent families of the town. They were not only "eminent ship builders," in the earlier period, but at times held important public office, three of the name serving as Sovereigns of Kinsale.[47]

In 1649, the inhabitants of the Town of Kinsale, declaring for the Commonwealth, John Chudleigh was of strategic assistance in the seizure of Kinsale Fort from the Royalists.[48] Chudleigh's most signal service to the Parliamentary cause, however, as recited in the records and histories of Ireland and on the monument of his son Thomas in Kinsale Church, was in 1652 as a participant in General Edmund Ludlow's reduction of Ross Castle, on an island in the Lakes of Killarney, in County Kerry. Effective use was made of boats built by Chudleigh at Kinsale, brought in parts overland and rebuilt by him on the lake. "Of good estate and good repute" wrote the Commissioners in referring to Chudleigh, at this time, in a letter to General Ludlow.[49]

---

[45] Chudleigh of Ashton, in J. L. Vivian, *Visitations of the County of Devon*, Part I (Exeter, 1895) 189–190; *Visitations of the County of Devon, 1564*, (Exeter, 1881) 52–54; *Visitations of the County of Devon, 1620*, Pub. Harleian Society, VI. (London, 1872) 59.

[46] George E. Cokayne, *Complete Baronetage*, I. 1611–1625 (Exeter, England, 1900) 206–207; Sir Bernard Burke, *General Armory*, (London, 1878) 193.

[47] Richard Caulfield, *Council Book of Kinsale* (1879), pages xcvi, 9, 10, 433, 434.

[48] Richard Caulfield, *Council Book of Kinsale* (1879), pages 357–358.

[49] *Ibid.*, page xcv. (where Caulfield erroneously refers to John Chudleigh as Thomas Chudleigh); C. H. Firth, ed. *Gen. Ludlow's Memoirs* I. (Oxford, England, 1894) 321, 526; Richard Bagwell, *Ireland under the Stuarts*, II. (London, 1909) 290–291, III. (London, 1916) 83; Robert Dunlop, *Ireland under the Commonwealth*, I. (Manchester, England, 1913) 213.

John Chudleigh having died in 1653, his widow, Joan Chudleigh, carried on his affairs,[50] and in 1661, the sons, John (died 1686) and Thomas Chudleigh (1639–1706) appear as conducting the business.[51] In his will of 1686, the son, John Chudleigh, is referred to as of London, Purser of the Royal Naval Ship "Bonaventure;" mention is made of his brother Thomas Chudleigh, who married Elizabeth Roberts, in 1666,[52] and his sisters Jane Crispin, of Ireland, and Joan,[53] who married Martin Peirse, in 1682,[82] both of the sisters being of Kinsale.[54]

Thomas Chudleigh, son of Captain John, and brother of Jane Crispin, continued at Kinsale in the family occupation, building among other ships, the Royal frigate "Kinsale." In the Church at Kinsale are still to be seen his gravestone and monument with a Latin inscription which is thus rendered in part:

> "Behold the venerable name which has delivered us.
> Together with his Father lies Thomas surnamed CHUDLEIGH
> Both built Ships for the Kings of the English
> The skill of the Father was conspicuous, alas, alas, his time was short." etc. etc.[55]

In a letter of May 21st, 1667, from the Navy Office in London, to his son William, then in Ireland, Sir William Penn sent messages to his cousin, Ensign William Penn (son of George Penn), Clerk of the Cheque at Kinsale, and to "Capt. Crispin" desiring him "to affoard him [Ensign Penn] his vtmost assistance."

---

[50] *Calendar of State Papers, Domestic, 1653–1654* (London, 1879), 529.

[51] *Calendar of State Papers, Ireland, 1660–1662* (London, 1905), 608–609.

[52] Herbert Webb Gillman. *Index to Marriage License Bonds of the Diocese of Cork, and Ross, Ireland, 1623–1750* (Cork, Ireland, 1896–7), 26.

[53] The will of Joan Pierce, of Kinsale, was dated 1724.—*Index to Irish Wills*, II. (London, 1910) 87.

[54] Wills at Somerset House, London, P. C. C., 39 Lloyd.

[55] Richard Caulfield, *Council Book of Kinsale* (1879), pages xcv-xcvi.

By 1669 Captain Crispin was living some little distance out from the Town of Kinsale, a letter of his to the Navy Commissioners of March 26th, 1669, being dated as "Near Kinsale." He writes, "I was constrained to leave my family and concerns by a costly and tedious journey to London."[56] His cousin, Ensign Penn, also, May 25th following, states that Captain Crispin lives at a distance and has been only twice in Kinsale Town.[57] At this habitation later in the same year, Crispin entertained his kinsman, William Penn, the future Founder of Pennsylvania, then a single young man of 25, who, on December 10th, 1669, having dined at the Fort at Kinsale, writes, "I Came to Cozen Crispins." There he lodged and then on the 11th, he adds, "I left C[ousin] Crisp[ins] and came to Immokilly he [Cousin Crispin] wth vs to ye first Ferry 7 miles."

August 9th, 1670, Philip Ford wrote from Cork to his master William Penn, after the latter's return from Ireland to England, "I sent a lett^r to Capt C[rispin] to Meet me at King Sayle fort who Accordingly did."

Sir William Penn having died in this same year, 1670, no reference to Captain Crispin's services at Kinsale have so far been found until 1676. Then, Ensign William Penn, Clerk of the Cheque at Kinsale, who was a first cousin of Captain Crispin's first wife, having died, about April of the latter year, Captain Crispin succeeded to that office, upon the recommendation of Robert Southwell (1607–1677), one of the most active and influential personages of Kinsale, Vice Admiral of the Province of Munster, the application to His Majesty the King, having been presented to the Royal Naval Board, May 13th, 1676,[58] by no less a person than

---

[56] *Cal. State Papers Domestic, 1668–1669* (Lond., 1894) 249–250.
[57] *Ibid.*, 343.
[58] Pepys Naval Papers, *Publications of the Navy Records Society*, XXXVI. (1909), 199, 203.

the noted diarist, Samuel Pepys (1633–1703), a leading naval official in London.

The action thus taken was entered upon the British Admiralty Journal, June 26th, 1676, as follows,—

"Navy Officers' report allowed of, touching Mr. Crispin's being entertained in the place of clerk of the check at Kinsale in Ireland, vacant by the late death of Mr. Penn, with the abatement of salary proposed by the said Officers during peace."[59]

Crispin next appears in the records as Muster Master and Clerk of the Cheque, in connection with the repairs of the Fortifications at Rinconnan, for the defence of Kinsale, commenced on March 4th, 1677/8. His duties are set out in the Orders and Instructions, as follows,—"He is to be constantly in attendance on the works, either in person or by deputy. He is to call over the names of day laborers. Not to take into work any person not capable of doing a good day's work, especially boys, very ancient men or maimed or disabled persons. Every Friday night he is to draw up a "faire muster rolle" of all the officers and laborers in such a way that the hours and the sum due are shown, leaving a margin to enable a receipt to be given."

From these Orders and Instructions, it appears that the workmen received 6^d for a 12 hour working day, commencing at 5 o'clock A.M., and finishing at 7 o'clock P.M., being allowed two hours for meals.

An interesting clause is that "All persons selling ale, beer or 'aquavitae' about the works shall not give a man credit for more than his earnings shall amount to, otherwise the excess will be their loss."

The Instructions to the Drummer as to beating the time were that "where dyalls (clocks) are wanting, he is to judge the true time by the tide, or by the engineer's watch."[60]

---

[59] Cata. *Naval Manuscripts in the Pepysian Library Magdalene College, Cambridge*, IV. (1923) 321.

[60] British Museum, Additional MS., 28085.

Four men were in charge of a pinnace, which they were to look carefully after, and not to take it from the works without the orders of the Engineer, or of Captain Crispin who had lent the boat for the service.

On April 3rd, 1678, Crispin is a witness to Articles of Agreement made between William Robinson and Captain Thomas Archer of the one part, and Thomas Chudleigh, of Kinsale, shipwright, his brother-in-law, of the other part, for the supplying by Chudleigh of 65 gun carriages for the Fortifications.[61]

Captain Crispin's duties in connection with the Fortifications probably occupied the whole of his time until his departure for America in 1681, when his residence was still in Kinsale.

At the time of Admiral Penn's death, the British Government owed him for expenditures in the naval service as Victualer 16,000 pounds. His heir William Penn, later the Founder, knew that Charles the Second was hard pressed for funds to keep up his expensive Court, and would find some difficulty in paying this large sum due to his father's estate. As, however, Charles and his brother, the Duke of York, were very friendly to William on account of their gratitude to, and affection for, the Admiral, by reason of the part he played in placing Charles on the throne, Penn thought Charles might be disposed to grant him some unoccupied land in North America in lieu of the debt. He thereupon petitioned the King, as above indicated, and was granted on March 4th, 1681, the Province of Pennsylvania, which was the largest stretch of territory ever granted to one man in America, covering as it does 40,000 square miles—much greater in extent than Ireland and not much smaller than England.

William Penn first sent his first cousin, Captain William Markham (also a first cousin by marriage of Captain Crispin), to Pennsylvania, as Deputy Governor,

---

[61] British Museum, Additional MS., 28085., f.188 &c., cited in Charles Smith, *Cork*, I. (1893) 238.

to receive the government from the Duke of York's representatives at New York. As a man of wide experience and sound judgment was required to assist in organizing and settling the new Colony, Penn immediately turned to his cousin, the trusted friend and associate of his father, Captain William Crispin, and persuaded him to come to America. That Penn intended him to occupy high office and position in Pennsylvania is made clear by the important appointments which he conferred upon him. Besides the appointments to public office Penn made Captain Crispin large grants of land in Pennsylvania, which later were laid out in and near Philadelphia. Thus he is listed as one of the "First Purchasers" of land in the Province, but he did not live long enough to have the purchase of 5000 acres laid out to him. After his death this amount was confirmed to his children in separate portions by the Proprietary's patents, in which it is stated to be of the latter's free gift. Captain Crispin's commission as Chief Justice of Pennsylvania is referred to in the following letter to Deputy Governor Markham:

Lond: 18th: 8mo—1681.

Cosen Markham/

. . . . I have sent My Cosen William Crispin to be thy Assistant, as by Commission will appear. his Skill, Experience, Industry & Integrety are well Known to me, & perticulerly in Court keeping &c: so y^t. it is my will & pleasure, that he be as cheif Justice, to Keep ye Seal, ye Courts & Sessions; & he shall be accountable to me for it. The proffitts redounding are to his proper behoof. he will show thee my Instructions, w^{ch}– will guide you all in ye business. ye rest is Left to your discretion, y^t. is, to thee, thy two Assistants & ye Councel.

. . . . . .

Pray be very respectfull to my Cosen Crispin he is a man my father had great Confidence in & vallue for. . . . . . .

Wm Penn

Three Commissioners headed by Captain Crispin were appointed by William Penn for "Settling the Colony of Pennsylvania," with authority to purchase land from the Indians, select a site for a city and carry out the numerous affairs connected with such an immense undertaking—affairs that could only be satisfactorily conducted by men of great courage, intelligence and foresight. The two other Commissioners were the Quakers, John Bezer and Nathaniel Allen. Their first instructions were issued September 30th, 1681. The next month Penn gave further instructions and added another Commissioner, William Haig,[62] likewise a Quaker; the commission to the four was dated October 25th, 1681, and refers to still other instructions of October 14th.

Two ships[63] carried the Commissioners and other passengers for Pennsylvania,[64]—the "John and Sarah," of London, Henry Smith, Master, and[65] the "Bristol Factor," of Bristol, Roger Drew, Master, both sailing in the fall of 1681.

William Penn's London lawyers charged him with the following items,—

Commission "to Wm. Crispin	0. 6. 8.
Like to ye same & Bezer	0. 6. 8.
Like to ye same & Allen	0. 6. 8.
Like to ye same & Hage	0. 6. 8.
Catalog of all the Purchas^{rs}	
2 large skins sent wth first ship	2. 0. 0.
A Charter Pty[66] int.[67] Smith & Crispin	0.10. 0"

One very important fact is brought to light in this account, namely, that Captain Crispin was joined with Bezer, Allen and Haig separately, which suggests that

---

[62] Of the Haigs of Bemersyde, Scotland, of whom the present head is the Second Earl Haig, 30th Laird of Bemersyde, whose father, Douglas Haig, the First Earl, was the celebrated Marshal Haig, Commander of the British Army in the World War.

[63] Considerable of this shipping information was supplied by Albert Cook Myers.

[64] Public Record Office, London, Port Book, E 190, Bundles 108 and 111.

[65] *Ibid.*, E. 190, Bundle 1144.

[66] *i.e.*, Party.

[67] int.—inter, *i.e.*, between.

they had authority to act only in conjunction with him, as Chief Commissioner. The last item is of special interest, for Henry Smith was master of the "John and Sarah." It would thus appear that Captain Crispin was in London, and had chartered this ship, on behalf of William Penn, to carry the Commissioners to Pennsylvania. It may therefore be assumed that he, as head of the Commission, sailed on this ship, carrying the Commissions and instructions, and taking with him his son Silas Crispin, who figures in the records of Pennsylvania as early as June 4th, 1682, when he was a juror at Upland Court.[68]

William Haig, doubtless, also was on board, for he was in London, in October, 1681, where he had a child born on the 4th of that month, a few weeks before the ship sailed.[69] He had arrived in Pennsylvania some time before March 11th, 1681-2, as on that date Lord Baltimore, in a Maryland letter, complains "that Penn sent over" Haig "this shipping" and that Haig had already made surveying observations on Elk River at the head of Chesapeake Bay, with respect to the disputed boundary between Maryland and Pennsylvania.[70]

On October 17th and 24th, 1681, customs duty was paid on various articles of clothing, to be sent to Pennsylvania in the "John and Sarah," for the account of John Moore and James Hayes,[71] and on January 19th, 1681/2, the Commissioners of Customs reported that merchandise was entered for export in this ship to Pennsylvania in October 1681.

The "John and Sarah" took passengers on board towards the end of October, 1681, and a few days after

---

[68] *Records of the Courts of Chester County, 1681-1697* (Phila., 1910) 15.
[69] MS. London Quaker Registers.
[70] *Maryland Archives*, V. (Baltimore, 1887) 349, 375-376.
[71] Public Record Office, London, Port Books, E. 190, Bundle 108.

sailed from Gravesend, as witnessed by William Penn himself. The ship was, however, delayed in the Downs, waiting for favourable winds, and doubtless for additional documents from William Penn. In the *London Gazette* of November 7th, 1681, there are two reports, probably relating to this, and other ships, bound for America and the West Indies; the first under date, Deal, November 5th, states that "The merchant ships in the Downs outward bound are preparing to sail though the wind is somewhat bare." Another entry dated the 7th states that the "weather has been very stormy." The issue of November 14th, contains a statement, dated the 11th that "All the merchant-men in the downs sailed . . . and there is at present not one ship there." The evidence would seem to indicate that the "John and Sarah" sailed from England early in November, 1681, and arrived in Pennsylvania possibly about January or February, 1681/2.

The "Bristol Factor" sailed from Bristol in October, 1681, arriving at Upland (now Chester) on December 11th, 1681, some little time before the "John and Sarah." On the "Bristol Factor" came the two other Commissioners, John Bezer and Nathaniel Allen, both of whom carried a large quantity of goods with them.

In the Port Books of Bristol, we find Thomas Coborne and Nathaniel Allen and Company, entered on this ship a quantity of wrought iron, nails, lead, and shot, gun-powder, shoes, sugar, haberdashery and felt hats—varied but useful commodities.

John Bezer carried wrought iron, serges, wearing apparel, gun-powder, cheese, stockings, soap, shot, &c. and also paid a duty of 6^d for two firkins of butter, presumably for use on the voyage.

Letters of administration on the estate of William Crispin, Gentleman, of Kinsale, who died intestate in parts "beyond the sea" ("transmarinus") were granted, July 7th, 1682, in Ireland, to John Suxbery[72] and John[73] Watts.[74]

The news of the death of his cousin, Captain Crispin, especially in the wintertime, would require some weeks for transmission to Penn. He must have had this information, however, by April 18th, 1682, as on that day he commissioned Thomas Holme, Surveyer General of Pennsylvania, in place of Crispin. It is safe to say, then, that William Crispin died about the time the "John and Sarah" reached America or American waters, in the early winter of 1681/2, at the age of 54. According to the statement of his great-grandson, William Crispin (1742-1797), of Philadelphia, Commissary General of Pennsylvania, during the Revolutionary War, he died in the Barbadoes, although no record of this has been found in the registers of the Island. Nevertheless, it was customary for the English ships bound for Pennsylvania to come by way of Barbadoes.

Thomas Holme sailed from England in the ship "Amity," April 23rd, 1682, and arrived at Upland, now Chester, Pennsylvania, August 2nd, 1682.[75]

There are on file in the Record Office in Chancery Lane, London, about 75 holograph letters written by Captain William Crispin to the English Government. The seal used by Captain Crispin on his letters in 1653 and prior thereto, is his crest, which is a "Demi griffin erased, with wings addorsed." On his papers after that date he used his arms which are "Three lions rampant." These arms (see frontispiece) have been

---

[72] The will of John Suxberry, of Kinsale, was probated in 1686.

[73] John Watts, of Kinsale, was one of the Trustees for the minor children of Captain Crispin, named by William Penn, 1687.

[74] Note made in 1913, by Albert Cook Myers, from the Prerogative Grant Book, Ireland, 1679-1684, pages 139-140, in the Irish Public Record Office, Dublin. This record with the other archives of the Record Office were destroyed in the Irish troubles of 1922, when a bomb blew up the building.

[75] Albert Cook Myers, *Immigration of the Irish Quakers into Pennsylvania, 1682-1750* (Swarthmore, Pa., 1902) 252-253.

confirmed by the College of Arms in England and the Office of Arms in Ireland. The heraldic description is as follows: Erminois, three lions rampant azure, armed and langued purpure. Crest.—A demi griffin erased with wings addorsed, azure. Motto.—*Dum clarum rectum teneam.*

Thus it will be seen that Captain Crispin played a very important part in the affairs of his country during the Commonwealth and the events which led up to the Restoration of Charles II., as is evident by his rapid promotion in the Navy, at a period when ability alone counted. He had entered the Navy at 15, was Purser at 22, Captain at 26, Rear Admiral and Colonel at 28. Also, that he was a man of courage, justice and resource is clearly shown by the fact that the great Founder considered him worthy to hold some of the highest offices in the formative period of what was to become the great Commonwealth of Pennsylvania.

(To be continued)

CAPTAIN WILLIAM CRISPIN

By M. JACKSON CRISPIN,
of New York City and of Berwick, Pennsylvania.

Captain William Crispin by his first wife, Rebecca (Bradshaw) Crispin, had issue:

1. WILLIAM, of whom nothing is known except that he was baptized on June 24th, 1653, as shown by the registers of the Church of St. Olave, Hart Street, London. He undoubtedly died young.

2. SILAS, concerning whom later.

3. REBECCA, married (first) on October 24th, 1688, at Ifield Friends' Meeting, in Sussex, England, Edward Blackfan, son of John Blackfan,[76] of Steyning, County Sussex, England.

Her cousin, William Penn, Proprietor of Pennsyl-

---

[76] John Blackfan, of Steyning, father of Edward, appears to have been a man of some position in his locality. He early joined the Society of Friends and suffered much persecution for his religion. Besse, in his "Sufferings" reports several instances. In 1659 John Blackfan was prosecuted in the Exchequer for twenty pounds for tithes of eight and a half acres, when all the corn that grew on his land was scarce worth half that amount. In 1662, he was committed to Horsham Gaol, on a writ *de excomminicate capiendo*, after prosecution in the Ecclesiastical Court for refusing to pay towards the repairs of the Steeple House. In 1663 he and the others were prosecuted in the Ecclesiastical Court for being absent from public worship, and he was excommunicated and some of the others imprisoned.

vania, his wife Gulielma Maria Penn, and their children Laetitia and Springett Penn attended the wedding and signed the wedding certificate.[76a] Edward Blackfan was a member of the Society of Friends, and like his father, came in for a share of the illtreatment inflicted upon that Society. In 1681, he was indicted, with others, at Horsham Assizes, for absence from the national worship, and in 1684, for being present at some Quaker meetings at Steyning, according to Besse, he "was fined £7.18. which, at the persuasion of some Justices and others, he paid in order to Appeal, but when the Sessions came on, he found so little encouragement in prosecuting the same, that he chose rather to lose his money, than to be put to farther Charge."

Edward Blackfan intended to go to Pennsylvania and is spoken of in Penn's letters in 1689 as being about to take official documents to the Provincial Council, but when on the point of sailing, he died in 1690. His widow, with their son William afterwards went to Pennsylvania, in the same ship with Thomas Chalkley and other Friends, about 1700. She was a member of the Free Society of Traders in Pennsylvania, subscribing to £50 of its stock. On her arrival, her relatives, the Penns, sent her to take charge of their Manor of Pennsbury, in Bucks County, where she lived a number of years.

Edward and Rebecca (Crispin) Blackfan had one child:

William Blackfan, married at Friends' Meeting, 2d month, 20th, 1721, Eleanor Wood of Philadelphia. From them descend the Blackfan family of Bucks County, Pennsylvania.

Rebecca (Crispin) Blackfan married (second) in 1725, Nehemiah Allen, of Philadelphia, son of Na-

---

[76a] The original marriage certificate now in possession of a lineal Pennsylvania descendant, Miss Elizabeth C. Blackfan, of Philadelphia.

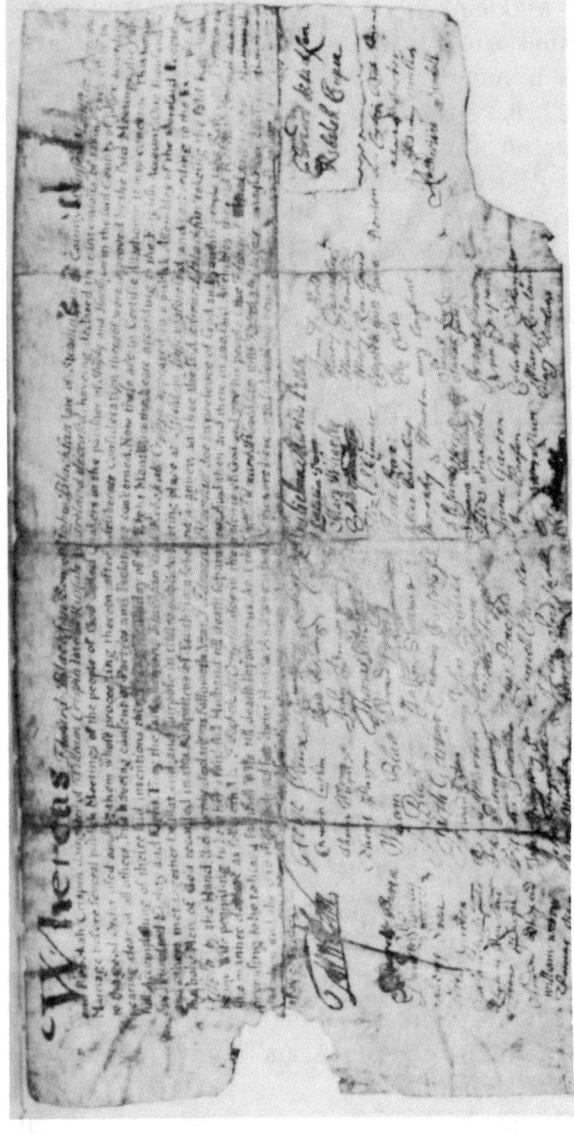

Original vellum certificate, in size 21¾ x 12½ inches, of the Quaker marriage of Edward Blackfan, son of John Blackfan, late of Steyning, County Sussex, England, Maulster, deceased, to Rebecca Crispin, daughter of William Crispin, late of Kinsale, Ireland, deceased; at Friends' meeting place, at Ifield, Sussex, 8 Mo. (October) 24th, 1688. Signed by the contracting parties, Edward Blackfan and Rebekah Crispin, and by the following witnesses: William Penn, his first wife, Gulielma Maria Penn, their children, Springett Penn and Laetitia Penn, and the following,—
Daniel Wharley, Henry Swan, Will: Garton, William Lickfold, Thomas Rowland, Thomas Parson, Andrew Shepard, William Weston, Thomas Bax, George Vaux, Edward Luckin, Thomas Wright, Thomas Parsons, William Blatt, Jn Blatt, Josiah Garton, Rhard Gates, Bennet Marton, John Humphrey, William Marden, John Humphrey, Jr., John Tugwell, Wm: Nicholas, Humphrey Killingbeck, Resta, Patching, John Downer, Thomas Patching, Edward Prior, John Cumber, John Shawe, Thomas Parsons, Jnr., John Michell, John Thaine, Nicho Hogge, Thos: Penefold, Daniell Chantler, Hen: Snashall, Edward Bax, Mary Wharley, Elis. Gouldney, Eliz: Skinner, Ann Bax, Alice Patching, Dorothy Marten, Sarah Hicokook, Susanna Standbridge, Eliz. Snashall, Jane Garton, Ann Parsons, Susanah Penfold, Mary Chandler, Mary Chandler, Mary Rowland, Elisabeth Gates, Eliz. Curtis, Mary Longhurst, Sarah Luckin, Sarah Gates, Joane Bourne, Ann Shepard, . . . , Mary Rowland, Mary Wooltren, Jane Benton, . . . Curtis, Rich Bourne, Charles Carter Henry Milles, Katherine Stodall.

Document owned (1929) by a direct descendant Miss Elizabeth C. Blackfan, of Germantown, Philadelphia.

thaniel Allen, previously mentioned as one of the Proprietary's Commissioners for settling the Colony in 1681, of whom her father, Captain William Crispin, had been one. She is not known to have had any issue by Allen.

4. RALPH remained in Ireland, and continued to live near Kinsale in County Cork.

An original vellum deed (in size 21 x 8¼ inches) of gift for 500 acres of land in Pennsylvania to Ralph Crispin, as signed by his cousin William Penn, "Sixth Month Caled July"[77] 25th, 1688, is in the collection of John Frederick Lewis, Esq., Vice President of The Historical Society of Pennsylvania. By his courtesy it is here printed and reproduced:

> William Penn Propriatary and Gover^r: of the Province of Pennsilvania and Countys Annexed To all persons to whome these presents shall come Greeting Know yee that I of my free Gift have Granted, and doe heareby give and Grant unto my Loveing Coszen Ralph Crispin the Son of Capt: William Crispin late of the Kingdome of Ireland Diceased five Hundred Acres of Lands within the said Province of Pennsilvania To have and to hould the afores^d five Hundred Acres of Lands, unto ye s^d. Ralph Crispin and his heirs to the onely use and behoof of him the said Ralph and his heirs and Assigns Yeilding and paying upon ye first Day of the first Month Cal'd March Yearly forever unto me and my heirs two shillings for Every one hundred Acres of the said five Hundred Acres of Lands as a Quit-rent for ye same, And I the said William Penn doe hereby nominate and appoint William Markham, Thomas Ellis, and John Goodson my Comm^{rs}. for Lands to Deliver Seizin thereof Accordingly, In Wittnes whereof I have hereunto sett my hand and Seale the Twenty fivfth Day of the Sixth Month[78] Caled July Anno: Do: one thousand Six Hundred Eighty and Eight and In the third yeare of the Raigne of King James ye Second over England etc
>
>   Wm Penn
>   [Red wax seal
>   impressed with
>   the Lesser Seal
>   of the Province of
>   Pennsylvania]

---

[77] Here is a contemporaneous error in the name of the month, for which William Penn is responsible: the Sixth Month in that period was not July but August.

[78] *Ibid.*

The verso of the document:
>   Sealed & Deliverd in
>   the P̃rsents of
>   Ro^t. Webb
>   Wm Penn^{79}

Know all men by these presents that I Ralph Crispin of Corke in the Kingdome of Ireland gent ffor and in consideration of the sume of Twenty seaven pounds st̃er to mee in hand paid before the perfection hereof by Ebinezer Pike the receipt whereof I doe hereby acknowledge and thereof and of every part thereof doe hereby exonerate acquitt and discharge the said Ebinezer Pike his Ex^r.s adm^{rs}. and assignes, Have and by these presents doe assigne make over Bargaine and sell unto the said Ebinezer Pike his heires and assignes all my right title Intrest and claime in the wth.in mencõned five hundred Acres of land in Pensilvania wth.in mencõned In witnesse whereof I have hereunto sett my hand and Seale this Twenty ffourth day of May Anno Dni One thousand Six hundred & Ninety and in the Sixth yeare of the Raigne of our Soveraigne Lord King James the Second &c

>   Raphe Crispin
>   Sealed and delivered in
>   the presence of us and
>   when the words (by Ebenezer
>   Pike) was Interlined
>   Wm Charters
>   Sam^{11} Hunt
>   Jo^n: Browne Notar P̃ubl
>   *Endorsed:*
>   William Penn
>   his Lease of 500
>   Accers of Land in
>   Pennsilvania
>   to R Crispin
>   & R Crispin to Ebenezer Pike

Ralph Crispin married, at Kinsale, first, in 1678, Anne Millner,[80] and second, in 1682, Anna Busted.[81] He died at Kinsale and was buried there on June 21st, 1730.[82] He left probably three children, as by deed,[83] dated May 10th, 1731, his son Silas sold a third part of

---

[79] This was yet another William Penn, possibly the son of Ensign William Penn, of Kinsale.
[80] Cork and Ross Marriage Licenses, index only, the originals being destroyed in the Irish troubles of 1922.
[81] *Ibid.*
[82] Parish Registers of Kinsale.
[83] Registry of Deeds, Dublin, No. 68,338,48381.

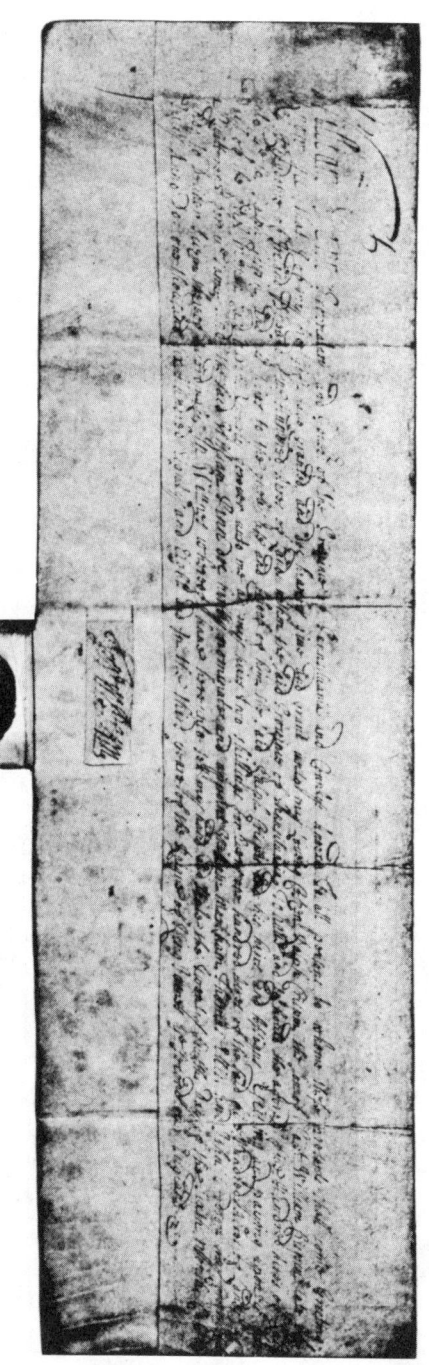

William Penn's Original signed Deed of Gift on Vellum, with his Lesser Seal of the Province, conveying to Captain William Crispin's Son, Ralph Crispin, 500 Acres of Land in Pennsylvania, in 1688.

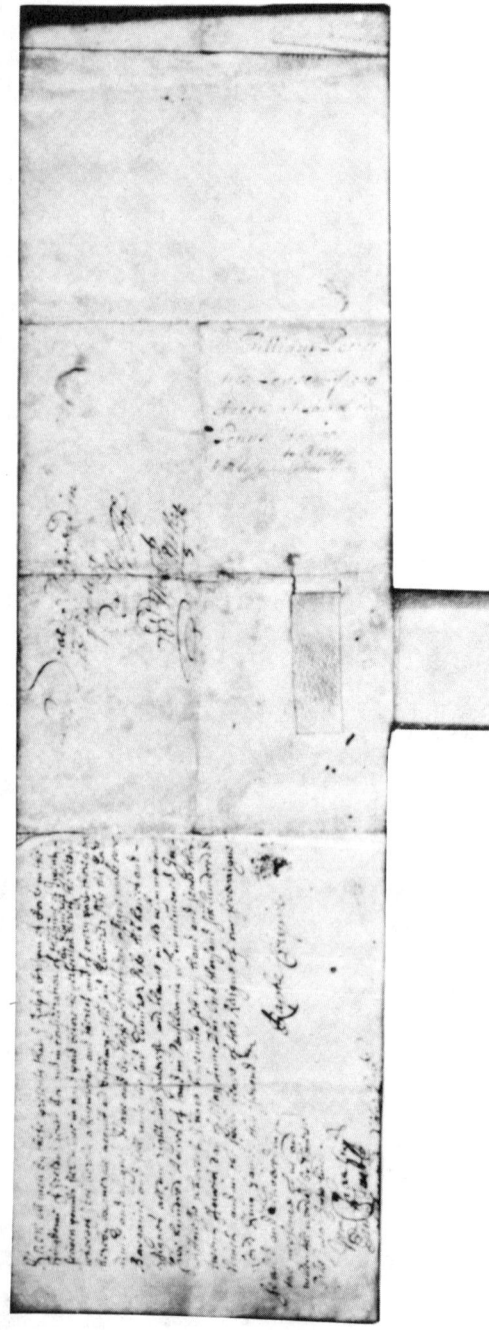

Verso of William Penn's Land Deed to Ralph Crispin, with Regrant to Ebenezer Pike, signed by Crispin, May 24th, 1690.

property, called Ballynrustigg in Kinsale, which evidently passed to him on his father's death. George Crispin, constable of Clontead parish in 1718,[84] who married Elizabeth Reynar in 1714,[85] and Rebecca Crispin who married John Watts in 1704[86] were probably children of Ralph. Although the will of Ralph Crispin was destroyed during the troubles in Ireland, in 1922, yet the following abstract of it was previously secured (for which reason it is recorded here):

Will of Ralph Crispin, of Killcaha,[87] Co. Cork, Gent. (Wills Diocese of Cork)

To son Silas Crispin 1/—

My worldly substance to be equally divided into three parts,—

To son Silas Crispin, one third of my substance and the same to be left in my executors hands until such time as he is lawfully divorced from Margret Goshin and after that to give him the lawful interest of it and no more till such time as he is married lawfully to another woman, but if said Silas Crispin do not as aforementioned, his part is to be taken from him and divided between the two parts as follows,—

To grand-daughter Ann Shaw, alias Watts, one third part of my substance.

To grandson Edward Watts, one third part.

To the three children of Ann Shaw, alias Watts, named John, Ralph and Ann Shaw £10 each, to be put to interest until they come to 21 years of age.

To sister Amy Wester, alias Crispin £6.

To son George Crispin's children by name, Ann, Elizabeth and Rebecca Crispin, Ballyrusligge, if they can prove any right to it under my hand and seal, provided they pay £100 if they have a right to the said lands, that is, the two thirds of the same, said three children to give sufficient security to make good all leases, and contracts whatsoever that I am obliged to, and if they have no right to said land I give and bequeath my granddaughter Ann Crispin £10, Elizabeth Crispin £5 and Rebecca Crispin £5, said sum of £20 to be put out to interest till they come to the age of 21 years.

To Ann Browne Crispin alias Busteed £5
To Uslye Upington alias Busteed £5
" Mary Condon als Crispin £15
" Mary Condon, daughter to John Condon and Mary Condon, alias Crispin £3

---

[84] Council Book of the Corporation of Kinsale.
[85] Cork and Ross Marriage Licenses.
[86] Ibid.
[87] Probably Kilcaha.

To grandson Ralph Crispin, the son of Thomas Crispin £5
To servant maid Nell Sheehy £2
" " boy Garrett Roch £2 together for Margaret Kewicke and Garrett Roch her son, a house and garden free for the term of 7 years.
To Teige Dally, the house he holds from Catherine Shaw at Brown's Mills, rent free for three years.
Executors, Nicholas Beamish, Sovereign of Kinsale and William Milard of Kinsale.
Dated 17th June 1730

Witnesses: Philip Ward
Tho. White
Dannell Murphy

Ralph Crispin (No seal)

Proved 13th March 1730 by Bartholomew Shaw and Edward Watts, principal legatees named in said Will, the executors having renounced.

5. RACHEL, m. Thomas Armstrong. William Penn granted her one thousand acres of land in Pennsylvania; he regranted this to her husband, by a deed dated 11th mo., 2nd, 1694, in which he acknowledged having some years before granted the same to Rachael Armstrong, by the name of Rachel Crispin "which grant is mentioned to be lost in the Wars of Ireland," and therefore repeated it to Thomas Armstrong; five hundred acres to be disposed of for the support of him, his wife Rachel, and their child born, or children to be born, and the other five hundred acres to Silas Crispin, Samuel Carpenter, and Lasse Cock, in trust for Rachel Armstrong, her child, &c. At the meeting of the Board of Property held 6th mo., 1st, 1733, Samuel Mickle, of Philadelphia, requested a warrant for this one thousand acres, which was granted him, as it was shown that Rachel and her heirs had sold to Henricus Chapman, of London, who sold to Mickle. Thomas Armstrong and Rachel his wife, Robert Swiney and Jane his wife (one of the daughters of the said Thomas and Rachel), by deed dated May 15th, 1724, for forty pounds granted the said one thousand acres to Henricus Chapman, of London, who, together with George Armstrong, son and heir of Thomas and Rachel Armstrong, by deeds of lease and release, dated July 6th and 7th, 1731, granted the said one thousand acres to

Samuel Mickle, of Philadelphia. At the meeting of the Board of Property held 4th mo. 15th, 1736, a patent was signed to Samuel Mickle for two hundred and fifty acres on a branch of the "Parkeawining," in right of Rachel Armstrong, formerly Crispin. On 8th mo. 2nd, 1731, James Buckley requested a grant of about two hundred acres on the branches of the Octoraro to build a mill. This was afterwards confirmed to him in right of Samuel Mickle's purchase "made of the children of Captain Crispin," the minutes of the Board have it, but Mickle's purchase was from only one child of Crispin's.

Thomas and Rebecca (Crispin) Armstrong had issue:

Jane Armstrong, m. Robert Swiney (probably Sweeney):

George Armstrong, "son and heir."

Another child, or children (at least one daughter), name or names unknown.

Captain William Crispin was married, secondly, in 1665,[88] at Kinsale, County Cork, Ireland, to Jane Chudleigh, daughter of John Chudleigh of that place, as has been shown. She was buried at Kinsale on March 28th, 1718.[89] They had issue:

6. JAMES, see below.

7. JOSEPH, died unmarried, between 1687 and 1698, between the ages of seventeen and twenty-one years.

8. BENJAMIN, married (between 1698 and 1702) Alice.....

9. JANE, m. (between 1687 and 1698) Greenslaid Lucomb. A Jane Crispin married by License in 1692 Robert Prince, possibly a first husband.

---

[88] Herbert Webb Gillman. *Index to Marriage License Bonds of the Diocese of Cork and Ross, Ireland, 1623–1750* (Cork), Ireland, 1896–7) 26, 34 —also Cork and Ross Marriage Licenses.

[89] Parish Registers of Kinsale.

10. ELEANOR, d. unm. between 1687 and 1698, aged between seventeen and twenty-one years.

11. ELIZABETH, m. between 1687 and 1698, ... Millard: he died before 1702.

An Elizabeth Crispin married at Kinsale, August 25th, 1691, to Garrett Condon,—possibly a first husband.

12. AMY, married at Kinsale, May 20th, 1699, Daniel Jones.

William Penn, of his free gift, granted 8th August 1687 to James, Joseph, Benjamin, Jane, Eleanor, Elizabeth, and Amy Crispin, children of William Crispin by his second wife Jane (Chudleigh) Crispin, all minors at this time, 3000 acres of land in Pennsylvania, and named as Trustees Thomas Chudleigh, Martin Pierce and John Watts.

Fifteen hundred acres was to to be sold for their "education, support, and settlement in life," and it was stipulated that if any child should die prior to the age of 17, that its portion was to revert to the Proprietary. No return of the laying out of this land was sent to the Trustees, and none was sold by them, but Jane Crispin, although left in straitened circumstances by her husband, had herself paid for the education of her children. Therefore, William Penn granted to her, "Jane Crispin of Kinsale, widow," November 22nd, 1696, this 1500 acres; an additional reason for this grant to her was, as stated in the deed, that Eleanor and Joseph had died after reaching 17 years and Jane, Elizabeth and James had married very well, while Benjamin and Amy were capable of supporting themselves. This land was afterwards inherited by her surviving children.

James Crispin married between 1687 and 1698 and removed from Kinsale to the Island of St. Christopher in the West Indies, where he became prominent in maritime affairs. He appears eventually to have obtained the entire 3000 acres above referred to, and while, according to the law of Pennsylvania, as eldest brother, he was entitled to two shares of it, each of his brothers and sisters receiving one share, it is not clear how he acquired the remainder of the property.

In an account of the disposition of this land among the Penn Papers in the possession of The Historical Society of Pennsylvania, it is stated that James' surviving brother and sisters Benjamin, Jane, Elizabeth, and Amy, by deed of May 10th, 1702, sold their rights to James, who died intestate, seized of three thousand acres, leaving issue. James Crispin's children were clearly considered the heirs of the whole three thousand acres, for about 1731 they sold all of their shares, aggregating this amount, to persons living in Pennsylvania, and their right was unquestioned until 1752, when a controversy arose about one of these sales. At this time, Thomas Penn wrote that he had in his possession a deed (Now owned by M. Jackson Crispin) of 1698, on which was endorsed a conveyance, dated July 30th, 1702, from Benjamin, Jane, Elizabeth and Amy, to Captain Arthur Smith, and that this appeared to be the original conveyance, thus they had not conveyed to their brother James. The reason for the conflict of these two conveyances is unknown; nevertheless it is certain that James Crispin's children were the actual owners of the property for their title was considered valid and accepted. It has been surmised that James Crispin had married a daughter (and possibly heiress) of Captain Arthur Smith, which could explain his possession of his brother's and sisters' rights, but as the name of his wife is at present unknown this is merely conjecture.

James Crispin was the Commander of the "St. George" Galley bound from Leghorne to London, loaded with a large cargo of merchandise. The "St. George" was attacked by two privateers and James Crispin so as to save the vessel, ran her ashore, on the island of Corsica, County of Laccindo in March 1711, which caused his ship to be badly damaged. Captain James Crispin, to save as much of the cargo, as possible, had to unload it in an unused barracks in the Gulf of St. Fiorenzo at Fornali nearby, and set up six cannon to guard it. While there, two large French privateers (galleys) strongly armed, and a galliot[90] came into the bay and sent boats ashore for provisions. Before landing they promised the Captain Commander of St. Fiorenzo that they would not make any attack on Crispin's ship. However, when they arrived on shore they told Crispin that unless he made

---

[90] A small galley.

them very good terms for his ship and cargo they would burn his galley. Crispin told them that he would defend his goods at all hazards and if they decided to come that he was prepared for them. They attacked him and the fight lasted from two-thirty to four-thirty in the afternoon. The Fort of St. Fiorenzo and the Tower of della Mortella joined with Crispin, and beat off the privateers in a hot fight. Crispin's battery fired so often that all of his six cannon were discharged every seven and a half minutes. Crispin's boat was repaired in due course and proceeded to its destination. Depositions concerning this matter were taken at Leghorne, and have been translated from the Italian.[91]

James Crispin had issue,—
Arthur Smith commanded merchant ships.
Prudence, m. ... Smith, of St. Christopher, 1752.
James, drowned off St. Christopher in a hurricane, 1731, died intestate, under 21 years, probably unmarried.
Richard, living in 1733.
Elizabeth, m. . Harris, living in St. Christopher, 1752.
Joseph, of St. Christopher. In Philadelphia, 1752.
Michael, living in Kingston, Jamaica, in 1751.
Joseph and Michael sold April 7th, 1752, to Thomas James, Jr., of the City of Philadelphia seven hundred and fifty acres of land, being their share of the three thousand acres given by William Penn, the Proprietor, to their grandmother, Jane (Chudleigh) Crispin.[92]

---
[91] Rawlinson MS. c. 683, Bodleian Library, Oxford.
[92] *Penna. Archives*, 3S. vol. 2, p. 188 (Board of Property Minutes).

(To be continued)

ERRATA*

First part of Captain William Crispin article, in April issue:
In the motto, frontispiece, and page 131, line 6, for *Clarum* read *Clavum*.
Page 100, line 22, delete *and*.
Page 115, line 11, for *Navy* read *Army*, as Robert Wadeson was Treasurer of the Army, not of the Navy.
Page 122, line 10, change footnote number *82* to *52*.

*For p. 131 see p. 221; for p. 100 see p. 186; for p. 115 see p. 203; for p. 122 see p. 212, all this volume.

CAPTAIN WILLIAM CRISPIN

By M. JACKSON CRISPIN
of New York City and of Berwick, Pennsylvania

SILAS CRISPIN I.

 Silas, youngest son of Captain William Crispin and Rebecca (Bradshaw) Crispin, was born probably in London, about 1655. He accompanied his father, it would seem, on the unfortunate voyage in the ship "John and Sarah" in the fall and winter of 1681-2. Captain Crispin having died on the way to America, it devolved upon the son, Silas Crispin, to succeed him and to establish the Crispin family in the New World. Silas was a settler in the Province quite some time before the coming of either Thomas Holme or William Penn. He came[93] to Pennsylvania a young, single man and doubtless at first made his home with his cousin, the Deputy Governor of the Province, Captain William Markham, then apparently living at Upland, now Chester. Crispin, as previously stated, appears in

---

[93] Silas Crispin did not return to England on the death of his father, as heretofore supposed; nor did he come to this country with Captain Thomas Holme, whose arrival was some months later.

the minutes[94] of the court of Upland, three times, on June 13th, 1682, as juror, his name with that of but two others of the twelve jurymen, together with the names of the justices, being preceded by "Mr", a significantly respectful differentiation of that day. Again, on coming to the same court, September 12th, 1682, as a witness, he and the Sheriff alone of all the court were given this designation.[95]

Crispin was with Governor Markham and William Haig in Bucks County, July 15th, 1682, when Markham and Haig in behalf of William Penn received from Idquahon, Janottowe, and other chiefs of the Lenni Lenape or Delaware Indians a deed of sale for the lands of the southern part of that County. This original vellum document, to which Silas Crispin's signature is affixed in bold chirography as a witness, is still in existence among the treasures of The Historical Society of Pennsylvania.

The destinies of Silas Crispin and his family line were now to be affected by the arrival, in early August, 1682, of William Penn's newly-appointed Surveyor General, Captain Thomas Holme (1624–1695) with his sons and marriageable daughters. Captain Holme, pending his laying out of the future City of Philadelphia,—where later he established his city house on the north side of Arch Street, near Front Street—, made his temporary home with the surveyor, Thomas Fairman, at Shackamaxon (Kensington), Delaware River, on the northern outskirts of the later city. Although the Holmes were Quakers and Silas Crispin, it is believed, was an Episcopalian, yet soon he came a courting the Captain's daughter, Hester Holme, and by 1683 had married her. Thereupon, it behooved him to establish an abode and an estate for his family.

---

[94] *Record of the Courts of Chester County, 1681–1697* (Philadelphia, 1910) 14–19.
[95] *Ibid.* 19–20.

The earliest catalogue or list of the First Purchasers of Pennsylvania lands, bought from William Penn in England, as to be laid out in the new Province, was engrossed on two vellum skins and signed by him in late October 1681, so that it might be taken overseas by Captain Crispin and his fellow Commissioners. Near the end of the second skin under section "XXIX" is the entry:

"William Crispin & Silas Crispin Acres of Kingsale in the Kingdom of 5000 Ireland Gent^s [96]

This record makes evident that the usual form of deeds of lease and release for 5000 acres of land *to be* laid out in Pennsylvania had been executed by Penn to the Crispins, in 1681, some time prior to their migration.

With the coming now of family responsibility, in 1683, Silas Crispin sought the execution of his deed and became for the first time an actual land owner in the Province. Upon this tract, the first issued to him, he located his habitation. His special knowledge of the county, gained by travel and influential association, enabled him to make a choice selection and his position as a member of the Proprietary governing family made easy his obtaining the title papers. Indeed, William Penn, himself, at that time here on his first American visit, signed Crispin's warrant for the tract, August 10th, 1683, as follows, by which Surveyor General Holme was directed to have the survey made:

William Penn Proprietary & Govern^r. of y^e
 Province of Pennsilvania & y^e
 Territories thereunto belonging
 At ye Request of Silas Crispin Purchaser of Five Thousand Acres of Land in this Province, That I would grant him to take up part thereof in ye County of Philadelphia. These are to will & require thee forth wth to survey or cause to be surveyed unto him Five hundred Acres in y^e

---

[96] Albert Cook Myers Collection.

sd County where not already taken up, according to yᵉ method of Townships appointed by me, & make returns thereof in to my Secretary's Office. Given at Philadelphia yᵉ 10ᵗʰ $\frac{6^{th}}{mo}$ 1683   Wm Penn
For Thomas Holmes
   Surveyʳ General.

Accordingly, on the 17th of the same month the tract was laid out, and June 4th, 1684, the return of the survey was formally recorded by Holme in the Land Office.[97]

The grant was a rectangle of 500 acres in what then was known as the upper part of Dublin Township (afterward Lower Dublin), Philadelphia County, on the line of the present Abington Township, Montgomery County. It was bounded on the northeast by Dr. Nicholas More's Manor of Moreland, on the southeast by John Mason's land, on the southwest by the Susquehanna Road and on the northwest (across the present Abington Township line) by William Stanley's land. It is shown on Thomas Holme's printed Map of Pennsylvania, of 1687.

To this plantation home Crispin brought his bride. There is a tradition in the family that their first child was born in the wigwam of an Indian chief. Howbeit, here, beginning with his daughter Sarah, March 31st, 1684, his children were born, and here he made his abode to the end of his days. The place now forms a part of the Pennypack Park, in the 35th Ward of the City of Philadelphia. It is, as the crow flies, ten miles northeast of the City Hall and nearly two miles north of the Roosevelt Boulevard.

In 1693 upon the petition of the inhabitants of the Township requesting the continuation and confirmation of a "ten year old road" from the Township to Walter Forrest's Mill,[98] which was on Poquessing

---

[97] MS. Survey and Warrant Book, No. 9, page 9, City Hall, Philadelphia.

[98] *Penna. Colonial Records, I* (Phila., 1852) 389.

Original Land Warrant signed by William Penn, Philadelphia, 6 Mo. (August), 10th, 1683, to his Cousin, Silas Crispin, for his 500 acre Tract in Philadelphia County. From the Pennsylvania State Land Office at Harrisburg.

Creek in Byberry, the road was begun "at the Bridge near the Dwelling House of Silas Crispin."[99] Thus it seems evident that the house stood on the bank of Pennypack Creek as it etches its picturesque way through the even yet well timbered hills of the region.

Over three miles down the Creek in the same Township, at present Holmesburg, Philadelphia, was Wellspring Plantation, the country estate of Crispin's father-in-law, Thomas Holme.

Crispin subscribed £50 for stock of the Free Society of Traders in Pennsylvania.[100] As executor of the will of his father-in-law, Captain Thomas Holme, he spent a great deal of time caring for the large interest in lands left by the latter, obtaining warrants for laying out lands not taken up at Holme's death, selling some of the tracts, and engaging in like business. In the deeds he is styled "Silas Crispin of Dublin Township, Gentleman."

On August 28th, 1689, the Provincial Council appointed Silas Crispin, Robert Turner, Benjamin Chambers, Joseph Fisher, Thomas Fairman and Robert Adams, with a surveyor, to lay out a cart road according to statute, they having petitioned to have a road laid out from Philadelphia to Bucks County. This was no doubt the present Bristol Pike and they probably followed to a great extent the rather indefinite trail previously known as the "King's Path." Again in 1703 and 1710 Crispin assisted in laying out roads near his home.[101]

In addition to his home plantation, Silas was granted 500 acres in Hilltown Township, Philadelphia County, forty acres in the "Liberties of Philadelphia" and three lots in the city. The Liberty land was just half,

---

[99] Land Records at Harrisburg, etc.
[100] *Penna. Mag.*, XI., 177.
[101] MS. Road Dockets, Philadelphia Court of Quarter Sessions, City Hall, Philadelphia.

and the area of the city lots approximately half of what was due under a purchase of five thousand acres, yet Silas appears to have been the only one of the children who had either, as the others all sold their rights before any land was actually laid out to them. The patents to all these are made out to "Silas Crispin, Purchaser," seemingly as part of his First Purchase of his father and himself. This five hundred acre tract in Hilltown Township, Philadelphia County (now Abington Township, Montgomery County), was about eight miles back from the Delaware River in a straight line along the hypothetical Susquehanna Road. The tract was rectangular, bounded northeast by Moreland, southeast by Lehnmann's land, southwest by the Susquehanna Road and northwest by land Captain Thomas Holme had taken up in right of Samuel Claridge. It is shown on Holme's map of 1687. Between 1686 and 1698 Silas Crispin sold this in separate portions to Cornelius Sturgis, John Meredith and Thomas Hood.

The forty acres of Liberty Land was rectangular, a short distance northeast of Germantown Road, beyond Isaac Norris' "Fairhill" plantation. He sold this to Nicholas Rideout in 1695, who sold it to Nicholas Waln. Silas Crispin's city lots, as already mentioned, were not the same as those allotted to his father on the original plan. A number of alterations had been made in the plan before the lots were surveyed. One was on the west side of Delaware Front Street, 162 feet south of Walnut. It was 42 feet on Front Street running back 155 feet on the north line and 201 feet on the south line, bounded on the west by a marsh. In 1684 he sold this to William Frampton. Another of his lots was on the southwest corner of High Street and Strawberry Alley, 40 feet (afterwards found to be 41 feet) on High Street and 80 feet on the Alley. He sold this about 1692 to Joseph Farrington. The other of Silas Crispin's lots was on the southeast corner of Sixth and High Streets, 66 feet on High and 306 feet on Sixth Street. This was patented to him in 1688 and the same year he sold it to Patrick Robinson. (Patrick Robinson exchanged thirty-nine and a half feet in breadth of this with Robert Greenaway, Captain of the Ship "Welcome," for the same amount adjoining the lot he (Patrick Robinson) had purchased from Crispin, as Holme's executor, farther east in the same square, the latter being twenty-six and a half feet, originally intended for twenty-six); these combined lots, sixty-six feet front, he sold to Lionel Britain. This exchange has made a good deal of confusion in the attempt to locate the lots from the records, some giving it as "Robert Greenway's exchange with Silas Crispin," while the deed shows Crispin to have sold the corner lot intact to Robinson, and the minutes of the Board of Property say that Robinson made the exchange with Greenway.

Silas Crispin's wife Hester died April 17th, 1696, and he married, second, 1697, Mary, daughter of Richard and Abigail Stockton, of Springfield Township, Burlington County, West New Jersey, and widow of Thomas Shinn of the same county and province. Her father, Richard Stockton, was an Englishman of good birth and some fortune, who settled in Flushing, Long Island, where he was a lieutenant of a troop of horse in 1665. He afterwards joined the Society of Friends and removed to Burlington County, New Jersey, and became ancestor of the Stockton family of that Province.

The final illness of Silas Crispin is thus mentioned in a holograph letter[102] of his first cousin, Robert Assheton[103] (1670–1727), Philadelphia Town Clerk,

---

[102] In the collection of the writer.
[103] Son of William Assheton, by his wife Frances Bradshaw (daughter of Ralph Bradshaw by his wife Rachel, daughter of Giles Penn).

to their first cousin, William Penn, dated Philadelphia, May 23rd, 1711:

"Cosin Crispin was Tapt yesterday for a Trapany or Dropsie has very bad how it will goe with him I cant tell but am in hopes heel recover it."

Silas Crispin died May 31st, 1711. His original will, in which he is styled "Gent," is preserved in the City Hall, Philadelphia. It is dated May 5th, 1711, and is in the handwriting of his cousin Robert Assheton, above mentioned, who signs as witness, along with his wife, Margaret Assheton, and Crispin's nephew, William Blackfan. Although "Weak in Body," Crispin signs his will with a strong clear hand. He made his wife, Mary, executrix, left her his plate, negroes, household goods, and the like, and directed her to sell a hundred acres, bought from Robert Pressmall, adjoining on the north east of his plantation, to pay debts and legacies. Among minor bequests to his son Thomas, were "ffour silver Spoons & one pair of silver buckles." To his granddaughter Sarah Loftus and his sister Rebecca Blackfan, he left sums of money. The will was proved August 7th, 1711, over the signature of the Deputy Governor Charles Gookin. The widow, Mary Crispin, however, renouncing her executrixship, July 5th, 1711, letters of administration, *cum testamento annexo*, were granted to the son, Thomas Crispin, April 19th, 1714.

The full text of the will is as follows:

In the Name of God Amen The ffith day of May In the year of our Lord One thousand seven hundred & Eleven I Silas Crispin of the Township of Dublin in the province of Pensilvania Gentl being Weak of Body but of sound memory do make this my last Will & Testam^t. in Manner ffollowing Impris my Just [debts] & ffuneral Expenses being paid out of my $\wp$sonal Estate All th[e] Rest residue & remaindr thereof whether live stock household goods ready Mony Debts plate Negros or of what Nature or kind it bee Not herein after $\wp$ticularly bequeathed I give & bequeath unto my Loving Wife Mary Crispin. Item I give devise & bequeath unto my sd Wife the One hundred Acres of Land adjoynyng to the North East End of my plantacon

Original Will of Silas Crispin, as signed by him, May 5th, 1711.

wch I purchased from Robert Prismall to be by her sold & disposed on towards the paym^t. of my Debts & the Legacies herein by me given & bequeathed Item I give & bequeath unto my Son Thomas Crispin One Mare Called Jewell with her Colt One ffeather bed Bedstead Rugg sheets blankets & pillows ffour silver Spoons & one pair of silver buckles. Item I give & bequeath unto my Granddaughter Sarah Loftus thirty pounds. Item I give unto my loving Sister Rebecca Blackfan three pounds And of this my last will I make my sd Loving Wife Sole Executrix In Witness whereof I have hereunto put my hand & Seal the day & year abovesd

              Silas Crispin

Sealed Signed published
& delivered by the sd
Silas Crispin as his last
will in the presence of
 Margaret Assheton
 William Blackfan
 Robt Assheton

Filed with the will is the inventory of Silas Crispin's estate, made September 6th, 1711 by John Hart and Michael Butcher. It is a long but quaint document affording an interesting exhibit of the household furnishings and plantation economy of that early day. A sumptuous item is "the Red bed and bedstead with all its furneture," appraised at £12. The livestock included 9 horses, 12 cows, a bull, 5 heifers, 6 calves, 38 sheep and 19 hogs.

His landed estate is not mentioned in his will, his own plantation going by the law of primogeniture to his son Thomas, while the other children of his first wife were heirs, through their mother, to Captain Thomas Holme's "Well Spring Plantation" and other large domains, Holme having acquired at different times upwards of 10,000 acres, of which at his death he possessed more than 2,100 acres. Crispin's children by his second wife were quite young at the time of his death and probably he expected them to be provided for by their mother whose family was wealthy.

After her husband's death, Mary Crispin returned to Burlington, New Jersey, where she had lived before her marriage. She was married, November 11th, 1714, at Springfield Quaker Meeting, to Richard Ridgway, Jr., of Springfield Township, who was her third husband.

Silas Crispin and Hester (Holme) Crispin had the following issue:

SARAH, born March 31st, 1684, married Lesson Loftus, of the City of Philadelphia.

REBECCA, born May 6th, 1685, married Joseph Finney, son of Samuel Finney, Provincial Councillor and Provincial Judge, and brother of Captain John Finney, Provincial Councillor and High Sheriff of Philadelphia County, of the family of Finney, of Fulshaw Hall, Cheshire, England.

MARIE, born October 1686, married John Collet, son of Richard and Elizabeth (Rush) Collet.

ELEANOR, born September 11th, 1687, married, November 23rd, 1708, John Hart, Jr., who was High Sheriff of Bucks County, and also Coroner and Justice in the same County, son of John Hart, Member of Assembly, by his wife Susanna Rush.

From their son, Colonel Joseph Hart, by his marriage with his first cousin, Elizabeth Collet, daughter of John and Marie (Crispin) Collet, descends James Watts Mercur (son of Ulysses Mercur, Chief Justice of Pennsylvania), of Wallingford, Pennsylvania, Trustee and Secretary of the Crispin Cemetery Corporation, and father of James Watts Mercur, Jr., Mrs. Thomas Cahall and Mrs. John Seaman Albert, of Wallingford, and of the Baroness Orazio Nicola Saitto, of Moylan, Pennsylvania.

WILLIAM, born October 3rd, 1689, died young.

ESTHER, born October 29th, 1691, married Thomas Rush, grandson of John Rush. The above mentioned John Collet, John Hart, Jr., and Thomas Rush were all grandsons of Captain John Rush, formerly of the Parliamentary Army of England, who came to Pennsylvania in 1683, and held a plantation in Byberry,

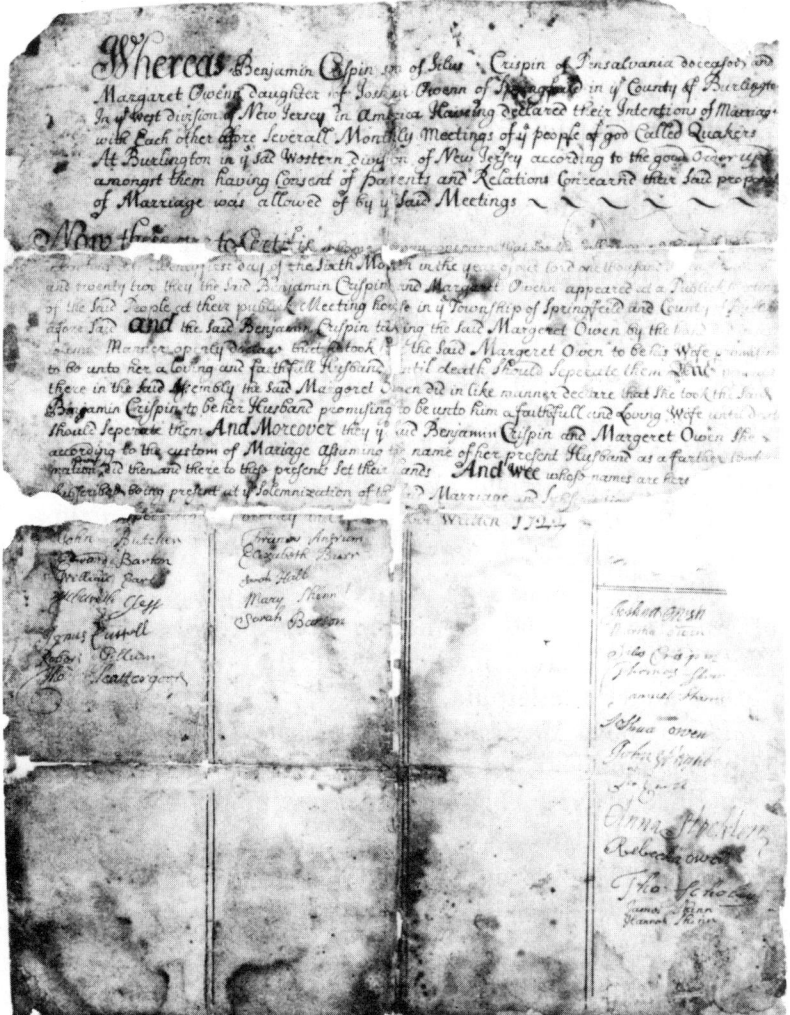

Original Certificate, owned by M. Jackson Crispin, of the Quaker Marriage of Benjamin Crispin, son of Silas Crispin, of Pennsylvania, deceased, to Margaret Owen, daughter of Joshua Owen, of Springfield, Burlington County, New Jersey, at Springfield Friends' Meeting House, 6 Mo. (August) 21st, 1722.

The signatures of the bride and groom are worn away but next below them in the relatives' column were the following witnesses: Joshua Owen, Martha Owen, Silas Crispin, Thomas Shinn, Samuel Shinn, Joshua Owen, John Wright, Tho Earl, Ann Stockton, Rebecka Owen. Tho: Scholey, James Shinn, Thomas Shinn. Other witnesses were: John Butcher, Edward Barton, William Earl, Zachariah Jess, Jonas Cattell, Robert Gillum, Tho. Scattergood, Frances Antrum, Elizabeth Burr, Sarah Hall, Mary Shinn, Sarah Barton.

for account of whom see *Pennsylvania Magazine,* Volume XVII, No. 3, pages 325–335.

THOMAS (See below).

SUSANNA, born April 14th, 1696, died young.

The above children removed from the immediate vicinity, Thomas Crispin alone remaining.

Silas Crispin and Mary (Stockton Shinn) Crispin had the following issue:

JOSEPH, born October 7th, 1698, married Elizabeth Barrett. Removed to Delaware.

BENJAMIN, born September 1st, 1699, married, August 21st, 1722, at Springfield Meeting, Margaret Owen, daughter of Joshua and Martha Owen, of Springfield Township.

ABIGAIL, born January 30th, 1701, married John Wright, of Springfield Township.

SILAS, born March 19th, 1702, died November 1749, married, November 9th, 1724, Mary Wetherill, daughter of Thomas and Ann (Fearson) Wetherill, of Burlington, and granddaughter of Christopher Wetherill, ancestor of the Wetherill family of New Jersey and Philadelphia.

MARY, born May 12th, 1705, married November 6th, 1727, Thomas Earl, of Burlington County, son of William Earl, of New England, ancestor of the Earl family of New Jersey.

JOHN, born December 11th, 1707.

THOMAS CRISPIN

Thomas Crispin, oldest surviving son of Silas and Hester (Holme) Crispin, was born June 22nd, 1694, on his father's plantation, in Dublin Township, later Lower Dublin Township, in Philadelphia County, which he inherited and made his home for the remainder of his life. He married, about

1716, Jane Ashton, daughter of Joseph Ashton, a Justice of the Philadelphia County Courts and a large landowner in Dublin Township. She was born about 1696; died 1749. They had issue: Silas (see below), Thomas, Joseph, Hannah, and Mercy. He and his sisters (of the full blood) inherited through their mother the estate of their grandfather, Captain Thomas Holme, which, as has been stated, included the Well Spring Plantation and a smaller tract adjoining, amounting in all to over 2100 acres, and which in 1723 was divided among the then living heirs.

One acre of ground, which was set aside by Captain Thomas Holme, in 1694, for a family graveyard was reserved for their use in common, and he was buried there in 1695. His grave is now marked by a marble shaft erected by the Trustees of the Lower Dublin Academy in 1863–4. Thomas Crispin and his wife were buried there in 1749, where their tombstones may be seen to this day, bearing their initials and the dates of their deaths. Thomas Crispin's descendants continued to use it and it became known as the "Old Crispin Burying Ground," later in 1831, the "Crispin Burial Ground Community," and since 1840, when it was incorporated, the "Crispin Cemetery Corporation." After 1800, there were practically no burials, although there were a few during the next fifty years, after which time they ceased altogether.

The heirs of Thomas Holme also set aside, in 1723, $1\frac{1}{2}$ acres of ground, to satisfy a clause in his will, for a charitable purpose, and on this ground was erected a log school house, which thus ante-dates the famous Germantown School. Out of this grew the Lower Dublin Academy which was chartered in 1794 and a new building erected. Both of these old buildings are now standing. The Thomas Holme Branch of the Free Library of Philadelphia, in Holmesburg, is the direct result of this donation.

The 300th anniversary of the birth of Thomas Holme was celebrated November 11th, 1924, elaborate exercises being held on this day in honor of the distinguished services rendered by him to the City of Philadelphia and to Pennsylvania. This commemoration, very appropriately, was inspired and directed by The Commonwealth of Pennsylvania, through one of its departments, The Pennsylvania Historical Commission, of which Albert Cook Myers was the Secretary-Director, and was participated in by high officials of the City and State, as well as by Holme's living descendants. On the preceding evening, the 10th, The Historical Society of Pennsylvania, held a meeting in honor of Holme, Mr. Myers delivering the address on the subject, with lantern slides. During the morning of the 11th, appropriate exercises were held at the Crispin Cemetery and in the afternoon a bronze tablet was unveiled (on a building at 113 Arch Street, on which site stood Thomas Holme's original Philadelphia residence), by Elizabeth Brockway Crispin, of New York City, whose line of direct descent from Thomas Holme is given in this article.

While preparing for the above commemoration, a permanent committee was formed, the purpose of which was to endeavor to have an ordinance passed by the Council of the City of Philadelphia to surround the Crispin Cemetery with a park to be named the Holme-Crispin Park, as a mark of respect to the memory of Thomas Holme. The members of this committee were: J. Harvey Gillingham, Chairman, George S. Webster, John A. Vogelson, Clement B. Webster, Walter Brinton, A. Zane Hoffman, William C. Reeder, John Stephenson Clark and M. Jackson Crispin. Eli Kirk Price attended all of the meetings subsequently held by this committee.

A number of meetings were held in Philadelphia from that time until October 19th, 1925, when the

Holme-Crispin Park was placed upon the City plan. After this date many meetings were attended by Messrs. Eli K. Price, Clarence K. Crossan, member of Council from the district in which the Crispin Cemetery is located, J. Harvey Gillingham, James Watts Mercur, John Stephenson Clark and M. Jackson Crispin, until May 7th, 1928, on which date a meeting was held at the Ritz Carlton Hotel attended by the gentlemen above mentioned. It was the opinion of Mr. Crossan that the time for action had arrived and consequently he presented an Ordinance to the City Council on May 10th, 1928, authorizing the City of Philadelphia to start proceedings to condemn for park purposes 37 acres more or less of land including the Crispin Cemetery.

Two days later on May 12th another luncheon was held at the Ritz Carlton Hotel at which were present the Hon. Harry A. Mackey, Mayor of Philadelphia, John H. Neeson, newly elected Chief Engineer and Surveyor of the Engineering and Survey Bureau, Messrs. Price, Crossan, Gillingham and Crispin. The entire matter was placed before the Mayor, who graciously expressed himself as being in favor of the plan and stated that he would be glad to give it his co-operation and approval. The first reading of the Ordinance occurred June 21st, 1928. It had been agreed to exclude the Cemetery property from the condemnation proceedings, which through an error had not been done, consequently, the Ordinance was recommitted to the Committee, June 28th, excluding the Cemetery. It was reported back by the Committee, September 27th, was amended and passed the second reading on October 4th, the third reading on October 11th and signed by Mayor Mackey, October 15th, 1928. After the signing of the Ordinance by the Mayor, it was discovered that the name of one of the streets recited in the boundary of the area was incorrect. This made it necessary for the City Council to pass an Amendment correcting the error, which was done on June 20th, 1929, by changing the name of Albion Street to Wilson Street, when the ordinance became a law. Hence, the Holme-Crispin Park, which is part of the Pennypack Park surrounding the Crispin Cemetery where Thomas Holme lies buried, has come into existence, thus recognizing the services of this distinguished man who drew up the plans and plotted the City of Philadelphia and the Province of Pennsylvania.

Mayor Mackey is to be heartily congratulated and most highly commended for his prompt support of this park, which action made its inception possible. The Trustees of the Crispin Cemetery will make appropriate improvements to this property and present it to the City of Philadelphia.

SILAS CRISPIN II.

Silas Crispin, son of Thomas and Jane (Ashton) Crispin, inherited the land of his father in Lower Dublin Township and lived there his entire life. This estate, part of the tract descending from Captain Thomas Holme, was known as "Bellevue." He married Martha Miles,[104] January 14th, 1749, daughter of Griffith Miles, of Radnor, Chester County, Pa., who was born 1727 and died before 1794. They had issue: Silas (see below), Joseph, an officer in the Revolutionary War, William, Sarah, Jane and Thomas. In 1794 he wrote an account of the family graveyard and other matters pertaining to the Crispin family. He died in 1800, and was buried in the Crispin Cemetery.

---

[104] From the original manuscript account book of James Hamilton, in the collection of The Historical Society of Pennsylvania.

SILAS CRISPIN, III.

Silas,[105] son of Silas and Martha (Miles) Crispin, was born, May 11th, 1767, in Lower Dublin Township, at "Bellevue," which he inherited from his father and he died there of lockjaw as a result of running a nail in his foot, August 13th, 1806, at the early age of 39. He married Esther Dougherty, 1788, who was born 1767, and died May 7th, 1838. They had issue: Martha, Benjamin (see below), Mary, Paul, Silas, Hester and Ann.

HON. BENJAMIN CRISPIN.

The Hon. Benjamin Crispin, son of Silas and Esther (Dougherty) Crispin, was born in 1792, on the ancestral estate of "Bellevue." He was educated in Lower Dublin Academy, with which his family was so closely identified. In 1822 he was commissioned a Lieutenant of Pennsylvania Militia. In 1823, he was appointed by the Governor of Pennsylvania, Justice of the Peace for the Townships of Byberry, Lower Dublin, and Oxford, Philadelphia County, and held that office until 1837. In 1828 he was appointed by the Court of Quarter Sessions of Philadelphia Director of Public Schools in his district. In 1837, he was elected a member of the General Assembly of Penn-

---

[106] While it is not definitely known, the facts all seem to indicate that Silas was the oldest son. He inherited his father's landed estate and was the sole executor of his will. It is highly probable that his father would name his first born "Silas" and there is plenty of evidence that he was a very old man at the time of his death in 1800. The late Oliver Hough in an article on the Crispin family, appearing in John W. Jordan's *Colonial and Revolutionary Families*, I. (New York, 1911) 365, designates him as the youngest son.

sylvania, and re-elected in 1838–1839. In 1840 he was elected to the State Senate and in 1843 was made Speaker of the Senate as the presiding officer of that body was then designated. When the whole of Philadelphia County was incorporated with the city in 1854, Mr. Crispin was elected the first Common Councilman from the 23rd Ward. On his retirement the Council presented him with a cane which is now in the possession of his family. He continued to manifest a deep interest in the schools, and on leaving the Council was again elected to the local school board. A new public school in Holmesburg was named after him in 1906, forty-two years from the time of his death. Benjamin Crispin was a founder of Emanuel Church, at Holmesburg, and served for twenty years, as one of its vestrymen, and eight years as accounting warden. He also represented the parish in the Diocesan Convention in 1854–56–58–60. He was one of the originators of and President of the Board of Trustees of the Holmesburg Athenæum Association and Chairman of its building committee, which in 1850 built the town hall called the Athenæum (In this building until 1908 was housed the Thomas Holme Library). In May, 1837, he was elected one of the Trustees of the Lower Dublin Academy and in 1838 its President, an office he held until his death twenty-six years later.

He was founder of the "Crispin Burial Ground Community" and principally instrumental in obtaining a charter for the "Crispin Cemetery Corporation" from the Legislature, while he was a State Senator in 1840, thus perpetuating the title to the heirs of Thomas Holme, under the care of a Board of Trustees, of which he was President. Mr. Crispin was of medium height but of quite stout build. He had a large—what might be called massive—head, though his features were not large. He was deliberate, rather slow in the manner of expressing himself and firm in his convictions.[106] He married, October 17th, 1816, Maria Foster, daughter of Amos and Eleanor (Thomas) Foster, of Collegeville, near Holmesburg. She was born 1800. They had issue,—Edward T., William, Benjamin Franklin (see below), Eleanor Jane, Thomas Holme, Silas (Colonel U. S. A.), and Charles H.

Colonel Silas Crispin was born at Holmesburg, Philadelphia County, Pa., on September 9th, 1828. He was educated at local schools and the Philadelphia High School. He was admitted as a cadet to the U. S. Military Academy at West Point, N. Y., July 1st, 1846, on appointment of the late Hon. Charles Jared Ingersoll, M.C. He graduated with distinction, being third in his class, on July 1st, 1850, and was then appointed a Brevet Second Lieutenant in the Ordnance Department, U. S. A. He was promoted from time to time, finally attaining the rank of Colonel of Ordnance on August 23rd, 1881. He served at Watervliet Arsenal, New York, Allegheny Arsenal, Pennsylvania, and St. Louis Arsenal, Missouri. He was in command of the Ordnance Depot, Leavenworth, Kansas, in 1860 and 1861.

During the Cival War, Colonel Crispin served for some time on the staff of Major-General George B. McClellan, and also in charge of the New York Ordnance Agency as a member of the Ordnance Board, Commandant of the New York Arsenal, and President of the Ordnance Board for five years. After the war he was sent to England by the Government to study the making of ordnance. He was the inventor of a breech-loading cannon called the "Crispin Gun," several of which were made by the government at a cost of $46,000 each. He was Commandant at the Frankford Arsenal Philadelphia, from June 1885 to June 1886, and the Benica Arsenal, California, from June

---

[106] Samuel C. Willits', MS. History of Lower Dublin Academy, 332.

1st, 1886, until a short time previous to his death, which occurred at New York City on February 28th, 1889. He was buried in Holmesburg, Penna., on March 8th. The interment was in the grounds connected with the Emanuel Protestant Episcopal Church. Colonel Crispin had never married.[107]

Benjamin and Maria Crispin began their married life at "Bellevue," the old Crispin homestead on the Welsh Road, but subsequently removed to Holmesburg, where they continued to reside the remainder of their lives. Benjamin died July 4th, 1864 and Maria died May 13th, 1882; both were buried in the cemetery adjoining the Emanuel Episcopal Church at Holmesburg.

BENJAMIN FRANKLIN CRISPIN I.

Benjamin Franklin Crispin was the third son of Benjamin and Maria (Foster) Crispin, and was born in Holmesburg, August 2nd, 1821, and died at his residence, 3258 Chestnut Street, Philadelphia, July 19th, 1898. He was educated at Lower Dublin Academy and other educational institutions. He was President of the Crispin Cemetery Corporation and the Lower Dublin Academy. He married, June 24th, 1845, Elizabeth Glenn, daughter of Robert and Sarah Glenn, of Holmesburg. She was born September 9th, 1825, and died in 1873. They had issue:

1. Benjamin Franklin (see below).
2. Robert Glenn, born at Holmesburg, Philadelphia, February 4th, 1849; received his early education at the Episcopal Academy, Philadelphia; 1872, went to Berwick, Pa., where he became connected with the Jackson

---

[107] The above sketch was written by the Hon. George Stephenson Clark, Holmesburg, Philadelphia, February 19th, 1901.

and Woodin Manufacturing Company (Now the American Car and Foundry Company). He was after a time a member of the firm of Bowman and Crispin. In 1902 he was elected Teller of the First National Bank of Berwick, which position he held at the time of his death, May 16th, 1913. He married on September 10th, 1873, at Berwick, Frances M., born at Berwick, Pa., December 4th, 1852, daughter of Seth B. and Louise F. (Doane) Bowman, of Berwick, Pa. Robert Glenn Crispin and Frances M. (Bowman) Crispin had issue,—a son born April 12th, 1875, died the same day.

3. William Henry, born Philadelphia, June 11th, 1851, died October 18th, 1924, married May 27th, 1875, Matilda, daughter of John Mitchell, of Philadelphia, in which city they resided for a few years, finally removing to Beverly, N. J., where he lived until a few years before his death. They had issue, Franklin Mitchell Crispin, born in Philadelphia, April 13th, 1876, married 1905, Emma Fowler, daughter of the late Joseph D. Weeks, of Pittsburgh, Pa., at one time Editor of "Iron Age."

4. Elizabeth Glenn Crispin, died unmarried, June 2nd, 1873, aged about eighteen years.

5. Maria Crispin, born August 10th, 1858, in Holmesburg, Philadelphia, married on October 10th, 1883, William Emerson Smith, a distinguished attorney of Berwick, Pa., who died January 7th, 1891. She is now (1929) living at Narberth, Pa. Of their four children, three died in childhood. A daughter, Elizabeth Crispin Smith, born June 26th, 1884, in Berwick, married, on December 9th, 1915, her first cousin, Charles Edwin Crispin, born December 22nd, 1917, in Flushing, L. I. They were divorced on May 22nd, 1922, and Elizabeth Crispin Smith Crispin and her daughter are living in Narberth with Mrs. Maria Crispin Smith. Charles Edwin Crispin, 2nd, married, second, Irene E. Sampson, on June 22nd, 1922. They are now (1929) living in New York City.

6. Charles Edwin Crispin, born at Holmesburg, November 14th, 1856, died in New York City, April 26th, 1926.

7. Louis Crispin, born at Holmesburg, December 30th, 1863, married 1881, Susan Church, of Laurelton, Pa. They lived at Laurelton for a few years after their marriage and then moved to New York City, where Mr. Crispin, who has been head of the Shipping Department of John Wanamaker for a number of years, now resides, his wife having died February 14th, 1912. They had issue, Charles Edwin Crispin, 2d, born at Laurelton, Pa., June 7th, 1882, who married Elizabeth Crispin Smith, daughter of Maria Crispin Smith, as above indicated.

8. Sarah Frances Crispin, born May 1st, 1846, married, June 4th, 1874, the Hon. George S. Clark, of Holmesburg, Philadelphia, who died September 29th, 1923. She is now living in Holmesburg. Mr. Clark was a son of a Civil War veteran, Colonel John Clark, of Holmesburg, and became one of the most prominent citizens of that town. In 1879, George S. Clark purchased the old Crispin homestead known as "Bellevue," which was part of the original plantation owned by Surveyor General Thomas Holme, from whom it had descended to the Hon. Benjamin Crispin. Both Mr. Clark and his wife were very active in all affairs relative to the Holme and Crispin families and were especially concerned with the preservation of the old Crispin Burying Ground, she at one time raising a fund among her relatives for fencing that property. They had issue,—

(1.) John Stephenson Clark, born August 1st, 1875, married Elizabeth, daughter of Jonathan and Mary Frances (Risdon) Rowland of Holmesburg. Mr. Clark succeeded his grandfather, B. F. Crispin, as Trustee of Lower Dublin Academy and Trustee of the Crispin Cemetery Corporation, and now resides in Holmesburg. He had issue one son, John Maxwell

Rodman Clark, born March 23rd, 1905, married June 2nd, 1928, Mary (Craig) Loper, of Holmesburg.

(2.) Benjamin Crispin Clark, born March 28th, 1877, died December 24th, 1878.

(3.) Arthur Douglass Clark, born August 14th, 1883,

(4.) Elizabeth Frances Clark, born September 16th, 1878, now a practicing surgeon in Philadelphia.

BENJAMIN FRANKLIN CRISPIN II.

Benjamin Franklin Crispin II., oldest son of Benjamin Franklin Crispin I., was born in Holmesburg, Philadelphia, July 21st, 1847, and died at his residence in Berwick, July 3rd, 1903; received his early education at the Lower Dublin Academy, later at the High Schools of Philadelphia.

He removed to Berwick, Pennsylvania in 1872 and immediately took a deep interest in its affairs. Mr. Crispin was one of the founders of the Berwick Rolling Mills and became connected with the First National Bank of Berwick in 1876, of which institution he was President for many years until the time of his death. He was the founder and first President of the Berwick Electric Light Company, was Vice-President of the Berwick Store Company, Limited, and trustee of the Jackson and Crispin Estate, whose large landed interests occupied much of his time. He was an ardent Republican, always active in that party and was for many years a director of the public schools. Mr. Crispin was a charter member of the Board of Trustees of the Young Men's Christian Association and a trustee of the Methodist Episcopal Church, where he was a regular attendant. He was President of the Mountain Grove Camp Meeting Association and associated himself with those who directed the church.

His long and efficient service to the public schools as director and advisor has been recognized by the presentation to the School District of an athletic field named in his honor. It is known as the Crispin Memorial Athletic Field, and consists of a trifle over 4 acres of land taken from the Borough Farm of the Jackson and Crispin Estate, situated within the borough limits and near the schools. It comprises a separate football and baseball field and also has a mile track. A brick club house has been erected sufficiently large to accommodate two football squads with separate quarters, completely equipped with showers and modern conveniences. A ticket office, Director's Room, and large basement is also provided for. Portable bleachers for the accommodation of 2000 people were purchased so as to make them available for both the football and baseball fields.

He married, June 14th, 1874, Margaret Jackson,[108] who was born November 19th, 1853, daughter of the Honorable Mordecai William Jackson[109] (1815–1894),

---

[108] Margaret Jackson Crispin married, second, on November 6th, 1907, the Rev. Richard H. Gilbert, a presiding elder in the Methodist Episcopal Church, who died on May 17th, 1924.

[109] Benjamin Doane (1770–1825), the maternal grandfather of Mr. Jackson, came to Berwick about 1790 and was the first of the family to settle there. He married, 1793, Hannah Sharpless Iddings, whose father, William Iddings, fought in the Revolutionary War *(Pennsylvania Archives,* 5S. V. 496). He was the son of Elijah and Sarah (Groves) Doane, and died while in the service of the Revolutionary army near Trenton. Benjamin Doane (Elijah^5, Israel^4, Daniel^3, Daniel^2, John^1) was directly descended from Deacon John Doane, one of the Pilgrim Fathers who came to Plymouth from England in 1629. He rendered distinguished services to that colony, of which he was one of the most influential personages. He was a member of the first Provincial Council of the Plymouth Colony, on which Council sat the celebrated Captain Myles Standish and John Alden, and was "Assistant to the Governor" in 1633. In 1634 he resigned from the Council to become Deacon of the Plymouth Church and in 1645 led in the establishment of the Puritan Church at Eastham of which he was chosen deacon.—A. A. Doane, *Doane Family* (Boston, 1902) 3, 4, 7, 246; Joseph Sharpless, *Sharpless Family* (Philadelphia, 1816), revised by Gilbert Cope, *Sharpless Family* (Philadelphia, 1887), 410–411.

a pioneer in that community, and one of the foremost business men of his day in central Pennsylvania. He[109a] founded, with William Hartman Woodin I., a partnership known as Jackson and Woodin, of Berwick, in 1849, now the American Car and Foundry Company.[110]

[109a] Mr. Jackson's son was General Clarence Gearheart Jackson, born in Berwick, Penna., March 25th, 1842. At the age of fourteen he entered Dickinson Seminary, Williamsport, Pa., where he graduated two years later with the highest honors of his class. He then entered Dickinson College, Carlisle, Pa., where at eighteen, he again led his class at graduation.

On August 2nd, 1862, he enlisted in the Civil War as Second Lieutenant of Co. H, 84th Regiment Pennsylvania Volunteers, at the age of twenty, and became First Lieutenant, January 2nd, 1863. At Chancellorsville, he was captured and taken to Libby Prison, where he remained many months. He, with companions, succeeded in escaping from prison, but was captured and brought back. Later, he was exchanged and appointed to a Captaincy. At the Battle of the Wilderness he was wounded, again taken prisoner and returned to Libby Prison. He was soon, however, included among six hundred officers who were taken to Charleston and placed under the fire of the Federal cannon from Fort Moultrie. They were taken to Columbia from Charleston and placed in a guarded field, with no roof to shelter them, where they dug underground cells for themselves, from which place he was finally exchanged. In 1870 he was appointed Major on the staff of General Osborne, later Colonel on the staff of Governor Hartranft, and was made Quartermaster General by Governor Hoyt in 1879.

General Jackson was one of the influential members and chief advisors of the Republican Party in the management of whose affairs he took a prominent part, representing it as a Delegate in State and National conventions. It was expected that he would receive the gubernatorial nomination of his party at the expiration of Governor Hoyt's term, but this was prevented by his sudden and unexpected death at the age of 38 in 1880. He was one of the substantial business men of Pennsylvania, having been interested in many enterprises. He was Trustee of Dickinson College and of the State Normal School at Bloomsburg. General Jackson's town honored him by naming its Grand Army Post No. 759, the Captain Clarence Gearhart Jackson Post.

[110] In 1860 Jackson and Woodin began the manufacture of coal and freight cars. In 1867–1868 the business was enlarged by building a wheel foundry, a pipe foundry, rolling mills and a large company store. They employed at that time 1300 men. In 1872 he and Mr. Woodin retired in favor of their eldest sons, General Clarence Gearhart Jackson and Clemuel Ricketts Woodin, who incorporated the business into

Mr. Jackson was a charter member and the first President of the First National Bank of Berwick, founder of the Berwick Company Store, now Berwick Store Company, Ltd., and was an Associate Judge in Columbia County, Pennsylvania. He was a trustee of Dickinson College and the State Asylum for the Insane at Danville.

Mr. Jackson married Margaret Gearhart, the great-granddaughter of Captain Jacob Gearhart[111] (1735–1813), of Revolutionary war fame, who had charge of the boats of George Washington troops when they crossed the Delaware. Captain Gearhart's eldest son

---

the Jackson and Woodin Manufacturing Company. General Jackson died in 1880, and the entire management of the Company devolved upon Mr. Woodin, who conducted its affairs in such an able manner that the growth steadily continued until 1899, when it became one of the most important units of the American Car and Foundry Company, known as its Berwick District. This plant now builds both freight and passenger cars and when working at capacity has employed 6300 men. In November 1907, 2530 freight cars of various types were built in 25 days or an average of 101 cars per day. During this month, 20 steel Interboro coaches were also erected and this department now has a capacity for building one and one-half passenger cars per day. Mr. C. R. Woodin's son, William Hartman Woodin II. is a very prominent and influential business man of New York City and is now President of the American Car and Foundry Company.

[111] Captain Jacob Gearhart came to New Jersey in 1735 from Strasburg, then a city of France, settled in Hunterdon County, N. J., and married, *circa* 1761, Catherine Kline; enlisted, in 1775, when the Revolution broke out and soon became Captain of the 2nd New Jersey Regiment. He was a man of brave and fearless spirit, who stood so high in the confidence of his superior officers that he was chosen by George Washington, with Cap. Van Tenyck, to take charge of the crossing of the Delaware, then filled with floating cakes of ice, on that eventful night of December 25th, 1776, when the Hessian camp of the English was attacked at Trenton. After the crossing had been accomplished the boats were placed in the charge of these two captains who were ordered to destroy them should the expedition prove a failure. Captain Gearhart saw service at Brandywine and Valley Forge, and after the war, *circa* 1785–95, settled in Northumberland County, Pennsylvania.—Office of the Adjutant General, Trenton, New Jersey; *Hist. and Biog. Annals of Columbia and Montour Counties, Pa.*, I. (J. H. Beers and Co., Chicago, 1915), 449, 450.

was Judge Jacob Gearhart[112] (1763–1841), of Northumberland County, a very influential man in Pennsylvania. Benjamin Franklin and Margaret (Jackson) Crispin had issue, Mordecai Jackson, Clarence Gearhart and Helen Jean, for accounts of whom see below.

MORDECAI JACKSON CRISPIN

Born at Berwick, Pennsylvania, May 13th, 1875, Mordecai Jackson Crispin was graduated from Berwick High Schools, 1892; then he entered Princeton College (now University) and was graduated from this institution in 1896, with the degree of Bachelor of Arts. He has always retained his legal residence in Berwick, but removed to New York City in 1900; he has been President of the First National Bank of Berwick since 1909 and President of the Crispin Cemetery Corporation since 1924. He was General Manager and Treasurer of the United States Metal

---

[112] Judge Jacob Gearhart, son of Captain Jacob Gearhart, entered his father's regiment in 1777, at the age of 14 years, and served until the end of the war, having become an ensign. He married, *circa* 1792, Margaret Runkle, of Hunterdon County, New Jersey, and followed his father to Northumberland County, Pennsylvania, about 1795. He was a very ardent and prominent Democrat, his house being the meeting place of men of importance the country over. It was there that Andrew Jackson, while President of the United States, requested Simon Cameron, then United States Senator from Pennsylvania, to get that delegation committed to the support of Martin Van Buren for President. Here also came Francis Asbury, the first Bishop of the Methodist Episcopal Church in this country, who preached in Judge Gearhart's barn. He was a Colonel of the Pennsylvania Militia, and a Presidential Elector in 1828 for Andrew Jackson. He was very fastidious in his dress, conforming to the colonial style, always wearing a ruffled shirt, swallow tail coat, and white fur top hat.—Ben. van D. Fisher, *The Runkle Family*, New York, 1899) 46, 64, 65; Department of the Interior, Bureau of Pensions, S.F.3392.

Arms of M. Jackson Crispin
Confirmed to him by the College of Arms in England

Quarterly of eight: 1 and 8, Erminois, three lions rampant azure, armed and langued purpure, *for Crispin;* 2, Sable, a lion rampant or, billetty sable, a bordure or, *for Crispin* (Tillieres) ; 3, Fusilly, gules and argent, on a chief of the second two lions passant combatant of the first, *for Crispin* (Bec-Crispin) ; 4, Gules, a griffin segreant or, on a chief of the second two pallets of the first, *for Crispin* (Devonshire) ; 5, Argent, two bendlets cotised between as many martlets sable, in the fesse point a cinquefoil gules, *for Bradshaw;* 6, Argent, a chevron azure, between three chaplets gules, within a bordure sable with ten roundels, *for Holme;* 7, Argent, on a fesse cotised sable three plates, *for Penn.* Crest—A demi-griffin erased with wings addorsed azure. *Motto—Dum clavum rectum teneam.* Crispin heraldic badge (not shown here) : A seven-headed hydra rampant vert.

[Reproduced in black and white in the interest of economy.]

and Manufacturing Company of New York City from 1900 to 1916, after which time he was associated with the American Car and Foundry Company in New York, until 1922, when he retired from active business. In 1916 he was a delegate from the 16th Congressional District of Pennsylvania to the Republican National Convention held in Chicago which nominated Charles Evans Hughes for President. He is a life member of the Board of Directors and President of the Crispin Memorial Athletic Field, of Berwick.

He married, first, Marie Brockway, June 7th, 1900, born at Beach Haven, Pennsylvania, July 2nd, 1874; died, New York City, October 27th, 1907. She was the daughter of Frank Eugene Brockway,[113] of Beach Haven, Pennsylvania, by his wife Cora, *née* Campbell, and was graduated from the Berwick High School and the Woman's College at Baltimore.

[signature: Elizabeth Crispin Trupcoveck]

They had issue, one daughter, Elizabeth Brockway Crispin, born January 3rd, 1905, at 17 East 11th Street, New York City, educated at Miss Marshall's School,

---

[113] Frank Eugene Brockway is a Civil War veteran, having been a Second Lieutenant in Battery F, First Regiment Pennsylvania Reserve Volunteers Light Artillery. His brother, Charles Brockway, a Captain in the same Regiment, in the hand to hand fighting at Gettysburg after the color-bearer had been killed grabbed the flagstaff shot off just below the colors. A "Louisiana Tiger" attempted to steal the horse of the color-bearer, but before he could draw his gun, Captain Brockway killed him with a stone. Their father, Beckwith Brockway, was born in New London, Conn., where his family had lived since their arrival in America. He removed from this locality to Luzerne County, Penna. and was Colonel of a Regiment of Militia at Berwick. The latter part of his life was spent at Harrisburg, Penna., where he was a State Librarian.

Briarcliff Manor, N. Y., Ely Court, Greenwich, Connecticut, Holton Arms School, Washington, D. C., and the Harcum School, Bryn Mawr, Pennsylvania; was married, January 30th, 1929, in St. Patrick's Cathedral, New York City, by Monsignor Lavelle, to Oliviero Tripcovich, of Trieste, Italy, younger son of the late Commendatore Diadato Tripcovich and Countess Gilda Tripcovich-Pozza. Mr. Tripcovich was graduated from the Royal University of Rome, and is a partner in the Tripcovich Shipping Company, of Trieste, in which city he and his wife now reside.

M. Jackson Crispin married, second, Erma Marchant, April 3rd, 1916, born July 10th, 1888, daughter of James Dwight Marchant, of Baltimore, Maryland, by his wife, Nannie *née* Mathews, of Mathews County, Virginia.

Clarence Gearhart Crispin, second son of Benjamin Franklin Crispin and Margaret (Jackson) Crispin, was born September 27th, 1879, was graduated from Wyoming Seminary, Wyoming, Pennsylvania, in 1898, and from Cornell University in 1902, with the degree of Mechanical Engineer. He retains his legal residence in Berwick, although is now living in New York City. He is President of Berwick Water Company, Berwick Store Company, Ltd., Multiplex Manufacturing Company and Vice-President of the First National Bank of Berwick. He is executor of the Estate of Frederick H. Eaton, Treasurer and Trustee of the Crispin Cemetery Corporation, and a life member of the Board of Directors of the Crispin Memorial Athletic Field, of Berwick.

He married, October 19th, 1904, Mae Lovely Eaton, born March 1st, 1892, daughter of Frederick Heber Eaton, deceased, a man very prominent in the business world of New York City, where he was a Director in many institutions. Mr. Eaton was President of the Jackson and Woodin Manufacturing Company of Berwick, from 1896 to 1899 and President of the American Car and Foundry Company from 1901 until the time of his death in 1916.[114]

They had issue: (1.) Benjamin Eaton Crispin, born in Berwick, Pennsylvania, October 10th, 1905, married, September 23rd, 1929, in Syracuse, New York, Laura Tenney Klock, daughter of Mabie Crouse Klock, of Syracuse, by his first wife, Nannie née Petersilia; and (2.) Frederick Eaton Crispin, born in Berwick, Pennsylvania, September 1, 1906, married September 18th, 1929, in Pittsburgh, Pennsylvania, Sara Louise Gwinner, daughter of Edward William Gwinner, of Pittsburgh, by his wife, Elizabeth née Minnemeyer. Both sons were educated at St. Paul's School, Concord, New Hampshire, and Princeton University; they are now in business with their father in New York City, and on January 8th, 1929, were elected directors of the First National Bank of Berwick. They are also life members of the Board of Directors of the Crispin Memorial Athletic Field.

Helen Jean Crispin Owens, born January 11th, 1886, at Berwick, Pennsylvania; educated, Berwick Schools, National Park Seminary, Washington, D. C., Merrill Van Lear School, New York City; married, June 8th, 1910, at Berwick, Pennsylvania, Charles Beland Owens, of Germantown, Kentucky, son of Theodoric Owens and Elizabeth Norris Owens. They removed to Toronto, Canada, after their marriage, where they are now living, and have issue,—Margaret Crispin Owens, born May 17th, 1911, and Elizabeth Crispin Owens born November 4th, 1914.

---

[114] Mr. Frederick H. Eaton was a director in the following institutions, —The American Agricultural Chemical Company, American Beet Sugar Company, Columbia Trust Company, Seaboard National Bank, Chairman of the Board of the American Car and Foundry Export Company, and a trustee of the Mutual Life Insurance Company of New York.

ERRATA

First part of Captain William Crispin article, in April issue:
Page 98. footnote 6, for *Vol. 12 (Paris, 1763)* read *Vol. X. (Paris, 1756)*. (For p. 98 see p. 184, this volume.)
Second part of Captain William Crispin article, in July issue:
Page 200 line 4, for *Millard* read *Hilliard*. (For p. 200 see p. 232.)
Page 200 line 9, for *Jones* read *Johnson*. (For p. 200 see p. 232.)

ADDENDA

First part of Captain William Crispin article, in April issue:
Page 98, line 22: Gilbert Crispin I. is called Count of Brionne by the Benedictine Monks of the Congregation of St. Maur, *Histoire littéraire de la France*, Paris, 1756, Vol. X. p. 192, by George Lipcomb* *County of Buckingham*, London, 1847, Vol. III. p. 466, and by John Mabillon, *Annals of the Order of Saint Benedict*, etc., Vol. IV. (Paris, 1707) pages 391 and 399. Sylvanus Urban, *Gentleman's Magazine*, London, January 1832, Vol. CII, p. 27, and James Anderson, *Royal Genealogies*, London, 1734, p. 671, table 398, made him the son of Ansgothus Crispinus, son of Crispina, the daughter of Rollon, 1st Duke of Normandy, and Grimaldi 1st, Prince of Monaco, and both of whom gave him the titles of Baron of Bec and Baron of Tillières. William of Jumièges, Jean Marx's edition, *Gesta Normannorum Ducum*, Paris, 1914, book 7. II (5). p. 117, and *Orderic Vitalis* (August Le Prévost's edition, Paris, 1852, Vol. IV. p. 369) call him Gilbert Crispin, châtelain of Tillières. Howbeit, he had the custody of Tillières *circa* 1042, when he defended the castle against Henry I., King of France.—Freeman's *Norman Conquest*, Vol. II. p. 133; Jumièges, opus citus, book 7. II (5) p. 117; *Orderic Vitalis*, opus citus, Vol. IV page 369.

Page 99, lines 4 and 6: William Crispin 1st and Gilbert Grispin II. with Robert are named in J. A. Giles' edition of *"Beati Lanfranci Miraculum quo beata Maria subvenit Willelmo Crispino Seniori, ubi de Nobili Crispinorum generi agitur"* (Paris, 1844, Vol. I. p. 348)—"The Miracle by which Blessed Mary came to the aid of William Crispin Sr., wherein the noble line of the Crispins is discussed" and also by many other historians, as the children of Gilbert Crispin 1st and Gonnor, sister of Foulke d'Aunou the Elder, and this must be taken as authoritative. Robert, the younger brother, after wandering through many countries, went to Constantinople where he acquired a high position and favor at court and was poisoned through jealousy by the Greeks.—J. A. Giles. opus citus, Paris, 1844, Vol. I. p. 341.

There has been naturally much discussion regarding the correct titles of William Crispin I. and Gilbert Crispin II.; the author chose to designate them as shown on Page 99 of the article for the reasons there given, substantiated by the references quoted. It it very difficult to be absolutely positive about matters of this kind at that early date, but it can be stated beyond any question of doubt that William Crispin I.

*for *Lipcomb* read *Lipscomb*

was Vicomte du Vexin (see J. A. Giles, opus citus, vol. I. p. 342), Seigneur de Neaufles, de Livarot, and de Blangy (Porée, page 99 of article) and that Gilbert Crispin II. was Seigneur de Tillières *(Orderic Vitalis,* opus citus, Vol. IV. p. 369). This is under investigation at the present time, with other points pertaining to this early branch of the family by that learned scholar and historian, the venerable Chanoine Porée, as well as by René Herval, whose book *"Falaise, Cité Normande"* has just been published, by Professor Leonce Macary, of the College of Falaise, and by Paul Gentil of Tillières.

The *"Miraculum quo beata,"* etc., is the most authoritative document on the origin of the Crispin family, and was written either by Gilbert Crispin (see Preface to Giles' edition of the *"Miraculum,"* already quoted), Monk of Bec, Abbot of Westminster Abbey *(circa* 1046–1117; J. Armitage Robinson, Dean of Wells, in *Gilbert Crispin Abbot of Westminster,* London, 1911, page 1) and son of William Crispin I. or by Milo Crispin *(circa* 1075–1150), Monk of Bec, leader of the choir at that Abbey for many years and a contemporary writer of Gilbert Crispin, Abbot, or by them jointly, both of whose works are considered among the best of their period.—*Histoire Littéraire de la France,* by the Benedictine Monks of the Congregation of St. Maur, Paris, Vol. XI. The identity of Milo Crispin is unknown, excepting that he was a descendant of William Crispin I. and must not be confused with Milo Crispin, lord of Wallingford.

The *"Miraculum"* states (Giles, opus citus, p. 342):

". . . et ideo dux Normannorum Willelmus qui postea rex Anglo-"rum fuit, praedictum Willelmum Crispinum, quia erat probatissimus "in re militari, collocavit in castro Melfia . . . et Viecasini vicecomitatum "jure haereditario custodiendum, et filius ejus post eum sicut usque hodie "videmus." (William Duke of Normandy who later became King of England, assigned the above William Crispin, who had a great reputation as a soldier, to take charge of a camp at Melfia *(i.e.* Neaufles) . . . and to guard the viscounty of Vilcasinus *(i.e.* Vexin) by hereditary right, and his son after him we see holding the same up to now.)

Page 99, line 7: The identity of Milo Crispin, favoured warrior at the Battle of Hastings, a Domesday Tenant in Capite, and the recipient of many honours and lands from the Conqueror, has not been definitely established, although J. R. Planché (London, 1874, Vol. I, p. 94), the *Gentleman's Magazine* (London, January 1832, Vol. CII) and James Anderson *(Royal Genealogies,* London, 1734) make him a brother of William Crispin, I. and Gilbert Crispin, II. and the author followed this genealogy on page 2 of the April number of this article. Milo most certainly was a direct descendant of Gilbert Crispin I., but whether he was a brother or half brother of William Crispin I. and Gilbert Crispin II., or a son of one of them is a question. The Reverend J. Armitage Robinson, Dean of Westminster Abbey, author of *Gilbert Crispin, Abbot* (page 17) names him son of Gilbert Crispin II., but does not give the reason why he thinks this is so. Milo married, *circa* 1084, Matilda, daughter and heiress of Robert d'Oilly, one of Duke William's chief commanders at Hastings, who gave to d'Oilly in marriage Aldrith, daughter and heiress of Wigo de Wallingford. After the death of d'Oilly, the Honour of Wallingford with vast possessions passed to Milo Crispin. The castle of Wallingford was at that period the strongest and most important fortress in all England. Lady Matilda manifestly must have been born after 1066, consequently when she married Milo Crispin, *circa* 1084, she was not more than 18 years old. If Milo was the full brother of William I. and Gilbert II. he was undoubtedly at the time of his marriage between 46 and 60; on the other hand, if he was the son of either William or Gilbert, his age would have been about 40, assuming that he was 20 years of age at the Battle of Hastings. He lived until 1107 (George Lipcomb, *"History and Antiquities of the County of Buckingham*, London, 1847, Vol. I., pp. 17 and 18), on which date he died Councillor to the King. Therefore, it would seem logical that he was their half brother or son rather than their full brother.

Page 99, line 11: The date of the death of Gilbert Crispin, Abbot of Westminster, is given as 1117, for he is known to have signed documents as late as that year. His tomb, however, in Westminster Abbey bears the date of 1114. J. Armitage Robinson, Dean of Westminster, thinks this inscription was placed on his tomb years, possibly centuries after his death, which would account for the inaccuracy.

Thomas Amory, Chief Commissioner of the Navy in Ireland, in 1666, wrote a letter to the Secretary of the Duke of Ormond, Lord Lieutenant of Ireland, a portion of which reads as follows:
"S^r

The Rumo^{rs} of the ffrench Invasion and some Preparations making ag^t them, hath created some active thoughts in my flegmatique nature; How agreeable they may be to better Judgments I know not, but bec., they are cheape, easy & probable I shall expose them to His Grace Censure wch is Apointing some persons to prepare fire-ships in Kinsale Harbo^r (& the same may perhaps be thought fit for other harbo^{rs} also as Corke, Waterford, Galway &c). The manner of doing it I have desired my agent Capt. Crispin to specify in the inclosed paper, and I suppose he wilbe the fittest person yo^u can have for preparing & managing thereof wherein my Endeavo^{rs} shall not be wanting if His Grace comand it. . . . I am now going for Kerry where I have not beene 11 days these 17 months & shal post thence If any com^{ds} follow mee: I am
S^r Yo^r humble serv^t
Tho. Amory

Corke 17 Jan^{ry} 1666 (1666/7).
Any ship that hath sailes to yard may be made a fire ship in 12 houres time, but they should laye at the Block house alwayes in a readiness.

Addressed: To the honb^{le} Sr George Lane Kt.
Sec^{ry} to his Grace the Lord Lieut
of Irelande
for his maj^{ty} service
present
Dublin."

October 25th, 1720. Administration of the estate of James Crispin, late of the parish of Stepney, Middlesex, and of the merchant ship "Tibington Galley," was granted to Elizabeth Crispin, the relict.
The entry is marked "Pts," signifying that the intestate died at some place out of England, but there is nothing in it to indicate the actual place.—Somerset House, P.C.C., Admon. Act Book for 1720, folio 212b.

Will of Elizabeth Crispin, of St. Nicholas, Deptford, widow. My daughter Elizabeth Harris, wife of Captain John Harris, of St. Christopher, commonly called St. Kitts, in the West Indies, to have a large diamond ring, silverware, etc. My grand-daughter Sarah Payne, a silver mug. My grand-daughter Sarah Crispin, a diamond ring. My niece Sarah Cooper a diamond ring. Residue of estate to my son Joseph Crispin, of "Patoxholine" (?), in Maryland, and my aforesaid son-in-law John Harris, of St. Kitts. John Chase, of Richmond, Surrey, to be executor.

Witnesses: Rebecca Debitt,   Dated 12 January 1750/1
Ann Weaver,
Edward Moore.   Elizabeth Crispin X
Proved 8 February 1750/1, by John Chase, esquire.
This is undoubtedly the will of the widow of James Crispin. In any event, she was the mother of Elizabeth (Crispin) Harris, of St. Kitts, and of Joseph Crispin, here described as of Maryland.
It will be seen that Elizabeth appears to have had a daughter who had married a ——— Payne.—Will at Somerset House, P.C.C., 40 Busby. 1751.

St. Annes, Sandy Point, St. Kitts, West Indies. Marriage, 1734, January 30, Richard Crispin and Sarah Fahie, by license.
This is the Richard Crispin referred to on page 202 of the second part of the Captain William Crispin article, in the July issue. The family of Fahie was of some standing in the island.

October 26th, 1630, Randall Bradshaw and Rachell Penne (By licence of the Vicar General), St. Gregory by St. Paul, London. Marriage Register, 1618–1635 (date of document)
The transition of Bradshaw's name from Raphe (Ralph) to Randall may arise from the possibility of the license having been in Latin, in which case the name would appear as Radulphus, accordingly the clerk, very much after the manner of his kind, reading as Randulphus, of which name Randall and Randle were accepted forms.

Ralph Crispin was the second child of Captain William and Rebecca (Bradshaw) Crispin, born probably at the home of his grandfather, Ralph Bradshaw, of Pendleton, Eccles Parish, near Manchester, Lancashire, England, whither doubtless the mother had gone during the absence of the father with the fleet in the West Indies; for the registers of Eccles Parish contain this entry: "Raph son of William Crispyne Gent baptized at Eccles 7 Feb 1654–5"
Other records from the same registers: "1635 July 28. Sara daughter of Raphe Bradshaw, gent. buried." "1667. October 30. M^r. Ralph Bradshaw of ye Pole, buried."

JACOB DUBS, OF MILFORD.

BY JOSEPH HENRY DUBBS, D.D.

On the 30th of September, 1732, the ship "Dragon," Charles Hargrave, master, entered the port of Philadelphia. On board were one hundred and eighty-five passengers, who in one record are termed "Palatines" and in another "Foreigners Imported." Most of them were, in fact, natives of Switzerland, from which country there was then an extensive emigration to America.

Among the passengers was a young Swiss gunsmith named Jacob Dubs. When the ship arrived at Philadelphia he was ill and could not personally appear to be qualified, so that the clerks had every opportunity to play havoc with his name. In one list it is written "Tups" and in another "Dubbs." The latter form has been generally adopted by his descendants; but the pioneer himself, as appears from extant autographs, was careful to write his name in all its original plainness.

Jacob Dubs was born August 31, 1710, in the hamlet of Aesch, parish of Birmensdorf, canton of Zurich, Switzerland. His parents, Jacob Dubs and Anna Glättli, of Bachstetten, had been married in the parish church of Birmensdorf, March 24, 1705. Two older sons, both successively named Hans Ulrich, had died in early infancy, and Jacob remained their only surviving child.[1]

The Dubs family had for many generations been settled at Birmensdorf and in the neighboring village of Affoltern. For a long time they had been gunsmiths, but in the earliest records they are called armorers.

Though so long resident in Switzerland, there was a tradition that the stock had been remotely of Bohemian

[1] Extract from the "Taufbuch" of the church at Birmensdorf.

origin. The name certainly comes from the Bohemian (Czech) word *dub*, which signifies an oak. More directly it is held to be derived from the name of a town near Prague, called Duba ("The Oaks"), or in German Eichen, or Aycha. In Bohemia the name is well known, though in the language of the country it is often written Dubsky. According to Merian ("Topographia Bohemiæ," p. 26), the families Von Eichen and Berka were originally named Dubs, the name first mentioned being a translation and the second derived from an estate. A branch of the Bohemian family, the tradition relates, became Hussites in the fifteenth century, and during the succeeding wars were compelled to flee to the Austrian province of Styria, where we find them settled in 1446. The head of the family there entered the military service, and distinguished himself in an expedition against the Swiss. He was knighted on the field of battle by the Emperor Maximilian I., who also gave him the privilege of occupying a clearing in the imperial forest. The arms granted on this occasion were carefully preserved by his descendants, and were recognized and approved by Frederick I., King of Prussia, in 1701. They appear in the "Europäische Wappensammlung," published by John Rudolph Helmers, Nuremberg, 1705, Vol. V. p. 38, and represent a silver lance with pennon on a blue shield, surmounted, as a crest, by three ostrich feathers (the Bohemian plumes), two silver and centre blue. The writer has in his possession an ancient engraved seal with these bearings.[1]

About the beginning of the Protestant Reformation a younger son, or grandson, of the Styrian knight removed to Switzerland. The motives of his removal it might now be difficult to determine, but it may perhaps be supposed that he was influenced by Hussite family traditions to cast his lot with the rising cause of the Reformation. At any rate, he became an earnest Protestant, while the family in Styria has remained Catholic to the present day.

[1] For the above facts the writer is mainly indebted to the late Dr. Jacob Dubs, President of the Swiss Confederation, who had made them the subject of careful investigation.

Having settled some six or eight miles from the city of Zurich, the Styrian immigrant became a manufacturer of weapons. In 1531, Zurich was unexpectedly invaded by the army of the Catholic cantons, and the artisan at once became a soldier. He fought bravely in the army of defence, but lost his life, with the Reformer Zwingli, in the fatal battle of Cappel, October 11, 1531. It is recorded in the ancient chronicle of the church at Affoltern that the armorer (*der Waffenschmied*) Dubs, of Birmensdorf, was slain at Cappel in defence of his faith. The fact is also stated by Henry Bullinger, the successor of Zwingli, in his "Reformation Geschichte" (reprint of 1840, Vol. III. p. 153); but in this case the author has got the name twisted and makes it Jacob Dupps.

The surviving children continued in their father's employment. The local records are full of notices of their successive generations, but their interest is purely genealogical. So far as the writer has been able to ascertain, they were a quiet and unpretentious people.

Jacob Dubs, the subject of our sketch, became, like his father, a gunsmith. He was fairly well educated and wrote an excellent hand. Family tradition has it that in his early boyhood his mother died. His father married a second time, and had another son; then he, too, passed away. By this time Jacob was of age, and after due consideration he determined to emigrate. Several of his cousins, "nearer or more remote," had already crossed the sea, and we may naturally suppose him to have been seized by the fever for emigration which had affected many of his neighbors. Gathering up his little patrimony, he left the old place to his step-mother and her son, and started on his way.

Arriving in Pennsylvania, it was but natural that he should seek the society of his countrymen; and we next find him at Great Swamp, in what was then Bucks County, where the Rev. John Henry Goetschius, of Zurich, had recently founded a congregation. On the oldest extant list of members his name appears.

Not far from the Great Swamp Church, in what is now Lower Milford Township, Lehigh County, Jacob Dubs fixed his home. The tract had hitherto been unoccupied, and, according to the earliest draft, all the surrounding land was vacant, except that Jacob Wetzel had just taken up a piece along its southern line. The earliest survey was made for Jacob Dubs by Nicholas Scull on the 28th of September, 1734. According to this survey, the "home farm" originally included one hundred and fifty acres, " with the usual allowance of six per cent.," but it was increased by subsequent purchases. A branch of the Perkiomen ran through the tract and furnished excellent water-power. One of the settler's first acts was to utilize this stream by the erection of a small forge, where he engaged in the manufacture of arms and iron implements. He was, first of all, a gunsmith, but it was said of him that he made everything " from a plough to a darning-needle." Men called him " ein Tausendkünstler," which was a rather polite way of saying that he was " a jack of all trades." At a later date he made, in his leisure hours, a musical instrument called " ein Flügel,"—a harpsichord, an instrument now superseded by the piano,—which was long in possession of his descendants. Though his various enterprises were continued by his son and grandsons, the fact remains that he laid the foundations of what were in their day a series of important business undertakings.

In 1734, Jacob Dubs was " duly qualified and invested with all the rights of a natural-born subject of Pennsylvania." A little later he was married to Veronica Welker, who was a native of the Upper Palatinate, but had relatives in America. George Welker, of Goshenhoppen, who speculated extensively in land, and whose name appears on many ancient deeds, was nearly related. She is said to have been a woman of some culture, and, when the neighborhood began to be settled, she gathered the children in her kitchen and taught them to read.

The following list of the children of Jacob and Veronica

Dubs is extracted, with the correction of a single date, from the records of the Great Swamp Church:

1. FELIX, born February 28, 1738; baptized by the Rev. J. H. Goetschius. Sponsors, Felix Brunner and his wife Barbara.
2. BARBARA, born April 5, 1744; baptized by the Rev. George Michael Weiss. Sponsors, Jacob Wetzel and Barbara Wetzel.
3. MARGARETHA, born 1746; baptized by the Rev. G. M. Weiss. Sponsor, Anna Maria Wetzel.
4. DANIEL, born October 5, 1748;[1] baptized by the Rev. G. M. Weiss. Sponsors, Daniel Christman and his wife Margaret.
5. ELIZABETH, born October 16, 1750; baptized by the Rev. G. M. Weiss. Sponsor, Elizabeth Huber.

That the family, like other pioneers, was exposed to dangers and privations will be readily understood. This is illustrated by a tradition related to the writer by a descendant. There were wolves in the woods near the house, and when Daniel was a little boy he often amused himself by imitating their barking. Once, while he was doing this, a wolf rushed out of the woods to attack him; but he escaped by running to the open window of the kitchen, and his mother drew him in.

Jacob Dubs was a man of peace, but when the Indians were making incursions into the Lehigh Valley, he joined a military company and followed the enemy beyond the Blue Mountains. They tracked the Indians for many miles, but there was no conflict.

In the welfare of the church the subject of this sketch was profoundly interested. He was chosen a ruling elder, and it has been mentioned as a somewhat unusual fact that in the same congregation this office was held by three generations of his descendants. The traditions of his domestic

[1] The church record gives this date October 28, 1748, but this is probably the date of baptism. On the united testimony of a family Bible and the inscription on his tombstone, the writer has ventured to correct it.

life have become faint, but it was no doubt very similar to that of the next generation, as described by a grandson, the late Rev. J. S. Dubbs, D.D., of Allentown.[1]

About the year 1759 the family was visited by a severe affliction. The eldest son, Felix, had grown up to be a bright young man, and was still unmarried. Having started for Philadelphia with a load of farm produce, he spent a night at North Wales, at the house of Matthias Schwenk, whose daughter Elizabeth was afterwards married to his brother Daniel. Rising early in the morning, while it was dark, Felix fell into the well, which, it seems, was not properly covered, and was drowned.

The daughters were all happily married. Barbara became the wife of Jacob Boyer, a man who was highly esteemed in the community. During the Revolution he sold his farm, and was paid in depreciated Continental money. Becoming financially involved, he removed to the West, and finally settled in Tennessee, where he is said to have many descendants. After some years he revisited his old home in Pennsylvania and paid all his old debts, with interest.

Margaretha became the second wife of Jacob Dillinger, and had three children. Her descendants are numerous.

Elizabeth was married to Jacob Haak, of Berks County, and from them many of the Haaks, Sells, Gabels, and other Berks County families derive descent. " Uncle Haak" must have been a rather peculiar person. He became wealthy, and in his later years lived in a style which his plain neighbors regarded as luxurious. He was an enthusiastic Freemason, and took great pleasure in entertaining the lodge of which he was master. Generally he was attended by a faithful negro slave, named Sam, who understood his peculiarities and did his best to humor him. When slavery was abolished in Pennsylvania, his master said, " Sam, you are a free man; you may go where you please !" The old man solemnly shook his head, and replied, " No, no, master,

[1] See life of Rev. Joseph S. Dubbs, D.D., in Harbaugh's "Lives of the Fathers of the Reformed Church," Vol. V. p. 241.

you can't get rid of me dat way. You ate de meat, you must pick de bone."

When the daughters were married, Daniel, the only surviving son of Jacob Dubs, remained with his parents at the homestead. As he had grown up to be a man of almost gigantic frame, and was of good mental capacity, his father's business naturally passed into his control. In 1772 the father sold his real estate to his son for three hundred and fifty pounds.

There is a tradition that in the last few years of his life Jacob Dubs spent much time in writing, and that his papers were put into the case of the old harpsichord, which was then out of order. Many years afterwards, a good woman, whose sense of neatness would not allow the preservation of ancient rubbish, destroyed these and many other papers unread.

The exact date of the death of Jacob Dubs the writer has not been able to determine. The church records are for several years incomplete, and his tombstone has crumbled so that its inscription has become illegible. The writer has the impression that he lived to the age of sixty-five, so that his death must have occurred in 1775, and this date cannot be far out of the way. His wife survived him several years. Both lie buried in the old church-yard of the congregation of which they were members, adjacent to the tomb of their son Daniel.

It may be interesting to add that, under the care of Daniel Dubs, the industries established by his father were greatly extended. After his marriage to Elizabeth Schwenk, he built for himself a large brick house, which is still standing in excellent condition. According to undisputed tradition, it was the first brick house built within the present limits of Lehigh County.

The forge erected by his father was enlarged, and became what would now be called a machine-shop. In those days they called it "die Schleifmuehle." Sickles were produced in large numbers, and screw-augers manufactured there not many years after their invention by Judge William Henry, of Lancaster. The business finally passed into the hands of his son John, who was no less skilful than his father. At this shop a large number of muskets were made for the government during the war of 1812.

The grist-mill was built about the beginning of the present century. It became especially well known for peculiarly fine buckwheat flour, which was a staple article in the Philadelphia markets.

To trace the history of the several industries established by Daniel Dubs would be impossible without access to original records, and these have apparently long since disappeared. There was, however, a tannery, as well as a saw-mill, an oil-mill, and, in fact, a whole cluster of enterprises, such as in those days were not infrequently conducted by a single man. In December, 1824, Daniel Dubs disposed of his real estate by selling it to three of his sons. John took the forge, Daniel, Jr., the mill, and Jacob the tannery. They had, in fact, been in possession of these interests at a much earlier period, and in 1815 a division was effected by written agreement, but it seems to have been discovered that a more formal act of transfer was a legal necessity.

Elizabeth Dubs, the mother of the family, passed away from life on the 20th of February, 1818. Her husband, Daniel, lived more than ten years longer, and died September 22, 1828. The following were their surviving children:

1. ANNA MARIA, born June 27, 1777. Married to Henry Eberhard. The late Michael D. Eberhard, of Allentown, was her son.

2. JACOB, born June 21, 1779; died May 17, 1852. He received a part of the home farm, and built a stone house which is still (1894) occupied by the widow and daughter of his youngest son. One of his grandsons, the Rev. Jacob G. Dubbs, is a minister in Lehigh County.

3. HENRY, removed to Hamilton, Butler County, Ohio, about 1825, and has many descendants. The wife of the Rev. F. W. Berleman, D.D., pastor of Salem Church, on Fairmount Avenue, near Fourth Street, Philadelphia, is a granddaughter.

4. DANIEL, born April 7, 1786. In 1836 he removed to

Montgomery County, Ohio. One of his sons, Daniel L., was a graduate of Heidelberg College, Ohio, and for some time a student at the Theological Seminary in Mercersburg. He became an officer in the army, and was fatally wounded at the battle of Fredericksburg.

5. JOHN, born September 5, 1788; died November 25, 1869. He lived all his life at the old homestead, which at his death passed to Aaron, his only son.

6. SOLOMON, born October 10, 1794; died May 24, 1880. He resided near Allentown, Pennsylvania, and has descendants.

7. JOSEPH S., born October 16, 1796; died April 14, 1877. He studied for the ministry, and was for more than thirty years pastor of Zion's Reformed Church, Allentown,—the church in which the historic bells of Philadelphia were concealed during the Revolution. His two sons are ministers. The elder, Alfred J. G., was until recently pastor of Salem Church, Allentown; the younger, Joseph Henry, is a member of the faculty of Franklin and Marshall College, Lancaster.

Concerning the industrial interests in which the family was so actively engaged, it may be said that, in the course of time, commercial methods changed and all such rustic manufactories declined. One by one the younger members of the family sought homes where conditions were more favorable, and now scarcely a trace is left of the toil of former days.

The last occupant of the homestead before it passed into the hands of strangers was Aaron K. Dubbs, who died June 22, 1874. In a published tribute his pastor, the Rev. Dr. C. Z. Weiser, says, "He was born in the quiet vale, surrounded by forests and watered by brooks, in which his father and grandfather had been born and had lived all their days, and in which his great-grandfather had set his tent-poles as the pioneer Dubbs, some time previous to 1734. Aaron's homestead had never been known otherwise than as the 'Dubbs' Place' since the days of the aborigines. It is one of the few family-houses, and on this account we delight to look at its roof-trees. The farm, house, barn, trees, fences,—everything,—were begun and preserved by the hands of the older or younger Dubbses. No wonder that Aaron loved it and all about it. He could not bring himself to part with it, though convenience and interest suggested it."

To the present generation, dwelling in other places, the story of the old home in Milford has become a tradition, and unless it is put in writing it must speedily disappear. Though it is not a history of great achievements, it deserves to be remembered by those who derive their lineage from the Swiss pioneer, as a record of honest toil and of devotion to duty.

PEDIGREE OF ROWLAND ELLIS, OF BRYN-MAWR, FROM HIS OWN MANUSCRIPT, 1697.*—Rowland Evans, Esq., of Haverford College Station, P. R. R., has kindly placed in my hands a sketch of his ancestor Rowland Ellis (after whose estate in Wales the present Bryn-Mawr is named), and also the following account of the descent of Rowland Ellis and of his second wife, written by himself some time prior to 1697. He was born at Bryn-Mawr, in Merionethshire, in 1650, and was the son of Ellis ap Rees ap Lewis. In 1686 he sailed from Milford Haven to Pennsylvania. Owing to rough weather the voyage lasted fully twenty-four weeks, during which time the vessel was driven into Barbadoes. He remained in the province only nine months, when he returned to Wales, leaving his young son, who had accompanied him, in the charge of his uncle John Humphrey. It was his intention to have sailed again for Pennsylvania the next spring, with his family, but he did not get back until June, 1697. This delay was probably caused by his succession to a property belonging to his cousin Lewis ap Owen, who having lost his life by an accident, and leaving no issue, Rowland Ellis became entitled under a settlement made by his grandfather, Rees, on the marriage of his uncle, Lewis ap Rees. On his departure from Wales he left his eldest daughter, and heiress by a former wife, in possession of his paternal estate. In Pennsylvania he resided during most of his life upon his plantation of some six hundred acres of land situate a little north of the present Bryn-Mawr Station. This farm is now known as the Morris property. Among other manuscripts left by this early Welsh Friend was the above-mentioned pedigree, a copy of which was made by Rowland E. Evans, uncle of Rowland Evans, Esq., through whom, as I have explained, it came into my possession. The manuscript has this endorsement by Rowland E. Evans: "The annexed pedigree is extracted from one in the hand writing of Rowland Ellis, except the names in parenthesis (") which are inserted in the original in a different hand. The original, it may be presumed from the omission of his daughter Catherine, was written prior to 1697, at which time her birth had happened, and if it had been written after that event, her name, as may be supposed, would not have been omitted. The part of the original not copied here is the pedigree of Rowland Ellis's first wife. The parts between brackets [ ] are additions here." As this genealogy is in the form of a chart it is, for convenience, here given much after the style of the ancient Welsh Heralds:

Rowland (Ellis) of Brin Mawr in Merionethshire, in Wales, born 1650, also described as of Dyffryden in 1677. He was son of Ellis, ap Rees, ap Lewis, ap Sion, ap Gruffydd, ap Howell. The mother of Rowland Ellis was Anne verch Humphrey, ap Hugh, ap David, ap Howell, ap Gronw(y). The mother of Anne verch Humphrey, was Elizabeth verch John. The mother of Elizabeth verch John, was Sibill verch Hugh Gwynn or Penarth. The mother of Sibill verch Hugh, was Jane verch Sir Hugh

---

*For more information on Ellis see Thomas Glenn's *Merion in the Welsh Tract* (1896; repr. Baltimore: Genealogical Publishing Co., Inc., 1970). See also Thomas Glenn's Welsh *Founders of Pennsylvania*, 2 vols. (1911, 1913, repr. Baltimore: Genealogical Publishing Co., Inc., 1970).

Owen. The mother of Humphrey ap Hugh, was Catherine verch Sion, ap Rhydderch Wyn Abergyno. The mother of Hugh ap David, ap Howell, was Mary verch Hugh Sion Bedo. The mother of Ellis ap Rees, ap Lewis, was Catherine verch Ellisa, ap David, ap Owen, ap Thomas, ap Howell, ap Mrhedydd, ap Gruffydd Derwas. The mother of Catherine verch Ellisa ap David, was Mary verch Sion, ap David, ap Gruffydd. The mother of Rees ap Lewis, was Ellin verch Howell Gruffydd. The mother of Lewis ap John Gruffydd was Elsbeth verch Dd Lloydd. Rowland Ellis married first Margaret daughter of Ellis Morris, descended from Gruffydd Derwas, and had issue: Ann, and Jane. He married secondly his cousin, Margaret, daughter of Robert ap Owen, ap Lewis, ap Sion, ap Gruffydd, ap Howell. The mother of Margaret verch Robert ap Owen, was Margaret verch Sion, ap Lewis, ap Tyddwr, ap Ednyved, ap Howell, ap Mrhedydd, ap Gruffydd Derwas. The mother of Margaret verch Sion ap Lewis, was Agnes verch Owen, ap Thomas, ap Owen, ap Thomas, ap Howell, ap Mrheydd, ap Gruffydd Derwas. The mother of Agnes verch Owen, ap Thomas, was Mary verch Ellisa (Byrin?) The mother of Robert ap Owen, ap Lewis, was Mary, verch Tudwr Vaughan, ap David Llwydd, ap Tyddwr. Vaughan, ap Gruffydd ap Howell [ap Gr. Derwas]. The mother of Mary verch Tudwr Vaughan, was Agnes verch Lewis ap Mrheydd. [The mother of Agnes, was Elin verch Robert ap Howell, ap David, ap Mevrig]. The mother of Owen ap Lewis, was Elin verch Howell Gruffydd. The mother of Lewis ap Sion Gruffydd, was Elsbeth verch David Lloyd.

Rowland Ellis had, by his second wife, five children: Elizabeth, Rowland, Ellin. (m. John Evans of Gwynedd), (Catherine).

A few explanations to the foregoing pedigree are desirable. Rowland Ellis was a descendant of the Nannau family, and it is in part the descent of that ancient house in Merionethshire that is here given. Humphrey ap Hugh was father, it appears, of John Humphrey of Llwyn-dv, the uncle of Rowland Ellis. According to Dwnn, II. 252, David ap Howell, ap Gronwy, ap Einion, married Mary, daughter of Howell ap Sion, ap Mer^{dd} ap Deio, descended from Aleth, Lord of Dyvet, the name of Bedo being dropped. This family was of Llwydiarth in Montgomeryshire. Hugh Gwyn's wife was Jane, sister, and not daughter to Sir Hugh Owen, Kt., son of Owen, ap Hugh of Bodean (Bodowen in Anglesea), who signed the visitation 8 Nov. 1588, (Dwnn, 205-6) and died 1613. Hugh Gwyn's daughter married John Powell of Llan Wyddyn. Other particulars will be found in the visitations of Lewis Dwnn II. 22, 241-235. Rowland Ellis was a descendant of Humphrey, Duke of Gloucester, son of John of Gaunt, through the Kynaston family, in the same line as Thomas Lloyd, Dep.-Governor of Pennsylvania.

THOMAS ALLEN GLENN.

PARENTAGE OF MAJOR JOHN FENWICK, FOUNDER OF SALEM, NEW JERSEY

BY EDWIN JAQUETT SELLERS
OF PHILADELPHIA.

Visitations of *Northumberland, 1615, 1666*, edited by Joseph Foster, 1876:

Page 51 contains the pedigree of Fenwick of Stanton from Flower's *Visitation of Yorkshire, 1563-4* (p. 121).

Page 52 gives the pedigree of Fenwick of Stanton from the Visitation of 1615.

The discrepancies in these pedigrees concerning the marriages with the Widdrington, Mitford and Corbet families are corrected in the account of the Fenwicks of Stanton in *The History of Northumberland*, by Rev. John Hodgson, 1832, Part II, Vol. II, p. 113, and at p. 112 of the same work is given the pedigree of Corbet of Stanton which shows that the manor of Stanton came to the Fenwick family by an heiress of the Corbet family marrying Sir Ralph Fenwick.

Hodgson's work, p. 113:

> William Fenwick, of Stanton, Esq., born 22 Sept., 1581, in 22 Eliz., 1638, is described as son of Richard and holding the manor of Stanton *in capite* of the king by knight's service. The House of Commons, 20 June, 1645, appointed him a commissioner of taxes for Northumberland. He died June 12, 1647. He married Elizabeth, daughter of Sir Cotton Gargrave, of Nostel, Yorkshire. Richard Fenwick and Margaret his wife, by indenture 8 Aug., 3 Jac. I, 1605, covenanted to acknowledge a fine to his son William Fenwick and his heirs of the manor of Longwitton and lands there and in Hartburn, Bolam, Harnham, Fernylam and North Middleton to the use of him "the said Wm. Fenwick and Elizabeth his now wife, being one of the daughters of Sir Cotton Gargrave, late of Nostal, in the county of York, knight, deceased, and to their heirs males, &c." (Stanton papers.)

They had

Edward Fenwick, of Stanton, Esq., born 29 Oct., 1606; called son and heir apparent of William Fenwick of Stanton in deeds dated 9 July, 1636, and 20 March, 1637, and to which he and his father were parties. (Stanton papers.) He died Aug. 14, 1689. He married Sarah Neville. She died at her daughter's house at Little Bavington 17 April, 1691.

Nine of their children are given, the eldest being Roger Fenwick, born 1632, a colonel in cavalry and slain in 1658.

Caecilia (sister of Edward and mentioned in Visitation of 1615.)

Margaret (sister of Edward and mentioned in Vist. of 1615.) William Fenwick's other children were born after 1615 as they are omitted in that Visitation.

Foster's *Visitations of Northumberland, 1615, 1666,* p. 54, Visitation of 1666, agrees with Hodgson's *History of Northumberland,* Part II, Vol. II, p. 17, concerning the following:

Sir William Fenwick, of Wallington, Knt., whose will was dated 1612, married, first, Grace, daughter and coheiress of Sir John Forster, of Edderston, Knt., and, second, Margaret, daughter of William Selby, of Newcastle, Esq. Her will was dated 1631.

By the first marriage they had

Sir John Fenwick, of Wallington, Knight and Baronet, who died circa 1658.

By the second marriage they had

Sir William Fenwick, of Meldon, who was buried 31, May, 1652.

Sir John and Sir William were, therefore, half-brothers but called *brothers* in deed of 1636 hereafter mentioned.

The Register of Admissions to Gray's Inn, 1521–1889, by Joseph Foster, 1889:

Page 94. 1597–8, Mar. 22. William Fenwick, gent., son and heir apparent of Richard Fenwick, of Stanton, Co. of Northumberland.

Page 147. 1617, Aug. 12. Edward Fenwick, son and heir of William Fenwick, of Stanton, Northumberland.

Page 221. 1638–9, Mar. 15. John Fenwick, second son of William Fenwick, of Stanton, Northumberland, Esq. (This refers to Major John Fenwick, of Salem, N. J., as will later appear.)

Page 232. 1641, June 28. Roger Fenwick, third son of William Fenwick, of Stanton, Northumberland, Esq.

It will be observed that William Fenwick, of Stanton, and three of his sons, Edward, John and Roger, were students of Gray's Inn.

A copy of the deed hereafter referred to was presented to the New Jersey Historical Society by the late Col. Robert G. Johnson. The following synopsis was made by Mr. Geo. B. Macaltioner, of Haddonfield, New Jersey:

> Indenture dated the 8th of July, 1636, between William Fenwick, of Stanton, Esq., of the Co. of Northumberland, and Edward Fenwick, son and heir apparent of the said William Fenwick, of the first part; Francis Neville, of Cheate, Esq., of the second part; and John Heron, of Burkley, in said Co. of Northumberland, Esq., and Edward Burdett, of Carron, Co. Northumberland, Gent., of the third part. The said parties of the first and second parts lease to the parties of the third part, in consideration of £500, the Manor of Stanton and certain other lands and messuages in Stanton in the parish of Horsley, Co. of Northumberland, during the lives of said William Fenwick and Elizabeth his wife and the said Edward Fenwick and Sarah his wife and after their deaths to the use of Roger Fenwick, son and heir apparent of the said Edward Fenwick, then to the use of William Fenwick, second son of the said Edward Fenwick then to the use of Peter Fenwick, the third son of said Edward Fenwick, then to the use of John Fenwick, the fourth son of the said Edward Fenwick, and then to the use, respectively, of the fifth, sixth, seventh, eighth, ninth and tenth sons of the said Edward Fenwick, then to the use of Sir John Fenwick, of Wallington, Co. of Northumberland, Knight and Baronet, and Sir William Fenwick his brother; said lease to be for the term of thirty years when the lease should cease. After the deaths of the children of the said Edward Fenwick the said lease is further conveyed to the use of John Fenwick, second son of the said William Fenwick, and his heirs and in case of default of issue to Roger Fenwick, third son of the said William Fenwick, and his heirs and in default of issue to Ralph Fenwick, fourth son of the said William Fenwick, and his heirs, and in default of issue to the right heirs of the said William Fenwick forever. (In Hodgson's account of Edward Fenwick, son of William and Elizabeth, previously given, mention is made of a deed of 9 July, 1636, which refers, evidently, to the foregoing deed, either the 8th or the 9th of July being an error.)

Binfield is a parish in the hundred of Cookham, County of Berks, 3½ miles northeast from Working-

ham. This place is situated in the midst of the tract called the Royal Hunt, in Windsor Forest. (Lewis' *Topographical Dict.*)
Visitations of Berkshire, 1532, 1566, 1623, 1665–6, published by the Harleian Society, Vol. LVII, p. 43:

List of those summoned to appear.
Cookeham Hundred, Binfield.
John Fenwick (No. app.) Summoned to Redding Assizes 1666/5.
Prisoner in Reading being a Quaker.

The following deed is in possession of Mr. William B. Goodwin, of Hartford, Conn., a descendant of the South Carolina branch of the Fenwick family:

This Indenture—tripartite—made the ninth day of November . . . one thousand six hundred sixty and eight, between John Fenwick of Binfield in the County of Berks, gentleman, of the first part, and Edward Fenwick and William Fenwick of Stanton in the County of Northumberland, gentlemen, of the second part, and Marke Milbank of the borough and County of Newcastle-upon-Tyne, esquire, of the third part. WHEREAS by a certain decree made in the High Court of Chancery between the said John Fenwick, complainant, and the said William Fenwick and William Boa of Cammo, in the County of Northumberland, gentlemen, and other defendants, bearing date the 29th day of June in the sixteenth year of the reign of our said sovereign lord King Charles II that now reigns, it was Ordered and Decreed that the said Edward Fenwick and William Fenwick should pay unto the said John Fenwick the sum of eight hundred pounds then in arrears and unpaid of a rent charge of fifty pounds per annum issuing out of the manor and Lordship of Stanton aforesaid with Thappiscombe in the said County of Northumberland and out of all the lands, tenements and hereditaments of the said Edward and William Fenwick in Stanton aforesaid and should continue the payment thereof as the same should grow due, and that the said William Boa who was seized of and to whom and his heirs the said rent charge was granted in trust for the said John Fenwick, should convey the said rent charge to the said then complainant, John Fenwick and his heirs, AND WHEREAS the said John Fenwick hath prosecuted the said Decree to a sequestration issuing out of the said Court of Chancery to sequester the said Manor and lands and premises to satisfy the same . . . and also the arrears incurred since the said decree with the growing annuity and to continue the same sequestration and growing payments till the same with the arrears and damages for non-payment and the cost of the said John Fenwick should be fully satisfied unto the said John Fenwick, his executors and assigns, which said moneys and arrears due upon the said decree and sequestration have been adjusted and settled between the said John Fenwick and the said Edward and William Fenwick, AND WHEREAS the said John Fenwick, together with William Fenwick of Nunriding, in the County of Northumberland, gentlemen, John Stangboy of Clemens Inn in the County of Middlesex, gentleman, and William Swinoe of Lincoln's Inn in the said County of Middlesex, gentleman, three of the sequestrators in the said commission of sequestration named, did, by their deed indented, bearing date this third day of April in the nineteenth year of the reign of our said sovereign lord Charles the second, that now is reigning . . . demise . . . unto the said William Fenwick, Thomas Spratt, James Fenwick, William Hull, Thomas Forster, Thomas Robinson, Nicholas Bartram, Henry Henderson and Richard Martyn, their executors, administrators and assigns, all that the said manor or lordship of Stanton with the appurtenances in the said County of Northumberland and all those several messuages, lands, (etc.) . . . situate . . . within the said Manor of Stanton . . . then in the possession of the said William Fenwick, Thomas Spratt, James Fenwick, William Hull, Thomas Forster, Thomas Robinson, Nicholas Bartram, Henry Henderson and Richard Martyn or any of them . . . TO have and to hold the said manor or lordship, lands, tenements and other the premises unto the said William Fenwick, Thomas Spratt, James Fenwick, William Hull, Thomas Forster, Thomas Robinson, Nicholas Bartram, Henry Henderson and Richard Martin from the Feast of Penticost then next ensuing the date of the said rented indenture unto the full end and terms of one whole year . . . and so from year to year so long as they, the said John Fenwick, William Fenwick, John Stangboy and William Swinoe, the said sequestrators, and the said William Fenwick should please, YIELDING and paying yearly unto the said John Fenwick, William Fenwick, John Stangboy and William Swinoe . . . for the use of the said John Fenwick, party to the said deed, the yearly rent of one hundred pounds of lawful money of England at the feast of St. Martyn the Bishop, in Winter, and the said feast of Penticost or within thirty days next after by equal portions as in and by the said rented indenture relation being thereunto had, may appear AND WHEREAS there is still due on the said Decree and sequestration the sum of One Thousand and Two Hundred Pounds besides the sum of Seven Hundred Pounds hereinafter mentioned to be paid for the consideration of the growing annuity which said seven hundred pounds is to be paid in such sort as hereinafter is mentioned AND WHEREAS the said William Boa in pursuance of the said Decree hath by indenture, tripartite, bearing date the first day of April, proximo, Quarterly, made between the said William Boa of the first part and the said Edward Fenwick and William Fenwick of the second part and the said John Fenwick of the third part, granted and assigned the said annuity or rent charge to the said John Fenwick, his heirs and assigns . . . NOW THIS INDENTURE WITNESSETH that the said John Fenwick by and with the direction of the said William Fenwick . . . as well for and in consideration of the sum of seven hundred pounds . . . to him, the said John Fenwick, in hand paid by the said William Fenwick and Mark Milbank at and before the sealing and delivery of these puissances . . . . HATH by the direction and appointment of the said Edward and William Fenwick, granted . . . unto the said Mark Milbank . . . ALL that the said annuity . . . of fifty pounds . . . issuing . . . out of all that the said Manor of Stanton and out of all and every the messuages lands (etc.) . . . of or belonging to the said William Fenwick and Edward Fenwick . . . together with all such power and authority upon default of payment of the said rent charge to enter into the premises charged thereon (etc.) . . . BUT it is nevertheless hereby declared and agreed by and between all and every the said parties to these powers, that these powers or the rent hereon to be levied by the said John Fenwick and Dame Mary, his wife, formerly called Dame Mary Rogers, nor anything herein conveyed, shall in any sort extend or be . . . made use of or construed to hinder or debar the said John Fenwick . . . or the said sequestrators . . . levying the said one thousand two hundred pounds or any part thereof and for that purpose the said Decree and sequestration is and are to stand and shall or may be prosecuted for payment . . . being all due before the rent charge was agreed to be granted and assigned for the said seven hundred pounds, which said seven hundred pounds was and is only given for the said growing rent charge and hath no relation to the said one thousand two hundred pounds, being former arrears and moneys due on the said decree and sequestration which the said John Fenwick . . . to have and receive over and besides the said seven hundred pounds. IN WITNESS WHEREOF the parties above named to these present Indentures interchangeably have set their hands and seals the day and year above written.

ED. FENWICK   W. FENWICK   JOHN FENWICK

(ENDORSEMENTS)

Signed sealed and delivered by the within named John Fenwick in the presence of us

> John Cudworth
> Rich. Nelson
> Jo. Stenyard
> Robert Fenwick

Signed sealed and delivered after the information of these words or the premises to be leased by the said John Fenwick and Dame Mary his wife formerly called Dame Mary Rogers in the prce. of us
       George Airey
       John Airey
       Gerrard Stokeld
Sealed and delivered by the within named Edward Fenwick in the presence of us
       James Fenwick
       Gerrard Stokeld

The pleadings of the bill of complaint filed by John Fenwick in the Chancery proceedings referred to would show the basis of the suit and his relationship to the Fenwicks mentioned. Probably, there was reference to the lease of 1636 previously mentioned.

The will of Major John Fenwick is recorded at Salem, N. J., in Liber. 2. fol. 103. The original will is in possession of the New Jersey Historical Society. The following are extracts therefrom:

"I John Fenwick late of Binfield in the Countie of Berks in the Kingdom of England Esq. the late absolute Lord or Chiefe propriate by law & survivorship of the province of Nova Caesaria or New Jersey and now of Fenwick's Coloney."

"& for want of such heires to *Roger Fenwick my nephew eldest sonn to my deceased brother Capt. Ralfe Fenwick* for life and after his decease to the heires male of his body lawfully begotten & for want of such heires to his brother for life & to his heirs male lawfully begotten and for want of such heires to his brother for life and to his heires male lawfully begotten & for want of such heires to the heires female of my sd grandchilde forever Elizabeth Adams totally excepted & her heirs forever."

Dated 7 August, 1683.
Proved 16 (6?) April, 1684.
Recorded 5 May, 1684.

Extracts from a letter of Edward Fenwick, of London, July 27, 1726, to his cousin Roger Fenwick, of Little Isle near Skibbereen, in the County of Cork, Ireland. A copy of this letter was obtained by Edward Fenwick of South Carolina, nephew of the writer of the letter, during a visit to the latter (the visit being referred to in the letter) and has been preserved by his descendants. The letter was printed in the appendix of *The Life of Commodore Josiah Tattnall,* by Charles C. Jones, Jr., Savannah, 1878. The extracts here given are quoted from a copy obtained from Mr. Wm. B. Goodwin of Hartford, Conn., a descendant of the nephew Edward Fenwick referred to in the letter:

"You were pleased to acquaint me that the original of your family's settlement in Ireland was by your grandfather, *Ralph Fenwick, who went into that Kingdom an officer in Cromwell's army,* and that your father, Charles Fenwick, died soon after the Revolution, leaving you a good estate". . .

"I perceive you have never been in England yourself". . .

"I shall only begin from the time of my great-grandfather, William Fenwick, who was born at Stanton the 22d, Sept., 1581, and died at the same place the 12th July, 1647. He left several children but his eldest son (my grandfather) was Edward Fenwick, born at Stanton 29th October, 1606, and died there the 14th August, 1689; and your grandfather *Ralph Fenwick* was a younger brother of this Edward Fenwick, my grandfather, who had eleven children. His eldest son was Roger Fenwick, born at Stanton the 18th March, 1632, but he was killed at the siege of Dunkirk at an assault in mounting the breaches at Mardike, 1658—he being then Colonel of a regiment of horse. After this Roger Fenwick's death, my grandfather's second son, William Fenwick, became his heir, and married and died soon after, but left a son named Roger Fenwick who inherited the Stanton estate after my grandfather's death. This Roger Fenwick also married, but died soon after, leaving a son John Fenwick, who now inherits the Stanton estate and is the first of the name and family. My father, Robert Fenwick, was the next son of my grandfather to William Fenwick above mentioned . . . .but he married a gentlewoman of the county by whom he had a considerable fortune. My father had eight children and I was his third son. . . . My eldest brother happened to be killed in a duel soon after he came to man's estate. My second brother went into the Army, a cornet in the House Service, in the last wars, and he also happened to be . . . wounded in the first engagement . . . and died soon after. I . . . went into the East Indies where I lived a merchant above eleven years . . . about eight years ago I married very happily and settled here in London, where I have lived ever since; but I have no children of my own living; neither are there any of my father's children living but myself and my youngest brother John Fenwick, who went into the West Indies about twenty years ago, and has acquired a very good estate in South Carolina, where he now lives in a a married state and has four or five children. The two eldest of them, a son and a daughter, are now in England under my care. . . ."

The letter is interesting as agreeing with the Visitations and Hodgson's account of the family, although written many years prior to the publication of those works.

The foregoing references show that Sir John Fenwick, of Wallington, Knight and Baronet, and his half-brother Sir William Fenwick, of Meldon, were of the eldest branch of the family. Sir John has been confused by several writers for John Fenwick, second son of William Fenwick, of Stanton, all of whom are mentioned in the deed of 1636 previously mentioned. John, the said second son, mentioned in the Admissions to Gray's Inn, is identified as John Fenwick, of Binfield mentioned in the Visitation of Berkshire, 1665-6, in the deed of 1668, which shows his interest in the Manor of Stanton, and as the testator "John Fenwick late of Binfield in the Countie of Berks" in the will of John Fenwick of Salem, New Jersey, which latter document establishes his death between 7 Aug., 1683, the date of the will, and its probate 16 (6?), April, 1684. The letter of Edward Fenwick of 1726 refers to Ralph Fenwick (son of William) as "being an officer in Cromwell's army" and, therefore, identifies the "deceased brother Capt. Ralfe Fenwick" mentioned by John Fenwick, of Salem, in his will.

Proceedings of the New Jersey Historical Society, Vol. IV, p. 53 (1849), contains a "Memoir of John Fenwick, Chief Proprietor of Salem Tenth, New Jersey," by Robert G. Johnson. The page numbers refer to that work:

P. 54. Col. Johnson confuses John Fenwick, of N. J., with the Sir John Fenwick, of Wallington, Knight and Baronet, in referring to the deed of 1636, which error was followed by the late John Clement, Esq., in his life of John Fenwick. William Fenwick, father of John of N. J., is also confused with Sir William Fenwick, of Meldon, half-brother of Sir John Fenwick of Wallington.

In referring to John Fenwick's first marriage, Col. Johnson says:

"It was previous to the year 1642, most probably 1641. She was Elizabeth, daughter of Sir Walter Covert, Knight, of Slaugham, in the County of Sussex." (Footnote:) "He had two sons and two daughters. The sons were Thomas and John —the daughters were Anna and Elizabeth. Thomas Covert being the eldest son, and heir apparently, gave to his two sisters a lease dated 30th January, 1639, for sixty years (at a rent of one pepper corn) of land called Sniderly, Hoggesland, and Denscombe, containing 700 acres. Also land called Rowle, Friende Betchlies, Sowlers, and Courtlands, containing 177 acres, situate in the parishes of Slaugham, Bolney, and Fineham, in the County of Sussex. Thomas Covert having died, John Covert, his brother and heir, confirmed the lease to his sisters. Anna Covert having died, her sister Elizabeth became the sole owner of the whole lease; and she having married one John Fenwick, they, husband and wife, conveyed the lease to a trustee for his benefit. This conveyance was dated 27 Nov., 1642. After that, to wit: on the 6th Dec., 1649, it was conveyed to other trustees, namely, Henry Brandreth, merchant, and Samuel Taylor, haberdasher, both of London, for the benefit of the said Elizabeth as long as she lived; and, in case of her death, for her husband John Fenwick if he should survive her. These trustees joined John Fenwick in a mortgage, with Elizabeth his wife, dated in 1651, for the sum of £950, loaned to them by John Goodwin, gentleman, of London.

"Neither have I ascertained at what time he married his second wife, Mary, who was connected with the Burdett family."

We have seen that the second wife was formerly "Dame Mary Rogers," consequently, she appears to have been a widow when she married John Fenwick.

"An Historical Account of the First Settlement of Salem, in West Jersey, by John Fenwick, Esq., Chief Proprietor of the same," by R. G. Johnson, 1839, page 46, letter from Mary Fenwick to John Fenwick, 27 Aug., 1678 (in possession of N. J. His. Soc.):

"I should have told thee first that I received thine sent by Sir Edmund Andross, and I came to London in January purposely to wait on him about giving thee liberty, as thou didst desire me; and the Earl of Carlisle, who is since going to be Governor of Jamaica, spoke to him in thy behalf, by my cousin Edward Burdet's means; and thy cousin Edward Burdet went to him himself," etc.

As Edward Burdet is mentioned as a cousin of both Fenwick and Mary his wife, Fenwick and his wife may have been cousins through a Burdet relationship, unless only one was a cousin of Burdet and the other called him cousin on that account. It will be recalled that in the deed of 1636 an Edward Burdett, of Carron, County of Northumberland, was one of the parties of the third part, consequently, as the date of that deed was prior to John Fenwick's marriage to "Dame Mary Rogers," John Fenwick may have been the cousin of Edward Burdet.

Johnson's "Memoir of John Fenwick," p. 54, et seq., refers to the Commission of Oliver Cromwell, dated 27th October, 1648, appointing John Fenwick a "Major under Colonel Thomas Barwis, in the regiment of cavalry, which was raised in the county of Westmoreland to assist the garrison of Carlisle." "The second commission was similar, requiring him as a Major of Cavalry to attend the decapitation of Charles 1st, which took place on 30th January, 1648." "So also John Bradshawe, the President of the judges of that court who passed sentence of death upon the King, and who was subsequently chosen President of that Parliament, specially appointed Fenwick Captain of a troop of horse, by him to be raised from volunteers, who were to act as a guard to that Parliament. . . . This commission was dated . . . 4th September, 1651." (This commission is in possession of N. J. His. Soc.)

Johnson, p. 60, gives the reference to the arrival of John Fenwick with his children at Salem 23rd June, 1675, in the *Griffin*, Capt. Robert Griffith.

P. 83. "He died December, 1683, aged about 65 years."

P. 85. "The names by which the farms (of John Fenwick in England) were distinguished, were those of Brockham and Worminghurst. His principal estate at Stanton he had leased to Colonel Nicholas Fenwick, his cousin, for the sum of £445 per annum. In his book ('Commonplace Book', in possession of Salem His. Soc.,) he charges money laid out for the house at Worminghurst—where I am inclined to think his family usually resided."

History and Genealogy of Fenwick's Colony, by Thomas Shourds, of Salem County, 1876, p. 9, states inaccurately that "His second wife was Mary Burdett, the daughter of Sir Walter Burdett." He assumed that the second wife was a Burdett and confused the name of her father with Sir Walter Covert, father of John Fenwick's first wife.

PARENTAGE OF MAJOR JOHN FENWICK, FOUNDER OF SALEM, NEW JERSEY

BY EDWIN JAQUETT SELLERS
OF PHILADELPHIA.

Sussex Archaeological Collections, Vol. XLII, p. 112:

Steyning Marriages, etc., during the Commonwealth, 1653 to 1658. Extracted from the Steyning Parish Registers. Entry of a marriage performed 29 May, 1654, by John Fenwick, Esq., one of the Justices of the Peace for the County of Sussex.

Synopsis of the Bill and Answer in the Chancery proceedings referred to in the indenture of 9 November, 1668 (*Pa. Mag.*, XLIX, p. 154):

Chancery Proceedings. Bridges. Bundle 37, No. 140. (Public Record Office, London):

John Fenwick *v.* Francis Nevill, Edward Fenwick and William Fenwick.

The Bill in Equity, dated 8 May, 1661, of John Fenwick, of Bray, Co. Berks, stated that about 25 years since William Fenwick, of Stanton, Co. Northumberland, Esq., his late father, deceased, and Edward Fenwick, son and heir apparent of the said Wm. Fenwick, elder brother of plaintiff, and Francis Nevill, of Chevett, Co. York, were seised in fee of the Manor of Stanton, Co. Northumberland, and of several messuages, lands and tenements in Stanton in the parish of Horsley in said county, of the yearly value of £600; that by indenture of 2 (?) July, 12 Charles I (1636) the said William Fenwick and Edward Fenwick of the first part, and Francis Nevill of the second part, sold to John Heron, of Birkley, Co. Northumberland, and Edward Burdett, of Carron in said county, of the third part, and their heirs the manor house and manor of Stanton, and other named lands, tenements and buildings in Stanton, for the purposes declared, to wit, that the said Francis Nevill, his heirs and assigns should have *pretence* and receive out of the rent and profits thereof the yearly rent of £50, and if the same should be unpaid for 20 days the said Edward and

William Fenwick should pay weekly to the said Francis Nevill, his heirs, etc., £5 as long as said rent should be in arrears, with right of distraint in the said Nevill; that, nevertheless, the said Edward and William Fenwick on 9 July, 12 Charles I (1636) by indenture sold to William Rea, of Camma, Co. Northumberland, gentleman, and Robert Watson, gentleman, of said county, and their heirs the said rent charges of £50, and although it was stated in said indenture that the same was in consideration of £700 to be paid the said Francis Nevill by the said William Rea and Robert Watson, neither of them did pay said sum nor any part thereof, whereupon the said Francis Nevill came to an agreement with the said Edward and William Fenwick, 4 June, 1640, made between the said Francis Nevill, of the first part, the said William Fenwick and Edward Fenwick, William Rea and Robert Watson, of the second part, and Sir John Fenwick, of Wallington, Co. Northumberland, Knight and Baronet, and the plaintiff John Fenwick, second son of the said William Fenwick, gent., of the third part, wherein in consideration of £830 the said Francis Nevill assigned to Sir John Fenwick and the plaintiff John Fenwick all his interest in the Manor of Stanton, Provided always that if the said Sir John Fenwick and the plaintiff John Fenwick, William and Edward Fenwick failed to pay the sum of £830 to Francis Nevill or his heirs that the said sale should be void and that no yearly rent of £50 should be paid until the said Francis Nevill had received the £830. That the said Sir John Fenwick, Edward Fenwick and John Fenwick the plaintiff became bound to the said Francis Nevill in the sum of £1400 for the payment of the said £830.

That the said Edward Fenwick importuned the said Sir John Fenwick and John Fenwick the plaintiff to suffer him to enjoy the said premises, rents, issues and profits, promising to pay the said £830, whereupon the said Edward Fenwick was allowed to enter into said premises. That the said Sir John Fenwick, William Fenwick and Robert Watson being dead, the said Edward Fenwick, Francis Nevill and William Rea combined with William Fenwick, son and heir of the said Edward Fenwick, to defraud the plaintiff John Fenwick of the said annuity and arrears of the same, and that they refused to produce the said agreements, indentures, etc.

The Answer of Francis Nevill, dated 27 September, 1661, stated that it might be true that there were such conveyances as claimed in the Bill, and that a statute was executed to secure the payment of £50 per annum but that he believed that no use was made of said statute. That Edward Fenwick, named in the Bill, having married about 36 years since one of this defendant's sisters; that this defendant, finding the estate of the said Edward oppressed with debts, in brotherly affection was willing to give same cost for the preservation of the same, but what was done he did not remember. That the said Edward Fenwick being oppressed by the dealings of his father William Fenwick, and the plaintiff, prevailed upon this defendant to preserve the Manor of Stanton, and sundry sums were disbursed for redemption of the said estate, of which there was still £500 unpaid to him, this defendant. That some estate was passed in trust to Sir John Fenwick, Bart., and the plaintiff John Fenwick, whereupon they became bound to pay several sums to this defendant, which they never did, but the said Edward Fenwick, after some great loss suffered by the said plaintiff by his undertaking to manage the estate, did re-enter the estate and undertake the payment of the said debts, whereof he has paid part and secured the rest.

(Chancery proceedings, Bridges, Bundle 39, No. 41, is a copy of the same suit.)

The Bill in the foregoing proceedings refers to indenture of 2 July, 12 Charles (1636). The 2nd is apparently an error, as an abstract of said deed is given on page 153 of this volume of the *Pa. Mag.* As the Bill states that the defendant refuses to produce the agreements, indentures, etc., the "2nd" was apparently, given upon memory, and the 8th would seem to have been correct.

The decree of sequestration obtained by John Fenwick is referred to in the deed of 1668 (page 154).

Col. Johnson in his *Memoir of John Fenwick*, p. 60, gives the date of arrival of John Fenwick and his children at Salem in the *Griffin*, Capt. Robert Griffith, as of 23rd June, 1675, which is error as to *June* and *Griffith* as the surname of the captain.

Dr. Carlos E. Godfrey, Director of the Public Record Office, Trenton, N. J., gives the following:

"During the winter I had occasion to employ Stevens & Brown of London to investigate the date of Fenwick's arrival at Salem. Under date of March 2, 1925, this firm writes, in part, the following:

'There are no shipping lists and few Custom House records extant for these early days, so that it is not possible to find from these the date on which the ship left London. The only thing is, to find from other records an approximate date, and though the Colonial Office papers

do not mention anything of the ship, the following items from the Treasury Books and Papers certainly indicate that she could not have sailed until about August:'
" 'May 28, 1675. Warrant from Treasurer Danby to Francis Hodges to seize and prosecute the ship *Griffin* of London, Robert Griffin master, with all her guns &c., which has lately landed in Ireland 20,000 wt. of Virginia tobacco contrary to the law and is now in the Thames. (Treas. Warrants not relating to money. VI. 50.)'
" 'July 9, 1675. Warrant from Treasurer Danby to the Customs Commissioners to discharge the seizure of the ship *Griffin* of London, Robert Griffin master, and to permit her to proceed on her voyage. (Treas. Out Letters, Customs, p. 7.)' "

The exact date of the ship's sailing, after being discharged, has not been obtained. The date of arrival is being investigated.

The deed of 1668, previously mentioned, refers to John Fenwick's second wife as "formerly called Dame Mary Rogers." The following is a synopsis of her will:

The will of Dame Mary Rogers alias Fenwick, of London, widow, dated 19 September, 1699, bequeaths to her grandchildren and great-grandchildren, Sir John Ashfield, Bart., Charles Ashfield, Esq., his son, Sir Edmund Denton, Bart., Edmund Denton, gent., Alexander Denton, John Denton, Mrs. Elizabeth Chamberlain, Richard Chamberlain, her son, Mrs. Carew Denton, Mrs. Mary Howell, Mrs. Bridget Howell, Mrs. Elizabeth Ashfield, Mrs. Anne Ashfield and Mrs. Lucy Ashfield, widow, to each as should be living at testatrix's decease the sum of £5. The residue of her personal estate was bequeathed to her granddaughter, Mrs. Mary Howell, late wife of Doctor William Howell, of London, deceased, whom she appointed sole executrix. Signed, Mary Rogers als. Fenwick. Witnesses, Anne Du Pratt, Mary Tyton, Martha Hind, James Tyton.
Proved at London 17 February, 1699/1700, by Mary Howell, widow and executrix. (P. C. C., 29 Noel.)

Burke's *Landed Gentry* (1858), p. 1030:

Sir Richard Rogers, of Bristol, and Eastwood, Co. Gloucester, born 1594, sheriff of Gloucestershire 1623; died 1635, leaving issue, by Mary his wife, youngest daughter of Sir Henry Marten, Judge of the Prerogative Court, and sister of the celebrated republican and regicide, Col. Henry Marten, two daughters, viz.,

Mary, who inherited Eastwood, married Sir Richard Ashfield, Bart., Sheriff of Gloucestershire, 1668.

Elizabeth (born posthumous) married Edmund Denton, Esq., of Hillesden, Bucks.

It was at the house of Lady Rogers that Col. Fiennes had his headquarters, when holding Bristol for the Long Parliament.

The date of the marriage of John Fenwick to Lady Mary Rogers has not been obtained.

For account of Sir Richard Ashfield, Bart., see *Complete Baronetage*, Vol. II (1902), p. 1, and Burke's *Extinct Baronetcies*.

For pedigree of "Denton of Hillesden," see *History and Antiquities of the County of Buckingham*, by George Lipscomb, Vol. III, p. 17.

PARENTAGE OF MAJOR JOHN FENWICK, FOUNDER OF SALEM, NEW JERSEY.

BY EDWIN JAQUETT SELLERS
OF PHILADELPHIA.

The writer is indebted to Alan Fenwick Radcliffe, Esq., Charterhouse, Godalming, Surrey, England, for reference to the records of which synopses are here given.

Major Fenwick's first wife was Elizabeth, daughter of Sir Walter Covert, of Maidstone, Kent County, and his wife (his second cousin), Anne, daughter of John Covert, of Ewhurst, Sussex County, and his wife Charity, daughter of Sir Martin Bowes, Jr.

For an interesting and ably compiled account of the Covert family, see "The Coverts," by the Rev. Canon J. H. Cooper, Vicar of Cuckfield, in *Sussex, Archaeological Collections*, published by The Sussex Arch. Society, Vol. XLVI, pp. 170–180, Vol. XLVII, pp. 116–147, and Vol. XLVIII, pp. 1–15.

Elizabeth Covert's and her sister Anne Covert's baptisms are quoted from Boxley Registers: "1610, bapt. Elisabeth Walteri Covert. 1613, Anne." (*Sussex Arch. Coll., Coll.* XLVIII, p. 1).

As Edward Fenwick, eldest brother of Major Fenwick, was born 29 Oct., 1606 (Hodgson's *His. of Northumberland*, Pt. II, Vol. II, p. 113), and as Elizabeth Covert was baptized in 1610, possibly Major Fenwick was born about 1608. His baptism has not been obtained.

According to the Covert pedigree by Canon Cooper, Sir Walter Covert and his wife Anne (née Covert) had issue.

   (a) Elizabeth, baptized at Boxley 1610; an executrix of her mother's will. (Married Major John Fenwick.)

(b) Anne, baptized at Boxley 1613; executrix of her mother.
(c) Walter, born 1615; died aged 8 years.
(d) Thomas, born 1618; died Sept. 1643; married Diana, daughter of George, first Lord Goring. She married afterwards George Porter.
(e) Sir John, born 1620; succeeded to Slaugham 1643; died May 1679; administration in P.C.C., May 1860; married Isabel, daughter of William Leigh, of Longborough, Co. Gloucester, widow of George Warmestry.

Anne Covert, wife of Sir Walter Covert, of Maidstone, Co. Kent, was heiress of her uncle Sir Walter Covert, of Slaugham, Sussex, as shown by Canon Cooper.

Synopsis of Dame Anne Coverts' will:

The twentieth day of September, 8 Chas. (1632). I Dame Anne Covert, widow late the wife of Sir Walter Covert Kt. late of Maidstone in the County of Kent. To be buried in or near the sepulchre where my said deceased husband's body was lately layed. Mentions eldest son Thomas Covert, her youngest son John Covert, her cousin Francklyn and his wife her near cousin (not named), her cousin Carkoredg and his wife (not named) her cousin, her father Mr. William Covert lately deceased, her daughters Elizabeth Covert and Anne Covert whom she appoints sole executors; she mentions also her deceased uncle Sir Walter Covert; she bequeaths the wardship of her sons to her kinsmen Sir Francis Barneham, Kt., her uncle Sir Thom. Colepeper, Kt., and her cousin James Francklyn. Signed, Anne Covert. Witnesses, Edw. Duke, Robt. Cooper, Fran. Seyar, Mich. Beaver.

Proved at London 13 November, 1632 by Elizabeth Covert and Anne Covert, daughters and executors of the said deceased. (P.C.C., London, Audley 111.)

John Fenwicke of Grays Inn co. Middlesex gentleman and Elizabeth his wife, executrix and one of the daughters of Dame Anne Covert, deceased, pltfs.

v.

Walter Francklyn and Sir John Henden, defendants.

Bill, dated 10 May 1644, for an accounting and possession of land. It mentions James Frankline of the Middle Temple, London, Esquire, deceased; Parsonage of Eboney in Kent the subject of suit; the said Elizabeth and Anne Covert her sister, since deceased; Walter Frankline, son and heir of said James Frankline; Sir John Henden, Bart., Sir —— Henden late one of the Barons of the Exchequer; that the said Lady Anne Covert died leaving the plaintiff and her sister very young, namely of about the age of 14 or 17 years (as Elizabeth was baptized 1610, she was 22 years old in 1632, date of Lady

Covert's will, and her sister Anne, who was baptized 1613, was 19 years old in 1632); that the said James Frankline died about four years ago. ; Walter Frankline was his son and executor; Bentley Lease in Sussex also subject of suit; that the said Walter Frankline refused and refuses to deliver the deeds or deliver possession of Bentley Lease to the plaintiff or her sister, or to the plaintiff now as sole executrix; the bill prays that Sir John Henden shall set forth what estate he has in the parsonage and that he may render an account and satisfaction.

(The proceeding does not contain any answers.)
(Chancery Proceedings, Mitford, 126/87. Public Record office, London.)

Synopsis of Will of Thomas Covert (d) aforesaid. I Thomas Covert, of Slaugham in the County of Sussex, Esquire, 30 July, 1642. To be buried in the newly erected Chapel adjoining the Parish Church of Slaugham. Mentions Diana his wife, Anne and Diana his daughters, mentions possibility of his wife being with child and disposition of his estate according to whether it be a son or daughter; bequeaths to his daughter Anne two silver dishes which the Earl of Holland, her godfather, gave her at christening, and to Diana the other daughter the great silver dish which the Countess Dowager of Devonshire, her godmother, gave her at christening. Mentions also a lease dated 6 March, 18 Chas. I (1642), by him to Sir William Culpeper of Wakehurst in co. of Sussex, Baronet, and William Hippisley, of London, Esquire, for forty years, in trust for his use, etc.; his wife Diana and Walter Burrell, Esquire, and William Fettiplace, gentleman, his two kinsmen, to be sole Executors and Executrix of his will. Residuary estate to his next heir male. Signed, Thomas Covert. Witnesses, Toby Hipplesley, William Devereux, William Cartwright, Ra: Bird, Robert Lanton, John Freer.

Proved at London 8 Oct., 1650, by the oath of Diana Covert, relict and of the Executors named in the will. Power reserved to Walter Burrell and William Fettiplace the other Executor. (P.C.C., London, 164 Pembroke.)

The foregoing will of Thomas Covert is given because he is referred to on page 160 of Vol. XLIX of the *Pennsylvania Magazine.*

Commission dated 22 May, 1652, from the Keepers of the liberty of England by authority of Parliament directed to Sir Thomas Handley, knt., John Burrell, John Oliver the younger, Richard Kidder, Richard Isted, William Cooper, John Viney, Edward Henshawe & William Bristow, gentlemen. Whereas John Fenwick, Esq., and his wife, plaintiffs, have exhibited their bill of complaint against Sir William Culpeper, Baronet,

William Hipplesley, Peter Courthopp, William Fettiplace, Walter Burrell, John Covert and Walter Francklyn, Esquires, defendants, who have failed to answer the said bill, the said Commissioners are commanded to take the answers of the said defendants to be made to the said bill, the tenor of which is sent them inclosed in these presents, and to send the same answers into the Court of Chancery in eight days after Holy Trinity next.

Bill dated 7 May 1652.

The plaintiffs, John Fenwick of Brockham co. Surrey, Esquire, and Elizabeth his wife, state that Sir Walter Covert late of Slaugham co. Sussex, knt., deceased, was seised to him and his heirs, during the lives of Walter Burrell and Walter Covert of lands in Cuckfield and other places in Sussex, which came to the said Sir Walter by lease or grant from Lord Burgaveny, or some other person, which were called Bentley Lease. After his death the same came to Lady Anne Covert as his *cousin* and heir, that is to say, daughter and heir to John Covert brother and heir to the said Sir Walter.

The said Dame Anne Covert, being so seised, and having issue Thomas Covert, John Covert, the plaintiff Elizabeth and Anne Covert, by her indenture dated on or about 9 September, 1632, granted the premises with all the deeds concerning them to James Francklyn then of Maidstone co. Kent, Esq., since deceased, and his heirs, during the lives of Walter Burrell and Walter Covert, in trust for the benefit of the said Elizabeth and her sister Anne equally, with power of revocation. The said Dame Anne soon after died, having appointed her two daughters executors of her will. The plaintiff Elizabeth obtained administration of her deceased sister's estate. The said James Francklyn took possession of the premises and received profits until his death. He made his eldest son Walter executor of his will, who, after his father's death, took possession and received profits. The said James and Walter Francklyn, or one of them, have made some estate thereof to some person or persons, under color of which the said Thomas Covert, although knowing of the trust, by himself and his agents, namely, Peter Courthorpe, Walter Burrell and William Fettiplace, during his life have received the rents and made some estate thereof to other persons. In July 1642 he (the said Thomas Covert) made his will and died possessed of sufficient estate to have made satisfaction to the plaintiffs. After his death Sir William Culpeper of Wakehurst co. Sussex, Baronet, and William Hipplesley of London, Esquire, pretending to be entrusted by Thomas Covert on behalf of John Covert, his brother and heir male, and for Anne and Diana the daughters and heirs of said Thomas Covert, have received the rents, although they know that Dame Anne Covert conveyed to them in trust for her said daughters.

The plaintiffs show that James and Walter Francklyn, Thomas Covert, George Porter and Diana his wife, Peter Courthorpe, Walter Burrell, William Fettiplace, William Culpeper, William Hipplesley, John Covert and Diana Covert have received the rents and concealed the deeds concerning the premises and have defaced the metes and bounds so that they cannot distinguish their land from lands of Thomas Covert. Although often asked in a friendly manner, they have refused to give up possession of the premises.

The plaintiffs pray for the help of the Court.

The joint and several answers of Peter Courthorpe, Esq., Walter Burrell, Esq., and William Fettiplace, gentleman, three of the defendants.

They believe that Sir Walter Covert was seised of land in Cuckfield as stated. They have never seen the said lease, except William Fettiplace, 4 or 5 years ago saw a box in which he believes it was, which was in the custody of a widow, whose name he does not remember, in Holborn, where the residue of the writings concerning the estate of Sir Walter Covert then were by the direction of Diana Porter wife of George Porter. None of these defendants have known of the lands called Bentley Lease. The said Sir Walter Covert being so seised of the said lands, about the 23rd of July, 1631, demised to Sir Thomas Pelham, Baronet, and to these defendants, all his manors and lands in Sussex, Surrey and Kent or elsewhere, except the Rectory of Ebony in Kent, for 21 years after the death of Sir Walter Covert at a yearly rent of a penny, if demanded, in trust for Dame Jane Covert his wife, with remainder as he might by will appoint.

About the 26th of July, 1631, the said Sir Walter Covert conveyed all his manors and lands in Slaugham, Twineham, Ashington, Washington, Thakeham, Worminghurst, Horsham, Shipley, Sullington, Hitchingfield, Ifield, Crawley, Cuckfield, Balcombe, Worth, Bolney, Russington, Woodmancoate, Hurst, Beeding, Warneham, Aldrington, Portslade, Hove, Rusfer, and Wivelsfield in Sussex to the use of the said Sir Walter and the heirs male of his body, and for want of such issue to the use of his cousin Thomas Covert, eldest son of Dame Anne Covert, and the heirs male of his body, with divers remainders, which deed defts. believe to be in the box at Holborn.

In January, 1632, Sir Walter Covert died without issue and left Dame Anne Covert his *cousin* and heir, she being daughter and heir to his deceased brother John Covert.

Defendants do not know that the lands called Bentley came to Dame Anne as his *cousin* and heir. After Sir Walter's death the said Sir Thomas Pelham waived his estate in the premises, whereupon these defendants entered into all the said lands, including Bentley, according to said trust, and took the profits until Thomas Covert attained the age of 21 which happened in

August 1639, when they accounted to him and by deed passed all their estate in the premises to him.

Answer of Walter Francklyn, Esq.

He says he knows nothing of the Bentley Lease. His father James Franklyn who died about eleven years since was a Counsellor at Law and held divers deeds. Defendant, as his father's executor, kept them till inquired for. About eight years since, the plff. John Fenwick spoke to him about some writing he believed in his custody, made for the benefit of his wife Elizabeth. Defendant found an indenture dated 19 Sept., 1632, made by Dame Anne Covert to James Francklyn thereby expressing that she had granted and confirmed to him lands in parish of Cuckfield co. Sussex, of which the said Sir Walter Covert was seised to him and his heirs during the lives of Walter Burrell and Walter Covert, in trust for the said Elizabeth and Anne her sister. He gave this deed to Mr. Beaver of the Middle Temple, an attorney at law, to deliver to John Fenwick, which he did, bringing back a receipt signed by the latter.

Defendant has never had a farthing benefit from the said lands nor does he know these lands. He has never accepted the said trust nor does he believe his father accepted it. Neither he nor his father, to his knowledge, ever made any estate of the said lands to any person.

(Chancery Proceedings. Bridges, 480/63. Public Record Office, London.)

Although the record of the foregoing proceeding does not show the disposition of the suit, yet the pleadings are of genealogical value as showing Major John Fenwick's marriage with Elizabeth Covert and distinguishing her father Sir Walter Covert, of Maidstone, Kent, from Sir Walter Covert, of Slaugham, Sussex, uncle of Dame Anne Covert, wife of Sir Walter Covert of Maidstone aforesaid. It also confirms the relationship of the Coverts referred to by Col. R. G. Johnson on page 160 of Vol. XLIX of the *Pennsylvania Magazine*.

The purpose of this and the two preceding articles concerning Major John Fenwick has not been intended as an account of his life. The writer desired merely to present the evidence establishing Major Fenwick's parentage and the names of his two wives and identification of the families from whom they descended.

CAPTAIN GERLACH PAUL FLICK, PENNSYLVANIA PIONEER
BY ALEXANDER C. FLICK, LITT.D.

I.
EUROPEAN BACKGROUND.

The family name Flick seems to have come from the Old German Flacco or Flecco. The German variations are Flack, Flak, Fleck, Flick, Fleek, Flock, Flook, Fluck, Flück, Fluch, Flüch, Flicker, Flickiger, Flickinger and Flickwir. Van Vleck may have been a Dutch spelling. The Anglo-Saxon form was Flagg and the modern English Flagg, Flegg and Flack. The French variations are Flec, Fleck, Flick, Flicky and Flieg. Today Flicks are found in Switzerland, Germany, Holland, France, England, the United States and other countries.[1]

Family tradition makes Switzerland the ancestral home of the American Flicks, where the name may have been derived from Flickwir, or from Flückiger, a village in Canton Berne.[2] A Flück family lived for many years in Brienz, Canton Berne.[3] Planches, *L'Armorial General* II, Pl. 333, gives the following coats of arms of two Flick families in Basle:

Flick
Bâle

Flick
Bâle

---

[1] Ferguson, The Teutonic Name System, 411.
[2] Letter of James B. Lux, 1926.
[3] Kuhns, Germans and Swiss—of Penn., 237.

Rietstaps, *Armorial General*, 681, prints a description of these two coats of arms. What relation, if any, these families have to the Flicks in the United States has not been ascertained.

In 1711 the political authorities of Bern, Switzerland, offered the Mennonites of that region free transportation down the Rhine river to a Dutch seaport in order that they might emigrate to the British colonies in North America, and also gave them permission to sell their property, on condition that they would promise never to return to Switzerland. Evidently, on account of their peculiar religious ideas and customs, these Mennonites were undesirable citizens. The Dutch ambassador to Switzerland, Johan Ludwig Runckle, seems to have taken an interest in them and was untiring in his efforts to facilitate their departure via Holland to the New World. Consequently, about this time, Swiss Mennonites crossed the Atlantic and began to settle in Lancaster county, Pennsylvania. Among them are found such names as Flückiger and Frick but no Flicks.[4] Favorable reports about their reception in Pennsylvania, and the religious toleration and economic opportunities found there, were sent back to Germany and Switzerland. As a result within a few

---

[4] Kuhns, Germans and Swiss—of Penn., 46–47, 57; Rupp p. 7–7 says that about the year 1672 relentless persecution drove "a large body of defenseless Mennonites" from the Cantons of Zurich, Bern and Schaffhausen to Alsace above Strassburg where they lived until 1708 when they emigrated to London and thence to Pennsylvania. They lived in the vicinity of Philadelphia for a few years and in 1712 purchased a large tract of land in Pequae, then Chester, now Lancaster County. This was the nucleus of a large Swiss, French and German settlement. The list of names from 1709 to 1730 contains no Flicks. *Ibid.*, 436–439. The Mennonites sent Martin Kendig to Germany and Switzerland to induce others to emigrate and so great was the influx that the Pennsylvania Provincial Government became alarmed. *Ibid.*, 9. That others than Mennonites crossed the ocean at an early date is shown by the fact that a Reformed Church was organized as early as 1717 at Goshenhoppen. German Reformed Messenger, Aug. 3, 1842. See Sheffer, Mennonite Emigration to Pennsylvania, Penna. Mag. of Hist. and Biog., II, 117.

years many Germans and Swiss who were not Mennonites but adherents of the Reformed Church followed them. It was in this later exodus that the Flicks first appear in America. The number of immigrants to Pennsylvania increased until in the year 1751 nearly 4000 Germans and Swiss arrived in that province.[5]

The social, economic and religious conditions in Europe and America which induced at least ten Flicks to seek new homes in Pennsylvania during the twenty-five years preceding the War of Independence were significant. The social inequalities in Europe under the old regime prevented ambitious young men from rising above the station in which they were born. The War of the Austrian Succession, which ended in 1748, left the common people of Europe in a wretched economic state. Employment was scarce and poorly paid, and the cost of living was high. Moreover there was little freedom of speech or opinion, and religious bigotry and intolerance were rampant. In sharp contrast to the difficulties and hard times in Europe came the encouraging news about America. There, it was reported, existed social equality, economic opportunity and religious freedom. The attractions of the New World had been spread over Europe and discussed at many a public gathering and family fireside. Thousands had already gone from Germany, Switzerland and other continental European countries to the English colonies over seas and had sent back glowing accounts of the new El Dorado—how an abundance of fertile land, with plenty of wood and good water, in a fine climate, could be had for the asking by those who were wise enough to make the venture. The emigration officers of that day were also very busy in eliciting business.[6]

Young Gerlach Paul Flick had his imagination fired by these alluring reports and with some of his brothers

---

[5] See Fisher, Making of Pa., 99 for European conditions.
[6] Fisher, Making of Pa., 105.

and kinsmen resolved to make the experiment. The journey to Holland and transportation across the Atlantic were comparatively expensive. The fares had to be paid in cash, clothing and food provided for the long journey, and some money taken along to get one started in the new home. Just how the necessary funds were obtained, whether by gifts from his parents or on loan, is not clear. Somehow the problem was solved and the start was made.

The Provincial Council of Pennsylvania after asking in 1717 for "the number and character" of foreigners in 1727 required masters of vessels to prepare a list of all immigrants, giving their occupation and European homelands. Such immigrants had to sign an oath of allegiance to the King of England and to swear fidelity to Pennsylvania.[7] To this wise provision we owe the preservation of the names of so many American pioneers, among them that of Gerlach Paul Flick and his relatives.

There were numerous complaints from the immigrants that they were robbed, swindled and mistreated in many ways.[8]

II.

IMMIGRATION OF THE FLICKS.

Emigrants bearing names which may have been related directly or indirectly to the Flicks arrived in Pennsylvania a generation before the Flicks themselves landed at Philadelphia. Johannes Flückiger, a Palatine, came September 15, 1729.[9] Theobald Fick followed in 1738[10] and Johann Henrich Fick in 1750.[11]

---

[7] Kuhns, German and Swiss—of Penn., 45–47.; *Min. of Prov. Council* III, 18, 299. The oath is printed in Rupp, 47.
[8] *Ibid.*, 105; Pa. Arch. 1" Ser. IV, 473.
[9] Rupp, Thirty Thousand Names of Immigrants, 61.
[10] *Ibid.*, 119.
[11] *Ibid.*, 232.

Johan Henry Fleck, a Palatine, reached Philadelphia October 25, 1738,[12] and after him Conrad Fleck November 9, 1738,[13] Peter Fleck in 1751,[14] Valentin Fleck in 1753,[15] Henry Fleck in 1753,[16] and Johan Wilhelm Fleck in 1771.[17] John Jacob Fleck, age 26, crossed the Atlantic on the ship *Lydia* in 1741.[18] Johannes Flück arrived October 20, 1744.[19] Lucas Flak came in 1747.[20] Matheis Flach landed in 1751.[21] Johan Adolph Flock followed in 1752.[22] Peter Flickinger reached Philadelphia in 1753.[23] John Christian Fleit came in 1772.[24] Gotthard David Flickwir arrived in 1772,[25] and Johan Matheis Flach landed in 1772.[26] John Flickwir served in the Revolution in New York in Col. Marinus Willett's Levies.[27] Insufficient data and the carelessness in spelling proper names makes it difficult to determine the relationship of these immigrants to one another and to the Flicks. All of them came via Holland from either Germany or Switzerland.

The first Flicks to reach Pennsylvania were Gerlach Paul Flick, the subject of this sketch, John Peter Flick, Johan Martin Flick and John Philip Flick on September 23, 1751, aboard the ship *Neptune,* which carried 154 passengers from Rotterdam via Cowes.[28] The first

---

[12] Rupp, Thirty Thousand Names of Immigrants, 61.
[13] *Ibid.*, 129.
[14] *Ibid.*, 254.
[15] *Ibid.*, 304, see map of his land.
[16] *Ibid.*, 320, Pa. Arch. 6, XIII, 131.
[17] *Ibid.*, 397.
[18] Pa. Arch. 2, XVIII, 212.
[19] *Ibid.*, 170.
[20] *Ibid.*, 177.
[21] *Ibid.*, 247.
[22] *Ibid.*, 410.
[23] *Ibid.*, 296.
[24] *Ibid.*, 400.
[25] *Ibid.*, 402.
[26] *Ibid.*, 410.
[27] N. Y. in the Rev., 89.
[28] Rupp's Thirty Thousand Names of Immigrants, 260. John Peter Flick arrived Sept. 25, 1754, Pa. Arch. 2 Ser. XVII, 341, 395. A James Flicke had been transported to Maryland as early as 1674.

three took the required oath of allegiance at Philadelphia on the same day.[29] These four Flicks were probably near relatives. Gerlach Paul Flick, a young man of 23, many years later mentioned a Philip Flick in his will, and named his second son Martin. During the quarter of a century subsequent to the coming of Gerlach Paul Flick and his three relatives to Philadelphia in 1751, six more Flicks sought homes in Pennsylvania —John Peter and Peiter,[30] on the ship *Neptune* in 1754;[31] Heinrich "von Rotterdam über Cowes" on the *Pallas* in 1763;[32] Johan Adam on the *Chance* in 1766;[33] Johan Wilhelm on the *Crawford* in 1769;[34] and John Wilhelm during the Revolution in 1777.[35] Andries Flick crossed from Amsterdam on the *Belvedere* in 1802.[36] It seems quite probable that some of these Flick immigrants brought their wives and children with them although, if so, the fact is not mentioned.

---

[29] Pa. Arch. 2 Ser. XVII, 341.
[30] It is possible that they were the same individual. The record is confusing. See Pa. Arch. 2 Ser. XVII, 397.
[31] Pa. Arch. 2" Ser., 395, 397.
[32] *Ibid.*, 458; Rupp, 355.
[33] Rupp, 373; Pa. Arch. 2" Series. XXIX, 475.
[34] Pa. Arch. 2" Ser. XVII, 491.
[35] *Ibid.*; Rupp, 491.
[36] Pa. Arch. 2" Ser. XVII, 584. Andries Flick may have been Andrew Flick, born near the Rhine River, Germany, in 1784, who "when a boy" came to Philadelphia, where he died in 1851 aged 67 years. He had a son, a sister Margaretha in Evansville, Ind., and a brother Louis who "kept a bakery on South Broad St., Philadelphia." Andrew Flick had four children: Margaretha, William, Andrew Jackson and Charles. Andrew Jackson, born in Philadelphia in 1813, died in Springfield, O., aged 83. He was married twice, had a daughter by his first wife, and three children by his second wife—Elizabeth, Charles Wallace and Claude Wilmot. Letter of May 20, 1928, from Mrs. Elizabeth Flick Edmonson, Harrisburg, Pa. Of the $180 passage money of Andries Flick $33.10 was advanced and the remainder was paid apparently by relatives upon his arrival at Philadelphia. Andreas Flick was godfather to John Schneider at Frederick, Md., in 1766. He and his wife Magdelein had two daughters, Catherine and Christina, confirmed in 1767 and 1770. Christina married Henry Bruer in 1797. Ger. Ref. Church Records, 128, 103; Eng. Luth. Church Records, 545; Nead, The Pa. Germans in Settling, Md., Lancaster, Pa., 1814.

Just what relationship these later arrivals sustained to the earlier ones is not apparent. Further study of the sources may throw more light on the later history of these contemporaries of Gerlach Paul Flick.

While searching for data about Gerlach Paul Flick the following items concerning the early Flicks in America were found and are given with the hope that they may be of some value to those who are interested in the collateral branches of the family:

1. Henry Flick. John Henry came to Philadelphia in 1751 with Gerlach Paul and Heinrich 12 years later.[37] Apparently John Henry settled in York county and was the executor of the will of John Ocker who died in 1761.[38] Heinrich seems to have settled in Philadelphia and was included in the return of the 5th Battalion, Philadelphia county Militia in July, 1777.[39] He served in Capt. John Jacons Company which was reported as needing shoes, stockings and blankets.[40] In 1774 he was a taxpayer of Philadelphia county owning 1 horse and 3 cattle and paying a tax of £2/13/4.[41] In 1779 he paid a tax of £4/[42] and in 1781 he paid a tax of 10/ as a "laborer."[43] A Henry Flick of Elk township, Cumberland county, served in the militia in 1789 and 1793.[44] Another Henry Flick was sponsor of Catherine Hinckle born in Bucks county May 23, 1812.[45]

2. Peter Flick. John Peter accompanied Gerlach Paul to America in 1751 and "Peiter" came in 1754.[46] One of them seems to have settled in Shenandoah Valley, Virginia, and was included in the census of 1785 as owning a dwelling and having a family of six.[47] The

---
[37] Pa. Arch. 2" Ser. XVII, 397.
[38] York Co. Wills, 409.
[39] Pa. Arch. 6" Ser. I, 341, 496, 511, III, 46; 1" Ser. III, 72.
[40] Ibid., III, 511, 971.
[41] Ibid., 2" Ser. XXV, 403.
[42] Ibid., 505.
[43] Ibid., XVI, 75, 214.
[44] Ibid., 6" Ser., V, 40, 190.
[45] Hinke, Tohickon Union Church, 515.
[46] Pa. Arch. 2 Ser. XVII, 397.
[47] Federal Census Va. 1790.

other located in Philadelphia and in 1777 was a "substitute" in the Philadelphia Militia.[48] A Peter Fleek enlisted in Capt. Craigh's Company, January 8, 1776. He was wounded. In May, 1818, he was living in Huntingdon Co., Pa., at the age of 65.[48a] A Peter Fleak was charged with stealing a horse in Augusta Co., Va., in 1785 and Wm. Jordan appeared against him as a witness.[48b]

3. Philip Flick. John Philip crossed the Atlantic in 1751 with Gerlach Paul and located in New Jersey where Thomas Andrews of Eversham, Burlington County, in his will dated July 17, 1755, mentioned him as a son-in-law and named him executor.[49] This may have been "the certain Philip Flick," possibly a brother, mentioned by Gerlach Paul in 1825 in his will as being dead and owing him £50. Another Philip Flick lived in Philadelphia and served in the Philadelphia Militia, 2″ Battalion, September 17, 1777.[50] He was a baker in Philadelphia and in 1779 paid a tax of £88 and £22.[51] In 1780 he paid £182/10 and £9/4. In 1782 he paid a tax of £3/6/6 and 15/9.[52] He must have died that year, for his estate paid an additional tax of 4/5.[53] On September 4, 1775, a Philip Flick married Mary Lowry.[54] Another Philip Flick had a wife Catherine and a daughter Margaret born February 3d and baptised April 3, 1778.[55]

---

[48] Pa. Arch. 6 Ser. I, 27, 199, 279.
[48a] Pa. Arch. 5 Ser. II, 95.
[48b] Abstract Records of Augusta Co., Va. I, 384.
[49] N. J. Arch. XXXI, 13; the following Flicks are mentioned in N. J. Index of Wills, Vol. I: Amy B., 1777, p. 308, Gloucester Co. William, 1821, p. 51, Index of Wills. Thomas, 1829, p. 51, Index of Wills. Henry S., 1834, p. 308, Gloucester Co. Ann W., 1834, p. 308, Gloucester Co. Sarah, 1849, p. 308, Gloucester Co. Joseph, 1866, p. 308, Gloucester Co. Charles, 1891, p. 225, Index of Wills, Union Co. Leonard, 1893, p. 225, Index of Wills, Camden Co.
[50] Pa. Arch. 6 Ser. I, 129.
[51] Ibid., 2 Ser. XIV, 475, 571.
[52] Ibid., XV, 210, 751; XVI, 321, 367.
[53] Ibid., XV, 429.
[54] Penn. Ger. Soc. V, 214.
[55] Ibid., 218.

4. Martin Flick. One Martin came to Pennsylvania in 1751 with Gerlach Paul and three other Flicks.[56] By September 11, 1758, he was married, for he and his wife Margaretha were sponsors at the baptism of Catharine Mehrkam on that date.[57] Another Martin was a son of Gerlach Paul Flick and served in the Revolution.[58]

5. Adam Flick. One Adam immigrated to Pennsylvania in 1766[59] and settled in Bedford County, Milford Township, where he paid a tax of 16/ in 1773 and 6/2 in 1776,[60] and in 1786 took out a land warrant for 140 acres.[61] He was included in the First Census as head of a family of 3 sons and 1 daughter, p. 24. He served in the Revolution[62] and performed militia duty in 1789.[63] Another Adam lived in Philadelphia where he was on the militia rolls in 1783–1790,[64] and paid a tax of £16 in 1779,[65] and £107/8 in 1780.[66] An Adam Flick was sponsor for Catherine Beitelman born in Bucks county February 7 and baptised March 21, 1810.[67] Another Adam took the patriot's oath in Washington county, Maryland, and also served in the Revolution.[68] Andrew and George, sons, as heads of families, were in the Census of 1790.

6. William Flick. Johan Wilhelm went to Pennsylvania in 1769 and John Wilhelm in 1771.[69] The first settled in Lancaster county, had a wife named Catherine[70]

---

[56] Rupp, 260.
[57] Pa. Arch. 6 Ser. VI, 11.
[58] See Part VII.
[59] Pa. Arch. 2 Ser. XVII, 475.
[60] Ibid., 3 Ser. XIII, 608; XV, 411.
[61] Ibid., XXV, 512.
[62] Ibid., 1" Ser. III, 72; 6" Ser. I, 639, 650.
[63] Ibid., 6" Ser. III, 40.
[64] Ibid., I, 639, 650.
[65] Ibid., XIV, 608.
[66] Ibid., XV, 411.
[67] Hinke, 413.
[68] Brumbaugh, 13.
[69] Rupp, 397.
[70] Brumbaugh, 13.

and 2 sons and 3 daughters.[71] He was a dyer in Lancaster county in 1779[72] and in 1782 paid a tax of £2/16/3.[73] He seems to have been on the payroll of Capt. John Reitzel's Company of Pennsylvania Militia.[74] The second married Elizabeth Hoffman October 5, 1778, in Christ Church, Philadelphia, and the next year paid a tax of £1.[75] He may have moved to Gloucester county, N. J., where his will was recorded in 1829.[76] A William Flick took the Patriot's Oath in Maryland and served in the Revolution.[77]

7. John Flick. Since so many of these early Flicks began their names with John and none of them apparently used it exclusively, it is difficult to know who was meant by this designation. In the year Gerlach Paul arrived at Philadelphia in 1751 a John Flick took up 100 acres of land in Lancaster county. It seems likely that he was the Revolutionary soldier who on August 2, 1776, was in the 4th Vacant Company of the German Regiment, Continental Forces, commanded by Lieutenant Colonel Lewis Weltner;[78] and also a private May 22, 1777, in Captain William Heyser's Company of the German Regiment commanded by Colonel Baron Arent.[79] He was recorded as a "freeman" in Lancaster county in 1779,[80] and in 1790 was included in the Federal Census as having 1 son and 1 daughter and as living in Donegal township. Another John Flick paid taxes in Philadelphia of £1/10 in 1779 and £56/ in 1780.[81] He may have moved to Washington county,

---

[71] Federal Census, Pennsylvania, 1790.
[72] Pa. Arch. 2″ Ser. XVII, 606.
[73] Ibid., 756.
[74] Pa. Arch. 6″ Ser. V, 357.
[75] Pa. Marriages Prior to 1810 I, 91; Pa. Arch. 2″ Ser. XVI, 475; 751.
[76] Index of N. J. Wills.
[77] Brumbaugh, 13; George Flick, Md. Arch. 18: 50, 206, and John Flick, Ibid., 208, 264, 285, may have been his sons.
[78] Pa. Arch. 4″ Ser. III, 804.
[79] Penn. Ger. Soc. XVII, 221, 225. Pa. Ar. 4″ Ser. III, 794.
[80] Pa. Arch. 2″ Ser. XVII, 522.
[81] Ibid., 2″ Ser. XV, 570; XVI, 475, 751.

Pennsylvania, and was included in the Federal Census of 1790 as being married but without any children. One of the John Flicks, probably of the second generation, was drafted in the War of 1812 at Dansville and saw service in the 81st Regiment in 1814.[82] The next year, 1813, John Flick had a survey of 38 acres made in Franklin county.[83] A John Flick was sponsor at the baptism of Absalom Benner born July 5, 1816, in Bucks county.[84] A John Flick from Elizabeth Town, Maryland, enlisted as a Revolutionary soldier in Washington county of that state.[85]

8. Jacob Flick. One served as a private in Captain Nathan Smith's Company from June 1, 1776, one month and fifteen days at Martha's Vineyard to defend the seacoast.[86] He was drafted for militia duty in Brothers Valley, Bedford county, in 1789.[87] Another Jacob served for six months at $20 in the War of 1812.[88] A Jacob Flick was also sponsor at the baptism of Jacob Eckert in 1815 in Bucks county.[89]

9. Daniel Flick was a Revolutionary soldier in the 1st Virginia Regiment[90] and may have been a son of one of the immigrants.

10. Christopher Flick, born in 1756, probably a son of an immigrant, went to Virginia as a boy, enlisted in the Revolutionary army from that state, and was in Colonel Crawford's Expedition to Ohio in 1782. He applied for a federal pension in 1835 from Orange county, Indiana.[91]

11. Michael Flick, probably an immigrant's son, in

[82] Pa. Arch 6" Ser. VII, 625; IX, 19; Jonas and Joseph Flick also served in the War of 1812, *Ibid.*, VIII, 562, IX, 200, X, 94.
[83] *Ibid.* 2" Ser. XXV, 18.
[84] Hinke, 418.
[85] Williams, Hist. of Washington Co., Md., I, 79.
[86] Mass. Soldiers and Sailors in the Rev., V, 786.
[87] Pa. Arch. 6" Ser. III, 43.
[88] *Ibid.*, VII, 205; VIII, 232, 699.
[89] Hinke, 417.
[90] Rev. Soldiers of Va. II, 112.
[91] Petition in Pension Bureau, Washington, D. C.

1773 paid a tax of 1/6 in Bedford county.[92] Another Michael was included in the Federal Census of 1790 as the head of a family in Philadelphia.

12. Thomas Flick made his will in Gloucester county, New Jersey, in 1829,[93] and may have been related to William Flick of that same county.

13. Among the women who bore the name Flick were the following: Elizabeth married Henry Carry in Christ Church, Philadelphia, June 22, 1771.[94] Another married Peter Becker August 22, 1776.[95] Another married Peter Tythe November 7, 1777.[96] And still another Elizabeth in 1835 witnessed a will in Philadelphia.[97] Mary Flick married William Stidhan September 29, 1785.[98] Margaret Flick married John Whetman in the Swedish Church, Philadelphia, July 31, 1777.[99] Catherine Flick married Ellet Howell at Trenton, New Jersey, December 27, 1777.[100] And Amy Flick made her will in New Jersey in 1777.[101] In all probability these Flicks were daughters of immigrants although some of them may have been widows of Flicks.

By the time of the American Revolution there were Flicks not only in Pennsylvania but also in New York, New Jersey, Maryland and Virginia. It seems more than likely that from Pennsylvania they scattered to the other colonies although it may be that some of them went directly. The exact relationship of these various branches cannot be determined until more public records, church records, family and cemeterial records, both in Europe and America are examined.

---

[92] Pa. Arch. 2″ Sed. XXII, 10.
[93] Index of N. J. Wills.
[94] Penn. Marriages Prior to 1810 I, 91. Cf. Pa. Arch. 2″ Ser. II, 103.
[95] *Ibid.*, 669.
[96] *Ibid.*, 524.
[97] Ger. Soc. of Penn. V., 311.
[98] Penn Mar. Prior to 1810 I, 39.
[99] *Ibid.*, 369.
[100] N. J. Arch. 1″ Ser. XXII, 148.
[101] *Index of Wills* I, 308.

The European ancestral home of the Flicks has not been determined with certainty. No printed primary sources contribute to the settlement of this point. The record of John Henry Fleck's arrival in Philadelphia in 1738 states that he came from the Pfalz, or the Palatinate, in Germany.[102] Doubt may be raised, however, as to whether this Fleck was a Flick. The only secondary work which mentions Gerlach Paul Flick and gives the family history of his son John Caspar and his descendants states that Gerlach Paul came from Germany.[103] The traditions preserved in other branches of Gerlach Paul Flick's family contend that German Switzerland was his European home. His affiliation with the Reformed Church, which was strong in Protestant Switzerland, strengthens this supposition. Further his marriage with a daughter of the Fabian family, which was of Swiss origin, increases the probability. It is also well known that in the eighteenth century a large stream of Swiss immigrants flowed into Pennsylvania. No doubt an examination of Swiss church and local records would throw much light on the problem. Many of the so-called Pennsylvania Dutch actually came from the German side of Switzerland.[104]

If the Flicks had their ancestral home in Switzerland, it seems certain that they settled on the Rhine River in Germany before going to America. Evidence of this is preserved in a letter written by Johann Christian Flick to his son Gerlach Paul Flick from Emmerichenhain near Wiesbaden on March 31, 1766. In the letter are mentioned three brothers of Gerlach Paul, namely, John Peter, Philip Henry and John Christian, Jr., and a sister, Anna Gertrude. John Jost Flick is also named but not as a brother. This letter

---

[102] Rupp, 125. A Conrad Fleck also arrived from Rotterdam and qualified Nov. 9, 1738. *Pa. Arch.* 2" Ser. XVII, 178.
[103] Kulp, Families of the Wyoming Valley.
[104] Fisher, Making of Pa., 89.

carries the family back to Europe and establishes what was in all probability the place from which Gerlach Paul Flick emigrated.[105]

III.

GERLACH PAUL FLICK IN BUCKS COUNTY, PENNSYLVANIA.

Gerlach Paul Flick was born on March 7, 1728, according to the records of Zion's Church (Stone Church) near Kreidersville, Northampton County, Pennsylvania.[106] The place of his birth may have been Emmerichenhain near Wiesbaden, Hesse-Nassau, Germany. This surmise is based on the fact that his father, Johan Christian Flick, Sr., wrote him a letter from that place in 1766. His mother's name is unknown but she, together with three brothers and a sister, were living at or near Emmerichenhain. It seems to be a reasonable conjecture, however, that Johan Martin and John Philip Flick, who accompanied him to Philadelphia were his brothers.

At the age of 23 he left home, made his way down the Rhine river to Rotterdam, Holland, to seek his fortune in the New World. In various ways he had learned of the unusual opportunities in the province of Pennsylvania to which he was going. As a rule the men who go from the older parts of the world to find homes in the newer are among the bravest, most intelligent and most venturesome. It took a good deal of pluck and self-confidence to sever family ties and neighborhood attachments and to encounter all the hardships and uncertainties incident to the establishment of a new place of abode across the broad Atlantic in a strange continent. What sort of financial adjustments and arrangements Gerlach Paul made for the long journey is

---

[105] Original letter in possession of Edward Paul Flick of Effort, Pa.
[106] These records when examined in 1928 were kept in the vault of the First National Bank at Northampton, Pa.

largely conjectural. Somehow he obtained his passage money, which enabled him to sail from Rotterdam in company with three other Flicks and in all likelihood with a number of neighbors for Philadelphia in 1751 on the ship *Neptune* under Captain Weir. No doubt, following the custom of that day, he and his companions carried their provisions with them for the long sea journey. Such supplies were partly brought from home and partly purchased before embarkation. The journey from Europe to America in the slow and small sailing ships of those days frequently consumed six weeks, and involved deprivations and hardships unknown today. No account of the ocean voyage has been preserved and hence its description must be left to the imagination. Mittelberger's "Journey to Pennsylvania in 1750" gives the nearest description we have of the amusements and hardships attending the crossing of the Atlantic at that time.[107]

A few facts about the sea trip have survived. The list of adult male passengers is known.[108] Among them was a pastor of the Reformed Church, John Egidius Hecker, from the village of Dillenburg in Nassau. He was two years older than Gerlach Paul Flick and had studied in the University of Herborn.[109] A warm friendship sprang up between these two young immigrants which was a determining factor in Gerlach Paul Flick's life. Some years later the families of these two men were more closely united by marriage.[110] Leaving Rotterdam probably in August, the *Neptune* after touching at Cowes, which afforded the passengers an opportunity to see something of England, landed at Philadelphia on September 23, 1751.[111] It was all a wonderful adventure for a young man seeking his fortune

---

[107] Fisher, Making of Pa. 102
[108] Rupp, 260.
[109] Hinke, 33.
[110] Rev. Henry Koch, grandson of Hecker, married Mary Hugus, granddaughter of Gerlach Paul Flick.
[111] Rupp, 260.

in a new quarter of the globe. Upon his arrival he immediately took the required oath of allegiance to the King of England and to the province of Pennsylvania.

The details of the career of Gerlach Paul Flick in Pennsylvania for the first few years are lacking. Influenced by relatives or acquaintances he early left the city of Philadelphia for the country and located in Bedminster Township, Bucks county, Pennsylvania, where Germans and Swiss had a settlement about the Tohickon Reformed Church. The first paster of this church and perhaps its founder was the Rev. John Conrad Wirtz, born in Zurich, Switzerland, in 1706, who came to Philadelphia with a Swiss colony in 1735. He served various rural churches, among them the Tohickon Reformed Church from 1745 to 1748.[112] There may have been some connection between the Flicks and Wirtz, although Wirtz had been succeeded by the Rev. John Jacob Riess when Gerlach Paul Flick settled there and became a member of the church.[113]

Apparently young Gerlach Paul found lucrative employment among the farmers and saved his earnings, for within four years after his arrival in the province he married Anna Catherine Fabian on October 28, 1755.[114] "After a three-fold proclamation" the ceremony was performed by the Rev. John Egidius Hecker, pastor of the Tohickon Reformed Church from 1755 to 1761, and special friend of the bridegroom. The marriage was recorded in the records of his church as the second performed by this minister.[115] At the time of his marriage Paul Gerlach Flick was 27 years old and Anna Catherine Fabian 19. She was a native American, having been born in 1736 and baptised June 20 in the Goshenhoppen Reformed Church as the daughter of Michael and Dorothea Fabian. Michael Fabian at

---

[112] Hinke, 3.
[113] *Ibid.*, 14.
[114] *Ibid.*, 212.
[115] *Ibid.*

the age of 30 immigrated from Rotterdam in 1732, landed at Philadelphia October 11 and settled in Goshenhoppen Valley, Montgomery county, Pennsylvania, where Anna Catherine was born.[116]

For about five years after his marriage Gerlach Paul Flick maintained his residence in Bedminster Township, where his first child, a daughter named Anna Margaret, was born August 18 and baptised October 14, 1756;[117] and his second child, a son named John Caspar, was born June 22 and baptised November 14, 1758.[118] Both births are in the Tohickon Reformed Church records.[119] On December 23, 1759, Gerlach Paul Flick and his wife acted as witnesses for the baptism of John Paul Neelig.[120] It is worthy of note that in the birth and baptismal record "Gerlach" and "Anna" were dropped and the more familiar "Paul" and "Catherine" used. With this incident the name of Gerlach Paul Flick disappears from the printed records of Bucks county in the year 1760, and it is quite evident that he had removed with his family to some other part of the province. When he went to Bucks county in 1751 it comprised all the territory north of Philadelphia county. The following year, March 11, 1752, Northampton county was formed from the northern part of Bucks.

IV.

GERLACH PAUL FLICK IN NORTHAMPTON COUNTY, PENNSYLVANIA.

After disappearing from Bucks county in 1760 Gerlach Paul Flick turned up in the newly organized Northampton county, which included all territory in

---

[116] Data of James B. Lux.
[117] Hinke, 81.
[118] *Ibid.*, 96.
[119] *Ibid.*
[120] Hinke, 105.

Pennsylvania north of the present northern boundary of Bucks until Lehigh county was formed from Northampton in 1812. In 1760 Northampton county was on the frontier, sparsely settled, and offered an abundance of free land and special opportunities to a young married man ambitious and willing to work. The frontier settlements were still menaced by hostile bands of Indians who roved about over the county. The roads were poor and few, and markets were far away.

The attention of Gerlach Paul Flick was called to the greater advantages of this newer region at an early date. Northampton county was organized only a year after his arrival in Philadelphia, and his friends and acquaintances had established new homes there. Several months before his marriage to Anna Catherine Fabian his father-in-law, Michael Fabian, on February 15, 1755, took out a land warrant for 25 acres in Northampton county.[121] This same year, whether before or after his marriage is not clear, Gerlach Paul Flick himself had a survey made of a tract of land in Northampton county, which would make it appear that at an early date he contemplated settling there. In 1773, eighteen years later, George Schwartz attempted to get control of this land on the claim that he had had the land surveyed earlier than 1755. The case was tried in November 1773 before the "Board of Property." The minutes of the Board show that the case was heard and dismissed, which was a victory for Gerlach Paul Flick.[122]

In 1757, apparently leaving his wife and child in Bedminster county, Bucks county, Gerlach Paul Flick went into Northampton county for employment of some kind, for on October 5th of that year at the "Forks of the Delaware" in Lehigh township near Easton, he joined others in signing a petition to the Governor and General Assembly of Pennsylvania asking for protec-

---

[121] Pa. Arch.
[122] *Ibid.*, 1" Ser. XXXII, 370.

tion against the Indians.[123] This petition, written in German and translated into English, stated that many of the settlers had fled from the county because of Indian attacks. It asked for arms for the pioneers and the construction of a road with small guard houses along it. Among the signers were a number of men who were actual settlers of the region which later was organized as Moor township. It seems very likely that Gerlach Paul Flick had gone to Northampton county to clear his land and to erect a log cabin for his little family. Again on October 28, 1784, he signed another petition at Easton for the appointment of Peter Caler as sheriff of Northampton county.[124]

It may be assumed that in 1760 Gerlach Paul Flick removed his family and such movable goods and livestock as he possessed to his farm in Lehigh township, Northampton county, for in 1761 he was recorded as a resident and as having paid a tax of £7 there.[125] That portion of Lehigh township in which he settled was organized in 1749 as Allen township and then was created into Moor township in 1765 and named after John Moor, a representative in the Pennsylvania General Assembly in 1761-2. No doubt Gerlach Paul Flick was one of the moving spirits in bringing about this change. Moor township was located in the northern part of Northampton county, was six miles square and contained 22,506 acres. It was well watered and wooded

---

[123] Pa. Arch. 1" Ser. III, 284; Frontier Forts I, 247. The fear of hostile outbreaks from the Indians in Northampton County is expressed in a number of letters and petitions from the inhabitants in that county. See Letter of Wm. Parsons to Governor Morris in 1755, Pa. Arch. 1" Ser., II, 515; petition of May 4, 1757, signed by 41 Germans, *Ibid.*, III, 151; petition from Lower Smithfield Township, *Ibid.*, 174; petition from Easton, July 25, 1757, *Ibid.*, 238; *Ibid.*, 321. See also Supreme Executive Council XII, 57, 62, 64, 248, 312, 236, 358, 677. See recommendations of Gov. James Hamilton to the Assembly for the protection of and relief of the inhabitants of Northampton Co. Pa. Arch. 4" Ser., 216-218.

[124] Pa. Arch. 6" Ser. XI, 266.

[125] Northampton County Papers Miscel. 1758-1767 (Pa. Hist. Soc.) p. 75.

and although hilly yet its gravel and shale soil was good for growing vegetables, fruit, rye and buckwheat. By 1740 the white settlers in that area numbered about 50, who increased during the next 30 years to 500. In 1770 there were 3 grist mills, and two saw mills in operation in the township. The village of Moortown was on the eastern border and Petersville was soon settled.[126] By 1830 the inhabitants of Moor township numbered 1645.

In such a frontier community, naturally, the records were meager but they are sufficient to present a fair outline of Gerlach Paul Flick's subsequent career. At that day few men thought of the wealth in the earth such as ores, coal and oil. It was what was on top of it that counted—farming and lumbering. Hence men gave their attention to crops, cheese-making, sawmills, gristmills, fulling mills, tanneries, blacksmithing, waggon-making, and the erection of buildings. From 1760 on Gerlach Paul Flick was a hard-working, highly respected farmer of considerable prominence in Northampton county. Later on he set up a mill and was known far and wide as "Miller Flick." Sometime between 1760 and 1770 Michael Fabian also moved into Moor township, or the neighboring Allen township. Both men took an active part in the Reformed Church at Kreidersville in Allen township. During this decade comparatively little is known of the activities of these two pioneers. On March 14, 1770, Gerlach Paul Flick witnessed the will of Michael Reubary of Moor township.[127] In erecting the new Stone Church at Kreidersville Gerlach Paul Flick contributed £4 on March 16, 1771, and Michael Fabian and his children £5.[128] His eldest child, Anna Margaret Flickin (feminine spelling) was confirmed in Whitehall Church at Egypt.[129]

---

[126] Haller, Hist. of Northampton Co. II, 485.
[127] Eyerman, 183.
[128] Records of Stone Church.
[129] Church Records in Harrisburg.

In 1797 he subscribed 18/9 and his son Caspar 15/ for the support of the Church.[130]

Like most men of that day Gerlach Paul Flick speculated in land which was both the evidence of wealth and one of the best means of increasing it.

On Nov. 22, 1766, Paul Flick filed application No. 2137 for a survey of land in Northampton Co. Philip Drum on Oct. 18, 1774, entered a "Caveat" against the survey on the claim that he had made improvements on a part of the land before the application was recorded. How the dispute ended is not clear.[130a]

In 1772 he was recorded on the tax records as the owner of 175 acres in Moor township on which he paid a property tax of £2/16.[131] In 1773 he had a survey made of a tract of 50 acres in Northampton county and took out a land warrant for it.[132] The same year in a suit before the "Board of Property" he won a clear title to another piece of land in the same county.[133] On April 14, 1774, Saul (Gerlach Paul) "yeoman" and William Beck bought the land on which Emanuel Church at Petersville, Moor township, was located and which adjoined Paul Flick's farm. On the death of Beck shortly thereafter he became the sole owner of the tract. On September 30, 1782, he sold 76 acres and 110 perches to Philip Drum, Casper Erb and Henry Bartholomew, trustees of the Church, for the use of the Reformed and Lutheran congregations for church and school purposes only.[134] The deed was recorded on November 7, 1785, in the county seat at Easton.[135] Meanwhile his friend, the Rev. John Egidius Hecker, who at an earlier

---

[130] Records of Stone Church, 24.
[130a] Pa. Arch. 3″ Ser. II, 581.
[131] Pa. Arch. 3″ Ser. XIX, 60.
[132] Ibid., XXIV, 77.
[133] Pa. Arch. 2″ Ser. XXXII, 370.
[134] Pa. Ger. Soc. I, 433, 551, 558, 561, gives the history of Emanuel Church at Petersville.
[135] County Court House, Land Records.

day had preached at various places in Northampton county, finally settled in Moor township in 1767 where in addition to several other congregations he ministered to Emanuel Church. He died in Moor township in November, 1773.[136] In 1774 Gerlach Paul Flick had a lawsuit with Philip Drum about a land application of November 21, 1766, in which Drum claimed that he had made improvements on the land before Flick filed his claim. How it was adjusted does not appear in the records.[136a]

In 1780 Gerlach Paul Flick was assessed on property in Moor township valued at £115.[137] His wife Catherine in 1781 paid a tax of £1/16, on a half lot valued at £600, in Philadelphia.[138] In 1782 he sold a parcel of land in Moor township to Daniel Schwartz. In 1785 he sold another tract in the same township to Philip Drum, and paid a tax of £1/3/4 on 175 acres, 2 horses and 4 cattle.[139] As administrator of the estate of Martin Herbster he sold a tract of land in Moor township to Daniel Schwartz on November 7, 1785. Land Records, F 1, 25. In 1786 he paid a Federal tax of £1/10/7 on 293 acres, 3 horses and 4 cattle, and witnessed the will of George Schwartz.[140] In 1788 he paid a similar tax of £1/1/2 on 175 acres, 4 horses and 4 cattle.[141] No doubt the unprinted records after 1788, if preserved, would show him paying taxes, buying land, operating his mill, performing the multitudinous duties of an active, prosperous farmer and participating in all the public affairs of the community. The printed records for the period from 1789 to 1825 contain but two references to his land deals. The will of Michael Schwart in 1801 mentioned the lands owned by Gerlach Paul

---

[136] Hinke, 33.
[136a] Pa. Arch. 3" Ser. II, 581.
[137] Hist. Northampton Co. (1877), 76.
[138] Pa. Arch. 3" Ser. XV, 667.
[139] Pa. Arch. 3" Ser. XV, 140.
[140] Pa. Arch 3" Ser. XIX, 249; Eyerman, 430.
[141] *Ibid.*, 352.

Flick;[142] and as late as November 19, 1819, he took out a land warrant for 46 acres in Northampton county.[143]

As old age approached, realizing that he was no longer able either to work his land himself with profit or to rent it advantageously he appears to have sold all of it. No doubt a careful search of the land records of Northampton county would reveal the dates of sale and the names of purchasers. After his death the inventory made of his property on February 18, 1826, by Peter Steckel and Abraham Stern, the two witnesses of his will, shows that it consisted of bonds, notes, book debts, farm implements and household goods. An inventory of his bonds, notes and book debts made a total of $8723.31 and the tools and home articles $161.12, or a total of $8884.43. For that day this sum was a modest fortune, the product of hard work and thrift in a new country. After all expenses were deducted, the proceeds of the sale were divided equally among his 11 surviving children.[144]

V.

CAPTAIN GERLACH PAUL FLICK'S MILITARY RECORD.

When Gerlach Paul Flick at the age of 23 came to Philadelphia in 1751 it is not unlikely that he had had some military experience in Europe. Although he must have had opportunities to serve in the French and Indian War after settling in America no evidence of such service has come to light. His eagerness to establish himself and his marriage in 1755 checked any such inclination.

The discussion of the issues between the colonists and the mother country found eager listeners among the Germans and Swiss of Pennsylvania, who for the

---

[142] Eyerman, 409.
[143] Pa. Arch. 3″ Ser. XXVI, 80. This may have been his son Gerlach Paul, Jr..
[144] Administration papers in Court House, Easton, Pa.

most part became champions of the American cause and proved their devotion in many ways. When the War of Independence began in 1775 Gerlach Paul Flick was 47 years old and had been in his adopted country 24 years. He had been married for 20 years and had a large family to support as well as a farm and a mill to manage. Located on the frontier he and his family lived in constant fear of massacre by the Indians, particularly after it became certain that most of them had allied themselves with the British in the pending struggle. It seems quite probable that in the years preceding the Revolution he had served in the militia of Northampton county organized to protect the frontier settlements against Indian outbreaks and thus had accustomed himself to the military tactics of the New World.[145]

In the American Revolution Moor township raised a company of 106 men under Capt. Adam Bruckhauer and Lieut. Timothy Reed, which was a credit for such a sparsely settled region.[146] John Caspar Flick, 18 years old when Lexington was fought, the eldest son of Gerlach Paul Flick, early enlisted as a private in the Revolution and saw much service.[147] Martin Flick, the second son, enlisted in New York during the whole period of the struggle for Independence.[148] Gerlach Paul Flick had adequate excuse for keeping out of the army but his heart was in the contest and he gladly volunteered. His name as a Revolutionary soldier ap-

---

[145] A company of militia was formed in Northampton county in October, 1763. Pa. Arch. 1" Ser. IV, 285. The Pennsylvania Council of Safety on December 17, 1776, authorized General George Washington to call out the Northampton County Militia for active service. *Ibid.*, V, 115. Again on August 5, 1777, the Executive Council ordered Northampton county to support General Washington with the Militia. *Ibid.*, 523. See petitions of the inhabitants of Allen township in 1779 for advice about Indian outbreaks. Pa. Arch. 1" Ser. VII, 284.

[146] Haller, Hist. of Northampton Co., II, 485.

[147] Pa. Arch. 3" Ser. XIX, 156, 258, 386; XXVI, 78, 80; Pa. Ger. Soc. XVII, 330, 221, 225; XXII, 235.

[148] Cal. N. Y. MSS. II, 356; Mass. Soldiers and Sailors of the Rev., V, 786; *N. Y. in the Rev.*, 21

peared first May 21, 1777, on the muster roll of Col. Cook Long.[149] A return of troops from Chester, Pennsylvania, on August 28, 1777, mentions his company and shows that he was a commissioned officer.[150] In June, 1777, and May 1, 1778, his name appears as Captain of the 8th Company, 4th Battalion, Northampton County Militia, commanded by Col. John Siegfried and Lieut. Col. Nicholas Kern.[151] From 1778 to 1783 he served as Captain of Rangers on the frontier.[152] in 1781 he commanded the 1st Company of the 3rd Battalion of Northampton County Militia,[153] under Lt. Col. Nicholas Kern.

Since General Sullivan's Expedition sent out in 1779 to punish the Indians of western New York marched from Easton to Wyoming not far from Captain Gerlach Paul Flick's home it is possible that he took part in it. He may have been in Schott's Rifle Corps, or in the Independent Rifle Company, or in the German Battalion, or even in Morgan's Riflemen, who were largely Pennsylvanians. President Reed of Pennsylvania on August 3, 1779, begged the people of Northampton county to turn out to protect the state against the enemy. Since the summons came in the midst of harvest the farmers strenuously objected and a near riot ensued. However cooler heads prevailed and matters were adjusted. The inhabitants stated that the county's quota was already in the field, and among those in service at the time was Gerlach Paul Flick. The 5th and 6th Battalions of the Northampton County Militia under Col. Nicholas Kern were at Wyoming July 30, 1784.[153a]

On the monument erected at Northampton, Pa., May

---

[149] Pa. Arch. 5th Ser. VIII, 304; Penn. Ger. Soc. XVII, 297.
[150] Pa. Arch. 5th Ser. VIII, 544.
[151] Pa. Ger. Soc. XVII, 297, 330.
[152] Pa. Arch. 3rd Ser. XXII, 301.
[153] Ibid., 5th Ser. VIII, 257.
[153a] Pa. Arch 1" Ser. VII, 616, 655; Pa. Ger. Soc. XVII, 330.

30, 1914, "to perpetuate the memory of Col. John Siegfried and the men who served under him in the Northampton County Militia during the War of the Revolution" the assertion is made that they participated in the battles of Assunpink, Brandywine, Germantown, White Marsh, Red Bank and Monmouth.

A military career on the frontier in the Revolutionary War was not ordinarily spectacular but it required unusual bravery, fortitude and resourcefulness. Gerlach Paul Flick possessed all these qualifications to an unusual degree. His contribution to American freedom will be better understood when the services of the military units which he led have been dug out of the records. It required an intelligent interest in an epoch-making movement and an exceptional courage and self-sacrifice to induce a man of middle age with a large family to support and a large farm to look after, to volunteer his services in the Revolution and to continue in the field for six years. His selection as captain also shows the high regard of his associates for his patriotism, his character and his ability. He neglected his own personal affairs and gave his time and energy gladly to create the new Republic of which he was a proud citizen. So far as known he never applied for a pension either to his state or the Federal Government. He must have taken considerable pride in the fact that two of his sons took up arms in defense of their native land. His youngest son, Gerlach Paul, Jr., was born the year Burgoyne surrendered at Saratoga. Whether any of his sons-in-law were soldiers in the Revolution has not been determined. At least four other Flicks who were immigrants like Gerlach Paul, several of whom were probably his brothers, and a number of their sons participated in the conflict.

At the conclusion of the Revolution Captain Gerlach Paul Flick returned to his mill and farm a man 55 years of age. He took a keen interest in the creation of the Federal Constitution of 1789[154] and voted for George Washington as the first President of the United States. Later he seems to have become a supporter of Jefferson. The inhabitants of Moor township bitterly opposed the House Tax which resulted in the Fries Rebellion of 1798–9, and Gerlach Paul Flick was unusually active in the hostile measures taken against it.[154a] State and local politics interested him greatly but he had no personal ambition to hold office although his high standing in Northampton county and his unusual military career would have brought him strong support had he cared to use them for political advancement. Although far advanced in years when the War of 1812 began, he followed its course with deep interest and rejoiced at its favorable conclusion.

In his home Captain Gerlach Paul Flick and his family spoke and wrote and read German, but all of them could use English in intercourse with neighbors who knew only that tongue. He himself, for that day, had received a good education in Hesse-Nassau and it had been supplemented by extensive travel and by service in the Revolutionary army. His scholarly taste is shown by the fact that he had 14 books in his library dealing no doubt with religion and history.

VI.

Captain Gerlach Paul Flick's Will.

Having accumulated a competence against his old age, Gerlach Paul Flick carefully guarded it and arranged for its distribution after his death among his children. On November 12, 1825, a little more than two

---

[154] No doubt he had taken an active part in organizing the "Constitutional Society of the Battalion of Northampton County" which looked out for the political rights and security of the inhabitants of the county. Pa. Arch. 1" Ser. VII, 284.

[154a] Davis, The Fries Rebellion, 1798–9, Doylestown, Pa., 1899, p. 38.

months before his death, he made a will which is still preserved in the Registry of Wills in the County Court House at Easton. It is written in English and signed in his own hand as "Paul Flick" instead of "Gerlach Paul Flick." The "Gerlach," probably a family name, was dropped as early as 1756, but has been retained throughout this paper to distinguish him from his third son, Paul Flick. The will written in another hand than his own is given here in full:

"In the name of God Aman. I Paul Flick of Moor township in the county of Northampton and State of Pennsylvania am old sick week of body but of perfect mind memory and understanding blessed be God Almighty for the same and knowing that it is appointed of all men to Die do publish this my last Will and Testament in manner and form following that is to say first is my will that all my Just Debts shall be paid after my Disease by my Executors hereinafter named second is my Will that all my reale as well as personel Estate Shall be sold by my executors after my Disease and the proceeds thereof shall be devided among my eleven children, shiere and shiere alike [excepting as hereinafter excepted] that is to say to my son Casper Flick one sheare to my son Martin one sheare one share to my son Paul one sheare to my daughter Margeretha intermarried to Jacob Gilbert to my daughter Catherine intermarried to Jacob Hugus one sheare to my daughter Anna Maria intermarred to Jacob Defenderfer one sheare to [my] daughter Suzanna intermarred to Peter Sholl one sheare to my daughter Elizabeth intermarried to George Greber one sheare to my Daughter Maria Magdelena intermarried to Peter Muffly one share to my daughter Sofya intermarried to John Reder one other sheare and as to my daughter Gertrante intermarred with Edward Greenemeyer her share shall remain in the hands of the executors and shall pay her the interest thereof during her natral life as also of the principal if she should stand in need of and after Desease what is left I give and devise to her son Daniel Sheikels and whereas I have paid in my lifetime fifty pounds for a certain Philip Flick who is since departed this life it is my will that this fifty pounds with the interest should remain in the hands of the children of said Philip [Flick] and should be diveided amongst them sheare and sheare alike and I do hereby impower my executors to make sign seal and execute such Deed or Deeds or other Instruments of Writing for my Real estate as I myself ought or chould have done in my lifetime and I do hereby Nominate Constitute and appoint my son Paul Flick and my sons in law Peter Sholl and John Reder sole Executors of this my last will and Testament hereby revoking disannul all former Wills by me made in witness whereof I have herunto set my hand and seal the twelfth day of November in the Year of our Lord one Thousand eight hundred and twenty five

(Signed) Paul Flick (Seal)

Signed sealed published and decleared by the above Testator and for his Last Will and Testament in the presents of us who at the instance and request of the Testator and in the presents of each other have hereunto subscribed our names as Witnesses

(Signed) Peter Steckel
Abraham Stern

Paul Flick
Peter Sholl Executors sworn Northampton Co.

Same day John Reder one of the Executors renounced all Letters Testamentary Granted Paul Flick and Peter Sholl the other two executors named in the will."

P. L. Eberle D. R.

It will be noticed that Gerlach Paul Flick does not mention his wife Anna Catherine in his will. Undoubtedly she died some years before, the date at present being unknown. He names 11 surviving children—3 sons and 8 daughters—and gives the names of all of them together with his sons-in-law. He showed no favoritism but divided his property "share and share alike" among his children but for some reason not quite clear provided that the portion going to Gertrante, presumably the youngest daughter, should be held in trust for her to be paid her as she needed funds, the remainder at her death to go to her son Daniel Sheikels, perhaps a son by a former marriage. A Philip Flick, very likely a brother who came to Philadelphia with him in 1751, is mentioned. The two eldest sons, John Caspar and Martin were not made executors, perhaps because they lived at some distance.

Captain Gerlach Paul Flick died January 20, 1826, at the age of 97 years, 10 months and 13 days, and was buried at Zion's Church (Stone Church) which he helped to build many years before at Kreidersville, Northampton county.[155] On February 4, 1826, his will was "exhibited and probated." At the public sale of his personal property 14 books were sold for $3., "one pair of specs" for 25 cents, "ten puter plates" for $1., and "one copper Kittle" for $4. An inventory of his property made on February 18, 1826, showed that Caspar Flick owed the estate one bond amounting to $1098.52 with interest; Col. Nicholas Kern owed a note and interest of $877.83; Martin Flick owed $443.54 and interest secured by one bond and three notes; Peter Muffly owed $247.39 with interest secured by three bonds; Paul Flick owed a "book debt" of $762.24 with interest; John Reder owed a "book debt" of $182.53 and interest; and many other persons owed notes and "book debts," the total amounting to $8723.31. The household goods and farm implements brought at public auction amounted to $161.12. The total sum

---

[155] His tombstone, a small brown stone slab about 18 inches high, has on one side the date 1826 and on the other side "P. Flick."

realized from the estate was $8884.43. When all expenses were paid it seems that each of the eleven children received $574.24. The savings of Captain Gerlach Paul Flick accumulated by a lifetime of hard work and thrift was a modest fortune for his day. It would be interesting to know the titles of the 14 volumes sold after his death, for they would give a clue to his intellectual equipment and to his literary taste. That this pioneer farmer and miller was a man of high standing in his community is attested by indisputabe evidence.

VII.
Captain Gerlach Paul Flick's Family.

So far as known no attempt has ever been made by any of Gerlach Paul Flick's descendants to write an account of either his life or that of his family. Hence the sources of information which might have been available at an earlier date have either disappeared altogether or have been so widely scattered that it is almost impossible to collect them. The colonial records of Pennsylvania preserve the date of his arrival in Philadelphia in 1751. The records of the Tohickon Union Church in Bedminster township, Bucks county, supply the date of his marriage and the birth of his two eldest children as well as the name of his wife. After his removal to Northampton county about 1760, however, there are few printed family or church records giving the dates of the birth or baptism of the nine later children. The records of Zion Church (Stone Church) at Kreidersville, Egypt Reformed Church and of Emanuel Church at Petersville might supply this information. The places of the burial of Gerlach Paul Flick, Jr., and wife and Peter Muffly and wife are known and the gravestones contribute data.

In the will of Gerlach Paul Flick the three sons are

mentioned in the order of seniority, and then the eldest daughter heads the list of girls. Knowing this arrangement it may be assumed that the eight daughters are named according to age. The Federal Census of 1790 contains the name of "Paul Flick" of Moor township as the "head of a family" with one son under 16 years of age and five daughters.[156] By 1790 he had been married 35 years and was 62 years old. Certainly all his 11 children had been born by that time. Assuming that the two eldest sons, Caspar and Martin, and the three eldest daughters, Margaret, Catherine and Anna Maria, were married and had homes of their own, that would leave Paul, aged 13, and Susanna, Elizabeth, Maria Magdelein, Sofya and Gertrante to make the six children still at home. The scanty information gleaned about the members of Gerlach Paul Flick's family will be summarized below, the order of his will being followed:

1. John Caspar Flick, born June 22, 1758, and baptised November 14, in Bedminster township, Bucks county, died in Northampton county in 1840 at the age of 82. Like his father he was a miller by trade. He served as a private in the Revolution and in 1794, was Captain of the 1st Company of the 4th Regiment of Northampton Co. Militia.[157] Caspar Flick in 1785 paid a tax of £2/16/3 on 193 acres, 1 horse and 2 cattle in Moor township; in 1786, 12/ on 133 acres, 1 horse and 2 cattle; in 1788, 3/4 on 1 horse and 1 cow. In 1786 he took out a warrant for 400 acres in Northampton county; in 1808 another tract of 50 acres; and in 1832 another tract of 12 acres.[157a] He had 12 children of whom all lived to be over 80. He was the father of John Flick, the founder of Flicksville, who was born January 1, 1783, and died at Flicksville, January 1,

---

[156] Federal Census, 1790, Pennsylvania, 177.
[157] Pa. Arch. 6″ Ser. IV, 394; V, 425, 431. He married Betsy Foulk.
[157a] Pa. Arch. 2″ Ser. XIX, 156, 253, 356; XXXIX, 78, 80.

1869. On May 27, 1810 he married Barbara Caster (Koester), who was born in 1780 and died 1858. His children were: (1) Elizabeth who was born in 1811, died 1887, married H. Shuman and had two daughters; (2) Bebra; (3) Catherine; (4) Joseph who went to Wisconsin; (5) Reuben Jay who became President of the Peoples Bank at Wilkes-Barre, was defeated for Congress, in 1882, died in 1890, and had 6 children; Liddon died 1905, Warren J. in Nevada, Helen F., Reuben J., Jr., Lydia and one other.[158]

2. Martin Flick was born about 1760 and may have been the third child. He was evidently named after John Martin Flick who came to Philadelphia in 1751 with Gerlach Paul Flick. On November 25, 1776, he enlisted for the period of the Revolutionary War as a private in Capt. James Gregg's Company, known also as the 3rd Company, of the 1st Regiment New York Line commanded by Col. Goose Van Scaick and Lt. Col. Cornelius Van Dyck.[159] Martin's name appears in the muster roll for March-June, 1780, and also in the muster roll dated at West Point January-April, 1781.[160] Col. Goose Van Schaick had been transferred from the 2nd New York Regiment to the 1st New York Regiment on November 21, 1776.[161] In the Battle of Monmouth he served as a brigadier general under Lord Stirling in 1778. He was in the Mohawk Valley in 1779 and was put in charge of the expedition against the Onondagan Indians. Martin Flick was one of the privates who invaded the Onondaga territory. Congress on May 10, 1779, publicly thanked Col. Van Schaick, his officers and men "for their activity and good conduct in the late expedition against the Onondagas."[162] In 1777 he

---

[158] See Nat. Enc. of Am. Biog. X, 35; Families of Wyoming Valley, II, 692; Wyoming Hist. and Geolog. Soc. X, 7, 14, 37, 285; XVIII, 25; Kieffer, First Settlers of the Forks of the Delaware, 360.

[159] N. Y. in the Rev., 21; Arch. of the State of N. Y., 177.

[160] Mass. Sol. and Sail. of the Rev. V, 786; Cal. N. Y. MSS. II, 356.

[161] Heitman I, 984.

[162] *Ibid.*

marched into Cherry Valley with 150 men against the Indians and Tories.[163] In 1781 with 800 men he pursued Sir John Johnson by way of Johnstown, N. Y.[164] For his services in the Revolution the State of New York on July 8, 1790, allotted Martin Flick 500 acres of land in the Military Tract, which was lot No. 26 in township 15, known as Fabius. He had the patent delivered to Caleb S. Riggs.[165] He had sold his New York bounty claim on June 26, 1790, to Benjamin Lay.[166]

After the Revolution he returned to Pennsylvania, for in 1785 he paid a tax of 10 shillings in Northampton county as a "single freeman."[167] On June 6, 1786, he took out two warrants for 400 acres each in that county.[168] The same year on August 20 "Mertain" Flick's name appears on the muster roll of Capt. John Rutter's Company of Northampton County Militia,[169] and on the muster roll of the 5th–7th classes of the 4th Battalion of the Northampton County Militia, which was called out on duty.[170] Nothing further is heard of him until 1826 when he was mentioned in his father's will.

3. Gerlach Paul Flick (second)[171] also called Paul Flick, Sr., and "Saw Miller Flick," third son but probably ninth child, was born in Moor township November 19, 1777, died September 14, 1856, and is buried

---

[163] Lossing I, 237. Upon returning from the Sullivan Expedition Col. Gansevoort found the 1st N. Y. Reg. at Fort Schuyler Sept. 24, 1779. Jour. of Lieut. Robert Parker in Pa. Mag. of Hist. 28:20.
[164] *Ibid.*, 290.
[165] Bal. Bk. 28, 129, 159.
[166] N. Y. Cal. of Land Papers, 819.
[167] Pa. Arch. 3" XXVI, 78, 79.
[168] Pa. Arch. 3" Ser. XXVI, 78, 79. He seems to have been enrolled in 1782 in the 1st Company, 3rd Battalion, of the Northampton Co. Militia along with "Gasper." *Ibid.*, 4th Ser. VI, 246, 260, 266, 279. On August 20, 1784, he was doing military duty at Wyoming, Pa. *Ibid.*, III, 883.
[169] *Ibid.* 6" Ser. III, 883.
[170] *Ibid.*, 790.
[171] Tombstone at Bath, Pa., Printed List of Names p. 8.

with his wife in the cemetery at Bath, Pennsylvania. In 1802 he married Maria Margaret Roeder who was born in 1782 and died in 1860. He ran a saw mill and plaster mill indicated on a map made in 1850 and now in the Pennsylvania Historical Society showing that the mills were located almost in the center of the southern border of Moor township. The Northampton county records state that between the years 1820 and 1852 he bought seven tracts of land. He died intestate and his son Stephen Flick and his son-in-law Abraham Leh were appointed administrators of his estate which realized at public sale $3790.[172] The petition of the administrators mentions 12 children—7 sons and 5 daughters—all living in 1856 except George, in the following order: (1) Lydia, born about 1802, married Jacob Donner and died about 1872 leaving six children, Caroline, Susan, Frank, Tihlman, Abraham, Paul, and Stephen. (2) John, the eldest son, born about 1804 and living in 1856, married Nancy ——— and had daughters Emelina and Helen. (3) Paul, born about 1806, died in 1859, unmarried. (4) Isaac, born about 1808, married Sarah Palmer about 1829, in 1841 went with his family and brother Abraham to Ohio, visited California in 1849, and removed to Illinois after the Civil War. His children were Mary, Abraham, Rebecca, Harrison, Elizabeth, Emaline and George. (5) Catherine, born about 1810, died about 1863, married Jeremiah Flick and had these children: George, Sarah, Susan, Abanton, Emma and Anne Eliz. (6) Henry, born about 1812, married Louisa Miller, and lived at Bath. He was the father of Quintus, Paul (unmar.), George and William Flick who married Louisa Bender in 1845 and had 14 children: James A., 1864; Mary E. S., 1867; Lydia S., 1869; Augustus F., 1870; Elmer A.,

---

[172] Orphans' Court Records, Easton, XVIII, 146. The records of the First Reformed Church at Easton, Pa., give the marriage of John Paul Flick to Maria Margaret Roeder, on Feb. 7, 1802. This was probably Gerlach Paul Flick Jr. Kieffer, 371.

1872; Hannah E., 1873; Sarah, 1876; Cora S., 1877; Lillian A., 1878; Mame V., 1880; Mackie R., 1881; Clara, 1884 Martha M., 1886, and Myce, 1890.[173] (7) Abraham, born April, 1813, in Moor township, died December, 1870, near Galion, Ohio, married Catherine Patterson of Philadelphia in 1836 and moved to Crawford county, Ohio, with his wife and three children and his brother Isaac in 1841. Children: Abraham Amandus, 1837; Mary Jane, 1838; Sabina Catherine, 1840; Lewis Paul, 1842; Enos Henry, 1845; Stephen, 1846; John Peter, 1848; Sarah Ann, 1850; and Hannah, 1853. About 1857 he visited his relatives in Pennsylvania and in 1859 his brother Stephen and his mother visited him in Ohio.[174] (8) Julianna, born July 15, 1817,[175] married Thomas Moyer. Children: Mary, Sarah, Abanton, John, Jane, Emma, Oliver and F. Rader. (9) Sarah ("Sally"), born September 26, 1822, baptised October 8 with Maria Siegfried, widow of John Siegfried, sponsor,[176] married Abraham Leh and had the following children: Ellen, Mary, James and Abraham. (10) Rebecca, born about 1819, and was unmarried, but had sons: Eugene Lowell, Charles B. and George Weitzel. (11) Stephen, born about 1825, was joint administrator of his father's estate, bought property in Bath in 1856, visited Ohio in 1857, and was father of Stewart, Flora, Margaret, Laura, Robert L., Gertrude, Edward, Paul, Emma and Harry Elwood. (12) George, born about 1806, was dead in 1856, married Elizabeth ——— and had five children—Levinda, Sybilla, George, William and Sarah, all of age in 1856, making him one of the older children. (13) Maria Margaret, born May 25, 1819, was named after her mother but since she was

---

[173] See Genealogical Record of the Schwenkfelder Families for details.
[174] The compiler of this paper traces descent through Abraham and Enos Henry Flick.
[175] Birth recorded in Egypt Reformed Church, Whitehall township, Lehigh county, Pa. Arch. 5th Ser.
[176] Pa. Arch. 6" Ser. VI, 100.

not mentioned in her father's administration papers was probably dead and without heirs.[177]

4. Margaretha, born August 18 and baptised October 6, 1756, in Bedminster township, Bucks county, married Jacob Gilbert and was living in 1826.[178]

5. Catherine, born about 1762 in Northampton county, married Jacob Hugus and was living in 1826. Their granddaughter Mary M. married Rev. Henry Koch, a grandson of Rev. John Egidius Hecker.[179] In 1819 Catherine was living at Greensburg, Pa., and had 4 sons and 7 daughters.[180] She died in Tuscarawas Co., Ohio, after 1834.

6. Anna Maria, born about 1764, married Jacob Defendorfer and was living in 1826.

7. Suzanna was born about 1766, married Peter Sholl and died about 1848.[181]

8. Elizabeth, born about 1768, married George Greber and made her will in 1844.

9. Maria Magdelein, born October 24, 1774, died February 9, 1859, was buried in Zion Cemetery, married Peter Muffly and had 2 sons and 4 daughters.[182]

10. Sofya, born about 1779, married John Reder and was living in 1826.

11. Gertrante, born about 1782, died November 8, 1846, married first apparently, —— Sheikels and had a son Daniel and secondly, Edward Greenemeyer. Died 1840. Theobald Sheffer on October 19, 1846, as executor of her estate in trust after the death of Peter Sholl, reported the balance in her account to be $546.15.[183]

---

[177] Same as footnote [175].
[178] Pa. Arch. 6" Ser. VI, 94.
[179] Fathers of the Reformed Church 299–303. 12, 1819. The 11 children signed their own names. Will of Jacob Hugus, Tuscarawas Co., O. Names of 12 children given.
[180] Letter of Jacob Hugus to Gerlach Paul Flick at Kernsville, Dec.
[181] Paul Flick's Will, Registry of Wills, Easton, Pa.
[182] Eyerman, The Old Graveyards of Northampton Co., 130.
[183] Registry of Wills, Easton, Pa., File No. 3734.

VIII.

CONCLUSIONS.

1. The first Flicks to leave Europe for America were Gerlach Paul Flick, John Peter Flick, Johan Martin Flick and John Philip Flick in 1751. They were followed by at least six more Flicks. Some of them undoubtedly brought their families with them. All of them sailed from Dutch ports and landed at Philadelphia.

2. Unfavorable social, economic and religious conditions induced them to leave the Old World. They came to Pennsylvania attracted by the favorable reports of the unusual opportunities and greater liberties sent home by those who had preceded them to that province. Although most of them settled in Pennsylvania, still some of them went to New York, New Jersey, Maryland and Virginia.

3. The coming of the Flicks was typical of what was happening in all the British colonies in North America. Young men of ambition and ability from the older communities over seas were settling on the frontiers of America, marrying into the families of older immigrants, establishing their own homes, clearing the land to make new farms, rearing families of future Americans, and rapidly becoming desirable citizens.

4. Captain Gerlach Paul Flick readily adapted his life to the new environment, emerged as a man of means and influence in his community, was perhaps the most conspicuous of the Flick pioneers, and left behind him an honorable reputation for industry, thrift, honesty, high morality, intelligence and good citizenship. Although nearly all of the Flicks took up arms, as did their sons, in defense of American rights in the Revolution, Gerlach Paul Flick and his son John Caspar

were the only ones who won for themselves the rank of an officer.[184]

5. Today the descendants of Captain Gerlach Paul Flick are found in all sections of the United States. If the four generations following him have kept up an average of five children for each family his descendants would now number more than 6000—a suggestion of how the present population of the nation has been created.

6. The problems connected with the biography of Captain Gerlach Paul Flick which remain to be solved are: (1) additional facts about his native land and his ancestors; (2) further details concerning his life in Pennsylvania; (3) a more specific account of his military services in the Revolution; (4) information about his children and their descendants. It is hoped that others will help to supply the data now lacking.

---

[184] The "Alphabetical List of Revolutionary Soldiers 1775–1783," which purports to give all the Pennsylvania Revolutionary soldiers' names, but two Flicks—Adam and Henry. Pa. Arch. 2" Series XIII, 1–250. This is manifestly an error as the later volumes in the Archives prove. For instance a Frederick Flick was enrolled as a Ranger on the Frontier from 1778 to 1783. *Ibid.*, Ser. XXIII, 268; and served in the Cumberland County Militia in 1780, 1781 and 1782. .*Ibid.*, 721, 741, 793. George Flick private in Capt. John Reynolds' Co. Pa. Ger. Soc. XXII, 221.

THE FOULKE FAMILY OF GWYNEDD, PA.*—In preparing the sketch of the genealogy of the Foulke family (descendants of Edward Foulke, of Gwynedd) in my *Historical Collections Relating to Gwynedd*, I failed to get either full or satisfactory details concerning the line of Caleb Foulke, Jr. Recently Mr. Frank Foulke, of New York City, a lineal descendant of Caleb, has supplied me with data enlarging and correcting what is given in my book. I therefore offer it in the PENNSYLVANIA MAGAZINE in the hope that it may reach some of those particularly interested in the subject.

The line to Caleb, Jr., is as follows :

1. Edward Foulke, of Gwynedd, original settler there, 1698.
2. Thomas, m. Gwen Evans.
3. William, m. Hannah Jones.
4. Caleb, m. Jane Jones (dau. of Owen, of Wynnewood, Lower Merion).
5. *Caleb, Jr.* He was twice married. His first wife, whom he m. 11th mo. 26, 1795, was Margaret, dau. of Thomas and Sibina Cullen, who died 7th mo. 23, 1809, buried at North Wales. (She had a sister who m. a Mr. Cottinger, of Baltimore.) His second wife was Sarah Hodgkiss, widow, of Germantown, whom he m. in 1814. By Margaret he had ten children, five of whom survived infancy, and are named below. By Sarah he had one daughter named Sarah, who died unm. 6th mo. 3, 1834. The five children were:

6. Louisa, b. in Philadelphia, 12th mo. 21, 1797 ; d. unm. in Jersey City, N. J., Oct. 24, 1886 ; buried at Gwynedd.
7. Jane, b. at Gwynedd, 8th mo. 30, 1799 ; d. in Philadelphia, June 20, 1845 ; m. Alexander Hall, and had one son who d. unm.
8. Ellen, b. in Philadelphia, 3d mo. 30, 1801 ; m. Samuel Hatfield (uncle to Dr. Nathan Hatfield, Sr.) ; d. in Jersey City, July 12, 1880 ; buried at Gwynedd.
9. William, b. at West Caln, Chester Co., Pa., 2d mo. 2, 1804 ; d. in Philadelphia, 12th mo. 2, 1847 ; m. at Hadley, Mass., Oct. 26, 1830, Lucy Dickinson, and had three children : (1) Charlotte, d. in infancy ; (2) Margaret, b. in Philadelphia, Jan. 13, 1833 ; m. in Philadelphia, Oct. 25, 1866, Arthur Johnes, of New York City (who d. March 27, 1880), and has two living children, William F., b. Jan. 15, 1868, and Lucy, b. June 8, 1870 ; (3) Edward D., b. February 14, 1837, in Philadelphia ; d. unm May 15, 1887.
10. Henry, b. at Berwick, Pa., 2d mo. 9, 1808 ; d. in New York, April 20, 1866. He m. Sept. 25, 1832, at the house of her brother, Jonathan Trotter, of Brooklyn (then mayor of that city, the second in service), Hannah Trotter, of Newcastle-on-Tyne, England.

(10). The issue of Henry and Hannah Trotter Foulke are as follows :
11. William Henry, b. in New York, July 1, 1833 ; m. Clara Hoyle of that city. No children.
12. Charles Trotter, b. in New York, March 6, 1837 ; m. Emma Gildersleeve, of that city, and has issue : Henry, b. Sept. 1, 1858 ; Jane, b. Nov. 19, 1860 ; Joseph S., b. Sept. 11, 1862 ; Frank, b. July 31, 1864.
13. Jane, b. in New York, May 18, 1844 ; m. in Philadelphia, May 7, 1863, John Potts Rutter, of Pottstown, Pa. He went to New York, 1864, became a member of the New York Stock Exchange in 1870 ; d. Nov. 6, 1887. No children.
14. Frank, b. in New York, Feb. 9, 1849 ; m. Mrs. Marguerite Staples Wood, *née* De Puy, of Delaware Water Gap, Pa. (The De Puys is the oldest family in that section.) No children.

*For more information on the Foulke family see Howard M. Jenkins' *Historical Collections Relating to Gwynedd*, published by the author, Philadelphia, 1897.

In comparing the foregoing with the account given in my book (page 241) there will be observed several corrections, but the most important is the addition of the fifth child (Henry) of Caleb, Jr., and Margaret, his children and grand-children being all that are now living of this branch of the family.

I add a few further details concerning the two sons of Caleb and Jane (Jones) Foulke (4th generation above). They were:

1. *Owen.* In my book few details are given concerning him. Besides being a partner with his father in business, he was a member of the Philadelphia bar, and was regarded as a man of more than ordinary talent. In 1798 he became a member of the City Troop. During the later years of his life he practised law in Sunbury, Pa. He was born in Philadelphia, 6th mo. 27, 1763, and died (and was buried) at Gwynedd, 8th mo. 30, 1808. He was, I believe, unmarried.

2. *Caleb, Jr.* (named above, No. 5), was born in Philadelphia, 8th mo. 7, 1770, and died in that city, 10th mo. 15, 1823. He was a merchant.

HOWARD M. JENKINS.

Avalon, Gwynedd, Pa.

OLD RECORDS OF THE FOULKE, SKIRM, TAYLOR, COALMAN, WOOLLEY, AND GASKILL FAMILIES.

[The Bible from which this record is taken, an old black-letter folio, was brought to this country in the year 1677, by Thomas Foulke, one of the Commissioners for the Province of West New Jersey,[1] who was born in Derbyshire[2] in 1624, and is now in the possession of one of his descendants, Mrs. Mary C. Gaskill, of Philadelphia. It is a reprint of the Cranmer edition of 1541, " Imprynted at London in Flete strete, at the signe of the Sunne, ouer agaynste the conduyte, by Edwarde Whitchurche. The XXIX. day of December the yeare of our Lorde, M.D. XLIX." During the last century it was rebound at the cost of twelve shillings and six pence, but unfortunately not until such a course was absolutely necessary, as the title-page of the Bible, the first two pages of Archbishop Cranmer's prologue, the last page of the contents, one page containing an exhortation, etc., the title-page of the second part, and the last four folios of the New Testament are all missing.[3]

This Bible is said to have been buried in the ground during the persecution of the adherents of the Reformed Church in the reign of Philip and Mary, and has numerous marginal notes showing the peculiarities of the sixteenth-century penmanship. Scattered through the Old Testament are the signatures of Richard Smallwood and Francis Berdesly, which evidently belong to the same period as the notes, and those of Thomas Foulke, Sarah Foulke, and Sarah Skirm, which can be assigned to a later date.]

Thomas Foulks[4] Senor Dyed June the 10th : 1714. Aged 90 years.

Mary Foulks[4] Dyed February the 16th : 1718. Aged 89 years.

Thomas Foulks[4] Son of Thomas Foulks Senor dyed August the 24th : 1739. Aged 75 years.

Elizabeth Foulks[4] Daughter of John & Anne Curtis dyed April 21st : 1731 aged 60 years & 2 months & 5 days.

[1] Smith's " History of New Jersey," p. 93.
[2] Besse's " Sufferings of the Quakers," Vol. I. pp. 138–40–41–42.
[3] Catalogue of Lea Wilson's Collection, pp. 31–33.
[4] Black-letter.

Writen[1] By Abraham Skirm February the 17th: 174¾.
Aged 14½ years the Son of Richard & Elizabeth Skirm.
Mary Folkes the Daghter of Thomas and Elizabeth Folkes was Born the 25th: of the first Month 1690.
Ann Folkes the Daghter of the Above Thos. And Eliz: Folkes was born the 12th: of the 12th: Month 1694.
Thomas Folkes the Son of the Above was Born the 1st: of ye 8th: Month: 1697. Departed this Life on the 21st: of 10 M: 1777 Aged 80 y: 2 M: 20 D.
Elizabeth Folkes the daughter of the Above was born the 31st: of ye 11th: Month 1700.
Sarah Folkes the Daughter of the Above was born the 25th: Day of the 2nd: Month 1702.
Isaiah Folkes the Son of the Above Thos. And Eliz^h: Folks was born the 23rd Day of the 5th: Month 1704.
Rebeckah Folkes the Daught^r. of the Above Said Was bo n the 3rd: of the 5th: Month 1706.
An Accompt of Mary Folkes who Married Joseph Mires An their Children.

An Accompt of Ann Folkes who Married Samuel Taylor and their Children which Are as Follows.
Mary Taylor   mary'd Godfrey Beck
Samuel Taylor
Thomas Taylor
Elizabeth Taylor "   Edward Rockhill
John Taylor[2]
Anne Taylor   "   Jonathan Quicksall
Rebeckah Taylor   "   William Steward
Susannah Taylor   "   Soloman Rockhill
Sarah Taylor   "   Richard Brown
Acsha Taylor   "   John Follswell
An Account of Thomas Folkes Who Married Mary the Daughter of and Joseph Pancost.

[1] Black-letter.
[2] Opposite the name of John Taylor is written that of John Skirm, who may have been the second husband of either Elizabeth or Anne.

An Accompt of Elizabeth Folkes Who Married Richard Skirm [of Burlington Co., N. J.] the Son of Abram Skirm & their Children
Abraham Skirm the Son of the Above was Born y^e 26th of 5th : Month About 7 of the Clock In the Afternoon 1729 one thousand Seven Hundred & Twenty Nine.
Mary Skirm wass Born y^e 17th of 3rd Month In the Year of Our Lord one Thousand Seven hundred & Thirty One.
Isaac Skirm Wass Born y^e 16th of the first Month 173$\frac{3}{4}$.
Joseph Skirm Was Born the 20th Day of the Seventh Month In the Year of Our Lord one Thousand Seven hundred & thirty five 1735
Elizabeth Skirm Was Born y^e 12th of the first Month 173$\frac{7}{8}$ Who Dyed———.
Elizabeth Skirm Was Born the 20th. of the 4th. Month 1741.
Richard Skirm Departed thiss Life the 6 Day of 6th. Month In Year 1746. Aged 64 years.
Elizabeth Skirm Departed thiss Life the 5th. of 2: 1765 aged 65 years.

An Accompt of Sarah Folkes Who Married Joseph Thorn the Son of———
There Children Viz^t:
Joseph Thorn
Elizabeth Thorn
John Thorn
Thomas Thorn
Michael Thorn
An Account of Rebeckah Folkes who Mar^d: Samuel Horsman the Son of———
Abram Skirm was married to Elizabeth Fowler the Daughter of John & Elizabeth Fowler on the 23rd Day of ye 3rd: Month In the year of our Lord 1750 Old Stile.

An Account of Abraham & Elizabeth Skirm's Children the Time of their Births.
Rebekah Skirm Daughter of the Above was Born on ye 15th. Day of 11 m: 1750

Anna Skirm was Born on the 9th Day 8 M: 1752.
Hannah Skirm was Born the 18th of 11 M. 1754.
Huldah Skirm was Born the 31st of 7 M. 1756.
John Skirm was Born the 10th of 7 M. 1758
Tacey Skirm was Born the 29th of 10 M. 1762
   The Above Departed this Life the 4th of the 4 M. 1837.
Abraham Skirm was Born the 20 of 9 M. 1765. Departed this Life on 27th. 6 M. 1784.
Sarah Skirm was Born the 16th 2 M: 1768. Departed this Life the 18 of 9th. M. 1836
Mary Skirm was Born the 25th of 3 M. 1771
Joseph Skirm was Born the 30th. of 7 M. 1774.
Abraham Skirm Son of Richard and Elizabeth Skirm Departed this life the 24 day of 4 M. 1785 aged 56 years.
Elizabeth Fowler was born the 5 da of 9 M. 1731.

   An Account of the Births of the Children of James and Anne [Skirm] Coalman.
Ruth Coalman was born on the 27 of the 3 Month 1774.
Huldah Coalman was born on the ——— of the ——— Month———
James Coalman was born on the 3 of the 5 Month 1777.
Elizabeth Coalman on 3rd. 3 Mo: 1780.
Anne Coalman was born 5th. 2 Mo: 1782
Nathaniel Coalman.
George Coalman was Born 10th of 3 Mo. 1786.
Nathaniel Coalman.

   An Account of the Births of James Woolley & Huldah [Skirm] his Wifes Children.
Elizabeth Woolley was born on 30th: of the first Month 1778.
Hannah Woolley was Born on the first Day of 8 Month 1781. Dyd the 9th of 7 M. 1783.
Deborah Woolley was born on 30th: of 9 M. 1783. Dyd the 6 of 10 M. 1784.
Mary Woolley was born on 13th. of 4 Mo. 1785.

John Tucker Woolley was born y⁰ 4 day of the 6 month 1787.
Ann Woolley
Huldah Woolley was born the 10th. of the 5 Month 1791.
Charlotte Woolley was born the 15 day of the tenth month 1793.
Edna Woolley was born the 31 day of 7 Mon. 1796.

Joseph Skirm & Elizabeth Anderson were married July 17th 1802. Elizabeth Anderson was born Feb. 24th 1776.
An Account of Joseph & Elizabeth Skirm's Children's Births.
Emlia Skirm was Born July 5th 1804 fifth of the week.
Abraham Skirm was Born February the 22 the Year 1806. Seventh of the week.
Charles C. Skirm was born October 22d 1808. Seventh of the week.
Malenia Skirm was born January 24, 1811. Fifth Day of the week.
Mary [Clark] Skirm was March the 20th 1814. First Day of the week.

Charles C. Skirm & Theodosia C. Lee. were married 22nd Nov. 1830.
Joseph. Skirm was born 22nd of August 1832.
Mary Elizabeth Skirm was born 28th day of February 1838.
Alethia Skirm was born 15th day of June 1841.

[The late] Joseph W. Gaskill [of Philad'a] & Mary C. Skirm were married the 3rd of the 10th Month 1832.
An account of Joseph W. & Mary C. Gaskill's Childrens' Births.
Edward M. Gaskill was born the 22nd of the 10th. Month 1833. Departed this life the 5th of the 11th Month 1841.
Anna Virginia Gaskill was born the 16th of the 11th Month 1835.
Charles Merwin Gaskill was born the 14th of the 8th Month 1838.

Edwin A. Gaskill
William H. C. Gaskill
Frank Gaskill
An Accompt of Richard Skirm's Brothers & Sisters In England [the children of Abraham Skirm].
Mary Skirm.
Richard Skirm.
Anne Skirm.
Sarah Skirm.
Abraham Skirm.
Isaac Skirm.
Rebeckah Skirm.

THE FRANKS FAMILY.—So much historical and personal interest centers around different members of the Franks family and so much that is not correct in regard to them has appeared in print, that I have put into shape some notes jotted down by me in the course of a search for a portrait of the wit and beauty, Rebecca Franks, afterward Lady Johnson, which was published for the first time as an illustration to *The American Woman*, by Miss Ida M. Tarbell, in *The American Magazine* for November, 1909.

It seems to be conceded that the American emigrant of the family was Jacob Franks, who came to this country according to one account, circa 1705, and according to another account, circa 1711. His father is variously stated to have been Aaron Franks and Naphtali Franks, of Germany, the former of whom it is claimed went to England, with George of Hanover, in 1714, to be crowned King of Great Britain, loaning him the jewels he wore in his crown on that occasion. Jacob Franks (1) was

born in 1688 and died in New York, January 16, 1769. In 1719 he married Belhah Abigail Levy, daughter of Moses Levy, and had 4 children, David, Phila, Moses and ——, if not more.
1. David Franks (2) b. in New York, September 28, 1720, removed to Philadelphia, circa 1738, and married there, December 17, 1743, Margaret Evans, daughter of "Peter Evans of the Inner Temple, gentleman, Register General of Pennsylvania." Mrs. Franks d. September 28, 1780, aged 60, and was buried in Christ Church yard.* David Franks died in England in 1794, having had 5 or 6 children, viz:
1. Abigail Franks (3), b. January 6, 1744/5; baptised in Christ Church, April 12, 1745; m. January 6, 1768, Andrew Hamilton, son of the Councillor of the same name who was brother of Governor James Hamilton, son of Andrew Hamilton, the great lawyer and elder brother of William Hamilton of the Woodlands. She died September 11, 1798, leaving one child, Ann (4), who married James Lyle, whose daughter Ellen (5) married Hartman Kuhn of Philadelphia.
2. Jacob (3), b. January 7, 1746/7; baptised at Christ Church, April 20, 1747; m. ——————. Jacob Franks was living in England in 1781, d. ——.
3. John (3), b. ——. d. ——. Styled of Ilesworth, Middlesex, England, Member of Parliament.†
4. Mary (3), b. January 25, 1748; baptised at Christ Church, April 10, 1748; d. August 26, 1774. On her tombstone in Christ Church yard she is called "Polly."
5. Moses (3), b. ——. d. ——.
6. Rebecca (3), b. 1760?; m. January 24, 1782, Henry Johnson, Colonel of the 17th regiment of Foot, who commanded Stony Point, when it was captured by Anthony Wayne and whose Orderly Book, which fell into the hands of Wayne on that occasion, is in the collection of the Historical Society of Pennsylvania. Colonel Johnson became a General in 1809 and was created a Baronet in December 1818, when his wife became Lady Johnson. She died March—, 1823. Her son Henry Allen Johnson m. Charlotte Elizabeth, daughter of Frederick Phillipse of New York, and their grandson is the present Colonel Sir Henry Allen William Johnson, b. 1855.
2. Phila Franks (2), b. June 19, 1722; m. ——. ——. 1742 Oliver Delancey of New York; d. 1811. They had 6 children, Susanna, Charlotte, Phila, Anna, Oliver and Stephen. Phila Franks is always stated incorrectly to have been a sister of Rebecca Franks, instead of her aunt.
1. Susanna (3) m. Lt. Gen. Sir William Draper
2. Charlotte (3) m. Field Marshal Sir David Dundas
3. Phila (3) m. Stephen Payne Galwey
4. Anna (3) m. John Harris Cruger
5. Oliver (3)

---

* The "copy" of Burials in Christ Church in the Historical Society of Pennsylvania, calls her "Rebecca," but her tombstone gives her name correctly.

† N. B. Jacob Franks probably changed his name to John, after he settled in England, as he is styled, the same as John, "of Ilesworth, Middlesex, England," in which case 2 and 3 are the same.

6. Stephen (3) m. ———— . His son was General Sir William Howe De Lancey who fell at Waterloo, where he was on Wellington's staff.

3. Moses Franks (2), b. ———— m. ———— Sarah ————. d. ————. Had issue Isaac (3) b. May 27, 1759; m. July 9, 1782 Mary Davidson and d. March 4, 1822. They had issue 4 children, 2 of whom died young and

1. Samuel D. (4), Judge of the Court of Common Pleas for the counties of Schuylkill, Lebanon and Dauphin, Penna.

2. Sarah Eliza (4) m. September 9, 1806, John Huffnagle.

N. B. David Solebury Franks, who was aide de camp to Benedict Arnold, is believed to have been also a son of Moses Franks (2), "Major David Franks," doubtless the same, was buried in St. Peter's Church yard October 7, 1793, and letters of Administration on the estate of David Solebury Franks were granted January 13, 1794, to Moses Franks. This last item would indicate his having been a son of Moses (2).

4. "Aunt Franks" is mentioned in the letter from Rebecca Franks to her sister Abby Hamilton, PA. MAG. OF HIST. AND BIOG., Vol. 22, and must have been either her father's sister or the wife of her uncle Moses.

CHARLES HENRY HART.

DELAWARE BIBLE RECORDS.

CONTRIBUTED BY REV. C. H. B. TURNER.

[The following records are copied from the Bible in possession of Mrs. John Wilson, of Delaware. The first record reads, "Eliz. Clarkson—her Book—was born in Cheshire, England, August 1st 1720. The gift of her Father, William Becket, Missionary at Lewes."] [1]

John Futcher son of William Futcher and Mary his wife was born May 7th 1744 and departed this life December 5th 177 [torn]

Thomas Futcher son of John Futcher and Sarah his wife was born on Wednesday the 21st day of May 1766. And departed this life 6th day of October 1769

William Futcher son of John Futcher and Sarah his wife was born on Saturday 9th day of January 1768. Departed this life December 18th 1836

Mary Futcher daughter of John Futcher and Sarah his wife was born July 19th 1769

[torn] Futcher son of John Futcher and Sarah his wife was born of Tuesday 18th day of December 1770

Susanah Futcher daughter of John Futcher and Sarah his wife was born of Thursday 11th day of January 1773

Elizabeth Futcher daughter of John Futcher and Sarah his wife was born on Wednesday August 23^{d}. 1775. Departed this life February 1776

Wm Futcher son of John Futcher was married 28th day of January 1795 [2]

[1] The will of the Rev. William Becket, bearing date 17 August, 1743, proved 29 August, 1743, recorded at Georgetown, Sussex County, describes him as "Missionary of the Gospel at Lewes," expresses his desire to be buried in the church yard of St. Peter's at Lewes, between the graves of his wives, makes bequests to his daughters, Elizabeth and Susanna, and states that his son-in-law, William Futcher, and his wife have already had their portion of his estate.

[2] William Futcher married Martha Little, January, 1795.

Sarah Futcher daughter of Wm Futcher and Martha his wife was born of the 9th day of December 1795

John Futcher son of Wm Futcher and Martha his wife was born on Sunday the 8th day of October 1797

Mary Futcher daughter of Wm Futcher and Mary his wife was born on the 5th day of February 1800. Departed this life January 23^d 1822—The wife of Wm Roades[1]

Peggy Futcher daughter of W^m. Futcher and Martha his wife was born Saturday the 10th Day of December 1803. Departed this life October 1806

W^m. Roades son of Wm Roades and Mary his wife was born December 13th 1821

Margaret Futcher daughter of John Futcher and Hetty Ann his wife was born of Thursday the 25th day of August 1825

Thomas Futcher son of John and Hetty Ann his wife was born September 20th 1826 and departed this life the same day

Mary West Futcher daughter of John and Hetty Ann his wife was born May 11th 1828

Erasmus Marsh Futcher son of John and Hetty Ann his wife was born January 1st 1830

William Futcher son of John and Hetty Ann his wife was born March 16th 1831 and departed this life the same day

Adaline Futcher daughter of John and Hetty Ann his wife was born August 25· 1832, and departed this life the same day

John Little Futcher son of John and Hetty Ann his wife was born March 17th 1834 and departed this life the same day

John Mitchelmore Futcher son of John and Hetty Ann his wife was born February 14th 1835

Martha Ann daughter of John and Hetty Ann his wife was born February 13th 1838

---

[1] William T. Rhodes married Mary Futcher, 18 January, 1821. Records of the United Presbyterian churches of Lewes, Rehoboth and Cool Spring, a copy of which is in The Historical Society of Pennsylvania. ED.

Joseph Franklin Futcher son of John and Hetty Ann his wife was born August 2^d. 1839

Becket Futcher son of John and Hetty Ann his wife was born April 23^d 1841 and departed this life the same day

Hetty Elinder Futcher daughter of John and Hetty Ann his wife was born February 6th 1843

Sarah Lamb daughter of Wm Futcher and Martha his wife departed this life March 3^d. 1848, aged 52 years 2 month——

John Little son of John Little and Sarah his wife was born June 6th 1771[1]

Margaret Little daughter of John and Sarah his wife was born July 3^d. 1773

Martha Little daughter of John and Sarah his wife was born June 27th 1774

[1] John Little married Sarah Gill, 20 December, 1770.

RECORD OF THE DESCENDANTS OF JAMES AND PHEBE GILLINGHAM.

Births.

John Hallowell, son of James and Phebe Gillingham, was born the 11th month (November) 1763. Died in infancy.

Martha, daughter of James and Phebe Gillingham, was born the 2nd of 2nd month (February) 1765.

Hannah Lewis, daughter of James and Phebe Gillingham, was born the 14th of 6th month (June) 1767.

James, son of James and Phebe Gillingham, was born the 14th of 5th month (May) 1768.

Esther, daughter of James and Phebe Gillingham, was born 1771.

One infant, the date of birth unknown, died in infancy.

Mary Gillingham, daughter of James and Sarah Gillingham, was born the 30th of the 6th month (June) in the year 1791, at 7 minutes before 12 o'clock at noon.

James Gillingham, son of James and Sarah Gillingham, was born on the 11th of the tenth month (October) 1795 at 5 o'clock in the morning.

Esther Gillingham, daughter of James and Sarah Gillingham, was born the 17th of the third month (March) 1798, at ½ past 12 o'clock noon.

George Washington Gillingham, son of James and Sarah Gillingham, was born the 17th of the 4th month (April) 1800, at 12 o'clock at noon.

William Cliffton Gillingham, son of James and Sarah Gillingham, was born the 10th of the 5th month (May) 1802 at 15 minutes before 12 o'clock at night.

Henry Bailie Gillingham, son of James and Sarah Gillingham, was born the 16th of the 2nd month (February) 1804, at ½ past 9 o'clock in the morning.

Sarah Ann Gillingham, daughter of James and Sarah Gillingham, was born the 10th of the 2nd month (February) 1806 at ½ past 2 o'clock afternoon.

Lewis Gillingham, son of James and Sarah Gillingham, was born the 5th of the 11th month (November) 1808 at 7 o'clock in the evening.

Elizabeth Waring Gillingham, daughter of James and Sarah Gillingham, was born the 12th of the 8th month (August) 1810 at 15 minutes before 8 o'clock morning.

Charles Gillingham, son of James and Sarah Gillingham, was born the 6th of the 8th month (August) 1812 at 15 minutes past 1 o'clock in the morning.

Mary Anna, daughter of John and Mary Hardwick, was born on the 4th of June, 1823.

Sarah Elizabeth, daughter of John and Mary Hardwick, was born on the 26th of February, 1825.

Charles, son of Mary Nicholson, was born on the 30th of June, 1831.

James, son of George W. and Maria Gillingham, was born on the 8th of November, 1823.

William, son of George W. and Maria Gillingham, was born November 29th, 1825.

Catharine Rapp, daughter of George W. and Maria Gillingham, was born December 8th, 1827.

Ann Maria, daughter of George W. and Maria Gillingham, was born June 2nd, 1830.

Still born daughter of George W. and Maria Gillingham, was born September, 1831.

George W., son of George W. and Maria Gillingham, was born August 8th, 1832.

Sarah, daughter of George W. and Maria Gillingham, was born May, 1834.

John D. Gillingham, son of George W. and Maria Gillingham, was born November 12th, 1835.

Still born child of George W. and Maria Gillingham born.

Caroline E., daughter of George W. and Maria Gillingham, was born November 1st, 1839.

Josephine, daughter of George W. and Maria Gillingham, was born March 10th, 1841.

Catharine Rapp, daughter of George W. and Maria Gillingham, was born March 1st, 1846.

William Cliffton, son of Henry B. and Sarah Gillingham, was born September 1st, 1826.

Henry D., son of Henry B. and Sarah Gillingham, was born March 1st, 1828.

George W., son of Henry B. and Sarah Gillingham, was born December 9th, 1829.

James, son of Henry B. and Sarah Gillingham, was born November 29th, 1831.

Elizabeth Rich, daughter of Henry B. and Sarah Gillingham, was born October 15th, 1833.

Lewis, son of Henry B. and Sarah Gillingham, was born October 8th, 1835.

Sarah Anna, daughter of Henry B. and Sarah Gillingham, was born July 29th, 1837.

Maria Louisa, daughter of Henry B. and Sarah Gillingham, was born May —, 1839.

Esther, daughter of Henry B. and Sarah Gillingham, was born September, 1840.

Emma Matilda, daughter of Henry B. and Sarah Gillingham, was born November 6th, 1842.

Thomas Conner, son of Henry B. and Sarah Gillingham, was born May 29th, 1845.

Charles Wood Gillingham, son of Lewis and Margaret Gillingham, was born March 20th, 1834.

Margaret Thompson, daughter of Lewis and Margaret Gillingham, was born February seventh, 1836.

Robert Rayburn, son of Lewis and Margaret Gillingham, was born February 6th, 1838.

Albert Bell, son of Lewis and Margaret Gillingham, was born February 6th, 1841.

Edward Augustus, son of Lewis and Margaret Gillingham, was born November 27th, 1842.

Anna Holbrook, daughter of Lewis and Margaret Gillingham, was born May 8th, 1845.

George G., son of John H. and Anne M. Geyer, was born December 3rd, 1855.

William, son of John H. and Anne M. Geyer, was born August, 1859.

John, son of John H. and Anne M. Geyer, was born ———.

Harry B., son of G. W. and Anne Gillingham, was born January, '57.

Sallie, daughter of G. W. and Anne Gillingham, was born January, '59.

George, son of G. W. and Anne Gillingham was born ———.

Harry B., son of H. D. and Mary A. Gillingham, was born December 5th, 1855.

Lizzie, daughter of H. D. and Mary A. Gillingham, was born December 3rd, 1859.

Sallie, daughter of H. D. and Mary A. Gillingham, was born December, 1861.

Lewis G., son of Frank and Maggie Carey, was born May 31st, 1859.

Robert, son of Frank and Maggie Carey, was born June 10th, 1862.

George F. L., son of Frank and Maggie Carey, was born August 29th, 1864.

James Junr, son of H. D. and Mary A. Gillingham, was born April, 1862.

Laura, daughter of Joseph and Lizzie R. Casper, was born October 21st, 1865.

Anne Gillingham, daughter of John A. and Anne H. Granville, was born August 12th, 1866.

Harry B. and T. Jefferson, twin children of Joseph and Lizzie R. Casper, were born February 28th, 1868.

Charles Arrison, son of Lewis and Addie Gillingham, was born March 3rd, 1866.

Wilbur, son of John H. and Anne M. Geyer, was born July 19th, 1868.

Sarah Maria, daughter of John D. and Sally Gillingham, was born October 2nd, 1871.

Lewis, son of Lewis and Addy Gillingham, was born June 10th, 1872.

T. Reeves, son of Ely and Caroline E. Lawrence, was born August 8th, 1872.

Anna M., daughter of John D. and Sally Gillingham, was born ——.

Anna Morgan, daughter of Ely and Caroline E. Lawrence, was born March 12th, 1874.

E. M., daughter of J. D. and Sally Gillingham, was born June, 1876.

Lewis, son of Albert B. and Jenny Gillingham, was born August 29th, 1877.

Emily B., daughter of General John G. and Ellen Palmer [Park], was born at Washington, D.C., December, 1868.

William Gillingham, son of Ely and Caroline E. Lawrence, was born November 17th, 1877.

Josephine, daughter of Joseph and Lizzie R. Casper, was born December 9th, 1877. Died December 11th, 1877.

Marriages.

John · Hardwick and Mary Gillingham, married the 22nd of September, 1813.

George Washington Gillingham and Maria Dornan were married the 2nd of January, 1823.

Henry Bailie Gillingham and Sarah Rich were married the 13th of November, 1825.

Lewis Gillingham and Margaret Thornton were married the 2nd of June, 1833.

John H. Geyer and Anna Maria, daughter of G. W. and Maria Gillingham, were married November 30th, 1854.

Frank Carey and Margaret T., daughter of Lewis and Margaret Gillingham, were married July 29th, 1858.

Joseph Casper and Elizabeth Rich, daughter of Henry B. and Sarah Gillingham, were married January 1st, 1862.

Deaths.

Phebe, widow of James Gillingham and daughter of John and Hannah Hallowell, died on the morning of the 4th of 4th month (April) 1819, aged 80 years and 9 months.

William Cliffton, son of James and Sarah Gillingham, died at St. Francisville, Louisiana, on the 13th of the 8th month (August) 1825, aged 23 years, 3 months, and 3 days.

Esther, daughter of James and Phebe Gillingham, died on the morning of the 5th of the 7th month (July) 1831, aged 60 years.

Martha, widow of Peter Blight and daughter of James and Phebe Gillingham, died on the 18th of the 3rd month (March) 1832, aged 67 years, 2 months, and 16 days.

Josephine, daughter of G. W. and Maria Gillingham, died —— 1841, aged —— weeks.

James, son of James and Phebe Gillingham, died on the morning of the 22nd of the 1st month (January) 1833, aged 64 years, 8 months, and 8 days.

Sarah, widow of James Gillingham and daughter of Henry and Jane Bailie, died on the evening of the 6th of 5th month (May) 1843, aged 72 years.

Mary Nicholson, daughter of James and Sarah Gillingham, died the 15th of November, 1849, aged 58 years.

George Washington, son of James and Sarah Gillingham, died on the 1st of December, 1864, between 11 and 12 o'clock at night, aged 64 years, 7 months, and 14 days.

Maria Gillingham, widow of George W. Gillingham, died on the evening of the 16th of November, 1865, in the 62nd year or her age.

Sarah Gillingham, wife of Henry B. Gillingham, died on the 6th of July, 1860, in the 57th year of her age.

Robert Rayburn, son of Lewis and Margaret Gillingham died July 5th, 1838.

Edward Augustus, son of Lewis and Margaret Gillingham, died August 24th, 1843.

Charles Wood, son of Lewis and Margaret Gillingham, died August 8th, 1852, aged 18 years.

James, son of G. W. and Maria Gillingham, died March 20th, 1844, aged 20 years.

Catharine Rapp, daughter of G. W. and Maria Gillingham, died November 25th, 1845, aged 17 years and 11 months.

Catharine Rapp, daughter of G. W. and Maria Gillingham, died Sept. —— 1846, aged 6 months.

Esther, daughter of Henry B. and Sarah Gillingham, died January, 184[3], aged 2 years and 4 months.

Josephine, daughter of G. W. and Maria Gillingham, died May, 1841, aged 10 weeks.

Lizzie, daughter of H. D. and Mary A. Gillingham, died February, 1860.

Sallie, daughter of H. D. and Mary A. Gillingham, died December, 1861.

Willie, son of John H. and Anne M. Geyer, died May, 1860, aged 9 months.

James, son of H. D. and Mary A., died June 19th, 1864, aged 14 months.

Edward Conch Cowden, died June 5th, 1864, aged 37 years.

John, son of John H. and Anne M. Geyer, died —— 1862, aged —— months.

Anne H., wife of John A. Granville, died August 30th, 1866, aged 21 years, daughter of Lewis and Margaret Gillingham.

T. Jefferson, infant son of Joseph and Lizzie R. Casper, died April 4, 1868.

Harry B., infant son of Joseph and [Lizzie] R. Casper, died August 11, '68.

Henry D., son of H. B. and Sarah Gillingham, died May 23rd, 1869, aged 42 years.

Lewis, son of James and Sarah Gillingham, died Sept. 13th, 1870, aged 61 years and 10 months.

Sarah A., widow of the late E. C. Cowden and daughter of H. B. Gillingham, died November 6th, 1873, aged 36 years.

George W., son of George W. and Maria Gillingham, died May 3rd, 1876, aged 43 years.

Esther, daughter of James and Sarah Gillingham, died March 10, 1882, aged 83 years, 11 mos., 24 days.

Henry B., son of James and Sarah Gillingham died August 25, 1882, aged 78 years, 6 mos., 10 days.

T. Reeves, son of Ely and Caroline E. Lawrence died July 20th, 1873, at Bridegton, New Jersey.

Eliz. R. Casper, daughter of H. B. and Sarah Gillingham, died Sept. 26, 1886, aged 52 years.

Anna Morgan, daughter of Ely and Caroline E. Lawrence, died January 26th, 1876.

Sarah, wife of H. B. Gillingham, died July 6th, 1860, aged 57 years.

Sarah Ann, daughter of James and Sarah Gillingham, died Jan. 18, 1892, aged 85 years, 11 mos., 9 days.

Emma M., daughter of H. B. and Sarah Gillingham, died Nov. 14/88, aged 46 years, 8 days.

Mary A., daughter of John and Mary Hardwick, died Oct. 10, 1887, aged 64 years, 4 mos., 7 days.

Thomas C. Gillingham, son of H. B. and Sarah Gillingham, died 4–18–99.

Kentmere Hall, near Staveley, Westmoreland, Seat of the Gilpin Family, 1206-1650.

THE GILPIN ANCESTRY.

To the Editor of The Pennsylvania Magazine of
History and Biography:

The memoir of Thomas Gilpin, published in the October number, 1925, cannot fail to be of great interest to your readers.

Permit me, however, to offer a few corrections. George Gilpin, Queen Elizabeth's Ambassador at the Hague, is stated therein to have left no descendants. This is an error. A search at the Hague disclosed the fact that his second wife Mary (Points) died there leaving a will, a copy of which is in the writer's possession. He left sons: Captain Philip and Gideon, and daughters Margaretta and Ann.

The genealogical details as to the English ancestry of the family, in light of more recent research, need considerable revision. As this involves the progenitors of the American pioneer, Joseph Gilpin, it may not be uninteresting to your readers to set forth the facts as disclosed by the records.

Respectfully,

ALFRED RUDULPH JUSTICE.

The early history of the Gilpin family is based chiefly on the researches of George Gilpin, Esq., son of William and Elizabeth (Washington) Gilpin, who about the year 1590, forwarded a copy of his MS. to his uncle, George Gilpin, Queen Elizabeth's Ambassador at the Hague; hence unusual reliance is to be placed on his statements concerning his relatives at this time and previous thereto. It was again, about the year 1650, the subject of careful research by Sir Daniel Fleming, Bart, of Rydal Hall, who was noted for his genealogical investigations of Westmoreland Families. (See Nicholson & Burns' Hist. of Westmoreland.) His manuscripts are now in possession of the Fleming family, at Rydal Hall.

1629, George Carlton, Bishop of Chichester, wrote a Life of Bernard Gilpin, the Apostle of the North, which contains much of interest concerning the family.

In 1713, William Gilpin of Scaleby Castle, Recorder of Carlisle, with the aid of his relative Alan Chambre, Recorder of Kendal, made a pedigree of the family.

1753, the Rev. William Gilpin of Boldre (1724–1804) wrote a Life of Bernard Gilpin, which is practically a second edition of Carlton.

Thomas Gilpin of Philadelphia (1729–1778), grandson of Joseph Gilpin, the progenitor of the Gilpins in America, visited England in 1753, and has left us the result of his investigations. It may be stated that he makes mention of the fact that Thomas Gilpin, the eminent Minister of the Society of Friends, was a son of Thomas Gilpin of Mill Hill, but does not state he was descended from Bernard and Dorothy (Airy) Gilpin.

Joshua Gilpin, son of Thomas (1765–1841) made copies of the early English accounts which are embodied in the "Memoirs of the Gilpin Family of Philadelphia."

Hon. Henry D. Gilpin, Attorney General of the United States, and Vice President of the Historical Society of Pennsylvania, was also a diligent student of the family history and his valuable library and collection of family papers are now in possession of the Historical Society of Pennsylvania.

The late William Jackson, F. S. A. of White Haven, England, compiled an elaborate pedigree chart of the Gilpin Family, which is inserted in the "Memoirs of Dr. Richard Gilpin," published by the "Cumberland and Westmoreland Arch. & Antiquarian Society," 1879. He had access to the Fleming MSS., and secured much additional data from various sources mentioned in a note to the Pedigree, page 155. This will be referred to later as the Gilpin Chart.

It has been stated by Joshua Gilpin, and accepted apparently without inquiry by William Jackson, F. S. A., and the error repeated by numerous writers since, that Thomas Gilpin of Mill Hill, was the son of Bernard and Dorothy (Airy) Gilpin and grandson of Martin and Katherine (Newby) Gilpin, and great-grandson of William and Elizabeth (Washington) Gilpin.

Referring to the MS. of the "Memoirs of the Gilpin Family of Philadelphia," Vol. 2, page 7, in the Gilpin room of the Historical Society of Pennsylvania, we have the following statement which forms the basis for the error:

"But the date, residence and tradition combine in fixing Thomas Gilpin, the son of Bernard Gilpin, as the Thomas Gilpin of Mill Hill." No other proof is offered.

The writer first became doubtful about this descent in attempting to check up the marriage and birth records chronologically, and it became clear that Thomas Gilpin of Mill Hill, b. circa 1586 and married 1608, could not have been the son of Bernard Gilpin, bapt. March 1, 1583/4, and whose parents were married in 1580.

Martin Gilpin, son of William and Elizabeth (Washington) Gilpin, b. circa 1554, d. December 18, 1629, buried at Kendal, Westmoreland. M. 1580, Katherine Newby, d. 1633/4 (Gilpin chart), daughter of Richard Newby of Strickland, parish of Kendal.

Will of Katherin Gilpin of Kirkie Kendall, widow, late wife of Martin Gilpin, deceased, dated 29 August 1632, pr. Arch. Richmond, 11 January 1633. "To be buried in my parish church of Kendal, as near my late father and my children as possible. Whereas: my son Barnard Gilpin was bound to my late husband for £10 payable on demand, one-half of which is due to me as executor of my late husband, the said £5 to be paid as follows: 20/ to his wife, 20/ to my daughter-in-law Isaac's wife. 20/ to his son Samuel, 20/ to my grandchild Thomas Bateman, and the £10 he is bound to pay me at hardimas next. I leave to Dorothy Bateman who hath been long with me for and towards her preferment, whereunto her father consented that I should dispose thereof to such of his children as I thought fitt." Whereas Henry Bateman owes me £10 which his father promised he would cause him (to) pay forth of his portion, of which £10, I leave to his father £5, and £5 I abate to the said Henry.

To Katherin, wife of Thomas Sands £5 forth of my goods. My part of pewther being half remaining in the house where I now dwell to be equally divided between them, my following grandchildren: Matithia, wife of George Warde. Dorithie Bateman, Marie Bateman, Katherin Sheepperd, Dorothie Gilpin, daughter of son Isaac, Elizabeth Gilpin, sister of said Matithia, Ann Dixon, daughter of Arthur Dixon. To my four sons in law, four of my silver spoons, one each, and the fifth to Dorothy Bateman.

To the said Dorothy Bateman, "the bedd clothes wherein I ly, viz, the fether bedd, the boulster, the coverlett and cadowe."

Residue of my goods to my four daughters, Grace, Dorothy, Marie and Alice, joint executors (No surnames given). Supervisors: my two sons Bernard and Isaac. Witnesses: William Helmer and Robert Crosfield.

Inventory of the goods of Katherin Gilpin, taken by William Helmer and William Rakestraw, 9 Jan. 1633, consisting of household effects, etc. Among the articles enumerated were: a laddle and a postnett, a morter and a pestell, chamber potts, Speets racks, and other small iron gear, brewing Knoppe; gile fatt gallons, carpets and guishions, wood and peats, one silver bole, one gilded salt, Silver buttons.

Summary of the value £XXX, XV/ VId.

A third part of wch goods at the least was given by the said Martin Gilpin to his children, and his said wife was but to have the use thereof during her life, albeit they were whollie prised (by mistaking) after her death. And her funeralls wth Pbate of her will are to be deducted amounting to ....beside her legacies.

No list of Debtors or Creditors.

14 James I

Richmond Archdy, Kendal Deanery.

Will of Richard Newby of Strickland in Parish of Kendal Co. West'm., yeoman, dated 2 March 1616/17, to be buried in Kendal church. To said church 10/. For poor of hamlets of Grayrigg, Lambrigg, Docker, Strickland Roger, and Strickland Kettle respectively £40—full particulars as to trusts. Copy of will to be kept in the reveotry at Kendal church. All lands in Dillaker and Strickland Roger of West'md. to my son Randall Newby for life remainder as to Dilliker, to Allen Gilpin, 4th son of Martin Gilpin and of Katherine his wife my Daughter, in tail, paying at Burneshead chapel Westm'd. to Helen Warde now wife of Anthony Warde only Daughter of my s'd son Randall, £20, in Default to Isaac Gilpin 2nd son of s'd Martin & Katherine in tail, in Default to Randall Gilpin 3rd son of s'd. Martin & Katherine in tail in Default to Bernard Gilpin, eldest son of s'd Martin & Katherine in tail in Default to right heirs of s'd. Allen Gilpin. All lands in Dilliker called Low Grayning Field late my brother Miles Newby's dec'd from Death of s'd son Randall as former lands. Lands in Strickland Roger where s'd. son Randall now Dwelleth to s'd Randall Gilpin in tail from Death of s'd. son Randall in Default to s'd Allen Gilpin in fee. Son Randal to abide by will considering great charge of children my Sd. Daughter Katherine hath, many of them being unprovided for otherwise than from me. To Sd. Isaac Gilpin my interest in messuage in Strickland Kettle whereon I lately dwelled & which was heretofore granted to me by Sd. Martin Gilpin, also £66, 13, 4. To Anne Tunstall £10, if Sd. Isaac & she marry one another. To S'd Allen Gilpin £120 to S'd Randall Gilpin £100 to my Daughter Katherine £10 & I forgive her £4 she owes me. To Grace Bateman her Daughter & wife of William Bateman £20 etc. & £6, 13, 4 d. to children of Sd. Grace equally. To Dorothy Crossfield wife of Robert Crossfield another Daughter of Sd. Katherine £26, 13, 4. To Mary Shepperd wife of William Shepperd another of her Daughters £26, 13, 4, to Alice Gilpin, youngest Daughter of Sd. Katherine, £20. To sd. Bernard Gilpin £10. To William Gilpin his eldest son £5. To his three younger sons 40/ a piece. To Dorothy Gilpin wife of Sd. Bernard 20/. To Mattithia their Daughter 40/. To Mrs. Choiter 10/. To sd. Helen Ward my said son Randall's Daughter £20. To her mother 20/. To Anthony Ward husband of Sd. Helen 20/. To my sister Holme 30/. I forgive her debts. To Dorothy & Elizabeth her daughters 30/ a piece. To John Wilkinson son of Robert Wilkinson, 10/. To Robert Brabyn my godson 10/. To Miles Newby 10/. To Martin Gilpin of Gill my godson 10/. To Henry Newby late servant to my son Randall 10/. To his brother Richard Newby 10/. To Thomas Crossfield, son of Sd. Robert Crossfield 20/. I forgive son Randall £20 I lent him long ago. To Sd. Robert Crossfield £20. £280 for which Thos. Harrington, gentleman, and his mother have mortgaged lands in Longsleddall to me & also £25 residue of £66 for which John Warriner hath m'tged me lands in Strickland Kettle, to my Executors half each, or in default, S'd Mortgaged lands to Daughter Katherine in fee & son Randall in fee equally. 10/ for amendment of highways below Chapel-in-the-Wood & Kendal. To friend James Rigge 10/, to William Bateman & William Shepperd 20/ a piece. To servants dwelling with my son in law Martin Gilpin & my son Randal 5/ a piece. Sums lent to Sd. Martin Gilpin or son Randall, I continue in their hands as executors. Rest of goods to my son in law Martin Gilpin & Sd. Katherin his wife, my daughter & sd. son Randall—half each & they three to be executors. Robert Crossfield to deside disputes. Supervisors, my son in law Martin Gilpin S'd Barnard Gilpin & Robert Crossfield. £20 to be abated of legacy to Allen Gilpin because the house in Kendal late Richard Seils was bought by me to his use & for £64 I lately lent my son Randall & Anthony Ward—they to apply £5 thereof to S'd Allen Gilpin. £5 to S'd Randal Gilpin & £54 among Sd. Randall Newby, Anthony Ward & their wives.

Witnesses: James Rigg, Miles Robinson, Robert Cressfield.

Inventory £1659, 14, 6d. Dated 19 Dec. 1617.

Bond 30 Jan. 1617 by Martin Gilpin of Strickland Roger, Co. Westmoreland, gentleman & Randall Newby of Same yeoman. Both sign.

Witns. Robt. Crosfield, Barnard Gilpin & John Houghton.

Martin and Katherine (Newby) Gilpin had issue: Bernard, Grace, Dorothy, Mary, Jane, Alice, Isaac, Randall and Allan.

Bernard Gilpin, eldest son of Martin and Katherine (Newby) Gilpin, bapt. March 1, 1583/4, at parish church of Kendal, d. April 21, 1636. M. circa 1603, Dorothy Airy.

Will of Bernard Gilpin of Strickland Roger in Kirkbie, Kendall, dated 12 April 1636. Pr. 28 May 1636, Deanery of Kendal, Arch. Richmond. To be buried in the parish church of Kendal.

Whereas: I have preferred my sonne Martin Gilpin to be an apprentice and synce the expiration of his said apprenticeshipp I have given him allowance and means for his further p'ferment. And whereas I have allso limmitted & appointed the some of twenty pounds to be paied to my brother Crosfield unto my sonne Francis Gilpin, forth of the price of Brabon tenement "these to stand for their child's portions."

To my son Arthur Gilpin £20 which legacy is to become void when he reaches the age of 21, if he then refuses to release his claim to a tenement in Strickland Roger, late Randall Gilpin's, upon reasonable request. To my son Randall Gilpin, 20 marks. To my son Alan Gilpin, £10. To my daughter Elizabeth Gilpin, 20 Nobles. To my son William Gilpin, my best cloke. My wife Dorothy Gilpin to be executrix & residuary legatee. My brother Robert Crosfield, my brother Isaac Gilpin, & George Warde, to be supervisors, and to have 10 Shillings apiece.

Witnesses: William Bateman, William Shepherd. (Other witnesses missing on account of the will being torn.)

Bond by Dorothy Gilpin, Francis Gilpin of Strickland Roger, yeoman, & William Baxter of Strickland Ketle, husbandman, (bearing signatures of the two last, and mark of the first named).

Inventory of the goods of Bernard Gilpin of Strickland Roger taken by Bartholomew Newbie, Hy. Bracken, Thos. Bracken, and Wm. Baxter, 22 April, 1636. Consisting of household and farm utensils, wearing apparel, pewter—silver spoons etc. and live stock 4 Cows—4 heiffers—143 sheep—2 Mares. A debt due from William Baxter £3, 7/. Summary £103, 5/ 10d.

Debts owing to sundry parties as follows: To Thomas Wilson, £14. To Thomas Burton, £13. To Arthur Dixon, 10/. To Isaac Gilpin, £3. To Henry Bracken,

£1, 8/. To William Gilpin's wife, £1. To Richard Towers, £4. For Servants wages, £1, 4/. To Margaret Warde, 8/. To Stephen Gurnell, 3/, 9d. To Edwin Mackrey, 8d. To Robert Tower, 3/. To Henry Holhead's wife, 4/. To John Nealson, 4/. To Richard Bland, £2, 1/. To George Warde, £4. To Francis Cholmely, £1. To Bartholomew Jennings, 3/, 9d. To Martin Gilpin, £2. Summary of debts, £59, 15/, 11d. Including Funeral Exp. & miscellaneous.

Barnard and Dorothy (Airy) Gilpin had issue: Matithia, William, Martin, Francis, Samuel, Arthur, Randall, Katherine, Elizabeth and Allan.

Grace Gilpin, daughter of Martin and Katherine (Newby) Gilpin, bapt. July 10, 1585. M. May 23, 1601, William Bateman, of Blees, Westmoreland.

Dorothy Gilpin, daughter of Martin and Katherine (Newby) Gilpin, of Strickland. M. September 6, 1606, at Parish Church of Kendal, Robert Crosfield. Robert Crosfield is mentioned in the will of Bernard Gilpin, of Strickland Roger, as my brother Crosfield, and received a legacy of £20. He was one of Bernard Gilpin's executors and a witness to the will of his mother-in-law Katherin Gilpin.

Mary Gilpin, daughter of Martin and Katherine (Newby) Gilpin, M. William Shepherd.

Jane Gilpin, daughter of Martin and Katherine (Newby) Gilpin, d. in infancy.

Alice Gilpin, daughter of Martin and Katherine (Newby) Gilpin, M. after 1616, Arthur Dixon. Arthur Dixon is mentioned as one of the creditors of Bernard Gilpin of Strickland Roger. His daughter, Ann Dixon, was left a legacy by her grandmother Katherin Gilpin, 1632, and is also named in the Inventory of Dorothy Gilpin, of Kendal, widow of Thomas Gilpin of Caton, Lancashire. He is stated to have had two other children, James and Martin. (Papers of Henry D. Gilpin's Collection.)

Isaac Gilpin, son of Martin and Katherine (Newby) Gilpin, of Strickland Kettle & Gilthroton, Westmoreland. M. Ann Tunstall, daughter of Ralph Tunstall of Coatham Mandeville, Co. Durham.

Randall Gilpin, son of Martin and Katherine (Newby) Gilpin; d. s. p.; M. Helen Wilson, daughter of William Wilson.

Allan Gilpin, son of Martin and Katherine (Newby) Gilpin, d. unmarried 1622.

The will of Allan Gilpin of Strickland Roger, parish of Kirby, Kendall, dated November 19, 1621, pr. May 11, 1622. (Arch. Richmond, Kendall Deanery.)

"I bequeath to my father £10 and to my mother £10, To my brother Barnard £10; and to my brother Randall £10. To my sisters Grace, Dorothy, Mary and Alice £10 each. Peggy Bateman, William Bateman's youngest daughter, £10, if she die before full age, the same to her sisters, Mary and Anne. To little Martin Gilpin, my brother Barnard's son 40/ and to little Dorothy Bateman, daughter of said William 20/. To the servants in my father's house 5/ each. To my three sisters-in-law, 10/, each. To Henry, son of William Bateman 20/. To Thomas Crosfield, 20/. To William Gilpin, son of brother Barnard 20/. To my brother Isaac, my ground in Dilaker, according to my grandfather's mind."

Executors: father, mother, and brother Barnard.

Overseers: brothers-in-law Robert Crosfield, William Bateman, and William Shepperd.

Witnesses: Bernard Gilpin and Randall Gilpin.

Having proved by these records that Thomas Gilpin of Mill Hill was not the son of Bernard and Dorothy (Airy) Gilpin, it remains to establish his parentage.

Referring to the Gilpin Chart, we find that Randal Gilpin who married Elizabeth Sykes, had four sons: Richard, Bernard, George and John.

Richard Gilpin married and had one son, who died without issue.

Bernard Gilpin married and had but one daughter, who died young.

George Gilpin married and had two sons: Thomas and Barnard.

John Gilpin, d. 1591. M. circa 1571, Thomazen Everard, daughter of John Everard of Gillingham, Norfolk, Gentleman, by his wife Dorothy Chancye and sister of Sir Edward Everard, of Gillingham.

The will of John Gilpin, of Gillingham, Norfolk and of St. Andrew Holborn, Gentleman, dated March 1, 1586, pr. May 10, 1591 (35 Sauberbe) mentions wife Thomazen, and my six small children and hers (names not given). The Gilpin Chart, however, mentions their names as Everard, John, Christian, Grace, Ursula and Theophila.

Referring to the children of Thomas Gilpin of Mill Hill, parish of Caton, it will be observed that he named sons: George, Francis, Everard, John and Darias. If he was the son of George, it is quite probable he would name his eldest son George, which was the case. On the other hand, if he was the son of John and Thomazen (Everard) Gilpin, he might name sons John and Everard, which was the case.

It is quite probable that Thomas of Mill Hill was a posthumous child of John and Thomazen (Everard) Gilpin, as John, in his will 1586, states his six children were young. Perhaps Thomas was brought up by his uncle George from childhood, which might account for his naming his eldest son George. It is significant that he had sons John and Everard.

Everard Gilpin, Gentleman, son of John and Thomazen (Everard) Gilpin. M. Sarah Quercy, daughter and heiress of Quercy of Boxcott, Suffolk; John Gilpin who married Martha Bray, daughter of John Bray of Surrey, was possibly a son; his widow Martha, married 2nd, Bernard Burton, Esq., one of the Privy Chamber of King James (Visitations of

Surrey) Admitted pensioner at Emmanuel, June 1, 1588, matriculated 1588. (Alumni Cantabrigienses, Vol. 2, p. 218.)

John Gilpin, Gentleman, son of John and Thomazen (Everard) Gilpin. According to the Fleming MSS. he died at Scanderoon, s. p.

Christian Gilpin, daughter of John and Thomazen (Everard) Gilpin, M. Elias Foxton, of Cambridgeshire, Gentleman, of Gray's Inn, son of William Foxton, Esquire, Alderman. (Visitations of Cambridge.)

Grace Gilpin, daughter of John and Thomazen (Everard) Gilpin, died single.

Ursula Gilpin, daughter of John and Thomazen (Everard) Gilpin, died single.

Theophila Gilpin, daughter of John and Thomazen (Everard) Gilpin. M. circa 1610, Francis Gilpin, bapt. March 25, 1585, died 1637, son of Richard and Elinor (Layton) Gilpin of Aldingham, Lancashire. (Visitations of Suffolk.) The will of Francis Gilpin of Wanstead, Essex, Gentleman, dated November 4, 1636, pr. June 19, 1637 (P. C. C. 98, Goare) mentions wife, Theophila, and a daughter Sarah. Issue: Sarah.

Thomas Gilpin, of Mill Hill, parish of Caton, Lancashire, perhaps son of John and Thomazen (Everard) Gilpin, b. circa 1586, d. 1628. M. February 11, 1608, at parish church of Caton, Dorothy Gibson, bapt. September 14, 1586, at Caton, Lancashire, daughter of Robert and Dorothy Gibson, of Mill Hill.

Concerning Thomas Gilpin of Mill Hill, parish of Caton, Lancashire, we have but little knowledge; the account from "Piety Promoted" states that he and his wife were Puritans, and people of good repute. His will, which follows, shows that his widow Dorothy, was executrix and that William Foxe was her bondsman. The latter also appears as the principal creditor of Thomas Gilpin.

Dorothy Gilpin mentions her son Everard Gilpin,

as living in London, and leaves a special sum for her overseers to use in placing Thomas in some "fitt calling" to earn his livelihood, and a similar provision for her daughter Jane; we know that Thomas was a Tallow Chandler. The writer found the will of William Fox, of St. Saviours, Southwark in Surrey, citizen and tallow-chandler of London, dated February 13, 1638/9, who mentions children Elizabeth, Anne, and Jane to inherit at the ages of 21 years. Nothing appears therein to indicate relationship to the Gilpins.

Will of Thomas Guilpine, of Caton, Lancashire, dated May 24, 1628, To be buried in Caton Church yard. To my wife Dorothy, one third of my entire residuary estate after the payment of debts. To my son Fraunce Guilpine; in full lewe of his child's part and portion of my goods; one greate ark standinge in the Barnne before the doore; one greate chiste att pke Barnnes; one steepinge Knopp standing in the kylne; a pr of my best bedstockes and all my husbandry geare. To the rest of my children, another third part equally among them. The residue to my wife Dorothy and my children: Evarard, Thomas, Ruthe, Jane and Dorothy, equally between them.

Executrix: wife Dorothy.

My special good and deare friends William Thornton, and William Barwick of the Greene, Supervisors.

Witness: Bernarde Pulley. No signature or mark.

Bond of Dorothy Guilpine, of Caton, widow, and William Foxe of Griffingham, Lancashire, yeoman; dated June 26, 1628. Mark of Dorothy Gilpin. Signature of William Foxe.

Inventory of the goods of Thomas Guilpine, late of Caton, deceased, taken by Edmund Bell, Thomas Padgett, Christopher Hodgeson, and John Berry, June 11th, 1628. One cow and calf, four beasts, thirty two sheep and 19 lambs, a horse, two mares and foale, farming utensils and household goods.

Total £94, 9/ 8d.

A list of debts owing as follows: To Elizabeth Baulderston, £IX. Richard Parkinson, £VI. George Waven, £III. Bryan Smith, £III, VI/. William Fox, £XX. Thomas Bennison, XXIVIJ/. Thomas Townson, XL/. John Hodgeson, £V. Maude Addamson, X/. William Bradgate, IIIJ/. For Servants wages, VI/. For Easter dues and School wages IIIJ/, VJd. To Mr. Bradshawe, William Wales and Marmaduke Hodgeson as appeareth by their leases about £XV. Summary £LXVJ, XIX/, VJd.

Will of Dorothy Gilpin of Kendal, widow, dated April 6, 1637, pr. May 13, 1637, Deanery of Kendal, Arch. Richmond. To be buried in Kendal Church. To four poor people of Kendal 5/ at the discretion of my overseers. To my eldest son Everard Gilpin, living in London, 20/ within a year. To my daughter, Ruth Gilpin, daughter of Jane Gilpin, and son Thomas Gilpin, £5 each, payable at the discretion of my overseers at times fittest for the placeing of them in some fitt course and callings for their livelyhood & preferment. To my daughter, Ruth Gilpin, "my litle bible." To my syster, Elizabeth Edmonson, one roofe bard, one smock, one white petticoate, one blacke cloth safeguard; on condition she pay Edward Bateman for a stone of lime for which I have passed my word for paiement. My *son John Gilpin,* Executor & residuary legatee. My friends and cousins, Allan Gilpin and Lawrence Belton, Supervisors.

Witnesses: H'y Masy, John Gilpin & Allan Gilpin (Signature).

Testator's Mark & Seal (A I C)
(P)

Bond by John Gilpin of Kendal, Mercer (Signature).

Inventory of the goods of Dorothy Gilpin of Kendal, by Anthony Shaw, Francis Hunter, Geo. Cocke & Edward Bateman, 21 April, 1637. In ready money X/. Apparel. Goods and wares in the shop. All the goods in the house. One cow. Owing to her, in good debts and desperat debts. Summary £XLIX, XVJ/, IIIJd.

Debts which she owes: To William Birkett, Mr. Stephen Watson of Yorke, Richard W. ———ilsoe, Isabel Nicholson, Thomas Towanson of Lancaster, Mr. Henry Bateman of Oldhutton, William Jenninges, William Edmonson, Arthur Dixon, Rowland Wright of Manchester, Thomas Blamer of Manchester, Alice Birkett, widow, John Burrows, Mr. Richard Forth, Joseph Edmondson, divers small debts. Summary £XXXVII, XIX/, Xd. Additional to son John Gilpin £XLIIJ.

Issue: George, Francis, Everard, John, Ruth, Darias, Thomas, Rebecca, Jane and Dorothy, all baptized at the parish church of Caton, Lancashire.

George Gilpin, son of Thomas and Dorothy (Gibson) Gilpin, bapt. September 27, 1609, buried May 4, 1614, at parish church of Caton, Lancashire.

Francis Gilpin, son of Thomas and Dorothy (Gibson) Gilpin, bapt. September 18, 1611, at Caton, Lancashire.

Everard Gilpin, daughter of Thomas and Dorothy (Gibson) Gilpin, bapt. November 25, 1613, at parish church of Caton, Lancashire. He was living in London at the date of his mother's will; doubtless so named to perpetuate the family name of Everard.

John Gilpin, son of Thomas and Dorothy (Gibson) Gilpin, bapt. December, 1615, at parish church of Caton, Lancashire. He was Executor and Residuary Legatee of his mother's will, probably named after Thomas Gilpin's father.

Ruth Gilpin, daughter of Thomas and Dorothy (Gibson) Gilpin, bapt. April 20, 1620, at parish church of Caton, Lancashire, mentioned in the wills of both her parents.

Darias Gilpin, son of Thomas and Dorothy (Gibson) Gilpin, bapt. February 3, 1621/2, at parish church of Caton, d. young.

Thomas Gilpin, son of Thomas and Dorothy (Gibson) Gilpin, bapt. August 24, 1622, at Parish Church of Caton, d. 12/3/1702/3 intestate. ("English Friends Records" and "Piety Promoted") M. circa 1650, Joan Bartholomew, bapt. August 28, 1625, died 3/21/1700/1, daughter of Thomas Bartholomew of Shillingford, Oxfordshire, Gentleman.

According to the biographical sketch of Thomas Gilpin, published in "Piety Promoted," "his parents were people of good repute in the country and were religious, being called Puritans, who educated their children very strictly. Shortly after his father's death (1632), his mother removed with her children to Kendal, Westmoreland, but a short distance from Caton, five of her ten children being dead, and Thomas, the youngest son being at that time about ten years of age. After he grew up in more years and his mother deceased, he ran into foolish and wanton delights as sports and pastimes, musik and dancing, and went to London where he served as an apprentice to a tallow-chandler."

During the Commonwealth period, he joined Cromwell's army and according to the "Memoirs of the Gilpin family," by Hon. Henry D. Gilpin, he fought at the battle of Worcester (1651) and arose to the rank of Colonel, and his brother-in-law Thomas West was a Major in the same regiment; Albert Cook Myers investigated this tradition, and has been unable to confirm the statement by any available data. There was a quarter-master Thomas West, in H. M. own regiment of foot guards in 1661, which was organized shortly after the Cromwellian regiments had been disbanded, but whether he was related to the West family into which two of Thomas Gilpin's children married, is unknown.

After leaving the army, Thomas Gilpin settled in Oxfordshire, and lived for a short time with his father-in-law in Shillingford, after which he resided in Warborough.

About the year 1654, while on a trip to London, he became a convert to the recently established faith of the Society of Friends, and in 1662, he became a Minister and made frequent visits to the neighboring counties. He is mentioned by Besse among the sufferers; he left a very small personal estate and died Intestate.

Admn. Bond of Thomas Gilpin of Warborough, Widower.

Isaac Gilpin of Warborough, Maulster.

Thomas Gilpin of Shillingford in Warborough, Agricola.

Thomas Fletcher of Oxon, Miller.

The said Isaac Gilpin, son of the deceased, to make an inventory and administer the said estate, 30th October, 1703. Then follows the Inventory, the chief part of which consists of a legacy left him by (——) Haynes of Banbury. (Signatures of Isaac Gilpin and Thomas Gilpin.) Isaac Gilpin. Thomas Gilpin.

Issue: Mary, Thomas, Isaac, Sarah, Rachel, Joseph and Richard.

Rebecca Gilpin, daughter of Thomas and Dorothy (Gibson) Gilpin, buried April 26, 1623, parish church of Caton.

Jane Gilpin, daughter of Thomas and Dorothy (Gibson) Gilpin, bapt. September 10, 1624, at parish church of Caton.

Dorothy Gilpin, daughter of Thomas and Dorothy (Gibson) Gilpin, bapt. October 14, 1627, at parish church of Caton. She is mentioned in her father's will, but is not named in her mother's will; she probably died between the dates of the two wills.

Mary Gilpin, daughter of Thomas and Joan (Bartholomew) Gilpin, b. 7/10/1651, died young.

Thomas Gilpin, son of Thomas and Joan (Bartholomew) Gilpin, b. 9/13/1653, died 11/13/1732. M. 1st 2/6/1684/5, at Thomas Elwood's house, Elizabeth West, died 7/19/1686, daughter of William and Elizabeth West, of Long Crendon, Bucks.

At the time of his marriage, Thomas Gilpin produced a Certificate from the Friends' Meeting at Turfield Heath, Oxfordshire. He married secondly Ann ——, whose death is recorded 2/28/1715, buried at Warborough 3/11/1715.

Isaac Gilpin, son of Thomas and Joan (Bartholomew) Gilpin, b. 1/9/1656–7. M. 4/–/1685, at Upperside Meeting, Bucks, Ruth Crook, of Chepping Wiccomb, Bucks, daughter of William Crook, of Minigrove, Oxfordshire.

(Minutes Upperside Bucks Meeting).

Sarah Gilpin, daughter of Thomas and Joan (Bartholomew) Gilpin, b. 2/8/1658. M. 4/7/1683, at Devonshire house, Richard Andrews, of Paternoster Row, London, Stationer, son of Richard and Esther Andrews, of Stratford, Essex. Richard Andrews, Sr., died 7/9/1683, aged 50 years, and was buried at Chequer Alley.

Sarah Andrews and her son Richard, after the death of her husband, Richard, Jr., lived with Moses West of Hertfordshire, whose daughter, her son Richard married. (A biographical account of Richard Andrews, will be found in "Piety Promoted").

Rachel Gilpin, daughter of Thomas and Joan (Bartholomew) Gilpin, b. 2/14/1660, d. 8/6/1684. M. 2/3/1682/3, at Haddenham, Co. Bucks, Thomas West, son of William and Elizabeth West of Long Crendon, Bucks.

They were the ancestors of Benjamin West, the Artist.

Joseph Gilpin, son of Thomas and Joan (Bartholomew) Gilpin, b. 4/8/1663, d. 9/9/1741. M. 12/23/1691, at Baghurst Meeting, Hannah Glover, d. 1/12/1757, daughter of George and Alice (Lamboth) Glover of Ichingswell, parish of Kingscleare, Southampton. He was the American pioneer.

Richard Gilpin, son of Thomas and Joan (Bartholomew) Gilpin, b. 1/2/1666/7, d. young.

Kentmere Hall, seat of the Gilpin family 1268 to about 1650.

The township of Kentmere is nine miles from Kendall and about four miles from Stavely, Westmoreland, and forms a narrow valley about two miles in length. The country is hilly. To the north are the hills of Patterdale, the source of the river Kent, which at one time spread out into a mere. The little lake thus formed has been drained and its bottom is now a fertile valley farmed by the tenant of Kentmere Hall.

The Hall consists of a pele tower of the usual rectangular type, 31 feet by 23 feet over the walls. At the southwestern angle there is a projecting turret running up to the height of the tower, containing garderobes. The tower presents a vaulted cellar on the basement, and three floors of single rooms, above which there is a boldly projected parapet, supported on heavy corbels. At the angles above the roof rise bartizan turrets, with battlements. The structure is very roughly but strongly built of the ragstone and cobbles with which the country abounds, and the design for defence is shown throughout. There is no entrance from the outside into the vaulted cellar, but from the interior of the hall, down a few steps through a pointed doorway. The only external entrance was on the first floor level by outside steps. The cellar has a narrow square window opening to the east.

On the first floor, there are three window lights, besides which there are two defensive loopholes or arrow slits which pierce the wall in a slanting or oblique direction, on the east front, so as to command the angles.

The original architectural features and details have been preserved without change or renovation. In the solar is a decorated window, it is of two lights trefoiled, under ogee heads, and surmounted by a moulded square dripstone; it dates from the fourteenth century. There are the remains of a fire place with a vent in the north wall. In the opposite corner to the garderobe turret, the semi-circular wall of the well-stair commences and is built into the room. This winding stone stair, much worn, leads up to the battlements.

The steps are built into the wall and overlap each other without a central pillar. The floor above comprises a single apartment with square headed windows, with dressed stone for the jambs, with mouldings. There is a door, now blocked, which communicated with the other part of the house. The old entrance is through a pointed arched doorway in dressed sandstone with the angle splayed, evidently of the late Decorated period. This leads into a passage $28\frac{1}{2}$ feet long which traverses the breadth of the building to the back door and to the down house in the back yard. The down house was a place where in ancient times the brewing and washing was done and used also as a receptacle for the "elding" or firewood.

To the right of the passage there is a long building placed transversely and about 25 feet in breadth with very substantial walls, now used for a stable.

The portion of the house to the left which constitutes the present farm residence contains on the ground floor what was formerly the dining hall and a low upper story of sleeping apartments.

The hall originally was about 30 ft. long and 14 ft. 2 in. in breadth and from it a pointed arched doorway led by a few steps into the vaulted cellar of the tower. The principal window was square headed, with a moulded drip stone and divided into four lights by molded mullions.

The description is from "The Old Manorial Halls of Westmoreland and Cumberland" by the late Dr. M. W. Taylor, F. S. A.

GENEALOGICAL NOTES REGARDING THE FAMILY OF GLEN, OR GLENN.

BY THOMAS ALLEN GLENN.

[No excuse, perhaps, is necessary for preserving here these notes in connection with a surname borne by over forty of those who arrived in the colonies from the earliest times to about the commencement of the Revolution. With the exception of two, these adventurers were kinsmen, and at least fifteen of them settled in Pennsylvania. In Scotland and Ulster, at the present day, however, the surname is somewhat uncommon, and those bearing it, for the most part, stand high in the communities to which they belong. This family was represented in the Darien expedition, with the first Dutch on the Delaware, and in the French and Indian Wars. General Forbes claimed near kinship with the Linlithgow branch. Some fifty of the name served, mostly as privates, and not with especial distinction, during the Revolution. The civil roll includes one Royal Governor, and two Governors of States. The information following is necessarily condensed; but it may prove of interest to descendants, and corrects some errors.]

At the close of the 13th century we find three families bearing the surname of Glen; two in Scotland, the other in England.

The English Glens, (Leicestershire) came, doubtless, from Nanancort, Balliwick of Quency, Normandy, where the name occurs 1170, and later.[1] It is claimed, however, that this family assumed the surname from Glen Magna. If so, individuals returned to Normandy in the service of the de Quencys, their lords.

In Leicestershire, 45 Hen. III., Galfridus de Glen and Winarch his wife are mentioned.[2] Walter de Glen, clericus, and Alan his brother appear 54 Hen. III.[3] On 18 July, 10 Edw. I., a commission of oyer and terminer was granted Nicholas de Stapleton on complaint that Adam, son of Geoffrey de Glen, and others, had broken

[1] Rot. Norm.
[2] Ex. E. Rot. Fin., ii., 346.
[3] Ibid., ii., 512.

into his house at Newton Harecourt, at night;[4] and, 20 Edw. III., John de Glen held lands in Humberston.[5] A John de Glen was in Sitheston, 33 Hen. VI.[6] Other references occur; but after the reign of Edward III. the house declined, descendants sinking to mere husbandmen. The name, now usually written *Glenn*, remains in Leicestershire.[7] Branches settled in Derbyshire,[8] Rutlandshire, London, and elsewhere. One Richard de Glenfield held lands in Glen Parva, 20 Edw. III., and in 32d of same was lord of that manor.[9] The arms of Glenfield and those of Glen of Leicestershire, are similar.[10] Thomas Glen, or Glenn, or Glean, in Philadelphia, 1684, was of this line probably from near Sproxton; and Nicholas Glen, a descendant, I believe, of the Rutland branch, was soon after in Maryland.

GLEN OF SCOTLAND.

Neither of the families of Glen of Scotland bore that surname before being seized of lands from which they assumed it; nor were they kinsmen.

A history of Scottish Parishes states that "The Glen," in Traquair, Peebles, gave its name to its ancient owners. This estate comprises an extensive glen, from whence its appelation, and in which stood the stronghold of its lords.[11] Before 24 Edw. I. "The Glen" belonged to Duncan de le Glen,[12] who died prior to 3 Sept. of that year, when his widow, Sara, subscribed allegiance. Duncan was the first of his race to be so called. The family was Celtic, Colban son of Duncan, under the

---

[4] Cal. Pat. Rolls, i., 47.
[5] Burton's "Leicestershire."
[6] Inq. P. M., William Lovell, 33 Hen. VI.
[7] A very respectable branch of this family has long resided at Sproxton.
[8] The name is found in Duffield and neighbouring parish registers. The Rutland branch, assuming arms, was disclaimed by the heralds.
[9] Burton.
[10] Ibid.
[11] Orig. Paroc. Scot., i., 44.
[12] Rot. Scot., i., 26^b.

designation of Colban de Glen, with Annabella his spouse, had a grant from Robt. I. of Quilts, Peebleshire (adjacent to "The Glen"), for payment of 20s. 8d yearly, half the service of a bowman in the King's army, and one suit yearly at the court of Peebles.[13] After 1329, Symon de Peebles, with consent of Andrew de Moray, Warden of the Kingdom, granted Henry de Douglass his lands of Quylt (Quilts) *which he had as heir to his sister Anabella*, who had been enfeoffed there by King Robert. This grant (undated), confirmed 1368,[14] proves that Colban died without issue; which is the last we hear of this family. What became of "The Glen," is not clear; but Gilbert Cokburn, Thomas Middlemarch, and Stewart of Traquair held it 1479–1488.[15] Colban, who was living 1329, held some appointment at Court, and the Queen left him a legacy.[16]

The second Scots family of Glen assumed that surname from the lordship of Glen, Renfrewshire, so called from a vale in Lochwinnoc, out of which flows the Black Cart Water. This lordship, comprising Bar, Brigend, Lynthills, Gaytflat, and other[17] lands, was granted by David I. to Walter the Steward. The first lords, therefore, were the Stewards, holding of the King *in capite*, who, by sub-infeodation, parcelled the lands among their retainers. Thus, in the grant of Pete Auchingowan in Lochwinnoc to the convent of Dalmunlin, on the Waters of Air, about the beginning of the 13th century, the pasture is described as "by the same bounds which Alexander the son of Hugh held the land of the Steward."[18]

Lord Richard de le Glen, before 12 Nov., 20 Edw. I. (1292), under the designation of Richard de le Glen *dño de le Glen et nam in Dño*, holding this lordship of the

[13] Mun. Vet. Com. de Mortoun, 27, 28; Robertson, 23.
[14] Ibid, 66, 67.
[15] Orig. Paroc. Scot., i., 44.
[16] Rot. Scac. Reg. Scot., i., 169, &c.
[17] Retours.
[18] Orig. Paroc. Scot., i., 95.

King *in capite, confirmed* to John de le Glen, his son (*fil' meo*), his lands called Gaytflat, in the tenure of the Glen, which Robert Nase and Cubinus formerly held of his (Richard's) predecessors, by the same bounds by which Richard his (i.e. Lord Richard's) uncle held the land of him (Richard) and his predecessors, hereditarily, John de le Glen and his heirs paying one penny yearly, on the Feast of the Pentecost, at the Court of the Glen.[19] Witnesses: Lord Robert Wishard, Bishop of Glasgow, Lord James, Steward of Scotland, Lord William Fleming of Barhushan, Knight, William Perel, Sheriff of Traquayr, Walter de Logan, William de Erth, John de Iethyn, Alexander Kirkintulack, and William de Ladel. Confirmed by Edward I., 12 Nov., 1292.[20] Two days after (14 Nov., 1292), the King, for 100 marks, granted Richard Freser custody of the lands and tenements which had belonged to Richard de le Glen, deceased, which he held of the King of Scotland *in capite*, and which because of his death are taken into the King's hand, holding the same for the legitimate heir of the said Richard.[21] This was the customary procedure.

I find no record of John having been proved heir to the lordship of Glen; but there is evidence to show that he was. The lordship became, finally, the property of the monastery of Paisley, the Glens holding the lands of Gaytflat, Bar, Brigend, and others under the Lord Abbots; but of this change of tenure, no account has been discovered. At the time of confirmation of the Gaytflat lands, Lord Richard was in Holy Orders, having probably assumed the monastic habit upon the approach of death. It is supposed that Lord Richard acquired "The Glen" through his mother, and that she was a daughter of one of the Stewards. From the grant of confirmation we find that Gaytflat had been the inheritance of Richard

---

[19] Rot. Scot., i., 11ᵃ & 11ᵇ.
[20] Ibid., i., 11ᵇ.
[21] Abbrev. Rot. Orig., Edw. I., 72, Ed. 1805.

the uncle of Lord Richard, who must have granted it to his grandnephew, John, whose father, as lord of the manor, confirmed the gift.[22] Further, we learn that the family surname had been Nase, or Ness, and that the immediate ancestors of Richard, the uncle, were Robert and Cubinus. The family of de Ness was from Ness, or Ness Strange, near Shrewsbury, and descended from the powerful Norman house of l'Estrange, the first of whom is said to have been Guy l'Estrange, younger son to the Duke of Brettaign. The de Ness accompanied Walter Fitz Alan from Shropshire to Scotland, and Henry de Ness held under the Steward in the lordship of Glen, 1180.[23]

It seems certain that John de Ness was father to Lord Richard, and indentical with John, constable of Dunoon, who was seized of lands in Kilmun. Descendants of John, son of Lord Richard, held estates in Kilmun, so late as 1373.[24]

John de le Glen must have been almost of age in 1292. During the revolt of Wallace he commanded the troops of Robert Wishart, Bishop of Glasgow, as appears by articles to be propounded before Pope Clement V. by King Edward, stating, among other things, that the said Bishop directed William Lydel, his Bailiff, to muster his forces, directing that they march under John de Glen *against the Prince of Wales.*[25]

We hear no more of John prior to Bannockburn. That he distinguished himself in this battle is, doubtless, true, for immediately after he had a grant from Robt. I. of the forfeited lands of Balmutache (Bulmato), Fife.[26] According to Scottish heralds John de le Glen married

---

[22] See grant *supra* where the words "*et' nam in Dno*" occur.
[23] Orig. Paroc. Scot. It may be well to explain that the possession of a lordship did not necessarily imply the fee of the lands which comprised it; but only the services or rents from the tenants, fines, &c., according to the custom of the manor.
[24] Hist. Com. Rep., 4, Appendix, 476.
[25] Docs. and Recds. ill. the Hist. of Scot., in Treas. Excheg.; Palgrave.
[26] Robertson, 25.

a co-heiress of Abernethy. He had Robert, and, probably, Roger. The latter had an annuity from the Crown of 100 shillings, 1329,[27] and, 25 Feb., 1332, rendered the accounts of the Provosts of Peebles;[28] he seems to have died s. p.

Robert, son of John de le Glen, married Margaret, illegitimate daughter of Robert Bruce.[29] Robert de Glen and "Margaret Bruce the King's sister," his spouse, had a grant from David II., undated, of Nether Pitedye, Kinghorn, Fife (adjoining Balmuto).[30] Robertson notes three other charters from David to this Robert de Glen, of the lands of Glasgow Forest, thanedom of Kintore, Aberdeen.[31] Wood[32] gives Margaret as legitimate, and says that she married, secondly, William, Earl of Sutherland. The latter did marry as his second wife, Margaret Bruce; but it is impossible that she was the widow of Glen, and an authority points out that the arms quartered by Glen, and attributed to the co-heiress of Abernethy, were not the Abernethy arms, but those of Scotland *with the Scottish mark of illegitimacy*,[33] which agrees with a tradition preserved in several branches of the family, and is conclusive.

Another tradition, traceable for four centuries, insists that Robert de Glen was one of those who accompanied the heart of Bruce to the Holy Land, and the Linlithgow line used two crests, one a martlet; the other an arm, the hand grasping a heart, in commemoration of that event.[34] Moreover, the Glens of Bar possessed the sword of Bruce, which a descendant carried to Ireland,

---

[27] Rot. Scacc. Reg. Scot., i., 209.
[28] Ibid., i., 411.
[29] Robertson, No. 43, p. 33; Rot. Scacc. Reg. Scot., i., cxxix, cxxx.
[30] Robertson.
[31] Ibid., No. 32, p. 38; 46, p. 39; 19, p. 62.
[32] Wood's "Peerage of Scot."
[33] Rot. Scacc. Reg. Scot., i., cxxix, cxxx.
[34] Iron seal in possession of a descendant. The arms of Linlithgow branch are identical with those of Bar.

1606, where it was seen a few years since, the inscription on the blade leaving no doubt as to its original ownership. Robert de Glen had issue, William, Robert and John. The order of births is uncertain; but John, perhaps was the youngest. William appears to have finally acquired all of his father's estates, including lands in the lordship of Glen, and in Kilmun, save Balmuto and adjacent property, which, probably by enfeoffment, vested in John, who was father of Sir John de Glen, of Balmuto. This Sir John was party to a deed dated after 1373, between Sir John de Glen de Balmuto, and Margaret his wife, and Sir John de Wemyess and Isabel his wife, touching lands of Sir John de Glen in exchange for lands of Sir John de Wemyess, the latter lying north of the Firth of Forth.[35] Sir John de Glen married Margaret, co-heiress of Sir Alrn Erskine (living 1364), by Isabel, co-heiress of Sir Patrick Inchmartin, whereby he acquired Inchmartin. Margaret was living 8 Sept., 1401, being, according to a retour of service of her and Isabel her sister of Inchmartin, heir to her mother in Auchlevin and part of Ardoyn.[36] Sir Michael Scot of Baheary, by a writ disposed of the lands and mill of Cambrune to Sir John Wemyess, 1400, and Sir John de Glen, lord of Balmuto, gets investment of part thereof by a precept from the Duke of Albany.[37] Among the lands held by Sir John de Glen were those of Lintrathen, Forfarshire. Sir John had co-heiresses: (a) Mariott, wife of Sir John Boswell of Balgregie, who thus acquired one third of Balmuto, and purchased the other two-thirds. His son, David, had a charter of confirmation from Jac. II., 24 Feb., 1439; (b) Margaret, wife of Sir Walter Ogilvy, treasurer to King James. Among the missing charters of Robt. III. is a confirmation of a grant by Sir John de

---

[35] Wood's "Peerage of Scot." Wood gives the date as between 1373 and 1428, the latter being the year of Sir John de Glen's death.
[36] Ibid.
[37] Writs of Far. of Bal.; Remarks on Ragmans Roll.

Glen to Walter Ogilvy, in marriage, of Ballhawell, Forfarshire; (c) Christian, wife of David Stewart; living 1464.³⁸

Robert de Glen, son of John and Margaret Bruce, entered the Church, becoming Rector of Liberton in Lanarkshire, the living being in gift of John, Lord of Maxwell, as appears by a charter of the latter, and Christian his wife, 12 Oct., 1357, to the monastery of Kilwynnyn, of patronage or advowson of the said church, with one acre of land, reserving the rights of Sir Robert de Glen, the Rector then instituted.³⁹ Confirmed by David II. This Robert de Glen de Liberton, witnessed a charter of David II. to Walter Byset, 30 Sept., 38 David II.,⁴⁰ and there was a payment to him of 53s. 4d. by order of the King, 1364.⁴¹

William de Glen died before 14 June, 1373, at which time Paul de Glen, his son and heir, was of age.

Paul Glenn (*sic*) son and heir of William de Glen, 14 June, 1373, granted Sir Archibald Campbell of Lochow the lands of Stronwhillan and Finniart in the barony of Kilmun, to be held of Paul Glenn and his heirs for service in time of war to the Superior, with three suits yearly at the Court of Kilmun.⁴²

John de Glen, succeeding Paul, entered the service of Robert Stewart of Lorn, by whom he was much trusted. Safe conduct was granted John de Glen and William de Balnawys *de Scotia s'viëntes de Robti Stewart de Lorn de Scotia*, at Westminster, 16 July, 7 Hen. VI. (1429), and also this John had safe conduct on several other occasions 9 to 10 Hen. VI.; Lorn being then a hostage in England.⁴³

---

³⁸ Wood's Peerage of Scot.
³⁹ Reg. Mag. Sig. i., No. 86, p. 34; Orig. Paroc. Scot., i., 36; Robertson, 75.
⁴⁰ Reg. Mag. Sig. i., No. 174, p. 57.
⁴¹ Rot. Scacc. Reg. Scot., ii., 168.
⁴² Hist. Mss. Com., Rep. 4, Appendix, 476. The name is given in the transcript as *Glenn*, and in an early survey of lands belonging to the Monastery of Paisley, the same spelling occurs; also in Accounts of the Lord High Treasurer, 1506.
⁴³ Rot. Scot., ii., 267ᵇ, 268ᵃ, 271ᵇ, 273,ᵇ 275ᵇ.

Thomas Glen, perhaps brother to John, was a prisoner of war in England, 6 April, 10 Hen. V.[44]

William Glen, son of John, appears to have held Gaytflat, as well as Bar, and adjacent lands. Under the designation of *Wilelmo Glen, armigeris* he is named as a witness to the donation of one third of the fishings in the Crocket—Shot, and lands, by Robert, Lord Lyle, to the Monastery of Paisley, dated at Paisley, 25 Sept., 1452.[45] This William was in the service of the Abbot, and, doubtless, rebuilt Bar. The lower walls of the castle are older than the upper works; the original sallyport, now walled up, as well as the vaults, are Norman, and it was, in all probability, the home of Lord Richard, before 1292. William Glen of Bar had issue, so far as known, Robert, John, William, and James. John Glen witnessed a confirmation of lands in Rengrew to William Cunningham, 4 Nov., 1483, a charter to the same person, 6 April, 1484, a grant *in re* William Cunnynghame of Cragenis, 23 May, 1499, and other charters relating to Auchinlech; one of William Cunningham and Margaret Auchinlech his spouse, 12 March, 1505.[46] William Glen, son of William, was one of the witnesses to a charter to Walter Lichtown of Houshawin (Howsane), 24 May, 1481.[47] He was also an arbitrator as to boundaries between Robert, Abbot of Paisley, Robert Symple of Fowlwod, and Richard Brown of Cultermayne, lord of Calderhawch in Lochquhywzok, 26 April, 1509.[48] The award was acknowledged before James Glen, brother to William, and *clericus de notarius imperiale et regali auctorifatibus*.

Robert Glen, heir of William of Bar, was a companion in arms, of Sir Unfridi Cunynghame of Glengarnock, and with him at Perth, 1494, where he witnessed a

---

[44] Ibid., ii., 232°.
[45] Reg. de Passelet, 250; reg. folio 25.
[46] Reg. Mag. Sig. (2d Ser.), i., 330, 390, 66, *note*, to 288, 627.
[47] Ibid., i., 309.
[48] Reg. de Passelet, 430-1.

charter by Cunynghame dated at Perth, 24 April, 1494; confirmed 2 May, 1500–1, 13 Jac. IV.[49] In 1500, Robert Glen, with Elizabeth, relict of John Browne (sic) of Cultermayne, compounded for wardship and marriage of the heir to the estates of the said John Browne, then in the Kings hand.[50] These lands afterwards passed to the Glens.[51] Robert Glen died 1506, and was succeeded by James.[52] The other children of Robert, so far as I can discover, were: Alexander, Robert, George, (Patrick?); and probably Marion, wife of Robert Shaw of Belgerry.[53]

James Glen, the heir, had a grant of confirmation from Robert, Lord Abbot of Paisley, of the lands of Bar, Brigend, and Lyntchils (Lynthills) in the lordship of Glen, and Regality of Paisley, 1506,[54] and in the same year made a pilgrimage to the tomb of St. James de Compostella. Accounts of the Lord High Treasurer contain this entry under 1506. "17 June, to James Glen quhen he passit [through Edinburgh] [on] his pilgrimage to Sanct James, xiiij s̄;"[55] it being then customary to present persons of note passing through certain towns a gratuity in lieu of entertainment. James and his kinsmen were at Flodden. In 1517 he was captain of a company of 102 footmen in the service of the Crown, and after entries in the Treasurer's accounts of pay for a term of service, viz., £30 to Captain Glen, and proportionate amounts to his Ensign, and men, follows a disbursement for "Supper for Capt. Glenny's (Glenn's) futband inlikewis that nycht to thair supper, (sic) thair wages beand spendit."[56] This James Glen "in Bar" was

---

[49] Reg. Mag. Sig. (2d ser.), i., 545; No. 2569.
[50] Accts. of the Lord High Treas. of Scot., ii., 14.
[51] Inq. Spec. &c. (Inqs. P. M.), 23 Jan., 1610, Alexander Glen.
[52] Crawfurd's Renfrewshire, 74; Nesbit, i., 351.
[53] Acta Dom. Conc. & Acta Dom. Aud., 1466–1495.
[54] Crawfurds "Renfrewshire," 74.
[55] Accts. of the Lord High Treas. of Scot., iii., 199.
[56] Ibid., v., 155.

on the assize as a Justice, 12 Feb., 1543,[57] and died 1544 (having been killed, supposedly, at the battle of Ancrum); when his son and heir, James, had a grant of confirmation from John, Abbot, of Paisley, with the consent of the convent, of his lands of Bar, Brigend, and others which his ancestors had held.[58]

In 1564, a feud long existant between the houses of Glen and Semple, became serious, the former by the appointment of Robert, Lord Semple to be Justiciary, and James Glen appealed to the Queen. At a Privy Council, 10 Oct., 1564,[60] the Queen's Letters were produced by James Glen, settling forth that whereas Robert Lord Sempill (sic) has obtained the commission of Justiciary upon all the inhabitants of the Barony and Sheriffdom of Renfrew within which jurisdiction "the said James and his barnis dwellis," which should not be, nor should Lord Sempill "haif ony commissioun or jurisdictoun upon the said James, his brethir (John) barnis freiendis, and servandis . . . . because it is noutourlie Knawin that the said Robert Lord Sempell beiris deidlie feid and inimytie aganis the said James, his barnis, brethir, kin, and freindis, and hes usit greit crudilitie and hostilitie upoun tham, ... in ony wyise, and specialie in caus criminall quhair he may dispone upoun thair lyffs." The commission of Lord Semple was suspended as to jurisdiction over James Glen, this action being subsequently confirmed, and James Glen, his children, brother, kin and friends made answerable to the Queen's Majesty, only, and exempt from any other process of law.

The brother of James—mentioned in the above proceedings, is supposed, I believe correctly, to have been that John Glen who settled at Stirling after the battle of Langside. A return of the inhabitants of Stirling,

---
[57] Reg. Mag. Sig. (2d ser.), ii., 767; under No. 3277.
[58] Crawfurd's "Renfrewshire," 74.
[60] Records of the Privy Council of Scot, anno 1564.

1544–1550, does not include the name; but the Kirk register shows that John Glen, son of John, of Cambuckenneth, married Elet, daughter of James Anderson of Sheok, 1589, that Thomas Glen, son of Thomas, and Bessie Abercrumbie of West Grainge, were married the same year, and that William Glen in Cabuskenth then espoused Jonet Sibbald.[61] They were, doubtless, grandsons of John. Stirling Register furnishes an unbroken pedigree to John Glen, who, about 1708, was lessee of Foot o'Green. He had: (a) Rev. John, born 1709; died 1792, father of Elizabeth, wife of Dr. Johnston of Virginia, ancestor to the Glen-Johnstons of Perth; (b) Archibald, born 1710, of who, presently; (c) James, died unm.; (d) Robert, born 1717, a tanner in Glasgow, Dean of his Guild, (e) William, born 1720, died in St. Petersburg, unm.; (f) Alexander, of Glasgow, father of Alexander, a magistrate there and others. The children of Archibald (born 1710), second son of John of Foot of Green, were: (a) John, born 1736, of Lumloch, Lanark, whose sons d. s. p; but a daughter was wife of Mr. Orr, Glasgow, mother of Sir Andrew Orr, Knight, Lord Provost of Glasgow. A brother of Sir Andrew went to St. Petersburg, and members of this Orr family settled in Philadelphia; (b) Robert, of Russia (a younger Robert d. inft.); (c) William, born 1744, of Forganhall, Falkirk, had George Glen of Liverpool and Oxford; (d) Alexander, born 1748, of Glasgow, married Jane Burns, and had, Archibald of West Indies; afterwards of Liverpool, William Glen, the poet, Robert of Trinidad, Alexander and James of Demerara, Thomas of Newfoundland, who left issue (in Canada) and a daughter Jean, died unm.; (e) Margaret, wife of Mr. Liddell, or Lytle, of Glasgow, some of whose family removed to Philadelphia; (f) Isabel, mother of Rt. Rev. David Anderson, Bishop of Prince Ruperts Land, and Thomas D., of Waverley Abbey, Mayor of Liverpool; (g) Catherine, wife of Wil-

[61] Old Stirling Register.

liam Kidston, Glasgow; (h) Mary, wife of Rev. Thomas Burns, Renfrew, whose daughter married General Harry Thomson, of Indian Army;[62] (i) three daughters died young.
James of Bar was kinsman to the Hamiltons, and, 4 Jan., 1565, with Robert Hamilton of Briggis, and James Hamilton, of St. Johns Chapel, executed a bond for the delivery, by John (Hamilton), Archbishop of St. Andrews, of the castle of St. Andrews to the King and Queen, upon six hours notice, under penalty of 5000 marks.[63]

James Glen commanded troop for Queen Mary, at Langside, and was forfeited, 1568; but restored by treaty of Perth, 1573.[64] Over the entrance to Bar Castle the motto "For God and my Queen," rudely carved, is legible. After Langside the Glens seem to have taken refuge with the Hamiltons, and there is evidence to shew that they were active in the plot to assassinate Moray, who was shot (1570) whilst passing through Linlithgow by Hamilton of Bothwell-Haugh.[65]

The children of James Glen of Bar, second of the name, were: James, William, Alexander, Archibald, David, Mary, and perhaps others. James, the eldest, Groom of the Chamber to Darnley, was killed at Kirk a Field. William and Alexander succeeded, in turn to the estates. Archibald is said to be identical with Archibald, Glen, Regent of the University of Glasgow, 1596, minister at Rutherglen, and, 1603, translated to Carmmunock; died 1614. He had sons, David, and Thomas, the latter (died 1635) a merchant in Glasgow, Master of Works there, 1625, father of Thomas, Ballie of the River and Firth of Clyde, 1638, 1639, 1642, 1646.[66] David Glen was of Glenlora, adjoining Bar, 1598-9;[67] of his issue I will

---

[62] "Literary Remains of William Glen."
[63] Recds. of Privy Council of Scot.
[64] Crawfurds "Renfrewshire."
[65] The account of personal estate of Margaret Cunningham, spouse of William Glen of Bar, 1598, shows transactions between the Glens and David Hamilton of Bothwell-Haugh, tending to confirm other evidence.
[66] "Literary Remains of William Glen." Corp. Recds. of Glasgow.
[67] Test. Dative of Margaret Cunningham, otherwise Glen, 1598.

speak presently. Mary, daughter of James of Bar, was, it is believed, one of the four Marys of the Queen.[68]

William Glen of Bar married Margaret Cunningham, who died May, 1589 (1598?)[69], the final decree regarding whose estate is dated 9 Jan., 1598–9, William being then alive. The account shows the joint debts of Margaret and her husband to exceed their assets by £390, including £20. for tithes and duties of Bar, due "my lord of Paisley and his chalmerlanes," being arrears for 88 years. No payments had, therefore, been made since 1608, although there was a grant of confirmation in 1644. As these arrears were against Bar, only, there would seem to have been a dispute as to their justice. William and Margaret had Isabel, executrix of her mother's will, afterwards wife of Thomas Boyd, Lavid of Pitcon, Ayr, who died 1617. Crawfurd gives also Sibilla, wife of James Semple of Milbank, and cites a charter from Robert, Lord Semple, 1603, of lands in Renfrewshire to James Semple of Milbank and Sibilla Glen his spouse ("a daughter of the house of Barr").[70]

William Glen of Bar died before 23 Jan., 1610, when his brother Alexander was proved heir, in lands of Auchiencruche, Calderhauche, Cruik, Jonishill, Langli, Knockernoch, and "an ancient estate in the parish of Lochwinzeoch."[71] Alexander died before 9 April, 1629, when Archibald Glen, his son, succeeded; and, in addition to the lands named, those of Bar, Brigend, Lynthillis, and Wester Kers, are mentioned in the inquisition.[72] Bar Castle passed to the Hamiltons; but Lynthillis descended

---

[68] Mary Queen of Scots had a number of ladies in waiting called Mary, as she was accustomed to replace those who married, died, or withdrew, by others of the same name.

[69] The date of her decease is given in proceedings as 1589; but the other dates on the same papers indicate that this is a clerical error for 1598.

[70] Crawfurd's "Renfrewshire."

[71] Inqs. P. M. Scot.

[72] Ibid. This was, no doubt, the same Alexander who had been a merchant in Edinburgh, and married Elisabeth, daughter and heiress of George Acheson, of Edinburgh, of the family of Acheson, Earls of Gosford, who died 1608.

to William Glen, living 1818, whose descendants held it for a long time, a continuous tenure, without the intervention of an heiress, of nearly 600 years, and a continuous land tenure in the same lordship for nearly 800 years. Captain Alexander Glen, of this house, is recorded as having expended his entire fortune for rations and pay for his men, and to have died of actual starvation, in the regular service of the later Stuarts.[73]

Lindsay Glen, who appears to have taken service with a merchant of Rotterdam, is known to have been a near relation to William Glen of Bar (died before 1610), perhaps a brother, and probably married a kinswoman of Gabriel Spreule, a Dutch trader, with whom the Glens of Bar had financial transactions. Alexander, son of Lindsay Glen, entered the service of the Dutch, was early on the Delaware, and afterwards at New Amsterdam. He founded Schenectady, and accounts of his career will be found in histories of that place. He is, however, erroneously called Alexander *Lindsay* Glen, whereas his baptismal name was Alexander. His father's name being Lindsay, the Dutch called him, after their custom, by the Dutch equivalent of Alexander son of Lindsay, as appears by New York Archives. Alexander was a headstrong, violent man, frequently engaging in disputes with the government. A descendant of Alexander, Dr. Jacob Glen, removed to Chestertown, Maryland, dying about the middle of the 18th century. His will mentions a rosary and crucifix, according to tradition, belonged to Mary Queen of Scots, and which Dr. Glen wished his descendants to retain as an heirloom, forever. The children of Dr. Glen wrote the name *Glenn*. A branch removed to Baltimore, some of them becoming eminent at the Bar, and Elias was Chief Justice of Maryland. Another of the Baltimore family went to Newark, New Jersey, dying there recently, aged over 106.

[73] Rep. of Rec. Com.

A family of Glen holding lands at Incherie, Fife, was probably from an illegitimate son of Sir John de Glen of Balmuto (died 1428). They were not numerous; but one of them, James Glen, a merchant-tailor, rose, to be Provost and Treasurer of Edinburgh. Robert, heir to Master Robert Glen of Inchkerie, was proved heir to his father, 1617.[74]

As stated, according to the best information at hand, the sons of Robert Glen of Bar (died 1506), were: James, Alexander, Robert, and George. Alexander, Robert, and George Glen, were, 4 Augt., 1542, joint tenants of the lands of Neither Glen, in the Lordship of Boghall, near Bar; all three were probably at the battle of Ancrum. Alexander Glen removed to Linlithgow before, or in, 1544-5, and entered the service of the Hamiltons. He was witness to a charter at Linlithgow, 6 Jan., 1545-6. The records of the Commissariot of Edinburgh, Retours of service of heirs, and parish registers, furnish data for a complete genealogy of the Glens of Linlithgow. Three of this line, James, George, and Andrew, represented Linlithgow in Parliament, 1625, 1641, 1652-63. Alexander Glen, of Linlithgow, who died before 22 Augt., 1722, owner of Bonnytoun and Loncroft, had (a) Andrew Glen, who left an only daughter Elizabeth, born 1739; died 1807, wife of George Ramsay, Earl of Dalhousie; (b) James Glen, Royal Governor of South Carolina; born about 1700, married Elizabeth, daughter of Sir William Wilson, of Eastbourne; died without issue before 26 Augt., 1777; (c) Dr. Thomas, married, 18 Sept., 1755, Isabella, widow of James Graham, Chief Justice of South Carolina; (d) John, and others.

Several other members of the Linlithgow family removed to the Carolinas. John Glen, who went out before the Governor, settled, finally, in Orange County, North Carolina, and married Sarah, daughter of Robert Jones, by Ann, daughter of William Duke. This Ann had been

[74] Inqs. P. M. Scot.

the wife of Captain Christmas, and Robert Jones was the son of Edward Jones of Shocco Creek, formerly of King and Queens county Virginia, and Abigail Shugan. John Glen, who is said to have been a clergyman who also practiced medicine, may have been married previously. His sons, whose descendants wrote the name *Glenn*, were: Warham, Thomas, William, Duke, Dr. John, and perhaps Edward. A daughter Ann seems to have married —— Downs. The sons were young men, but probably all of age, 1761, and resident in Orange County, North Carolina. Dr. John Glen was educated abroad; he had Thomas, James, born 1775; removed to Baltimore, Maryland, 1799, John, and William. The descendants of Duke Glen, or Glenn, removed to Atlanta, Georgia. The late Luther Judson Glenn, whose widow was living 1900, was a grandson of Duke, and son of Thomas.

William Glen, a cousin of the Governor, settled in Charleston, South Carolina, his descendants intermarrying with the Drayton and Bulloch families. A grandson of William, Dr. James Glen, practiced medicine in Philadelphia, in the early part of the 19th century. Archibald Glen, of the Linlithgow line, was also early in the Carolinas.

THE IRISH BRANCH.

In 1605–6, Sir James Hamilton and Montgomery, having secured large grants of land in Ulster, prepared to plant a colony of Scotsmen in that country. Among those interested in this undertaking were Rev. Patrick Hamilton of Dunlop, near Bar, husband of Elizabeth Glen, daughter of David of Glenlora, and Thomas Boyd of Pitcon, husband of Isabel Glen, daughter of William of Bar. Rev. Patrick Hamilton secured lands mostly in the parish of Hollywood, Down, which Sir James, his brother, had obtained by a patent, 3 Jac. I., and, with James and John Glen, who from evidence so far secured are considered, I believe rightly, to have been younger sons of David of Glenlora, and a few others from the neighbourhoods of Dunlop and Bar, removed to Ireland, 1606.[75] These brothers were ancestors to most of this surname in that country.

James Glen had lands from Rev. Patrick Hamilton, in East Hollywood, Down, and, 15 Nov., 15 Jac. I., a grant was made to him and other "Scotsmen," that they enjoy the "privileges of English subjects."[76] Robert Glen (died 1767), Sheriff, and Mayor of Waterford,[77] was probably a descendant; also David Glen (or Glenn), who removed to North Carolina about 1770, and some of those who were earlier in Pennsylvania, of whom, probably, James, the progenitor of a family at Tacony, and Frankford. John Glen removed from Down to Lifford, Donegal, acquiring denization, 17 Augt., 14 Jac. I.[78] His children, born 1606–1620: John Glen (perhaps eldest son), merchant at Londonderry, died 1686. Admon. to John Glenn (sic) eldest son, 28 Dec., 1686, to use of widow (unnamed), himself, and other children of deceased,[79] who were: Ninian, and probably George, James, and David.

John, son of John Glen (or Glenn), of Londonderry, died s.p., 1700, and will, 1700 (admon. C. T. A. granted Jane his widow, 22 June, 1700),[80] mentions children of brother Ninian Glen, named in a suit *in re* this will, John, James, Joseph, and Mathew, all of age, 1700.

James Glen, son of Ninian seems to be identical with James of Boytown, Tyrone, whose will of 13 Sept., 1740, was proved 23 May, 1747.[81] This James married, secondly, widow of one Caldwell, mother of David Caldwell, executor of his stepfather's will; but who, 1747, was in

---

[75] Hamilton MSS.
[76] "Cal. Patent Rolls, James I." 339.
[77] "History of Waterford."
[78] "Cal. Patent Rolls, James I.," 337.
[79] Derry Diocese Wills, Dublin, 1677–1745, 44; P. R. O.
[80] Prerogative Will, 1700, Dublin; P. R. O.
[81] Derry Diocese Will, 1747, Dublin; P. R. O.

Pennsylvania. John and William Glen (or Glenn), half brothers to David Caldwell, also removed to Pennsylvania. William is believed to be the William Glenn(sic) buried at Presbyterian Church near Media, Philadelphia; born 1730. John was born 1727-8, and removed from Pennsylvania to Virginia.

George Glen, supposedly brother to Ninian, died at Cloney, Aghlow(Aghloo), Antrim, 1701-2; his grandchildren then adults. Will 3 March, 1701-2; proved 13 March.[82] Issue: Benjamin, John, ——(daughter), wife of Robert Paton;——(daughter), wife of —— Christy; Hannah, wife of —— Mur(Muir); Abigail, wife of —— Glendinning;——(daughter), wife of Duncan McClockey; Margaret. Their mother was Jean Merton.

John Glen, first of Lifford, left other sons. Thomas Glenn(sic) of Tircullen, Aghanlow, gentleman (grandson doubtless of the first John of Lifford) and Margaret Calwell of Drummon, Tamlatard, had license to marry, 1683.[83] John Glen of Money Gobbin, Antrim (perhaps brother to Thomas), died 1698[84], leaving James, Thomas, William, John, Robert, Joseph, and Agnes (or Ann). James, the eldest, of age 1698-9, d.s.p. in the West Indies, before 1747, Joseph d.s.p. in Delaware, before 1747, Robert removed to Delaware, 1747, Agnes married Arthur Glen, of Cappah. In the year last mentioned the family was living at Donagheady, Tyrone. The wife of John Glen (died 1698) was Janet (or Jane) McCrea, living 1747.[85]

Archibald Glen, Diocese of Clogher,[86] died intestate, 1685, and was, no doubt, the Archibald who was an officer under Charles I., in the Irish wars, and who, with William Glen, Ensign, received lands in compensation for

---

[82] Derry Diocese Will, 1701.
[83] Pub. Rec. Off. Dublin.
[84] Prerogative Grant.
[85] Power of Atty. to Robert Glen, recorded at Wilmington, Del., U.S.A.
[86] Diocese of Clogher Will.

awards for arrears of pay, 1666. Patrick Glen of Donacava (Donaghacavey), Tyrone, probably another son of John of Lifford, died 1682.

A family of Glen (later spelling, Glenn), supposedly descended from the Linlithgow line, appears in Londonderry, about the middle of the 18th century. James, John, and Robert Glenn(sic) are named in city records, 1756, and some of the name are buried in Derry Cathedral, of whom William Glenn, of Londonderry, merchant, died 1796, aged 61 years. One of this line, William, died without issue, in Baltimore, Maryland, at the close of the 18th century.

William Glen, of Machreymonoch, Ballywillen, died 1730, leaving issue: Joseph, John, Ana, and Martha. The sons were then married, and had children. Thomas, supposedly brother of William, witnessed the latter's will, 22 Sept., 1730; proved 18.[87] Patrick Glen, of Aughereagh, died 1775.[88] William Glen, of Calhirneman, Galway, gentleman, died 1777.[89] William Glenn(sic) A.M., was 1675, Prepend of Kilchrist.[90]

Many of the Ulster Glens removed to America, and almost all of these, as well as most of those who went direct from Scotland, added an additional *n* to their surnames.

---

[87] Diocese of Connor Will.
[88] Diocese of Clogher, Admon. Bond.
[89] Pub. Rec. Office, Dublin.
[90] "Irish Parishes."

GRAHAM FAMILY RECORDS.—Kept by James Graham, and contributed by Mrs. Harry Rogers.

Births.

Gallant, Son of Samuel & Isabella Graham was born on the 12th day of June A.D. 1769.

Ann, Daughter of James & Ann Robinson was born on the 26th day of March A.D. 1770.

James, Son of Gallant & Ann Graham was born on the 29th day of Jany. A.D. 1794.

Samuel, Son of Gallant & Ann Graham was born on the 6th day of July A.D. 1796.

Mary, Daughter of Gallant & Ann Graham was born on the 20 day of December A.D. 1797.

Samuel, Son of Gallant & Ann Graham was born on the 29th day of Jany. A.D. 1800.

Ann, Daughter of Gallant & Ann Graham was born on the 24th day of September A.D. 1801.

Martha, Daughter of Gallant & Ann Graham was born on the 27th day of August A.D. 1804.

John, Son of Gallant & Ann Graham was born on the 2d day of September A.D. 1806.

Elizabeth, Daughter of Gallant & Ann Graham was born on the 7th day of July A.D. 1808.

Elizabeth, Daughter of Robert & Ann James was born on the 13th day of Aug. A.D. 1802.

Anna Mary Belknap, Daughter of James & Elizabeth Graham was born on the 19th day of Novemb. A.D. 1827.

William Crowell, Son of James & Elizabeth Graham was born on the 26th October A.D. 1829.

Edwin Pinkerton, Son of James & Elizabeth Graham was born on the 16th November A.D. 1832.

Helen Bruster, Daughter of James & Elizabeth Graham was born on the 29th July A.D. 1836.

Marriages.

Gallant Graham and Ann Robinson were married on the 18th day of April A.D. 1793.

Mary, Daughter of Gallant & Ann Graham was married to Isaac Campbell on the 12th January 1813.

Ann, Daughter of the above G & A Graham was married to Robert F. James Nos. 22d 1825.

James, Son of Gallant & Ann Graham was married to Elizabeth James on the 12th September 1826.

John, Son of Gallant & Ann Graham was married to Margaretta Jaquette on the 9th January 1832.

Deaths.

Samuel, Son of Gallant & Ann Graham departed this life July 30th 1797, aged 1 year & 24 days.

Gallant Graham departed this life on the 19th day of November 1810, aged 41 years 5 months & 7 days.

Elizabeth, Daughter of Gallant & Ann Graham departed this life on the 14th day of April A.D. 1811 aged 2 years 8 months & 7 days.

Mary, Daughter of Gallant & Ann Graham, and wife of Isaac Campbell departed this life on the.15th July 1819 aged 20 years, 6 months & 25 days, and Henry her Son departed to Join her on the 6th day of August Same year, aged 2 years and 6 months.

William Crowell, Son of James & Elizabeth Graham departed this life on the morning of Jany. 19th 1832 aged 2 years, 2 months & 25 days.

Births.

Martha Isabella, Daughter of James and Elizabeth Graham was born on the 10th day of August A.D. 1838.

Theodore Alexander, Son of James and Elizabeth Graham was born on the 27th day of October A.D. 1841.

Henry Rodman, Son of ditto was born on the 14th day of October A.D. 1844.

Deaths.

Martha, daughter of Gallant and Ann Graham departed this life on the morning of December 6th 1839, aged 35 years, 3 months & 9 days.

John, Son of Gallant & Ann Graham departed this life on the 5th day of April 1842 aged 35 years 7 mos. and 3 days.

Samuel, Son of Gallant & Ann Graham died on the 6th day of December 1843 aged 43 years 10 mos and 7 days.

Ann, Relict of Gallant Graham departed this life on the night of the 4th June 1851 aged 80 years 2 mos and 9 days.

Margaretta, widow of John Graham departed this life December 19th (Sabbath) 1852 aged 40 years.

Tho⁸ R. only son of the above died Nov. 15, 1855, aged 19 years.

James, son of Gallant & Ann Graham departed this life on the evening of the 21st of January 1860 aged 65 years, 11 mos. 23 days.

Marriages.

Anna Mary Belknap daughter of James and Elizabeth Graham was married by Rev. Jn° L. Grant, October 1, 1849 to Abraham Harris.

Married on the Morning of September 1, 1850 in the First Reformed Presbyterian Church by T. W. J. Wylie, D.D. Edwin Pinkerton Graham and Mary Hendrey Milax of Philadelphia and at the same time, Martha Isabella Graham and Henry Montgomery of Belfast, Ireland.

Ann Pinkerton & Robert B. James married in 1788 at Trenton N. J.

RECORDS OF THE HALL FAMILY, OF BRISTOL, PENNSYLVANIA.

Jn°: Hall his Holy Bible Bought of Fra^s. Knowles Cost 12/ in Philad^a the firs day of y^e twelfth month 17$\frac{12}{13}$.[1]

Jn° Hall Born y^e: 12th: of the Sixth Month 1686.[2]

1708 } Jo^n and Rebecca [Radcliffe] Hall Took each
y^e 21st 4 mo. } other in mariage.

1709 } Priscilla Hall Daughter of Jn° & Rebecca Hall
March 25 } was born & died 8^{br}. 2 1710.

1711 } Bob^t Son of Jn° Hall & Rebecca Born and Died 9^{br}
7^{br} 22^d } 22^d 1716.

1714 } Rebecca Daughter of Jn° & Rebecca Hall Born And
7^{br} 7th } Died 1738/9.

1714
11th: 8th m° } Rebecca Hall wife of Jn° Hall Deceased.[3]

1717 } Jn°: Hall Son of Jn° & Sarah [Baldwin][4] Hall
Decemb^r 1 } Born And Died 8^{br} 1734.

1719 } Robt. Son of Jn°. & Sarah Born And Died De-
July 5th } cemb^r 13th 1722.

1722
April 22^d } Mary Daughter of Jn° & Sarah Born.

1724 } Elizath. Daughter of Jn° & Sarah Hall Born.
May 20th } Died 9^{br} 13th 1728.

1726
March 29th } Sarah Daughter of Jn°. & Sarah Born.

1728 } Robt. Son of Jn° & Sarah Born. Died 9^{br} 24th
April 11th } 1729.

1730 } George Son of Jn° & Sarah Born. Died 7^{br} 12:
July 27th } 1731.

---

[1] This Bible is now owned by Augustus R. Hall, Esq., of Philadelphia, who has courteously allowed to be made copies of the very complete family records which it contains.

[2] See Note A. [3] See Note B. [4] See Note C.

1732 Decembr 28th } Joseph Hall Son of Jn° & Sarah Born.

1735 May 17 } Ruth Daughter of Jn° Hall & Hann[a] [Atkinson] Born.

17— y[e] 11 mo[th] 12 day } Lidia Daughter of Jn°. & Hannah Born. Died Aug[t] 23[d] 1823.[1]

1741 9th mo[th] 25th } Meribah Hall [wife of —— Annis, and] Daughter of John & Hannah Hall Born.

1744 ye 10th 29th } Jane Hall Daughter of John & Hannah Hall Born. Died February 10th 1826.

1760 9th y[e] 12th : m° } Han[a] Hall wife of Jn° Hall died.[2]

1768 } John Hall husband of above Hannah Hall Deceased the 10th 11th month.[3]

Joseph Hall and Hannah [Allaire] Hall was married the 12th of the 10th month Anno Dom. 1755 at Trenton in New Jersey.[4]

John Hall Son of Joseph & Hannah Hall was Born the 8th 12th month Anno Dom. 1755 in Trenton.

Alexander Hall son of Joseph & Hannah Hall was born Anno Dom. 1759 at Trenton.

Joseph Hall Son of Joseph and Hannah Hall was Born the 17th of the 2[d] month Anno Dom. 1761 at Trenton.

Thomas Hall Son of Joseph and Hannah Hall was Born the 16th Day of the 4th month A.D. 1763 at Trenton.

Achsah Hall Daughter of Joseph & Hannah Hall was Born the 10th day of the 4th mo. Anno Dom. 1767 in Bristol.

Achsah Hall departed this life the 17th day of the tenth month 1771.

[1] Lydia Hall married, first, in 1763, Henry Wilson; and, secondly, Jonathan Pursell. She had issue by the former: Joseph, born June 24, 1764; John, born October 4, 1766; Isaac, who removed to Philadelphia in 1793.

[2] See Note D.

[3] See Note E.

[4] Hannah Allaire, widow of Joseph Hall, married, secondly, June 11, 1782, William Bidgood, Senior, of Bristol township, who died shortly afterwards without issue by her.

Joseph Hall the husband of Hannah Hall Deceased the 15th Day of the First Month 1777.[1]

John Hall Son of Joseph Hall Dec^d the 19th of Seventh Month A.D. 1782.

Joseph Hall Son of Joseph & Hannah Hall Dec^d the 27 of the 9 month aged 22 years & 8 months 10 Days.

Alexander Hall departed this Life The 18th of the 10th month 1783 Aged 24 Years & 3 months.

Thomas Hall and Sarah [Atkinson of Bristol] was married the 17th of the 5th month Anno Dom. 1790.

Harriet Hall Daughter of Thomas & Sarah Hall Born the 28th of the Third Month Anno Dom. 1791 in Bristol.

John Hall Son of Thomas & Sarah Hall Born July 30th 1792.

Joseph Son of Thomas & Sarah Hall Born June 2^d 1794.

Sarah Wife of Thomas Hall Died Sept 18th 1794.

Thomas Hall & Rebecca [Church] married Feby 11th 1797.

Merribah Daughter of Thomas & Rebecca Hall Born Novem^r 26th 1797.

Edward [Church] Son of Thomas and Rebecca Hall Born Febru^y 17th 1799.

Robbert Son of Thomas & Rebecca Hall Borne August 28th 1800.

Sarah [Church] Daughter of Thomas & Rebecca Hall Born 18th Octo^{br} 1802.

Samuel Scotten Hall Born Jan 2^d 1805.

[Benjamin] Shepherd Hall Born August 23^d 1806.

I [saac] Wilson Hall Born Sepr 18th 1808.

Mary Smith Hall Born June 4th 1811.

Meribah Hall Daughter of Thomas & Rebecca Hall departed this life on the fifteenth day of May 1818 between 10 & 11 o'clock in the morning.

Lydia Pursell departed this life August 23^d 1823 about 4 o'clock in the morning.

---

[1] Joseph Hall removed to Trenton, New Jersey, in 1755, but returned to Bristol Borough in 1763, being elected second burgess in the following year, and a member of the common council in 1765.

John Hall Son of Thomas & Sarah Hall departed this life on the 3ᵈ day of March 1825 about 4 o'clock in the morning.

Jane Scotten departed this life February 10ᵗʰ 1826 about 7 o'clock in the evening.

Samuel Scotten Hall, son of Thomas and Rebecca, and Christianna Stockton,[1] daughter of William and Ann, were married June 9th, 1831.

Rebecca wife of Thomas Hall died February 21st, 1837 in the 70th year of her age.[2]

Thomas Hall husband of the above died April 16th, 1844 in the 82d year of his age.

Mary Smith Wallace died August 24th, 1858 in the 48th year of her age.

Harriet Westphal died December 29th, 1866 in the 76th year of her age.

Samuel Scotten Hall died September 18th, 1875 in the 71st year of his age.

Christianna, widow of Samuel Scotten Hall died March 23d, 1883.

Sarah Church Spain died March 24th, 1887 in the 85th year of her age.

Joseph Hall and Olivia Gardiner were married January 3d, 1822.

A daughter of Joseph and Olivia Hall was born November 14th, 1822 and buried the same day.

John Augustus Rattaux (Augustus R.) son of Joseph and Olivia Hall was born at Paterson, New Jersey, October 27th, 1824.

Henrietta Idel, daughter of Joseph and Olivia was born at Mount Holly, New Jersey, June 25th, 1828 and died November 12th, 1828.

Olivia, widow of Joseph Hall and daughter of the late

---

[1] Mrs. Hall was a descendant of John Stockton, of Springfield township, Burlington County, New Jersey, second son of Richard Stockton, the founder of the family. A full account of her ancestry will appear in the "White Ancestry."

[2] See Note F.

Abraham and Olivia Gardiner, of Burlington, New Jersey,[1] died June 13th, 1848.

Augustus R. Hall and Caroline Alford were married September 14th, 1847.

Olivia, daughter of Augustus R. and Caroline Hall was born September 1st, 1848 and died October 16th, 1858.

Zachary Taylor, son of Augustus R. and Caroline Hall was born July 9th, 1850.

Joseph Augustus, son of Augustus R. and Caroline was born June 15th, 1852 and died June 25th, 1873.

Harry Basil, son of Augustus R. and Caroline Hall was born December 26th, 1854.

Walter Ferdinand, son of Augustus R. and Caroline Hall was born December 4th, 1856.

Willis Edward, son of Augustus R. and Caroline Hall was born July 20th, 1860.

Caroline Alford Gardiner, daughter of Augustus R. and Caroline Hall was born September 15th, 1864.

Zachary Taylor Hall and Sophia Roberts were married November 13th, 1879.

Evans Roberts, son of Zachary Taylor and Sophia Hall was born August 16th, 1880.

Haslett Gardiner, son of Zachary Taylor and Sophia Hall was born December 14th, 1882.

Zachary Taylor son of Zachary Taylor and Sophia Hall was born August 7th, 1884.

Walter Ferdinand Hall and George Annie Benners Stouffer were married May 18th, 1882.

Catharine Benners, daughter of Walter Ferdinand and George Annie Benners Hall was born April 15th, 1883.

[Note A.]

John Hall was the only surviving child of Robert Hall, of St. Margaret's Parish, in the city of Westminster, England, who (with his wife, Elizabeth, and their two children, Elizabeth and George, both of whom died

[1] Abraham Gardiner was the second son of Thomas and Susanna (Elton) Gardiner, and a descendant of Thomas Gardiner, Jr., the first Speaker of the General Assembly of East and West New Jersey. A full account of his ancestry will appear in the " White Ancestry."

in early childhood) immigrated to Pennsylvania, taking up a tract of five hundred acres on the Neshaminy Creek, in Middletown township, Bucks County. Tradition credits him with having been a passenger on the "Welcome," or on one of the vessels of Penn's fleet, which left England August 31, 1682, and arrived at New Castle, on the Delaware, October 27, 1682. In a register of children of members of the Middletown Monthly Meeting, born in England, the birth of his son George is recorded as having taken place April 18, 1682, though the English records place his birth on the same date in September of that year. The latter is probably the correct date, as in the register of births of the Middletown Monthly Meeting his youngest child, the original owner of the Bible from which the preceding records are taken, is incorrectly styled Robert, Jr., it being clearly proved by the entry in the family Bible and a deed recorded at Doylestown, in Bucks County, that his name should be John.[1]

Robert Hall was elected one of the Representatives of the county of Bucks in the Provincial Assembly, March 10, 168⅔, re-elected in 1687 and 1688, and appointed coroner of the county in 1685, being the first incumbent of that office, which he retained until his decease, March 28, 1688. He married, first, October 17, 1678, Sarah Buterton, of Hounsditch, London, who died on the 16th of the next month; and, secondly, May 26, 1680, Elizabeth, daughter of George and Elizabeth White, of Bucklebury, County Berks, England, who married, secondly, in 1690, Stephen Newell, of Bucks County, Pennsylvania.

The Whites of Bucklebury, a parish near Reading, in the county of Berks, appear to have occupied a good position among the yeomanry of the neighborhood, and were probably related to the heraldic family of the same name residing at Fifield in the same county, but originally of Reading, one of whose members was Sir Thomas White, Kt., Lord Mayor of London in 1554, and founder of St. John's College, Oxford, as the names of George and Francis were great favorites with both families.

Humphrey White, of Bucklebury, was the second son of Maud White, "late, whilst she lived, of Sparshalt, within the county and archdeaconry of Berks, widdow," who died in 1634. He died in 1639, his will being dated and proved in that year, and still preserved among the probate records of the archdeaconry of Berks. He left a widow, Joan, and seven children,—Simon, Roger, Humphrey, Thomas, George, Joan, Elizabeth.

George White, of Bucklebury (youngest son of Humphrey and Joan), was among the early converts to Quakerism, and a frequent sufferer, both in person and estate, for his religious belief, being excommunicated in 1678, twice imprisoned, the last time in 1684, for refusing to take an oath, and having considerable sums of money taken from him in 1683 and 1686 to satisfy claims for corn-tithes. His daughter Elizabeth, who married Robert Hall, having settled in Pennsylvania, he obtained a certificate from the Monthly Meeting of Friends at Newberry, intending to remove

[1] Book IV. p. 104.

to that province, but was prevented by his imprisonment, as appears by the certificate, which was dated 8th month 19, 1683, and signed by fifteen persons on the 21st of that month, when he was confined in the jail at Reading. It was not until the year 1687 when his certificate was again read at a monthly meeting held at Ore on the 21st of the 4th month, and signed by the members then present, that, having some time previously purchased fifteen hundred acres in Pennsylvania, he immigrated to that province with his entire family, settling in Middletown township, Bucks County, where he died September 15, 1688, leaving a widow, Elizabeth, who died in 1699, her will being dated September 11, and proved November 10 of that year. They had nine children,—John, their eldest son; Humphrey, buried December 9, 1675; Elizabeth, wife of Robert Hall; Sarah, wife of —— Huett; Peter, born August 3, 1663, married Elizabeth English; William, born May 5, 1666; Francis, of Middletown township, born May 10, 1668; Joseph, born April 13, 1670; Benjamin, born April 19, 1676.

[Note B.]

James Radcliffe, of Chapel Hill, in Rosendale, County Lancaster, England (probably brother to John Radcliffe, born in 1657, son of Richard and Alice Radcliffe, of Rosendale), married, June 1, 1673, the widow Mary Rawthorpe at her own house in Olden; became a minister of the Society of Friends, and in 1685 immigrated to Bucks County, in Pennsylvania, where he died March 29, 1690, leaving four children,— Richard, born June 8, 1675; Edward, born October 14, 1678; Rachel, born April 16, 1682; Rebecca, first wife of John Hall, born January 11, 1684.

[Note C.]

John Baldwin, yeoman, settled in Philadelphia County prior to July, 1686, but shortly after that date removed to Makefield township, in the county of Bucks, finally settling in the town of Bristol in the latter county, where he died in November, 1714, having married, December 19, 1689, Sarah, daughter of Samuel and Mary Allen, who was born at Chew Magna, County Somerset, England, July 17, 1667. They had five children,—Mary; Sarah, married, in January, 1715, John Hall; John; Richard; Joseph.

Samuel Allen, of Chew Magna, arrived at Chester, in Pennsylvania, December 11, 1681, being a passenger on the ship "Bristol Factor," and settled on the Neshaminy Creek, in Bucks County, from whence he removed to Philadelphia, where he died in November, 1710.

[Note D.]

In the latter part of the seventeenth century four persons of the name of Atkinson settled in Pennsylvania, viz.: Thomas, of whom hereafter; his brother John; James, who arrived at Philadelphia from Ireland in December, 1682; and Christopher, who settled in Bucks County in 1699, bringing a certificate for himself and family from the Monthly Meeting at Lancaster, in England.

Thomas Atkinson, of Newby, County York, England, an early convert to Quakerism and a preacher in that Society, immigrated to Pennsylvania in 1682, settling in Northampton township, Bucks County, where he died in October, 1682, leaving a widow, Jane, and three sons, —Isaac, William, and Samuel.

William Atkinson (second son of Thomas and Jane) resided in the borough of Bristol, served one term as a member of the common council, and was eleven years collector of the excise. He was for thirty-three years an elder of the Falls Monthly Meeting, holding that office at his decease, October 29, 1749. He married, first, April 6, 1704, Mary, daughter of Richard Hough, a native of Macclesfield, County Chester, England, and one of the representatives of Bucks County in the Provincial Assembly. She died November 11, 1720, and he married, secondly, June 5, 1722, Margaret, daughter of Henry and Margaret Baker, who died in December, 1748, aged fifty-five years. William Atkinson had eleven children, six of whom were by his first wife. Their births are recorded in the registers of the Falls Monthly Meeting. His second child, Hannah, was born January 25, 1706, and in May, 1734, became the third wife of John Hall.

[Note E.]

John Hall, of Bristol (who had been previously referred to in the Bible and in Note A) was an active member of the Falls Monthly Meeting, frequently serving as a delegate to the Quarterly Meeting, and an influential inhabitant of the town, being one of the principal persons instrumental in obtaining from the crown a charter, dated November 14, 1720, erecting Bristol into a royal borough, and constituting Joseph Bond and John Hall burgesses. He served as chief burgess for the ensuing seven years, and was again elected to that office in 1733, '38, '39, '40, '41, '45, '46, and '61; serving as a member of the common council in 1747, '48, and '62. In 1717 he represented Bucks County in the Provincial Assembly, and was commissioned sheriff and justice of the peace, serving the county in the latter capacity for seven years, and being again commissioned sheriff in 1718, '20, '21, '22, and '33. He was also collector of the excise for six years. In 1740 he went to the Assembly again and remained there as the representative of his county for eight consecutive years, being re-elected in 1749 and '50. He was by trade a cooper, and was also at one time interested in Langhorn's Mills, in Middletown township, his partners in that venture being Charles Plumley, of Middletown, and Edward Roberts, of Bristol,—the latter a miller.

[Note F.]

Joseph Church, of Bristol, was probably the son of Edward Church, of the same place, spoken of as old and infirm in 1777. He served as a member of the common council in 1760, '62, and '63, and died in December, 1784, leaving two sons, Edward and Joseph, both of whom are mentioned in his will, which was dated November 1, 1784, and proved January 7, 1785.

Edward Church, of Bristol, died shortly after his father, having married, in 1765, Sarah, daughter of Thomas and Prudence Antrim, of Burlington County, New Jersey, who died in May, 1797, her will being dated June 29, 1795, and proved May 30, 1797. They had three children, William, Samuel, and Rebecca, the latter of whom married Thomas Hall, of Bristol, who in 1806 removed to Burlington, New Jersey.

HALL—BRADING—CARMICKE.—The following entries are copied from an old Breeches Bible in the possession of Captain P. G. Watmough, Chestnut Hill, Philadelphia:

Wm Hall the first sun of William Hall and Sarah his wife wass borne one the 22 day of October in 1701 it being betweene 3 & 4 aclock in thee morning and one the 4th called Wednes Day

Sarah Hall thee Eldest Daughter of William Hall & Elizabeth his first wife wass borne thee 18 day of Aprall in thee year 1689 ☉ in ♋ die ol hoe 4 and Departed this Life on Thursday the 27th Oct abt 11 aclock at night 1748

Hanna Hall thee 3 daughter of William and Elizabeth wass borne one the 20 day of March in the yr 1692

Elizabeth Hall thee 4 daughter of William & Elizabeth wass born one thee 31 day of Desember 1694 of a monday about 3 aclock in thee after noone

Elizabeth Hall died the day before —— day in ye year *1699*

Ann Hall the 5 daughter of William Hall and Elizabeth wass born one ye 9 day of Desember in the yeare of our lord *1699* it being one a tuesday a boute 4 in the morning & departed this life one ye 15 day of Feborray 170½, on a fasst day

[1] Sarah Hall Borne the 18th Day of Aap^{rll} 1689 and Departed this Life on Thursday 27th Octob^r ab^t 11 aclock at night in the year *1748*.

[1] Hanna Hall the 3 Daughter of William Hall and Elizabeth his wife was Borne on ye 20 day of March in 1692

[1] Elizabeth Hall ye forth Daughter of William Hall and Elizabeth wife was Borned Desamber ye 31d in ye yeare *1694* of a Monday a bout three aclock in ye after noone

Nathaneill Brading Aidged aboute Thirtysix: years of age Died ye ninth Day of January aboute Three or four a Clock In ye morning In ye year of our Lord 1712–13

Laus Deo In Salem

On the 16th Day of 8^{br} Anno Domine 1713 Peter Carmicke and Sarah Brading Daughter of Wm Hall of Salem towne wear Maried together By ye Rev^d Mr Boise

On Tuesday the 17th day of Augt. in the forenoon at eleven John Carmicke eldest son of Peter & Sarah his wife was Borne Anno y^r *1714* on the 25th 9th our Son John recd Baptism by ye rev^d Mr Mansell who was his Godfather 1715 & Departed the 27 May 1754

On Thursday 14th Feby: Eliz: eldest Daughter of Peter & Sarah was borne about a quarter of eight at night 1716 & Apll 14th 1719 she was Baptised by ye Rev^d Mr Gerard who was her Godfather

On Saturday Stephen Second son of Peter and Sarah was Borne abt. twelve at noon 1718–9 Jan 31st and Apll. 14th 1719 he was Baptized by ye Rev^d Mr Gerard & my Son Jo^n was his Godfather

On Monday 15th day of Jan. 1721-2 abt. 10 at night Sarah second Daughter of Peter & Sarah was Borne & on the 11th day of March was Baptiz^d by ye Rev^d Mr Hodgson & Doc. Reily & Mary Saill stood for her 1721-2

On Monday ye 26 of 8th 1724 abt. 3 in ye morning Clementina ye third Daughter of P. & Sarah was borne and on ye 24th of 9th she was Babtiz^d & Mr Hodgson who was her Godfather. On ye 15th Jany 1724-5 she Departed this Life & on May 24 1728 my wife Sarah was Delivrd of a Dead Girl by Doctors Graham & Griffeth Owen after a terrible Labour of 3 days &c.

[1] These appear to be duplicate entries, in another part of the Bible.

GENEALOGICAL SKETCH OF GENERAL W. S. HANCOCK.

BY HOWARD M. JENKINS.

Winfield Scott Hancock, senior major-general in the army of the United States, and who, in 1880, received one hundred and fifty-five electoral votes for President of the United States, died at Governor's Island, New York, on the 9th of February, 1886.

General Hancock was entirely of Pennsylvania blood. He was born near Montgomery Square, in Montgomery County, and both his parents were natives of this State. Upon his mother's side his progenitors were Pennsylvanians back to their immigrant ancestors. Upon the paternal side his line is apparently not traceable beyond his grandfather, Richard Hancock, a seaman, who made his home in Philadelphia in the close of the last and beginning of the present century.

The mother of General Hancock was Elizabeth Hawksworth. About 1730, Peter Hawksworth and his wife, Mary, came from England to Pennsylvania, and settled in what is now the township of Hatfield, in Montgomery County. (Hatfield had not then been created a separate township, nor had Montgomery County been set off from Philadelphia.) The tradition is that they came from Birmingham. Peter purchased a tract of land, and in his will, made February 26, 1767, he left to his " dearly beloved wife, Mary," the plantation he then lived on, including fifty-three acres. He mentions in the will his " three sons, by name Edward, John, and Peter," and his " three daughters, by name Sarah, Ann, and Rachel." He left his wife executrix, but before the probate of the will (March 22,

1769) she died, as appears from the fact that John Jenkins,[1] who had married his eldest daughter, Sarah, subsequently took out letters of administration "with the will annexed" upon his estate.

It is traditional in the family that Peter and Mary Hawksworth were buried in the church-yard of St. Thomas's Episcopal Church, at Whitemarsh. Their age is not known.

Of their three sons, Edward probably died unmarried. Peter was twice married, but need not be farther traced at present, and JOHN married Elizabeth Jenkins. She was the second daughter and fourth (and youngest) child of Jenkin Jenkin and Mary, his wife, immigrants from Wales, about 1729, who settled also in what is now Hatfield township, and who therefore preceded by a short time the arrival of the Hawksworths at that place.

JOHN HAWKSWORTH was born in 1733, and died in February, 1777. He was a member of the Baptist Church of Montgomery[2] (the township adjoining Hatfield on the southeast), and was probably buried there. In 1761 he had purchased from his father a farm in Hatfield, which the father (Peter) had bought in 1749 from John Jenkins. Upon this he no doubt lived. It is upon the authority of one of his sons that he served as a soldier in the "French and Indian" war, and that he had been in the army of the Revolution during the operations of the period before his death, this being caused (at the early age of forty-four) by disease contracted in the service.

The children of JOHN and Elizabeth Jenkins Hawksworth were seven in number: Mary, EDWARD, John, Elizabeth, Ann, Sarah, and Peter. John died unmarried; Peter, known as "Colonel Peter," from his position in the militia

---

[1] John Jenkins was the son of Jenkin Jenkin, the immigrant. His marriage with Sarah Hawksworth made a double connection between the two families, the other being that stated in the narrative,—John Hawksworth (brother of Sarah) with Elizabeth Jenkins (sister of John).

[2] This church was formed in 1719, the fourth of the Baptists in Pennsylvania, its predecessors being Cold Spring, Pennepack, and Philadelphia.

forces of Pennsylvania, was captain of a company in the war with England in 1814, and was absent for some time in the service. He held some civil positions, and left a family. EDWARD, who in his lifetime appears to have adopted the present spelling of the name (Hoxworth), was born September 22, 1760, and died January 11, 1847. He was, like his father, connected with the Baptist Church at Montgomery. His home was in Hatfield, on a farm partly inherited from his father, and partly purchased from his brothers and sisters. "He entered the Revolutionary army," says a genealogical sketch by his nephew, the late William J. Hoxworth, of Macungie, "when a boy about fifteen years of age, and served under various commands until independence was established, and received a pension to the end of his life. He was a member of the company of which John Jenkins[1] was lieutenant, which company had in charge part of the Hessian prisoners taken at Trenton, December 26, 1776. He was a small-built man, but exceedingly lithe and active. In his younger days he would leap over an ordinary-sized horse without touching, and after he had reached threescore years and ten was able to do a full day's work in the harvest-field without apparent weariness."

EDWARD married MARY Hoxworth, who was born in 1760, and died in 1823. She was his first cousin, being the eldest daughter of his uncle, Peter (son of Peter, the immigrant), by his first wife. They, EDWARD and MARY, were the grandparents of General Hancock. They had in all nine children,—Ann, Ellen, John, Israel, Mary, Margaret, Edward, ELIZABETH, and Sarah. ELIZABETH was born December 8, 1801, and died January 25, 1879. She married BENJAMIN FRANKLIN HANCOCK.

Returning now to the male line, Richard Hancock, of Philadelphia, the seaman, is said to have been one of the victims of the British enforcement of the arbitrary "right of search," to have been taken from an American vessel,

[1] This was John Jenkins, second, son of the John heretofore mentioned. His daughter Sarah married "Colonel Peter" Hoxworth, mentioned above.

and subsequently to have been imprisoned several years in England—conjecturably at Dartmoor—before he secured his release. He was twice married. By his first wife he had two daughters, Eliza and Ann, of whom nothing further is known to the writer. By his second wife, Anna Maria Nash (who was born at Edinburgh, Scotland, June 28, 1777), he had also two children, BENJAMIN F. and Sarah. The latter was born in 1802, and was living at least as late as 1821. She married H. E. Reynolds, but her further record, if there be any, has not been found.

Both Benjamin F. and Sarah were born in Philadelphia, and it was during their infancy that their father was impressed by the British and so long detained. After his release (or escape) he returned, but going on a subsequent voyage, died of ship fever. His wife, left with the two children, was obliged to labor for her own maintenance, and presently, after the rule of the time in such a case, found "places" for the children. She died, it is stated, about 1822.[1]

BENJAMIN FRANKLIN HANCOCK was born October 19, 1800. The earlier years of his childhood were spent in Philadelphia, as already stated, and then he was placed to be brought up with 'Squire John Roberts, of Montgomery, a prominent citizen and active man of business. His large farm near Montgomery Square, an inheritance from his father, Eldad Roberts, he had removed to about 1794, having previously been a storekeeper at Spring House, a few miles southward, on the road from Philadelphia to Bethlehem. Supposing BENJAMIN to have gone to Montgomery at the age of ten, 'Squire John was then a man of sixty. He had been appointed a justice of the peace in 1791 by Governor Mifflin, and he continued in commission until his death in 1823. With him the orphan lad doubtless found a comfortable

[1] I have a letter written by her on the 1st of January, 1821, to 'Squire John Roberts, in which she speaks of a recent illness, and desires the payment of a small sum due her. She mentions a number of family and other details, and sends her "love to Benjamin." This was a year or so before her death.

home, and received a fair education at the "Free School," which had been founded at an earlier date at Montgomery Square,[1] and which afforded, indeed, opportunities superior to those usually found in the rural parts of Pennsylvania at that time. Some of the teachers were men of good qualifications, and the neighborhood contained some persons of literary culture.[2] During the war with England, in 1814, though but a lad, he entered the service, and made a "tour of duty," probably with the company, which must have been recruited from the neighborhood, under command of Captain Peter Hoxworth (the "Colonel Peter" named above).

BENJAMIN F. HANCOCK married ELIZABETH HOXWORTH. The home of her parents was in the south corner of Hatfield township, and therefore but a few miles distant from 'Squire Roberts's farm. It is a tradition that the marriage was displeasing to the 'Squire, and upon the ground of difference of religious views.[3] Whatever measure of truth there may

[1] One of the teachers here for several years (1804 to 1819), a man of good parts, was William Collum, who must have been B. F. Hancock's preceptor. He made the calculations for almanacs published at Doylestown by Asher Miner, and removed subsequently to Philadelphia. Others of his pupils contemporaneously with Mr. Hancock were Samuel Aaron, afterward famous as a teacher and preacher, who was born in the adjoining township of New Britain, and Samuel Medary, afterward conspicuous in the public affairs of Ohio, and Territorial Governor, for a time, both of Minnesota and Kansas. When Winfield S. Hancock was appointed a cadet at West Point, in 1840 (by Hon. Joseph Fornance), it chanced that Mr. Medary was a member of the Board of Visitors, so that Mr. B. F. Hancock, who had accompanied his son to the Academy, met his old friend and companion, and presented the youthful soldier to him, even before the Academy officials.

[2] Among these at the time of the Revolution and later (he died in 1801) was Dr. Charles Moore, whose home was at Montgomery Square. His wife, Milcah Martha (née Hill), was a woman of fine intelligence and cultivation. She removed, after the death of her husband, to Burlington, N. J., where she died in 1831. A small circulating library was established at Montgomery Square before 1800, which continued in existence for about half a century. Among those who had presented books to it in its early years was Mrs. Ferguson, of Horsham, the daughter of Dr. Graeme, of Graeme Park.

[3] Though this is a matter of no consequence, I think it not very likely. The difference may have been caused by political divergences, the Hox-

have been in this, it is certain that 'Squire Roberts's will contained a small bequest for Mr. Hancock, which was paid him by the executors, in January, 1824 (the 'Squire having died in June of the previous year), together with an allowance, the amount of which had been determined by arbitrators, " for services rendered the deceased."

Mr. Hancock's education was sufficient to qualify him as teacher at the " Free School," which, as already related, he had attended as a pupil. He obtained that position, and occupied for a home the dwelling-house end of the school building. This was the birthplace of General Hancock, who, with his twin brother, Hilary Baker, was born February 24, 1824. The building still stands. It is a two-story stone building, at the hamlet of Montgomery Square, on the turnpike,—the old road from Philadelphia to Bethlehem. Here Mr. Hancock remained as a teacher for a short time after the birth of the twin children, and then, having begun to read law under the direction of John Freedley, Esq.,[1] of Norristown, removed to that borough, and was admitted to the bar in 1828. There he resided, engaged in the practice of his profession, until his death, February 1, 1867. His third son, John, was born at Norristown, March 23, 1830. He and his wife were buried in Montgomery Cemetery, on the banks of the Schuylkill, at that borough, where the remains of their distinguished son have now also been placed.

WINFIELD S. HANCOCK, then a lieutenant in the United States Army, married, January 24, 1850, Almira DuBois, daughter of Samuel and Almira DuBois Russell, of St. Louis, Mo., and she survives him. Their children were:

(1.) Russell, born October 29, 1850; died December 30, 1884; married, April 30, 1872, Elizabeth Gwynn, daughter of Nicholas and Elizabeth (Greathouse) Gwynn. They had

---

worths being Democrats of Jeffersonian enthusiasm, while 'Squire John was a Federalist. Party feeling in those days had not so subsided as would be inferred from the phrase " the era of good feeling," applied to Monroe's time.

[1] He represented his district in Congress from 1847 to 1851.

four children,—Ada Elizabeth, Gwynn Richard, Almira; and Winfield S., Jr., who died in infancy.

(2.) Ada Elizabeth, born at Fort Myers, Florida, February 24, 1857, died unmarried, March 18, 1875, at New York, and buried at Norristown, Pa.

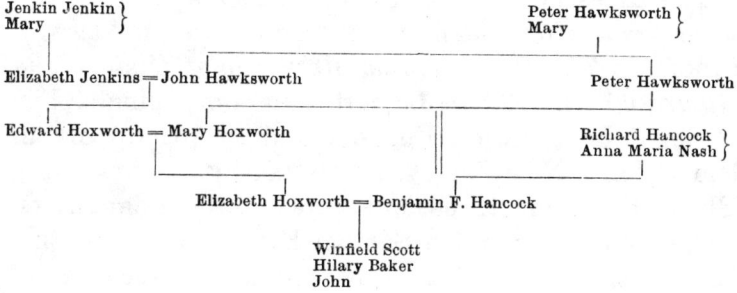

ENGLISH ANCESTRY OF SAMUEL HEDGE SON-IN-LAW OF MAJOR JOHN FENWICK OF SALEM COLONY, NEW JERSEY

By the REVEREND A. H. HORD, Registrar of the Diocese of Pennsylvania

The ancestry of Major John Fenwick and of his two wives, was, for the first time fully presented, with proofs, in *The Pennsylvania Magazine of History and Biography*,[1] by Edwin Jaquett Sellers of Philadelphia. Major John Fenwick, Founder and Proprietor of Salem Colony, New Jersey, left issue, by his first wife, Elizabeth Covert, three daughters. Of these daughters, Anna Fenwick married Samuel Hedge, who was Surveyor General, April 30, 1678; Clerk and Recorder of Fenwick's Colony, and a Member of the New Jersey Assembly, in 1682. The ancestry of Samuel Hedge was recently discovered by the writer, and the evidence on which his pedigree is based is as follows:

A lady living in Philadelphia, who is a direct descendant of Samuel Hedge and his wife, Anna Fenwick, inherited and now owns a silver spoon[2] on the handle of which are engraved the coats-of-arms impaled of two families. As to these arms nothing was known by the owner, but Mr. Sellers identified one of them as certainly the arms of the Weld family, described in Burke's "General Armory" as *Azure a fess nebulé between three crescents ermine*. The name of the other family represented in this impalement remained a mystery until sometime later the writer, while looking over the pages of the published "Calendar of Wills, Court of Husting, London,"[3] found

---

[1] XLIX. 151, 256; L. 267.

[2] To ascertain the date when this spoon was made, the writer took it to the well-known jewelers, The Bailey, Banks & Biddle Company of Philadelphia, where, after careful examination, the spoon was pronounced "a very fine specimen of James 2nd spoon bearing the hallmark of the London Assay Office of 1686–7."

[3] Part II., 1358–1688, p. 777.

the will of Elizabeth Weld, dated October 14, 1676, in which she mentions her grandsons, Samuel Hedge and Thomas Hedge, and her granddaughter, Elizabeth Medley. Starting with this knowledge, the pedigree was worked out.

Elizabeth Weld was the wife of "John Weld, Goldsmith," of the Parish of St. Mary Woolnoth, London. "John Weld and Elizabeth Glanfield, both of this Parish," were married, March 4, 1622.[4] Elizabeth Glanfield was probably the daughter of John Glanfield, son of "Francis Glanfield, Goldsmith," as the only reference to the name Glanfield in this parish register is the baptism on December 4, 1597, of "John, son of Francis Glanffeild, Goldsmith."

John Weld and Elizabeth his wife, had the following children, whose baptisms are recorded in the Registers of St. Mary Woolnoth:

> Elizabeth Weld, dau. of John Weld, Goldsmith, baptized, August 14, 1623.[5]
> John Weld, son of John Weld, Goldsmith, baptized, July 25, 1624.[6]
> Thomas Weld, son of John Weld, Goldsmith, baptized, December 5, 1628.[7]

Elizabeth Weld, daughter of John and Elizabeth Weld, married Samuel Hedge. The Register of St. Mary Woolnoth[8] records that "Samuel Hedge of St. Peter's the Poor and Elizabeth Weld of this parish" were married, March 4, 1640. Concerning the Parish of St. Peter le Poor, in which Samuel Hedge lived, Stow, in his "Survey of London," writes that it was "sometimes peradventure a poor parish but at this present [1598] there be many fair houses possessed by rich merchants and other."

---

[4] *Register of St. Mary Woolnoth, London*, p. 142.
[5] *Ibid.*, p. 35.
[6] *Ibid.*, p. 36.
[7] *Ibid.*, p. 38.
[8] *Ibid.*, p. 149.

Of the children of Samuel Hedge and his wife, Elizabeth Weld, we know the names of three who are mentioned (as already stated), in the will (1676) of their grandmother, Elizabeth Weld. The names of these children are:

> Elizabeth Hedge, who married John Medley. "April 18, 1666, John Medley, of St. Mary Woolchurch, London, Skinner, Bachelor, about 23, and Elizabeth Hedge, Spinster, about 19 daughter of Samuel Hedge of St. Peter's le Poor, Painter-Stainer."[9]
> Thomas Hedge. He was probably the "Thomas Hedge of St. Saviour's, Southwark" who married "Mary Johnson of St. Botolph's, Bishopsgate,"[10] December 20, 1662.
> Samuel Hedge, son of Samuel Hedge and Elizabeth Weld, was evidently the Samuel Hedge who came to the Colony of New Jersey with Major John Fenwick, as Shourds[11] states that "Samuel Hedge 2nd was the son of Samuel Hedge, a merchant and citizen of London".

Samuel Hedge, senior, was evidently a man of considerable prominence. He was "Master" (1663) of the Painter Stainers Company,[12] which is described as "an old gild of painters of heraldic emblazonments."[13] To be elected to the office of "Master"—the highest dignity in a London Company—was at that time quite an honor in the city of London. Samuel Pepys, Secretary of the Admiralty and noted diarist, was, as a mark of distinction, elected Master of the Clothworkers Company. Samuel Hedge probably belonged to an old London family, as the names of Christopher Hedge (1568) and John Hedge (1570) appear in a "List of Scholars of St. Peter's College, Westminster who were elected to Trinity College, Cambridge."[14]

---

[9] *Marriage Licenses issued by the Vicar-General of the Archbishop of Canterbury, 1660 to 1668*, p. 172.
[10] *Ibid.*, p. 225.
[11] *History and Genealogy of Fenwick's Colony*, p. 13.
[12] Whitebrook, *London Citizens in 1651*, pp. 7, 23.
[13] *Century Dictionary.*
[14] Compiled by Joseph Welch.

The pedigree given identifies the two families whose arms are impaled on the spoon of 1686. According to the laws of heraldry, the impalement of two arms necessarily signifies the marriage of two families. The marriage of Samuel Hedge and Elizabeth Weld is thus represented in the engraving on the spoon. The engraving of the Weld arms on the spoon corresponds in every respect to the Weld Arms as delineated in various books on British heraldry and as described in Burke's "General Armory." Moreover, Thomas Weld of the parish of St. Mary Woolnoth, London, who seems to have been nearly related to "John Weld, Goldsmith," of the same parish, signed his pedigree in the Visitation of London, 1664, thereby proving his right to these arms.[15]

The arms of Hedge engraved on the spoon are described in the language of heraldry as *Ermine, three lozenges conjoined in fess argent, within a bordure engrailed sable.* These arms are not found in Burke's "General Armory," but it is a well-known fact that the arms of some old English families were never recorded in the College of Heralds. The writer is acquainted with several of these unrecorded arms that do not appear in Burke—among them being the arms of a distinguished prelate of the time of Charles II., which are carved on a monument in the Poet's Corner in Westminster Abbey, recorded in the archives of the Abbey, and impaled with the arms of another family on a tablet in an old English church. That the arms impaled with the Weld arms on the silver spoon are those of the Hedge family is further indicated by the fact that they are what are described in heraldry as "Canting Arms"—that is, they are "such as have an allusion to the name of the bearer."[16] Thus, the

---

[15] *Miscellanea Genealogica et Heraldica*, New Series, I. 113.

[16] See "Dictionary of Terms used in Heraldry" in Burke's *General Armory.*

name Hedge is canted in the arms on the spoon (1) by three lozenges arranged point to point in a horizontal line, or in fess, across the center of the shield like a fence or *hedge;* and (2) by the engrailed bordure, or border around the shield, which may also represent a *hedge.* It is reasonable to assume that Samuel Hedge, ''Master'' of a guild of painters of heraldic emblazonments, was entitled to the arms engraved on his silver.

"John Weld, Goldsmith," of St. Mary Woolnoth Parish, London, grandfather of Samuel Hedge of New Jersey, was descended from an ancient and honorable family. The pedigree of the Weld family is traced to Edric, nephew of Edric, Duke of Mercia, husband of Edina, daughter of King Ethelred 1003 A. D.[17] Among his descendants may be mentioned William Weld, Sheriff of London, 1352; Sir Humphrey Weld, Lord Mayor of London, 1610;[18] Thomas Weld of Lulworth Castle, Dorset, created a Cardinal of the Roman Catholic Church in 1829,[19] and Mary Weld (granddaughter of Thomas Weld of St. Mary Woolnoth, London, who signed his pedigree in the Visitation of 1664), who married John Kennedy, Earl of Cassilis.[20]

The family to which these persons belong bore the same arms that are engraved on the silver spoon, now two hundred and forty-six years old, which was owned by Samuel Hedge of the Colony of New Jersey. Samuel Hedge, therefore, on his mother's side was descended from a family that was equal in the antiquity of its descent to the family of Fenwick.[21] John Fenwick made "his friend William Penn, one of his executors and trustee for his three eldest grandsons"—one of whom was Samuel Hedge, Jr.

---

[17] Burke, *Commoners of Great Britain*, 1836, I. 197; II. 677; III. 334.
[18] *Ibid.,* I. 198.
[19] *Ibid.,* I. 197.
[20] *Miscellanea Genealogica et Heraldica*, New Series, I. 114.
[21] *American Historical Register*, III. 221–223; Shourds, *History and Genealogy of Fenwick's Colony.*

RECORDS OF THE HILL FAMILY OF MASSACHUSETTS.

CONTRIBUTED BY CHARLES AUSTIN ROBINSON.

David Hill, son of Joseph and Phebe Hill, of Holliston, was married to Mercy Holbrook, daughter of Luke and Mercy Holbrook, of Bellingham, on the twenty-first day of April, 1785.

The dates of the births of their children and their names are as follows, viz.:

Sylvester Hill, born Wednesday, April 12, 1786.
David Hill, Jr., born Sunday, September 23, 1787.
Amos Hill, born Monday, July 6, 1789.
Artemon Hill, born Tuesday, January 23, 1792.
Solon Hill, born Tuesday, February 4, 1794.
Phebe Hill, born Wednesday, August 14, 1799.
Paulina Hill, born Friday, March 4, 1803.
Solon Hill (2d), born Wednesday, June 12, 1805.
Charles Austin Hill, born Tuesday, July 10, 1810.

Record of Deaths.

Solon Hill, son of David and Mercy Hill, departed this life February 23, 1799.

Phebe Hill, daughter of David and Mercy Hill, departed this life October 29, 1799.

Paulina Hill, daughter of David and Mercy Hill, departed this life March 17, 1806.

David Hill, husband of Mercy Hill, died November 4, 1813.

Mercy Holbrook, mother of Mercy Hill, died December 3, 1813.

Luke Holbrook, husband of the above, died November 3, 1775.

Rachel Holbrook, daughter of the last named, died November 7, 1775.

Sena Abbee, another daughter of above, died September 7, 1815.

Harriot (Fales) Hill, wife of David Hill, Jr., died August 19, 1817.

Sylvester Hill, son of David and Mercy Hill, died June 14, 1820.

Dinah Holbrook, daughter of Luke Holbrook, died January 8, 1827.

Jerusha Lethbridge, daughter of Luke Holbrook, died July 4, 1833.

Solon Hill (2d), son of David and Mercy Hill, died September 1, 1833.

Lucy Jencks, daughter of Luke Holbrook, died July 24, 1833.

Mercy Jones, relict of David Hill and daughter of Luke Holbrook, died July 28, 1841, aged seventy-three years.

David Hill, second son of David and Mercy Hill, died January 3, 1847.

Amos Hill, third son of David and Mercy Hill, died October, 1869.

Artemon Hill, fourth son of David and Mercy Hill, died February 6, 1870, at New Orleans, Louisiana.

David Hill, Jr., son of David and Mercy (Holbrook) Hill, was married to Harriot Fales, daughter of Nehemiah and Sarah (Whiting) Fales, of Dedham, Massachusetts, on the 14th day of February, 1813.

The dates of the births of their children, and their names, are as follows, viz. :

Emily, born April 23, 1814.

Caroline, born December 7, 1815.

Harriet Fales, born August 7, 1817.

Emily Hill, of Philadelphia, daughter of David, Jr., and Harriet (Fales) Hill, was married to Daniel M. Robinson, of Philadelphia, September 19, 1836. The date of the births of their children and their names are as follows, viz. :

Charles Austin Robinson, born September 18, 1837.

Alice Ada Robinson, born January 8, 1839; died May 30, 1839.

Harriet Lucretia Robinson, born May 29, 1840.

Emily Nevins Robinson, born September 28, 1841; died April 20, 1842.

Adèle Nevins Robinson, born September 28, 1841.

Edward Louis Robinson, born May 21, 1843; died January 13, 1847.

Horace Percy Robinson, born December 24, 1846; died August 10, 1878.

Charles Austin Robinson, son of Daniel M. and Emily (Hill) Robinson, of Philadelphia, was married to Deborah Blight, youngest daughter of George Waln and Mary Valeria (Sergeant) Blight, of Philadelphia, March 10, 1864.

The dates of the births of their children and their names are as follows, viz.:

George Blight Robinson, born June 27, 1865.

Charles Norris Robinson, born October 20, 1866.

Roberts Coles Robinson, born October 25, 1867.

HILL RECORDS.—From a Bible in possession of Mrs. C. T. Glover, 300 Park Ave., Baltimore, Md.

Levi Hill son of George and Ruth Hill was born July 15, 1764.
Leah Simpler his first wife.
Sarah W McIlvaine the daughter of Andrew and Comfort McIlvaine was born April 6, 1778.
Nancy Hill the daughter of Levi and Leah Hill was born Jan 29, 1792.
Joshua Hill son of Levi and Sarah Hill was born Sept. 7, 1803.
David Hill son of Levi and Sarah Hill was born Feb 7, 1806.
Charlotte Hill the daughter of Levi and Sarah was born Nov. 21, 1808.
Maria Hill the daughter of Levi and Sarah was born April 27, 1812.
Robert Hill son of Levi and Sarah Hill was born July 6, 1814.
Sarah Hill the daughter of Levi and Sarah was born June 23, 1817.
Joshua Hill born Sept. 7, 1803.
Marid Hill . . April 27, 1812.
Mitchel Hill departed this life November 25, 1826.
John Williams Hill son Mitchel Hill and Sophia his wife was born June 20, 1825,
Nancy their first daughter born January 29.

THE DESCENDANTS OF SARAH HOLME, DAUGHTER OF THOMAS HOLME.

U. S. Navy Yard.
League Island Pa.
February 22, 1920.

To the Editor of Pennsylvania Magazine:

Looking through Volume XVIII Pennsylvania Magazine for the year 1894-95, I encountered an advertisement requesting information concerning the descendants of Richard Holcomb, who married Sarah Holme the daughter of Thomas Holme, who laid the plan for the City of Philadelphia.

This advertisement I have learned was inserted by the late Mr. Oliver Hough when he was collecting material for his article on Thomas Holme, Penn's Surveyor-General, which article continued through several numbers of the Pennsylvania Magazine.

The will of Thomas Holme contained the following item:

> "Item.—I give and bequeath unto the children of Richard Holcomb by my daughter Sarah, the sum of thirty pounds to be paid of the thousand acres of land next beyond Hilltowne of this countie upon the said lands are sold."

It is evident that Mr. Hough did not succeed in obtaining the information he sought, as though he deals with descendants of other children of Thomas Holme, he states that it is not known if Sarah Holme or her children ever came to America. This statement has been repeatedly copied in various monographs relating to

WASHINGTON'S HEADQUARTERS AT HOLCOMB'S

Thomas Holme, or of Holmesburg, or in genealogical works such as the Crispin family.

The will of Thomas Holme, now on file at the City Hall is in a ragged and mutilated condition. If any inventory or accounting was ever made of the estate by the sole executor, Silas Crispin, it is now missing. Consequently it is impossible to tell by this means in just what manner the executor made settlement with the children of Richard Holcomb of the one thousand acres in Hilltowne.

Hilltowne was later known as Abington. The "thousand acres of land next beyond Hilltowne" was a part of a tract of 2500 acres that Holme purchased from Samuel Clarridge (then residing in Ireland) the deed dated May 18 1686 (E5 p 528 Phila. Co.) this tract is shown on Thomas Holmes map of 1686 lying to the northward of the Squehanna Road, labeled "Samuel Clarridge" and lying between the land of "Silas Crispin" and "Perce & Comp." The total amount of land covered in the deed is 5000 acres and the sum paid for all this land by Holme was fifty-seven pounds, nine shillings.

The Holcomb children came to Hilltowne or Abington shortly before the year of 1700. There were two brothers, Jacob and John Holcombe. They were both born in Tierton, Devonshire, England and their father Richard Holcomb died while they were young. Both of their parents being Friends they were brought up in this sect, and throughout their lives in America both are identified as prominent and consistent members of the Abington, Falls, and Buckingham Friends Meetings.

After the death of Richard Holcomb, Sarah (Holme) Holcomb, married John Hurford. John Hurford had a son named John by a previous marriage. All of this family came to America and settled in Hilltowne, or Abington as it is now known. One of the early minutes of the Abington meeting notes the marriage of John

Hurford Junior. "28 10mo 1702 A certificate granted John Hurford jun In order to his proceeding on in marriage with one of ye county of Chister" Of this second marriage of Sarah (Holme) Holcomb to John Hurford, Sr. two children were born, namely Grace who married Robert Thomas of North Wales, Gwynedd in 1722 and Samuel Hurford who married Hannah Sermon of Abington in 1731. Samuel had no descendants. By his will (No 118 Book O pg 158 Phila. Co.) dated, "23rd 3mo called March 1765" he gives "sixty pounds to be divided between all the children of my half brother John Hurford" and the bulk of his estate including his silver watch, silver shoe buckles, silver knee buckles, silver stock buckle, and certain real property to the children of his sister Grace, namely, John Thomas, Samuel Thomas, and "to my nieces husband Lewis Roberts." He also left a legacy to his "kinsman Joseph Hallowell" who married Elizabeth daughter of his half brother Jacob Holcombe. Joseph Hallowell was a descendant of John Hallowell of Abington who 15th 6mo 1696 purchased of Silas Crispin, executor of the estate of Thomas Holme, 630 acres of the land in Hilltowne for 58 pounds 16 shillings. At this date John Hallowell was living in Darby Pa.

John and Sarah Hurford continued to reside at Abington until 1720 when they removed to Buckingham and located on a farm adjoining Jacob Holcombe. Their certificate of removal from Abington meeting is dated "25th of ye 5 1720" they were growing aged and feeble as one might infer from this extract from the Buckingham minutes "6 mo 3 1725. Jacob Holcombe by request of his aged parents John and Sarah Hurford to have an evening meeting at their house by reason of their inability to get to the public meeting place every other first day meeting" And here they still lived in 1726 when the map referred to in Volume I page 256 Davis History of Bucks County was prepared, which notes them as residing between the houses of Jacob Holcombe and Mercy Phillips.

About the year of 1700 Jacob Holcombe, one of the children of Richard Holcomb and Sarah (Holme) Holcomb removed to Buckingham township and was one of the early settlers of what is now Solebury Pa. The early records of the township as well as the records of Buckingham meeting testify to his public spirit. He was one of the first ministers of the meeting, the first book of minutes was transcribed in his handwriting and he was one of the committee to build the second meeting house in 1729. He was petitioner and later commissioner to lay out the road now known as the Old York Road and also the road from Solebury along the Delaware. He traveled to England; Connecticut; Rhode Island; Long Island N. Y.; and Maryland on Missions to Friends meetings at those places. A testimonial from Buckingham meeting concerning Jacob Holcombe may be found in the "Collection of Memorials concerning Divers deceased Ministers and others of the People called Quakers etc." published 1787. Jacob married Mary Woolridge of Falls meeting 1712 and had eight children. 1 Thomas who married Hannah Pownall 6mo 3 1741–2 Sarah, (named after his mother) married Thomas Lewis 7 mo. 6 1736; 3 Rebecca; 4 Mary, married Jacob Walton 3mo 1 1749; 5 Elizabeth, married Joseph Hallowell of Philadelphia 4 mo 13 1745; 6 Susanna, married John Van Duren of Gwynedd; 7 Hannah; and 8 Sophia.

Jacob Holcombe and his brother John located on tracts of land on either side of the Delaware along the course of what became the Old York Road and at the crossing which during Revolutionary time was known as Coryells Ferry, but now known as the city of Lambertville on the New Jersey side and New Hope on the Pennsylvania side. I append a photostat of a part of the two maps prepared in 1881–83 by Mr. Walter F.

Hayhurst and the late Mr. Ruben Pownall Ely, both of Lambertville N. J. These maps have an index or title brief cap size of some 200 pages and the originals are owned by the daughters of Mr. Ely now residing in Lambertville.

In addition to the tract of 500 acres, a part of the Heath tract shown on the map, Jacob Holcombe purchased from James Logan 25 March 1709 the two tracts shown in his name, one containing 320 acres, the other 500 acres. These he promptly sold to John Scarborough and at the same time purchased from John Scarborough another tract containing 510 acres, the money consideration in each of these deeds being mentioned as £300 silver money. Jacob Holcombe sold on December 3 1717 to Thomas Canby (who also came from Abington) 444 acres of this 510 acre tract. Jacob had still another tract of 500 acres which was patented to him April 12 1712. He died 30th 6mo 1748. In his will (Bucks Co No 597) he disposes among other items, a silver spoon to his grandson Jacob marked with his fathers initials "R. H." This Jacob was a son of Thomas Holcombe and he married Esther Livesey, daughter of Jonathan and Katherine Livesey of Lower Dublin township 19th 6mo 1768.

The remaining son of Richard Holcomb and Sarah (Holme) Holcomb, named John Holcombe continued to reside at Abington Pa until 1705. On November 16 1705 he purchased of Richard Wilson of Bucks Co Pa., a tract of 350 acres of land on the New Jersey side of the Delaware about opposite to the tract owned by his brother Jacob. He is designated in this deed as "John Holcombe of Abington, county of Philadelphia and Province aforesaid, yeoman" Near the southwestern border of this purchase was later to be the crossing of the York Road from Philadelphia to New York. This purchase was the first of a series of purchases amounting to nearly 1500 acres and shown on the Lambertville map. He married Elizabeth Woolrich of Abington Meeting "28th ye second mo 1707." John Holcombe was prominent in the affairs of Old Amwell and early Hunterdon County N. J. He was twice a justice of Burlington County before Hunterdon County was set off from it in 1713, having been appointed justice February 14 1710 and March 17 1713. He was one of the first justices of Hunterdon County being a member of the first court which met at Maidenhead N. J. June 14 1714. He served as Freeholder, Overseer of the Poor; Collector; Surveyor of Roads; etc. All his life he lived a consistent member of the Buckingham Friends Meeting and left a legacy to this meeting upon his death. A few years before his death he built a large stone house on the hillside with a commanding view of the river. This house is still standing and was twice used by Washington as his Headquarters while his army was at Coryells Ferry. John Holcombe had six children. 1 John who died in early life unmarried; 2 Samuel born 1711 and who married Eleanor Barber (most of the Holcombes of New Jersey and Pennsylvania are descendants of this Samuel); 3 Grace who married Phillip Calvin; 4 Mary, married Samuel Furman; 5 Julia Ann, married Daniel Howell; 6 Richard named after his grandfather. He was born March 10 1726, was twice married and died 1783.

John Holcombe died August 1743 and lies buried in the ancient plot of the Friends Burying Ground, Lahaska (Buckingham). He has a large number of descendants, now scattered through New Jersey, Pennsylvania, Ohio, Indiana, Iowa and many other states. The late Ruben Pownall Ely of Lambertville compiled in 1886 a 500 page manuscript of over 1600 descendants of John Holcombe of the first six generations, not half bearing the name of Holcombe, but through the female line, the names of many old and respected families of New Jersey and Pennsylvania.

One more matter before closing and that is in reference to the statement made above that the Holcombe house has the distinction of having been twice used by General Washington as his headquarters. I am aware that where he stopped is expressed doubtfully in many quarters. This has seemed to me to be due to the fact that both the Pennsylvania and New Jersey sides of the river were for a time called Coryells Ferry. Today being Washington's birthday, it does not seem amiss to say a few words about this historic crossing.

John Wells, whose tract is shown on the New Hope map next to Jacob Holcombe's, both as parts of a tract patented to R. Heath in 1710, appears to have been operating a ferry here before 1715. There was occassion for a ferry here as "Heaths mill at the ferry" was built in 1707, and the Old York Road was opened from Philadelphia to the Delaware in 1711. This ferry became known as "Wells ferry" and in 1719 the Pennsylvania Assembly passed an act granting to John Wells the privilege of operating a ferry for seven years. This license was renewed in 1726 by the Lieutenant Governor for a further term of seven years. In the year 1733 the proprietaries, John, Thomas, and Richard Penn extended the license for another seven years.

As stated above the York Road was opened to the Delaware in 1711. Gradually the trail had been blazed through the wilderness. In August 1693 the road had been laid out from Philadelphia as far as Cheltenham. By 1697 it was further extended to Mooreland by surveys made by Nicholas Scull. Then on the 27th of January 1710 the inhabitants of Buckingham and Solebury petitioned the council of Pennsylvania for a convenient Road to begin at the Delaware opposite John Reading's landing, from thence the most direct and convenient course to Buckingham meeting house; and thence through the lands of Thomas Watson, by the house of

Stephen Jenkins and Richard Wells, and so forward the most direct and convenient course to Philadelphia. A jury composed of Thomas Watson, John Scarborough, Jacob Holcombe, Nathaniel Bye, Matthew Hughes, Joseph Fell, Samuel Cart, Stephen Jenkins, Thomas Hallowell, Griffith Miles, Job Goodson, and Isaac Norris were to lay out the road and return their report in six months. And this was the extention of the York Road through Pennsylvania, the first crossing at the Delaware being at Reading's Ferry, later called Howell's ferry, and still later Mitchell's ferry. But the traffic early began to split and turn off at Well's ferry four miles below, so that what is known as the York Road in New Jersey begins at Lambertville courses through what is now Mount Airy, Ringoes and Readville to New Brunswick that common meeting point of the various old roads from Burlington and the Falls of the Delaware (now Trenton) for ferrying the Raritan River. This was one of the early wagon roads of the State of New Jersey (not the earliest) and followed an old Indian path. In a deed for land at Ringoes, N. J. dated August 25 1726, this road is described as "the Kings Highway that is called York Road" And so it is called even today.

In the meantime there had settled upon the Jersey side of the river one Samuel Coate the land he settled is described in the deed to John Holcombe as then (1705) belonging to Robert Eaton, "formerly Hugh Howells" Coate seems to have bought the land from Robert Eaton and here he established a ferry which became known as "Coates ferry" No clear brief of the title of this land seems to exist. It was originally a 400 acre tract surveyed to Benjamin Field in 1700. It is alluded to as a Henry Clarks, and as Hugh Howells. On Oct 15 1728 John Coate sold to John Purcell 200 acres of this tract, and on August 4 1732 John Coate then of Bethlehem N. J. sold of John Holcombe 30 acres of this tract. This deed refers to a post in William Coates and a post in Henry Coates land. John Purcell on Feb. 8 1732 sold his tract to Emanuel Coryell and one of the courses is described as "a post standing by the Kings Road that leads to the Ferry over the aforesaid River Delaware to John Wells." This deed is the first recorded evidence of the coming of Emanuel Coryell to Amwell in West New Jersey. The next year, January 7 1733, King George II granted to his "loving subject" Emanuel Coryell "the sole privilege of keeping a ferry at the place called Coates ferry opposite Wells ferry the Pennsylvania side and three miles up and three miles down the said river Delaware and to his heirs and assigns forever." On the Jersey side a small settlement grew up. Here on a site now the southwest corner of Ferry and Union Sts. Lambertville, Emanuel Coryell built a stone tavern, which after standing about 100 years was torn down shortly before the Civil War. John Coryell the eldest son of Emanuel Coryell in 1760 shortly after the death of his father, bought the Wells ferry property on the Pennsylvania side from the widow of Benjamin Canby, and his tavern like the tavern on the Jersey side was known as Coryells tavern. Thus Elizabeth Drinker in her diary Aug (or Sept.) 1771 speaks of going to Coryells tavern on the York Road where Mr. Drinker was to meet "the commissioners for improving and clearing the navigation of the River." Down to 1770 the ferry was generally known as "Wells ferry" Whether prior to 1760 Emanuel Coryell and John Wells were rival ferrymen or whether they jointly operated under a common interest there is no data at hand to determine.

New Hope took its name from a flour mill which came into possession of the Parrys. Since the days of the Heath mill there had been a mill here and in 1790 the Parry mills caught fire ad burned down. At about this same time, 1790, they bought the mills on the Jersey side near "Wells falls" known as the Prime Hope mills and when they rebuilt their mills on the Pennsylvania side, they named them New Hope. About these mills a small settlement grew which by 1810 was known as New Hope. As for the name Lambertville on the Jersey side, it chanced that in 1814 the Hon. John Lambert, United States Senator from New Jersey, secured for his nephew and namesake the appointment of first postmaster here and had the post office designated as Lambertville. This was a disappointment to some of the Coryell family who wanted the place named Georgetown and failing were pleased for a while to call it "Lambertvillany."

In the year 1811 the ferry rights all rested in the New Hope Delaware Bridge Co. organized this year and chartered by Pennsylvania and New Jersey in 1812. And now after another 100 years, January 1920 the bridge is taken over by the two states, the toll house closed and a free passage between the two towns of the two states established.

It is a fact that at the time of the Revolution both sides of the river were known as Coryell's Ferry.

In July 1777 filled with apprehension as to the destination of Howe's fleet, Washington marched across New Jersey. His center, with which his headquarters were attached headed for the crossing at Coryell's Ferry, his right was to cross the river at Howell's Ferry four miles above, while his left marched to Trenton to cross at one of the two ferries at that point. Upon reaching the river, Washington decided to wait more definite news of Howe's movements, and selected the stone house built by John Holcombe for his headquarters. In the manuscript division of the Library of Congress at Washington there are copies of some ten letters of Washington's correspondence written at Headquarters Coryell's Ferry bearing date July 29, 30, and 31 1777. From Colonel Pickering's Journal the year 1777 we find the following notes of the march; "26 to Morristown, 27th to Reading eighteen miles from Coryell's ferry over the Delaware 28th Marched to the ferry and quartered at a hearty old Quaker's named Oakham." The "hearty old Quaker named Oakham" was Richard Holcombe son of John Holcombe the first settler on the Jersey side of the ferry.

June 1778 when the army left Valley Forge for that memorable march across New Jersey, in pursuit of the enemy retreating from Philadelphia and on the eve of the battle of Monmouth, once again Washington established headquarters in this house. The line of march led from Valley Forge to Crooked Billet now Hatboro, and thence along the York Road to Coryell's Ferry. Washington arrived on the Jersey side about 3 oclock in the afternoon of June 21 1778 and went directly to the house of Richard Holcombe upon the hillside to the north of the ferry. It was raining and progress of the troops was much delayed so that Washington remained at the house for two days. Copies of seven letters are on file at the Library of Congress prepared at headquarters here on this occasion, namely June 22 & 23 1778. I also found among Washington's Headquarters accounts kept by Capt Caleb Gibbs, a receipt signed by Richard Holcombe for subsistence and entertainment of Washington and his staff on the occasion of this visit.

June 21st & 22, 1778 } His Excell'cy Gen. Washington To Richd Holcombe   Dr.

To 38 dinners @ 3/9 ....£7 " 2 " 6—
To bread butter & other necessaries 1 " 17 " 6—
To Trouble &c. made in the house.. 1 " 17 " 6

Near Coryells Ferry   £10 " 17 " 6
       June 22d 1778.
Rec'd ye above account in full
                           Richard Holcombe

Washington kept an exact account of his headquarters and secret service expenses. Though Congress had fixed the pay of the Commander-in-Chief at five hundred dollars a month, Washington in his address to Congress when accepting this commission said, "As to pay, I beg leave to assure the Congress that, as no pecuniary consideration could have tempted me to accept this arduous employment at the expense of my domestic ease and happiness, I do not wish to make any profit of it. I will keep an exact account of my expenses. Those, I doubt not, they will discharge, and that is all I desire." John Adams, who was present, writing to a friend said of the incident "He declared, when he accepted the mighty trust, that he would lay before us an exact account of his expenses, and not accept a shilling of pay." Washington's account book noting his advances for headquarters expenses about Germantown, the Brandywine and Valley Forge is entered sometimes in dollars and sometimes in pounds which latter currency he calls "lawful money."

As better reflecting the times than anything I could write I am attaching two photostats of original letters of Washington addressed by Washington to the President of Congress and among the papers of the Continental Congress now on file with the manuscript division of the Library of Congress, and both written from Headquarters at Coryell's Ferry.

I am sorry for this long delay in answering Mr. Hough's inquiry, which may really be of very little interest to anyone else. It was not until I was ordered here in command of the Naval Hospital at League Island during the Great War that I had occasion to learn of the wealth of material in the possession of the Historical Society of Pennsylvania.

Very respectfully,
Richmond C. Holcomb.
Comdr. (M. C.) U. S. Navy.

HUDSON FAMILY RECORDS.

BY HOWARD WILLIAMS LLOYD.

[As a sequel to Mr. Thomas Allen Glenn's article, "William Hudson, Mayor of Philadelphia, 1725–1726" (PENNA. MAG., Vol. XV. p. 336), the following records from the Bible of William Hudson, Jr., will be of interest. This Bible, printed in Oxford, England, 1723, is now in the possession of one of his descendants, Mrs. Fanny C. de Martinez, of Buenos Ayres, South America. Through the kindness of Mrs. Harris Graffen, Camden, New Jersey, another descendant, Mr. Lloyd was enabled to make this copy.—ED. PENNA. MAG.]

Jane Hudson, wife of William Hudson, departed this life in true peace y[e] 15th day of May, 1759, aged 59 years, 6 months and 13 days. Lived a wife 41 years, 6 mos. and eleven days.

William Hudson departed this life y[e] 22nd of the 7th month, 1762, on the 5th day of the week, about 10 in the morning, aged 66 years, 3 mos. & 22 days.

Mary Hudson departed this life 1st of July, 1795.

Susanna Hudson departed this life on the 1st day of the week, at 9 o'clock in the morning, on the 20th day of July, 1817, aged 85 years, 1 month & 10 days, and was buried in Friends' Burial Ground, on Arch Street, between Third & Fourth Sts., on the 21st July, at 5 o'clock in the afternoon.

William Hudson was born March 31st day, 1696.
Jane Hudson was born October y[e] 21st, 1699.
They were married October y[e] 29, 1717.

Sarah Hudson was born July y[e] 30th, 1718.
Mary Hudson was born 12 m°. 22, 1719[20].
Elizabeth Hudson was born 12 m°. 20, 1721[2].
Rachall Hudson was born 11 m°. 6 day, 1723[4].
Jane Hudson was born March y[e] 4 day, 1725[6].
William Hudson was born 8th 29 day, 1728.

Susannah Hudson was born 8th 30 day, 1729.
Susannah, ye 2, was born June ye 10 day, 1733.
Margerat Hudson was born ye 2 mo 16 day, 1734.
Margrat, ye second, was born July ye 17 day, 1735.
Samuell Hudson was born 8th ye 6, 1736.
Hannah Hudson was born 9th 14 day, 1739.

Susannah Hudson dyed ye 12 mo 25 day, 1731, of smallpox.
William Hudson dyed ye 1 mo. 1 day, 1731, of smallpox.
Margaret Hudson dyed ye 5 mo. 7 day, 1734.
Margaret, 2d, dyed ye 6m. 3 day, 1735.
Jane Hudson, ye 6m. 22 day, about 2 o'clock in the morning, in the year 1768.
Sarah Langdale dyed Aug. 5 day, 1780.
Elizabeth Morris dyed ye fifth mo. 22 day, 1783.
Samuel Hudson died ye 2d of November, 1793.

The time of ye births of John and Sarah Langdale's children:

Rachel Langdale, { Born ye 7th 3d (March?), 1737 8
                  { Died November, 1773.
Josiah Langdale, ye 18th 10th, 1739.
William Langdale, { Ye 22d 5 mo. (July), 1741
                  { Died 19th (August?) following.
John Langdale, ye 22d 7th mo, 1742; died 23 Dec., 1765.
Margaret Langdale, ye 9th 7th mo, 1744; died.
Jane Langdale, ye 17 5 mo, 1746; died.
Wm. Hudson Langdale, 22d 9th, 1747; died Dec., 1772.
Elizabeth Langdale, ye 13th 11 mo, 1749 50.
Margaret Langdale, ye 3 mo, 1752.
Jane Langdale was born 1 mo 3, 1755.
Samuel Langdale, 16th 10 mo, 1759.

William Hudson, my father, was born at ye City of York, in England, ye 3 day 4 m., 1664.

Mary Hudson, my mother, was born in ye City of London ye year 1673, ye 4 mo 19 day.

William & Mary Hudson were married ye redy? 12m, 1689? [12 mo. called Feb. 28, 1688].

Mary Hudson departed this life 16 d⁷ 12ᵐ, 1708⁹, in the 37 year of her age, being 36 years, 4m. 19 days old, who dyed of her 14ᵗʰ child.

William Hudson departed this life yᵉ 16ᵗʰ day 10 mo., 1742, being 78 years & 6 mo. 13 days old.

Rebekah Rawle, born February, 1773.
Robert Turner Rawle, born February, 1775.
William Hudson Rawle, born February, 1778; died August following.

HUSBAND—PRICE—HAINES.—Families. In an old Bible belonging to Israel B. Haines, of Canonsburg, Pennsylvania, are found the following records:

William Husband & Mary His Wife—ages of Our Children
First Born:
Hannah was born 27th day of March 1722
Hermon was born 3rd day of October 1724
William was born 7th day of March 1727
John was born 31st day of March 1729
Thomas was born 10 day of March 1731
Mary was born 20th day of May 1734
Joseph was born 15th day of February 1736/7
Catharine was born 23rd day of Decemʳ 1738
Margery was born 27th day of   1741
Ann was born 29th day of   1745
Sarah was born 26th day of September 1748
The 4 day of the 9 month 1775
    Josiah Haines

[Note.—This was doubtless the date of marriage of the above Ann and Josiah Haines.]

David Price (son of John Price & Abigail his Wife) and Ann Husband (Daughter of William Husband & Mary his Wife) was married by John Hamilton Rector of North East Church Cecil County & Province of Maryland upon the fourteenth Day of November In the year of our Lord one Thousand and Seven hundred & Sixty five 1765

                      Recorded by David Price.

Abigail Price (first Born) Daughter of the above Named David Price & Ann his Wife, was Born the 24th day of August about Two o clock in the afternoon being the first Day of the Week Anno Domini 1766

William Price (second child) son of the above Named David Price & Ann his wife was Born the first Day of November being the first Day of the Week about Two o clock in the Morning In the year of our Lord 1767.

Mary Price (Third Child) Daughter of the above Named David Price & Ann his Wife was born the Twenty fifth Day of January being the fourth Day of the Week about Two o clock in the Morning In the year of our Lord 1769

David Elisha Price (fourth Child) son of the above Named David & Ann his Wife was born the Twenty fifth Day of December being the Third day of the Week about two o Clock in the morning in the year of our Lord one Thousand seven hundred & Seventy 1770

Ann Price (fifth Child) Daughter of the above named David Price & Ann his Wife was born the fifteenth day of June about four o Clock in the Morning in the year of our Lord 1772 one Thousand Seven hundred & Seventy two.

Margery the Sixth Child was Born the 18th day of November Anno Dom. 1773 about 3 o'Clock in the afternoon.

David Price Departed this Life at Redstone the Seventh day of November anno Domini 1773

Jane Haines Daughter of Josiah Haines & Jane his Wife, was born the fourth Day of eight month in the year 1772

Hermon Haines Son of the same Josiah Haines & Ann His Wife was born the 22nd Day of the 6th mo: 1776

Catharine Haines Daughter of the same Josiah and Ann Haines was born the 22nd Day of the 12th mo: 1777

Lydia Haines Daughter of Josiah and Ann Haines was born the fourteenth Day of the 10th mo: at 7 O clock in the evening, in the year 1779

Sarah Haines Daughter of Josiah and Ann Haines was born the 17th Day of the 7th mo: at 3 O clock in the morning in the year 1781.

Marget Haines Daughter of Josiah and Ann Haines was born the 12th Day of the 3rd mo. at 7 O clock in the evening, in the year 1783

Joseph Haines Son of said Josiah and Ann Haines was born the 5 Day of the 3 Month at or near abought 4 O Clock morning in the year of our Lord 1785.

Elizabeth Haines last Child and Daughter of Josiah & Ann Haines was born the 22d Day of the 3d mo: March about 10 °Clock in the Evening & Seventh Day of the week in the year of our lord One thousand seven hundred and eighty eight. 1788

The above Ann Haines Departed This Life on Feb^r 17th Ann. dom. 1813 Aged 68   3 °Clock.

Andru Vaneman his Wife Elizabeth Vaneman Departed this Life on august 24 1813 Daughter of Josiah Haines and Ann his Wife.

Josiah Haines Departed this Life on Feb^r 6th Ann. dom. 1822 in the ninetyeth year of his Age.

Joseph Haines Departed this Life one the 18 day of aprel 1832

Margaret Haines departed this life on the 21st of April 1853 aged 75 years 3—17

Hermon Haines died July 29th 1865 aged 89 years and 7 days. Buried in the family burial ground on his farm, North Strabane Township Washington County Pennsylvania.

Note by Redick McKee of California }
July 4 1867

Note.—Ann Husband, daughter of William and Mary first married David Price, son of John and Abigail; and second Josiah Haines, son of Isaac and Catharine (David) Haines. She died in Washington County, Penna.

Josiah Haines was three times married, first to Mary Cock, daughter of Benjamin and Ann (Brinton) Cock; second to Jane Garrett daughter of Joseph and Mary (Sharpless) Garrett; and third to Ann Price, *née* Husband.

Abigail Price married Hon. Isaac Weaver, once Treasurer of Pennsylvania, and who also served in both houses of the Legislature.

Mary Price married Craig Ritchie, a prominent citizen of Canonsburg in its earlier history.   TH. MAXWELL POTTS.

Canonsburg, Pa.

HUTTON, PLUMSTED AND DEVEREUX FAMILIES.

BY GREGORY B. KEEN, LL.D.

The following entries are copied *literatim* from a quarto Bible printed at Oxford in 1776 acquired by Benjamin Hutton in 1785, now belonging to his descendant William H. Klapp, M.D.

JOHN S. HUTTON.

An account of John Strangeways Hutton by Charles Willson Peale is given in "The Columbian Magazine" for Sept. 1792, and reproduced in Watson's Annals of Philadelphia, with a portrait from an oil painting by Peale, in the possession of a descendant of his son John Hutton. He was the son of John Hutton and was born in Bournesdoures (incorrectly transcribed by Watson as Bermuda), Scotland, and became a resident of New York City, and grandson of Arthur Strangeways, or more probably Strangways, (a well known English surname) of New York City who died in Boston at the age it is said of 101 years. He married 1st. Catharine Cheeseman of New York city, by whom he had eight children, and 2ndly. in 1735, Ann, daughter of John Van Laer, Jr. of Philadelphia and Prescilla Preston, whose father William Preston, son of Henry and Jane Preston was baptized April 30, 1650, as appears in Register of St. Andrew's Parish, New Castle upon Tyne, and married September 10, 1672, Ann Taylor, daughter of Edmund and Margaret Taylor, who was baptized July 18, 1651, as appears by the Register of North Sheald upon Tyne. William and Ann Preston left England, with their children, June 10, 1683, and arrived in Pennsylvania August 20, 1683. He died September 19, 1717, She died December 4, 1732. (Statements copied from the old Preston folio bible Printed in 1599 in the possession of the family.) John Strangeways and Ann Hutton are buried in the Third Presbyterian Churchyard of Philadelphia. The inscription on their tombstone is as follows: "In Memory of ANN HUTTON, who died November 14th, 1788, Aged 72 years. Also, of JOHN HUTTON, who died December 23d, 1792, Aged 108 years and 4 months." The great longevity attributed to John Strangeways Hutton does not accord with the date of the marriage license in New York of John Hutton and Kathrine Stranguish (no doubt Strangways) October 28, 1695, presumed to be his parents. According to the article in the "Portfolio" Hutton had seventeen children by his second wife, five more than are indicated in the bible of Benjamin Hutton.

Their son George Hutton married (Register of Christ Church) August 11, 1760, Mary Moore. Their daughter Mary Hutton married John McMullin of Philadelphia who left descendants of this and other surnames, among whom were the wives of the late Major-General William Scott Ketchum and Colonel Franklin Foster Flint.

Their son John Hutton married (Register of St. Paul's Church) October 6, 1764, Elizabeth Merritt. He died December 6, 1791, and his wife died April 11, 1823, in the 80th. year of her age. They are buried in St. Peter's Protestant Episcopal Churchyard, Philadelphia. They left descendants living in that city. including their grandson Adjutant Lieutenant John Galt Hutton, who served in the War of 1812, and others mentioned in the "Descendants of Joran Kyn".

Their son Benjamin Hutton married Rebecca Plumsted, whose descendants are mentioned in "Chronicles of the Plumsted Family" by Eugene Devereux, and Keith's "Provincial Councillors of Pennsylvania."

Their son Nathaniel Hutton married Eleanor Dempsey. Their son Nathaniel was the father of Benjamin Henry Hutton of New York, who was the father of Major Charles Gordon Hutton, Anne Hutton, who married Count Moltke-Whitfield (Denmark) and Adèle Hutton, who married Marquis de Porte of France. Their son James Hutton removed to Washington, whose son William Rich Hutton lived in New York, and whose son Nathaniel Henry Hutton resided in Baltimore.

Mary Hutton born April 23 on Sunday at 1 o'clock in the afternoon in the year 1737

George Hutton born in Febr. 30th (*sic*) at 1 o'clock in the morning in the year 1738.

Sarah Hutton born in April 24th at 8 o'clock at night year 1741.

Sarah Hutton departed this Life August 17th in the year 1742.

John Hutton born in March 12th on Saturday at 6 o'clock in evening and in the year 1743.

Joseph Hutton born in August 22nd about 6 o'clock in the evening.

Benjamin Hutton, Senr. born on January 15th on Wednesday about 11 o'clock at night in the year 1746.

Sarah Hutton born 15th Day Novr. in the year 1748.

Elizabeth Hutton born Sept. 8 Day on Friday evening and in the year 1749.

Ann Hutton born Febr. 17 about 2 o'clock in the morning in the year 1751.

Benjamin Hutton born May 4th on Monday about 3 o'clock in the afternoon in the year 1752.

Presila Hutton born in August 11th in the year 1754.

Nathaniel Hutton born Febr. 15th in the year 1756.

The children of John Strangeway Hutton.

John Strangeways Hutton died on Thursday the 20th day of December 1792 Aged one hundred & eight years & four months.

Thos. Plumsted married Mary Coates Augst. 16th 1762 at 9 A. M.

Clement Plumsted Son of Mary and Thos. Plumsted was born September 6th at one Quarter past 7 o'clock in the Evening 1763.

Rebecca Plumsted the daughter of Mary and Thomas Plumsted was born March 8th. 1765 at one Quarter after 7 o'clock in the Evening.

Thos. Plumsted died October 29th 1776.

Mary Coats daughter of Warwick and Mary Coats was born October 8th 1741.

Benjamin Hutton married Rebecca Plumsted August 1st 1780.

Mary Plumsted died the 15th of August 1780.

Mary Hutton the Daughter of Benjamin and Rebecca Hutton was born August 9 1781 at 4 o clock in the afternoon.

Sarah Hutton the daughter of Benj. and Rebecca Hutton was born the 15th day of September ½ past 6 in the afternoon 1783.

Sarah Hutton Daughter of Benjamin & Rebecca Hutton Died August 30th 1786.

Thomas Hutton The Son of Benj. Hutton & Rebecah Hutton was born April the 11th day 1786.

Benj. Hutton the Son of Benj. Hutton and Rebecca Hutton was born the fifth day of August 1788.

Benjamin Hutton the Son of Benjamin and Rebecca Hutton Died September 16th 1789.

Ann Hutton the Wife of John Strangeways Hutton Died the 14th November.

Elizabeth Hutton Daughter of Benjamin and Rebecca Hutton Born October 31st 1791 half after 4 o Clock in the morning and Died 20th Day of August in the Year 1792 at ½ past 10 o Clock in the Evening, Aged 9 Months and 20 Days.

Eliza Hutton Daughter of Benjamin and Rebeccah Hutton was born December 21st. 1794.

Ann Hutton daughter of Benjamin & Rebecca Hutton was born Novm the 18 1797

Elenor Hutton the daughter of Benjamin and Rebeccah Hutton was born April 24th 1799, 3 o clock wednesday morning.

Clement Hutton Son of Benjamin & Rebecca Hutton was born Jany. 20th 1801

Thos. Hutton Son of Benjamin & Rebeccah Hutton died 22 February 1803—also the 27th April their Daughter Ellenora.

Clement Hutton died the 10th May 1803.

Elenor Hutton, the daughter of Benjamin and Rebecca Hutton was born Friday July 19th 1804 at Twelve o Clock at night.

Robert Burton married Eliza Elliott Hutton March the 4th 1815.

Mary Ann Burton, daughter of Robert and Eliza Burton was born December the 16th 1815 at half past 4 in the morning.

Ann Maria Burton, daughter of Robert and Eliza Burton was born December the 5th 1816.

John Devereux married Mary Hutton September 22d 1799.

John Devereux the Son of John & Mary Devereux was Born August 10th at Half past 6 in the morning 1800.

James Devereux the Son of John & Mary Devereux Was Born April 17th at 6 in the morning 1803.

Mary Ann Devereux the Daughter of John & Mary Devereux Was Born the Fifth of February 1806 at 5 A. M.

Benjamin Hutton Senr. Departed this Life August 20th 1809.

R. P. Devereux the Daughter of John & Mary Devereux was Born Oct. 16, 1808.

B. H. Devereux, Son of John & Mary Devereux was Born Sept. 17, 1817.

THE JONES FAMILY OF BETHLEHEM TOWNSHIP.

BY THE REV. J. H. DUBBS, D.D.

The early history of Bethlehem, the chief seat of the Moravians in Pennsylvania, has recently received considerable attention. Even its environs have not been neglected, and in the charming volume of the late Rev. W. C. Reichel, entitled "The Crown Inn," we have an interesting account of the Moravian farms lying south of the Lehigh River. We are, therefore, following an excellent precedent in giving our readers some account of the Jones family, whose farms adjoin the ancient town on the east, and who at a comparatively recent period held all the land between Bethlehem and Freemansburg, besides other valuable property in the immediate vicinity.

This tract, consisting of five hundred acres, was purchased by John Jones, from Patrick Graeme, of Philadelphia, on the 4th of April, 1750.[1] It is believed that Jones was the first actual occupant, and that the land had been taken up by Graeme solely for purposes of speculation.

According to the Bethlehem "church-book," and the inscription on his tombstone, John Jones was born at Skippack, now Montgomery County, in June, 1714. "His father," says Mr. Reichel, "had emigrated from Wales with other persons of excellent and worthy character, descendants of the ancient Britons, principally from Radnor, Bryn Mawr, and Haverford, in Merionethshire." This company founded a settlement in Montgomery County, and, in 1690, purchased a tract of forty thousand acres from William Penn. We need not say that these lands subsequently passed into the hands of Germans,

---

[1] This date is taken from the will of John Jones, on record at Easton. In the same document the name of the original proprietor is written *Green*, which has been shown from other sources to be an error. Patrick Graeme was a brother of Dr. Thomas Graeme, a well-known physician, in the early history of Philadelphia, son-in-law of Sir Wm. Keith.

so that the Welsh settlement has long since utterly disappeared.

Of the early history of Griffith Jones, the father of John, we know little or nothing. His wife, Sarah, had been previously married to Israel (?) Morris, by whom she had three sons, Israel, Daniel, and John.

The will of Griffith Jones, of "Skyppack," is on record at Philadelphia. It does not appear that he was possessed of much property. He says: "I give and bequeath unto my dear wife Sarah Jones, whom I do make and ordain my sole executrix, full power to settle upon and improve my land late purchased of Anthony Morris upon Matchin,[1] to the bringing up of my three children, viz., John, Ann, and Mary, until the expiration of my son John's age of twenty-one, and then to be the said John's and his heirs forever, he paying to his sisters Ann and Mary the sum of ten pounds current money of the province aforesaid." His wife was to have all the personal property, and his stepsons, Daniel and John Morris, were each to receive a legacy of five pounds, "if in case they shall live with and help my said wife Sarah improve my said lands until they be of the age of twenty-one."

From this document it appears that Griffith Jones died in July or August, 1720. His widow did not long survive him. Her will, dated December 25, 1720, was proved April 7, 1721, so that her death must have occurred between these two dates. By this will she divides her estate into four parts, one of which she gives to her "friend" and executor Griffith Jones, "for his trouble" in settling her estate, and the remaining three parts to her children, Ann, John, and Mary Jones. Concerning this "friend," Griffith Jones, we have no information. There is a family tradition that John Jones had a brother Griffith, and it is not impossible that he may have been a son by a former marriage, who, for some reason, had been omitted from his father's will.

The Morris boys were not greatly enriched by their mother's legacies. Israel and Daniel were to receive her "two flax

---

[1] Methachen—a stream in Montgomery County.

heckles, Israel to have the best, when they come to the age of twenty, Israel to pay his brother John Morris twenty shillings."

From all this we see that John Jones was, at the time of his parents' death, between six and seven years old. Where he spent his childhood and early youth cannot now be certainly ascertained, but subsequent events render it probable that he found a home with relatives in the Welsh settlement at Upper Merion, which was familiarly known as "Over Schuylkill." This may account for the erroneous family tradition that he was born at the latter place. His opportunities of acquiring an education must have been limited, but he learned to write a beautiful hand and to express himself in good English. He also learned the trade of a blacksmith, and is said to have been an excellent workman, though in his later years he devoted himself almost exclusively to agricultural pursuits.

At an early age John Jones was married to Eleanor Godfrey, a daughter of Thomas Godfrey, of Tredyfryn Township, Chester County.[1]

Thomas Godfrey, according to the traditions related by his daughter, was descended from a highly respectable family in the county of Kent, in England. She always insisted that the family name had once been something else, but that at some remote period the younger members of the family had assumed their father's Christian name as a surname. This story always appeared to me to be more than doubtful, until I found, in Burke's "Commoners," the statement that the Godfreys are said to be descended from Godfrey le Fauconer, Lord of the Manor of Hurst, in the reign of Henry II., which renders it not impossible that a portion of the family assumed as a surname the hereditary official title of Fauconer or Falconer, while others were more modestly satisfied to be called Godfrey.

[1] There were at least two Thomas Godfreys in the neighborhood of Philadelphia at this time: Thomas Godfrey, of Tredyfryn, mentioned above, and Thomas Godfrey, of Bristol township, the grandfather of the inventor of the quadrant. There is no evidence that they were related.

Thomas Godfrey was married in England to his wife Jane, whose maiden name is no longer remembered. Two other couples were married at the same time, all having been three times announced in church, "to be married to go to the new world." The date it is impossible to fix with exactness, but it must have occurred about 1704 or 1705.

A few months later the youthful pair sailed for America. The voyage was tempestuous; they were driven to the West Indies; and eight months are said to have elapsed before they reached their destination. Their first child was born on sea, and was named Seaborn, but died before the end of the voyage.

In America the Godfreys grew prosperous and wealthy. Besides the daughter born on sea, they had eight children, of whom Eleanor was the third.[1] Thomas Godfrey died in 1756. His wife Jane lived to a great age, and died in 1771. In her will she bequeaths "five pounds to the vestry of the church at Radnor, two pounds to St. Peter's Church at Great Valley, and two pounds to the minister who shall officiate at her funeral."

John Jones and his wife Eleanor began housekeeping in New Providence, Montgomery County, probably on the land inherited from his father. Here, according to the Bethlehem church records, their oldest son Levi was born on the 24th of August, 1737, and their second son Jesse on the 28th of February, 1740; both were baptized by the Rev. Mr. Currie.[2] Others of their children, Jonathan, Peter, and Thomas, were also born at this place, but the date of their birth has not been entered on the records.

The decade of years extending from 1740 to 1750 is the most interesting period in the religious history of Pennsylvania. The preaching of Whitefield in 1740, the visit of Zin-

[1] The names of these children were: (1) William, whose son Thomas received a special legacy in his grandmother's will; (2) Elizabeth married ——— Thomas, and removed to North Carolina; (3) Eleanor married John Jones; (4) Sarah died unmarried; (5) Rebecca married ——— Hulen; (6) Lucy married ——— Jones; (7) Hannah died unmarried; (8) John died without issue.

[2] Rector of Radnor.

zendorf in 1741, the arrival of Muhlenberg in 1743, and of Schlatter in 1746, with the subsequent organization of the Reformed Synod in 1746, and of the Lutheran Ministerium in the following year, all these are events which may justly be regarded as important epochs in the history of our religious denominations. The Moravian itinerants, taking advantage of the general interest in religion, traversed the country, and gathered many into their fold. One of their best friends was Henry Antes,[1] who is known as "the pious Reformed layman of Frederick Township." On his farm, in June, 1745, the Brethren established a boarding-school for boys, which was continued with various fortunes until September, 1750, when it was finally discontinued. Among their first scholars was Levi Jones, the son of John, and during the succeeding years we find on the records of the school entries recording the admission of his younger brothers.

Under these circumstances it is easy to see how the Jones family became Moravian. In 1749 they were induced to remove to Bethlehem, probably settling on the land which John Jones subsequently purchased. Here they built a massive stone house, which stood until 1835, when it was taken down by one of their descendants and a modern mansion erected on its substantial foundations. The old house is described as having been an edifice of a very superior order. Hidden away behind the wainscoting there were curious secret closets, and in the cellar was a receptacle for valuables, known only to the initiated, which could only be discovered by removing a stone in the wall.

The blacksmith-shop erected by John Jones is, I believe, still standing. Here he did a great deal of work for the

---

[1] Rev. George Whitefield, the most celebrated pulpit orator of modern times, preached at the house of Henry Antes, April 23, 1740, to a great multitude of people. Mr. Seward, who accompanied Whitefield, says in his "Journal," pp. 12–13: "They were Germans where we dined and supped, and they prayed and sung in German as we did in English, before and after eating." What a magnificent subject for a painter! Whitefield preaching English to the Germans of Frederick Township, who, while most of them probably failed to understand the sermon, could not help feeling the power of his transcendent eloquence.

Indians, especially during the time when the Moravian Indian converts occupied the village of Nain in the vicinity of Bethlehem. The book in which all these transactions were recorded with scrupulous exactness was in existence a few years since, but we believe it has been destroyed by some one who did not appreciate its value.

Three children, John, Sarah, and Joseph, were born in Bethlehem Township, so that the whole number was now eight, or, as in after years, Joseph Jones used to puzzle his auditors by saying: "There were seven brothers, and each of us had a sister." Joseph Jones, the youngest of the children, was born on the 22d of April, 1755.

The Jones house was a place of considerable importance during the Indian wars. Again and again it was crowded with refugees fleeing from the frontier. On the 7th of July, 1757, an Indian boy, the son of the old chief Tattamy, was recklessly shot by a white boy at Craig's settlement, while on his way to Easton with a party of friendly Indians. Dangerously wounded, the Indian boy was brought to the Jones house to be nursed, while his companions encamped around the house, breathing threats of the direst vengeance in case of the death of their young chieftain. It was a matter of the greatest importance that his life should, if possible, be saved, and Dr. Bodo Otto was engaged, at the expense of the government, to give him his undivided attention.

For more than a month young Tattamy lingered between life and death. The Indians could wait no longer, so they hurried away to their hunting-grounds, greatly to the relief of the family which had entertained them. Three days afterwards the young chief died, and was buried in the graveyard on the opposite side of the river. Several Indians of minor consideration who died about this time were buried on the hill behind the barn, in a small inclosure which, we believe, has entirely disappeared.

John Jones soon became a man of wealth and consideration. In 1752 he was appointed, by Act of Assembly, one of the commissioners to secure a piece of land to build a court-house and prison for Northampton County, at Easton, "to accommodate the public service, and for the ease and convenience of the inhabitants." He did not, however, long remain a member of the Moravian brotherhood. Shortly after the purchase of his farm he voluntarily withdrew, and for a long time worshipped with the Lutheran Church. The reason of this change it would now be hard to determine. There is, however, a probable tradition that it was occasioned by his refusal to dispose of his property to the Society, which was desirous of extending its possessions in his direction. It is pleasant to know that he renewed his old ties shortly before his death, which occurred on the 2d of June, 1781. He was buried in the beautiful graveyard at Bethlehem.

The children of John Jones were scattered far and wide. Long before his death Joseph alone was left at the paternal homestead. Jonathan lingered until 1767, when he removed to Rowan County, North Carolina. Peter made his home in Northumberland, Pennsylvania. Levi was collector of excise for Northampton County before the Revolution. John went to New Orleans and was married there. Desirous of visiting his aged parents, he engaged passage for his bride on a ship, and then, from motives of economy, started to make the journey alone by land. His wife reached Bethlehem safely, but John never arrived. He was supposed to have been murdered on the way. No wonder that his mother often mournfully inquired, "Where, oh! where is John?"

It would be easy to enter more fully into particulars with reference to the immediate descendants of John Jones. In his will—a formidable document of ten folio pages, recorded at Easton—all of those living at the time of his decease are fully enumerated. To this paper we would refer any of the family who may be desirous of making further researches.

By the terms of this will, Joseph Jones, "in consideration of his most dutiful behaviour to his parents," was made the sole heir of his father's landed estate, including farms in Saucon and Williams Townships, and comprising nearly eight hundred acres of excellent land. He had, however, to pay out a considerable number of legacies, and in those days "land was cheap but money dear."

Eleanor Jones survived her husband more than twenty-one years. She remained to the last in full possession of all her faculties, and was regarded with most profound respect and affection. Her name became a favorite in the family, and even now there are many among her descendants who are called Eleanor.

Joseph Jones was married in 1775 to Hannah Horn, of Upper Merion, whose brother had previously married Sarah Jones. We need not say that the first years of their married life fell in troubled times. In 1777, when their eldest child Eleanor was an infant, Joseph Jones was required by the authorities to take a wagon load of flour to camp, for the relief of the army. He left home in good spirits, expecting to return in a few days; but when the flour was out they loaded him with candles, and he was compelled to follow the army for many months. One day during his absence a company of French soldiers came to his house, and by signs demanded food and lodging. They were, I presume, a part of the suite of General Lafayette, who had been wounded at the battle of Brandywine, and was at this time under surgical treatment at Bethlehem. These French soldiers were polite and respectful, but it is not surprising that Mrs. Jones was afraid of them. At night she crept into a closet hidden by the wainscoting, in deadly fear lest her hiding-place should be discovered by the crying of her child. One night she heard a noise in the garden, and, looking out of the window, saw that a party of Tories were engaged in stealing a row of hives full of honey. Without a moment's hesitation she called "Messieurs!" at the top of her voice, and in a few moments the soldiers came running down stairs. Unable to make herself understood, she pointed to the window, when they raised their muskets and fired a volley through the panes. Next morning the hives were found scattered along the garden-walk, stained with blood, but whether any one of the thieves was seriously wounded was never discovered.[1]

---

[1] As these stories are probably unknown to most of the present members of the Jones family, it may be well to add that they were related to the writer many years ago by the eldest daughter of Joseph Jones—the very

Joseph and Hannah Jones had seven children: (1) Eleanor married David Lerch, of Sussex County, New Jersey; (2) John married Sybilla Beil; (3) Mary died unmarried; (4) Sarah married William Hagy; (5) Elizabeth married Samuel Heller; (6) Joseph married Mary Butz; (7) Hannah married John King. All of them are now deceased, but most of them have numerous descendants.

In June, 1805, Hannah Jones died, and for more than five years her husband remained a widower. In 1809 he built a fine stone mansion a few rods west of the old homestead. It is still standing, and is in the possession of one of his grandsons.

In September, 1810, Joseph Jones was married the second time, to Mrs. Maria Nitschman, a widow. She was a sister of Bishop Jacob Van Vleck, father of the late Bishop Wm. Henry Van Vleck, of the Moravian Church. By this marriage he had no children.

Though never in public life, Mr. Jones was a man of great influence. He had read much, and was widely known as an excellent surveyor. His flow of spirits was remarkable, and many stories are still related which illustrate his keen sense of humor. In short, he was an excellent example of a good-humored intelligent country gentleman. He died on the 17th of December, 1824, in the 70th year of his age.

The Jones family-tree is still green and vigorous, and to enumerate its more recent branches would prove a difficult task. We have merely attempted to save a few fragments of family history that seemed in danger of being lost, leaving the completion of the work to others who are more immediately interested. The collection of these materials has proved a pleasant employment, and the motives of the work have been their own abundant reward.

child that slept with her mother in the closet; and as she had heard them from her parents, there can be no doubt of their substantial accuracy.

GENEALOGICAL RECORDS OF THE JONES FAMILY OF WALES AND PENNSYLVANIA.

CONTRIBUTED BY LEWIS JONES LEVICK.

[The following records have been copied from the Welsh Bible of the Jones family, and no rearrangement has been made.]

John the Son of Thomas and Anne Jones was born the 14th day of the 10th month 1703 about the 9th or 10th hour in the afternoone being the third day of the week.

Katherine daughter of Thomas and Anne Jones was born the 26th day of the 12th month 1704 about the 2d or 3d hour in the morning the 2d day of the week.

Elizabeth daughter of Thomas and Anne Jones was born the 28th day of the 10th month 1706 about ye 8th hour in the afternoone the 7th day of the week.

Katherine the daughter of Thomas and Anne Jones was born the 9th day of the 9th month 1708 about the 11th hour in the afternoone ye third day of the week.

Evan son of Thomas and Anne Jones was born the 16th day of ye 9th month 1709 about ye 10th hour in ye afternoone ye 4th day of ye week.

Anne daughter of Thomas and Anne Jones was born ye 25th day of the 12th month 17 $^{10}/_{11}$ about ye second hour in the morning the first day of ye week.

Mary the daughter of Thomas and Anne Jones was born ye 12th day of ye 11 month 1713 halfe an hour past the 3d hour in the afternoone the 3d day of ye week.

Sarah the daughter of Thomas and Anne Jones was born the 18th day of the 2d month 1716 about the 6th hour in the morning. It being the fourth day of the week.

Our dear father Thomas Jones of [erased] the county of [erased] In [erased] departed this Life the 4th day of the 8th month 1727 In the 57 y^r about 10 month of his age.

Ruth the daughter of Evan and Prisella Jones was born

the 7th day of ye 4th mo. 1741 about ye 7th hour in ye afternoon it being ye first day of ye week.

1764 Lewis Jones his Book Bought of Ruth Jones Daughter of Evan Jones deseased for five Shilings.

My Dear husband Lewis Jones Departed this Life the 3 day of ye 4 month 1778 being ye 6 Day of the Week & was buried ye 5 of the month aged 72 years 10 months & 27 Days.

Our dear Mother Katharine Jones Departed this Life the 9th Day of the 1 M° 1794 about 6 o'clock in the morning aged 85 years 2 mo & 20 Days.

Joseph Jones my Son Departed This Life the 12th day of ye 8 month 1783 abought half past 7 in the Evening aged 40 years 1 month & 25 Days.

Ruth Lewis the daughter of Evan Jones Departed this life 28 day of 5 month 1785. Ageed 44 years 1 month & 21 Days.

Dear Mother Katharine Jones departed this life the 9th Day of the 1 M° 1794 about 6 o'clock in the morning.

Our dear Father Thomas Jones departed this Life ye 4th day of ye 8 mo 1727 being the fourth Day of the week & was buryed the 6 day following aged about 57 years & 10 month.

Our dear Mother Ann Jones departed this Life ye 14th day of ye 9th mo 1732 being the third day of the week & was buryed the 16 of ye said month aged about 59 years.

My dear Wife Elizabeth Jones departed this Life ye 8 day of the 2d mo 1735 being the third day of ye week & was buryed the 11th day of ye sd. month aged about 47 years & 5 months.

Ann a born Daughter of William Horn and ye sd. Elizabeth was born ye 24th day of 9th mo 1731/2 about five o'clock in ye morning. William Horn Departed this life on 20 day of ye 12 mo 1731/2.

Our Sister Mary Jones departed this Life ye 23 day of ye 2 mo. 1740 being the fourth day of the week & was

Buried the 25th of ye sd mo aged about 26 years & three months.

My dear Wife Priscilla Jones departed this Life ye 25th day of the 10th mo 1742 being the Seventh day of the week & was Buried the 27th day of ye sd mo aged about 23 years and some months.

The 4th day of ye 12 mo following my daughter Ruth went to my father in Law John Jones to live.

Our Brother Eavan Jones Departed this Life the 28th Day of the 5th mo 1748 being the 5 Day of the week and whas buried the 30 of the said mo aged 38 years and 8 months.

Our Sister Elisabeth Jones Departed this Life the 3d of ye 8 month 1765 being ye 7 day of the week and was buried the 4 day of ye month aged 58 years 8 months & 25 days.

John Jones Son of David & Catharine Jones his Wife was Born 31 Day of the 9 Mounth 1697.

James Jones the Son David & Catharine Jones his Wife was Born the 31 day of 5 mounth 1699.

Susanna Jones Daughter of David & Catharine Jones his Wife was Born the 24 day of the 9 Mounth 1702.

John Jones Son of David & Catharine Jones his wife was born the 16 day of the 2 Mounth 170 $^3/_4$.

Lewis Jones Son of David & Catharine Jones his wife was born th. 27 of the 2 mounth 1705.

David Jones Son of David and Catharine Jones his Wife was born the 14 of the 5 Mounth 1706.

David Jones Son of David & Catharine Jones his Wife Departed this Life the 24 of the Sixth Mounth 1729.

Isaac Jones Son of David & Catharine Jones his Wife was born the 1 day of th. 7 Mounth 1708.

Alce Jones the Daughter of David & Catharine Jones his Wife was born the 1 day of the 4 Mounth 1710. Alce Departed this Life the 24 day of the 10 Mounth 1710.

Ellin the Daughter of David & Catharine Jones was born the 11 day of the 11 Mounth 1713.

Elizabeth Departed this Life 11 of the 10 Mounth 1714.

Jacob Jones Son of David & Catharine Jones was born the 30 of the 2 Mounth 1716.

Ellin Departed this Life the 6 of 12 Mounth 1764.

David Jones Son of Lewis Jones and Catharine his Wife was born ye 29 of ye 8 mo 1733.

Seth Jones Son of Lewis Jones and Catharine his Wife was born ye 8th of ye 12 mo 1735/6.

Seth Jones Departed this Life ye 10th of ye 2 mo. 1736.

Ann Jones Daughter of Lewis Jones and Catharine his Wife was born 10th of ye 12 mo 1736/7.

Thomas Jones Son of Lewis Jones and Catharine his Wife was born ye 9th of ye 4 mo. 1739.

Isaac Jones Son of Lewis Jones and Catharine his Wife was born ye 12 of ye 9 mo 1741.

Isaac Jones Departed this Life ye 7th of ye 7th mo 1742.

Joseph Jones Son of Lewis Jones and Catharine his Wife was born ye 17th of ye 4 mo 1743.

Thomas Jones Departed this Life ye 14th of ye 5 mo 1745.

Lewis Jones Son of Lewis Jones and Catharine his Wife was born ye 17th of ye 8 mo 1745.

David Jones departed this life 6 mo the 20 1810 about half past 10 o'clock in the evening aged 76 Years 7 Months & 13 Days.

Joseph Jones Departed this Life ye 12th of ye 8 mo 1783.

Ann Jones departed this life 10 m 21st 1814 aged 77 years 8 Months & 21 Days.

Jane Jones departed this life 4 mo 9th 1815 aged 72 years 9 mo and 22 Days.

John the Son of Thomas and Ann Jones departed this Life the 12th day of the 2^d month 1706 about ye 6th or 7th hour in the morning being the 6th day of the week and was buryed the 14th day being the first day following.

> The holy bible Containing the old and new Testament being the writtings of ye prophets and apostles as were moved by the holy Ghost.

Katherine ye Daughter of Thomas and Anne Jones departed the 16th day of the 4th month 1706 abt ye 11th hour (the first day of the week) in the morning & was buryed the next day following.

Our Dear father John Thomas of Llaithgwm in the Commott of Penllyn in the County of Meirioneth in North Wales departed this Life the 3d day of ye 3^d month 1683 being the 5th day of the week & was buryed at friends burying place at Havodbadog in the said Commett and County ye 5th Day of the said month.

Our dear Sister Sydney Jones departed this Life the 29th day of the 7th month 1683 as we were a coming from ye said place to Pennsilvania on board ye ship Morning Star of Chester Thomas Hayes Master.

Our Dear Sister Mary Jones departed this Life the 18th day of ye 8th month 1683 at Sea in the said Journey.

Our Relations hereafter written departed this Life at our house called Gelli y Cochiaid (excepting Hugh Ro:) in the Township of Meirion in ye County of Philadelphia in the Province of Pennsilvania and they (& he also) were buryed at friends burying place by ye meeting house in ye said Meirion.

Hugh Roberts the son of Brother Robert Roberts & Sister Katherine was born ye 31st day of ye 11th month 169$\frac{4}{5}$ at our sd house & departed the 4th day of the 5th month 1697.

Our dear sister Katherine departed this Life ye 12th day of ye 5th month about noone 1697 & she was buryed next day.

Our dear Mother Katherine Tho. departed this Life the 18th day of ye 11th month about 2^d or 3^d hour in ye morning (as we thought) & she was buryed next day 1697.

Our Dear Brother Evan Jones departed this Life the 27th day of the 12th month 169$\frac{7}{8}$ being something past midnight (as we thought) abt ye first hour in ye morning.

Our Nephew John Rees son of Brother Rees Evans & Sister Elizabeth departed this Life the 23^d day of the 3^d

month 1700 at 12th hour in ye night on board ye Ship called ye Tyger of Bristol John Hort Commander.

father in Law Griffith John departed this Life the 7th day of the 5th month 1707 being the Second day of the week and was buryed the next day at Meirion Burying place by the meeting house.

William Miller a Servant Lad departed this Life ye 14th day of ye 1st mo 174½ it being ye first day & was buried the next day aged about 19 years. he was four days sick with Itch and fever.

THE WIFE AND CHILDREN OF SIR WILLIAM KEITH

By CHARLES P. KEITH, Litt.D.,
President of The Genealogical Society of Pennsylvania

The picture reproduced facing this article, date and artist unknown, has been preserved among descendants of Governor Keith and his wife as a portrait of the latter, who was properly styled Dame Ann Keith or Lady Keith from his becoming a baronet. The photograph was sent over by the family with copies, not *literatim,* of letters and parts of letters, which we will quote, hoping that they will be found interesting supplemented by data from other sources. The portrait is indeed different from the rough and almost comic sketch in the possession of the Historical Society, attributed to John Watson, a Scotch artist, who died at Perth Amboy in 1760, who, by the way, is not known to have been related to Watson the Annalist.

It is to be regretted that Sir Robert's inquiry in one of his letters as to his mother's progenitors is not answered. We cannot verify the statement in one of her letters that she was "born of a noble family and once heiress to a very large fortune." Her maiden name was Ann Newbury, and she was born in 1675. The late William J. Buck found a memorandum, that Ann Morgan, evidently her mother, was born in England in 1625, so fifty years old at this daughter's birth, and died in 1697, aged 72.

Ann Newbury first married Robert Diggs, who is spoken of as a Counsellor, by whom she had a daughter Ann, born July 22, 1700, at St. Alban's, England, who married in Philadelphia Dr. Thomas Græme[1]. There is some suspicion that Governor Keith's father had hid at the Græme family seat, Balgowan, Perthshire, after the battle of Sheriff Muir in that county. Græme came with Keith and his family to Pennsylvania. Dr. Græme and his wife Ann Diggs had three children who survived their grandmother, *viz.*, Thomas, Collector of Port of Newcastle, and two daughters, Ann and Elizabeth. Ann Græme married Charles Stedman from Scotland, sea captain, merchant and ironmaster, who built the house now numbered 244 South Third Street, Philadelphia, subsequently known as the "Powel House." Elizabeth Græme had an unhappy career; jilted by Benjamin Franklin's son, William, who was afterwards Governor of New Jersey, she sought solace in literature, becoming quite a poetess; in middle age married Henry Hugh Fergusson, a Scotchman, who went to England during the Revolutionary War, and never returned, she dying in 1801, childless, poor, and unpopular from her connection with British attempts to induce Washington and Joseph Reed to forsake the American cause.

When a young widow, Mrs. Diggs, *née* Newbury, made her second marriage, which probably in the end depleted any fortune she had, and which at the time could not have been looked upon as prudent, however distinguished. She married William Keith, heir apparent to a baronetcy, who had embroiled himself with the exiled king and his party, having spent some years at St. Germain's, in the hope, says Bishop Burnet's *History,* of becoming Under-Secretary for Scotland in the event of James II.'s restoration. Returning to Eng-

---

[1] Charles P. Keith, *Provincial Councillors of Pennsylvania*, pp. 157–166.

land, where he was admitted to the Inner Temple on July 3, 1704, he had been used by the enemies of the Duke of Athol to give evidence of the latter's connection with Fraser's scheme. The only post that young Keith received from the Tories when in power was Surveyor of the Customs for the southern district of America, and this was lost at the accession of George I. Meanwhile Keith's father, the third baronet of the line, contracted great debts, increased by his joining in the insurrection of 1715, so that at his death, his estate was insolvent. For the eldest of his three children, the Lieutenant Governorship of Pennsylvania would have been a sufficient support; but a high style of living, unsuccessful speculations, and a political course antagonizing the leading men, not to mention slips in morality, caused the loss of the earlier savings and subsequently expected stipends, and sent him back to England in unsuccessful search of better fortune. He was Lieutenant-Governor of Pennsylvania and Delaware from his arrival, May 31, 1717, until superseded on June 22, 1726, and left America in 1728, never to return. His wife and second son neither accompanied nor followed him. There was no quarrel; in fact the letters of all the family indicate union of affection and interests, not lessened by there being two illegitimate children of Sir William, a boy and a girl, of the former of whom the fate is unknown, but the latter, after the death of a *fiancé,* died unmarried. The sons Robert and James were sent for by their father to be put to school. Lady Keith pities herself in after life as "deprived & stript of a tender husband," and says that she would "most joyfully rather have endured death than have parted with him." After for a short time making a home with her son, she lived at Horsham on the plantation taken from the widow of Samuel Carpenter, the Treasurer, in satisfaction for the money voted to the Queen's use. There Sir William had built the house, which is still standing. By deed dated April 23, 1731, Keith conveyed this with 934 acres 10 perches to his eldest surviving son and others in trust with power to sell for Lady Keith, and to pay her the proceeds. They soon sold 100 acres. After repeated attempts to dispose of the balance to one of the family, they put it up at public sale on August 12, 1737, and Turner, who bought it for £750 Pennsylvania money, conveyed it in December following to Dr. Græme, from whom what is left is known as "Graeme Park," although Sir William once called it "Fountain Low." It is now (1931) owned and occupied by Welsh Strawbridge, who lives in a more modern house upon the place. Watson's *Annals,* perhaps on the authority of William Rawle[2], gives a deplorable account of Lady Keith's last years, incorrectly calling her this Governor's "widow," and saying that she "lived and died in a small wooden house in Third Street between High Street and Mulberry Street, there, much pinched for subsistence, she eked out her existence with an old female, and declining all intercourse with society or her neighbours. The house itself was burnt down in 1786." It seems unlikely that Dr. Græme and his wife and children, surviving her, left her to starve. She died July 31, 1740, aged 65 years, according to the tombstone in Christ Churchyard.

If Watson's account is true, very remarkable is the following letter dated the month before the Lady's death.

Letter of Lady Anne Keith (more properly Ann Lady Keith) to her daughter Mrs. Jane Yeeles, Philadelphia, June, 1740.

My dearest child
I must now let you know I have lately received a very long tender & affectionate letter from your dear Father, who enjoys a great share of good health blessed be God he also wrote a very kind letter of thanks to Doctor Graeme for his respect & care

---

[2] *The Pennsylvania Magazine of History and Biography,* XXIII. 533.

of me. I have likewise heard from your brother Robert, who was then in France with General Keith who had gone there in hopes of finding relief from a wound he received in an engagement with the Turks, for which he can have no cure & that I am under great apprehension of your brother losing so great & generous a friend who is not only so, but like a Father too, as your Brother writes me. he desires his affectionate love to you & says he can never forget the affection you always expressed for him. He is your own brother indeed, he has a most noble & generous way of thinking, & expresses ye so great a duty & regard for his Parents & so much tenderness & concern for me in particular that it is moving indeed & I can but think myself Blest with such children but oh! then what must be my trial never to hope to have the happiness of seeing them more O my dear how does he revive the memory of my dear son William My dear daughter I can only recommend you & yours to the great God . . .

Sir William and Lady Keith had the following children, with possibly others who died in early childhood:

1st. William, mentioned in the *Votes of Assembly* as secretary to his father, went to Jamaica, where he married a widow named Barham, and d.s.p. before December 5, 1727, at "Mesopotamia," Westmoreland, Jamaica.

2nd. Alexander Henry, possibly the Henry Keath in a list of "departed saints of the law," was styled eldest surviving son and heir apparent of Sir William in deed of 1731; was collector of port of New Castle, Delaware, as early as 1729; died without issue about October 5, 1741, buried at Christ Church, October 6; married Thomasine, daughter of Anthony Palmer, afterwards President of the Council of Pennsylvania, which marriage was objectionable to Lady Keith, probably because Thomasine's prospective inheritance would not be sufficient to support a baronet; Thomasine Keith founded Palmer Burying Ground for Kensington.

3rd. Jane, born about 1708, marriage ceremony performed by the well-known non-juror, Dr. Richard Welton, out of which fact Keith's enemies made political capital; she died before September 5, 1760; married (date from *American Weekly Mercury*) December 10, 1724, William Yeeles of St. Elizabeth, Goshen, Jamaica.

Issue of William and Jane Yeeles:

>Deborah married, in 1747, William Senior of Westmoreland, Jamaica, and was ancestress of several officers in Army and Navy.
>Jane.
>Mary married ——— Brooke.
>Thomas died 1753.
>Catherine.
>Arabella.
>Elizabeth married John Merrick Williams of Jamaica, and was ancestress of Valentine Rowe, Col. R. E., lately deceased, and his daughters, of Torquay, England.

4th. Robert, born 1714, who succeeded as the fifth baronet, when he had already served in the Russian army under the patronage of his kinsman James Keith, and had followed him into the Prussian service, where the said kinsman became a Field Marshal. Robert married Margaritha Albertina Conradina von Suhm (misprinted Suchen in Burke's *Extinct Baronetcies*). In later life, Sir Robert entered the Danish army, and was Colonel commandant at Rendsburg, and became a General. He died in 1771.

Issue of Sir Robert and wife; besides two daughters who died infants:

>Frederick William Henry Ferdinand, born 7.10.1751 (this means October 7); four of the Prussian royal family were sponsors at his baptism; became the sixth and last baronet; rose from ensign to major in Danish army; died unmarried, 8.11 (or November 8), 1798.
>Robert George James, born 16.10. (October 16), 1752; captain Danish army; died unmarried 12.1. (Jan. 12?), 1791.

5th. James, born on shipboard May 10, 1717, while his parents were coming to Pennsylvania; baptized at Christ Church, Philadelphia, June 19, 1717; went with

Robert to their father in England; entered the British navy; was later in Prussian army; appears to have died childless before November 3, 1753, from Sir Robert's saying at that date, "I am the only representative of the family."

Although there are letters from Sir Robert of later date, the following is selected to close this article:

Sir Robert Keith to Mrs. Yeeles

Potsdam Nov. 3, 1753

My dear sister.

It was with the greatest pleasure I received your kind letter, as it had been so long that I had not heard any news of yourself & family; tho' I must own on perusing it my joy was much abated by the account it gave me of the death of your only son & the more so as I had already been informed how hopeful a youth he was. I am by the blessing of God myself the father of two boys & tho' their infancy does not permit me to guess whether they will answer my expectations by their conduct when of riper years, Yet I know what I & their Mother should have felt had we lost either of them; a loss that we lately much apprehended as they both were ill of the small-pox. The oldest who among the many names by which he was baptized is known by that of Frederic (after the King of Prussia who was his chief Godfather) was before this accident but sickly through this misfortune of having had two different nurses, so that when he was seized with the snall Pox we thought we should have lost him and this apprehension greatly afflicted his mother whose darling he is: but God be praised, our fears are happily over, as he is now in good health. He is two years and one month old and as sprightly a child as one can find, so you may judge how dear he is to us. The youngest is called Robert: he is one year & two months old, is entirely recovered and a very fine boy, but I think my wife's health affected and the Phisicians have frighten me by telling me she may fall into a consumption; and I can assure you that I have so good a wife that to lose her would be an affliction insupportable, but I hope in God, not to live to know such a loss. I have the greater obligation to her as she could have had much better matches by far when she married me. She even lost by her marriage a Pension, which the King gave her, as daughter of a man for whom he had a great friendship besides her own fortune. She has several relations to whose inheritance she will have an undoubted right. I shall not neglect to send you our pictures. I would willingly have a picture of my Father & Mother. I wrote last year to our sister G. [Græme] beging her to yield me those two large pictures at full length which were at Horsham, and as I am the only representative of the family I think she can not refuse me, but as she has not yet answered my letter, I am afraid my demand has not been agreeable. I own, as I have no picture of either Father or Mother I should be very thankful to her for such a present as they are very good ones. There is one thing I would willingly know, therefore if you are not sufficiently informed beg you will endeavor to get as particular an account as you can from Sister G. the thing is, I am desirous to know what family our dear Mother was of. I know she was a young widow of a Councillor Diggs when my Father married her, but I would willingly know her maiden name, who & what her Father & Mother were, in what part of Britain they were settled, whether people of landed estate or otherwise. There are particulars I am entirely ignorant off and about which I should not have troubled myself were I not settled in this country, but as it is, I would willingly be informed on account of my dear children . . . my reasons are these. Here is a Protestant order called the order of St. John into which a number of Nobility enter as it sometimes when the turn comes procures a Revenue of 500 and even 1000£. In order to be entered one must prove one's Nobility both of Father & Mother's side for eight Generations. I can easily get my children's Nobility proved of the Father's side, as the family of Keith is known throughout all Europe . . . but I must equally prove it of my Mother's side, and as I should be glad to enter my son into this order I should wish to be informed of these particulars . . . the only difficulty I have to get my Genealogical Table drawn and when I know the family of which my Mother was I shall write to England for further particulars. My wife's family is one of the ancientest in Germany so that I have on that side no difficulty.

When you write address your letter thus: Sir Robert Keith Bar^t Colonel & Adjutant General to his Majesty the King of Prussia Potsdam. Mr. James Stephens is my correspondent at Hamburgh.

My wife makes you many compliments. I have promised her to excuse her to you for not writing at this time, but as she has not yet learned English I told her I would write for her & give you a particular account of our family. I have however made her write to my niece Mrs. S———— She first wrote her letter in French. I translated it & then she copied it. I beg you will write me in what part of the Island you live & particularly how to address you, for tho' I have the means of Geo. Barclay yet perhaps I may find a nearer way by direct shipping from Hamburgh. My kindest compliments to Mr. Y———— Adieu my dear Sister. God Almighty grant you & your family long life & all manner of happiness, such are the sincere wishes of, my dearest sister, Your most affectionate brother & obedient . . . Servt.

ANCESTRY AND CHILDREN OF ISAAC LEA.

John Lea, b. 1661, d. 1726, m. 1698 Hannah Hopton.
Isaac Lea, b. 1699, d. —, m. 1721 Sarah Fawcett.
James Lea, Sr., b. Mar. 26, 1723–4, d. Oct. 2, 1798, m. 1741 Margaret Marshall.
James Lea, Jr., b. Mar. 28, 1759, d. Sep. 30, 1825, m. Apl. 18, 1781 Elizabeth Gibson, mentioned in this sketch.
Isaac Lea, writer of this sketch, b. Mar. 4, 1792, d. Dec. 8, 1886, m. Mar. 8, 1821 Frances Anne, daughter Mathew Carey.

- Matthew Carey Lea, 1st, b. 1822, d. same year.
- Matthew Carey Lea, 2d, b. Aug. 8, 1823, d. Mar. 15, 1897.
- Henry Charles Lea, b. Sep. 19, 1825, d. Oct. 24, 1909, m. 1850 Anna Caroline Jaudon, "Niece and Ward" mentioned in sketch.
- Frances Lea, mentioned in this sketch, b. Mar. 6, 1834, d. Feb. 25, 1894.

James Lea, Jr. Born March 28, 1759 in Wilmington, Del., m. at Centre Meeting, Newcastle Co., Del. March 28, 1781 Elizabeth, daughter of Thomas and Hannah (Ring) Gibson, b. Chad's Ford, Pa. Jan. 23, 1762, d. Cincinnati Mar. 13, 1833. He was a merchant owning a fleet of eight or ten ships engaged in Irish and West Indian trade, but was ruined by the embargo of Dec. 7, 1807 and moved to Pittsburgh, and thence by boat down the Ohio River to Cincinnati in 1822, where he again built up a prosperous business, but was again ruined, this time by the acts of a near relative whom he had taken into this business. J. L., Jr. died at Cincinnati Sep. 30, 1825. He was distinguished for hospitality and charity.

Isaac Lea, son of James Lea, Jr. was born in Wilmington Mar. 4, 1792. In 1807 he moved to Philadelphia, receiving a certificate to So. District, Philadelphia Aug. 10, 1809. He engaged in the wholesale importing business of his eldest brother, John Lea. In 1814 he joined a volunteer rifle company which offered its services to the Governor and held itself in readiness to march at any time. The English army was then in possession of Washington, and the need seemed urgent, but in the following Autumn the Governor disbanded the company. For this volunteering he lost his birthright in the Society of Friends. He married at St. Joseph's Roman Catholic Church, Philadelphia, on March 8, 1821 Frances Anne, daughter of Mathew Carey. His wife subsequently became a Protestant. She died May 29, 1874. I. L. entered the publishing house of his father-in-law in 1821 and became a member of the firm of M. Carey & Sons, then the most extensive publishers in the United States. The firm (now Lea & Febiger) is in its 142d year. I. L. retired from successive firms in 1851. In 1828 be became a member of the "Wistar Association," of which he was Dean from 1841 to 1861. In 1832 and again in 1852 he went to Europe to meet the learned men there in his special branches, Geology, Mineralogy and Conchology. From 1851 his life was devoted entirely to scientific research and writing. He was most prolific, his printed works numbering 279. He was made Doctor of Laws by Harvard University in 1852. His contributions to science have been universally recognized by the best scientists at home and abroad as of great importance. The issues of the Academy of Natural Sciences and the American Philosophical Society for sixty years justify this. More than fifty American and foreign learned Societies conferred the honor of membership on him. He was a most lovable man. I. L. died Dec. 8th, 1886.

ANCESTRY AND CHILDREN OF ELIZABETH GIBSON, Wife of James Lea, Jr.

Thomas, m —.
John, b. 1655, d. 1698, m. Elizabeth —.
John, b. 1699, d. 1754, m. Christina Harlan, b. 1687, d. 1764.
Thomas, b. 1723, d. 1814, m. 1751 Hannah Ring. The Thomas Gibson mentioned in this sketch.
Elizabeth, b. 1762, d. 1833, m. 1781 James Lea, Jr.
Isaac Lea, b. 1792, d. 1886, writer of this sketch, and 10 others.

Thomas Gibson, son of John and Christina (Harlan) Gibson, was born at Lurgan, Ireland, April 18th, 1723 and came to Pennsylvania with his parents at the age of six years. He married at Concord, Pa., September 27th, 1751, Hannah, daughter of Nathaniel and Lydia (Vernon) Ring of Bradford, Chester Co. He moved to Connellsville, Pa. and died there 1814.

Elizabeth Gibson, daughter of above, was born at Chad's Ford, on the Brandywine, January 23d, 1762. She married at Centre Meeting, Newcastle Co., Del., April 18th, 1781 James Lea, Jr. She died at Cincinnati, March 13th, 1833. "Benevolent and cheerful, she was always happy in doing good to others and will be remembered with enduring affection by her numerous posterity." She had eleven children. Of them Isaac was the writer of this sketch. His love of nature pervades it. Hannah Gibson Lea and Elizabeth were two of his sisters. Frances Lea was his daughter.

"Anna J., niece and ward" was Anna Caroline Jaudon, daughter of Susan Gibson Lea, another sister of Isaac Lea. Susan Gibson Lea married William Latta Jaudon. Their daughter, "Anna J." married Henry Charles Lea May 27th, 1850.

SOME OF THE DESCENDANTS OF EVAN ROBERT LEWIS, OF FRON GÔCH, WALES.

[The following is a copy of a manuscript genealogy of the descendants of Evan Robert Lewis (*i.e.*, Evan son of Robert son of Lewis), of Fron Gôch, a large farm near Bala, Merionethshire. It exemplifies very well the Welsh system of surnames, by which the son took his father's Christian name as his surname, so that a number of persons bearing different surnames were frequently descended from a common ancestor in the male line. Thus the descendants in the male line from Evan Robert Lewis, no later than 1750, were known by the surnames of Owen, Evan, Jones, Williams, and Griffiths; but such surnames indicated no relationship to families of the same name. The genealogy here printed was presented to the Historical Society of Pennsylvania by Mr. George Vaux in 1891, having been found among the papers of Eleanor Long in 1887. It is a copy of one of those compiled about the year 1797 by Cadwalader Evans from data furnished him by older members of the family and from family papers, some of which were brought from Wales in 1698. There are several copies of this genealogy extant, which vary more or less in information. The one here printed is the most accurate that the writer has seen, except that in possession of Rowland Evans, Esq., which has been added to from time to time, and also has appended the pedigree of Evan Robert Lewis from papers brought from Wales, and which was amplified by the late Rowland E. Evans. The pedigree runs thus: Evan (*i.e.*, Evan Robert Lewis) ap Robert ap Lewis ap Griffith ap Howell ap Enion ap Deikws Ddu ap Madog ap Evan Gôch ap David Gôch ap Trahairn Gôch O'Lyn. Additional information regarding the families descended from Evan Robert Lewis may be found in Jenkins's *Gwynedd* and Glenn's *Merion*. The genealogy here presented also gives the Pennsylvania descendants (in the female line) of Ellis Williams, of Cai Fadog.]

Ellis Williams of Cai fadog had four Daughters, viz: Margaret, Douse, Gwenn & Ellin.

The said Ellin married John Morris of Brin Gwin in Denbighshire, by her had one daughter named Ellin who married Cadwalader ab Evan late of Gwynedd deceased.

Gwenn, another daughter of the said Ellis Williams had three children who came to Pennsylvania viz:

1. Ellis Pugh late of Gwynedd deceased.
2. Ellin, married to Edward Foulke, late of Gwynedd, dec^d.
3. Jane, married to Wm John of Gwynedd, also deceased.

Hence it appears that Thomas Foulke & John Evans were Second Cousins, as being each of them great grand children of Ellis Williams abovenamed.

Evan Robert Lewis was an honest sober man—lived in Fron Gooh [Fron Gôch]. He had five Sons, vizt 1. John ab Evan. 2. Cadw^r ab Evan. 3. Owen ab. Evan. 4. Griffith ab Evan and 5. Evan ab Evan.

John ab Evan had three sons and three daughters by his first wife, vizt (a.) Cadwalader. (b.) Robert. (c.) Griff. (d.) Margaret. (e.) Gwen. (f.) Catharine.

The Second Son (b.) Robert came to Pennsylvania and settled at Abington and left Issue.

(c.) Griffith, the youngest son of the said John ab Evan came also to Pennsylvania, had issue two Sons and one Daughter, viz: Evan Griffith late of Gwynedd dec^d and John Griffith late of Merion dec^d. Their sister married Thomas Jones, late of Merion deceased.

The said (1) John ab Evan had issue by a second wife vizt (g.) William John. (h.) Rowland John and (i.) Gainor John. William the eldest Son settled in Gwynedd and left issue. (d.) Margaret their sister died on Sea and left issue two daughters, viz: Gwen who married Thomas Foulke of Gwynedd and Gainor who married Robert Humphrey also of Gwynedd.

Hence it appears that the said Gwen & Gainor were second cousins to John Evans of Gwynedd late deceased, as he was Grandson to Evan ab Evan (5) they Grand daughters of John ab Evan (1) who was a Brother of the said Evan ab Evan (5).

(2.) Cadw^r ab Evan son of the said Evan Robert Lewis died without issue.

(3.) Owen ab Evan had three Sons and two Daughters vizt Robert,^{1} Owen,^{2} and Evan,^{3} Jane^4 and Ellin.^{5} Robert,^{1} one of the Sons, came to Pennsylvania and settled in Merion, and left Issue four Sons and two daughters, viz: Robert, Owen, Evan and John, Gainor & Elizabeth.

Jane,^{4} one of the Daughters of the said Owen ab Evan came here married Hugh Roberts who had issue three Sons vizt Robert, Owen, and Edward—The two latter lived and died in Philadelphia. Robert settled in Maryland. Each of them left Issue.

Ellin,^{5} one of the Daughters of the said Owen ab Evan [wife of Cadwalader Thomas] died in Wales, but her Son John Cadwalader lived and died in Philad^a, the late Doctor Cadwalader being his Son and the present John Dickinson his Grandson.

(4.) Griffith ab Evan had four Sons and one Daughter viz: Hugh,^{1} Edward,^{2} Robert,^{3} David,^{4} & Catharine.^{5} Hugh,^{1} one of the Sons, came here, settled in Gwynedd, died there, and left a numerous issue.

Edward,^{2} second son of the said Griffith ab Evan, died in Wales. His son Griffith Edward came here with two of his Sisters viz: Jane and Margaret. Jane married to John Jones of Montgomery and Margaret to David George of Blockley.

Robert,^{3} another son of the said Griffith ab Evan died at Sea. Two of his Daughters arrived here. Catharine one of them was married to William Morgan of Montgomery. The other sister died single.

Catharine,^{5} the only daughter of the said Griffith ab Evan, came here, was married to Jno Williams of Montgomery, left issue, died at a very advanced age.

(5.) Evan ab Evan, youngest Son of the said Evan Robert Lewis, had issue by his first Wife two Daughters^a and by the latter wife four Sons and one Daughter viz. Thomas[1], Robert[2], Owen[3], Cadwalader[4] & Sarah[5]. One of his Daughters[a] by the first wife had issue two Sons. Robert Jones, one of the Sons settled in Gwynedd and was a County Magistrate many years and left issue. His Brother Cadw^r died at Sea and left issue.

Thomas, eldest Son of the said Evan ab Evan arrived in Pennsylvania with his Brethren[2,3,4] & Sister[5] with many other of their Relations in July 1698, and settled in Gwynedd, having taken up the whole township between them. The said Thomas[1] lived to a very advanced age, and left issue four Sons and two Daughters, viz. Robert, Evan, Owen & Hugh, Lowry and Sarah.

Robert[2], the second Son of Evan ab Evan died in Gwynedd, had two Sons Evan and Hugh and three daughters, viz. Lowry, Ann and Mary, who were all married and left issue.

Owen ab Evan[3], third Son of Evan ab Evan did not arrive to great age, left issue Evan, Robert, Thomas, John, Cadw^r, and Elizabeth, who have all left issue except John and Cadw^r.

Cadwalader ab Evan[4], youngest Son of the said Evan ab Evan, arrived to great age and left issue one Son and one Daughter, viz. John Evans, late of Gwynedd, deceased, and Sarah married to John Hank.

Sarah[5] the Daughter of the said Evan ab Evan had issue by Evan Pugh two Sons and four Daughters.

GENEALOGICAL RECORDS, copied from a Bible in the possession of Mrs. George E. Vichers, Lewes, Delaware, and contributed by Rev. C. H. B. Turner. The family surnames include those of Manlove, Master, Mason, Bibbe, Broxson, Kellam, Burroughs, Polk, Shaw, Chipman, and Brown.

William Manlove Senior was born December ye 25. 1691.

Willm Manlove departed this life on ye 15th day of March in ye afternoon, about one hour before sun setting Anno Domini 1761.

(William Manlove. His Book Bought in Phildelphia in ye year 1729. The price of this book is £1.15.0.)

Ruth Manlove departed this life the 5th day of April 1746.

Sarah Masten the wife of William Masten departed this life February the 27th about One Oclock the afternoon 1776.

Mary Mason the wife of Joseph Mason departed this life November 5th about One Oclock in the afternoon 1779.

The ages of the children of William Manlove and Mary his wife:

Nathaniel Manlove was born ye 6th day of January 1717 & departed this life April 27th 1729.

William Manlove Jr. was born April 29th 1721 about midnight.

Mary Manlove was born ye 27th day of October 1723 about four in the afternoon.

Ruth Manlove was born December 10th 1726 about 11 Oclock in the evening.

Sarah Manlove was born September ye 28th 1730 about 8 Oclock at night.

Edmund Bibbe was married to his wife Mary October ye 1st 1709

William Manlove was married to his wife Mary December ye 6th 1716.

Mary Manlove daughter of Mark Manlove and Ann his wife was born April ye 18th 1712.

Thomas Manlove son of Mark Manlove and Ann his wife was born June ye 27th 1714.

Elizabet Manlove daughter of Mark Manlove and Ann his wife was born October ye 7th 1716.

Ester Bibbe was born November ye 16th 1710.

Matthew Bibbe was born January ye 19th 17$\frac{11}{12}$.

Mary wife of *William Manlove*, above, departed this life December ye 1st day about 5 Oclock in the afternoon Anno. Dom. 1757.

John Masson Brown was born August. ye 5ᵗʰ 1728 about Two Oclock in the afternoon.

Sarah Chipman was born ye 30ᵗʰ day of October Anno Dom. 1757.

William Shaw departed this life ye 25ᵗʰ day of May Anno Dom 1758.

Elizabeth Polk daughter of Ephraim Polk and Mary Polk was born the 29ᵗʰ day of March 1739.

William Burroughs the son of John Burroughs and Ester Burroughs was born the 2ᵈ day of January 173$\frac{4}{5}$.

The above *William Burroughs* departed this life on the 14ᵗʰ day of April 1797.

Esther Burroughs the daughter of John Burroughs and Esther Burroughs was born the 8ᵗʰ day of January 17$\frac{4 3}{4 9}$.

William Masten the son of W. M. Masten and Sarah his wife was born the 7ᵗʰ day of February about 10 Oclock in the morning A. D. 175$\frac{2}{3}$.

Thomas Broxson was born in ye year of one thousand seven hundred and thirty six ye 27ᵗʰ day of December.

Joseph Broxson born in ye year one thousand seven and forty one ye 17ᵗʰ day of November.

An account of the births of the children of Joseph Mason and Mary his wife:

Sarah was born April ye 7ᵗʰ 1744.
Mary "   " March ye 13ᵗʰ 1748.
Jacob "   " Decbʳ ye 19ᵗʰ 1754.
Charles & Elias were born March 24ᵗʰ 1760.
Joseph was born Decbʳ 24ᵗʰ 1763.
Joseph died April 16ᵗʰ 1851 aged 57 years & 4 months.

Willian Masten son of John Masten & Hannah his wife was born January 15ᵗʰ day 1711.

John Masten departed this life December 20ᵗʰ day 1771.

William Masten son of Willian Masten & Sarah his wife was born February 7ᵗʰ day 1751.

Mary Masten was born November 17 day 1754.

Sarah Masten was born January 25ᵗʰ day 1756.

Deborah Masten was born October 8ᵗʰ day 1760.

John Masten was born November 1ˢᵗ 1763.

David Masten. was born February 6ᵗʰ day 1767.

Charles Mason & Catharine Stayton his wife were married May 6ᵗʰ 1815.

Jacob Mason son of Charles Mason & Catherine his wife was born April 20ᵗʰ 1816.

James L. son of Charles & Catherine Mason was born April 1ˢᵗ 1818.

William S. son of Charles & Catherine Mason was born October 16ᵗʰ 1821.

Josepn H. son of Charles & Catherine Mason was born February 20ᵗʰ 1823.

Catherine, only daughter of Charles & Catherine Mason was born July 4ᵗʰ 1830.

William S. Mason departed this life October 1876.

Joseph H. Mason departed this life——— 1852.

An account of the times of the births of the childrem of Charles Mason and Betty his wife.

Mary was born upon Sunday the 11ᵗʰ day of May 1783.
Rachel was born upon Sunday the 31ˢᵗ day of October 1784.
Jacob was born upon Friday the 28ᵗʰ day of December 1786.
Charles was born on Saturday the 13ᵗʰ day of September 1788.

The above *Betty Mason* departed this life upon Saturday the 19th day of November about 8 O'clock in the morning 1791.

The above Charles Mason Senior departed this life upon Sunday the 30th day of September 1810, being aged 50 years 6 months and 6 days.

The above *Jacob* son of Charles and Elizabeth Mason departed this life January 20th 1825.

Charles Jr. son of Charles & Elizabeth Mason departed this life August 21st 1858.

Elias Mason was married to Magdalen Owens on the 6th day of March 1783.

The births of the children of Elias Mason and Magdalen his wife are as follows:

Joseph was born October 23rd 1785.

Elias was born November 30th 1787.

Elizabeth was born January 28th 1790.

The above *Elias Mason Senr* departed this life December 17th 1793.

Stephen Sturgis was married to *Sally Mason* October 12th 1807.

The above *Sarah Mason* departed this life June 9th 1847.

An account of the times of the births of the children of George Cullen and Sarah his wife is as follows Vizi.

John Cullen was born June 7th 176—

Charles Mason Cullen was born January 19th 176—

Piercy Cullen was born September 17th 1773   *Margin of lear*

Sarah Cullen was born September 14th 1—   *missing.*

Jonathan Cullen was born   31st 17—

Piercy Cullen departed this life May 24th 178—

Sarah Cullen, younger, departed this life December 8th 1794.

The above named *Charles W. Cullen* was married to *Elizabeth Dickerson* on the 26th day of January 1797.

Elisha D. Cullen son of the above named Charles & Elizabeth his wife was born April 23d 1799.

An account of the children of Thomas Kellam and Mary Mason his wife:

Thomas Kellam and Mary Mason were married the 15th day of December 1802.

Elizabeth W. Kellam was born the 24 day of April 1804.

Joseph Mason and Mary his wife were married the 20th day of November 1807.

(James W. Mason M. D. one among the descendants of those whose births and marriages are recorded in this book will be 38 years of age the 27th day of this present month, February 1835.

                        Cincinnati Ohio February 5th 1835.

The widow Cullen gave me this book when I was in Lewistown Del. in ye year 1832. J. M. M.)

James W. Mason departed this life (margin destroyed——) Cincinnati Ohio at 7 O'clock in the morning.

This bible was presented to me by Sarah Mason, widow of Joseph Mason (the younger); she resided in Cincinnati, Ohio, where she died April 14th 1843. aged 74.

Joseph Mason, her husband, died April 16th 1821, aged 57 years.

                        James W. Mason,
                        Son of Charles Jr.

Inscription of fly page of Bible:
Printed & sold by Richard Ware at ye Bible & Sun in Amen Corner.

GENEALOGICAL RECORDS OF THE MARSHALL FAMILY OF LEWES, DELAWARE, 1737–1839.

CONTRIBUTED BY REV. C. H. B. TURNER.

[Extracts from a Bible belonging to Jacob Marshall of Lewes, Delaware, which was printed in London by Charles Bill, and the Executrix of Thomas Newcomb, deceased, Printers to the King and Most Excellent Majesty, Anno Dom. 1698.]

Jacob Marshall, the son of Jacob Marshall and Mary Wovs, born April 9, 1737, at three o'clock in the morning, Sunday.

Isaac Marshall, the son of Jacob Marshall and Mary Wovs, was born in the year 1738, September 27, on Thursday.

Abraham Marshall, the son of Jacob Marshall and Mary Wovs, was born in the year 1741, on February the fourth day about one o'clock in the morning on Thursday.

Bathsheba Marshall, the daughter of Jacob Marshall and Mary Wovs, was born in the year 1743, on December the 25, about four o'clock in the morning, on Sunday.

Moses Marshall, the son of Jacob Marshall and Mary Wovs, was born March the seventh day, 1745, on Friday, about seven o'clock in the morning.

William Marshall, the son of Jacob Marshall and Mary Wovs, was born in March 1748, on the 28th day, about ten o'clock at night on Monday.

November 31, 1751, John Marshall was born, the son of Jacob Marshall and Mary, Monday at three o'clock in the morning.

Mary, daughter of Jacob and Mary Marshall, born November 12, 175–.

Aaron Marshall, the son of Jacob Marshall and Mary Marshall, was born 7 July, 1758.

29 December, 1757, Elizabeth Davis was born, the daughter of Samuel and Elizabeth Davis. And departed this life 10 July 1828, aged seventy years and six months and twelve days; was married to Aaron Marshall Senr on the seventeenth day of February, 1780.

Jacob Marshall, the son of Aaron Marshall and Elizabeth Marshall, was born 27 December 1780, at 15 minutes apast 1 o'clock in the morning.

Samuel Marshall, the son of Aaron Marshall and Elizabeth Marshall was born November the . . . th day, 1782, about 6 o'clock in the morning.

Moses Marshall, the son of Aaron Marshall and Elizabeth Marshall, was born the 15th day of November, 1784, on Friday, about 11 o'clock in the morning.

Martha Marshall, the daughter of Aaron Marshall and Elizabeth Marshall, was born the 29 day of August 1786, about 11 o'clock in the morning.

16 November, 1788, was born Mary Marshall, the daughter of Aaron Marshall and Elizabeth Marshall.

30 December, 1790, was born Aaron Marshall, the son of Aaron Marshall and Elizabeth Marshall, on Thursday about 7 o'clock in the morning.

20 April, 1793, was born Davis Marshall, the son of Aaron Marshall and Elizabeth Marshall, on Saturday night, about 10 o'clock.

22 February, 1796, was born Hester Marshall, the daughter of Aaron Marshall and Elizabeth Marshall.

15 August, 1796, Hester Marshall, the daughter of Aaron Marshall and Elizabeth Marshall, departed this life.

29 August, 1797, was born Isaac Marshall, the son of Aaron Marshall and Elizabeth Marshall, and departed this life in one month and one night after.

22 October, 1798, was born Elizabeth Marshall, the daughter of Aaron Marshall and Elizabeth Marshall, and departed this life three weeks after.

Jacob Marshall, the son of Aaron Marshall and Elizabeth Marshall, departed this life the 1st day of September, 1800.

Jacob Marshall, the son of Aaron Marshall and Elizabeth Marshall was born April 9th 1801, about 9 o'clock at night.

John Marshall, the son of Aaron Marshall and Elizabeth Marshall, was born November the seventh 1805, before breakfast.

Aaron Marshall Senr. died July 18th 1839, over 81 years old. Entered by his grand-son Samuel Marshall.

1 June, 1766, Abraham Marshall was born, the son or Isaac Marshall and Hannah Marshall.

William Marshall, the son of John Marshall and Elizabeth Marshall was born November, . . day, 1774, on Friday.

DELAWARE BIBLE RECORDS.—The following records have been copied from the Bible belonging to Mrs. Louisa Moarshall, Lewes, Delaware:

John Marshall son of Wm Marshall and Kitty his wife (Catherine Maull) b. 11–10–1802.

Eliza Rodney West daughter of William and Mary West b. 9–29–1806

Burton Marshall son of John and Eliza Marshall b–5–23–1824. at 3 P. M

William Marshall son of John and Eliza Marshall b. 7–5–1825, at midnight

Charles M. Marshall son of John and Eliza Marshall b–7–14–1826. at 7 A. M.

Helen Mar. Marshall daughter of John and Eliza Marshall b. 8–4–1829, at 7 P. M.

Elizabeth R. Marshall daughter of John and Eliza Marshall b. 6–2–1843

George Herbert de Orton b. 9–25–1874

Edgar Marshall de Orton b. 8–24–1877

William West, father of Eliza Rodney West, b. 10–15–1771 d. 12–1–1816

Mary, wife of Wm West and mother of Eliza R. West, b 7–30–1776 d 4. 28–1845

John Marshall was married to Elizabeth Rodney West, Sept. 3^d 1823 by John Finley. Departed this life 3–8–1868

William Marshall, the father of John Marshall, was born 11–4–1774. d 6–21–1850, ¼ past 10 P. M.

John Marshall son of John Marshall and Eliza Rodney his wife. b. 1–1–1831. 4 P. M., Married Lizzie P. Morris 1–26–1853

Catherine M. Maull wife of Wm Marshall d. 11–27–1874, aged 95 years

James W. Marshall son of John and Eliza Marshall was b–11–13–1832. at 11 P. M.

Elizabeth Marshall daughter of John and Eliza Marshall b. 8–6–1834, at 6 P. M

William Marshall son of John and Eliza R. Marshall b. 4–26–1836 at 12 P. M. d–3–2–1866

David A. son of John and Eliza R. Marshall b. 9–28–1838.

Frances Almira Boggs Marshall daughter of John and Eliza Marshall b 12–5–1840, at 1 A. M. d. 11–15–1845

Burton Marshall son of John and Eliza R. Marshall d. 8–17. aged 2 months and 25 days

William Marshall son of John and Eliza R. Marshall d. 9–5 aged 2 months

Elizabeth daughter of John and Eliza R. Marshall d–7–31—aged 11 months, 25 days

Elizabeth R. de Orton daughter of John and Eliza Marshall d. 1–27–1880 at 6 P. M.

George de Orton (her husband) d. 8–16–1880

Eliza Rodney Marshall d. 7–22–1882 in the 76th year of her age

Helen Mar. Marshall d–11–9–1851.

"Elizabeth Rodney youngest daughter of the late Hon. John Marshall and beloved wife of George de Orton"

(Newspaper cutting pasted in Bible.)

SKETCH OF COLONEL EPHRAIM MARTIN, OF THE NEW JERSEY CONTINENTAL LINE.

COLONEL EPHRAIM MARTIN was born in Central New Jersey, probably in Somerset or Middlesex County in the year 1733, and died at New Brunswick, New Jersey, at the home of his son, Squire Martin, February 28, 1806, in his 73rd year. He was buried at Stelton, New Jersey, in the old Baptist Cemetery, where the tombstone is still standing with the date of his death and the year of his age inscribed on it.

Ephraim Martin was one of the early settlers in Sussex County, New Jersey, and was a landholder there in Newton township in the year 1761. He was appointed Coroner of Sussex County at the Council held at Burlington, New Jersey, February 21, 1774; he was a member of the Committee of Safety of Sussex County, organized at the outbreak of the Revolution, and was appointed leader of a company "to set right certain Tories" in that neighborhood.

At the outbreak of hostilities, he raised a regiment of militia in and about Sparta, which was known as the Second Establishment of State Militia.

He was chosen Member from Sussex County to the Provincial Congress at Trenton, October 20, 1775; also of the Congress which met in May, 1776. This was the Congress which changed the constitution of New Jersey from that of a colony to that of a state.

He was Colonel of a battalion of the State Militia ordered to reinforce the defences of New York early in 1776. Anthony Wayne's Orderly Book, under the date of April 6, 1776, headquarters New York, notes that Colonel Martin's regiment was assigned to the Brigade of Lord Sterling. (See PENNSYLVANIA MAGAZINE OF HISTORY AND BIOGRAPHY.)

Ephraim Martin was commissioned by the State of New Jersey on June 14, 1776, as Colonel of a regiment of New

Jersey Militia in General Nathaniel Heard's Brigade. He was described as of Sparta, Sussex County, New Jersey.

He was wounded August 24, 1776, by a musket ball in the breast, at the outposts previous to the battle of Long Island, which occurred August 27, 1776; he doubtless accompanied Washington in his retreat from the Island across New Jersey in the autumn of 1776.

On November 28, 1776, he was appointed, by the State of New Jersey, Colonel of the Fourth Battalion in the Second Establishment of the New Jersey Continental Line. This establishment was not fully completed with its full quota of officers in General Maxwell's Brigade until February 17, 1777.

In the meantime, Colonel Martin's regiment continued as a part of General Nathaniel Heard's Brigade of New Jersey Militia. As such it took part in the operation around Trenton, December 25, 1776, though the Brigade failed to get across the Delaware in time to take part in the actual fighting, being stationed opposite Trenton in order to keep the Hessians from crossing the river into Pennsylvania.

His regiment took part in the Battle of Princeton, January 5, 1777, and followed Washington into camp at Morristown; and it also took part in the skirmish at Elizabethtown Farms, where his son Absolom, who was his paymaster, had his arm broken.

In the Orderly Book of Major William Heth (see Virginia Historical Collections, Vol. X, New Series, 1891, page 365) it is noted that Colonel Martin was field officer for the day on June 21, 1777, at Camp Middlebrook.

In Maxwell's Brigade Colonel Ephraim Martin's regiment followed Washington in his march to the Brandywine, where it was the first to meet the enemy at Iron Hill in Pencader Hundred, Delaware, and he was wounded at the battle of the Brandywine. "He wore a cocked hat and barely escaped death, having been struck in the forehead by a passing bullet which only grazed it but stunned him, cutting through the hat and making a furrow in his forehead." (See Martin Genealogy, p. 315.)

He was probably at the attack on the Chew House in the battle of Germantown, but he was certainly with Washington at Valley Forge during the winter of 1777-78. In the Valley Forge Orderly Book, of General George Weedon, it is noted that on the 16th of October, 1777, headquarters Worcester Township, Colonel Martin, of Jersey, is in the list of field officers for the day. A similar mention of Colonel Martin as field officer for the day occurs under the date of May 14, 1778.

The Muster Rolls of the Continental Army, by William Bradford Junior, preserved in the collection of the Historical Society of Pennsylvania, show the name of Ephraim Martin as Colonel of the Fourth New Jersey Regiment in the abstracts for July, 1778, again for October, 1778, and still again for January, 1779.

The records of the New Jersey office show that Colonel Ephraim Martin's regiment accompanied Washington across Jersey in 1778. He was stationed in the reserve at Princeton on occasion of the battle of Monmouth, June 28, 1778. He was still in the service in November, 1779.

New Jersey asked in this year that the Continental Congress should reduce its quota from four regiments to three with a corresponding reduction in men and officers. The Congress agreed to this and appointed a committee to carry through this reduction. The Legislature of New Jersey on September 26, 1780, approved the arrangement made by Congress for this reduction and Ephraim Martin as the supernumerary Colonel resigned from the service after serving for nearly six years, if we count from his first raising of a militia regiment.

Ephraim Martin removed to Somerset County and entered the Upper House of the New Jersey Legislature as representative from that county, where with some interruptions he continued to sit until his death, in 1806. He had several brothers; three sons; and many nephews in the Revolutionary Army, and played in the field and in the cabinet an important part in the life of his state for a quarter of a century.

In Somerset County he lived in Bernardstown; was a member of the old Baptist church at Mount Bethel, in which he was elected deacon June 21, 1786.

His son Ephraim, Junior, was born in 1760, at Sparta, Sussex County, New Jersey; enlisted in his father's regiment in September, 1777, and served throughout the war. In 1789 he removed to Mecklinberg County, North Carolina, and later to Campbell County, Georgia, where he died, in 1840.

Martha Martin, daughter of Ephraim Martin, Junior, and Mercy Alward, was born May 18, 1779, and married Samuel Stites of Somerset County, New Jersey, September 14, 1794.

Their daughter, Anna Stites, was born December 10, 1796. She married Anthony Wayne Casad of Fairfield, Ohio, later of Lebanon, Illinois, February 6, 1811.

Their daughter, Amanda Keziah Casad, was born at Lebanon, Illinois, August 18, 1827, and married Colin D. James November 27, 1850.

Their living children are as follows:

1. Edmund Jones James, b. Jacksonville, Illinois, May 21, 1855; for thirteen years Professor in the University of Pennsylvania; for the past six years President of the University of Illinois.

2. Ella Amanda, b. Jacksonville, Illinois, April 10, 1857, m. (1) Edwin J. Bickell, (2) Temple R. Noel.

3. Benjamin Brown, b. July 4, 1860, at Island Grove, Illinois, now Professor of Physics, Milliken University, Decatur, Illinois.

4. John Nelson, b. April 15, 1865, Normal, Illinois. Teacher in the Pennsylvania State Normal School, Indiana, Pennsylvania.

5. George Francis, b. Aug. 18, 1867, Normal, Illinois; at one time lecturer in the University of Pennsylvania; now Dean of the College of Education, University of Minnesota.

6. Clara Belle, b. at Normal, Illinois, April 12, 1871, m. Cheeseman A. Herrick, President of Girard College, Philadelphia.

SOME ADDITIONAL INFORMATION
Concerning
EPHRAIM MARTIN, ESQUIRE, COLONEL OF THE FOURTH NEW JERSEY REGIMENT
OF
THE CONTINENTAL LINE.[1]

BY EDMUND J. JAMES.

In the Historical Register of the Officers of the Continental Army published by F. B. Heitman, Washington, D. C., 1893, the statement is made on page 39 that Colonel Ephraim Martin, commissioned November 28, 1776, never joined his regiment. Heitman further says, that the rolls of this regiment are very incomplete and that it was broken up about July, 1778. In the alphabetical list in the same book, under Martin, page 286, the following statement is found: "Ephraim Martin was colonel of a New Jersey regiment on the 14th day of July, 1776; was wounded at the battle of Long Island August 27, 1776; appointed colonel of the fourth New Jersey regiment November 28, 1776, but never joined the regiment."

This is a good illustration of the inaccuracy of many of Heitman's statements. An inaccuracy which, in this case, he could easily have corrected if he had taken the trouble to drop a note of inquiry to the office of the Adjutant General of New Jersey, or if he had consulted the roster rolls of the Continental Army, by William Bradford, Jr., which show that Ephraim Martin was colonel of the fourth New Jersey regiment for the months of July

---

[1] See sketch of Colonel Ephraim Martin of the New Jersey Continental line in the PENNSYLVANIA MAGAZINE OF HISTORY AND BIOGRAPHY for October, 1910, page 480 and following. *

*(For p. 480 see p. 494, this volume.)

and October, 1778, and for January, 1779, for which months the abstracts have been preserved.[2]

The facts concerning Ephraim Martin's military record, so far as they are contained in the files of the Adjutant General's office at Trenton, New Jersey, have already been given in the article published in a previous number of this Magazine referred to above.

It appears from this record that Martin was in command of his regiment with Washington's army during the years of 1777 and 1778 and part of 1779 at any rate. He was in the battle of Princeton, 1777; at Morristown; at the battle of the Brandywine, where he was wounded; at Germantown; at Valley Forge; at Monmouth; and, in general, as a constituent, first of Heard's and then of Maxwell's brigade, his regiment took part in all the important movements of Washington's army from the middle of 1776 through the years 1777 and 1778, being stationed at Princeton in November and December, 1778.

The legislature of the state of New Jersey, in 1778, petitioned Congress to reduce the quota of New Jersey from four regiments to three, on the ground that four regiments were more than New Jersey's share.

Congress accepted this view, as will be seen by the following report of a committee, to whom was referred the representation of the state of New Jersey, praying a reduction of their quota.

"The committee to whom was referred the representation of the state of New Jersey beg leave to report:

"That having considered the same, it appears to your committee that so much of the representation as relates to the supporting that state with a body of Continental troops is properly cognizable by, and ought to be submitted to, his Excellency, the Commander-in-Chief. And as to that part of the representation praying a reduction of their quota we beg leave to submit the following resolution.

---

[2] These roster rolls are preserved in the library of the Historical Society of Pennsylvania, at Philadelphia.

"Resolved, That the state of New Jersey be requested to complete only three regiments of infantry in the manner recommended by the resolutions of the 26th day of February last, and that the committee of Congress lately at camp, do arrange the officers of the said state accordingly."[3]

On March 9, 1779, Congress called for eighty battalions of infantry, of which New Jersey was to furnish three, to be organized in accordance with the action referred to in the above report taken by Congress on May 27, 1778.

It appears that the fourth New Jersey regiment of the Continental Line was broken up in February, 1779, or shortly thereafter[4] and certain officers were declared supernumerary.

I have not been able to find out who actually undertook this rearrangement, whether a committee of the New Jersey legislature, or a committee of Congress. It was presumably the latter, for on Monday, April 26, 1779, there was presented and read to the legislature of New Jersey a

"Memorial and Remonstrance of Sundry Officers of the New Jersey Brigade left out as supernumerary in a late arrangement of the said brigade, setting forth that they have been illegally deprived while new officers have been made, and praying redress of such grievances."

This Memorial was read a second time April 27, 1779, and referred to a committee of conference. This committee made a report on April 29th and it was resolved that a remonstrance should be made to Congress upon the

---

[3] See Papers of the Continental Congress, 20, I, Folio 315, in the Library of Congress.

[4] Although the state did not take definite action providing for three regiments until June 9, 1779. The arrangement of officers in these regiments evidently continued to make trouble, as the Congress of the United States appointed a committee in the summer of 1780 to make an arrangement for the officers of the first, second and third regiments of the New Jersey Line, which arrangement was approved by the New Jersey legislature September 26, 1780.

practice of appointing officers without the participation of the authority of the state.

Seemingly, however, nothing came of this remonstrance. From this time on, all references are to "the *three* regiments of this state in the service of the United States," instead of the *four* as hitherto. Various references are to be found in the acts of the legislature of New Jersey to the "late arrangement" by which the four regiments were reduced to three. Thus on April 30 a resolution was passed that the sum of 200 pounds be paid for "cloatheing," to each officer, who at the time when the "late arrangement" of the Brigade in this State in the service of the United States was made, did belong, or for one year previous thereto, had belonged to the said Brigade.

Presumably Ephraim Martin was declared "supernumerary" in this "late arrangement," although I have not been able to find any definite statement to this effect. He may have resigned from the service altogether, though the Adjutant General's office at Trenton wrote me that Ephraim Martin was "Super-numerary from February 11, 1779, until the close of the war."

If this is correct, and it is so presumably, Martin was in the Continental army from the time of his commission November 28, 1776, until February 11, 1779, a little over two years and two months.

He had been in active service, however, for a little more than one year and four months before in the State troops and State militia.

In the library of the New Jersey Historical Society at Newark, in a volume entitled "Provincial Congress Papers, 1776," there is an unpublished paper numbered 126 containing the following information.

"July 26, 1775. The officers chosen in the towns of Upper Hardwick, Newtown, Wantage, and Hardiston, agreeably to the direction of the Provincial Congress, met by appointment at the house of Ephraim Martin to chuse field officers."

Then follows the list of captains, the first and second lieutenants and ensigns for thirteen companies.[5]

And the further statement that the following field officers were chosen:

    Ephraim Martin, Colonel;
    Daniel Harker, Lieutenant-Colonel;
    John B. Scott, Major;
    Aaron Hankinson, Second Major.

It will thus be seen that Martin's official connection with the Revolutionary Army began July 26, 1775, as colonel of the second Sussex County regiment of militia.

According to another paper, numbered 125 in the same volume, the first Sussex regiment had been organized four days before, that is, July 22, at the home of Abram McKinney by the election of William Maxwell as colonel.

That Martin was not idle in his new office is evident from the following extract from *Holt's Journal* of December 28, 1775:

"December 26. This morning about four hundred of the militia of Sussex County, New Jersey, under the command of Colonel Ephraim Martin and Marsh Thompson assembled in Newtown and from thence proceeded in good order and regularly in quest of tories, a considerable number of whom, inhabitants of that county, had entered into a combination and agreement not to comply with any congressional measures. We hear about forty are taken, most of whom have recanted, signed the association, and professed themselves sons of liberty, being fully convinced of their error. Two or three who remained incorrigible are to be presented to the Congress to be dealt with."

When, on June 3, 1776, Congress called on New Jersey for 3300 troops to reinforce the army in and about New

---

[5] These officers had already been chosen by the respective companies, in accordance with a law of the state of New Jersey, of June 3, 1775, providing that one or more companies should be raised in each township which should choose their own officers. These companies were to be grouped into regiments and the company officers of such regiments when organized were to choose the field officers of the same.

York, the state of New Jersey ordered out, June 14, 1776, five battalions of eight companies each, under Brigadier General Heard for this service. Colonel Ephraim Martin was in command of one of these battalions, consisting of four companies from Morris County and four from Sussex County, and they took part in the operations on Long Island, where Ephraim Martin was wounded in the breast at an outpost on the day before the battle of Long Island. He had already received his commission as colonel in the state troops of New Jersey, dated June 14, 1776.

When Congress in 1776 called for eighty-eight battalions of infantry and assigned four battalions as New Jersey's share, the State decided to recruit three of the battalions from the State regiments which had already been sent to the north of Albany and to recruit the fourth battalion from Heard's brigade at New York.[6]

Of this fourth battalion Ephraim Martin was appointed colonel and received his commission as of November 28, 1776. He resigned his commission in the State troops when he entered the Continental Line.

At some time during the war Martin removed his residence from Sussex County to Somerset County; possibly while the army was encamped about Morristown. Mrs. Colonel Martin seems to have bestirred herself also in behalf of the American cause as appears from the following extract from the *Pennsylvania Packet* of July 8, 1780:

"July 4, 1780.—The ladies of Trenton are promoting a subscription for the relief and encouragement of those brave men of the Continental army, etc." The committee consisted of ladies in the various counties. The following were from Somerset County:

> Lady Stirling,
> Mrs. General Morris,
> Mrs. Colonel Martin,
> Mrs. Attorney General Pattison,
> Mrs. R. Stockton.

Compare Notes, etc., of the General Assembly of New Jersey, September 30, 1776.

Martin did not long remain out of the service of the state. He was elected a member of the Council, *i.e.*, the upper house of the New Jersey legislature, for Somerset County, on October 12, 1779, and was present, as the minutes show, during the session which began October 26th of that year. He was a member of the Council from Somerset for ten years continuously, from 1781 to 1790.

He moved later to New Brunswick and represented Middlesex County in the Council in the years 1795, 1797 and 1800 to 1805, inclusive. He had been, it will be remembered, a member of the Provincial Congress in 1775 and in 1776 from Sussex County. He thus had the honor of representing three separate counties in the State legislature for an aggregate period of more than twenty years, at a time when it was an honor to be a member of the legislature.

While in Somerset County he lived in Bernardstown and was a member of the old Mt. Bethel Baptist church, where he was elected deacon in 1786. He joined the Baptist church of Piscataway, established in 1689, and located at Stelton, two and one-half miles east of New Brunswick, on May 27, 1795, by letter from the Mt. Bethel Baptist church. This probably indicates very closely the time at which he changed his residence from Somerset County to Middlesex County. It is noteworthy that if he moved to New Brunswick in 1795 he was immediately elected the delegate from Middlesex County in the State Council.

When Ephraim Martin died, on February 28, 1806, in the seventy-third year of his age, the following note appeared in the *New Jersey Journal*, published at Elizabethtown in the issue for March 11, 1806:

"DIED.

"On Friday morning last, Ephraim Martin, Esquire, a leading member of the legislative Council of this state, after a long and painful illness, in the seventy-third year of his age."

The following is extracted from a sermon on the occasion of his death:

"For several years he served his country on the tented field and in the public councils with faithfulness and to the best of his abilities, as none who knew him will doubt, for which his memory is deservedly cherished by all.

"As a citizen and a neighbor he was peaceable, just and benevolent, and duly exemplary in his deportment. When among his neighbors it was his delight to converse on the subject of religion. When at home he trained his family with a pious care and conversed much with his Bible and his God."

Ephraim Martin left a will dated October 24, 1805, with a codicil of November 21, of the same year, disposing of considerable property. The will is on file in the Surrogate's office, New Brunswick, New Jersey, Book A, page 146. In this he mentions sons: Squire, Absalom, Jeremiah and Ephraim; grandchildren: Ephraim, son of Squire and "seven other children of Squire;" Ebenezer and Martin, children of Absalom; Abner, Jeremiah and Susannah, children of Jeremiah; Ocey, Ephraim and Patty (wife of Samuel Stites), Polly, wife of Cutter, and Elizabeth, all children of Ephraim; and Katherine Kennan, niece of his wife, to whom he leaves certain property, on account of her care of him and his wife during their illness. He does not mention his wife otherwise in the will.

His wife must have died before him, though her headstone in the old Piscataway town cemetery connected with the St. John's Protestant Episcopal church in Piscataway, on the road from New Brunswick to Woodbridge, two or three miles from the former place, shows her death later. The stone, which is still standing, contains the following inscription:

"IN MEMORY OF KATHERINE, WIFE OF COLONEL EPHRAIM MARTIN, WHO DEPARTED THIS LIFE OCTOBER 5, 1806, IN THE SEVENTY-SECOND YEAR OF HER AGE.

FORBEAR, MY FRIENDS, YOUR FOND COMPLAINT,
YOU HAVE NO CAUSE FOR TO LAMENT;
FOR CHRIST, MY SAVIOR, SUMMONS ME
AT HIS COMMAND I MUST OBEY."

It is somewhat peculiar that she was buried in one cemetery and he in another, not far away. His body lies in the Baptist cemetery at the old Piscataway Baptist church, located at Stelton, two and one-half miles east of the court-house in New Brunswick. It contains the following inscription:

"IN MEMORY OF COLONEL EPHRAIM MARTIN WHO DEPARTED THIS LIFE THE 28TH DAY OF FEBRUARY, 1806, IN THE SEVENTY-THIRD YEAR OF HIS AGE.
FAREWELL, VAIN WORLD, I AM GOING HOME
MY SAVIOR SMILES AND BIDS ME COME,
WHILE ANGELS BECKON ME AWAY
TO SING GOD'S PRAISE IN ENDLESS DAY."

It is of interest to note that Sussex County was greatly stirred on behalf of the cause of the colonists, although it was still a new and only partially settled region. It furnished more than its quota of men to the militia, state, and continental troops, though it was far removed from the scene of conflict. This was doubtless owing to the activity of men like Maxwell and Martin, who seemed to be indefatigable in recruiting men.

A diligent search was made in Sussex County, as in other counties of the state, for materials for munitions of war. A note is made in one of the newspapers of the time of the discovery of "a supply of flint exceeding promising, on a hill near Colonel Martin's and the brook called Beaver Run in Sussex." The Sharpsborough Iron Works were not far from Colonel Martin's farm;[7] and were important enough, as a possible source of supply, to lead the New Jersey legislature to exempt the workmen from military duty by law of October 10, 1777.

Martin seems to have had his full share of trouble and difficulty in keeping his regiment fully manned. Many men deserted for the sake of enlisting in other regiments in order to obtain the bounty, and patriots who disdained to accept bribes from the British commanders did not hesitate to desert from the northern army and enlist in

---

[7] See advertisement of "a farm for sale one mile from Sharpsborough Iron Works in Sussex County and an equal distance from Colonel Ephraim Martin's estate in Hardiston." *Pennsylvania Journal*, June 19, 1776.

the southern, or vice versa, for the sake of the emolument.

Martin advertised in the *Pennsylvania Journal* of February 19, 1777, for the return of deserters from the fourth New Jersey battalion under his command who had left the regiment on or about December 15, 1776. Again in the *Pennsylvania Gazette*, for February 19th and March 12th, 1777, for deserters who had left his regiment stationed at Morristown about February 1, 1777; a similar advertisement for deserters at Salem May 13, 1777, and finally in the *New Jersey Gazette* for December 2, 1778, and in a later issue of 1779, for troops who had left his headquarters at Princeton on or about November 20, 1778.

Colonel Ephraim Martin was not the only one of his family in the Revolutionary War. His son Absalom was paymaster in his father's regiment, having been commissioned in the Continental line on the same date as his father, November 28, 1776. He had his arm broken in a fight at Elizabethtown. When the arrangement was made by which the four New Jersey regiments of the Continental line were consolidated into three, Absalom entered the first regiment as lieutenant, and was later promoted to a captaincy. He served until the close of the war and had been in the militia before he entered the Continental line.

Colonel Ephraim Martin's third son, Ephraim, Jr., served almost continuously in the militia in which he became first sergeant. In his application for a pension, file No. 31, 840, in the pension rolls of the Revolutionary War, in the War Department, at Washington, Ephraim Martin stated that he was of Sussex County, New Jersey, aged seventy-two years, his application being dated 1832; that he had enlisted September, 1777, at the age of seventeen under Captain Beckwith; then one month under Captain McCoy in the regiment of Colonel Freelinghausen and Major Davidson, and was stationed at Elizabethtown to guard the stores. He then enlisted in the company of Minute men under Captain McCoy and was appointed first sergeant, fought at Connecticut Farms, where Mrs. Caldwell was murdered, was in the skirmish with the British at Springfield on their retreat to Staten Island about June 1, 1780. Volunteered again in the company of Captain Manning, under Colonel Webster, and stationed in Middlesex County. Had a brother Absalom Martin, who was wounded at Elizabethtown; had a brother Squire Martin living at New Brunswick, New Jersey. He stated further that he was born in September, 1760, in Sussex County, was the third son of Colonel Ephraim Martin of the New Jersey Line, who afterwards removed to Somerset County. That in 1789, he, Ephraim, Jr., had moved to Mecklinburg County, North Carolina, and afterwards to Campbell County, Georgia.

The name of Squire Martin (another son of Colonel Martin) does not appear, so far as I can ascertain, in the list of the New Jersey militia or line in the Adjutant General's office at Trenton. But Sergeant John Martin, of Piscataway, Middlesex County, New Jersey, in his application for a pension states that he enlisted in June, 1776, in Middlesex County, New Jersey, for five months under Captain John Webster and Lieutenant Squire Martin in the regiment of Colonel Forman sent to New York. If this is correct, and this is the Squire Martin mentioned in Ephraim's will, Ephraim Martin, Sr., had three sons in the Revolutionary War.

In Paper No. 126 of the Provincial Congress Papers, above referred to, it is stated that Edmond Martin was captain of a company from Hardiston and John Martin was first lieutenant of another company from the same place. This, it will be remembered, was the home of Colonel Ephraim Martin also, who was elected Colonel of the Second Sussex regiment at the meeting at his house on July 26, 1775. In Paper 229, of the same volume, it is stated that Captain Isaac Martin was elected Major in the Second Sussex regiment.

What relation these three parties were to Colonel

Ephraim does not appear from the records of this meeting, but some light is thrown upon the fact from another Revolutionary pension record.

Reuben Martin, of Wayne County, Ohio, applied for a pension in 1834 at the age of eighty-five years. He speaks of serving in Sussex County in the company of his brother, Captain John Martin, commanded by another brother, Colonel Edmond Martin; was under this Colonel Martin in the battle of the Brandywine, where he was wounded and at Germantown, and was at Middle Brook May 10, 1778, under the same brother. He states that there were two brothers Martin in Washington's army, both colonels, one was Edmond.

Reuben's memory had evidently served him here a trick. There were indeed two colonel Martins in Washington's army during a portion of the Jersey campaigns, and at the battle of the Brandywine,—*viz.*, Ephraim Martin of New Jersey, who was wounded, and Alexander Martin of North Carolina, who was subsequently tried by court-martial for cowardice at this battle, but was acquitted.[8]

He was probably a cousin of Ephraim Martin.

Edmond Martin was later (1780) a member of the legislature from Sussex County, but does not figure in the army rolls except as captain of a company of Sussex County militia.

If Reuben's memory as to relationships was otherwise correct, it would appear that Ephraim, Edmond, John and Reuben were brothers, and of these the first three were officers in the second Sussex County of militia, and

---

[8] This Alexander Martin of North Carolina was Lieutenant Colonel of the second North Carolina regiment September 1, 1775; was appointed colonel May 7, 1776; was court-martialed October 30, 1777, for cowardice at the battle of the Brandywine; although he was acquitted he resigned from the service November 22d and returned to his native state. He later became governor of North Carolina and a member from that state in the United States Senate.

the fourth served four campaigns, 1777, 1778, 1779 and 1780, much of the time under his brother, Colonel Ephraim. He was sixteen years younger than the colonel.

As there were many other Martins in the Revolutionary forces, militia, state and line from Sussex, Somerset and Middlesex, it is quite possible that Colonel Ephraim Martin had many nephews and cousins in one and another of the New Jersey regiments, but the military records, so far as I know, do not give further information on this point. A Jacob Martin was captain in the fourth New Jersey continental line, commissioned November 28, 1776.

There are a few other references to Colonel Ephraim Martin which have come under my eye.

In Paper No. 128 of the Provincial Congress Papers, above referred to, under date of October 28, 1775, Ephraim Martin unites with William Maxwell in recommending certain persons in Sussex County to the Provincial Congress for commissions in the New Jersey militia.

In the *Pennsylvania Journal*, of March 19th, is a letter from Haddonfield, dated March 17, 1777, concerning an engagement which had occurred on March the 8th, which runs partly as follows:

"March 9.—Yesterday the British, supposed to be about three thousand strong, came out from Amboy and posted themselves on Punk Hill. They brought artillery and a number of wagons. They met near Carman's Hill and Woodbridge. Colonel Martin was sent by General Maxwell to the support of the Americans."

In the first report of the Cincinnati Society, of New Jersey, with the by-laws and rules of the Society, published at Trenton, New Jersey, 1808, is to be found a list of the field officers, captains and staffs of the New Jersey line, as organized in November, 1776, and February, 1777, comprising the Jersey brigade in command of Brigadier General Maxwell. Ephraim Martin is given as commander of the fourth regiment, and on page 9 of the same book he is mentioned as among those who received wounds during the Revolution.

Colonel Ephraim Martin's name appears in various deeds on file in Somerset and Middlesex Counties,—one at Somerville (Deed Book B, 471), dated December 17, 1800, of lands to "Colonel Ephraim Martin of the County of Middlesex;" a second deed of these same lands, dated March 5, 1801 (Deed Book B, 593), from Ephraim Martin and Katherine, his wife, of Middlesex, to Rune Runyon. Land was surveyed in Sussex County to Ephraim Martin December 26, 1761, in Hardiston Township of Sussex County, March 1st, 1785, and June 22, 1785. Lands in the same township of Hardiston were also surveyed for Edmond Martin about the same time. Edmond Martin of the County of Sussex, deeded on April 3, 1771, to David Newman lands situated in Hardiston on both sides a brook called Beaver Run (recorded in the city of Perth Amboy, Book A. B. No. 6, page 152).

Ephraim Martin, junior, probably the same person as Colonel Ephraim Martin, was a member of the grand jury in Sussex County in the year 1767.

Luther Martin of Maryland was probably a relative of Colonel Ephraim Martin.

The ancestry of Colonel Ephraim Martin is, in my opinion, not definitely known, but the following is given by one of our most careful genealogists as probable. Indeed, he considers it as reasonably well established. It will be noted, however, that the list does not include any of the brothers named by Reuben in the pension application noted above, except Ephraim, and it is quite possible that Colonel Ephraim and his brothers were children of Edmond, son of James, son of Joseph, son of John, one of the original associates in the Piscataway purchase at Woodbridge; possibly some one of the readers of this Magazine may possess accurate information on this point.

Genealogy of Colonel Ephraim Martin.

1. John Martin — Born 1620, died July 5, 1687 (was at Dover, N. H. 1648), came to N. J. as original settler in 1666, taking grants with Woodbridge settlers; colonized Piscataway Township.
Married, 1646, Esther Roberts, born 1628, died Dec. 6, 1687; daughter of Thomas Roberts, Governor of N. H.

Children:
 I. John, will May 25, 1703
 II. Mary—b. 1649; d. after 1696; m. Hopencee Hull
 III. Martha
 IV. Lydia
 V. Joseph
 VI. Benjamin
 VII. Thomas
 VIII. James

2. Joseph² (John¹) — Born 1657, died 1723; constable in 1690. Married, Nov. 25, 1697, Sarah Trotter, died after 1700, daughter of William Trotter, d. 1687, and his wife Catherine Gibbs

Children:
 I. James
 II. Joseph
 III. Abigail
 IV. David
 V. Joshua
 VI. Moses

3. James³ (Joseph,² John¹) — Born Dec. 14, 1680, died after 1721; married, Sept. 4, 1701, Hannah Smith, daughter of John Smith of Woodbridge, N. J.

Children:	I. Edmund—b. Mar. 21, 1701 II. William—b. Mar. 21, 1701 Twins III. Abigail—b. Jan. 14, 1703 IV. James, b. Nov. 8, 1705 V. Ephraim, b. Jan. 25, 1708 VI. Hannah, b. Jan. 13, 1711 VII. Anna, b. Jan. 4, 1714 VIII. Grace, b. May 6, 1717 IX. Rosanna, b. April 29, 1719 X. Rosanna, b. Mar. 22, 1721
4. Ephraim[4] (James,[3] Joseph,[2] John[1])	Born Jan. 25, 1708, died 1771; married about 1730 Keziah Runyon, born 1713
Children:	I. Jeremiah, b. 1731, d. 1804; married 1752–3 Elizabeth Person Caldwell II. Ephraim (Colonel) III. Humphrey, b. 1735, d. 1805; married Experience Piatt, 1756 IV. Nathaniel, b, 1736–7; married 1756–8 Mary Clarkson
5. Ephraim[5] (Ephraim,[4] James,[3] Joseph,[2] John[1])	Born in Middlesex County, 1733, died in New Brunswick Feb. 28, 1806; married Catherine
Children:	I. Squire II. Absalom III. Jeremiah IV. Ephraim
6. Ephraim[6] (Ephraim,[5] Ephraim,[4] James,[3] Joseph,[2] John[1])	Born in Sussex County, Sept., 1760, died in Campbell County, Georgia, 1840. Served in the Revolutionary War. Married Mercy Alward

Children: I. Ocey
    II. Ephraim
    III. Martha ("Patty"), b. May 18, 1779; m. Samuel Stites Sept. 14, 1794; d. Dec. 16, 1838
    IV. Polly
    V. Elizabeth (Cutler)

7. Martha Martin (Ephraim,⁶ Ephraim,⁵ Ephraim,⁴ James,³ Joseph,² John¹)

Married Samuel Stites

Children:
    I. Keziah, b. April 2, 1795; d. Jan. 19, 1829; m. July 4, 1813, John Brake. Lived near Trenton, Illinois
    II. Anna, b. Dec. 10, 1796; d. 16th of July, 1838; m. 6th of Feb., 1811, Anthony W. Casad°
    III. Mary, b. 5th of Jan., 1799; m. 5th of Jan., 1817, William Lewis
    IV. Mercy, b. 28th of Apr., 1801; d. Nov., 1808
    V. Sarah, b. 12th of Feb., 1803; d. 7th of Mar., 1805
    VI. Ephraim M., b. Jan., 1805; d. Dec., 1805
    VII. Squire M., m. Abigail Cravens 23d Apr., 1826
    VIII. John, b. 16th of Oct., 1808; d. 1846, Ridge Prairie, Ill.; m., 1828, Katherine Mace
    IX. Martin, b. 8th Jan., 1811; m. 1830, Scott, who was born June 6, 1810; d. May 16, 1869; lived at Ridge Prairie, Ill., both died in Minn.

° See page 483 PENNSYLVANIA MAGAZINE OF HISTORY AND BIOGRAPHY, October, 1910. (For p. 483 see p. 497, this volume.)

X. Charlotte, b. July 22, 1813; d. Dec. 18, 1813

XI. Isaac, b. Dec. 19, 1814; m. Martha Thompson; lived in St. Clair Co., Ill.

XII. Indiana, b. June 9, 1817; m. Reuben Rutherford, Oct. 20, 1836; lived at Trenton, Ill.

XIII. Emma, b. 15th of Apr., 1820; m. 24th Sept., 1840, Ora M. Curtis, lived near Trenton, Ill.

XIV. Samuel, b. Mar. 23, 1823; d. 1835[10]

The Samuel Stites, referred to in the above genealogy as the son-in-law of Colonel Ephraim Martin, was born October 31, 1776, near Mt. Bethel, Somerset County, New Jersey, and died August 16, 1839, at Trenton, Illinois. He was the son of Anna Butler (born 1752, died January 27, 1824, daughter of Amos) and Isaac Stites of Mt. Bethel, Somerset County, New Jersey (born 1754, died 1830), who was the son of William Stites of the same place, born 1719, died 1810;[11] son of William Stites of Springfield, New Jersey, born at Hempstead, Long Island, 1676, died at Springfield, New Jersey, 1727, refers to himself in his will as "late of Long Island Colony"; son of Richard Stites, born 1640 in England, died in 1702 at Hempstead, Long Island; son of John Stites, surgeon, born in London, 1595, died in Hempstead, Long Island, 1717.

The last three items are based on the record in a family Bible which belonged to William Stites of Springfield, New Jersey, great-grandson of William Stites, senior (1676–1727). The age of John Stites, surgeon, is rather

[10] Compare statement of Littell "Early Settlers of the Passaic Valley."

[11] This William Stites is referred to by James Manning, President of Brown University, in his diary, as living at Dead River when he visited him in 1780.

remarkable, to say the least, and lends color to the supposition that he may stand for two generations.

I have not been able to trace the Stites family to any locality in England.

In the history of Long Island by Benjamin F. Thompson, New York, 1843, Volume II, in the footnote on pages 53 and 54, there is a statement that "Edmund Titus, born in England in 1630, came from Massachusetts to Long Island in 1650 in company with one William Stites, then upwards of one hundred years old, who, it is said, came on foot from Seekonk to this place, Hempstead, where he lived to the great age of one hundred and sixteen years."

The records of the town of Hempstead themselves contain numerous references to Richard Stites of Westbury, Hempstead, Long Island. This Richard Stites, according to statements made in deeds contained in the town records of Hempstead, had sons William, John, Benjamin and Henry. Henry Stites is mentioned in a deed made February 28, 1700, as of Cape May in the bounds of West Jersey.

This family was prominent in the localities in which they lived in New Jersey during the eighteenth century, and many of the references in the current genealogical lists to Stiles should be to Stites instead. John, who was born 1706, and died 1782, son of William Stites (born 1676, in Hempstead, Long Island, died 1727, Springfield, New Jersey), was mayor of Elizabethtown. His daughter, Margaret, was the wife of James Manning, first president of Brown University. John's nephew, Benjamin, junior, was the founder of Columbia, now a part of Cincinnati, and the family has played a prominent part in the pioneer life of New Jersey, Kentucky, Ohio and Illinois.

JAMES MILES AND SOME OF HIS DESCENDANTS.

BY THOMAS ALLEN GLENN.

The following brief account of James Miles of Llanfihangel Helygen (the Church of St. Michael by the Willows), Radnorshire, and some of his descendants, is based partly on notes furnished by the late Mr. George K. Miles, of Pittsburgh, and partly on data gathered by myself. In placing the results of his researches in my hands, Mr. Miles expressed his desire that the information should be printed. After consideration, I am of opinion that Mr. Miles' wishes can best be carried out by the inclusion of the material in the PENNSYLVANIA MAGAZINE. The Miles family is traceable for many generations in Llanfihangel Helygen, and neighbourhood, and, in the sixteenth century, was of considerable importance, and probably of Flemish descent.

Among that large number of Welsh emigrants who left their native shores in the last quarter of the seventeenth century to seek homes in the province of Pennsylvania, came James, Samuel (and Margaret his wife), Richard, Griffith, David and Ann Miles. James Miles, the father of Richard, Griffith, David, and Ann, was born in the parish of Llanfihangel Helygen,[1] Radnorshire, 1622. He had a deed, dated 19–20 June, 1682, for 100 acres of land to be surveyed to him in Pennsylvania. Authorities differ as to time of their arrival in America; but the following would seem conclusive:

(Pa. Arch. Sec. Ser. ed. 1893–Vol. XIX. p. 462) "Min-

---

[1] Llanfihangel Helygen, formerly written Llanvihangel Helygen, appears in Pennsylvania records concerning this family, including a Family Bible, in various forms.

utes of the Board of Property—of the Province of Pennsylvania." "Upon an Affid't made by Benjamin Chambers before a Justice that Sam'l Miles, who now appeared before ye Board, Came a Serv't into this Province to ye Society in the year 1682, [1683] 'tis ordered upon his h'ble Req't and Suit that a Warrant be granted him for his headland." (6 mo. 27, 1705.)

JAMES MILES brought a Certificate of Removal to the Philadelphia Monthly Meeting from the Redstone Monthly Meeting, held "in the Parish of Llanvihangell Helygen,"¹ Radnorshire, Wales, dated 5 mo. 27, 1683. It is not known whether his wife accompanied the party —nor her name. James was afterward baptized (as an adult) in the Baptist Church, as appears by the Pennepak records. Date of his death and place of burial unknown.

SAMUEL MILES, son of James, brought a Certificate of Removal to the Philadelphia Monthly Meeting, from Redstone Meeting, Radnorshire, Wales, dated 5 mo. 27, 1683. He married in Wales, 25th day of 4th mo., 1682, Margaret James (at the parish of New Church, in the house of Ann Thomas). He, and his wife (Margaret James, Spinster) were purchasers of land from Richard Davies, before emigrating to America. A Patent to Samuel confirming various lots, for 352 acres, bears date 5 mo. 6 day, 1705. Samuel and Margaret settled first in Philadelphia; but afterwards removed to Radnor. Their first-born daughter Thamer (called also Thamer James) b. 8 mo. 21—1687, was "the first white child born in Radnor." Samuel was baptized (records of the Seventh Day Baptist church of Providence) 6 mo. 9, 1698, and died, 1708. (Abstract of Will, PENNA. MAG. Vol. XV. p. 202). Will dated June 24, 1707; proved April 28, 1708, mentions as legatees: Wife (name not given), and children, Phebe, Tamar, Ruth, and two (not named), and testator's brother Richard. The widow was taxable in Radnor as late as 1715.

Children of Samuel and Margaret Miles were:
Tamar (Thamar, or James) b. 8 mo. 27 1687; d. mo. 27, 1770; m. 3 mo. 6, 1708, Thomas Thomas (son of William), Her dau. m. Nathan Lewis.
Phebe, b. 4 mo. 20, 1690; (rem. to Haverford); m. 2 mo. 13, 1715, Evan Evans.
Ruth, b. 1 mo. 28, 1693; d. prior to 1736; m. 11 mo. 3, 1715/16, Owen Evans.

RICHARD MILES, son of James, was a purchaser (in Wales) of land from Richard Davies, (deed dated June 19, 1682, 100 acres;—recorded in Phila., 1 mo. 12, 1684). He also held 49½ ft front on south side Chestnut Street, in 1683. In the above deed he is described as of parish of Llanvihangel Helygen, in the County of Radnor, weaver. He married (by Friends' Ceremony) 4 mo. 28, 1688, at the house of John Evans in Radnor, Sarah Evans. The Certificate designates him as "of ye township of Radnor, Taylor."

He was probably one of the Keithian Quakers, who later became Baptist. Richard and his wife were baptized, shortly before 1701, (by William Beckingham) in Upper Providence, and meetings were often held at his house. In June, 1706, a conference was held there by deputies from the Pennepak and Welsh Tract churches, to adjust some differences in ordinances of the church. Griffith and David Miles attended this conference.

In April, 1711, the Great Valley Baptist church was formed, with Richard Miles, Sarah his wife, and daughters Joan and Jane, among the constituent members.

"From this time on, he and his family were identified with the Baptists. His five sons-in-law were Baptists of standing and influence. After his death (or more probably after the death of his oldest son Richard Miles, 1734) his widow Sarah seems to have gone to Plymouth township, where her son-in-law John Davis "of Plymouth" lived.

In her will dated October 6, 1750; pr. Aug 25, 1756, she describes herself as "of Plymouth."

The will of Richard Miles is dated August 29, 1713; proved Dec. 23, 1713. Signed with his mark "being Sick of body but of sound and perfect mind and memory." Witnesses: Thomas Thomas (husband of niece Tamar), Ruth Miles (niece), and William Meredith. Richard's brother-in-law, William Davies, and John Powell "my Daughter's father-in-law" were to be Tutors and Guardians over the children until they became of age.

Children of Richard and Sarah (Evans) Miles were:
Richard, m. Phebe Davis.
- JAMES, m. Hannah Pugh (sist. Jonathan), dau. of David and Catharine Pugh. Constable in Radnor 1701; Supervisor 1702; Pat. 174 acres land, in 1703 (Oct 26).
- Evan, m. Mary, landlord of the "Unicorn," Tredryffryn.
- John, m. Rebecca James, (sist. Evan James) dau. David of Radnor; who settled there in 1682.
- Jane, m. John Davis "of Plymouth."
- Sarah, m. Rev Benjamin Griffith, b. "Llanllwny,"[1] Wales, 1688; emigrated to America 1710; half-bro. of Rev. Abel Morgan.
- Hannah, m. Jonathan Pugh, (bro. Hannah;—see above).
- Abigail, m. Rev John Davis, (Second pastor at Great Valley Baptist church).
- Joanna, m. Joseph Powell, (son of John Powell, named in Richard's will); he and Joan were constituent members the Brandywine Bapt. church).

Children of James and Hannah (Pugh) Miles were:
Enos, m. Sarah Pugh,

---

[1] Carmarthenshire.

NATHANIEL, (Capt in Augusta Regt. at Ft. Halifax, Pa., with 30 men, July 1, 1756.) m. Hannah Jones, (sist. John "of Radnor" Gr. dau. Thos John Evan; arrived in Phila. Apr 16, 1682— (30 weeks fr. London).
Richard, m. Mary Pugh,
Samuel, (Of Revolutionary fame—Mayor Phila., 1790.) m. Catharine Wistar,
Sarah, m. Samson Davis (her cousin)
James, m. Susanna Rock, (he and Richard, his bro., rem. to Brush Valley, Centre Co., Pa., where Samuel held much land).

Children of (Capt.) Nathaniel and Hannah (Jones) Miles:
Sarah, m. George Siters (or Siders)
Catharine, m. Meyers.
NATHANIEL, (Blacksmith by trade; resident of Tredyffrin & Vincent townships) m. Mary Frick, (descendant of Jacob Frick,)

Children of Nathaniel and Mary (Frick) Miles:
Rebekah, m. Moses V. Williams,
Catherine, m. Willis Davis,
Sarah, unm.
NATHANIEL (III) m. SARAH PHILIPS,
Jacob, m. Dinah Walkinhood.
John, m. Margaret Kelly.
Joseph, (twin) m. Mary Ann Frits.
Hannah, (twin) m. John Simes.
Mary, d. in infancy.
James, unm.
Eliza M. m. Thomas J. Grover.

Children of Nathaniel and Sarah (Philips) Miles were:
EDWIN, (twin) m. SUSAN EVANS JONES,
Emma, (twin) m. George W. Keiter.
Mary, m. Lewis Heffelfinger,

Lewis, m. Isabella Innes Kinzie,
Martha Frame, m. Thos Davenport Davis.
Sarah, m. William Leonard,
Catharine D. m. George R. Stiteler,
Owen Philips, m. Hannah P. Shirk,
George Baugh, m. Helen R. Yountz,

Children of Edwin and Susan Evans (Jones) Miles, of Pittsburgh, Pa.
Amanda M. m. James Buchanan Dewhurst.
George Keiter, unm.
Nathaniel, m. Jennie C. Overholt.
Sarah Elizabeth, unm.

GRIFFITH MILES, son of James, (b. in Wales, 1670—), married by Friends' Ceremony, at the house of David Price at Radnor, "in a public assembly," 8 mo. 20, 1692, Bridget Edwards, daughter of Alexander and [?Bridget] Edwards, of Radnor, Pa. The subscribing witnesses were 30 in number, among whom were— James, Richard, Samuel and Margaret Miles; and Ann Davis.

Griffith Miles was baptized (as an adult) 1697; and Bridget in 1709 (Pennepak Church records). Both died in 1719; she in Jan'y. The will of Griffith Miles is dated Mar. 28, and proved in Phila. June 13, 1719. Many particulars concerning his branch are to be found in "Annals of Miles Ancestry"—C. H. Banes, 1895.

Children of Griffith and Bridget (Edwards) Miles were:
Hester, b. Sep 28, 1693.
Martha, b. Oct 12, 1695.
Margaret, b. Apr 9, 1698; m. John Carl,[1]
Griffith, b. Dec 3, 1700; m. 1721–, Sarah ———; and
   d. June, 1727.
Samuel, b. Sept 1703.

---
[1] Some accounts state that *Martha* married John Carl.

John, b. Apr 26, 1709; m. Ann Davies, (dau. Mirick Davies; and d. June, 1747.

In his will (dated Mar 28, 1719) Griffith describes himself as "Yeoman, of the township of Bristol, in the county of Philadelphia. Griffith Miles' branch of the Miles family first settled in Lower Dublin township, Philadelphia county; but, about the year 1800, removed to Bucks county.

DAVID MILES, son of James, was a witness at marriage of his brother Richard in 1688, and at the marriage of James and Jane Edwards, in 1692, and at the marriage of William Thomas and Elizabeth Philips, 1694 (where the names of Samuel, Griffith and Sarah Miles also, appear). He was baptized (as an adult) in Philadelphia (as shown by Pennepak church records), 7 mo. 9, 1697.

The records of the Welsh Tract church show that David and Alice Miles joined that body in the year 1709. Her name appears as a witness at marriage of Phebe Miles (dau. Samuel & Margaret) 2 mo. 13, 1716, with Evan Evans. David does not appear to have been a purchaser of land, and no record of will or administration has been found. In list of deaths among the records of the Welsh Tract church—the name "Dafydd Miles—1710" is given, and in the graveyard of Pennepak Baptist church a "very old piece of rough stone, with no date, bears the name D. Miles." Als Mils is among the signers, Feb 4, 1716, of a Confession of Faith (at Welsh Tract Church), showing that she survived her husband by some years. None of their descendants are known, other than "Niece Sarah Miles, daughter of David Miles" who inherited under the will of her uncle Richard,—"one oack Chest wch is now in the house of my Brother in Law, William Davies."

ANN MILES, daughter of James, (b. in Wales—) married William Davies (or Davis) of Radnor township, who came to America about the year 1685, and purchased a lot on Walnut Street Philadelphia, from John Jones. In the same year he bought a plantation in Radnor. He was originally, a member of the Society of Friends; but later became a member of the Church of England. The first English services in the vicinity were held in his house. Afterwards in a log cabin built upon his plantation, which burned down early in 1700, and replaced by the present St David's Church, at Radnor. He was a member of the Pennsylvania Assembly, 1712 and 1714. Later he removed to Caernavon township (now Lancaster county), and the records of the Bangor Church shew numerous descendants. Ann (Miles) Davies died in 1734; William died 1739.

MORTON OF CALCON HOOK.

BY THOMAS ALLEN GLENN.

[The following notes are from notes made some years since, a brief of title to lands in Ridley, and from a Ms. pedigree. The accuracy of the latter is not vouched for by the compiler of this genealogy; but as the pedigree is of interest because of its relation to a signer of the Declaration of Independence, it is hoped that corrections and additions will be made.]

(1) MÂRTON MÂRTONSON (*i.e.* Mârton son of Mârton, or Morton) a native of Sweden; of full age and on the Delaware, 1655; died after 24 May, 1703. He was probably born about 1625, and his father, Mârton, about 1595–1600.

>Deed, 1694–5, 12 Mar. Andrew Jansen to Mârton Mârtonson, for a tract of land at Amosland.

Mârton is called in various documents and records, of Amsland, Amosland, Ammesland, and Millkill, in Ridley.

Issue:
- (2) i. Mârton.
- (3) ii. Mathias.
- (4) iii. Andrew; d. 1722. Admon. 8 Nov., 1722. This Andrew had a deed from his father, 24 May, 1703, for land in Amosland.
- (5) iv. Lace.

(2) MÂRTON MÂRTONSON (otherwise Morton Mortonson, and Morton Morton), of Calcon Hook, Co. Chester, eldest son.

>Patent, 1701, 20 Oct. Wm. Penn by his commissioners, to Mârton Mârtonson, for land on the east side of Schuylkill, adjoining lands of Andrew Peterson Longacre and Otto Erick Cock, being 1200 acres. [Exemplification Book I., 565 etc., Phila.]

Deed, 1708, 7 Augt. Morton Mortonson of Calcon Hook, Co. Chester, yoeman, to John Mortonson [alias Morton], his son, of Calcon Hook, for 300 acres of the above 1200 acres. [Deed Book C., 42–46 etc., West Chester.]

Deed, 1708, 7 Augt., same to Andrew Mortonson [otherwise Morton], his son, for another 300 acres of the above 1200 acres [West Chester.]

Deed, 1708, 7 Augt. same to Lawrence Mortonson [otherwise Morton.] his son, two tracts of land; one of 60 acres, the other of 100 acres, in Co. Chester [West Chester.]

The Will of Morton Mortonson [otherwise Morton], dated 1 Nov., 1718; proved at West Chester, 1 Jan., 1718–19. He married Margaret ———; living and acknowledged a deed 27 July, 1716.

Issue:
- (6) i. Marton, b. 17 June, 1675; d. s. p. before 1718.
- (7) ii. Lawrence, b. 5 Oct., 1678.
- (8) iii. Andrew, b. 8 Sept., 1681.
- (9) iv. John, b. 1 June, 1683.
- (10) v. Jacob, b. 24 May, 1686; d. s. p. before 1718.
- (11) vi. Margaret, b. 27 Mar., 1687–8; m. George Culin.
- (12) vii. Mathias, b. 8 Sept., 1690; m. Bridget ———; d. before 9 Dec., 1736.
- (13) viii. David, b. 20 Feb., 1695; Admon. 11 Nov., 1738; m. Eleanor, dau. Justea Justea, of Kingsessing, yeoman. [See his will proved at Phila., 17 Feb., 1721. D.; p. 208.]

(3) MATHIAS MARTONSON, 2d son of Mârton Mârtonson(1) (otherwise Mortonson and Morton), was of Amosland, yoeman. His descendants assumed the surname of Morton.

Deed, 1703, 24 May. Mârton Mârtonson to Mathias Mârtonson [otherwise Morton], his son, for 350 acres of land, which the grantor had by deed from Andrew Jansen, 12 Mar., 1694–5.

Mathias died intestate before 15 Mar., 1717–18.

Issue:
- (14) i. Andrew.
- (15) ii. Morton.
- (16) iii. John.
- (17) iv. Peter
- (18) v. Mathias.
- (19) vi. Mary, m. John Stalcope.
- (20) vii. Christianna, m. Samuel Peterson.
- (21) viii. Catherine (?); d. young.

(7) LAWRENCE MÂRTONSON (otherwise Mortonson, and Morton), born 1675; of Calcon Hook, Co. Chester. He died 1713–14. Wife Bridget ———, who survived him.

Issue:
- (22) i. Tobias; a witness to will of Andrew Morton, his cousin; proved at Phila., 18 June, 1748. (Perhaps others.)

(8) ANDREW MÂRTONSON (otherwise Mortonson, or Morton), 3d son of Mârton Mârtonson, born 1681; of Calcon Hook; called "Andrew Morton senior."

Deed, 1708, 7 Augt., Mârton Mârton to this Andrew, his son, for 300 acres of land, as cited *supra*.

Grantor in a deed 1727.

Grantor, with Anne his wife, in a deed 12 June, 1741.

Issue:
- (23) i. Morton.
- (24) ii. Andrew.

(9) JOHN MÂRTONSON (otherwise Mortonson, or Morton), 4th son of Mârton Mârtonson, born 1683; of Calcon Hook. He married, 1723–4, Mary, daughter of John Archer.

Deed, 1708, 7 Augt., Mårton Mårtonson, of Calcon Hook, to this John, his son, for 300 acres of land on Schuylkill, as cited *supra*.

John Morton is later called "of Ridley" in the county of Chester, yeoman. Will dated 6 Feb., 1724; proved 20 of 12 mo., 1724–5 [will Book A. 1, 166, West Chester.]

Issue.:
(25) John, b. 1724–5; m. Mary Sketchley.

(15) MORTON MORTON, 2d son of Mathias Mårtonson, married Christianna Wabraven.

Issue:
- (26) i. Mathias.
- (27) ii. Jonas.
- (28) iii. Andrew.
- (29) iv. Sarah.
- (30) v. John.
- (31) vi. Anna.
- (32) vii. Cornelius.
- (33) viii. Susanna.
- (34) ix. Christiana.
- (35) x. John.

(23) MORTON MORTON, "eldest son and heir" of Andrew Morton of Calcon Hook. He was of full age, 1726, and 1748, had a bequest of Swamp land in New Jersey, from his brother Andrew. Married Lydia, daughter of Andrew, son of Mathias Mårtonson. She was under age 25 Feb., 1729–30; died 19 Sept., 1756. Morton Morton and Lydia his wife quit claim to Jonas Morton, son of Andrew, for land of said Andrew, father to said Jonas and Elizabeth.

Issue:
- (36) i. George, m. Elizabeth Morton.
- (37) ii. Morton, m. Mary Been.

(14) ANDREW MORTON, 2d son of Mathias Mårtonson, was of full age 1727, and called "of Calon Hook," and "of

Darby," yeoman. He owned a farm "at Darby Marsh on Calcon Hook Island," a cedar swamp in "the Jerseys," and "a lot at Wicco that hath a building on it." Will dated 16 Mar., 1747–8; proved at Philadelphia, 18 June, 1748. Married, first, Mary ———, secondly, Amy, or Eamey, ———.

Issue:
- (38)   i. George.
- (39)   ii. Hannah, unm. 1770.
- (40)   iii. Ann, unm. 1770.
- (41)   iv. Eleanor, m., 25 Augt., 1763, Garrett Boon.
- (42)   v. Amy, d. 12 Dec., 1751.
- (43)   vi. Elizabeth, m., 12 Nov., 1763, George Morton; living 1770.

(38) GEORGE MORTON, eldest son of Andrew, probably by first wife, was of Ridley, and Kingsessing, and married, 17 Jan., 1766, Ann Robinson; she married secondly, before 1800, Andrew Boon. George Morton was under age 16 Mar., 1748–8; died 1782. Admon. to Charles Justice, 13 May, 1782.

Deed, 1775, 23 Jan. George Morton, of Kingsess, Phila., and Ann his wife, to Andrew Boon, of Calcon Hook, for land on Calcon Hook, which grantor had by deed of Benjamin Urian, of 8 July, 1772.

Issue:
- (44)   Mary, b. 1776, m., 1ˢᵗ, 19 Sept., 1795, George Higgins; m., 2dly, 24 Sept., 1800, John Bishop, son of Christopher, of Gloucester Co., N. J.

OWEN OF MERION.*

BY THOMAS ALLEN GLENN.

I. Owen ap Evan, of Fron Gôch,[1] near Bala, in the comot of Penllyn, Merionethshire, Wales, was born probably prior to his father's removal from Rhiwlas, which event may have occurred subsequent to 1636. He was the son of Evan Robert Lewis, of Fron Gôch, a Welsh gentleman of small fortune, but " of an ancient and honourable family," who was born circa 1585,[2] and is described as " a sober honest man." Owen ap Evan had several brothers, of whom John ap Evan was father of William John, of Gwynedd, and of Griffith John,[3] of Merion, early settlers of Pennsylvania. Further on it will be noticed that Robert Owen in his will mentions his " cousin Griffith John," thus confirming the account given in the old manuscript from which the above statement is partly taken. Evan ap Evan, another son of Evan Robert Lewis, was father of the Evans brothers who settled at Gwynedd, for a detailed account of whose descendants see H. M. Jenkins's " Historical Collections of Gwynedd." The children of Griffith John called themselves " Griffiths," and those of William, " Williams." The descendants of Owen ap Evan assumed the surname of Owen. Owen ap Evan died at Fron Gôch prior to 1678. From records extant it appears that his wife's name was Gainor John, and that she was probably living until 1682. Owen and Gainor had issue,—five children:

[1] Called also Vron and Tron Gôch, the Red Slope.

[2] Old manuscript pedigree. Dwnn Visit. Wales, 1601 (Meyrick).

[3] Described in Welsh documents as " Griffith John de Gwerevol;" he came with Robert Owen in 1690. His certificate was from the Quarterly Meeting of Friends at Tyddyn y Garreg, Merionethshire, and bears the same date as that of his relative.

*Modified and expanded versions of this article appeared in Thomas Glenn's *Merion in the Welsh Tract* (1896, repr. Baltimore: Genealogical Publishing Co., Inc., 1970) and his *Welsh Founders of Pennsylvania*, 2 vols. (1911, 1913, repr. Baltimore: Genealogical Publishing Co., Inc., 1970).

1. Robert, b. circa 1657; m. Rebecca Owen.
2. Owen, supposed to have d. s. p.
3. Evan, living 1690.
4. Jane, m. Hugh Roberts.
5. Ellin, m. Cadwalader Thomas ap Hugh.

II. Robert Owen,[1] son of Owen ap Evan, of Fron Gôch, and Gainor, born at Fron Gôch, Merionethshire, Wales, circa 1657; died in Merion Township, Philadelphia County, Pennsylvania, 10th mo. 8th, 1697, and was buried in the ground of the Merion Friends' Meeting on the 10th of same month. His brother-in-law, Hugh Roberts, says of him: " He was one that feared the Lord from his youth, being convinced of the truth when about seventeen years of age . . . travelling several times through his native country, Wales, where he was of good service. In 1690 he came into Pennsylvania, where he lived about seven years, visiting this and the adjacent provinces, and was also very useful in the meeting where he resided . . . a man of peace, hating all appearance of contention, endued with wisdom and authority, yet merciful unto the least appearance of good in such as he had to do withal."

Regarding his earlier life in Merionethshire many particulars have been obtained. The following from " Besse's Sufferings of Friends," Vol. I. p. 755, is the first mention we have of him as a Quaker: " Anno 1674, on the 3d day of the month called May, John David, Robert David, Robert Owen, Cadwallader Thomas, and Hugh Roberts were taken by the Sheriff with a process and committed to Dolgelly Goale, being indicted at sessions some time before for their being absent from National Worship." " Robert

[1] There was another Robert Owen and Jane, his wife, of Dolsereu, near Dolgelly, Merionethshire, who came to Pennsylvania in 1684, on the " Vine," and settled on Duck Creek, New Castle (now Delaware), where a son, Edward Owen, had previously located. Robert and Jane died in 1685. They had nine sons, all of age before their arrival here, of whom I can name only Lewis, who came with them, but returned to Wales; Dr. Griffith Owen, who accompanied them, and died in Philadelphia; Edward, who remained on Duck Creek and left descendants.

Owen, of Vron Gôch," was one of those Quakers fined for meeting at Llwyn y Braner, in the parish of Llanvawr, May 16, 1675 (PENNA. MAG., Vol. V. p. 359), together with his two sisters, Elin, who afterwards married Cadwalader Thomas ap Hugh, and Jane, wife of Hugh Roberts. His younger brother, "Evan Owen ye son of a widdow called Gainor, whose late husband was Owen ap Evan of Vron Gôch," was also present at a meeting, "though but 9 or 10 years old."

Robert was appointed one of the overseers of the will of John Thomas, of Llaithgwm, which document is dated 9th February, 1682,[1] and was executed in Wales, but probated in Pennsylvania in the year 1688. He is described therein as "Robert Owen late of fron goch neer Bala in the County of Merionyth." Subsequent to this date I find him a resident of the parish of Llanddervel in Merionethshire.[2] On the 8th day of the 6th month (August), 1690, the Quarterly Meeting of Friends held at Tyddyn y Garreg, Merionethshire, granted a certificate of removal to this Robert Owen. This certificate is of record in Book 1st, pp. 286–87 of the Merion, Radnor and Haverford Meeting, and is as follows:

To oᵉ Friends & Brothers in the Province of Pennsylvania.

These are to certifie, as occasion shall require, unto whom it may concern in the behalf of oᵉ dearly beloved friende & Brother Robt. Owen & Rebecca his wife & their dear & tender children. That they are faithfull & beloved friends, well known to be serviceable unto Friends & brethren since they have (become convinced), of a Savory & Blameless conversation. Alsoe are psons Dearly beloved & Respected of all sorts. His testimony sweet & tender, reaching to the quicking seed of life, of a meek, quiet & gentle Behavior; we cannot alsoe but bemoan the want of his company, being

[1] Will Book A, Philadelphia.

[2] He appears as a witness to sundry deeds executed in Merionethshire in 1682, and recorded in Philadelphia, 1684, in Deed Book C I, for land in Pennsylvania, viz.: "John Thomas, of Llaethgwm, Merioneth, yeoman," to "Edward Jones, of Bala Chyrurgeon," dated 1st April. "Edward Jones, of Bala, to Hugh Roberts, of the township of Ciltalgarth, yeoman," dated the last day of February.

he was near and dear unto us & seasonable in intention for Pennsylvania many months before his removal, now seeing it remaineth still on his mind, & in order therein unto finding his way clear & freedom in the truth according to the measure manifested unto him, we thought it o^e duty to commend him unto you as o^e dear & faithfull friend & brother, and hereby desiring their faithfull services in the truth may increase & abound among you to their endless joy without end.

Att o^e quarty. Meeting att Tyddyn y Garreg in Merionethshire the eight of the sixe month in the year 1690.

Ellis Morris	David Jones
Hugh David	Evan Owen
Rowland Ellis	Regnald (Rowland?) Humphrey
Jn. Evan	
Hugh Rees	Margaret David
Rowland Owen	Jonett Johnes
Lewis Owen	Elizabeth Jones
Owen Lewis	Ellin Ellis
Griffitt Robt.	Jane Robt.
Evan Rees	Margaret Robt.
Robert Vaughan	Ann Rowland
Rees Thomas	Gainor Jones.
Rees Evan	

Some time before this, about 1678, Robert Owen had married, according to Friends' ceremony, Rebecca Owen, daughter of Owen Humphrey (or Humphreys), Esquire, a gentleman who "had a good and indefeisible estate of inheritance" called Llwyn-du, in the township of Llwyngwrill and parish of Llangelynin, Talybont, Merionethshire, which he had succeeded to in or about 1646. The agreement concerning a marriage settlement was executed on the 6th of 1st month, 1678, between Gainor John, mother of Robert Owen, and Owen Humphrey. The bond of this contract, "Owin Humphrey de Llwundu" to "Robt Owen de vron goch com^t Penllin, gener." (gentleman), dated as above, is extant. The witnesses were, Rowland Ellis, Edward Vaughan, John

Thomas, Owen Thomas, Hugh Robert, Rowland Owen, and Humphrey Owen; the last two were brothers of Rebecca, as were John and Joshua Owen, who afterwards removed to Pennsylvania and lived with Robert Owen or with their uncle, John Humphreys. After his coming to Pennsylvania his name is of continual occurrence as executor, administrator, or trustee, or as a party to some agreement. He is described in one of these documents, dated 30th May, 1696, as "Robert Owen, of Merioneth, in the County of Philadelphia, in the Province of Pennsylvania, Yeoman," and is grantee in a deed from Thomas Lloyd,[1] dated "the fifth day of the sixth month, Anno Dom. 1691," for a tract of land containing four hundred and forty-two acres, situate in "the Township of Merion" in Philadelphia County, the consideration being one hundred pounds. This "plantation," as it was then called, lay west of the present Wynnewood Station, on the Pennsylvania Railroad, and extended to near the present village of Ardmore. It was confirmed to Evan Owen, eldest son and heir of Robert, by patent[2] from Penn's Commissioner, dated 8th February, 1704, "Together with the Messuage or Tenement, Plantation, . . . Houses, Barns, Buildings, Gardens, Orchards, Woods, Underwoods, Ways, Waters, Meadows, Water-courses, Fishings, Fowlings, Hawkings, Huntings, Rights, Liberties." By a deed dated 31st December, 1707,[3] "Evan Owen, of the Township of Merion, in the County of Philadelphia, and Province of Pennsylvania, yeoman, son and heir of Robert Owen, late of Merion, yeoman, deceased," conveyed this farm, devised to him by his father, to his brother-in-law, "Jonathan Jones, of Merion, yeoman." A manuscript by Owen Jones, grandson of Robert Owen, says,[4] "He purchased a large tract of land about nine miles from the city of Philadelphia, in the township of Lower Merion. Here he built a large commodious dwelling-house, and resided in it during the remain-

---

[1] Deed Book E2, Vol. V. p. 174, etc., Philadelphia.
[2] Patent Book A, Vol. III. p. 241, Harrisburg, Pennsylvania.
[3] Deed Book E4, Vol. VII. p. 40, etc., Philadelphia.
[4] "Memoir of Charles J. Wister."

der of his life. He had children, viz., Gainor, Evan, Owen, Elizabeth, John, and Robert, some of whom were born in Wales." This house is yet standing, and compares favorably with many of the modern dwellings erected near it. The date is carved upon a corner-stone, "1695." Robert Owen was a justice of the peace for Merion, and by 1695 had, says this old manuscript, "gained the confidence of the people in general, which they manifested by making choice of him to represent them in the Assembly of the Province of Pennsylvania (elected again, 1697) . . . which position he filled with much reputation. It pleased Divine Providence to remove his beloved wife in the year 1697 (died 8th mo. 23d, buried 25th), which severe trial he survived but a few weeks."

Robert, as already stated, outlived his wife—whom he had loved long and tenderly—but a short time, and was buried beside her. Among the eminent Friends whose bones lie near his, scarcely one has left a more stainless, and none a more honored, name. His will, dated "10th mo. 2d day, 1697," was probated May 16, 1705.[1] He left his plantation in Merion to his eldest son, Evan Owen, and speaks of his other children without mentioning their names. He appoints as overseers John Humphreys, Hugh Roberts, John Roberts, Griffith John, Robert Jones, Robert Roberts, Robert Lloyd, and Rowland Ellis, and appoints his "cousin Griffith John above named" as sole executor. The witnesses were Joshua Owen, Robert Jones, and Rowland Ellis. John Owen, described elsewhere as "ye 2nd son of Owen Humphreys of Llwyn-du," in Merionethshire, and brother to Joshua, above named, subsequently acted as an appraiser. Robert Owen's important services as a minister among Friends must not be overlooked. He was one of the founders of the Merion Meeting, and a trustee thereof, as appears by a deed dated 20th 6th mo., 1695, Edward Rees, of Merion, yeoman, to Robert Owen, Edward Jones, Cadwallader Morgan, and Thomas Jones, of Merion, yeomen, in trust, for one-half acre of land in Merion, "for the purposes of the Merion

[1] Register of Wills' Office, Philadelphia.

Meeting." As early as 28th June, 1692, Robert Owen, with Thomas Lloyd, Nicholas Waln, Dr. Griffith Owen, Hugh Roberts, John Symcock, William Byles, and others, the then ministers at or near Philadelphia, signed the communication of the Meeting of Friends in Philadelphia, to the Monthly Meetings of Friends in Pennsylvania, and East and West Jersey, setting forth their displeasure and sorrow at the action of Keith, who was making himself obnoxious to Friends about this time. Perhaps the last documents, executed the year of his death, 1697, that in any way concerned Robert, are an agreement of his with one Evan Harry concerning the estate of Cadwallader Lewis, deceased, of which Robert Owen was appointed by the court administrator, "Letters of Attorney,[1] Richard Davies of Cloodie Cochion, Welchpoole (Montgomeryshire), gentleman," to Robert Owen et al., his "true and lawful attys.," dated 1st mo. 8th, 1696/7, and a letter from him to Hugh Roberts, then travelling in Wales, dated 24th of 2d mo., 1697. So far as can be ascertained at this late day, Robert and Rebecca Owen had but eight children; or, if there were others, their early decease in Wales renders their existence of little interest. Of these eight, the first four—Evan, Gainor, Elizabeth, and Jane—were born in Merionethshire, and are the "tender children" mentioned in the certificate of removal. The rest were born in Merion Township, Philadelphia County, Pennsylvania, as appears by the record of their births in the "Book of Births" of the Radnor Monthly Meeting, and there mentioned as children " of Robert and Rebeckah Owen." Their births are also noted in records of said Meeting as " Births in Merion Meeting." The eight were:

1. Evan, b. circa 1682; m. Mary Hoskins.
2. Gainor, m. Jonathan Jones.
3. Elizabeth, m. David Evans.
4. Jane.
5. Owen, b. 12 mo. 21st, 1690; m. Anne Wood.
6. John, b. 12 mo. 26th, 1692; m. Hannah Maris.
7. Robert, b. 7 mo. 27th, 1695; m. Susanna Hudson.

[1] Exemplification Book 4, p. 677, Philadelphia.

8. Rebecca, b. 1 mo. 14th, 1697; d. inft.; buried 9 mo. 21st, 1697.[1]

II. Jane, daughter of Owen ap Evan, of Fron Gôch, and Gainor, born at Fron Gôch, 1653/4; died in Merion Township, Philadelphia County, Pennsylvania, 7th mo. 1st, 1686, and buried 3d of same month. She married, in Merionethshire, 1672/3, " Hugh Roberts, of the township of Kiltalgarth, parish of Llanvawr, Merionethshire, yeoman." He was a prominent minister among Friends, and afterwards a Provincial Councillor of Pennsylvania. Their certificate of removal from the comot of Penllyn, is dated " ye 2nd of 5 mo., 1683," and they settled upon about six hundred acres of land in Merion. All of their children, except Elizabeth, were born in the township of Kiltalgarth, but a record of their births has been preserved in the archives of the Merion, Pennsylvania, Monthly Meeting of Friends. They were as follows:

1. Robert, b. 11 mo. 7th, 1673; m. 1st Catharine Jones; 2ndly, Priscilla Johnes.
2. Ellin, b. 10 mo. 4th, 1675.
3. Owen, b. 10 mo. 1st, 1677; m. Ann Bevan.
4. Edward, b. 2 mo. 4th, 1680; m. 1st Susannah Painter; 2ndly, Martha Hoskins; 3dly Maria Cox.
5. William, b. 3 mo. 26th, 1682; d. 1697 in Penna.
6. Elizabeth, b. 12 mo. 24th, 1683.

II. Ellin, second daughter of Owen ap Evan, of Fron Gôch, and Gainor, born at Fron Gôch, circa 1660; died in Merionethshire prior to 1697. She married, subsequent to 16th May, 1675, Cadwalader Thomas ap Hugh, of the township of Kiltalgarth, in Llanvawr, Merionethshire. He was the son of Thomas ap Hugh, ap Evan, ap Rees Gôch, ap Tudor, ap Rees, ap Evan Coch, of Bryammer, in the parish of Gerrig y drudion, Denbighshire, derived from Marchwerthian, Lord of Issallt, who bore Gules, a lion rampt.,

[1] " Burials at Merion Meeting," in Records of Radnor Monthly Meeting of Friends.

arg., armed, and langued azure. Cadwalader Thomas died prior to 9th February, 1682, as appears by the will of his brother, John Thomas, of Laithgwm, "gentleman," dated as above, and proved in Philadelphia, 1688. Cadwalader had issue by Elin, two sons:

1. Thomas Cadwalader, living 9th Feb., 1682.
2. John Cadwalader, born prior to 1682; removed to Pennsylvania and became ancestor to the Cadwalader family of Philadelphia. He was a member of the Provincial Assembly, and his son, Dr. Thomas Cadwalader, was a Councillor.

III. Evan Owen, eldest son and heir of Robert and Rebecca, born in Merionethshire, Wales, 1682/3; died at Philadelphia, Pennsylvania, 1727. Letters were granted on his estate to Mary, his widow, 27th October, that year. He married, 10th mo. 11th, 1711, Mary, daughter of Dr. Richard Hoskins. The record of their marriage says, " Evan Owen, son of Robert, of Merion Township, Philadelphia County, yeoman, deceased, and Mary Hoskins, daughter of Richard, practitioner of physick, deceased. . . . Philadelphia Meeting." The witnesses were Owen, John and Robert Owen, Gainor Jones, John and Martha Cadwalader, and forty-seven others. Evan Owen, having sold his Merion land to his brother-in-law, Jonathan Jones, removed to Philadelphia, and was admitted to the freedom of the city in April, 1717; neither he nor his brother Robert, who was admitted with him, gave any occupation. He (Evan) became a member of Common Council, 1717, and was appointed a justice of the peace of the Philadelphia County Courts, 1723, serving until his decease. He was justice of Court of Common Pleas, Quarter Sessions, and Orphans' Court, commissioned 18th February, 1723. Became associate justice of the City Court and alderman, 6th October, 1724. Justice of Orphans' Court from 5th December, 1724; was a master of the Court of Equity, 1725; treasurer of Philadelphia County from 1724 to his death. Became a member of the Provincial Assembly, 1725, and Provincial Councillor of Pennsylvania,

1726, being a justice of the Court of Chancery the same year. While serving as a member of the Assembly, Evan Owen was, as we have seen, called to the Provincial Council, the lieutenant-governor expressing a desire to have another Quaker at the board, and Preston and Fishbourne, whose advice was asked, recommended him. He asked to be excused until the expiration of the sessions of the Assembly, but appears to have qualified, as there is a note to the minutes of the first meeting he afterwards attended, which was during Gordon's term, that he had qualified in Keith's time. Perhaps Evan's most important trust was as a trustee of the Society of Free-Traders, who had purchased several thousand acres in Pennsylvania. The records of the Arch Street, Philadelphia, Monthly Meeting show the births of four children of Evan and Mary, and the death of one. They were:

1. Robert, d. 10 mo. 9th, 1712.
2. Robert, b. 10 mo. 12th, 1712; d. s. p.
3. Martha, b. 4 mo. 12th, 1714.
4. Esther, b. 9 mo. 18th, 1716; m., 1743, William Davis.[1]
5. Aurelius, b. 1 mo. 1st, 1718; d. 5 mo. 2d, 1721.

III. Gainor Owen, daughter of Robert and Rebecca, born in Merionethshire, died in Pennsylvania. She married, 8th mo. 4th, 1706, Jonathan, son of Dr. Edward Jones, of Merion, by Mary, daughter of Dr. Thomas Wynne, of Bronvedog, near Calwys, Flintshire. Gainor is described as being "much beloved by her neighbours, a friend to the poor." They had eleven children; surname Jones:

1. Mary, b. 14th 5 mo., 1707; m. Benjamin Hayes.
2. Edward, b. 7th 7 mo., 1708; d. unm.
3. Rebecca, b. 20th 12 mo., 1709; m. John Roberts.
4. Owen,[2] b. 19th 9 mo., 1711; m. Ann Evans.
5. Ezekiel Jones, supposed by his father to have d. s. p.
6. Jacob, b. 14th 5 mo., 1713; m. Mary Lawrence.
7. Jonathan, b. 29th 4 mo., 1715; m. Sarah Jones.

[1] Register of Christ Church, Philadelphia.
[2] He was colonial treasurer of Pennsylvania.

8. Elizabeth, m., 1758, Jesse George.
9. Martha, b. 6th 3 mo., 1717.
10. Hannah, b. 28th 11 mo., 1718/9.
11. Charity, b. 4th 8 mo., 1720.

III. Elizabeth Owen, daughter of Robert and Rebecca, born in Merionethshire, Wales; died at Philadelphia, Pennsylvania, 22d 10th mo., 1753. She married David Evans, of Philadelphia, "gentleman," deputy sheriff of Philadelphia, 1714–21. His will is dated Sept. 27, 1745. They had six children; surname Evans:

1. Evan, d. prior to 1762; issue, Sidney, David, Rebecca.
2. Rebecca, d. unm.
3. Sidney, m. 4 mo. 26th, 1759, Joseph Howell, of Chester.
4. Sarah, d. unm. Will d. 14 July, 1762; proved 21 Dec.
5. David, d. 11 mo. 18th, 1725.
6. Margaret, d. unm. 4 mo. 12th, 1734.

III. Owen Owen, second son of Robert and Rebecca, born in the township of Merion, Philadelphia County, 21st 12th mo., 1690; died at Philadelphia, 5th 8th mo., 1741. Will dated 4th 5th mo., 1741; proved 11th August, 1741. He married, 13th 3d mo., 1714, Anne Wood, who died 2d mo. 4th, 1743. He was high sheriff of Philadelphia from 4th October, 1726, and coroner, 1729 to 1741. The *Pennsylvania Gazette*, August 6, 1741, says, "Yesterday died after a long illness, Owen Owen, Esquire; formerly High Sheriff, and for many years Coroner of this city and county." Owen and Anne had five children:

1. Robert.
2. Jane, m., 1760, Dr. Cadwallader Evans, who d. s. p., 1773.
3. Sarah, m. John Biddle; d. 1 mo. 1st, 1773.
4. Tacey, m., 1744, Daniel Morris, of Upper Dublin, Pa.
5. Rebecca, d. unm., 10th Dec., 1755.

III. John Owen, third son of Robert and Rebecca, born in Merion Township, Philadelphia County, 12th mo. 26th,

1692; died in Chester County, 1752. Will proved 23d January that year. He removed from Philadelphia to Chester in 1718. He married, 8th mo. 22d, 1719, Hannah, daughter of George Maris, Provincial Councillor and a colonial justice of Pennsylvania, the marriage being recorded as follows in the books of the Chester Monthly Meeting of Friends: "John Owen, son of Robert, of Merion, Philadelphia County, yeoman, deceased, and Hannah Maris, daughter of George of Chester, yeoman." The witnesses were Evan, Robert and Owen Owen, George Maris, Sr., and forty-four others.

John Owen was high sheriff for the county of Chester, 4th October, 1729–31; 3d October, 1735–37; 4th October, 1743–45; 8th October, 1749–51. He was elected a member of the Provincial Assembly of Pennsylvania at periods extending from 1733–1748; was collector of excise for Chester, 1733–37, and for many years one of the trustees of the Loan Office of Pennsylvania. He had issue by Hannah, his wife,—five children:[1]

1. Jane, m. Joseph West.
2. George, m., 1751, Rebecca Hains; d. at Philada. s. p., 1764. Will proved 28th Sept. that year.
3. Elizabeth, m. James Rhoads.
4. Rebecca, m. 8 mo. 22d, 1754, Jesse Maris.
5. Susanna, m. Josiah Hibbard.

III. Robert Owen, fourth son of Robert and Rebecca, born in Merion Township, Philadelphia County, 7th mo. 27th, 1695; died circa 1730. He married, 11th mo. 10th, 1716/17, Susanna, daughter of William Hudson, mayor of Philadelphia and a justice of the Orphans' Court, by Mary, his first wife, daughter of Samuel Richardson, Provincial Councillor and a justice of Pennsylvania. The following is an abstract of the original record of their marriage certificate:[2] "Robert Owen, son of Robert, late of Merion,

[1] For descendants, see "History of Maris Family of Pennsylvania."
[2] Philadelphia (Arch Street) Friends' Monthly Meeting Records, Book A, p. 91, No. 188.

Philadelphia County, yeoman, deceased, and Susanna Hudson, daughter of William, of the city of Philadelphia, . . . at Philadelphia Meeting." The witnesses were William, Hannah, Samuel, William, Jr., John, Hannah, and Rachel Hudson, Evan, Mary, John, and Owen Owen, and fifty others.

Along with his brother Evan, the Councillor, Robert Owen was admitted to the "freedom of the city" in April, 1717, and continued to reside there until his decease. His widow married, 3d mo. 2d, 1734,[1] John Burr, of Northampton, Burlington County, New Jersey, and died at Philadelphia, 3d mo. 4th, 1757.[2]

Robert Owen is grantee in a deed[3] dated "24th May, in 4th year of the reign of our sovereign Lord George, King of Great Britain, and in the year of our Lord 1718," for a lot of ground " fronting 28 feet on Walnut St., and in length to formly the 30 foot cartway under the bank of the Delaware, called King Street, 58 feet" and " with North and West, the Smithshop & ground of Robert Jones, Eastward by Samuel Carpenter's Warehouse."

Robert and Susanna had three daughters, whose births are thus noted in the original book of record of the Arch Street, Philadelphia, Monthly Meeting of Friends:

1. "Mary Owen, daughter of Robert & Susanna Owen, was born in Philadelphia ye 3d day of ye $\frac{3}{mo}$: 1719." She d. young.

2. "Hannah Owen, daughter of Robert & Susanna Owen, was born in Philadelphia ye 16th day of ye $\frac{3}{mo}$: 1720." She m. 1st, John Ogden; 2ndly, Joseph Wharton.

3. "Rachel Owen, daughter of Robert & Susanna Owen, was born in Philadelphia ye 19th day of ye $\frac{6}{mo}$: 1724." Living unm. 1740.

IV. Mary, first daughter of Jonathan and Gainor Jones, born in Merion Township, 14th 5th mo., 1707; married at

---

[1] Philadelphia (Arch Street) Friends' Monthly Meeting Records, Book A, p. 131, No. 259.

[2] She was born 12th mo. 17th, 1698/9.

[3] Deed Book F1, p. 251, etc., Philadelphia.

Merion Meeting, 10th mo. 2d, 1737, Benjamin Hayes, son of Richard, of Haverford, "yeoman." They had one child: Elizabeth, b. 7th mo. 16th, 1738.

IV. Rebecca, second daughter of Jonathan and Gainor Jones, born in Merion Township, 20th 12th mo., 1709; married at Merion Meeting, 3d mo. 4th, 1733, John Roberts, son of Robert Roberts, of Merion. They had ten children; surname Roberts:
1. Jonathan, b. 1 mo. 30th, 1734.
2. Gainor, b. 11 mo. 30th, 1735/6.
3. Alban, b. 7 mo. 7th, 1738.
4. Elizabeth, b. 6 mo. 18th, 1740.
5. Mary, b. 5 mo. 3d, 1742; d. unm. Will proved 1771.
6. Tacey, b. 7 mo. 2d, 1744.
7. John, b. 9 mo. 16th, 1747.
8. Robert, b. 10 mo. 8th, 1749.
9. Algernon, b. 11 mo. 24th, 1750/1.
10. Franklin, b. 11 mo. 27th, 1752.

IV. Jonathan Jones, fifth son of Jonathan and Gainor, born in Merion Township, 29th 4th mo., 1715; married at Merion Meeting, 11th mo. 8th, 1742, Sarah, daughter of "Thomas Jones, of Merion, deceased, yeoman," son of John Thomas, of Llaithgwm, Merionethshire, Wales, descended from Evan Coch, of Bryammer, Denbighshire. (See PENNA. MAG., Vol. IV.) They had three daughters:
1. Mary, b. 11 mo. 23d, 1744/5.
2. Gainor, b. 8 mo. 4th, 1742.
3. Katharine, m. Lewis Jones, of Blockley.

IV. Hannah Owen, second daughter of Robert and Susanna, born in Philadelphia, 3d mo. 16th, 1720; died January, 1791, in said city. Will dated 28th November, 1786; probate January, 1791.[1] She married first, 8th mo. 23d,

---

[1] Will Book W, p. 65, Philadelphia.

1740,[1] John Ogden, of Philadelphia (widower), son of David Ogden, of Chester. John Ogden died 6th February, 1742, being then of the "Township of Myamensing and Passyunct, Philadelphia County." Will dated 31st January, 1742; probate 12th February, same year.[2]

Hannah married secondly, 6th mo. 7th, 1754, Joseph Wharton, of Walnut Grove, Southwark, Philadelphia. In her will, dated as above, Hannah leaves to her " son William Ogden," among other bequests, " my Silver Tankard," and directs that her executors " sell my Charriott, and apply the Amount of the same toward payment of my debts." She also mentions her grandfather, William Hudson, and her children by her second husband, Wharton. By her first husband, John Ogden, she had one son:

William Ogden, b. prior to 31st January, 1742; m. 1st, Marie Pinniard, 2ndly, Tacey David.

By her second husband, Joseph Wharton, she had a large family, the most distinguished of whom was Robert Wharton, mayor of Philadelphia, captain of the City Troop, etc. For an account of them and their descendants, see " History of Wharton Family," in PENNA. MAG., Vol. II.

V. William Ogden,[3] only son of John, by Hannah Owen (his second wife), born in Philadelphia County prior to 31st January, 1742; died in Camden, New Jersey, 13th May, 1818. He married first, 1st mo. 11th, 1769, Marie Pinniard, of French descent. She died 7th mo. 14th, 1775, aged twenty-three years. He married secondly, Tacey David, daughter of Benjamin and Ann David; the latter daughter of Hugh Evans, of Gwynedd. She died 11th September, 1809. William Ogden had by his first wife two children:

1. Hannah, b. Dec., 1770; m. 1st Captain William Duer; 2dly, Samuel Cuthbert.

---

[1] Philadelphia (Arch Street) Friends' Monthly Meeting Records, Book A, p. 172.

[2] Will-Book G, p. 31, Philadelphia.

[3] He was commissioned notary public for the State of New Jersey subsequent to 1801.

2. Joseph, b. 7 mo., 1775; d. 10 mo. 20th, 1778.
He had by his second wife two children:
1. Ann, m. Hezekiah Niles, of Baltimore.
2. Robert Wharton, of Camden.

VI. Hannah Ogden, eldest daughter of William by Marie (his first wife), born in Philadelphia County, December, 1770; died at Philadelphia, 29th July, 1827; buried in the ground of the Third Presbyterian Church, Pine Street, said city. She married first, in Christ Church, 10th April, 1795, Captain William Duer, who was lost at sea, 1800/1.[1] She married, secondly, in Christ Church, 27th January, 1810, Samuel Cuthbert, "gentleman," son of Thomas. He died January, 1839. Hannah had by Captain Duer three children:
1. Harriet, b. 1796; d. unm. at Phila. 7th May, 1851.
2. Mary Ann, b. 1798; m. 5th May, 1825, Lewis Washington Glenn, son of James, of Maryland, and had issue,— William Duer, d. s. p. in Cairo, Egypt, 1876; Edward, of Ardmore, Lower Merion; Hannah Cuthbert, m. A. W. North, who d. s. p.
3. William, d. at Phila., 25th March, 1802.

By Samuel Cuthbert she had two daughters:
1. Frances Duer, d. infant.
2. Elizabeth Frances, d. unm.

[1] Letters of administration granted on his estate, 25th November, 1801, to Hannah Duer. Sureties, William Ogden, "gentleman," and Robert Ralston, "merchant."

GENEALOGICAL GLEANINGS, CONTRIBUTORY TO A HISTORY OF THE FAMILY OF PENN.*

BY J. HENRY LEA, Fairhaven, Mass.

[The following fragments, comprising items gleaned at odd moments during a very busy year passed in special investigations among the English Records, are submitted with some diffidence, as they are, at best, but *disjecta membra* and can do little more than point out the path which the (let us hope not distant) future historian of the family should tread in his researches. A stray handful only, gathered from a field full of promise to that patient investigator whose time and means may permit an exhaustive examination of the ground.

The name of Penn is a very ancient one in England, dating in fact not only behind the Norman, but even the Saxon Conquest, as the word, a distinctly native British appellation, which signifies a Top, Hill, Crest, or Summit, occurs in this sense in many different and widely-separated parts of the Kingdom, and no doubt, as the use of surnames became general, gave local rise to several altogether distinct families whose only connection is in the coincidence of their common cognomen. It is not very uncommon to find it used with its translation as an *alias* (*i.e.*, Hill *alias* Penn), for an example of which see the Register of South Littleton, Worc. (page 58), as also the Will of William Penn, of Charlestown, Mass., 1688, cited by Savage.[1] The name is most frequent, as we might expect would be the case, in Cornwall,[2] Devon, and Wales, where the indigenous population made their last stand against the invaders.

Of these families one of the most ancient was that of Penn Manor,[3] co. Bucks, which claims to antedate the Conquest and from which, it has been claimed, our Founder's family was derived—a claim which, like so many other traditional ones, will not bear the light of investigation, and which the proofs, hereafter given, utterly refute, as will be shown later. In the Northern part of Bucks, at Stony Stratford, was another family of Penn which may have been, and probably were,

[1] Savage's Genealogical Dict., vol. III., fo. 389.

[2] " By Tre, Ros, Pol, Lan, Caer & Pen,
  You may know the most of the Cornish men."
  Heraldic Journal, vol. IV., fol. 11.

[3] " Penn, as its name signifies, stands on very high ground" (see Lyson's *Magna Britanica*, vol. I., pt. 3, fo. 618). See for Pedigree of Penn of Penn, Notes and Queries, 5th Series, vol. I., fo. 265, and Lipscomb's Bucks, vol. III., fo. 287.

*Only the material in this article that appeared in 1890 has been published as a book.

cadets of the former, but no proof has yet been discovered to connect them.

At Codicote, in Hertfordshire,[1] a family were long seated which probably descended from John Penn, Citizen and Mercer of London, whose will was proved in 1450; certain it is that his son Ralph was of that co. and died there childless in 1483, but whether the John Penn of Codicote who died in 1557 was descended from one of Ralph's brothers, John or Thomas, is as yet a matter of conjecture only; a search of the Wills in the Commissary Court of London, Essex, and Herts would probably set this point at rest.

In Worcestershire there have been Penns from a very early period (the name occurs there in the reign of Edward III) in the district about Bromsgrove, where we find them in considerable numbers. A most interesting MS. has been preserved written by one John Penn (tmps. Commonwealth), a member of this family, which throws much light on the history of the Penns of Worcestershire.[2] The arms which he there claims are the same as those borne by the Founder differenced by " in cheife a lyon passant gules" and in his time "wass standing thus in the beginning of our late warrs in the said church (*i.e.*, Churchill, near Starbridge) window and there remaineth if it be not ruinated by the late usurpers." One of the daughters of this family, in 1713, married the poet Thomas Shenstone. Another colony, perhaps quite distinct from the former, flourished at Pershore, Littleton, Chipping-Campden, &c., on the borders of Worcester, Warwick, and Gloucester; Francis Penn of Bobbington, Staffordshire, 1613, may have been of this latter family.

Salop also furnishes its quota and a pedigree is given of a Penn family of Stockton, in that county, which extends 15 generations previous to the seventeenth century; the Arms being again identical with those of our Founder.

Northampton, Kent, and Sussex also furnish names which are not yet identified with any of the other pedigrees, while the Hampshire family and their London branches are very probably an offshoot of the Wiltshire stock, as may be also the Penns of Fifehead, Somerset.

The Wiltshire family will of course be of the greatest interest to us, as it is certainly that of our illustrious Founder, and it gives the writer much satisfaction to be able to cast a ray of light on what has hitherto been a somewhat obscure page of genealogical history.

It has been generally assumed that the William Penn of Minety, with whom the existing pedigrees commence, was a cadet of the Penns of

---

[1] A very full pedigree of this family, with copious extracts from the Parish Registers, is given in Clutterbuck's Herts, vol. II., fo. 306, which has been reprinted in Coleman's pamphlet on the Penn Family.

[2] Herald & Genealogist, vol. VII., fo. 131.

[3] Harl. MS. N° 1241, fo. 128 op. cit.; Herald & Genealogist, vol. VII., fo. 144.

Penn, co. Bucks, and this belief seems to have been based on a tradition (as untrustworthy as such traditions usually are) which is embodied in a letter of John Penn, Sen., Esq., to Dr. Smith, of Penna.[1] (query, if Dr. George Smith, the Historian of Delaware County ?), in which it is stated that the father of William Penn of Minety was a younger son, named William, of David and Sibel (Hampden) Penn of Penn, who was a monk in the Abbey of Glastonbury in Somerset, and after the dissolution, being granted lands in the Forest of Braydon, Wilts, by Henry VIII, he married and became the progenitor of the Wiltshire Penns.

This statement, in view of the especial fury which the iconoclastic monarch displayed towards Glastonbury and its inmates, more than almost any other of the religious houses which he spoiled, would be naturally received with suspicion, as it would not seem plausible, to say the least, that he should have hanged the Abbot and distributed his mangled body among the surrounding towns, while at the same time rewarding with rich gifts one of his late retainers. Moreover, the Abbey was not attacked until 1539, while in 1538, as the documents hereafter cited will show, the Penn family was already fully established in the County.

Awbrey says, "The Penns have been here a long time, but, I think, only Yeomen. In Braden Forest, in parish of Brinckworth,[2] is Penn's Lodge, yet so called. At Rodburne there were Penns which —— Power of Stanton Quinton married." [3]

To this we have to add that David Penn of Penn, in his will (1570), while reciting his children, makes no mention of any son William, nor does his eldest son John (1596) name such a brother or descendants of such brother. It is then among the sturdy yeomanry of Wilts that we have to look for the ancestry of that most illustrious scion of the race, the Founder of Pennsylvania.

But in the absence of further proof, which only a patient and thorough investigation of the Wiltshire Records and Registers will yield, it is idle to speculate further on the conjectural kinship of the various Penns of

---

[1] Commonplace Book of John Penn, Jun., Esq. in Penn MSS. in Lib. Hist. Soc. Penna., Phila., op. cit. Notes & Queries, 5th Series, vol. I., fo. 265. He is followed in this error by Mr. Stratford (Worthies of Wilts, fo. 145)wh o says "Awbrey was mistaken in making William Penn a Wiltshire man," and repeats substantially the above tradition.

[2] The Register of Brinkworth only exists from the year 1653. The Vicar, Rev. William de Quetteville, very kindly made a thorough search of the records from that date, but failed to find a single entry of the name of Penn, while the writer was equally unsuccessful with the Bishop's Transcripts at Sarum, of which twelve fragmentary years exist previous to 1653, the earliest being 1572.

[3] Awbrey's Wiltshire Collections, Jackson's Edition, fo. 270.

Wilts during the sixty years that elapse between their first appearance in these notes and the death of William Penn of Minety, with whom the authentic pedigree begins, and, waiting such proof, the writer suspends all further comment, although the temptation is strong to build up a conjectural pedigree out of the scanty material already at hand.

In conclusion the writer wishes to express his feeling of deep obligation to the many and kind friends in England who have done so much to aid him in his researches and among whom the word "*America*" has ever proved an "*Open Sesame!*" to the vast Antiquarian treasures of the realm. To Mr. J. C. C. Smith, the Superintendent of the Literary Enquiry Department at Somerset House, in particular, he would express his thanks for an unfailing courtesy and patience, as also to Mr. G. H. Rodman, in charge of the District Probate Courts at same place; likewise to his friends Mr. William Brigg of Epping Forest and Mr. Eedes of London, to whose kindness in furnishing abstracts of a number of wills overlooked by him in the Prerogative Court of Canterbury he owes the practical completion to the eighteenth century of the records of that most important of all the English Courts.

To the Historical Society of Pennsylvania, which has generously defrayed a considerable portion of the expense of these collections, his thanks are also due.

Such as they are, then, these notes are submitted, and if they have the effect of arousing the dormant interest in the Family of our Founder that should animate every true Pennsylvanian and lead some other and more competent worker into the field, the writer will feel himself well repaid for his labors.]

PREROGATIVE COURT OF CANTERBURY. PENN WILLS
from 1383 to 1700.[1]

1450—John Penne, Citizen & Mercer of London; to be buried in St. Albans, Wode strete, London; wife Alice, sons Ralph, John & Thomas Penne; daus Alice, Mary & Margaret. Wit. wife's father Thomas ffereby; Exrs. John Lok & Wilton Grand Proved 7 Sept., 1450.[2]—Rous 11. 12

1483—Raufe Penne of Co. of Hertf., Gentilman; to be

---

[1] The Wills of the Prerogative Court of Canterbury date from 1383, but before 1400 are somewhat fragmentary; the Admons. date only from 1559, none being preserved before that date.

[2] Probably the John Penn who was Sheriff of London 1410, vide Bakers' Chronicle, fo. 168. Undoubtedly the ancestor of the Penns of Codicote, Herts. A John Penn was also M. P. for Weymouth in 1413, 1420, and 1422, but probably not identical. Her. Jnl. IV., fo. 11.

buried in church of Adenhm betwene Edmude Broke & the Chauncell vnder the Arch; all feoffees that be enfeoffid in all my goodes and landes maners rents and s'uices wt the apprtenncs that be in the Counties of Hertf., Midd. and Surr', that they in goodely hast aftyr my deceese do make astate and relese to myn exrs. her'aftyr named a sufficient Sur' and laufull astate of and in all the seid maners londes rents and s'uices wt their apprtennce to thentente to pforme my Will &c.; all profits of all my lands to go to the ordennce of a chapell on Coppidthorn hill till it be fynyshed for the ease of the neyghbours that fer to ps church; a yerely obite in Aldenhm church; exrs. to ordeyne & make sure for eu'more as moche londe to the yerely value of xx s. for to kepe & repayre the Church wey betwene Illestre & Rylond gate; Richard Howell shall haue the grete Whits for euyrmor to hym & hys heyres; to sell my lond in london and Lamehith; to euerich of my cosyns fferbeis x li.; to John Peke for t^{r}me of hys liefe v marke a yer & all hys costs that he doth abought me; same to Richd: Grotemore; euerich of my god children x s.; myn executors John Verney, John Peke, Humfry Conyngesby and Richard Grotemore; John Verney & Humfrey Conyngesby Resid. Legatees; And I the seid Raufe the last day of Septembyr the yer of our Lord mlcccclxxxv ratefie and conferme the same. Probatum fuit coram nobis ac p. nos approbatum et in sinuatum testm. (no date given)—Logge 27.

1504—Richard Pen, Citizen & Taillor of London; to be buried in the Chapel of St. Ann, Church of St. Brides, Flete strete; brothers John & Richard Pen; sister Lewce; nephew Thomas Everton; wife deceased; Proved 2 April 1504.—Holgrave 5

1558—Thomas Penne of Stonestreteforde, co. Bucks, Tanner; to be bur. in Church of St. Gyles at Stonestreteforde; sons Roger, John & Thomas Penne; dau. Marye; Exrs. sons Roger & John; Overseer Jordeyne Thomas; dat. 11 Sept., pro. 13 Feb 1558—Welles 37

1559—John Penne, Esquire, of Codycote, co. Herts.; to be bur. in Church of Codynte; to churches of C. & Welwyn; daus. Elen, Elizabeth & Dorothye each 40 li at marriage; son Robert's wif; son Robert Penne my mylle of Codynte; son William; wife Lucy Residuary Legatee & Extrix. Wit. Michael Hogkin; Signed John Pen; dat. 15 Aug. 1556; pro. 6 May 1559 by wid. second grant 10 Oct. 1560 to Gyles Penne—Chayney 16

1570—David Penne of Penne in the countie of buck, Esquior; to be bur. decentlie in Penne Chan'cell among myne auncestors; Exrs. to remove the bodie of my wife where she in nowe buried and burie her in the same place where I shalbe buried; legs. to poor of Penne & other Townes nere adioyninge; I giue and bequeathe for the tearme of xxx yeares nexte to begynne ymmediatlie after my deathe to my executors & theire assignes to paie my debtes my manno^r howse of Penne with all the Demeane groundes belongeinge vnto the same; if sonne Thomas Penne doe order hymselfe frome henceforthe honestlie and be ruled by my executors in the choseinge of his wyfe and reforminge of his oder lewde mannors then I giue vnto hym ymmediatlie after my deathe by the space of Tenne yeares £11-6s-8d.; dau. Marie Peckham & dau. Margett Gyfforde to either of them foure of my beste bowles & cuppes of siluer; to George Peckham, my dau. Peckham's son the nexte best bowle; to son Edward Penne the Tenthe beste bowle or cuppe of siluer; myne olde sarvaunte Edwarde ffowkes; Exers. welbeloued brother Richard Hampden esquio^r, sonne-in-law George Peckham, cosen Nich'as Weste & sonne-in-lawe Thomas Gifforde.

Codicil dat. xxiij Jan. 1564—Legs. of furniture &c. to das. Mary Peckham & Margaret Gifford & sons Edward & Thomas Penne to Thos. Tempeste my downe geldinge; to Anne Playcer for her paines that she hath taken with me in my sicknes., the beste bedd; legs. to Ellis Tiler, Roger Clerck, Richard Sexten, John Bovindon of Penstrete, Margerie Cockley, Andrew Deane, William Parsley & John

Cutler; my grounde called Bentles in the pishe of Agmondeshm; to Davide Easte my sister's sonne xl s.; to Henrie Easte my sister's sonne xx s.; William Nasshe xl s.; all my landes over & above xxtie marckes of annuitie by the yeare graunted to my sonne Thomas Pen I will & bequeathe to my eldest sonne John Pen; This being written by the concent of me David Pen being sick in bodie but being pfecte in memorie thankes be gyven to god the xxvth. daie of Januarie Anno d'n'i 1564. p. me DD Pen. Wit: John Cheyne de bois, John Cheyne of Agmondshm, Thos. Tempest. dat. 5 Jan 1564; Adm. granted 13 June 1570 to son John Penn, the exors. having renounced.—Lyon 18.

1572—Anthony Penne Esquier of London; wife Julyan; bro. William; sister Cisley; Michael, Clement & Baptist Hickes; Proved by widow Julyan Penn, 17 July 1572. —Daper 24.

1573—Gilbert Pen of fforburie, parish of Bromsgrove, co. Worcester; mother; wife Johanna; son-in-law William Chaunce. Proved 2 June 1573 by widow Johanna Pen. —Peter 20

1575—John Pen of ffifhed, co. Somerset, Yeoman; to be buried in Cathedral Church of Wells; sons John, Henry & Edward Pen; daus. Agnes, Mary & Alice; dau.-in-law Jesse Taylor; sist. Ellner Strowde; wife Agnes; Proved 14 May 1575 by widow.—Pyckeringe 20

1579—Edward Pen of ffyfehed, co. Somerset. sisters Agnes & Mary Pen; sist. Ales Chamber; Joane Comb; Proved 18 Dec. 1579 by bro John Pen.—Bakon 49.

1579—Henry Pen of ffyfehed, co. Somerset; to be buried in Cathedral Church of Wells; sisters Agnes, Mary & Ales; bros John & Edward Pen; Exr. bro. Edward Pen; Admon. 18 Dec. 1579 to bro. John Pen, bro. Edward being decd. —Bakon 49.

1584—Richard Penne, Citizen & Butcher of London; son William Penne; wife Margaret; wives' brothers; sons Adam & William; daus Alice, Barbara & Margarett; Proved 26 Mch. 1584 by widow.—Butt 34

1586—Anthony Penne of Pedmore, co. Worcester, Gent.; mother Eliz.; bro. Humphrey's 4 children Roger, Henry, Ursula & Martha; sist. Ann Combye's children William, Joane, Katherine & Philip; sist. Joice Taylor's child. Anthony, Agnes, Mary Margaret & Elizabeth Taylor; sist. Mary Pearman, wife of Hugh Pearman & their child. Anthony, John, Nicholas, Jane & Anne Pearman; bro. Francis Penne's child.; Edmund & Eliz.; bro. Gilbert Penne; son-in-law John Cartwright; bro-in-law John Harle; wife Elizabeth; Exrs. bros. John & Francis; Overseer, bro. Humphrey. Pro. 12 Nov. 1586 by John and Francis Penne. —Windsor 58

1591—Anthony Penne, Citizen & Mercer of London; to be buried in the Church of St. Mary Magdalen in Milk street; mother Mrs. Julian Penne; bros. Clement & Michael Hickes; sister Elizabeth, wife of bro. Baptist Hickes. Pro. last of August, 1591.—Sainberbe 64

1591—Gilbert Penn of the Fenn, parish of Belbroughton, co. Worcester Sythsmith; sons William, John & Oswald Penn; dau. Elizabeth; wife Margarett; bro. William; bro.-in-law John Wakeman of Bewdley. Pro. 18 Dec. 1591 by widow Margarett.[1]—Sainberbe 94

1592—Will of William Penne of Minety, Gloucester, Yeoman.[2]

---

[1] A note in reference to this Gilbert Penn, scythesmith, will be found in Herald & Genealogist, VII., 131, demonstrating that the trade is not one incompatible with a gentleman, and giving instances.

[2] His monumental inscription at Minety Church in Chancell near South door reads, according to Awbrey (fo. 270), as follows:

"William —enn dyed the 12 of March in the year of our Lord 1591."

The writer learns from Rev. Mr. Edwards, Rector of Minety, that this stone has now quite disappeared.

IN THE NAME OF GOD AMEN The first day of May in the two and Thirtieth Year of the Reign of our Sovereign Lady Elizabeth by the Grace of God Queen of England ffrance and Ireland Defender of the ffaith &c Et Anno Dominij Millesimo quin gentesimo Nonagesimo I Willm Penne of Myntie in the County of Glouc Yeoman being at this present time whole in Body and of good and perfect remembrance (laud and praise be vnto Almighty God) Do ordain and make this my last Will and Testament in manner and form following viz. ffirst I commit and bequeath my Soul to my Lord and Sauior Jesus Christ by whose Death and Merits and precious Bloodshedding I hope to be saved And my body to be buried within the Parish Church Chancele or Church Yard of Mintij where my ffriends shall think meet Item I give and bequeath vnto the poor people dwelling within the said Parish Twenty Shillings to be distributed by my Overseers after my Burial according to their Discretions Item I give and bequeath vnto Giles Penn, William Penn, Marie Penn, Sara Penn and Susanna Penn being the Children of my late Son William Penn deceased Twenty Pounds apeice To be paid vnto them by my Executor as they shall come to and be of the age of Twenty one Years apeice or at the day of any of their Marriages (if any of them happen to be married before) So that such Marriage or Marriages be made to the liking and with the Consents of my Overseers Provided always that if any of the said Children shall fortune to departe this Life before the Age of Twenty one Years Then my Will is that their portion or portions so dying shall be equally divided among the Rest that shallbe living Item I give and bequeath vnto Margaret Penn Widow late Wife to William Penn my Son deceased the Sum of Ten pounds to be paid vnto her Yearly during her natural Life by my Executor at the ffeast of the Annunciation of the Virgin Mary and

It is much to be regretted that the Parish Registers should have perished before 1668. In the Bishop's Transcripts at Sarum there are five fragmentary years before that date, beginning with 1607, which were carefully searched but without result.

StMichael the Archangel by equal portions if she shall and do so long keep herself sole and chaste and vnmarried The same payment to begin after my death at such time as my Heir shall come to and be of the full age of Twenty one Years Provided always that if at any time the said Margaret shall happen either to marry or otherwise to miscarry and not to continue an honest Life Then my Will is that the foresaid Ten pounds shall surcease and be no longer paid vnto her by my Executor But that then vpon either such Marriage of her or other disordered Life being known my Will is that my Executor shall pay and deliver vnto her the Sum of Twenty Pounds in money and also a good Bed with all manner of Furniture therevnto belonging and so she quietly to depart from my Executor Item my Will is that the said Margaret Penn my Daughter-in-Law and my Overseers shall have the whole Charge Rule and Government of my Heir and of all the Rest of the Children which were the Sons and Daughters of Willm Penn my Son deceased and of all such Lands and Tenements and Hereditaments and of all such Goods and Chattells as I shall leave at my Death till such time as my Heir shall accomplish and be of the full Age of Twenty one Years and that the said Margaret Penn shall continue with the said Children and help to breed them vp during the time aforesaid And that she shalbe maintained of the whole and shall do and vse all things in the House for the vse and benefit of my Executor in such manner of wise and sort as she did in my own days vsed to do for me so that her doings and Dealings therein be done with Consent and Advice and good liking of my Overseers provided always that if the said Margaret Penn shall fortune to marry or otherwise not to live sole and chaste as beforesaid before such time as my Heir shalbe of the Age of Twenty one Years Then my Will is that my Executor with the Advice and Consent of my Overseers shall pay and deliver unto her the said sum of Twenty Pounds and the said Bed with all the ffurniture to the same as aforesaid and that therevpon the said Margaret quietly to depart and have no more Rule and Authority of any of my said Sons Children or of any Thing to them belonging But my Overseers only to do all Things concerning the Children according to their own Discretions and according to my true meaning herein expressed as my faithful Trust is in them ffinallie the Rest of all my Goods and Chattels Moveable and vnmovable not bequeathed my Debts and Legacys being paid and my ffuneral discharged I give and bequeath to George Penn being the eldest Son of Willm Penn my late Son deceased whom I do make my sole Executor of this my last Will and Testament With Condition that he the said George Penn shall perform and do all Things herein contained by and with the advices and consents of my Overseers Mr Robert George of Cirencester and Richard Lawrence of Withingeton in the County of Glouc: Gent and ffrancis Bradshaw of Wokesey[1] in the County of Wiltshire Gent whom I desire to be my Overseers And I give to them hereby lawfull authority to see that all Things herein mentioned be by my said Executor with their helps and Consents performed And I give to every of them for their Pains so taken in and about the Premises ten Shillings to be paid by my said Executor In witness whereof to this my said last Will and Testament I the said William Penne have put my Hand and Seal the day and Year first above written Item I further give to Richard Bidle one Cow Item I give to his Daughter Katherine Bidle one Heifer of two years of Age Also I give to my Daughter Ann Greene one Heifer and to Elizabeth Greene one Heifer each of them to be two Years old Item I give to Willm Mallibroke one Yearling Heifer And likewise I lastly give to Alice Thermor my old white Mare These being Witnesses—ffrancis Bradshaw Gent, Willm Taylor and Richard Munden with Others.

Probatum fuit superscriptum Testamentum apud London coram Venli Viro Magro Wilimo Lewin Legum Doctore ad exercendum Officium Magri Custodis sive Commissarij Curiae Proerogativae Cant et Etimo deputat Vicesimo primo

---

[1] Oaksey, often written Wokesey.

Die Mensis Aprilis Anno Dni 1592° in Psona Georgij Penn Executoris in Testo dicti Defuncti nominat Cui Commissa fuit, adstrationum omnium et singulorum bonum et Creditum ejusdem Defti De bene et fidelitur ad strand eadem juxta juris in eo Qto exigenciam et tenorem dicti Testamenti ad Sancta Dei Evangelia in Debita nostris forma personala juratj.

Wm: Legard, Pet: St. Eloy, Hen: Stevens Deputy Registers.—Harrington 31.

1596—John Penn of Penn, co. Bucks, Esq.; sons William, John, Griffyth, Edward & Francis Penn; bros. Thomas & Edward Penn nephew Edward Penn; dau. Martha; sist. wife of John Eden; Mr. John Walliston; friend Nowell Sotheston. Proved 6 Oct. 1596.—Drake 71

1596—William Penn of Kings Sutton, co. Northants.; sons Thomas, Michael, William & John Penn; dau. Margarett; wife Margaret (*enceinte*); bro. Richard; sisters Dorothy and Johan Penn; mother Christian; mother-in-law Agnes Caddie; Pro. 18 Oct. 1596 by widow.—Drake 70

1599—John Penne of Great Sherston, co. Wilts,; sons John, Robert, Thomas & William Penne; dau. Joane Penne; Pro. 20 June 1599 by John & Joan Penne.—Kidd 56

1607—Julian Penn of London, widow. Will dated 20 Aug. 34 Eliz. To be buried in parish church of Mary Magdalen in Milke streete "as nere to my late husbandes Anthony Pen & Robert Hickes as convenyently yt may be;" my mansion house vpon St. Peters hill where I now dwell to eldest son Michael Hickes, with remainder to son Baptist Hickes, remainder to my right heirs; my house called the White Beare in Cheapside wherein my son Baptist Hickes doth now inhabite & all houses in Bredstreete &c to said son Baptist; to son Clement Hickes "one blacke leather chiste;" to Julyan Hickes my goddau. & to her mother my son Baptist his wife; To Mary Hickes one other of the daus. of said Baptist £50; To the child that my dau. Baptist his wife now goeth withall "yf it be a male childe" £100 & if a female £50 &c Sons Michael & Baptist exrs. Witnesses—Andrew Sumner, ffrancys Mynne. Codicil dat. 1 Sept. 1592 with several small legacies. Pro. 29 Jan 1607 by Sir Baptist Hickes knt one of the exor., reservation to Sir Michael Hickes knt the other exor.—Windebanck 4

1609—William Penne of parish of Belbroughton & diocese of Worcester; will dated 6 June 1609. To daughter Bridget £100; To daus Elizabeth, Dorothie & Anne 100 marks each; To son Gilbert £100 to be paid to him at Michaelmas in 1612; To dau. Anne Westwood one sylver spoone; same to daus. Joane & Margerie To son Oswald all my waynes, Tumbrells, yokes, Towes, Harrowes &c. Residue to son Henry whom I make exor. (No signature) Witnesses—John Hemming, Oswald Penn & Joyce Tollye her marke. Proved 23 Aug 1609 by exr.—Dorset 79

1610—Edward Penn of Middleton, co. Northants, Yeoman; bro. Thomas of Banbury; sons John, Thomas, Edward, William & Mathew; daus. Margarett & Elizabeth. Proved 9 Oct. 1610 by bro John Penn.—Wingfield 84

1611—Robert Penn of Westerleigh, co. Gloucester; dau. Eleanor; son Robert Penn to whom he bequeaths the living of Sherston, co Wilts; dau. Agnes; wife Ann. Pro. 21 Jan. 1611.—Wood 1

1613—Francis Penne of Bobbington, co. Staff., Gent.; to be buried at Bobbington; daus. Mary, Anne, Margarett & Magdalen; sist.-in-law Margarett Gray; son Edward; wife Constance; Overseers bro.-in-law John Brodock & John Duke, Gent. Pro. 31 Dec. 1613.—Capel 114

1616—Oswald Pen of Belbroughton, co. Worcester, Yeoman; only child William Pen; sisters Ann & Dorothy;

Proved 4 May 1616; Admon. de bonis non granted in 1630 to Ann, widow of William Pen.—Cope 47

1617—William Penn of Kings Sutton, co. Northants.; bros. Henry, William, Richard, Thomas & Michael; sist. Margery, Margaret & Elizabeth. Proved 13 Oct. 1617.—Weldon 99

1618—Johane Peene late of Tovill in parish of Maydstone, co Kent, widow; (*nuncuptative will*) In the monethes of Julye & August 1617 declared that her sonne Thomas Peene should haue her howse & all the goodes therein as yt was hers after her decease & as greate a share in money besides as any other of her children for that she meant he the saied Thomas Peen shoulde giue entertaynment to all the rest of her children, which wordes or like in effect were vttered within the tyme aforesayed at the house of Robert Jackson situate in ffanchurche streete, London, in the p'nce of Barbara Jackson wife of the sayed Robert & Elizabeth Winterborne & dyvers others. Admon. gr. 19 Aug. to son Thomas Peene.—Meade 79.

1618—Thomas Penne of Stony Stratford, co. Bucks., Gent.; sons Michael, Thomas & William Penne; dau. Catherine; grson. Thomas Franklin; grdau. Grace Michell; Thomas, son of bro. Edward Penne; wife Grace, Extrx. Pro. 10 Oct. 1618.—Meade 98

(To be continued.)

GENEALOGICAL GLEANINGS, CONTRIBUTORY TO A HISTORY OF THE FAMILY OF PENN.

BY J. HENRY LEA, Fairhaven, Mass.

PREROGATIVE COURT OF CANTERBURY. PENN WILLS
from 1383 to 1700.

1621—Will of Lawrence Penn of Stebenheathe als Stepney, co Middx, gent.; da 17 Sept 1620; pr 1 Mch 1621; wife Christian all household stuff in dwelling at Stepney; mother Julian Penn annuitie of £15 per ann. for life to be yssuing as foloweth, viz. Nyne pds for dwelling ho. afsd in S., sixe pds out of farm Lands in psh of Petersfield, co South.; to Neiphue & godsonne Lawrence Penn the 3d son of my brother Richard Penn, & his heirs male, fee simple of farm lands in Tything of Sheete, in psh of Petersfield, co South. & a mortgage now held on same by Mistress Marye Hyndsey of Lond. widow, to be discharged, & for want of such issue to John Penn, one other son of my bro Rich. & his hrs male & for want of such yssue remaynder to Richard Penn one other of the sons of sayed bro. R. P., with remaynder to William Penn, son of my bro Wm. P. & his hrs male & for want of suche yssue to my right heirs forever; brothers Richard, Thomas & William Penn 20 marks apeece to be raysed out of certain Corne, Horses &c remayninge in hds of sayed bro Richard P. which are in full discharge of my promises heretofore made in that behalfe vnto my late father William Penn decd.; to Thos. Orchard & Sara Orchard sonne & dau of Edward O., bro vnto my sayed wife 20/s apeece; Richard Budd, esq., the kinges' Majesties' Auditor of Co. of Southampton sole Exr.; Witnesses—Thos. ffludd, Richard Penn (his mark), Rich Philipp, Rob. Evelye.

Codicil: same date. wife Christian lease which I have to come of ffarme called Reade ffarme in psh of warnring Campe, co Sussex. Wit: Thos. ffludd, Rich Penn (mark) Robt. Evelyn, Rich. Phillip.—Dale 72

1628—Thomas Peene of Ryd, co Sussex, Yeoman; to be bur at Ryd; bro. William; sist. Margarett Harvey; Thomas, son of bro. William; son Thomas Peene; Pro. 28 June 1628.—Clarke 39

1634—John Penn of Arundell, co. Sussex, Mariner; wife Ursula; bro. Jacob; sister wife of William Cornelison; sister Elizabeth Sansum; Proved 8 Oct. Admon. de. ibons non of widow Ursula in 1637.—Seager 90.

1637—William Penn of Canterbury, co. Kent; bro-in-law Richard Keeling; godsons William Allen & Michael Page; sole Extrx Good Friend & Mistress the Right Honble. Margarett Lady Wotton. Pro. 25 May 1637.—Goare 66
Limited Admon. gr. in May 1667.

1637—Ursula Penn of Arundell, sick of body &c. Will dated 23 Dec 1636   To be buried in Arundell churchyard; To Anne Gibbons dau. of George G. of Littlehampton decd., my now dwelling house called the Blew Anker, if she die without heirs of her body remainder to Mary Goble dau. of Thos. Goble of Anckton in the psh. of Felfame; To poor of Arundell 20s. at burial; To repairs of Schoolhouse commonly called Marygate 20s.; To Godchild the dau. of Peter Foster 50s.; John Wade 40s.; Anne Wade my Godchild £3; Benjamin Ellyott 5s.; Godchild Mary Bishop 40s.; James Humfrey 20s.; William Turner £3 & his wife Jane 40s. & to their children £5 each; John Walter 10s.; Jane Rewell 10s.; Sister Elizabeth Clarke 30s. & to her children 20s. each; Alice Bell £10; godchild Mary Thorne 40s.; Ursula Sandon £5; my kinsmen Thomas & William Humfrey 40s. each; John Emery 40s.; Anne Emery 20s.; Thomas Druett my peace ring & to his son my godson 40s.;

To wife of Robt. Roberts 40s.; To Mary wife of Thos. Goble £5 & to my goddau. Marie Goble £5; Mary Lutard £5; My godchild the dau. of Kewell (altered from Rewell) of Littlehampton 20s. Mr. Edward Southcott of Chichester £20; Mrs. Robertes 20s. for a ring; Alse wife of Edward Laslatt £4; Alse wife of John Masters of Chichester £4; Richard Robertes 20s.: John Willard £3; Richard Moth 40s.; Mary wife of Thos. Russell £13/6/8.; Elizabeth Crowch 20s. for a ring; Anne wife of Henry Stoner 10s.; widow Browing 30s.; Mary wife of John Moore 20s.; my brother Robert Lawnsone £5; father-in-law Richard Studder £5 which he owes me; John Thorne £10; To Mr Christopher Minshall three Angells for a ring; Richard Wooldridge 10s. for a ring; John Strong senior 40s.; Susan Walter dau. of Samuell Walter £10 at age of 18 or marriage; Mary Carter dau. of John Carter 5s.; my wearing apparel to widow Browing, widow Clarke, Mary Bishop, Mary Moare & Elynor Bishop; Residue to John Hale, son of George Hale, & Thomas Philpott of Arundell, to be Exors; friends Wm. Voakes & Richard Colden Overseers, 20s. each; Mr. Westwood 40s.; Sara Stringam junr. 20s.; Witnesses—peter Foster & John Carter. The mark of Ursula Penn. Proved 2 May 1637 by Thomas Philpott, John Hale the other Exor. having renounced.—Goare 80

1638—Robert Penn of Sherston, co. Wiltes., Yeoman; bro-in-law Wm: Knapp the younger of Redborne in psh. of Malmesbury, Wiltes Yeoman, & Elliner his wife all my landes &c in Didmarton & Oldburie, co. Gloucester & ground called Mussels in Luckington for their lives & aft. their dec. to hrs of said Wm. Knapp on bodie of said Ellianor begotten, the sd. Wm. K. to enter into bond of £120 vnto Ethelbright Howell of Sherston Magna co Wilts yeoman & John Boy of Luckington yeoman for payment of £60 in 1 year aft. my dec. & in consideration of sd. land called Mussells to pay to sd. Boy £10 to be employ. by him for benefit of his dau Johanna at 15 years of age; to William, John, Joseph, Anne & Johanna Boy child. of sd Joh

Boy 5s. each; to Elizabeth wife of Ethelbright Howell xx s;
to John, Henry & Katherine child. of said Eth. Howell 5s.
each; to Joane, Richard, Julyan & Eliz. child. of William
Lawrence of Westerlie 5s. each; to Wm., Anne, Marie, &
Susanna Knapp, child. of bro-in-law Wm. K. 5s. each; to
Wm. Boy son of sd. John Boy my best coat; Israel
Holborn 5s.; Gabriell Humfrie my best Cloak; to Henrie
Howell my best suit of wearing apparel; mother Anne Penn
Res. Leg. & Extrx. Signed Robti Penn. Wits: Nicholas
Waddington, ffrauncis Goodenough, Nicholas Gastrell. Dat.
15 Mch. 1637. Pro. 18 July 1638 by Extrx.—Lee 86

1639—Richard Penn of Peterfeild, co. Southants., Yeoman; sons Lawrence & John Penn; dau. Magdalen.—Harvey 166

1640—Will of Anne Penn of Sherston Magna, co. Wilts;
to sister Gillian, wife of William Lawrence of psh of Westerlay, co. Gloucester, my second gowne & petty cote & wast
cote; child. of Wm. Lawrence above named every one of
them a pewter platter, i. e. to Richard, Jone, Gillian & Elizabeth L.; child. of brother-in-law Ethelbright Howell of S.
M. every one of them a pewter platter, i. e. John, Henry &
Katherine Howell; to child. of bro.-in-law John Booy of
Luckington, every of them a pewter platter, i. e., William,
Anne, John, Joseph & Joanne Booy; to grchild. the sons &
daus of William Knapp & Ellen his wife, every on of them
a pewter platter, i. e. Anne, Marie, Susan, William & Sara
Knapp; Residuary Legs Anne & Susan Knapp, my grchild.;
Executor son-in-law Wm. Knapp; Witness—Nicholas Waddington, Clarke. Dat. 17 Jan. 1639; pro. 11 Dec. 1640.—
Coventry 163

1641—Thomas Penne of Stretton-super-ffosse, co. Warwick, Yeoman, "weak of body"; Nuncupative will dated
30 Sept 1640; To be buried in Stretton churchyard; dwelling house & 2 cottages in Stretton to wife Margaret for life,
after her decease to be divided between my 2 daus. Christian

Penne & Anne penne, also bedding & furniture to said daus. after wife's death; wife Margaret Penne Residuary Legatee & sole Extrix.; Wit. Tho: Brownent, minister; Robert Gressingham, Joice ffisher, Elizabeth Longe, Marie Gressingham, Anne Boyse & Jane Savage. Pro. 12 Feb. 1640 (1640-1) by Margaret Penne the relict.—Evelyn 21

1641—John Penn of Penn, co. Bucks; To be buried in Church of Penn; names wife Sarah; sons William & John Penn; cozen Sibell; uncle Francis; proved 21 Oct. 1641 by relict.—Evelyn 121

1642—Henry Penn of London., gent., weak in body &c. (described in Probate Act as of the parish of St. Andrew, Holborn, co. Middx.) Will dated 10 Oct. 1642; To be buried at discretion of Exor.; To wife Elizabeth Penn £300 due to me by her bro. Richard Hull upon a statute in the penalty of £600 in full performance of an Obligation wherein I stand bound to her brother Richard Hull & George Hull; To said wife all my goods now remaining in the house of Sir Thomas Hampson, Bart in Shoe Lane commonly called the Statute Office; said Sir Hampson, Bart., to be sole Exor.; Witnesses—daniel Evance, Nathaniel Humfreys, Elizabeth penn, John Longs, John Taylor. Proved 5 Nov. 1642 by Sir Thos. Hampson, Bart.—Cambell 120

1643—Edward Penn of Stony Stratford, co. Bucks, gent.; will dated 28 March 1643; To be buried in Church or Chapel of St. Giles on the west side of Stony Stratford near my wife; son Edward Penn 5s.; son John Penn 5s.; godson & grandchild Edward penn, son of Thomas Penn 50s.; to the rest of my grandchildren 2/6 each.; to Anthony Norman senr. of Shenley £3/6/8.; To Joane now wife of Thomas Lovell of Stonistratford 20s.; Bequests to servants; Residue of lands, goods & tenemts. to eldest son Thomas Penn sole Exor.; Overseers friends Anthony Norman & Richd. Abbott of Stonistratford. Witnesses—Richd. Abbott, Jane (sic) Lovell, Dorcie Densce. Pro. 29 Apr. 1643 by son Thomas Penn.—Crane 32.

1645—Henry Penn of Stony Stratford,[1] co. Bucks, gent., sick of body; will dated 15 July 1644; To be buried in St. Giles Church where my father John penn lies buried; to poor of the West side of Stony Stratford 20s. in bread at my death; to my grandchild peter Penne the Copyhold Close & 2 houses at the Bridgefoot at age of 21 paying to his brother Arthur Penn £5 in the meanwhile my son Matthias penn shall receive the rents in consideration of which he shall pay his brother Nathaniel Penn 40s. per ann. & my dau. Sarah penn 20s. per ann. till my said grandchild peter is of age; my said son Matthias penn sole Exor., to whom residue; Overseers—Thomas Simcocks & Robert Garner; Witnesses—John Reball, Erasmus Simons, William Dudley, Mary Dudley. Proved 27 Feb. 1644 (1644–5) by son Mathew penn.—Rivers 44

1646—George Penn of Westerham, co. Kent, Yeoman; Legacies to Catherine, Benjamin & John Bonwicke; Proved 24 Apr. 1646.—Twisse 51

1649—Edward Penn of St. Giles-in-the-Fields, Middx., gent.; will dated 15 Feb. 1648;. To be buried in parish I shall die in; to niece Annie Harper £5; cousin Martha Harper £5; to Doctor Atherton £5; Mr. Francis Shelley £5; Mris. Anne Penn £5; to Thomas Penn, Edward penn, Ursula penn & Civill witney, children of the sd. Anne Penn £15 amongst them; I release to Sir Thomas Shirley knt. £100 which he owes me by Bond & it to be

---

[1] Mr. P. S. P. Conner, the writer of the article in "Notes and Queries" (5 S. 1. 265), referred to by Mr. Lea, sends us the following extract from a letter of William Penn, the Founder, in regard to the Penns of Stony Stratford:

"Let Stephen Gould, my servant, and now the Governour's Clerk, [have] six pounds. He is an ingenious lad, a good scholar, and something of a lawyer, being about two years in Counsellor Poordan's service as clerk, a man of 800 or 900 per annum. His mother was a Stony Stratford Penn, old Arthur's daughter, that was housekeeper at Chelsea College. His father's side, gentleman of 300 or 400 per annum, but left his father upon a religious account." (Penn to James Logan: London, 29, 7 mo., 1708. "Penn and Logan Correspondence," vol. ii. p. 294.)—ED. PENNA. MAG.

divided between him & his children; to Geffrey Minshall of Sutton, co. Chester, gent., my lands called parke & Fulford grove, parke meade & Downesall, in the parish of Upton-St.-Leonards, co. Glouc. (which lands were demised to me by Henry Lygon of London Esq. in 1640) & I also give the said Geffrey Minshall £100 & I make my sister Mris Martha Harpur & the said Geffrey Minshall my Exors. Witnesses— John day, Andrew Giffard, Thomas Button & Wm. Minshall. Proved 7 Mar. 1648 (1648–9) by Martha Harpur, power being reserved to Geffrey Minshall.—Fairfax 29

1650—Robert Penn of Radway, co. Warwick, Yeoman; Legacies to sons William, Richard, Zackary & John Penn; daughters Mary & Anne; grandson Robert Penn; granddau. Elizabeth; brother Giles; wife Elizabeth; Proved 25 May 1650.—Pembroke 79

1653—John Penn, son of William Penn[1] of Harborow in the parish of Hagley, co. Worc., sick in body &c.; Will dated 22 Apr. 1651; To brother Richard Penn my right & title to a Lease of 1000 years made by Thos. Blunt & George Tokey, Esqrs. to my grandfather Thomas Cookes & his brother Wm: Cookes decd., dated 1 May 4 & 5 phil. & Mary, lately given me by the will of my uncle William Cookes, & also my messuage &c in Romsley in the parish of Halsowen, Salop, commonly known as Smiths ground, & 30 acres of land in the Common Fields of Romsley now in the tenure of Fortune powell; my brother Gervase penn £5; to Wm. penn, son of my brother Wm. penn, to Anne penn, & Mary penn, daus. of my brother Thomas Penn, & to Thos. Dickins & Mary Dickens, son & dau. of my brother-in-law Thomas Dickins & my sister Mary his wife, 40s. each; said brother Richard penn sole Exor.; Wit. William penn, Edmond Kettell & Thomas Penn; Proved 13 May 1653 by brother Richard penn.—Brent 66

[1] " William Penn of Bromsgrove, gent., married Margaret, daughter of Henry Cookes (of the Bentley family) she was living in 1683."—Grazebrook's article on Penn MS. in Her. & Gen., VII. 131.

1654—William Penn of Drayton, co. Worcester; Legacies to sons Wm. & John Penn; daughters Ann & Mary; wife Margaret; Proved by relict 26 Sept 1654.—Alchin 228

1654—Thomas penn of Haddon, co. Huntington, Grazier, weak in body; Will dated 12 Feb. 1653; I suppose my wife to be with child & I give such child £300 if a son, at age of 21, & if a dau. at age of 21 or day of marriage; to niece Anne Penn of Glapthorne, co. Northamp. £40; to Edward Penn & Thomas Penn the two sons of Robert Penn of Chasterton, £20 each at ages of 21; to William Cole son of Thomas Cole of Haddon £20 at age of 21; to sons-in-law William Burton & Savige Burton each £100 at ages of 21; Residue of goods & chattels to Cicely my wife, sole Extrx.; Wit.—Kenelme Collins, Robt. Savig; Proved 20 Mar. 1653 (1653–4) by Cicely penn the relict.—Alchin 152

1654—Edmund Penn of Littleton Packington,[1] co. Warwick, Gentleman; Legacies to sons Thomas, Francis & Humphrey Penn; daughter Constance; grandson Edward Wilson; wife Elizabeth.—Alchin 291

1654—Frances Pen of Send, co. Surrey, widow, weak in body &c.; Will dated 11 Dec. 1653; To be buried in the churchyard of Send; my late husband John Pen bequeathed to his 2 daus. Julian & Frances pen £10 each. The said Julian is since dead & her portion is due unto her sister Frances penn, & in consideration of the said £20, I devise to my said dau. Frances my lease of the tenement & lands belonging in which I now dwell & which I have by devise from Sir Richard Weston late of Sutton in the parish of Workinge (sic) co. Surrey, decd., & Dame Grace his wife, & also £30 which is in the hands of the said Sir Richard Weston & Dame Grace, as by a certain writing signed by him, ap-

---

[1] Littleton Packington is probably in the southwest part of Warwick, or in Worcester. I do not identify the place, but a group of Littletons (North, South, Middle, &c.) are in Worcester close to the Warwick border (*vide* Register of South Littleton, page 58).

peareth. I give her all my house hold goods; to grandchild Francis Potter £50 & to grandch. Damaris potter £40 at their ages of 21; Richard Forbench, gent., Wm. Bowell, yeoman, Edward Worsfold, mealman, & Thos. Ryde, yeoman, all of Send, to be my Exors in Trust. Wit.—John Bowell, Nicholas Hunt. Proved 20 Mar. 1653 (1653–4) by the Exors. named in the will. Signed by mark.—Alchin 359

1655—Thomas Penn of Codicote, co. Hertf., Gentleman; To be buried in his own chapel; Legacies to wife Alice; sons, John, ffrancis, William, Simon, Jonathan & Robert Penn; daus. Ellen & Alice; grandson Thomas Kirke; Proved 29 Jan. 1655.—Aylett 28

1655—Symon[1] Penn of St. Clements Lane, London, Surgeon; Legacies to mother Alice; sister Eleanor; brother ffrancis.—Aylett 32

1656—Gilbert Penne of Cakborow, co. Worcester, Yeoman; aged 80 years; brother John Penn's sons John, William & Gilbert Penn; daughters of same Margarett, Elizabeth & Mary; Proved 15 May 1656.—Berkley 179.

1657—Oswald Penn of Romford in the parish of Hornchurch, Essex, Baker, in perfect health &c.; Will dated Feb. — 1651; To be buried at discretion of my Extrx.; eldest daughter Sarah Penne £25 at age of 18 or marriage; youngest dau. Marie Penn £25 at 18 or marr; sister Mary, now wife of Wm. Collins of Bewdley, co. Worc., Yeoman, 10s.; Overseers friends James Jetur of daggenham, Essex & Christopher wilson of Romford & to each 5s.; Residue to wife Sarah, sole Extrx.; Proved 19 June 1657 by Sarah penne the relict. No witnesses named.—Ruthen 246

1657—William Penn of Cosgrave, co. Northampton, gent.; Will dated 19 Aug. 1657; To grandchild William Thorne a messuage on East side of Stonie Stratford, co.

---

[1] Evidently the son of preceding.

Bucks, wherein Jane Purchase, widow; my house in Stonie Stratford in which Thomas Fisher now dwells to be sold by my Exors. & out of the money which it fetches to Rockingham & Charles Bason 2 of the sons of my late wife Ellen by her former husband William Bason, £5 each to bind them apprentices, & the overplus to be equally divided between the said Rockingham & Charles, Richard, Robert & John, being all the sons of my said wife & her former husband. Residue of my goods &c to the aforesaid Rich., Robert, John, Rockingham & Charles Bason at ages of 21; Exors., my friends Richard Rockingham the elder & the said Richard Bason, eld. son of my said wife; Whatever debts I owed before my marriage with my said wife Ellen are to be paid by my son Gabriel penn out of the profits of a lease which I took of Sir Edward Longside & have since assigned to the said Gabriel. Signed with mark; Wit.—Thos. Tresham, Richd. Collins, Thos. Hearne & John Mansell; Proved 15 Sept. 1657 by Richard Bason, power reserved to Richard Rockingham.—Ruthen 361

1658—Giles Penn of Middle Aston, co. Oxon., husbandman, weak in body Will dated 3 Aug. 1657; To wife Elizabeth Penn, household stuff, &c.; grandchild Lawrence Middleton £10; son Robert Penn £8/10/; grandchild Elizabeth Middleton £10; daughter Jane Southam 20s.; dau. Anne Hanwell 20s.; Overseer son-in-law William Hanwell; to the 3 children of my son Giles Southam, a sheep each; & the 2 children of my son William Hanwell, a sheep each; & the 4 children of my son Robert Penn, a sheep each; son Giles Penn sole Exor.; Signed with mark. Wit. Wm. Hanwell & Joane Martin.—Wootton 59

1658—Walter Penn of Hanbury, co. Worc., Yeoman, in good health &c. Will dated 13 Feb. 1654; Thomas Vernon, gent, 2nd. son of Edward Vernon of Astwood in the parish of Hanbury, Esq., by deed 16 June 1647, for £200 paid to Edwd. Laser D. C. L. & Richd. Mence (or Meuce) for the uses therein mentioned & whereas I have reserved

£50 of the said sum of £200 to be disposed by my last will, I give to Anne penne, dau. of my son Wm. penne decd., £25, to make up the sum of £75, (named in above deed) to £100; To Mary Hatton & Anne H., daus. of my son-in-law Mathew Hatton & Elizabeth his wife, £5 to make up the sum of £75 (named in af sd. deed) to £80; To dau. Elizabeth Hatton £5; my sister Anne Bucknell 20s.; To John Penne son of my brother Wm. Penne 40s.; my son-in-law Mathew Hatton 20s. & my wearing apparel; to the af sd. Mary & Anne Hatton a moiety of all my goods &c.; Residue to the af sd. Anne Penne, sole Extrx.; Overseers my friends Edwd. Lake, Dr. of the Civ. Law, my cousin Wm. Chaunce & the sd. Mathew Hatton; Wit.—Richd. Vernon, junr., John Elvins, Thos. Meuce & Wm. Heywood. Admon 25 May 1658 to Mathew Hatton, father and guardian of Mary & Anne Hatton, minors, grandchildren of the testator.— Wootton 317

1659—Henery Penne the Seniour of the parish of Wittersham in Isle of Oxney co. Kent, yeoman; To poor of Wittersham 20s.; sister Catherine Martine one silver Bowl; bro. Geo. Martine £10; brother Eastland's children 20s. apiece; servant John Brummell 10 ewe sheep; uncle Henry Peene £40; to child which my wife is now great withall £100 at 21 & if it die under that age then £50 to my wife Elizth. & the other £50 amongst my sisters' children i. e. bro. Eastland's & bro. Martine's children; my father-in-law Isaacke Cloake of Eboney & Rich. Couchman of Beckley Overseers; wife Elizth. Extrx.; Wit.—Margarett Gilbard her marke & John Whatlow; Proved 27 Jan. 1658-9 by the Extrx.—Pell 26

1659—Katherine Penne of Worcester (no abstract).—Pell 245

1666—John Penn the elder of Boddicott, co. Oxon., yeoman; Will dated 21 Jan. 1663; To be buried in church or churchyard of Adderberry, co. Oxon.; To eldest son

Thomas messuage &c. in Boddicott wherein I now inhabit (except the estate & interest of Margery my loving wife settled upon her for her Jointure before our intermarriage); to dau. Anne Penn £200 of which £100 is to be paid by said son Thomas to the overseers of my will for her benefit within six months of my decease & the other £100 to be paid in same way twelve months after my decease & "if it shall please God to restore my said daughter Anne Penn to her former sences" said money to be paid to her; to son Samuel Penn & dau. Alice Crafts 12d. apiece; to son John Penn all moveable goods &c & I appoint him Exor.; Richard Crafts of Hornton, co. Oxon yeoman, & Robert Baily of Combrooke, co. Warw., yeoman, to be Overseers; Wits. —W. Style, Phill. Style, Tho: Nicholls, Steuen Danyell; Proved 26 Nov. 1666 by Exor.—Mico 168

1670—William Penn of the Parish of St Mary Whitechappell; Will dated 11Oct. 1669; To sister Joane Penn 40s. which her husband oweth me; to sister Ann Major 40s.; to brother Samuel's child Judith Penne 40s.; to sister Sarah £16; to brother Thomas Penne 5s.; to brother Robert Penn 5s.; to godson Willm: son of Mathew Penn 5s.; to cozen Wm: Penn son of bro. Thos. Penn 5s.; to cozen Wm. Major 5s.; to cozen Richard Penn son of Thos. Penn 5s.; to cozen Mathew Penn son of bro. Mathew Penn 5s.; to cozen Susanna Arrow 5s.; to sister Sarah a Table &c.; to bro. Mat. Penn of parish of St. Mary Whitechapel, gardiner, all residue; Wits.—James Roberts, Nicholas Snelson; Admon. with will annexed granted 24 Jan. 1669-70 to Matthew Penn the brother and legatary above named.—Penn 8

1670.—Sir William Penn of London, Knight; Will dated 20 Jan. 1669; To be buried in Parish Church of Redcliffe (i.e. St. Mary Redcliffe, Bristol,) "as nere vnto the body of my dear mother deceased as the same conveniently may be"; to have a monument for self & mother; wife Dame Margaret Penn; son William Penn; younger son Richard

Penn £120 per ann. until 21 years of age & then £4000; daughter Margaret wife of Anthony Lowther; nephews James & John Bradshaw & William & George Markham; cozen William Penn son of George Penn late of the Forest of Brayden, co. Wilts, Gentlemen, deceased; Proved 6 Oct. 1670 by son William Exor.—Penn 130

MONUMENTAL INSCRIPTION IN ST. MARY REDCLIFFE—BRISTOL.

Sir William Penn, Knight, born at Bristol 1621, of the Penns of Penns Lodge, in the county of Wilts. He was made captain at 21, rear admiral of Ireland at 23, vice admiral of England at 31, and general in the first Dutch wars at 32, whence returning in 1655 he was chosen a parliament-man for Weymouth 1660, was made commissioner of the admiralty and navy, gouvernor of the forts and town of Kingsale, vice-admiral of Munster and a member of that provincial council, and in 1664 was chosen great captain commander under his Royal Highness in that signal and most evidently successful fight against the Dutch fleet. Thus he took leave of the sea, his old element, but continued his other employs till 1669, when through bodily infirmities (contracted through the care and fatigue of public affairs) he withdrew, prepared his mind for his end, and with a gentle and even gale in much peace arrived and anchored in his last and best port at Wanstead, in the county of Essex, 16 September, 1670, being then but 49 years of age and 4 months. To whose name and merit his surviving lady erected this remembrance.[1]

1671—Chevall Penn of Wellwyn, co. Hertford, gent.; Will dated 7 Dec 1667; To my two daus. Mary Penn & Sarah Penn £100 each at 21 or marriage, to be paid by Thos. Penn my son, the said £200 being laid out & disbursed by me for the building of the mills in the parish of Coddicott, co. Herts,

---

[1] The above inscription, on a stately mural monument in the south transept, adorned with the armor and faded fragments of the banners of the deceased, is placed at such a height on the wall as to make the reading of the inscription, even with a glass, a very difficult task, but the writer believes that the transcript here given is correct. It will be noticed that the inscription contradicts the statement of Wood (Ath. Ox. II. 1050) that the admiral was born at Minety. The writer found no trace of the monument to his mother, Margaret (Gilbert) Penn, provided for in the admiral's will, q. v. An account of this tomb has been printed in Notes and Queries, 5th Series, XI., fo. 457. *An exhaustive search of the Parish Registers of St. Mary Redcliffe should be made.*

now in the occupation of John Chalkley; to wife Elizth. for life one close of arrable land in parish of Wellwyn called Thomas Croft, after the decease of my mother Alice Penn & after sd wife's decease to my sd. two daus. Mary & Sarah; Residue to sd. wife Elizth.; Bro. Jonathan Penn Exor.; said son Thomas to be a "dutifull sonne to his mother-in-law"; Wits.—Ro: Vaughan, Nath. Manestey, William Hill; Pro. 21 Jan 1670–1 by the Exor.—Hene 8

1673—Richard Penn of Walthamstow, Co Essex, younger son of Sir Wm. Penn late of Wansteed in Essex, Knt., deceased; Dated 4 April 1673; To be buried in Walthamstow & to poor of that place £10; To mother Dame Margaret Penn £40 yearly for life; To sister Margaret Lowther, wife of Anthony Lowther, Esq. £50 & to said Anthony Lowther £30, 2 guns & a pair of pistols, at the selection of brother William Penn; To servant Geo. Homond £10; Mourning for mother, bro. & sister Anthony & Margaret Lowther, & their children, servant George & mother & sisters servants; To sister (*in law*) Gulielma Maria Penn £50 in token of love; Mother Dame Margaret Executrix; Wit: Richard Newman, George Haman, Michaell Lee.; Proved 11 April 1673 by Extrx named in Will.—Pye 49.

1691—William Penn of Petworth, co. Surrey; died abroad; Emma Markin of Petworth sole legatee & Executrix; Proved 30 Sept. 1691.—Vere 147

1692—Oliver Penn of Stoney Stratford, co. Bucks; brother William Penn of London, Innholder, & his son Oliver; daughter Mary Busby; grandchildren Catherine, Olive, Mary, John & Elizabeth Busby; wife Anne; kinswoman Sarah wife of Henry Honour; Proved 25 July 1692.—Fane 132

1696—William Penn of Penn Place, co. Bucks, Esq.; To father William Penn; sisters Martha, Elizabeth & Henrietta Penn; Exor. Sir Nathaniel Curson; Proved 15 June 1696. —Bond 100

1697—Oswald Penn, Mariner, of H. M. Ship Shrewsbury; Will dated 1 June 1695; wife Mary Penn of Christ Church, Southwark, named Atty. to receive Prize Money & sole Legatee & Exrx; Proved by Relict 8 Apr. 1697.—Pyne 81.

1698—Giles Penn of St Marys, Whitechapel; Susan Butler sole Legatee & Executrix; Proved 26 Mar. 1698.—Lort

1699—Sarah Penn of Penn, co. Bucks, widow; son Roger; 3 daughters Martha-Elizabeth, Catherine & Henrietta; Proved 16 Jan. 1699.—Pett 12.

I WILLIAM PENN, Esqr. so called Cheife proprietor & Gouernour of the Province of Pensiluania and the Territoryes thereunto belonging being of sound mind and understanding for which I bless God doe make and declare this my last Will and Testament.

my eldest Son being well provided for by a Settlement of his Mothers and my ffathers Estate I giue and deuise the Rest of my Estate in manner following

The Gouernment of my Prouince of Pensiluania and Territoryes thereunto belonging and all powers relateing thereunto I giue and devise to the most Hono'ble the Earle of Oxford and Earle Mortimer and to William Earle Powlett so called and their Heires upon Trust to dispose thereof to the Queen or any other person to the best aduantage they can to be applyed in such a manner as I shall hereinafter direct.

I give and devise to my dear Wife Hannah Penn and her ffather Thomas Callowhill and to my good ffriends Margarett Lowther my dear Sister and to Gilbert Heathcote Physitian, Samuel Wildenfield, John ffield, Henry Couldney all liueing in England and to my ffriends Samuel Carpenter, Richard Hill, Isaac Norris, Samuel Preston and James Logan liueing in or near Pensiluania and their heires All my lands Tenements and Hereditaments whatsoeuer rents and other profitts scituate lyeing and being in Pensiluania and the Territores thereunto belonging or else where in

America upon Trust that they shall sell and dispose of so much thereof as shall be sufficient to pay all my just debts and from and after paymt thereof shall conuey unto each of the three Children of my son William Penn, Gulielma-Maria, Springett and William respectiuely and to their respectiue heires 10000 acres of land in some proper and beneficiall places to be sett out by my Trustees aforesaid All the rest of my lands and Hereditamts whatsoeuer scituate lyeing and being in America I will that my said Trustees shall conuey to and amongst the Children which I haue by my present wife in such proporcon and for such estates as my said Wife shall think fitt but before such Conueyance shall be made to my Children I will that my said Trustees shall conuey to my daughter Aubrey whom I omitted to name before 10000 acres of my said Lands in such places as my said Trustees shall think fitt.

All my p'sonall estate in Pensiluania and elsewhere and arreares of rent due there I giue to my said dear Wife whom I make my sole Executrix for the equall benefitt of her and her Children. In Testimony whereof I haue sett my hand and seal to this my Will which I declare to be my last Will reuoking all others formerly made by me.

Signed Sealed and Published by the Testator William Penn in the presence of us who sett our names as Witnesses thereof in the p'sence of the said Testator after the Interlineracon of the Words aboue Vizt: whom I make my sole Executrix.

Sarah West, Robert West, Susanna Reading, Thomas Pyle, Robert Lomax,   (Signed)   Wm Penn.

This Will I made when ill of a feauour at London with a Cleur understanding of what I did then but because of some unworthy Expressions belying Gods goodness to me as if I knew not what I did doe now that I am recouered through Gods goodness hereby declare that it is my last Will and Testament at Ruscomb in Berkshire this 27th of the 3d Month called May 1712.

Wm Penn.

Witnesses p'sent Eliz. Penn, Tho: Pyle, Tho: Penn, Eliz. Anderson, Mary Chandler, Josiah Dee, Mary Dee.

Postscript in my own hand.

As a further Testimony of my loue to my dear Wife I of my own mind giue unto her out of the rents of America vizt: Pensiluania £300 a year for her naturall life and for her care and charge ouer my children in their Education of which she knows my mind as also that I desire that they may settle at least in good part in America where I leaue them so good an Interest to be for their Inheritance from Generacon to Generacon which the Lord p'serue and prosper. Amen.

Probatum fuit hujusmodi Testamentum apud London (cum Codicillo annexo) coram venerabili viro Gulielmo Phipps Legum Doctore Surrogato Venerabilis et egregij viri Johannis Bettesworth Legum etiam Doctoris curiae Proerogativae Cantuari Magistri Custodis sive Comissarij legitimo constituti Quarto die mensis Nouembris Anno Domino Millesimo Septingen'mo Decem Octavo per Affirmaconem sive Declaraconem solennem Hannae Penn viduae Relictae dicti defuncti et Executricis unicae in dic to Testamto: nominatae Cui commissa fuit Administratio omnium et singulorum bonorum jurium et creditorum dicti defuncti declaracone praedicta in praesentio Dei Omnipotentis juxta Actum Parliamenti in hac parte editum et provisum de bene et fidelitur administrando eadem per dictum Executricem prius facta.

Decimo Sexto die mensis ffebruarij Anno D'ni 1726 emt. Com'o Johanni Penn Armo. filio et Ad'stratori cum Test'o annexo bonor' &c Hannae Penn viduae def'tae dum vixit Relictae Ex'tricis unicae et Legatariae Residuariae nominatae in Tes'to dicti Gulielmi Penn def'ti hen' &c ad ad'strandum bona jura et Credita dicti def'ti juxta tenorem et effectum Tes'ti Ipsius def'ti per dictam Ex'tricem modo etiam demortuam inad'strata de bene &c jurat.

Tenison 221.

PREROGATIVE COURT OF CANTERBURY. PENN ADMONS.
1559 to 1700.

1598—Richard Pen late of the town of Salop, decd., Admon. issued 10 Feb. 1597–8, to Willm. Pen, his son.—Act Book 1592–98, fo. 239

1606—Anne Penne late of Barston, co. Warwick, decd., Admon. 25 June 1606 to Thos. Penne her brother.—1605–10, fo. 43

1606—Richard Penne late of City of Westminster, decd., Admon. 11 Nov. 1606 to John Penne his brother.—1605–10, fo. 56

1612—Richard Pen late of parish of St. James, Clerkenwell, co. Midd., Admon. 6 Jan. 1611–12 to Bridgett Pen, relict.—1611–14, fo. 46

1615—Richard Penne late of Stanwell, co. Midd., decd., Admon. 3 April 1615 to John Jordaine one of the creditors. —1615–18, fo. 11

1619—William Penne late of Bromsgrove, co. Worc., decd., Admon. 12 July 1619 to Elizth. Penne, relict. Admon. de bonis non in Nov. 1626 (q. v.).—1619–22, fo. 29

1622—Edward Pen late of Pen, co. Bucks, decd., Admon. 16 July 1622 to Willm. Pen his brother.—1619–22, fo. 187

1626—John Penn late of Gregory Stoke, co. Somerset, bachr., decd., Admon. 3 May 1626 to Agnes Penn alias Middleton & Margt. Penn alias Pococke, his sisters.—1625–27. fo. 81

1626—William Pen of Bradford in parish of Belbroughton, co. Worcester decd., Admon. 11 Nov. 1626 to Anne Pen the relict.—1625–27, fo. 117

1626—William Penn late of Bromsgrove, co. Worcester, decd., Admon. "de bonis non" 20 Nov. 1626 to Gervase Penn his son, Elizth. Penn, the relict, being dead not having fully administered. (Former grant July 1619.)—1625-27, fo. 116

1631—Sibill Winscombe alias Penn late of parish of St. Andrew, Holborn, co. Midd., decd., Admon. 30 June 1631 to Francis Penn next of kin.—1631-33, fo. 36

1632—Henry Penn late " in partibus transmarinus" bachr., decd., Admon. 7 June 1632 to Giles Penne his father.—1631-33, fo. 107

1632—George Penn late of Brinckworth, co. Wilts, decd., Admon. 15 Dec. 1632, to Elizabeth Penn the relict.—1631-33, fo. 138 b.

1641—John Penn late of Corton, co. Suffolk, decd., Admon 7 Nov. 1641 to his mother Elizabeth Penn.—1641, fo. 83

1646—Paul Pen late of Stonystratford, co. Bucks, decd., Admon. 9 June 1646 to Matthew Penn, his kinsman.—1646, fo. 64

1646—William Penn late of Chadesley Corbett, co. Worcester, decd., Admon. 12 Sept. 1646 to Ellianor Penn, the relict.—1646, fo. 108

1648—William Penn late in partibus vltramarinus decd., Admon. 25 Aug. to Susanna Penn, the relict.—1648, fo. 90

1648—Thomas Penn late in partibus transmarinus, bachelor, decd., Admon. 26 Dec. to father Matthew Penn.—1648, fo. 144

1649—Samuel Penn late of parish of St. Clements Danes,

co. Midd., decd, Admon. 9 June to Thomas Penn, his father.—1649, fo. 66

1649—Oswald Penne late of Belbroughton, co. Worcester, bachelor, decd., Admon. 13 July 1649 to William Penn his brother.—1649, fo. 80

1650—James Penn late of the City of Oxford, decd., Admon. 13 Sept., to Willm. Farr, principal creditor.—1650, fo. 138

1654—Michaell Pen late of Stonie Stratford, co. Bucks, decd., Admon. last day of Feb. 1653-4, to Anne Pen, the relict.—1653-54, II, fo. 21

1656—Humfrey Penne late of Hagley, co. Worcester, decd., Admon. 18 June to Katherine Penne, the relict.—1656, fo. 139

1657—Thomas Penn late of Twickenham, co. Midd., decd., Admon. 17 July to Grace Penn, the relict.—1657, fo. 168

1657—Alice Penne late of the City of Worcester, decd., Admon. 5 Oct. to Marke Penne, her husband.—1657, fo. 238

1658—William Penne late of Bromsgrove, co. Worcester, decd., Admon. 18 May to Dorothy Penne, the relict.—1658, fo. 117

1660—Thomas Penne late of the City of Oxford, decd., Admon. 23 Oct. to Alice Pen, the relict.—1660, fo. 145

1671—Thomas Pen late of parish of St. Giles, Cripplegate, London, decd., Admon. 1 Feb. 1670-71 to Elizabeth Pen, the relict. Admon. de bonis non 15 June 1671 to Edward Astell, uncle & guardian assigned to Beate Pen, daughter of said Thomas Pen, Elizabeth Pen, the relict, having died.—1671, fos. 19 & 72

1681-2—Margaret Penn. 13 March 1681-2 Letters of Admon. issued to William Penn, Gent., natural & legit. son of Margarete Penne late of Waltham Stow, co. Essex, widow, deceased intest.—Act Book, fo. 31.

1689—Thomas Penn—Jan. 31, 1689-90, Com. issued to John Armstrong principal Creditor of Thomas Penn late of psh. of St. Olaves, Southwark, in com. Surry, but on the Queen's ship Advice on seas deceased & admon. granted as above. Hanna Penn the Relict first renouncing.—Act Book fo. 14

1691—George Penn—Dec. 15, 1691, Com. issued to George penne the natural and legit. son of George penne Sen: late of Toller Wilm in co. Dorset, deceased intestate &c., Elizabeth penne, the widow, first renouncing.—Act Book fo 224

1693—Stephen Pen—May 17, 1693, Com. issued to Roger Grier, prin. Creditor of Stephen Pen, late in the Island of Barbadoes, deceased unmarried & intestate.—Act Book fo 78

1698—Elizabeth Penne—Jan. 6, 1698—Com. issued to Elizabeth Parker (wife of John Parker) nat. & legit. daughter of Elizabeth penne, late of Evershott, in com. Dorset, widow, deceased intestate, &c—Act Book fo 17

" —Richard Penn—Sept. 30, 1698, Com. issued to Judith Penn, Relict of Richard Penn, late of Shotteswell, in co. Warwick, deceased intestate &c.—Act Book fo 167

1700—Thomas Penn—Oct. 8, 1700, Com. issued to Thomas Penn natural & legit. son of Thomas Penn, late of the City of Bristol, deceased intestate, &c.—Act Book fo 201

The following will, cited in the *Heraldic Journal*, Vol. IV., folio 110, as occurring among the Suffolk wills, may be properly introduced here:

1679—Katherine Penn, widow of James Penn; Will dated 25 Oct. 1679; names only her kinsmen James Allen & his sons James, John & Jeremiah; Witnesses—Humphrey Davis & John Fayerweather. Seals with Arms—Party per chevron Ar. & Erm., in chief 2 leopard's heads erased. Crest—A leopard's head erased. These arms are identified by the writer in the Journal as those of the Alleynes, Baronets, formerly of Barbadoes.

(To be continued.)

GENEALOGICAL GLEANINGS, CONTRIBUTORY TO A HISTORY OF THE FAMILY OF PENN.

BY J. HENRY LEA, Fairhaven, Mass.

WORCESTER PROBATE COURT.[1]

1493—Wm. Penne of Halesowen or Hagley[2] (no abstract). File 1493—N° 1.

1526—Hugh lee of Bromsgrove; will dated xvj May 1526; to be buried in Church of our ladye at B.; Trustees, for wife Alys & child., Nicholas Barnysley of Barnysley, co. Worc., gentl. & William Chaunce of same; (inter alia child.) dau. Elizabet Pen, wiffe to Phylyp Pen, & Gilbert Pen, son of sd. Phylyp; &c., pro. iij Apr. 1528. File 1526—N° 96.

1552-3—Richard Penne (no abstract). File 1552-3—N°—.

1557—Edmund Penne of Bidford (no abstract). File 1557—N° 50.

---

[1] At the time of the writer's examination of the Worcester Calendars the idea of collecting Penn material had not suggested itself to him, and the fragments above given were preserved by a mere accident. As the county was evidently rich in Penns, from the evidence in the Prerogative Court, there can be no doubt that a thorough search of this District Court would yield considerable results.

[2] In the Visitation of Worcestershire in 1634
  William Penn of Hagley
  Francis Pen of Belbroughton
occur among the Disclaimers, alleging that they are no gentlemen and claim no right to bear arms. (Brit. Mus. Ad. MS. 19,816, art. 2.) The will of Richard Penn, of Hagley, dated 1470, beneficiary to Cath. of Worc., and to parishes of Hagley, Clent, Pedmore, Belbroughton, Churchill, etc., is quoted by Nash, the county historian, "Herald and Genealogist," Vol. VII. fo. 131.

PENN MONUMENTAL INSCRIPTIONS AT PENN, CO. BUCKS.[1]

In Memorium Gulielmi Penn Armigeri ex desiderio suo extra in Coemeterio sepulti qui obiit duodecimo die Maij Anno Dom. 1693. Anno aetatis suae 64 hoc posituum.

Heere lyeth the Bodyes of William Pen, Esq and of Martha his Wife, by whom hee had issue one Sonne and two Daughters. Shee dyed the 19th. day of November Anno Dni 1635. Hee dyed the 9th. day of January Anno Dni 1638.

Hic jacent corpora Johannis Pen Armigeri quond'm Domini hujus Manerij de Pen qui obiit—die Octobris Anno salutis 1597 et aetatis suae 63 et Ursulae uxoris eius Que obiit anno salutis — et aetatis suae - Horum terreno clanduntur membra sepulchro sed capiunt animas sydera sola pias Quos univit, mortis seperare potestas Non voluit, junctos cerimus hoc tumulo.

Heere lyeth interred the Bodye of John Pen of Pen Esquire, who married Sarah the Daughter of Sr : Henry Drury, Knight, by whome hee had Issue five Sonnes and five Daughters. Hee departed this life the second of July A° Dni 1641.

Here lies the Body of Mrs. Henrietta Penn, sister of Roger Penn, Esq., who died Jany. ye 17th. 1728.

Here lies the Body of Roger Penn, Esq., Lord of this Manor, who died unmarried March ye 17th. 1731 in the 55th year of his age.

—— lies the Body of Mrs. —— Penn, Sister to Roger Penn, —— who died Augst. 12th. 1728.

Here lies the Body of Elizabeth Catherine Penn, Sister to Roger Penn, Esq., who died Feby. ye 20th. 1——.

[1] From Lipscomb's "History of Bucks," Vol. III. fo. 287.

William, Son of the Honble: Thomas Penn, Esq., Proprietor of Pennsylvania & of the Rt. Honble: Lady Juliana Penn, his Wife, died Feb. 14, 1753, aged 7 months.

Near this place lies the Body of —— daughter of Sr: Nathaniel Curzon of Kedleston, Bart., by Sarah his Wife, daughter of William Penn, Esq. who died Jan. 19 1701, aged 29 years. Also Christopher Curzon, Doctor of Civil Law, younger son of same, who died Feb. 4, 1713, aged 32 years.

PEWSEY (WILTS) REGISTER.[1]

Baptisms.

1568—m—— Pen the son of Richard Pen was baptized the sixt of January.

1569—William Pen the sone of Richard Pen was baptized the 6 of December.

1572—Richard Pene the son of Richard Pen was bapt. the xx of Aprill.

1573—John Pen the son of Richard Pen was bapt: the same 17 of January.

1576—Richard Pen the sone of Richard Pen was bapt: the x of October.

1578—Gregory Pen the sone of Richard Pen was bapt: th 22 of march.

1582—Jone Pen the daughter of Richard Pen was bapt: May 7.

1601—Ellenor Pen the daughter of Richard Pen was bapt: Aprill 12.

1604—Thomas Pene the sone of Richard Pene was bapt: July: 29.

1606—Daniel Pene the sonn of Mathew Pene was bapt: ffebru: 22.

---

[1] The register dates from 1568, and is in beautiful preservation. The writer's most cordial thanks are due to the Hon. and Rev. Mr. Bouverie, Rector of Pewsey, for the great courtesy shown by him and the facilities afforded for making the examination of this important Register full and thorough. Most valuable items were obtained from it for the family in whose behalf the search was made.

1607—Richard Pene the sone of Richard Pene was bapt: June x.

1611—Agnis Pene the Daughter of william Pene was bapt: ffebru: 26.

1612—Jane the daughter of mathew Pene was bapt: Deceb: 20.

1612—Elizabeth the daughter of Gregory Pene was bapt: Jana: 24.

1641—Jane the daughter of Williā Penn was baptized sixth of march.

1642—wenifrinte the Daughter of Richard Penn was bapt August the 4.

1644—William the sonne of William Penn was bapt: March the 2.

1650—Christian the daughter of John Penn was baptized the 7th of Aprill.

1650—Sarah the daughter of William Penn was baptised the 19th. of July.

1652—Hester the daughter of Richard Penn was bapt the 13th. of Aprill.

1652—Ann the daughter of John Penn was bapt the 17th of octob:/August.

1662 [1]—elner the daughter of John Penn was bapt the 14 of September.

1653—Daniell penn the sonn of Richard penn was bapt the 15 of october.

1655—John penn the sonn of John penn was bapt the 15 of april 1655.

1657—Richard the soon of Richard penn was bapttized 4 of october.

1658—philipe the sone of John penn was bapt the 8 of february 1658.

1660—Thomas the soone of John penn was bapt the first of nouember 1660.

1662—Ellenor the daughter of John Penn was bapt Sept: 14th.

---

[1] Misplaced and duplicate entry. See foot of page.

1665—James the Sonn of John & Edey Penn bapt May th ffifteenth.

1668—Elizabeth Penn ye Daughter of John Penn & Edith his Wife was baptized March ye 7th.

Weddings.

1604—Roger Deare and Jone Pene were maryed Janua: 21: 1604.

1626—John Adams and Agnis Pen were maryed Octo: 9.

1641—Richard Pen & Christian Colman were married August th 28.

1676—William Harding & Elizabeth Penn both of this Parish were married June the twelfth.

Burials.

1568—Michael Pen the sone of Richard Pen was buryed Janu: 23.

1573—Richard the Sone of Richard Pen was buried march: 28.

1574—Catherine Pen was bury—noub: 21.

1605—Alice Pene the wife of Richard Pen was buryed Janu: 20.

1606—Richard Pene was buried Janu: 5.

1623—Jone the Daughter of Richard Pen was buryed Jan: 14.

1649—Cicely the wyfe of Richard Penn was buryed the 18th of Octbr:

1654—widow penn was buried the 19 Nouember.

1657—Richard penn was buried the 24 of september 1657.

1663—Jean Penn was buried Octob: 4th.

1665—Doritey the wife Richard Penn buried May the siuenth.

1665—William Penn buried Deasember the sixt.

1669—Jacob Pen son of Richard Pen of Kepnet Tithing buried April.

1670—John Penn & Edith his wife buried August the seventeenth.

1688—Richard Penn was buried the Third of March (Affidavit not made till March the thirteenth).[1]

1694—Penn—Richard Penn was Buried September the third (in woollen).

REGISTER OF ST. MARY'S-MARLBORO' (WILTS).[2]

Baptisms.

1603—Richard the sonne of John Pen was bapt the ixth of December.

1605, June—Mariar the daughter of John Pen the fourth day.

1608-9, March—Amy and Elizabeth the daughters of John Pen the 26.

1623—Alice daughter of Robert Pen   Septamb 14.
1641—Mary daughter of John Pen octobr: 3.
1648—Margaret daughter of John Penn Aprill 18.

Weddings.

1637—John Pen & Susan Auste August 19.

Burials.

1625—Mary wife of John Pen January 12.
1641—John Pen sonne of John Pen March 27.
1656—Elizabeth ye daughter of John Penn March ye 21.
1657—John Penn   octobr: th 29.
1673—John Penn   August 28.

HIGHWORTH REGISTER.[3]

1636—Robert Penne sonn of Richard Penne buried 20 January 1636.

MALMESBURY ABBEY (WILTS) REGISTER.[4]

1606, Aug.—The xvij daye was baptized Elizabeth Penn the Daughter of Thomas Penn of Rodborn.

---

[1] Affidavit of burial in woollen only, according to act of Parliament in 1679.

[2] The register dates from 1602.

[3] Searched from 1627 to 1650 only. Records date from 1539.

[4] The Malmesbury Abbey Registers, which include the Chapelry of Rodborne, commence in 1590, and are in a fine state of preservation. No

1610-1, January—The xxiiijth. daye was baptized Joane Penne the Daughter of Tho: Penn.

1613, Maij—Anna Penn, daughter of Tho: bap: 29.

1615, Deceb:—Janet ye daughter of Thomas Penn of Rodborne bap: 30.

1619, September—The 16 day was baptized william Penne the sonne of Thomas Penne.

1619, October—The 23rd. was buried Joane Penn of Rodbourne.

1622, December—The 2th. day was buryed Elizabeth Pen the daughter of Thomas Pen of Rodburne.

1626, July—Baptized the 23 George Sonne of Tho: Penne of Rodborne.

1646—Buryed the 18th. ffebruarie 1646 Thomas Penn of Rodborne.

SHERSTON MAGNA (WILTS) REGISTER, FROM THE TRANSCRIPTS[1] AT DIOCESAN REGISTRY, SALISBURY.

1605—Editha Penne sepulta fuit xij die Julij Anno pd.

REGISTER OF ALLHALLOWS PARISH, BARKING, LONDON.

Baptisms.

1644, October 23—William, son of William Penn and Margarett his wife of the Tower Liberty.[2]

---

search was made for Penns after the burial of Thomas, in 1646, and other entries may exist, as the family were still seated there in 1665 (see will of Thomas Penn, in Archdeacon of Wilts Court). In one of his manuscripts Awbrey mentions "old Mr. Penn of Rodburne, an ingeniose man and a good chymist," temps Jac. I., as of the same family as the founder of Pennsylvania and Admiral Sir William Penn.—JACKSON'S "Awbrey's Wilts," fo. 280.

[1] These transcripts are very fragmentary and defective. The Register at Sherston has perished previous to 1653. The earliest year in the Transcripts is 1605. Although searched to 1812, no other Penns were found.

[2] This e⋯ ⋯t of the baptism of the Founder is taken from "Collections Relating to the History of the Parish of Allhallows, Barking, in the City of London," by Rev. Joseph Maskell, folio 68. It has been previously cited in PENNA. MAG., Vol. VIII. folio 108.

BIDFORD (WARWICKSHIRE) REGISTER.[1]

Baptisms.

1688, Sept. 3—John son of William Pen.
1690, June 10—William son of William Pen.
1692, Sept. 17—Robert son of William Penn.
1694, Feb. 10—Elizabeth, dau. of William Penn.
1705, Oct. 7—Sarah dau. of Ann Penn.
1720, Feb. 23—Mary dau. of Elizabeth Penn.

Marriages.

1731, Apr. 27—Edward Price and Elizabeth Penn.
1742, Sept. 2—Thomas Court and Sarah Penn.

Burials.

1666, Mch. 8—John son of William Pen.
1669, Dec. 26—William Pen.
1695, Sept. 21—Elizabeth Pen, widow.
1695, Nov. 3—William Pen.
1747, Oct. 25—Anne Penn, widow, of Brome.

SOUTH LITTLETON (WORCESTER) PARISH REGISTER.[2]

Baptisms.

1554, Jan. 10—Alys, dau. of Wyllyam pen, tayler.

1576, Oct. 17—Phyllyppe, dau. of Wm: and Joane Hyll, commenly called Pen.

1580, Apr. 9—Alyce, dau. of Wm: and Jone Hyll, commenly called Pen.

1588, Nov. 24—Elsabeth Hyll, commenly called Penne, dau. of Wm: and Joane Hyll.

---

[1] The Bidford Register dates from 1655 for marriages and 1664 for baptisms and burials. The above extracts, which are evidently fragmentary, appear to have been taken from the bishop's transcripts. They, as well as the four following register extracts, are taken from Coleman's "Notes," pp. 12-14. Bidford lies close to the Worcestershire border, about fourteen miles southeast of Bromsgrove and four north of Littleton. Brome is about one mile west of Bidford.

[2] The registers exist from 1538, but are defective—the baptisms after 1644 and the burials after 1610—according to the government report.

1734, Oct. 6—Mary, dau. of Samuel and Mary Penn.
1736, Nov. 14—William, son of Samuel and Mary Pen.
1738, Mch. 11—Anne, dau. of Samuel and Mary Penn.
1741, June 14—John, son of Samuel and Mary Penn.

Marriages.

1562, Nov. 21—Jhon Marshall and Margery Hyll otherwise called penne.

1566, Oct. 26—Michael Roberts and Jone Hyll otherwise called penne.

1581, Nov. 21—Thomas Marshall and Elnor Hyll commenlye called Pen.

1587, Oct. 2—Wm: Tayler and Alice Hyll commenlye called Pen.

Burials.

1553, Oct. 31—Thomas son of Wyllyam penne, tayler.
1559, July 3—Sybyll Hyll als penne.
1564, May 14—Margarete Hyll als pen.
1588, July 15—Wyllyam Hylle the elder, commenly called Pen, a tayler.
1594, Jan. 24—Ales, wife of Wm: Hill als Pen.
1736, May 27—John Penn.
1741, Aug. 15—Samuel Penn.

BLOCKLEY (WORCESTER) REGISTER.[1]

Baptisms.

1665, May 2—Nathaniel son of Giles Pen of Dorne.

1719, June 7—Anna filia Gulielmi Penn et Annae ux. de Blockley.

Marriages.

1713, Sept. 29—Gulielmus Pen et Anna Wilks de Blockley.

---

[1] The register dates from 1538. Blockley, although under the jurisdiction of Worcester, is geographically in Gloucester, being a detached part of Oswaldslow Hundred, about a mile south of Chipping-Campden, Gloucester.

STANTON (GLOUCESTER) REGISTER.[1]
Baptisms.
1629, Sept. 20—Wm. son of Wm. Penne.
1631, July 24—Maria filia Gulielmi Penne.
1633, Sept. 1—Johannes filius Gulielmi Penne.
1636, May 1—Richard son of Wm. Penne.
1638, Jan. 20—Anna filia Gualteri Penne.

Burials.
1629, May 21—Richardus Penn, puer.
1640, May 7—Gulielmus Penne, Textor.
1696, Mch. 23—Maria Penn, vetula inupta.
1729, May 4—Johannes Pen, coelebs.

CHIPPING-CAMPDEN (GLOUCESTERSHIRE) PARISH REGISTER.[2]
Baptisms.
1660, Sept. 14—Thomas son of Wm. Pen.
1661, Dec. 1—Anthony and Wm. sons of Wm. Pen.
1664, Nov. 1—John son of John Pen.
1666, July 1—Sarra dau. of John Pen.
1668, Feb. 8—John son of John Pen.
1671, Apr. 9—Wm. son of John Pen.

Marriages.
1695, Oct. 14—Wm. Pen and Mary Adkinson.

Burials.
1681, May 18—William Pen.

REGISTER ST. HELEN'S—WORCESTER.[3]
1630—Anne, daughter of John Penn baptized 4 July.
1632—Henry Penne & Elizabeth Redinge married 20 August.

[1] The existing register only dates from 1653, showing that Mr. Coleman's extracts, in this case at least, must have been taken from the transcripts. Stanton is in the northeast part of the county, close to the Worcestershire border and about seven miles west of Blockley and about the same distance from Chipping-Campden.
[2] The register dates from 1616.
[3] Cited by H. S. Grazebrook, Esq., in "Herald and Genealogist," VII. 131.

WILTS LAY SUBSIDIES IN THE PUBLIC RECORD OFFICE.

1576—Rodbourne—Edmond Pen in goods iiij li vjs viijd. (198.294).

1581—Rodbourne—Edmond Pen bon. iiij li iiijs. (198.296).

1587—Sharston Magna—John Penne goods xxs. iiijd. (198.324).

1587—Malmesbry borough—Willms Pene[1] goods iij li—viijd. (198.324).

1587—Rodborne—Edwardus Penne goods iij li—viijd. (198.324).

1599—Rodborne— —— Penne goods iij li — — (198.331).

1600—Luckington — William Penn goods iij li viijs. (198.333).

1609—Rodborne—Thomas Peine (Seassors[2]) terris, xxs; 1—iiijd. (199.366).

1609—Luckington—Willms Penn terris xxs; js—iiijd. (199.366).

1623—Rodborne—Thomas Penn Lands xxs.; 4s. (199.378).

1625—Sherston Magna—Agnes Pen Goodes. iijli xls. (199.382).

1625—Rodborne—Thomas Pen Lands xxs. (199.383).

1629—Sherston Magna—Agnet Penne Vid. goods iijli viijs. (199.399).

1629—Rodborne—Thomas Penn lands xxs. iiijs. (199.399).

1641—Allington (Calne) Willms Pen gen., Goodes iiijli xxs iiijd. (199.406).

WILTS MUSTERS IN PUBLIC RECORD OFFICE.

1538—The Certyfycatt of the vewe of abull men, as well Archars as Byllmen, takyn the x daye of Apryll, in the xxxth yere of the reyne of our Soverayne Lorde, King Henry the VIIIth by the Grace of God Kynge of Englonde

---

[1] This William Penn, of Malmesbury, I believe to have been the William, father of William, of Minety, who died before his father, and was grandfather of Admiral Sir William Penn.

[2] Query if assessor—*i.e.*, of taxes—is not intended by this?

& of ffraunce, defender of the ffayth, Lord of Irelonde & in the erth mooste suppreme hed of the Church of Englonde; by Sir Henry Longe, Knt., John Hamlyn, Esq., & Wyllm Stump, Commyssyoners:

Brynkworth.
Roger Pen archar.

(A. 6. 12.)

1633—Bond of Richard Cusse[1] of Wotton basset, in com. Wilts, Mercer to the Bishop & Sir John Prouden, clerk, in £100 that there be not nor hereafter shall be any let or impediment etc. etc but that Richard Cusse & Susan Penn of the Parish of Brinkworth, spinster, may lawfully marry together. Sworn before ffran : Roberts, ntr. pbu. 2 August, 1633.

Marriage Bonds in Diocesan Registry Office at Salisbury 1628 to 33.

WILTSHIRE PROBATE COURTS.

Archdeacon of Sarum's Court.

1538—John Penne of Patney Will & Inventory (Will has perished).

Consistory Court of Sarum.
(Searched 1593 to 1744.)

1616–17—Thomas Pen de Aldrington   Test.   121

1632—Henry Penn of Broad Chalke, Wilts., sick & weak &c; will dated 4 June 1632; To be buried in Broadchalke Churchyard; To my daughter Alice Penn, bedding, household stuff, & also my biggest coffer at my son, Ralph Penn's house; household stuff &c to my daughter Sarah Smalwell,

---

[1] The name of Cusse is an ancient one in Wiltshire. A pedigree from the Visitation of 1623 is in Harl. Manuscripts 1165, folio 97. In the Parish Register of Christian-Malford, Wilts, the writer met with a member of this family bearing the somewhat contradictory appellation of "Christian Cuss."

This Susan Penn is unquestionably the daughter of William and Margaret (Rastall) Penn, and the aunt of Admiral Penn, father of the founder.

wife of John Smalwell, to my sons Ralph Penn & Thomas Penn, my godson Henry Penn & my grandchild John Penn; Residue to my son Thomas Penn & my daughter Alice Penn, joint Exors; The mark of Henry Penn; John Streat & Thos. Moxam, overseers, to whom 12 d. each; Wit: Wm. Archer, Thos. Moxam, John Streat, Henry Davis; Inventory taken 30 June 1632, total not given, but about £20; proved 28 July 1632, by the Exs.

1646—Ralph Penn, late of Broadchalke, Wilts., Yeoman, decd. Admon. Bond of Mary Penn of Broadchalke, relict of the above, & John Smalwell of Broadchalke, Yeoman, 22 May 1646. Inventory taken 2 May 1646, total 171 li. 7 s. 10 d., The mark of Marie Pen, Jo: Smalwell, Jo: Lawes.

Sub Dean of Sarum's Court.

1587—John Penn, late of the parish of St. Martin in the City of New Sarum, deceased. Admon. 7 July 1587 to his son John pen Senr (sic) Inventor 35s. 8d.

Chantor & Treasurer's Court.

1697—Mary Penn of Highworth. Will (abstract not received).

Peculiar of Dean of Sarum.

1699—Jsabella Penn of Hurst. Will (abstract not recd).

Archdeacon of Wilts' Court.

1601—Will of Edmund Towerman of Rodborne, co. Wilts. dated 20 Dec. 1601; Overseers Wm: Knapp, Thos. Powle & Thos. Penn. Witnessed by William Penne, the writer.
Reg. Book A. fo. 144.

1619—Joane Penn of Rodburne in the parish of Malmesbury, co. Wilts., widow; will dated 13 July 1619; no date of Probate; To the children of Nathaniel Butt & Mary Butt £20 to be employed to the use of Mary Butt, my daughter, for her maintenance & that of her children, by the hands of my daughter Alice Power of Stanton Quinton.[1] To Thomas Butt & George Butt, two of the said children, an ox & a steer when of age; To Edith Batten's children 30s. among them; To Wm. Cox 40s.; To Margery Bayley 20s.; To my son William Penn, all my goods & chattels unbequeathed, he to be sole Exor. if at the time of my death he shall come into England to take possession thereof, but if he shall be dead, or not come into England as aforesd., then I bequeath the said residue to my daughter Alice Powell & make her Extrix. (No signature.) Wit. Thos. Penn, Elizth. Penn, John Smith; Inventory of goods taken 25 Oct. 1619 by Richd Jaques, gent., Thos. Cox, Zacharias Power & Wm. Tanner, yeomen (no total given, but in all about £60).

1628—George Penn of Brinkworth. Will (abstract not received).

1630—Will of George Jones, Yeoman, of Grittenham, co Wilts; dated 20 ffeb. 1629; proved 7 Oct. 1630: Overseer George Penn, gent.   File 30 N° 12.

1634—Will of Robert Sargent of Gritlington, co Wilts— Yeoman; dated June 1634; no date probate; bequest "to Joanne Penne, wife of John Penne, 3 ackers of Barley, shonting vpon ould mead."

File 40 N° 34.

1637—Will of Richard Cromwell of Startley, Parish of Broad Somerford, co. Wilts, husbandman; dated 8 Aug. 1637; Witnessed by Elizabeth Penne.   File 49 N° 14.

1665—Thomas Penne of Rodborne in Parish of Malmesburie, co Wilts, Yeoman; nuncupative will dated 20 Maye 1657; proved 5 June 1665; To all his children then living

---

[1] Compare with Awbrey's statement, already cited (page 287), that "at Rodbourne there were Penns, which —— Power of Stanton Quinton married." Jackson's "Awbrey's Wilts' Collections," folio 270. It is probable that the Zacharias Power who assists in taking the inventory was the husband of Alice.

1/s. apeece; wife Anne Penne Sole Residuary Legatee & Extrx.; Witnesses Wm: Gale & John Winkworth, sen. Inventory taken 22 May 1657 by David Alexander & Jeremy Godwine :—Sum to'l is 71 li 3s. 0d. File 57 N° 32.

1665—Will of Elizabeth Penne of Rodborne, Widow; da 11 Apr 1664; pr 4 June 1665; dau Joane wife of Walter Wastfield 6 pounds & to all her child. 40/s. to be div. among them & to sd dau Joane table & bed linen & clothing; child. of son-in-law John Sparrow 12/d apeece; Elizabeth dau. of said J. S. "one greene rugg"; grchild Mary Symmons 1 Iron Pott, bed linen, clothing, &c. & 10 pounds at 21 years, with remainder to grchd. Jane Penne, eld. dau. of my son Thomas Penne, dec'd; grchd Mary Penne, dau of William Penne dec'd., 20/s at end of 7 years after my decease "if she shall not recover any lands in Ireland," but if she recover such lds this legacy to be void; to all child. of son Thomas Penne dec'd 20/s apeece! to dau-in-law Anne Penne of Rodburne Residuary Legatee & Extrx; Overseers—Friends John Auth of ffowlesweeke & Richard Winkworth of Somerford Magna; Witnesses—William Gale, Jeremie Godwin. Signed with mark.

Inventory taken 14 Nov. 1664 by John Handy, William Gale & Jeremiah Godwin. 24 li—13s—2d.

File 57 no. 48.

1682—Eliza Penn of Pewsey. Bond. (abstract not rec'd).

1689—Richard Penn of Pewsey. Will & Inv. (abstract not rec'd).

Marriage Licenses at Diocesan Registry—Worcester.

1580, Jan. 27—Thomas Penne & Mary Bradshaw of Worcester.

1584, Sept. 20—Thomas Penne & Ann Vizar of St. Nicholas Psh. Worcester.

1681, July 2—John Clarke & Mary Pen both of Clent.[1]

[1] The above from a communication by Rev. Thomas P. Wadley, in Marshall's "Genealogist," VI. folio 177.

Somerset Wills.

1606—James Bysse of Croscombe, Somerset. Will not dated. Proved 14 Feb. 1606/7 by relict Christian. Legacy to daughter Joyce Penn.

Pre. Ct. Cant. Huddlestone 21.

1608—Christian Bisse of Croscombe, co. Somerset. Will dated 30 Jan. 1608; Proved 10 Aug. 1609. Legacy of £10 to daughter Joyce Pen. Proved by son Robert. Wells Registry.

ST. MARY REDCLIFFE—BRISTOL.[1]

Baptisms.

1607, ffebruarie 24—Rachell daughter to Gyles Penne.

1610, Maie 26—Elianor the daughter of George Penne.

1610, Decembr 23—Catherine the daughter of williā Penne.

Marriages.

1600—Giles Penne and Joan Gilbeart were married the vth. Daye of Nouember.

Burials.

1612, Nouember 24—Elianor the daughter of Mr Giles Penne.

1628, Awgust 12—Mattha Pen Daughter to m'gery Pen Wydow.

1651, ffebe: 23—Ann Pen.

1670, Octobr 3—S^r willam penn In Led.

NOTE.—The writer must express his most cordial thanks to the Vicar, Rev. C. E. Cornish, and the curates, Messrs. Ramsay and Seavey, for the facilities shown him in the examination of these important registers.

---

[1] First Vol. Reg. 1559–1677.

GENEALOGICAL GLEANINGS, CONTRIBUTORY TO A HISTORY OF THE FAMILY OF PENN.

BY J. HENRY LEA, FAIR HAVEN, MASSACHUSETTS.

DEAN AND CHAPTER OF WESTMINSTER. 1504 to 1750.

1517—Will of Anthony Legh of psh. of St. Margarets, Westminster; Dated 1 october mvxvij, ix Hen. viij, Pro. 6 ffeb. 1517; bequeathes (*inter alia*) to godson Antony penne xl s.—Reg. Wyks fo. 129.

1538—Robert Pen; Will dated xxvj Sept. xxx Hen. viij; sons John and Anthony Exrs.; dau. Cecylly my Covent Seall of Abbey of Westminster & xx nobles & a ryng with a dyamond wch was hyr mothers & my best bedd & cou^{r}lett; dau. Elizabeth xx^s & h^r dau. Anne a Ryall; son William the bedd he lyeth on; sons John & Anthony Res. Legs.; owes to m^r ffysher iiij s. but he saith that it is vj s. but I confesse but iiij s. & that is all the dettes I owe in the worlde; m^r Subdean of the kyngs Chapell with all my fellows haue eu^{r}y man a penny; Wit. m^r byrd, m^r barker, m^r Radys, m^r bury, m^r Colman, m^r Raffe of the vestry; Pro. xvj Oct. mvxxxviij by Exrs.—Reg. Bracy 66.

1685—Probate on Will of Johanna Pen, late of parish of St. Margarets, Westminster, widow, granted 18 February 1685 to Mary Wise, dau & sole Executrix named in the will. (*Will filed but not Reg.*)—Act Book, fo. 78.

1698—Probate on Will of John Penn late of St. Margarets in the city of Westminster, granted 11 May 1698 to Robert Hater, the Executor named in the Will. (*Will filed but not Reg.*)—Act Book, fo. 87.

Other Names in Calendar of which no Notes were taken.

1715—Ralph Penn　　Jan.　　Filed　Act Book fo. 63

1720—Elizabeth Penn 2 Mar.　　"　　"　　" 106

1739—William Penn　May　　"　　"　　" 95

1740—John Penn　　May　　"　　"　　" 99

Admons.

1614—William Penn　　　Feb.　　Act Book, fo. 23

1648—Joanna Penn　　T. Aug.　　　"　　" 13

1673—Gulielmus Penn　　Jan.　　　". 　" 83

1678—Peter Penn " Reno."　(*So entered in index.*)

1722—George Penn　　　July　　Act Book, fo. 115

" Ad° et Ren°" in Index　Inv 84.

ARCHDEACONRY OF WILTS.

1630-1—Chri'ri' Tucke ats Pen de Charleton. Compos Georgii Pen Sup.[1] Admon. bonor. Bundle 29, no. 63.

ARCHDEACONRY COURT OF LONDON. 1564 to 1719.[2]

1588—Richard Penn. 22 July Commissued for Admon. of goods of Richard Pen late of St. Andrew Wardropp, to Isabelle Pen his relict. Inv. Ex. sm. 58*.—Act Book, fo. 9.

---

[1] An exhaustive search both by others and myself having failed to bring to light the documents referred to in the entry before given from this court (PENNA. MAG., Vol. XIV. p. 294)*as "1628—George Penn of Brinkworth, Will," it seems probable that this was an error, and the George above referred to is the one intended. No doubt identical with the George of Brinkworth, whose Admon. in 1632 has been already given.—P. C. C., Act Book, fo. 138b.

[2] The earlier indices of this important court, which date from 1368 (with some chasms), were not examined.

*For p. 294 see p. 595, this volume.

1593—Thomas Penn. 26 Nov. 1593 Commission issued for Admon. of goods of Thomas (*Humphrey first written & interlined*) Penn late of St. Botolph without Aldersgate, to Rose Penn his relict. Inv. Ex. summ iiij^{oo} vj^{li} ij^s x^d.—Act Book, fo. 135.

1639—Christian Penn of St. Andrew in Holborne, co. Middx., Widdowe, in good health; Will dated 6 Nov. 1628, 4 Chas.; To kinswoman Sara Orchard £100 in 12 mos. yf shee bee then livinge, & all househ. stuffe & wearinge apparell &c.; kinsman Thomas Orchard, bro. of said Sara £5; goddau. Christian Kinge £10; Mrs. Susan Linsey wife of my Exr. a ring of gold of £3; Mr. William Linsey Res. Leg. & Exr.; Wit. Anthony ffish, William Studwy, Thomas ffitzhushe & John Comberford. Pro. 6 Nov. 1639 by Exr. (*See pro. Act infra.*)—Reg. Book 8, fo. 310.

6 Nov. 1639 Probate on will of Christiana Penn, widow, of St. James Clerkenwell, co. Middx., granted to William Linsey, the Exr. named in the will. Inv. Ex. 24^{li} 14^s 11^d.—Act Book, fo. 45.

1665—Robert Penn. 7 October 1665 Probate on Will of Robert Penn of St. Trinity, London, granted to Grace Certaine, the Executrix named in the will. (*Will filed but not Reg.*)—Act Book, fo. 136.

1687—Samuel Penn. 4 Nov. Commission issued to Mary Penn, relict of Samuel Penn, late of St. Leonards Shoreditch, London, deceased intestate, to admr. &c.—Act Book, n. f.

1707—Elizabeth Penn ats Edis Ad° Jan. (*No notes taken.*)—Act Book, n. f.

DEAN AND CHAPTER OF ST. PAUL'S. 1535 to 1725.

1591—Agnes Penne, wyfe to Thomas Penne of Graies Jnne Lane & parishe of St. Andrewes, in Holborne, co. Middx., Late wief & Extrx. of Thos. Ensar of same parish

& Co., Late Citizen & Butcher of London, dec'd.; Languishinge Weake & sicke in bodye; makes will with consent of husband Thomas Penne; Dated last Sept. 1691 33 Eliz.; To be buried in Ch. or Chyd. of St. Andrews; sonne Thomas Ensar a peyer of best flaxen sheets, a flaxen tablecloth, Doz. best Napkyns, all my childbedd lynen & 2 golde Ringes whereof thone ys a Hooped or weddinge ringe & one other Ringe sett wth a stone called a Cornelion, at age of xxj yeares; forgyve to George Ralfe half the debt he oweth to my husbande; Husband Thomas Penne Res. Leg. & sole Exr.; Wit. John nashe scr., margarett Hoddys wydowe, william walker. John Evans his marke, Confirmed by mee Thomas Penne; Pro. 2 Dec. 1591 by Exr. named in will.—Book B, fo. 361.

1686—John Penn. 29 Dec. Commission issued for Admon. of estate of John Penn, late of St. Giles, Cripplegate, but dec'd. intestate, to his widow, Bridgitt Penn, &c.—Adm. Act Book, fo. 98.

1718—John Penn. 3 Feb. 1717–8, Commission issued to Mary Penn, relict of John penn of precinct of purpool in parish of St. Andrews Holborn, co. Middx., to administer &c.—Act Book fo. 101.

1722—Thomas Penn. 11 Apr. Commission issued to Elizabeth Penn relict of Thomas Penn of St. Giles, Cripplegate, to administer &c.—Act Book, fo. 147.

SUNDRY GLEANINGS.

1516—Will of William Scott of Busshey, co. Herts.; Dated 17 Mar 1516, pro.—June 1516; son Richard Prin. Leg. & Exr. with John Hodell Anne Pen one heifer; daus of Jordan; dau Marion; wife; son John; Archdeaconry of St. Albans—Reg. Walingford fo. 162.

1681—William Penn. Nov. 15 Commission issued to Ellinora Penne, Widow of William Penne, late of parish of

St. Sepulchre, London, decd intestate, to admr. &c. Commissary of London.—Act Book 24, fo. 2.

1706—Will of Bernard Lee of psh of Arberfild, co. Berks., yeoman, in reasonable health but well stricken in years; Dated 24 July 1701 13 Wm. 3, pro. 13 Apr 1706; wife Christian; daus. Ann, Mary, Elizabeth & Christian; sons Bernard & James; Wit. Edw: Penn, Susanna Standen, Margarett penn, John May, Phebe Knight. Adm. to son James & dau Christian (no Exr. being named), with bond of John Sale of Arborfeild, Clerk, & Henry Dame of Soning, yeoman in £1000. Dean of Sarum Filed Will.

1721—Richard Penn. 22 May Commission issued to Richard penn father of Richard Penn, Junr., late of parish of St. Mary Rotherhith in co. Surrey, but in the merchant ship Le Cadogan at Newfoundland, deceased intestate, to admr. &c. Commisary Court Surrey.[1]—Act Book, fo. 92.

FRIENDS' RECORDS AT DEVONSHIRE HOUSE, LONDON, E. C. BRISTOL QUARTERLY MEETING.

Births.[2]

1701/2—1 mo. 9—Thomas Penn born at dwelling house of Thomas Callowhill son of William & Hannah Penn.

1703—5 mo. 30—Hannah Margerita Penn born at Thomas Callowhills in James Parish, daughter of William and Hannah Penn.

1704—9 mo. 7—Margaret Penn born at Thomas Callowhills in James parish daughter of same.

1705—11 mo. 17—Richard Penn born at Thomas Callowhills son of same.

---

[1] This court, which was searched from its commencement in 1662 to 1726, contains no other entries of the name of Penn than the above.

[2] Marriages and burials of this Quarterly were not examined, and no doubt contain other entries.

FRIENDS' RECORDS AT DEVONSHIRE HOUSE, LONDON,
E. C. BUCKS QUARTERLY MEETING.

Births.

1672—11 mo. 23—Gulielma Maria Penn, daughter of William & Gulielma Maria Penn, born at Rickmansworth, Herts. Upperside Mo. M.

1673—12 mo. 28—William & Mary Penn, twins, children of William & Gulielma Maria Penn, born at Rickmansworth. Upperside M. M.

1675—11 mo. 25—Springett Penn son of William & Gulielma Maria Penn born at Walthamstow, Essex, parish of Rickmansworth.

Marriages.

1672—2 mo. 4—William Penn of Walthamstow, Essex, & Gulielma Maria Springett of Penn, married at Kings Charitywood, Herts. Upperside Mo. M.

1688—5 mo. 30—Richard Dell of Chesham & Mary Penn, spinster, of Coleshill, Amersham parish, Herts., daughter of Thomas & Martha Penn of Adderbury, Oxon., married at Amersham, Upperside Mo. M.

Burials.

1672—1 mo. 17—Gulielma Maria Penn daughter of William and Gulielma Maria Penn of Rickmansworth, buried at Jordans, Upperside Mo. M.

1674—3 mo. 15—William Penn son of the same buried at Jordans, Giles Chalfont parish.

1674—12 mo. 24—Margaret Penn daughter of the same buried at same place.

1689—9 mo. 20—Gulielma Maria Penn of Worminghurst, Sussex, but died at Hammersmith in Middx., daughter of same, buried at Jordans.

1693—12 mo. 23—Gulielma Maria Penn of Worminghurst, Sussex, but died at Hoddesden, Herts., wife of William Penn, buried at Jordans.

1696—2 mo. 10—Springett Penn of Worminghurst, Sussex, but died at Lewes, Sussex, son of William and Gulielma Penn, buried at Jordans.

1708—11 mo. 24—Hannah Penn died at Kensington, Middx., daughter of Wm. & Hannah Penn, buried at Tring, Upperside Mo. M.

1718—5 mo. 30—(*died*) William Penn buried at Jordans 6 mo. 5th. 1718.

1726—6 mo. 20—Hannah Penn wife of William Penn buried at Jordans, Upperside Mo. M.

MARRIAGE ALLEGATIONS, 1615 TO 1675, AT DIOCESAN REGISTRY, SARUM, WILTS.

1628—last of October—Appared personally Robert walker of Sherret in parish of Pewsey, co. Wilts., husbandman, aged xxxiiij yeers & humbly craved License to marry with Elinor Penn of the same place spinster, aged xxx^{ty} yeers.

1635—12 May—Appeared personally Edward keene of Blackeboreton, co. Oxon., yeoman, aged xxvij years, & humbly craved License to mary wth Elinor Penn of Brinckworth, co. Wilts., spinster, aged xxiiij years, & hath express consent of parents.

TRANSCRIPTS OF WEST KINGTON, CO. WILTS., AT DIOCESAN REGISTRY, SARUM.

1754—Nov. 27—Ann Penn buried.

TRANSCRIPTS OF CASTLE CARY, CO. SOMERSET, AT DIOCESAN REGISTRY, WELLS.

1607—Julie xxjth. was marye Pen the wife of Walter Pen Buryed.

1621—Julie—The xvjth. daye was Walter Pen buried.

REGISTER OF ST. MARY MAGDALEN, TAUNTON, SOMERSET.[1]

Christenings.

1589—Nov.—Johane the daughter of Richard Penn 8 daie.

1592—Jan.—Katherine Daughter of Richard Penn 28 daie.

Buriynges.

1615—ffeb.—Robert Peen 7.

REGISTER OF FROME, SOMERSET.[2]

1629—Nov. 30—Steeven Peene sepultus.

REGISTER OF MELKSHAM, WILTS.[3]

Baptisms.

1666—Sarah ye daughter of Thomas Pen baptized Dec. 22.

1669—Hester the daughter of Thomas Penn Baptized Octob: 9th.

1672—(no.)—35—John the sonn of Thomas Pen baptized Jan. 24th.

1675—(no.)—26—Joan the daughter of Thomas Penn february 12.

Marriages.

1692—Richard Joanes & Sarah penn botht of this parish May the 7.

Burials.

1678—Jone Penn widow Buried October 27.

1692—Thomas Penn December 27.

---

[1] Searched from 1558 to 1656 inclusive.
[2] Searched from 1558 to 1653.
[3] Examined from commencement, 1568, to 1750 inclusive.

REGISTER OF ST. DUNSTAN-IN-EAST, STEPNEY, LONDON.[1]

Baptisms.

1615—July 30—James sonn of william Pen of wapinge wale of ix daies ould.

1619—July 11—William sonne of William Penne of Wappynwall smyth & Martha his wife ten days old.

—Sept. 15—Abigall daughter of Roger Penne of Wappingwall smyth & anne his wife, 4 days old.

1624—July 18—Henry sonn of Roger Penne of Shadwell smith & Agnes his wife.

1627—Apr. 18—William sonn of Roger Penne of Whitehorse streete smith & Anne his wife at 8 days.

1629—May 13—Sara daughter of Roger Penne of Whitehorse street smith and Agnes ux. at 7 days.

1632—Apr. 20—George sonn of Roger Penn of Whitehorse street smith & Anne ux. at 4 days.

1633—Jan. 31—Edward sonn of George Penne of Prusons Iland shipwright & Marg^t 4 days.

1636—June 8—John sonn of George Penne of Prusons Iland shipwright & Margaret ux. 3 days.

REGISTER OF ST. THOMAS, SARUM, WILTS.[2]

1610—Sept.—Tamson Pen 15. (*Buried.*)

[1] The very voluminous registers of this large and important parish were examined for baptisms and marriages, from their beginning, in 1568, to 1609, and for baptisms alone to 1638, the above names being all the Penns found in this portion of the registers.

[2] Vol. I. of register, from 1571 to 1653, examined,—the above being the only entry of the name of Penn found.

REGISTER OF ST. MARTIN'S, SARUM, WILTS.[1]

Baptisms.

1602—May 23—William Pen filig Nicholas Pen.

—ffeb. 11—Thomas Pen filig Richard Pen.
(*Chasm* 1604–1630.)

Marriages.

1580—Nov. 13—william Pen dux' Elizabeth Rowland vge.

1582—May 12—John Pen duxit Alis michell vid.

1598—May 24—Nicholas Pen duxit Alis Cholles.
(*Chasm* 1607–1630.)

Burials.

1579—Sept. 20—Annis Pen vxor John Pen.

—Oct. 2—John Pen maritg Agnis Pen.

1581—may 16—Elinor Penne filia John penne.

—Sept. 29—Annys Penn vxor william Pen.

1588—may 29—Jone Pen filia John Pen.

1602—Maye 26—william Pen filig Nicholas Pen.

1604—Aug. 7.—Annis Pen filia Nicholas Pen.
(*Chasm* 1604–1630.)

REGISTER OF ST. EDMUNDS, SARUM, WILTS.[2]

Baptisms.

1580—Nov. 5—Katherine daughter to wyllim penne.

1591—June 6—John sonn to wyllm Penne.

[1] Vol. I. of registers, from 1559 to 1653. Vol. II. searched from 1653 to 1681, but no further Penn entries found.

[2] Vol. I. of registers contains baptisms and marriages from 1560, and burials from 1559 to 1653 inclusive.

1593—Dec. 19—wyllyams D: to wyllym Penne.

1596—Aug. 27—wyllym Penne ye son of wyillym Penne.

1618—Jan. 31—willm S: to Stephen penne shoemaker.

Weddings.

1567—July 21—John Darbye & margaret Penne.

1571—Jan. 23—Davye Johnsson & margaret Penne.

1580—Nov. 27—John Penne & Agnis maleye.

1582—Jan. 22—Thomas penne & Tomson okeford.

1584—July 14—wyllym Oallyver & mercy Penn.

1589—Nov. 3—Anthonye penne & Jone Abbyat.

1602—Sept. 9—John Browne & Tompson penne.

Buryals.

1580—Sept. 13—Jane Penne.

—Sept. 24—Henry Penne.

1595—marche 24—wyllyam Penne.

1596—March 31—Jone Penn.

1604—May 29—willmas Penne d: to willm Penne.

—June 8—William Penne the Son of John Penne.

REGISTER OF ST. THOMAS, BRISTOL.

1621—Aprill 23—Willm Pen sonn of gilles penn. (*Baptized.*[1])

[1] This most important entry of the baptism of Admiral Penn, father of the founder, I owe to the courtesy of my esteemed friend and correspondent, Rev. Charles H. Pope, of Kennebunkport, Me., who found it while engaged in a research on his own family. He adds, "It seems to me there were other Penn entries at St. Thomas, though I cannot affirm

BRISTOL DEEDS IN POSSESSION OF THE HISTORICAL SOCIETY OF PENNSYLVANIA.

1661—Indenture made 26 June, 1661, 13 Chas. II, between Thomas Callowhill of Bristoll, Button Maker sonn & heir of John Callowhill, late of said City, Gent., deceased, of the first part, and Dennis Hollister of the same, Grocer, Thomas Speed of the same, Merchant, Walter Clement of Alveston, co. Glouc., Gent., & Thomas Goldney of the same City, Grocer :—Witnesseth, that in consideration that a marriage had been had between the said Thomas Callowhill & Hanna his wife, one of the daughters of the said Dennis Hollister, & for a provision of livelyhood for the said Hanna in case she survive the said Thomas & for preferment of such children as it shall please God to send said Thomas & Hanna &c, said Thomas Callowhill is to deed certain properties to the parties of the second part in trust &c &c.

1682—Indenture made 25 Jan. 1682, 30 Chas. II (*sic*), between Simon Clement of the City of Bristoll, Merchant, & Mary his wife, of the first part, and Thomas Callowhill, Linendraper, & Thomas Jordan, Grocer, both of the same City, of the second part—In consideration of 5s. paid to said Simon Clement he sells to said Thos Callowhill & Thos Jordan all that one third part of the corner house in St. Mary Port street adjoyning to High street in said Bristoll, now in tenure of said Thomas Jordan for terme of one whole year, to only intent that said Thomas Callowhill & Thomas Jordan may accept & take a tenant &c.

1711—Indenture made 27 Nov. 10 Anne, between Thomas Callowhill of City of Bristol, Linnen Draper, & Hanna his wife of the one part, & Charles Harford of same City, merchant, & Richard Champion of said City, merchant, of the other part—whereas, by an Indent. quinque ptite made between the said Thomas Callowhill & Hanna his wife of the first part, Thomas Jordan of same, Grocer, & Lydia his wife

it." The registers of this parish date from 1552 for baptisms, 1553 for burials, and 1558 for marriages, and seem well worthy a careful examination.

of the second part, Simon Clement of same, Merchant, & Mary his wife of the third part, Phebe Hollister of same, Spinster, of the fourth part (which said Hanna, Lydia, Mary & Phebe were daughters & coheirs of Dennis Hollister, late of said city, Grocer, dec'd.), & Walter Clement of Alveston, co. Glouc., Gent., & Nathaniel Haggatt of Bristoll afsd., Esq., of the fifth part &c &c.[1]

[1] These valuable deeds give us the first clue, as far as the writer is aware, to the name and parentage of the mother of Hannah Callowhill, the second wife of the founder, and likewise supply us with the name of her paternal grandfather, John Callowhill, also unknown hitherto. The writer's examination of these interesting volumes was very hasty, as his time was limited. No doubt some Philadelphia antiquary, with leisure to scan thoroughly every document, may find much more to repay his search.

GENEALOGICAL GLEANINGS, CONTRIBUTORY TO A HISTORY OF THE FAMILY OF PENN.

BY J. HENRY LEA, FAIRHAVEN, MASSACHUSETTS.

PREROGATIVE COURT OF CANTERBURY.

[The list of Penn Wills in this important court, which was printed in the PENNA. MAGAZINE for April, 1890, and subsequent numbers, was the result of a general gathering by several hands, and, as a natural result, many wills were overlooked, which would not have been the case had a regular and systematic search of the Calendars been undertaken. This search the writer was about to undertake, waiting only till the time could be found for the tedious task, when his friend, Mr. H. W. F. Harwood, who had just completed the same search for the name of Penny (taking incidentally all Penns), very kindly placed his note-book at his disposal, giving an exhaustive list of the name by which the following wills have been checked and may be relied upon as giving all Penns in this court to the year 1700.]

1592—William Penne of Minety, Glouc.

[Following this will, given in the first part of these Gleanings,[1] occur the names of "Wm: Legard, Pet: St. Eloy, Hen: Stevens Deputy Registers." These names are not in the original register and are those of officials in the Probate Court a century later, and were probably appended to an official transcript made for some of the family at that time.]

1655—Thomas Penn—Jan. 29, 1655–6 Letters of Admon. issued to Richard Stratton, principal Creditor of Thomas Penn late of Stratford in parish of Passenham, co. Northton., but intestate dec'd, to admr. &c.—Act Book, fo. 11.

1659—Katherine Penne of Hagley, co. Worc., widow, sick in bodie. Dated 18 March 1658. To dau. Rebecca Titterre £10; dau. Sibell James £10; Sarah Lench, dau. to

[1] PENNA. MAG., April, 1890, Vol. XIV. pp. 58–61.*
*For pp. 58-61 see pp. 554-557, this volume.

my son-in-law Thomas Lench £30 a bedd chest, Trunk &c in 2 years; eldest son of my son Joseph Browne £5; eldest son of my son Gabriel Browne £5; cos. Humphrey Penne of Romesley in parish of Hales Owen, co Salop, gent. 10s; Margaret Goodier of Hagley, widow, £1; Margaret Cardale of Hagley, spinster, £1; Mary wife of William Cardale £1; Ffrances wife of Richard Allchurch of Stourbridge, co. afsd., Chandler, £1–4–0; dau. Sibill James all rest of household goods; master John Addenbrook of Bewdley, gent., £1; Wm. Bardale of Hagley £1; Thomas Lane 2s.; Thomas Watkis 1s.; to poor widows of Hagley 12d. each; son-in-law Thomas Lench £5; Residuary Legatees the son of my dau. Sibill James, dau. of my dau. Rebecca Tetterie, ch. of my son Joseph Browne & ch. of my son Gabriel Browne; Executors Mr. John Addenbrook of Bewdley, co. worc., gent., & William Cardale of Hagley, yeoman; Witness Ellenor Price & Margaret Goodier; Signs by mark; Codicil 19 Mar 1658, nuncupative, has no new names; Pro. 27 June 1659 by Exrs.—Pell, 245.[1]

1661—John Penn of Kilkewydd in psh. of fforden, Co. of Mountgomery & Dioc. of Hereford; dated 2 Mar. 13 Chas. II, 1660; To be bur. in psh. Church of Chirbury; to my now wife Margarett £13–13–4; to kinsman James Alderson £20; to nephew Robert Davis the like sum of £30 (*sic*); to nephew Richard Roberts £20; to my sister Elizabeth Davis £10 if alive, otherwise to her dau. Katherine H. Humphreys; to neece Katherine Lloyd, wife of Richard Lloyd £5; to children of my kinsman John Roberts of Willmington £5; to my nephew Cessar Roberts £10 he oweth to 4 of his children, Cessar, Richard, Thomas & Mary; to cosin Richard Penne 40s.; to kinsw. Mrs. Hanna Harris £5; to Anne, dau. of Thos. Lloyd £8–13–4; to Johane, dau. of Richard Griffithes of Wallope 40s.; to Elizabeth, wife of Oliver Watters 40s.; to zachews Jones & Elizabeth Jones each

[1] The above will was omitted in former paper (see PENNA. MAG., Vol. XIV., No. 2, July, 1890, folio 170), the abstract having been received too late for incorporation.

50s.; to Nicholas and Peter Jones each 20s.; to servant Wynefred Purcell 40s.; & a Wainscot Bed & furniture after decease of my wife; to servt. Reynald Kerver 40s. & all apparell; to Nicholas Wyne, gent. £5; to Richard Jones, gent., 20s. for a ring; to brother law Thomas Edwards, gent. 10s. for ring; to Jane wife of Thos. Lloyd the same; to Magdalen Rogers 30s.; to George sonn of George Purcell 10s.; to Thomas sonn of Thomas Jenkes 10 groates; to children of my 2 Nephews Robert Davis and Richard Roberts £10; to poor of fforden & Chirbury £4; to Mrs. Anne Griffithes & Mrs. Mary Griffithes my best feather Bed &c.; to wife Margarett my best kine & all household goods that were hers before marriage; to Robt. Davis, Rich. Roberts & Katherine Lloyde all brass & pewter; to Jane wife of Thos. Lloyd a Truckle bed; to nephew Robt. Davis all bills, bonds &c & he Res Leg & Exor.; Wit. Thomas Lloyd, Thomas Lloyd the younger & Richard Jones; bequest to James Alderson changed to £20 before signing; Wit. William Draper, RLL, Richard Jones. Pro. 15 ffeb. 1661 by Exor. named in will.—Laud, 24.

1670—Sir William Penn of London, Knt. Will dated 20 Jan. 1669; To be buried in Parish Church of Redcliffe in the City of Bristol "as nere vnto the body of my dear mother deceased as the same conveniently may be"; To have erected a handsome and decent tomb for my mother & myself to be erected by Exr.; Wife Dame Margaret Penn £300 & all jewells not otherwise bequeathed & use for life of one moiety of plate, hou. stuff, coaches & coach horses & all cows; To younger son Richard Penn £4000, my fawcett dyamond ring & all swords, guns & pistols to be paid at 21 years of age & until then £120 per ann.; To granddau. Margaret Lowther £100; Nephews James Bradshaw & William Markeham each £10; Nephews John Bradshaw & George Markeham each £5; Cozen William Penn, son of George Penn, late of the Forest of Brayden in the Co. of Wilts., Gent., deceased, £10; To Cousin Eleanor Keene £6 per ann. for life; To late servant William Bradshaw 40s.

for ring; To servant John Wrenn £5; To poor of Redcliffe & St. Thomas parishes, Bristol, each £20; To eldest son William Penn my gold chain & medall with all residue of plate, hou. stuff & personal estate unbequeathed & remainder goods to wife at her decease; son William Executor; Mourning to wife, son Richard, dau. Margaret Lowther & son-in-law Anthony Lowther & Dr. Whistler & his wife &c; Any differences between Executor & wife to be referred to final judgement of my worthy friend Sir William Coventry of St. Martin-in-the-Fields, co. Middlx Wit. R. Langhorne, John Radford & William Markham. Pro. 6 Oct. 1670 by Executor named in will.

Marginal Note:—Quinto Aprilis 1671° Recepi Testum orile dñi Willimi Penn defti e Reg^{ro} Curiae Praerogativae Cantuar p me Wm Penn. Testibus Car Tuckyr Ri: Edes.—Penn, 130.[1]

1672—Robert Pen. Mar. 12 Commission issued to Michael Pen, brother of Robert Pen late of St. Michaels Cornhill, London, bachelor, but intestate decd. &c.—Act Book, fo. 26.

1673—Thomas Penn of Barner Gardner, co. Surry, Gardner, sicke in body dated 18 May 24 Chas. II, 1672; To my sonns Thomas, John and Joseph Penne & daus. Mary & Elizabeth Penn all my Coppyhold & all goods &c. for the bringe of them upp according to discretion of my Exors & goods to be divided between Thomas, John, Mary & Elizabeth; to sonn Joseph all said Copyhold lands, he paying his sister Mary & Elizabeth each £10; to Ellen Stephens 10s. for ring; friends John Smith & Thomas Singould to see will fulfilled; brother William Blind & sister Mary Watson, widdow & Cittizen of London, to be Exors.; Wit. Matt: Preston, John Farmare, Thomas Singnell & Moses Burnham; Pro. 7 May 1673 by Exors.—Pye, 63.

[1] An abstract of this important will (not taken by the writer) has been already printed (see PENNA. MAG., Vol. XIV., No. 2, July, 1890, folio 171), but as several omissions of importance occur in the former, it has seemed best to reproduce it here in full.

1673—William Penn of Brodford in psh. of Bellbroughton, co. Worcester, Gent., in bodily health; dated 6 Aug., 20 Chas. II, 1668; To my dau. Margarett Penn all lands in Bellbroughton & Kingsnorton or elsewhere in co. Worc., & she Res. Leg. & Extrx.; to wife Mary Penn a rent charge of £15 yearly for her life; Wit. Humfrey Perrott, Elizabeth Barcroft, her mark, & William Perrott. Pro. 27 Nov. 1673 by Margarett Harris *alias* Penn the Extrx. named in the will.—Pye, 149.

1676—Richard Pen of St. Paul Shadwell in co. Middx., marriner, outward bound on a voyage to sea; dated 5 May 1675, 27 Chas. II; I appoint kinsman Richard Pen of same place, waterman, to be my lawful attorney to demand all debts, wages, &c. & he to be my Res Leg & Exor.; Wit. Tho: Somerby, Not. Pub. & Theop: Haydock his servant; Pro. 3 ffeb. 1676 by Exor.—Hale, 23.

1677—Bartholomew Penn. Sept. 24 Com. issued to John Penn, father of Bartholomew Penn late in partibus transmarinus, Bachelor, dec'd to administer &c.—Act Book, fo. 111.

1679—Elizabeth Pen. Dec. 22 Com. issued to William Carver Grandfather (*Avo ex filia*) & Curator assigned to Elizabeth Pen junior, the daughter of Elizabeth Pen late of Petersfeild, co. Southton., widow, to admr. during minority of said Elizabeth Pen junior.—Act Book, fo. 173.

1680—Edward Penn. June 2 Com. issued to Dorothy Pen, neece of Edward Penn late of Affrica, in Guinea a Bachelor deceased intestate, to admr. &c.—Act Book, fo. 93.

1683—Robert Penne. June 14. Com. issued to Dorathy Penne widow, relict of Robert Penne late of St. Botholph Aldgate, co. Middx., to admr. &c.—Act Book, fo. 86.

1683—John Penne of Bodicote, co. Oxon., yeoman, weake in body; dated (*blank*) Mar. 1682; To Aunt Grant of Bodicote £5 & to her 7 children £5 apeece, that is to say, to my couzins William & Samuel Grant, Bridgett Judd of Adderbury, Alice Dodivell of Banbury & Jane & Elizabeth Grant of Hornton; to couzin Leonard Bradford of Sutton & his sonn & dau. £5 apeece; to coz. Thomas Heynes of Sibbord £5; to coz. Thomas Penne of Cittie of Oxford £5; to coz. Joanna Richeson of Pillerton £5; to coz. Askill of Geden £5; to coz. Elizabeth Penne £4 per ann. for life by hands of my bro. Thomas Penne; to poor of Bodicott £5; brother Thomas Penne sole Exor.; Wit. Elizabeth wrighton, Richard Smith & Samuel Huckell; Pro. 5 Dec. 1683 by Exor.— Drax, 143.

1683—Rachel Penn. Dec. 18. Com. issued to Hanna Luested (wife of John Luested) sister of Rachel Penn late of psh. of St. Olaves Southwark, co. Surry, Spinster, (*solute*) dec'd., to admr. &c. Inv. ex. xxxv^{li}.—Act Book, fo. 181.

1684—Thomas Penn. Mar. 22. Com. issued to Samuel Penn, brother of Thomas Penn late of Bodicote, co. Oxon., Bachelor, decd., to admr. &c.—Act Book, fo. 43.

1686—Susanna Penn. Dec. 6. Com. issued to Thomas Penn husband of Susanna Penn late of Kenver (?) in co. Stafford., to admr. &c.—Act Book, fo. 184.

1686—Anthonie Penne. Dec. 6. Com. issued to Dorathe Penne widow, the relict of Anthonie Penne late of psh. of St. James in Liberty of Westminster (*infra Litatem Westm^r*) in co. Middx., decd to admr.—Act Book, fo. 186.

1686—Samuel Pen, Merchant, sometime of Bodicott, co. Oxon.; dated 5 Dec. 1686, 2 Jas. II; The house &c in Bodicott which was my fathers (subject to trust for my sister Ann Penn) to my neece Mary Askell (or whatsoever her Christian name may be), wife of Mr. Michaell Askell of Geydon in co. Warwick, for life, remainder to my friends Capt. Robert Smith & John Broome of London, Hosier, in trust for her sonnes &c; The farme at Bodicott called

Knights, purchased by my brother John Penn, to said Michael Askell & my friend William Barnes the elder of Bodicott, yeoman, for life of my sister Ann Penn on trust for said sister for life, rem. to neece Mary Askell; House & land near Long Marston, co. Glouc., to my cozen John Penn of Oxford, Shoomaker, for 99 years, rem. to his heirs, rem. to neece Mary Askell; to coz. John Penn of Oxford £200; to Thomas Haines sonn of Charles Haines of Sibford, co. Oxon., £100; to kinswoman Mary ffrogley and her 3 ch. Richard, Jane & Mary £10 apeece; to kinswoman Joane, dau. of Michaell Penn decd., £10; to Aunt Jane Grant, widow, £5 & to her 6 ch. William Grant, Jane Lyornes, Elizabeth Trusse, Alice Aldington, Bridget Judd & Susanna Grant £10 apeece; to kinswoman Elizabeth White of Dodington £5; to 2 children of Leonard Bradford decd., Elizabeth & her brother, £5 apeece; to servt. Richard Smith £10 & to servt. Jane Aris £3; £100 to be divided by my Exor. among such of my Mothers relations whose names are or have been Herne (of the same family of the Hernes of which my Mother was one) who shall be found in low condition or want; to Elizabeth Righton, widdow, 20s.; to Wm. Barnes afsd. £10; to Capt. Robert Smith 50 guineas; to John Broome £100; to James Wallis of London, Merchant, 50 guineas; to poor of Bodicott £5; to dau. of my neece Mary Askell £1000 at 21 or marr.; neece Mary Askell & her ch. Res Legs; Michaell Askell Exor.; James Wallis & John Broome Overseers; Wit. Charlis Beswick, George Young, Jeremy Mount Att^{r}ney in King street nere Guildhall; Pro. 14 Dec. 1686 by Exor.—Lloyd, 169.

1690—James Penn of Herst, co. Berks, Butcher, very sick & weake; dated 17 June 1 Wm. & Mary, 1689; To sonn in law Thomas Chanler one shilling; sonn in law Henry Creed the same; to grandchild James Chanler £6 & to his bro. & sist., 2 other of my grch., 40s. apeece; to Joane Creed, wife of Robert Creed decd., & her 2 ch. 1s. apeece; to my brother Thomas Penn's widdow & all her ch. 1s. apeece; to bro. George Penn's widdow & her ch. the same; to Simon Wincleoll & his wife & ch. the same; to Thomas Harbert & his wife & ch. the same; to sonn in law Joseph Geats the same; to dau. in law Mary Geats same; sonn in law Benjamin Geats same; wife Isabell Res Leg & Extrx; Wit. Thomas Draper, his mark, Thomas Simonds & Robert Brant; Pro. 23 July 1690 by Extrx.—Dyke, 113.

1697—William Penn of City of London, Marriner, now in Petuxant River in Maryland, sick & weak; dated 20 Sept. 1696; to my 3 sisters £50 sterling apeece; my wife Res. Leg. & Extrx.; Wit. Robert Marsham, Jn° Wight & Tho: Greenfeild; Pro. 18 Nov. 1697 by Elizabeth Penn the relict & Extrx named in the will.—Pyne, 249.

[The three wills which follow have been already printed in Mr. H. F. Waters's invaluable " Gleanings,"[1] but may well be reproduced here as in continuity with the history of the Founder's family, as also the will of Mary Pennington, from a later number of the same collection.[2]]

1726—Hanna Penn, widow, Relict of William Penn late of Ruscombe in co. of Berks., Esq.; Dated 11 Sept. 1718; Refers to will of husband dated 27 May 1712 & to Trust under said will as to disposal of all lands &c in Pennsylvania &c, legacies to his dau. Aubrey & the 3 children of his son William & the conveyance of the rest of said lands &c in America amongst his children by the now Testatrix his second wife; All said lands, tenements & personal estate to be divided as near as may be into 6 equal parts whereof to my eldest son John Penn & his heirs three sixths or one full half he to pay his sister Margaret £2000 at her marriage or age of 21 years & remaining half unto my 3 other sons Thomas, Richard & Dennis Penn respectively, each one sixth part of the whole divided as aforesaid, with remainder of deceased children to the survivors; Wit. Susanna Perrin,

[1] New Eng. Hist. and Gen. Reg., April, 1890, Vol. XLIV. pp. 190–192.
[2] Ibid., July, 1892, Vol. XLVI. p. 305.

Mary Chandler, Hannah Hoskin, Thomas Grove & S. Clement.

Admon. with will annexed issued 16 Feb. 1726 to John Penn, Esq., natural & lawful son & principal legatee named in the Will of Hanna Penn late of the Parish of St. Botolph Aldersgate, London, widow, deceased &c to administer according to tenor of Will.—Farrant, 49.

1746—John Penn of Hitcham, co. Bucks., Esq.; Dated 24 Oct. 1746; Personal estate in England to William Vigor of Lond., merchant, Joseph Freame, citizen & banker of same, & Lascelles Metcalfe of Westminster, Esq., as Exrs. in trust & also all moneys and effects in America which, before my death shall be heard of in the City of Philadelphia, shall have been collected or remitted by agents there to any part of Europe on own acct. or jointly with my bros., all which to be part of English personal estate; To afsd Exrs all lands &c in & near the City of Bristol & the co. of Gloucester to be applied to charges of trust, debts, funeral & legacies; Sister Margaret Freame annuity; Servant John Travers £100; each of English Exrs one hund. guineas; old servants Thomas Penn & Hannah Roberts; Jane wife of Henry Aldridge of White Walthan, Berks.; nephew John Penn to be educated; nephews & nieces Hannah Penn, Richard Penn & Philadelphia Hannah Freame; bro. Thomas Penn; nephew John Penn my share of mannor of Perkassie, tract of Liberty land & High Street Lot (claimed under deed by late father or will of late grfather Thos. Callowhill); brother Richard Penn all property in New Jersey in America & sd bro. Exr. for New Jersey; My moiety of inheritance of Pennsylvania & the 3 lower Cos. of Newcastle, Kent & Sussex upon Delaware in America to bro. Thomas Penn for life, rem. to his sons in order of age, rem. to bro. Richard with rem. to his sons John & Richard, rem. to latter & his male issue, rem. to neice Hannah only dau. of sd brother Richard & her male issue, next in entail to be sister Margaret Freame & her issue & niece Philadelphia Hannah Freame, next nephew (of the half blood) William

Penn of Cork in Kingdom of Ireland, Esq., then to Springett Penn his eldest son & his male issue, rem. to Christiana Gulielma Penn, only dau. of said William Penn, next to grand nephew (of the half blood) Robert Edward Fell, only son now living of Gulielma Maria Fell, dec'd, then great niece Mary Margaretta Fell, eld. dau. of sd Gulielma Maria, then another great niece Gulielma Maria Frances Fell only other living dau. of said Gulielma Maria Fell, dec'd. &c; Bro. Thomas Penn to be Exr. for Province of Pennsylvania & the 3 lower Counties of Newcastle, Kent & Sussex upon Delaware. Proved 13 Nov. 1746.—Edmunds, 332.

1775—Thomas Penn of Stokehouse, co. Bucks., Esq.; Dated 18 Nov. 1771; Wife Lady Juliana Penn & son-in-law William Baker of Bayford Bury, Herts., Exrs for personal estate except in America; Recites an Indenture tripartite dated 15 Aug. 1751 in consideration of then intended marriage; James Hamilton, Esq., Revd. Richard Peters & Richard Hockley, Esq., all of City of Philadelphia, certain lands in Pennsylvania in trust; Mr. Duffield Williams of Swansea, co. Glamorgan, £20 per ann.; sons John & Granville Penn; daus. Sophia & Juliana; Recites Agreement entered into with late brother dated 8 May 1732, 31 Jan. 1750 & 20 Mar. 1750; Nephew Richard Penn, Lieut. Gov. of Pennsylvania, & Richard Hockley, Esq., Exrs for Province of Pennsylvania; Codicil dated 11 July 1772, names dau. Juliana as advanced in marriage; 2nd. Codicil dated 18 July 1772 to Mrs Harriott Gordon of Silver Street Golden Square £20 per ann. & Grace Armagh & Mary Clarke each £10 per ann.; 3rd Codicill 23 June 1774; Pro. 8 Apr. 1775.—Alexander, 166.

1682—Mary Pennington, dated "att my house att Woodside in Amersham psh. & co. of Bucks this Tenth day of the third moneth called May One thousand six hundred eighty," but signed & sealed 5 July 1680; Refers to personal estate "which I had before marriage to my deare husband Isaac Pennington which he made over for my use by a deed before marriage to my cousin Elizabeth Dallison." I have taken unto me the debts of my husband by administering after his death. As for my daughter Penn though she be very near to me and hath deserved well of me in her own particular and upon her worthy father's account, yet she hath a large proportion of this world's substance and these my latter children have not anything but what I give them, the Lord having seen it good to strip their dear and pretious father and left him without a capacity to do anything for them, and if so my estate not being great I can only signify my naturalness to my dear daughter Penn and hers by some little things for them to remember me by, and I do believe the witness of God in her will answer to the righteousness of it. To my son William Pennington £500 sterling, £100 to bind him to some handsome trade that hath not much of labor, because he is but weakly, & the other £400 to be paid him at the age of 22 years; to son Edward Pennington the like sums upon the like conditions; to my daughter Mary Pennington £30 a year till she marr & then £300; to my dear son William Penn £50 & to my friend Thomas Elwood the like sum; to my cousin Mary, wife of William Smith £50; I give £20 towards a meeting house when friends of Chalfont meeting think it convenient to build one; to Martha Sampson £2 a year for life; To Martha Cooper *als* Heywood £3 a year for life; to my daughter Gulielma Maria Penn her choice of a suit of damask except that suit marked I ^P_M; to her son Springett Penn my great platt with the Springett's and my coat of arms upon it and the silver two eared cup made in the fashion of his mother's golden one; to her daughter Letitia Penn my silver chafin dish & skimmer with a brasile handle & that large nun's work box & a little basket of nun's work & a purse & a girdle of black plush & a black straw basket which her father brought me out of Holland &c &c; to my son William Pennington my dear husband's watch; Other bequests to son Edward Pennington & dau. Mary, to cousin Mary Smith the elder & her daughter Mary; to son John Pennington my house & land at Woodside & all my husbands houses in Kent (upon conditions); Reference to will of my mother the Lady Prewed "that is annext to my fathers Sir John Prewed," also to "my mother's sister the Lady Oxenden"; I would have my son John Pennington lay mee in friends burying ground at Jordans very neare my deare and pretious husband Isaac Pennington" My son John to be executor and my dear son William Penn and my loving friend Thomas Ellwood to be overseers; Proved 11 October 1682. —Cottle, 121.

[The testatrix was daughter and heir of Sir John Proude and wife of Sir William Springett, who died in 1643, having had issue by her a son, John Springett, who died young, and a daughter, Gulielma Maria Springett, the first wife of the Founder and the legatee named in the will of her mother, who had remarried to Isaac Pennington.

The following Pennington Admon is interesting as showing a member of that family dying in America five years before the founding of Pennsylvania, whether connected or not with William Penn's step-father-in-law the writer is ignorant.]

1679—James Pennington. Feb. the last day. Com. issued to Mathew Travers, principal creditor of James Pennington late of the psh. of St. Bartholomew Royal Exchange, London, but in Maryland in partibus transmarinus decd. intestate, to admr. &c, Sara Pennington, the relict, having renounced.—Act Book, fo. 20.]

[The wills which follow, of Dennis Hollister and Thomas Callowhill, are most valuable as confirming and extending the knowledge of the ancestry of Hannah Callowhill, the second wife of the Founder, which was obtained from the deeds printed by the writer in the last number of these Gleanings.[1]]

1676—Will of Dennis Hollister of Bristol, Grocer, in perfect health. Dated 1 Sept. 1675; To only sonn Dennis all

[1] PENNA. MAG., Vol. XVI., No. 3, October, 1892.

corner house & shopp in Mary Part in Bristoll aforesaid where I now dwell & certain furniture, linnen, " best silver belly pott with its cover," all shopp Jmplements &c, £600 & a caudle cupp with leggs & a cover; To dau. Hannah, wife of Thomas Callowhill new house late built in ffryers Orchard in parish of Jamesses in suburbs of Bristol & stable & houses in same lately purchased in which one Hannah Hollister & Jeane Partridge, Widdow, now dwell, & Warehouses in Peters parish with remainder, as to the last, to my granddau. Sarah, eldest dau. of my said dau. Hannah Callowhill, remainder, if she die without heirs, to my granddau., Hannah Callowhill, after said dau's decease remainder of houses in ffryers bought of Henry Lloyd to granddau. Bridgett Callowhill, remainder as to new house in ffryers to sonn-in-lawe Thomas Callowhill for his life with remainder to my grandsonn Dennis Callowhill eldest sonn of my said dau., remainder to grandsonn Thomas Callowhill second sonn of same, & to said dau. certain linnen, silver, &c &c and £200 over her marriage portion & to Thomas Callowhill, her husband, £10; To dau. Lydia Jordan wife of Thomas Jordan new house late builded at fframton Cotterill, co. Glouc., late bought of Humphrey Hooke, Knt., with remainder to her husband for life, remainder at his death or marriage to my granddau. Bridgett Jordan, eldest dau. of my said dau. remainder to grdu. Lidia Jordan, second dau. of same, and to my said dau. Lydia Jordan certain furniture &c, & £200 & to her husband £10; To dau. Mary Hollister new house in Mary part Streete in Bristol & outlet or pavement over Kitchen of house wch I now dwell in & wch was devised to sonn Dennis, & certain furniture &c & £500, silver beare bowle & a little silver bottle; To dau. Phebe Hollister moyety of Jnn called White Hart in Broadstreet in Bristol, one fourth of which was my Wives inheritance & one fourth late bought of Ann Yeomans decd., & other fourth late bought of Edmond ffrench sonn & heire of Elizabeth ffrench also decd., & other fourth late bought of Henry Rowe & Judith his wife, which said Judith, Elizabeth, Ann & my wife were the daus. & coheires of Edmond

Popley, Merchant, dec'd., also to my said dau. Phebe certain furniture &c and "lesser belly pott," and £500; To grandchildren Dennis, Thomas & Hannah Callowhill £20 apeece; To granddaus. Sarah & Bridgett Callowhill £15 apeece; To grchil. Bridgett & Lidia Jordan £20 apeece; To kinswoman Lydia that late served me & is now become the wife of Edward Hackett £100 over what I have given her towards her marriage; To Beloved ffriends George ffox, William Dewsbery, Alexander Parker, George Whitehead & John Storye £10 a peice and to Thomas Briggs, John Wilkinson of Westmerland, James Pooke, Steeven Crispe & John Wilkinson of Cumberland £5 a peece as a toaken of my love to them & the service they have done for the Lord & for his people & to be paid only to the above named who hath often lodged at my House & eaten bread at my table & are well known to my Executors; To Mary Goulding, Wife of Tho: Goulding of Bristol, Grocer, and to Magdalene Love, Wife of John Love of same £20 & to said Tho: Goulding & John Love £10 for certain poor people; To each of my Brothers a peece of old gold of 20s. value; To each of Brothers' & Sisters' children the same except Samuell sonn of my brother Thomas Hollister and Nathaniel Tovie, only sonn of my sister Margery Tovie, dec'd., who because they are ill husbands & like to misspend it, nothing, but to Samuell Hollister's wife for benefitt of his children & to Nathaniel Tovie's children that are in England at my decease; To Nem Dawson, Widdow, 40s. p. ann. for life; To Joanne Pillerne, Widdow, £3; To Margaret Price, Widdow, 40s.; To Mary Evans, Widdow, 20s.; To servant Joseph Smith £5; To all other domestick Servants 20s. apeece; To dau. Phebe house & lands called Old feilds at Vrcott in parish of Almesbury in co. Glouc^r for rest of tearme of yeares; friend Alexander Parker, Geo: Whitehead, Walter Clements & John Story to be Overseers & to each 40s.; Only sonn Dennis Hollister & two sonns-in-lawe Tho: Callowhill & Tho: Jordan Executors;—" in testimony that this is my absolute Will contayned in these 5 sides & this little peece of paper written every word with my owne hand & subscribed in the margent of every side with my owne name." Wit: J. Chauncey, John Eckly & Rich: Hawkesworth.

Codicil dated 6 July 1676, being sicke & weake, considering that since making my will it hath pleased God to take out of this World my sonn Dennis & severall others, I revoke all Legacies to all who are now dead; To daus. Hannah, Lydia & Mary my house at corner of Mary Port Street where I now dwell & keepe shop; I do confirm to dau. Phebe the Jnn called White Hart in Bristol and revoake house & lands called Oldfeild in parish of Almondsbury & give same to my four daus. for tearme; To dau. Hannah Callowhill's three children, Hannah, Thomas & Elizabeth messuage & lands at Westerleigh held of Dean & Chapter of Wells; My grandchild Lydia Jordan being dead her £20 to grandchild Bridgett Jordan; To sonn-in-lawe Thomas Jordan £150 towards the purchase of the fee simple of house & lands at fframpton Cottrell given to my dau. Lydia Jordan; Revoake such part of bequest of 20s. each to the children of brother & sister as refers to Cosen Lydia, now wife of Edward Hackett, having otherwise provided for her, & to cos. Samuell Hollister, sone of my bro. William Hollister £10; To servt. Joseph Smith £5 more; To servt. Dorcas (*blank*) £5; To Dennis sonn of Abel Hollister £10 to bind him an Apprentice; To Samuell Hollister, grandsonn of brother William & sonn of Jacob Hollister £5; To Mary Hollester dau. of Jacob Hollester aforesd £10 more than what I have bestowed in placeing her; To sonn-in-lawe Thomas Jordan best bay gelding; To sonn-in-lawe Thomas Callowhill best horse beast & to both of them £50 apeece; To my four daus. all overplus of estate; Thomas Speed to be an Overseer in place of John Story; To servt. ffrances (*blank*) £5; Wit: J. Chauncey,[1] John Eckley & Rich:

---

[1] Ichabod Chauncey, the second son of Rev. Charles Chauncey, President of Harvard College from 1654 to 1671. He graduated at Harvard, was chaplain in the regiment of Sir Edward Harley, at Dunkirk, and had some clerical function in England, but, being persecuted for his non-conformity, became a physician and settled at Bristol, where he

Hawksworth. Proved 21 July 1676 by Exors named in will.—Bence, 91.

1712—Will of Thomas Callowhill of City of Bristoll, Linnen Draper, in health of Body; Dated 28 November 1711; I am possessed of the residue of term of 1000 years in certain garden whereon I have erected certain buildings adjoyning my now dwelling in parish commonly called St. James granted me by Edward Baugh, Whitetawer, since dec'd., & residue of 1000 years granted by Edward Baugh, Jr., of tenmts, garden, malt house, &c, erected on same garden & other term of 1000 years lately granted me by my dau. Hanna of all messuage &c on South side of Quaker's Meeting house in place called the ffryers now or late in occupation of Simon Barnes, Daniell Kindall & William Timbrell, I bequeath all same to kinsmen Brice Webb of said City, Linnen Draper, & Charles Harford of same, Merchant, on trust for wife Hanna *als* Anna for her life with remainder to my granddau. Margarett Penn, dau. of Hannah Penn, my daughter, by William Penn, Esq., her husband, for her life, remainder to grandson John Penn, son of said dau., for rest of term; By an indenture 27 instant month between me and Brice Webb & Charles Harford, Linnen Drapers, & Richard Champion, Merchant, I have conveyed to them lands in said City, in Co. of Somerset, & other places in England & in Pennsylvania, to uses therein menconed, confirm said deed save that said Trustees may sell any part of a Close called Barrs Leaze *als* Brick Leaze adjoining my now dwelling, & said trustees to grant to said dau. Margaret Penn or John Penn afsd 4 messuages in street called Broad Meade in parish of St. James, being part of wives Joynture, wherein Richard Hooper, John Hide & Edward Cullimore now dwell; And whereas I have an In-

died July 25, 1691, aged fifty-six, and was buried at St. Phillip's Church in the same city. His will, which is dated March 19, 1688, with codicil September 26, 1690, was probated February 17, 1691/2, at P. C. C. (Savage I., 368; Pedigree of Fam. of Chauncey by Stephen Tucker, Somst. Herald, Lond., 1884, p. 7.)

terest in the province of Pennsylvania as a security for £1000 due to me from said William Penn & am interested in lands in Caldecott in co. Monmouth as security for £160 due from Mary Herbert, spinster, sole heir of ffrancis Herbert, Esq., dec'd., & am possessed of residue of 90 years granted by Samuell Price & others of Society of Merchants of said City of the tenth part of the whole of several messuages &c neare the hot well in parish of Clifton, co. Glouc., & am interested in one sixteenth part of Brass works in ptnershipp with James Peters, Jeoffry Pinnell & others, now carried on about Terren, co. Salop, & am also interested in a twentieth part of Copperworks with same partners at Colebrooke Dale, co. Salop, & also one sixteenth of certain Packett Boats now Trading for the port of Bristoll to New York & other places in America, in partnership with Brice Webb, Richard Champion & others, I give to said Brice Webb & James Peters all right in lands &c given me by said William Penn of lands in Pennsylvania afsd. & in Caldecott by said Mary Herbert, & lands at Hot Well, Brass & Copper Works & Packett Boats in trust for uses hereafter menconed, to dispose of same & settle moneys so raised on my dau. Hanna & her children. In the first place to pay to said William Penn & Hanna his wife £26 yearly in satisfaction of Rents of Estate at ffrenchan & Hambrooke which I promised them, & residue to paymt. of £800 & Interest due to said Brice Webb & others by Deed dated 5 July last past between me & said Brice Webb, Charles Harford & Richard Champion, residue to said John Penn of houses at Hot Well &c, & residue of Brass & Copper Works & Packett Boats to Thomas Penn, another sone of said Hanna Penn & all remainder to said Margaret Penn; My brother Walter Duffield is bound by two obligations, viz., one dated 12 Jan. 1694 for paymt. of £25, & other dated 13 Aug. 1674 for £14-10-0, he to pay Executrix £25 only; If sister Elizabeth Iaveling pay to Executrix in one year what she owes her bonds to be discharged; To neices Elizabeth Iaveling, Duffield Iavelin, Sara Gurman & Mary Gurman a peice of gold apeece of 23s. 6d.; To late servt. Elizabeth

Weekes a peice of like value; To housemaids a guiney apeice; To tenant Simon Barnes 10s.; To Ancient friend George Whitehead of London & Benjamin Coole, Paul Moon & John Pope, my friends in Bristoll, 2 broad peices of gold of 23s. 6d.; To old servt. & friend John Isgar best suit of Clothe & Beaver Hatt; To poor of parish where I dwell £5 in hands of Charles Weeks, Gardiner there, for Coles; To bind sonn of any poor friend an Apprentice £10; Wife Hanna *als* Anna Res. Legatee & Executrix; Brice Webb & Charles Harford Overseers & to them 2 broad peices of gold apeice; Will written on 2 peices of parchment, the greater containing 63 lines & the lesser 9 lines. Wit: Nicholas Taylor, Ben: Bisse & Jo^n Gregory. Proved 24 Dec, 1712 by Hanna Penn (wife of William Penn) dau. of dec'd., the Executrix, Hanna *als* Anna Callowhill having died before Executing. On 19 Oct 1738 Com. issued to John Penn, Esq., son & Admrr. with Will annexed of Hanna Penn, widow, dec'd., while living dau. & only child (*sic*) & administratrix with will annexed of Thomas Callowhill, to administer goods &c left unadministered by said Hanna Penn &c.—Barnes, 232.

[In this connection the following extracts, for calling my attention to which I have to thank Mr. Henry Gray, the genealogical bookseller of Leicester Square, may be of interest. The name of Callowhill is a very uncommon one, and it may well be that the earlier members of this family were among the progenitors of Thomas Callowhill, of Bristol. At the least it may serve as a clue to the origin of the Bristol family.]

PARISH REGISTER OF KNIGHTWICK,
Co. *Worcester*.[1]

1620—Charles sonn of Thomas Callowhill & Alice his wyfe was baptized the vij day of Maie anno suprascript.

[1] "Parish Registers of Knightwick and Doddenham, County of Worcester, from 1538 to 1812." Edited by Joseph Bonstead Wilson. London, 1891.

the same buryed the xiiijth daye of June anno suprascripto.

Katherine the Daughter of William Callowhill & (Margerie) his wyfe was buryed the xxvjth day of October anno suprescripto.

Gulielmus Callowhill sepel iebatur quinto die Novembris Anno superscripto. (*From Bishop's Transcripts.*)

1615—Margerie the daughter of William Callowhill & Margerie his wyfe was baptized the xviij of October Anno p. dicto.

1618—Thomas the sonn of William Callowhill & Margery his wyfe was baptized the twenty nynth of March Anno p. dicto.

1634—James the sonn of Richard Callowhill & Anne his wife was baptized the xxviijth day of Julye anno praedicto.

1637—Thomas Callowhill & Allice Brooke were married October the Third Anno praedicto.

1638—Mary the daughter of Thomas Callowhill & Allice his wife was baptized June the third: Anno p. dict.

Mary the daughter of Thomas Callowhill ye younger & Allice his wife was buryed June ye Twenty.

1640—ffravncis Callowhill & Bridgett Perry were married the 7th day of february Anno supra dicto.

1641—Thomas the sonn of ffravncis Callowhill & Bridgett his wife was baptized the 7th day of November 1641.

Allice the wife of Thomas Callowhill the younger was buried Aprill 26th.

1642—William the sonn of William Callowhill was baptised ffebruary the 20th Anno supra dicto.

1644—John the sonn of William Callowhill was baptised Aprill 7th.

1662—Elijah y'e' son of Wm: Callowhill (and Dorathy his wife) was bapt. June the tenth Anno p. dicto.

1663—Anne ye daughter of James Callowhill & Margery his wife was bapt. December y'e' 22^d. (*Transcripts.*)

1674—Tho: Callowhill, Churchwarden.

1675—Thomas Callowhill was buried March y'e' 10th anno pr. dicto. (*Transcripts.*)

PARISH REGISTER OF DODDENHAM.

1713—Hannah Gulielmi & Mariae Callowhill εβαπτισθιν.

1718—Dec. 21—Gulielmus Gulielmi et Mariae Callowhill ’ΕΒΑΠΤΙΣΘΙΝ.

1702—John Jones of City of Bristoll, Linnendraper, in health of body; dated 13 Dec. 1699; To ffather Cha: Jones, 2 Jacobus, & to mother Ann Jones the same; to that brother or sister whom parents may think most worthy in one years time 100 guineas; to ffatherlaw William & motherlaw Ann Smith each 2 guineas; to use & benefit of people called Quakers inhabiting the City of Bristoll £200 to be disposed by father Chas. Jones, William Smith, Charles Harford Senior, Benjamin Cool & Cornelius Sarjant; to ffather & mother Jones each 4 Jacobuses more; to meeting people that are poore that belong to Congregation where Andrew Gifford doth preach, at disposal of sd. And. Gifford & John Bowman Cooper or Henry Parsons Grocer in Thomas St.; to parish of Thomas, the place of my nativity £20 to be given to poor in bread & apparell by Henry Parsons in Thomas St. & Richard Taylor Jronmonger in Ratcliffe St.; to parish of Nicholas wherein I now live £20 to be distributed by William Bush Draper & Alderman Wallis to poor as before; to (*blank*) Read, he that preaches in the publick place of worship of sd. psh. £10; to late erected Hospitalls Boys & Maides but most· especially to the ancient thereof £100 at discretion of Major Wade, Thomas Callowhill, Edward Martindale and my father Chas. Jones; to William ffallowfield that commonly lyes at Charles Harfords & often hath preached very well in our meeting house one guinea & £50 sterling; to Jeremy Hignell Cooper in Temple St. £50; to John Pope Senior that lives over against the Glass hous without Lowfords Gate £25; to Benjamin Coole Senr, that lives on Michael hill in this City £50; to Uncle Char: Harford one guinea; to bro. Charles Jones, bro. Michael Jones & bro. Mathias Jones each £100; to sister Sarah that is married to ffrancis Roach £200; to sister Elizabeth that is married to Edward Harford £200; to Peter Young my brother law £50; to ffrancis Roach my brother law the same; to Peter & Ann Young children of my sister Young each £500; to brother Charles Jones more £600 if he agree with Exors. on the account of the late brigantine Expedition; to bro. Michael Jones £600; to sister Roach the same; to sister Elizabeth married to Edward Harford the same; to kinsman Mathias Jones Senr of London £100; to John Keinton that was my apprentice £60; to servant Jane Persevell £10; to servant Martha Gifford £5; to John Horwoods wife £5; to 6 or 12 bearers who carry me to the grave each 20s.; to Arthur Thomas Pewterer £5; to cousin Thomas Dickson £3; to Charles Harford Jr. £3; to Elias Osborne, Richard Yeomans, Robert Priest & Arthur Taylor each one guinea; to Arthur Sawyer same; to aunt Smith £5; to William Pope my porter £10; to sister Roach my part of ship called Susannah; to cousin Widow Low of this City £5; to cousin Martha married to William Stafford £100; to cousin Mary married to William Penn £100;[1] cousins Peter & Ann, children of sister, & Rachell daughter of my brother Michaell, & 2 youngest children of sister Harford to be Res. Legs. & these 5 Exors.; Wit. William Rushton, Richard Hawkesworth & Richard Vickris, Jr.; Pro. 4 Aug. 1702.—P. C. C. Herne, 136.

[1] William Penn, eldest son of the Proprietor of Pennsylvania, by his first wife, Gulielma Maria Springett, and from whom the Penns of Shanagary, Ireland (now represented by the Gaskell-Halls), were descended, married Mary Jones. This valuable will gives, as far as the writer is aware, the first clue to her identification.

FAMILY RECORDS CONTAINED IN THE BIBLE OF JONATHAN PLATTS.

The following entries were transcribed by Mr. Clarence Almon Torrey, of the University of Chicago, from a bible (printed by Matthew Carey, in 1811), in the possession of his mother, Mrs. Susan Almira Roe Torrey, and formerly belonging to Jonathan Platts. From various sources Mr. Torrey determines the maiden names of the married women mentioned in the entries to be these: wife of Jonathan Platts, Rebecca Keen; wife of Enos Veal, Letitia Platts; wife of Jesse Keen Platts, Rachel Martindale; wife of Watson Roe, Eleanor Platts; wife of David Platts, Letitia Gilman; wife of Jonas Keen, Mary Hall. The Benjamin Keen, son of the last named, born September 1, 1759, was, no doubt, the person commissioned June 4, 1783, Lieutenant in Captain Platts's Company, Second Battalion, Cumberland County, New Jersey, Militia, and not the Benjamin Keen, son of Mounce Keen, mentioned in PENNSYLVANIA

MAGAZINE vol. iii. p. 447. Mr. Torrey supplies these data, hoping to elicit further information as to his family from some reader of the MAGAZINE.

BIRTHS.

Jonas Keen sen[r] was Born August 31st 1728.
Mary, wife of Jonas Keen, was Born April 2d 1728.
Jesse Keen was Born January 25th AD 1757.
Benjamin Keen was Born September 1st AD 1759.
Jonas Keen was Born September 23 AD 1762.
Rebecca Keen was Born July 4th AD 1765.
Jacob Keen was Born October 13th AD 1769.
Ephraim Keen was Born January 18th AD 1771.
Mary Keen was Born September 28th AD 1772.
Jesse Keen (son of Jonas Keen Ju[r]. and Phebe his wife) was born October 26th AD 1784.
Benjamin Keen (son of Jesse Keen and Margarett his wife) was Born February 9th AD 1787.
Lydia Keen (Daughter of Benjamin Keen & Laodamia his wife) was Born December 24th AD 1788.

DEATHS.

Jonas Keen sen[r] Departed this life February 13th AD 1787, being 58 y 5 mo 12 days.
Mary Keen Departed this life February 2d AD 1797, being 68 y & 10 mo old.
David Platts sen[r] Departed this life July 2d AD 1805.
Jonas Keen Platts Departed this life December 5th 1798.
Lettitia Sheppard, formerly widow, of David Platts Departed this life May 4th AD 1814 aged seventy-three years and thirteen Days.
Lettitia G Veal Departed this life July 1st 1824 aged 24 years & 22 days.
Rebecca P Veal Departed this life August 29 1823.
Jonathan Platts Departed this life June 22d 1838 aged 66 years 6 months 15 days.
Rebecca Platts, widow of Jonathan Platts, Died Aug 6th 1850 Aged 85 years 1 month and 2 days.

MARRIAGES.

Jonathan Platts & Rebecca his wife were married April 15th AD 1794.
Enos Veal & Lettitia his wife Married April 19th AD 1817.
Jesse Keen Platts & Rachel his wife were married July 23d 1818.

> In vain does Hymen with religious vows,
> Oblige his slaves to wear his yoke with ease,
> A privilege alone that love allows,
> Tis love alone can make our fetters please.

Watson Roe & Eleanor his wife were married Nov. 23. 1820.
Benjamin Keen Platts & Jane his wife were married February 19th 1824.
David R Platts & Sarah his wife were married September 3d 1833.
David Platts & Lettitia his wife were married January 25th AD 1763.
Jonas Keen and Mary his wife were married May 9th 1756.
Jonathan J Platts & Tabitha his wife were married December 3d 1833.

BIRTHS.

David Platts son of Moses Platts was born March 25th AD 1739.
Lettitia wife David Platts was Born April 21st AD 1741.
Rachel Platts Daughter of David & Lettitia Platts was Born May 25 AD 1764.
Lettitia Daughter of David Platts & Lettitia his wife was Born August 6th AD 1767.
Jonathan Platts Son of David and Lettitia Platts was born December 7th AD 1771.
David Platts son of David & Lettitia his wife was Born September 12th AD 1774.
Eleanor Platts Daughter of David and Lettitia his wife was born May 25th AD 1776.
David Platts son of David & Lettitia Platts was Born February 18 AD 1781.
Jesse Keen Platts son of Jonathan & Rebekah Platts was Born February 3d AD 1795.
Benjamin Keen Platts son of Jonathan & Rebekah Platts was Born January 25th AD 1797.
Jonas Keen Platts son of Jonathan & Rebekah Platts was Born November 13th AD 1798.
Lettitia Gilman Platts Daughter of Jonathan & Rebekah Platts was Born June 9th AD 1800.
Eleanor Platts Daughter of Jonathan & Rebekah Platts was born September 21 AD 1802.
David Rittenhouse Platts son of Jonathan & Rebekah Platts was Born March 29th 1805.
Jonathan Jarmin Platts son of Jonathan & Rebekah Platts was Born May 16th AD 1811.

PORTER FAMILIES OF CHESTER COUNTY AND YORK COUNTY, PENNSYLVANIA.—In Egle's "Notes and Queries," 1897, p. 121, substantially identical with the version originally contained in the "Sketch of the M'Creary Family," by Miss Harriet M'Creary, Gettysburg, Pennsylvania, 1882, it is stated that these Porters were descended from John Porter, colonist, of Windsor, Connecticut, through his eldest son, John Porter, Jr., the connecting link, according to Miss M'Creary's account, being set forth as follows:

"3rd Generation—Samuel, fourth son of John and Mary (Stanley) Porter, was born March 5th, 1664. He left Connecticut and went southward—settled in the southern part of Chester County, Pa., where his family appear to have been prosperous and respectable, and were considered wealthy farmers in their day. And when the country west of the Susquehanna River was thrown open to settlers two of his grandsons, Nathaniel and William Porter (brothers) crossed the river and settled in York (now Adams) County. Nathaniel, who was several years older than his brother, had married Sarah Maffitt, a lady of Scotch parentage, of Cecil County, Md."

In the "National Illustrated Magazine," Vol. I., No. 7, Washington, D.C., 1884, the biographer of Governor James D. Porter, of Tennessee, says of Samuel that he "settled in Chester County, Pa., married and reared a large family; his son William, born 1695, owned and lived upon his father's homestead."

That this pedigree is not correct is shown by a search of the records deposited in the State Library at Hartford, Connecticut. "Samuell sonn of John Porter was borne: march 5–1664" ("Connecticut Colony Land Records," Vol. I. folio 54, "Windsor children's age"); "Samuel Porter Dyed November 16th 1694." (Ibid., p. 50); Agreement dated January 12, 1688, regarding the lands of "o^r father John Porter of Windsor," signed by John Porter, James Porter, Nathaniel Porter, and Samuel Porter; "An agreement between ye brethern of Samuell Porter deceased of Windsor concerning ye devition of his estate," signed by John Porter, Timothy Lomas, Joseph Porter, "wth ye consent of his guardean Jno Moore." James Porter, Hezekiah Porter, Enoch Drake, Thomas Lomas, Nathaniel Porter, Nathaniel Lomas; "A Speciall Court held at Hartford Decemb^r 25, 1694." . . . "An Inventory of the estate of Samuel porter was exhibited in court & oath made by John porter that there was a True presentment of the estate of the deceased so far as at p^{r}sent he knows & If more comes to knowledg he will cause it to be aded to the Inventory. This Court Grants administration on the estate to James & Nathaniel porter who are to pay the debt in the first place & the remaynder of the estate is to be distributed to each of the brothers & sisters by equall proportion and [?] heyden & return strong are to distribute the estate to the legatees the lands to be wholly to the sonns & If any land fall to the sons more then their portions comes to they are to pay to their sisters what they shall be appoynted by the said Strong & Heyden;" "windsor december 19 : 1694. An Inventory taken of the Estate of Samuel porter deceased." Real and personal amounting to £210. "The Legatees or those next of kind The Bretheren & sisters of samuel porter John Porter James porter Nath Porter Hezekiah porter Joseph Porter Sarah drake Hannah Loomys Rebecka Loomys Ruth Loomys." ("Hartford Probate Records," Vol. V. p. 278, and Reverse End, p. 196.)

Accepting the above evidence as conclusive, the authentic pedigree begins with William Porter, who married Mary Price, daughter of Thomas and Ann Price. There appears to be no evidence that he "owned and lived upon his father's homestead." His first land warrant (Churchman Papers) was dated May 10, 1734, and was for land located in Elk Township, a little west of Lewisville, Chester County. In 1688 a "William Porter was among the witnesses who signed the marriage certificate of Henry Hollingsworth of New Castle, Pa." (PENNA. MAG., Vol. XXII. p. 376); "1718. William Porter. Kennett. Servant—unmarried" appeared on the list of taxables; and April 16, 1727, William Porter was a witness to the will of William Reynolds, of West Nottingham. Probably the last-mentioned William Porter was the only one identical with the subject of this note.

William Porter was commissioned a captain for the French and Indian War, February 8, 1747–8, in the Associate Regiments of Chester County ("Penna. Archives," Second Series, Vol. II. p. 506). His will, probated at West Chester August 3, 1749, does not mention a son Nathaniel, but there was one of that name who had a brother William, who was a son of James Porter, of West Nantmeal.

William Porter, "heir at Law" of William and Mary Porter (Deed Book Z, p. 429, West Chester, Pennsylvania), married Sarah Piersol, daughter of John and Alice Piersol, of Chester County, and not Sarah Percival, as in pp. 72, 73 and Chart, "The Ancestry of Benjamin

Harrison," by Charles P. Keith, Esq. They were great-great-grandparents of Benjamin Harrison, President of the United States.

Further information concerning the ancestry and descendants of the various Porter families of Chester County and York County, Pennsylvania, and of Delaware and Maryland, will be appreciated by the undersigned.

PORTER FARQUHARSON COPE.

4806 CHESTER AVENUE, PHILADELPHIA.

A SKETCH OF SOME OF THE DESCENDANTS OF OWEN RICHARDS, WHO EMIGRATED TO PENNSYLVANIA PREVIOUS TO 1718.

BY LOUIS RICHARDS, READING, PA.

The surname of Richards is of Welsh origin, and from that nationality, it may be generally asserted, the great majority of those who bear it in this country are descended. In Wales it occurs with great frequency, and from thence has been borne into other parts of Britain, and especially England, where it is almost equally common. It was at first a Christian name, merely, from which the *s* was omitted, the latter being added when it came to be used as a patronymic.

The earliest families of Richardes in New England were of Puritan stock, their ancestors emigrating hither from old England at various dates during the seventeenth century. In a "Genealogical Register of the Descendants of Several Ancient Puritans," vol. iii., compiled by the Rev. Abner Morse, A.M., Member of the New England Historic Genealogical Society, and published in Boston in 1861, several thousands of the name are traced out, through many generations, from the emigrant founders. Of the twelve original ancestors whose posterity is sketched, the earliest mentioned is Thomas Richards, who, it is stated, was born about 1590, and came to Dorchester in 1630, ten years after the landing of the Pilgrims.

Among the colonists who came over at the invitation of William Penn, at the date of the foundation of the province in 1682, or within a few years subsequently, were, as is well known, a number of Welsh, to whom the Proprietor granted a tract, or barony as it was termed, of forty thousand acres west of the Schuylkill. The original warrant was issued in 1684. and the territory it embraced was mainly included in the townships of Newtown, Goshen, Uwchlan, Tredyffrin, and Whiteland in Chester County; Haverford and Radnor, originally also in Chester, now in Delaware County, and Merion, formerly Philadelphia, now Montgomery County. Gwynedd Township, Montgomery, originally in Philadelphia County, was also settled by people of this nationality, about 1698. The broad fertile region known as the Great Valley, in Chester County, a large part of which was included in the Welsh grant, began to be extensively populated by them in 1711. The names given to most of the townships mentioned unmistakably suggest the circumstances of their origin. A considerable proportion of the early Welsh settlers were Friends, a large number of them were Baptists, and a few adhered to the Church of England. They were a hardy, sober, and vigorous race, possessing means, enterprise, and energy, and constituted a valuable accession to the original population of the province, to which they gave some of the most distinguished men in its early history. Their native language continued to be employed to some extent, it is said, down to about the period of the Revolution. At the present day they have become largely merged in other nationalities more numerously represented in later immigrations. Their descendants are recognized by their names, and the localities in which they originally settled in any considerable numbers are invariably found to be English-speaking communities.

Among the early records of Philadelphia and Chester Counties, which date back to 1683, are to be found the names of several Richardes, who located within their limits—all undoubtedly of Welsh, or, more immediately, English origin. Joseph Richards was a member for the county of Chester of the first Assembly convened by Penn in 1682, and purchased 500 acres of land in Aston Township the same year. He died in Chichester in 1710, and a son and a grandson bearing the same Christian name, succeeded, respectively, to the ownership of a portion of his estate. Solomon Richards was also a "first purchaser," and drew for city lots in Philadelphia in 1682. One Richard ap Richard was a landowner in Whiteland Township in 1710. Others of the earliest of the name mentioned in the Chester County records were Nathaniel, who was a landholder in Aston Township in 1692, and died there in

1700; Guenlyon, of Haverford, who died in 1697; Rowland, of Merion, who purchased in Tredyffrin in 1707-8, and died there in 1720—a grandson of whom had the same name; William, whose estate was administered upon in 1716, and Thomas, of Tredyffrin, who died in 1739. The ancient records of Philadelphia County mention, among others, Philip and John Richards, whose wills were probated respectively in 1698 and 1711, and both of whom were residents of the city.

1. OWEN RICHARDS, a few of whose descendants it is proposed to trace, emigrated to Pennsylvania from Merionethshire, a county of North Wales. According to tradition, he sailed from the port of Chester, England, and landed at Philadelphia, accompanied by his wife, three sons, James, William, and John, and a daughter, Elizabeth. There is no means of ascertaining the exact date of his arrival, but it was certainly before the year 1718, and probably not earlier than 1710 or 1715, though the last two dates mentioned are merely conjectural. There is some reason to think that he may have resided for a time in Tredyffrin, Whiteland, or some other Welsh portion of Chester County before referred to, and some of the earliest of his name already mentioned may have been, and probably were, his kindred. Both suppositions are without any record evidence to support them, but they are rendered at least plausible from the fact that certain names which appear in some land transactions of his in another county, a few years later, are unmistakably those of original residents of Chester.

The first positive trace of him discoverable is by his purchase, December 22, 1718, of 300 acres of land in Amity Township, then Philadelphia, now Berks County, from one Mouns Justice, at that time a resident of the Northern Liberties. The latter was one of several Swedes to whom a warrant for a tract of ten thousand acres was granted by the Proprietary, through his Commissioners of Property, in 1701. These Swedes belonged to the congregation at Wicaco, and their pastor, Andreas Rudman,.who was one of the grantees, probably negotiated the purchase. Possession was taken under the warrant, and patents for these lands in severalty were issued in 1704 and 1705. Out of the Swede tracts, collectively, the township of Amity was formed, and it constitutes the location of the earliest settlement within the limits of the present county of Berks, which was erected in 1752. Justice's patent is dated in 1705, and was for 700 acres. The portion of the tract purchased from him by Owen Richards, it has been ascertained, lies close to the present village of Weaverstown, about three miles from the Schuylkill, a considerable part of it being at this date in the possession of the heirs of Daniel McLean. The land is rolling and of good quality for agricultural purposes. A small tributary of the Monocacy Creek runs through it.

In 1726, Owen, together with one David Harry, from Chester County, also a Welshman, bought 250 acres of land in Oley Township from John Banfield, 100 acres of which were a portion of a larger tract which had been patented to John Longworthy, of Radnor, in 1714. This land is in the southeastern corner of the township, on the Manatawny Creek, about half a mile from a well-known tavern called the "Yellow House." Richards and Harry resold this tract the same year to John Ellis, of Springfield, Chester County, and in 1735 it passed to Jacob Hill, remaining in the possession of the Hill family for a century and a quarter.

Owen Richards doubtless resided in Amity Township, on the property purchased by him from Justice, from 1718 until his death, the date of which is uncertain, though records show that it did not occur previous to 1734. In 1729 he sold one-half of this tract to his eldest son James, in consideration of £7, and "natural love and affection." The remaining portion, which he probably occupied, it is likely passed to his heirs, as no conveyance of it by him, or recital thereof, is to be found of record. When and where his first wife died is unknown. It cannot be affirmed, indeed, with any confidence, that she ever saw America. The records of Christ Church, Philadelphia, show that he was married in 1727 to a second wife, Elizabeth Baker. She survived him, and died in 1753, without issue, aged about eighty years. She was buried, as was doubtless also her husband, in the ground of the Episcopal church at Douglassville, on the Schuylkill, in Amity Township, anciently a Swedish church known as "St. Gabriel's at Morlatton," the organization of which dates back to about the time of the original Swedish settlements before referred to. Its oldest existing records begin in 1736.

The descendants of Owen Richards have frequently been confounded with those of another family of the same name, but of German derivation, residing in Berks, Montgomery, and some other adjoining counties. The latter were originally called *Reichert*, their first ancestor in this country being Johann Frederick Reichert, a native of the Kingdom of Wurtemburg, who patented lands in New Hanover Township, originally Philadelphia, now Montgomery County, in 1720, and died there in 1748. Their name has been anglicized for over a century, having been changed to Richards, as is said, by English schoolmasters, out of preference for their own tongue. Of this stock, which is a very numerous one, were John and Matthias Richards, grandsons of Frederick, both early members of Congress from Pennsylvania, a son of the latter, Judge Matthias S. Richards, of Reading, the late George Richards, of Pottstown, formerly a State Senator from Montgomery County and a son of John, and his brother, Mark Richards, for many years a well-known merchant of Philadelphia. A number of families who still write their name Reichert are found in various portions of Berks and neighboring counties. These are also of German descent, and of Palatinate origin.

The children of Owen Richards, of whom any trace or tradition remains, appear to have been—

2. JAMES, of whom no information is obtainable beyond the record of his purchase from his father of the 150 acres in Amity in 1729, and the sale by him of the same tract in 1741 to Peter Weaver. In the deed conveying away this land he is styled "labourer," and he was a single man at that date. He probably left no descendants.

3. WILLIAM.

4. JOHN, who appears to have resided in Amity, or vicinity, for some years, though the records do not show that he was a landowner. His wife's name was Sarah, and the names of two of their children, as

appears by the Register of St. Gabriel's Church, were Edward and Susannah, the former baptized in 1737 and the latter in 1739. Another child (name not given—probably an infant) was buried in 1736. The tradition is that he eventually removed to Virginia, where some of his descendants remain at the present day. From him, it is said, "Richards' Ford," on the Rappahannock, takes its name, and from his posterity proceeded a family of the name who settled in Kentucky.

5. ELIZABETH, of whom nothing whatever is traceable. It is likely that she d. unm.

3. WILLIAM, through whom all of the family who here follow are traced, was without doubt born in Wales, and had probably about arrived at manhood at the date of his father's emigration. He appears at one time to have been possessed of considerable estate, but closed life in comparative poverty. In 1735, he bought from one Michael Waren, 150 acres of land in Amity; which had also been a part of the Mouns Justice tract. It adjoined the 150 acres acquired by his brother James from Owen, but did not constitute any part of the latter's original purchase. In 1740, William, together with his wife Elizabeth, sold 53 acres of his land to Peter Weaver —the same who the following year purchased the whole of James's. One of the witnesses to the deed of conveyance is Rowland Richards. What disposition he made of the balance does not appear. It may have been comprised in a tract of 184 acres situated in the same vicinity, which he mortgaged in 1747 to the executors of Samuel Powell, Jr., for £140, the debt being repaid by his assignee, Jacob Roads, in 1751, presumably out of the proceeds of the sale of the land. The mortgage contains no recital of title. To his occupation of tiller of the soil, he at one time added the functions of constable of the township. In the first volume of the Pennsylvania Archives, first series, is published at length a deposition which he gave in 1738, containing a diverting account of his rough experience, as one of His Majesty's peace officers, with some violators of the ancient provincial laws against the obstruction of the navigation of the river Schuylkill by the erection of racks for the taking of fish—a subject of ab-

sorbing importance in the primitive days of river transportation, when grain was conveyed to Philadelphia by rafts.

He died in Oley Township in January, 1752. His will, dated December 26, 1751, is on file in Philadelphia, and mentions the names of all his children. The inventory of his personal estate amounted to £207 7s. 10d. Pennsylvania currency. The appraisers were Ellis Hughes—without doubt a Welshman—and George Boone, for many years a prominent provincial magistrate of Oley, who belonged to a family of Quakers of that neighborhood, and was the uncle of Daniel Boone, the pioneer of Kentucky. Nearly one-half of the sum total of the appraisement is made up of obligations for moneys due the decedent by various persons, while the character and valuations of the different chattels enumerated seem to indicate that at the time of his death he was a small tenant farmer, whose resources had been run down to the verge of exhaustion.

The witnesses to his will were James and Jane Norrell and Benjamin Longworthy. His wife Elizabeth and Peter Weaver were appointed executors, but the latter renounced. He directs all his personal property and movables, "within and without," to be sold, and gives his wife the use of the proceeds for life, but adds that " if she thinks proper to alter her condition, she shall have her thirds according to law"—a favorite mode of restriction upon widows in those days. He enjoins that his son William " is to live with his mother for the space of one year, and then be put out to a trade which he likes." His daughters Ruth and Sarah were " to be to the care and discretion of their mother," each receiving £5 Pennsylvania currency, and the latter, in addition, the testator's " chest of drawers at Cornelius Dewees's." His son Owen and his daughters Mary Ball and Margaret were each given five shillings Pennsylvania currency—a slender patrimony! His son James received £10 and a mare. The residue of his estate was given to William upon his coming of age, and after his mother's decease.

Of his seven children it would appear that but three, Mary, Owen and James, had attained their majority at the date of the will. The following notices of them are given in the supposed order of their ages:—

5. MARY married John Ball, who resided in Douglass Township, Berks County, and acquired land in Amity in 1754. One of their children was Joseph Ball, who became a prominent merchant and extensive landowner and capitalist of Philadelphia, accumulating a large fortune. He was interested in various business enterprises in that city, among which was the Insurance Company of North America, established in 1792, of which he was one of the original directors, and President in the years 1798 and 1799. In his early manhood he was employed as manager of the iron works at Batsto, Burlington County, New Jersey, then owned by Col. John Cox. He was there in that capacity during the earlier part of the Revolutionary War, and in 1779 became proprietor. The works were extensively employed in the manufacture of shot and shell for the Continental service. In the 4th volume of Pennsylvania Archives, first series, pp. 757, 761, 762, a correspondence of Mr. Ball and Col. Cox with the Committee of Safety of Philadelphia in May, 1776, shows that the ammunition then being furnished to the Committee was, by their special order, hauled by teams from Batsto to Cooper's Ferry (now Camden), instead of being transported by the usual less expeditious mode of conveyance by water. He took the oath of allegiance to Pennsylvania September 10, 1777, under a law passed by the Assembly to insure fidelity to the interests of the State on the part of its citizens. During the struggle for liberty he was a decided patriot, and advanced liberally of his rapidly accumulating means in aid of the cause. After the close of the War, it is said that he was extensively embarked in the schemes for the restoration of the public credit set on foot by Robert Morris, the financier of the Revolution, by means of which he, in common with many others, suffered considerable pecuniary loss. Mr. Ball died in 1821, aged 73 years, leaving a widow, Sarah, but no issue, and his vast estate passed to an immense number of collateral heirs, occupying many years in process of distribution.

6. OWEN was baptized, according to the records of St. Gabriel's Church, before mentioned, together with his brother James and sister Ruth, September 20, 1737. He appears to have been a farmer by occupation, and is assessed in Amity Township as a tenant from 1756 to 1760, and in Union Township from 1766 to 1773, after which no further trace of him is to be found in the county records. He removed, probably about the commencement of the Revolutionary War, to Northumberland County, or some other of the then so-called western portions of the State. A person of his name, pre-

sumably the same individual, appears on the list of privates of Capt. Gray's Company, Fourth Pennsylvania Regiment, Continental Line, in 1777. The names of his children, as given in a tabulated list of the heirs of his nephew, Joseph Ball, were William, John, Mary, Elizabeth (Barr), Eleanor (Hamilton), Jane (Stevens), and Sarah (Roberts).
7. JAMES.
8. RUTH married Daniel Kunsman. Nothing is known of her family record excepting the names of her children, which were Rebecca (Hoffman), Elizabeth (Miller), Mary (Seiler), Catharine (Canstatter), and William.
9. WILLIAM.
10. MARGARET married Cornelius Dewees. The Deweeses, as I am informed by one of their descendants, were of Huguenot stock, the name being originally written De Wees. Several of them are found among the list of landholders in Philadelphia County as early as 1734. Margaret died in 1793. Her children were William, Owen, David, Cornelius, Mary (Patterson), and Samuel.
11. SARAH married James Hastings, and resided for a considerable portion of her life in Virginia. She died, probably about 1825, leaving three children, Howell, William, and John.

7. JAMES was b. about 1722, and was baptized, as above stated, in 1737. He was engaged all his life in farming, and resided first in Amity, and subsequently in Earl and Colebrookdale Townships, Berks County, being assessed as a property owner in the last-mentioned district from 1768 to 1797. He owned 150 acres of land at the head of Ironstone Creek, about two miles northwest from the present borough of Boyertown, upon which he resided. He served for a short period during the Revolutionary War, and his name appears on the roll of Captain Tudor's Company, Fourth Pennsylvania Continental Line, as a Sergeant, enlisted May 10, 1777. He was a man of immense frame, and great physical strength, and his long life of rugged toil was varied with many lively episodes of conflict and adventure. Disposing of his property in Berks to certain of his sons, he removed, with perhaps some of his youngest children, in 1797 or '98, to the North Branch of the Susquehanna, near Danville, then Northumberland County, where he d. in 1804, aged upwards of eighty.

His wife's name was Mary, and his children were William, Frederick, Elizabeth, James, Owen, Mary, Sarah, Hannah, and John. Of the daughters, Hannah d. unm.; Elizabeth m. Enoch Rutter; Mary, Henry Fox, and Sarah, Henry Schmale. Descendants of several of these children remain, both in Berks and on the Susquehanna. William, the eldest son, was b. Jan. 27, 1754, and m. Mary, daughter of John William and Elizabeth Miller, of Earl Township, by whom he had four children, William and Elizabeth, both of whom d. young, James, b. March 27, 1782, and John, b. June 5, 1784. William Richards d. about 1786, and his widow in 1838, at an advanced age.

James Richards, last mentioned, was distinguished for the fervor of his religious convictions, and the purity of his character and life. He m. 1811, Ann Hunter Smith, dau. of John Smith, Esq., of Joanna Furnace, Berks County, and Elizabeth, his wife, and was the father of the late John S. Richards, Esq., for many years a prominent and well-known member of the Bar of Reading. James d. September 21, 1828, and his widow, April 25, 1857. John Richards m. 1st, 1811, Rebecca, dau. of Michael and Susanna Ludwig, who d. January 19, 1840, and 2d, 1841, Louisa, dau. of Ephraim and Elizabeth Silvers, who d. January 26, 1880. He had seven children. He was a native of Colebrookdale Township, Berks County, and removed to New Jersey in 1808. He was engaged for forty years in the iron manufacturing business, principally at Weymouth and Gloucester Furnaces, Atlantic County, of the latter of which he became a proprietor in 1830. In 1836–37 he was a member of the Legislature of New Jersey for the county of Burlington, but, with this exception, declined all public positions, his predilections being wholly in the line of business life. He resided from 1848 to 1854 at Mauch Chunk, Pennsylvania, where he continued the iron manufacture, retiring in the latter year to an estate called "Stowe," in the vicinity of Pottstown, Montgomery County, where he d. November 29, 1871, in the 88th year of his age. He possessed in a marked degree the characteristics of energy and self-reliance, and was a fair example of the success which, in spite of the lack of early advantages, usually attends the exercise of these qualities when joined to principles of strict business integrity.

9. WILLIAM was b. September 12, 1738, and was baptized at St. Gabriel's Church, Feb. 23, 1739. At the time of his father's death he was in his fourteenth year, and in accordance with the directions of the will of the latter that he should be taught such a trade as he preferred, was sent to Chester County, and placed, it is believed, at Coventry Forge, on French Creek, to learn the occupation of a founder. Coventry was built by Samuel Nutt, an Englishman of enterprise and fortune, about 1718 or 1720. At the time William went there, it was under the management of John Patrick, also an Englishman, who was early associated with Nutt in that capacity. In 1764, William m. Mary, dau. of John Patrick and his wife Anna, dau. of Oliver Dunklin. She was b. June 24, 1745, and had a brother Samuel, who was b. in 1743, and m. Rachel Gibbs, and a sister Esther, b. in 1747, who m. Ezekiel Leonard. After the death of his first wife, John Patrick m., 1755, Abigail Hockley. In 1748, he purchased from the heirs of his father-in-law, Oliver Dunklin, 150 acres of land in Amity Township, before mentioned, which he disposed of in 1750 to Henry Van Reed, from Holland, the ancestor of the well-known family of that name in Berks, in the possession of one of whose descendants the premises still remain. John Patrick d. in East Nantmeal Township, Chester County, in 1765. His son Samuel was also a forgeman, and an agreement is still in existence, bearing the date of 1767, in which he undertook to blow the Cornwall Furnace, then in Lancaster County, for the proprietors, Peter and Curtis Grubb, at "five shillings per ton for pigs," and "forty-five shillings per ton for stoves." At a later date he was engaged at an establishment called the Forest of Dean Furnace, in Orange County, New York.

William Richards was subsequently employed at Warwick Furnace, another well-known establishment, on French Creek in the vicinity of Coventry, built by Samuel Nutt's widow, Anna Nutt, in 1737. About the year 1768, he went to

Batsto Iron Works, New Jersey, before mentioned, as founder, his family continuing to reside in Pennsylvania. In 1774, he purchased a tract of 210 acres in East Nantmeal Township, Chester County, from the heirs of his father-in law, John Patrick, who had bought it in 1763 from the heirs of Samuel Savage. He sold this farm to one Jacob Weimands in 1775, and was subsequently, in 1778, the owner of another tract of 151 acres in West Whiteland Township, afterwards known as the "Ship Tavern" property, situated on the Lancaster Turnpike, near the present station on the Pennsylvania Railroad called Whiteland.

In June, 1775, he was commissioned by the Assembly of Pennsylvania as "Standard Bearer to the Second Battalion of Associators of Chester County." On August 13, 1776, as appears from his private diary, he joined the Revolutionary forces, his family being then resident at Valley Forge, on the Schuylkill, where he was in camp with the army during the memorable winter quarters in 1777–78. The length of his entire term of service is not known, but it probably extended over the greater part of the active period of the war. In January, 1781, he accepted the position of resident manager of Batsto, tendered him by Col. Cox and Mr. Charles Pettit, succeeding his nephew, Joseph Ball. He shortly afterwards acquired an interest in this large and then celebrated manufacturing establishment, and about the year 1784 became sole owner. He rebuilt the works, and made extensive additions and improvements, his operations expanding from time to time with his increasing prosperity. His domain extended over many thousands of acres, and he acquired what was then regarded as a princely fortune.

He was a man of unbounded enterprise and untiring energy, of great firmness of character and tenacity of purpose. These qualities well fitted him to be a leader, rather than a follower of men. A large community gradually grew up around him, in the midst of which he lived in a style suited to his wealth, commanding the respect and confidence of his dependants, who in turn prospered under his judicious supervision. In person he was six feet four inches in height, of gigantic mould, and great physical strength—his robust frame being a fitting tenement for his vigorous and active mind. A miniature profile engraving of him by St. Mémin, accompanying this sketch, taken in advanced life, portrays him as of calm and reflective features, equally indicative of force of character and benignity of disposition. Surmounting his long thick hair is a flat circular comb, such as the then prevailing fashion warranted as a masculine ornament.

His first wife, Mary Patrick, by whom he had eleven children—seven sons and four daughters—d. November 24, 1794. He was m. in 1796 to Margaret Wood, a daughter of Isaac Wood, of Moorestown, Burlington County, New Jersey, who was b. in 1767. Eight children—seven sons and one daughter—were the result of this union. In 1809 he relinquished the iron works at Batsto to his son Jesse, and removed to Mount Holly, Burlington County, where he became a landowner, and though past threescore and ten, thoroughly identified himself with the growth and development of that place. In this new home, surrounded by his numerous family, he d. on the 31st of August, 1823, in the eighty-fifth year of his age. He was a member of the Protestant Episcopal Church, and his remains rest in St. Andrew's Cemetery, belonging to that denomination, near Mount Holly, beside those of his second wife, who survived him until December 21, 1850. The spot is marked by a plain high marble tomb, inscribed with the date of his decease and age.

The children of William and Mary (Patrick) Richards were—

12. ABIGAIL, b. June 1, 1765; d. May 14, 1794.
13. JOHN, b. June 1, 1767; d. November 30, 1793.
14. SAMUEL, b. at Valley Forge May 8, 1769. He was for many years an extensive iron manufacturer in the State of New Jersey, and a prominent and esteemed merchant and resident of Philadelphia. He m. 1st, 1797, Mary Morgan, dau. of William Smith, merchant of that city. She d. in 1820, and he m. 2d, 1822, Anna Maria Witherspoon, dau. of Burling Martin, of New York, who survived him. Mr. Samuel Richards had eleven children. Two of those by his first marriage were Sarah Ball, the widow of the late Stephen Colwell, merchant of Philadelphia, and Thomas S., also a large iron works proprietor, who m. Harriet, dau. of General Francis Nichols. Mr. Richards d. January 4, 1842.

15. ELIZABETH, b. August 26, 1771. She m. 1799, the Rev. Thomas Haskins, of Maryland, and had three children. Her husband d. June 29, 1816, and Mrs. Haskins, September 24, 1857.
16. REBECCA, b. August 7, 1773. She m., 1794, John Sevier, of Tennessee, and had seven children. She d. May 10, 1809.
17. WILLIAM, b. July 1, 1775; d. December 21, 1796.
18. JOSEPH, b. October 6, 1777; d. March 26, 1797.
19. THOMAS, b. February 10, 1780. He was a merchant of Philadelphia, and m., 1810, Ann Bartram, by whom he had nine children. He d. October 17, 1860—the date upon which it had been arranged to celebrate his golden wedding, and the marriage of his daughter.
20. JESSE.
21. CHARLES, b. August 9, 1785; d. May 11, 1788.
22. ANNA MARIA, b. February 8, 1789; m., 1810, John White, of Delaware, and had three children. She d. May 2, 1816.

The children of William and Margaret (Wood) Richards were

23. BENJAMIN WOOD, b. Nov. 12, 1797.
24. CHARLES HENRY, b. April 9, 1799; d. April, 1802.
25. GEORGE WASHINGTON, b. May 6, 1801; d. June, 1802.
26. AUGUSTUS HENRY, b. May 5, 1803; m. Rebecca, dau. of the Hon. John McLean, of Ohio; was a member of the Philadelphia Bar, to which he was admitted in 1826; had two children; d. in 1839.
27. WILLIAM, b. January 16, 1805; m., 1831, Constantia Marie Lamand, and had five children. He inherited in a very striking degree the physical constitution of his father; was of remarkably large and massive build, and possessed the strength of a giant. He d. April 19, 1864.
28. GEORGE WASHINGTON, b. May 3, 1807. He was a merchant of Philadelphia, and subsequently engaged extensively in the cotton manufacture, and was active in the directory of prominent railroads in Pennsylvania and New Jersey, and for many years of the Franklin Fire Insurance Company of Philadelphia. He m., 1829, Mary Louisa, dau. of Louis Le Guen; had eight children; d. April 22, 1874.
29. JOSEPH BALL, b. November 9, 1811; d. January 30, 1812.
30. MARY WOOD, b. March 6, 1815; d. September 19, 1860.

20. JESSE. He was b. at Valley Forge, December 2, 1782, and succeeded his father, as before stated, in the management of Batsto. In 1829 he rebuilt the works, and, in 1846, the furnace having been abandoned, established extensive glass

B. W. Richards
1797-1851.

manufactories, which he carried on successfully until his death, June 17, 1854. He greatly enlarged and improved the Batsto estate, which, toward the close of his proprietorship, comprised about forty thousand acres. This property he left to his children, who occupied it and carried on the glass manufacture for a considerable period. It passed a few years since into the ownership of Mr. Joseph Wharton, of Philadelphia.

Jesse Richards was a member of the Assembly of New Jersey for Burlington County at the Sessions of 1837–38 and 1838–39. He m., 1810, Sarah Ennals Haskins, dau. of the Rev. Thomas Haskins, before mentioned, by his first wife, Martha Potts,—Mr. Haskins having previously m., as his second wife, Elizabeth Richards, sister of Jesse. Mrs. Richards d. Oct. 14, 1868, in her eightieth year. They had seven children. One of the eldest, Thomas Haskins Richards, a graduate of Princeton, was a member of Assembly in 1841–42 and 1842–43, and member of the Senate for Burlington County in 1847, '48, and '49.

23. BENJAMIN WOOD. He was b. at Batsto, November 12, 1797, and graduated at Princeton in 1815, in his eighteenth year. Whilst at college he received very deep religious impressions, and decided to enter the ministry of the Presbyterian church, but the extremely delicate condition of his health at that period compelled him to abandon this intention, and to seek the restoration of his physical strength by travel. After an extended tour through the southern and southwestern States, he returned, greatly re-invigorated, and went to Philadelphia in the year 1819, and entered upon mercantile pursuits. Becoming interested in municipal affairs, he was elected to membership of the City Councils. His capacities for public service, and the confidence of his fellow-citizens, led to his selection in 1827 as a member of the Legislature, in which he served for one year. While in the Assembly he evinced a particular zeal in the cause of public education, procuring the first appropriation from the State for the establishment of public schools in Philadelphia. He was an active promoter of the common school system, after-

wards adopted, and was one of the original members of the City Board of Controllers. Under an Act passed in 1829, he was appointed one of the Canal Commissioners of Pennsylvania. In April of that year, he was chosen Mayor of Philadelphia, to fill the unexpired term of George M. Dallas, who had resigned. The office was at that time elective by the City Councils, and the period of service one year. In October following, William Milnor was chosen for the succeeding term, but Mr. Richards was again elected in October, 1830, and re-elected in 1831, serving until October, 1832, when he was succeeded by John Swift.

His public spirit led him to take an active part in the organization and promotion of a number of the leading benevolent and educational institutions of the city. He was one of the founders of the Blind Asylum, an early manager of the Deaf and Dumb Asylum, a member of the Philosophical Society, and a trustee of the University of Pennsylvania. He took considerable part, at one period, in Federal politics, and was appointed by President Jackson a director of the United States Bank, and a director of the Mint, but resigned these positions upon being elected Mayor. He was the chief magistrate of the city at the death of Stephen Girard, and after the expiration of his term, became a director of Girard College.

While travelling in Europe in 1833 for the restoration of his then seriously impaired health, his attention was directed to the subject of rural public cemeteries, more especially in consequence of a visit which he made to that of Père la Chaise at Paris, and upon his return he wrote much for the journals of the day to direct public attention to the desirability of establishing some worthy institution of this character for the city of Philadelphia. Having secured the active co-operation of several other prominent citizens in this project, the result was the purchase and organization, in 1835, of the beautiful cemetery at Laurel Hill. In 1836, he originated and founded the Girard Life Insurance, Annuity, and Trust Company—one of the earliest of a numerous class of institutions of the city since grown to great business magnitude and importance—and was its President from its organization until his death.

The qualities which prominently entered into the elements of his character were great benevolence of heart, profound convictions of right and justice, and unflinching moral courage. These, combined with a strong degree of intellectual force, and a disposition to employ his talents and energies for the good of his fellows at large, constituted what may be truthfully termed a highly successful life, the impress of which has been deeply engraven upon the institutions of his adopted city. In person Mr. Richards was of tall and imposing figure, and of peculiarly symmetrical and attractive features. In the earlier part of his public life he was considered one of the handsomest men in Philadelphia, and a portrait of him, by Inman, which hangs in the Mayor's office, and from which the accompanying picture was taken, confirms the justice of the compliment. He was m., in 1821, to Sarah Ann, dau. of Joshua Lippincott, and left seven children—four sons and three daughters. He d. July 12, 1851, aged fifty-three years. His wife d. March 19, 1862. His remains are interred at Laurel Hill.

Thus imperfectly, from very meagre materials, have been compiled a few facts which may prove of interest to some of those to whose descent they more or less immediately relate. It may be added that the inquiries which led to their development were originally stimulated by some researches of the writer for other purposes into the records of the county of Berks, where, as it has appeared, the scene of the narrative opens. It is due to him to remark, in conclusion, that the natural feeling of hesitation with which a publication of this mass of personal details was at first regarded, has only been overcome by the reflection that the subject-matter, at least, is in harmony with the character and design of the medium through which it is presented—a consideration which it is hoped will be accepted as a sufficient apology for the propriety of a work of this nature, which, under any circumstances, usually proves a perilous undertaking.

A RECORD OF THE RICHARDS FAMILY FROM AN OLD WELSH BIBLE.
—The title-page and that part of Genesis to the beginning of Chapter VI. are missing; the rest appears to be intact and in a good state of preservation.

The title-page to the New Testament part is as follows:
"Testament Newydd ein Harglwydd an Hiachawdwr IESU GRIST. Rhuf. I. 16. Nid oes arnaf gywilydd o Efengyl Grist, oblegid gallu Duw yw hi, er Iechydwrideth i bob vn a'r sydd yn credu.

"Printiedig yn Llandain gan Charles Bill, a Thomas Newcomb, Printwyr i Ardderchoccaf, Fawrhydi y Brenin ar Frenhines 1690."

On the pages set apart for records of family events there are entries in several different handwritings. Here is a transcript.

"Josuah Richards was born the 20th of December 1720.

"Rowland Richards son of Sam'l and Elizabeth Richards was Born ye 29 of 10th mo'th 1728.

"Catherin Richard her book 1716. Samuel Richard his hand 1716.

"Rowland Richards his Book so saith Sam'l Rich'ds.

"Rowland Richards dyed the Eight day of November in ye year 1720, Aged 60 years 6 months & 8 days.

"Abijah Richards son of Rowl'd Richards & Mary his wife was born the 23d of the 5th mo 1753.

"Ebenezer Richards was born the 18th of the 7th mo 1754.

"Abigail Richards daughter of Rowl'd Richards and Lydia his wife was born the 17th of the 10th mo 1764.

"Samuel Richards was born the 27th of the 11th month 1765 & departed this Life the 29th of the 12th mo 1787 aged 22 years 1 month and 2 days.

"Elizabeth Richards was born the 13th of the 11th mo 1767 & departed this Life the 17th of the 2nd mo 1788 aged 20 years 3 months & 4 days.

"Susannah Richards was born the 16th of the 10th mo 1769 and departed this Life the 9th of the 2 month 1788 Aged 18 years 3 months 3 weeks and 3 days.

"Eli Richards was born the 16th of the 9th mo 1771.

"Hannah Richards was born the 30th of the 1st mo 1774.

"Lydia Richards was born the 24th of the 3rd month 1776 and departed this Life the 28th of the 7th month 1777 aged 1 year 4 months and 4 days.

"Townsend Richards was born the 25th of the 3rd mo 1785 and departed this Life the 5th of the 3rd month 1788 Aged 3 years 11 months 1 week 1 day.

"Mary Richards was born the 12th of the 9th mo 1780.
"Lydia Richards was born the 18th of the 10th mo 1782.
"Sarah Richards was born the 24th of the 8th month 1784.
"Catharine Richards was born the 30th of the 7th mo 1786.
"Sitnah Richards was born the 5th of the 1st mo 1789 [Sidney?]
"Ebenezer Richards departed this Life the 9th of the 3rd month 1775 Aged 20 years 7 months 3 weeks.
"Eli Richards departed this Life the 25th of the 8th month 1804 Aged 33 years 11 months 9 days.
"Eli Mullin son of John Mullin & Lydia his wife was born the 19th of the 12th month 1806.
"Roland Richard in his 86 year of his age went up seven stories in the Stone Mill in Cyty of Cincin'ti conducted by Samuel Test and departed this Life at the House of David Holloway in Cincin'ti on the 21 Day of the 5 month 1815 aged 86 years & 6 months & 21 Days.
"Lidia Richard Departed this Life at the House of David Holloway near Richmond in the State of Indiana on 25 Day of 6 month 1835 in the ninety first of her age."

Written on the margin of one of the pages is "Gainor Richards her hand 1720."

On the fly-leaf at the end of the book are the following entries:

"Rowland Richard Died ye Eight day of the 9th month 1720 aged sixty years and six months.
"Catharine Richard his wife Dyed the 20th Day of ye fifth month 1758 aged ninety years one m'th.
"Samuel Richard Dyed the 30th of the seventh m'th 1760 aged 59 and 9 months."

Bound with the Bible are a number of pages of psalms other than those to be found in all Bibles. The title-page to this part of the book reads as follows:

"Llyfer y PSALMAU, wedi Eu Cyfieithu A'i Cyfansoddi Ar Fesur Cerdd, yn Gymraeg. Drwy waith Edmund Prys Archdiacon Merionnydd.
"Printiedig yn Llandain gan Charles Bill, a Thomas Newcomb Printwyr i Ardderchoccaf Fawrhydi y Brenin ar Frenhines 1690."

A few notes respecting the above Richards family may not be out of place here.

Merion Friends' Meeting Book has recorded the births of the following children of Rowland and Catherine Richard: "Rowland, 2nd Mo: 22nd., 1690, Margaret, 8th Mo: 5th., 1692, Gainer, 11th Mo: 13th., 1693, John, 9th Mo: 9th., 1695, Elizabeth, 7th Mo: 22nd., 169–, Samuel, 8th Mo: 7th., 1700." Two daughters not in the above list were Sarah and Ruth. Rowland and Catherine Richard were residents of Tredyffrin Township, Chester County, in 1715. The son Samuel, born in 1700, married Second month 21, 1726, Elizabeth, daughter of Owen Evans, of Gwynedd. From this alliance descends the present owner of the old Bible, Mrs. Thomas Woodnutt, of Philadelphia (formerly Hannah Morgan). Through her kindness this copy has been allowed to be made.

HOWARD WILLIAMS LLOYD.

ROHRER RECORDS, from a scrap book in possession of Howard O. Folker, 1343 West Somerset Street, Philadelphia, whose wife, Annie M. Folker, inherited it in 1890 from her cousin, Amos W. Rohrer Henning, of Niagara Falls, N. Y. On the fly-leaf of book, in the handwriting of Mrs. Jacob Henning, is the following:

"This scrap book was commenced about the year 1832 by Mrs. Susan Henning, Suspension Bridge."

BIRTHS.

John Rohrer; born March, 1696, in Alsace, previous to the Revolution a province of France.
Maria Souder, his wife; born February 24, 1716, in Manheim, Germany.
The children of John and Maria Rohrer were eight in number:
 Jacob Rohrer, born June 26, 1734.
 John Rohrer, born Feb. 2, 1738.
 Christian Rohrer, born Oct. 23, 1741.
 Elizabeth Rohrer, born Nov. 17, 1744.
 John Rohrer, born March 18, 1746.
 Maria Rohrer, born Jan. 18, 1749.
 Susannah Rohrer, born March 16, 1756.
(But seven named.) All the above seven born in Lancaster County, Pa.
Maria Neff, born in Lancaster County, Pa., August 16, 1752.
The following are the children of John Rohrer and Maria Neff, nine in number, all born in Lancaster County:
 Henry Rohrer, born Oct. 20, 1773.
 Barbara Rohrer, born Sept. 28, 1775.
 John Rohrer, born March 14, 1778.
 Maria Rohrer, born Nov. 18, 1780.
 Henry Rohrer, born Aug. 3, 1786.
 Magdalena Rohrer, born Aug. 19, 1788.
 Elizabeth Rohrer, born Feb. 20, 1791.
 Ann Rohrer, born July 4, 1796.
(But eight named.)
Magdalena, the daughter of John Schenk, born the 24th of December, 1781, in Lancaster County, Pa.
The children of John Rohrer and Magdalena Schenk:
 Barbara, born Oct. 3, 1802.
 Mary Ann, born Oct. 15, 1804.
 Magdalena, born Aug. 27, 1806.
 John Schenk, born June 10, 1808.
 Henry Neff, born Feb. 2, 1810.
 Amos Kaufman, born May 14, 1812.
 Susan Ann, born June 4, 1814.
 Reuben Souder, born Feb. 12, 1816.

Samuel Franklin, born Oct. 15, 1817.
Martin Musser, born Feb. 16, 1819.
Felix Columbus, born May 7, 1821.
Ann Eliza, born July 18, 1824.
The above children all born in Lancaster County, Pa.
Rebecca Shin Eastlack; born in Philadelphia, May 6, 1815.
Earl Penn, son of John S. and Rebecca S. E. Rohrer; born June 5, 1838, in Lancaster City, Pa.
Helen Eliza; born May 11, 1840, daughter of John S. and Rebecca S. E. Rohrer.
Jacob Henning; born December 8, 1816, in Annville, Lebanon County, Pa.
Amos William Rohrer Henning, son of Jacob and Susan Ann Rohrer Henning; born May 5, 1842, in Annville, Lebanon County, Pa.

DEATHS.

Maria Rohrer, the wife of John Rohrer, died the 11th day of May, 1769, in her 54th year.
John Rohrer, died the 23d of November, 1771, aged 75 years.
Henry Rohrer, son of John Rohrer, died the 26th day of August, 1777, aged 4 years.
Barbara Rohrer, daughter of John Rohrer, died the 12th of September, 1777, aged 2 years.
Magdalena Rohrer, daughter of John Rohrer, died the 12th of April, 1790, aged 2 months.
Henry Rohrer, son of John Rohrer, died the 10th of May, 1798, aged 14.
Jacob Rohrer, died the 19th of April, 1803, aged 68 years.
Christian Rohrer, died the 27th of June, 1804, aged 8 years.
John Rohrer, died the 10th of January, 1814, aged 68 years.
Elizabeth Rohrer, died the 12th of July, 1818, aged 27 years.
Martin Musser Rohrer, son of John and Magdalena Schenk Rohrer, died June 19, 1820, aged 16 months 12 days.
Mary Ann Rohrer, daughter of John and Magdalena Schenk Rohrer, died the 6th of May, 1822, aged 17 years 6 months 21 days.
Mary Rohrer, wife of John Rohrer, died July 1, 1825, aged 72 years 10 months 16 days.
Barbara Harman, wife of Samuel Harman and daughter of John and Magdalena Schenk, died December 19, 1827, aged 25 years 2 months 16 days.
Ann Eliza Rohrer, daughter of John and Magdalena Schenk Rohrer, died August 17, 1829, aged 5 years 29 days.
Magdalena Rohrer, wife of John Rohrer, died January 30, 1837, aged 55 years 1 month 7 days.
Catharine S. Reigart, daughter of John Reigart, deceased, and Ann Rohrer, deceased, died January 25, 1839, aged 17 years.
John Rohrer, Esq., died on the 30th of January, 1840, aged 61 years 10 months 16 days.
Helen Eliza Rohrer, died on the 12th of September, 1842, aged 2 years 4 months 1 day.
Felix Columbus Rohrer, died on the 13th of December, 1842, in Philadelphia, aged 21 years 7 months 6 days.
Samuel F. Rohrer, died on the 19th day of January, 1888, at Marionville, Pa., aged 70 years 3 months 4 days.

Susan Ann Henning, wife of Jacob Henning, died December 9, 1877, at Suspension Bridge, N. Y.
Jacob Henning, died September 5, 1888, at Suspension Bridge, N. Y.
Amos W. R. Henning, only son of foregoing, died June 10, 1890, at Suspension Bridge, N. Y. [Last of his line.]
Emma Edwards Henning, wife of Amos W. R. Henning, died at Suspension Bridge, N. Y., October 2, 1889.
Died at Annandale, the residence of her son, Col. S. C. Stambaugh, Mrs. Mary Stambaugh, in the 89th year of her age. She was a Miller on the paternal side and a Carpenter on the maternal, two of the oldest and largest families in the old County of Lancaster; and she was the last of the last generation.
Died April 3, Maria de Welden, wife of A. N. Brennaman. She was a daughter of the late Baron Xavier de Welden, of Wurtemburg, Germany, and a niece of the late Baron Lui de Welden, a Grand Marshal of the Austrian Empire.
Mrs. Martha, wife of Martin Miller, of Pine Grove Township, aged 46 years 9 months and 16 days.
In Lancaster, in the 27th year of his age, Reuben S. Rohrer.
On the 16th inst. [no year] in Lancaster, Mrs. Laura M. Carpenter, wife of Dr. Henry Carpenter, and daughter of Martin Miller, Esq., of Oil City, Venango County, in the 37th year of her age.

MARRIAGES.

John Rohrer was married to Maria Souder in the year 1732.
John Rohrer was joined in marriage with Maria Neff the 8th of December, 1772.
John Schenk married to Barbara Kaufman in the year 1779.
John Rohrer, Esq., married to Miss Magdalena Schenk, daughter of the Rev. John Schenk, the 14th of April, 1801.
Barbara Rohrer, daughter of John and Magdalena Rohrer, married to Samuel Harman, October 2, 1823.
Magdalena Rohrer, daughter of John and Magdalena Rohrer, married to Martin Mill, November 11, 182 [mutilated].
Married on Thursday evening, October 6, 1836, by the Rev. Mr. Clempon, at Philadelphia, John S. Rohrer, M.D., of Lancaster, Pa., to Miss Rebecca Eastlack, daughter of Thomas Eastlack, Esq., of Burlington, N. J.
Married June 3, 1885, Amos W. R. Henning, of Niagara Falls, N. Y., to Miss Emma, daughter of Mr. and Mrs. Dr. Edwards, of East Eagle Street, Buffalo, N. Y.
Samuel Franklin Rohrer, County Superintendent of Schools, Forest County, Pa., married at Clarion to Miss Clarine L. Blood, daughter of the Hon. Cyrus Blood, deceased, both of Marion, Forest County, Pa.
At the residence of Dr. A. J. Rohrer, in Mountville, Lancaster County, Henry Carpenter, an eminent physician of Lancaster City, was married by the Rev. Dr. Greenwald to Miss Laura Miller, formerly of Venango, Pa. There were present distinguished persons of Columbia, Lancaster and elsewhere; among the number, Hon. Thaddeus Stevens and Ex-President James Buchanan.
Earl Penn Rohrer, son of John S. and Rebecca S. E. Rohrer, married to Mary Louisa, daughter of Adaline and Alexander Hamilton.

DESCENDANTS OF JOHN RUSH.

[The following genealogy is taken from a chart presented to the Historical Society of Pennsylvania, in 1880, by Robert Bethell Browne, of Jeansville, Luzerne County, Pennsylvania, it being a copy of a record compiled by General James Irvine in the year 1800, and placed by him in the family Bible of his cousin, Frances Bethell, mother of R. B. Browne. A few additional notes are now added.—ED.]

1. JOHN RUSH commanded a troop of horse in Cromwell's army. At the close of the war he married Susanna Lucas, at Hortun, in Oxfordshire, June 8, 1648. He embraced the principles of the Quakers in 1660, and came to Pennsylvania in 1683, with seven children and several grandchildren, and settled at Byberry, thirteen miles from Philadelphia. In 1691 he and his whole family became Keithians, and in 1697 most of them became Baptists. He died at Byberry in May, 1699. His sword is in the possession of Jacob Rush, and his watch now belongs to General William Darke, of Virginia. He had issue (as appears by a record in his own handwriting now in possession of Dr. Benjamin Rush), viz.:

1. Elizabeth, *b.* June 16, 1649.
2. William, *b.* July 21, 1652.
3. Thomas, *b.* November 7, 1654; *d.* in London, 18th of Fourth month, 1676.
4. Susanna, *b.* December 26, 1656.
5. John, *b.* 1st of Third month, 1660.
6. Francis, *b.* 8th of Second month, 1662.
7. James, *b.* 21st of Seventh month, 1664; *d.* and was buried at Banbury, 24th of First month, 1671.
8. Joseph, *b.* 26th of Tenth month, 1666.
9. Edward, *b.* 27th of Ninth month, 1670.
10. Jane, b. 27th of Twelfth month, 1673–74.

2. ELIZABETH RUSH, eldest daughter of John and Susanna Rush, married Richard Collet, May 27, 1680, as appears by a certificate of a Quaker Meeting in London, now in the possession of Mary Peart. They came to Pennsylvania in

the same ship with William Penn in the year 1682, and settled in Byberry upon five hundred acres of land, two hundred of which are now owned by Captain Decator and one hundred by two of his great-grandchildren, Elizabeth Messer and Mary Peart. They lost their first child, aged two years, by the fall of a tree. They had afterwards the following issue:

11. John Collet.
12. Mary Collet.
13. Rachel Collet, *m.* Benjamin Peart.

3. WILLIAM RUSH, eldest son of John and Susanna Rush, married first in England and afterwards a second wife. [According to some authorities, the name of his first wife was Aurelia.] He died at Byberry in the year 1688, five years after his arrival in the country.

Issue by first wife:

14. Susanna, *m.* John Webster and [John?] Gilbert.
15. James, *m.* Rachel Peart; *d.* 1727.
16. Elizabeth, *m.* Timothy Stephenson, by whom she had no issue. He afterwards married Rachel Rush, widow of his brother-in-law, James Rush, by consent of the Synod of New York. No issue.

By second wife:

17. Sarah (first called Aurelia), *m.* David Meredith.
18. William, *m.* 1711-12, Elizabeth Hodges.

5. SUSANNA RUSH, second daughter of John and Susanna Rush, married in England, John Hart, born at Whitney, in Oxfordshire, November 16, 1651. He was a member of the first Assembly called by William Penn in 1683. He was educated a Quaker, but became a Keithian in 1691 and a Baptist in 1697, being a preacher among each of these sects, and much respected for his piety. They had issue:

19. John Hart.
20. Joseph Hart.
21. Thomas Hart.
22. Josiah Hart.
23. Mary Hart.

These married into the Crispin, Miles, Paulin, and Dungan families, from whom have descended a numerous issue in Philadelphia and Bucks counties. John Hart was shot dead by accident in Virginia. His brother Thomas, who lived in Virginia, had nineteen children before he removed from thence to South Carolina, where many of the family are settled. [See, also, Hart Genealogy, by Davis, 1867.]

6. JOHN RUSH, third son of John and Susanna Rush, married and had issue:

24. John, m. ——.
25. Thomas, m. ——.

11. JANE RUSH, youngest daughter of John and Susanna Rush, married John Darke, son of Thomas Darke, and had issue:

26. John Darke, b. in 1698.
27. William Darke, b. in 1700; m. ——.
28. Joseph Darke, b. in 1702; m. ——.
29. Samuel Darke, b. in 1706; m. ——.
30. Mary Darke, b. in 1709; m. ——.

The other sons and daughters of John and Susanna Rush died single or childless, or if they had children, they died young.

14. RACHEL COLLET[3] (Elizabeth,[2] John[1]) married Benjamin Peart, youngest son of Bryan Peart. [The will of Bryan Peart, "of Throughfare to Duck Creek," is dated January 1, 1705–06; proven at New Castle, April 18, 1706. He mentions his daughters Anne Steather and Margaret as living in Maryland; his wife, Jane, and other children, William, Benjamin, Ralph, and Rachel. The will of Jane Peart, widow of Bryan Peart, "late of Haurskip, in Yorkshire, whitesmith," was dated April 28, 1708, and proven at Philadelphia, December 7, 1709. Children: Benjamin, Ralph, William, Ann, Margaret, and Rachel, and son-in-law, James Rush.] Benjamin and Rachel Peart had issue:

81. Thomas Peart, *m.* ——.
82. William Peart, who had seven children (not named).
83. Elizabeth Peart, *m.* twice.
84. Mary Peart (living in 1800), unmarried.
85. Bryan Peart, *m.* ——.

15. SUSANNA RUSH[3] (William,[2] John[1]) married first, John Webster, and secondly, —— Gilbert, by whom she had no issue. [John Gilbert, of Byberry, died intestate, and letters of administration were granted at New Castle, September 14, 1744, to Susanna Gilbert, his widow. He had property in New Castle County. Some authorities state that Susanna had children by both husbands.] By John Webster she had issue:

86. A son.
87. Phœbe Webster, who *m.* William Lockhart.

16. JAMES RUSH[3] (William,[2] John[1]) married Rachel Peart, the youngest daughter of Bryan Peart. He lived on a farm on Poquestion [Poquessing] Creek, where he died in 1727.
Issue:

88. John, *m.* Susan (Hall) Harvey.
89. William, had children, William and John.
40. Joseph.
41. James.
42. Thomas.
43. Rachel.
44. Ann, *m.* John Ashmead.
45. Elizabeth, *m.* Edward Cary.
46. Aurelia, *d.* young.

18. SARAH RUSH[3] (William,[2] John[1]) was called Aurelia till her marriage and baptism. She married David Meredith and lived to be about eighty-six years old, when she left upward of one hundred descendants. [They resided in Whiteland Township, Chester County, Pennsylvania, where David died in 1754.]

Issue:

47. Susanna Meredith, m. —— Hayes.
48. David Meredith, m. [Elinor] Garrett; [died, 1755].
49. Rebecca Meredith, m. John Jenkins.
50. William Meredith, m. [Margaret? daughter of Walter?] Lloyd.
51. Rachel Meredith, m. —— Connolly.
52. Joseph Meredith, went to Cape Fear and never returned.
53. John Meredith, m. —— Cloyd.
54. Mary Meredith, m. —— Bean [Bane].
55. Hannah Meredith, m. —— Guest.

There were several other children, who died young. One of them, a son, was lost and perished in the woods.

19. WILLIAM RUSH[3] (William,[2] John[1]) was married, March 1, 1711–12, to Elizabeth Hodges, at a Quaker Meeting held at the house of his brother, James Rush, in Byberry, as appears by a certificate now in possession of James Irvine. He died January 31, 1733, at Boston, in New England, and his widow in Philadelphia, April 15, 1755.
Issue:

56. Mary, b. February 9, 1712–13; m. George Irvine.
57. William, b. February 26, 1717–18; m. Esther Carlisle.
58. Joseph, b. January 3, 1719–20; m. Rebecca Lincoln.
59. Elizabeth, b. January 6, 1721–22; d. same day.
60. Elizabeth, b. February 12, 1722–23; d. December 8, 1754.
61. Francis, b. November 5, 1725; d. August 27, 1726.

25. JOHN RUSH[3] (John,[2] John[1]) married Sarah ——, and had issue:

62. William, b. February 26, 1703.
63. Mary, b. January 10, 1713; m. —— Norwood; had son, John.
64. John, b. April 11, 1717.
65. Joseph, b. August 19, 1722; m. and had issue.
66. Sarah, b. October 14, 1725.
67. Benjamin, b. September 5, 1730.

26. THOMAS RUSH[3] (John,[2] John[1]) married and had issue:

68. John, who married, but left no issue.
69. Thomas, d. young.
70. Mary, m. —— Crow; settled in Virginia.
71. Rebecca, m. J. English, and had issue.
72. Elizabeth, d. unmarried.
73. Esther, d. unmarried.

28. WILLIAM DARKE[3] (Jane,[2] John[1]), born in 1700; married and had issue:

    74. John Darke.
    75. Ann Darke, who *m.* and had issue: a son, who was drowned; Esther, who *m.* a Bembridge, and had a son Henry; and Rachel, who *d.* single.

29. JOSEPH DARKE[3] (Jane,[2] John[1]), born in 1702; married and had issue:

    76. Jane Darke, *b.* May 9, 1734.
    77. William (now General) Darke, *b.* May 6, 1736.
    78. Mary Darke, *b.* June 13, 1738.
    79. John Darke, *b.* March 10, 1741.
    80. Joseph Darke, *b.* September 20, 1744.
    81. Martha Darke, *b.* September 17, 1750.

30. SAMUEL DARKE[3] (Jane,[2] John[1]), born in 1706; married and had issue:

    82. Sarah Darke.
    83. Jane Darke.
    84. Samuel Darke.
    85. Mary Darke.
    86. Lydia Darke.
    87. Thomas Darke.
    88. William Darke.

31. MARY DARKE[3] (Jane,[2] John[1]), born in 1709; married [name not given] and had issue:

    89. Elizabeth, *b.* in 1734.
    90. John, *d.* young.
    91. Edward, *b.* in 1738.
    92. Robert, *b.* in 1740; killed by the Indians; left seven children.
    93. William, *b.* in 1742.

32. THOMAS PEART[4] (Rachel,[3] Elizabeth,[2] John[1]) married and had issue:

    94. William Peart.
    95. Edmond Peart.
    96. John Peart.

97. Thomas Peart.
98. Bryan Peart.
99. Rachel Peart.
100. Elizabeth Peart.
101. Rachel Peart.

34. ELIZABETH PEART[4] (Rachel,[3] Elizabeth,[2] John[1]) married first, —— Millard, and secondly, —— Messer. She is now living, July 14, 1800, and is nearly eighty years of age.
Issue:

102. Mary Millard.
103. Elizabeth Millard.
104. Rachel Millard.
105. Mary Millard.
106. Jonathan Millard.
107. Thomas Millard, who *m.* and had twelve children.

108. Ann Messer.

36. BRYAN PEART[4] (Rachel,[3] Elizabeth,[2] John[1]) married [(Swedes' Church record), November 30, 1752, Elizabeth Walton, born Third month 27, 1725, daughter of Benjamin and Rebecca Walton, of Byberry. He died December 27, 1757, and his widow married again (Christ Church record), August 17, 1760, Benjamin Gilbert, and they with their children were taken captives by the Indians in 1780. She died in Fallowfield Township, Chester County, Eighth month 5, 1810]. Bryan Peart left three children:

109. Benjamin [*b.* 1753; *d.* 1840; *m.* Elizabeth Jones].
110. Rebecca [*b.* 1754].
111. Thomas [*b.* 1756; *d.* 1831; *m.* Mary Roberts].

39. JOHN RUSH[4] (James,[3] William,[2] John[1]) married Susan Harvey, formerly Hall, daughter of Joseph Hall, of Tacony.
Issue:

112. James, *d.* single, at sea.
113. Rachel, *m.* Angus Boyce, by whom she had a son, Malcolm Boyce; and by a second husband, J. Montgomery [Rev. Joseph. See "A Sketch of the Life of the Rev. Joseph Montgomery," by John Montgomery Forster, Harrisburg, 1879], had a son John. She died in 1798.

114. Rebecca, *m.* [June 11, 1761] Thomas Stamper, and had issue: Joseph and Susanna Stamper. She died of the yellow fever in 1793.
115. Benjamin (M.D.), *m.* Julia Stockton.
116. Jacob, *m.* M. Rench.
117. Stephenson, *d.* young.
118. John, *d.* young.

45. ANN RUSH[4] (James,[3] William,[2] John[1]) married John Ashmead, and had issue:

119. William Ashmead, *m.* ——.
120. John Ashmead, *m.* Mary Mifflin.
121. Rachel Ashmead, *m.* J[ames] Hood.
122. Benjamin Ashmead.

By second husband [Samuel Potts]:

123. James Potts [*b.* June 17, 1752; *d.* July 28, 1822; *m.* Sarah Wessell. See "Sketch of Major James Potts," by Thomas Maxwell Potts, Canonsburg, Pennsylvania, 1877].

46. ELIZABETH RUSH[4] (James,[3] William,[2] John[1]) married Edward Cary, and had issue:

124. Elizabeth Cary.
125. Jesse Cary.
126. Ezra Cary.
127. Ann Cary, *m.* —— Gouge.
128. Rachel Cary.
129. Sarah Cary.

50. REBECCA MEREDITH[4] (Sarah,[3] William,[2] John[1]) married John Jenkins, and had issue:

130. David Jenkins, *m.* and had seven children.
131. Margaret Jenkins, *d.* young.
132. John Jenkins, *m.* —— Douglas, and had eight children.
133. Isaac Jenkins, *d.* single.
134. George Jenkins, *m.* and had one child.
135. William Jenkins, *m.* and had two children.
136. Jenkin Jenkins, *d.* young.
137. Rebecca Jenkins, *m.* and had six children.
138. Joseph Jenkins, *m.* —— Morgan, and had thirteen children.
139. Benjamin Jenkins, *d.* young.

57. MARY RUSH[4] (William,[3] William,[2] John[1]) married (May 24, 1733) George Irvine, who died October 2, 1740. She died January 5, 1766.
Issue:

140. Elizabeth Irvine, *d.* March 2, 1801 [aged sixty-seven].
141. James Irvine (General), *d.* [Philadelphia, March 28, 1819, aged eighty-four].
142. Susanna Irvine, *d.* young.
143. Mary Irvine, *d.* single.

58. WILLIAM RUSH[4] (William,[3] William,[2] John[1]), born February 26, 1717–18; married Esther Carlisle.
Issue:

144. John, *b.* November 9, 1742; *d.* young.
145. Joseph, *b.* May 8, 1745; *d.* young.
146. William, *b.* October 13, 1746; *d.* young.
147. John, *b.* November 10, 1748; *d.* young.
148. Elizabeth, *b.* December 8, 1750; *m.* R. Bethell.
149. Hanna, *b.* and *d.* same day.

William Rush married second wife, Frances Decowe, and died November 30, 1791.
Issue by last wife:

150. Abraham, *d.* young.
151. Francis, *d.* young.
152. Joseph, *b.* August 20, 1761; *m.* S. Massey, of South Carolina.
153. Sarah, *m.* Joseph Kerr.

59. JOSEPH RUSH[4] (William,[3] William,[2] John[1]), born January 3, 1719–20; married first [September 19, 1750, Christ Church record], Rebecca Lincoln [probably daughter of Abraham Lincoln, of Springfield Township (now), Delaware County, Pennsylvania].
Issue:

154. Elizabeth, *m.* William Allen.
155. William, *m.* Martha Wallace.
156. Mary, *m.* Joseph Tatem.
157. Abraham, *d.* young.

By second wife, Elizabeth Hilton:

158. Catharine, *m.* John Cochran.
159. Joseph, *d.* single.
160. Susanna.
161. George, *d.* young.
162. Esther, *d.* young.
163. Rebecca, *d.* young.
164. Benjamin, *m.* Deborah Jones.
165. Esther, *m.* John Loughrey.
166. Sarah.
167. James Irvine.

116. BENJAMIN RUSH [5] (John,[4] James,[3] William,[2] John [1]) [the celebrated physician, signer of the Declaration of Independence, etc., born near Poquessing Creek, 1741] married Julia Stockton. [He died in Philadelphia, 1813.]
Issue:

168. John.
169. Emila.
170. Richard.
171. Susanna.
172. Elizabeth.
173. Mary.
174. James.
175. William.
176. Benjamin.
177. Benjamin.
178. Julia.
179. Samuel.

117. JACOB RUSH [5] (John,[4] James,[3] William,[2] John [1]) married M. Rench, and had issue:

180. Rebecca.
181. Sarah.
182. Mary.
183. Louisa.
184. Harriet.

120. WILLIAM ASHMEAD [5] (Ann,[4] James,[3] William,[2] John [1]) married and had issue:

185. John Ashmead.
186. Thomas Ashmead.
187. William Ashmead.
188. James Ashmead.
189. Mary Ashmead.
190. Ann Ashmead.

121. JOHN ASHMEAD[5] (Ann,[4] James,[3] William,[2] John[1]) married Mary Mifflin, and had issue:

191. John Ashmead.
192. Benjamin Ashmead.
193. Ann Ashmead.
194. Joseph Ashmead.
195. William Ashmead.
196. Mary Ashmead.
197. Eliza Ashmead.

122. RACHEL ASHMEAD[5] (Ann,[4] James,[3] William,[2] John[1]) married, 1768, James Hood [son of Thomas and Rebecca Hood, of the Northern Liberties, Philadelphia].
Issue:

198. Mary Hood [*m.* August 11, 1792, Samuel Boys, and had fourteen children].
199. James A. [*d.* unmarried about 1806].

149. ELIZABETH RUSH[5] (William,[4] William,[3] William,[2] John[1]), born December 8, 1750; married R. Bethell.
Issue:

200. William Bethell.
201. Robert Bethell.
202. Frances Bethell [*b.* June 21, 1783; *d.* April 29, 1855].

GENEALOGICAL RECORDS COPIED FROM THE BIBLE OF THOMAS SAY.

MARGARET PASCHALL departed this life the 17th day of January 172$\frac{8}{9}$. It being upon Friday about 12 o'clock at noon, and was buried at Sunday f . . . .

THOMAS PASCHALL JR., departed this life the 17th day of January 172$\frac{8}{9}$ about 10 o'clock at night.

SETH FLOWER, departed this life the 18 day of January about 10 o'clock at night.

SAMUEL PASCHALL, departed this life the 11th of February 172$\frac{8}{9}$ about 9 o'clock in the morning.

ELIZABETH FLOWER, died 19th of July 1706.

My Mother died on the 2nd of September 1707 about 12 o'clock at night, and was buried by her son William Paschall, (being 71 years and 9 months old).

WILLIAM SAY my husband died the 23rd of 8^{ber} 1714, being $\frac{3}{4}$ after 10 o'clock at night.

WILLIAM SAY JR., was born the 17th day of January 1696.

JOANNA SAY, was born the 5th of April 1700—1 hr. 28 m. P.M. Friday.

MARY SAY, was born the 17th of 10^{ber} 1701—5 hours 30 P.M. Saturday.

PASCHALL SAY, was born 24th of 10^{ber} 1703 A. M. on a Friday.

ELIZABETH SAY, was born the 13th of 7^{ber} 1706 8 hr P.M. Friday.

Thomas Say, was born the 16th of 7ber 1709 1 hr. 20 m. P.M. Friday new style is the 27th of 9 month.

Thomas Paschall Sen^R., departed this life the 13th of 7ber 1718 about 4 o'clock in the morning in the 83d year of his age and was buried upon his wife.

Mary Clunn, (late Say), departed this life the 25 of Oct. 1723 about half past 10 o'clock in the morning—Friday.

Elizabeth (late Paschall) Jenkins, departed the 18th day of January 1725-6 aged about 93 years on a Tuesday.

Paschall Say, departed this life at Jamaica the 22nd of October 1726 10 hr. 00 m A. M.

Joanna Flower, (late Paschall), departed this life the 11th day of January 1727-8; 25 m: to 10 o'clock at night on a Thursday buried the ☉ following aged about 26 years.

Mary Paschall, (late Say), was born the 21st day of December 1674 in the city of Bristol.

Elizabeth Edgar, (late Say), departed this life 8ber 1729 8 hr 25 m P.M. on a ☉

Benjamin Paschall, departed this life the 16 day of May 1730 at 11 hr 10 m of Sunday was taken the 7th in the morning and was buried Monday following in his own burying ground.

Joanna Holmes, (late Say), departed this life the 11 day of July 1730 between 1 & 2 o'clock in the afternoon and was buried the Sunday following by her Sister Mary in our own burying ground.

Mary Paschall, departed this life the 19th day of July 1734—45 m. past 5 o'clock in the afternoon on Friday & was buried the 20th day following by her husband in our own burying ground aged about 60 years.

Susannah Catherine Sprogell, was born between the 10th & 11 day of October 1713—Thomas *Say* was married to S. C. *Sprogell* the 15 " of 3 mo. called (old Stile) April 1735 15 m : past 12 at night 6th day.

Catherine Say, was born the 3 of 10 mo old Stile called December 1736 14 m past 1 on Friday.

Susannah Say, was born the 24th of 8 mo old Stile called November 1738 58 m. p. 12 a Friday.

Catherine Say, departed this life 27th of 12 mo | old Stile | called February 1738-9 12 m to 4 in the morning and was buried 1st (of the 1 mo) March.

Thomas Say, was born the 19th of 6th mo : (old Stile) called September 1740—25 m . p : 11 a Friday (Son of Thoˢ).

Elizabeth Say, was born the 24 of 7 mo O.S. called October 1742—18 m. p. 1 in the day—A 1st day.

Catherine Say, was born the 19th of 10 mo : O. S. called January 1744-5 4 m. p. 4 in the morning of 7th day.

William Say, was born the 3rd of 11 mo (O. S.) called January 1746-7; 20 m. p. 8 in the morning of 7th day.

Catherine Say, departed this life the 6th of 7 mo. 1747 at 4 in the morning of a 1st day.

Elizabeth Say, departed this life 29th of 8 mo 1747— 4 m. after 6 in the evening on 5th day.

William Say, departed this life 23d of 12 mo 1748-9; 53 minutes after 7 in the evening on a 5th day.

Joanna Say, was born the 7th of 4 mo called June 1749 about 45 m after 10 in the evening—on a first day.

Susannah Catherine Say, departed this life the 18th of the 4 mo called June 1749 about 45 m after 10 in the evening on a first day.

Catherine Sprogell, departed this life the 16th of 8 mo October 1749: 20 m after 1 of a third day aged 73 years and was buried by her husband.

Johanna Say, departed this life the 24th of 5th mo: 1750; 32 m after 11 in the night 3rd day.

James Wilson, was married to my daughter Mary Say the 15th of 5 mo: May 1753.

George Wilson, the son of my daughter Mary was born the 1st of 3 mo March 1754 about 4 m. before 4 of a 6th day.

Thomas Say, was married to Rebekah Budd at Mount Holly the 3rd of 10 mo October 1753, 15 m after 1 in the day at Mount Holly Meeting house.

Benjamin Say, the son of Thomas & Rebekah his wife born 28 of the 8 mo. 1755—35 m after 3 in the afternoon a 5th day.

Susannah Wilson, the daughter of my daughter Mary was born the 13th day of April 1756 about ¼ after 6 in the morning a 3d day.

Rebekah Say, daughter of Thomas Say and Rebekah his wife was born the 26th of 4 mo 1758 about 58 m after 4 in the afternoon 4th day.

Susannah Say, was married to James Carmalt 20th of 6 mo: 1758 at Uptown Meeting.

Thomas Wilson, the son of my daughter Mary was born the 27th of the 8 mo August 1758 a little before 10 o'clock a first day.

HANNAH CARMALT, the daughter of James Carmalt was born the 19th of the 11 mo 1759 a first day about 5 oclock.

THOMAS WILSON, departed this life the 31st of the 3rd mo 1759 36 m after 10 oclock 7th day & buried by his Grandfather Wilson.

REBEKAH SAY, daughter of Thomas Say departed this life the 26th of 10 mo 1759 about 38 minutes after 12 in the day.

THOMAS SAY JR., departed this life the 9th ot the 11 mo 1759 about 38 m p. 5 in the afternoon a 6th day and was buried by his Grandmother Paschall a 1st day (19 years and 1 mo old).

MARY WILSON, daughter of James Wilson & my daughter Mary was born the 26th of the 9 mo 1760 after 1 oclock in the day a 6th day.

THOMAS SAY CARMALT, son of my daughter Susannah was born 29th of the 10 mo 1760 about $\frac{1}{2}$ an hour after 2 oclock in the afternoon a fourth day.

REBEKAH SAY, daughter of Samuel Atkinson was born the 13th of the 5 mo July 1760 old stile the 24th of the 7 mo new stile between 6 & 7 oclock in the morning.

REBEKAH CARMALT, daughter of my daughter Susannah was born the 27th 11 mo 1762 about 25 m after 9 oclock at night a 7th day.

REBEKAH WILSON, daughter of James Wilson & my daughter Mary was born the 4th of the 12 mo 1762 about 6 m after 9 oclock a 6th day evening.

MARY WILSON SENR., wife of James Wilson & daughter of Thomas Say departed the 16 of 12 mo 1762 about 6 m after 10 oclock in the afternoon on a 5th day & was buried the first day following in Friends Ground by her son Thomas (was 27 years 7 mos & 18 days old.)

MARY WILSON, daughter of James Wilson departed this life the 4th of the 4 mo April 1764 about 15 m past 7 oclock in the morning 4th day aged 3 yrs 6 mos & 22 days & buried next her mother in Friends Ground.

ELIZABETH BUDD, daughter of my wife Rebekah was married to Moses Bartram at Uptown Meeting House the 10th of the 7 mo July 1764 about 40 m after 11 oclock.

JONATHAN CARMALT, son of James & of my daughter Susannah was born the 17th of April 1765 about 23 m after 2 o'clock in the afternoon on a 4th day.

JAMES CARMALT, the husband of my daughter Susannah departed this life the 15th day of the 8 mo 1765 at 2 oclock in the afternoon on a 5th day & buried the next in my burying ground.

SUSANNAH LIVINGTON, daughter of John Livington & my daughter Susannah was born the 16th of the 3 mo 1772 about 45 m after 5 in the afternoon.

JOHN LIVINGTON, son of John Livington & my daughter Susannah born the 26th of the 3 mo 1774 about 45 m after 5 in the afternoon.

My daughter SUSANNAH LIVINGTON, departed this life the 17th of the 7 mo called July 1778 & was buried on her mother in my Burying Ground.

BENJAMIN SAY, was married to Ann Bonsall the first day of the 10 mo called October 1776 at the Bank Meeting House Phil^a.

POLLY SAY, daughter of Benjamin & Ann Say was born the 17th of the 11 mo called November 1778 about $\frac{1}{2}$ past 12 oclock on 3rd day.

THOMAS SAY, son of Benjamin & Ann Say was born on the 27th of 6 mo called June 1787. about ¼ of an hour after 4 oclock in the morning being the 4th day of the week.

BENJAMIN SAY, son of Benjamin & Ann Say was born on the 10 day of the 12 mo called December 1790 about ½ an hour after 8 oclock in the morning on the 6th day of the week.

REBEKAH ANN SAY, daughter of Benjamin & Ann Say was born on the 24th day of the 8 mo called August 1793 about 20 m after 4 oclock in the morning it being on the 7th day of the week.

POLLY SAY, daughter of Benjamin & Ann Say, departed this life on the 13 day of the 10 mo called October 1793 at ¼ after 8 in the morning on the 1st day of the week of the malignant fever & was buried in our Family Burying Ground on the same day.

ANN SAY, wife of Benjamin Say departed this life on the 15th day of the 10 mo called October 1793 about 11 oclock A M. on the 3rd day of the week of the malignant Fever & was buried in our Family Burying Ground on the same day.

HANNAH MATLACK, wife of William Matlack grand daughter of Thomas Say departed this life on the 27th of the 11 mo 1793 about 3 oclock at night & was buried along side of her Mother in our Family Burial Ground (of the dropsy).

REBAKAH SAY, wife of Thomas Say departed this life after a tedious spell of illness on the 26th day of the 6 mo June 1795 on the 6th day of the week about 11 oclock in the morning and was buried in the Family Burial Ground on the first day following aged nearly 79 years.

THOMAS SAY, departed this life on the 27th day of the 3 mo March 1796 about 2 oclock in the morning on the 1st day of the week of a complicated complaint & was buried on the 3rd day following in the Family Burial Ground aged 86 years & 6 mos:—

great, great, great, grand father to Clara Mitchell Carey.

REBEKAH, daughter of Samuel Atkinson and Ruth, his wife, was born the 13th day year of our Lord 1716, between 6 and 7 o'clock in the morning. (Dr. Say's mother.)

DESCENDANTS OF DR. WILLIAM SHIPPEN.

COMPILED BY CHAS. R. HILDEBURN.

On page clxxxv of "Letters and Papers relating chiefly to the Provincial History of Pennsylvania, with some Notices of the Writers," the editor, Mr. Balch, after referring to a preceding page on which the following pages on which the pedigree of Dr. William Shippen I have no further information than such as is already in print. The following table of Dr. Shippen's descendants has been prepared to supply the omission, and to correct the confusion which has arisen from Lanman (Dictionary of Congress), Alexander (History of Princeton College), and others having confounded the elder Dr. Wm. Shippen with his son Dr. Wm. Shippen, Jr.

William Shippen, of Hilham, Yorkshire, England.

Edward Shippen, youngest son, born Philadelphia, Oct. 1, 1712, == **Elizabeth Lybrand,** first wife.
emigrated to Boston, Mass., 1669, and removed to Philadelphia, 1693.
== **Abigail Gross,** first wife.

Joseph Shippen

Dr. William Shippen,[1] youngest son born Philadelphia, Oct. 1, 1712, married Sept. 19, 1735,[2] died Germantown, Nov. 4, 1801.[3] He early applied himself to medicine, and soon attained eminence in his profession[10]. He was one of the founders of the Second Presbyterian Church, 1742; was a member of the first Board of Trustees of the College and Academy of Philadelphia, 1749; one of the founders and many years a Trustee of the College of New Jersey; Physician to the Pennsylvania Hospital, 1753–78.[12] Vice-President of the American Philosophical Society, 1768;[3] elected member of the Continental Congress, Nov. 16, 1778,[14] and re-elected Nov. 13, 1779,[14] and throughout both terms was most constant in his attendance.[13]
== **Susannah,** eldest daughter of Joseph Harrison, of Philadelphia, by his wife Katherine Noble, born Philadelphia, June 30, 1711; died between June 4, 1774, and Jan. 10, 1775.[21]

Prof. William Shippen,[1] M.D., born Philadelphia, Oct. 21, 1736;[3] married in London[4] circa 1760; died Germantown, July 11, 1808.[3] &[5] Graduated at College of New Jersey, 1754;[6] delivering the Valedictory for that year. Studied with his father till 1758,[9] when he went to England and studied anatomy under Dr. John Hunter, and midwifery under Drs. Wm. Hunter and McKenzie.[3] Graduated M.D. of the University of Edinburgh, 1761, and after a short visit to France returned to Philadelphia in May, 1762.[10] On Nov. 16, 1762, he commenced the first course of lectures on anatomy delivered in America. The introductory was given at the State House. He continued to lecture on Anatomy and Midwifery until Sept. 23, 1765, he was elected Prof. of Anatomy and Surgery in the Medical School of the College of Philadelphia,[3] of which he was the founder. On July 15, 1776, he was appointed "Chief Physician for the Flying Camp."[13] In March, 1777, he laid before Congress a plan for the organization of a Hospital Department, which, with some modifications, was adopted,[13] and on April 11, 1777, he was unanimously elected "Director General of all the Military Hospitals for the Armies of the United States;"[3] he resigned Jan. 3, 1781.[13] On the reorganization of the College of Philadelphia as the University of Pennsylvania, he was elected May 11, 1780, Prof. of Anatomy, Surgery, and Midwifery; he resigned in 1806.[21] He was one of the originators of the College of Physicians, 1787, and President 1805, till his death.[19]
== **Alice,** youngest daughter of Col. Thomas Lee, Gov. of the Province of Virginia, by his wife Hannah Ludwell, and sister of Richard Henry, Henry Lightfoot, and Arthur Lee, born in Virginia, June 4, 1736;[3] died in Philadelphia, March 25, 1817.[3]

Joseph W. Shippen,[1] born Philadelphia, Oct. 17,[3] 1737;[3] died, unmarried, at Oxford, Sussex Co. N.J., Sept. 13, 1795.[3]

John Shippen, M.D., born Philadelphia, Jan. 23, 1740;[3] graduated at Coll. N. J., 1758;[3] studied under his father, and afterwards at the University of Rheims,[18] Fr., where he received his degree of M.D. Soon after his return he commenced, April 5,[5] 1770, a course of lectures on Fossils," etc. He died unmarried, Baltimore, Md., Nov. 26, 1770.[1]

Susanna,[1] born Philadelphia, Oct. 23, 1743; married at Abington, Ct., Sept. 24, 1769;[3] died Germantown, Oct. 12, 1821.[3]
== **Rev. Samuel Blair,** D. D., son of the Rev. Samuel Blair, by his wife Frances Van Hook, born in Chester Co., Penna., 1741, died in Germantown, Sept. 23, 1818. Graduated at the College of New Jersey, 1760, and was a tutor there 1761–4; licensed to preach 1764; installed Pastor of the Old South Church, Boston, Mass., September, 1766; resigned Oct. 10, 1769. Elected President of the College of New Jersey, but declined in order to secure the election of Dr. Witherspoon, 1767. Resided in Germantown, 1769, till his death.[20]

See page 681.

AUTHORITIES.

[1] Named in father's will.
[2] Named in grandfather's will.
[3] Records of the First Presbyterian Church.
[4] Records of the Second Presbyterian Ch.
[5] Records of Presb. Church, Germantown.
[6] Records Presbyterian Church, Abington.
[7] Newspaper of the period.
[8] MSS in the possession of Ed. Shippen, M.D.
[9] Tombstone.
[10] Thacher's Medical Biography.
[11] Wood's History of the Univ. of Penna.
[12] Wood's Centennial Address, Penn. Hosp.
[13] Journal Continental Congress.
[14] Colonial Records, Vols. XI–XII
[15] Cat. Coll. Nova Caesaria.
[16] Hodge's Obstetrics.
[17] Carson, Hist. Med. Dept. Univ. Penna.
[18] Charter, By-Laws, etc., Coll. Physicians.
[19] N. E. Gen. and Hist. Mag., XXV.
[20] Sprague's Annals Am. Pulpit, Vol. III.
[21] Deeds.

679

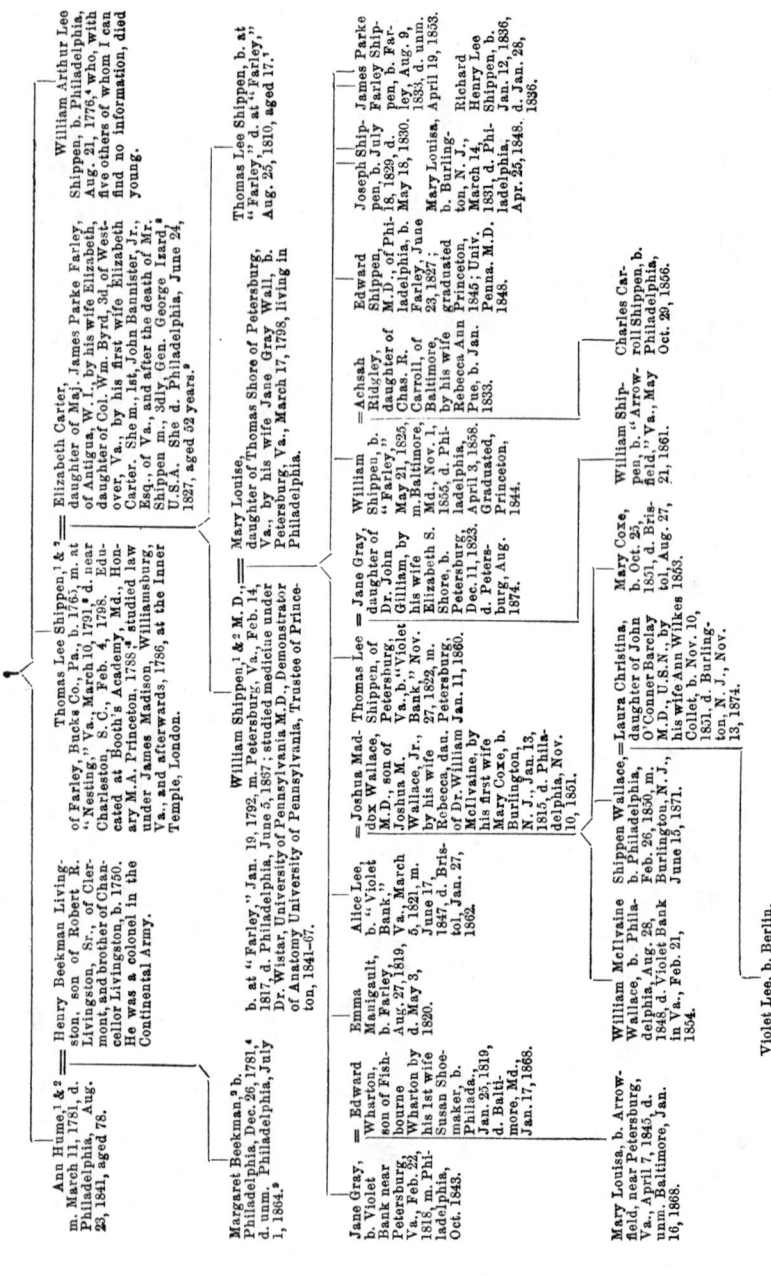

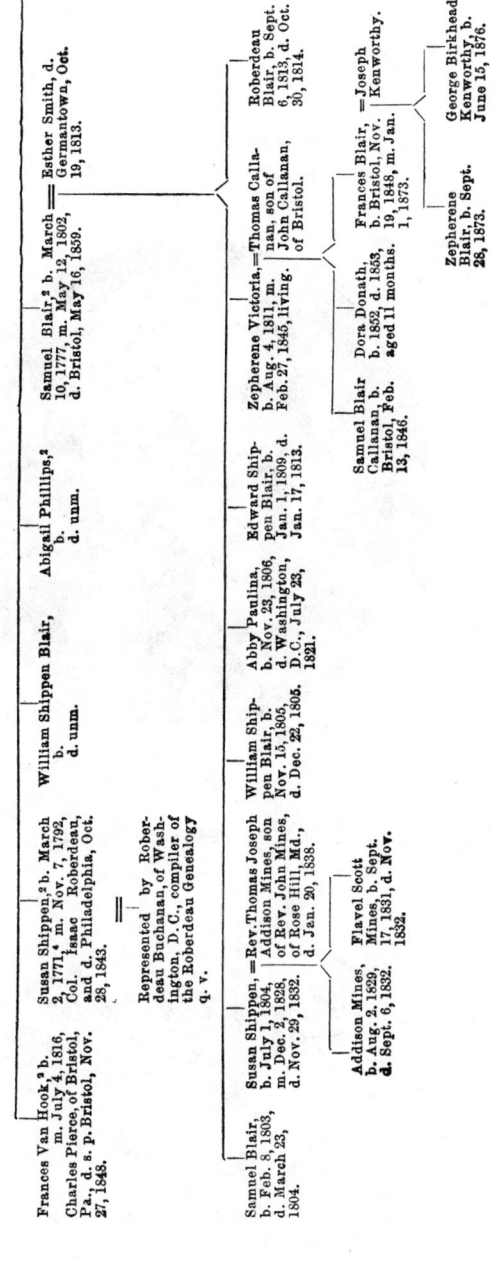

COL. JOSEPH SHIPPEN.

THE ENGLISH ANCESTORS OF THE SHIPPEN FAMILY AND EDWARD SHIPPEN, OF PHILADELPHIA.

BY THOMAS WILLING BALCH.

Among those who in the second part of the seventeenth century left England for the New World, not to escape political or religious persecution, but to better their fortune, was Edward Shippen, of Methley, in the West Riding of Yorkshire.[1]

In the month of September, 1902, the writer of this paper, after visiting the College of Arms in London and collecting the information in the collections there concerning the Shippen family of Yorkshire, went to Methley.

When "Letters and Papers relating chiefly to the Provincial History of Pennsylvania, with Some Notices of the Writer," [2] by Thomas Balch, were privately printed in 1855,

[1] In collecting some of the information embodied in this paper the writer received most courteous aid from the Rev. Henry Armstrong Hall, Rector of Methley, and also from Dr. John Woolf Jordan, Librarian of The Historical Society of Pennsylvania.

[2] In preparing this article free use has been made of "Letters and Papers," etc., which were printed in 1855 at the request of The Histori-

Mr. Balch was not able to state, from the then accessible information, from what place in Yorkshire Edward Shippen, the founder of the family in America, had come, nor who his mother was, nor anything further of his father than that his name was William. It was known from deeds in this country that Edward Shippen was born in the year 1639. In the "Memoirs" of James Logan, Edward Shippen is made to say that "Alethey" was, at the time of his birth, the residence of his father. This, however, was "presumed to be a misprint, or an error of the copyist, there being no such place, as far as ascertained."[1] Nor could it be said with certainty in 1855 whether the Shippens were of English origin or whether they had emigrated to Yorkshire from the Netherlands, and in the "Letters and Papers" the then available evidence as to the original nationality of the family, whether of English or Dutch origin, was merely marshalled.

To-day, with the additional facts that have become accessible in the course of half a century, it can be stated, as it could not in 1855, that the Shippens were of English origin, and did not come into Yorkshire over the North Sea from the Low Countries during the persecutions of the Duke of Alva.

There is a family tradition, confirmed by a letter of Edward Shippen, "of Lancaster," written in 1741,[2] that the

cal Society of Pennsylvania. Owing to the great quantity of letters in that work written by or to members of the Shippen family, it has been spoken of often as "The Shippen Papers."

[1] "Letters and Papers," etc., p. vi.

[2] This letter of Edward Shippen, "of Lancaster," is dated from Chester, Pennsylvania.

"DEAR SIR :—

"If you should happen to see Mr. Ralph Peters, be pleased to ask him whether he can put me in a way to dispossess my Cousin Margaret Jeykil (formerly Shippen) of a Small Estate in Hillam at Yorkshire (which I have been told has been in our Family five hundred years). It is a Copy hold. I have heard it yields ten or fifteen pounds per an.

Shippens were settled at Hillam, a hamlet in the ancient parish of Monk Fryston, in Yorkshire, as early as the thirteenth century. There is nothing further known to prove this tradition, and it may be true. In any case, at the dawn of the Reformation the Shippens were established at Hillam, in the parish of Monk Fryston. The Rev. Henry Armstrong Hall, rector of Methley, one of the neighboring parishes to that of Monk Fryston, writes,—

"The order of Thomas Cromwell, for keeping parish registers, was promulgated in 1537, and the registers of Monk Fryston commenced in 1538; so near the commencement as September of the following year

---

My Grandfather [Edward Shippen the emigrant] who reaped the benefit of it many years, Gave it by will to my Uncle Edwd Shippen & told him at the time of making his will if it was not for the aversion he always had to entailing Estates, he would entail Hillam Estate on his family. Some Short time afterwards my Uncle died & leaving but one child & heir viz: The above mentioned Margaret gave it by will to my father J. S. & the male heirs of his body.

"My Uncle Thomas Story in England not knowing I imagine of the devise of my uncle but hearing of his Death took the trouble upon him to get my Said Cousin entred Tenant; as soon as my father heard of this he wrote to Tho. Story & told him exactly how the thing was, upon which Tho. Story wrote him an answer & let him know that as Margt Shippen was a near relation he might be contented to let her have the benefit of it for a while as her mother was poor, & the Child had nothing left her that she could then command but Sayes he you may have the possession at any time on paying a fine of five pounds & producing the will. And about two years ago I Sent my Grandfathers & my Uncle's will to Mr Peters with the Mayors & Notary Publicks Seal. If you can Serve me in this affair you will do me a Singular favour   I heartily wish you a good Voyage & am

      "Dear Sir
       "Your Sincere friend
        "& humble Servt
         EDWD SHIPPEN

"P.S.
"I would Sell Said Estate for one hundred & fifty pounds Sterling without Charge   E S
"Chester the 9th 7br 1741"

(1539) there is the entry, 'Jenet Shippen christened the XXIIth day,' and between this date and 1678 there are about forty Shippen entries, the latest of which are in 1622–3 and 1624–5. There were Shippens, however, in many of the villages adjacent to Monk Fryston, and to this day there is a farm-house called Shippen in the parish of Barwick-in-Elmet,[1] six or seven miles to the northwest of Monk Fryston. The word 'shippen' is in every-day use in agricultural Yorkshire, at the present time, and denotes a partly covered cattle-yard, and there are persons bearing the name Shippen still to be found in Leeds and the neighborhood.

"Monk Fryston is in the West Riding of Yorkshire, and lies about thirteen miles southeast of Leeds and fifteen miles south of York. Here William Shippen—the father of the emigrant—appears to have been born about the year 1600, but by some mischance his name is not to be found in the Monk Fryston registers. What is certain is that he migrated to Methley,—the 'Alethey' above mentioned,—a village about seven miles to the west of Monk Fryston, and that there, on July 16, 1626, he married Mary Nunnes or Nuns."

William Shippen, in his new home at Methley, became a man of local prominence, for in 1642 he was overseer of the poor, and in 1654 overseer of highways. He died in 1681 at Stockport in Cheshire, where he was living with his son William. His wife, Mary Nunes, the daughter of John Nunes, of a substantial yeoman family, long established at Methley, and of Effam Crosfeld, his wife, was baptized at Methley on October 11, 1592, and buried there May 25, 1672. John Nunes and Effam Crosfeld were married at Methley October 17, 1584. William Shippen himself spent his declining years with his son William, rector of Stockport, and died there in 1681. William and Mary (Nunes) Shippen had six children, all born at Methley:

Robert Shippen, baptized May 20, 1627.
Mary Shippen, " June 24, 1629.
Ann Shippen, " November 21, 1630.
Dorathe Shippen, " February 9, 1631.
William Shippen, " July 2, 1637.
Edward Shippen, " March 5, 1639.

[1] Elmet or Elmete was the great forest which in Saxon days stretched across mid-Yorkshire. Leeds, Barwick, Sherburn, and probably Monk Fryston were all villages in the forest.

Of these, Robert, Ann, and Dorathe died young at Methley, and Mary married, in 1663, William Chapman, of the neighboring town of Normanton. Of the two remaining children, William remained in England and Edward came to America.

I. William Shippen, baptized at Methley July 2, 1637; studied and graduated at University College, Oxford, receiving his B.A. in 1656 and his M.A. in 1659. "He was afterwards Proctor of the University, 1664, and at length Rector of Stockport in Cheshire; and author of 'The Christian's Triumph over Death,' a sermon preached at the funeral of Richard Leigh, Esq. He is D.D., not of this University, if I mistake not, but by diploma of Dr. Wm. Sancroft, Archbishop of Canterbury."

He died in 1693, and was buried under the chancel of the church. The Rev. William Shippen had four sons:

1. Edward Shippen, born in 1671, M.A. and M.D., Brasenose College, Oxford, who subsequently succeeded his brother Robert as Professor of Music at Gresham College. He was a physician, and is supposed to have married Frances, daughter of Peter Leigh, of Lynne.[1]

2. William Shippen, born in 1673 and died in 1743; he was buried in St. Andrew's Church, Holborn, London. Educated at Westminster and Brasenose College, Oxford, he was called to the Bar from the Middle Temple in 1693. He sat in five Parliaments from 1716 to his death in 1743. He was the incorruptible leader of the Jacobites. In his speeches he spoke his mind clearly and fearlessly, and to such purpose that on one occasion, for reflecting on the policy of the King, he was confined in the Tower of London. It was of him that Pope wrote,—

> "I love to pour out all myself, as plain
> As downright Shippen, or as old Montaigne."

---

[1] Burke's "Landed Gentry," London, 1850. See under Tatton, of Withenshaw, p. 1355.

Lord Dover, in his edition of the letters of Sir Horace Walpole, brother of Sir Robert Walpole,[1] says of Shippen,—

"'Honest Will Shippen,' as he was called, or 'Downright Shippen,' as Pope terms him, was a zealous Jacobite member of Parliament, possessed of considerable talents, and a vehement opposer of Sir Robert Walpole's government. He, however, did justice to that able Minister, for he was accustomed to say, 'Robin and I are honest men; but as for those fellows in long perriwigs,' (meaning the Tories of the day) 'they only want to get into office themselves.' He was the author of a satirical poem, entitled 'Faction Displayed,' which possesses considerable merit."

Sir Robert Walpole said of Shippen, "Some are corrupt, but I will tell you of one who is not; Shippen is not."[2]

On one occasion the Prince of Wales, to show his satisfaction with a speech of Shippen, sent the sturdy Jacobite leader, by General Churchhill, Groom of his Bedchamber, a thousand pounds sterling, which Shippen refused.[3]

William Shippen married Frances Stote, daughter of Sir Richard Stote.[4] Of Shippen and his wife Lord Mahon says,[5]—

[1] "Letters of Horace Walpole, Earl of Oxford, to Sir Horace Mann," edited by Lord Dover, London, 1833, Vol. I. p. 45, note.

In a letter dated at Somerset House, December 10, 1741, Sir Horace Walpole writes to Sir Horace Mann,—

"On Tuesday we had the Speech; there were great differences among the party; the Jacobites, with Shippen and Lord Somerset [afterwards fourth Duke of Beaufort] at their head, were for a division, Pulteney and the Patriots against one; the ill-success in the House of Lords had frightened them: we had no division, but a very warm battle between Sir R. [Walpole] and Pulteney."

[2] "Walpoliana," Vol. I. p. 38.

[3] "A Century of Anecdote from 1760 to 1860," by John Timbs, London, 1864, p. 127.

[4] Burke's "Landed Gentry," London, 1850. See under Bewicke, of Close House, p. 92.

[5] "The History of England from the Peace of Utrecht to the Peace of Versailles, 1713–1783," by Lord Mahon, Boston, 1853, Vol. III. p. 30.

"Shippen, whom the public voice still proclaimed as the great leader of the Jacobites, was thought by them so weak as to be left out of all their consultations. Shippen, at this time, was sixty-eight, and his energy, perhaps, much impaired. But, as it seems to me, even his earlier reputation grew much more from his courage, his incorruptibility, his good humored frankness of purpose, than from any superior eloquence or talent. Horace Walpole, the younger, describes his speeches as spirited in sentiment, but generally uttered in a low tone of voice, with too great rapidity and with his glove held before his mouth—certainly not the portrait of a great orator! It is said that he had some skill in poetry, yet it does not seem that he was known or prized by any eminent men without the House of Commons. His father was Rector of Stockport, and his paternal inheritance had been small; he acquired, however, an ample fortune by marriage. His wife was extremely penurious, and, as a relation gently expressed it, 'with a peculiarity of temper, and unwilling to mix in society; she was much noticed by Queen Caroline, but steadily declined all connection with the Court. Shippen himself, like Pulteney, was not free from the odious taint of avarice; when not attending Parliament, he lived chiefly in a hired house on Richmond Hill, and it is remarkable, that neither of these distinguished politicians, though each wealthy, possessed that chief pride and delight of an English gentleman—a country seat.'"

Apropos of this view of Lord Mahon, we find in "Letters and Papers" this criticism:[1]

"Whether or not, Lord Mahon, who claims to present a fair and impartial narrative to his readers, has done full justice to Shippen, may be a question. That Shippen possessed, in a high degree, all the virtues ascribed to him by the historian, is, of course, unquestionable. The courage and integrity which animated him in such dangerous and agitated times, were truly noble; such as neither danger could daunt, nor temptation undermine, nor discouragement diminish. With what a fine spirit does he protest against a standing army, though his earnest efforts against 'a burden heavy and dangerous to the people' had so often failed. 'Sir; I now stand up to make my anniversary oration against a standing army. I have made one and twenty already, of which fifteen have never been seconded, and this will probably be the sixteenth.' Not the less, though, was he bound to do his duty.

"But courage, integrity and good temper, though sufficient to render him a prominent actor amongst the Jacobites, were not enough to con-

---

[1] Page x. *et seq.*

stitute him their leader in a body like the House of Commons; that too, during a long service of many years, with such men as Walpole, Pulteney, Stanhope, Barnard, as associates and antagonists. He must have had, as the debates fully show, both the sagacity and the eloquence of an accomplished statesman.

"Perhaps Lord Mahon's judgment was warped by the fact, that Shippen was at the head of the commission appointed to examine and sift General Stanhope's accounts, as Envoy and as Commander-in-Chief. However candid or correct his recital may be as to other matters, it loses those characteristics whenever the individual or the subject touches the house of Stanhope or the American Revolution. His partiality for his family is a weakness excusable in the eyes of many, and harmless, except where it presents his story to the injury of others. Such is the case as to the character which he has drawn of this 'Parliament man;' and though not disposed to use his own words, and say 'that it implies not merely literary failure, but moral guilt;' we may at least protest against the manner in which he appears to 'lower the fame of a political adversary.'"

Shippen's character and conduct are well illustrated in the report of the proceedings in Parliament, when he was sent to the Tower.

"In this speech, Mr. Shippen overshot himself so far in his expressions, as to give too much advantage against him, to such as perhaps were not over-backward to lay hold of it: His words that gave the offence were to the following purpose, *'That the second paragraph of the King's speech seemed rather to be calculated for the meridian of Germany, than Great Britain; and that 'twas a great misfortune, that the King was a Stranger to our language and constitution.'* These expressions gave offence to several members, and in particular to Mr. Lechmere, who having taken them down in writing, urged, 'That those words were a scandalous invective against the King's person and government, of which the house ought to shew the highest resentment, and therefore moved, That the member who spoke those offensive words should be sent to the Tower.' Mr. Lechmere was seconded by Mr. Cowper, brother of the Lord Chancellor, and back'd by Sir Joseph Jekyll, and some others: Upon which Mr. Robert Walpole said, 'That if the words in question were spoken by the member on whom they were charged, the Tower was too light a punishment for his rashness; but as what he had said in the heat of his debate might have been misunderstood, he was for allowing him the liberty of explaining himself.' Mr. Snell, Mr. Hutchinson, and some other gentlemen, spoke also in behalf of Mr.

Shippen, intending, chiefly, to give him an opportunity of retracting or excusing what he had said; which Mr. Shippen not thinking proper to do, several speeches were made upon the question, Whether the words taken down in writing were the same as he had spoken? A gentleman having suggested, That there was no precedent of a censure passed on a member of the house, for words spoken in a Committee, Sir Charles Hotham produced instances of the contrary; and, on the other hand, Mr. Shippen having maintained what he had advanced, it was, at last, resolved by a majority of 196 votes against about 100, That the words taken down in writing were spoken by Mr. Shippen. It was then about nine o'clock in the evening, and it being moved and carried, That the Chairman leave the chair; Mr. Speaker resumed his place, and Mr. Farrer reported from the said Committee, 'That exceptions having been taken to some words spoken in the Committee, by William Shippen, Esq., a member of the house, the Committee, had directed him to report the words to the house.' Which being done accordingly, and candles ordered to be brought in, Mr. Shippen was heard in his place, and then withdrew. After this it was moved, that the question might be put, 'That the words spoken by William Shippen, Esq., (a member of this house) are highly dishonorable to, and unjustly reflecting on his Majesty's person and government.' Which occasioned a debate that lasted 'till past 11 o'clock; when the question being put, was carried in the affirmative by 175 voices against 81; and thereupon ordered, 'That William Shippen, Esq., be, for the said offence, committed prisoner to his Majesty's Tower of London, and that Mr. Speaker do issue his warrant accordingly.'" [1]

Of a speech by Shippen in the Commons (1720) the Countess of Cowper writes in her diary,—

"Shippen upbraided Walpole terribly in Debate with having chid the Committee of Supply for fear of such an indiscreet method as this to raise Money, and now with moving and helping the Court to it in this manner. He spoke long, and very well—the better for being in the Right." [2]

Something of his political views are expressed in the following speech in the House of Commons:

[1] "Debates in Parliament, 1717–21" (December 4, 1717), p. 20.
[2] "Diary of Mary Countess Cowper, Lady of the Bedchamber to the Princess of Wales, 1714–1720," London, John Murray, 1854; May 5, 1720, p. 160.

"For my part I am not ashamed nor afraid to affirm, that thirty years have made no change in any of my political opinions; I am now grown old in this house, but that experience which is the consequence of age has only confirmed the principles with which I enter'd it many years ago; time has verified the predictions which I formerly utter'd, and I have seen my conjectures ripen'd into knowledge. I should be therefore without excuse, if either terror could affright, or the hope of advantage allure me from the declaration of my opinions; opinions, which I was not deterred from asserting, when the prospect of a longer life than I can now expect might have added to the temptations of ambition, or aggravated the terrors of poverty and disgrace; opinions, for which I would willingly have suffered the severest censures, even when I had espoused them only in compliance with reason, without the infallible certainty of experience. Of truth it has been always observed, Sir, that every day adds to its establishment, and that falsehoods, however specious, however supported by power, or established by confederacies, are unable to stand before the stroke of time: Against the inconveniences and vexations of long life, may be set the pleasure of discovering truth, perhaps the only pleasure that age affords. Nor is it a slight satisfaction to a man not utterly infatuated or depraved, to find opportunities of rectifying his notions, and regulating his conduct by new lights. But much greater is the happiness of that man, to whom every day brings a new proof of the reasonableness of his former determinations, and who finds, by the most unerring test, that his life has been spent in promotion of doctrines beneficial to mankind. This, Sir, is the happiness which I now enjoy, and for which those who never shall attain it, must look for an equivalent in lucrative employment, honorary titles, pompous equipages, and splendid palaces. These, Sir, are the advantages which are to be gained by a seasonable variation of principles, and by a ready compliance with the prevailing fashion of opinions; advantages, which I indeed cannot envy, when they are purchased at so high a price." [1]

3. Robert Shippen, born in 1675. He received his M.A. July 22, 1693, was Fellow of Brasenose, and Professor of Music at Gresham College; he held several preferments. In 1710 he became Principal of Brasenose, and in 1718 Vice-Chancellor of Oxford University. He is buried in Brasenose Chapel, where there is his bust and an epitaph in Latin by Dr. Frewin, of which the following is a free translation:

[1] "Debates in Parliament, 1741-2," pp. 102, 103.

"Robert Shippen, Professor of Sacred Theology
Who amongst the Mertonians
Well Versed in the knowledge of Literature
And the rules of Philosophy
Was first a Fellow of this College
Afterwards for Thirty Five Years
Warden
Meanwhile five times vice-Chancellor of the University.
A man, if ever such there was,
Prompt, diligent and faithful
In promoting the interests & advantage of his friends
Careful, expert and unwearied
In enlarging the revenue & emoluments of the College
Watchful, bold and resolute
In maintaining and defending the rights & privileges of the University.
Died 24 November A.D. 1745—Aged 70 years.
Most deeply lamented by his friends, the College and the University."

"William Seyborne Esquire
A nephew by a sister
To his greatly revered Uncle
And who honored him living and dead,
Hath erected
This memorial of his love and duty."

The tablet is about eight feet in length, surmounted with a bust of Robert Shippen, terminating with the shield of the Shippen coat of arms. There appears to have been a certain degree of intimacy between Robert and his American cousin, Joseph. His book-plate is preserved in the American branch of the family (see opposite page).[1]

4. John Shippen, baptized by his father at Stockport, July 5, 1678. He was a merchant in Spain and British consul at Lisbon; died unmarried in September, 1747; and is buried in St. Andrew's, Holborn, London.

5. The Rev. William Shippen also had a daughter named Anne; for Edward Willes, one of the Judges of the Court

---

[1] There is also a copy in The Historical Society of Pennsylvania.

of King's Bench in 1767, married Anne Taylor, daughter of Anne, sister of William Shippen, M. P.[1]

II. Edward Shippen, the emigrant, was baptized on March 5, 1639, at Methley, not far from the manufacturing city of Leeds; the Loidis-in-Elmet of Saxon days, now the sixth city of the United Kingdom, with a population of nearly half a million. The name Methley probably originally meant the middle pasture land between the rivers Calder and Aire. To-day Methley Church is almost, with the exception of the steeple, which is an eighteenth-century addition, as it was when Edward Shippen lived at Methley. He came over to America and settled in Boston in 1668. There he engaged in mercantile pursuits with much success, as it appears that, upon his removal to Philadelphia, some twenty-five years later, he was computed to be worth at least ten thousand pounds sterling,—a sum by no means inconsiderable in those days, particularly in a new country. In 1669 he was a member of the Ancient and Honorable Artillery Company, showing that he was still at that time a member of the Protestant Church of England. Two years later he married Elizabeth Lybrand, a Quakeress; this marriage led him to become a Quaker. Owing to his new religion, he was subjected to severe persecution. In 1677 he was twice "publickly whipped." In various ways he was subjected to great annoyance, until finally, about 1693-4, Edward Shippen decided to take refuge in Pennsylvania.

It would seem to have taken him about a year to perfect the disposal of his estate in Boston and transfer it to Philadelphia. In this latter city his wealth, his fine personal appearance, his house on Second Street, styled "a princely mansion," his talents, and his high character speedily obtained for him such position and influence that on July 9, 1695, he was elected Speaker of the Assembly; in 1699 he

[1] Burke's "Landed Gentry," London, 1850. See under Willes of Astrop House, p. 1592.

was made Chief-Justice;[1] and on October 25, 1701, William Penn named him in the Charter as the mayor of the city of Philadelphia.

"Penn, as is well known, gave the most anxious consideration to his selection of officers to govern the new city.[2] He thoroughly appreciated the importance of a correct choice. It was, to borrow a military phrase, the base-line of his operations. The success of his whole enterprise turned upon it; the consciousness of which, apart from any other motives, political or philanthropic, was sufficient to stimulate him to the utmost caution and deliberation in his choice of incumbents. In Shippen he found a man of courage, energy, integrity, intelligence, and sagacity; whose unspotted moral character was ample earnest to the citizens that the executive power would be exercised with the strictest justice and fidelity; whose active business habits and bravery equally assured them of the chief magistrate's resolution and promptness, whilst his high social position gave dignity to the office."

From 1702 to 1704 Edward Shippen was President of the Governor's Council, and for about six months, when there was no Governor in the Province, he was acting Governor. In 1704 he contracted his third marriage, which led to his separation from the Society of Friends. After that, apparently, he retired from public life, except that he continued to advise upon public affairs, as is shown by Penn's letter, dated 24th 5th month, 1712, where Edward Shippen is addressed, in connection with Isaac Norris, Thomas Story, and others. Edward Shippen died at Philadelphia October 2, 1712.

"No one could wish to detract in the slightest degree from Penn's merits; but we are taught to render 'honor to whom honor is due.'[3] In doing so, we must needs say that a great, if not the greatest, portion of the glory of building up the Commonwealth which was 'founded by deeds of peace' is due to Shippen, Norris, and Logan, and men like them; the men who, here, in the new country itself, fostered commerce, developed the resources of the Province, set the best of examples, by

---

[1] "Pennsylvania Archives, Second Series," Vol. IX. (1879) p. 629.
[2] "Letters and Papers," etc., p. xvii.
[3] "Ibid., p. xviii.

disdaining no proper toil in their respective vocations, yet neglected not the refinements and graces of letters and polite society."

Edward Shippen married in 1671 his first wife, Elizabeth Lybrand, of Boston; they had eight children, from whom are descended the Shippen family in America.

He married at Newport, Rhode Island, in 1690, his second wife, Rebecca Richardson, widow of Francis Richardson, of New York. They had a daughter, Elizabeth, born in 1691, who died the following year, about which time Mrs. Shippen also died.

Edward Shippen married in 1704 his third wife, Elizabeth James, widow of Thomas James, of Bristol, England (her maiden name was Wilcox); they had

John Shippen, who died an infant.

William Shippen, who died in 1731, about twenty-five years of age.

Among the descendants of Edward Shippen and his first wife, Elizabeth Lybrand, many reached to positions of influence and distinction both under the Colonial and the State governments. In 1727 their son Joseph Shippen joined Franklin in founding the Junto,[1] "for mutual in-

[1] The association consisted of Benjamin Franklin, Joseph Shippen, Hugh Roberts, William Coleman, Philip Syng, Enoch Flower, Joseph Wharton, William Griffiths, Luke Morris, Joseph Turner, Joseph Trotter, Samuel Jervis, Samuel Rhodes, Joseph Brintnall, Nicholas Scull, William Parson, and Thomas Godfrey. Hazard's "Register," Vol. XV. p. 184. See also Sparks's "Franklin," Vol. I. p. 83.

Joseph Shippen married Abigail Grosse, of Huguenot descent, at Boston, July 28, 1702. She died at Philadelphia June 28, 1716. Their children were:

1. Edward, born in Boston, July 9, 1703, known as "of Lancaster."
2. Elizabeth, born in Philadelphia, and died young.
3. Joseph, born in Philadelphia, known in the family as "Gentleman Joe."
4. William, died young.
5. Anne, born August 5, 1710, married Charles Willings.
6. William, born October 1, 1712, known as Dr. William Shippen, *the Elder*.
7. Elizabeth, born September 28, 1714, and died young.

formation and the promotion of the public good." It was the forerunner of our now numerous learned societies, such as The Historical Society of Pennsylvania (1822) and the American Philosophical Society (1743). Of the emigrant's grandsons, Edward Shippen, designated as "of Lancaster," to distinguish him from others of the same name, was much esteemed and respected throughout the Province. Among his other services to the community may be mentioned that he "laid out" Shippensburg, and that in 1744 he was elected mayor of the city of Philadelphia. He was also one of the founders, in 1746, of the College of New Jersey, now Princeton University, and for twenty years was one of its trustees. He served as a county judge both under the Provincial and the State governments, subscribed to the University of Pennsylvania, and was an accomplished French scholar, a rare thing in those days. He was elected a member of the American Philosophical Society, March 8, 1768. Of his sons, one, Edward Shippen, who was also a member of the Philosophical Society, became in 1791 a Justice of the Supreme Court of Pennsylvania, and afterwards, in 1799, by appointment of Governor McKean, Chief-Justice of the Commonwealth. Another son, Joseph Shippen, who graduated at Princeton in 1753, rose to the rank of lieutenant-colonel in the Provincial army. As such he took part in General Forbes's expedition that captured Fort Duquesne. After the troops were disbanded he visited Europe, and on his return was made Secretary of the Province. He took an interest in the fine arts, was elected, January 19, 1768, a member of the American Philosophical Society, and was one of the gentlemen who aided Benjamin West to visit and study in Europe. On June 16, 1786, he was appointed Judge of the Court of Common Pleas of Lancaster County.[1]

And, *en passant*, it is worth remembering, for the truth of history, that the Chief-Justice's two daughters, Margaret, known as "Pretty Peggy," and her sister Sarah, were not

[1] "Pennsylvania Archives, Second Series," Vol. III. (1875) p. 738.

present at the much-talked-of Meschianza Ball. The young ladies were invited, their names were on the programme, and their dresses were actually prepared, but at the last moment their father refused his consent to their appearing at the dance, and although they were in a "dancing fury," they spent the night in tears in their own room in the big brick house on Fourth Street.[1]

Another Joseph Shippen, a brother of Edward Shippen, "of Lancaster," was a subscriber to the First Philadelphia Assembly dances in 1748.[2] Owing to the gay, luxurious life that he led, and which, as appears from his brother's letters, wasted his patrimony, he was known in the family by the name of "Gentleman Joe."

Another grandson of the emigrant who gained distinction was William Shippen, generally known as Dr. William Shippen, *the Elder*. He was born at Philadelphia October 1, 1712, and died there November 4, 1801. He inherited his father's desire to explore the domains of physical science, and no doubt the Junto had its influence in shaping his course in life. Conscious of the deficiencies for medical education in America, and animated by a patriotic desire to remedy them, Dr. Shippen trained his son, known as Dr. William Shippen, *the Younger*, for that profession, sent him to Europe for further study, and on his return (1762) encouraged him to commence a series of lectures on anatomy in one of the large rooms of the State-House. Dr. William

---

[1] On this point see "The Pennsylvania Magazine of History and Biography," Vol. III. (1879) p. 366, note 2; "Two or Three Old Letters;" "The Pennsylvania Magazine," etc., Vol. XXIII. (1899) p. 187. Miss Elizabeth Footman, then a girl of only sixteen, and on intimate terms with the Misses Shippen, and who afterwards married their brother Edward, said repeatedly in after-life that of her own knowledge she knew that Margaret and Sarah Shippen were not at the fête, but spent the night as described above.

[2] The assemblies were first given in 1748 under the management of four directors: John Swift, who was also the secretary and treasurer; John Inglis, John Wallace, and Lynford Lardner. Swift and Lardner were born in England, and Inglis and Wallace in Scotland.

Shippen, *the Elder*, and Dr. William Shippen, *the Younger*, were both elected at the same time in November, 1767, members of the American Philosophical Society. Dr. Shippen, *the Elder*, was elected on November 20, 1778, by the Assembly of Pennsylvania, a member of the Continental Congress.[1] At the end of the year, November 13, 1779, he was re-elected. An examination of the records shows that Dr. Shippen, in spite of his advanced years, was steadily at his post, and that his vote and conduct were those of an honest, intelligent, high-minded, patriotic gentleman, who thought only of his country's welfare. Dr. Shippen, *the Elder*, was also a vice-president of the American Philosophical Society, one of the first physicians to the Pennsylvania Hospital,[2] and one of the founders of the Second Presbyterian Church, and a member of it for nearly sixty years.[3]

---

[1] By some strange perversity which seems to attend the various members of the Shippen family, Dr. William Shippen, *the Younger* (the son), has been substituted by some writers for Dr. William Shippen, *the Elder* (the father), as a member of the Continental Congress. The "Journals of Congress" prove that it was the elder Dr. Shippen that sat in the Continental Congress.

"Wednesday, November 25, 1778.

"Mr. Roberdeau, Mr. Clingan and Mr. Searle, three delegates from Pennsylvania, attended, and produced the credentials of the delegates of the state, which were read, and are as follows:

"'In general Assembly of Pennsylvania, Friday, November 20, 1778.

"'The order of the day being called for and read, the house proceeded by ballot to the election of delegates in Congress for the ensuing year, when the following gentlemen were chosen, viz. Daniel Roberdeau, William Clingan, Edward Biddle, John Armstrong, William Shippen, the elder, Samuel Atlee, and James Searle, Esq.'"—"Journals of Congress: containing their Proceedings from January 1, 1778, to January 1, 1779," Vol. IV. p. 485.

[2] "The Early History of Medicine in Philadelphia," by George W. Norris, M.D., Philadelphia, 1886, p. 21.

[3] In reference to the religious belief of the Shippens, see a letter of Edward Burd to William Rawle, dated at Philadelphia, December 17, 1825, from which it appears that some of the Shippens were Quakers, others Episcopalians, and the rest Presbyterians.—THE PENNSYLVANIA MAGAZINE OF HISTORY AND BIOGRAPHY, Vol. XXIII. (1899) p. 202.

The name of Shippen is woven in the history of Philadelphia. Almost at once upon Edward Shippen's arrival in this city, seeking a refuge from religious oppression in Massachusetts, he took a leading and influential part in the public affairs of the town; and in subsequent years the family bore an important rôle in shaping the development of the city. The mayors it has given to Philadelphia set a high standard of honor in that office. Not long since an honorable bearer of the name went to his long rest. The present Bainbridge Street formerly was called Shippen Street. Without disturbing this memorial to the memory of a gallant officer who a century ago helped forward the commercial freedom of the high seas and also proved incidentally that the United States were a world power at that time,—a fact which in the last few years seems to have been forgotten,—may it not be suggested that it would be appropriate for the present city fathers to perpetuate the name of the mayor named by William Penn in the City Charter of 1701 in one of the *new* avenues or boulevards with which it is proposed to encircle and beautify the greater city of the future?

NOTES ON THE STEELMAN FAMILY OF CINNAMINSON TOWNSHIP IN BURLINGTON COUNTY AND GREENWICH TOWNSHIP IN GLOUCESTER COUNTY, NEW JERSEY.

COMPILED BY PROF. ARTHUR ADAMS.

The earliest record of the Steelman Family in New Jersey, that I have been able to find, is in connection with a sale of land on the north-east side of Penisaukin Creek to Philip Waller by Charles Steelman in 1666.* There are other references to this Charles Steelman; he held various township offices, such as Overseer of the Highways. From a deed made by his son Charles in 1730, we learn that his wife was a daughter of Hance Monsier; probably she is the "Mrs. Ella" referred to in Rudman's list of the parishioners of Old Swedes' Church in Philadelphia made in 1697–1698. The deed recites that Hance Monsier left land to Charles Steelman by will, but no such document can be found of record.

From the deed made by the younger Charles Steelman, we learn something in regard to the children of the first Charles. This deed (Trenton Deeds, D–D 206), is dated 25 May, 1730; it is of sufficient interest to justify a brief abstract: Charles Steelman of the County of New Castle upon Delaware River, son and heir of Charles Steelman late of Sinnaminson, Burlington County, New Jersey, deceased, by and with the advice and consent of John Bird of New Castle and Margaret his wife and of David Enuxson and Eleanor his wife of the same county, sisters of the aforesaid Charles Steelman, sells to Philip Wallis of Evesham in Burlington County, for £30, a small tract of land in Chester Township on the east side of Penisau-

---

* The compiler has seen no record of this deed; a friend sent the data without giving or being able to give any explicit reference for it.

kin Creek. The land was purchased of William Biddle by Hance Monsier, grandfather of the said Charles Steelman, by deed of 10 April, 1688, and was bequeathed by Hance Monsier to Charles Steelman the father of the grantor. It is evident then that Charles Steelman the elder died sometime between 1688 and 1697. We know from Rudman's list that, in addition to the children mentioned in this deed, he had a son Eric.

Children:
    i. Charles, b. c. 1679; went to New Castle; nothing further known.
2. ii. Eric, b. c. 1681.
    iii. Margaret, m. John Bird.
    iv. Eleanor, m. David Enuxson.

2. Eric Steelman (Charles[1]). He is first mentioned in Rudman's list with his brother Charles as a son of Mrs. Ella, "mother of the Steelmans now," where his age is given as sixteen (1697.) He bought land in Greenwich Township, Gloucester County, of Justa Lock 9 July 1715. He married Britta or Bridget ——. Letters of Administration on his estate were granted to Bridget Steelman and Tobias Bright 12 May 1731. From documents relating to the estate, we learn that Eric Steelman had at least the children whose names are here given.

Children:
3. i. Hance.
4. ii. James.
    iii. Mary.
    iv. Catherine.

3. Hance Steelman (Eric[2], Charles,[1]). From various deeds we learn that Hance was the eldest son. He filled local offices, such as Overseer of the Highways and Constable, with satisfaction to his neighbors and credit to himself. He married Alse or Alice Jones, a daughter of the widow Catherine Jones. She was housekeeper for

John or James Boles; when he died he left his property to her daughters; his will is dated 4 March 1715. From a deed (Woodbury Deeds, TT 268), it appears that Hance married *Alse* and his brother James married *Rebecca* [Jones] Boles.

The will of Hance Steelman is dated 7 May 1755 and was proved 29 December 1760. His wife is mentioned, but not by name. He gives his son James the homestead and ten acres of cedar swamp nearest the Delaware; to his son Hance he gives the plantation he lives on and ten acres of cedar swamp adjoining that given to James; to his son Charles he gives half of the homestead plantation —250 acres; to his sons John and Daniel he gives the residue of his real estate equally. The executors named are Alexander Randall and his son John.

Children:
5. i. James, b. 17 November 1719.
6. ii. Hance.
7. iii. Charles.
8. iv. John.
v. Daniel, d. intestate and s. p.

4. James Steelman (Eric[2], Charles[1].) From the deed cited in connection with Hance[3] Steelman, it is evident that this James married Rebecca Jones, or as his son James speaks of her, Rebecca Boles. So far as is known, they had only one child.

Child:
9. i. James.

5. James Steelman (Hance[3], Eric[2], Charles[1]). According to the record of Trinity (Racoon) Church, Swedesboro, James was born 17 November 1719. In addition to the homestead given him by his father, he became the owner of the lands of his brother Daniel on his decease intestate and without children, he being the eldest brother. His first wife was Magdalen Peterson; she dying in her

forty-ninth year, was buried in Racoon churchyard 12 January 1771. He married, second, Catherine, daughter of Nicholas and Elizabeth (Lock) Keen. She was born 4 April 1747, and they were married 12 February 1772. Her second husband was Ephraim Seeley, whom she married 17 December 1788; letters of administration were granted to her on his estate 31 January 1801. James Steelman was one of the trustees to whom the charter of Trinity (Racoon) Church, Swedesboro, was granted in 1765.

James Steelman's will is dated 3 April 1786 and was proved 22 January 1788. He speaks of a wife but not by name. To his son James, besides other land, he gives ten acres of meadow land on Repaupo Creek; to his son Isaac he gives the rest of the Repaupo land and about two acres lower down the creek then in the tenure of Andrew Steelman; to his sons John and Andrew he gives the homestead plantation; he mentions three daughters—Sarah, Elizabeth, and Jemima; the executors named are Thomas Clark and his son-in-law Daniel Sutherland. Letters of guardianship were granted to Ebenezer Adams for Jemima, John, and Andrew Steelman 22 January 1788; similar letters were granted to the same person the same date for Elizabeth Steelman. The birth of the son Isaac is recorded in the register of Racoon Church.

Children:
- 10. i. James.
- ii. Sarah, b. December 1761, m. Daniel Sutherland.
- 11. iii. Isaac, b. 15 June 1764, bap. 9 July 1764.
- iv. Elizabeth, m. James Code.
- v. Rebecca, b. 5 February 1773.
- vi. Jemima, b. 31 May 1776, bap. 10 June 1776, m. Isaac S(L)aymon.
- 12. vii. John, b. 5 November 1778.
- 13. viii. Andrew, b. 15 June 1781.

6. Hance Steelman (Hance[3], Eric[2], Charles[1]). The will of this Hance Steelman is dated 4 November and was proved 15 December 1761. He speaks of his wife, but does not mention her name; it is probable, however, that it was Sarah, for letters of administration were granted to his brother James Steelman and to Sarah Steelman. To his son John, who is spoken of as under age, he leaves the homestead. He speaks of young children, specifically of young daughters, but does not mention their names. Charles Steelman was a witness. A John Steelman who died in 1774 speaks of his mother Sarah Steelman and of his sisters Johannah and Catharine. As he seems to be a young unmarried man, he is doubtless John son of Hance, and so we are able to determine the names of two of the unnamed daughters. The land given to the two sisters seems to be the land given to Hance junior by Hance senior and by him to his son John.

Children:
   i. John; will dated 14 December 1773 and proved 21 January 1774; unmarried; property left to sisters.
   ii. Johannah.
   iii. Catharine.

7. Charles Steelman (Hance[3], Eric[2], Charles[1]). He married Brigitta Dalbo 17 March 1756 (Records of Old Swedes' Church, Philadelphia). Charles and Britta Steelman of Greenwich Township 10 October 1764 sell a plantation on the westerly branch of Repaupo Creek to James son of Hance Steelman; Charles derived title from Alse Jones through his father Hance Steelman. Letters of administration were granted to Felix Fisher and Daniel Sutherland on the estate of Charles Steelman 4 February 1785. Nothing further known of him.

8. John Steelman (Hance[3], Eric[2], Charles[1]). This John Steelman married Mary ——. John and Mary Steelman 6 June 1769 sell land in Greenwich Township near Rep-

aupo Creek. The land was left by Hance Steelman to his sons John and Daniel by will of 7 May 1755; Daniel died intestate and his interest went to his eldest brother James, who released it to John 7 February 1769. The will of John Steelman is dated 21 January 1775 and was proved 11 August 1775. He mentions his wife but does not give her name; nor does he mention the names of his children who are said to be under age. Letters of administration were granted to Mary Steelman the date of the probate of the will.

Children:
    i. Sarah, b. September 1764, bap. 10 September 1764 (Racoon Church Record).
    ii. Mary, m., first, ——— Miller; second, 19 March 1803 John Ernest Christian Bethausen, practioner of physic. He was the son of Charles Christian and Rosina Maria Bethausen, now or late of Berenberg, Germany. They were married by the Rev. Nicholas Collin, who carefully noted her parentage in the records of Old Swedes' Church, Philadelphia. (Old Swedes' Church Records, p. 263.)

9. James Steelman (James[4], Eric[2], Charles[1]). This James moved to Great Egg Harbor, where he made a deed 18 May 1789, in which he signs himself James Steelman, Senior. He sells a plantation in the forks of Repaupo Creek in Greenwich Township to William Beaston, tracing title from James Boles through his mother Rebecca Steelman formerly Rebecca Boles. Nothing further has been learned concerning him.

10. James Steelman (James[5], Hance[3], Eric[2], Charles[1]). He married Eleanor ———. Letters of administration were granted 2 January 1790 to Eleanor Steelman and James Code on the estate of James Steelman. 17 January 1795 Felix Fisher of Greenwich Township was appointed guardian of Sarah and James Steelman, children

of James Steelman the younger of Greenwich Township, both under fourteen; the mother Eleanor was the wife of John Kerns.

Children:
  i. Sarah, b. probably in 1785, if the record in the Racoon Church register refers to her: "buried 6 December 1798, Sarah, daughter of James Steelman, Jr., aged thirteen years."

14. ii. James Boles, bap. 4 July 1790

11. Isaac Steelman (James[5], Hance[3], Eric[2], Charles[1]). Isaac was born 15 June 1764 and was baptised 9 July 1764 (Racoon Church Record). He married Elizabeth ———. It would seem that he died about 1828. Isaac Steelman and Elizabeth his wife 11 October 1790 sold land in Greenwich Township to Meshack Fish of Waterford Township. The land was conveyed to Eric Steelman by Justa Lock 9 July 1715, and Eric Steelman dying intestate, the land descended to his eldest son Hance, who left it by will of 7 May 1755 to his sons John and Daniel. Daniel died without issue and his part went to his eldest brother James, who by his will of 3 April 1786 gave the land to his son Isaac, the grantor, to whom it was confirmed by decree of the Supreme Court at Trenton in November 1789 (Woodbury Deeds, B 96). The only child of whom trace has been found is a daughter Elizabeth. She made a deed 6 October 1830, in which she speaks of herself as of Philadelphia, and by which she sells land in Greenwich Township that had been left to her by her grandfather James Steelman. She mentions her father Isaac Steelman (Woodbury Deeds, B[3] 120).

Children:
  i. Elizabeth, moved to Philadelphia.

12. John Steelman (James[5], Hance[3], Eric[2], Charles[1]). According to the records of Racoon Church, John son of James and Catharine (Keen) Steelman was born 5 Novem-

ber 1778. No record of his marriage has been found unless he be the John Steelman who was married to the widow Hannah Hendrickson by the Rev. James Feltus, Rector of Trinity Church, Swedesboro, 6 January 1803. John Steelman's will is dated 27 August 1825 and was proved 5 October 1825. He does not mention a wife. He speaks of his eldest son Hiram, and provides that if the property he received from his father is entailed to him, he shall have no more of his real estate; but if it prove not so, that all is to be divided between his children equally.

Children:
- 15. i. Hiram.
- ii. Elizabeth.
- 16. iii. James B.
- iv. Sarah.

13. Andrew Steelman (James^5, Hance^3, Eric^2, Charles^1). Andrew son of James and Catharine (Keen) Steelman was born 15 June 1781 (Racoon Church Records). It appears from a deed dated 10 August 1811 (Woodbury Deeds, Q 251) that he married Sarah daughter of Daniel England; she had a sister Susannah who married Joseph Cooper. Andrew must have been married before 18 January 1804, because she joined in a deed on that date. Nothing further known.

14. James Boles Steelman (James^{10}, James^5, Hance^3, Eric^2, Charles^1). He was baptised 4 July 1790 (Racoon Church Record). His lands in Greenwich Township were sold by the Sheriff to John Steelman 23 March 1813 (Woodbury Deeds, B 223). The inventory of the estate of James B. Steelman is dated 11 May 1815, and John Kerns, doubtless his step-father, was appointed administrator. It does not appear whether or not he was married.

15. Hiram Steelman (John^{12}, James^5, Hance^3, Eric^2, Charles^1). 17 December 1827 Hiram Steelman, son of John and grandson of James Steelman, sold land in Greenwich Township to John B. Miller (Woodbury Deeds,

UU 319). Hiram Steelman and Sarah Shoulders were married at Lower Bridge 18 August 1835 by Samuel G. Ogden. The compiler has heard of at least two children.

Children:
i. James, deceased a few years since, lived at Daretown, N. J.
ii. A daughter, living.

16. James B. Steelman (John[12], James[5], Hance[3], Eric[2], Charles[1]). From a deed (Woodbury Deeds, K[4] 453), we learn that this James B. Steelman married Judith L., daughter of William Casperson. The deed is dated 5 December 1849. Nothing further known.

* * * * * * * * * * * * * * * * * * *

DATA NOT PLACED

Woodbury Marriages

31 June 1828 Charles Steelman to Martha Russell of Woolwich Township.

10 March 1810 James Steelman to Mary Sweeten, both of Woolwich Township.

16 March 1803 Andrew Steelman to Sarah Seeley by the Rev. James Feltus, Rector of Trinity Church, Swedesboro.

Trenton Guardianship Record

28 January 1788 letters of guardianship for the person and estate of Elizabeth Steelman were granted to Ebenezer Adams. It is probable that she was a daughter of James[5] Steelman by Magdalen Peterson his first wife. On the same date letters of guardianship were granted to the same person on the person and estate of three children of the second marriage, namely, Jemima, John, and Andrew Steelman.

RECORDS FROM THE TAYLOR FAMILY BIBLE.—*Births.*—Jacob Hollinshead, son of William and Mary Hollinshead, was born the 16th day of the 10th. month 1732.

Mary Hollinshead, daughter of Hugh and Anna, was born the 30th day of the 7th. month 1737.

Anna Hollinshead, daughter of Jacob and Mary Hollinshead, was born the 25th day of the 3rd month 1772.

Wm. Taylor Father of Othniel Hart Taylor was born at Cambridge England June 11. 1772.

Mary Alice Gazzam, wife of Wm. Taylor and mother of Dr. O. H. Taylor was born at Cambridge England June 11. 1774.

Marmaduke Burrough was born Nov. 30 1797.

Jehu Burrough son of Isaac Burrough and Abigail Jennings b. Oct. 10. 1769.

Abigail Burrough was born Feb. 22. 1799.

Evelina C. Burrough was born Oct. 24. 1800.

Sarah M. Burrough was born June 11. 1802.

Jehu Burrough was born June 11. 1803.

Othniel Hart Taylor was born at Philadelphia May 4. 1803.

Wm. Rivers first son of Othniel Hart Taylor and Evelina C. Taylor was born Jan. 5 1833 at S. W. cor. 10th and Race Streets Philadelphia.

Othniel Gazzam Taylor was born June 24, 1834 (son of O. H. & E. C. Taylor) at Race St Second door below 11th Street South Side Philadelphia.

Marmaduke Burroughs, third son of O. H. and E. C. Taylor was born Aug. 17. 1835 Race St. 2nd door below 11th South Side Philadelphia.

Henry Genet, fourth son of O. H. & E. C. Taylor was born at Shodack Rensselaer Co. opposite Albany New York (Residence of Gen'l Genet) July 6. 1837.

Clarence Wills 1st son of M. B. and A. C. Taylor was born July 11. 1862 Camden N. J. 312 Market St.

Evelina Constance Taylor 1st daughter of M. B. & A. C. Taylor born Dec. 5. 1865 at 310 Market Street Camden.

Annie Taylor was born Sept. 3. 1871 at 310 Market Street Camden Second daughter M. B. & A. C. Taylor.

Henry Genet Taylor Jr. 1st son of Henry Genet & Helen Cooper Taylor was born July 19. 1883 at 312 Market St. Camden N. J. ¼ past 5. P. M. Thursday.

Richard Cooper Taylor, second son of H. Genet & Helen Cooper Taylor was born at 312 Market St. Sept 29. 1884 9.45 P. M. Camden.

Helen Elizabeth Taylor 3d child H. G. & H. C. Taylor was born at 305 Cooper St. Camden at 11.45 A. M. Feb. 27. 1887.

Marriages.—Jacob Hollinshead married Mary Hollinshead.

William Hollinshead married Hannah ———.

Isaac Burrough son of Sam'l B. married 1st Deborah Jennings daughter of Isaac Jennings of the Province of New Jersey April 3. 1742.

Isaac Burrough was married to 2nd Abigail Heulings.
" " " " " 3rd Elizabeth Wallace.

Jehu Burrough married Ann Hollinshead daughter of Jacob & Mary Hollinshead Feb. 10. 1797.

Jehu Burrough second son of Jehu and Ann Burrough was married to Anna Earl of Burlington Co. New Jersey, Jan'y. 1831.

Evelina Constance Burrough 2nd daughter of Jehu and Ann Burrough was married to Othniel Hart Taylor M.D. of Philadelphia. Feb. 16. 1832.

Marmaduke Burrough 2nd son of O. H. & E. C. Taylor was married Tuesday Sept. 3rd 1861 to Agnes Caroline daughter of Dr. Joseph & Rebecca C. Crain of Cumberland Co. Pa. by Rev. Joseph Garrison at St. Paul's Church Camden where said marriage is recorded.

Henry Genet Taylor, M.D. 4th son of O. H. & E. C. Taylor was married on Thursday Oct. 23, 1879 to Helen daughter of Alexander & Hannah C. Cooper by Rev. Dr. Foggo and Rev. J. F. Garrison at Christ Church Phila.

William Taylor father of O. H. Taylor was married at Mary's the

Great Church, Cambridge England June 11. 1774, where said marriage is recorded.

Deaths.—Isaac Burrough died November 30. 1796.
Jehu Burrough his son died March 10. 1803 aged 34 yrs 5 mos.
Jacob Hollinshead died Dec. 19. 1819 aged 88 yrs 1 m. 18 d.
Mary Hollinshead his wife died Aug 7. 1814 aged 77 yrs. 7 days.
Sarah Burrough daughter of Jehu & Ann died July 8 1802 aged 4 w. 2 d.
Abigail Wallis Burrough daughter of Jehu & Ann died Feb. 10. 1826.
Jehu Burrough Sr. son of Jehu & Ann died Sept. 24. 1836. 33 y. 3 m. 13 d.
Anna Relict of Jehu Burrough Sr. died Oct 7 (6. P. M.) 1846, 74 y. 6 mo. 12 d. at 312 Market St. Camden.
William Taylor father of O. H. Taylor—died at Bergen, Hudson County N. J. at the residence of his son Dr. Benjamin C. Taylor Apr. 4. 1849 in the 77th year of his age.
Mary Alice Taylor mother of Dr. O. H. Taylor died at Greenbush, opposite Albany N. Y. August 31. 1831 in the 57th year of her age.
Marmaduke Burroughs M. D. 1st. son of Jehu Sr. and Anna died Feb. 10. 1844, at Mount Holly—77 years.
Othniel Hart Taylor husband of Evelina C. Taylor died at 312 Market St. Camden Sept 5. 1869 aged 66 yrs.
Wm. Rivers son of O. H. & E. C. Taylor died Aug. 31. 1833 aged 8 mos. and was interred in St. Stephen's burial ground cor. 13th & Cherry Streets—Phila.
Evelina Constance daughter of M. B. & A. C. Taylor died Feb 3. 1870.
Evelina Constancia Taylor daughter of Jehu & Ann Burrough and relict of O. H. Taylor M. D. died at her residence in Camden Sept 18. 1878 aged 78 years.
Othniel Gazzam Taylor, 2nd son of Othniel H. and Evelina C. Taylor died at his residence 312 Market St. Camden N. J. March 14. 1886 aged 52 years, 2 mos. (11.30 P. M.)
Marmaduke Burrough 3rd son of O. H. & E. C. Taylor died at 310 Market Street Jan. 15. 1890 at 5.45 A. M. aged 54 yrs, 5 mos.
Agnes Crain Taylor relict of Marmaduke B. Taylor died July 17. 1890 at 1 P. M. at 305 Cooper St. Camden aged 48 years & born Oct. 28, 1841.

Pedigree of the above-mentioned Hollinshead family as shown by various wills and deeds:
Will of John Hollinshead, Jr. Recorded Secretary of State's Office, Trenton, Book 4, page 221.
Extracts: "I John Hollinshead Jr. of Wisham, County of Burlington, Province of New Jersey," &c. Item 1 devises to son Joseph, "plantation where I now live given to me by my father as appears by deed of gift, except 5 acres of meadows to go to my son Benjamin," &c. Item 2 devises to "my son Benjamin all the land and plantation I purchased of my Uncle, Aunt, and Cousin William Hollinshead as may appear by deed of sale also five acres of meadows to my son Benjamin out of that meadow lying beween my dwelling house and the little house where William Hollinshead Jr. formerly dwelt."
Item 3 devises to "my son John 100£ to be paid by my Executor when he attains full age."
Item 4 devises to daughter Martha £71 6s. when eighteen years old.
Item 5 specifies that in case son Joseph and son Benjamin die before twenty-one years old the executor is to pay surviving brother £40.

Item 7.—" It is my mind that the white Indian Peter remain with thy family, and that there be what is necessary allowed him from me estate."

Item 8 devises everything, including all personal estate and negroes and mulattoes to my widow as long as she remain single; if she marries, everything to revert to sons.

Item 9 nominates brother-in-law Abraham Haines Executor, and my beloved wife Executrix, and is dated December 14, 1739.

[Signed] JOHN HOLLINSHEAD, JR.

Witness: JOHN HOLLINSHEAD,
SAML. ATKINSON,
EDWARD HOLLINSHEAD.

Probated March 12, 1740.

Letters testamentary granted Hannah Hollinshead, Abraham Haines relinquishing Executorship May 2, 1740. Inventory of personal Estate filed £458 7 1."

Extract from deed dated December 10, 1718, William Hollinshead (Sr.) to John Hollinshead. Recorded Book B. B. B. page 406. Secretary of State Office, Trenton. Consideration £8 for $2\frac{30}{100}$ acres. "Whereas John Hollinshead father of y^e William and y^e John in and by hys last will and testament duly recorded in y^e Surrogates office at y^e towne of Burlington left all hys land to hys two sons William and John."

Will.—William Hollinshead Jr. of Chester township, County of Burlington. Book 4, page 291, Secretary of State's Office. Let or be recorded that I William Hollinshead, Jr. of Chester Township in the County of Burlington and in the Province of New Jersey &c.

1st.—I will and order that my father and mother shall have a maintenance out of the plantation whereon I now dwell during their natural life, the remainder I give to my beloved wife during her widowhood.

Item.—I give and devise the remainder and reversions of my aforesaid plantation, unto my son Jacob and to his heirs and assigns forever.

Item.—It is my will that my son Jacob shall pay to my two daughters vizt.: Mary and Jerusha, each of them 10£ apiece in three years after the same shall come into his possession.

Item.—I give and devise unto my son Anthony all that my land and plantation where Thomas Harley now dwells. Containing 130 acres and which was given me by my father by one deed of gift unto my son Anthony his heirs and assigns forever. And I hereby order that my son Anthony shall pay unto my daughter Bathsheba 10£ in three years after the same comes into his possession.

Item.—I nominate my beloved wife (Hannah) my sole executor of this my last Will and Testament and after my just debts are paid and discharged to whom I give all my personal Estate.

In witness whereof I hereunto set my hand and seal this Seventh day of July in the year of our Lord one thousand seven hundred and forty-one.   WILLIAM HOLLINSHEAD.

Witness: GRACE RUDDEROW,
THOMAS GILL,
SAMUEL ATKINSON.

Affirmed at Burlington August 11. 1741.

JOSEPH ROSS, Sur.

HANNAH HOLLINSHEAD
Letters Test. granted.

Extract from Deed showing whom William Hollinshead, son of Jacob Hollinshead, married.

Deed, William Pine and Judith, his wife, daughter of Daniel Lippincott, to William Hollinshead and Hope, his wife, daughter of Daniel Lippincott, and George Githens. Dated September 9, 1793 Recorded at Mt. Holly at Clerk's Office, Book D., p. 232. Recital.of property shows that by the will of Daniel Lippincott dated February 10, 1781, and recorded at the Secretary of State's Office, left certain lands to his daughter Hope, wife of William Hollinshead.

Extracts from the will of Jacob Hollinshead, of the township of Chester, county of Burlington, State of New Jersey. Dated April 29, 1817. Recorded Surrogate's Office of Burlington County. Book B, page 621. Proved January 12, 1820.

Item 1 devises to his son Enoch the plantation he is now on and in possession, including two acres of meadow "if he pays his brother Jacob $400 one year after my decease."

Item 2 devises to his three daughters, Zillah, Ann, and Jerusha, the same farm he now lives on, beginning at a stone corner to Clayton Hollinshead's land, and runs from thence S. 46° 15″ E. 9 ch. 45 l. to a stone corner to Enoch Hollinshead's; from thence N. 48° 15′ E. 21 ch. 15 l. to James Borden's line; thence along Borden's line N. 24° and 30″ W. 2 ch. 86 l. [or 26 l.?] to a stone corner to Clayton Hollinshead's; thence S. 65° W. 23 ch. 68 l. to the place of beginning, containing 13 acres 29 perches. "To be equally divided between them by my executors and their survivors."

Item 3 devises to his son William the remainder of the farm he now lives on during his life and to be divided among his children after his decease.

Item 4 devises to his daughters Mary and Elizabeth 4 acres on the plantation he now lives on the S. E. cor. next to Clayton Hollinshead's, to begin in the middle of the road from Moorestown to Mount Holly.

Item 5 devises to his son Thomas all the residue of the farm after paying daughters Zillah, Jerusha, Ann Elizabeth and Mary, $50 each.

Item 6 devises all the personal estate to son Hugh Hollinshead and 5 daughters, Zillah, Jerusha, Ann, Elizabeth and Mary.

Item 7 names Benjamin Hollinshead and George French as Executors. No codicil.

CATHARINE TENNENT (Vol. VI. pp. 374 and 498).—*Catharine Tennent*, widow of the Rev. Wm. Tennent, of Freehold, New Jersey, was descended from *Johannes Pieterse Verbrugge*, or *van Burgh* (Bridges in English), from Haarlem in Holland, born 1624, who was a trader in Nieu Amsterdam and Beaverwyck at a very early date, and in 1657 sent down from the latter place three hundred beaver skins. After his marriage van Burgh made the former his place of residence, where he became a prominent merchant and magistrate. He married in Nieu Amsterdam, 29 March (24 April ?), 1658, Catrina Roelofse (daughter of Roelof Jansen van Maesterlandt and his wife, the noted Anneka Janse), widow of Lucas Rodenburgh (vice-director of Curacoa, 1646–57, in which latter year he died). His children were all born in Nieu Amsterdam. His will is dated 22 December, 1696, and he died 1697. (See Valentine's *Manual*, 1861-4-6.) He had issue:

1. Helena, baptized 4 April, 1659, died young.
2. Helena, baptized 28 July, 1660, married 25 (26 ?) April, 1680, Tennis de Kay.

3. Anna, baptized 10 August (September?) 1662, married 13 June (2 July), 1684, Andries Gravenraedt.
4. Catharine, baptized 19 April, 1665, married Hendrick van Rensselaer.
5. Peter, baptized 14 July, 1666, married 2 November, 1688, Sarah Cuyler.
6. Maria, baptized 20 September, 1673, married Stephen Richards.
7. *Johannes* married 9 July, 1696, Margaret Provoost.

Captain Peter van Burgh was Mayor of Albany, New York, 1699, 1700–21–3. He had a house lot on the north side of State Street, west of Pearl, and near the stockade, next to the lot of his father-in-law, Hendrick Cuyler. He was buried in the church, 20 July, 1740. (See Pierson's *First Settlers of Albany, N. Y.*) He had issue, one daughter:

Catharine, baptized 10 November, 1689, married 19 September, 1707, Philip, eldest son of Robert Livingston, of Albany, born at that place, 1686, died in New York city, 1749. They had issue, six sons and three daughters. The youngest son, William, born 1723, was for many years Governor of New Jersey. (See Holgate's *American Genealogies*, Livingston family.)

Captain *Johannes van Burgh*, of New York city, was captain of the sloop *Constant Abigail*, captured off the coast of England by a French privateer. (*Doc. Col. Hist. N.Y.*, vol. iii. p. 430.) By the census of New York for 1706, he was living in that city. His will, recorded N. Y. Sur. Office, Liber 10, p. 45, is dated 14 November, 1705, in which he styles himself "mariner," and names his wife Margareta, son Johannes, daughters Johanna and Catharine, and brother Peter van Burgh, and brother-in-law David Provoost (see *N. Y. Gen. and Biog. Record*, vol. 6, p. 5, 1876). Issue:

1. Johanna, baptized 16 April, 1697, married 20 August, 1720, Gerardus Duyking.
2. Johannes, baptized 6 August, 1699.
3. *Catharine*, baptized 16 August, 1704, married first, 1719, John Noble; married secondly, 23 August, 1738, Rev. Wm. Tennent; she died at Pittsgrove, Salem Co., New Jersey, 1787.
4. David, baptized 12 September, 1708.
5. Elizabeth, baptized 25 March, 1712.

After her first marriage, *Catharine* went with her husband to England, and two children were soon born: one died young; the other, Mary Noble, married first Robert Cumming, of Freehold, New Jersey, and married secondly a Mr. Wyncoop, of Bucks Co., Pa. The husband, John Noble, went to the West Indies on business, and while there was taken with the fever and died. During his stay, he met an old New York friend, Mr. Boudinot, who wrote the circumstances of John's death to his father in England. John had a bachelor uncle named Stokes, of Stoke Castle, near Bristol, who urged the widow to make his house her home; but she preferred to return to her family in New York, which she did in 1723, a short time after the receipt of the news of her husband's death, when she went to live with her husband's brother, Mr. Isaac Noble, a wealthy merchant, who, as well as Mr. Boudinot, were elders in the Huguenot church of that city. This Mr. Isaac Noble was the means of bringing together the Rev. Mr. Tennent and his widowed sister, resulting in the marriage, as related by Mr. Elias Boudinot in his life of the Rev. Wm. Tennent. Her second husband died 8 March, 1777. His son, Rev. Wm. Tennent, who was pastor of a church in Charleston, South Carolina, came north upon the death of his father, and after settling affairs, took his father's papers, and with his mother started to return to Charleston. They travelled by means of private conveyances, and with them were the widow of the Rev. Dr. Findley and Capt. Schaff, and two servants. When about fifty miles from Charleston, her son was suddenly taken sick and died; and his father's valuable papers were lost sight of, and have not since been found. The bereaved widow soon decided to return, and went to live with her daughter Mary, now the wife of Matthew Wyncoop, of Bucks Co., Pa., but in a few years she too died, and Mrs. Tennent then went to the home of her granddaughter, Anna (Cumming) Schenck, the wife of the Rev. Wm. Schenck, then the pastor of the Pittsgrove, Salem Co., New Jersey, church, where he remained from 1780 to 1787, and where this worthy old lady, having survived two husbands and all of her children, died about 1787, in the 84th year of her age, and was buried in the church burying ground at that place. A record of these facts respecting Mrs. Tennent was left some years since by Miss Catharine van Burgh Schenck, who was born 7 January, 1775, and died at Franklin, Ohio, 4 July, 1871. She had a vivid recollection and a profound love for her great-grandmother, from whom she derived her name. No record of the death of Mrs. Tennent, nor any tombstone to her memory has yet been found in New Jersey, but the statement as to her death at Pittsgrove, and her age at the time, is undoubtedly correct.

By her first husband, John Noble, she had issue:

Mary, b. Bristol, England, married first, 1746, Robert Cumming; secondly, Matthew Wyncoop.

―――, d. young.

By her second husband, Rev. Wm. Tennent, she had, besides several children who died young, issue:

Dr. John, b. Freehold, N. J., d. in West Indies, æt. about 33 years.

Rev. William, b. Freehold, N. J., d. near Charleston, S. C., Sept.-Oct. 1777, æt. 37 years.

Dr. Gilbert, b. Freehold, N. J., d. at Freehold, N. J., before his father, aged 28 years (see *Life of Rev. Wm. Tennent*, by Hon. Elias Boudinot, N. Y., T. Whittaker, 2 Bible House).

General Robert C. Schenck, of Washington, D. C., has a very fine portrait of Mrs. Tennent, painted in England while yet Mrs. Noble, and which presents a lady of great beauty.

Mr. John N. A. Griswold, of New York city, brother of Mrs. Secretary Frelinghuysen, has the portraits of both Catharine van Burgh and her husband, John Noble, and also of Johannes, brother of Catharine. Catharine was nearly related to Sir John van Burgh, and to Charles and Philip van Burgh, commanders of men-of-war in the English navy.

With this much of the record given, can any one give information as to the fate of the papers of the Rev. William Tennent, of Freehold, N. J., which were lost sight of at the time of the death of his son? or give information respecting Mr. Isaac Noble, the brother of Catharine's first husband, or of his family or descendants?

Washington, D. C., March 17, 1883. A. D. S.

THE WASHINGTON PEDIGREE; CORRIGENDA AND ADDENDA.

BY CHARLES H. BROWNING.

I.

THE MOTHER OF MR. LAWRENCE WASHINGTON, A GRANDFATHER OF GENERAL WASHINGTON.

There has never been a controversy as to who was the mother of Mr. Lawrence Washington, the eldest son of Colonel John Washington, of Washington parish, Westmoreland County, Virginia, and the grandfather of General George Washington. In fact, there has never been any doubt as to her name, and whose daughter she was. Ask any of the many "Colonial Dames" and "Colonial Warsmen," lineal descendants of Mr. Lawrence Washington, who she was, and these concerned will readily reply: "Ann Pope." To them there is no question about it, because they had used her father, Colonel Nathaniel Pope, of Virginia, as a "claim," either original or supplementary, with the consent of their Society's Genealogist.

But the fact is, the ladies and gentlemen of Washington blood are not descended from Colonel Pope, because his daughter Ann, tho a wife of Colonel John Washington, was not the mother of Colonel Washington's son and heir Lawrence, their ancestor, and I hope that herein I shall convince them, and the pedigree examiners, that they have erred in this item of the Washington genealogy, by telling how I know it. But I have to admit that the alleged "examiners" all over the Union, are, in a way, not to be blamed altogether for the mistake, because they naturally relied upon the many printed Washington pedigrees and could have believed the writers of them had personally substantiated all their statements before publishing.

As will appear hereafter, young Captain John Washington, who had been living in Virginia, first in Northumberland Co., and next in Westmoreland Co., for several years, returned from a short visit to England, before April, 1655.

It may have been before going on this voyage, or immediately upon his return from his visit to Tring, a market town, in Hertfordshire, that he married his first wife, a young widow, with one child, and also a resident of Westmoreland, when he was about 24–26 years of age. The exact date and place of this wedding are still conjectural, but the lady's maiden name is certainly unknown at this writing, so far as I am aware. However, this latter item would only be nice to know, for it does not affect my story. The lady whom Captain (and he may have been a Major, as will be explained) John Washington married as his first wife (but not in the sense that he was going to accumulate wives), was Mrs. Ann Brett. She was the widow of Mr. Henry Brett, sometime a merchant of Plymouth, Devonshire, but at the time of his decease a land owner and resident of Westmoreland Co., Va., who died intestate, and Washington administered his estate, after he married Mrs. Brett, as appears from the following Court items.

Westmoreland Court Order Book, under date of 28 Sep., 1670, is a Statement of Account of Henry Brett's Estate, "exhibited by Lt. Col. John Washington, who married Ann, the relict of Mr. Henry Brett, late of ye county dec'd." A commission reported "We have examined ye whole Inventory & Debts of ye said Henry Brett, and Wee Doe find that Mrs. Ann Brett Washington hath paid beyond the Assatts," &c.

And *ibid,* under 31 May, 1671, find that Mrs. Ann (Brett) Washington's son, Samuel Brett, a merchant at

Plymouth, gave power of attorney "to execute a discharge to Lt. Col. Washington, who intermarried with Mrs. Ann Brett, ye relict and Admin'trix of Henry Brett, of Plymouth, merchant, dec'd."

These items, while they confirm the marriage of John Washington and the Widow Brett, his first wife, do not tell us when Mr. Brett died, nor when Mrs. Washington died, but this happened certainly before Feb. 1658–59, as will appear. In their short married life, they had three children, namely Lawrence, John and Ann, as also will be shown.

It was probably after this 1671 item, when Samuel Brett* testified that Washington had administered the estate of Brett Sr. so satisfactorily that he ran in debt to Washington thru some trading account, and Lawrence Washington, as his father's executor, had to sue his half-brother for balance of the account, £21.4.5 ster. This suit was brought against Samuel's Virginia attorney, as Brett was then a merchant at Bristol, 14 June, 1682, before a Westmoreland County Court, of which Lawrence was one of the Justices. Sometime later, Samuel's lawyer, as defence, brought a counter claim against the estate of John Washington for £100 ster., to pay for damages to a sloop, belonging to Samuel, which Washington had used to take his cattle, horses, &c., over to Maryland, in April, 1676, "as may more largely appear" below. The jury decided in favor of Lawrence.

A very short time after his first wife died, leaving him with three young children, John Washington married his second wife, who was Mrs. Ann Brodhurst, the widow and relict, and apparently the second wife, of Walter Brodhurst, who removed from Maryland to Northumberland Co., where he was the sheriff in 1652,

---

* There was a Samuel Brett, who married in 1647, in St. Andrew parish, Plymouth, who may have been brother to Henry, who named his son for him.

and a burgess next year, and then was seated in Westmoreland, when it was formed from Northumberland, and the daughter of Lieut. Colonel Nathaniel Pope, of Westmoreland Co., a near neighbor to Washington.

In this way it appears as if Ann Pope, a young woman, was the second wife of Walter Brodhurst, and that his first was one of the daughters of Lt. Col. Thomas Gerrard. Brodhurst and Gerrard had been neighbors in Maryland and removed together to Northumberland Co., 1650. Gerrard in his will, dated 1 Feb. 1672–3, says he married twice, and had issue by each wife. He had five daughters (and several sons, one John, of whom hereafter), but named only two, and a lot of grandchildren through them, but named only two, Gerrard Tucker and Gerrard Peyton, a son of daughter Frances, who was the wife of several prominent Virginians, and then became the third wife of Lt. Col. Washington. Possibly Brodhurst's son, Gerrard, was also one of his unnamed grandchildren, and well enough off not to need a special legacy.

Brodhurst's will, dated 26 Jan., 1658–9, proved by the witnesses at his house, and presented in Court, 12 Feb. following by his widow, Ann, born Pope, as its executrix. According to the will, she was so to act, excepting as to his land he desired "my son Gerrard" to have. His arrangement for his widow was not generous. As long as she remained his widow and unmarried, she was to have the use of his land, cattle, horses, &c., but for this she should pay rental to his will overseers, Col. Gerrard, possibly his first father-in-law, and Col. Pope, his second father-in-law, who should use the money for the up-keep and education of his children. From this, it looks as if Gerrard was to look after the welfare of his namesake, if not his grandson, Gerrard Brodhurst, and Pope to do the same for his daughter's son, Walter. That young Gerrard Brodhurst may have had some trouble in getting some of his inheritance from his father's estate, appears through a quit-claim deed, dated 20 Sep. 1668, from "Mrs. Ann Brodhurst" (whom we have reasons to imagine was then "Mrs. John Washington"), by which she assigned 500 acres of land, which, after 1675, lay in Stafford Co., to her stepson, Gerrard Brodhurst.

The exact date of the marriage of John Washington and Mrs. Brodhurst is unknown, and so is that of the death of Mr. Brodhurst. Both dates remain hypothetic. Mr. Brodhurst's will, which was dated 26 Jan. 1658–9, was not filed till in Nov., 1659, and the inventory of his personal estate on 17 April, 1661, therefore, we got no information from these sources, or only that Washington seems to have lost no time in getting a second wife to mind the infants of his previous one, and look out for his comfort. However, there is a suggestive, tho not convincing, item extant which shows Major Washington must have married Mrs. Brodhurst around Feb., 1658–9, which I shall bring up.

There are two good items extant that approximate the time of their wedding. One, dated 12 Feb., 1658–9, a recorded paper in which Ann's father, Lt. Col. Pope, styled her "my daughter Ann Pope Brodhurst."

The other item, dated 11 May, 1659, also signed with his "mark" by Lt. Col. Pope, is a power of attorney concerning some land, addressed to his daughter Ann, in which he calls her "My daughter Ann Pope *alias* Washington."

Therefore it may be seen that John Washington and his second Ann, another widow with a son, married early in the year 1659, and before May, certainly, if the "young son" baptised on 4 Oct. was her first child and not the last one of the first wife of Col. John.

In the Spring of 1659, John Washington went on one of his trading voyages abroad, and returned to Virginia in Sep. On the 29 Sep., 1659, the Governor of Maryland wrote him a letter, which he received by messenger in Westmoreland Co., at his home, in which the Governor requested him to attend a Maryland Court on the following 4 Oct., to testify in a criminal case, instituted by Col. Washington, concerning the brutal hanging by the sailors of a woman passenger, believed by them to be a witch, and that she had hoodooed their ship, in which Washington was coming over to Virginia, and caused it several times to get on the wrong course. (See Neill's "Virginia-Carolorum," pp. 257-8).

In reply to this request, Col. Washington wrote to the Governor, by his messenger, a note dated 30 Sep., 1659, saying (*ibid*), that it was impossible for him to attend that Court on 4 Oct. following, "because then, [4 Oct. 1659], God willing, I intend to gett my young son baptised. All ye company and Gossips being already invited." [The full text of this letter may be read in vol. XVI, p. 264, this mag.].

Thus, we have virtually the record of the date of the baptism of John, Jr., the youngest son of Col. John Washington, for we may presume he was baptised on 4 Oct., 1659. This being a child of Col. John's first wife, deceased, and born in 1658, before Feb., 1658-9, there may be many causes imagined why he was not baptised before this, or during his mother's lifetime. There are at least two probable reasons worth suggesting. The child's mother may have died giving birth to it, and its father had not yet arrived home from his voyage. John, Jr., was 17 years of age when his father made his will, in which he desired that Thomas Pope, the lad's step-uncle, should "have the care of his bringing up" and educating.

When Col. Washington made his will, dated either 11, or 21 (writing indistinct), Sept., 1675, he named as executors his then wife (Anne [Pope] Brodhurst), his brother Lawrence, who predeceased him, and "my son Lawrence." The date of his death has not been found. The will was proved, and filed in Westmoreland County Court 10 Jan., 1677-8, by his son and heir, Lawrence (Ann Pope, his wife, not acting for reason hereafter explained), he being the heir, and then of age and naturally had livery of his inheritance, and succeeded his father.

This is another of the reasons why Lawrence could not have been the child of Ann Pope ("her second son" it has been printed), because she and Col. John were married early, probably, in Feb., 1658-9, and Lawrence would have been only 18 or 19 years old in 1677-8, and not of age. Whereas he was born early in 165—, (1655-6), hence was the son of Col. John's first wife, Mrs. Ann Brett.

But the proof that Lawrence, John, and Ann, were the children of Col. John by his first wife is more convincing through the following extracts from the wills of Col. John Washington and his sons, Lawrence and John. See Mr. Ford's "Washington Wills," which may be assumed are reliable copies of the originals (tho his footnotes to them are not always that), or, better, Dr. Toner's copies printed in Waters' "Gleanings in English Wills," pp. 524, &c., and W. and M. Quart., *XIII*, p. 145, will of John Jr.

Col. Washington wrote into his will, on 11 (or 21) of Sept., 1675: "My body to be buried in ye plantation where I now live, by the side of My Wife yt is already buried."

As his second wife (frequently mentioned in this will, and named as one of its executors), Mrs. Ann Brodhurst ("Ann Pope that was") was living, and presumably with him, when he wrote this desire, Col. John could have only referred to his first wife, the Widow Brett, as being the wife, "yt is already buried," before May, 1659. However, his wife, Widow Brodhurst, survived Col. John and died in England, as below.

Lawrence Washington, Col. John's eldest son and

heir, in his will, dated 11 March, 1697–8, desired to be buried "by the side of my father and mother."

Therefore, Col. John Washington was buried as he wished to be, beside his first wife, "already buried" there, in the Washington graveyard, on the homestead plantation, Westmoreland Co., and his son Lawrence was buried next to them, and near several half-brothers and half-sisters.

John Washington, Jr., Col. John's second son, and last child by his first wife, in his will, dated Washington parish, 22 January, 1697–8 (proved 23 Feb. following), desired that his body be "buried by my father and mother and brothers."

These I presume were step-brothers (brother Lawrence being alive), because Mrs. Brett-Washington could not have had more than three children in her short married life with Col. John, unless there were "twins, or better."

Here, we have the proof in two wills that Lawrence and John Jr. were sons of Col. John's first wife, and you will see by the Colonel's will that his daughter, Ann, was also her child, and that their own mother, the wife of Col. John, was buried in the plantation graveyard, before Sep., 1675.

Since, as related below, Washington's second wife (Ann Pope), died in Salop, England, while among her first husband's relatives, and was buried there by them, and there is not the slightest hint of contemporary record, nor likelihood probably, that her body was disinterred and brought to Virginia, by Lawrence's or John Jr.'s order, Lawrence and John were buried by the side of Mrs. Ann Brett-Washington, and were not the sons of (Mrs. Ann Pope) Brodhurst-Washington, and were only step-sons.

Taking up Col. John Washington's will again, read what he says of his children:—"My wife (i. e. his then wife, Ann Pope, who survived him) to have the "bringing up of my daughter, Ann Washington, until my son. Lawrence comes of age."

This item shows the Colonel's particular consideration for his own, and not his and his then wife's, Ann Pope, children. Lawrence at that writing was about 19 years old, and may be presumed to have been so manly and educated that he required no further "bringing up" by anyone, nor was a guardian suggested for him during his minority, in the event that his father might be killed in the Bacon war, or rebellion, or in the coming conflict with the Indians, both threatened at this time, and the Colonel realized he would soon be in active military duty as a commander, hence he made his will.

[It is a rather remarkable coincidence about the two brothers, John and Lawrence Washington, the immigrants, and worthy of note here, that John's will was dated 21 Sept., 1675, and filed in Court on 10 Jan., 1677–8, and that of Lawrence being dated 27 Sep., 1675, was filed in the same Court on 6 Jan., 1677–8.]

Even then, his father realized that young Lawrence would be competent to look after his own young sister, and it would be more natural that he should do so, rather than to be continued at the command of her step-mother, especially at so important period of her young life when there would be wooers acoming. Therefore, it may be assumed, that when his father died, Lawrence, as the head of the House, not only took charge of his sister, without their step-mother having to resign her, he being then of age, which was the condition in the will. Should he not have been of full age, the Court would have been obliged to appoint someone to administer the Colonel's estate until he was, and the Court Order Book shows no such order, hence, again, he could not have been Ann Pope's child.

I think nothing more is needed to identify young Ann as, like Lawrence and John, Jr., a child of Col. John by his first wife, Widow Brett, than the following item from her father's will. After having given "to my daughter Ann" two tracts of land, containing 1200 and 1400 acres each, he says:—"I give to my say'd Daughter, wch was her mother's desire, and my promise, ye Cash in ye new parlour, & the Diamond ringe, & her Mother's rings, & the white quilt & the white curtains & vallians."

There is still another important item to record here, suggesting about when Lawrence was born, and showing he must have been the child of his father's first wife, and could not have been the son of Ann Pope, the second wife, whom Col. John did not marry till after Jan., 1658-9, and before 11 May, 1659.

In 1679, Mr. Lawrence Washington was appointed one of H. M. Justices of the C. P. Court, the Westmoreland County Court. (ex V. H. M., I., 250), and was still a member in 1682-3 (ex W. & M. Q., IV., 87), and in 1685, when he is styled Captain, (W. & M. Quart., Vol. XV, p. 186), and probably was a captain when young. If Lawrence had been any child, or the first, of Col. Washington by his second wife, Ann Pope, married possibly in Feb., 1658-9, he would have been too young, not even of age, to be a Justice. But as the son of Col. Washington by his first wife, Mrs. Ann Brett, he was 23 or 25 or more years of age, and quite eligible to sit on the Bench, in 1679-80.

II.

WAS COL. JOHN WASHINGTON A BIGAMIST?

Such a query as this is not intended to be a malicious dissemination, as it is intended only as the title of a case stated, the hypothesis being:—When a man and woman live together, and he has acknowledged her as his wife, and, at a certain date, there is evidence that they were then living together in harmony, but in less than eight months afterwards he openly marries another woman, and the former presumed wife goes abroad, and centuries afterwards there is not found any record of the decree of divorce, legally separating the man from the departed woman, who had been living with him as his wife for about seventeen years, what is the inference?

In our present-day life, we may, under these circumstances, assume the discarded woman was only a "common-law wife," a concubine, and that theirs had not been a legal union, and consequently their issue was illegitimate.

But as to this suppositious statement, and also the query, we are advised, as a counter to it, that we should not judge actions of centuries ago by our present-day methods. Therefore, we should allow there was a separation legally confirmed, a divorce, legally granted and duly recorded somewhere, which evidence has not been discovered up to this time.

As already stated, Major John Washington, of Washington parish, Westmoreland Co., of the church of which he was elected a vestryman in July, 1661, married, when 30 years of age, his second wife, the widow, Ann (Pope) Brodhurst, possibly in Feb., 1658–9, or even later, before May, 1659.

This union, as you shall see, took place before the 11th of May, 1659, when it was acknowledged by Ann's father, but the wedding day is not of record. Ann's former husband signed his will on 26 Jan., 1658–9, and it was presented in Court for probate 12 Feb., 1658–9, but some testamentary proceedings here and in England, in the P. C. C., where it also had to be filed, delayed its filing here till the Nov. term of the Court, 1659. Also on the same date, 12 Feb., 1658–9, Ann's father, Col. Pope, executed a deed to her for land, in which he called her "my daughter Ann Pope Brodhurst," hence, it may be presumed she did not marry John Washington till after this date.

But it looks as if Ann shed her weeds for a veil a very

short time after 26 Jan., 1658–9, or after she had buried Brodhurst, as her father, Lt. Col. Nathaniel Pope, also a planter in Westmoreland Co., in a power of attorney to her about some land, dated 11 May, 1659, as above, styled her "My daughter Ann Pope, *alias* Washington." In his will (which he "marked," for possibly Col. Pope could not write, as all of his extant papers bear only "His Mark"), dated a few days later, or on 16 May, 1659, written just before going to England (proved in Virginia 20 April, 1660), he gave, or rather forgave, "to my son-in-law, John Washington," a debt of eighty pounds money, which John, he said, owed him.

And there is a recorded grant of 700 acres of land in Westmoreland, to Mrs. Ann Pope *alias* Washington, dated 13 June, 1661. [With no intention to suggest anything like it in this case, it may be remarked here that in England, Ireland, and the B. W. I., when there are papers of court record in which the woman living with a man as his wife, "but not parsoned" or married to him, she is described this way in old records, "Mary Smith *alias* Jones," her name and the surname of the man, to identify her.]

After this union, the next great event in the lives of John and Ann was, so far as I know, the christening of John's last child by his first wife (Widow Brett), on 4 Oct., 1659, referred to before, the date of whose birth is unknown.

On the 20th of this month and year, as "Mrs. Ann Brodhurst (she being Major Washington's wife on 11 May, we have seen), she was present in the Westmoreland Court, and as "the relict (but not the widow, because she had married again since his decease), and adm'trix of Mr. Walter Brodhurst, dec'd," sued a Capt. Lefebur for "accommodation," which was "for four months' house roome and dyett of his family." Judgement in favor of "Mrs. Ann Brodhurst," which was only the half measure of her then identity, but may have then been the legal way.

From now on till he died 17 years later, John Washington, being a man of affairs, was constantly employed in duties as a county justice, a coroner (in August, 1661, when coroner, he and his jury reported to the County Court on their burial of a suicide, saying they had obeyed the Law, and had buried him at a certain spot, "with a stake driven through ye middle of him in his grave"), a burgess and a member of the General Assembly, and commander of the county militia, having been commissioned Lt. Col. 29 Mar., 1673; on 17 Mar., 1674–5, he had been on a commission to employ Indians, and reward them for work, but on 31 August, 1675, this scheme to pacify the savages having failed, he was ordered to organize an expedition against the Indians, and set out to drive them out of the sea-board, and his activity was one of the causes for Bacon's Rebellion, which Col. Washington was active in helping to put down, and it was suppressed early in the Spring of 1677.

You have seen that Col. Washington dated his will on 21 Sep., 1675, and named his then wife as a co-executor. In a general way it could be said "he provided for his wife handsomely," should she survive him. She did survive him, as will be shown. His was but a perfunctory will, so far as she was concerned; a rather cold one. Beside the "widow's third," her dower right in his real estate, which the law guaranteed a wife, and a one-fourth share in his personal estate, he made no mention where, nor how, she should live, which a testator of his time always did for his wife, nor did he mention her in any endearing term as was also the custom. His brother Lawrence, who made his will almost at the same time, was more generous and considerate for his second wife.

By his second wife, Col. Washington seems to have

had several children, possibly four, according to wills. Two evidently died before he wrote his will, as he says two were buried in the Washington graveyard. And his son Lawrence says he has "brothers and sisters" buried in the same ground, and John, Jr., his brother, also says "brothers" buried there. Apparently they died young and unmarried.

Col. Washington we have seen married as first and second wives, two widows, each a "Mrs. Ann B.," and each had a son. Now, you will find that he married, thirdly, while his second wife was living, another widow, and that he was her fourth husband. She, too, survived Col. John, and was his joint-widow and co-relict with his alleged second wife, Ann Pope.

The evidence that Col. Washington did have a third wife, while Ann Pope was alive, may be found in the Westmoreland Co. Court Order Book of the date. This is the customary "Marriage Contract," dated 10 May, 1676, "of Lt. Col. John Washington and Mrs. Frances Appleton, the widow and relict of Captain John Appleton." All of this county.

As the proof that this contract was carried out, there is the following item, also from this Order Book, under date, 26 November, 1677.

"It is ord'r yt Jno Garrard have out of ye Estate of Cap't Jno Appleton, deceas'd, now ye estate of Coll. Jno. Washington, who intermarried with ye Relict of ye sd Appleton, tenn goode breeding cows," &c.

The petitioner and beneficiary under this Court Order was the eldest brother of the lady whom Col. Washington had married the year before, and he surely knew they had married. He had served under Lt. Col. Washington, in the expedition against the Indians, in the Autumn of 1675. He was present at the Court of Inquiry as to the particulars of it, and on 14 June, 1677, testified as to the conduct of his commander, Washington, present in Court, and exonerated him and the Virginia troops he commanded, from the charge of participating in the execution of Indians when attending a conference with the commanders of the troops.

Col. Washington apparently raised no objection to this order of the Court. Nor did he alter his will, after he married, between its date and filing, Mrs. Frances (Garrard) Speke-Peyton-Appleton, and became her fourth husband.

Col. Washington and Widow Appleton were old friends and neighbors, and he had known all of her husbands intimately, having long served in the same regiment with them. He became her attorney after the death of Captain Appleton, who, was high sheriff of Westmoreland, 1673–4, and was a subscribing witness to Washington's will, but died before 9 May, 1676, when the inventory of his personal estate was filed by his widow. As the latter's attorney, he is of record of having been in Court several times on her behalf.

It is evident that the Widow Appleton was clear and free to marry, in May, 1676. But how about Col. Washington? His second wife, Widow Brodhurst, certainly has to be reckoned with. She must be allowed an exit, for I do not wish to asperse his character, nor hers. He was a gentleman, that must be remembered, and Mrs. Appleton there is no reason to suppose was not his equal. Both seemed rather fond of marrying, and we must admit that the Colonel was no "laggard in love," but he must have been sensible along with this habit, and would scorn to take the risk of a bigamist. Still the query:—How can a man with a wife (his own, of course), marry another woman? The Colonel certainly had a wife of his own, in Sept., 1675, who outlived him, but in the following May, he married another lady, and polygamy had ceased for ages to be fashionable, and was not revived till a couple of centuries later, therefore, how did he get rid of her?

That Mrs. Ann (Pope) Washington, formerly Mrs.

Walter Brodhurst, was alive after Sept., 1675, and survived Col. John Washington, who died before 10 Jan., 1677-8, and after 14 June, 1677, may be seen thru the following items:

Whether it was before, or after, May, 1676, or before, or after, Col. Washington died, and it matters little here when it was, Mrs. Ann (Pope) Brodhurst-Washington went to England to visit her son, Walter Brodhurst, Jr., and her Brodhurst kin residing at Lilleshall, in Salop. And, as it is learned from an English Court record, she hoped to collect a legacy, due her over twenty years from the estate of her Brodhurst father-in-law.

Before sailing, or after reaching England, it matters little which, she executed a power of attorney, dated 18 March, 1677-8, and signed it "Ann Washington," and in which she is described "the widow and relict of Captain John Washington," and qualified Mr. Caleb Butler, a Westmoreland Co. Justice, to collect and remit to her certain debts due her in Maryland and Virginia. This document was filed in this County Court, on 30 March, 1678. As there are only twelve days between the date of writing and of filing this "Power," and considering the time it required then for a ship to cross from England to Virginia, the paper was signed in Virginia, hence, Ann Pope Brodhurst-Washington went to England after, or on the 17 March, 1677-8, which was, of course, after Col. Washington was buried by the side of his first wife, the mother of Lawrence, John, Jr., and Ann.

Ann Pope's description of herself in this paper was rather impertinent; however, we are thankful for the preserving of it, because it tells us that Col. Washington's second wife was alive when he married his third wife, and that Ann Pope survived him.

And, since there is no item yet found showing that Ann had been in England between Sept., 1675, and

March, 1678, this paper also shows that she was divorced from John by a Virginia County Court, or by the General Court. Which of them instituted the suit would be interesting to know, but no one has come across such an item. The action would have been in their home-county, and the Westmoreland Court Order Books, or daily minutes of the proceedings of the courts in session, are perfect and complete, as are also those of the General Courts of these days, as Bacon's Rebellion had ended. Therefore, where's the evidence that John and Ann were divorced?

There is evidence that Washington was a busy man, sometimes in the Assembly, and again in the field with his troops, even up to his third wedding-day, but we know that a great many things can and do happen in eight months, so it may have been in this time, between when Col. John signed his will and then went on his expedition against the Indians, and the filing of the marriage contract, that it was Ann who got busy with the divorce court, and the Colonel made no defense. However, whilst this could have happened, there is no proof that it did. It does not seem possible that the divorce was granted, or even arranged before John wrote his will, because of its contexture. Howsoever, whatsoever, it happened, and Col. Washington was free to marry, and did so about May, 1676, and, as you may have noticed, in no clandestine manner either, because his intention to marry the Widow Appleton was spread upon the Court minutes that anyone might read. And there was his marriage license, too.

No one thinks that Ann Pope, who had been living seventeen years with John Washington, minding her step-children and her own, and possibly being homely in disposition, would not have protested, to put it mildly, in this month of May, 1676, if she did not know that Col. John was free to do as it pleased him when it came to marrying even a thrice relict and widow.

Judging from the arrangement Ann Pope made in March, 1678, about her personal affairs in the colonies, it looks as if she did not intend returning to America. And there was no particular reason why she should delay her departure, or return. Her use as an executor of Washington's will had automatically ceased, when Lawrence entered upon his inheritance, and with him, only a step-son, as the head of the House of Washington in Virginia, as his father's heir. And, too, she had been relieved by him of the "care of bringing up" of his sister Ann, and the bringing up of John, Jr., had been entrusted to her brother, Thomas Pope. But more than anything, she may have realized that she was not a *persona grata* amid the Washingtons and neighbors. Therefore, she went to England.

She died shortly after she reached her destination. The exact date of this event I do not know. Nor do I know when she landed, but of course, it was after 18 March 1677–8.

She was buried, probably at Lilleshall parish church, certainly before 12 April, 1678, because on this date, her son, Walter Brodhurst, Jr., of Lilleshall, Shropshire, was appointed by the Litchfield Diocesan Court, which had jurisdiction over wills, estates, orphans, &c., in the Archdeaconery of Salop, to administer on the personal estate of "his mother, Misstress Ann Washington *alias* Brodhurst, (*sic*), of Washington parish, Westmoreland County, Virginia."

If Ann Pope was divorced from Col. Washington, and there are reasons to hope she was, it was more likely to have been after Washington signed his will than before. The cause of it, of course, I do not know, but, for a conjecture, it may have been because of the will. But what we are also interested in is the suggestion all thru it that John had really married Ann Pope, and he knew, if she survived him she would be his widow and relict before the law, for, wherever he gave land to a child he excepted Ann's dower right.

When the Bacon uprising got afoot, Col. Washington hired a sloop and sent his cattle, horses, &c., into Maryland to save them from raiders. When the rebel commander learned this he issued a warrant dated 21 Oct., 1676, ordering one of his officers, one Mannering, to go to Washington's plantations and prevent their removal, or "to cease ye sloope yt shall in anytime attempt yt takeing of goods belonging to sd Washington or any other delinquent yt are fleed fayle not hereof." Subsequently, Mannering, was captured and parolled on giving bond dated 19 June, 1677. Before a commission investigating the conduct of many of those who had been rebels, a Mr. Arminger made an affidavit, dated 26 July, 1677, telling of Mannering's visit in Oct., 1676, to Col. Washington's house, and said "Madam Washington sd to ye sd Mannering, 'if you were advised by your wife, you need not acome to this passe' "; that is, being in disgrace. As this visit occurred in Oct., 1677, it was Mrs. Frances Washington speaking.

Simply because the usual records of the lawful marriage of Col. John Washington and Ann Pope Brodhurst, and the decree of their divorce cannot be found, it would not be fair to assume, or presume she had not legally married John (early in 1659), when I have cited contemporary items suggesting, if not actually proving, she had. And it would be unfair to both John and Ann to doubt they were legally separated (between Sep., 1675, and May., 1676), for John's third marriage was no secret, as contemporary items cited show. Therefore, it may be assumed that John Washington was not a bigamist. The ancient "Scotch verdict" is more appropriate to the question of John's marriage (and divorce) with Ann Pope, than to this conclusion.

III.

THE LEGITIMATION OF COL. JOHN WASHINGTON.

When Mr. Waters discovered the evidence proving that Col. John Washington, of Virginia, was "the eldest son of the Rev. Lawrence Washington, A.M., (Oxon)," sometime the rector of the Purleigh parish church, Essex, England, it was the consensus of genealogists he had accomplished something worthwhile.

But when Mr. Stanard subsequently discovered the evidence proving that Col. John Washington was born in the year 1629, he started a lot of genealogical trouble because his find either made a mare's nest of Mr. Waters' discovery, or that Col. Washington was born out of wedlock, thus placing him in the illegitimate class.

The following are the facts as to both of these statements. My intention is to try to legitimate Col. Washington, and you will see what is required to do so. Contemporary circumstantial evidence, based on incidents, or presumptive evidence, in this case would not be sufficient, being secondary, to overcome the demonstrative internal evidence. There must be material evidence and proof that the Rev. Mr. Washington married before his eldest son and first child was born.

The will of a Mr. Andrew Knowling was found by Mr. Waters and printed in his valuable book, "Gleanings in English Wills," pp. 364 and 386, of vol. I. it is dated at Tring, in Hertfordshire, 13 Jan., 1648-9, and signed with his "mark." He had considerable property, and had married the widow of John Roades, the mother of children by her first husband.

It was through the finding of Mr. Knowling's will, that Mr. Waters claimed he was enabled to bring to a positive conclusion, in 1889, the search for the parents of Col. John Washington, which quest had been going on intermittingly since in 1791, and then identified Col.

John's father in the family of Washington of Sulgrave, therefore, what I say of Col. John's pedigree is on Waters' information.

In his will, Knowling mentioned relatives of his wife, and her children, his step-children. Among the latter was "Mrs. Amphillis Washington," who had six children, also named by Knowling. But while he named many persons, he did not mention the name of Amphillis' husband, nor mention him in any way, which seems rather strange. However, one may imagine a lot of reasons, and in a case of this kind, one guess may be as good as another, and mine is, Knowling was a Cromwellian, and Mr. Washington was a rabid Royalist, and the Civil War was at its worst then, and the king was executed only seventeen days after Knowling made his will.

The names of the six Washington children as given by Knowling, were so suggestive of the Virginia Washingtons, that it started Waters on his quest for their father's name is interestingly told by him.

By the address of Knowling's will, he was first attracted to Tring. Here he found two of these children were baptised at the parish church as the children of "Mr. Lawrence Washington." He decided, as this father was styled "Mr.," he was a minister. Eventually, as he found that a "Rev. Lawrence Washington" had been employed at the Church Court at Wheathampstead, near Tring, at the time Knowling made his will, and later, he felt sure he had found the husband of Amphillis, and the father of her children, which idea was strengthened by the fact that one of them was designated in the will as "Lawrence Washington the younger," as though to distinguish him from his father of the same name, the others being named in it as John, William, Elizabeth, Margaret and Martha Washington.

From the records of the University of Oxford and one of its colleges, Brasenose, it was easy to get information as to the early life, some of it anyway, of the Rev. Lawrence Washington, which is proper to repeat in this article. He was born in 1602, at Brington Manor, Northamptonshire, and entered Brasenose College as a student, when 17 years of age, but did not sign as such till 2 Nov., 1621. He graduated and received the A.B. degree 10 May, 1623, and on 27 May, 1623, he was elected to the Darbie Fellowship in Brasenose, and became a Fellow for ten years of this college, from which he received the A. M. degree, 1 Feb., 1625–6. In the following year he was appointed his college lector, and on August 26, 1631, he was elected the proctor of the University of Oxford.

On 10 March, 1632–3, "his grace for the B.D. degree was passed on," and on 4 April, 1633, "he informed Brasenose College that he was to be inducted in a benefice." And, on 30 Nov., 1633, he resigned his Fellowship in Brasenose College, having previously resigned as the University proctor.

The Rev. Mr. Washington, on 14 March, 1633–4, entered upon his duties as the rector of the church of the parish of Purleigh, in the deanery of Malden, Co. of Essex. Thus, Mr. Washington was removed to the most easterly of the tier of adjoining counties, Oxford, Bucks, Herts and Essex, with which you shall see he was associated.

What was the influence Mr. Washington had to have this living, a fairly good one, given to him by Jane Horsmanden, of Purleigh, is not in evidence. Nor is the reason, when he entered into it, why he did not take his wife and family with him to the rectory, than to place them nearly a two days' horseback journey away from him in the village of Tring, in Herts. May be she preferred it; her mother and step-father having resided there, and some relatives were still there. Mr. Washington, too, must have been acquainted with the place, and this may have been the residence of

Amphillis since the birth of her first child. Mr. Washington's acquaintance with the place may be accounted for this way. A distant relative by marriage, of his father, Sir Robert Anderson, Knt., resided in a manor house near Tring, which he bought from Sir Francis Verney, in 1607, and Lawrence may have visited him when a college student, as Sir Robert, who was buried at the Tring church, in 1632, in his will, dated 5 Oct., 1630, remembered him with a legacy: "to my cousin, Lawrence Washington, of Bras Nose College, forty shillings," which was a generous gift, since it was only Sir Robert's wife who was a cousin of Lawrence's father, and it suggests he knew Lawrence well.

There is little information about Mr. Washington after he became the rector of Purleigh till his last year. There was a case in the Chancery Court, under date of 20 Oct., 1640, which shows that an Oxford storekeeper had entered suit, away back in July, 1633, against "Mr. Lawrence Washington, clerk, of Purleigh," for £69.18, balance due for furniture and clothing sold to him "when a student at Braz Nose College." Washington's defence was that he had paid the man all he had owed him in installments, in May, 1633, and May, 1636. Our particular interest in this case, rather an interesting one, but too intricate to go into here, is the title description of the defendant, because it clearly identifies the Purleigh rector with the student and Fellow of Brasenose, for there is no record of any other Lawrence Washington having attended any college of Oxford University, 1619–1634.

In Nov., 1643, the Rev. Mr. Washington was ejected from his charge, the parish church of Purleigh. This happened during the Civil War, and was one of Cromwell's measures for silencing "Rabid Royalists." This was the primal objection or charge as to our minister, but it was printed that he was "a drunkard and tavern loafer," and not fit to have charge of a parish, however, the Rev. Washington had plenty of company under such charges. What Mr. Washington did after this to support himself and his alleged (by Mr. Waters) family, a wife and six children, does not appear.

Along in 1649, it may be imagined that his wife was in need of some assistance, as on 15 August, 1649, the Committee on aid to "Plundered Ministers," victims of Cromwell, ordered the then rector of Purleigh parish, Washington's old charge, "to pay one-fifth of the tithes "to Mrs. Washington, the [former] rector's wife."

Early in 1648–9, Mr. Washington is found employed as the surrogate in the office at Wheathampstead, Herts, of the Archdeacon's Court. And as surrogate, 29 Jan., 1648–9, he wrote the bond of the guardians of two orphans, his alleged wife's nieces, daughters of a tallow chandler, legatees in the 1649 will of Mr. Knowling, and signed it with his full name, and also his Oxford degrees, and then official position. This was the only connection "the Rev. Lawrence Washington, clerk," had with the will of his alleged (Waters) wife's step-father.

When the commission aided "Mrs. Washington," it is possible it also did something for the former rector. A salaried position may have been found for him in or near Malden, Essex, as "he died and was buried here at All Saints' Church," its register entry being:—"Mr. Lawrence Washington, buried 21 Jan., 1652." It was too far away for him to be buried at Tring. No particulars of his death are known.

As evidence that the Rev. Lawrence Washington, 1602–1652, A.M., B.D., (Oxon), of Tring and Purleigh, was a son, the fourth, of Lawrence Washington, Esq., lord of Brixton, or Brington manor, Northamptonshire, and his wife, Margaret Butler, married at Aston le Wells, 3 August, 1580, I shall use a few of the interesting wills collected by Mr. Waters, for his book. q. v.

But first we have the record of Lawrence, Jr.'s matriculation at Brasenose College, 2 Nov., 1621:— "Laurent Washington, Northamp., gen. fil., an. nat. 19." Which is, he was 19 years old, and the son of a gentleman of Northants.

Then next, we find this item connecting him definitely with the Washingtons of Brington:—Robert Washington, brother to the lord of Brington, (died in 1616), was buried at Brington, 10 March, 1621-2. His widow, Elizabeth Washington, died 19 March, 1622-3, leaving a will, dated 17 March, 1622-3, in which she named many legatees, principally her late husband's nephew and nieces, called "cousins," the children of his deceased brother Lawrence, among them Sir William, Mrs. Mewce, Alice and Frances Washington, "my cousin Pill," and "To my cousin, Lawrence Washington, who is nowe at Oxford, my husband's seal ringe."

The will of the above mentioned Mrs. Elizabeth Mewce, widow, residing in County Middlesex, near London, dated 11 Aug., 1676, of her legatees are her sisters:—Lady Washington, Mrs. Alice Sandys, and Mrs. Frances Gargrave, and her husband, Mr. Robert Gargrave, and their five children; her uncles, Mr. Robert Washington, brother of Mr. Washington, of Brington, and Mr. Francis Pargiter, father-in-law of Sir John Washington; her nephews, William Pill and Roger Thornton; and her nieces, Mrs. Margaret Stevenage, and two children; Mrs. Frances Collins, Mrs. Elizabeth Rumball, and Mrs. Penelope Thornton, and five children.

The will of Lady Dorothy (Pargiter) Washington, widow of Sir. John Washington (a son of Mr. Lawrence Washington, of Brington), dated 6 Oct., 1678, mentions Mrs. Penelope Thornton aforesaid, as her daughter, and this assures us that Mrs. Mewce was a daughter of the lord of Brington manor, Northants.

No brother or sister of Lawrence Washington in their extant wills mentions him after he became a clergyman, or his wife and children. It was a large family, some children died young, some unmarried, some adults died intestate. Those who left wills were well off, and may not have felt any interest in the struggling minister, who, himself, seems to have been a rather independent character, even when a student, of the classics or of theology, and certainly when ejected.

This brings me up to an interesting time of the Rev. Lawrence Washington's early life, while a student, especially as to when, where, or how he made the acquaintance of "Amphillis Roades, or Roads; the mother of his children." But as to when and where they were married, I am sorry I can only say that to be able to answer this question, the most expert of genealogical searchers, most persistent men and women, plodders in old records, for years, have looked, and looked, and looked in vain, to find even some slight clew, or item, relative to it. Yet some day, such an item may turn up. Many have in the years many of these same genealogists have been dead, that have given a new twist to their statements and deductions, especially in the "Washington Genealogy." "WATCH YOUR STEP," is a well-known sign everywhere. "Watch your genealogical 'step'," should be a good one to hang before him and her on their desks when writing Family History.

In 1620, Sir Edward Verney (he and Thomas Washington, a brother of the Rev. Lawrence, served together in the household of Prince Charles), brother to Sir Francis mentioned before, purchased the large manor of Middle Claydon, in Co. Bucks, which was near to the University of Oxford, in the next county, and died in 1643, leaving a will, dated 26 March, 1639. Among his sundry legatees he gave "to my servant, John Roades, at Middle Claydon, an annuity of ten pounds for life."

John Roades was above an ordinary "servant," yet

he was such. He was evidently the head-farmer, or the superintendent of the manor, because he is of record as being Sir Edward's bailiff, or deputy sheriff, in 1639. His son, William Roades, was a witness to Sir. Edward's will, and succeeded his father as chief farmer of this manor, before 1648, as Andrew Knowling, aforesaid, had married his mother, widow of the said John Roades, before Jan., 1649, when Knowling made his will, and made William, his step-son, and brother of Mrs. Amphillis Washington, his step-daughter, legatees, therefore, William was uncle to Col. John Washington, and John Roades was one of his grandfathers, his other being, of course, the prominent Lawrence Washington, Esq., the lord of the manor of Brixton, or Brington. William Roades made his will 19 Sep., 1657, and was buried on the 29th, at Finmoor Hill, about 2 miles from Middle Claydon), but did not mention his sister, Amphillis Washington, nor her husband, nor their issue. In fact, neither did Amphillis' sister, Mrs. Elizabeth Fitzherbert, in her will, dated 23 Feb., 1684, (her step-nephew, John Freeman, was her executor, having married at Luton, 4 April, 1668, Esther, a daughter of Amphillis' brother, William Roads), but which is not surprising, because this Washington family was nearly all dead.

When Lawrence Washington was an Oxford student, the son and heir of this Sir Edward Verney was also. It is quite possible they were well enough acquainted for young Verney to take Washington home with him on holidays, or week-ends (anyway, Lawrence's elder brother, Thomas, had been a page with Sir Edward in the household of Prince Charles, while in Spain, in 1623, and Lawrence was not a stranger), and when at Middle Claydon he met Amphillis Roades, the farmer's daughter, in some natural way that young people have, and we may imagine what happened next, as we know the sequel. [Sir Edward had a younger son, of whom it is related in "Virginia Carolorum," pp. 108–111, that he "married beneath him," and as punishment, his parents shipped him to the Virginia colony].

This romantic affair at Middle Claydon certainly happened before the year 1629, as it was in this year, or in 1628–9, or in 1629–30, Amphillis gave birth to her first child, who was named John, whom you have seen became our Virginia Colonel (who had some romances of his own), who was about five years old when his father became rector of Purleigh.

As evidence of the date of Col. John Washington's birth-date, there is the following Court item. Some years ago (but years after the "true Washington pedigree," authenticated, signed and printed, in sundry ways), Mr. Stanard, editor of the Va. Mag. of His., discovered and printed this good newsy item: "In a deposition dated 1674, and recorded in the Westmoreland County Court Order Book, Col. John Washington stated he was then forty-five (45) years of age."

This is not exactly all the facts connected with this important item. The affidavit was a part of the court proceedings when the will of a Richard Cole was presented in Court for probate. Washington's deposition, beginning:—"Col. John Washington, aged 45 years, or thereabouts, declared," &c.

This deposition is undated, but it could be no later than the date of the item that follows it; but as it is recorded between two items both dated, that is, next after one dated "5 Jan'y, 1675", (1674–5), and followed by one dated "12 Feb'y, 1674–5," it may be presumed that John was then aged 44–45, or 45–46, and born in 1628–29, or in 1629–30, or, as a compromise, in 1629.

Richard, or "Dick" Cole, at the proving of whose will Washington testified, was a queer character (see W. M. Quart., IV, p. 30). His abusive tongue spared few of his acquaintances. Of John Washington, it is reported he said: "He's an ass, negro-driver," whom he would have up before the governor and council, "as a Companie of Caterpillar fellowes," who "live upon my bills of export," or foreign exchange.

But not everyone was glad to know what this item told. For one, Dr. Tyler, the editor of the W. and M. Quar., who asked the appropriate question:—"As John Washington was born in 1629, what becomes of the Washington Pedigree, saying that John was the son of the Rev. Lawrence Washington, who was the proctor of Oxford University, in 1631, presumably unmarried then."

The approximation of the birth-date of Col. Washington is a more serious discovery than a gratifying one, for it opens up controversy over an unpleasant question. But it is only one of the peculiar situations that turn up in genealogy once in a while to puzzle its writers, for a genealogist's work is not one of all thrills; he is often up against ugly propositions which have to be handled with consideration.

Dr. Tyler, as above said, only thought that John's 1629 birth-date ruined Mr. Waters' claim to have discovered John's parentage and his long line of paternal ancestry, this, because the Rev. Lawrence Washington, 1602–1652, could not have been the proctor of the University of Oxford and also have a wife, which was contrary to University rules, at the time, seeing that John was born while his alleged father was the proctor.

In order to have authoritative information upon this alleged University rule, and an opinion on the speculation which was started by the acquaintance with it, a vital one to Col. John's pedigree, but more so to the morality of his parents, I stated the case to one of the Oxford Uni. officials, who should be familiar with its laws and customs, ancient as well as modern.

He replied confirming in the main Dr. Tyler's statement, by giving a different version as proof, saying: "Mr. Lawrence Washington, on 27 May, 1623, was elected to a Darbie Fellowship at Brasenose, and, as a Fellow, he would necessarily be unmarried." "He resigned his Fellowship on 30 Nov., 1633." "The Proctorship is a University office; not a College office. Lawrence Washington was elected the proctor of the University on 26 August, 1631, he being at that time a Fellow of Brasenose College," [and "necessarily" a bachelor, of course.]

We have from this first-hand information, Lawrence Washington, being, so far as the college was aware, an unmarried man in the ten years he was a privileged student at Brasenose, he being a Fellow, was the father of a child born before 30 Nov., 1633, when he resigned from the Fellowship, and before 23 June, 1635, when his apparently second child was baptised Lawrence.

Therefore, it may be assumed this Brasnose Fellow married clandestinely the farmer's daughter, and had a child by her while she resided at . . . . I know not where, while he passed himself off in college as a bachelor, and pursued his theological studies, and prepared himself for the ministry, on the principle, "Let not thy right hand know what thy left hand doeth."

Lawrence certainly married out of his social class, which was no crime, nor even a novelty in his class, yet it was not a match that would please his aristocratic family, which was allied to many families holding prominent positions in the social world. It may have been because of this mesalliance that Lawrence seems to have been "dropped" by his family. But I have no excuse for the Roades people ignoring him.

Of the six children of Lawrence and Amphillis Washington (for she was twice styled "Mrs. Washingon" in 1649, as above):

1. John Washington, born "*circa* 1629," as above. He went to Virginia, probably after his father's death, in 1652, as he was apparently a Captain of Northumber-

land Co. militia, before he was commissioned Major in the Westmoreland regiment, 4 April, 1655, and, in spite of higher ranks attached, was sometimes called Captain, and even so by his second wife, after his death, in her document of 1678. It used to be thought that he was the John who was at Bermuda in 1654, as stated in the will of Theodore Pargiter, but as Pargiter calls him "cousin John Washington in Bermuda," it seems more reasonable to place him as Sir John's second son John, since his mother, mentioned above, was Theodore's sister.

Another reason why it may be presumed with confidence that John Washington came to Virginia to reside, possibly earlier than 1652, or when he was 21, is suggested by the following: Whenever he came, he settled in the thriving county of Northumberland, a large county (which included the site of Washington city), and in that part of it from which the new county of Westmoreland was formed by an Act of Assembly in 1652-3, and was represented by two Burgesses in the Assembly of 1654. By another Act, 1654-5, it was ordered that original parishes should be relayed, surveyed and renamed. The old parish in which Captain Washington had his residence was renamed in his honor Washington parish, which surely should be almost convincing that John Washington had lived here years, and was not only a popular citizen, but a man, tho young, noted as a leader in public affairs.

2. Lawrence Washington, "the younger," as called in Mr. Knowling's will. He was their first child of record in the Tring parish register:—"Christened, on Our Lady's Day, 1635, Layaranc sonn of Layrance Washington." He was named as the residuary legatee of his estate by Mr. Knowling, his mother's step-father, in his will, 1649, he being Mr. Knowling's god-son. It has been thought that he was sometime a merchant at Luton, in Bedfordshire, before his removal to Virginia,

where he certainly was in May, 1659, as he was one of the subscribing witnesses, with his brother John, to the will of Col. Pope, at this date.

There was a Lawrence Washington, a merchant, at Luton, with whom Virginians had some dealings, and he could have been the son of Amphillis, the merchant being identified otherwise, but there is no positive evidence connecting Amphillis' son, Lawrence, with Luton as a merchant such as there is which identifies this son, and his brother, John, with her. There is evidence that he returned shortly to England and went to Luton, where he married at the parish church, 26 Jan., 1660, his first wife, Mary, daughter of Edmund Jones, of Luton, and brought her to Virginia, several years later, (some accounts say in 1667), and after the baptism of their child, recorded at the parish church, Luton, "Mary Washington, daughter of Mr. Lawrence and Mary," 22 Dec., 1663. Mary is mentioned in the wills of her grandfather Jones, 8 March, 1682, and her father, 1675.

Apparently, aside from these items connecting him with Luton, it is presumed he was influenced to settle there by the following two original, or further, reasons, (1), his mother's sister, Mrs. Elizabeth Fitzherbert, of Much Maltham, Essex, had acquaintance and interests in Luton, and (2), his cousin, Mrs. Esther Freeman, his uncle William Roades' daughter, resided at Luton.

Lawrence's earliest grant of Virginia land of record, is for 700 acres (in Stafford Co.), dated 27 Sep., 1667; his brother John was granted 5000 acres, same date and locality. Lawrence became a planter, died in Virginia, a few days before his brother John died, leaving a will and issue by two wives.

3. Elizabeth Washington. She was baptised at the Tring church, 17 August, 1636, and entered on the register as "daughter of Mr. Layarance Washington." [This is the only instance found (unless the "Mr. Law-

rence Washington," buried at Malden, Essex, in 1652, is proved to have been the husband of Amphillis, which has not been done yet, is another), where Amphillis' husband is styled "Mr."]. She is named in the will, 1697, of Mrs. Martha Hayward, of Virginia, as "my eldest sister, Mrs. Elizabeth Rumbold, in England."

It is not known when or where she married, nor has the name of her husband been found. It may be she did not marry in London, as her sister Margaret did, as she is not in the printed London marriage license lists. It is quite possible that her husband may have been a Hertfordshire man, because there were in her day, and from early times, Rumbold families in Herts. However, families of Rumbold, Rumbould, Rumboldz, Rambold, Rombolde, &c., are of record in Elizabeth's time in many English shires. Nothing further of her is known.

For a good reason, as will appear below, it is proper to notice here some of the Rumbold families in Herts. In 1316, a Nicholas Rumbaud, served on a jury at an Inq. P. M., and 1437, a James Rumbolde served in this county on the same kind of a jury. In 1567, a John Rumbold bought a farm in North Mimms parish from the Crown, and in 1606, John and Robert Rumbold were tenants of Clothall manor, and in 1670, there was a Rumbold family living in Walkhorne parish, and so on.

A member of a Rumbold family of Herts, long residing at the purchased manor of Woodhall, was created a baronet. An early member of his family, William Rumbold, was "controller of the great wardrobe," to Charles I., and surveyor-general of all the customs of England. Another Hertfordshire Rumbold worthy was that Colonel Richard Rumbold, born in 1622, who resided at "Rye House," a farm in Stanstead-Abbot parish, this county. He was one of the gentlemen who was captured after much trouble in finding him, tried and executed, after being found guilty of high treason, in 1683, for conspiring to murder King Charles II., and his brother James. His home, where he assembled his fellow conspirators, gave name to this historic plot. His son, Thomas Rumbold, Generosus'' (the keeper of the Rose Tavern, at Cambridge), was buried at Royston parish church, Herts.

4. Margaret Washington. There is no record of her baptism at the Tring parish church, but she was born in or about 1638–9, as learned from her marriage license, from which we also learn she was living in the parish of St. Giles-in-the-Field, Middlesex county, near London, when she married.

The printed abstract of her marriage license runs:— Margaret Washington, age 24 years, of St. Giles in the Field, Middlesex, and George Talbott, of the same, bachelor, gent., age 26 years. To be married at the same parish. Nothing further is known of her, excepting she is mentioned in the will of Mrs. Martha Hayward, as "my other sister, Mrs. Margaret Talbut," in England, (1697).

5. William Washington. He was baptised at the Tring church, 14 Oct., 1641. His father's name was not recorded. This is all that is known of him. He may have died young and unmarried, tho not again mentioned in the church register, beginning in 1584.

A careless blunder is made in Burke's "Visitations of Seats and Arms," in England (1852), in saying that Sir William Washington, of Packington manor, was this William, and "brother to John and Lawrence Washington, the Virginia immigrants." He was the brother of Sir John, the Rev. Lawrence, Mrs. Mewce, et al.

6. Martha Washington. Her birth and baptism not of Tring parish church record. From her statements in her will, 1697, she was apparently the youngest daughter and last child of Lawrence and Amphillis.

Col. John Washington, of Virginia, mentions her particularly in his will, 1675, saying:—"To my sister, Martha Washington, ten pounds out of the money I have in England, and whatever she should be owing to me for transporting herself into this country, and a year's accommodation after coming, and 4000 pounds of tobacco and cask." She came to Virginia and married a Mr. Hayward, and died here, leaving a will, written in Stafford Co., Va., 6 May, 1697, and proved 28 Dec. following. This will was found by Mr. Ford among papers at the Federal Dept. of State, and, as stated below, was of great value to Mr. Waters, in completing his Washington pedigree.

After giving legacies to a number of Virginia cousins, she enjoined her executors "with all convenient speed send to England to my eldest sister, Mrs. Elizabeth Rumbold, a Tunne of good weight Tobacco." [This commodity at that time was equivalent to our money, and was the only "cash" the colony had in circulation.] She also instructed that her executors:—"Doe likewise take freight and for England to my other sister, Mrs. Margaret Talbut, a Tunne of good weight of Tobacco."

An extant letter of John Washington (a son of Lawrence, the immigrant), dated Virginia, 22 June, 1699, to his half-sister, Mrs. Mary Gibson, of Hawnes, Bedfordshire (her father had given her all of his estate in England, by his will), mentions a letter from her to "my aunt Howard," as the surname Hayward was pronounced in Virginia.

By this, to me, accurate arrangement of the succession of the recorded issue of Lawrence and Amphillis Washington, it seems that the hiatus between the birth dates of their first child, John, "born in 1629," and Lawrence, their first child of church record, born in 1635, appears somewhat irregular (but then "you can never tell!" The unexpected happens as regularly as the expected), compared with the records of the rest of the brood.

Mrs. Amphillis (Roades) Washington, died at home, in the village of Tring, and was buried at Tring parish church, 16 Jan., 1654-5, according to the church record, and it is possible that all of her children were at the funeral.

On 8 Feb., 1654-5, about a month after the funeral, letters of administration on the personal estate of Mrs. Washington, by the Archdeacon's Court, at Wheathampstead, Herts, "to John Washington, the eldest lawful and natural son of Amphillis Washington, late of Tring, dec'd." "He being first sworn, deposed," &c. This valuable item settles three things. Amphillis' son John was then of full age, 21 years, as was necessary, so that he could qualify as administrator. That he was present in person in this Diocesan Court, on this date, 8 Feb., 1654-5, and that he must have returned shortly to Virginia, to personally receive his commission, on 4 April, 1655, promoting him from a captain to a major of the Westmoreland regiment, at the time that Thomas Speke (the first husband of Washington's third wife), was appointed its colonel, and Nathaniel Pope (Washington's second father-in-law), its lieut. col. The appointment of John Washington to be the major of the first regiment organized in this new county, shows he had been well established in the county of Northumberland, from which it was formed, for several years at least, and was a man of affairs, and popular in the county, where shortly the parish in which he resided was given his surname. It was not remarkable that he should have been in England when his mother died, it was only a coincidence, and this was his first trading voyage abroad, under Col. Pope, a business he followed on his own account for many years after this, and in this way, "came to Virginia" in several different years.

You have seen that Lawrence Washington, A. B., 1623, A. M., 1626, remained at the University as a theological student, preparing for the ministry, and received the B. D. degree, 10 March, 1632-3. And that from 27 May, 1623, when he was elected, till 30 Nov., 1633, when he resigned it, he was a Fellow of Brasenose College, and "necessarily unmarried." The college Fellowships of Lawrence's time, were still governed by feudal and monkish requirements and regulations, which had been enforced ever since there were colleges and fellowships in Great Britain and the continent. These ancient fellowships, regulations and customs were unchanged at Oxford University till in 1852, when they were revised and modified to conform more with modern customs and comforts.

Under the olden time Fellowship rules, to be elected a Fellow, the candidate had to be a graduate of the college that controlled the Fellowship he desired to join, and agree to continue to be a student in some special course. The advantages it would give a Fellow over ordinary students and the undergraduates were many, because he had more privileges. Another important feature was he was a co-partner in the Fellowship fund, and even in the college revenue, which was a great help to a poor student. Such advantages made them the aristocrats of the college world. Tho freer in his movements, he still had to conform with the fundamental college laws, as well as those of his Fellowship. The one law, passed on for centuries, that particularly interests us, is the one that a college student, an undergraduate or a post-graduate, must be and remain a bachelor while connected with the University and his college. Naturally, this was the *sine qua non* of the Fellowships, for the Fellow was only a higher grade college student, therefore, a Fellow was "necessarily unmarried." And one other rule was, should a Fellow while pursuing his studies, and enjoying the Fellowship, receive a salaried position, he must resign from his Fellowship, and should a Fellow marry, he also must resign. Since the ancient laws have been made more liberal, students may marry, and a married man can become, by special permission, members of a Fellowship, also Fellows may marry, if they get the permission, but not otherwise. A married Fellow, at Cambridge, is called a Fellow Commoner, and at Oxford, a Gentleman Commoner. These married Fellows are obliged to pay extra "to common," that is to dine with the regular Fellows at their table, the latter being known as the Dons of the college, while the married students who are Fellows, are Demi Dons.

Lawrence Washington we know was a Fellow. Was he married while a Fellow? When he got a salaried position he resigned from the Fellowship, for he could not hide that fact. We have seen that in paying his debts, he was an honorable man, and in this other matter he had nothing to conceal.

If it was not that it was certainly possible for Lawrence Washington, B. D., after he resigned from his Fellowship, to marry and have a child born to him, before Lawrence, Jr., was born, then the 1629 bugaboo deserved the prominence I have given it. But even with Mr. Washington's schedule satisfactory, there seems to be no way of being able to eliminate the ugly thing *toto cœlo* as I should like to, by exposing it as fake item, a forgery and counterfeit, and the figuring on it is after all, only amusement, but it is certainly the proper thing to do.

For instance, John Washington's undated deposition, in which he gives his then age, I have said, has position in the Order Book of the Court, between two dated items, showing it should have been dated Feb., 1673–4. In this deposition, made under oath presumably, he says his age is "45, or thereabouts." We understand "thereabout" to mean near to, or close to. He might have said, if pushed for a definite answer, aged 44 or 43, (and may have gone further up the gamut of age); but what consolation does this bring? It only places his birth in either 1628–9, or 1629–0, or 1630, or 1631, according as reckoned by O. S. or N. S. In any of these years, Lawrence Washington was "necessarily unmarried."

Again, it may have been in 1674 that "thereabouts" meant time within the fourth decade, "between 40 and 50 years of age," and "45" was the compromise date. But John, in 1674, should have been only 40, to satisfy us. Since it was possible for Mr. Washington to have married openly in Dec., 1633, and son John to have been born in August, 1634, and followed by the birth of his brother Lawrence, Jr. (tho we do not have the date of his birth; only that of his baptism), in June, 1635. With John "born August, 1634," he would be old enough in 1655, to have gone to Virginia, become a militia captain, the supercargo for Pope, of Virginia, and his mother's administrator, and we would have been satisfied. But this "Again" idea is too utopian to be accepted seriously. The Court matter in which Col. Washington's name appeared, was not a personal one, nor had his age any bearing whatever on it, therefore, his statement of his age was not a false pretense, as the giving of his age was only a matter of form.

Probably the last chance of the reduction of "45" might be found in the original entry in the Court record. But this has been tried, and "45, or thereabouts," is the correct reading of the entry.

Now what, may I ask, will enable us to exclaim: "Colonel, you were wrong. You were only 39, or 40 years old in Feb., 1673–4?

In conclusion, I have this to say to Washington descendants, there are some features apparent in what I have reported, which are worthy of more prominence, but as they wipe out the stigma the Rev. Lawrence seems to be under, they separate them, for a while probably, from the long Washington pedigree.

While here is proof aplenty that Lawrence was a son of the lord of Brington, and became a Fellow, a proctor, a B. D., &c., at Oxford, and then the rector of Purleigh, 1634–1643, and a diocesan surrogate, 1648–9, there is no proof that this minister was the husband of Amphillis Roades, or that he was the father of the children baptised at Tring church, or that he had ever resided there, or that he was the Lawrence Washington buried at Malden church.

It is only assumed that the Lawrence Washingtons who are styled "Mr." once only on the Tring parish register, and once on that of Malden, are identical with the rector of Purleigh, because a minister was thus entitled in the records of that period, but that is not enough, for to his name it was the custom to write the suffix "clerk" (especially if a B. D., Oxon.), his legal appellation in the Church of England. This may be seen in the above-mentioned Chancery suit, 1640, where he is "Mr." and "clerk." The designation of "Mr." was not sufficient to identify a man as a cleric, because, for one reason, the school teacher was styled "Master" then, and this title was abbreviated into "Mr."

Nor is there proof that the father of the children baptised at Tring, was the Lawrence Washington buried at Malden. The latter was buried in 1652, and you have read there was a Mrs. Washington whom a Commission made a beneficiary of the church and parish the Rev. Lawrence Washington was ousted from by the Cromwellians. As it was in August, 1649, it was decided to aid "the wife of the Rector" who had been "plundered," and you have seen he was a surrogate in the previous Jan. I should not be surprised if it was found sometime that this lady asking aid was then his widow, and that the former rector died between Jan.,

1648–9, and August, 1649, and that the lady was not Amphillis.

It can be seen there is good proof that the Virginians, Col. John, Lawrence and Martha Hayward, were children of Mrs. Amphillis Washington of Tring, and that "Mr. Lawrence Washington," also of Tring, 1635–41, (and several years later, it may be assumed, because two children were born after 1641), was their father, but proof is certainly required to establish that he and the minister were one and the same man.

In 1893, Mr. Waters was positive he had finished at last his many years' quest satisfactorily, by placing, as he expressed it, the right keystone in his "Washington arch," when he used the information found in the Martha Hayward will. In 1886, he had no hope nor expectation he ever would complete his undertaking, which was to justify his theory that the Rev. Lawrence Washington of Purleigh, was the husband of Amphillis, and the father of Col. John of Virginia, for he knew, as well as any of the critics of his Washington work, its weakness, namely, the lack of proper proof positive to establish beyond doubt that "the Rev. Lawrence Washington, clerk," of Purleigh, and the "Mr. Lawrence Washington" of Tring, were identical. This was his theorem, and the following items his sole proof, which he was sure made a perfect "keystone" to bind and make his perfect "arch."

One of these items is from the will of Mrs. Martha Hayward, sister of Col. John Washington, in which she mentions "my sister, Mrs. Elizabeth *Rumbold,* in England." The other item being from the will of Mrs. Mewce, a sister of the Rev. Lawrence Washington, in which she mentions "Elizabeth *Rumball,* my niece."

Mr. Waters was quick to jump at the pleasant conclusion that the two named Elizabeths were the same person, because "their surnames were the same," altho written differently, one "Rumbold," the other "Rumball," one being the accidental perversion of the other, but he did not go so far as to venture which should be the correct surname for both.

Being self-convinced of this, he sees that Amphillis' "Mrs. Elizabeth Rumbold," being the niece of Mrs. Mewce, "Mrs. Rumbold" only could have been the daughter of Mrs. Mewce's brother, the rector of Purleigh, therefore this clergyman was the husband of Amphillis and the father of her six children.

From this deduction, the material, the "keystone" was made, and it completed the "Washington Arch," and that's all there is to this great genealogical discovery. The conjunction of the two will items is the only "proof" that the Rev. Lawrence Washington was the father of Colonel John Washington. Should it be indisputable, it leaves the clergyman and the colonel each with a "skeleton." Otherwise, in which of the numerous Washington families of England belonged the "Mr. Lawrence Washington," of Tring, Herts, 1636, who married Amphillis Roades about 1628, and was alive about 1642?

Incidentally this is the place to mention that about the time of these occurrences, there was a Washington family owning and residing at Beaches manor, in Brent-Pelham parish, Herts. The lord of this manor was Adam Washington, a barrister of Lincoln's Inn, who bought this manor in 1640, owning at the time two others in the county. His wife, living in 1659, was Elizabeth, daughter of Francis Floyer, lord of Brent-Pelham manor, high sheriff of Herts, in 1648. Their daughter Margaret Washington, of Euen parish, Herts, aged 20, her parents dead, had license to marry, in 1679, William Wright.

I wish for the memory of Mr. Waters, that his deduction had been as plausible as pleasing, but we can't get away from the fact that for centuries there have been two distinct families in England, often in the same county, called, the one Rumbold, the other Rumball; the niece was born to one, and the sister married into the other.

Because there were, and are, so many families of each of these surnames, and for want of space, I shall mention only a few instances of Rumball (having done the same for Rumbold), they being suitable to this review. As mentioned of Rumbold, Rumball, too, has had many variations, or corruptions, as Rombold;—Rumboll, Rumbell, Rumble, and even Rumbello, to match Rumbold's Romboldus.

William Rumball and wife Elizabeth had a son baptised at St. Paul's, Covent Garden, London, 22 Feb., 1662–3. "Mr. William Rumball" was buried at this church ("he died of ye Plague"), 6 July, 1665. Richard Rumball, of Great Buddon parish, Essex, widower, age 50, had license to marry, 16 May, 1661. Richard Rumball, and wife Elizabeth, had a daughter baptised 17 June, 1683, at Christ Church, New Gate, London. Buried at this church, 20 Oct., 1685, Mrs. Elizabeth Rumball, and on the 23d, Richard Rumball. Edmund Rumball, of Christ Church parish, London, aged 25, had license to marry, 15 June, 1675. John Rumball, Gent, of Shefford, Bedford, widower, age 50, had license to marry in London, 6 April, 1665.

Edward Rumball, of Fullham, Essex, Esq., age 25, had license, dated 13 Sep., 1687, to marry Lady Anne Villiers, of St. Margaret parish, Westminster, (London), age 19, daughter of the Rt. Hon. George Villiers, Lord Viscount of Grandison. The Viscount was a near relative of George Villers, Duke of Buckingham, whose half-sister Lady Anne Villiers, was the wife of Sir William Washington, of Kensington and Thistleworth, Middlesex, brother to Sir John, Rev. Lawrence, Mrs. Mewce, &c.

John Newdigate removed with his family from London to Boston, Mass., in 1632. His son and heir, Nathaniel Newdigate, returned to London, became a merchant, and died there leaving a will, dated 22 Sep., 1668. He named his wife, Isabella, his ex'trix, and his brothers-in-law, Sir John Lewis, Edward Rumball, of the Savoy, a precinct of the Strand, London, and Edmund White, merchant of London, overseers. Among his legatees—"To Edward Rumball, and his wife, Anne, ten pounds a piece." "To my niece, Mary Rumball, five pounds." Isabella and Anne, mentioned, and Joan, wife of Sir F. Holles, were sisters of Sir John Lewis.

If it is admitted as a fact that there was always a Rumbold family and a Rumball family, it proves that "niece Rumball" was not "sister Rumbold." This agreed upon, then there is no known proof that the clergyman of Purleigh was the Mister of Tring. Therefore, the clergyman was not the father of the colonel, hence, the latter was, no doubt, born in wedlock. Otherwise, if the niece and the sister were identical, it has to be believed, through the evidence, that the colonel was illegitimate, unless we prefer to think the Fellow lived a double life, a bachelor at the University, and a married man and father somewhere else. It would not be fair to Amphillis to say she never was married, since a record of her marriage has not been found, because the circumstantial evidence of the Tring parish church register is in her favor. However, it only shows her husband was a "Mr." Lawrence Washington. Who he was it is charitable to those concerned, to say he has never been identified, therefore, the authoritative Royal Descent line of the Rev. Lawrence Washington remains in abeyance so far as Colonel John Washington of Virginia is concerned, because there is no proof he was the son of the clergyman.

THE WASHINGTON PEDIGREE.

BY G. ANDREWS MORIARTY, JR., A.M., LL.B.

(A reply to an article by Mr. Charles H. Browning in the October 1921 number of THE PENNSYLVANIA MAGAZINE OF HISTORY AND BIOGRAPHY.)

In the October issue of THE PENNSYLVANIA MAGAZINE OF HISTORY AND BIOGRAPHY there appears a long article by Mr. Charles H. Browning, the author of "Americans of Royal Descent" and other works, entitled "The Washington Pedigree; Corrigenda and Addenda," in which he proceeds to throw new light upon the Washington pedigree as hitherto published. As to the greater part of this I do not profess to pass an opinion because it was not of interest to me, but when I came to the third part, entitled "The Legitimation of Col. John Washington," in which Mr. Browning, to his own satisfaction, demolishes the pedigree constructed with great care many years ago by my old friend, Fitz Gilbert Waters, I felt some curiosity to examine the matter carefully in order to see whether the able author of "Americans of Royal Descent" had really anything to add to the work already compiled by the ablest and most careful antiquary that this country has hitherto produced.

The result of this investigation has not tended to change the opinion that I formed many years ago regarding Mr. Waters' Washington pedigree and I fear, to use the language of Lord Coke's daughter, Mrs. Sadler, in her letter to Roger Williams that there is great danger that Mr. Browning's "new lights may become dark lanterns," for the arguments used by him to disprove Mr. Waters' work are unconvincing.

The Washington pedigree as compiled by Mr.

Waters states that the father of the emigrant to Virginia, John Washington, was Rev. Lawrence Washington, a younger son of Lawrence Washington, of Sulgrave and Brington in Northants. This Lawrence Washington was an M.A. of Oxford and was from 27 May 1623 to 30 November 1633 a Fellow of Brasenose College at that University when he resigned as a Fellow. For this latter date I have no authority but Mr. Browning himself, but I assume that Mr. Browning is correct when he says that he notified the college authorities of his resignation on that date. Mr. Browning states that from 14 March 1633/4 to November 1643 he was rector of Purleigh in Essex, and at the latter time he was ejected from his living by the Parliamentary authorities. The first date as given by Mr. Browning is incorrect as will be seen by reference to "Waters' Gleanings" giving the original document. He was instituted to the living of Purleigh on 14 March of 1632/3, one year earlier than the date given by Mr. Browning. He paid his composition on 22 of March 1632/3. On 4 of April 1633 "he informed Brasenose College that he was to be inducted in a benefice" and on 30 November 1633, according to Mr. Browning, he notified the Fellows of his resignation. He also appears to have been acting as Surrogate in the Archdeaconry of Herts on 29 January 1649/50. It would seem, therefore, extremely likely that as soon as he became assured of the living in the Spring of 1633 he took steps to marry and with this in mind informed the college authorities that he had received a living. It would also seem most probable that he thereupon married and that shortly after, within a few months, he sent in his resignation as a Fellow of Brasenose. I do not believe that so long as he resigned his Fellowship within a few months after marriage that there was any hard and fast enforcement of the rule requiring the actual resignation to take place before the marriage. It seems that Rev. Lawrence Washington made sure of a living before resigning his Fellowship, that he married at once after his induction and that John Washington was born in January 1633/4 and he may have been so born even if marriage did not take place until after November 30, 1633, when we consider the social customs of seventeenth-century England. All this, however, is not at all vital to the argument that I propose to put forward, which will show that nothing has been produced to show that John Washington could not have been born anywhere between 30 November 1633 and August 1634.

Mr. Waters in a long and carefully prepared analysis of the evidence, that I shall not now go into, except so far as is necessary in considering Mr. Browning's new finds, because it is easily available to everyone in "Waters' Gleanings," identified this Rev. Lawrence Washington with the Lawrence Washington, who married Amphillis, the daughter-in-law of Andrew Knolling Gent. of Tring and had issue John, Lawrence, William, Elizabeth, Margaret and Martha. Of these children Lawrence was baptized at Tring 23 June 1635, Elizabeth was baptized there 17 August 1636, and William was baptized there 14 October 1641.

Mr. Browning admits that this Lawrence Washington, who married Amphillis, was the father of the emigrants to Virginia, John and Lawrence, but he denies that he is identical with the Rev. Lawrence Washington, M.A., the son of the Lord of the Manor of Brington.

Let us now examine what evidence he produces to destroy this identification. Briefly stated his argument comes down to this: Col. John Washington, the emigrant, deposed in Westmoreland County, Va., "aged 45 years or thereabouts," in an undated deposition, which Mr. Browning dates between 5 January 1675 (1674/5) and 12 February 1674/5, because he finds it between two items of those dates. From this he argues that John Washington must have been born in 1629 and, as at that time Rev. Lawrence Washington was still a Fellow at Brasenose, and hence unmarried, he cannot be the father of this John. Moreover, he observes that the second son, Lawrence, was not baptized until 23 June 1635, some six years later, which is a large gap between the first and second child in a seventeenth century family.

We must now examine this new and important discovery with the greatest care, as, if his arguments are correct, the mass of evidence so carefully collected by Mr. Waters and all forcing one to the conclusion that the two Lawrences are identical is seriously shaken. In the first place the deposition referred to is undated, but Mr. Browning boldly dates it between 5 January 1674/5 and 12 February 1674/5 because it lies between two items of these dates. With regard to this conclusion I would suggest that Mr. Browning take to heart his own admonition regarding "Washington Genealogy" and "Watch His Step," because while his conclusion as to the date is probably correct, it is by no means certain that it is so. If Mr. Browning is personally familiar with original records of the seventeenth century he must surely know that the transcribers often put in items of a later date between items of an earlier period provided there was sufficient space left between two entries, as was often the case. If he will examine the printed first volume of the town records of Portsmouth, R. I., he will find entries of the early nineteenth century wedged in between entries of the seventeenth century in this earliest book of Portsmouth records that commence about 1638. Of course it may be that the nature of the records upon the same page with the deposition in the Westmoreland Order Book, referred to by Mr. Browning, conclusively shows that the undated deposition must be dated between the two dates assigned to it by Mr. Browning but there is nothing set forth in his article to show this. I do not quarrel with the date assigned by him to the deposition, but merely wish to point out that he cannot positively assert, on the evidence so far presented by him, that his assigned date is correct; in other words I would suggest that he exercise some caution in arriving at a positive conclusion.

Now let us assume that the date assigned to the document in question is correct, namely between 5 January 1674/5 and 12 February 1674/5, then John Washington was born in January or February 1629/30 or *thereabouts*. Mr. Browning assumes that he must limit the period in which John Washington was born to 1628/30. Surely a person versed in seventeenth-century depositions knows that the deponents almost invariably stated their ages a year or so out of the way and frequently even three or four years out of the way. If Mr. Browning will take the trouble to examine the printed Court Files of Essex Co. Mass., and abstract the depositions taken therein and compare the various depositions made by the same persons or will compare the ages given therein with the records of the deponents' births or baptisms he will find the above statement to be true. I refer to the printed Essex County Quarterly Court Files, because there are to be found in compact and convenient form a greater number of seventeenth-century depositions than anywhere else in print. I would refer him at random to the deposition of William Beale of Marblehead "aged about 22 years" on 28 March 1654 and to his deposition aged "about 38 years" November 1666 and to that made by him in June 1667 "aged about 38 years" (Cf. Marblehead Vital Records printed by the Essex Institute Vol. III, page 32 and Essex Quarterly Court Files Vol. 1, p. 331, Vol. III, pp. 368 and 419). Here we have one man stating that he was born about 1632, about 1628 and about 1629. Likewise William Nick of Marblehead deposed in June 1661 "aged about 35 years" and again 22:1: 1666/7 "aged about 35 years" and again in March 1669 "aged about 35 years," and again in March 1669 "aged about 35 years," and in September 1670 "aged about 40 years" (Cf. Printed Marblehead Vital Records, Vol. III, p. 38).

Since this is so, what is to prevent John Washington having been born between 30 November 1633 and August 1634? Rev. Lawrence Washington was certainly instituted into the living of Purleigh on 14 March 1632/3. Why should he not have married at once or at any rate soon after 30 November 1633 and had his eldest son born by August 1634 or even earlier, for it was extremely common for the first child of seventeenth-century marriages to be born a few months after marriage, as our early New England Court Records amply prove,* for surely a deposition of a man aged about 45 or thereabouts in 1674/5 covers a range from 1627 to 1634 viewed in the light of other contemporaneous depositions.

Mr. Browning's next point is a most remarkable one and one that it was absolutely necessary for him to make in order, deposition or no deposition, to shake the Waters pedigree because it was the point that absolutely clinched the identification of Lawrence Washington, the father of the Virginia emigrants, with the Rev. Lawrence Washington. Among the children of Lawrence and Amphillis Washington were Elizabeth and Martha. Martha went to Virginia and married a Mr. Hayward or Howard. She made her will in Stafford Co. Va. on 6 May 1697, proved 8 December 1697 in which she leaves to her eldest sister Mrs. Elizabeth *Rumbold* a "Tunne of good weight Tobacco." Now the will of Elizabeth, widow of Francis Mewce, the

---

* A sensible admission. Everyone will hope for some more satisfactory conclusion.—(Ed.)

known sister of Rev. Lawrence Washington, of Brasenose and Purleigh, dated 11 August 1676, proved 12 December 1676, leaves "to my neice Mrs. Elizabeth *Rumball* five pounds." Here was a difficult piece of evidence for Mr. Browning to meet, as it tied the two families together and in order to do away with it he was forced to argue that Elizabeth Rumball and Elizabeth Rumbold were two different persons. Surely a person who has been investigating original records as long as Mr. Browning has not failed to note the many varieties of spelling family names that characterized the seventeenth century. To cite one instance in the preceding century we find the name Nansiglos spelled Nansicles, Nansigles, Nantigles, Nansiglas, etc. Surely this is no better than Rumball and Rumbold. I really cannot help feeling that he was straining to meet a fact which had to be disproved in order to give his argument any standing. But it is further evident that he is not entirely familiar with the records of the Rumbold family of Herts whose history he alludes to in his article (page 352). For his further information permit me to refer him to the Herts Genealogist and Antiquary Vol. 3, page 149, where he will find in the Herts Feet of Fines, a fine of *"John Roomball alias Rumboulde* for lands in Weston, Trinity term 36 Elizabeth (1594).

For a similar use of the alias to denote a variant of the same name I can refer Mr. Browning to "The Visitation of Oxon and Bucks 1574" (unpublished) preserved at the Herald's College pp. 104 and 104b where in the pedigree of Gifford of Middle Claydon we find that Roger Gifford married Mary, daughter of William Nansiglas alias Nansicles.

For a further example of the spelling of seventeenth-century names I can refer Mr. Browning to the Suffolk County Ship Money Returns for 1639 edited by my old friend Vincent B. Redstone, Esq., F.S.A. of

Woodbridge in that County. He will there find our New England name of Tarbell spelled Torball and Torbould, and the old Essex name of Corball appears as Corball, Corbell, Corbold, Corboul, Corbowl, Corboll, Corbull.

Examination of Mr. Browning's "Magna Charta Barons" Philadelphia 1898, page 162, under the name of Converse shows that he is not always so rigid upon the spelling of seventeenth-century names. There he states that the name of Edward Converse the early settler of Woburn was Edward Converse or Conyers and that he was a member of the gentle Conyers family of Northants through whom he deduced his descent from a Magna Charta baron. As a matter of fact Edward Converse was a yeoman and has been proved beyond all doubt to have been a member of a very respectable yeoman family of Essex living in the vicinity of Navestock and his ancestry has been traced back for a number of generations in this good old yeoman stock, but the baronial descent assigned to him by Mr. Browning has faded away in the light of critical research.*

One other point of great significance should be noted. Mrs. Hayward in Virginia mentions her sister Margaret Galbut (Talbut) in England. This Margaret was the sister of the Virginia emigrants and as Margaret Washington of St. Giles-in-the-Fields spinster, aged 24 she had license to marry George Talbot of the same 27 February 1662/3 (Chester's London Mar. Lic. p. 1312). Now Margaret, the known sister of Rev. Lawrence Washington, married 1st Samuel Thornton of St. Giles-in-the-Fields whose will dated 9 January 1666, proved 2 May 1666, was witnessed by Elizabeth Mewce and *Margaret Talbot* (P.C.C. Carr 41). It seems most

---

* Logically this is a plea that Mr. Browning show leniency in his conclusion concerning the Washington matter similar to that accorded certain others of so-called Royal Descent for whose records Mr. Moriarty has little respect. Otherwise it has no place in the article.—(Ed.)

likely that Margaret Washington the sister of the emigrants was living, at the time of her marriage, in the family of Samuel and Margaret (Washington) Thornton in the Parish of St. Giles-in-the-Fields, London.

To give genealogical work any value absolute accuracy is required, but there are times when rigid and literal interpretations of seventeenth-century expressions and statements instead of producing that accuracy produce the opposite result and it is only by long and personal familiarity with the original records of the sixteenth and seventeenth centuries that one can acquire a knowledge of the looseness with which language was then used that will enable him to give it a proper interpretation.

[Several communications have been received with regard to an article entitled "The Washington Pedigree," and the above, by Mr. G. Andrews Moriarty, Jr., is printed because it is the most painstaking and detailed of the arguments presented. The interested reader is referred in the matter of John Washington's birth, *first*—to Colonel Washington's deposition (undated, but about 24th June, 1674), *second*—to a legal paper dated 5th January, 1674-5, and *third*—to a legal paper dated 12th February, 1674-5. (Westmoreland Co. Va. Court Records.) Washington's deposition was made to prove the validity of Mr. Cole's will, and the Will Book says this will was probated 24th June, 1674. Richard Cole died in 1674. John Washington at about this date gave his age as 45 years, and therefore he was born in 1629 or thereabouts, when his alleged father was a divinity student, a Fellow of Brasenose College, Oxford, and presumably unmarried. The Year-Book of the Society of Colonial Wars, 1898, has John Washington born in 1629 and the date is therefore not a new matter.—EDITOR.]

THE WHARTON FAMILY. [+]

BY ANNE H. WHARTON.

THOMAS WHARTON,[2] who emigrated to Pennsylvania at an early date, was the son of Richard Wharton,[1] of Kellorth, in the Parish of Orton (or Overton),[*] Westmorelandshire, England. His parents were members of the Church of England, and on the 16th of October, 1664, he was baptized in All Saints Church, Orton. At what period he adopted the tenets of the Friends I am unable to discover, but at the time of his marriage he was certainly in full membership with their Society. The marriage took place January 20, 1688-9, O. S., at the Bank Meeting House in Philadelphia, where he and Rachel Thomas, in the quaint phraseology of their marriage certificate, " having declared their Intentions of taking each other in marriage before several public meetings of the People of God, called Quakers," . . . " according to the good order used amongst them, whose Proceedings therein, after a deliberate Consideration thereof, were approved by the said Meetings: They appearing Clear of all others. Now these are to Certify all whom it may concern, that for the full accomplishing of their said Intentions, this Second day of the Eleventh month, called January, in the Year One thousand Six Hundred, Eighty and Eight. They" . . . " appeared in a public Assembly of the aforesaid People and others mett together for that end and purpose . . . and (according to the Example of the holy men of God recorded in the Scriptures of Truth) in a Solemn manner, he the said Thomas taking the said Rachel by the hand, did openly declare as followeth—Friends, in the presence of God and before you his people do I take Rachel Thomas to be my wife and do promise to be a faithful and loving husband, until death separate us." After recording a similar declaration on the part of Rachel, the certificate

---

[*] See Clark's British Gazetteer, London, 1852.
[+] An expanded version of this work was published in 1880.

proceeds—" And the said Thomas Wharton and Rachel Thomas, as a further Confirmation thereof, did then and there to these Presents set their hands,   THOMAS WHARTON.
RACHEL WHARTON."

Among the witnesses were Micah and James Thomas, Sen., also Samuel Richardson, William Salway, and William Southeby, about that time members of the Provincial Council, John White, then speaker of the Assembly, and William Bradford, the celebrated printer.

Rachel Thomas was born Sept. 1, 1664, in Monmouthshire, Wales. She survived her husband nearly thirty years, and died in Philadelphia, June 10, 1747.

Thomas Wharton was principally engaged in mercantile pursuits, and was unambitious of political distinction; he was, however, on October 6, 1713, elected a member of the Common Council of the city of Philadelphia, and gave an active attendance to his duties in that position until his death. He remained during his life an earnest member of the religious denomination to which, in his youth, he had attached himself. He died in Philada. July 31, 1718, leaving a considerable estate to be divided between his children.

Thomas and Rachel Wharton had eight children, all b. in Philada.

3. JOSEPH, b. Nov. 25, 1689; bu. July 24, 1690.
4. RICHARD, d. unm. Philada. Mar. 5, 1721.
5. MARY, d. unm. Philada. Jan. 10, 1763, aged 67.
6. JAMES.
7. THOMAS. m. Christ Church, Philada. Sept. 12, 1728, **Mary Curry.** In his will, proved 1730, he styles himself " Mariner," and bequeathes all his estate to his wife. She m. 2dly, in 1736, Richard Grafton.
8. RACHEL, d. unm.; bu. Aug. 7, 1735.
9. JOHN, m. Mary Dobbins.
10. JOSEPH, b. Aug. 4, 1707; m. 1st, **Hannah Carpenter;** and 2dly, Hannah Ogden.

9. JOHN WHARTON[3] (Thomas,[2] Richard[1]) m., Chester Co., Nov. 2, 1727, Mary, dau. of James Dobbins. She was b. 1696, and d. Philada. Jan. 10, 1763. After his marriage he resided for

many years in Chester Co., of which from 1730 to 1737 he was annually selected coroner. He had five children.

11. JAMES, bu. Philada. May 4, 1785, aged 53 years; m. 1st, Mary Hogg; and 2dly, Christiana Redd.
12. THOMAS, b. Chester Co., 1735; m. 1st, Susannah Lloyd; and 2dly, Elizabeth Fishbourne.
13. JOHN, d. Oct. 22, 1799, aged 67; m. Rebecca Chamless.
14. RACHEL, m. William Crispin.
15. MARY, m. —— Baxter.

10. JOSEPH WHARTON³ (Thomas,² Richard¹), b. Philada. Aug. 4, 1707; m. 1st, Philada. March 5, 1729-30, Hannah, dau. of John Carpenter,* by his wife, Ann Hoskins. She was b. Philada. Nov. 23, 1711, and d. July 14, 1751. He m. 2dly, June 7, 1752, Hannah, wid. of John Ogden, and dau. of Robert Owen, by his wife, Susannah Hudson.† She was b. Phila. March 16, 1720-1, and d. Jan. 1791. He was a very successful merchant, but towards the close of his life retired from business, and lived at his country seat, Walnut Grove, which soon after his death was made famous as the scene of the Meschianza. He d. in Philada. and was bu. in Friends Ground, July 27, 1776. By his 1st wife he had eleven children, all b. in Philada.

16. THOMAS, b. Jan. 15, 1730-1; m. Rachel Medcalf.
17. SAMUEL, b. May 3, 1732; m. Sarah Lewis.
18. JOSEPH, b. March 21, 1733-4; m. Sarah Tallman.
19. RACHEL, b. June 7, 1736; bu. Jan. 6, 1736-7.
20. JOHN, b. Jan. 17, 1737-8; d. 1770.
21. WILLIAM, b. March 12, 1740; m. Oct. 15, 1767, Susannah, dau. of Jacob Medcalf by his wife Susannah Hudson, b. June 6, 1734. He d. s. p. Will proved, Philada. Jan. 21, 1805.
22. GEORGE, b. March 13, 1741-2; bu. March 17, 1741-2.
23. CHARLES, b. Jan. 11, 1743-4; m. 1st, Jemima Edwards; 2dly, Elizabeth Richardson; and 3dly, Hannah Redwood.
24. ISAAC, b. Sept. 15, 1745; m. Margaret Rawle.
25. CARPENTER, b. Aug. 30, 1747; m. Elizabeth Davis.
26. BENJAMIN, b. Feb. 12, 1749-50; d. Sept. 8, 1754.

* Son of Samuel Carpenter, many years a member of the Provincial Council, and Treasurer of the Province, by his wife, Hannah, dau. of Abraham Hardiman.

† Daughter of William Hudson, sometime Mayor of Philada., by his wife, Elizabeth, dau. of Samuel Richardson. Richardson was a member of the Provincial Council, 1688-93.

By his 2d wife he had seven children.

27. MARY, b. April 3, 1755; m. William Sykes.
28. ROBERT, b. Jan. 12, 1757; m. Salome Chancellor.
29. BENJAMIN, b. April 29, 1759; d. April 9, 1764.
30. JAMES, b. Jan. 3, 1761; d. Jan. 9, 1761.
31. RACHEL, b. Aug. 27, 1762; m. William Lewis.
32. HUDSON, b. Feb. 21, 1765; d. Aug. 10, 1771.
33. FRANKLIN, b. July 23, 1767; m. Mary Clifton.

11. JAMES WHARTON[4] (John,[3] Thomas,[2] Richard[1]) m. 1st, Mary, dau. of Peregrine Hogg, sometime of Philada. but finally of London, Mercer, by his wife Mary Fitzwater.* She was bu. Philada. April 13, 1772, aged about 35 years. He m. 2dly, Sept. 14, 1773, Christiana Redd, who d. before him. During the Revolution he was the proprietor of a rope-walk, and furnished a large portion of the cordage for the vessels of the State Navy. He was bu. in Friends Ground, Philada. May 4, 1785, aged 53 years. Of his seven children all but the last named were certainly by his first wife.

34. REYNOLD, m.
35. JAMES.
36. REBECCA, d. unm. Aug. 31, 1807, aged 46.
37. PEREGRINE, b. Feb. 14, 1765; m. Jane Brown.
38. GEORGE, m. Mary Doughty.
39. MORRIS.
40. DEBORAH CLAYPOOLE, m. Philada. May 7, 1795, Isaac H. Jackson.

12. THOMAS WHARTON,† Junr.[4] (John,[3] Thomas,[2] Richard[1]), b. Chester County, 1735; m. 1st, Christ Church, Philada. Nov. 4, 1762, Susannah, dau. of Thomas Lloyd,‡ by his wife, Susannah Kearney.§ She d. Oct. 24, 1772, and he m. 2dly,

---

* Daughter of George Fitzwater, who, with his parents, Thomas and Mary Fitzwater, of Hamworth, Middlesex, Eng., was among the companions of Penn on his first visit to Penna. in 1683.

† A biographical sketch of Gov. Wharton will be published hereafter.

‡ Son of Thomas Lloyd, and grandson Thomas Lloyd, President of the Council, 1684 to 1688, and again 1690 to 1693.

§ Daughter of Philip Kearney, of Philada., by his wife Rebecca, daughter of Lionel Britton. In the "Hill Family," by J. J. Smith, Philada., 1854, she is said to have been Susannah *Owen;* but Susannah, wife of Thomas Lloyd and daughter of Philip Kearney, is a party to a deed from Rebecca Kearney, et al., to Edmund Kearney, and in the will of Joanna Kearney, who was also a party to the deed, Susannah Wharton is named as a niece of the testatrix.

Dec. 7, 1774, Elizabeth, dau. of William Fishbourne,* by his wife, Mary Tallman. She was b. Sept. 1752, and d. Philada. April 24, 1826. He d. at Lancaster, May 22, 1778. By his first wife he had five children.

41. LLOYD WHARTON, m. Mary Rogers and d. s. p.
42. KEARNEY, d. Jan. 4, 1848, aged 82; m. Maria Salter.
43. WILLIAM MOORE, d. Aug. 14, 1816, aged 49; m. 1st, Mary Waln; and 2dly, Deborah Shoemaker.
44. SARAH NORRIS, d. 1836, aged 64; m. 1st, Dr. Benjamin Tallman; and 2dly, Samuel Courtauld.
45. SUSANNAH, bu. Philada. Feb. 2, 1773.

By his 2d wife he had three children.

46. Mary, b. Sept. 7, 1775; d. unm. Philada. June, 1799.
47. THOMAS FISHBOURNE, b. Nov. 10, 1776; d. unm. Philada. Jan. 1865.
48. FISHBOURNE, b. Aug. 10, 1778; m. 1st, Susan Shoemaker; and 2dly, Mary Ann Shoemaker.

13. JOHN WHARTON[4] (John,[3] Thomas,[2] Richard[1]) m. Philada. June 24, 1761, Rebecca Chamless. He was a shipbuilder in Philada., and during the Revolution, built for the Pennsylvania Navy two men-of-war, the Experiment and the Washington. He was a member of Continental Navy Board, 1778–1780. He d. Philada. Oct. 22, 1799, aged 67 years. His children were

49. CHAMLESS, b. 1769; d. April 20, 1775.
50. CHAMLESS, d. unm. Philada. Oct. 22, 1802, aged 22 years.

14. RACHEL WHARTON[4] (John,[3] Thomas,[2] Richard[1]) m. Friends Meeting, Philada. Dec. 10, 1762, William Crispin, son of Silas Crispin, of Burlington, N. J. He was a commissary of the American Army. Collector of Excise. He d. Philada. April 24, 1797, aged 60 years. They had six children.

51. WILLIAM.
52. SARAH, m. William Levis.

* His father, William Fishbourne, a member of the Provincial Council, 1723 to 1731, was born in Talbot County, Md., where his parents, Ralph and Sarah (Lewis) Fishbourne, then resided. William Fishbourne, the elder, settled in Philada. before 1700, and in 1702 married Hannah, daughter of Samuel Carpenter—see note, page 326. (For p. 326 see p. 773, this volume.)

53. ESTHER.
54. RACHEL.
55. MARY.
56. THOMAS, bu. Sept. 23, 1781, aged 3 years.

16. THOMAS WHARTON[4] (Joseph,[3] Thomas,[2] Richard[1]), b. Phila. Jan. 15, 1730–1; m. Friends Meeting, Philada. Rachel, dau. of Jacob Medcalf, by his wife Hannah Hudson. She was b. Feb. 21, 1729–30. "He was a merchant of great wealth and influence, and of the sect of Quakers. In the enterprise of Galloway and Goddard to establish "The Chronicle," a leading newspaper, he was their partner; and the parties supposed that Franklin, on his return from England, would join them. Previous to the Revolution, Franklin and Mr. Wharton were correspondents. In 1774, Washington records that he "dined with Thomas Wharton." (*Sabine's Loyalists.*) Like many other Friends, he was at first actively opposed to the oppressive measures of the British Government, and a signer of the non-importation agreement in 1765; but when the colonies resorted to arms his sympathy was entirely withdrawn from their cause. His prominence among the Friends, the majority of whom had pursued a similar course in regard to the active prosecution of the Revolution, made him an object of suspicion to the authorities of the newly arisen commonwealth, and in Aug. 1777 he and several other Friends were arrested, who, on their refusing to sign a parole, were in the following month exiled to Virginia. In April, 1778, they were allowed to return to Philada. Mr. Wharton, however, was proscribed as an enemy to his country, and lost his estate under the Confiscation Act of Penna. He d. near Philada. in the winter of 1782.

(To be continued.)

THE WHARTON FAMILY.

BY ANNE H. WHARTON.

Issue all b. in Philada.

57. HANNAH, b. Sept. 3, 1753; m. James C. Fisher.
58. MARY, b. Jan. 22, 1755; m. Philada. May 17, 1780, Owen, son of Owen Jones, by his wife Susannah Evans, b. in Philada. March 15, 1744–5. By her he had one child; bu. in Friends Ground, Jan. 22, 1784. Mrs. Jones d. soon after, and he m. 2dly, Hannah Foulke, and d. s. p. His will was proved May 14, 1825.
59. RACHEL, b. Nov. 29, 1756; d. Nov. 8, 1759.
60. JOSEPH, bu. Aug. 1, 1766, aged 6 years.
61. JACOB, bu. Dec. 21, 1769, aged 9 years.
62. MARTHA, d. unm.; bu. April 7, 1788, aged 24 years.
63. FRANKLIN, bu. Aug. 1, 1766, aged 4 mo.
64. SUSANNAH, d. unm. June 5, 1786. The following obituary appeared in the "Pennsylvania Mercury," of June 9, 1786, which we give as a curious specimen of a certain style of composition:—

"On Monday last, the 5th of June, the amiable, the blooming Miss Susannah Wharton, in the bud of life, resigned her breath. Amongst the many sacrifices that are hourly made at the altar of the grim monster, few possessed more real accomplishments than this lovely victim. Born under the smiles of nature—educated in the paths of prudence and virtue—she rose like the sun —illuminating with her knowledge, and cherrishing with her philanthropy.

"To a mild, condescending disposition, she added those generous sentiments, which characterize the worthy part of her sex, and mark the Christian. In her pastime she was chearful, in her devotion she was serious. A perfect consistency was seen in her conduct.

"If the frailty of her companions was the topic of conversation, she spoke but to vindicate; when their virtues were admired she joined with a fervency that testified her liberality. In the common occurrences of life she was neither too much elevated, nor too much depressed; she turned with a smile from the casualities of human life to Nature's God, and into His hands she resigned herself with pleasure. No motives influenced her conduct, but the happiness of her fellow-creatures. The heart-rending sighs, the sorrowful looks of all who knew her, manifest their loss. The effusions of esteem in one of her acquaintance has given birth to this imperfect sketch of her character. It wants no aid of the pen to be beloved—she need only to have been known."

65. WILLIAM HUDSON, bu. Sept. 13, 1781, aged 10 years.

17. SAMUEL WHARTON[4] (Joseph,[3] Thomas,[2] Richard[1]), b. May 3, 1732; m. Sarah, dau. of Stephen Lewis, by his wife Rebecca

Hussey. Mr. Wharton was one of the signers of the Non-Importation Resolutions of 1765, a member of the City Councils of Philada., of the Committee of Safety of the Revolution, and of the Colonial and State Legislatures. He was a prominent member of the Ohio Company, whose plan of forming a settlement on the Ohio River was projected by Sir William Johnson, Governor Franklin, and others. In 1767, Dr. Franklin, then in England, mentions his correspondence with Mr. Wharton on this subject. Lord Hillsborough, in his "Report of the Lord's Commissioners for Trade and Plantations," in which he considered the "humble memorial of the Hon. Thomas Walpole, Benjamin Franklin, John Sargent, and Samuel Wharton, Esquires, in behalf of themselves and their associates," strenuously opposed the passing of the bill confirming the grant of land (known as Walpole's Grant), in reply to which Dr. Franklin put forth his powers to such purpose that the petition was finally granted, June 1, 1772. In consequence, however, of revolutionary troubles the project was not realized.

Mr. Wharton was a partner in the house of Messrs. Baynton, Wharton & Morgan, one of the most respectable commercial associations in the Colonies. At one time, the Indians destroyed upwards of £40,000* worth of their goods; as indemnification for which depredation, the chiefs made over to the firm all the lands which, at present, compose the State of Indiana. "Mr. Wharton, being an accomplished gentleman and scholar, was deputed by his partners to pass over to England for the purpose of soliciting a confirmation of this grant, in which he so far succeeded that the day was appointed by the Minister for him to attend at Court, and kiss the King's hand on receiving the grant.‡ Unfortunately, however, in the interim, some of his correspondence with Franklin, in furtherance of the Revolution, was discovered, and instead of the consummation he expected, he was obliged to fly for his life, and was fortunate in reaching the shores of France in

* Penna. currency.

‡ The Penna. Gazette announced Mr. Wharton's appointment as Governor of the new province of Pittsylvania.

safety, where he was joined by his old friend Dr. Franklin."*
In 1780, Samuel Wharton returned to Philada., and on Feb.
9, 1781, he took the oath of allegiance to the State of Penna.
He was a member of the Continental Congress during the
years 1782 and 1783. In 1784, he was appointed a Justice
of the Peace for the District of Southwark, he having, a short
time before, retired to his country seat, in that suburb, where
he anticipated ending his days in peace and quietness. His
will was admitted to probate, March 26, 1800. His children
were—

 66† STEPHEN, d. Philada. March 24, 1755.
 67. SAMUEL LEWIS, b. Philada. Feb. 14, 1759; m. Mrs. Rachel Musgrave.
 68. HANNAH, d. Philada. April 6, 1764, aged 2 years.
 69. REBECCA, m. June 7, 1798, Chamless Allen, and d. s. p. Soon after
  he m. 2dly, Rachel, widow of Samuel L. Wharton.
 70. MARTHA, m. Samuel B. Shaw.
 71. RICHARD, d. unm.

 18. JOSEPH WHARTON⁴ (Joseph,³ Thomas,² Richard¹), b.
Philada., March 21, 1733–4; m. Philada., June 18, 1760,
Sarah, dau. of Job and Sarah Tallman, b. Aug. 25, 1740, and
d. before her husband. Before the Revolution, Mr. Wharton
was an active and successful merchant; but losses during the
war, and a series of reverses attending his mercantile ventures,
after the establishment of peace, obliged him to retire from
business.

 The following is an obituary notice, which appeared in
Poulson's "Advertiser," Dec. 30, 1816:—

 Died, on the 25th instant, in the eighty-third year of his
age, Joseph Wharton, Esq., long a respectable inhabitant of
this city, and deeply and sincerely lamented by those who
enjoyed the advantage of his friendship.

 The protracted term of life, and the lingering illness through
which this gentleman had passed, had neither impaired the
original vigour of his mind, nor lessed the uncommon warmth
of his affections. His understanding, naturally quick and
powerful, was improved to an extent little common with the
past generation. Few men, perhaps, possessed such an intimate acquaintance with the language and literature of Greece

 * "Daily Advertiser."   † 66a. Joseph living 1770.

and Rome, and still fewer have, like him, retained an undiminished attachment to them, at an advanced stage of existence, and while suffering under an accumulation of physical evils. In the early part of his life he had enjoyed the peculiar good fortune of an intercourse with many of the most celebrated literary men of Europe. In latter years disease and misfortune caused his retirement from the world, but lessened not his zeal for the welfare of society, his duties toward which he discharged with exemplary propriety. It only remains perhaps to add, that he was a sincere and devout believer in the great truths of our religion, and closed a well-spent life in the firm persuasion of a removal to a better state of being.

He had nine children, all b. in Philada.

72. JOSEPH TALLMAN, b. July 16, 1761; d. Dec. 17, 1762.
73. SARAH, b. Nov. 20, 1763; d. Aug. 27, 1764.
74. THOMAS PARR, b. Nov. 18, 1765. He d. unm., and in the "Daily Advertiser," Dec. 3, 1802, the event is thus noticed:—

"Died on Wednesday, the 1st instant, in the 37th year of his age, Thomas Parr Wharton. A vigorous and highly-cultivated understanding, united to a just and benevolent disposition, rendered the deceased peculiarly agreeable and dear to his friends and family. A series of misfortunes taught him the uncertainty of all human pursuits and attachments as the means of happiness, and a tedious and painful illness became, in the hands of a kind Providence, the means of conveying to him the knowledge of his Redeemer, in whose mercy alone he placed his hopes of acceptance beyond the grave; his last words were, 'I die in peace.'"

75. HANNAH, b. Nov. 4, 1767; m. William Chancellor.
76. NANCY, b. Aug. 2, 1770; m. James Cowles Fisher (his 1st wife was Hannah Wharton, No. 57) and d. s. p. Jan. 1852.
77. SARAH, b. April 23, 1772; m. Jonathan Robeson.
78. MARTHA, b. Feb. 18, 1774; d. unm. March, 1861.
79. RACHEL, b. Aug. 8, 1775; d. Jan. 29, 1784.
80. ELIZA, b. Sept. 18, 1781; d. unm. April 7, 1869.

23. CHARLES WHARTON[4] (Joseph,[3] Thomas,[2] Richard[1]), b. Philada. Jan. 11, 1743; m. 1st, March 12, 1772, at Christ Church, Jemima Edwards, who was bu. in Philada. Nov. 13, 1772, aged 21 years. He m. 2dly, at Friends Meeting (Oct. 22, 1778), Elizabeth Richardson, who d. May 23, 1782, aged 30 years. His third wife was Hannah, dau. of William Redwood, by his wife Hannah, dau. of Samuel Holmes. They were m. at Friends Meeting, Oct. 13, 1784. She was b. in Newport, R. I., Sept. 25, 1759; d. Philada. April 11, 1796.

Mr. Wharton was a most successful merchant, and extensively engaged in the importing business of the city. He took the oath of allegiance to the State of Penna. July 3, 1778; and d. in Philada. March 15, 1838. His children, all by his third wife and b. in Philada., were—

81. JOSEPH, b. Aug. 17, 1785; d. unm. June 27, 1803.
82. WILLIAM, d. infant, March 8, 1788.
83. SARAH REDWOOD, b. June 1, 1789; m. William Craig.
84. WILLIAM, b. June 27, 1790; m. Deborah Fisher.
85. CHARLES, b. Sept. 20, 1792; m. Anne M. Hollingsworth.
86. HANNAH REDWOOD, b. Nov. 15, 1794; m. Thomas G. Hollingsworth.

24. ISAAC WHARTON[4] (Joseph,[3] Thomas,[2] Richard[1]), b. Philada. Sept. 15, 1745; m. Friends Meeting, Philada. Nov. 14, 1786, Margaret, dau. of Francis Rawle, by his wife Rebecca Warner. He died, Philada. March 31, 1808. His children were—

87. FRANCIS RAWLE, b. Jan. 11, 1788; m. Juliana M. Gouverneur.
88. HANNAH MARGARET, b. July 17, 1789; d. unm. Philada. Oct. 14, 1875.
89. THOMAS ISAAC, b. May 17, 1791; m. Arabella Griffith.
90. JOSEPH, b. April 29, 1793; d. unm. 1822.
91. REBECCA SHOEMAKER, b. Sept. 1, 1795; m. Joseph R. Smith.

25. CARPENTER WHARTON[4] (Joseph,[3] Thomas,[2] Richard[1]), b. Philada. Aug. 30, 1747; m. Christ Church, April 13, 1771, Elizabeth Davis, who d. May, 1816. He d. April 6, 1780, leaving issue—

92. JOHN, m. Nancy Craig.
93. THOMAS CARPENTER, m. June 21, 1806, Ann, dau. of William Green, by his wife Mary, dau. of Ellis Lewis, and d. s. p. She d. 1857.

27. MARY WHARTON[4] (Joseph,[3] Thomas,[2] Richard[1]), b. April 3, 1755; m. Friends Meeting, May 17, 1786, William Sykes, son of Samuel and Elizabeth Sykes.

94. JOSEPH, d. Philada. March 26, 1789.
95. ELIZABETH, d. Philada. Dec. 6, 1791.
96. WILLIAM, d. Philada. Sept. 1, 1791.
97. ROBERT WHARTON, b. July 26, 1796; m. 1st, Mrs. Frenaye, and 2dly, Lucy, dau. of Lemuel Lamb. He d. s. p.

(To be continued.)

THE WHARTON FAMILY.

BY ANNE H. WHARTON.

28. ROBERT WHARTON[4] (Joseph,[3] Thomas,[2] Richard[1]) was born, Jan. 12, 1757, at his father's country seat in Southwark. Although his future career proved him to be possessed of abilities of a superior order, Robert Wharton early evinced a decided distaste for learning; consequently, at the age of fourteen, his studies were relinquished, and he was apprenticed to a hatter. During his mayoralty, he frequently alluded to this portion of his life, remarking that he greatly respected those who were masters of a trade, which sentiment being generally known, it became convenient for those, who desired to avoid the penalties of the law, to declare themselves hatters. Pleasant as this may have been, as a matter of conversation in later years, Mr. Wharton, after serving his time, left his trade to enter the counting-house of his half-brother, Charles.* While in this position, he gratified his taste for field sports, and became a member of the "Gloucester Fox Hunting Club," instituted in 1766, of which he was President when it disbanded in 1818. In 1790, Mr. Wharton became a member of the "Schuylkill Fishing Company, of the State in Schuylkill." In 1812, on the death of Samuel Morris, the venerable Governor of the Company, he was elected to fill the unexpired term, to which honorable position he was re-chosen for sixteen successive years, when, in consequence of the increasing infirmities of age, he tendered his resignation of office and membership.†

Mr. Wharton was a member of City Councils from 1792 to 1795. His more prominent career began in 1796, when he

---

* Robert Wharton's name appears in the Philada. Directory of 1785 as flour merchant, Water, between Walnut and Spruce Streets.

† Memoir of the Schuylkill Fishing Company.

was appointed alderman for the city, under the mayoralty of Hilary Baker, Esq. During this year a formidable riot occurred, which threatened to interfere seriously with the commercial interests of Philadelphia, as sailors, in large numbers, took part in the melée, and held possession of the wharves on the Delaware. Robert Wharton was empowered by Mr. Baker to act in his stead, and in meeting and quelling this insurrection, he signally displayed the executive ability and great personal courage, which were his distinguishing characteristics.

Another incident, which took place during Mr. Wharton's term of office as alderman, speaks most eloquently of his disregard of danger in the discharge of his duty. In 1798, the yellow fever broke out in the Walnut Street Prison, where several hundred persons were confined. Mr. Smith, the jailer, resigned his position, as did several deputy jailers, upon which Mr. Wharton volunteered his services as jailer, taking up his residence in the prison and fulfilling all the duties of the office. While the fever raged within the prison walls, some of the more desperate of its inmates planned an insurrection, in order to escape from confinement and the much dreaded pestilence.* Being warned of the danger, Mr. Wharton, armed with a fowling-piece, and accompanied by several keepers provided with muskets, prepared to meet the insurgents. His company consisted of not more than seven or eight men, one of them being a colored prisoner, detailed for outside prison work, who entreated Mr. Wharton to permit him to bear arms in his service; after kneeling and taking the most solemn oath to defend the supporters of the law, this man was provided with a musket, and acquitted himself so bravely that he was subsequently pardoned. Passing through the first gate of the prison, Mr. Wharton turned the key of the gate which communicated with the cells in the west wing of the building, by which forethought he secured himself from trouble from that quarter; and entering the second gate, with

---

* "The mutiny occurred in the yard, some of the prisoners, taking advantage of the visit of the physician, escaped from their cells and called upon the convicts in the yard to assist them."—*History of the Yellow Fever*, 1798.

his handful of men stood ready to meet the convicts, who advanced armed with crow-bars, pickaxes, etc. The order was given to halt and surrender, and, being disregarded, Mr. Wharton gave the order to his own men to fire, which was immediately obeyed. Fire-arms, as usual when opposed to an undisciplined rabble, proved an all-sufficient argument, and the rioters finally yielded, two of their number having fallen mortally wounded. One of these men sent for Mr. Wharton, when dying, and said, "It is well for you that you conquered us, for if successful, we intended to plunder and burn the city." This prisoner had been wounded in two places, one ball being from Mr. Wharton's fowling-piece, the other from a musket; an autopsy proved that the ball which entered the vital part was a musket ball; this is Mr. Wharton's own account of the affair,* although he was wont to add that he should not have hesitated to kill the man, as he was discharging his duty, and had taken aim with that purpose in view. Upon the assembling of the grand jury of the "Court of Oyer and Terminer" in the next year, Robert Wharton, who was then Mayor of the city, addressed the foreman, by letter, and requested an investigation of the circumstances connected with the rebellion in the prison, in these words: "Permit me, Sir, through you to request that the grand jury will be pleased to investigate the transaction; for although the verdict of the Coroner's inquest was clear and satisfactory, as far as laid with them, yet it certainly is a matter of too much importance (as the lives of two fellow creatures were taken) to last without a minute enquiry being made by your highly respectable body." The grand jury made a special presentment to the Court in Feb. 1799. . . After relating the circumstances they presented "Robert Wharton and all his associates, as doing an act which was of imperious necessity and their duty as officers, men, and citizens, were not only fully justified, but which we further present as highly meritorious and deserving the thanks of their fellow citizens."

* Communicated by his nephew, Mr. G. W. Wharton.

The Court received this document and ordered it to be put upon record.*

The City Councils met Oct. 16, 1798, when Robert Wharton was unanimously elected Mayor of Philadelphia, succeeding Hilary Baker, who died of yellow fever Sept. 25, 1798. Mr. Wharton held this honorable position during the following years: 1798–99; 1806–07; 1809–10; 1814–19; 1820–24. Of the success and popularity of Mayor Wharton's several terms of administration, it is needless to dwell, his frequent re-elections to office proving the esteem in which he was held by his fellow-citizens. Many incidents are related of him, of his suppressing insurrections, preventing escapes from prison, and of ferreting out plots and counter-plots against the established authorities, all indicative of constant vigilance, keen insight into character, great presence of mind, and a singular intrepidity of spirit; qualities, which gained for him the confidence and affection of the people, and which, added to a good share of common sense and a jealous care of all that nearly concerned the interests of the city which he governed, have caused Mr. Wharton to be acknowledged, by thinking men, then and since, as one of Philadelphia's best mayors.

The following, which appeared in one of our journals, Jan. 13, 1829, proves that the earnestness in vindicating the law, which distinguished Mr. Wharton as a young man, was not wanting in later years.

On the evening of the 9th inst., about 4 o'clock, whilst the fire was raging at the warehouse of Mr. Albrecht, directly opposite the dwelling of the subscriber, in Third Street below Spruce, the front door of his house was repeatedly and violently assaulted by a mob of from ten to fifteen persons, who insisted on entering to obtain, as they said, victuals and drink. At that time a number of citizens, firemen, and others, whose presence on the occasion was known to be for useful purposes, had been admitted into the subscriber's house to partake of refreshment. Though frequently cautioned to desist, the mob persisted, and so far succeeded in the first instance as to prevent the door being shut, notwithstanding the efforts of several gentlemen to close it. The undersigned was then compelled to resort to

* Philada. Gazette, March, 1799.

more efficient means of defence. He threw open his door, and armed with an instrument of defence, he advanced to meet these lawless intruders: he again admonished them to desist, and assured them he would, at all hazards, defend his house from their intrusion. They were for a moment checked, but one of them, more resolute than the rest, swore he would enter, and at the head of his associates advanced for the purpose; a severe blow received by him at the threshold of the door, stopped, however, their progress. The door was then closed and fastened. Shortly after they renewed the attack, and by violence, split and started one of the panels of the door. A gentleman in the entry heard them propose to set fire to my house, and they immediately introduced fire under the door, which was extinguished by the same individual. The undersigned deems it a duty he owes to his fellow-citizens, as well as to himself, publicly to state these circumstances, and to offer a reward of Twenty Dollars for the discovery and conviction of all or any of the individuals concerned in the outrage.

ROBERT WHARTON.

In politics he was an ardent federalist. The following is an extract from a letter written to his brother, Colonel Franklin Wharton, in 1808.

" Our city as to traffic is almost a desert, wharves Crowded with empty Vessels, the noise and buz of Commerce not heard, whilst hundreds of labourers are ranging the streets without employ, or the means of getting bread for their distressed Families, this is the blessed fruit of Creeping within our Own Shell—not so in the days of Washington, when difficulties approached, our Country assumed a bold attitude, gave employ to our brave seamen, mechanics, and others, and convinced our opponents we were not to be Dragooned into their Views."

Mr. Wharton was elected a member of the City Troop, June 19, 1798, and became its Captain Aug. 15, 1803, "without having served in any of the intermediate grades." Subsequently, on the formation of a regiment of cavalry by the city and county of Philadelphia, he was elected its Colonel, and was then, June 14, 1810, placed upon the Honorary Roll of the Troop. In 1811, Colonel Wharton was elected Brigadier-General of the 1st Brigade Pennsylvania Militia. In 1814, when the troop went into active service, although fifty-seven years of age, he volunteered, and served in the field as a private soldier, under his former lieutenant, Captain Ross. In October, of the same year, when a Committee of Councils of Philadelphia waited on him to inform him of his recent re-election as mayor of the city, they found him in camp, busily engaged, taking his turn as company cook. It was only upon their earnest solicitation that he was induced to accept his discharge and return to Philadelphia.*

Mr. Wharton was vice-president of the Washington Benevolent Society, his name being first on the list of original subscribers. He was m. Philada. Dec. 17, 1789, by Bishop White, to Salome dau. of William Chancellor, by his wife, Salome Wistar. He d. in Philada., March 7, 1834. He had two children, who d. before him.

    98. JOSEPH, b. May 31, 1791; d. June 4, 1791.
    99. ROBERT OWEN, m. Charlotte Musgrave, and d. s. p. She afterwards m. Tyler.

31. RACHEL WHARTON[4] (Joseph,[3] Thomas,[2] Richard[1]), b. Aug. 27, 1762; m. Dec. 13, 1781, William son of Robert Lewis, by his wife, Mary Pyle, and d. 1836. He d. Nov. 6, 1801, aged 53. They had seven children.

    100. JOSEPH WHARTON, b. Jan. 27, 1783; d. Oct. 20, 1805.
    101. ROBERT MORTON, b. Aug. 20, 1786; m. Martha R. Stocker.
    102. WILLIAM, b. Sept. 15, 1788.
    103. WHARTON, b. July 23, 1791; m. Frances Cuthbert, and d. s. p. Nov. 8, 1857.
    104. FRANKLIN, b. June 12, 1794; d. June 26, 1794.
    105. HANNAH OWEN, b. June 6, 1795; m. Richard Wistar.
    106. ANNA MARIA.

33. FRANKLIN WHARTON[4] (Joseph,[3] Thomas,[2] Richard[1]), b. July 23, 1767; m. at Christ Church, Philada. Oct. 1, 1800, Mary dau. of William Clifton. She d. in Washington, Aug. 31, 1813. He was appointed Colonel Commandant of the U. S. Marine Corps, under the administration of James Madison.

Colonel Wharton died in New York, Sept. 1, 1818, and was buried in the churchyard of old Trinity. The following is

---

* "His 'First Troop City Cavalry.'"

the announcement of his death in the Washington "National Intelligencer."

"At New York, on the 1st instant; Lieutenant-Colonel Franklin Wharton, Commandant of the Marine Corps, and for many years a resident of the headquarters of the corps in this city. His conduct through life was marked with every virtue that could dignify the man; and the sincere affection of his numerous relatives and friends bears ample testimony to the amiable and honorable qualities of his heart. He has left six sons to lament the loss of a father whose paternal care and kindness were most exemplary. Respected and beloved by those who knew him well, the society of Washington will long lament, in the decease of Colonel Wharton, the loss of one of its most benevolent and hospitable members."

He had eight children.

107. CLIFTON, b. Oct. 22, 1801; m. Oliveretta Ormsby.
108. GEORGE WASHINGTON, b. May 12, 1803; m. Emmeline D. Stout.
109. FRANKLIN, b. June 3, 1804; m. 1st, —— Baylor; 2dly, —— Walker; 3dly, Octavie Coycault.
110. WILLIAM LEWIS, b. Dec. 17, 1805; m. Ellen J. Brearley.
111. ELLEN CLIFTON, b. May 18, 1807; d. Jan. 7, 1808.
112. ANNA MARIA, b. 1808; d. Aug. 22, 1809.
113. ALFRED, b. June 1, 1810; m. Adelaide C. Passage.
114. HENRY WILLIAMS, b. Sept. 27, 1811; m. Ellen G. Nugent.

34. REYNOLD WHARTON^5 (James,^{4} John,^{3} Thomas,^{2} Richard^1). His name appears in Philada. Directory, 1785, as shipbuilder, Front St., Kensington. He had two sons, who are named in their grandfather's will.

115. JAMES.
116. JOSEPH.

37. PEREGRINE HOGG WHARTON^5 (James,^{4} John^3 Thomas,^{2} Richard^1), b. Feb. 14, 1765; m. Jane, dau. of Benjamin Brown, b. May 17, 1776. He d. May 27, 1811. They had ten children.

117. ANTHONY MORRIS, b. June 19, 1794; d.
118. PEREGRINE, b. Dec. 2, 1795; d. Dec. 7, 1795.
119. WILLIAM, b. Nov. 13, 1796.
120. FREDERICK AUGUSTUS, b. August 13, 1798.
121. HENRY, b. Sept. 4, 1800; d. March 5, 1804.
122. LEWIS, b. Oct. 24, 1802.
123. MARY ANN, b. Aug. 17, 1804; m. Samuel P. Griffitts.

124. CLEMENTINE, b. Oct. 26, 1806; d. May 1, 1810.
125. CHAMLESS, b. Dec. 16, 1808; d. Dec. 18, 1808.
126. JANE, b. Nov. 12, 1809; d. infant.

38. GEORGE WHARTON[5] (James,[4] John,[3] Thomas,[2] Richard[1]), m. Mary, dau. of James Doughty. She d. Oct. 31, 1832, aged 55 years, 9 mo. They had nine children.
127. JANE, m. 1st Daniel Morris; 2dly, Thomas Pickering.
128. CHARLES DOUGHTY, b. Feb. 27, 1798; m. Maria Donnel.
129. JOSEPH, m.
130. GEORGE, d. infant.
131. MARGARET DOUGHTY, m. David Stuart.
132. REBECCA LOUISA, d. unm.
133. GEORGE, m.
134. WILLIAM.
135. EDWIN, d. infant.

42. KEARNEY WHARTON[5] (Thomas, Junr.,[4] John[3] Thomas,[2] Richard[1]), m. Nov. 11, 1795, at Magnolia Grove, her father's house on the Delaware, Maria dau. of John Salter, by his wife Elizabeth Gorden. She d. June 16, 1867, aged 92. Mr. Wharton was elected President of the Common Council of Philada. Oct. 16, 1798. In 1799, his name is affixed to an address from the Select and Common Councils, on the subject of supplying the city with wholesome water, and subsequently to "An Ordinance Providing for the raising of a Sum of Money on Loan," for the same purpose.* He d. Jan. 4, 1848, aged 82, and was bu. at Oxford Church. He had six children.
136. THOMAS LLOYD, b. 1799; m. Sarah A. Smith.
137. LLOYD, b. Feb. 25, 1801; m. Margaret A. Howell.
138. JOHN SALTER, d. unm. Aug. 10, 1835, aged 36.
139. ELIZABETH SALTER, b. 1803; m. Thomas Morris.
140. GEORGE SALTER, d. unm. Aug. 7, 1844, aged 33.
141. JAMES SALTER, b. 1817.

* "True American," Feb. 1799.

(To be continued.)

THE WHARTON FAMILY.

BY ANNE H. WHARTON.

43. WILLIAM MOORE WHARTON[5] (Thomas, Junr.,[4] John,[3] Thomas,[2] Richard[1]), b. June 24, 1768; m. 1st, Mary Waln, and 2dly, Aug. 13, 1804, Deborah Shoemaker, who was b. Dec. 18, 1783; d. July, 1851. He d. Aug. 14, 1816. By his first wife he had four children.

142. MARY WALN.
143. REBECCA, b. Aug. 6, 1793.
144. SUSAN, m. Colin Campbell.
145. SARAH, b. 1797; bu. Feb. 25, 1800.

By his 2d wife he had eight children.

146. MARY MOORE, b. May 25, 1805; d. unm. July, 1868.
147. DEBORAH MUSGRAVE, b. April 29, 1806; d. unm. July, 1871.
148. WILLIAM MOORE, b. June 10, 1807; d. unm.
149. DANIEL CLARK, b. July 9, 1808; m. Anne W. Morgan.
150. JOHN HALOWELL, b. July 9, 1809; d. July 26, 1809.
151. SARAH NORRIS, b. Feb. 11, 1811; d. July 5, 1811.
152. KEARNEY, b. March 4, 1812; d. unm. Feb. 1, 1843.
153. ELIZABETH SHOEMAKER, b. June 16, 1813; m. William J. McCluney

44. SARAH NORRIS WHARTON[5] (Thomas, Junr.,[4] John,[3] Thomas,[2] Richard[1]), m. 1st, Benjamin Tallman, M.D., of Haddonfield, N. J., who d. s. p. She m. 2dly, Samuel son of Samuel Courtauld, of London, by his wife Louisa Perine Ogier. He d. 1821, aged 69. She d. 1836, aged 64. They had three children.

154. LOUISA, b. Oct. 7, 1800; d. unm. Aug. 27, 1860.
155. AMELIA WHARTON, b. Aug. 10, 1803; m. June 26, 1843, Milton Smith.
156. SARAH LLOYD, b. Feb. 1806; m. July 28, 1830, Milton Smith.

48. FISHBOURN WHARTON[5] (Thomas, Junr.,[4] John,[3] Thomas,[2] Richard[1]), b. Aug. 10, 1778; m. 1st, May 10, 1804, Susan Shoemaker, who d. Nov. 3, 1821; and 2dly, Jan. 20, 1832,

Mary Ann Shoemaker, sister of his first wife. She d. Nov. 4, 1858. He d. Dec. 3, 1846. By his first wife he had eight children.

    157. THOMAS, b. May 4, 1805; d. unm. March 7, 1830.
    158. GEORGE MIFFLIN, b. Dec. 26, 1806; m. Maria Markoe.
    159. FISHBOURN, b. Feb. 13, 1809; d. unm. Jan. 3, 1842.
    160. HENRY, b. Dec. 24, 1810; d. young.
    161. JOSEPH, b. March, 1812; d. unm. Aug. 30, 1838.
    162. DEBORAH, b. Feb. 29, 1816; d. Dec. 28, 1816.
    163. WILLIAM, b. Nov. 14, 1817; d. young.
    164. EDWARD, b. Jan. 25, 1819; m. Jane G. Shippen.
    165. ELIZABETH FISHBOURN, b. Jan. 14, 1821.

By his 2d wife he had two children.

    166. SUSAN, b. April 9, 1837.
    167. PHILIP FISHBOURN, b. April 30, 1841.

52. SARAH CRISPIN[5] (Rachel,[4] John,[3] Thomas,[2] Richard[1]), m. William Levis. They had two children.

    168. EDMUND, m. Elizabeth Thompson.
    169. WILLIAM, m. Elizabeth A. White.

57. HANNAH WHARTON[5] (Thomas,[4] Joseph,[3] Thomas,[2] Richard[1]), b. Sept. 3, 1753; m. Jan. 5, 1785, James Cowles son of William and Sarah Fisher. They had one son.

    170. WILLIAM WHARTON, b. Oct. 1, 1786; m. Mary P. Fox.

67. SAMUEL LEWIS WHARTON[5] (Samuel,[4] Joseph,[3] Thomas,[2] Richard[1]), b. in Philada. Feb. 14, 1759; m. May 30, 1782, by Rev. William White, to Rachel, widow of Israel Musgrave, and dau. of James and Rachel McCulloch. He d. Oct. 27, 1788. They had three children.

    171. SAMUEL LEWIS, b. May 25, 1783; m. Dorcas Clark.
    172. WILLIAM, d. May 6, 1786, aged 6 mo.
    173. HANNAH CARPENTER, d. infant.

70. MARTHA WHARTON[5] (Samuel,[4] Joseph,[3] Thomas,[2] Richard[1]), m. Samuel B. Shaw, whose will, dated Feb. 27, 1822, was offered for probate Dec. 1, 1835. She d. Nov. 3, 1821, aged 53. They had two children.

    174. SARAH LEWIS.
    175. SAMUEL WHARTON.

75. HANNAH WHARTON[5] (Joseph,[4] Joseph,[3] Thomas,[2] Richard[1]), b. Nov. 4, 1767; m. June 24, 1790, William son of William Chancellor, by his wife Salome Wistar. She d. April 13, 1847. They had six children.

    176. WILLIAM, d. infant.
    177. WILLIAM, b. 1792; d. unm. May 18, 1876.
    178. CHILD, bu. March 7, 1794.
    179. SARAH WHARTON, b. 1797; m. Edward Twells.
    180. HENRY, b. 1804; m. Caroline Clapier.
    181. WHARTON, d. unm. 1866.

77. SARAH WHARTON[5] (Joseph,[4] Joseph,[3] Thomas,[2] Richard[1]), b. April 23, 1772; m. Jan. 22, 1795, by Bishop White, at her father's house, 81 South Third Street, to Jonathan Robeson. He was commissioned, by President Adams, Lieut.-Vol. Light Dragoons Provisional Army of the U. S., July 17, 1798.* In Feb. 1799, he was appointed one of twelve commissioners to receive subscriptions for shares in a loan for the purpose of supplying the city of Philadelphia with wholesome water.† He d. Sept. 5, 1799, aged 44. She d. Aug. 27, 1847. They had three children.

    182. SARAH WHARTON, b. Nov. 26, 1795; m. Charles F. Logan.
    183. JOSEPH, b. July 13, 1797; d. April 12, 1798.
    184. ELIZABETH, b. Feb. 14, 1799; d. unm. July 3, 1872.

83. SARAH REDWOOD WHARTON[5] (Charles,[4] Joseph,[3] Thomas,[2] Richard[1]), b. June 1, 1789; m. Nov. 19, 1808, William‡ son of William Craig, by his wife Mary Johns. She d. June 15, 1837. He d. July 14, 1869. Their children were—

    185. MARY JOHNS, m. James Hall.
    186. WHARTON, m. Sarah A. Kruger.
    187. NANCY WHARTON, d. unm. Dec. 26, 1867.
    188. JOSEPHINE, m. Samuel Rodman son of Charles Waln Morgan, by his wife Sarah Rodman.

84. WILLIAM WHARTON[5] (Charles,[4] Joseph,[3] Thomas,[2] Richard[1]), b. June 27, 1790; m. at old Pine Street Meeting, June

---

* "History of the First Troop Philadelphia City Cavalry."
† "Daily Advertiser."
‡ Mr. Craig m. 2dly, Beulah, dau. of William Rawle.

4, 1817, Deborah, b. Oct. 24, 1795, dau. of Samuel Rowland Fisher, by his wife Hannah Rodman. He d. Jan. 15, 1856.

189. HANNAH, b. March 6, 1818; m. Robert Haydock.
190. RODMAN, b. Jan. 26, 1820; m. Susan D. Parrish.
191. SARAH, b. Dec. 10, 1821; m. Abraham Barker.
192. CHARLES WILLIAM, b. Dec. 23, 1823; m. Mary Lovering.
193. JOSEPH, b. March 3, 1826; m. Anne Lovering.
194. MARY, b. Jan. 17, 1828; m. Joseph Thurston.
195. WILLIAM, b. May 19, 1830; m. Anna Walter.
196. SAMUEL FISHER, b. Aug. 11, 1832; d. Feb. 22, 1843.
197. ANNE, b. March 30, 1834; d. unm. Nov. 20, 1863.
198. ESTHER FISHER, b. Jan. 20, 1836; m. Benj. R. Smith.

85. CHARLES WHARTON[5] (Charles,[4] Joseph,[3] Thomas,[2] Richard[1]), b. Sept. 20, 1792; m. June 15, 1815, Anne Maria dau. of Jehu Hollingsworth, by his wife Hannah Shallcross.* She was b. March 29, 1796; d. Jan. 24, 1865. He d. May 23, 1864. They had five children.

199. CHARLES, b. Feb. 26, 1816; m. Mary M. Boggs.
200. ELIZABETH, b. Feb. 12, 1818; m. Charles Illius.
201. REDWOOD, b. June 15, 1821; d. July 19, 1821.
202. ANNE MARIA, b. July 28, 1824; m. April 2, 1844, Patrick Julius, son of John Lachaussèe Bujac, by his wife Celeste Robin. He d. s. p. Jan. 3, 1854.
203. EDMUND, b. May 13, 1831; d. unm. Dec. 26, 1856.

86. HANNAH REDWOOD WHARTON[5] (Charles,[4] Joseph,[3] Thomas,[2] Richard[1]), b. Nov. 15, 1794; m. Oct. 14, 1813, before Robert Wharton, to Thomas Gilfillan Hollingsworth (brother of Mrs. Charles Wharton), b. April 16, 1791; d. Oct. 19, 1864. She d. June 11, 1854. Their children were—

204. CHARLES WHARTON, b. Oct. 27, 1814; d. Jan. 10, 1853.
205. HANNAH REDWOOD, b. Jan. 29, 1816; d. unm. Feb. 3, 1868.
206. ELIZABETH SHALLCROSS, m. Charles A. Lyman.
207. WILLIAM WHARTON, b. Dec. 14, 1827; m. Caroline Newbold.
208. FANNY REDWOOD, b. Aug. 8, 1833; m. Crawford Arnold.

87. FRANCIS RAWLE WHARTON[5] (Isaac,[4] Joseph,[3] Thomas,[2] Richard[1]), b. Jan. 11, 1788; m. April 5, 1826, Juliana Matilda dau. of Isaac Gouverneur, of New York. He d. Feb. 10, 1862. She d. March 7, 1870. They had seven children.

* Daughter of Joseph Shallcross, by his wife Orpah Gilpin.

209. ALIDA GOUVERNEUR, m. June 25, 1856, John Teakle son of Rev. James Montgomery, D.D., by his wife Eliza Dennis. He was b. April 3, 1817.
210. FRANCIS RAWLE, b. April, 1828.
211. ROBERTSON, b. Sept. 29, 1829; d. unm. March 31, 1863.
212. EDWARD, b. Dec. 9, 1830; d. unm. May 27, 1873.
213. GOUVERNEUR, b. May 23, 1832; d. unm. March 15, 1850.
214. MARGARET, b. Oct. 2, 1833; d. March 24, 1849.
215. ALFRED, b. Sept. 5, 1835; m. Susan Budd.

89. THOMAS ISAAC WHARTON[5] (Isaac,[4] Joseph,[3] Thomas,[2] Richard[1]), "the second son of Isaac Wharton, was born at the family residence on Third Street, on May 17th, 1791. He graduated at an early age at the University of Pennsylvania, and shortly after graduating began the study of law in the office of his uncle, Mr. William Rawle, then a lawyer of large practice in Philadelphia, and previously district attorney under Washington's administration. In the war of 1812 Mr. Wharton served as a captain of infantry, and was engaged, with his company, in the duties at Camp Dupont. At the close of the war he began the practice of law in Philadelphia, and in the twenty-fifth year of his age married Arabella, second daughter of Mr. John Griffith, a merchant of Philadelphia, son of the attorney-general of New Jersey of the same name, and brother of Judge William Griffith, a judge of the Circuit Court of the United States, and author of several law treatises. Mr. Wharton was a diligent and discriminating student, and at an early period of his life was distinguished for his literary taste and skill. He was one of the contributors to the Portfolio, under Mr. Dennie's management, and he became afterwards one of the editors of the Analectic Magazine. It was to law, however, that his studies were principally given; and in this department they bore ripe fruit. To him, in connection with his uncle, Mr. Rawle and Judge Joel Jones, the codification of the civil statutes of Pennsylvania was committed; and the code they reported, a document much in advance of the legislation of the day, is marked by the impress of their wisdom, learning, and skill. He was the author of the first editions of Wharton's Digest, and of the six volumes of Wharton's Reports. In addition to these works, several historical and

literary addresses are in print bearing his name; addresses marked by strong sense, clear thought, and a nervous and elegant style. Mr. Wharton's chief labors, however, were given to his profession, in which he acquired, chiefly as counsel on matters of title, a large and commanding practice. In politics he was attached to the Whig party during its existence, and was a personal and political friend of Mr. Clay. On the dissolution of the Whig party, his attachments and constitutional principles led him to unite with leading members of that party in union with the Democratic. He died on April 7th, 1856, leaving behind him the reputation not only of high legal abilities, but of spotless integrity and of undaunted courage in the performance of duty. Of purity and unselfishness in domestic relations no truer example could be found."—F. W.

Thomas Isaac Wharton m. Arabella Griffith, Sept. 11, 1817; her mother was Mary Coré. She d. Feb. 27, 1866. Their children were—

216. MARY GRIFFITH, b. Aug. 24, 1818; m. George D. Bland.
217. FRANCIS, b. March 7, 1820; m. 1st, Sydney Paul; and 2dly, Helen E. Ashhurst.
218. EMILY, b. Oct. 12, 1823; m. Charles Sinkler.
219. HENRY, b. June 2, 1827; m. Katharine J. Brinley.

91. REBECCA SHOEMAKER WHARTON[5] (Isaac,[4] Joseph,[3] Thomas,[2] Richard[1]), b. Sept. 1, 1795; m. Nov. 12, 1817, Jacob Ridgway son of James Smith, by his wife Ann Ridgway, b. Oct. 10, 1791; d. Sept. 2, 1865. She d. July 16, 1846. They had five children.

220. MARGARET WHARTON, b. April 4, 1819; m. George H. White.
221. CAROLINE RIDGWAY, b. Oct. 24, 1820; m. Feb. 25, 1851, Samuel son of Joseph and Mary Pleasants, and d. s. p. Sept. 27, 1858.
222. ANNA RIDGWAY, b. April 30, 1822; m. William E. Evans.
223. EMILY SOPHIA, b. June 3, 1824; m. James C. Worrell.
224. JAMES CHARLES, b. Jan. 6, 1827; m. Nov. 7, 1869, Heloise dau. of Francis Martin Drexel, by his wife Catharine Hookey.

92. JOHN WHARTON[5] (Carpenter,[4] Joseph,[3] Thomas,[2] Richard[1]) m. April 22, 1809, Nancy, dau. of William Craig, by his wife Mary Johns. She was b. July 6, 1781.

225. WILLIAM CRAIG, b. May 7, 1811; m. Nancy W. Spring.
226. MARY CRAIG, b. Aug. 24, 1814; m. James S. Wadsworth.
227. THOMAS CARPENTER, b. April, 1819; d. unm.

101. Robert Morton Lewis[5] (Rachel,[4] Joseph,[3] Thomas,[2] Richard[1]), b. Aug. 20, 1786; m. Feb. 23, 1815, Martha Rutter dau. of John Clement Stocker and Mary Katharine,—b. March 11, 1789. He d. Feb. 18, 1855. Their children were—

    228. Clements Stocker, b. May 6, 1816; d. Aug. 26, 1816.
    229. Robert Wharton, b. June 22, 1817; d. July 12, 1817.
    230. Mary Stocker, b. Oct. 14, 1818; d. unm. 1858.
    231. Margaretta Stocker.
    232. Julia Wharton, b. Aug. 2, 1823; m. Lawrence Lewis.

105. Hannah Owen Lewis[5] (Rachel,[4] Joseph,[3] Thomas,[2] Richard[1]), b. June 6, 1795; m. Richard, son of Richard Wistar. She d. Jan. 30, 1857. They had six children.

    233. Sarah, m. 1st, Joseph Hopkinson; and 2dly, James Gillilan.
    234. Rachel, d. inf.
    235. Rachel Lewis, m. Alexander E. Harvey.
    236. Richard.
    237. William Lewis.
    238. Frances, m. Lewis A. Scott.

107. Clifton Wharton[5] (Franklin,[4] Joseph,[3] Thomas,[2] Richard[1]), b. Oct. 22, 1801; m. Aug. 21, 1838, Oliveretta, dau. of Oliver and Sarah Ormsby, of Pittsburg. They had five children.

    239. Clifton Ormsby, b. Aug. 19, 1839; m. Jane E. Page.
    240. Oliver Franklin.
    241. John Burgwin, d. young.
    242. Josephine, m. Pressly N. Chaplin.
    243. Mary Etta, d. young.

108. George Washington Wharton[5] (Franklin,[4] Joseph,[3] Thomas,[2] Richard[1]), b. May 12, 1803; m. Dec. 3, 1829, Emmeline Davis dau. of Robert Stout, by his wife Elizabeth Evans. Their children are—

    244. Mary Clifton, b. June 3, 1831; d. unm. May 5, 1858.
    245. Franklin, b. Feb. 11, 1833; d. April 7, 1846.
    246. George Washington, b. June 27, 1835; m. Josephine O. Page.
    247. Robert Stout, b. Nov. 2, 1837.
    248. Elizabeth, b. April 13, 1840; d. unm. Aug. 10, 1872.
    249. Emmelene Barclay, m. George O. McMullin.
    250. Clifton Lewis, b. June 8, 1848; m. Letitia Irwin.

109. FRANKLIN WHARTON[5] (Franklin,[4] Joseph,[3] Thomas,[2] Richard[1]), b. June 3, 1804; m. 1st, —— Baylor; 2dly, Walker; 3dly, Madam Octavie Coycault, née Duvergé. By his 1st wife he had one son.

   251. EDWARD CLIFTON, b. Nov. 1827; m. twice.

By his 3d wife he had two sons.*

   252. LOUIS DUVERGÉ, b. June, 1844; d. unm. Feb. 1876.
   253. FRANKLIN NICHOLAS, b. 1847.

110. WILLIAM LEWIS WHARTON[5] (Franklin,[4] Joseph,[3] Thomas,[2] Richard[1]), b. Dec. 17, 1805; m. Nov. 9, 1829, Ellen Jones dau. of Col. David Brearley; and d. Oct. 4, 1846. He had four children.

   254. CLIFTON TUCKER, b. July 31, 1834.
   255. DAVID BREARLEY, b. Aug. 7, 1836.
   256. AMANDA JONES, b. Oct. 16, 1840; m. Frederick H. Gibson.
   257. WILLIAM LEWIS, b. April 10, 1842; m. Jane A. Cavanna.

113. ALFRED CLIFTON WHARTON[5] (Franklin,[4] Joseph,[3] Thomas,[2] Richard[1]), b. June 1, 1810; changed his name to Alfred Wharton Clifton. He m. Dec. 22, 1829, at Princeton, Adelaide Charlotte dau. of John and Mary Passage, and d. March 30, 1854.

   258. FRANKLIN WHARTON, b. Oct. 18, 1830; d. 1849.
   259. ANNA HOWELL, b. June 16, 1832; d. May 18, 1835.
   260. MARY, b. Dec. 11, 1833; m. Henry P. Ross.
   261. ALFRED CLIFTON *Wharton*, d. unm. Aug. 24, 1865, aged 30.
   262. CLIFTON WHARTON, b. Feb. 22, 1837.
   263. FRANCES ANNA, m. June 8, 1874, Henry son of Henry Freedley, of Norristown, Pa., by his wife —— Pawling.
   264. ADELAIDE CHARLOTTE, b. Feb. 9, 1846; d. June 3, 1852.
   265. ROSA, b. Feb. 29, 1848; d. June 3, 1852.
   266. HENRIETTA, b. Aug. 23, 1851; d. unm. Aug. 1874.

114. HENRY WILLIAMS WHARTON[5] (Franklin,[4] Joseph,[3] Thomas,[2] Richard[1]), b. Sept. 27, 1811; m. Jan. 13, 1841, Ellen G. Nugent. Their children are—

   267. HENRY C., b. Nov. 1842; d. unm. April, 1870.
   268. GEORGE, d. 1859.
   269. ELLEN CLIFTON, m. William Moore Wharton.

         * Their eldest child, Octavie, d. infant.

THE WILLIAMS FAMILY.

[The following record of the Williams Family is copied from a Memorandum in a Bible in the possession of Mrs. Deborah M. Cresswell, of Merion, formerly of Philadelphia, a descendant of Thomas Ellis.]

Edward ap John of Cynlas in the Parish of Landerval near Bala or Pennlyn, Merionith-shire North Wales in Gt. Brittain. A free holder of about £24 per annum a man of good repute and careful to bring up his children in the fear of the Lord according to the Church of England anno 1670.

William ap Edward son of Edward ap John & —— his wife born the   day of   anno   Married

Katherin second daughter of Robert ap Hugh whose wife was one of the first of those people called Quakers in that part of Great Brittain.

Elizabeth daughter of William ap Edward and Katherin his wife born the 14th of 3 month 1672.

Katherin daughter of William ap Edward and Katherin his wife born the 29th of the 11th month 1676.

Their mother died soon after Katherins birth.

William ap Edward married anno 1681

Jane daughter of John ap Edward a respectable religious family inclining to join the people called Quakers S^d Jane having some time before joined them and in the Spring of the year 1682 s^d W^m ap Edward and Jane his second wife and daughters Elizabeth and Katherin took Shipping with a number of their friends and relatives Edward Rees, Edward Jones and others leaving their native country clear of debt and in love and good report and esteem among them and arrived safely in the river Schuylkill in Penn^a the 13th of 6 mo called August [1682] in the ship Lyon John Compton master from Liverpool. The town of Philadelphia then not known being a bank of woodland containing a few caves and two log houses occupied by Sweedes and a few English families.

In about three or four months after, their worthy proprietor Wm Penn arrived with a number of families to settle this uncultivated wooden country & after several meetings and councils held it was concluded to fix the city and a plan thereof agreed upon where it was and now remains to be built and soon after in the fall of 1682 S^d William ap Edward with his family Edwd Jones, Ed. Rees, Robert Davis and many others settled on the west side of schuylkill Six or seven miles distant from the city, there dug caves, walled them and dwelt therein a considerable time where they suffered many hardships in the beginning, the next season being wet and rainy about [the time of] their barley harvest they could not get their grain dry to stack before it swelled and began to sprout—rendering it unfit for bread. They were in their necessities supplied by the natives (Indians) with venison and wild fowl. Their first cows to milk were obtained from New Castle Del., and divided among the neighbours and not having inclosures for them they were obliged to tie them with rope of grapevine some to a tree or stake driven in the ground there then being plenty of grass and sweet weeds. The Lord blessed them and enabled them to bear their difficulties for a time and blessed their labour with great success in raising grain and every support they could wish for—

Love friendship and unity abounded among them and they cheerfully assisted one another as loving brethren.

To return to the family s^d William ap Edward after living some time or years in their cave in merion township bought about 200 acres of land in Blockley township adjoining to David Jones & others and there made improvements until he died anno Sept. 1749.

S^d William ap Edward's daughter Elizabeth married Thomas Lloyd of Merriam township and was blessed with many children and lived & died in love and esteem with their neighbours.

Katherin married near Salem New Jersey and died without issue.

S^d William ap Edward and Jane his second wife had four children namely

Sarah born the 29th of the Eighth month 1685. married Thomas Lawrence son of David Lawrence the elder whose wife was Eleoner daughter of Thomas Ellis (Register-General under Wm. Penn) who arrived in Penna. anno 1683, and settled in Haverford in Chester County about 12 miles west of Philadelphia They were blessed with five children David, Rachel, William, Daniel and Sarah who were all of them married except William.

Ellen born the 19th of fourth month 1691 married Henry Lawrence brother of s^d Thomas Lawrence and they were blessed with many children who were also married & were blessed with many children Sarah Jane married David Lewis. Ellen married David Jones of Radnor. Mary married Jacob Jones of Merriam but had no children Hannah married Evan Jones son of John Jones carpenter of North Wales & had three children Margaret, Henry and Hester.

Mary the youngest born the 11th of eleventh month 1694 married Richard Preston Tanner of Philadelphia and had but one child Rachel who died in minority.

Edward their only Son was born the 7 day of second month 1689 and wrote his name Edward William married anno 1714.

Eleanor daughter of David Lawrence the elder and the grand daughter of Thomas Ellis aforesaid anno 1683 and had five children namely

Sarah daughter of Edward and Eleanor William was born the 13th day of fourth month 1720—Married Joshua Humphreys of Haverford son of Daniel Humphreys one of the first settlers there and had children Clement, Joshua, Hannah, Daniel and Jane.

Edward son of Edward and Eleanor Williams was born the 24th of seventh month 1722—Married Hannah daughter of William Garret of Darby township and had two daughters Hannah and ——

Joseph son of Edward and Eleanor William born the 21st. of third month 1724. Married Hannah daughter of Jonathan Jones of Merrion and had three Daughters, Rebecca, Eleoner and Sarah.[1]

Jane daughter of Edward & Eleoner William was born the 21st of seventh month 1732 married Evan Thomas and had children Edward Eleoner, Joseph and Jonathan.

S^d Edward William and Eleonore his wife departed this life, Edward in the ninth month 1749 aged 60 Years. Eleoner in same month about the same age.

Daniel (Founder of Williamsport, Pennsylvania also signer of the Non-Importation Act of 1765) eldest son of Edward and Eleonor William was born the 12th day of second month 1717 (Died Nov. 29th 1794) added s to his name and married the 27 of first month (March) at Philad^a Jane Oldman daughter of Thomas Oldman of Philadelphia and grand daughter of Thomas Oldman of Lewiston near the Capes of Delaware and Grand daughter of Samuel Garrets of Darby township Chester County Penna. and lived in the greatest love and affection until 8 Mo. 1780 s^d Jane departed this life in the morning having had fifteen children two whereof died in their minority, viz.

Mary daughter of Daniel and Jane Williams was born the 11th of 11th month 1747 about three o'clock in the morning being the first day of the week. Departed this life second month sixth 1749.

Daniel and Jane Williams, Twins, son and daughter of Daniel and Jane Williams were born the 29th day of 7 mo. 1748 between the hours of 10 & 11 o'clock in the morning being the fifth of the week. Departed this life Daniel the 12th of 5 mo. following & Jane on the 14 of same month being in the space of two days together 1749.

Edward son of Daniel and Jane Williams was born the

---

[1] Sarah married Edmund George. The late Jesse George was one of their children.

Rebecca married Amos George. Three of their grandchildren—John, Joseph, and Jane—are still living at the old homestead at Overbrook Station, Philadelphia.—D. M. C.

15th day of 3 month (called May) 1750 about six o'clock in the morning being the 3ᵈ of the week.

Ennion son of Daniel and Jane Williams was born on the 3ʳᵈ day of April 1752 being the sixth of the week about eight oclock in the evening.[1]

Sarah daughter of Daniel and Jane Williams was born the 16th day of March 1754 at about eight oclock in the evening Departed this Life . . .

George son of Daniel and Jane Williams was born the 16th day of March, 1756 Departed this life the 15ᵗʰ day of May, 1756.

Mary (the second of that name) Daughter of Daniel and Jane Williams was born on the 17th day of May 1757. Departed this life in July following.

Deborah daughter of Daniel and Jane Williams was born the   day of   month   Married John Field of Philadelphia.

Departed this life the 31ˢᵗ day of 5 month 1802 and was interred at Merrion.

Joseph son of Daniel and Jane Williams was born on the 21ˢᵗ day of 7 month called July 1762 Departed this life November 26th 1765 of small pox.

Daniel son of Daniel and Jane Williams was born the 23 of ninth month called September 1763 Departed this life the 10th day of November 1765 of small pox.

Samuel son of Daniel and Jane Williams was born the 10th third month called March 1766 at 2 oclock in the morning Departed this life May 1769.

Daniel son of Daniel and Jane Williams was born the 4th day of the ninth month called September 1770 at half past 10 oclock at night Being the third son of that name and fifteenth child.

Departed this life the 18th day of 8 month 1797.

Hannah daughter of Daniel and Jane Williams was born

---

[1] Ennion Williams, Major of the First Battalion of the Pennsylvania Rifle Regiment, commanded by Colonel Samuel Miles. He was commissioned March 3, 1776, and resigned Feb. 4, 1777. He was at the battles of Long Island, Trenton, and Princeton.

on the   day of 9 month 1760. Departed this life on the day of   month.

Sarah daughter of Daniel and Jane Williams was born on the third day of the 12th month called December 1764 at Eleven oclock at night being the second of that name and 13th child married on the fourth day of 6th month 1799 at Friends North Meeting house Philadelphia to John Moulson who was born the 31st day of 5 month (May 1761) at $6\frac{1}{2}$ P.M. son of Saml. M. and Dinah Moulson of St. Johns England.

Samuel Moulson son of John and Sarah Moulson was born in Norfolk Virginia on the 13th day of fourth month 1800 between the hours eleven and twelve at night.

Departed this life on the 26th day of 7th mo. following at half past twelve oclock at night 1800

Deborah Moulson daughter of John and Sarah Moulson was born the fifth day of the ninth month 1801 between the hours of five and six oclock in the afternoon near Paradise Creek Virginia.   was a prominent speaker in Friends meeting.

John Moulson Jr son of John and Sarah Moulson was born on the 21st day of the fourth month 1803 between the hours of two and three oclock in the morning near Paradise Creek Virginia—died Decr 15th (Sunday) 1861 buried Dec 17th in the Union Cemetery 6th & Federal

John Moulson Senr. departed this life on the 9th day of 1st Month 1824 of Typhus fever and was interred in Friends burial ground corner of fourth and arch sts Philadelphia in the 64th year of his age.

John Moulson Jr. son of John and Sarah Moulson married at Frankford near Philadelphia by the Rev^d. Thomas Biggs on the 26th day of November 1826 unto Ellen Mary Lalanne Born the 28th day of February 1808—Daughter of Dominique Périgué and Don Minequette Duchesne Lalanne of the City of $Philad^a$ died May 24th 1865. buried 6th & Federal.

Edward Williams Moulson son of John and Ellen Mary Moulson was born on the third day of September 1827 at half after nine o'clock in the evening at No. 298 High st. Philadelphia one door below 9th st. Departed this life on the 21ˢᵗ day of October 1829 at 20 minutes before nine oclock in the evening at the same place of Dropsy of the Brain being the fourth day of the week—was interred the next day in Plot T No. 6 of the Union Burial Ground corner of Federal and Sixth streets southwark Philadelphia —the deed for sᵈ plot being in his name. in the middle of the plot aged 2 Years 1 month 18th days.

Ennion Williams son of Daniel and Jane Williams Departed this life second month twelfth 1830 at 11 oclock in the morning after five days illness of Pleurisy aged near 78 Years.

Francis Edward Moulson son of John and Ellen Mary Moulson was born on the (8ᵗʰ) eighth day of June in the year of our Lord Eighteen hundred and Thirty one (1831) at about twenty minutes after one oclock in the morning being the fourth day of the week at Bristol Pennᵃ—died August 9ᵗʰ 1866 buried at 6th & Federal Philadelphia.

Sarah Moulson daughter of Daniel & Jane Williams departed this life after an illness of nine days of pleurisy at about 9 oclock on the morning of the 16th day of the Eleventh Month (November) in the year 1832 being the sixth day of the week and on the following first day was interred in the family plot T No. 6 (on the southern side of the Union Burial Ground before mentioned. Aged 68 years.

Sarah Williams Moulson daughter of John & Ellen Mary Moulson was Born on the 23ᵈ day of the 12ᵗʰ month (December) in the year 1833 at about Eight oclock in the evening being the sixth day of the week at No. 96 south fifth st. Philadᵃ.

Deborah Moulson daughter of John and Ellen Mary Moulson was born on the 10ᵗʰ day of the first month (January) in the year of our Lord Eighteen hundred and thirty six at about 10½ oclock in the evening being the first of the week at No. 210 south Third st. Philadelphia (Tenth day of January 1836).

Ellen Mary Moulson daughter of John and Ellen Mary Moulson was born on the 26th day of the third month (March) Eighteen hundred and thirty eight at about oclock in the   being the second day of the week at No. 160 south Second st. 3ᵈ door below Spruce st.

Deborah Moulson daughter of John and Sarah Moulson Departed this life on the 26th day of fourth month (April) at half after twelve oclock P.M. being on the sixth day of the week Eighteen hundred and thirty nine at No. 160 south Second st. of disease of the Lungs being sensible to the last moment and was interred in the grave of her mother on the south side of Plot T No. 6 of the Union Burial Ground on the following sabbath afternoon And at the same time and in the same grave was interred Ellen Mary Moulson who departed this life on the 28th of the fourth month Eighteen hundred and thirty nine at about a quarter before two oclock in the morning (of effusion of Water on the Brain) and the first of the week—daughter of John and Ellen Mary Moulson—aged one year one month and two days.

Ellen Mary Moulson daughter of Jno. and Ellen Mary Moulson was born sept. 18. 1840.

Died Dec. 16 1843.

Ellen Mary Moulson daughter of John and Ellen Mary Moulson was born May 26 1848.

Sarah Williams Moulson born 23ᵈ Dec. 1833 married Robt. M. C. Rae and died 29th March 1853 leaving one male child called Robert born July 17th 1852.

GENEALOGICAL GLEANINGS OF THE WILSON, OR WILLSON'S, OF ULSTER.

BY THOMAS ALLEN GLENN.

Among those Scotch-Irish who emigrated from the Province of Ulster to Pennsylvania, Virginia, North Carolina, and other American colonies, at various times prior to the War of the Revolution, were many bearing the surname of Wilson, or, as frequently written in Scotland and Ireland, Willson. The following abstracts of Ulster Wilson wills, may be of interest to descendants.

Diocese of Derry Wills.

Will of John Wilson of Strabane in Co. Tyrone, gentleman. Dated 20 Dec., 1620. No date of probate.

The testator desires to be buried in the Parish Church of Lechpatrick, and appoints his son Robert to be sole executor and overseer of his (testator's) "other children." He also names sons William Wilson and John Wilson, and provides for his wife Barbara Moore.[1] Witnesses: John Browne, James Coghrane, James Gibb, Robert Cadwalader, W. Cunningham.

Will of Claud Willson of the parish of Donagheady, Co. Tyrone. Dated 13 Dec., 1636. Proved 21 Dec., 1636, by Agnes, widow and relict, James Hamilton of Dowlette, gentleman, and John Hamilton of Moyagh, gentleman.

The testator desires to be buried in the Parish Church of Donagheady, and bequeaths all of his personal estate to his wife and children (names not given).

---

[1] At this time, and later, it was the custom in Scotland, Ulster, and Wales, for women to retain their maiden name after marriage.

Wife Agnes, James Hamilton of Dulette (*sic*), gentleman, and John Hamilton of Moyouhe (*sic*), gentleman, to be executors. Witnesses: Thomas Wilson, ———— Hardie.

Will of George Willson. No place named. Dated 31 May, 1640. Proved Dec., 1640, by Katherine Willson relict of the deceased.

The testator names children: John Willson, and Mary Willson. He also mentions his mother, Elizabeth McGee, brother James Willson, sister Margaret Willson, and wife Katherine, who is executrix. Witnesses: John Kilver, Susane Holding, Constans Killver (*sic*).

Will of James Willsone, of Londonderry, weaver. Dated 17 March, 1664. Proved 8 May, 1665, by Margaret, widow and relict of the deceased.

The testator mentions his wife (executrix), and son James Willsone. Witness: Thomas Brown.

Will of William Wilson of the parish of Bouevah, Co. of Londonderry. Dated 22 April, 1692. No date of probate.

The testator mentions his son-in-law James Boyle, husband of his daughter Elizabeth. Daughter Katherine Wilson, and grandchild Agnisse Boyle, daughter of the said James Boyle.

The testator mentions "the will of my son Robert late deceased."

Wife Jannett Wilson, executrix, and testator's friend Richard Griffith, Rector of Drumchose, to be overseer. Witnesses: Charles Sterling, Patrick ————.

Will of Thomas Wilson of Strabane, merchant. Dated 26 Dec., 1693. No date of probate.

The testator desires to be buried in the Churchyard of Strabane, and he bequeaths to his wife Agnes Wilson alias Stewart the house and land called Burnes tenement, for life, and then to testator's son John Wilson. The testator leaves bequests to his other sons, Thomas and Francis Wilson. Son John Wilson to be "administrator," and testator's friends Mr. John Crawford and Mr. William Homes to be overseers. Witnesses: William Homes, John Crawford.

Will of Robart Wilson of Minemer in the parish of Maghera, barony of Loghlin, Co. Londonderry. Dated 28 Dec., 1714. Proved 12 July, 1715.

The testator mentions his son Hugh Wilson, and daughter Mary Wilson.

"I order that whatever can be made of the interest left to me by my father in the Co. of Antrim be managed and truly divided between my son and daughter."

The testator appoints his brother Hugh Speer, and friend Mr. William Montgomery, gentleman, executors. Witnesses: Nath. Paterson, Ann Speer.

Will of David Willson of Newtownlimavaddy. Dated 23 June, 1715. Proved 25 April, 1716.

The testator appoints his wife, Margret (*sic*) Willson, executrix, and mentions daughters Margret and Elizabeth Willson. Overseers: Mr. John Stirling, and John Alexander. Witnesses: Ro. McCausland, Tho. Blair.

Will of John Willson of Fyfin in the parish of Urny, Co. Donegal. Dated 6 April, 1706. Proved 23 April, 1724.

The testator desires to be interred in the Parish Church of Urny, and bequeaths the "interest of my part of the land of Fyfin unto my three full sisters that are unmarried equally to be divided." Witnesses: James Mayes, James Thomson.

Will of Patrick Wilson of Donaghmore. Dated 4 Feb., 1727–8. No date of probate.

The testator desires to be buried in the churchyard of Donaghmore. He mentions sons John Wilson, and Joshua Wilson; son-in-law James Cochran, and wife Cathrin Olivent. Executors: Andrew Willson, and Archibald White. Witnesses: Thomas Willson, John Willson.

Will of James Wilson of Stoancarlidagh in the parish of Drumragh, Co. Tyrone. Dated 20 April, 1741. Proved 2 March, 1742, by Robert Wilson, one of the witnesses.

The testator bequeaths to his eldest son, John Wilson, £20. Unto second son, David Wilson, "one moyetie or half of my farm;" unto each of his sons-in-law, viz. Hugh Wilson, James Anderson, John Young, Edward Young, John Hetheringtown, and William Christie, the sum of £3. due by bond; to "my youngest son Robert Wilson, and eldest son John, the other moyetie of my farm." Executors: John Christie of Mullaghbane, Co. Tyrone, and testator's second son, David Wilson. Witnesses: John Rodger, and Robt Wilson Junr.

Will of Archibald Willson of the Laugh. Dated 2 March, 1745–6. Proved by executors named, 5 April, 1746.

The testator desires to be buried in Donaghmore, and leaves bequests as follows:

To elder Brother Daniel, £15.; to brother John, £14.; to brother Thomas, £14.; to John Heris (Harris), a relative, £5.10.0.; to Jean Heris, £3.10.0.; to Nancy Heris, £2.10.0.; to Thomas Heris, £2.10.0.; to Samuel Heris, £1.2.0.; to John Anderson, £5.0.0.; to Margrat Anderson, £2.10.0.; to Martha Anderson, £2.10.0.; to Archibald Anderson, £3.10.0; to Rebeckah Anderson, £2.10.0. Executors: Archibald Whit (White), and Moses Lindsay. Witnesses: John Willson, and John Marshal.

Will of James Willson of Killymuch in the parish of Tamlaght O'Crilly, Co. Londonderry. Dated 27 March, 1745. Proved by executors named, 29 July, 1747.

The testator desires to be buried in the churchyard of Tamlaght O'Crilly. To "wife Margret the fifth part of all my goods and chattels, all the rest and residue to my four children to be divided into four equal parts. If there is another child property to be divided into six parts, and a sixth part to each of my five children." Wife and children to "enjoy my house and farm" (which went to his heir). The testator mentions his son William, and appoints as executors, his brother, John Willson, and brother-in-law, William Hamilton. Witnesses: Hugh Hill, Edward Marks, and John McPeake.

Will of James Willson of Kern in the parish of Dunboe, Co. Londonderry. Dated 30 March, 1747. Proved by the oath of Andrew Walker, witness, and the execution committed to John Dunn and Thomas Boyd, sons-in-law of the deceased and next of heir, 27 July, 1747.

The testator desires to be decently buried at the discretion of his son John. All money owing, the testator bequeaths to his daughter Margrat Willson otherwise Boy (*sic*), "except what James Lewes is owing, that I allow to my daughter Mary, with what my son John Dunn is owing to me that I allow him to keep in his own hands for his part. Son John (Dunn) to be at the cost of funeral. Witnesses: Andrew Walker, and Joseph Wardon.

Will of Andrew Wilson Senior of Banagher. Dated 22 Nov., 1748. Proved by the oath of Andrew Wilson, a witness, and execution granted to Henry Wilson, the executor, 28 Nov., 1748.

The testator bequeaths his lands in the town of Deryviear to Henry Wilson, together with all houses and tenements thereunto appertaining, except the tract of land in possession of James Moore. Witnesses: William McClosky, Thomas Hason, and Andrew Wilson.

Diocese of Connor Wills.

Will of John Willson of Belley Lagon. Dated January, 1727. Proved by John Willson and John Allen, 5 March, 1728.

The testator bequeaths the lease of the farm on which he lives to his sons Robert and John Willson, and mentions his wife and "children." The farm in Belley Lagon to wife during life, and after her decease to testator's son John. Executors: Testator's wife, Andrew Willson, John Allen, and George Willson. Witnesses: James Steuart, John Morrons, and Thomas Willson.

Will of John Willson of Aghohill. Dated 5 March, 1738–9. Proved at Aghohill, 22 Jan., 1739.

The testator bequeaths to his wife Jean two parts of all stock, both of money, goods, chattels, and the house and land. "And also I leave the third part of the remaining third to my brother's son Robert, and the remainder of the first third part to be equally divided amongst my brother Samuel and his children, and my sister-in-law Elizabeth and her children, and also my brother Robert's daughter Margaret to run equal with the rest of my nephews in the remaining part of the first third." Witnesses: Robert McClure, Francis Hilles, and Andrew McClure.

Will of John Willson of the parish of Ballinderry. Dated 13 Feb., 1747–8. Proved 12 March, 1747–8.

The testator mentions his brothers, Isaac, Samuel, and Henry Willson; sisters, Mary McCoy, and Anne Erwin. Executors: Testator's father (name not given), and brother Samuel Wilson. Witnesses: Thomas Sefton, William Maxwell, and James Cook.

Will of John Willson of Largy in the parish of Killead, Co. Antrim, farmer. Dated 1 June, 1737. Proved by Andrew Willson, one of the executors, 19 November, 1751.

The testator bequeaths to his sons John and Andrew all of his freehold land in Largy, share and share alike. He mentions son Samuel, son-in-law Alexander Young, daughter Esther Willson alias Coaplin, and daughter Margaret Willson alias Bell. Executors: Testator's sons, John and Andrew Willson. Witnesses: Joseph Ewen, Langford Shoen, and Fran. Shoen.

Will of Hugh Willson of Killade. Dated 8 March, 1750–1. Proved by oath of Isabel Wilson, widow of said deceased, 24 Oct., 1751.

The testator mentions his son Hugh Willson, wife, and "son-in-law." Witnesses: George Grice, and Will. Brayen.

Bond. Dated 24 Oct., 1751. Isabell Willson, and Hugh Willson, both of the parish of Killade, and John Cumberland of Lisburn, all in Co. Antrim. £40. For good admon. by said Isabell widow and relict of Hugh Willson of Killade, deceased, of estate of her said husband. Witness: Henry Marmion, Not^y Pub.

Prerogative Wills.

Will of Sir John Wilson of Wilson's Forte, Co. Donegal, Knt. and Bart. Dated 13 April, 1636. Codicil 15 April, 1636.

The testator desires to be buried in the Church of Raphoe, and he bequeaths the Manor of Wilson's Forte, and the lands of Killcaddan which he holds on lease from the Lord Bishop of Derry, to his (testator's) father, William Wilson, Esq., for life, and after his decease to testator's brother Andrew Wilson; provided the said William and Andrew pay unto testator's only daughter Anne Wilson her yearly maintenance for twelve years. If said Andrew die without issue male, before said Anne, then said estate to revert to the said Anne Wilson, subject to a jointure to the widow of Andrew.

In case both the said Andrew Wilson and Anne Wilson die without issue then said estate to revert to testators nephew Andrew Hamilton, and for want of issue, then to the heirs male of John Hamilton, brother of Andrew, then to the heirs male of Francis Hamilton, another brother of Andrew, then to the heirs male of Francis Hassett, son of Francis Hassett of Rosbegg, Co. Fermanagh, then to testator's general heirs forever.

The testator mentions his niece Anna Hamilton, sister of Andrew, John, and Francis, and his (testator's) sister, Rebecca Wilson. Executors: Testator's father, William Wilson, Esq., and . . . . Nicholas Loftus of Dublin. Testator's father-in-law, Sir Thomas Butler, Knt., to be supervisor. Witnesses: Charles Atkinson, Thomas Pamantur, Nicholas Pamantur, John Pitts, Donatus O'Syell, and John Vaughan.

Codicil by which the testator leaves certain bequests viz.: to Neale Donnell, "son unto my brother (sic) Colvagh Donnell" £5; to Mary Donnell, "daughter unto my said brother-in-law Colvagh Donnell, £30."

Will of John Wilson late clerk of the Forge of Inisrush, Co. Londonderry, gentleman. Dated at Antrim, 13 June, 1696. Proved by Richard Wilson brother of said deceased, 18 July, 1696.

The testator bequeaths to his eldest brother, Richard Wilson all of his right title and interest in the fourth part of the forge of Inisrush, Co. Derry, he paying to testator's youngest brother David Wilson, £200. To said brother Richard testator's fourth share of a Decree of £160. recovered against Randle, Earl of Antrim, some time before the late war at the suit of John Wilson late of Ballow and the testator, as executors of Robert Wilson late of Ballow, who bequeathed the said sum of £160 as a legacy to testator and his (testator's) three brothers, James, Richard, and David, to be equally divided. The testator mentions his sister, Sara, wife of Mr. James Hartson. Testator's brother Richard to be sole executor. Witnesses: Ja. Shonnan, and Jonathan Hammond.

Will of John Wilson of Strabane in the parish of Camus, Co. Tyrone, merchant. Dated 16 June, 1735.

Proved by Anne Wilson widow and relict, saving the rights of Patrick and Thomas Wilson, sons of decd.

The testator desires to be buried in the churchyard of Strabane, and mentions wife Ann, sons Patrick, Thomas, and John Wilson; daughters Martha, Ann, wife of Richard Hughes, and Isabella Wilson. Nieces, Sally, daughter of Richard Hughes, and Elizabeth Willson (*sic*) deceased. Executors: Testator's wife, and sons Patrick and Thomas. Overseers: George Gladstanes, Esq. of Lisburn in the parish of Clogher, Rev. Victor Ferguson, and Mr. Hugh Brown of Strabane, merchant. Witnesses: Victor Ferguson, Patr. Caldwell, and John Ferguson.

Will of John Wilson, Rector of Kilcar, Co. Donegal, Clk. Dated 24 Feb., 1740–1. Proved 16 Augt., 1743, by Isabella Wilson, widow and relict of decd., saving the right of the other executors.

The testator bequeaths unto his wife one third part of his personal estate "above the £200 I am obliged to leave her by marriage settlement. The other two thirds for use "of my surviving children." All other effects to be divided amongst my children, Thomas, John, Nicholas, Sarah, and Hannah. Executors: Testator's wife, and Rev. John Robertson of Donegal. Witnesses: Ed. Scanlan, Eliz. Walter, and Nich. Dogherty.

Will of John Willson, mariner on board His Majesty's Ship the *Lyme,* now lying at Spithead. Dated 1 Nov., 1743. Proved 27 May, 1748.

The testator bequeaths all of his estate to his mother Margaret Willson of the parish of St. Catherine's, Dublin, and he appoints her sole executrix. Witnesses: Chas. Calford, and Peter Yearworth.

Letter of testator to his mother in which he mentions his brother [? in law] Tho⁵ Hooks, sisters Mary and Elizabeth, and uncle Johnston.[2]

---

[2] I include this will because it relates to an Ulster family, although resident in Dublin.

GENEALOGICAL GLEANINGS OF THE WILSON, OR WILLSONS, OF ULSTER.[1]

BY THOMAS ALLEN GLENN.

Diocese of Derry Wills.

Will of Hugh Willson in Broglashow. Dated 5 Dec., 1721. Proved 9 August, 1722, by Thomas Martin, John Cross (*sic*), and John Willson.

To testator's wife (name not mentioned) one third part of all my goods & household furnishing & only one cow to Mary Willson daughter to George Willson & all the rest of my worldly goods to be equally divided between my son John Willson & my son (*sic*) John Corss (*sic*) & my son (*sic*) Thomas Martin.

Witnesses: John Scot, George Clenden.

Diocese of Ardagh (searched to 1800).[2]

*George Wilson, Lehery, 1722.

Alexander Wilson, Lisserdowland, Co. Longford, 1765.

Mathew Wilson, Fagharoe, 1769.

William Wilson, Augherickard, 1768.

William Wilson, Cloncoose, 1787.

William Wilson, Drumbruckless, Co. Cavan, 1790.

Will of George Wilson of Lehery, Co. Longford. Dated .... Proved 1722, by Jona Wilson, executrix.

Testator desires to be buried in the Church of Lanesboro, and refers to lands in the Co. of Longford.

Sons John and James, three unmarried, and one

---

[1] And borderland. Many of the descendants of the Ulster Wilsons moved to adjacent places, and a number to the south of Ireland.

[2] * before a name indicates that an abstract of the will is given.

married daughter. Wife (no name mentioned), executrix.
Witnesses: Jean Kelly, Arth. Forbes.

Diocese of Kilmore Wills (searched to 1800).

Admon. (C. T. A.) of Thomas Wilson of the parish of Killersherdine deceased granted to George Wilson and Ann Wilson (widow and relict of the deceased), 25 April, 1711.[3]

*Ann Wilson, Corabagh, Co. Cavan, 1716.
*William Wilson, Drumwhose, Killisherdin, 1743.
*Samuel Wilson, Derryhow, Drumlane, 1746.
*Andrew Willson, Poles, Anageliff, 1752.
*Thomas Willson, Billis, 1763.
John Wilson, Proudstown, Co. Meath, 1792.

Ardagh Admon. Bonds.

William Wilson, Lisardoolin, Templemichael, 1720-1.
Samuel Wilson, Derryhow, 1746.
Mathew Wilson, Farraghroe, Killoe, 1771.
Alexander Wilson, Clonbroney, 1799.

Kilmore Admon. Bonds.

John Wilson, Cornacary, 1759.
Thomas Wilson, Billys, 1763.
George Wilson, Drominiskin, 1768.
Robert Wilson, Drewlamon, 1777.
Thomas Wilson, Belisses, 1800.

Meath Admon. Bonds.

Mark Wilson, Parsonstown, Meath, 1778.

Will of Ann Wilson (*alias* Boyers) in the Co. of Cavan living in the land of Corabagh [widow of Thomas Wilson deceased]. Dated 20 April, 1716. Proved 14 May, 1716.

---

[3] Will missing.

Daughter Mary and her (the latter's) husband Thomas Wilson.

Sons of testatrix, viz.:
Thomas Wilson, and
Hugh Wilson.[4]

Daughters: Sarah, Elizabeth, and Mary (above named, wife of Thomas Wilson).

Lease of Corabagh[5] to testatrix's son Hugh Wilson.

"If Sarah Wilson and Elizabeth Wilson marry without the consent of their uncle Hugh Wilson and Thomas Wilson their natural[6] brother their portions shall not be given to them nor their husbands."

Trustee, "George Wilson who is Exor [of will of testatrix's late husband, Thomas] along with me."

Exor., son Hugh Wilson.

Witnesses: Thomas Wilson, David Campbell, Hugh Wilson.

Will of William Wilson of Drumwhose, in the parish of Killisherdin, Co. Cavan, Linendraper. Dated 13 April, 1742. Proved by James Moore and James Trenor, exors., 20 April, 1743.

Wife Sarah to have lease of house in town of Cootehill, and lands belonging thereto, she to educate testator's children.

Son Adam Wilson under age of 21 years. Daughters, Lidia, Jane, and Elizabeth.

Exors., Brother-in-law James Trenor of Dung, in the parish of Drumgoon, Co. Cavan, Linendraper.

Brother-in-law James Moore of Manor of Corvoggy in said Co., farmer, Kinsman John Boyle of Cootehill, gent., to be director.

---

[4] He was born 1689 (about), and removed to Pennsylvania. See PENNSYLVANIA MAGAZINE, vol. xxxvii, page 507.

[5] Near Cootehill.

[6] *i.e.* natural born, *not* illegitimate as the word is generally understood. The records of this period frequently contain the words "natural and legitimate."

Witnesses: James Hamilton, John Reed, Robert Hicks.

Will of Captain Samuel Wilson of Derryhow in the parish of Drumlane, Co. Cavan, gent. Dated 21 Sept., 1745. Proved by Rebeckah Wilson, relict, 16 Augt., 1746.

The testator desires to be buried in the Church of Drumlane.

Wife Rebeckah Wilson, Lease of Derryhow, and she executrix.

Daughter Rebeckah Anderson "now in America." Grandson Samuel Stephens, and his sister Frances Baker. Nephew Tom Wilson.

Witnesses: Jos. Ingham, Francis Halliday, Richard Moore.

Will of Andrew Willson of Poles in the parish of Anageliff, Co. Cavan. Dated 24 April, 1752. Proved by Robert Wilson, 18 May, 1752. The testator desires to be buried in the Churchyard of Anageliff.

Wife to have money due from a bond of her father James Johnston.

Daughter Elizabeth Wilson.

Testator's father Robert Wilson, and mother Mary. Lands of Poles and Lisdromin.

Children of Samuel Ramsay by testator's sister Mary.

Cousin Robert Wilson.

Uncle James Wilson.

Exors., Mr. James Cottingham, testator's father Robert Wilson and Michael Collum of Stragetly.

Witnesses: A. Evans, Robert Ramsay, John Reily.

Will of Thomas Willson of Billes. Dated 6 Sept., 1762. Proved by the widow, 28 March, 1763.

Testator mentions his wife Uphemia, sons Charles

and Thomas, and daughter Elizabeth. Testator was possessed of freehold farm lands, a mill, and other property.

Exors., Robert Byers, and John Bran.

Indexes to the Act of Settlement.
(Grants).
1666–1684.

John Willson, Waterford.
Nicholas Willson, Clonmell.
Sir Ralph Willson, Limerick.
Rowland Willson, West Meath.
Samuel Willson, Meath, Kings County.
William Willson, West Meath.

Certificates of the Court of Claims.

John Wilson, vi. 24.
Nicholas Wilson, vi. 8.
Rowland Wilson, vi. 17.
William Wilson, vi. 57.
Samuel Wilson, vi. 44.
John Wilson, xi. 58.

Certificates for Adventurers and Soldiers.

Mr. Willson, xxiv. 35.
Ralph Willson, xxvii. 48.
Robert Willson, xxiv. 30.
Samuel Willson, xv. 79.
David Wilson, xxviii. 48.
Edith Wilson, xxix. 81.
John Wilson, xvii. 41, xxiii. 29, 30, 43.
Nicholas Wilson, xxv. 48.
Sir Ralph Wilson, v. 40.
Robert Wilson, xxl. 82.
Rowland Wilson, xiii. 61, xxx. 60.
Susan Wilson, xiii. 61.

*Thomas Wilson, xxix. 83.
William Wilson, xi. 41.

Decrees of Innocents.

*Thomas Wilson, ix. 86.

1668, 2 Jan., the Kings Inn, Dublin. Award to Thomas Wilson, one time an officer in His Majesty's service in Ireland, of lands in Ireland in lieu of arrears of pay. The said lands being part of those seized and set apart by reason of the late horrid Rebellion or Warre which began or broke out in this Kingdome of Ireland upon the twenty-third day of October, 1641. The said Thomas Wilson being an officer as aforesaid during this war, had in common with other officers, a grant of said lands, 7 May, 1659, which is confirmed (Certif. for Adventurers &c., xxix., 83).

14 Carl. 11., 6 Nov. Claim of George Gouldsmith and Hester his wife, to town and lands of Kilbeg in the Co. of West Meath, and Barony of Moycashell, setting forth that Thomas Wilson, esquire, being seized of said town and lands grant the same with his daughter the said Hester to the said George Gouldsmith as a marriage portion, in the year 1650. Claim allowed 4 Augt., 16 Carl. 11. (Decree of Innocents, Roll ix., 86). The decree did not release the remainder of the estate of the said Thomas Wilson, forfeited.

Muster Rolls and Hearth Tax, Raphoe and Derry.

Mr. William Wilson,[1] Raphoe, 1618.
William Wilson, tenant, Raphoe, 1630.
James Wilson, tenant, Raphoe, 1630.
Robert Wilson, tenant, Raphoe, 1630.
John Wilson, tenant, Raphoe, 1630.

---

[1] Father of Sir John Wilson of Wilson's Fort. Mr. William Wilson survived his son, and was living after 1636.

Alexander Wilson, tenant, Raphoe, 1665.
Richard Wilson, Raphoe, 1665.
Humphrey Wilson, 1665.
John Wilson, Derry, 1630.
Gabrael Wilson, Derry, 1630.
James Willsone, Derry, 1663.
James Willsonn, Derry, 1663.
Robert Wilsonn, Derry, 1663.
Andrew Wilson, Derry, 1663.

WILTBANK FAMILY RECORD.

[Copied from Wiltbank Bible, in possession of St. Peter's Church, Lewes, Delaware.]

Judge John Wiltbank, departed this life, 1792
Mary Wiltbank wife of John Wiltbank, departed this life, 1795
Cornelius Wiltbank son of Judge John and Mary Wiltbank died 9 November, 1813
Ann Wiltbank, wife of Cornelius Wiltbank, departed this life 9 April, 1801.
Esther Wiltbank wife of Cornelius Wiltbank, departed this life, 1 November, 1802
John Wiltbank, son of Cornelius and Ann Wiltbank was born 23 January, 1795; married Eliza Paynter, A.D. 1817; died 13 February, 1830
Cornelius Wiltbank, son of John and Mary Wiltbank, departed this life 9 November, 1813
Ann Hudson, wife of Henry Hudson, and daughter of Cornelius and Ann Wiltbank, departed this life 24 January, 1812.
Mary Metcalf, wife of Thomas Metcalf, and daughter of Cornelius and Ann Wiltbank, departed this life 29 October, 1814.
Thomas Metcalf, son of Jehu and Esther Metcalf, departed this life, 1 November, 1814 (He survived his loving wife only two weeks)
Robert Wiltbank, son of Cornelius and Ann Wiltbank, departed this life on Sunday, the 22 January, 1815, at the house of his grandfather, Judge John Wiltbank, "Dover," Delaware was buried at the family burial ground on Wednesday, 25 January, 1815, (at Tower Hill Farm near Lewes).

John Wiltbank, son of Cornelius and Ann Wiltbank, departed this life on Saturday morning, 13 February, 1830, aged thirty-five years, twenty-one days. Sermon delivered by Rev. John Mitchell from Luke 12, 37. Buried in Family Ground near Lewes.

John and Eliza Wiltbank's first son was born 5 September, 1818; and departed this life 15th of the same month.

Samuel Paynter Wiltbank, son of John and Eliza Wiltbank was born 19 April, 1820

John Cornelius Wiltbank, son of John and Eliza Wiltbank was born on Tuesday, 15 July, 1823

Alfred Stockley Wiltbank, son of John and Eliza Wiltbank, was born on Saturday, 12 September, 1829

John Cornelius Wiltbank, departed this life 9 September, 1829

Alfred Stockley Wiltbank and Hannah Richards Wolfe were married by Rev. John L. M'Kim, 28 January, 1852

Samuel Rowland, John Paynter and Alfred Stockley, children of Alfred S. and Hannah R. Wiltbank, all died in infancy

Frank Comly Wiltbank, son of Alfred and Hannah R. Wiltbank was born 9 July, 1859

Alfred Stockley Wiltbank, M.D. son of John and Eliza Wiltbank, departed this life 7 August, 1860

Comly J. Wiltbank M.D. departed this life 23 December, 1886.

Samuel Paynter Senr. was born 20 October, 1736

Samuel Paynter, son of Samuel Paynter Senr, was born 25 August, 1768

Elizabeth Rowland was born 9 December, 1779

Samuel Paynter Junr. and Elizabeth Rowland were married by the Rev. James Wiltbank, at the house of Mr Cornelius Wiltbank, on Wednesday, 16 March, 1796, at four o'clock. That and the next day were remarkably stormy days, but it is hoped that prudence and economy may render the married life a happy one.

Mary Paynter, daughter of Samuel and Elizabeth Paynter, was born

Mary Paynter and Simon K. Wilson, M.D. were married.

Samuel I Wilson, son of Simon K. Wilson, and Mary Paynter was born July 1820; died in 1849.

Mary P. Wilson, wife of Simon K. Wilson, M.D., and daughter of Samuel and Elizabeth Paynter, departed this life 12 November, 1820

Eliza Paynter, daughter of Samuel and Elizabeth Paynter, was born 8 December, 1798; died 14 November, 1857, at Lewes, Delaware

John Wiltbank and Eliza Paynter were married by the Rev. James Wiltbank, on Thursday, 7 August, 1817

Samuel Rowland Paynter, son of Samuel and Elizabeth Paynter, was born

Sarah Paynter, daughter of Samuel and Elizabeth Paynter, died 10 August, 1820.

John Parker Paynter, son of Samuel and Elizabeth

Alfred Stockley Paynter, son of Samuel and Elizabeth Paynter, died aged five years.

Elizabeth Paynter, wife of Samuel Paynter, departed this life 10 November, 1820, aged forty years

Samuel Paynter departed this life on 2 October, 1845 in the 78th year of his age.

"With unfeigned regret that we announce the death of Ex Governor Samuel Paynter at his residence at the Dracot Bridge, Sussex County Delaware, on the 2nd inst. in the seventy-eighth year of his age"—Delaware Journal October 1845

Comly I Wiltbank was baptized by the Rev. Walter Franklin at St. Peter's Church, Lewes, Delaware, 4 August, 1844, making the seventh generation baptized in that church; Sponserd his great-grandfather Ex Governor Paynter of Delaware and grandmother, Eliza P. Wiltbank. He was born 12 May, 1844

J. Comly Jones married, 10 September, 1821 by the Rev. Mr Meyer, Mary Hillborn, daughter of Joseph and Rachel Roberts

Rachel Roberts Jones, daughter of Comly and Mary H. Jones was born 7 May, 1824

Samuel Paynter Wiltbank was married to Rachel Roberts Jones 4 August, 1842, by the Right Reverend Bishop H. M. Onderdonck

Mary Elizabeth Wiltbank, daughter of Samuel Paynter and Rachel Roberts Wiltbank, was born 1 August

Died at Philadelphia on the 10th day of June, 1845, J. Comly Jones aged forty-nine years

Died on the 23rd February, 1850, Charles B. Jones in the seventeenth year of his age

Died on 7 June, 1860, Mary R. Jones, in the nineteenth year of her age

Died in Philadelphia on 7 August, 1860 Dr A. S. Wiltbank of Lewes, Delaware

NOTES ON THE WOODS FAMILY, OF BEDFORD, PENNSYLVANIA.

BY JOSEPH L. DELAFIELD.

GEORGE WOODS: Came of a family of Scotch origin resident in Ireland. He emigrated to America from the northern part of Ireland before 1733, probably with John Woods, who appears to have been his brother. He took the oath of allegiance in Philadelphia in 1740 and settled in Tuscarora, prior to 1754. He was taken captive by the Delaware Indians in 1756, confined in Fort Duquesne, now Pittsburgh, apportioned by the French commander to Chief John Hudson of the Seneca tribe, and later released by him. He was a Presbyterian and had married, before coming to America, Rosanna Hall. By 1762 he had moved to Fort Bedford, now Bedford, where his children and their families had probably preceded him. By occupation he was a packer and Indian trader and owned large trains of horses for transporting merchandise of all kinds from Harris Ferry, now Harrisburg, to Fort Pitt, now Pittsburgh, and the intervening settlements. They had issue:

Thomas Woods.
Rebecca Woods.
George Woods.

SECOND GENERATION.

THOMAS WOODS: Followed the occupation of his father, having commenced to trade prior to 1743 and settled in Bedford probably before 1761. Deputy Sheriff Bedford Co. 1771. His first wife, who had emigrated with him from the North of Ireland, having died shortly after their arrival in Bedford, he married secondly the Jean Woods famous for her competent management of her husband's tavern, during his absence on the trails with his pack trains. He died in 1798, apparently without issue.

REBECCA WOODS: Married George Nixon, probably before emigrating to America, and settled in Bedford, about 1761. They had issue:

Rebecca Nixon.

GEORGE WOODS: A surveyor by profession, his name appears on the records of Lancaster County prior to 1749, after which the records of Cumberland County show that, with his countrymen, many of whom were probably companion emigrants prior to 1733, he was moving westward up the Juniata Valley. In about 1753 he married Jane McDowell, a daughter of Dr. William McDowell, d. 1769, of Peters Township, then in Cumberland County, who had settled in that region in about 1730. In 1755, the date of the birth of his eldest child, he was in Tuscarora, from whence he pushed steadily westward, leading the eventful life of a frontier surveyor in a country harassed by Indian wars, until in about 1759 he located in Bedford. Most of the early surveys in the upper Juniata Valley were made by him. His services to the community in which he lived and to the country in general, may be briefly stated as follows;— Appointed Justice by Commission from George III, King of England, in 1771-3-4; one of a committee appointed by an Act of the General Assembly of the Colony of Pennsylvania in 1771 to purchase a site for the Court House and Jail at Bedford; appointed by an Act of the General Assembly in 1771 to mark definitely the boundaries of Bedford County; Treasurer of Bedford County in 1773-4; member of the General Assembly from Bedford County in 1773; sole Deputy from Bedford County to the Provincial Convention at Philadelphia in 1774 to act on the refusal of the Governor to call a General Assembly; member of the Committee of Correspondence, Bedford County, 1774-5; Colonel Second Battalion Bedford County Militia 1776, in which capacity he served until the end of the Revolution; member Supreme Executive Council Bedford County 1777-8-9; Bedford County Lieutenant 1784-5; surveyed and laid out in 1784 the City of Pittsburgh; member Committee on Navigation Susquehanna River 1785; State Councillor for Bedford Co. 1787; member State Board of Property 1788-9; presiding Justice of the Quarter Sessions 1790; Justice of the Orphans Court 1790; presiding Justice of the Court of Common Pleas, the highest Court in Bedford County in 1790. He was a stanch Presbyterian, to which Church his children and his grandchildren adhered after him. Living to a ripe old age, he died after 1795, possessed of considerable property and honored by the respect and good will of the community in which he had spent a long and useful life. They had issue:

Jane Woods.
Henry Woods.
Mary Woods, b. 1759, d. Oct. 28th, 1840, unmarried.
George Woods.
John Woods.
Ann Woods.

THIRD GENERATION.

REBECCA NIXON: m. first Thomas Fannegan, secondly Isaiah Davis. She had issue:

Alexander Davis, b. 1814, resided at Everett, Bedford County.

JANE WOODS: b. 1755, d. June 12th, 1813, m. 1775 David Espy, b. 1730, d. June 13th, 1795, son of George and Jean (Taylor) Espy. A man of mark in Bedford County prior to and during the Revolution. An attorney by profession, he entered public life, was Deputy of the Provincial Convention in Philadelphia in 1775, member of the Council of Public Safety 1776; Colonel Bedford County Militia 1776, Prothonotary Bedford County 1778 to 1790; Justice Bedford County 1778. They had issue:

David Espy, b. 1777, d. 1818, unmarried, Captain Bedford County Militia.
Mary Elizabeth Espy.
George Espy, b. 1781, d. 1855, unmarried.

HENRY WOODS: Resided at Bedford and Hazelwood, Allegheny County, where he kept a handsome establishment and was active and useful in public life; Lieutenant Bedford County Militia, 1779, and elected to Congress 1799, d. 1826. He had issue:

Henry Woods.
John George Woods.

GEORGE WOODS: b. 1764, d. August 25th, 1807, a surveyor by profession and a man of distinction in Bedford, where he made his home when not in Pittsburgh or at Steubenville, Ohio. He ran for Congress on the Federalist ticket about 1806. Assisted his father in the survey of the City of Pittsburgh in 1784 and surveyed and laid out the City of Cincinnati. He married Anna McDowell, a daughter of Dr. John and Martha (Johnston) McDowell, of Philadelphia. They had issue:

Anna Woods.
Margaretta Woods, m. John S. Dike, d. without issue.
Mary Lythe Woods, died unmarried.

JOHN WOODS: One of the first men admitted to practice law at the Bar of Pittsburgh. He rose rapidly to distinction in his profession and helped create and maintained by his example the high standard which is so rightly attributed to the Bench and Bar of that City. He assisted his father in plotting the City of Pittsburgh; was a Presidential Elector in 1796, a State Senator in 1797 and represented Allegheny in Congress from 1815 to his death in 1817, leaving issue, a daughter who married Judge Henry M. Breckenridge of Pittsburgh and Carlisle.

ANN WOODS: b. Jan. 20th, 1771, d. Sept. 11th, 1805, m. Jan. 13th, 1791, James Ross, b. July 12th, 1762, d. Nov. 27th, 1847, son of Joseph and Jane (Graham) Ross, resided in Pittsburgh and at the Meadows, Allegheny County. Senator Ross served as a young man in the Revolutionary

Army; was one of the most prominent members of the First Pennsylvania Constitutional Convention; represented his native state in the United States Senate from 1794 to 1803; for three years in 1799, 1802 and 1805 he was the candidate of the Federal party in Pennsylvania for the office of Governor, was chairman of the committee named by Washington to compose the Whiskey Insurrection; was legal adviser and an intimate friend of General Washington. They had issue:

George Woods Ross, b. April 16th, 1792, d. Feb. 10th, 1814, unmarried.

James Ross, b. July 21, 1794, d. July 30th, 1795, unmarried.

Mary Jane Ross.

James Ross, b. May 23rd, 1799, d. Nov. 7th, 1851, unmarried.

Mary Ross, b. Sept. 21st, 1801, d. Aug. 5th, 1802, unmarried.

FOURTH GENERATION.

MARY ELIZABETH ESPY: b. 1779, d. Nov. 28th, 1815, m. July 10th, 1807, John Anderson, M. D., b. May 1st, 1770, d. March, 1840, son of Thomas and Margaret Alice (Lyon) Anderson, who acquired large properties in Bedford, where he resided in the homestead erected by Col. Espy, and towards the latter part of his life devoted himself to the development of the now famous Bedford Mineral Springs. He was Prothonotary of Bedford County. They had issue:

George Woods Anderson.
Espy Lyon Anderson.
Ann Jane Anderson, died young, unmarried.
Mary Woods Anderson.
Elizabeth Stewart Anderson, b. 1814, d. 1865, unmarried.

HENRY WOODS: Collector of the Port of Pittsburgh and Sheriff of Allegheny County. Resided at Hazelwood,

Allegheny County. He married Rachael E. Keller, daughter of Daniel Keller of Pittsburgh. They had issue:
Henry Woods, d. unmarried.
Mary Woods.
Rachael Woods, d. unmarried.
Prudence Woods, d. unmarried.
Ida Woods, d. unmarried.

JOHN GEORGE WOODS: Resided at Hazelwood, Allegheny County, m. Mary Ann Piper, d. 1792, she married secondly Dr. George W. Duffy of Philadelphia. He had issue:
Lucy P. Woods, married Col. Richard Penn Smith, resided on Staten Island, New York.
Florence Woods, married Dr. Hilton, resided in Philadelphia.
William Woods.

ANNA WOODS: m. Dr. Nathaniel Dike of Steubenville, Ohio, and had issue:
Virginia Dike.
George Dike, d. unmarried.
William Lythe Dike, d. unmarried.

MARY JANE ROSS: b. June 28th, 1797, d. Sept. 27th, 1825, m. Oct. 7th, 1816, Edward Coleman, son of Robert and Ann (Old) Coleman, of Lancaster and Philadelphia, b. July 4th, 1792, d. June 6th, 1841, (he married secondly Ann C. Griffith of Philadelphia, by whom he had no issue) served as a member of the Assembly and of the Senate of the State of Pennsylvania. They had issue:
Anne Ross Coleman.
Harriet Coleman.
Mary Jane Coleman, b. Aug. 21st, 1825, d. March 25th, 1847, unmarried.

FIFTH GENERATION.

GEORGE WOODS ANDERSON: A physician by profession, b. June 27th, 1808, d. June 20th, 1877, m. Caroline Mossell and had issue:

Perry Woods Anderson, b. June 18th, 1856, d. Jan. 1st, 1886, unmarried.

George Mossell Anderson, b. July 27th, 1858, m. Oct. 6th, 1886, Kathleen O'Neill, b. Nov. 8th, 1864. They reside at Bedford.

ESPY LYON ANDERSON: b. March 28th, 1810, d. May 12th, 1866, m. Feb. 26th, 1835, Louisa H. Watson, b. May 18th, 1817, d. Oct. 3rd, 1884. They had issue:

John Anderson, b. Aug. 2nd, 1837, d. unmarried.

Major William Watson Anderson, b. July 29th, 1839, d. Jan. 17th, 1856, unmarried.

Dr. James Ross Anderson, b. Sept. 14th, 1841, d. Jan. 19th, 1873, unmarried.

George Espy Anderson.

Mary Espy Anderson.

Eliza Watson Anderson, b. 1848, m. Irwin Beatty of Harrisburg, no issue.

Louisa Harrison Anderson.

Edward Harrison Anderson, b. April 15th, 1855, d. Feb. 1883.

MARY WOODS ANDERSON: b. 1812, d. Dec. 25th, 1872, m. Jan. 11th, 1843, Frank Johnston of Pittsburgh, b. Oct. 31st, 1816, d. Sept. 10th, 1863, son of Alexander Washington and Ann (Poyntell) Johnston. They had issue:

Alexander Johnston, b. Oct. 21st, 1843, d. May 5th, 1876, unmarried.

Ross Johnston.

Mary Espy Johnston.

VIRGINIA DIKE: m. Thomas S. Blair of Tyrone, and had issue:

George Blair.

Thomas Blair.

Anna Dike Blair.

ANNE ROSS COLEMAN: b. Nov. 7th, 1818, d. Dec. 2nd, 1895, m. Dec. 12th, 1837, George Woolsey Aspinwall, b.

Jan. 10th, 1814, d. June 19th, 1854, of Philadelphia, and had issue:
Mary Jane Aspinwall, b. Sept. 22nd, 1840, d. Feb. 28th, 1842, unmarried.
Emily Aspinwall, b. March 15th, 1843, d. Aug. 10th, 1844, unmarried.
Georgina Aspinwall, b. May 1st, 1845, d. July 21st, 1873, unmarried.
Harriet Coleman Aspinwall, b. Jan. 1st, 1849, d. Feb. 28th, 1850, unmarried.
Edward Aspinwall, b. 1855, d. June 30th, 1869, unmarried.

HARRIET COLEMAN; b. July 5th, 1820, d. May 3rd, 1848, m. Dec. 7th, 1841, Eugene A. Livingston, son of Robert L. and Margaret M. (Livingston) Livingston, of Clermont and New York City, (he married secondly Elizabeth Rhodes Fisher of Philadelphia, by whom he had issue), b. Aug. 30th, 1813, d. Dec. 22nd, 1893. They had issue:
Eugene Livingston, b. Jan. 8th, 1845, d. Dec. 31st, 1862, unmarried.
Mary Coleman Livingston.

SIXTH GENERATION.

GEORGE ESPY ANDERSON: b. Oct. 30th, 1843, d. April 30th, 1885, m. June 3rd, 1869, Rebecca Johnson. They had issue:
Mary Espy Anderson.
Espy Lyon Anderson.
Thomas Johnson Anderson.
Louisa Anderson.

MARY ESPY ANDERSON: b. July 17th, 1846, d. Feb. 29th, 1890, m. M. Edward Middleton of Philadelphia. They had issue:
Lillian Middleton.
Edwin Middleton.

Louisa Harrison Anderson: b. June, 1850, m. William O. Hickok of Harrisburg. They had issue:
William Orville Hickok.
Ross Anderson Hickok.
Louisa Hickok.

Ross Johnston: b. Sept. 1st, 1848, d. March 11th, 1885, resided at Pittsburgh, m. Sept. 18th, 1879, Anna Dike Blair. They had issue:
Virginia Blair Johnston, m. J. Frazer Harris and have issue.

Mary Espy Johnston: m. Dec. 27th, 1877, Prof. William Milligan Sloane of Princeton and New York City, b. Nov. 12th, 1850, son of James Renwick W. and Margaret (Milligan) Sloane, and have issue:
Mary Renwick Sloane, m. Joseph L. Delafield.
James Renwick Sloane.
Francis Johnston Sloane.
Margaret Milligan Sloane.

George Blair: Resident at Newcastle. He has issue:
Virginia Blair, m. Henry Thornton.
Cust Blair.
George Blair.

Thomas Blair: Resident at Chicago, m. Emma Parker. They have issue:
Margaretta Blair.
Thomas Blair.

Anna Dike Blair: m. 1st Ross Johnston and 2nd Harvey Childs, of Pittsburgh, and has issue:
Virginia Blair Johnston.
Harvey Childs.
Blair Childs.

MARY COLEMAN LIVINGSTON: b. Aug. 17, 1847, m. Dec. 1st, 1868, Maturin L. Delafield, of New York City, b. Feb. 17th, 1836, son of Joseph and Julia (Livingston) Delafield, and have issue:

Maturin Livingston Delafield, m. Lettice Lee Sands.
Joseph Livingston Delafield, m. Mary Renwick Sloane.
John Ross Delafield, m. Violetta Susan White and have issue.
Julia Livingston Delafield, m. Frederick William Longfellow, and have issue.
Edward Coleman Delafield, m. Margaretta Stockton Beasley, and have issue.
Mary Livingston Delafield.
Harriet Coleman Delafield, m. Jarvis Pomeroy Carter, and have issue.
Eugene Livingston Delafield, m. Margaret Nevius Woodhull, and have issue.

ZANE FAMILY.—Copies of memoranda relative to the Zane family, in possession of George Vaux, of Philadelphia.

These memoranda all bear the marks of being very ancient, but there is nothing to indicate when they were prepared. There are five in all, one of them being written on the back of the title-page of a New Testament, which has evidently been torn from a Bible. The printed date has unfortunately been lost from the lower part of the page.

Robert Zane came from Ireland to America in the year [date torn off] landed at Elsinburra near Selam in West Jersey and stayd there about 4 years, in which time he tuck a canew and went in sarch of a settlement & padled along the side of the river & up the creeks till at last he chose a place up Newton Creek in gloster County, which place is cald

Newton. here he settled having only one child whose name was Nethaniel and was about 2 years old when they landed.

afterwards he marred one of Hinry Willises Daughters by whom he had Sons & Daughters Namly Nathan, Robert, Ester, Elnathan & Rachel. Ester marred Joshua Delaplan & left 2 sons namly Joshua & Joseph in New York. Rachel marred Joshua Pine on long Island and after his Death marred Jonathan Peasley by him she had one daughter named Elizabeth.

And Nathan had 3 children Elizabeth Nathan & Nethaniel. Elizabeth married somewhere in Merland & I never knew her Nathan died before he marred a sober young man. Robert marred in the Jerseys and has many children Sons & Daughters

My grandfather afterwards marred

Robert Zane of Newtown came into America in ye year 1673 he was 3 times married—his last wife was Hinrey Willises Daughter by whom he had 5 children namely Robert Nathan Elnathan Hester & Rach[el]

Nethaniel Zane of Newtown in West Jersey was by his first wife: who she was and from whence thers no ac[count] he Died the last day of the 12th month 1728/29 aged 55 years and left 8 children namely Margrit, Abegall Josep, Hannah, Jonathan, Ebenezear, Isaac and William which were all liveing when the younges (namely W^m) was about 34 years old. Isaac was boarn ye 3 day of the 3 mo 1711 and married ye 15 of ye 11 mo 1734 Sarah Elfreth the daughter of Hinrey Elfreth and had 8 children by the time he was 40 years old Namely Hannah, Phebe (who died between 3 & 4 years old) Isaac (he also Died under 2 years old) John, Isaac, Danel (Died under 2 years old) Phebe (she Died under 2 years old) Danel the 5th son was boarn about the time of this was writ

After the Deth of the above s^d Nethanial Zane grace his widow who was a Daughter of William Rakestraw married David Price at Merian and she died the 6th Day of the 10th month 1741

The Time of births of the children of Isaac & Sarah Zane
1 Hannah was bornd ye 23d of ye 10th mo 1734/5
2 Phebe the 16th 2d m^o 1737 and died ye 26th 2nd m^o 1740
3 Isaac the 23 of the 10th mo 1738/9 & died ye 6th of ye 3d m^o 1740
4 John the 9 of the 12th m^o 1740/1
5 Isaac the 26 of ye 4 mo 1743

[The following is written on the back of the title-page of a New Testament as mentioned above. It is in a very dilapidated condition.]

1733 ye 3 mo Isa^c Zane his book
Isaac and Sarah Zanes Book

The birth and Nativaty of hannah Zane was the 23 of the 10th month in the year of our Lord 1734/5

The Birth of Phebe Zane was the 16 day of ye 2 month 1737 at ¼ before 2 of ye clok in ye morning

Birth or Nativaty of Isaac Zane was the [torn off] day of ye 10 month about 8 a clok ad night the year of our Lord 1738/9

Phebe Zane Died the 26th day of ye 2 mo 1740 3 yers & 10 days and her departure was nere half an hour after 6 o clok after noon

Isaac Zane died about half a houer after one o clock at knight betwe^n ye 5th & ye 6th day of ye 3 mo 1740 aged [torn off] year & 5 mo & 13 days

[Jo]hn Zane the son of Isa^c & Serah Zane was bornd about 2 a clock at night betwen the 8th & 9th of y^e [torn off] month 1740/1

The birth or nativity of Isaac Zane the 26th of the 4th month 1743

[The remaining paper, as follows, though containing early dates, was probably prepared later than the others.]

Magrett Zane Daughter of Nathaniel Zane and Grace his wife Was Born the 1 day of 9 month 1698
Abigall Born 17 day of 5 month July 1700
Joseph Born 1 day 6 month Augt 1702
Hannah Born 19 day No^r 1704
Jonathan Born 29 day Sep^t 1706
Ebeneazear Born 7 day Dece^m 1708
Isaac Born 3 day 3 month 1710
William Born 26 day 11 month 1712

Deborah Zane Daughter of Joseph Zane & Mary his Wife Was Born 22 day of Augt 1729
Ester Born 27 day 12 Month 1730
Nathaniel Born 8 day 3 Month 1732
Elizabeth Born 9 day 7 Month 1735
Hannah Born 27 day 1 Month 1738
Rodah Born 8 day 3 Month 1740

APPENDIX

ACHEY–STIEGEL GENEALOGICAL NOTES.—Copied by Luther R. Kelker, of Harrisburg, Penna., from an old German Hymn Book.

Thomas Achey, Heidelberg Twp. Lancaster Co., Penna. Born Nov. 9, 1769. Witnesses present at his baptism were Thomas Filbert and his wife Catherine. He died Nov. 20, 1838.

Christine Stiegel, his wife, (daughter of Anthony Stiegel and Christine Neip), born Oct. 27, 1771. Witnesses present at her baptism, were her grandparents John Neip and his wife Agatha.

They were married August 9, 1789, and had issue:
Christine, b. Dec. 21, 1790, d. Feby. 23, 1821.
John, b. March 25, 1792.
Catherine, b. March — 1793, d. Dec. 15, 1821.
Samuel, b. May — 1795.
Thomas, b. May — 1797.
Henry, b. Aug. 20, 1799, d. Nov. 12, 1831.
Peter, b. March 26, 1802, d. March 9, 1827.
Charles, b. June 10, 1805, d. March 28, 1839.
Anthony, b. Oct. 20, 1807, d. July 12, 1826.
Frederick, b. May 12, 1809.
Filbert, b. March 14, 1812, d. Feb. 4, 1832.
Lydia, b. Aug. 14, 1815.

JAMES ANDERSON OF YORK COUNTY, PENNA.—

James Anderson, of Maryland, md. Sept 1774, *Mary Boyd,* b. in Ireland, 1756. They had issue:
Anna, b. Aug 1776.
Margaretta, b. Feb. 2, 1780.
George, b June 29, 1782.
Maria, b. Aug. 14 1784.

YORK COUNTY, PENNA., GENEALOGICAL NOTES, 1780.—
James and *Elizabeth (Boyd) Anderson*, md. September 1774, had issue :
    Anna, b. Aug. 1776.
    Margaret, b. Feb. 2, 1780.
    George, b. June 29, 1782.
    Maria, b. Aug 14, 1784.
PETER BINKELE, b. March 2, 1704 in Switzerland, md. Feb. 2. 1725.
Maria Werle, b. Oct. 28, 1704 in Alsace, d. Sept. 1748, and had issue :
    Maria b. Dec. 26, 1725.
    Catherine, b. March 25. 1727.
    Peter, b. June 25, 1728. d.
    Christmann, b. Sept. 27, 1729. d.
    Anna, b. June, 26, 1731. d.
    Sarah, b. Feby. 24 1733.
    Margaret, b. July 24, 1735.
    Christina, b. Feb. 21, 1738.
    Elizabeth, b. Feb. 16. 1740. d.
    Anna Barbara, b. May 26, 1741. d.
    John, b. March 26, 1743
    John Adam, b. Aug. 13, 1744.
Married second *Anna Margaret Ginger*. Feb. 3, 1749. She was b. Jany. 18, 1722, in Wurtemberg. Issue :
    Elizaeth, b. Dec. 8, 1749.
    Christian, b Jany. 28, 1751.
    John Peter, b. Jany, 30, 1753.
    Anna Maria, b. Feb. 22, 1755. d. 1759.
    Frederick, b. Nov. 4, 1757.
    Joseph, b. July 9, 1761.

RECORD OF THE ANTHONY FAMILY OF PHILADELPHIA,* from the Gesang Buch of Jacob Anthony. 1774.—[See Hildeburn No 3023.]

Jacob Anthony was born 13 October, 1764.

Sukey Anthony was born February 1766.

Michael Anthony was born the 16th of April and christened the 22nd of April and departed from this world the 15th of June, 1788.

John Anthony was born the 28 July, 1789 and christened the 16th of August, 1789, and departed the 27th of July, 1790.

Jacob Anthony was born 7 June, 1792, died 30 September, 1798.

Joseph Anthony was born the 25th July, 1795.

Sally Anthony was born the 30th October, 1797.

William Anthony was born 15 January, 1801.

Catharine Sherer, of Bustleton, wife of Joseph Anthony, died August 1752.

Jacob Anthony was married 15 July, 1787 to Susanna Cart.

John Anthony born 16 April, 1788.

Peter Anthony was born the 28th November, 1804, and christened March the 3rd, 1805.

Jacob W. Anthony, born 17 August, 1820, died 16 February, 1897, son of Joseph Anthony. Mary Abel, wife of Jacob W. Anthony, born 26 March, 1826, died 12 November, 1901, daughter of John Abel, by his wife Mary Himes. Her grand-father was Frederick Himes and his wife Sarah McCoombs.

Henry P. Anthony, son of Joseph Anthony, born 26 August, 1823.

Joseph H. Anthony, born Sunday, 18 October, 1845.

Caroline R. Cramp, wife of Joseph H. Anthony was born 18 November, 1849.

*The Pennsylvania Gazette of October 14 1772, has the following advertisement: JACOB ANTHONY *Turner and Instrument Maker at the Sign of the German Flute and Hautboy &c. on the East-side. the upper End of Second-Street, a little Way above Vine-Street, near the Vendue-House,* Begs leave to acquaint the Public that he makes and sells all Sorts of Musical Instruments, and German Flutes of all Sorts, common Flutes, Hautboys, Clarinetts, and Soldiers Fifes; he also mends old Ones; and makes all Sorts of other Turner's Work.

BARTOW GENEALOGY.—Thomas Bartow, merchant of Philadelphia, [son of Thomas Bartow, b. 22 Oct. 1709 at West Chester, New York, d. Bethlehem 5 Dec. 1782] was born at Perth Amboy N. J. 1737. Married 23 June 1768, Sarah daughter of Daniel and Elizabeth (North) Benezet. Their children were:
Elizabeth, b. 24 March 1769, md. Christian Reich.
Mary, b. 16 June 1770, md. George Peter.
Thomas, b. 4 July 1771.
Sarah, b. 1 July, 1773, md. William Geddes Latimer.
Susannah, b. 10 July 1775, md. John David.
Daniel, b. 16 July 1777.
Anna, b. 14 May 1779, md. Joseph Drinker.
Helene, b. 1783, md. John Sergent.
John Benezet, b. 16 Aug. 1787.
Benjamin, b.23 April 1789, d. 9 Nov. 1790.   B.

BARTOW.—Thomas Bartow, Jr., was born in Perth Amboy, New Jersey, in 1737; died in Philadelphia, January 26, 1793. He was a son of Thomas Bartow, Sen., born October 22, 1709, in Westchester County, New York; died in Bethlehem, Pennsylvania, December 5, 1782. He filled many civil offices under the Colonial government. Thomas Bartow, Jr., married, June 23, 1768, Sarah, daughter of Daniel and Elizabeth (North) Benezet, born in Philadelphia, February 23, 1746, and died July 14, 1818. Their children were:
Elizabeth, born March 24, 1769; married Christian Reich. *Mary*, born June 16, 1770; married George Peter. *Thomas*, born July 4, 1771. *Sarah*, born July 1, 1773; married William Geddes Latimer. *Susanna*, born July 10, 1775; married John David. *Daniel*, born July 16, 1777. *Anna*, born May 14, 1779; married Joseph Drinker. *Helena*, born ——, 1783; married John Sergent. *John Benezet*, born August 16, 1787. *Benjamin*, born April 23, 1789; died November 9, 1790.

BATTLE—PRICE.—Copy of entries in Book of Common Prayer, which belonged to James and Mary Price of Christiana Mills, New Castle County, Delaware, and is now in the possession of Mr. William J. Williams of Philadelphia. It is deficient in title-page, but the Psalter, bound with it, was "Printed by J. Barber, for J. Holland, at the Bible and Ball, and W. Taylor at the Ship, both in St. Paul's Church-yard, 1707." The record, other than that of the Battell family is not consecutive.

CHRISTIANNA MILLS.

Mary Battell, daughter to William Battell* and Parnellah his wife, was born the 27th of September, at eleven o'clock in the day in the year 1723.
French Battell was born the 16th day of July, 1725.
Aves Battell was born the 25th day of June, 1727.
Sebeller Battell was born the 6th day of April, 1729.
Elizabeth Battell was born the 30th August, 1730.
In another hand Mary Price, March the 29th, 1752.

* William Battell married 19 June, 1718, Parnel French [Records of Immanuel Church, New Castle], daughter of John French. The will of the latter, dated 22 November, 1728, probated 12 December, of the same year, and on file in the Registry of Wills of New Castle County, styled him "Colonel John French of New Castle upon Delaware, gentleman." In it, Colonel French named wife Eves, daughters Mary and Sybilla French, sons-in-law Robert Robertson and Captain William Battell and grand-children Mary Battell, Avis Battell and Mary Robertson, also a "beloved grand-son." Colonel French was a familiar figure in Colonial Pennsylvania, serving successively as Sheriff of New Castle County, Register of Wills, Master of the Court of Chancery, Justice of the Supreme Court, and a member of the Governor's Council at the time of his death. M. A. L.

NEW CASTLE, December 9, 1749.

Robert, son of Mary Mackys was born on the 9th of this inst, about . . . o'clock in the morning.
Mary Price departed this life 25 April, 1777.
Ruth Price, daughter of James Price and Mary his wife, was born January 5th, 1753, about 12 o'clock in the day in New Castle Hundred.
Ruth Price departed this Life the 27th Day of October in the year 1753, in the tenth month of her age.
Aves Price was born on Wednesday at eleven o'clock in the morning, 26 March, in the year 1755 in Penn Cader Hundred, New Castle County.
M. James Price, April the 22nd, 1759.
Mary Price was delivered of a son the 18th of October, 1766, which died the 24th of the same month.
William Price was born in the year of our Lord, 9 April, 1761, in Penn Cader Hundred in New Castle County.
James Price departed this life March ye 25th at midnight, 1802.
William Price Departed this life March ye 24th about 4 o'clock in the afternoon, in the year of our Lord, 1803.
Esther Price departed this Life September ye 16th in the year of our Lord 1773.

Records on the back of the Marriage Certificate of William Blackfan, Jr. and Esther Dawson.

Elizabeth Blackfan Daughter of William Blackfan Juneor & Esther His Wife was Born the 23^d Day of ye Second Month about Eight o'Clock Mor^n In ye year of our Lord 1759.

Rachel Blackfan Daughter of William Blackfan & Esther His Wife was Born the 29th Day of ye 8th Month about 5 o'Clock In the afternoon, in the year of our Lord 1760.

John Blackfan Son of William Blackfan & Esther His Wife was Born the 20th Day of 2^d Mo. Between 8 & 9 o'Clock in ye afternoon in ye year of our Lord 1762.

Hannah Blackfan Daughter of William Blackfan and Esther his Wife was Born ye 17th day of 7th Month near 2 o'Clock in ye Morning in ye year of our Lord 1764.

Sarah Blackfan daughter of William Blackfan & Esther his Wife was born ye 26th day of the 10th Month in the afternoon in ye year 1766.

Agness Blackfan daughter of William Blackfan & Esther his Wife was born ye 10th day of 3^d Month in the afternoon in the year 1769.

Thomas Blackfan born the 8th day of 2nd M^o 1771 in the afternoon.

William Blackfan was born the 15th day of the first month 1773 Deceased the 4th day of the 4th Month 1773.

William Blackfan was Born the 23^d of the 7th month 1774.

Aaron Blackfan was born the 8th day of the 11th month 1776 Deceased the 29th day of 3^d Month 1777.

William Blackfan Deceased the 9th d. of 8th month 1777.

Jesse Blackfan was born the 17th day of 2nd mo. 1779.

BUCK FAMILY RECORD.—In a prayer-book, printed at Edinburgh, 1783, are the following entries, in a fair hand, relating to the family of Buck, at one time residing in Bridgeton, New Jersey. The book also contains a printed book-plate of "E. Buck," probably done in the present century:

"Joseph Buck was Born 1. May 1758
"Ruth Seeley Novr 15. 1763
"Joseph Buck and Ruth Seeley were married 19th March 1783
"John Buck was Born 1. April 1784
"Maria Buck Sept 25. 1785
"Sarah Buck 11 August 1787
"Jane Buck 4. October 1789
"Hanah Buck 25 October 1791
"Naomi Seeley Buck 13 Sept. 1793
"Ephraim Buck 23^d Feby 1795
"Joseph Buck 23 Decr 1796
"Naomi Seeley Buck died Septr 26th 1798 4 o'clock A.M.
"Maria Buck died same Day at 5 o'clock in the afternoon"
On a fly-leaf in a childish hand,—
"Jeremiah Buck September 8th 1803
"Joseph Buck Sen. died May 15th 1803
"Ruth Ogden died——"

CARTER—SUTTON—MORRIS—HILL—RIDGWAY. — According to a memorandum made by me in February, 1870, the following is a copy of entries in a Bible of 1698 (imprint not recorded in my note) that had once belonged to William Carter:

William Carter, son of Joanas & Dority his mother (*sic*) was born the 20th day of the 4th month called June 1651 & was baptised at one day ould.

William Carter came to Pensilvania the 9th month 1682.

Philadelphia 26th 6th month 1721, William Carter married Mary Sutton, widow.

William Morris son of John and Mary Morris born 27th 4th month 1735, at Spring Mills in White Marsh Township.

Anthony Morris son of John and Mary Morris born at Spring Mills in White Marsh the 10th day of 8th month and 6th day of the week.

And departed this life 9th mo. 2d day, 1740 and was buried at Plimouth Meeting.

The following endorsement, in the handwriting of Mrs. Margaret Morris, *née* Hill, is upon the marriage certificate of William Morris and Margaret Hill, who were married at Philadelphia, 21st Ninth Month, 1758:

Richard Hill Morris & John Morris, Twins, were born Sep. 28. 1759. R. H. M. died Aug. 29. 1760. Deborah Morris was born Nov. 29th 1760. Richard Hill Morris was born Sep. 5th 1762.

Mary Morris was born June 19th 1764. Died Feb. 14. 1765.

April ye 14th 1766.

On this sorrowful day my dearly beloved companion & husband W. Morris departed this life (after an illness of 12 days) & is I trust, at rest in the bosom of his & my glorious Redeemer. He was aged 30 years & 9 mos.

And now Lord! what wait I for? my hope is in thee.

Gulielma Maria Morris was born August 18th 1766. The last dear Pledge of the fondest & happiest Love that ever was experienced by Mortals. M. M.

I copy the following from a "Trenton Bible" (printed by Isaac Collins):

Mary Oldden Ridgway (*sic*) was born on 4th Day the 17th Feby 1808, 17 minutes past 10 o'clock in the evening.

Mary Oldden Ridgway Died 26th of November 1809 at 1 o'clock & 50 minutes in the Morning, aged one year nine months & nine Days.

James Ridgway was born 3d day the 28th Nov. 1809 ¼ past 7 o'lk in the evening.

Elizabeth Ridgway was born 2d day the 8th April 1811 15 minutes past 9 o'clock in the evening.

Rebecca Ann Ridgway was born the twenty fourth day of September 1813 about fifteen minutes before nine in the morning, on the Sixth day of the week.   T. S.

THE CHEVALIER FAMILY OF PHILADELPHIA.—Peter Chevalier, perhaps the son of Peter Gerardus Chevalier and Belitije Claerhout, his wife, who was baptized at the Reformed Dutch Church in New York Jan. 1, 1695, removed from New York to Philadelphia about 1720, and resided here until his death, which probably occurred in 1769, as his estate was administered by his two sons Nov. 6, 1769. He had by wife Elizabeth six children: I. Judith, m. April 24, 1735, Joseph Worrell. II. Susanna, born Aug. 21, 1721; m. July 35, 1739, Valentine Standley, of Philadelphia, "Potter," and had issue. III. Jane, baptized Dec. 6, 1723 (date of birth not recorded), m. May 6, 1740, Garland Anderson, and had issue. IV. Elizabeth, born Oct. 9, 1726; m. Dec. 17, 1747, John Baynton, and had issue. V. John Chevalier, born May 29, 1729; died between 1778 and 1786. He m. Feb. 13, 1760, Eleanor, dau. of Thomas Berkley, by his wife Jane, dau. of the Hon. Anthony Palmer, whose will was proved Jan. 27, 1789. They had eight children: 1. Peter Chevalier, bapt. Dec. 14, 1760 (date of birth not stated), died young. 2. John Chevalier, born June 29, 1762, living in 1786, died before July 19, 1802. 3. Jane Chevalier, born Aug. 1764, died unm., will proved July 6, 1796. 4. Elizabeth, born Oct. 10, 1767, m. 1786 John Shaeffer. 5. George Chevalier, born Oct. 1, 1769; administration granted July 15, 1790. 6. Thomas Chevalier, named in his mother's will, m. Susanna Evans, and had one child, John Barkley Chevalier, who was living in 1796. Letters of administration were granted to Susanna, widow of Thomas, Dec. 13, 1793. 7. Samuel Chevalier, born April 7, 1776; will proved April 25, 1816, in which he mentions his wife Susanna and four children, viz., Elizabeth Chevalier, William Wagner Chevalier, Susan Chevalier, and Samuel Chevalier. 8. Andrew Chevalier, born Aug. 29, 1778, died young. VI. Peter Chevalier, born March 25, 1730-1; m. May 16, 1759, Mary, dau. of James Renaudet, by his wife Belitije Mooglandt. His will was proved Nov. 10, 1778. They had seven children: 1. Isabella, born Nov. 17, 1760, m. George Turner, and had issue. 2. Peter Renaudet Chevalier, born Dec. 12, 1761, was graduated at the University of Pennsylvania in 1780, m. Jane Harriet, who died in 1847, aged 87 years. He died before June 1, 1805, leaving a dau., Ann Renaudet Chevalier, born May 28, 1792. 3. James Chevalier, born Aug. 6, 1765, living 1778, dead in 1805. 4. Susannah Chevalier, born Dec. 12, 1767; m. —— Francis, and had issue. 5. Morris Chevalier, born Aug. 6, 1769; died young. 6. Richard Chevalier, named in his father's will, dead in 1805. 7. William Chevalier, named in his father's will; executor of his mother's will in 1816.   C. R. H.

CLOWES FAMILY RECORD.—From original, now in possession of M^{rs}. Watson, of Milford, Delaware, and said to have been copied from the diary of the Rev. William Beckett.

[In the Episcopal burying-ground of Jamaica is the grave of Samuel Clowes, the first lawyer settled upon Long Island, who died 27 August, 1760; that of his wife Catherine Donne, who died 7 August, 1740, and that of his son, Samuel, a lawyer also, who died 19 May, 1759. Thompson's History of Long Island says of him, that he was born at Derbyshire, England, March 16, 1674, and was instructed in mathematics by Flamstead, for whose use the Greenwich Observatory was erected; that he came to New York in 1697, accompanied Lord Cornbury to Jamaica in 1702, and was forthwith appointed clerk of the county, which he held until 1710, when his professional business compelled him to resign it. If his will, printed in the Collections of the New York Historical Society, Volume XXIX, pp. 423–4, be correctly transcribed, he was born in 1664, as at the making thereof, 24 July, 1750, and "written with my own hand," he begins with, "I, Samuel Clowes, of Jamaica, in Queens County, Gent., being now 85 years and 5 months old, and infirm of body, but Praised be God, of sound mind." His son, Samuel Clowes, Junr., was for many years Surrogate of Queens County, his son, Peter Clowes, was a physician in practice in Broadkill Hundred, Sussex County, Delaware, before 1735, and was elected high-sheriff of that county in 1748, and his son, John Clowes, to whose family this record appertains, was commissioned Justice of the Peace of Sussex County in 1752.]

Samuel Clowes the oldest on this record was born in 1684, and died in 1760, being seventy-six years old. He was buried at Jamaica, where his tomb still stands. He was alternately a Lawyer and Judge. His wife's name was Catherine. They left six sons. Peter, their first, left no children who settled in Lewestown, Delaware. John their son left sons. Caleb the third son left no children. Joseph no children. Samuel, their fifth son, left no children. Gerardus, their sixth son left three sons, whose names are Samuel, Timothy and John Clowes, all of these lived on Long Island, at Hampstead, and at the City of New York. Many of the above-named persons' descendants were still living in 1823, in those places; a few of [whose] names we will give here: Thomas, Samuel, Isaac, Gerardus, John, Joseph, Benjamin, Timothy, Theodore, Edward, Charles and William.

John Clowes, second son of the aforesaid Samuel Clowes, settled in the State of Delaware, anno domini 1727, August the twenty-fifth, at five o'clock. John Clowes was married to Mary, his wife, at Lewes Town, in the County of Sussex in Delaware, by the Rev. William Beckett, missionary from the Society for propagating the gospel.

On 1728, June 28th, at four o'clock in the morning, was born William Clowes, eldest son of the said John and Mary his wife, was born at Broadkill in the County of Sussex, and was Christened by the above Becket, privately at Lewestown on the 28th August, Mr Becket, Jonathan Bayley, Jane and Mrs Becket his sponsors.

1730, November 5th, at eleven in the morning, John Clowes their second son was born at Lewistown, and there Christened by the same Mr Beckett, on the 11th of December following. His Sponsors were: Mr Ryves Holt, John Welbor and Mrs Holt.

1732, August 28th at one o'clock in the morning, their first daughter, Aletta Clowes was born at Lewes, and on the 5th September was Christened by the said Mr Becket privately, being very sick and on the sixth inst died at eight o'clock in the morning, and was buried in the Churchyard at Lewestown.

1733, September 16th, at five o'clock in the morning, David Clowes, the third son was born at Lewistown and christened there by Mr Becket, 28 April, 1734; his sponsors Mr Rives Holt, Mr Peter Clowes and Mrs Comfort Clowes.

1736, July 9th, at nine in the morning, Catherine Clowes, their second daughter was born at Lewistown and there christened by the said Mr Becket the fifth of September following. Her sponsors were Daniel Nunez, Mrs Mary Nunez and Mrs Eliza Price

1737, December 31st at six in the morning, their fourth son, Samuel Clowes was born at Lewestown and there christened on the 5 March following. His sponsors were Simon Kollock, Edward Naws and Mrs Comfort Kollock. He lived until 19th March, 1758 and was buried at Broadkill in the burying-ground of his mother's relations, lamented by his relations

1739, February 7th at five in the morning, their third daughter Mary Clowes was born at Lewes and there christened by Mr Beckett on 27th of April following. Her sponsors were Cornelius Wiltbank, Margaret Kollock and Mrs Hester Phillips.

1742, May 19th, at seven in the evening, the fourth daughter, Lydia Clowes was born at Lewestown, and there christened by Mr Beckett, on the first of August, following. Her sponsors were Ryves Holt, Mrs Catherine Holt and Mrs Nunez.

1747, March 12th at ten o'clock in the morning the fifth son, Gerardus Clowes was born at Parkton, on the Broadkill, Sussex County, and was Christened by the Rev. Mr Usher, Missionary at Lewestown on the eighteenth of September following. His sponsors were the said Mr Usher, Mr Daniel Nunez and his own mother.

1766, October 26th, the eldest son William departed this life of pleurisy, and was interred at Eliza Staton's at Broadkill, where his former wife was buried. his four children: First was Catherine. Second was Mary. Third, Lydia born 15 November, 1762. Fourth, John, born 18 March, 1765. In 1763, March 14th, the fifth son Gerardus Clowes perished to death in a most violent storm of snow on Accoqunamen Beach, being drove in a vessel there, and was decently buried there, in an old Burying Ground much lamented by all his Friends.

1769, April 24th, at twelve o'clock in the day, John Clowes Esqr., second son of the aforesaid Samuel Clowes departed this life on the ninth day of pleurisy aged sixty-six years and nine days. The corpse was laid in an open grave on the 27th inst., and on the fifth of June was interred in a new vault, built at his request at Heaveloes Landing. Mr Andrews preached his Funeral [Sermon].

1770, February 5th, at eleven o'clock at night, Mary Clowes widow of the above John Clowes departed this life on the eighth day of her illness, with pleurisy aged about sixty-three years, and on the eighth instant was enterred in the aforesaid Vault. Mr Lyons Preached her Funeral Sermon.

1770, May 25th, at nine o'clock in the morning David Clowes departed this life of a disorder that had continued nearly four years, and on the 27th instant was interred in the aforesaid vault. Mr Lyon Preached his Funeral Sermon. He left but one Child, a daughter. She was born at Nanticoke on the 22nd day of April, 1767, and called Hannah Clowes. [She died] 1783, December 9th at twelve o'clock at night. Died of quinsey and was interred in the above Vault.

1781, November 25th on Sunday, at three o'clock in the morning Lydia Clowes, fourth daughter of John and Mary Clowes and wife of Lott Clark, departed this life of nervous fever, and on the 27th her remains were laid in the vault, and on the 4th December, Mr Tillney

preached her funeral sermon. She left six children three by her first and three by her last husband, viz: Shephard Conwell, born 23 July, 1765. Gerardus Conwell, born 12 November, 1767. John Conwell, born 29 January, 1770.
Milicent Clark, born 29 September, 1776
Anna Clark, born 27 April, 1778
Charlotte Clark, born 12 February, 1780.

1790, February 24th, at five o'clock in the morning, on Wednesday, John Clowes Esqr, judge of the Court, died the ninth day of his sickness with a violent pleurisy and inflamation of the Lungs, aged 59 years, 3 months and 18 days and was buried at the south-side of the Vault. Mr Wilson preached his funeral sermon. He objected to being laid in the Vault. He left his beloved wife and three children out of ten. He was a son of the above mentioned John Clowes, who died in 1769 and grandson of the aforesaid Samuel Clowes who died in 1760.

Catherine Clowes, second daughter of John and Mary, born July 9th at nine in the morning, 1736 and now the widow of John Young has but one child living, viz: John, born on the 28th February, 1772. Mary Clowes, the third daughter of John and Mary Clowes, born February 7th at five o'clock, now the wife of John Sheldren Dorman has four children, viz three sons and one daughter:

 Gerardus Dorman, born 23rd August, 1772
 Nehemiah Dorman, 31 July, 1774
 Elizabeth Dorman, born 29 July, 1776
 John Dorman, 22 May, 1779.

Mary Dorman, wife of John Sheldren Dorman, departed this life about three o'clock on Tuesday morning, 18 January, 1791

1758, September 7th, John Clowes Junr was married to Mary Draper, by the Rev. Mathias Harris at John Spencer Esqr's, her step-father, in the afternoon of the above. Mary Draper, daughter of Isaac and Sarah Draper was born the 10th day of November in the year 1739. The above Sarah Draper after the death of Isaac Spencer married the above said John Spencer. Her maiden name was Hines.

1759, August 17th, on Friday, was born Sarah Clowes, between 12 and one o'clock, daughter of John and Mary baptized on Monday privately by the Rev. Mathias Harris; and on Thursday, the first day of January 1767 at two o'clock in the afternoon was seized with a choking-fitt which ended her life in 9 or 10 hours. She was buried at John Heaveloe's Landing.

1762 March 22nd, on Monday, between one and two o'clock in the afternoon was born Samuel Clowes, son of John and Mary Clowes, baptized on Saturday following by the Rev. Mathias Harris at Pilott-town.

1764, on Sunday the 7th of October at two o'clock in the afternoon, was born John Clowes, son of John and Mary Clowes was baptized on Sunday, 29 September, 1765, at St Georges Chappell by the Rev. Mathias Harris, and on Sunday 21 September, 1766, departed this life at half past four in the afternoon with a flux of four days continuance.

1767 on Tuesday, the seventh of April at half past nine in the morning was born Aletta Clowes, daughter of John and Mary Clowes, and was baptized the 13th of May at home by the Rev. Mathias Harris.— Note. He baptized eighty-five children here this day, forty-six girls and thirty-nine boys.

1769, on Monday, the 12th of June, at half after eight in the morning, Sarah Clowes was born, daughter of John and Mary Clowes, and on Monday, the 18th September, following was baptized by the Rev. John Andrews.

1771, on Tuesday, 16 July, at eight in the morning was born John Clowes, son of John and Mary Clowes, and on Monday, the 5th August following was baptized by the Rev John Lyons, and on the 7th inst his body was interred in the vault at Haveloes Landing

1780, November 21st the first son Samuel was lost in the Delaware Bay, in a violent storm of wind together with all the others on the vessel. We heard on the 3rd June following that he was buried on the Murderkill Beach, and on digging down to the body believed it to be his.

1772, on Thursday the 20th August, at half after three in the afternoon, was born Isaac Clowes, son of John and Mary Clowes, and was baptized by the Reverend John Lyons, the 28th November following.

1775, on Thursday, the 2nd day of February, at twelve o'clock, was born Peter Clowes, son of John and Mary Clowes, and on the 22 May following he was baptized by the Rev. Samuel Tingle. He was a pious and good man, and a Doctor of Medicine. He lived thirty-one years and seven months and died of a billious fever leaving one son Ezekiel William Clowes

1777, on Friday, the 12th of September, at one o'clock in the morning, was born John Clowes, son of John and Mary, and was baptized by the Rev. Samuel Tinley on Saturday, 28th November, in 1778, at our own house. The reason why the Baptism was delayed, it was the time that Toryism prevailed. It was dangerous to go to Church and the Parson seldomed called on us then.

1780, on Friday, the 17th of May was born at 11 o'clock in the morning, was born Mary Clowes, daughter of John and Mary, and was baptized by the Rev. Samuel Tinley, on Saturday, 26th August, at our house, myself from home, and on July 17th, 1781, she was taken with the diorea which continued with her till the 3rd of September, when she died, and on the 4th her remains were laid in the Vault.

1784, January 27th. our third son John departed this life of trial and Probation at twelve o'clock of a malignant quinsey, or the Putrid Sore Throat of only three days continuance on the 29th. We laid his remains in the Vault.

1789, December 9th, the second daughter, Sarah, wife of John Clarke, died on the fourth day of her sickness on Wednesday, at ten o'clock in the morning with a violent head-pleuriser or inflamation of the Brain. On the 11th we laid her in the ground at the south-end of the Vault. Mr Wilson preached her funeral sermon on the 14th. She was aged twenty years and six months lacking three days. She left one daughter, born October the 4th, 1787, by the name of Joanna Clark, married Martin Duwaeli in 1809, and the said Sarah Clark left one son by the name of John Clark, born the 6th day of December 1789 and departed this life in January, 1812.

CLOWES—CLARKE GENEALOGICAL RECORDS. [Copied from the Bible in the possession of a lady residing in Broadkill Hundred, Delaware, by Rev. C. H. B. Turner.]—

1783 Catherine Clowes within mentioned now the widow of John Young has but one child living (viz) John Young born 28^t July 1772

Mary Clowes within mentioned now the Wife of John K. Dorman, has living four children (viz) 3 boys and 1 girl

Gerhardus Dorman born 23^d of Aug. 1772   Nehemiah born 31. July 1774

Elizabeth Dorman born 29 July 1776.   John Dorman born 22^d May. 1779

Miers Clarke was married to Aletta Clowes in the year 1785

Miers Clarke was born the 2 of May in the year 1761

Mary Clarke daughter of Miers & Aletta Clark was born August 28 about 3 oClock in the afternoon, on Sunday in the year 1786

Was Baptized by the Rev Lydenham Thorne

Miers Clarke departed this life December 17^t 1810

1792 May 9 Wednesday about 9 in the morning was born Sarah Clarke Daughter to Miers Clarke his wife

1794 Sept. 10th on Wednesday about 9 oClock at night was born Hannah Clarke daughter to Miers Clarke and Aletta his wife

1798 Oct. 24th on tuesday was born Elizabeth Clarke, about 11 in the morning.   Daughter to Miers Clarke and Aletta his wife

1800 July 18th about 5 in the morning on Friday was born Lidia Clarke Daughter to Miers Clark and Aletta his wife

1803 febbruary the 1st at 2 in the afternoon was born tuesday Ester Clarke Daughter to Miers Clarke and Aletta his wife

1805 febbruary the 6th on Wednesday morning about 1 oClock was born Anna Clarke Daughter to Miers Clark and Aletta his wife

1807 April 30 between 12 in the morning was born Aletta Clarke Daughter to Miers and Aletta Clarke

Mary Clowes Died the 6th of August 1813 aged 73 years, 8 months, & 26 days

Sept. 7. 1758 John Clowes J^r. was married to Mary Draper by the Rev. Matthias Harris at John Spencer's Esq. about 1 in the afternoon

Mary Draper Daughter of Isaac & Sarah Draper was born the 10th day of November 1739

On frayday the 17th day of Aug. anno Domi. 1759 Between the Hours of 12 & 1 in the morning was born Sarah Clowes Daughter to John & Mary Clowes and was Baptized Munday Privately by the Reverend Matthias Harris. On thursday the 1st day of July 1761 about 2 Oclock in the afternoon she was Siezed with a choaking fitt which ended with her life in about 9 or 10 hours afterwards and she was buried at John Havelaves on Saturday following

1808 May 12th at 4 Oclock in the afternoon James Walker was married to Mary Clarke by Rev^d Mr. William Hickman

1809 Aug. 16th on Monday was born James Miers Walker son of James & Mary Walker.   He died March 10. aged 27 years. 4 months, 8 days

Miers Clarke was born May 2. 1761. Departed this life December 17 1810

1815 Joanna Truitt March 17th on Friday Daughter to John and Sarah Truit

Sarah Pinner daughter of Miers Clarke and Aletta his wife died in North Carolina Jan. 3. 1871

COATE[S], LEEDS, AND STEELMAN FAMILY RECORD.—On the fly-leaf to the New Testament in a Bible, printed by Thomas Basket, London, 1758, in the possession of Mrs. Chalkley S. Leeds, Atlantic City, New Jersey, the following is recorded:

John Coate [sic], Born January ye 2d. 1747–8 ye 7th day of ye week at 11 o'Clock in the Morning.

Mary Coate Born September ye 26th 1749 ye 3rd day of ye week 10 o'clock in ye Morning.

Daniel Leeds Born July ye 25th 1752 ye 7th Day of ye week at 1 o'clock in the afternoon.

Jeremiah Leeds Born March ye 4th 1754 ye 3rd day of ye week about Noon.

Vincent Leeds Born July ye 30th 1756 ye 7th day of ye week about Noon.

Dorothy Leeds Born July ye 30th 1756 ye 7th Day of ye week at 7 o'clock afternoon.

Sarah Leeds wife of John Leeds was Born September 19th 1721/2 old stile these are their children.

Mrs. Jeremiah Leeds, the mother of Chalkley S. Leeds, was a Millicent Steelman. The following family record is from a book formerly belonging to her called "The Young Man's Companion."

Peter Steelman the son of Isaac Steelman and Mary Steelman his wife was born the 28 day december in the year of our Lord 1779.

Jesse Steelman the son of Isaac Steelman and Mary Steelman his wife was born the 21th day of September 1781.

Hannah Steelman the daughter of Isaac Steelman and Mary Steelman his wife was born the 25th day of August 1783.

Judith Steelman the daughter of Isaac Steelman and Mary Steelman his wife was born the 13 day of March 1785.

Sarah Steelman the daughter of Isaac Steelman and Mary Steelman his wife was born the 12th day of July 1788.

Melesent Steelman the daughter of Isaac Steelman and Mary his wife was born the 30th day of August 1792.

Isaac Steelman the son of Isaac Steelman and Mary Steelman his wife was born the 5th day of March 1795.

"THE FAMILY RECORD OF HERCULES AND SARAH COOKE, Transcribed from a Rare folio Edition of THE BIBLE: London: Printed by John Baskett, Printer to the Kings most Excellent Majesty. MDCCXXII. (1722).

"(1) Hercules Cooke Was Borne The two and Twentieth day of July, in the Year of Our Lord god 1697.

"(2) Sarah Cooke The Wife of Hercules Cooke Was Borne The two and Twentieth Day of May In The Year of Our Lord God Anno D'mi 1710

"(3), ffranies Cooke The Daughter of Hercules and Sarah Cooke Was Borne July 27th In the Year of Our Lord Christ 1730

"(4) Elizabeth Cooke The Daughter of Hercules and Sarah Cooke was Borne the Tenth Day of September in The Year of our Lord 1732

"(5) RICHARD Y COOKE the Son of Hercules and Sarah Cooke was borne the Sixteenth Day of June In the Year of our Lord God A'no Domi. 1734.

"(6) William Cooke the Son of Hercules and Sarah Cooke Was Borne The one and Twentieth Day of August In ye year of our Lord 1736.

"(7) MARY COOKE the Daughter of Hercules and Sarah Cooke, Was Borne December the 16th in the Year of our Lord Crist, 1738.

"(8) JOHN COOKE the Son of Hercules and Sarah Cooke Was Borne the Twenty sixth Day of January in the year of our Lord 1740.

"(9) SARAH COOKE the Daughter of Hercules and Sarah Cooke Was Borne the Twentieth Day of August in yᵉ year of our Lord. 1742.

"I. HERCULES COOKE departed this Life Sept. yᵉ 30th in yᵉ year of our God 1760."

CORELL.—Jacob Corell, born December 3, 1713, at Meshfeld, in the Palatinate, married, December 14, 1749, Magdalena Schwartz, born February 28, 1723, at Giffengen, Switzerland, and came to York County in 1744. Issue:
1. *Mary Magdalen*, born January 24, 1751.
2. *John Philip*, born June 17, 1752; died 1758.
3. *John Jacob*, born September 12, 1755; died 1758.
4. *Maria Elizabeth*, born November 14, ——.
5. *Ann Catherine*, born August 11, 1757.
6. *John Jacob*, born July 5, 1759.
7. *Susanna*, born February 19, 1761.
8. *Anna Maria*, born April 21, 1764.

DILLWYN GENEALOGICAL NOTES.—Extracted from Genealogical Memoranda of the Ancestors of William and Sarah Dillwyn and their families, compiled in 1809 by W. Dillwyn and copied by I. N. D. in 1825, with a few additions.

William Dillwyn and Sarah Fuller, of West Chillington, in Sussex, were among the earliest settlers of Philadelphia. They had one son and two daughters, of whom only the son, John, survived minority.

John Dillwyn married, first, Mercy Pierce. Their issue was Mary, who died in minority, and Sarah, born 9th month, 1720, who in 1751 married Thomas Davis, of Philadelphia. Thomas Davis was from New Penrith, in Cumberland. He died 11th month 25, 1757, without issue. John Dillwyn married, second, Susanna Painter. He was born in 1693, and died 7th month 19, 1748. Susanna was born 1st month, 1712, and died 6th month 1, 1784. They were married in Philadelphia 12th month 7, 1733. Of their twelve children but four survived infancy, namely:

George, b. 2 26, 1738; m., 1759, Sarah, dau. of Richard Hill, of Madeira, and had no issue. George was a minister of the Society of Friends, and resided in Burlington, New Jersey.

Lydia, b. 7 21, 1740; d. 8 6, 1753.

William, b. 10 2, 1743; m. 5 19, 1768, Sarah Logan, dau. of John Smith, of Burlington, who died 4 23, 1769, leaving issue a daughter Susannah, b. 3 31, 1769; m. 4 16, 1795; Samuel, son of Samuel Emlen, of Philadelphia, who was born at Bristol, England, 9 4, 1766, where his mother died the 11th, and was buried the 18th of 1st month, 1767; Samuel Emlen, Sr., b. at Philadelphia 3 15, 1729/30; m. Elizabeth Ward, of Philadelphia. The father and son were in England 1784/5.

Ann, b. 2 4, 1746; m. 10th month, 1785, John Cox, whose first wife was Hannah, the 2nd daughter of John Smith, who left him a daughter, married 1st month, 1804, to Dr. David. John and Ann Cox had issue one daughter, Susanna, b. 7th month, 1788; m. 10 20, 1808, Dr. Joseph Parrish, of Philadelphia.

The said William Dillwyn married, secondly, 11 27, 1777, Sarah, the only daughter of Lewis and Edith Weston, of London, who was born in London 3 20, 1751. They had issue sons and daughters, namely:

Lewis Weston, b. 8 21, 1778; m., 7 13, 1807, Mary, dau. of John Llewellyn, of Penllyne, in Glamorganshire. They had issue three sons and three daughters, viz.: Fanny Llewellyn, b. 5 19, 1808; John, b. 1 12, 1810; William, b. 7 11, 1812; d. 4 27, 1819; Lewis Llewellyn, M. P., b. 5 19, 1814; Mary, b. 3 8, 1816; Sarah Llewellyn, b. 8 9, 1818.

John Crook, b. 7 18, 1780; d. 6 5, 1781.

Judith Nichols, b. 8 26, 1781; m. Paul Benan, of Tottenham.

Ann, b. 9 11, 1783; m., 9 27, 1810, R. Dykes Alexander, of Ipswich, in Suffolk.

Lydia, b. 4 11, 1785; m., 4th mo., 1823, Dr. John Sims, of London.

George, b. 3 14, 1790.

William Dillwyn, the second of the name in America, and compiler of the above memoranda, was the son of John Dillwyn, of Philadelphia, who, dying of yellow fever in 1748, when his children were young, the time and place of birth of his father are not known. He may have been a native of Brecknockshire, in South Wales.

Sarah Fuller's mother having died, her father married a second wife, who, after his death, married John Barnes, one of the early settlers of Pennsylvania, who at his decease gave most of his property to his nominal daughter.

John Dillwyn, the compiler's father, was born and died in Philadelphia. His widow married, 10th month, 1756, Peter Worrell, of Lancaster, where they lived from 1759 to 1763, when they removed to Burlington, West New Jersey, where they both died, she, 6 1, 1784; he, 3 23, 1786.

Until the autumn of 1763 I resided in Pennsylvania, and afterward in New Jersey, with the exception of a journey to New England in 1764, and two voyages to South Carolina in 1773 and 1774. I then, in the 5th month, embarked at Philadelphia for Bristol, and in the 11th month, 1775, returned to Burlington, during the hostilities which terminated in the independence of my native country.

In the 5th month, 1777, after passing both the hostile armies with a flag of truce, I embarked at New York and returned via Cork, Swansea and Bristol to London, since which time I have been an English resident.

Samuel and Susanna Emlen lived at West Hill, Burlington, New Jersey, in a house afterward occupied by Richard Smith, a cousin of S. E. and later by Eliza K., widow of Joseph Gurney, of Norwich, England.

DODD-HOLLAND and other family records, copied from Bible of Mrs. Charles Jones, Lewes, Delaware, and contributed by Rev. C. H. B. Turner.

William Dodd the son of Wm Dodd and Elizabeth his wife was Born September the 14th 1775

Elenore Bruce Daughter of Alexander Bruce and Ester his wife was Born May the 26th 1778

Eliza Turner Dodd Daughter of Wm Dodd and Elenore his wife was Born September the 17th 1799

Maria Dodd the Daughter of Wm Dodd and Elenore his wife was Born October the 24th day Anno Domini 1801

Comfort Bruce Dodd daughter of Wm Dodd and Elenor his Wife was Born Feb. 11th 1804

Hannah Dodd Daughter of Wm Dodd & Elenor his Wife was Born December the 25th Day Anno Domini 1805

Elenor Bruce Dodd Daughter of Wm Dodd and Elenor his Wife was Born April the 14th 1808

Joseph Hazlett Dodd son of Wm Dodd and Elenor his Wife was Born October 6th 1810

Amy Dodd Daughter of Wm Dodd & Elenor his Wife was Born April the 22th Anno Domini 1814

William Alexander Dodd the Son of Wm Dodd and Elenor his Wife was Born August the 11th day Anno Domini 1820

Ebenezer the Son of John Holland & Elizabeth his Wife was Born Sept 4th 1801

Maria Holland the Daughter of Ebenezer Holland and Eliza T. Holland his wife was Born June the 18th 1827

Ann Robbins Holland the Daughter of Ebenzer Holland & Eliza his Wife was Born January the 7th 1829

Hetty Elenor Holland Daughter of Ebenezer Holland and Eliza his Wife was Born June 21th 1831

Hannah Newbold Holland the Daughter of Ebenezer Holland and Eliza his Wife was Born March 22, 1833

Joseph Holland the Son of Ebenezer Holland and Eliza his Wife was Born September the 12th 1835

Tabitha Holland Daughter of Ebenezer Holland and Eliza his Wife was Born February the 11th 1837

William Dodd Holland the Son of Ebenezer Holland and Eliza his Wife was Born March the 22nd 1839

John Paynter Holland the Son of Ebenezer Holland and Eliza his Wife was Born August the 6th 1841

Albert Bruce Holland the Son of Ebenezer Holland & Eliza his Wife was Born January the 4th 1846

Hannah N Lank the Daughter of John C. Lank and Hannah his Wife was Born November the 14th 1859

Mary Alif Daughter of Joseph Aylif and Amy his Wife Departed this life May the 14th Day about 6 oclock in the morning, Anno Domini 1803. Supposed to be about Seventy years of Age

Hannah Newbold the wife of James Newbold departed this life August the 15th in the year of Our Lord 1825 Supposed to be 73 years 2 months old

William Dodd departed this life March the 31st in the year of Our Lord 1838.

Aged 62 years 6 months & 16 days

Eleanor Dodd Departed this Life April the 3ᵈ day in the year of Our Lord 1840

Aged 61 years 10 mo. & 23 days

Wallace W. White and Tabitha Holland were married December 24 1862

John P. Holland and Maggie A. White were married December 29ᵗʰ 1868

Maggie A. Holland, wife of John P. Holland, departed this life August 18, 1869

Ebenezer Holland & Eliza T. Dodd were Married May the 3ᵈ 1826

Hannah N. Lank the Daughter of Ebenezer Holland and Eliza his Wife Departed this life the 24 Day of December 1859. Age 26 years 9 months 2 days

DRINKER GENEALOGICAL NOTES.—The marriage certificate of Henry S. and Hannah (Smith) Drinker contains the following endorsements on the same:

"Henry S. Drinker of the City of Phila son of Henry Drinker of same place—Merchant, & Elizabeth his wife—
to
Hannah Smith dʳ of James Smith Jʳ of sᵈ city Merchant & Esther his wife—11ᵗʰ of 12ᵐᵒ 1794—at Philad—

"The within named Henry S. Drinker was born at Philadelphia on the 30ᵗʰ day of October 1770.

"Hannah Smith was born on the 26ᵗʰ of the 11ᵗʰ month 1773 at 40 minutes after 10 °Clock P.M. at Houghton in Springfield, New Jersey.

"William Drinker was born at Clearfield in Bristol Township in the County of Philadᵃ on the 14ᵗʰ day of the 10ᵗʰ month 1795 at one °Clock P.M.

"Henry S. Drinker Jʳ was born at North Bank in Falls Township Bucks County on the 15ᵗʰ day of the 7ᵗʰ month 1797 at 11 °Clock P.M. and died at yᵉ same place January 4ᵗʰ 1798.

"Esther Drinker was born at North Bank on the first of November 1798 at ( ) °Clock in the evening.

"James Drinker was born at Philadelphia (his mother being there on a visit) on the first day of April 1800. He died at North Bank on the 1ˢᵗ day of November 1801.

"Elizabeth Drinker was born at North Bank on the 11ᵗʰ day of December 1801 at 11 O'Clock P.M.

"Sarah Drinker was born at North Bank on the 9 day of May 1803, at ½ past 11 O'Clock A.M.

"Henry & Hannah Drinker (Twins) were born at North Bank on the 11ᵗʰ day of August 1804 at 5 °Clock A.M.—Henry came first.

"Henry Drinker died at his residence in Montrose, February 5ᵗʰ 1868.

"Hannah Drinker died at 1224 Spruce St. April 11ᵗʰ 1869, Philᵃ.

"Elizabeth Drinker Paxson died at the house of her son in law Wm. H. Cooper in Montrose Susquehanna Co. Pennᵃ on the 11 day of July 1874."

DUER FAMILY BIBLE RECORDS.—In a family Bible, a thick 4to, bearing the imprint: New York. Collins, Perkins and Co., 1807, recently sold at a book auction, the following record of marriages, births and deaths were found by the writer:

Marriages.

John Duer and Susanna Norris were married on the nineteeth day of September, one thousand, eight hundred and eleven. 1811.

Edward Norris Duer and Eleanora A. Fite were married on the sixteenth day of November, one thousand, eight hundred and forty-one. 16th Nov., 1841.

John Duer, Jr., and Henrietta D. Adgate were married on the ninth day of September, eighteen hundred and forty-five. Sept. 9th, 1845.

Dr. Thomas S. Herbert and Elizabeth Duer were married on the fifth day of November, eighteen hundred and forty-six. November 5th, 1846.

Births.

Edward Norris Duer, son of John and Susanna Duer, was born on the 22d day of August, 1812.

Charles Duer, 2d son of John and Susanna Duer, was born on the 20th day of September, 1814.

John Duer, 3d son of John and Susanna Duer, was born on the 16th day of March 1816.

Mary Duer, daughter of John and Susanna Duer, was born on Friday morning the 10th day of April, 1818.

Elizabeth Duer, 2d daughter of John and Susanna Duer, was born on the 7th day of November, 1819.

Mary Caroline Duer, 3d daughter of John and Susanna Duer, was born on Sunday, the 2d of September, 1821.

The infant female child, not named, was born on Sunday the 8th day of June, 1823, and died on Thursday morning, the 26th of the same month, aged eighteen days.

Andrew Adgate Duer, son of John Duer, Jr., and Henrietta D. Duer, was born on the 3d of December, 1846.

Isabel Duer, daughter of John Duer, Jr., and Henrietta D. Duer, was born on the 28th of April, 1848.

Douglass Henry Duer, son of John Duer, Jr., and Henrietta D. Duer, was born on the 11th day of April, 1851.

Edith Duer, 2d daughter of John Duer, Jr., and Henrietta D. Duer, was born on the 5th of January, 1853.

Deaths.

John Duer, Sr., born in Bucks County, Pa., on the 1st day of July, 1773, and removed to Baltimore in 1795, died on Christmas day, 1860, at 4 o'clock P. M., in his eighty-eighth year. Dec'r 25, 1860.

Susan Duer, wife of John Duer, died on Sunday, the 4th of July, 1824. Aged forty-one years and four days.

Charles Duer died on the 14th day of October, 1815. Aged one year and twenty-four days.

Mary Duer, daughter of John and Susanna Duer, departed this life the 29th day of Dec'r, 1820, aged two years, eight months and nineteen days.

Elizabeth Norris departed this life on the 21st Sept'r, 1852, aged seventy-one years.

Elizabeth Duer Herbert, daughter of John and Susanna Duer, died on the 9th day of Dec'r, 1854, aged thirty-five years, one month and two days.

JAMES B. LAUX.

DUNGAN GENEALOGICAL NOTES, from Bible in possession of Ethel Duval, Philadelphia.—

Thomas Dungan, was born the 16th day of March, 1738.
Elizabeth Dungan, was born the 22d. day of January, 1740.
Sarah Dungan, was born the 25th day of August, 1742.
[Torn] Dungan, was born the 3rd. day of March, 1745.
John Dungan, was born the 12th day of March, 1747.
[Torn] Dungan, was born the 24th of September 1749.
William Dungan, son of Thomas Dungan and Elizabeth his wife, born 17 May 1766.
Thomas Dungan, son of Thomas and Elizabeth Dungan, was born 23rd March 1794.

DUNTON GENEALOGICAL NOTES.—William Dunton, of Philadelphia, was married to Mary Stadler, May 14, 1772, and had issue:
Jacob, b. Aug. 14, 1773.
Thomas, b. Dec. 14, 1774.
William, b. May 18, 1776.
Sarah, b. May 14, 1778; md. Francis Hunt.
George, b. Aug. 23, 1780.
Elizabeth, b. March 31, 1783.
Margaretha, b. Feb. 25, 1785.
Amelia, b. Oct. 22, 1787.
Maria, b. April 4, 1790.
William, b. Dec. 13, 1792.
Anna, b. Nov. 28, 1794.

Jacob, son of William and Mary Dunton, md. first Bridget ———, and had issue:
William, b. Feby. 28, 1796.
John, b. June 24, 1797.
Jacob, b. April 27, 1800.
Isaac, b. May 26, 1802.

Married second, Ann McCarty, Oct. 2, 1806, and had issue:
Anna Maria, b. June 8, 1807.
Abraham, b. July 29, 1808.
Wilson, b. March 30, 1812.

George, son of William and Mary Dunton, md. Mary ———, and had issue:
John Lewis, b. Feby. 19, 1807; md. Susan B. Pierson, 1830.
Sarah Ann, b. Sept. 14, 1808; md. John E. Murray, 1828.
William Washington, b. Dec. 9, 1810.
Mary Amanda, b. May 22, 1813.
Margaret Susan, b. Aug. 11, 1815; md. Joseph H. Gregory.
Joseph F., b. March 13, 1818 } twins.
Susannah Elizabeth, b. March 13, 1818
Amanda Amelia, b. May 9, 1821.

BIBLE RECORDS OF COL. WILLIAM EDMONDS, OF FAUQUIER CO., VIRGINIA.—The following was copied from the family Bible of Colonel William Edmonds of Fauquier County, Virginia, many of whose descendants reside in Philadelphia and vicinity. Colonel Edmonds served in the Revolutionary Army; and was also Captain of a Company for Fauquier County, Virginia, in the French and Indian War in 1761. He was born in 1734 and died in 1818.

The Bible referred to was published at Oxford, England, in 1768 by S. Wright and W. Gill, printers to the University. EMMA B. BELT.

William Edmonds & Elizabeth Blackwell were married ye 17th day of March in ye year of our Lord 1764 (on Saturday) by ye Revd James Craig.

William Edmonds Jr. was born on Fryday ye 10th of May in ye year of our Lord 1765, Ja⁸ Bell, Wm Bell, Franke Bell & Hannah Blackwell godfathers & godmothers.

Franke Edmonds was born on Fryday ye 1st day of August in ye year of Our Lord 1766. Saml. Blackwell, Ja⁸ Blackwell, Anne Pickett & Anne Edmonds, godfathers & godmothers.

Sarah Edmonds was born on Sunday ye 4th day of Octr in ye year of our Lord 1767. Sarah Blackwell & ye Rev^d Ja⁸ Craig, godfather and godmother.
Dyed 17th Decb^r 1828.

Elias Edmonds was born on Thursday ye 10th of Nov. in ye year of our Lord 1768, Elias Edmonds Jr. Bennitt Price, Mrs. Billy Edmonds & Judith Price, godfathers & godmothers.
(the above died 1st April 1811)

Mary Edmonds was born on Thursday ye 17th of April in ye year of our Lord 1770. Col. Wm Blackwell, Jo⁸ Fantleroy, Mrs. Elizabeth Blackwell & Judith Edmonds, godfathers & godmothers.
(Died June 1837)

Elizabeth Edmonds was born on Sunday ye 2nd of June in ye year of our Lord 1771. Francis Attswell, Tho⁸ Keith, Judith Hubbard & Betty Edmonds, godfathers & godmothers.
Dyed ye 16th of April 1773.

Betty Edmonds was born on Saturday ye 20th of February in ye year of our Lord 1773. Hancock Lee, Joseph Blackwell, Elizabeth Hewitt, Susannah Yates, godfathers & godmothers.

John Edmonds was born on Tuesday ye 6th of June in ye year of our Lord 1775. John Blackwell, son of Joseph, Geo. Pickett, Miss Betty Edmonds & Frankey Edmonds, godfathers & godmothers.

Lucy Edmonds was born on Monday ye 10th day of May in ye year 1777. John Barker godfather & Eliz^th, her mother, godmother.

James Edmonds was born on Tuesday ye 16th of February, ye year of our Lord 1779. W^m Ed. & Eliz^th, father & mother to the above, godfather & godmother.
Died March 1845.

Catey Edmonds was born on Tuesday ye 20th Feby in ye year of our Lord 1781. Wm Edmonds Jr godfather, Nancy Taylor & Elizth Taylor, godmothers.

Judith Edmonds was born on Sunday ye 28th Decr in ye year of our Lord 1783. Robert Green, godfather & [undecipherable.]

Susannah Eliza Green was born January 9th 1789.
Robert Green was born February 23rd 1790.

The above were the two oldest grandchildren of Wm Edmonds, whose oldest daughter, Frankey, married her cousin, R. Green. [Note made by grandson Gust. R. B. Horner, Surg. U.S.N., Feby 27, 1848.]

Names of servants of Wm Edmonds, of Fauquier Co., Va.

Manuel	Dick	Hannah
James	Anthony	Myma
Dan¹	Franke	Dinah
Harry	Cati	Agga
Toney	Jane	Grace
Sam	Willey	Willm Ben
Ben	Phillis	Abram.
Phill	Fanny	

EMLEN FAMILY: ENTRIES REGARDING CORRECTED.—

Samuel Emlen did not marry a Ward; nor did Dr. Physick marry *the Daughter* of Emlen, of Burlington.—

In William Dillwyn's account of his family (see PENNA. MAG., Vol. xxviii, p. 248) he states that his daughter Susannah married "Samuel, son of Samuel Emlen of Philadelphia," which is quite correct, and that the latter's wife was Elizabeth "Ward"—which is a mistake. The said Samuel Emlen of Philadelphia, the well known minister of Friends, born, as Mr. Dillwyn correctly states, on the 15th of the 3d month, 1729–30, married twice: *First*, on the 16th of the 7th mo., 1761, Elizabeth Moode, daughter of William Moode of Phila., and, *Secondly*, on the 1st of the 2d mo., 1770, Sarah, daughter of Asher Mott, fourth son of Gershom Mott, High Sheriff of· Monmouth Co., New Jersey, in 1697, and a member of the Provincial Assembly. (See Phila. Friends' Monthly Meeting Records; Marriages.)—By his *first* wife, Elizabeth Moode, Samuel Emlen, of Phila., had the said Samuel who married Susannah Dillwyn: By his *second*, Sarah Mott, he had Deborah, who died unmarried, and Elizabeth who married, on the 18th of Sept., 1800, Philip Syng Physick, M.D., of Phila.

The statement, which I have seen somewhere, that Dr. Physick's wife was a daughter of Samuel Emlen "of Burlington" is, of course, incorrect; the Samuel of Burlington being he who was the husband of Susannah Dillwyn and, in truth, half-brother to the said Elizabeth, not her father.

P. S. P. CONNER.

ROWLANDSVILLE, MARYLAND.

The Fischel Family of York County, Pennsylvania, and North Carolina.—

John Adam Fischel, b. Sept. 19, 1730, Esenheim, in the Palatinate, came with his parents to Pennsylvania in Sept. of 1752. Married March 2, 1757, *Ursula Catherine Thomas*, b. in Wurtemberg, April 15, 1738, who came to Pennsylvania in 1739. They had issue:
  Anna Maria, b. April 4, 1758.
  Catherine, b. July 21, 1760.
  John, b. March 31, 1762.
  John Jacob, b. May 22, 1765.
  John Adam, b. Nov. 4, 1768.
  Eva, b. July 15, 1770.
  Anna Margaret, b. Dec. 2, 1772.
  Henry, b. July 25, 1774.
  Conrad, b. Aug. 26, 1777.

In October of 1779, the parents with their children, settled in Western North Carolina.

Fishels Buried at the Roth Church, near Spring Grove and La Botte, York County, Penna. This church, also known as Trinity Reformed Church, is one hundred and thirty-five years old, and it is asserted that some twenty years ago the Church Board ordered the destruction of their records. In addition to the Fishels, a great many of the following families are buried in its cemetery: Roth, Wiest, Spangler, Stover, Miller, and Stambaugh.

Frank L. Crone.

Fishels.

Daniel, died Sept. 16, 1899, age 80 years, 9 months, and 2 days. (Father of Samuel Fissel who lives at LaBotte.)

George, died Feb. 7, 1904, age 74 years, 6 months, and 22 days.

Franklin, son of George and Saretta, died June 4, 1898, age 28 years, 9 months, and 27 days.

Alexander, died July 27, 1915, age 60 (?).

Sarah, wife of Alexander, died Jan. 11, 1896, age 21 years, 8 months, and 21 days.

George W., died May 29, 1910, age 56 years, 9 months, 29 days.

Amanda S., wife of George, died April 2, 1879, age 24 years, 5 months, and 4 days.

Michael S., died July 12, 1878, age 37 years, 6 months, and 16 days.

Sarah, wife of George, died Jan. 1, 1875, age 79 years, 6 months, and 26 days.

Anne M., daughter Alexander and Sarah, died April 12, 1875, age 16 years, 1 month, and 21 days.
Catherine, died Oct. 15, 1891, age 71 years, 3 months, and 15 days.
Zachariah, died June 4, 1908, age 80 years, 5 months, and 18 days.
John, died March 5, 1866, age 71 years, 7 months, and 1 day.
Mary M., died July 15, 1874, age 78 years, 11 months, and 20 days.
Infant son of Michael and Mary, died Nov. 27, 1866.
Christina, wife of Henry, died June 7, 1846, age 68 years.
Sarah, wife of Samuel, Aug. 15, 1827—Sept. 5, 1869.
John Henrich, Sept. 16, 1766, Jan. 5, 1830.
Johannes, June 14, 1791, April 24, 1814.
Michael, Feb. 11, 1770—Nov. 30, 1815.
Magdalena, wife of Michael, Nov. 10, 1775—Dec. 20, 1841.
Anna Barbara, May 13, 1704, April 3, 1823.
Daniel, April 10, 1797—May 18, 1831.
Margaret, June 16, 1806—Nov. 29, 1830.
Leah, died Jan. 4, 1826, age 13 years, 4 months, and 5 days.
David, March 16, 1807—March 18, 1830.
George F., died Feb. 22, 1832, age not known.
Salinda, died Feb. 28, 1832, age 6 mo. 21 days.
Henrich, Aug. 2, 1793—March 6, 1814.
Jacob, 1818—Aug. 22, 1823.
Michael, died March 20, 1864, age 55 years, 9 months, and 8 days.
Sarah, wife of Michael, died July 30, 1883, age 70 years, 9 months, and 14 days.
Mary, wife of David, Dec. 28, 1796—Aug. 8, 1872.
Amanda, daughter of Michael and Sarah, died Aug. 1, 1871, age 21 years, 6 months, and 4 days.
Savilla, Daughter Michael, died Oct. 4, 1853, age 17 years, 11 months, and 10 days.
"Hier ruhen die gebeine von Frederich Fishel er trat in diese welt am 26ten Horning und verlies dieselbe an 27ten Aprill, 1817 seines altes 30 jahren, 2 monaten, und 1 tag."

FAMILY RECORDS OF THOMAS FRANKLIN, JR.—Thomas Franklin, Jr., son of Thomas Franklin, of the city of New York, and Mary, daughter of Samuel Rhoads, of Philadelphia, were married 15th of Second month, 1764, at Philadelphia. (For certificate of marriage, see Book B, p. 90.)

"Elizabeth Franklin Daughter of Thomas and Mary Franklin jun' was born March the fourteenth in the Year of our Lord 1765 at half an hour past three in the afternoon.

"Elizabeth Franklin took the small Pox November the thirteenth 1765 and had it very favourably.

"Benjamine Franklin son of Thomas and Mary Franklin Jun' was born January the twenty fifth [sic] in the [sic] of our Lord one thousand seven hundred and sixty seven at one °Clock in the morning.

"Benjamine Franklin inoculated for the small Pox April ye 18th 1767 and had it very favourably.

"Elizabeth Franklin Died July the twenty eighth [sic] in the Year of our Lord one thousand seven hundred and sixty seven about 3 °Clock in the morning aged two Years and four months.

"Ann Franklin Daughter of Thos and Mary Franklin jun' was born January the Sixth one thousand seven hundred an [sic] sixty nine about nine °Clock in the Evening.

"Ann Franklin inoculated for the Small Pox April the 23, 1769 and had it very favourably.

"Thomas Franklin son of Thos & Mary Born the 12th Octr 1770 at two o'clock after noon.

"Thomas Franklin son of Thomas & Mary Franklin Jun' died July the 20th 1771 at Philadelphia about five °Clock in the morning aged 9 months.

"Walter Franklin son of Thomas & Mary Franklin jun' Born the Seventh day of May 1773 about 8 °Clock in the morning was Inoculated for the Small Pox November 1773 and had it favourably.

"Samuel Franklin Son of Thomas and Mary born August the 6th one thousand seven hundred seventy four at one oclock after noon.

"Mary Franklin the wife of Thomas Franklin departed this Life on first Day morning ab^t 15 Minuts [sic] after 6 Oclock the 2^d of ye 5mo 1779 after ten weeks Linguering [sic] Illness which Shee bore with Christian patients [sic]. Apprehending her time short amongst us all in a Christian like Cherefullness & expressed a Desire if it was her makers will to live a little longer for the sake of her Dear Babes.

"Benjamin Franklin Died in Phil^a 14th of ye 6mo 1781 after 60 hours Illness with the Chollick.

"Walter & Samuel Franklin had the measels in Philadelphia in the 5th m^o 1785.

"Israel & Ann Pleasants first child and son Samuel Born 19 Feby 1789 half after 5 o'clock A.M.

"Thomas Franklin departed this Life on the night of Fourth Day the Eleventh of January in the year of our Lord one Thousand seven hundred and ninety seven at 20 minutes past 11 o'clock."

GARDNER BIBLE RECORDS. Contributed by Mrs. A. W. Hand, Cape May, N. J.

John Gardner, son of William & Elizabeth Gardner. Born September 4th, 1751. Old stile. Died June 17, 1810.

Hannah Gardner, daughter of William & Elizabeth Gardner. Born August 8th, 1753. Married June 29th, 1773. Died October 10, 1793.

Mary Scott, daughter of William & Isabella Scott. Born November 5th, 1755. Died March 8, 1805.

John Gardner & Mary Scott were married March 31, 1774.

Elizabeth Gardner, daughter of John & Mary Gardner. Born January 30th, 1775. Died May 17th, 1781.

John Macpherson Gardner, son of John & Mary Gardner. Born October 18th, 1775. Died August 29th, 1815.

Sarah Gardner, daughter of John & Mary Gardner. Born March 8th, 1779. Died April 3rd, 1783.

[torn.] Born July 24th, 1781. Died February 16th, 1786.

Elizabeth Gardner, daughter of John & Mary Gardner. Born November 19th, 1783. Died March 14th, 1786.

Hannah Gardner, daughter of John & Mary Gardner. Born January 29th, 1786.

Robert Gardner, son of John & Mary Gardner. Born April 4th, 1788.

Hannah Rollinson, grandmother to John Gardner. Died September 7th, 1789. Aged 79 years.

William Gardner, son of John & Mary Gardner. Born March 23d, 1791. Died October —, 1794.

Isabella Gardner, daughter of John & Mary Gardner. Born December 1st, 1793.

Susan Oliphant Gardner, daughter of John & Mary Gardner. Born November 23rd, 1796. Died August —, 1798.

John M. Gardner and Sophia B. Gassaway. Married the 1st of November, 1805.

John Thomas Gardner, son of J. M. & S. C. Gardner. Born August 12, 1809.

Robt. Gardner & Esther Maria Wagner. Married October 28th, 1810.

Margaret Wagner Wass Borne the 7th of June, 1776.
William Wagner Wass Born the 15 of October, 1781.
Mary, the daughter of Francis & Hannah [line torn] (illegible).
Esther M. Wagner Wass Born March 12th, 1787.
John Wagner 13th of October, 1793.
John M. Gardner and Sophia C. Gardner.
Catharine Deprefontaine was born January 16th, 1828.
Amanda Deprefontaine was born June 27th, 1830.

GERHARD GENEALOGICAL NOTES.—Frederick Gerhard, born March 26, 1714, at Langenselbot, Hesse Darmstadt, was married January 23, 1737, to Elizabeth Fisher. In the Summer of 1739, they sailed from Rotterdam on the ship Samuel, Captain Hugh Percy, for Philadelphia, where they made their home. Mrs. Gerhard died there, leaving a son, Peter, born October 28, 1737. Soon after the death of his wife, Frederick Gerhard removed to Heidelberg Township, Berks County, where, February 14, 1740, he married a widow, whose maiden name had been Barbara Rieger, and with her had five sons and four daughters.

Conrad, son of Frederick and Barbara Gerhard, was born November 22, 1740. In 1768, he married Rachel, daughter of Isaac Martens and

Rachel (Bogart) Ysselstein, born in Bucks County, June 8, 1741. She died at Philadelphia, May 31, 1801. They had issue:
  Rachel, b. Jany. 15, 1770.
  Elizabeth, b. March 2, 1772.
  William, b. April 10, 1774.
  Mary, b. Feby. 4, 1776.
  John, b. Oct. 17, 1778.
  Eleanora, b. Nov. 17, 1780.
  Thomas, b. Jany. 31, 1782.

After the death of his wife, Conrad Gerhard married second, Elizabeth Jungman, November 9, 1802.

William, son of Conrad and Rachel Gerhard, b. April 10, 1774, married Sarah Wood, Oct. 6, 1808, and had issue:
  William Wood, b. July 23, 1809.
  Benjamin, b. June 3, 1811.
  Thomas, b. Oct. 2, 1813.
  Louisa, b. Sept. 25, 1816.

GRAY—EMERSON—DRAPER—FOWLER GENEALOGICAL RECORDS.
[Copied from the Bible of a descendant, by Rev. C. H. B. Turner, Lewes, Delaware.]—

John Gray was born October the 17. 1750 son to Allen Gray and Sarah his wife

Anne Wells was born August the 28th 1758 Daughter to Benjamin & Elizabeth his wife

John Gray & Anne was married September 21, in the year of our Lord 1774

Sarah Gray was born April 30th 1776 Daughter to John Gray and Anne his wife

Benjamin Gray was born January 28. 1778 son to John & Anne his wife

Elizabeth Gray was born February 6. 1780 daughter to John Gray & Anne his wife

Allen Gray was born March 22. 1782 son to John Grey & Anne his wife

John Gray son to John Gray & Anne his wife was born May 17. 1783

William Gray was born February 25. 1785 son to John Gray and Anne his wife

Susanna Gray was born March 30th 1787. Daughter to John Gray and Anne his wife

James Grey was born July 6. 1789 son to John Gray & Anne his wife

Thomas Gray was born Sept. 9. 1791 son to John Gray & Anne his wife

John Gray and Susanna his wife was married January 30th 1794

Mary Gray was born Oct. 14. 1795 Daughter to John Gray and Susanna his wife

Samuel Draper was born October 27th in year 1811 son to John Draper & Susa his wife

William Draper was born August 7 year 1813

Elisa Draper was born October 24th in year 1814

Sally Ann Draper was born April 14 year 1817

Ebenezer Fowler and Susan his wife was married June 30. 1808

Susan Annay Fowler was born March 29. 1809 Daughter to Ebenezer and Susannay his wife

John Fowler was born April 21. 1811 son to Ebenezer Fowler and Susanna his wife

Susan Gray Daughter of William Gray & Unity his wife was born August 5. 1815

Ann Emerson Gray Daughter of William Gray & Unity his wife was born November 27. 1816

Sarah Gray Daughter of the aforesaid William & Unity was born Aug. 7. 1819. about 6 Oclock in the evening

Deaths

Elizabeth Gray wife of William Gray departed this life January 22. 1811 in the 24th year of her age

Ann Emerson Gray Daughter of William & Unity Gray departed this life Sept. 10th 1817 aged 9 months & 13 days

William Gray husband of Unity Gray departed this life June 6th 1828 aged 43 years, 3 months & 9 days

Unity Gray relict of William departed this life Feb. 14. 1863

Mariam Gray departed this life July 12. 1812

Benjamin Gray departed this life June 26, 1781

Sarah Gray departed this life February 14. 1790

James Gray departed this life October 6. 1790

Anne Gray wife to John Gray departed this life Aug. 21. 1792

John Gray Sen. departed this life April 1. 1797

John Draper departed this life December 7. 1806

Unity Emerson daughter of Vincent Emerson and Mary his wife was born the 21st day of 11th month 1776. 14 minutes past 12 Oclock in the morning

Peniel Emerson son of Vincent and Mary his wife was born the 4th day of the 8th month ¾ after 3 Oclock in the morning in the year 1779

Anna Emerson daughter of Vincent Emerson & Mary his wife was born the 9th day of the 2d month, 12 minutes past 6 Oclock in the afternoon of the year 1783

Marriages

William Gray and Elizabeth his wife was married the 14th day of March. 1806

William Gray and Unity his wife was married the 25th day of May 1811

Births

Rebecca Gray Daughter of William Gray & Elizabeth his wife was born August 15. 1807

Mariam and Ann twin Daughters of William Gray and Elizabeth his wife were born Aug. 18. 1810

Mary Gray Daughter of William Gray and Unity his wife was born June 25. 1812

Ann Eliza Gray Daughter of William Gray & Unity his wife was born November 29. 1813

GUEST—MORRIS—POWELL (vol. vii. p. 351).—In the year 1600 there lived in Birmingham, England, a gentleman named T. Chanders who had a daughter Elizabeth, who married William Bailyes of the same place. They had two daughters, Alice and Elizabeth. Alice married George Guest. Elizabeth married William Hard.

George Guest and his wife came to America (Philadelphia) from Birmingham, England, in the year 1681, and first lived in a cave on the Delaware River, near Chestnut Street wharf, at which time they learned that her sister Elizabeth and her husband intended to come also and prepared to welcome them in the cave till they could build. Afterwards they built a house (Blue Anchor Inn) on Dock Creek, where they received William Penn when he first landed in Philadelphia, the house being unfinished at the time. George and Alice Guest had issue: George Guest, John Guest, and Phœbe Guest (born 7 mo. 28, 1685) who married Anthony Morris in 1705.

Elizabeth Guest, born in Birmingham, England, in 1675, came to America with her parents, married Arthur Holton 10 mo. 5, 1695, died 4 mo. 12, 1757, and had issue Mary Holton, who married Samuel Hudson, and had issue: Elizabeth Hudson, who married ——— Jones; Hannah Hudson, who married Joseph Howell, and had issue, Arthur Howell, a celebrated minister among Friends; and Mary Hudson, married 2 mo. 15, 1746, to John Head, merchant of Philadelphia.

Alice Guest survived her husband and died August, 1705; her sister, Elizabeth Hard, a widow without issue, was living in Philadelphia at the time of her decease.

Anthony and Phœbe Morris had fourteen children: 1. Anthony, born 1705, married Sarah Powell; 2. James, b. 1707, m. Elizabeth Kearney; 3. John, b. 1709, m. Mary Sutton; 4. Samuel, d. 1710; 5. Samuel, b. 1711, m. Hannah Cadwalader; 6. Mary, b. 1713, m. Samuel Powell; 7. Joseph, b. 1714-5, m. Martha Fitzwater; 8. Elizabeth, b. 1716, m. Ben. Shoemaker; 9. Benjamin, b. 1717, died unmarried; 10. Phœbe, b. 1721, d. unm.; 11. Susanna, b. 1722, d. unm.; 12. Deborah, b. 1723-4, d. March, 1793; 13. Benjamin, b. 1725; 14. Unnamed.

With respect to when Samuel Powell came to America, and where he came from, and the maiden name of his wife Abigail, I am not able to give any information. Samuel Powell and Abigail his wife had three children: Sarah, who married Anthony Morris; Samuel, m. Mary Morris; and a third, m. Joshua Emlen.

Anthony and Sarah Morris had six children: Samuel, Deborah, Anthony, Israel, Sarah, and Thomas.

Samuel and Mary Powell had three children: Abigail, Samuel, and Mary.

Joshua Emlen and wife had only one child, Samuel, who married ——— ——— and had two children: Samuel, who m. Susan Delroy, and had no issue; and Elizabeth, who m. Philip S. Physick, and had four children: Philip, Emlen, and two girls, one of whom married Dr. Jacob Randolph, and the other, Commodore David Conner, U. S. N.   A. S. M.

FAMILY OF WILLIAM GUEST, OF WEST JERSEY.—William Guest, born in Dublin, Ireland, 12th September, 1713; came to America and settled in West Jersey, where he died, 10th October, 1783. He married Christina (maiden name Halton, born at Greenwich, 31st December, 1713), widow of Andrew Arihard, 12th February, 1736. (By her first husband she had one child, *Christina*, born 13th October, 1733.) She died 29th November, 1789. Their children were:

Elizabeth, b. 16 Dec. 1736.
James, b. 18 Nov. 1738, d. 1789.
William, b. 14 March, 1740.
Henry, b. 14 March, 1742.
Isaac, b. 17 Dec. 1743.
Nathaniel, b. 14 Oct. 1746, d. Jany. 1750.
Joseph, b. 5 Jan. 1749.
Catherina, b. 29 Nov. 1751.
Mary, b. 8 Oct. 1752.
Benjamin, b. 10 July 1755, d. 7 Nov. 1758.
Sarah, b. 9 Oct. 1758.

CAPTAIN JOHN HEWSON.—Captain John Hewson was the son of Peter Hewson, a Woollen draper of London, by his wife, Catherine, a woman of great beauty said to have preserved her faculties and her charm till the age of 96. Descended from Colonel John Hewson, the Regicide, sometime Governor of Dublin and a Member of Cromwell's House of Peers, he early imbibed the extreme political views of his celebrated ancestor and was a source of considerable anxiety to his family, who strongly recommended his migration to the Colonies.

He was a Cotton-spinner and Calico-printer of considerable means, and Benjamin Franklin, while on a visit to one of Mr. Hewson's relatives, hearing of great Republican tendencies and the family's anxiety concerning them, urged upon him the claims of Philadelphia as the best place to establish a factory and introduce his industries into the New World.

Dr. Franklin had recently been engaged in the surveys relative to the changing of the Point-no-point Road on the estate of Mr. Wm. Ball at Richmond, and offered to use his influence to secure a lease from him of a good house and sufficient land abutting on Kensington for the erection of a factory. Mr. Hewson accepted the suggestion and emigrated to Philadelphia in 1774. The village which sprang up around the factory was called "Balltown." The factory was subsequently used for Dyott's Glass Works and Morris' Iron Foundry, and is now incorporated in the Cramp Company Ship Yards.

At the outbreak of the War of the Revolution, Mr. Hewson raised a Company of Volunteers in Kensington, principally from his own workmen, and served with some distinction, having a price set on his head and his property confiscated. He was twice married, his first wife, Mary, dying a few months after his arrival in America. In 1775 he married Zebiah Smallwood of Gloucester Co., N. J., whose mother was Margaret Cheesman, a sister of Captain Cheesman who fell with his commander while acting A.d.c. to General Montgomery at the storming of Quebec. His eldest surviving daughter by his second marriage, Esther, married Joseph Ball, nephew and heir of Wm. Ball of Richmond Hall, mentioned above.

Captain Hewson was a great favourite of General Washington who was a frequent visitor at his house, and Mrs. Esther Ball, who died in 1863, and who was some twelve years of age when the General and his wife last dined with her father, had a fund of personal reminiscences of them, which she used to relate with considerable gusto.

Portraits of Captain John Hewson and his wife are in the possession of Mr. Samuel Van Dusen of New York.

John Hewson Son of Peter and Catherine Hewson of London was born in England in 1747 and married in 1766—Mary—by whom he had five children:

John, b. 13 Oct. 1767 at Westham, Essex.
Sarah, b. 26 Jan. 1769 at Westham, Essex. m. Mr. Wm. Alcock.
James, b. 3 Apl. 1771 at Crayford, Kent.
Mary, b. 12 Feb. 1773 at Bromley, Middlesex, m. Mr. Labrie.
Jonathan, b. 7 Oct. 1774 at Kensington, Philadelphia, d. 27 July 1776.
Mary Hewson died three days after the birth of this child, aged 29.

In 1775 John Hewson married Zebiah Smallwood of Gloucester County, N. J., and by her had 12 children.

Peter, b. 13 Jan. 1776, d. 2 Aug. 1779.
Catherine Washington, b. 15 Nov. 1777, d. 20 July 1778.
Esther, b. 23 June 1779 (born after her father's return from captivity) m. 1st Thomas Connell, and 2nd Joseph Ball. d. 25 June 1868.
Ann, b. 1781.
Peter, b. 13 Jan. 1783, d. 1790.
Catherine, b. 26 Dec. 1785.
Zebiah, b. 1 Feb. 1787.
Robert, b. 10 Feb. 1789.
Margaret, b. 17 Feb. 1791, m. 1st Mr. Van Dusen, 2nd Mr. Sturdevant.
Priscilla and Phoebe, b. 1794, d. 15 days after birth.
William, b. 22 Oct. 1795.

R. BALL DODSON.

HINCHMAN—HARRISON—BLACKWELL—BENEZET.—There was recently upon the shelves in Leary's Old Book-Store, in Philadelphia, an old Bible, printed in 1715, at Oxford, in which was entered the following family record:

"Jacob Hinchman & Abigail Harrison was married the 5th Day of June Anno Dom. 1740.

"Mary Hinchman, the Daughter of Jacob Hinchman, and Abigail his wife, was born ye 26th Day of May, Between the hours of Ten & Eleven of the Clock in the Morning in the year of our Lord Anno Dom. 1742.

"Robert Blackwell the Son of Jacob Blackwell was born 5 of May, Anno Dom. 1748.

"Maria Benezet the Daughter of John and Hannah Benezet was born the 19 of March anno Dom. 1748.

"Ann Bingham Blackwell was born September th' 13 in the year of our Lord 1784. Died Ap. 17. 1789."

On some of the front pages are found the following names written: "Peter Watson," "Benjamin Watson," "Rebekah Harrison," and "Robt Blackwells."

THOMAS MAXWELL POTTS.
Canonsburg, Pa.

HOEFFNER–SÜRER NOTES.—Extracts from the *Baptismal Register* of Nicklashaus and Höhefelder, Germany.—
1704, April 24.—Anna Eva, daughter of John George and Apollonia Hoeffner. Godmother, Anna Eva, daughter of Wendel Woekenweins of Höhefelder.
Marriage Register.—1730. Aug. 29. John William Sürer, son of John William Sürer, and Anna Eva Hoeffner, daughter of John George Hoeffner.
Baptismal Register, Oberbeineldsches Church.—1731, May 24. Maria Barbara, daughter of John William and Anna Eva Sürer. Godmother, Maria Barbara, daughter of John William Hoeffner.
1744, Oct. 16.—Ottilia, daughter of Anna Eva, widow of John William Sürer, and named after Ottilia, single, daughter of Martin Endresen.

HUNSICKER.—On the fly-leaves of a copy of Saur's Bible, Germantown, 3d ed. 1776, is the following record:
Diese bibel gehöret Henrich Hunsicker dem Jungen zu und ist Mir Kauft worden von meinem Vatter d/ 5 Abrill 1803.
D: 11 January 1782 ist Henrich Hunsicker gebohren des abends um 9 uhr Soli Deo gloria.
Den 11 October 1804 ist Henrich Hunsicker verheirat mit Maria Detweiler.
Maria Detweiler was born February 14th Satterday evening at 9 o'clock in the year of our Lord 1784.
15 Februarius 1806 ist unser dogter Catharina Hunsiker auf diese welt geboren des abens um 11 uhr.
22 October 1807 ist unser Sohn Johanes Hunsicker auf diese welt gebohren des nachmittags um 3 uhr.
Den 15 martz 1810 ist unser Sohn Henrich Hunsicker auf diese welt gebohren des nachmittags um 2 uhr.
Den 13 martz 1812 ist unser Sohn Danyel Hunsicker auf diese welt gebohren des morgens um 8 uhr.
Den 3 September 1814 ist unser Dogtter Maria Hunsicker auf diese welt geboren des abens um 8 uhr.
Den 11 September 1817 ist unser Sohn Pilzus Hunsicker auf diese welt geboren des abens um 11 uhr und ist gestorben den 21 februarius 1 uhr.
12 April 1818 ist unser Dogter Ester Hunsicker auf diese welt geboren des morgens um 5 uhr.
This 3 Day of March 1821 Was our Son Wailloim Hunsicker Was Born in the four noon at 11 Clock.
This 8 Day of March 1823 Whas our Dauchter Elizabath Hunsicker Was Born in the Afternoon at 5 oclock.
Unto uz a child waz given Unto uz a Daughter was Born the 10th Day of December 1826 at 1 oclock and became the name Suzanna Hunsicker.
T. S.

HYNES FAMILY DATA—While browsing through a collection of Americana about to be sold at auction in New York City some time ago, I found the following record of births on a blank page in the body of a copy of the "Votes and Proceedings of the House of Representatives of the Province of Pennsylvania, beginning the Fourth Day of December, 1682. 2 parts in 1. Folio, unbound. Phila.: Printed and sold by B. Franklin and D. Hall at the New Printing Office, near the Market, 1752."
William Hynes was Born the 11th Day of March A. D. 1750.
Elizabeth Hynes was Born the 6th Day of June A. D. 1753.

John Hynes was Born the 22nd Day of May A. D. 1772.
Isaac Hynes was Born the 4th Day of October A. D. 1773.
Jacob Hynes was Born the 1st Day of September A. D. 1775.
Elizabeth Hynes was Born the 14th Day of July A. D. 1777.
Samuel Hynes was Born the 21st Day of July A. D. 1779.
Martha Hynes was Born the 20th Day of January A. D. 1782.
Ann Hynes was Born the 25th Day of April A. D. 1784.
Sarah Hynes was Born the 28th Day of October A. D. 1786.
William Hynes was Born the 31st Day of December A. D. 1788.
Hannah Hynes was Born the 11th Day of January A. D. 1792.
Prescilla Hynes was Born the 12th Day of April A. D. 1796.

On the margin of the page on the right hand were the following figures placed opposite the following seven names, as if to indicate the age of the persons so marked at the time of their deaths. This is mere speculation however: William Hynes (father) 80; Elizabeth Hynes (mother) 77; John Hynes, 75; Elizabeth Hynes, 65; Ann Hynes, 74; William Hynes, 64; Hannah Hynes, 69.

JAMES B. LAUX.

SOME GENEALOGICAL NOTES OF THE IRELAND FAMILY OF NEW JERSEY.—

Marriages.

1727, Sept. 18.	Joseph Ireland to Ruth Cordury, of Gloucester Co.
1732, July 28.	Jemima Ireland to Steven Morress, of Gloucester Co.
1737, Sept. 3.	Deborah Ireland to Nehemiah Nicholson, of Great Egg Harbor.
1744, Dec. 15.	Reuben Ireland to Deborah Gandy, of Gloucester Co.
1746 —	Ruth Ireland to Henry Woodward, of Gloucester Co.
1751, Dec. 2.	Jane Ireland to William Harkins, Jr.
1758, July 24.	Hezekiah Ireland to Mary Dickson, both of Great Egg Harbor.
1760, Aug. 11.	Sarah Ireland to Elias Smith, both of Great Egg Harbor.
1761, March 7.	Sarah Ireland to Willoch Paulin.
1762, July 23.	Mary Ireland to Aaron Butcher, of Cumberland Co.
1765, April 22.	Mary Ireland to James Hollinshead.
1767, April 21.	Joseph Ireland to Mary Townsend.
1770, Feb. 17.	Dorcas Ireland to Peter Halter, of Salem.
1771, July 15.	Daniel Ireland to Phebe Steelman, of Gloucester Co.
1771, Nov. 4.	Ruth Ireland to Daniel Edwards, of Salem.

1773, Nov. 3. Lydia Ireland to James White, of Pittsgrove.
1773, Dec. 16. Ann Ireland to Jacob Duffel, of Cumberland Co.
1776, April 24. Joseph Ireland to Judith Johnson, of Cumberland Co.
1776, May 1. Micajah Ireland to Prudence Bacon, of Cumberland Co.
1777, March 5. Mary Ireland to Joshua Smith, of Cape May.
1777, July 31. Phoebe Ireland to John Miller, of Cumberland Co.
1777, Dec. 13. Jonathan Ireland to Mary Gwin, of Gloucester Co.
1778, Nov. 25. Deborah Ireland to Owen Shepherd, of Cumberland Co.
1778, Dec. 3. John Ireland to Elizabeth Price, of Gloucester Co.
1781, July 2. Amos Ireland to Elizabeth Cordury, of Gloucester Co.
1784, June 26. Rebecca Ireland to Richard Adams, of Gloucester Co.

Abstracts of Wills.

Amos Ireland, of Great Egg Harbor, proved Jany. 14, 1745; children, Amos, Katherine, Sarah. Son Extr. Invent. filed £170.3.8.

Jacob Ireland, of Hopewell, Cumberland Co., proved Jany. 21, 1752. Wife Mary; children Jacob, Ananias, Isaac, Amos. Extrs. wife and Jacob Gouldin.

John Ireland, of Great Egg Harbor, proved June 2, 1765. Wife Rebecca; children Daniel, Thomas, Jonathan, James. Extr. Gideon Scull. Invent. filed £136.18.1.

Daniel Ireland, of Great Egg Harbor, proved Feby. 17, 1768. Wife Mary; children Ruth, Phoebe, Rhoda. Extrs. Reuben and Thomas Ireland.

Job Ireland, of Cumberland Co., proved Jany. 30, 1784. Wife Elizabeth; children, Daniel, Joseph, John, Ruth (Edwards), Elizabeth, Dorcas. Extr. wife Elizabeth.

KEAN-MACOMB FAMILY RECORD.—From the entries in a New Testament printed at Philadelphia by W. W. Woodward, 1809, I have copied the following data, taking the liberty of rearranging them in order:

"Thomas Kean, sen., d. Oct. 26, 1802, of malignant fever, aged 55 years.

"Mary Potter, wife of Thomas Kean, b. March 13, 1750; d. March 14, 1817.

"Children of Thomas Kean, sen., and Mary (Potter) Kean:

"I. Margaret, b. May 9, 1779; d. Sept. 12, 1781.

"II. Alexander, 'first son,' b. Jan. 18, 1781; d. August, 1798.

"III. Matthew, b. March 20, 1782; m. Elizabeth Wilson Macomb (b. Oct. 13, 1783), on Monday evening, May 8, 1815, the Rev. Doctor Read performing the ceremony; she d. Jan. 20, 1818, four hours after having given birth to a son, James Macomb, aged 34 yrs., 3 mos., 7 days. He m. 2d, Elizabeth Lewden Robinson (née Lewden?), July 27, 1824, the Rev. E. R. Gilbert performing the ceremony; she d. July 6, 1856, aged 74 yrs., 7 mos. Issue: 1. Thomas, b. Nov. 16, 1816; d. Aug. 8, 1831; 2. James Macomb, b. Jan. 20, 1818; d. Aug. 11, 1831.

"IV. Mary, 'second daughter,' b. July 5, 1784; d. Nov. 17, 1852.

"V. Thomas, 'third son,' b. Feb. 5, 1786; d. Aug. 18, 1802.

"VI. John, 'fourth son,' b. May 31, 1788.

"VII. Jane, 'third daughter,' b. May 31, 1792 (?); d. Sept. 7, 1792.

"VIII. William, 'fifth son,' b. March 28, 1792 (?); d. Nov. 7, 1813.

"IX. Margaret Jane, 'fourth daughter,' b. Jan. 12, 1794; m. Thomas Wilson, Dec. 12, 1812; d. March 25, 1826."

KING FAMILY RECORDS.

Copied from the Bible owned by Mrs. Edward P. Allen, of Stratford, Conn., and the Registers of the Moravian and Christ P. E. Churches, Philadelphia.

Family Bible.

Thomas King and Rebeckah, married October ye 31, 1703.
William King, ye son of Thomas King and Rebeckah, born October ye 30, 1704.
Thomas King, born October ye 27, 1705.
John and Mary King, born December 23, 1707.
John King, born August ye 25, 1711.
Rebeckah King, born December 29, 1712.
Ann King, born December ye 8, 1714.
Samuel King, the son of Thomas and Rebeckah King, born Sept. ye 27th at between 3 & 4 o'clock in ye morning in ye year of our Lord 1718.
Ann King (Daughter of Thomas King), who was born 1714, married Captain Topp, by whom she had issue Thomas and Ann, who both died without issue. She was likewise married in 1747, to George Sharswood by whom she had issue: George and James born 1748, and William 1751; James and William now living 1810.
Samuel King, was born Sept. 24, 1718. Ann Evans, was born Mch 25 1720 and were joined in Marriage August 31st 1739.
James son of Samuel and Ann King b. July 27, 1751.

Moravian Church, Baptisms.

Susannah King, daughter of Ann King, a widow, b. Nov. 26, 1754; baptized March 13th 1759—(died not very long after.)

Register of Members of Moravian Church, 1757.

Ann King, adult,
Anna King,   ⎫
Samuel King, ⎪
James King,   ⎬ Children.
John King,   ⎪
Susannah King.⎭

Moravian Church, Burials.

Samuel King died March 28th, 1795, buried March 30th, 1795, in the Moravian Ground (not a member, but by request of friends); born July 27th, 1745, 49 yrs. 8 mo. left a widow and three children.
Ann King, died April 5, 1909, buried April 7, 1909; born in Pembrokeshire Wales, March 25, 1790—married Samuel King and had five sons and three daughthers; 25 grandchildren and 32 great-grandchildren; eldest son and youngest daughter buried in Moravian ground; eldest daughter and youngest son living.
James King, died Dec. 31st 1832, buried Jan. 2, 1833 born in Phila July 27th, 1751; Oct. 11, 1772 married Cornelia England; had 4 sons and 5 daughters.

Christ Church Marriages.

Samuel King and Ann Evans, Aug. 31, 1739.
James King and Cornelia England, Oct. 11, 1772.

Baptisms.

Ann, d. Samuel and Ann King, Nov. 29, 1741. 2 weeks, 1 day.
Samuel, s. Samuel and Ann King, b. July 27, 1745; Oct. 27, 1745.
John, s. Samuel and Ann King, b. July 4, 1748; 1748.

LAKE—LEAK—HEATH.—The following records have been copied from an old Dutch New Testament, printed in Amsterdam, 1715:
1721, Sept. 25, b. Jacobus Lake.
1745, May 2, b. James Leak Jr.
1747, Aug. 21. b. John Stryker Lake.
1750, Oct. 11. b, Dinah Leak.
1769, Oct 24, John Heath married Dinah Lake.
1770, Feb. 10 b. Lewis Heath.
1773, Jany. 7, b. Margaret Heath.
1775, Feb. 21, b. Ann Heath.

LEOSER GENEALOGICAL RECORDS.—The following items of Pennsylvania genealogy were found by the writer in a family Bible, the property of the late Col. Charles McK. Leoser of New York City whose library was recently sold at auction:

Marriages.

Jacob Leoser and Sarah Bull Smith were married June 2. A.D. 1814, by the Rev.'d Levi Bull of Chester County.

Thomas Smith Leoser and Mary Hillegas Rhiem were married November 7th, 1838 by the Rev. William Suddards in Philadelphia.

Births.

Jacob Leoser was born January 3rd A.D. 1787.
Sarah Bull Smith daughter of John Smith Esq. and Elizabeth Bull his wife was born October 7. A.D. 1795
John Smith Leoser was born September 28th A.D. 1816.
Thomas Smith Leoser was born May 27th A.D. 1818.
Elizabeth Stringer Leoser was born May 29th 1820.
Annette Old Leoser was born Septr 14th A.D. 1823.
Charles McKnight Leoser son of Thomas and Mary Leoser was born Aug. 4th 1839.
Christian Leoser was born Sept. 9th A.D. 1840.
Sidney Harvey Leoser was born May 1st A.D. 1842.
Thomas Smith Leoser was born October 22. A.D. 1843.

Deaths.

Jacob Leoser departed this life Septr 4. 1823.
Thomas Bull Smith departed this life February 27. A.D. 1825.
John Smith Esq. died April 2. 1815.
Jas. Richards died Sept. 4. 1828.
Elizabeth S. O'Brien died in London England June 1. 1834.
Mary C. Smith died March the 5th 1835.
Mrs Elizabeth Smith died March 23. 1835.
Mary M. Smith died Feb. 1. 1837 aged 21 years.
Annette O. Leoser died July 11. 1838 aged 14 years and 10 months.
Sarah B. Leoser departed this life Nov. 15th 1845, aged 50 years 1. mo & 8 days.
Thomas S. Leoser jr. died Feb'y 15. 1846 aged 2 years, 3 months & 24 days.
John Smith Leoser died February 12th 1848 aged 31 years, 4 mos. 15 days.

Elizabeth Stringer Leoser died April 11th 1849, aged 28 years, 10 mos. & 22 days.

Thomas Smith Leoser died Sept 12th 1849, aged 31 years, 3 mos. & 16 days.

A parchment certificate of membership in the Masonic Order was also found in the Bible with the seal of Lodge F. & A. A. Y. M No. 62 of Reading Penn[a] bearing data of August 7th 1816 and granted to Jacob Leoser, signed by David C. Baum w.m. John C. Neidly s.w. John E. Ruhl J.w. and by Henry Betz Sec'y.

A parchment certificate of membership in the Royal Arch Chapter No. 152 of Reading was also found bearing date of May 1st 1840 and granted to Thomas S. Leoser   Signed by J. L. Stichter h.p., Daniel Herr k. William B. Hetzel. s. John K. Souder t and bearing seal of the Chapter.

Jacob Leoser was evidently a resident of Reading and his family of old Berks County stock.

JAMES B. LAUX.

LOXLEY FAMILY RECORDS.—

"Elizabeth Loxley the first Daughter of Benjamin & Catharine Loxley was Born the 8th Day of January About 10 minutes aft. . . . the Clock in the Afternoon in the Year 1762.

"Mary Loxley the Second Daughter of Benjamin & Catherine Loxley Was Born the 29th Day of May about 12 of the Clock in the Day. Departed this Life on Friday May 4th 1787.

"Jane Loxley the third Daughter of Benjamin & Catherine Loxley Was born the 16th of February about 2 of the Clock in the Mor. . . .

"John Loxley the first son of Benjamin & Catherine Loxley Was Born the 2[d] Day of August About 2 of the Clock in the Morn. . . . 1766.

"Catherine Loxley jun[r] the 4th Daughter of Benjamin & Catherine Loxley Was Born July the 17th about 2 of the Clock in the Morning 1767.

"Stephen Loxley 2[d] Son of Benj'n & Catherine Loxley was Born the 12th of August, 1768, about 6 a Clock in the Afternoon.

"Elizabeth Loxley the 5th Daughter of Benjamin & Catherine Loxley was Born the 9th Day of June about 2 o'Clock in the Year 1770.

"John Loxley the third Son of Benjamin & Catherine Loxley was Born the 12th of April 1772 about 1/2 after . . . the afternoon.

"Jane Loxley The Wife of Benj[n] Loxley Departed this life the 22[d] Day of September about 11 Clock at Night aged 55 years
1760.

". . . Loxley Son of Benjamin & Catherine Loxley Departed this Life . . . Day of August About 8 of the Clock in the Morning after an Ilness of About 5 Weeks Flux &cc—in the Year 1767.

"Elizabeth Loxley Daughter of Benjamin & Catherine Loxley Departe . . . this Life October the 16th about 10 of the Clock in the Morning of ye Hives after an Ilness of about 6 Days in the Year 1767.

"Catherine Loxley, 4th Daughter of Benj[n] & Catherine Loxley Departed this Life the 26th of July 1768 at 7 a Clock in the Evening of the Small pox & Lax Cutting teeth.

"Stephen Loxley 2[d] Son of Benj[n] & Catherine Loxley Departed this Life July 23 at 6 a Clock in y' Ev'g. . . . of Cutting teeth Lax & vomiting.

"Benjamin Loxley 2[d] Son of Benjamin Loxley & Jane Loxley was born June y' 6th at 8 a Clock in ye Evening, 1746.

"Abram Loxley 3[d] Son of Benj[n] & Jane Loxley was born ye 16th of January at 2 a Clock in ye morning 1750

"PHILA**D** Sep**r** ye 22**d** 1760

"This Book I Bought before I was married, and I give & Bequeath it to My Son Benjamin Loxley & to his heirs & Assigns forever as my last legacy & I give him to ye care of his Father Benj'n Loxley . . . with my . . . Hoping our Almighty Father will Protect them Both

"Witness.
  JANE BAYLY
  HANNAH WATKINS.
          her
         JANE J LOXLEY
         mark

"Jane Loxley the Wife of Benjn Loxley Departed this life the 22^d of September at Night between the Hours of 10 and 11 aged 55 Years, 1760.

"Thursday Nov. 5th 1772. Benjamin Loxley Jr. was Married to Miss Polly Barnes the Daughter of Mr. Barnaby Barnes of Philada. Mar. 4th 1774 my spouse died in Childbed & was interr'd in the Buriall Ground of the Baptist Society in Philadelphia—aged—

"Satterday July 14th 1781 Benjn Loxley Junr was Married.—Miss Polly Pryor Daughter of Norton Pryor.

"Richard the son of Benjamin & Mary Loxley was born Wednesday July 31st 1782 about half an hour after 12 in the morning.

"Jane the Daughter of Benjn & Mary Loxley born Thursday March third about 9 in the Morning 1785.

"Departed this Life September 18th 1786 about 9 in the Morning.

"Benjamin Loxley the second son of Benjn & Mary Loxley was born August 5th about 4 in the morning 1787.

"Departed this life Sunday Ev. March 9, 1834 aged 46 years 7 mo 4 days.

"Mary Pryor Loxley 2^d Daughter of Benjn & Mary Loxley was born July 4th 1789 about 12 min after 7 in the morning

"Richard Loxley the eldest son of Benjamin and Mary Loxley departed this life on Saturday morning April 5th 1851 aged 68 years 8 months & 5 days."

[Note pinned on original Document.]

"Susannah Margaret Wiperton was born the 6th day of January 1717 at Lunbach and departed this life the 18th day of April 1784 on the first day of the week about 10 Minutes after 8 oClock in the Evening and was interred the 20th in the Southeast corner of Friends burial ground Arch Street."

LUCKEN—LUKEN—FAMILY RECORDS.—Miss Annie M. Daniels, of Swarthmore, Pennsylvania, contributes the following records of the Luken family, copied from the Bibles of Jan Lucken, who settled in Philadelphia County in 1683, and Abraham Luken. The latter is in the collection of the Historical Society.

From Bible of Jan Lucken.

1684 the 28th of ye 7th mo. Elizebeth Lucken Born.
1686 the 10th of ye 5th mo. Elase Lucken was Born.
1688 the 22^d of ye 12th mo. William Lucken was Born.
1689 the 19th of ye 7th mo. Sarah Luken was Born.
1691 the 27th of ye 9th mo. John Lucken was Born.
1693 the 18th of ye 11th mo. Mary Lucken was Born.
1696 the 30th of ye 1st mo. Peter Lucken was Born.
1698 the 25th of ye 5th mo. Hannah Lucken was Born.
1700 the 13th of ye 8th mo. Mathias Lucken was Born.
1703 the 16th of ye 7th mo. Abraham Lucken was Born.
1705 the 3^d of ye 9th mo. Joseph Lucken was Born.

1742 Mary Lucken Dyed in ye Lord.
1744 John Lucken Dyed in ye Lord.
1771 27th Day of March Susanna Lucken ye Wife of Joseph Lucken Departed this Life a half an Hour past tenn in the fournoon.

From Bible of Abraham Luken.

Margret Luken Daughter of Abraham Luken and Elizabeth his Wife Was Born the 24th Day of May Between 7 & 8 o'clock in yᵉ afternoon. 1772.

Jonathan Luken Son of Abraham Luken and Elizabeth His Wife Was Born the 29th Day of September at 2 o'clock in yᵉ afternoon. 1773.

Enes Luken Son of Abraham Luken and Elizabeth his Wife Was Born the 30th Day of July at a Half an hour Past Six in the morning. 1775.

Abraham Luken Departed this Life the first Day of June one thousand Seven hundred and Seventy Six and was Buried the Third Day of June. 1776.

Margret Luken Daugter of Abraham Luken and Mary his Wife Was Born the Twelft Day of February.
this is the tru Date, 1727.

John Luken Son of Abraham Luken and Mary his Wife Was Born the Seventeenth Day of October, 1729.

Matthias Luken Son of Abraham Luken and Mary his Wife Was Born the Eighteenth Day of September, 1731.

William Luken Son of Abraham Luken and Mary his Wife Was Born the Twenty third Day of February, 1733.

Abraham Luken Son of Abraham Luken and Mary his Wife Was Born the Twenty first Day of November, 1734.

David Luken Son of Abraham Luken and Mary his Wife Was Born the Twenty seventh Day of February 1737.

Joseph Luken Son of Abraham Luken and Mary his Wife Was Born the Fourteenth Day of May 1739.

Mary Luken Daughter of Abraham Luken and Mary his Wife Was Born the Twenty second Day of March 1741.

Job Luken Son of Abraham Luken and Mary his Wife Was Born the Twenty eight Day of July 1743.

Mary Luken Departed this Life in December The Ninth Day at Six a Klock and forty minits at Night In the Year 1751.

LUCKEN GENEALOGY.—In the list of the children of Jan Lucken, of Germantown, PENNA. MAG., Vol. xxxiii. p. 270, the second child is called "Elase." The real name is Elsje (Alice its English equivalent), and in her father's will Alitze Conrad. She married John Conrad, third son of Tunis Kunders; d. 5, 29, 1706.

Elizabeth, m. Edward White; d. 9, 25, 1717.
William, m. Elizabeth Tyson, dau. Renier Tyson; d. 9, 27, 1710.
  Issue:
William, m. 1st, Martha Pennington; 2d, Elizabeth Pennington.
John, m. 1st, Debora Fitzwater; 2d, Dorothy Griggs.
Mary, m. Joseph Coombs.
Sarah, m. John Lukens, son of Peter.
Renier, m. Jane Perry.
Mathew.
Jacob.
Elizabeth, m. Thomas Potts.
Joseph, m. Sarah Powel.

John, *m.* Margaret Cursted (Kuster); *d.* 12, 25, 1711. No issue. His widow appears to have married Thos. Rose.
Mary, *m.*, 1712, John Gerrit (Jarrett); *d.* 10, 29, 1712.
Peter, *m.* Gainor Evans; *d.* 10, 28, 1719, and had issue:
  John (Sur.-Gen.), *m.* Sarah Lukens, dau. of Wm., 8, 31, 1741.
  Abraham, *m.* Rachel Iredell; *d.* 1, 25, 1745.
  Joseph, *m.* Elizabeth Spenser; *d.* 9, 19, 1751.
  Mary, *m.* John Palmer; *d.* 4, 24, 1745.
  Benjamin, *m.* Alice Cadwalader, Sept. 10, 1755.
  Hannah, *m.* Robt. Iredell; *d.* 2, 29, 1745.
  Evan, *m.* Martha Dungan.
  Peter, *m.* Jane Cadwalader, Jan. 29, 1760.
  Anna, (an Anna, *m.* Isaac Cleaver, Jr.; *d.* 4, 18, 1751).
  Gaynor, *m.* Jesse Dungan.
Hannah, *m.* Sam'l Dan'l Pastorius, son of Francis Daniel Pastorius.
Mathias, *m.* Bnn Johnson, dau. of Derrick; *d.* 7, 24, 1721. Issue:
  John, Dirk, Daniel, Mary, Hannah, Ann, Rebecca, and Sarah.
Abraham, *m.* Mary Maule; *d.* 2, 29, 1727; *m.* 2d, Elizabeth Walker. (Issue, published in a late number, three children by his second wife: Margaret, Jonathan, and Enos.)
Joseph, *m.* Susanne Maule, sister of Abraham's wife; *d.* 7, 30, 1728.

THEODORE COOPER.

35 BROADWAY NEW YORK.

LYNN—MARSHALL.—Joseph Lynn Senyore was born the 14th of June in the year of our Lord 1691.

Joseph Lynn Senyore was married the 25th of December in the year of our Lord 1712—

Joseph Lyn Juner was born the 22nd day of Aprell in the morning betwixt 8 or 9 of the clock in ye year of our Lord 1716.

John Lyn was born the 17th of September at half an hour after 11 at night in the year of our Lord 1718.

Elizabeth Lyn was born ye 13th of June at 26 minutes after 9 in the Morning in the year of our Lord 1720, and the Second day of the week.

Martha Lyn was born the 29th of May at 50 minutes after Eleven in the morning and in the year of our Lord 1722.

Esther Lyn was born the 19th of February at 35 minutes after one in the morning and in the year of our Lord 1724.

Susanah Lyn was born ye 20th of September between two and three in the morning and in the year of our Lord 1725.

The Second Susanah Lyn was born the 18th of December between two and three in the morning and in the year of our Lord 1726.

Seth Lyn was born the 29th of September 3/4 after eleven at night and dyed the 27th of November following.

Martha Lyn wife of —— departed this Life 16th of August 1736 at 8 Oclock in the evening.

Joseph Lyn Senr was married to his Wife Sarah the 25th of May 1737.

Jeremiah Lyn was born the 22nd of February about 4 of the Clock in the morning, in the year 1738.

Sarah Lyn was born the 8th of October about half an hour after 6 in the Evening in the year 1739.

Hannah Lynn was born the 8th of August about 4 of the Clock in the morning in the year 174–.

Joseph Lynn Senr departed this life October ye 12th 1742, aged 51 years and 3 month, 28 days.

Sarah Lynn wife of Joseph Lynn departed this life ye 4th of June 1759 at 6 in the morning, aged 52 years 11 months and 28 days.

Hannah Lynn departed this life ye 11th of January 1760 aged 18 years 4 months and 22 days at half an hour after 3 afternoon and Sixth day of the week.

Sarah Marshall was born December 11th 1762.

McCULLOCH—ROACH.—John McCulloch, born March 29, 1754, died September 27, 1824, and Mary Roach, born August 15, 1756, were married May 5, 1777. They had issue:

John, born February 13, 1778; died March 11, 1778.
Margaret, born March 21, 1779.
Mary, born October 11, 1780; died August 10, 1781.
William, born April 6, 1782; died March 9, 1816.
Ebenezer, born December 5, 1783.
Annie, born March 22, 1786; died July 24, 1791.
Mary, born June 16, 1788; died March 4, 1789.
Elizabeth, born July 8, 1790; died December 16, 1810.
John, born November 15, 1791.

[Inscription on tombstone.]

In Memory of
JOHN McCULLOCH
Bookseller,
A Native of Glasgow.
Born Mar. 29, 1754,
Died Sept. 27, 1824.

He was eminently useful as a member of the Associate Presbyterian Church of this City, in which he was an Elder during thirty-eight years.

"The memory of the just is blessed."

MASON.—The following family record is from an old Bible in possession of the undersigned, printed in London in 1755:

"Joseph Mason and Mary Hewlett was maried in Aldergate Church, October 19, 1758.

"Susannah, Daughter of Joseph & Mary Mason was Born on Sunday the 29 of July 1759, between 4 & 5 o'clock in the morning. And she died the 7 of September, 1759.

"Mary, Daughter of Joseph Mason & Mary Mason was Born on Sunday the 7 of September 1760, between 4 and five in the evening. She died 27 of September 1760.

"William, Son of Joseph & Mary Mason was Born on Sunday the 1st of November 1761 between 11 & 12 in the morning.

"Thomas, Son of Jos. & Mary Mason Born on Sunday ye 26 of february 1764 between 1 & 2 in the Day, & Died March ye 10, 1764. Intered in St. James, Dublin.

"Jo, son of Jo and Mary Mason was born Jun 1."

The above-mentioned couple, Joseph and Mary (Hewlett) Mason, must have had another child, as a daughter (Anne?) married in Ireland —— McFaden, and was the mother of William McFaden, who immigrated to Philadelphia about the middle of the last century, and was in his day one of its prominent citizens, a member of Common Council, 1805, etc., and resided on Chestnut Street where the *German Demokrat* office now stands. He commanded several privateers during the Revolutionary War for John Maxwell Nesbitt & Co., of Philadelphia. I have his letter of marque, spy-glass, chronometer, etc. The mother immigrated to America a number of years later and brought with her the Bible from which the above is copied.

FRANK D. GREEN.

"ACCOUNT OF THE OFFSPRING OF WILLIAM MAUL AND BETHIAH GUTHRIE, ANCESTORS OF THE LOGAN FAMILY;" the original manuscript being in the possession of Mrs. Gulielma Howland, Wilmington, Delaware.

An Acco^t of the Numerous ofspring of Willm Maul & Bethiah Guthrie his Wife father to the great grandmother of James Logan Secretary of ye Province of Pensilvania.

Willm Maul was son to —— Maul of Panmure & Arburthnet, daughter to the Viscount Arburthnet. He had 3 brothers 1 Maul of Panmure whose son was created an Earl by K. James ye 1st of Eng^{ld} & is in an florishing condition at this day (2^d James Maul of Guldie.) (3. henry Maul of Skrein(?) he married Bethiah Maul daughter of ye Laird of Lunnen chief of Guthries & —— Henderson daughter to the Laird of Jordell. She had to her 2^d brother Mr Alexander Guthries Heritable Clark of Edinburgh whose son sold it for an Estate of 4000 Marks per Anno her 1st Sister —— Guthry was married to the Right honble ye Earl of Belleary of whom this present Earl is descended & another sister married upon one Henderson a rich merchant in Edinburgh He had by his wife bethiah Guthrie a son who dyed young & 7 daughters all honourably married 1 Marrion 2 Bethiah 3 Margaret 4 Isabel 5 hellenor 6 Janet 7 Bessie.

1 Marrion was married to Sr Alex Seton brother to the Laird of Touch. He was a L^d of ye Session (his Title My Lord Killereich) his son was Sr Alex who bought the Estate of Greddon in the Mers & Willm Min^r of Greddon Sr Alex had to his son Sr Walter who bought the lands of Abercorn & he had a son of the same name now alive who sold Abercorn and has another Estate & is an Advocate & married his own Cousin youngest sister to Maj^r General Murray in holl^d He has a sister Lady barbowrie near Edinburgh. These are the Most considerable of her Offspring:

2^d Bethiah was marrd to James Murray a brother of Philiphaugh a rich Merch^t in Edinburgh he bought ye Estate of Skirlen. He had by her 3 sons all Knights 1 Sr James Murray of Skirlen 2^d Sr Robt Murray of Priestfield provost of Edinburgh. 3 Sr Patrick Murray of Deuchars and a Daughter Bethia married to Elleis of Stenmelns. Sr James had a son of the same name his Lady was Hamilton a daughter of Prestons whose offspring yet enjoys the Estate & the Honour. Sr Robert has a son now a Major Genl in holl^d & has a fine Scotch Regem^t & had the hon^r to save the Duke of Malbour.

to Mr Robt Row Min^r of Abercorn by whom she had children 4 now alive & y^n Mr. Row dying she marr^d Mr Luke Greenshield now Min^r at Dunagan in Ireland who has only by her James now Min^r at Tynan in the County of Armaugh writter of this acco^t Eliz is yet alive having Survived all her brothers sisters & Cousin Germans by her Mother & is about 80 years of Age 1706 and is the only Surviving Grandchild of Wm Maul & Bethiah Guthrie. 5 Helenor was marr^d upon Sr Morison of Prestongrange who bore him Sr Alex W^m & Robert (Sr Alex Succeeded him & Married Colt Rougheads daughter by Whom he had several Children W^m now Laird & a Daughter marr^d to Sr Bennet of Grubbet —— Marr^d to my Ld Direleton.) Helen had 5 Daughters 1 Bethiah 2 Kath^n 3 Bessie 4 Nicholas 5 hellenor Bethia was marr^d to Sr Robert Spotswood Ld President of the Session son to Prime Spotswood who has a grandson John an Advocate & Laird of Spotswood Kath^n Marr^d Sr Hume of Wedderburn an Accient Knight after Wedderburns death she Marr^d the Laird of [MS. ends].

[*The material missing between the bottom of the previous page and the top of this page was not included in any subsequent issue of the magazine.*]

MEADE FAMILY.—Mrs. Ellis, niece of General George G. Meade, furnished the following record in a recent letter to one of our members.
ROBERT MEADE, *b.* in Ireland, *d.* Phila., Aug., 1754; *md.* Mary ——. Their children were:
GARRETT, GEORGE, and CATHERINE: the last *d.* June 20, 1810; *md.* Nov. 23, 1761, Thomas Fitzsimons, who was *b.* in Ireland in 1741, *d.* in Phila., Aug. 26, 1811 (no issue).
GEORGE MEADE son of Robert Meade, *b.* Feb. 29, 1741, *d.* Philada. Nov. 9, 1808; *md.* May 5, 1768, Henrietta Constantia Worsam, dau. of Hon. Richard Worsam, member of the King's Council for the Island of Barbadoes. She was *b.* in England in 1748, *d.* Aug. 27, 1822, *bu.* in Edgebarton, England. Their children were:
CATHERINE, *b.* Feb. 20, 1769, *d.* Jan. 17, 1799, in London, unmarried.
ELIZABETH, *b.* Jan. 20, 1770; *md.* Thomas Ketland, Jr., of Birmingham, England. She *d.* 1837, in Leamington, England.
HENRIETTA CONSTANTIA, *b.* Aug. 15, 1772, *md.* Dec. 22, 1796, John Ketland, of Birmingham, England, *d.* June 27, 1801. He *d.* 1801, in Philadelphia.
RICHARD WORSAM, *b.* June 23, 1778, *d.* June 25, 1828; *md.* Jan. 1801, Margaret Coats Butler.
CHARLOTTE, *b.* Sept. 9, 1781, *d.* Dec. 25, 1801; *md.* Oct. 2, 1800, William Hustler; left one son Thomas Hustler, of Ackland Hall, England, and left issue (see Burke's "Landed Gentry").

George Meade had four other children, who died young and unmarried, so that Richard Worsam Meade and Charlotte Hustler are the only two leaving issue.
Richard Worsam Meade's children were:
HENRIETTA, *md.* Alexander J. Dallas; no living issue.

CHARLOTTE HUSTLER, *md.* Col. James D. Graham, had issue, Col. William M. Graham, Duncan Graham, U.S.N., and Mrs. John G. George.

ELIZABETH, *md.* Alfred Ingraham, and had issue, three sons, Francis, Edward, Thos. Rockhill, and Mrs. Maury, Mrs. Brunson, Mrs. Ellis, Mrs. Lyman.

RICHARD W., U.S.N., *md.* Clara F. Meigs, and had issue, Admiral R. W. Meade, Robert Meade, Mrs. Sands, Mrs. Clara Meade.

MARIA, *md.* Gen. Hartman Bache, and had issue, Mrs. Albert Bache, R. Meade Bache, and Henrietta Borie, who left son Hartman.

SALVADORA, *md.* 1st Thomas McLaughlin, U.S.N.; 2^d. Judge Peterson, issue: Mrs. Van Wyck, Mrs. Canell, Emily Paterson.

GEN. GEORGE G. MEADE, *md.* Margaretta Sergeant and had issue, John Sergeant Meade, Col. George Meade, Margaret Butler Meade, Spencer Meade, Sarah Wise Meade (*md.* John B. Large), Henrietta Meade, William Meade.

MARIAMINE, *md.* Capt. Thomas Huger of South Carolina, and had issue, Thomas, Chapman, Charlotte (Mrs. Parker), Mrs. Lafitte, Mrs. Prioleau.

I find that Elizabeth Meade married Thomas Ketland in 1790; he returned to England about 1811; he died some years before his wife at Ackland Hall, the seat of the Hustlers; she died at Leamington, England. General Meade's son George might have known more about the Ketlands, but I believe he said very little was known of them except that two of them married Meades and left no children.

MILLER RECORDS.—The following records have been copied from the Bible of Benjamin and Hannah Miller.

BIRTHS.

Ruth Miller was Born the 29th day of January 1772.
Joseph Miller was born the 7th day of January 1774.
Rebecah Miller was Born the 13th day of December 1776.
Mary Miller was born the 22nd day of October 1778.
Pamela Miller was Born the 19th day of September 1781.
Abner Miller was Born the 23d day of May 1787.
Benjamin Miller Jr. was Born the 6th day of Aprile at 12 o'Clock 1792.

DEATHS.

Rebecah Miller Departed this life the 15th day of March 1777.
Benjamin Miller Sen: departed this life Feby. 15. 1840.
Hannah Miller departed this life March 19. 1840.
Benjamin Miller Jr. departed this life June 26. 1840.
Ruth Martin departed this life Jany. —— 1850.
Abner Miller departed this life July 8. 1851.
Mary Chamberlain departed this life July 22. 1852.
Pamela Miller departed this life June 21st 1868.

MORRIS—WALTON. (From a MS. book written about the year 1835.) —" Catherine Morris Daughter of Samuel Castner and mother of Elizebeth Walton Was born the 5th of August In the Year of our Lord 1734. The 2nd day of the week. Departed this life the 25th of November 1816.

"Age 82 Years 3 months and 20 days.

"Elizebeth Morris Daughter of Reese Morris and Catherine his wife was born the 20th of June In the year of our Lord 1752.

"Elizabeth Morris was Married to Samuel Walton November the 7th In the year of our Lord 1776."

Dates of birth of her children from same book are

1. 24th October 1777
2. 29 November 1779
3. 1 May 1782
4. 14 November 1784
5. 29 October 1786
6. 15 October 1790
7. 26 February 1794
8. 20 June 1796

In back of book, among other entries of like nature, is "Elizabeth Walton will be 91 years old if she should live till the 20th of June next 1843."

T. S.

NORMAN FAMILY GENEALOGICAL NOTES; copied from a Bible in possession of Purnell Norman, Lewes, Delaware. On title page, "Thomas Norman's Bible, presented by his friend O. Dudley A. Q. Master Sargent in the 32d. regiment U. S. A. 1814."

C. H. B. TURNER.

Thomas R. Norman & Miriam Bennett were married June 7th 1798.

Thomas R. Norman son of John & Anne Norman was born October 22d 1774.

Mariam Bennett daughter of Pernal and Mariam Bennett was born February 20th 1779.

John B. son of Thomas R. and Mariam Norman was born November 18th 1799.

Mills R. son of Thomas R. & Mariam Norman was born August 4th 1801.

Joshua L. son of Thomas & Mariam Norman was born December 10th 1803.

Patience, daughter of Thomas & Mariam Norman was born February 20th 1806.

Annes daughter of Thomas R. & Mariam Norman was born September 30th 1808.

Eliza daughter of Thomas R. & Mariam Norman was born September 22d 1810.

Mary daughter of Thomas R. & Mariam Norman was born April 18th 1813.

Purnal Norman son of Thomas R. & Mariam Norman was born January 18th 1816.

Mary Norman daughter of Thomas R. & Mariam was born April 29th 1818.

Thomas L. Judge Norman son of Thomas R. & Mariam was born March 18th 1821.

Mary daughter of Thomas R. & Mariam Norman died September 13th 1814.

Thomas L. Judge, son of Thomas R. & Mariam Norman died July 11th 1823.

Thomas R. Norman died March 27th 1863.

Mariam B. Norman died September 27th 1857.

George Orton son of William & Hannah Orton died 2-5-1830.

John Bennett Norman died 9-24-1853.

RECORD OF THE ORMSBY FAMILY.—

1. George Ormsby, was born August 1, 1773.
2. Sarah Ormsby, was born *Aprail* 11, 1777.
3. John Ormsby, was born Oct. 3^d 1789.
4. Catharine Ormsby, was born Aug. 27, 1791.
5. William Ormsby, was born Feb. 18, 1794.
6. Edward Ormsby, and *Rachel, was* born January 2, 1797.
7. Eleanor Ormsby, was born June 1, 1799.
8. Henry Ormsby, was born February 18, 1801.
9. Margaret Ormsby, was born Aug. 4, 1802.

G. P. P.

OSBORN-RENAUDET-CHEVALIER GENEALOGICAL RECORDS.—The following data are taken from a Bible, printed in the year 1715, presented to Dr. Francis West by Mrs. Chevalier, who with her daughter lived for some time and died at Christ Church Hospital, Philadelphia; now in the possession of Mrs. Cooper Smith, Philadelphia.

George Lucas Osborn marryed to Jane Renaudet in Philadelphia, Dec. 5th. 1735.

ditto was born in Antigua, March 21st 1713. Jane, his wife born in N. York, April 1st 1710.

My son George was born in Philadelphia, Sept. 20th 1736. died in Antigua March 26th 1738.

My daughter Ann was born in Antigua, January 22nd 1739/40. Baptized by Mr Byam

My daughter Elizabeth Priscilla was born in St Christophers, June 26th 1741 Baptise by Rev John Merac.

My son James was born in St Christophers, Oct. 17. 1742 Died Nov. 26th 1743. by Do.

My son Fraser Mathews born in St Christophers Decem. 17th, 1743. by Do

My Son Robert was born in St Christophers February 19.th 1744/5. by Do

My Daughter Mary Grace born in Do. March 28.th 1746 by Do

My Daughter Jane Frances born in Do. Septem r. 23. 1748 by Do

My Son George Renaudet born in Do. Decem r. 30. 1749 Baptised by the Reverend Mr John Merac.

My Son Peter James born in Philadelphia April 6th 1751. died in St Croix Septem r 25.th 1753 Baptised by the Reverend Mr. Jenny Oct. 20 1751

My Daughter Sabella was born in ditto Septem r. 2 1752 OStile Baptised by Mr. Jenny Oct 31 1752.

My Son John Adrian born in St Croix February 14th. 1755. Baptised by the Revnd Mr Cicel Good Child.
John A^d Baptised by Domine Beker Dutch Chu^l,

My Daughter Russel Lillie was born in St Croix Novem^r. 22 1756 Do
My Daughter Ann was Married to Nathaniel Lillie in St Croix June 26th. 1760; and my Grand Daughter, Jane Harriett Lillie the daughter of Nathaniel & Ann Lillie was Born in St Croix on Fryday the 21st Day of August 1761 and was Baptised the 20th. day of September following By The Rev^d Mr. Goodchild.
George Lucas Osborn Departed this Life the 12th. Day of May 1762 in St Croix in the 49th. Year of his Age.
Ann Lillie Daughter of Geo. & Jane Osborn departed this Life in St Croix the 17th. Day of December 1763 In the 23^d year of her Age
Mary Lillie Daughter of Nathl & Ann Lillie was born in St Croix on Friday the 3^d Day of Sepr. 1762 & was Baptised the 4th. Day of October following by the Rev^d. Mr. Goodchild.
My Daughter Elizabeth Priscilla was married to Lucas Benners in St Croix 23 Aug 1767.
Jane Benners Daughter of Lucas & Elizth Priscila Benners was born at St Croix January 24 1768 between 9 and ten o'clock in the Morning & Baptised by the Rev^d Mr. Cicel Good Child February 2 1768/69.
Jane Benners Daughter to Lucas & Elizth Prissilla Benners Died of the Small Pox in St Croix March the 29. 1771: was 2 years & 2 months old.
Mary Lillie Died in Philadelphia Mar^h 26 1773 of the Smallpox Aged Nine Years & Seven Months was interd in Christ Church Buriel ground March 27 1773 Fryday—Buried Saturday.
Mathew Frasure married to Miss Mary Puppen.
Ann Renaudet Chevalier was born in Philadelphia on Monday the 28th. of May 1792, was Baptized by the Reverend Bishop White.
Jane Osborne Departed this Life in Philadelphia, January the 6th.
Aged 88
1803
Ann Renaudet Chevalier daughter of Peter Renaudet Chevalier and Jane Harriet Chevalier was born in Front Street between Sassafras & Vine Streets in Philadelphia on Monday the 20th. of May in the year of our Lord Anno Domini 1792, and Baptized by the Reverend William White, Bishop of Pennsylvania.

On a separate sheet of paper found in the same Bible is the following:—

Departed this life, Saturday, August 14th. 1847, Mrs. Jane Harriet Chevalier, in the 87th year of her age. She was born in the Island of St Croix, Friday August 21st, 1761.

She was the first grandchild of George Lucas, and Jane Osborn.

"Let me die the death of the righteous and let my last end be like his."

PAYNTER–JACOBS–TRUXTON–GREEN–THOMPSON NOTES.—

Albert J. Paynter died June 10th 1828. aged 28 yrs. 6 mo. 15 da.
Jane wife of Wm Paynter died Aug 10th. 1813. aged 30 yrs 9 mo 20 da.
Wm Paynter died March 19th 1845. aged 71 yrs 1 mo 25 da.
Elizabeth Jacobs died Dec 24th 1783. in the 20 year of her age.
Albert Jacobs died March 4th 1786 in the 28 year of his age.
Thomas Truxton son of Wm and Elizabeth Truxton died March 9th 1861. Born May 17th 1802.
Ann Green departed this life June 10th 1830. aged 23 yrs. 5 mo. 15 da.
Jane Eliza Green departed this life Dec. 15th 1829. aged 2 yrs 3 da.
Jane Paynter departed this life Dec 9th 1832. aged 27 yrs 9 mo. 2 da.
Jane C. Thompson daughter of John M. and Sarah Thompson. departed this life Oct 11th 1813. aged 13 mo.
James son of John M. and Sarah Thompson departed this life Oct 18th 1845. aged 5 yrs. 5 mo.

C. H. B. TURNER.

Lewes, Del.

JOHN BENEDICT PETER, son of Rudolph and Anna Peter, was born at Eggelbach in der Pfalz, January 1, 1730, and baptized four days later. Came to Pennsylvania on the ship Bennet Galley, Capt. John Wadham, and was qualified at Philadelphia, August 13, 1750. He married Elizabeth Ruevel, June 20, 1753, in Philadelphia. She was a daughter of George and Catharine Ruevel and was born in Germany, February 2, 1736, and came to Pennsylvania in 1752. Issue:

JOHN, b. Oct. 13, 1754, d. Aug. 15, 1756.
JOHN, b. Nov. 26, 1756.
ELIZABETH, b. Jany 28, 1759, d. Dec. 6, 1759.
ELIZABETH, b. Nov. 11, 1760.

PIERSON FAMILY. Contributed by James B. Laux, Esq.

In an old quarto Bible with the imprint of Matthew Carey, Philadelphia, May 8, 1805. bearing ample evidence of use or abuse, found by the writer recently in a second-hand book collection the following interesting genealogical data appears:

Benjamin Pierson, born October 3rd, 1701.
Patience Pierson, born October 4th, 1707.
Were married . . .

Births of their children:

Elijah Pierson, August 24th, 1728.
John Pierson, May 13th, 1731.
Sarah Pierson, September 20th, 1733.
Benjamin Pierson, March 30th, 1736.
Moses Pierson, September 20th, 1738.

Keziah Pierson, June 15th, 1741.
Patience Pierson, Jany. 6th, 1744.
Aaron Pierson, October 3rd, 1746.
Daniel Pierson, April 25th, 1750.

Daniel Pierson, born April 25th, 1750.
Prudence King, born September 8th, 1762.
Were married February 19, 1784.

Births of their children:

Clarissa H. Pierson, born September 19th, 1785.
Charles Edwin Pierson, born September 1st, 1787.
John Alfred Pierson, born May 3rd, 1789. Died February 19, 1811.
William Horace Pierson, born February 12th, 1791. Died November 10, 1820.
Elizabeth Ann Pierson, born March 19th, 1793. Died June 12, 1794.
Henry Alexander Pierson, born November 23rd, 1795.

Marriages.

Clarissa H. Pierson and Samuel W. Davis, March 6th, 1815.
Henry Alexander Pierson and Ellen Waring, March 29th, 1831.
Charles Edwin Pierson and Ann M. Shaw.

Charles Edwin Pierson was born Nov. 15th, 1808.
Daniel Waring Pierson, son of Henry A. and Ellen W. Pierson was born January 15th, 1832, died Tuesday morning, March 21st, 1865, at 2 o'clock.

The name of Daniel Pierson is written on a fly leaf of the Bible.

POWELL.—Copy of entries made by Samuel Powell, the first, of Philadelphia (died Sixth month 27, 1756), in his Bible, printed in the year 1683, and now in the possession of one of his descendants, Mrs. Charles Penrose Keith, of Philadelphia.

Samuel Powell's wife was Abigail, the daughter of Barnabas Willcox, of Philadelphia.

Sam^{el} Powell & Abigail his wife were married the 19th day of the 12th month *1700* in Philadelphia.

Ann Powell the Daughter of s'd Sam^{el} & Abigail was Born the 10th day of the 2nd month *1702* about 2 o'clock after noon.

Sam^{el} Powell the Sonn of ye s'd Sam^{el} & Abigail was Born the 26th day of ye 12th month *1704*, 1/2 past 11 of o'clock night.

Deborah Powell the Daughter of s'd Sam^{el} & Abigail Powell was born the 24th day of the 8th month *1706* in the house of my Aunt Ann Parsons.

Ann Powell the Second of y^{t} name was born the 24th day of ye 8th m^{o} *1708* near 10 at night.

Ann Powell the first of yt name departed this Life ye 10th day of ye 10th m^{o} *1707*.

Ann Parsons departed this Life ye 24th ye 6 m^{o} *1712* about nine in ye Morning.

Sarah Powell ye Daughter of Samuel & Abigail Powell was born ye 29 of ye 4th m^{o} *1713* about 5 in ye morning.

My Deare Wife Abigail Powell Departed this Life ye 4th day of ye 7th m^{o} 1713.

Ann Powell ye Second of ye name Departed this Life ye 26th day of ye 8th m^{o} *1714* Aged 6 years & 2 days.

Correct copy.
P. S. P. CONNER.

PRICE-SHUTE-COURTNEY-COOPER-RUDOLPH GENEALOGICAL NOTES, from Bible in possession of Mrs. Edward Esher.—

Mary Price the Daughter of Joseph and Sarah Price, was Born Sunday July y⁰ 3ʳᵈ 1743, about a Quarter after Six of the Clock.

The 27 Day of 7 month 1755, about 10 minits after 10, it being the first Day of the weak, was born Sammuel Shute Son of Henry and Mary Shute.

John Shute, the son of Henry & Mary Shute, was born the 8ᵗʰ day of July 1758.

Sarah Shute, the Daughter of Henry Shute was born April the 3rd day in 1760.

Hannah *alias* Anne Shute, the Daughter of Henry and Mary Shute, was born January 18, 1762.

Elizabeth Shute, the Daughter of Henry and Mary Shute, was born the 18th day of February 1764.

Mary Courtney, the Daughter of Hercules and Mary Courtney, was born the 24ᵗʰ day of March 1767.

George Cooper and Elizabeth Shute were married Oct. 3, 1780, by Wᵐ White, Rector of Christ Church & St. Peters.

John Rudolph was Married to Elizabeth Shute, by the Rev Mʳ Keaton, the 16th. day of September 1794, at St Mary's Church, on Fourth Street Philadelphia.

NOTES ON THE PRICHETT OR PRICKETT FAMILY, OF NEW JERSEY.— The name of *Prichett* is to be found at an early date in Burlington County, New Jersey; it is evidently the same as that of Prickett in the Bible records given below, in which the same Christian names also occur. In Clement's "First Settlers in Newton Township, New Jersey," there is a list of marriages which do not appear in the index. On p. 406, Evesham Meeting, Burlington County, 1721, we find the marriage of Zachariah *Prichett* to Mary Troth; 1758, Jacob Prichett to Elizabeth Phillips; 1759, Brazilla *Prichett* to Sarah Sharp. See also p. 137, where it is stated that Sarah Cowperthwaite, daughter of John Cowperthwaite, married Josiah Prichett some time before 1781; he dying, she became the third wife of John Gill, of Haddonfield, in 1781. On p. 81 there is also mention of a Diana Pritchett, who married Joseph Collins probably before 1750. See also Stryker's "Officers and Men in the Revolutionary War," pp. 269 and 726, and Clarke's "Burial Inscriptions of Christ Church, Philadelphia;" "Christ Church Records, Burials," PENNSYLVANIA MAGAZINE, Vol VI. p. 348. A Josiah Prickett, from Burlington, was one of the founders of Cranberry, New Jersey, 1697; he sold out the following year (Barber and Howe's "History of the Colony of New Jersey," p. 320). This family may be descended from John Prickett, apparently of Gloucestershire, a persecuted Friend, in 1660 (see Besse's "Sufferings").

FAMILY RECORD.

Marriages.

Josiah Prickitt and Mary C. Prickitt was maried the 9ᵗʰ Day of November 1823.

Births.

Josiah Prickitt son of Jacob and Mary Prickitt was born the 6th Month 14th. 1796.

William L. Prickitt son of Josiah and Mary C. Prickitt was born 11th. Month 3rd 1824.

Mary C. Prickitt daughter of Joseph and Ann Prickett was born 8th. Month 6th 1802.

Rachel L. Prickitt Daughter of Joseph Prickitt and Ann his wife was born September 1st 1806.

Joseph Prickitt Son of Zachariah and Mary his wife was born the 2nd Month the 13th Day 1766.

Ann Coverley Daughter of Job Coverley and Rebecca his wife was born the 2nd Month the 18th Day 1778.

Joseph Prickitt Son of Joseph Prickitt and Ann his wife was born the 2nd. month 19th Day 1800.

William L. Prickitt Son of Joseph Prickitt and Ann his wife was born the 12th Month the 16th Day 1808.

Edward D. Prickitt Son of Joseph Prickitt and Ann his wife was born January 16th 1816.

Wilkins Prickitt Son of Edmund D. Prickitt and Rachel his wife was born December 28th 1847.

Ellen Virginia Prickitt was born 12 mo 1st 1860.

Deaths.

Josiah Prickitt departed this life the 7th Month 10th 1825.

William L. Prickitt departed this life the 7th Month 28th 1825.

Mary C. Prickitt departed this Life the 18th of december 1839.

Rachel L. Prickitt Departed this life the 7th of march 1837.

Ann Prickitt wife of Joseph Prickitt departed this Life 25th of January 1843.

Joseph Prickitt Senr Departed this Life the 1st Month the 31. Day 1826.

Joseph Prickitt Junr Departed this Life the 12th Month, the 27th Day 1830.

William L. Prickitt Departed this Life the 1st Month the 28th Day 1823.

Jacob L. Wilkins Departed this Life 8th Mo 23rd 1853.

Rachel B. Prickitt wife of Edmond Departed this life August 10th 1858.

Edmund D. Prickitt departed this life April 16th. 1877.

FAMILY RECORDS EXTRACTED FROM THE BIBLE OF ANNA RAGUET, NEWTOWN, PENN., contributed by Mrs. Israel H. Johnson.—

Marriages.

James Michael Raguet (son of Michael Raguet & of Anne Gilminot). Born at Ricey Bas in the province of Burgundy near Bar sur Seine in France on the 6th September 1756. Came to America in the month of June 1783. Married to Anna Wynkoop second daughter of Henry Wynkoop, Esq. of Bucks County State of Pennsylvania on the 18 August 1790, & Anna Dyed on the 23rd July 1815. Married on the 17th June 1817 to Mary Harbeson—Daughter of Benjamin Harbeson Deceased of Philadelphia.

Claudine Raguet married Sylas Vansant Son of Garret Vansant on the 2 of March 1817.

Henry Raguet married Mercy Ann Towers daughter of Robert Towers (deceased) of Philadelphia on the 25th of April 1818.

James Raguet married Margaretta Thompson daughter of Samuell Thompson Esqr of Zanesville Ohio on the 14th of July A. D. 1821.

Deaths.

Susannah Raguet died suddenly the 21 May 1793, greatly regretted by her fond parents who were almost inconsolable.

Anna Raguet died 23 July 1815. In Philadelphia. Adorned with every virtue and lovely in the light of faith, never will thy death and long suffering be forgotten by thy bereaved family; who knew too well thy pure soul, thy heavenly mind to wish even for an instant to recall thee to Earth.

James Raguet died suddenly in Philadelphia on the 9th of February 1818. "In haste to meet his God his anxious spirit flew."

James Raguet son of Silas & Claudine Vansant died at Dr. Plumly's on the last day of February 1820 wanting five hours of being five months old. After a violent disease of three days constant pain. Never did a child live 5 months who gave less trouble than did this little Angel.

Catherine Daughter of Henry & Mercy Ann Raguet Died 5th July 1821 aged 8 months.

Silas Vansant died 3rd December 1841. Aged 46.

C. Vansant died 1st December 1842 aged 48 years.

Births.

Susannah Raguet born July 22nd, 1791, called for her grandmother Wynkoop.

Claudine Raguet born March 30th, 1796, named after her aunt in France.

Henry Raguet born 20th February 1796. Named after his grandfather Wynkoop.

James Raguet born 24th July 1793. Named after his uncle in France.

James Condy Raguet born the 17th May, 1823. (son of Henry & Mercy Raguet).

Henry Wynkoop, son of Henry & *Mercy Ann Raguet* born

Mercy Jane, daughter of Silas & *Claudine Vansant* born June, 1825.

Juliet, daughter of Silas & Claudine Vansant born 26th March, 1827.

Anna Elizabeth, daughter of Silas & Claudine Vansant born November 28, 1817, 3 o'clock in the morning. Called for both grandmothers.

Anna, daughter of Henry & Mercy Ann Raguet, born 25th January, 1819, named for her grandmother Raguet.

James Raguet, son of Silas & Claudine Vansant, born 30th September, 1819, called for his grandfather.

Catherine, daughter of Henry & Mercy Raguet born the 16th of October, 1820, named for her cousin Catherine Raguet.

Mary W., daughter of Silas & Claudine Vansant, born 8th of January, 1821, called for her aunt Wirts.

Wm. Henry, son of Silas & C. Vansant born 2nd August, 1823, called for Wm. H. Raguet.

In the year 1787 Nicholas Raguet a younger brother of James was killed by the Indians on the River Ohio on his way to Kentucky.

In the year 1792-3 Claudius Paul Raguet, an elder brother of James, died at Bordeaux in France greatly lamented by his brother James, of which he was always a faithful friend.

James Watall, the son of Silas and Claudine Vansant, was born December 9th, 1833.

GENEALOGICAL NOTES OF THE FAMILY OF ZACHARIAH RICE.— *Zachariah Rice* or *Reiss*, was born in Germany, 1731, and arrived at Philadelphia, on the ship "Edinburgh," September 16, 1751. He resided in Chester and Perry Counties, died August 19, 1811, and is buried at Church Hill, Juniata County, Pennsylvania. *Abigail Hartman,* his wife, was born about 1741 in Germany, and arrived at Philadelphia, August 15, 1750, on the ship "Royal Union." She died November 6, 1789, and is buried at St. Peter's, Pikeland, Chester County, Pennsylvania.

They had issue:

John, born about 1758; married Elizabeth Hench; died January 2, 1837, and is buried at Church Hill, Juniata County, Pennsylvania.

Elizabeth, born November 8, 1760; married Jacob Hipple; died October 24, 1823, at Marietta, Pennsylvania.

Peter, born 1764; married Mariah Foose; died February, 1839, and is buried at Church Hill, Pennsylvania.

Anna Mariah, born 1765; married Benjamin Sheneman; died October 24, 1834, in Chester County, Pennsylvania.

Jacob, born January 15, 1767; married, first, Catharine Foose; second, Barbara Landis; died April 1, 1838, at Loysville, Pennsylvania.

Catharine, married Henry Strauch; died in Ohio.

Margaret, married John Hench.

Conrad, born 1770; married, first, Elizabeth Foose; second, —— Stowe; died October 3, 1856; buried at Emmanuel Church, Perry County, Pennsylvania.

Benjamin, married Nancy Diller, and lived in Cumberland County, Pennsylvania.

George, born 1772; married Catherine Geirich; died January 5, 1841; buried at Church Hill, Pennsylvania.

Sallie, married John Weimer; died June 18, 1855.

Zachariah, born 1774; married Mary Knerr; died January 19, 1846, at Landisburg, Pennsylvania.

Susan, married, first, Stoffel Bower; second, Jacob Hench; died January 12, 1856, in Juniata County, Pennsylvania.

Mary, married Daniel Kabel; died 1822, at Charlestown, Virginia.

Henry, married Margaret Thomas; died September 21, 1853, at Landisburg, Pennsylvania.

Polly, married Benjamin Wallack, Peru, Indiana.

Betsy, married Alexander Martin; last heard of in Indiana.

The descendants of Zachariah Rice, computed in August, 1900, numbered eight thousand seven hundred and thirty-six.

J. M. HARTMAN.

MOUNT AIRY, PHILADELPHIA.

RIDGWAY.—Family records of births are sometimes found in unusual places. On several occasions I have seen them in frames hung upon the wall of the reception-room, and in one case painted on the side of the barn, the latter being probably a duplicate copy.

In my library is a book of nearly one thousand pages, printed in 1679, entitled "The Testimony of Truth Exalted by the collected labours of that worthy man, good scribe and faithful minister of Jesus Christ, Samuel Fisher, who died a prisoner for the Testimony of Jesus and Word of God, Anno 1665."

In said book is the following record of a Ridgway family:

Lott Ridgway was born August the 9. 1718, at nine o'clock at night, son of Josiah Ridgway and Sarah his wife.

Lott Ridgway departed this life December the 30. 1784, aged 66 yrs, 4 mos and 3 weeks.

The Time of Birth & Names of the Severall Children Born unto Lot Ridgway by Susanna his Wife.
  I. Samuel Ridgway, Born about 5 in the morning, First day of the Week Feb^{ry} 10. 1751.
  II. Caleb Ridgway, July 29: 1752, about 10 in the morning.
  III. Barzillai Ridgway, Born May 21 :: about 2 in the afternoon 1754.
  IV. Hephzibah Ridgway, Born November 20, 1755, about 5 at Night.
  V. Lott Ridgway, Born May 24 about Nine aClock at Night 1757.
  VI. Daniell Ridgway. Born December 4th 1758, about 4 in the morn.
  VII. Beaula Ridgway, Born the 4th day of ye week, May the 28th, about break of day 1760.
  VIII. Richard Ridgway, Born October 2ond about midnight 1762, on 6th day of the week.
  IX. Freedom Ridgway. Born December 18th on ye 1st day of ye week, in ye evening 1763.
  X. Susannah Ridgway Born July 18th on ye 6th day of ye week in ye morning 1765.

Mount Holly, New Jersey.   BARCLAY WHITE.

Notes to above.—Hepzibah Ridgway married —— Tonkin (probably Edward). Beulah Ridgway married Jacob Lamb ; second wife ; no issue. Susannah Ridgway married John Dobbins, Sen., of Mount Holly.

                                                                B. W.

GENEALOGICAL NOTES OF THE ROSE FAMILY OF IRELAND AND AMERICA.—The following short diary and genealogical records of the

Rose family have been copied from a small vellum-bound volume, formerly the property of Thomas Rose.

Left Dublin 25th Feb. 1746; made y⁰ Land Wed. 3ᵈ April; got in y⁰ Bay Thursday [*illegible*]. Came along side of Philadelphia Sat. 11th facing the great and main St. called Market street. Went on shore directly and found Mr. George Miller, by whom I was handsomely rec'd. and entertained. Set out for Burlington the Tuesday following, being y⁰ 14th. Arrived there in the evening, met with a brotherly, friendly reception. Matilda, bro. Joseph's eldest daughter was born at Burlington, in New Jersey, the third of November 1741, $\frac{1}{2}$ an hour after 10 at night and Baptized by the Rev. Mr. David Cowell, the 5th 7ber 1744. Sarah Ann Ursula Rose, 2ᵈ daughter to brother Joseph, was born 27th May 1744. Mr. Bliss at Bordentown.

1744/5 January 23.—This day I entered the 47th year of my age, being 46 years old. It is the most melancholy birthday yᵗ I remember, being worse yⁿ a prisoner at large, confined to my Bro. Joseph's house at Burlington, New Jersey, in America; not having handled one single Penny since the 4th day of November last, and yᵗ was a Shilling bill, having no acquaintances nor no friend of no sort.

February 7 to 9th.—A great frost and y⁰ 9th a deep Snow.

William Rose and *Sarah Crutchly alias* Chapman, were married in St. John's Church, Dublin [Ireland] March 27th 1694. He died January 8th 173$\frac{1}{2}$ æt 68; she died 27th 10ber 1728, æt 53. Mrs Grace Chapman, mother of above Sarah, died 25th 10ber 1698.

Sarah Rose, daughter to the above, was born between 5 and 6 in the morning, being Friday, March 13th 169$\frac{5}{8}$. She married 8th July 1732, the Rev. David Syme, Minister of the Gospel, in the town of Catherloch. When I left their house, which was February 7th 174$\frac{6}{7}$, she had living isssue :

    Sarah Syme, born 8ᵇᵉʳ 1 1733,
    Ann Syme, born March y⁰ 27th 1735,

Ann Rose, was born May 14th 1698, and married y⁰ 30th of June 1716, to Mʳ Josiah Jackson of Glassceily; and died y⁰ 21ˢᵗ August 1733, and left seven children :

    Grace,
    Ann,
    Susannah,
    Sarah,
    Josiah,
    Samuel,
    Katherine,

whereof Ann and Samuel are since dead.

William Rose, was born June 22ᵈ 1700, and died 1 year and 4 months old.

Thomas Rose, was born at 2 in the morning January 23ᵈ 170$\frac{1}{2}$.

John Rose, was born February 14th 170$\frac{2}{3}$. Died on Good Friday 1730, at Philadelphia.

Joseph Rose, born about 9 on Saturday night, April 8th 1704. Left Dublin August 21ˢᵗ 1729, and arrived at Philadelphia 21ˢᵗ 9ber following. Married Mrs. Ursula Wood, relict Abraham Wood, and had by her—

    Matilda, born November 3ᵈ 1741, at Burlington N. J.
    Sarah Ann Ursula, born May 27th 1744.

Joseph Rose died at Lancaster, Penna., February 14th 1776. He was admitted to Supreme Court, April 26th, 1750. [His wife died in 1794.]

Benjamin Rose, was born July 25th 1705, at 6 Wednesday night.

Catherine Rose, was born June 27th 1707, died æt 2 years 6 months.

Grace Rose, was born January 23d 1708, died young.

William Rose, was born September 9th 1713, died 1716.

Catherine Rose, was born March 24th 1714 [?]. Married June 29th 1732, James Wall, of Knockrigg, County Wicklow. When I left her house February 11th 174$\frac{2}{3}$, she had the following children living:
> *James,*
> *Pierce,*
> *Ann,*
> *Oliver Cromwell,*
> *Lydia.*

Nathaniel Rose, was born April 21st 1715; died in 5 months.

Samuel Rose, was born October 2d 1717, about 5 p.m.

ROTHROCK.—Philip Rothrock, born August 14, 1714, at Beiselhein, in the Palatinate. Came to Pennsylvania in 1733, and settled on the Skippack, in Philadelphia County, and later removed to York County. He married, first, Catherine Kuntz, March 22, 1740, who died November 10, 1777, aged fifty-seven years and six months, and had issue:
1. *Jacob*, born May 25, 1741.
2. *Anna Maria*, born September 25, 1742; died ——.
3. *John*, born February 18, 1744.
4. *Catherine*, born September 30, 1745; died ——.
5. *Philip,* }
6. *Peter,* } born October 22, 1746. Settled in North Carolina.
7. *George*, born October 29, 1748. Resided in Baltimore, Maryland.
8. *Valentine*, born August 31, 1750; died ——.
9. *Valentine*, born October 17, 1751. Settled in North Carolina.
10. *Benjamin*, born November 9, 1753.
11. *Joseph*, born May 11, 1755.
12. *Catherine*, born May 18, 1757.
13. *Anna Maria*, born March 1, 1759.
14. *Frederick*, born September 30, 1760. He married, second, September 21, 1781, Eleonora (maiden name Maquinet), widow of —— Galatin, born August 14, 1724, in Schwarzenau, Witgenstein. No issue.

JACOB ROTHROCK, son of Philip and Catherine Rothrock, was born May 25, 1741, in Skippack, Philadelphia County. He married, April 21, 1765, Barbara Weller, born April 16, 1747, in York County, Pennsylvania, and had issue:
1. *Eva Elizabeth*, born March 1, 1766.
2. *Catherine*, born December 12, 1767; died 1768.
3. *Eva*, born August 5, 1769.
4. *George*, born April 28, 1771.
5. *Catherine*, born November 17, 1772.
6. *Jacob*, born September 21, 1774.
7. *Susanna*, born November 24, 1776; died December, 1776.
8. *John*, born April 27, 1778.
9. *Maria*, born July 31, 1781.

In December of 1782 the family removed to Baltimore, Maryland.

JOHN ROTHROCK, son of Philip and Catherine Rothrock, born February 18, 1744, married, first, May 1, 1767, Dorothy Gump, born October 11, 1749, died December 18, 1775, and had issue:
1. *George*, born January 27, 1768; died 1768.
2. *John*, born June 13, 1769.
3. *Daniel*, born August 27, 1771.
4. *Catherine*, born February 13, 1774; died ——.

He married, second, Charity Worley, November 5, 1776, and had issue:
1. *Elizabeth*, born September 16, 1778.
2. *Anna Maria*, born February 17, 1780.
3. *George*, born May 24, 1781.
4. *James*, born May 22, 1782.
5. *Charity*, born September 17, 1783.
6. *Susanna*, born April 20, 1785.
7. *William*, born September 23, 1786.

SCUDDER, ANDERSON, AND WIKOFF FAMILY RECORDS.—The following entries are taken from a 16mo Bible printed in London by "John Baskett, Printer to the King's Most Excellent Majesty, and by the assigns of Thomas Newcombe, and Henry Hills deceas'd 1715." The earliest records in the name of Anderson would seem to be an evidence that it was brought to this country by that Scotch family who settled in New Jersey at that date. The volume is at present in the possession of Miss Wikoff, of Camden, who has kindly allowed these records to be copied. The families were of Monmouth County, N.J. Several of them served in the Revolution with distinction, especially "Col. Nathaniel Scudder [physician], long a member of the N.J. Assembly; member of the old Congress 1777–9; killed in a skirmish with an invading party of the enemy at Shrewsbury, N.J., Oct. 15, 1781." For an interesting account of Colonel Scudder and the Andersons see Wickes's "History of Medicine and Medical Men in New Jersey."

Nathaniel Scudder was born on Thursday the 10th Day of May O. S. 1733 at nine oClock in the Morning. Died 16 Octr 1781.

Isabella Anderson was born on Wednesday the 6th day of July O. S. 1737, at 4 oClock in the Afternoon. Died Decem^r 24, 1782.

Nathaniel & Isabella Scudder were married on Wednesday the 23^d Day of March 1757 in the Evening. They both died in the Morning of the above mentioned Days.

John Anderson Scudder was born on Thursday the 22^d day of March 1759, at 3 oClock in the Afternoon

Joseph Scudder was born on Friday the 12th Day of February 1762 at 7 oClock in the Morning

Hanna Scudder was born on Tuesday the 16th Day of August 1763, at 2 oClock in the Afternoon

Kenneth Anderson Scudder was born on Wednesday the 21st Day of August 1765, at 8 oClock in the Evening.

Lydia Scudder was born on Tuesday the 27th Day of October 1767, at ½ past 1 °Clock in the Morning

A nameless Male Infant was born on the 13th & died on the 17th Day of July 1770, aged 4 Days.

Scriptam A.D. 1788.

William Wikoff was born the 16th day of March 1755 in the evening. Died 8th of May in the morning 1824

Hanna Scudder was born on Tuesday the 16th day of August 1763, at 2 °Clock in the afternoon.

William & Hanna Wikoff were married on Wednesday the 17th day of October 1787 in the evening.

Nathaniel Scudder Wikoff was born on monday the 11th of August 1788 at 10 °Clock in the evening

Sally Wikoff, was born on tuesday the 17th of November 1789 at 4 °Clock in the morning

[On another page occurs a duplicate entry, in another hand, of Isabella Anderson's birth, and below as follows, apparently referring to one of the Anderson family]:

"Lydia was born august the 26th 1740 on a tosday at seven a cloke in the afternoon."

[On a fly-leaf at the end, in the same hand as the first entries]:

"Matilda Wikoff was born on Saturday the 31st day of March 1792 at two °Clock in the afternoon.

"Ann Wikoff was born on Fryday the 5th of July 1793 at 5 oClock in the afternoon

"Charlotte Wikoff was born on Wednesday the 15th April 1795 at 11 oClock in the night.

"Lydia Scudder Wikoff was born the 18th of Sept'' in the year of our Lord 1798. She died 11th May 1801

"Amanda Wikoff was born the first of February 1806 at 2 °Clock in the morning.

"Our Father Jacob Wikoff, died 5th March 1812."

COPY OF FAMILY RECORDS IN THE SELDEN BIBLE (contributed by Mrs. Harry Rogers).—

Births.

George Selden was born 27th February 1763.

Olive Selden was born 11th July 1775.

Adelaide Louisa Selden daughter of George & Louisa S. Selden was born April 12th 1821.

George Shattuck Selden son of Geo. & Louisa Selden was born December 3rd A.D. 1822.

Mary Elizabeth Selden daughter of George & Louisa Selden was born May 2nd A.D. 1824.

Marriages.

George Selden was born August 17th 1796 and married to Louisa Sophia Shattuck born April 24th 1801—on the 21st February 1820.

Geo. Selden was married to Olive West 9th May 1795.

George was born wednesday 17th August 1796.

Maria was born friday 20th April 1798.

Olive was born friday 12th Sept. 1800.

Samuel West was born sunday 3rd June 1810.

Elizabeth Ely was born friday 17th March 1815.

Maria Selden was married to John Tribbey 21st Feby 1815.

Olive Selden was married to Archimedes Smith 18th of May 1818.

Deaths.

George Selden died 27th of May 1817.

Elizabeth Ely Selden daughter of George & Olive Selden died December 16th 1824.

John Tribbey died 24th Dec. 1822.

SITGREAVES.—Sarah Sitgreaves was born in England in 1667/8, and died the 13th of the 1st month, 1727/8.

William Sitgreaves, son of said Sarah, was born near Preston, in Lancashire, England, 17th of 2d month, 1704. He married Mary Cook in England, 26th of 4th month, 1728, and embarked with his wife for America, in the "Watts Galley," William Wallis, master, 7th of 7th month, 1729; arrived in Philadelphia 27th of 9th month, 1729. He died 1st of 12th month, 1747/8, and was buried at John Shaw's, Core Sound, North Carolina.

Mary Cook was born in London 24th of 11th month, 1707/8, and died at Georgetown, in Winyaw, in South Carolina, the 13th of 9th month, 1734.

Their first child died in England and was buried in Wapping Meetinghouse yard, London, in 1728/9.

Their second child, William Sitgreaves, was born 14th of 12th month, 1729/30, in Philadelphia. He married Susannah Deshon, in Boston, September, 1756, and died in Philadelphia, the 20th December, 1800.

Thomas Sitgreaves, son of said William and Mary, was born 25th of 9th month, 1731, in Philadelphia.

Sarah Ann Sitgreaves, daughter of said William and Mary, was born the 4th of 4th month, 1733, in Philadelphia, and died in 1734.

William, the first child of William and Susannah Sitgreaves, was born in New-Berne, North Carolina, 1757, and died an infant.

Their second child, William Deshon Sitgreaves, was born in Philadelphia, 1759, and died the same year.

John Sitgreaves, their third child, was born in Philadelphia, February 11, 1763, and died September 3, 1798, at Germantown. He lies buried in the burial-ground of the German Baptist congregation of that place.

Samuel Sitgreaves, their fourth child, was born in Philadelphia, 16th March, 1764, and died at Easton, April 4, 1827.

Juliana Sitgreaves, their fifth child, was born in Philadelphia, May 15, 1765.

Kitty (*sic*, should be Hitty) Sitgreaves, their sixth child, born in Philadelphia, September 16, 1766.

Charlotte Sitgreaves, seventh child, born in Philadelphia, January 8, 1769.

Clement, eighth child, born in Philadelphia, August 21, 1770; died July 31, 1771.

William, ninth child, born in Philadelphia, December 23, 1772.

Harriet, tenth child, born in Philadelphia, January 10, 1774; died February 19, 1778.

Moise Yats (or de Jats) was born in Clerac, in Agenois, in France, the 12th March, 1649. He came from England to Virginia with Lord Culpepper in 1680, having left France on account of the persecution of the Huguenots.

Susanna Horrian Maviniere, wife of the said Moise de Jats (or Deshon), was born in France, September 27, 1668, at Marennes, and died at Boston, July 6, 1756.

Moses Deshon, seventh child of the said Moise and Susanna, was born in Boston, April 28, 1710; he married Persis Stevens, daughter of Erasmus Stevens, June 3, 1731, and died in Boston, September 22, 1779.

Persis Deshon died in Boston, 21st July, 1738, aged about twenty-six years.

Susanna Deshon, daughter of said Moses and Persis, was born in Boston, June 22, 1735, and died in Philadelphia, June 30, 1808.

L. A. S.

GENEALOGICAL NOTES OF GENERAL WALTER STEWART AND HIS CHILDREN.—We are indebted to Miss Mary Trumbull Morse, of New York City, for the following genealogical notes of General Walter Stewart and his children:

From the Stewart Family Bible.

"*Deborah McClenachan* and *Walter Stewart* were married the 11th of April 1781 by the Reverend Doctor White.

"Their eldest son *William* was born the 27th Decemb'r 1781 at 7 o'clock in the morning, was christened by the Rev'd Doctor White: His Godfathers were General Washington and J. M. Nesbitt Esqr: His Godmother Mrs Hayfield Conyngham.

"*Robert* their second son was born Saturday 14th February 1784 at 2 o'clock A.M. His Godfathers were his Uncle Adam Stewart & Alexander Nesbitt, his Godmother Miss Patty McClenachan; Christened by the Rev'd Doctor White.

"*Anne* their third child was born in London-Derry, Ireland. July the 22nd 1786. Christened by the Rev'd Doctor Graham.

"*Walter* their fourth child was born in London July the 6th 1787. Christened by the Rev'd ——.

"*Henry* their fifth child was born December 27th 1788, at 6 o'clock P.M. Christened by the Rev'd Doctor White.

"*Mary Ann* their sixth child was born March the 3rd 1791. Christened by the Rev'd Doctor White.

"*Caroline* their seventh child was born May the 5th 1794. Christened by the Rev'd Doctor White, departed this life Dec'r 4th 1795 of a Dropsy on her brain. Was interred in St. Paul's Church Burial Ground Dec'r 5th. Service read by Bishop White.

"*Washington* their eighth child was born August 24th 1796, at 2 o'clock A.M., two months and ten days after his Father's decease.

"The Father of the above children departed this life June 14th 1796 of a billious fever, was interred in St. Paul's Burial Ground, June 16th 1796. Service was read by Bishop White."

From a Memorandum-Book.

"Married Deborah McClenachan, Oldest daughter of Blair McClenachan & Ann Darrach of Germantown, Pa. on April 11th 1781.

"Deborah McClenachan was born on June 4th 1763.

"Their Family consisted of

"1 *William* Stewart born Dec. 27, 1781. Lost at sea summer of 1808.
"2 *Robert*   "   " Feb. 14, 1784. Died Apr. 19th 1806 at Canton, China.
"3 *Anne*   "   " July 22, 1786. Married Philip Church.
"4 *Walter*   "   " July 6, 1787. Died 1807 at Port Alajon near Gibraltar.
"5 *Henry*   "   " Dec. 27, 1788. Died spring of 1823 in Mexico.
"6 *Mary Ann* "   " Mar. 3, 1791. Died Aug. 25, 1844 in Philadelphia.
"7 *Caroline* "   " May 5, 1794. Died Dec. 4th 1794.
"8 *Washington* "   " Aug. 24, 1796. Died April 1826 at Coquimbo, S. Am."

JAMES STRATTON, son of Benjamin Stratton 3d and Sarah Austin, was born in Cumberland County, New Jersey, 20th August, 1755. His preceptor was Dr. Isaac Watts Harris, of Pittsgrove. He graduated M.D. at the University of Pennsylvania and became a successful and distinguished physician, and President of the Medical Society of New Jersey. His residence, known as "Stratton Hall," a large brick mansion, and farm, situated on the north side of Raccoon Creek, near Swedesborough, remained in the possession and occupancy of the family until after the death of his son, ex-Governor Charles C. Stratton, in 1859. Dr. James Stratton died here 29th March, 1812. He married, 1st, July 15, 1779, Anna Harris, daughter of Benjamin Harris, of Bound Brook, Somerset County, N. J., by whom he had,—

1. *Benjamin Harris*, b. April 18, 1780; d. August 29, 1795.
2. *Sarah*, b. September 30, 1781; d. February 12, 1852. Married, September 5, 1799, Edward Carpenter, son of Thomas Carpenter, of Carpenter's Landing, descendant of Samuel Carpenter, first Treasurer of Pennsylvania, member of the Provincial Council, etc., and left issue.
3. *Anna Harris*, b. December 12, 1782; d. May 15, 1810. Married, May 5, 1803, Dr. John L. Stratton, of Mount Holly, N. J., and left issue.

Dr. Stratton married, 2d, January 1, 1787, Mary Creighton, b. December 9, 1762; d. April 30, 1847, daughter of Hugh Creighton and Mary French, née McCullough, of Haddonfield, N. J., by whom he had,—

1. *Maria*, born, November 17, 1789; d. April 12, 1857. Married, 1st, May 9, 1812, Erkurius Fithian, M.D., son of Joel Fithian and Elizabeth Beatty, of Roadstown, N. J. She married, 2d, December 31, 1814, Daniel Powell Stratton, son of Levi Stratton and Abigail Harris. She left issue by second marriage.
2. *James Creighton*, b. November 16, 1792; d. July 26, 1793.
3. *Samuel Creighton*, b. May 10, 1794; d. October 25, 1860. Graduated from Rutgers College; ordained priest, Episcopal Church. Married, 1st, November 17, 1824, Margaret Sheppard Ker, daughter of George Ker and Sarah Parker, of Albemarle County, Virginia, and, 2d, Elizabeth Hood, daughter of John and Sarah Hood, of Philadelphia. He left issue by first marriage.
4. *Charles Creighton*, b. March 6, 1796; d. March 30, 1859. Graduated from Rutgers College; was twice a Representative to Congress and Governor of New Jersey. Married, February 1, 1854, Sarah Taggert, daughter of Joseph Taggert, of Philadelphia. No issue.
5. *Harriet*, b. January 4, 1798; d. May 20, 1850. Married, November 12, 1817, Dr. Joseph Fithian, son of Amos Fithian and Rachel Leake, of Cumberland County, New Jersey. No issue.
6. *Isabella*, b. July 10, 1799; d. July 1, 1847. Married, February 20, 1817, Benjamin Matlack Howey, son of Isaac Howey and Abigail Matlack, and left issue.
7. *Frances*, b. March 24, 1802; d. unmarried, February 2, 1890.
8. *Abigail*, b. January 9, 1804; d. April 27, 1805.

JOHN WALKER.—Dr. Egle has a pedigree of John Walker, of Northumberland County, Pennsylvania, in "Notes and Queries," 3d ser., I. 357, 4th ser., I. 130, which places him as the son of James Walker, *d*. Paxtang Township, will proved November 10, 1784, and to them is given a long pedigree.

But as said James Walker and his second wife, Barbara McArthur, were married January 25, 1776 (Paxtang and Derry Records), and John Walker was killed in 1782, described as "an old man," and had a son born in 1758, who had a son born in 1787, he could not have been of the lineage Dr. Egle gave him. It is true that James and Barbara Walker had a son "John," but he was alive in 1784, a minor, according to his father's will. So he could not have been the John murdered in 1782, as stated in the "Notes and Queries."

This John Walker was the old gentleman who was murdered by Indians on August 8, 1782, while on a visit to the home of Major John Lee, who resided where the town of Winfield, in Union County, now stands. An account of this Indian raid may be found in Meginniss's "History of the West Branch Valley," pages 273, 361, and Linn's "Annals of the Buffalo Valley," written up from a letter from Colonel Butler, August 25, 1782, to Colonel Magaw, at Carlisle, and discovered among the latter's papers, and a letter dated Fort Augusta, August 13, 1782, in the *Pennsylvania Gazette*, August 28. Mr. Walker resided at the mouth of Pine Creek, on the West Branch. He had nine children by his wife Jean, who was accidentally killed in May, 1788, daughter of Benjamin Powell. Of these:

1. *Benjamin Walker*, b. October, 1758; d. La Porte, Indiana, 1846; m. March, 1784, Ann Crawford, d. 1836, and had ten children.
2. *William Walker*, d. Lycoming County, Pennsylvania, 1789. He had John and William, of Vigo County, Indiana, 1820.
3. *Henry Walker*, alive September 26, 1796.
4. *Joseph Walker*, alive February 4, 1793.
5. *John Walker*, alive August 30, 1791.
6. *Samuel Walker*, alive August 30, 1791.
7. *Jean Walker*, alive August 20, 1791.
8. *Sarah Walker*, d. after 1810. She was the eldest daughter, according to a deed of 1794, and probably the eldest child. She m. William Morrison, Jr., 1747–1810 (see "Morrison Family History"), and had issue.
9. (Name unknown. Mr. Walker's estate was administered September 13, 1782, by his widow Jean and son Benjamin Walker, and was divided into nine-ninths. Eight of these parts are accounted for by the children named above. The other ninth may have been for the widow or for another child.) As to how the Walker boys avenged their father's murder, see Meginniss's "Historical Journal," II. 90, 114, and Court Records of Northumberland County, Pennsylvania.

C. H. BROWNING.

DATA FROM THE WEST FAMILY BIBLE, printed in Edinburgh in 1722, by James Watson, printer to the King's Most Excellent Majesty. Cum Privilegio.   Now in the possession of Mrs. Cooper Smith, or Philadelphia.

William West the son of Willm West and Ann Osborn of Urlar, near Sligo in Ireland, born the 1st. June 1724.

Mary Hodge alias West, the Daughter of William Hodge of Philad^a. Born the 7th. Day of Novb^r. 1737,   Polly was married to William West 18th. Augt. 1757 and had issue :—

    Mary West born the 13th. Novr. 1758
    William West Jr. born the 1st. Feb^ry. 1760.   Died 5th Jan^ry. 1763.
    Fran^s. West Born the 14th. Septr. 1761 at 6 o'clock in the morning.
    John West Born the 26th. Novemb^r. 1762 at 11 o'clock in the morning.
    a son – – – Born the 24th. August 1765.   died 10th. Octr. 1765.
    William Hodge West Born 24th. Decr. 1766 at 5 in the afternoon.
    James West Born the 22nd. Novr. 1768 at 4 in the morning.
    Ann West Born the 19th. Novr. 1769 at 4 in the morning.
    And^w. West Born the 14th. Feb^ry. 1771.   Died Aug. 1772.
    Benjn. Fuller West Born the 29th. Augt. 1772 at 9 o'clock in the morning.
    Harry West Born the 1st. Aug. 1774 at 10 at Night.   Died Feb^ry. 7th. 1775   6 in the evening.
    Helen West Born Fryday the 4th. April 1777 at 4 o'clock in the afternoon.

Francis West the son of William West of Philadelphia
Mary Nixon alias West, the Daughter of John Nixon of Philadelphia was married to Francis West January the 10 1793 & had issue :
    * Mary West born the 4th. of Nov. 1793 at 9 in the morn^g.
    Elizabeth West born September the 28th. 1795 at 11 A. M.
    William West born March the 16 1797 at 8 P. M.
    John West born October the 24 1798.
    Ann West born July the 12th. 1800.
    James West born May 16th. 1802.
    Helen West born March 25 1804.   6 P. M.
    Caroline West born November 24th. 1805.   died
    Francis West born March 5th. 1810. ½ past 3 A. M.
    Caroline West January 5 1812

        * Mary West died February 13th. (Tuesday) 1838.

ANCESTRY OF BENJAMIN WEST.

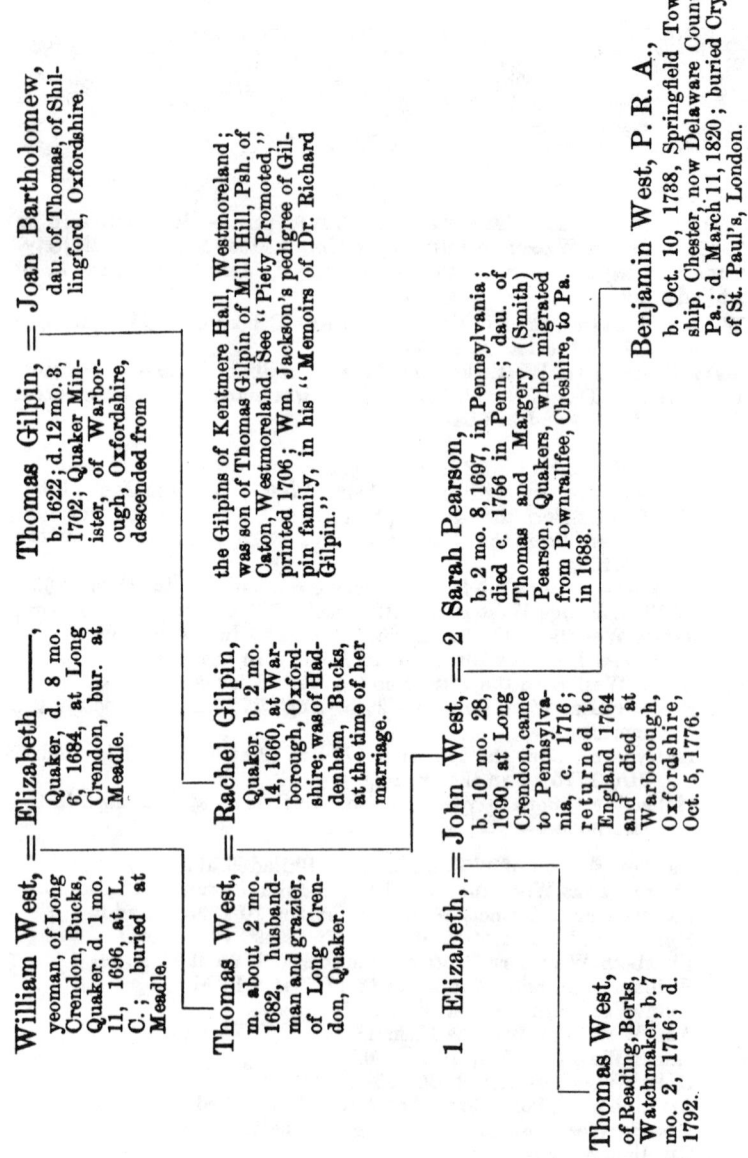

ALBERT COOK MYERS.

WRIGHT—BATTEN, family records, in the possession of Miss Emily Robbins, Swedesboro, Gloucester county, New Jersey.

Susanna Wright daughter of Ezekiel & Mary Wright, was born Sept. 25, 1749.

Edith Wright daughter of Ezekiel & Mary Wright, was born Jan. 1, 1750.

Jacob Wright was born Jan. 10, 1753.
Catharine was born Jan. 1, 1754.
Ezekiel was born Jan. 24, 1757.
Enoch was born Oct. 16, 1758.
Israel was born Jan. 20. 1761.
Mary was born Sept. 6, 1764.
Jemima was born Feb. 2, 1769.
Ezekiel Wright departed this life Apr. 11, 1771.

Zara Batten son of Edward & Edith Batten was born Oct. 25, 1770.
Mary Batten March 20, 1773.
Jemima was born Nov. 17, 1775.
Edward was born Feb. 24, 1778.
Edith was born Aug. 3, 1780.
Ann was born Mar. 11, 1782.
Catharine was born Dec. 17, 1785.
Edward Batten departed this life May 7, 1787.

W. M. MERVINE.

INDEX

(?), Alexander 389
(?), Ann 174, 384
(?), Bridget 858
(?), Elizabeth 180
(?), Francis 864
(?), Hannah 864
(?), Hugh 389
(?), Mary 174, 858, 864
(?), Sarah 174
(?)ilsoe, Richard W. 381
Aaron, Samuel 423
Abbott, Richard 564
Abbyat, Joane 608
Abel, John 841
  Mary 841
Abercrumbie, Bessie 398
ab Evan. See Evan.
Acheson, Elizabeth 400
  George 400
Achey, Anthony 839
  Catherine 839
  Charles 839
  Christine 839
  Filbert 839
  Frederick 839
  Henry 839
  John 839
  Lydia 839
  Peter 839
  Samuel 839
  Thomas 839
Adam, mulatto 51
Adams, Pres. 792
  Ebenezer 705, 710
  Elizabeth 291
  John 446, 586
  Richard 872
  Robert 240
  Thomas 44, 45
Adamses, (?) 47
Addamson, Maude 380
Addenbrooke, John 612
Adgate, Henrietta D. 857
Adkinson. See Atkinson.
Airey, George 291
  John 291
Airy, Dorothy 373
Albert, Mrs. John Seaman 246
Albrecht, (?) 785
Alcock, Wm. 869
Alden, John 261
Alderson, James 612, 613
Aldington, Alice 617
Aldridge, Henry 619
  Jane 619
Aldrixman, Peter 136
Alexander, David 596
  John 808
  R. Dykes 854
Alford, Caroline 413
Alif, Mary 855
Allaire, Hannah 410
Allchurch, ffrances 612

Allchurch, Richard 612
Allen, Chamless 779
  Mrs. Edward P. 873
  James 581
  Jeremiah 581
  John 581, 810, 811
  Mary 415
  Nathaniel 217, 219, 223, 225
  Nehemiah 223
  Samuel 415
  Sarah 415
  William 561, 668
Alricks, Peter 137
Alward, Mercy 497, 513
Amory, Thomas 210, 271
Anderson, Ann Jane 830
  Anna 839, 840
  Archibald 809
  Rt. Rev. David 398
  Edward Harrison 832
  Elet 398
  Eliz. 576
  Eliza Watson 832
  Elizabeth 353
  Elizabeth Boyd 840
  Elizabeth Stewart 830
  Espy Lyon 830, 832, 833
  Garland 845
  George 839, 840
  George Espy 832, 833
  George Mossell 832
  George Woods 830, 831
  Isabella 895, 896
  James 398, 809, 839, 840
  Dr. James Ross 832
  John 809, 830, 832
  Louisa 833
  Louisa Harrison 832, 834
  Lydia 896
  Margaret 840
  Margaret Alice Lyon 830
  Margaretta 839
  Margrat 809
  Maria 839, 840
  Martha 809
  Mary Espy 832, 833
  Mary Woods 830, 832
  Perry Woods 832
  Rebeckah 809, 818
  Sir Robert 740
  Thomas 398, 830
  Thomas Johnson 833
  Maj. William Watson 832
Andrew, mulatto, 51
Andrews, Mr. 847
  Esther 384
  Rev. John 849
  Richard 384

Andrews, Sarah 384
  Thomas 315
Andros, Gov. 134
  Sir Edmund 132, 133, 295
Annis, (?) 410
Antes, Henry 461
Anthony, Henry P. 841
  Jacob 840, 841
  Jacob W. 841
  John 840
  Joseph 840, 841
  Joseph H. 841
  Michael 840
  Peter 840
  Sally 840
  Sukey 840
  William 840
Antrim, Prudence 417
  Randle, Earl of 813
  Sarah 417
  Thomas 417
Antrum, Francis 247
ap David. See David.
ap Hugh. See Hugh.
ap John. See John.
ap Lewis. See Lewis.
ap Owen. See Owen.
ap Rees. See Rees.
ap Richard. See Richard.
Appleton, Capt. 732
  Widow 734
  Mrs. Frances 731
  Frances Garrard Speke Peyton 732
  Capt. John 731
Arbuthnet, (?) 880
  Viscount 880
Archer, John 527
  Mary 527
  Capt. Thomas 215
  Wm. 594
Arent, Col. Baron 317
Arihard, Andrew 868
  Christina 868
Aris, Jane 617
Armagh, Grace 620
Arminger, (?) 736
Armstrong, George 230, 231
  Jane 231
  John 580, 700
  Rachel 230
  Rachel Crispin 231
  Rebecca Crispin 231
  Thomas 230, 231
Arnold, Benedict 356
  Crawford 793
Arrow, Susanna 571
Asbury, Francis 264
Ashfield, Mrs. Anne 300
  Charles 300
  Mrs. Elizabeth 300
  Sir John, Bart. 300

Ashfield, Mrs. Lucy 300
  Sir Richard, Bart. 301
Ashhurst, Helen E. 795
Ashmead, Ann 669, 670
  Benjamin 667, 670
  Eliza 670
  James 670
  John 663, 667, 670
  Joseph 670
  Mary 670
  Rachel 667, 670
  Thomas 670
  William 667, 669, 670
Ashton, Jane 249
  John 74
  Joseph 249
  Robert 153
  See also Assheton.
Askell, Mary 616, 617
  Michael 617
  Michaell 616
Askill, Coz. 616
Aspinwall, Edward 833
  Emily 833
  George Woolsey 832
  Georgina 833
  Harriet Coleman 833
  Mary Jane 833
Assheton, Margaret 243, 245
  Robert 242, 243, 245
  William 242
  See also Ashton.
Astell, Edward 579
Atherton, Dr. 565
Athol, Duke of 475
Atkinson/Adkinson.
  Mrs. 33
  Abigail 61, 64
  Agnes 7
  Alice 89, 92
  Ann 6, 87, 88, 93, 96
  Anne 61, 63, 87
  Anne Hollingsworth 28
  Archibald 61, 63
  Cephas 110, 111
  Charles 813
  Christopher 1, 2, 41, 63, 65, 66, 71, 83, 87, 88, 89, 90, 91, 92, 93, 95, 96, 97, 98, 99, 100, 101, 102, 110, 111, 112, 113, 116, 415
  Deborah 89, 92
  Edward 7
  Elizabeth 61, 63, 111
  Ezekiel 109, 110, 111
  George 7
  Hann. 410
  Hannah 33, 40, 77, 89, 92, 93, 107, 416
  Isaac 14, 15, 19, 20, 24, 25, 26, 27, 28, 29, 30, 39, 40, 41, 42, 43, 68, 71, 77, 134, 416
  James 2, 46, 61, 64, 415
  Jane 3, 12, 14, 15, 17, 18, 19, 20, 24, 29, 30, 42, 64, 71, 72, 81, 159, 416
  Jennet Cowgill 62
  John 1, 2, 3, 4, 5, 6, 7, 8, 9, 10, 14, 17, 18, 19, 29, 41, 51, 53, 63, 65, 66, 71, 83, 87, 88, 89

Atkinson, John (cont'd)
  90, 91, 96, 97, 98, 100, 101, 102, 104, 105, 106, 108, 109, 110, 111, 116, 118, 415
  John B. 1
  John L. 110
  Joseph 37, 38, 39, 40, 54, 57, 58, 59, 60, 61, 62, 63, 71, 89, 92, 114
  Margaret 41, 42, 88, 89, 90, 91, 92, 93, 94, 95, 99, 117
  Widow Margaret 88
  Margaret Baker 41
  Margaret Fell 91, 92, 114
  Mary 40, 56, 61, 63, 98, 99, 100, 101, 104, 107, 109, 110, 111, 116, 118, 591
  Mary Hough 39, 40, 54, 56, 58, 77
  Mary Smith 111, 118
  Myles 6
  Phebe 107
  Phebe Taylor 107
  Rachel 38, 39, 41, 42, 63
  Rebecca 41, 42, 51, 53, 54, 56, 57, 78
  Rebekah 678
  Richard 6
  Robert 6, 7, 86
  Ruth 44, 45, 46, 47, 51, 53, 78, 678
  Ruth Stacy Beakes 53, 54
  Sampson 93
  Samuel 2, 14, 15, 19, 20, 38, 41, 42, 43, 44, 45, 46, 47, 48, 50, 51, 52, 53, 54, 78, 81, 134, 416, 675, 678, 714
  Sara 102
  Sarah 27, 28, 29, 40, 61, 63, 93, 411
  Sarah Hough 71
  Sarah Pawley 56
  Stacy 46
  Susanna 107
  Susanna Hynde 101, 102, 108
  T. 65
  Thomas 1, 2, 3, 10, 11, 12, 13, 14, 15, 16, 17, 19, 20, 24, 29, 30, 41, 42, 46, 47, 50, 51, 53, 64, 65, 72, 81, 86, 91, 106, 108, 110, 111, 116, 134, 159, 160, 415, 416
  Timothy 2
  William 1, 2, 14, 15, 19, 20, 25, 27, 28, 30, 31, 32, 33, 34, 35, 36, 37, 38, 39, 40, 41, 42, 48, 49, 51, 53, 54, 55, 56, 57, 58, 59, 60, 61, 68, 71, 72, 77, 83, 84, 86, 87, 88, 89, 93, 96, 97, 98, 99, 101, 102, 103, 104, 106, 107, 108, 110,

Atkinson, William (cont'd)
  111, 116, 117, 134, 416
Atlee, Samuel 700
Attswell, Francis 859
Auchinleck, Margaret 395
Auste, Susan 587
Austin, Sarah 899
Auth, John 596
Ayers, Robert 130
Aylif, Amy 855
  Joseph 855
Bache, Mrs. Albert 882
  Gen. Hartman 882
  R. Meade 882
Backhouse, Jannet 98
Bacon, Prudence 872
Bailie, Henry 364
  Jane 364
Baily, Robert 571
Bailyes, Alice 867
  Elizabeth 867
  William 867
Bainbridge, Sarah 78, 79
Baines, Edward 85
Baker, Ann Mary 164
  Elizabeth 640
  Francis 818
  Henry 27, 33, 40, 41, 62, 68, 70, 71, 72, 76, 77, 108, 116, 133, 142, 155, 161, 416
  Hester 72
  Hillary 785
  Hillery 783
  Margaret 20, 33, 40, 41, 72, 76, 108, 416
  Margaret Hardman 72, 77
  Mary 33, 40, 41
  Nathan 71, 72
  Phebe 33, 71, 72, 77
  Rachel 71
  Rachel Warder 164
  Rebecca 71
  Samuel 29, 37, 69, 71, 164
  Sarah 71
  William 620
Balch, Mr. 684
  Thomas 683
  Thomas Willing 683
Balderston, Joseph 60
Baldwin, John 58, 415
  Joseph 415
  Mary 415
  Richard 415
  Sarah 77, 415
Ball, Esther 868
  John 644
  Joseph 644, 645, 648, 868, 869
  Mary 643
  Sarah 644
  Wm. 868
Balnawys, William de 394
Baltimore, Lord 218
Banckson, Mary 38
Bane, (?) 664
Banfield, John 640
Bankson, Daniel 40
Bannister, John 680
Barber, Eleanor 440
  J. 842
Barbowrie, Lady 880
Barclay, George 480

Barclay, John O'Connor 680
  Laura Christina 680
Barcroft, Elizabeth 615
Bardale, Wm. 612
Barham, Mrs. 477
Barkar, Henry 161
Barker, Mr. 598
  Abraham 793
  John 859
Barkstead, Joshua 130
Barnard, (?) 690
Barneham, Sir Francis 303
Barnes, Barnaby 876
  John 854
  Polly 876
  Simon 626, 628
  William 617
Barnham, Moses 614
Barnysley, Nicholas 582
Barr, Elizabeth 645
Barrett, Elizabeth 248
Barrow, John 65
Bartholomew, Henry 328
  Joan 382, 902
  Thomas 382, 902
Barton, Edward 247
  Sarah 247
Bartow, Anna 841
  Benjamin 841
  Daniel 841
  Elizabeth 841
  Helena 841
  Helene 841
  John Benezet 841
  Mary 841
  Sarah 841
  Susannah 841
  Thomas 841
Bartram, Ann 650
  Moses 676
  Nicholas 289
Barwick, William 379
Barwis, Col. Thomas 295
Basket, Thomas 851
Baskett, John 852, 895
Bason, Charles 569
  John 569
  Richard 569
  Robert 569
  Rockingham 569
  William 569
Bateman, Anne 376
  Dorothy 370, 376
  Edward 380, 381
  Grace 372
  Henry 370, 376, 381
  Marie 370
  Mary 376
  Peggy 376
  Thomas 370
  William 372, 373, 374, 375, 376
Bates/Beatts.
  (?) 164
  Jeremiah 163
  Job 164
  John 163, 164
  Sarah 164
  William 163
Battell, Aves 842
  Avis 842
  Elizabeth 842
  French 842
  Mary 842
  Parnellah 842
  Sebeller 842
  William 842
  Capt. William 842

Batten, Ann 903
  Catherine 903
  Edith 595, 903
  Edward 903
  Jemima 903
  Mary 903
  Zara 903
Baugh, Edward 626
Baulderston, Elizabeth 380
Baum, David C. 875
Bax, Ann 224
  Edward 224
  Thomas 224
Baxter, (?) 773
  William 374
Bayley, Edward 61
  Jonathan 846
  Margery 595
  William 104
Bayliss, James 174
Baylor, (?) 788, 797
Bayly, Jane 876
Baynes, Elizabeth 98
Baynton, (?) 778
  John 845
Beach, Capt. 195
Beakes, Abraham 79, 80
  Edmund 44, 53, 79, 81
  Elizabeth 80
  Elizabeth Worrilow 81
  Grace 160
  Johannah 160, 161
  John 80, 160
  Mary 79, 80, 160
  Mary Waln 80
  Nathan 81
  Rebeckah 161
  Ruth 43, 44, 53, 81
  Ruth Stacy 20, 52
  Samuel 79, 80, 133, 160, 161
  Sarah 81
  Stacy 50, 81
  Stephen 79, 80
  Walter 81
  William 44, 52, 78, 79, 80, 81
Beaks, Samuel 158
  Stephen 158
  William 140, 155
Beale, William 766
Beamish, Nicholas 230
Bean, (?) 664
Bear, John 200
Beasley, Margaretta Stockton 835
Beaston, William 707
Beatham, Thomas 116
Beatts. See Bates.
Beatty, Charles 116
  Elizabeth 899
  Irwin 832
Beaver, Mich. 303
Beck, Godfrey 350
  William 328
Becker, Peter 319
Becket, Mr. 847
  Mrs. 846
  Elizabeth 357
  Jane 846
  Susanna 357
  William 357
  Rev. William 357
Beckett, Rev. William 845, 846
Beckingham, William 519
Beckwith, Capt. 507
  William 4

Bedant, Abigail 120
  John 120
Been, Mary 528
Beil, Sybilla 465
Beitelman, Catherine 316
Beker, Domine 885
Bell, Alice 561
  Charles 490, 656
  Edmund 379
  Franke 859
  Ja. 859
  Margaret 811
  Thomas 655
  Wm. 859
Belleary, Earl of 880
Bells, Ann 127
Belt, Emma B. 859
Belton, Lawrence 380
Bembridge, (?) 665
Benan, Paul 854
Bender, Louisa 342
Benezet, Daniel 841
  Elizabeth North 841
  Hannah 869
  John 869
  Maria 869
  Sarah 841
Benner, Absalom 318
Benners, Eliz. Priscilla 885
  Jane 885
  Lucas 885
Bennet, Sr. 881
  Edm. 140
Bennett, Aaron 124
  Abigail 124
  Abraham 162
  Arcady 124
  Elizabeth 124, 125
  Elizabeth Rockards 124
  Harriot 124
  Hester 124, 125
  John 124
  Joseph Smith 124
  Mariam 883
  Miriam 883
  Nehemiah 124, 125
  Patience 124
  Pernal 883
  Sarah Bell 124
Bennison, Thomas 380
Benton, Jane 224
Berd, Ra. 304
Berdesly, Francis 349
Berkley, Eleanor 845
  Thomas 845
Berleman, Rev. F. W. 280
Berry, John 379
Besse, (?) 64
Beswick, Charles 617
Bethausen, Charles Christian 707
  John Ernest Christian 707
  Rosina Maria 707
Bethel, R. 668
Bethell, Frances 660
  Francis 670
  Helen 178
  John 154
  R. 670
  Robert 670
  William 670
Bettesworth, Johannis 576
Betz, Henry 875
Bevan, Ann 537
Beyle, Roger 126
Bezer, John 217, 219
  Ruth 174

Bibbe, Edmund 487
  Ester 487
  Matthew 487
Bickell, Edwin J. 497
Bickerdike, Mary 81
Bickett, Alice 381
Biddle, Edward 700
  John 540
  William 703
Bidgood, William 60, 410
Bidle, Katherine 556
  Richard 556
Biell, William 127
Biggs, Rev. Thomas 803
Biles, Alexander 129
  Ann 158, 160, 161, 164
  Charles 127, 128, 129, 132, 140, 163, 164
  Dorothy 126
  Elizabeth 80, 128, 129, 158, 163, 164
  George 15, 24, 30, 44, 128, 134, 158, 160
  Grace 160, 164
  Hannah 165
  Jane 14, 15, 21, 22, 23, 33, 34, 156, 164
  Joanah 158
  Joanna 80
  Johannah 128, 157, 158, 160, 161
  John 128, 129, 158, 160
  Langhorne 163, 164
  Margaret 163
  Martha 160
  Mary 128, 158, 160
  Phebe 160
  Rebecca 128, 131
  Rebeckah 158
  Sarah 129, 160, 163, 164
  Thomas 127, 133, 160, 163, 164
  William, 14, 15, 21, 22, 23, 24, 27, 30, 31, 43, 66, 67, 80, 127, 128, 129, 130, 131, 132, 133, 134, 135, 136, 137, 138, 139, 140, 141, 142, 143, 144, 145, 146, 147, 148, 149, 150, 151, 152, 153, 154, 155, 156, 157, 158, 159, 160, 161, 162, 163, 164
Biley, Henry 127
Bill, Willen 127
  Rev. William 127
Bills, Elizabeth 127
  Thomas 127
  William 127
Bingley, William 104, 115
Binkele, Anna 840
  Anna Barbara 840
  Anna Maria 840
  Catherine 840
  Christian 840
  Christina 840
  Christmann 840
  Elizabeth 840
  Frederick 840
  John 840
  John Adam 840
  John Peter 840
  Joseph 840

Binkele, Margaret 840
  Maria 840
  Peter 840
  Sarah 840
Bird, John 702, 703
  Margaret 702
Birkett, William 381
Birtwistle, Henry 74
  Mary 74
Bishersle, Henry 100
Bishop, Christopher 529
  Elynore 562
  John 529
  Mary 561, 562
Bispham, Joshua 51, 53
Bisse, Ben 628
  Christian 597
  Robert 597
Blackborne, Robt. 192, 195
Blackburne, Robert 196
Blacket, Sir Edward 11
Blackfan, Widow 223
  Aaron 843
  Agness 843
  Edward 222, 223, 224
  Elizabeth 843
  Elizabeth C. 223, 224
  Esther 843
  Hannah 843
  Jesse 843
  John 222, 224, 843
  Rachel 843
  Rebecca 243, 245
  Rebecca Crispin 223
  Sarah 843
  Thomas 843
  William 223, 243, 245, 843
Blackshaw, Martha 158
  Nehemiah 37
  Randal 15
  Randall 61
  Sarah 61
Blackwell, Ann Bingham 869
  Elizabeth 859
  Mrs. Elizabeth 859
  Ja. 859
  Jacob 869
  John 859
  Joseph 859
  Robert 869
  Sam'l 859
  Sarah 859
  Col. Wm. 859
Blackwells, Rob. 869
Blair, Abby Paulina 681
  Abigail Phillips 681
  Anna Dike 832, 834
  Cust. 834
  Edward Shippen 681
  Frances Van Hook 681
  George 832, 834
  Roberdeau 681
  Samuel 681
  Rev. Samuel 679
  Susan Shippen 681
  Thomas 808, 832, 834
  Thomas S. 832
  Virginia 834
  William Shippen 681
  Zepherene Victoria 681
Blake, Admiral 189
  Capt. Benjamin 200
Blakes, Catherine 62
Blakey, William 38, 60

Blamer, Thomas 381
Bland, George D. 795
  Richard 375
Blatt, John 224
  William 224
Blight, Deborah 433
  George Weber 433
  Martha 364
  Mary Valeria Sergeant 433
  Peter 364
Blind, William 614
Bliss, Mr. 893
Blood, Clarine L. 659
  Cyrus 659
Blunston, Jno. 145
Blunt, Thos. 566
Boa, William 288, 289, 290
Boggs, Mary M. 793
Boid, Jane 159
Boise, Rev. Mr. 418
Boles, James 704, 707, 708
  John 704
  Rebecca 707
  Rebecca Jones 704
Bond, James 108, 112
  Jane 19
  Joseph 416
Bonsall, Ann 676
Bonwicke, Benjamin 565
  Catherine 565
  John 565
Boon, Andrew 529
  Garrett 529
  Squire 166, 167
Boone, Anne 167, 169
  Benjamin 166, 167
  Catherine 167
  Daniel 643
  Deborah Howell 167
  Dinah 169
  George 166, 167, 168, 169, 170, 643
  Hannah 169, 170
  James 166, 167, 168, 169, 170
  John 166, 167, 168, 169, 170
  Joseph 166, 167
  Joshua 167, 169
  Judah 167, 169, 170
  Martha 167, 169
  Mary 166, 167, 168, 169, 170
  Mary Foulke 169
  Moses 167, 169
  Nathaniel 169
  Rachel 167, 169
  Samuel 166, 167
  Sarah 167
  Sarah Uppey 166
  Susanna 167
  Susannah 170
Booy, Anne 563
  John 563
  Joseph 563
  William 563
Borden, James 715
Borie, Hartman 882
  Henrietta 882
Borradail, John 162
Borradaile, John 31, 59
Borrodaile, John 54
Boswell, David 393
  Sir John 393
  Mariott Glen 393

Boudinot, Mr. 716
  Elias 716
  Hon. Elias 717
Bourne, Joane 224
  Rich. 224
Bouverie, Hon and Rev.
  Mr. 584
Bovindon, John 551
Bowater, Ann 174
Bowden, Mordecai 25, 30
Bowell, John 568
  Wm. 568
Bower, Stoffel 891
Bowes, Charity 302
  Sir Martin 302
Bowman, Francis M. 258
  John 630
  Louise F. Doane 258
  Seth B. 258
Boy, Anne 562
  Johanna 562
  John 562, 563
  Joseph 562
  Margrat 810
  William 562, 563
Boyce, Angus 666
  Malcolm 666
Boyd, Mary 839
  Thomas 400, 403, 810
Boyer, Jacob 278
Boyers, Ann 816
Boyle, Agnisse 807
  Elizabeth Wilson 807
  John 817
  Thomas 807
Boyles, William 138
Boys, Samuel 670
Boyse, Anne 564
Bracken, Henry 374
  Hy. 374
  Thomas 374
Bradford, (?) 617
  Elizabeth 617
  Leonard 616, 617
  William 496, 772
Bradgate, William 380
Brading, Nathaniell 418
Bradshaw, Frances 242
  Francis 556
  James 572, 613
  John 572, 613
  Mary 596
  Ralph 189, 210, 242, 272
  Randall 272
  Raphe 272
  Rebecca 189, 190
  Sara 272
  William 613
Bradshawe, Mr. 380
  John 295
Brabyn, Robert 372
Brake, John 514
Bran, John 819
Brandreth, Henry 294
Brant, Robert 618
Braxson, Joseph 488
  Thomas 488
Bray, John 377
  Martha 377
Brayen, Will 812
Brearley, Col. David 797
  Ellen J. 788
  Ellen Jones 797
  Sarah 129
Breckenridge, Judge Henry
  M. 829
Brennaman, A. N. 659
  Maria de Welden 659

Brett, Widow 724
  Ann 719, 720
  Henry 719, 720
  Samuel 719, 720
Brettaign, Duke of 391
Brigg, William 549
Briggs, Thomas 624
Brigham, Charles 15
Bright, Tobias 703
Brinley, Katherine J. 795
Brintnall, Joseph 697
Brinton, Walter 250
Bristow, William 304
Britain, Lionel 242
Brittaine, Lyonell 155
Britton, Lionel 80, 774
  Rebecca 774
  Thomas 566
Brock, Elizabeth 156
  John 142
  Thomas 32
Brockway, Beckwith 266
  Charles 266
  Frank Eugene 266
  Marie 266
Brodhurst, Mrs. Ann 722
  Ann Pope 720, 721, 728, 729, 732
  Gerrard 721, 722
  Walter 720, 721, 729, 733, 735
Brodock, John 558
Broke, Edmude 550
Brooke, (?) 478
  Allice 629
Brooks, Edward 69, 70
  Jno. 156
Broome, John 616, 617
Broughton, Thomas 203
Browing, Widow 562
Brown, (?) 171
  Benjamin 788
  Hugh 814
  Jane 774, 788
  John 61
  John Masson 488
  Richard 350, 395
  Samuel 61
  Thomas 807
Browne, Elizabeth 396
  Gabriel 612
  Hester Baker Yardley 68
  Honour 72
  James 72
  Jo. 226
  John 396, 608, 806
  Joseph 612
  Robert Bethell 660
  William 72
Brownent, Tho. 564
Browning, C. H. 900
  Charles H. 718, 762
Bruce, Alexander 855
  Elenore 855
  Ester 855
  Margaret 392
  Robert 392
Bruckhauer, Capt. Adam 331
Fruer, Henry 313
Brummell, John 570
Brunner, Barbara 277
  Felix 277
Brunson, Mrs. 882
Bryarly, John 130
Buchanan, James 659

Buchanan, Roberdeau 181, 681
Buck, E. 843
  Ephraim 843
  Hanah 843
  Jane 843
  Jeremiah 843
  John 843
  Joseph 843
  Maria 843
  Naomi Seeley 843
  Sarah 843
  William J. 473
Buckley, James 231
  Phineas 60
  Ruth 62
  William 34
Bucknell, Anne 570
Budd, Elizabeth 676
  Rebekah 674, 676
  Richard 560
  Susan 794
  Thomas 53, 54, 78
Bujac, John Lachaussee 793
  Patrick Julius 793
Bull, Elizabeth 874
  Rev. Levi 874
  Richard 54
Bullinger, Henry 275
Bunting, Job 62, 71, 77
  Priscilla Burgess 118
  Rachel Baker 62
  Samuel 38, 39, 60, 118
Burd, Edward 700
Burdet, Edward 295
Burdett, Edward 287, 295, 297
  Mary 294, 296
  Sir Walter 296
Burgaveny, Lord 305
Burgess, Daniel 38, 118
  Samuel 38
Burgoyne, (?) 333
Burnet, Gov. William 162
Burns, Jane 398
  Rev. Thomas 399
Burnyeat, John 65
Burr, Elizabeth 247
  John 542
Burrell, John 304
  Walter 304, 305, 306, 307
Burrough, Abigail 712
  Abigail Wallis 713
  Ann 713
  Ann Hollinshead 712
  Anna 713
  Evelina C. 712
  Evelina Constance 712
  Isaac 712, 713
  Jehu 712, 713
  Marmaduke 712
  Marmaduke, M. D. 713
  Samuel 712
  Sarah 713
  Sarah M. 712
Burroughs, Ester 488
  John 488
  Mary 68
  William 488
Burrows, John 381
Burton, Ann Maria 456
  Anthony 32, 33, 59, 160
  Bernard 377
  Eliza 456
  Mary Ann 456

Burton, Robert 456
  Savige 567
  Thomas 374
  William 567
Burtons, (?) 33
Bury, Mr. 598
Busby, Catherine 575
  Elizabeth 573
  John 573
  Mary 573
  Olive 573
Bush, William 630
Busted, Anna 226
Butcher, Aaron 871
  John 93, 247
  Michael 245
Buterton, Sarah 414
Butler, Col. 900
  Amos 515
  Anna 515
  Caleb 733
  Capt. Gregory 203, 207
  Margaret 741
  Margaret Coats 881
  Susan 574
  Thomas 203
  Sir Thomas 813
Butt, George 595
  Mary 594
  Nathaniel 594
  Thomas 595
Butz, Mary 465
Byam, Mr. 884
Bye, Nathaniel 442
Byers, Robert 819
Byle, Josias 126
  Walter 126
  William 126
Byles, Daniel 126
  John 126
  Josiah 126, 127
  Rev. Mather 127
  William 130, 138, 142, 536
Byley, Henry 127
Byrd, Mr. 598
  Elizabeth Carter 680
  Col. William 680
Byset, Walter 394
Bysse, Christian 597
  James 597
Caddie, Agnes 557
Cadwalader, Alice 878
  Hannah 867
  Jane 878
  John 485, 538
  Martha 538
  Robert 806
  Thomas 538
  Dr. Thomas 538
Cahall, Mrs. Thomas 246
Caldwell, (?) 404
  Mrs. 507, 508
  David 404, 405
  Elizabeth Person 513
  Patr. 814
Caler, Peter 326
Calford, Chas. 814
Callahan, Dora Donath 681
  Frances Blair 681
  John 681
  Samuel Blair 681
  Thomas 681
Callowhill, Alice 628, 629
  Anna 626, 628
  Anne 629, 630
  Bridgett 623, 624, 629
  Charles 628

Callowhill, Dennis 623, 624
  Dorathy 630
  Elijah 630
  Elizabeth 625
  Francis 629
  Gulielmi 630
  Gulielmus 629, 630
  Hanna 609, 626, 628
  Hannah 610, 622, 623, 624, 625, 630
  James 629, 630
  John 609, 610, 629
  Katherine 629
  Margerie 629
  Margery 630
  Mariae 630
  Mary 629
  Richard 629
  Sarah 623, 624
  Thomas 574, 602, 609, 619, 622, 623, 624, 625, 626, 628, 629, 630
  William 629, 630
Calvin, Phillip 440
Calwell, Margaret 405
Cameron, Simon 264
Campbell, Sir Archibald 394
  Colin 790
  Cora 266
  David 817
  Henry 407
  Isaac 407
Canby, Benjamin 443
  Lydia 111
  Samuel 70
  Sarah 70
  Thomas 439
Canell, Mrs. 882
Canstatter, Catharine 645
Caper, Joseph 363
Captain Cumbansh, Indian 134
Cardale, Margaret 612
  Mary 612
  William 612
Carey, Clara Mitchell 678
  Frances Anne 481
  Frank 362, 363
  George F. L. 362
  Lewis G. 362
  Maggie 362
  Mathew 481
  Matthew 632, 886
  Robert 362
  Samson 58
  Samuel 58
  Sarah 58
Carkocedg, (?) 303
Carl, John 522
Carleton, Tho. 65
Carlisle, Earl of 295
  Esther 664, 668
Carlton, George 368
Carmalt, Hannah 675
  James 675, 676
  Jonathan 676
  Rebekah 675
  Susannah 675, 676
  Thomas Say 675
Carmicke, Clementina 418
  Eliz. 418
  John 418
  Peter 418
  Sarah 418

Carmicke, Stephen 418
Caroline, Susan 342
Carpenter, Annie Eliza 171
  Benjamin 172
  Catharine F. 171
  Catharine H. 172
  Comfort H. 171
  Edward 899
  Elizabeth 171, 172
  Hannah 772, 773, 775
  Dr. Henry 659
  James 171, 172
  James H. 172
  Jas. Henry 171
  Jane 171
  John 773
  John Dean 171, 172
  Jos. 171
  Mrs. Laura M. 659
  Louis Marshall 171
  Lydia 172
  Margaret 172
  Margaret Staton 171
  Mary 171, 172
  Mary Quinn 171
  Mary Rodgers 171, 172
  Nancy 171, 172
  Robert Howard 171, 172
  Samuel 38, 60, 230, 475, 542, 574, 773, 775, 899
  Thomas 899
  Thos. H. 171, 172
  Thos. Howard 171
Carroll, Achsah Ridgely 680
  Charles R. 680
Carry, Henry 319
Cart, Samuel 442, 840
Carter, Charles 224
  Dority 844
  Edward 93
  Isabel 92, 93, 95
  Jarvis Pomeroy 835
  Joanas 844
  John 93, 95, 562
  Lydia Walley 93
  Mary 562
  Robert 93
  William 844
Cartwright, John 553
  William 304
Carver, William 615
Cary, Ann 667
  Edward 663, 667
  Elizabeth 667
  Jesse 667
  Rachel 667
  Sarah 667
Casad, Amanda Keziah 497
  Anthony W. 514
  Anthony Wayne 497
Casper, Eliz. R. Gillingham 365
  Harry B. 363, 365
  Joseph 362, 363, 365
  Josephine 363
  Laura 362
  Lizzie R. 362, 363, 365
  T. Jefferson 363, 365
Casperson, Judith L. 710
  William 710
Cassell, Arnold 55, 56, 57
  Israel 55, 56
  Johannes 56
  Lydia 55

Cassell, Lydia Fordham 56
  Rebecca 55
  Susanna de la Plaine 56
  Veronica 57
Caster, Barbara 340
Castner, Samuel 882
Cattell, Jonas 247
Cavanna, Jane A. 797
Certain, Grace 600
Chadsey, Francis 173
Chadwick, Jane 39
Chalkley, John 573
  Martha 115
  Thomas 115, 223
Chamber, Ales 552
Chamberlain, Mrs. Elizabeth 300
  Mary 882
  Peter 104
  Richard 300
Chambers, Benjamin 240, 518
Chambre, Alan 368
Chamless, Rebecca 773, 775
Champion, Richard 609, 626, 627
Chancellor, Henry 792
  Salome 774, 787
  Sarah Wharton 792
  Wharton 792
  William 780, 787, 792
Chancye, Dorothy 377
Chanders, Elizabeth 867
  T. 867
Chandler, Widow 173
  Ann 173, 174
  Betty 174
  Charity 173, 174
  George 172, 173, 174
  Hannah 174
  Isaac 174
  Jacob 173, 174
  Jane 173, 174
  John 173, 174
  Lydia 174
  Margaret 174
  Mary 174, 224, 576, 619
  Moses 174
  Phebe 174
  Rachel 174
  Ruth 174
  Samuel 174
  Sarah 174
  Susannah 174
  Swithin 173, 174
  Thomas 173, 174
  William 173, 174
Chanler, James 617
  Thomas 617
Chantier, Mary 224
Chantler, Daniell 224
Chaplin, Pressly N. 796
Chapman, (?) 174
  Abraham 176
  Ann 176
  Benjamin 176
  Mrs. Grace 893
  Henricus 230
  Isaac 176, 177
  Jane 175, 176
  John 76, 175, 176
  Joseph 35, 176, 177
  Mara 176
  Margaret 176
  Mary 176
  Sarah 176, 893

Chapman, William 687
Charles I, K. of Great Britain 295, 405
Charles II, K. of Great Britain 184, 208, 210, 215, 221, 288, 289, 429
Charters, Wm. 226
Chase, John 272
Chaunce, William 552, 570, 582
Chauncey, Rev. Charles 625
  Ichabod 625
  J. 625
Cheeseman, Catherine 453
Cheesman, Capt. 868
  Margaret 868
Chevalier, Mrs. 884
  Andrew 845
  Ann Renaudit 845, 885
  Elizabeth 845
  George 845
  Isabella 845
  James 845
  Jane 845
  Jane Harriet 885
  John 845
  John Barkley 845
  Judith 845
  Morris 845
  Peter 845
  Peter Gerardus 845
  Peter Renaudet 845, 885
  Richard 845
  Samuel 845
  Susan 845
  Susanna 845
  Susannah 845
  Thomas 845
  William 845
  William Wagner 845
Cheyne, John 552
Child, Mary Atkinson 63
  Cephas 63, 101
  Rev. Cicil Good 885
  Isaac 63
  Mary 116
  Rachel 63
Childs, Blair 834
  Harvey 834
Chipman, Sarah 488
Choiter, Mrs. 372
Cholles, Alis 607
Cholmely, Francis 375
Christie, John 809
  William 809
Christman, Daniel 277
  Margaret 277
Christmas, Capt. 403
Christy, (?) 405
Chudleigh, Capt. 211
  Jane 210, 231
  Joan 212
  John 211, 212, 231
  Capt. John 210, 212
  Thomas 211, 212, 215, 232
Church, Edward 416, 417
  Joseph 416, 417
  Philip 898
  Rebecca 411, 417
  Samuel 417
  Susan 259
  William 417
Churchill, Gen. 688
Claerhout, Belitije 845
Clapier, Caroline 792

Clark, Capt. 200
  Aletta 850
  Anna' 848
  Arthur Douglass 260
  Benjamin Crispin 260
  Charlotte 848
  Dorcas 791
  Elizabeth Francis 260
  George S. 259
  George Stephenson 257
  Joanna 849
  John 849
  Col. John 259
  John Maxwell Rodman 259, 260
  John Stephenson 250, 251, 259
  Lott 847
  Milicent 848
  Sarah 849
  Thomas 705
Clarke, Col. 207
  Widow 562
  Anna 850
  Elizabeth 561, 850
  Ester 850
  Hannah 850
  John 596, 849
  Lidia 850
  Mary 620, 850
  Miers 850
  Sarah 850
Clarks, Henry 442
Clarkson, Eliz. 357
  Mary 513
Clarridge, Samuel 436
Clay, Mr. 795
Claypoole, (?) 177
  Elizabeth 177
  George 177, 178, 179
  Helen 177
  Helena 178
  James 177, 178, 179
  Jehu 178, 179
  John 177, 178
  Joseph 177, 178, 179
  Josiah 177, 178, 179
  Mary 177, 178, 179
  Nathaniel 177, 178
  Norton 178
  Prissilla 177
  Rebecca 178, 179
  Samuel 177
Cleaver, Isaac 878
  John 105
Clement V, Pope 391
Clement, Judge 1
  John 294
  Mary 609, 610
  S. 619
  Simon 609, 610
  Walter 609, 610
Clements, Walter 624
Clempson, Rev. 659
Clenden, George 815
Clerck, Roger 551
Clerk, William 197
Clifton, Adelaide Charlotte 797
  Alfred Wharton 797
  Anna Howell 797
  Clifton Wharton 797
  Frances Anna 797
  Franklin Wharton 797
  Henrietta 797
  Mary 774, 787, 797
  Rosa 797
  Thomas 787
Clingan, (?) 700

Clingan, William 700
Cloake, Isaac 570
Clough, George 37, 38
Clowd, William 173
Clowes, Aletta 846, 848, 850
  Benjamin 846
  Caleb 846
  Catherine 846, 847, 850
  Charles 846
  Comfort 846
  David 846, 847
  Edward 846
  Ezekiel William 849
  Gerardus 846, 847
  Hannah 847
  Isaac 846, 849
  John 846, 847, 848, 849, 850
  Joseph 846
  Lydia 847
  Mary 846, 847, 848, 849, 850
  Peter 846, 849
  Samuel 845, 846, 847, 848, 849
  Sarah 848, 849, 850
  Theodore 846
  Thomas 846
  Timothy 846
  William 846, 847
Clows, Margery 39
Cloyd, (?) 664
Clunn, Mary Say 672
Clymer, Ann 181, 182
  Catherine 180
  Chris 181
  Christopher 180
  Daniel 180
  Daniel Cunyngham 181
  Edward Tilghman 182
  Elizabeth 180, 181
  George 180, 181
  Henry 181
  John 180
  Julian 181
  Margaret 180, 181
  Meredith 181
  Richard 180, 181
  Sarah 180
  William 180, 181, 182
  William Coleman 181
Coalman, Anne 352
  Anne Skirm 352
  Elizabeth 352
  George 352
  Huldah 352
  James 352
  Nathaniel 352
  Ruth 352
Coaplin, Esther 811
Coate, Ann 53
  John 442, 851
  Mary 851
  Samuel 442
Coates, Henry 443
  Mary 455
  William 443
Coats, Mary 455
  Warwick 455
Coborne, Thomas 219
Coch, Evan 543
Cochran, James 808
  John 669
Cock, Ann Brinton 451
  Benjamin 451
  G. C. 197

Cock, Lasse 230
  Mary 451
  Otto Erick 525
Cocke, Geo. 380
Cockley, Margerie 551
Code, James 705, 707
Coghran, James 806
Cokburn, Gilbert 389
Coke, Lord 762
Colden, Richard 562
Cole, Mr. 770
  Richard 745, 770
  Thomas 567
  William 567
Coleman, Ann Old 831
  Anne Ross 831, 832
  Edward 831
  Harriet 831, 833
  Mary Jane 831
  Robert 831
  William 697
Colepeper, Sir Thom. 303
Collet, Ann Wilkes 680
  Elizabeth 246
  Elizabeth Rush 246
  John 246, 661
  Marie Crispin 246
  Mary 661
  Rachel 661, 662, 665, 666
  Richard 246, 660
Collett, Jeremiah 72
  Sarah 72
  Tobias 109
Collin, Rev. Nicholas 707
Collins, Mrs. Frances 742
  Isaac 844
  Joseph 888
  Kenelme 567
  Mary 568
  Rich'd 569
  Wm. 568
Collison, Robert 35
Collum, Michael 818
  William 423
Colman, Mr. 598
  Christian 586
Colwell, Stephen 649
Comb, Joane 552
Combe, Joan 553
  Katherine 553
  Philip 553
Comberford, John 600
Combye, Ann 553
  William 553
Comly, Joan 20
Compton, John 798
Condon, Garrett 232
  John 229
  Mary 229
  Mary Crispin 229
Connell, Thomas 869
Conner, Comm. David 867
  P. S. P. 565, 860, 887
Connolly, (?) 664
Conrad, Alitze 877
  John 877
Constable, Thomas 117
Converse, Edward 769
Conway, Philip 133
Conwell, (?) 172
  Gerardus 848
  John 848
  Shephard 848
Conyers, Edward 769
Conyngesby, Humfrey 550

Conyngham, Mrs. Hayfield 898
Cook, Arthur 16, 140, 142
  James 811
  Mary 178, 179, 897
Cooke, Elizabeth 852
  Francis 178
  ffranies 852
  Hercules 852
  John 852
  Mary 852
  Richard Y. 852
  Sarah 852
  William 852
Cookes, Henry 566
  Margaret 566
  Thomas 566
  Wm. 566
Cool, Benjamin 630
Coole, Benjamin 628, 631
Coombs, Joseph 877
Cooper, (?) 91
  Alexander 712
  George 888
  Hannah C. 712
  Helen 712
  Rev. J. H. 302
  Joseph 91, 709
  Martha 621
  Robt. 303
  Sarah 272
  Theodore 878
  William 90, 91, 304
  Wm. H. 856
Cope, Gilbert 174, 261
  Porter Farquharson 636
Cordury, Elizabeth 872
Core, Mary 795
Corell, Ann Catherine 853
  Anna Maria 853
  Jacob 853
  John Jacob 853
  John Philip 853
  Maria Elizabeth 853
  Mary Magdalen 853
  Susanna 853
Cornbury, Lord 131, 846
Cornelison, William 561
Cornish, Rev. C. E. 597
Cornthwait, Margret 98
Corss, John 815
Coryell, (?) 444
  Emanuel 443
  John 443
Cottinger, Mr. 347
Cottingham, James 818
Cotton, Jane 101
Couchman, Rich. 570
Couldney, Henry 574
Couper, Wm. 91
Court, Thomas 589
Courtauld, Amelia Wharton 790
  Louisa 790
  Samuel 775, 790
  Sarah Lloyd 790
Courthopp, Peter 305
Courthorpe, Peter 306
Courtney, Hercules 888
  Mary 888
Coventry, Sir William 614
Coverdale, Lydia 172
Coverly, Ann 889
  Job 889
  Rebecca 889
Covert, Anna 294

Covert, Anne 302, 303,
    304, 305, 307
  Dame Anne 307
  Lady Anne 305
  Diana 304, 306
  Elizabeth 294, 302,
    303, 307, 426
  Dame Jane 306
  John 294, 302, 305,
    306
  Sir John 303
  Thomas 294, 303, 304,
    306
  Walter 303, 307
  Sir Walter 294, 296,
    302, 303, 305, 306,
    307
  William 303
Coward, Ellen 98, 100
  Henry 100
Cowden, Edward Couch 365
  Sarah A. 365
Cowell, Rev. David 893
Cowgill, Catherine 62
  Edmund 61, 62
  Ellen 61, 62, 113,
    114
  Jane 61
  Jennet 40, 61, 63
  Jennett 62, 114
  John 61, 62, 71, 77
  Mary 63
  Rachel 77
  Ralph 61, 62, 63, 83
  Susan 63
Cowles, James 791
  William 791
  William Wharton 791
Cowper, Countess of 691
  Mr. 690
Cowperthwaite, John 888
  Sarah 888
Cox, Col. 648
  Ann 853
  Hannah 853
  John 853
  Col. John 644
  Maria 537
  Susanna 853
  Thos. 595
  Wm. 595
Coxe, Mary 680
Coycault, Octavie 788
  Mme. Octavie Duverge
    797
Crafts, Alice 571
  Richard 571
Craig, Rev. James 859
  Josephine 792
  Mary Johns 792
  Nancy 781, 795
  Nancy Wharton 792
  Wharton 792
  William 781, 792, 795
Craigh, Capt. 315
Crain, Agnes Caroline
    712
  Dr. Joseph 712
  Rebecca C. 712
Cramp, Caroline R. 841
Crapp, Priscilla 178
Cravens, Abigail 514
Crawford, Ann 900
  John 808
Creed, Henry 617
  Joane 617
  Robert 617
Creighton, Hugh 899

Creighton, Mary 899
Cressfield, Robert 373
Cresson, Susanna 57
Cresswell, Deborah M.
    798
Cripps, Cadwallader 201
Crispe, Sleeven 624
Crispin, (?) 208, 242,
    436
  Capt. 200, 202, 204,
    207, 209, 212, 213,
    215, 217, 218, 220,
    221, 271
  Col. 204, 256, 257
  Mr. 214, 255, 260
  Abigail 248
  Alice 231
  Amy 232, 233
  Ann 229, 253
  Ann Browne Busteed
    229
  Arthur Smith 234
  B. F. 259
  Benjamin 231, 232,
    233, 247, 248, 253,
    254, 255, 257, 259
  Benjamin Eaton 268
  Benjamin Franklin 256,
    257, 260, 264, 267
  C. 199
  Charles Edwin 258,
    259
  Charles H. 256
  Clarence Gearhart 264,
    267
  Edward T. 256
  Eleanor 232, 246
  Eleanor Jane 256
  Elizabeth 229, 232,
    233, 234, 272
  Elizabeth Brockway
    250, 266
  Elizabeth Crispin
    Smith 258
  Elizabeth Glenn 258
  Esther 246, 776
  Esther Dougherty 253
  Francis M. Bowman 258
  Franklin Mitchell 258
  Frederick Eaton 268
  George 229
  Gilbert 270
  Gilbert, I, 270
  Gilbert, II, 269, 270,
    271
  Gilbert, Abbot of
    Westminster 271
  Gilbert, Abbot of
    West Monastery 185
  Gilbert, Baron of Til-
    lieres 185
  Count Gilbert 184, 185
  Gilbert, Count of Bri-
    onne 269
  Count Gilbert, Baron
    of Tillieres 184
  Hannah 249
  Helen Jean 264
  Hester 253
  Hester Holme 242, 246,
    248
  James 231, 232, 233,
    234, 272
  Jane 212, 231, 232,
    252
  Jane Ashton 252
  Jane Chudleigh 232,
    234

Crispin, John 186, 248
  Joseph 231, 232, 234,
    248, 249, 252, 272
  Louis 259
  M. Jackson 183, 186,
    222, 233, 235, 247,
    250, 251, 265, 267
  Margaret Jackson 261,
    264, 267
  Maria 257, 258
  Maria Foster 257
  Marie 246
  Martha 253
  Martha Miles 253
  Mary 243, 245, 248,
    253, 776
  Mary Stockton Shinn
    248
  Mercy 249
  Michael 234
  Milo 270, 271
  Milo, Lord of Walling-
    ford 185
  Mordecai Jackson 264
  Paul 253
  Prudence 234
  Rachel 230, 776
  Ralph 225, 226, 228,
    229, 230
  Raphe 226
  Rebecca 222, 224, 229,
    246
  Rebecca Bradshaw 210,
    222, 235, 272
  Richard 234, 272
  Robert 269
  Robert Glenn 257, 258
  Sarah 246, 252, 272,
    775, 791
  Sarah Frances 259
  Silas 45, 106, 218,
    222, 226, 229, 230,
    231, 235, 236, 239,
    240, 241, 242, 243,
    244, 245, 246, 247,
    248, 249, 252, 253,
    256, 436, 437, 775
  Col. Silas 256
  Susanna 248
  Thomas 230, 243, 245,
    248, 249, 252, 776
  Thomas Holme 256
  William 183, 186, 187,
    188, 189, 190, 195,
    196, 198, 199, 201,
    204, 210, 216, 217,
    219, 220, 222, 224,
    232, 237, 246, 252,
    256, 269, 773, 775
  William, I, 270, 271
  William I, Count of
    Vexin 185
  Capt. William 183,
    186, 187, 188, 191,
    192, 193, 194, 197,
    200, 202, 203, 205,
    206, 216, 220, 222,
    225, 227, 231, 234,
    235, 269, 272
  William, Marshal of
    France 185
  William Frost 190
  William Henry 258
Crispina, (?) 269
Crispinus, Ansgothus 269
Croasdale, Agnes 113
  Agnes Hathornthwaite
    62, 114

Croasdale, Bridget 62
  John 117
  Thomas 62, 113
  William 38
Croasdel, John 176
Croft, Thomas 573
Cromwell, (?) 191, 200, 208, 209
  Oliver 207, 295
  Richard 595
  Thomas 685
Crone, Frank L. 861
Crook, Henry 74
  Ruth 384
  William 384
Crosfeld, Effam 686
Crosfield, (?) 374
  Robert 370, 373, 374, 375, 376
  Thomas 376
Cross, John 815
Crossan, Clarence K. 251
Crossfield, Dorothy 372
  Robert 372, 373
  Thomas 372
Crouch, Elizabeth 562
  William 130
Crow, (?) 664
Cruger, John Harris 355
Crutchly, Sarah 893
Cubinus 390, 391
Cudworth, John 290
Cuff, John 132
Culin, George 526
Cullen, Charles Mason 489
  Elisha D. 489
  George 489
  John 489
  Jonathan 489
  Margaret 347
  Piercy 489
  Sabina 347
  Sarah 489
  Thomas 347
Cullimore, Edward 626
Culpeper, William 306
  Sir William 304
  Sir William, Bart. 304, 305
Culpepper, Lord 897
Cumber, John 224
Cumberland, John 812
Cumming, Robert 716, 717
Cunningham, Margaret 399, 400
  W. 806
  William 395
Cunyngham, Mary 181
Cunynghame, Sir Umfridi 395
Currie, Rev. 460
Curry, Mary 772
Curson, Sir Nathaniel 573
Cursted, Margaret 878
Curtis, (?) 224
  Anne 349
  Elizabeth 1, 224
  John 349
  Ora M. 515
  Thomas 1
Curzon, Christopher 584
  Sir Nathaniel 584
  Sarah Penn 584
Cusse, Richard 593
Cuthbert, Elizabeth
  Frances 545
  Frances 787
  Frances Duer 545

Cuthbert, Samuel 544, 545
  Thomas 545
Cutler, (?) 514
  John 103, 108, 551, 552
Cutter, (?) 505
  Polly 505
Cuyler, Hendrick 716
  Sarah 716
Dakins, Capt. 209
  Rear Admiral 200, 202
Dalbo, Brigitta 706
Dalboo, Lasse 138
Dalhousie, Earl of. See Ramsay, George
Dallas, Alexander J. 881
  George M. 653
Dalles, Mary 121
  Ruth 121
Dallison, Elizabeth 621
Dally, Teige 230
Dame, Henry 602
Danby, (?) 300
Daniels, Annie M. 876
Dankers, Jasper 132
Danyell, Steven 571
Darbye, John 608
Dark, William 155
Darke, Ann 665
  Jane 665
  John 662, 665
  Joseph 662, 665
  Lydia 665
  Martha 665
  Mary 662, 665
  Samuel 24, 662, 665
  Sarah 665
  Thomas 662, 665
  William 662, 665
  Gen. William 660, 665
Darlington, Elizabeth 92
Darlinton, Abraham 92
Darrach, Ann 898
d'Aunou, Foulke 269
  Gonnor 269
David II, K. of Scotland 392, 394
David, Dr. 853
  Ann 544
  Benjamin 544
  Hugh 533
  Hugh ap 284
  John 531, 841
  Margaret 533
  Robert 531
  Tacey 544
Davidson, Maj. 507
Davies, Ann 523
  Ann Miles 524
  Mirick 523
  Richard 518, 519, 536
  William 520, 523, 524
Davis, Alexander 828
  Ann 522
  David 140
  Elizabeth 491, 612, 773, 781
  Henry 594
  Humphrey 581
  Isaiah 828
  John 519, 520
  Rev. John 520
  Phebe 520
  Robert 612, 613, 799
  Samson 521
  Samuel 106, 107, 491
  Samuel W. 887
  Susanna 106
  Thomas 853

Davis, Thos. Davenport 522
  Gen. W. W. H. 135
  William 523, 539
  Willis 521
Davison, Sarah 100
  Tho. 100
Dawes, David 91
  Janney 70
Dawson, Esther 843
  Nem. 624
Day, John 566
Dd Lloydd, Elsbeth verch 284
Dean, Mary 171, 172
Deane, Admiral 189
  Col. 189
  Andrew 551
  Col. Richard 191
Deare, Roger 586
Debitt, Rebecca 272
De Burgh, John 10
  Serlo, Baron of Tonsburgh 10
Decator, Capt. 661
Decowe, Francis 668
de Douglass. See Douglass.
Dee, Josiah 576
  Mary 576
de Erth. See Erth.
Defenderfer, Jacob 335, 344
de Glen. See Glen.
de Glenfield. See Glenfield.
de Iethyn, John 390
de Jats, Moise 897
de Kay, Tennis 715
Deke, John S. 829
de Ladel. See Ladel.
Delafield, Edward Coleman 835
  Eugene Livingston 835
  Harriet Coleman 835
  John Ross 835
  Joseph 835
  Joseph L. 834
  Joseph Livingston 835
  Julia Livingston 835
  Mary Livingston 835
  Maturin L. 835
Delancey/De Lancey
  Anna 355
  Charlotte 355
  Oliver 355
  Phila. 355
  Stephen 355, 356
  Susanna 355
  Gen. Sir William Howe 356
de la Plaine, Susanna 57
Delaplan, Joseph 836
  Joshua 836
de la Glen. See Glen.
de Logan. See Logan.
Delroy, Susan 867
de Martinez, Mrs. Fanny C. 447
de Moray. See Moray.
Dempsey, Eleanor 454
de Ness. See Ness.
Dennie, Mr. 794
Dennis, Eliza 794
Densce, Dorcie 564
Denton, Alexander 300
  Mrs. Carew 300
  Edmund 300, 301
  Sir Edmund, Bart. 300

Denton, John 300
de Orton. See Orton.
de Peebles. See Peebles.
de Porte, Marquis 454
Deprefontaine, Amanda 864
   Catharine 864
de Quetteville, Rev. William 548
de Radeclyve, Richard 73
Derleton, Lord 881
Derwas, Gryffydd 284
Deshon, Moses 897
   Persis 897
   Susannah 897
de Stapleton. See Stapleton.
Detweiler, Maria 870
Devereux, B. H. 456
   Eugene 454
   James 456
   John 456
   Mary 456
   Mary Ann 456
   R. P. 456
   William 304
Dewees, Cornelius 643, 645
   David 645
   Margaret 645
   Owen 645
   Samuel 645
   William 645
De Wemyess. See Wemyess.
Dewhurst, James Buchanan 522
Dewsberry, William 624
Dewsbury, William 74
Dickerson, Elizabeth 489
Dickins, Mary 566
   Thomas 566
Dickinson, John 485
   Lucy 347
Dickson, Mary 871
   Thomas 631
Diggs, Councillor 480
   Ann 474
   Anne Newbury 474
   Robert 474
Dike, George 831
   Dr. Nathaniel 831
   Virginia 831, 832
   William Lythe 831
Diller, Nancy 891
Dillinger, Jacob 278
Dillwyn, Ann 853, 854
   Fanny Llewellyn 854
   George 853, 854
   John 853, 854
   John Crook 854
   Judith Nichols 854
   Lewis Llewellyn 854
   Lewis Westor 854
   Lydia 853, 854
   Mary 853, 854
   Sarah 853
   Sarah Llewellyn 854
   Susannah 853, 860
   W. 853
   William 853, 854, 860
Dilworth, Tho. 98
Dinsdale, Ralph 116
Dixon, Ann 370, 375
   Arthur 370, 374, 375, 381
   James 375
   Martin 375
Doane, A. A. 261
   Benjamin 261

Doane, Daniel 261
   Elijah 261
   Israel 261
   John 261
   Sarah Grove 261
Dobbins, James 772
   John 892
   Mary 772
Dockery, Thomas 98
Dodd, Amy 855
   Comfort Bruce 855
   Eleanor 856
   Elenor 855
   Elenor Bruce 855
   Elenore 855
   Eliza T. 856
   Eliza Turner 855
   Elizabeth 855
   Hannah 855
   Joseph Hazlett 855
   Maria 855
   William 855
   William Alexander 855
Dodson, R. Bruce 869
Dodwell, Alice 616
Dogherty, Nich. 814
d'Oilly, Matilda 270, 271
   Robert 270
Donne, Catherine 845
Donnel, Maria 789
Donnell, Colvagh 813
   Mary 813
   Neale 813
Donner, Abraham 342
   Caroline 342
   Frank 342
   Jacob 342
   Paul 342
   Stephen 342
   Tihlman 342
Dorman, Elizabeth 848, 850
   Gerardus 848
   Gerhardus 850
   John 171, 848, 850
   John K. 850
   John Sheldren 848
   Mary 848
   Nehemiah 848, 850
   Samuel 171
Dornan, Maria 363
Dottery, Thomas 100
Dougherty, Esther 253
Doughty, James 789
   Mary 774, 789
Douglas, (?) 667
Douglass, Henry de 389
Downs, (?) 403
Dove, Robert 16
Dover, Lord 688
Downer, John 224
Doyle, Edward 27
Drake, Enoch 635
Draper, Elisa 865
   Isaac 848, 850
   John 865, 866
   Mary 848, 850
   Sally Ann 865
   Samuel 865
   Sarah 848, 850
   Susa 865
   Thomas 618
   William 613, 865
   Lt.-Gen. Sir William 355
Drexel, Francis Martin 795
   Heloise 795

Drinker, Mr. 443
   Elizabeth 443, 856
   Esther 856
   Hannah 856
   Hannah Smith 856
   Henry 856
   Henry S. 856
   James 856
   Joseph 841
   Sarah 856
   William 856
Druett, Hannah 119
   Thomas 561
Drum, Philip 328, 329
Drury, Sir Henry 583
   Sarah 583
Dubbs, Aaron 282
   Aaron K. 281
   Rev. J. H. 457
   Rev. J. S. 278
   Rev. Jacob G. 280
   Rev. Joseph S. 278
Dubs, Alfred J. G. 281
   Anna Maria 280
   Barbara 277, 278
   Daniel 277, 278, 279, 280
   Daniel L. 281
   Elizabeth 277, 278
   Elizabeth Schwenk 280
   Felix 277, 278
   Hans Ulrich 273
   Henry 280
   Jacob 273, 275, 276, 277, 279, 280
   Dr. Jacob 274
   John 280, 281
   Joseph Henry 281
   Joseph S. 281
   Margaretha 277, 278
   Solomon 281
   Veronica Welker 276, 277
Dudley, Mary 565
   O. 883
   William 565
Duer, Andrew Adgate 857
   Charles 857
   Douglass Henry 857
   Edith 857
   Edward Norris 857
   Elizabeth 857
   Hannah 545
   Harriet 545
   Henrietta D. 857
   Isabel 857
   John 857
   Mary 857
   Mary Ann 545
   Mary Caroline 857
   Susan 857
   Susanna 857
   William 545
   Capt. William 544, 545
Duffel, Jacob 872
Duffield, Ann 224
   Walter 627
Duffy, Dr. George W. 831
Duke, Edw. 303
   John 558
   William 402
Dumer, Elizabeth 54
   John 54
Duncan, Colban son of 388
   William 156
Dundas, Field Marshal Sir David 355
Dungan, (?) 858

Dungan, Clement 25, 27, 30, 77
  Elizabeth 858
  Jeremiah 16, 77
  Jesse 878
  John 77, 858
  Martha 878
  Sarah 858
  Thomas 25, 27, 30, 77, 858
  Rev. Thomas 68
  William 15, 25, 30, 858
Dunklin, Oliver 647
Dunn, John 810
Dunton, Abraham 858
  Amanda Amelia 858
  Amelia 858
  Anna 858
  Anna Maria 858
  Bridget 858
  Elizabeth 858
  George 858
  Isaac 858
  Jacob 858
  John 858
  John Lewis 858
  Joseph F. 858
  Margaret Susan 858
  Margaretha 858
  Maria 858
  Mary 858
  Mary Amanda 858
  Sarah 858
  Sarah Ann 858
  Susannah Elizabeth 858
  Thomas 858
  William 858
  William Washington 858
  Wilson 858
Dupps, Jacob 275
Du Pratt, Anne 300
Duval, Ethel 858
Duwaeli, Martin 849
Duyking, Gerardus 716
Dymock, Sarah 27
  Tobias 27
Dyvet, Aleth, Lord of 284
Earl, ANna 712
  Thomas 247, 248
  William 247, 248
Eastburn, Samuel 35
Easte, Davide 552
  Henrie 552
Eastlack, Rebecca 659
  Thomas 659
Eastlake, Rebecca Shin 658
Eastland, (?) 570
Eaton, Frederick H. 267, 268
  Frederick Heber 267
  Mae Lovely 267
  Robert 442
Eberhard, Henry 280
  Michael D. 280
Eberle, P. L. 336
Eckert, Jacob 318
Eckly, John 625
Ecroyd, John 100
Eden, John 557
Edes, R. 614
Edgar, Elizabeth Say 672
Edina of England 430
Edmonds, Anne 859
  Betty 859

Edmonds, Mrs. Billy 859
  Catey 860
  Elias 859
  Eliz. 859
  Elizabeth 859
  Franke 859
  Frankey 859, 860
  James 859
  John 859
  Judith 859, 860
  Lucy 859
  Mary 859
  Sarah 859
  William 859, 860
  Col. William 859
Edmondson, Elizabeth Flick 313
  Joseph 381
Edmonson, Elizabeth 380
  William 381
Edric 430
Edric, Duke of Mercia 430
Edward III, K. of England 547
Edward, Edward 800
  Elizabeth 798, 799
  Griffith 485
  Jane 485, 798, 800
  John ap 798
  Katherine 798, 800
  Margaret 485
  Mary 800
  Sarah 800
  William ap 798, 799, 800
Edwards, Dr. 659
  Rev. 553
  Alexander 522
  Bridget 522
  Daniel 871
  Emma 659
  James 523
  Jane 523
  Jemima 773, 780
  Ruth 872
  Thomas 613
Eedes, Mr. 549
Egle, Dr. 899
  Dr. William H. 135
Elfreth, Henrey 836
  Jeremiah 55
  Sarah 836
Eliot, (?) 151
Elizabeth I, Q. of England 367
Ellers, (?) 880
Ellet, Ann 30
  William 30
Ellis, Mrs. 881, 882
  Ann 284
  Catherine 283, 284
  Eleanor 800
  Elizabeth 284
  Ellin 284, 533
  Ellis 106, 107
  Jane 284
  John 640
  Rowland 533, 535
  Thomas 225, 798, 800
  William 159
Ellisa, Catherine verch 284
  Mary verch 284
Ellwood, Thomas 621, 622
Ellyott, Benjamin 561
Elvins, John 570
Elwood, Thomas 384

Ely, Elizabeth 896
  Ruben Pownall 439, 440
  W. S. 133
  Warren S. 79
Emerson, Anna 866
  Mary 866
  Peniel 866
  Unity 866
  Vincent 866
Emery, Anne 561
  John 561
Emlen, Deborah 860
  Elizabeth 860, 867
  Joshua 867
  Samuel 853, 854, 860, 867
  Susanna 854
Emley, Mary 44
  William 44, 81
Empson, Cornelius 140, 145
Endresen, Martin 870
  Ottilia 870
England, Cornelia 873
  Daniel 709
  Sarah 709
  Susannah 709
Engle, Sara Atkinson 102
English, Elizabeth 415
  J. 664
  John 129
  Joseph 15, 19, 20, 133
Ensar, Thomas 600, 601
Enuxson, David 702, 703
  Eleanor 702
Erb, Casper 328
Erskine, Sir Alrn 393
  Margaret 393
Erth, William de 390
Erwin, Anne 811
Esher, Mrs. Edward 888
Espy, Col. 830
  David 828
  George 828
  Jean Taylor 828
  Mary Elizabeth 828, 830
Ethelred, K. of England 430
Evan, Anne 486
  Cadwallader 484, 486
  Cadw'r 486
  Cadw'r ab 484
  Catherine 484, 485
  David 485
  Edward 485
  Elizabeth 485, 486
  Ellin 485, 537
  Evan 485, 486
  Evan ab 484, 485, 486
  Evan ap 530
  Gainor 485
  Griff. 484
  Griffith ab 484, 485
  Gwen 484
  Hugh 485
  Jane 485, 537
  Jn. 533
  John 485, 486
  John ab 484, 530
  Lowry 486
  Margaret 484
  Mary 486
  Owen 485, 486
  Owen ab 484, 485, 486
  Owen ap 530, 532, 537
  Reese 533

Evan, Robert 484, 486
  Sarah 486
  Thomas 486
  Thos. John 521
Evance, Daniel 564
Evans, Gov. 133, 147, 154
  A. 818
  Ann 539, 873
  Cadwallader 483
  Cadwallader ab 483
  Dr. Cadwallader 540
  David 536, 540
  Elizabeth 470, 656, 796
  Evan 519, 523, 540
  Gainor 878
  Gwen 347
  Hugh 544
  John 284, 484, 486, 519, 601
  Gov. John 148, 149, 150
  Lowry 101, 107
  Margaret 355, 540
  Mary 624
  Owen 519, 656
  Peter 355
  Rebecca 540
  Rees 470
  Rowland 283, 483
  Rowland E. 283, 483
  Sarah 519, 540
  Sidney 540
  Susannah 777, 845
  William E. 795
Evelye, Rob. 560
Evelyn, Robt. 561
Everard, Sir Robert 377
  John 377
  Thomazen 377
Everton, Thomas 550
Ewen, Joseph 812
Fabian, Anna Catherine 323, 324, 325
  Dorothea 323
  Michael 323, 325
Fahie, Sarah 272
Fairfax, Edward 5
Fairman, Thomas 106, 236, 240
Falconer, (?) 459
Fales, Harriot 432
  Sarah Whiting 432
ffallowfield, William 630, 631
Fannegan, Thomas 828
Fantleroy, Jo. 859
Farley, Elizabeth Byrd 680
  Elizabeth Carter 680
  Maj. James Parke 680
Farmare, John 614
Farr, William 579
Farrer, Mr. 691
Farrington, Joseph 241
Fauconer, (?) 459
  Godfrey le 459
Fawcett, Sarah 481
Fayerweather, John 581
Fell, Christopher 66, 91
  Gulielma Maria 620
  Gulielma Maria Frances 620
  Joseph 442
  Margaret 66, 83, 88, 91
  Richard 65
  Robert Edward 709

Feltus, Rev. James 709, 710
Fen, Capt. Henry 200
Fenwick, (?) 295
  Ann 426
  Caecilia 286
  Charles 292
  Edward 286, 287, 288, 289, 290, 291, 292, 293, 297, 298, 299, 302
  Elizabeth 287, 305, 307
  Elizabeth Covert 303
  James 289, 291
  John 286, 287, 288, 289, 290, 291, 292, 293, 294, 295, 296, 297, 298, 299, 300, 301, 303, 305, 307, 430
  Maj. John 47, 286, 291, 297, 302, 307, 426, 428
  Sir John 286, 287, 293, 298, 299
  Margaret 285, 286
  Mary 290, 291, 294, 295
  Dame Mary 300
  Col. Nicholas 296
  Peter 287
  Capt. Ralfe 291, 293
  Ralph 287, 292, 293
  Sir Ralph 285
  Richard 285, 286
  Robert 290, 292
  Roger 286, 287, 291, 292
  Sarah 287
  William 285, 286, 288, 289, 290, 292, 293, 294, 297, 298, 299
  Sir William 286, 287, 293, 294
Ferguson, Mrs. 423
  John 814
Fettiplace, William 304, 305, 306
ffereby, Thomas 549
Fick, Johann Henrich 311
Field/ffield
  Benjamin 45, 118, 442
  John 574, 802
  Robert 45
  Sarah 118
Filbert, Catherine 839
  Thomas 839
Findley, Rev. Dr. 716
Finney, Capt. John 246
  Joseph 246
  Samuel 246
Fischel. See Fishels.
ffish, Anthony 600
Fishbourne, (?) 539
  Elizabeth 773, 775
  Ralph 775
  Sarah Lewis 775
  William 775
Fishels/Fischel
  Alexander 861, 862
  Amanda 862
  Amanda S. 861
  Anna Barbara 862
  Anna Margaret 861
  Anna Maria 861
  Anne M. 862
  Catherine 861, 862
  Christina 862

Fischel, Conrad 861
  Daniel 861, 862
  David 862
  Eva 861
  Franklin 861
  Frederick 862
  George 861
  George F. 862
  George W. 861
  Henrich 862
  Henry 861, 862
  Jacob 862
  Johannes 862
  John 861, 862
  John Adam 861
  John Henrich 862
  John Jacob 861
  Leah 862
  Magdalena 862
  Margaret 862
  Mary 862
  Mary M. 862
  Michael 862
  Michael S. 861
  Salinda 862
  Samuel 862
  Sarah 861, 862
  Saretta 861
  Savilla 862
  Zachariah 862
Fisher/ffisher
  Deborah 781, 793
  Elizabeth 864
  Elizabeth Rhodes 833
  Felix 706, 707
  James C. 727
  James Cowles 780
  John 69
  Joice 564
  Joseph 141, 240
  Samuel 54, 892
  Samuel Rowland 793
  Sarah 791
  Thomas 569
Fissel, Samuel 861
Fite, Eleanora A. 857
Fithian, AMos 899
  Erkurius 899
  Joel 899
  Dr. Joseph 899
Fitzabeth, Deborah 180
Fitz Alan, Walter 391
Fitzherbert, Mrs. Elizabeth 744, 749
ffitzhushe, Thomas 600, 881
Fitzwater, Debora 877
  Deborah 180
  George 180, 774
  Martha 867
  Thomas 774
Flack, Johan Matheis 312
  Matheis 312
Flak, Lucas 312
Flamstead, (?) 846
Fleak, Peter 315
Fleck, Conrad 312, 320
  Henry 312
  Johan Henry 312
  Johan Wilhelm 312
  John Henry 320
  John Jacob 312
  Peter 312
  Valentin 312
Fleek, Peter 315
  John Christian 312
Fleming, Sir Daniel, Bart. 367
  Lord William 390

Fletcher, Gov. 142, 144
  Hannah 69, 82
  Mary 69
  Thomas 383
Flick, Abanton 342
  Abraham 342, 343
  Abraham Amandus 343
  Adam 316, 346
  Amy 319
  Amy B. 315
  Andreas 313
  Andrew 313, 316
  Andrew Jackson 313
  Andriess 313
  Ann W. 315
  Anna Catherine 336
  Anna Gertrude 320
  Anna Margaret 324
  Anna Margaret Fabian 327
  Anna Maria 335, 339, 344
  Anne Eliz. 342
  Augustus F. 342
  Bebra 340
  Casper 328, 335, 337, 339
  Catherine 313, 315, 316, 319, 329, 335, 339, 340, 342, 344
  Charles 313, 315
  Charles Wallace 313
  Christina 313
  Christopher 318
  Clara 343
  Claude Wilmot 313
  Cora S. 343
  Daniel 318
  Edward 343
  Edward Paul 321
  Elizabeth 313, 319, 335, 340, 342, 343, 344
  Elmer A. 342
  Emaline 342
  Emelina 342
  Emma 342, 343
  Enos Henry 343
  Flora 343
  Frederick 346
  George 316, 317, 342, 343, 346
  Gerlach Paul 310, 311, 312, 313, 314, 315, 316, 317, 320, 321, 322, 323, 324, 325, 326, 327, 328, 329, 330, 331, 332, 333, 334, 335, 336, 337, 338, 339, 340
  Capt. Gerlach Paul 308
  Gertrante/Gertraute 335, 337, 339, 343, 344
  Gertrude 343
  Hannah 343
  Hannah E. 343
  Harrison 342
  Heinrich 313, 314
  Helen 342
  Helen F. 340
  Henry 314, 342, 346
  Henry Elwood 343
  Henry S. 315
  Isaac 342, 343
  Jacob 318
  James A. 342
  Jeremiah 342

Flick, Johan Adam 313
  Johan Christian 321
  Johan Martin 312, 321, 345
  Johan Wilhelm 313, 316
  Johann Christian 320
  John 317, 318, 339, 342
  John Caspar 320, 324, 331, 337, 339, 345
  John Henry 314
  John Jost 320
  John Martin 340
  John Peter 312, 313, 314, 320, 343, 345
  John Philip 312, 315, 321, 345
  John Wilhelm 313, 316
  Jonas 318
  Joseph 315, 318, 340
  Julianna 343
  Laura 343
  Leonard 315
  Levinda 343
  Lewis Paul 343
  Liddon 340
  Lillian A. 343
  Louis 313
  Lydia 340, 342
  Lydia S. 342
  Mackie R. 343
  Magdelein 313
  Mame V. 343
  Margaret 315, 319, 339, 343
  Margaretha 313, 316, 335, 344
  Maria Magdalena 335
  Maria Magdelein 344
  Marua Margaret 343
  Martha M. 343
  Martin 313, 316, 331 335, 337, 339, 340, 341
  Mary 319, 342
  Mary E. 342
  Mary Jane 343
  Michael 318, 319
  Myce 343
  Nancy 342
  Paul 328, 335, 336, 337, 339, 341, 342, 344, 344
  Paul Gerlach 323
  Peiter 313, 314
  Peter 314
  Philip 313, 315, 336, 337
  Philip Henry 320
  Quintus 342
  Rebecca 342, 343
  Rueben J. 340
  Reuben Jay 340
  Robert L. 343
  Sabina Catherine 343
  Sarah 315, 342, 343
  Sarah Ann 343
  Saul 328
  Sofya 335, 339, 344
  Stephen 342, 343
  Stewart 343
  Susan 342
  Susanna 339
  Suzanna 335, 344
  Sybilla 343
  Thomas 315, 319
  Warren J. 340
  William 313, 315, 316, 317, 319, 342, 343

Flicke, James 312
Flickinger, Peter 312
Flickwir, Gotthard David 312
Flickwis, John 312
Flint, Col. Franklin Foster 454
Flock, Johan Adolph 312
Flower, Elizabeth 671
  Enoch 697
  Joanna Paschall 672
  Seth 671
Floyer, Elizabeth 759
  Francis 759
Fluck, Johannes 312
Fluckiger, Johannes 311
ffludd, Thos. 560, 561
Folker, Annie M. 657
  Howard O. 657
Folkes. See Foulke.
Follswell, John 350
Foose, Catherine 891
  Elizabeth 891
  Mariah 891
Footman, Elizabeth 691
Forbench, Richard 568
Forbes, Gen. 698
  General 387
  Arth. 816
Ford, Philip 213
Fordham, Benjamin 56
Fornance, Hon. Joseph 423
Forrest, Walter 238
Forster, Grace 286
  John 286
  Thomas 289
Forth, Richard 381
Foster, Amos 256
  Eleanor Thomas 256
  Joseph 286
  Josiah 862
  Maria 256
  Peter 561, 562
Fothergill, John 115
Foulke/Folkes/Foulks/ffowkes
  Ann 350
  Anne 169
  Betsy 339
  Caleb 347, 348
  Charles Trotter 347
  Charlotte 347
  Edward 347, 484, 551
  Edward D. 347
  Elizabeth 350, 351
  Elizabeth Curtis 349
  Ellen 347
  Frank 347
  Gwen 484
  Hannah 777
  Hannah Trotter 347
  Henry 347, 348
  Hugh 169
  Isaiah 350
  Jane 347
  Jane Jones 348
  Joseph S. 347
  Louisa 347
  Margaret 347, 348
  Mary 167, 169, 349, 350
  Owen 348
  Rebeckah 350, 351
  Sarah 347, 349, 350, 351
  Thomas 347, 349, 350, 484
  William 347

Foulke, William Henry 347
Foulks. See Foulke.
ffowkes. See Foulke.
Fowler, Ebenezer 865, 866
  Elizabeth 352
  Emma 258
  John 351, 866
  Susan 865
  Susan Annay 865
  Susanna 866
  Susannay 865
Fox, Anne 379
  Elizabeth 379
  George 83, 624
  Henry 646
  Jane 379
  Mary P. 791
  William 379, 380
Foxe, William 378, 379
Foxton, Elias 378
  William 378
Frampton, William 241
Francis, (?) 845
  Elizabeth 95
Franklin, (?) 776
  Dr. 778, 779, 868
  Gov. 778
  Ann 863
  B. 871
  Benjamin 149, 474, 697, 778, 863, 868
  Benjamine 863
  Elizabeth 863
  Mary 863
  Samuel 863
  Thomas 559, 863
  Walter 863
  Rev. Walter 824
  William 474
Frankline, James 303, 304
  Walter 303, 304
Francklyn, (?) 303
  James 303, 306, 307
  Walter 303, 305, 306, 307
Franks, Aaron 354
  Abigail 355
  David 355
  David Solebury 356
  Jacob 354, 355
  John 355
  Margaret Evans 355
  Mary 355
  M oses 355, 356
  Napthali 354
  Phila. 355
  Rebecca 354, 355, 356
  Samuel D. 356
  Sarah 356
  Sarah Eliza 356
Fraser, (?) 475
Frasure, Mathew 885
Freame, Joseph 619
  Margaret 619
  Philadelphia Hannah 619
Frederick I, K. of Prussia 274
Freedley, Henry 797
  John 424
Freelinghausen, Col. 507
Freeman, Mrs. Esther 749
  John 744
Freer, John 304
Frenaye, Mrs. 781
French/ffrench
  Edmond 623

French, Elizabeth 623
  Eves 842
  George 715
  John 842
  Col. John 842
  Mary 842
  Mary McCullough 899
  Parnel 842
  Sybilla 842
Freser, Richard 390
Frewin, Dr. 692
Freylinghausen, Mrs. 717
Frick, Jacob 521
  Mary 521
Frits, Mary Ann 521
ffrogley, Jane 617
  Mary 617
  Richard 617
Frost, Edmund 95
  Isaac 95
  John 95, 114
  Joseph 95
  Margaret Atkinson 95
  Samuel 95
  Thomas 95
Fuller, Sarah 853, 854
Furgusson, Henry Hugh 474
Furman, Samuel 440
Furnis, John 54
Futcher, (?) 357
  Adeline 358
  Becket 359
  Elizabeth 357
  Erasmus Marsh 358
  Hetty Ann 358, 359
  Hetty Ellinder 359
  John 357, 358, 359
  John Little 358
  John Mitchelmore 358
  Joseph Franklin 359
  Margaret 358
  Martha 358, 359
  Martha Ann 358
  Mary 357
  Mary West 358
  Peggy 358
  Sarah 357, 358
  Sarah Lamb 359
  Susannah 357
  Thomas 357, 358
  William 357, 358, 359
Galatin, (?) 894
  Eleanora Maquinet 894
Galbut, Margaret 769
Gale, William 596
Galloway, (?) 776
Galwey, Stephen Payne 355
Gamp, Dorothy 895
Gandy, Deborah 871
Gansevoort, Col. 341
Gardiner, Abraham 413
  Olivia 412, 413
  Susanna Elton 413
  Thomas 413
Gardner, Elizabeth 864
  Hannah 864
  Isabella 864
  J. M. 864
  John 864
  John M. 864
  John Macpherson 864
  John Thomas 864
  Mary 864
  Robert 864
  S. C. 864
  Sarah 864
  Sophia C. 864

Gardner, Susan Oliphant 864
  William 864
Gargravé, Sir Cotton 285
  Elizabeth 285
  Mrs. Frances 742
  Robert 742
Garner, Robert 565
Garrard, Jno. 731
Garret, Hannah 800
  William 800
Garrets, Samuel 801
Garrett, Ellinor 664
  Jane 451
  Joseph 451
  Mary Sharpless 451
Garrison, Rev. Joseph 712
  Mary L. 121
Garton, Jane 224
  Josiah 224
  Will. 224
Gaskill, Anna Virginia 353
  Charles Merwin 353
  Edward M. 353
  Edwin A. 354
  Frank 354
  Joseph W. 353
  Mrs. Mary C. 349
  Mary C. Skirm 353
  William H. C. 354
Gassaway, Sophia B. 864
Gastrell, Nicholas 563
Gates, Elizabeth 224
  Rhard 224
  Sarah 224
Gazzam, Mary Alice 712
Gearhart, Capt. Jacob 263, 264
  Judge Jacob 264
  Margaret 263
Geats, Benjamin 618
  Joseph 618
  Mary 618
Geirich, Catharine 891
Genet, Gen. 712
Gentil, Paul 270
George I, K. of Great Britain 354, 474, 542
George II, K. of Great Britain 443
George, Amos 801
  David 485
  Edmund 801
  Jane 801
  Jesse 540, 801
  John 801
  Mrs. John G. 882
  Joseph 801
  Robert 556
Garard, Rev. Mr. 418
  Stephen 653
Gerhard, Mrs. 864
  Barbara 864
  Benjamin 865
  Conrad 864, 865
  Eleanora 865
  Elizabeth 865
  Frederick 864
  John 865
  Louisa 865
  Mary 865
  Peter 864
  Rachel 865
  Thomas 865
  William 865
  William Wood 865

Gerrard, Col. 721
    Frances 721
    John 721
    Lt. Col. Thomas 721
Gerit, John 878
Geyer, Anne M. 362, 363, 365
    George G. 362
    John 362, 365
    John H. 362, 363, 365
    Wilbur 363
    William 362
    Willie 365
Gibb, James 806
Gibbons, Anne 561
    George 561
    P. E. 35
Gibbs, Capt. Caleb 445
    Catherine 512
    Rachel 647
Gibson, Dorothy 378
    Elizabeth 481, 482
    Frederick H. 797
    Hannah Ring 481
    John 482
    Mrs. Mary 752
    Robert 378
    Thomas 481, 482
Gifford, Andrew 566, 630
    Margaret 551
    Martha 631
    Roger 768
Gifforde, Thomas 551
Gilbard, Margaret 570
Gilbeart, Joan 597
Gilbert, (?) 92, 663
    Benjamin 666
    Rev. E. R. 872
    Jacob 335, 344
    John 661, 663
    Joseph 90
    Mary 90
    Rachel 111
    Rev. Richard H. 261
    Samuel 115
    Sarah 90
    Susanna 663
    Thomas 90
Gildersleeve, Emma 347
Gill, John 888
    Sarah 359
    Thomas 714
    W. 859
Gilliam, Jane Gray 680
    Dr. John 680
Gillilan, James 796
Gillingham, Addie 363
    Albert B. 363
    Albert Bell 362
    Ann Maria 361
    Anna Holbrook 362
    Anna M. 363
    Anna Maria 363
    Anne 362
    Caroline E. 361
    Catharine Rapp 361, 364
    Charles Arrison 363
    Charles Wood 364
    E. M. 363
    Edward Augustus 362, 364
    Elizabeth Rich 361, 363
    Elizabeth Waring 360
    Emma M. 365
    Emma Matilda 362
    Esther 360, 362, 364, 365

Gillingham, G. W. 362, 364
    George 362
    George W. 361, 365
    George Washington 360, 363, 364
    H. B. 365
    H. D. 362, 364, 365
    Hannah Lewis 360
    Harry B. 362
    Henry B. 361, 362, 364, 365
    Henry Bailie 360, 363
    Henry D. 361, 365
    J. Harvey 250, 251
    James 360, 361, 362, 363, 364, 365
    Jenny 363
    John D. 361, 363
    John Hallowell 360
    Josephine 361, 364
    Lewis 360, 361, 362, 363, 364, 365
    Lizzie 362, 364
    Margaret 362, 363, 364, 365
    Margaret T. 363
    Margaret Thompson 362
    Maria 361, 363, 364, 365
    Maria Louisa 362
    Martha 360
    Mary 360, 363
    Mary A. 362, 364, 365
    Phebe 360, 363
    Robert Rayburn 362, 364
    Sallie 362, 364
    Sally 363
    Sarah 360, 361, 362, 364, 365
    Sarah Ann 360
    Sarah Anna 361
    Sarah Bailie 364
    Sarah Maria 363
    Sarah Rich 363
    Thomas C. 365
    Thomas Conner 362
    William 361
    William Clifton 360, 361, 364
Gillum, Robert 247
Gilman, Letitia 632
Gilminot, Anne 889
Gilpin Alan 374
    Alice 370, 372, 373, 375, 376
    Allan 373, 375, 376, 380
    Allen 371, 372, 373, 376
    Ann 367
    Arthur 374, 375
    Barnard 373, 375, 376, 377
    Bernard 368, 369, 370, 371, 372, 373, 374, 375, 376, 377
    Christian 377, 378
    Darias 377, 381, 382
    Dorothie 370
    Dorothy 372, 373, 374, 375, 376, 378, 380, 381, 383
    Dorothy Airy 368, 369, 375, 376
    Dorothy Gibson 381, 382, 383
    Elinor Layton 378

Gilpin, Elizabeth 370, 374, 375
    Elizabeth Washington 367, 369
    Everard 377, 378, 380, 381
    Francis 374, 375, 377, 378, 381
    George 367, 376, 377, 381
    Gideon 367
    Gill 372
    Grace 370, 373, 375, 376, 377, 378
    Henry D. 375, 382
    Hon. Henry D. 368
    Isaac 370, 371, 372, 373, 374, 376, 383, 384
    Jane 373, 375, 379, 380, 381, 383
    Joan Bartholomew 383, 384, 385
    John 376, 378, 380, 381
    Joseph 367, 368, 383, 384
    Joshua 368, 369
    Katherine 373, 375
    Katherine Newby 369, 371, 372, 373, 375, 376
    Margaretta 367
    Marie 370
    Martin 369, 370, 371, 373, 374, 375, 376
    Mary 373, 375, 376
    Mary Points 367
    Matithia 375
    Mattithia 372
    Orpah 793
    Capt. Philip 367
    Rachel 383, 384, 902
    Randal 373
    Randall 371, 372, 373, 374, 375, 376
    Rebecca 381, 383
    Richard 376, 378, 383, 385
    Dr. Richard 368, 902
    Ruth 380, 381
    Samuel 370, 375, 378
    Sarah 378, 383, 384
    Theophila 377, 378
    Thomas 367, 368, 369, 375, 377, 378, 379, 380, 381, 382, 383, 384, 385, 902
    Thomazen Everard 377, 378
    Ursula 377, 378
    William 367, 368, 369, 372, 374, 375, 376
    Rev. William 368
Ginger, Anna Margaret 840
Githens, George 715
Gladstaner, George 814
Glan, Gabriel 122
Glanffield, Francis 427
Glanfield, Elizabeth 427
    Francis 427
    John 427
Glattli, Anna 273
Gleen, Gabriel 121
Glen, Adam de 387
    Agnes 405
    Alan de 387
    Alexander 396, 398,

(Glen, Alexander, cont'd)
    399, 400, 401, 402
  Capt. Alexander 401
  Ana 406
  Andrew 402
  Ann 405
  Annabella de 389
  Archibald 398, 399,
    400, 403, 405
  Arthur 405
  Benjamin 405
  Catherine 398
  Colban de 388, 389
  David 399, 403, 404
  Duncan 388
  Duncan de le 388
  Elizabeth 398, 402,
    403
  Galfridus de 387
  Geoffrey de 387
  George 396, 398, 402,
    404, 405
  Isabel 398, 400, 403
  Dr. Jacob 401
  James 395, 396, 397,
    398, 399, 402, 404,
    405
  Dr. James 403
  Jean 398
  John 395, 397, 398,
    402, 403, 404, 405,
    406
  John de 388, 391, 393,
    394
  John de le 390, 391
  Rev. John 398
  Sir John de 393, 394,
    402
  Joseph 404, 405, 406
  Lindsay 401
  Margaret 398, 405
  Margaret Bruce 394
  Margaret Cunningham
    400
  Margaret de 393
  Martha 406
  Mary 399, 400
  Mathew 404
  Nicholas 388
  Ninian 404, 405
  Patrick 396, 406
  Paul de 394
  Richard de le 390, 391
  Lord Richard 395
  Lord Richard de le
    389, 391
  Robert 395, 396, 398,
    402, 404, 405
  Robert de 393, 394
  Robert de le 391, 392
  Sir Robert de 394
  Roger de le 392
  Sara de le 388
  Sibilla 400
  Thomas 388, 395, 398,
    399, 405, 406
  Dr. Thomas 402
  Walter de 387
  William 395, 398, 399,
    400, 401, 403, 405,
    406
  William de 393, 394
  Winarch de 387
  See also Glenn.
Glendinning, (?) 405
  Abigail Glen 405
Glenfield, Richard de
  388
Glenn, Ann 403

Glenn, David 404
  Duke 403
  Edward 403, 545
  Elias 401
  Elizabeth 257
  Hannah Cuthbert 545
  James 403, 404, 406,
    545
  John 403, 406
  Dr. John 403
  Lewis Washington 545
  Luther Judson 403
  Paul 394
  Robert 257, 406
  Sarah 257
  Thomas 388, 403, 405
  Thomas Allen 284, 387,
    447, 517, 806
  William Duer 545
  Warham 403
  William 403, 405, 406
  See also Glen.
Glenny, Capt. 396
Glover, Alice Lambeth
  385
  Mrs. C. T. 433
  George 385
  Hannah 384
Gohle, Marie 562
  Mary 561, 562
  Thomas 561, 562
Goddard, (?) 776
Godfrey, (?) 459
  Capt. 195
  Dr. Carlos E. 299
  Eleanor 459, 460
  Elizabeth 460
  Hannah 460
  Jane 460
  John 460
  Lucy 460
  Rebecca 460
  Sarah 460
  Seaborn 460
  Thomas 459, 460, 697
  William 460
Godolphin, Jo. 197
  Joseph 196
Godsalm, Ellin 98
Godwin, Jeremiah 596
  Jeremie 596
Godwine, Jeremy 596
Goetschius, Rev. J. H.
  277
  Rev. John Henry 275
Goldney, Henry 109
  Thomas 609
Goodchild, Rev. Mr. 885
Goodenough, ffrauncis
  563
Goodier, Margaret 612
Goodson, Vice-Admiral
  200, 202
  Job 442
  John 225
Goodwin, John 294
  William B. 288, 292
Gookin, Charles 154
  Deputy Gov. Charles
    243
Gordon, (?) 539
  Elizabeth 789
  Mrs. Harriott 620
Goring, Diana 303
  George, 1st Lord 303
Goshin, Margret 229
Goucon, Elizabeth 98
Gouge, (?) 667
Gould, Stephen 565

Gouldin, Jacob 872
Goulding, Mary 624
  Tho. 624
Gouldney, Eils 224
Gouldsmith, George 820
  Hester 820
Gouverneur, Isaac 793
  Juliana M. 781
  Juliana Matilda 793
Gove, Richard 157
Graeme, (?) 479, 480
  Dr. 423, 476
  Ann 474
  Elizabeth 474
  Patrick 457
  Thomas 474
  Dr. Thomas 457, 474
Graffin, Mrs. Harris 447
Grafton, Richard 772
Graham, Dr. 418
  Rev. Dr. 898
  Ann 407, 408
  Anna Mary Belknap
    407, 408
  Duncan 882
  Edwin Pinkerton 407,
    408
  Elizabeth 407, 408
  Gallant 407, 408
  Helen Bruster 407
  Henry Rodman 408
  Isabella 402, 407
  James 402, 407, 408
  Col. James D. 882
  John 407, 408
  Margaretta 408
  Martha 407, 408
  Martha Isabella 408
  Mary 407
  Samuel 407, 408
  Theodore Alexander
    408
  Tho. R. 408
  William Crowell 407
  Col. William M. 882
Grand, Wilton 549
Grant, Aunt 615
  Elizabeth 616
  Jane 616, 617
  Rev. Jn. L. 408
  Samuel 616
  Susanna 617
  William 616, 617
Grantham, Lord 11
Granville, Anne Gilling-
  ham 362
  Anne H. 362
  Anne H. Gillingham
    365
  John A. 362, 365
Grave, John 65
Gravenraedt, Andreis 716
Gray, Capt. 645
  Allen 865
  Ann 866
  Ann Eliza 866
  Ann Emerson 866
  Anne 865, 866
  Benjamin 965, 866
  Elizabeth 865, 866
  Henry 628
  James 865, 866
  John 865, 866
  Margaret 558
  Mariam 866
  Mary 865, 866
  Rebecca 866
  Sarah 865, 866
  Susan 866

Gray, Susanna 865
　Thomas 865
　Unity 866
　William 865, 866
Greber, George 335, 344
Green, Ann 886
　Elizabeth 98
　Frank D. 880
　Jane Eliza 886
　John 25
　R. 860
　Robert 860
　Susannah Eliza 860
　Tho. 98, 130
Greenaway, Robert 242
Greene, Ann 556
　Elizabeth 556
Greenemeyer, Edward 335, 344
Greenfield, Tho. 618
Greenshield, James 881
　Luke 881
Greenwald, Rev. Dr. 659
Gregg, Capt. James 340
Gregory, Jo'n, 628
　Joseph H. 858
Gressingham, Marie 564
　Robert 564
Grey, James 865
Grice, George 812
Grier, Roger 580
Griffin, Robert 300
Griffith, Ann C. 831
　Anne 168, 169
　Arabella 781, 794, 795
　Rev. Benjamin 520
　Evan 484
　John 484, 794
　Richard 807
　Capt. Robert 295, 299
　Judge William 794
Griffithes, Mrs. Anne 613
　Johane 612
　Mrs. Mary 613
　Richard 612
Griffiths, William 697
Griffits, Samuel P. 788
Griggs, Dorothy 877
Grimaldi I, Prince of Monaco 269
Griswold, John N. A. 717
Gross, Abigail 679, 697
Groteman, Rich'd 550
Grove, Thomas 619
Grover, Thomas J. 521
Growden, Joseph 143
　Lawrence 164
Growdon, Joseph 94, 142, 144
Grubb, Curtis 647
　Peter 647
Gruffydd, Elin verch Howell 284
　Ellin verch Howell 284
　Howell 284
　John 284
　Lewis ap John 284
　Lewis ap Sion 284
　Sion 284
Guest, (?) 664
　Alice 867
　Benjamin 868
　Catherina 868
　Elizabeth 867, 868
　George 867
　Henry 868

Guest, Isaac 868
　James 868
　John 867
　Joseph 868
　Mary 868
　Nathaniel 868
　Phoebe 867
　Sarah 868
　William 868
Guilpine, Dorothy 379
　Evarard 379
　Fraunce 379
　Jane 379
　Ruth 379
　Thomas 379
Gumley, Deborah 68
　John 68
Gunson, Ann 100
　Wm. 100
Gurman, Mary 627
　Sara 627
Gurnell, Stephen 375
Gurney, Eliza K. 854
　Joseph 854
Guthrie, Bethiah 880
Guthries, Alexander 880
Guthry, (?) 880
Guy, John 24, 27
Gwin, Mary 872
Gwinner, Edward William 268
　Sara Louise 269
Gwyn, Hugh 284
　Jane Owen 284
Gwynn, Elizabeth 424
　Elizabeth Greathouse 424
　Hugh 283
　Nicholas 424
　Sibill verch 283
Gyfforde, Margett 551
Haak, Jacob 278
Hacket, Lydia 625
Hackett, Edward 624, 625
　Lydia 624
Hage, (?) 217
Haggatt, Nathaniel 610
Hagy, William 465
Haig, Douglas 217
　Earl 217
　Marshal 217
　William 217, 218, 236
Haige, William 31
Haines, Abraham 714
　Ann 450
　Catherine 450
　Catherine David 451
　Charles 617
　Elizabeth 450
　Hermon 450
　Isaac 451
　Israel B. 449
　Jane 450
　Joseph 450
　Josiah 449, 450, 451
　Lydia 450
　Marget 450
　Nehemiah 45
　Sarah 450
　Thomas 617
Hains, Rebecca 541
Hale, George 562
　John 562
Hall, (?) Wilson 411
　Lieut. 200
　Achseh 410
　Alexander 347, 410, 411
　Ann 418

Hall, Augustus R. 409, 412, 413
　Benjamin Shepherd 411
　Bob 409
　Caroline 413
　Caroline Alford Gardiner 413
　Catherine Benners 413
　Christianna 412
　D. 871
　Edward 411
　Eliza 409
　Elizabeth 413, 418
　Evans Roberts 413
　George 409, 413, 414
　George Annie Benners 413
　Hanna 418
　Hannah 58, 410, 411
　Hannah Allaire 410
　Harriet 411
　Harry Basil 413
　Haslett Gardiner 413
　Henrey 122
　Henrietta Idel 412
　Henry 121, 122
　Rev. Henry Armstrong 683, 685
　James 792
　Jane 410
　Jn. 409, 410
　John 2, 31, 32, 33, 39, 40, 58, 77, 410, 411, 412, 413, 414, 415, 416
　John Augustus Ratlaux 412
　Joseph 410, 411, 412, 666
　Joseph Augustus 413
　Lidia 410
　Lydia 410
　Mary 122, 409, 632
　Mary Smith 411
　Meribah 410
　Merribah 411
　Olivia 412, 413
　Priscilla 409
　Rebecca 409, 411, 412
　Rebecca Radcliffe 409
　Rob. 409
　Robbert 411
　Robert 413, 414, 415
　Rosanna 826
　Ruth 410
　Samuel Scotten 411, 412
　Sarah 247, 409, 410, 411, 412, 418
　Sarah Baldwin 409
　Sarah Brading 418
　Sophia 413
　Thomas 410, 411, 412, 417
　Walter Ferdinand 413
　William 122, 418
　Willis Edward 413
　Zachary Taylor 413
Hallowell, Hannah 363
　John 363, 437
　Joseph 437, 438
　Thomas 442
Halter, Peter 871
Halton, Christina 868
Haman, George 573
Hamilton, (?) 880
　Deputy Gov. 149
　Abby 356
　Adaline 659

Hamilton, Alexander 659
  Andrew 355, 812, 813
  Ann 355
  Anna 813
  Eleanor 645
  Francis 812, 813
  James 252, 399, 620, 806, 807, 818
  Gov. James 326, 355
  Sir James 403
  John 806, 807, 812, 813
  John, Archbishop 399
  Rev. John 449
  Mary Louisa 659
  Rev. Patrick 403
  Robert 399
  William 355, 810
Hamlyn, John 593
Hammond, Jonathan 813
Hampden, Richard 551
Hampson, Sir Thomas 564
Hancock, Gen. 421, 424
  Mr. 424
  Ada Elizabeth 425
  Almira 425
  Ann 422
  B. F. 423
  Benjamin F. 422, 423, 425
  Benjamin Franklin 421, 422
  Edward 128
  Eliza 422
  Gwynn Richard 425
  Hilary Baker 424, 425
  John 424, 425
  Richard 419, 421, 425
  Russell, 424
  Sarah 422
  Gen. W. S. 419
  Winfield S. 424, 425
  Winfield Scott 419, 425
Hand, Mrs. A. W. 864
  Silvea 121
Handley, Sir Thomas 304
Handy, John 596
Hank, John 486
  Sarah 486
Hankinson, Aaron 502
Hannum, Capt. William 200
Hanwell, Anne 569
  William 569
Harbert, Thomas 618
Harbeson, Benjamin 889
  Mary 889
Hard, Elizabeth 867
  William 867
Hardie, (?) 807
Hardiman, Abraham 773
  Hannah 773
Harding, William 586
Hardman, Margaret 33
  Margaret 71
Hardwick, John 361, 363, 365
  Mary 361, 365
  Mary A. 365
  Mary Anna 361
  Sarah Elizabeth 361
Harford, Charles 609, 626, 627, 628, 630, 631
  Edward 631
  Elizabeth 631
Hargrave, Charles 273
Hargreaves, Alice 74

Hargreaves, Henry 74
  John 74
Harker, Adam 58
  Daniel 502
  John 60
  Mary 82
Harkins, William 871
Harlan, Christina 482
Harle, John 553
Harley, Sir Edward 625
  Thomas 714
Harman, Barbara 658
  Samuel 658, 659
Harper, Anne 565
  Martha 565, 566
Harriet, Jane 845
Harrington, Thos. 372
Harris, (?) 234
  Abigail 899
  Abraham 408
  Anna 899
  Benjamin 31, 58, 899
  Elizabeth 272
  Hanna 612
  Dr. Isaac Watts 899
  J. Frazer 834
  John 809
  Capt. John 272
  Margaret 615
  Rev. Mathias 848
  Rev. Matthias 850
Harrison, Abigail 869
  Benjamin 635, 636
  James 76, 139, 140, 155
  Joseph 679
  Capt. Leon 200
  Phebe 76
  Rebekah 869
  Susannah 679
Harry, David 640
  Evan 536
  John 245, 246, 661, 662
  Joseph 661
  Col. Joseph 246
  Josiah 661
  Mary 661
  Thomas 661, 662
Hartley, Jeremiah 55
  John 86
Hartman, Abigail 891
  J. M. 891
Hartranft, Gov. 262
Hartshorne, Richard 60
Hartson, James 813
  Sara 813
Harvey, Alexander E, 796
  Margarett 561
  Susan Hall 663, 666
Harwood, H. W. F. 611
Haskins, Sarah Ennalls 652
  Rev. Thomas 650, 652
Hason, Thomas 810
Hassett, Francis 813
Hastings, Howell 645
  James 645
  John 645
  William 645
Hater, Robert 598
Hatfield, Dr. Nathan 347
  Samuel 347
Hatton, Anne 570
  Elizabeth 570
  Mary 570
  Mathew 570
Hattsell, Capt. 195, 198
Hattswele, Capt. 195

Haward, Lieut. 200
Hawkes, Capt. 200
Hawkes, William 173
Hawkesworth, Richard 625, 631
Hawks, William 173
Hawksworth, Ann 419, 420
  Edward 419, 420
  Elizabeth 419, 420
  Elizabeth Jenkins 420
  John 419, 420, 425
  Mary 419, 420, 425
  Peter 419, 420, 421, 425
  Col. Peter 420
  Rachel 419
  Rich. 625, 626
  Sarah 419, 420
Hayden, (?) 635
Haydock, Robert 793
  Theop. 615
Hayes, (?) 664
  Benjamin 539, 543
  Elizabeth 543
  James 218
  Richard 543
  Thomas 470
Hayhurst, Alice 113
  Cuthbert 112, 113, 114
  Margery 113
  Mary 20
  Walter F. 438, 439
  William 77, 103, 113, 114
Haynes, (?) 383
Hayward, Mr. 752, 767
  Mrs. 769
  Martha 750
  Martha Washington 751, 758
Hayworth, Abraham 75
Head, John 867
Heard, Brig.-Gen. 503
  Gen. Nathaniel 495
Hearne, Thos. 569
Heath, Ann 874
  John 874
  Lewis 874
  Margaret 874
  R. 441
  Sir Robert 151
Heathcote, Gilbert 574
Heathcott, George 77
Heaton, Grace 114
Heaveloe, John 848
Hecker, (?) 322
  John Egidius 322
  Rev. John Egidius 323, 328, 344
Hedge, Christopher 428
  Elizabeth 428
  John 428
  Samuel 426, 427, 428, 429, 430
  Thomas 427, 428
Heffelfinger, Lewis 521
Heister, Maria C. 182
Heller, Samuel 465
Helmer, William 370
Hemming, John 558
Hench, Elizabeth 891
  Jacob 891
  John 891
Henden, Sir John 303
Henderson, (?) 880
  304
  Henry 289
Hendrickson, Hannah 709

Henning, Amos W. R. 659
  Amos W. Rohrer 657
  Amos William Rohrer 658
  Emma Edwards 659
  Jacob 658, 659
  Mrs. Jacob 657
  Mrs. Susan 657, 659
  Susan Ann Rohrer 658
  Henry II, K. of England 186
  Henry VIII, K. of England 548
  Henry I, K. of France 184, 269
  Henry Plantagenet, Count of Anjou 182
Henry, Judge William 279
Henshawe, Edward 304
Herbert, Elizabeth Duer 857
  Francis 627
  Mary 627
  Dr. Thomas S. 857
Herbster, Martin 329
Heris, Jean 809
  John 809
  Nancy 809
  Samuel 809
  Thomas 809
Heron, John 287, 297
Herr, Daniel 875
Herrick, Cheeseman A. 497
Heston, Dorothy 114
  Aebulon 114
Heth, Maj. William 495
Hetherington, John 809
Hetzel, William B. 875
Heulings, Abigail 712
Hewes, Elizabeth 160
  Matthew 160
Hewitt, Elizabeth 859
Hewlett, Mary 879
Hewson, Mr. 868
  Ann 869
  Catherine 868, 869
  Catherine Washington 869
  Esther 868, 869
  James 869
  John 869
  Capt. John 868, 869
  Col. John 868
  Jonathan 869
  Margaret 869
  Mary 868, 869
  Peter 868, 869
  Phoebe 869
  Priscilla 869
  Robert 869
  Sarah 869
  William 869
  Zebiah 869
Heynes, Thomas 616
Heyser, Capt. William 317
Heywood, John 44
  Martha 621
  Wm. 570
Heyworth, Abraham 74
  Susan 74
Hibbard, Josiah 541
Hickes, Baptist 552, 557, 558
  Sir Baptist 558
  Clement 552, 553, 557
  Elizabeth 553
  Julyan 557

Hickes, Mary 558
  Michael 552, 553, 557, 558
  Sir Michael 558
  Robert 557
Hickman, Rev. William 850
Hickok, Louisa 834
  Ross Anderson 834
  William O. 834
  William Orville 834
Hicks, Robert 818
Hicokook, Sarah 224
Hide, John 626
Higgins, George 529
Hignell, Jeremy 631
Hildeburn, Chas. R. 679
Hill, Ales 590
  Amos 431, 432
  Artemon 431, 432
  Caroline 432
  Charles Austin 431
  Charlotte 433
  David 431, 432, 433
  Emily 432
  George 433
  Harriet Fales 432
  Harriot Fales 432
  Hugh 810
  Jacob 640
  John 145
  John Williams 433
  Joseph 431
  Joshua 433
  Leah 433
  Levi 433
  Margaret 844
  Maria 433
  Marid 433
  Mercy 431, 432
  Mercy Holbrook 432
  Mitchel 433
  Nancy 433
  Paulina 431
  Phebe 431
  Richard 853
  Robert 433
  Ruth 433
  Sarah 433, 853
  Solon 431, 432
  Sophia 433
  Sylvester 431, 432
  William 573, 590
Hillborn, Abigail 91
  Elizabeth 92
  Margaret 90, 91, 92, 95
  Margaret Atkinson 92
  Samuel 91, 92, 95
  Thomas 92, 95
Hilles, Francis 811
Hills, Henry 895
Hillsborough, Lord 778
Hilton, Dr. 831
  Elizabeth 669
Himes, Frederick 841
  Mary 841
Hinchman, Abigail 869
  Jacob 869
  Mary 869
Hinckle, Catherine 314
Hind, Alice 98
  Martha 300
  Mary 98
  Richard 101
Hines, Sarah 848
Hippisley, William 304
Hipple, Jacob 891
Hipplesley, Toby 304
  William 304, 305, 306

Hockley, Abigail 647
  Richard 620
Hoddys, Margarett 601
Hodell, John 601
Hodge, Mary 901
  William 901
Hodges, Capt. 204
  Elizabeth 661, 664
  Francis 300
  Capt. Robert 200
Hodgison, Christopher 379
  John 380
  Marmaduke 380
Hodgkiss, Sarah 347
Hodgson, Mr. 418
  Rev. Mr. 418
  Martha 98
Hodhsan, Marg't 100
Hoeffner, Anna Eva 870
  Apollonia 870
  John George 870
  John William 870
  Maria Barbara 870
Hoffman, A. Zane 250
  Elizabeth 317
  Rebecca 645
Hogg, Mary 773, 774
  Peregrine 774
Hogge, Nicho. 224
Hogkin, Michael 551
Holborn, Israel 563
Holbrook, Dinah 432
  Luke 431, 432
  Mercy 431
  Rachel 432
  Sena Abbee 432
Holcomb, Richard 434, 436, 439
  Richard C. 446
  Sarah Holme 436, 437, 438, 439
Holcombe, Elizabeth 437, 438
  Grace 440
  Hannah 438
  Jacob 436, 437, 438, 439, 441, 442
  John 436, 438, 439, 440, 442, 444, 445
  Julia Ann 440
  Mary 438, 440
  Rebecca 438
  Richard 438, 440, 445
  Samuel 440
  Sarah 438
  Sophia 438
  Susanna 438
  Thomas 438, 439
Holden, Robert 75
Holding, Susane 807
Holhead, Henry 375
Holland, Earl of 304
  Albert Bruce 855
  Ann Robbins 855
  Ebenezer 855, 856
  Eliza 856
  Eliza T. 855
  Elizabeth 855
  Hannah Newbold 855
  Hetty Elenor 855
  J. 842
  John 855
  John P. 856
  John Paynter 855
  Joseph 855
  Maggie A. 856
  Maria 855
  Tabitha 855, 856
  William Dodd 855

Holles, (?) 151
　Sir F. 761
　Joan 761
Holliday, Francis 818
Hollingsworth, Ann Maria 793
　Charles Wharton 793
　Elizabeth Shallcross 793
　Fanny Redwood 793
　Hannah Redwood 793
　Henry 635
　Isaac M. 781
　Jehu 793
　Thomas G. 781
　Thomas Gilfillan 793
　William Wharton 793
Hollinshead, Ann 712, 715
　Anna 711
　Anthony 714
　Bathsheba 714
　Benjamin 45, 713, 715
　Clayton 715
　Edward 45, 714
　Elizabeth 715
　Enoch 715
　Hannah 712, 714
　Hope Lippincott 715
　Hugh 711, 715
　Jacob 711, 712, 713, 714, 715
　Jerusha 714, 715
　John 713, 714
　Joseph 713
　Martha 713
　Mary 711, 712, 713, 714, 715
　Thomas 715
　William 711, 712, 713, 714, 715
　Zillah 715
Hollisshead, James 871
Hollister, Abel 625
　Dennis 609, 610, 612, 625
　Hannah 623
　Jacob 625
　Mary 623, 625
　Phebe 610, 623, 624, 625
　Samuel 625
　Samuell 624
　Thomas 624
　William 625
Holloway, David 656
Holme, (?) 242, 372
　Surveyor Gen. 237
　Ann 87
　Dorothy 372
　Elizabeth 372
　Hester 236
　John 16
　Sarah 434
　Thomas 87, 220, 235, 240, 249, 250, 252, 255, 259, 434, 436, 437
　Capt. Thomas 236, 241, 245, 249, 252
Holmes, Joanna Say 672
　Samuel 780
　Thomas 238
Holt, Mrs. 846
　Catherine 847
　Rives 846
　Ryves 846, 847
Holton, Arthur 867
　Mary 867

Holworthy, Richard 183
Homes, William 808
Homond, Geo. 573
Honour, Henry 573
　Sarah 573
Hood, Elizabeth 899
　James 667, 670
　James A. 670
　John 899
　Mary 670
　Rebecca 670
　Sarah 899
　Thomas 241, 670
Hooke, Sir Humphrey, Kt. 623
Hookey, Catherine 795
Hooks, Thos. 814
Hooper, Richard 626
Hoopes, Eleanor 156
　Isabel 80
　Joshua 37, 66, 80, 156
　Margaret 80
Hooten, Thomas 44
Hopkines, Mr. 207
Hopkinson, Joseph 796
Hopton, Hannah 481
Hord, Rev. A. H. 426
Horn, Ann 467
　Elizabeth 467
　Hannah 464
　William 467
Horner, Gust. R. B. 860
Horsman, Samuel 351
Horsmanden, Jane 739
Hort, John 471
Horwood, John 631
Hoskin, Hannah 619
　Rolf 136
Hoskins, Ann 773
　Martha 537
　Mary 536, 538
　Dr. Richard 538
　Robert 138
Hotchkin, Rev. S. F. 69
Hotham, Sir Charles 691
Hough, Mr. 446
　Benjamin 56
　Elizabeth 68
　John 68
　Joseph 68, 77
　Margery 34, 40, 68, 156
　Margery Clows 29, 39, 68, 72
　Mary 20, 33, 39, 68, 416
　Oliver 42, 82, 83, 183, 253, 434
　Richard 15, 29, 33, 39, 66, 67, 68, 70, 72, 77, 145, 155, 156, 416
　Sarah 20, 29, 68, 77
Houghton, John 373
Howard, Mr. 767
Howe, (?) 444
Howell, Arthur 867
　Mrs. Bridget 300
　Daniel 440
　David ap 284
　Deborah 563
　Elizabeth 563
　Ethelbright 562, 563
　Henrie 563
　Henry 563
　Job 16
　John 563
　Joseph 540, 867

Howell, Katherine 563
　Mary 300
　Mrs. Mary 300
　Richard 550
　Dr. William 300
Howells, Hugh 442
Howey, Benjamin Matlack 899
　Isaac 899
Howland, Mrs. Gulielma 880
Hoxwcrth, Ann 421
　Edward 421, 425
　Elizabeth 421, 423, 425
　Ellen 421
　Israel 421
　John 421
　Margaret 421
　Mary 421, 425
　Capt. Peter 423
　Col. Peter 421, 423
　Sarah 421
　William J. 421
Hoyle, Clara 347
Hoyt, Gov. 262
Hubbard, Judith 859
Hubberthorne, Richard 112
Huber, Elizabeth 277
Hubershe, Mary 98
Hubert, Capt. 200
Huckell, Samuel 616
Hudson, Ann Wiltbank 822
Hudson, Elizabeth 447, 867
　Elizabeth Richardson 773
　Hannah 448, 542, 776, 867
　Henry 822
　Jane 447, 448
　John 542
　Chief John 826
　Margaret 448
　Margerat 448
　Margret 448
　Mary 447, 448, 449, 541, 867
　Rachall 447
　Rachel 542
　Samuel 448, 542, 867
　Samuell 448
　Sarah 447
　Susan 773
　Susanna 447, 536, 541, 542
　Susannah 448
　Thomas 100, 134
　William 447, 448, 449, 541, 542, 544, 773
Hues, William 173
Huett, (?) 415
Huffnagle, John 356
Huger, Chapman 882
　Charlotte 882
　Thomas 882
　Capt. Thomas 882
Hugh, Cadwalader Thomas ap 531, 532, 537
　Humphrey ap 284
　Katherine 798
　Mary 101, 107
　Mary verch 284
　Owen ap 284
　Robert ap 798
　Rowland 107
　Sibill verch 283
　Thomas ap 537

Hughes, Ann 814
  Charles Evans 266
  Ellis 643
  Matthew 80, 158, 442
  Richard 814
  Sally 814
Hughs, Ellis 106, 107
  Hannah 106
  Thomas 107
Hugus, Jacob 335, 344
  Mary 322
  Mary M. 344
Hulen, (?) 460
Hull, George 564
  Hopencee 512
  Richard 564
  William 289
Hume, Sr. 881
Humfrey, James 561
  Thomas 561
  William 561
Humfreys, Nathaniel 564
Humphreis, Capt. 196
Humphrey, D. of Gloucester 284
Humphrey, Anne verch 283
  Gainor 484
  John 224, 283, 284
  Owen 533
  Regnald 533
  Robert 484
  Rowland 533
Humphreys, Capt. 195
  Clement 800
  Daniel 800
  Hannah 800
  Jane 800
  John 534, 535
  Joshua 800
  Katherine H. 612
  Owen 533, 535
Hunfrie, Gabriel 563
Hunloke, Thomas 48
Hunsicker, Danyel 870
  Elizabath 870
  Ester 870
  Henrich 870
  Johanes 870
  Maria 870
  Pilzus 870
  Suzanna 870
  Waillaim 870
Hunsiker, Catharine 870
Hunt, Francis 858
  Nicholas 568
  Sam 226
Hunter, Francis 380
  Dr. John 679
  Dr. Wm. 679
Hurford, Grace 437
  John 436, 437
  Samuel 437
  Sarah 437
Husband, Ann 449, 451
  Catherine 449
  Hannah 449
  Hermon 449
  John 449
  Joseph 449
  Margery 449
  Mary 449, 451
  Sarah 449
  Thomas 449
  William 449, 451
Hussey, Rebecca 777, 778
Hustler, Thomas 881
  William 881
Hutchinson, (?) 690
  John 38, 60

Hutton, Adele 454
  Ann 453, 455
  Anne 454
  Benjamin 452, 453, 454, 455, 456
  Benjamin Henry 454
  Maj. Charles Gordon 454
  Clement 456
  Elenor 455, 456
  Eliza 455
  Eliza Elliott 456
  Elizabeth 455
  Ellenora 456
  George 453, 454
  James 454
  John 452, 453, 454
  Adj.-Lieut. John Galt 454
  John S. 452
  John Strangeways 452, 453, 455
  Joseph 454
  Mary 454, 455, 456
  Nathaniel 454, 455
  Nathaniel Henry 454
  Presila 455
  Rebecca 456
  Rebeccah 455, 456
  Sarah 454, 455
  Thomas 455, 456
  William Rich 454
Hyll, Alice 590
  Elnor 590
  Elsabeth 589
  Joane 589
  Jone 590
  Margarete 590
  Margery 590
  Phylyppe 589
  Sybyll 590
  Wm. 589
Hylle, Wyllyam 590
Hynde, Alice 89, 97, 98, 99, 101, 102, 103, 108, 115, 116, 117, 119
  Elizabeth 100
  John 100
  Lydia 97, 100, 101
  Mary 89, 97, 98, 99, 100, 101, 102, 108
  Richard 100, 101
  Roger 101
  Susannah 88, 100, 101
Hyndsey, Marye 560
Hynes, Ann 871
  Elizabeth 871
  Hannah 871
  Isaac 871
  Jacob 871
  John 871
  Martha 871
  Prescilla 871
  Samuel 871
  Sarah 871
  William 871
Iavelin, Duffield 627
  Elizabeth 627
Iddings, Hannah Sharpless 261
  William 261
Iden, Dorothy 118, 119
Idquahon, Indian 236
Iethyn, John de 390
Illius, Charles 793
Inchmartin, Isabel 393
  Sir Patrick 393
Indian Peter 714
Ingersoll, Charles Jared 256

Ingham, Jos. 818
Inglis, John 699
Ingraham, Alfred 882
  Edward 882
  Francis 882
  Thos. Rockhill 882
Inman, (?) 654
Ireland, Amos 872
  Ananias 872
  Ann 872
  Daniel 871, 872
  Deborah 871, 872
  Dorcas 872
  Elizabeth 872
  Hezekiah 871
  Isaac 872
  Jacob 872
  James 872
  Jane 871
  Jemima 871
  Job 872
  John 872
  Jonathan 872
  Joseph 871, 872
  Katherine 872
  Lydia 872
  Mary 871, 872
  Micajah 872
  Phoebe 872
  Rebecca 872
  Reuben 871, 872
  Rhoda 872
  Robt. 878
  Ruth 871, 872
  Sarah 871, 872
  Thomas 872
Iridell, Rachel 878
Irvine, Elizabeth 668
  George 664, 668
  James 664
  Gen. James 660, 668
  Mary 668
  Susanna 668
Irwin, Letitia 796
Isaac, (?) 370
Isted, Richard 304
Izard, George 680
Jackson, Gen. 263
  Mr. 262, 263
  Pres. 653
  Andrew 264
  Ann 893
  Barbara 559
  Gen. Clarence Gearheart 262
  Grace 893
  Isaac H. 774
  Josiah 893
  Katherine 893
  Margaret 261
  Mordecai William 261
  Robert 559
  Samuel 893
  Sarah 893
  Susannah 893
  William 74, 368, 369
Jacobs, Albert 886
  Elizabeth 886
Jacons, Capt. John 314
James II, K. of Great Britain 225, 226, 474
James, Ann 407
  Benjamin Brown 497
  Clara Belle 497
  Colin D. 497
  David 520
  Edmund Jones 497
  Elizabeth 407

James, Elizabeth Wilcox
    697
  Ella Amanda 497
  Evan 520
  George Francis 497
  John Nelson 497
  Margaret 518
  Rebecca 520
  Robert 407
  Robert B. 408
  Robert F. 407
  Sibell 611, 612
  Thamar 519
  Thamer 518
  Thomas 234, 697
Janney, (?) 38
  Abel 37, 78, 132, 164, 165
  Ann 160, 164
  Bettie 164
  Betty 164
  Charles 164
  Elizabeth 164
  Elizabeth Biles 164
  Elizabeth Stacy 164, 165
  Hannah 163, 164
  Isaac 56
  Jacob 139, 156
  Joseph 158, 160
  Margery Heath 158
  Martha 160
  Rachel Pownall 164
  Randle 56
  Rebeckah 160
  Thomas 22, 37, 56, 140, 141, 142, 155, 156, 157, 158, 164, 165
  William 56
Janoltowe, Indian 236
Janse, Anneka 715
Jansen, Andrew 525, 527
  Catherine Roelofse 715
  Roelof 715
Jaques, Rich'd 595
Jaquette, Margaretta 407
Jarrett, John 878
Jasper, Anne 190
Jaudon, Anna Caroline 481, 482
  William Latta 482
Jefferis, Anne 174
  Benjamin 174
  Charity 174
  George 174
  James 174
  Jane 174
  John 174
  Mary 174
  Patience 174
  Robert 174
  Thomas 174
  William 174
Jefferson, Thomas 334
Jeffrys, Capt. 178
Jekyll, Sir Joseph 690
  Margaret Shippen 684
Jencks, Lucy 432
Jenconson, Elizabeth 98
Jenkes, Thomas 613
Jenkin, Jenkin 420, 425
  Mary 420, 425
Jenkins, Mr. 84, 85, 86, 87, 88, 94
  Benjamin 667
  Charles Francis 83
  David 667

Jenkins, Elizabeth 420, 425
  Elizabeth Paschall 672
  George 667
  Howard M. 348, 419
  Isaac 667
  Jenkin 667
  John 420, 421, 664, 667
  Joseph 667
  Margaret 667
  Rebecca 667
  Sarah 421
  Stephen 442
  William 667
Jenninges, William 381
Jennings, Abigail 712
  Bartholomew 375
  Isaac 712
  Rebecca 177
Jenny, Mr. 885
  Rev. Mr. 884
Jervis, Samuel 697
Jess, Zachariah 247
Jetur, James 568
Joanes, Richard 605
John of Gaunt, D. of Lancaster 284
John, Elizabeth verch 283
  Gainor 484, 530
  Griffith 530, 535
  Margaret 484
  Rowland 484
  William 484, 530
Johnes, Arthur 347
  Jouett 533
  Lucy 347
  Priscilla 537
  William F. 347
Johns, Mary 792, 795
Johnson, Col. 293
  Bnn. 878
  Derrick 878
  Henry 355
  Henry Allen 355
  Col. Sir Henry Allen William 355
  Sir Henry, Bart. 355
  Mrs. Israel H. 889
  Sir John 341
  Judith 872
  Mary 428
  Col. R. G. 307
  Rebecca 833
  Lady Rebecca Franks 354, 355
  Robert G. 293
  Col. Robert G. 287
  Sir William 778
Johnsson, Davye 608
Johnston, (?) 814
  Dr. 398
  Alexander 832
  Alexander Washington 832
  Ann Poyntell 832
  Frank 832
  James 818
  Mary Espy 834
  Mary Johnston 832
  Ross 832, 834
  Virginia Blair 834
Jones, (?) 460, 867
  Mr. 465
  Mrs. 464
  Alce 468
  Alice 703

Jones, Alse 703, 704, 706
  Ann 458, 467, 469, 630
  Ann Duke 402
  Anne 466, 469
  Cadw'r 486
  Catharine 469
  Catherine 468, 537, 703
  Cha. 630
  Charity 540
  Charles 631
  Mrs. Charles 855
  Charles B. 825
  Charles C. 292
  Comly 825
  Daniel 232
  David 468, 469, 533, 799, 800
  Deborah 669
  Eaven 468
  Edmund 749
  Edward 403, 532, 535, 539, 798, 799
  Dr. Edward 539
  Eleanor 460, 464, 465
  Elizabeth 465, 466, 467, 468, 533, 540, 612, 666
  Ellen 468
  Ellin 469
  Evan 466, 467, 470, 539, 800
  Ezekiel 539
  Gainor 533, 538, 542, 543
  George 174, 595
  Griffith 458, 471
  Hannah 347, 465, 521, 540, 801
  Henry 800
  Hester 800
  Isaac 468, 469
  J. Comly 824, 825
  Jacob 469, 539, 800
  James 468
  Jane 347, 469
  Jesse 460
  John 92, 95, 115, 457, 458, 459, 460, 461, 462, 463, 465, 466, 468, 469, 485, 521, 524, 630, 800
  Jonathan 460, 463, 534, 536, 538, 539, 542, 543, 801
  Joseph 462, 463, 464, 465, 467
  Josiah 862
  Katharine 543
  Katherine 466, 467, 470
  Levi 460, 461, 463
  Lewis 467, 468, 469, 543
  Margaret 92, 800
  Martha 540
  Mary 458, 465, 466, 467, 470, 539, 542, 543, 631, 749
  Mary H. 825
  Mary R. 825
  Mathias 631
  Mercy 432
  Michael 631
  Nicholas 613
  Owen 347, 534, 777
  Peter 460, 463, 613
  Prsicilla 468
  Rachel Roberts 825

Jones, Rachell 631
  Rebecca 539, 543, 704
  Richard 613
  Robert 402, 403, 486, 535, 542
  Ruth 466, 467
  Sarah 402, 458, 462, 464, 465, 466, 539, 543
  Seth 469
  Susan Evans 521
  Susanna 468
  Sydney 470
  Thomas 460, 466, 467, 469, 470, 484, 535, 543
  Zacheus 612
Jordaine, John 577
Jordan, (?) 601
  Bridgett 623, 624, 625
  John W. 253
  John Woolf 683
  Lidia 624
  Lydia 623, 625
  Thomas 609, 623, 625
  Wm. 315
Jordell, Laird of 880
Judd, Bridget, 617
  Bridgett 616
Julyan, Eliz. 563
Jungman, Elizabeth 865
Justea, Eleanor 526
  Justea 526
Justice, Alfred Rudulph 367
  Charles 529
  Mouns 639, 640, 642
Kabel, Daniel 891
Kaufman, Barbara 659
Kean, Alexander 872
  James Macomb 872
  Jane 872
  John 872
  Margaret 872
  Margaret Jane 872
  Mary 872
  Mary Potter 872
  Matthew 872
  Thomas 872
  William 872
Kearney, Edmund 774
  Elizabeth 774
  Joanna 774
  Philip 774
  Rebecca 774
  Susannah 774
Keath, Henry 477
Keaton, Rev. Mr. 888
Keeling, Richard 561
Keen, Benjamin 632, 633
  Catherine 705
  Elizabeth Lock 705
  Ephraim 633
  Gregory B. 452
  Jacob 633
  Jesse 633
  Jonas 632, 633
  Laodemia 633
  Lydia 633
  Margaret 633
  Mary 633
  Mounce 632
  Nicholas 705
  Phebe 633
  Rebecca 632, 633
Keene, Edward 604
  Eleanor 613
Keinton, Charles 631

Keites, George W. 521
Keith, (?) 454, 476, 536, 539
  Gen. 477
  Gov. 473, 474
  Lady 472, 475, 476
  Alexander Henry 477
  Dame Ann 473
  Lady Ann 477
  Lady Anne 476
  Charles P. 473, 474, 636
  Mrs. Charles Penrose 887
  Frederic 479
  Frederick William Henry Ferdinand 478
  George 21, 22, 156, 157
  James 475, 478
  Jane 477
  Robert 475, 477, 478 479
  Sir Robert 473, 478, 479, 480
  Robert George James 478
  Tho. 857
  Thomasine Palmer 477
  William 474, 475, 477
  Sir Wm. 457, 473, 475, 476, 477
Kelker, Luther R. 839
Kellam, Elizabeth W. 489
  Thomas 489
Keller, Daniel 831
  Rachael E. 831
Kelly, Jean 816
  Margaret 521
Kendig, Martin 309
Kennan, Katherine 505
Kennedy, John 430
  Nathan 84
Kenworthy, George Birkhead 681
  Joseph 681
  Zeįherene Blair 681
Ker, George 899
  Margaret Sheppard 899
Kern, Col. Nicholas 337
  Lieut.-Col. Nicholas 332
Kerns, Eleanor 708
  John 708, 709
Kerr, Joseph 668
Kerver, Reynald 613
Ketchum, Maj.-Gen. William Scott 454
Ketland, John 881
  Thomas 881, 882
Kettell, Edmund 566
Kewell, (?) 562
Kewicke, Margaret 230
Kidder, Richard 304
Kidston, William 398 399
Killereich, Lord 880
Killingbeck, Humphrey 224
Killver, Constans 807
  John 807
Kindall, Daniell 626
King, Ann 873
  Anna 873
  James 873
  John 465, 873
  Mary 873
  Prudence 887
  Rebeckah 873

King, Samuel 873
  Susannah 873
  Thomas 873
  William 873
Kinge, Christian 600
Kinsey, (?) 91
Kinzie, Isabella Innes 522
Kirkbride, (?) 17
  Hannah 164
  Joseph 16, 33, 37, 38, 60, 67, 78, 130, 156, 161, 164
  Sarah Fletcher 164
Kirke, Thomas 568
Kirkintinlack, Alexander 390
Kite, Nathan 18
Klapp, William H. 452
Kline, Catherine 263
Klock, Laura Tenney 268
  Mabie Crouse 268
Knapp, Anne 563
  Ellen 563
  Elliner 562
  Marie 563
  Sara 563
  Susan 563
  Susanna 563
  Wm. 562, 563, 594
Knerr, Mary 891
Knight, Phoebe 602
Knolling, Andrew 764
Knowles, Fra. 409
Knowling, (?) 748
  Mr. 741
  Andrew 737, 744
Koch, Rev. Henry 322
  Rev. Henry M. 344
Koester, Barbara 340
Kollock, Comfort 847
  Margaret 847
  Simon 847
Kruger, Sarah A. 792
Kuhn, Hartman 355
Kunders, Tunis 877
Kunsman, Daniel 645
  William 645
Kuntz, Catherine 894
Kuster, Margaret 878
Kyn, Joran 454
Labrie, Mr. 869
Ladel, William de 390
Lafayett, Gen. 464
Lafitte, Mrs. 882
Lake, Beaston 121
  Caroline 121
  Charles D. 121
  Daniel 121
  David R. 120
  Dinah 874
  Edward 570
  Elizabeth 121
  Jacobus 874
  John R. 121
  John Stryker 874
  Rebecca 121
  Robert 121, 122
  Samuel 121
Lalanne, Dominique Perigue 803
  Ellen Mary 803
  Don Minequette Duchesne 803
Lamand, Constantia Mariae 650
Lamb, Jacob 892
  Lemuel 781
  Lucy 781

Lambert, Elizabeth 158, 163
  Capt. John 200
  Hon. John 444
  Mary 158
  Thomas 44, 81, 130, 158, 163
Lancaster, James 112
Landis, Barbara 891
Lane, Bernard 62
  Sir George 271
  Jennet 62
  Thomas 612
Langdale, Elizabeth 448
  Jane 448
  John 448
  Josiah 448
  Margaret 448
  Rachel 448
  Samuel 448
  Sarah 448
  William 448
  Wm. Hudson 448
Langhorn, Jer. 161
Langhorne, Grace 158
  Jeremiah 163
  R. 614
  Sarah 158, 163
  Thomas 158
Lank, Hannah 855
  Hannah N. 855, 856
  John C. 855
Lanning, John 26
Lanton, Robert 304
Lappewins, Indian 134
Lardner, Lynford 699
Large, John 60
  John B. 882
  Sarah 62
Laser, Edw'd 569
Laslatt, Alse 562
  Edward 562
Latimer, William Geddes 841
Laux, James B. 857, 871, 875, 886
Lavelle, Msgr. 267
Lawes, Jo. 594
Lawnsone, Robert 562
Lawrence, Anna Morgan 363, 365
  Caroline F. 363, 365
  Daniel 800
  David 800
  Eleanor 800
  Ellen 800
  Ely 363, 365
  Gillian 563
  Hannah 800
  Henry 800
  Joane 563
  Jone 563
  Julyan 563
  Mary 539, 800
  Rachel 800
  Richard 556, 563
  Sarah 800
  Sarah Jane 800
  T. Reeves 363, 365
  Thomas 800
  William 134, 563, 800
  William Gillingham 363
Lawson, Vice Adm. 209
  Deborah 98
  Rear Adm. John 191
  Vice Adm. John 200
Lay, Benjamin 341

Laynfall, Thomas 101
Lea, (?) 565
  Elizabeth 482
  Frances 481, 482
  Hannah Gibson 482
  Henry Charles 481, 482
  Isaac 481, 482
  J. Henry 546, 611
  James 481, 482
  John 481
  Matthew Carey 481
  Susan Gibson 482
Leak, Dinah 874
  James 874
Leake, Rachel 899
Lechmere, Mr. 690
Ledew, Rachel 122
Lee, Alice 679
  Alys 582
  Ann 602
  Arthur 679
  Bernard 602
  Christian 602
  Hancock 859
  Henry Lightfoot 679
  Hugh 582
  James 602
  Maj. John 900
  Mary 602
  Michael 573
  Richard Henry 679
  Theodosia C. 353
  Gov. Thomas 679
Leeds, Chalkley S. 851
  Mrs. Chalkley S. 851
  Daniel 851
  Dorothy 851
  Jeremiah 851
  Mrs. Jeremiah 851
  John 851
  Sarah 851
  Vincent 851
Lefebur, Capt. 729
Legard, Wm. 557, 611
Legh, Anthony 598
Le Guen, Louis 650
  Mary Louisa 650
Leh, Abraham 342, 343
  Ellen 343
  James 343
  Mary 343
Lehnmann, (?) 241
Leigh, Frances 687
  Isabel 303
  Peter 687
  Richard 687
  William 303
Lelius, Conradius 177
Lench, Sarah 611
  Thomas 612
Leonard, Ezekiel 647
  William 522
Leoser, Annette O. 874
  Annette Old 874
  Charles McKnight 874
  Col. Charles McKnight 874
  Christian 874
  Elizabeth Stringer 875
  Jacob 874, 875
  John Smith 874
  Mary 874
  Sarah B. 874
  Sidney Harvey 874
  Thomas 874
  Thomas S. 874, 875

Leoser, Thomas Smith 874, 875
Lerch, David 465
LeRoy, J. Rutgers 177
l'Estrange, Guy 391
Letelier, Peter 55
  Sarah 55
Lethbridge, Jerusha 432
Leverett, Capt. John 204
Levick, Lewis Jones 466
Levis, Edward 791
  William 775, 791
Levy, Belhah Abigail 355
  Moses 355
  James 810
Lewis, Agnes verch 284
  Anna Maria 787
  Cadwallader 536
  Charles 181
  Clements Stocker 796
  David 800
  Evam Robert 483, 484, 530
  Franklin 787
  Hannah 787
  Hannah Owen 796
  Sir John 761
  John Frederick 225
  Joseph Wharton 787
  Julia Wharton 796
  Lawrence 796
  Margaretta 796
  Mary Stocker 796
  Nathan 519
  Owen 533
  Owen ap 284
  Rees ap 284
  Robert 787
  Robert Morton 787, 796
  Robert Wharton 796
  Ruth 467
  Samuel 85
  Sarah 771, 777
  Stephen 777
  Thomas 438
  Wharton 787
  William 514, 774, 787
Lichtown, Walter 395
Lickfeld, William 224
Liddell, Mr. 398
Lightfoote, Capt. 200
Lillie, Ann 885
  Jane Harriett 885
  Mary 885
  Nathaniel 885
Lincoln, Abraham 668
  Rebecca 664, 668
Lindsay, Moses 809
Linsey, Susan 600
  William 600
Lions, Capt. Richard 200
Lippincott, Daniel 715
  Joshua 654
  Sarah Ann 654
Little, John 359
  Margaret 359
  Martha 357, 359
  Sarah 359
Livesey, Esther 439
  Jonathan 439
  Katherine 439
Livingston, Chancellor 680
  Eugene 833
  Eugene A. 833
  Henry Beekman 680
  Margaret Beekman 640
  Margaret M. Livingston 833

Livingston, Mary Coleman 833, 835
  Philip 716
  Robert 716
  Robert L. 833
  Robert R. 680
  William 716
Livington, John 676
  Susannah 676
Llewellyn, John 854
  Mary 854
Lloyd, Anne 612
  David 146, 148, 149, 284
  Elizabeth verch 284
  Henry 623
  Howard Williams 447, 656
  Jane 613
  Katherine 612, 613
  Margaret 664
  Richard 612
  Robert 535
  Susanna 774
  Susannah 773
  Thomas 82, 284, 534, 536, 612, 613, 774, 799
  Walter 664
Lock, Justa 703, 708
Lockhart, Wulliam 663
Lofland, William 125
Loftus, Lesson 246
  Nicholas 813
  Sarah 243, 245
Logan, (?) 151, 696
  Charles F. 792
  James 134, 146, 152, 439, 565, 574, 684, 880
  Walter de 390
Lok, John 549
Lom, Swen 138
Lomas, Nathaniel 635
  Timothy 635
Lomax, Robert 575
Lon, Temperance 122
Long, Col. Cook 332
  Eleanor 483
  H. 172
  Dr. W. S. 42
Longacre, Andrew Peterson 525
Longe, Elizabeth 564
  Sir Henry 593
Longfellow, Frederick William 835
Longhurst, Mary 224
Longs, John 564
Longside, Sir Edward 569
Longworthy, Benjamin 643
  John 640
Loomys, Hannah 635
  Rebecka 635
  Ruth 635
Loper, Mary Craig 260
Lott, mulatto 51
Loughrey, John 669
Love, John 624
  Magdalene 624
Lovell, Joane 564
  Thomas 564
  William 388
Lovering, Anne 793
  Mary 793
Lovet, Edmund 64
Lovett, Edmond 37
  Edmund 60
Low, Widow 631

Lowell, Charles B. 343
Lowry, Mary 315
Lowther, Anthony 572, 573, 614
  Margaret 573, 574, 613, 614
Loxley, (?), 875
  Abram 875
  Benj. 875
  Benjamin 875, 876
  Catherine 875
  Elizabeth 875
  Jane 875, 876
  Jane J. 876
  John 875
  Mary 875, 876
  Mary Pryor 876
  Richard 876
  Stephen 875
Lucas, Edward 37
  George 885
  Robert 138
  Susanna 660
Lucken, Abraham 876, 878
  Alice 877, 878
  Anna 878
  Benjamin 878
  Daniel 878
  Dirk 878
  Elase 876, 877
  Elizabeth 876, 877
  Elsye 877
  Enos 878
  Evan 878
  Gaynor 878
  Hannah 876, 878
  Jacob 877
  Jan 876, 877
  John 876, 877, 878
  Jonathan 878
  Joseph 876, 877, 878
  Margaret 878
  Mary 876, 877, 878
  Mathew 877
  Mathias 876, 878
  Peter 876, 878
  Rebecca 878
  Renier 877
  Sarah 877, 878
  Susanna 877
  William 876, 877
Luckin, Edward 224
  Sarah 224
Lucomb, Greenslaid 231
Ludlow, Gen. Edmund 211
Ludwell, Hannah 679
Ludwig, Michael 646
  Rebecca 646
  Susanna 646
Luested, Hanna 616
  John 616
Luff, John 132
Luken, Abraham 876, 877
  David 877
  Elizabeth 877
  Enes 877
  Job 877
  John 877
  Jonathan 877
  Joseph 877
  Margret 877
  Mary 877
  Matthias 877
  Sarah 876
  William 877
Lukens, John 877
  Peter 877
  Sarah 878
Lundy, Rich. 25, 30

Lunnen, Laird of 880
Lutard, Mary 562
Lux, James B. 308, 324
Lybrand, Elizabeth 679, 695, 697
Lydel, William 391
Lye, Anne 126
Lygon, Henry 566
Lyle, Ellen 355
  James 355
  Robert, Lord 395
Lyman, Mrs. 882
  Charles A. 793
Lyn. See Lynn.
Lynn/Lyn
  Elizabeth 878
  Esther 878
  Hannah 878, 879
  Jeremiah 878
  John 878
  Joseph 878, 879
  Martha 878
  Sarah 878, 879
  Seth 878
  Susanah 878
Lyon, Mr. 847
Lyons, Capt. 209
  Mr. 847
  Rev. John 849
Lyornes, Jane 617
Lytle, Mr. 398
Macaltioner, Geo. B. 287
Macary, Prof. Leonce 270
Mace, Katherine 514
Mackey, Mayor 251, 252
  Harry A. 251
Mackrey, Edwin 375
Mackys, Mary 842
  Robert 842
Macomb, Elizabeth Wilson 872
Maddox, John 26
Madison, James 680
Maffitt, Sarah 634
Magaw, Col. 900
Mahon, Lord 688, 689, 690
Major, Ann 571
  Wm. 571
Maleye, Agnis 608
Mallibroke, William 556
Manesty, Nath. 573
Manlove, Ann 487
  Elizabet 487
  Mark 487
  Mary 487
  Nathaniel 487
  Ruth 487
  Sarah 487
  Thomas 487
  William 487
Mann, Sir Horace 688
Mannering, (?) 736
Manning, Capt. 508
  James 515, 516
Mansell, Rev. 418
  John 569
Marchant, Erma 267
  James Dwight 267
Marchwerthian, Lord of Issallt 537
Marden, William 224
Maris, George 541
  Hannah 541
  Jesse 541
Markeham, George 613
  James 613
Markham, Gov. 143, 236

Markham, Deputy-Gov. 216
  George 572
  William 225, 572, 614
  Capt. William 215,
    235
Markin, Emma 573
Markoe, Maria 791
Marks, Edward 810
  Thomas 162
Marmion, Henry 812
Marriott, Thomas 38, 60
Marsden, Richard 73
Marshal, Catherine F. 171
  John 809
Marshall, Aaron 491, 492
  Abraham 490, 492
  Bathsheba 490
  Burton 493
  Charles M. 493
  D. J. 172
  David A. 493
  Davis 491
  Eliza 493
  Eliza A. 172
  Eliza Rodney 493
  Elizabeth 492, 493
  Elizabeth Davis 491
  Elizabeth R. 493
  Elizabeth R. de Orton
    493
  Frances Almira Boggs
    493
  Hannah 492
  Helen Mar 493
  Hester 492
  Isaac 490, 492
  J. A. 172
  Jacob 490, 491, 492
  James W. 493
  Jhon 590
  John 490, 492, 493
  Kitty 493
  Margaret 481
  Martha 491
  Mary 491
  Mary Q. 172
  Moses 490, 491
  Samuel 491, 492
  Sarah 879
  Thomas 590
  William 490, 492, 493
Marsham, Robert 618
Marston, Edward 178
Marten, Dorothy 224
  Col. Henry 300
  Sir Henry 300
Martens, Isaac 864
  Rachel 864
Martin, (?) 570
  Capt. 197, 198
  Mrs. Col. 503
  Squire 494, 505, 508,
    513
  Abigail 512, 513
  Abner 505
  Absolom 495, 505, 507,
    508, 513
  Alexander 891
  Col. Alexander 509
  Anna 513
  Benjamin 512
  Burling 649
  Catherine 513, 570
  David 512
  Ebenezer 505
  Edmond 511
  Capt. Edmond 508
  Col. Edmond 509
  Edmund 513

Martin, Elizabeth 505,
    514
  Ephraim 497, 505,
    507, 508, 511, 513,
    514
  Col. Ephraim 494, 495,
    496, 498, 499, 501,
    502, 503, 504, 505,
    506, 507, 508, 509,
    510, 511, 512, 513,
    515
  Geo. 570
  Grace 513
  Hannah 513
  Humohrey 513
  Capt. Isaac 508
  Capt. Jacob 510
  James 511, 512, 513,
    514
  Jeremiah 505, 513
  Joane 569
  John 26, 508, 511,
    512, 513, 514
  Capt. John 509
  Sgt. John 508
  Joseph 511, 512, 513,
    514
  Joshua 512
  Katherine 505, 511
  Luther 511
  Lydia 512
  Martha 497, 512, 513
  Martin 505
  Mary 512
  Moses 512
  Nathaniel 513
  Ocey 505, 514
  Patty 505
  Polly 514
  Reuben 509, 511
  Richard 289
  Rosanna 513
  Ruth 882
  Susannah 505
  Thomas 512, 815
  William 513
Martindale, Edward 630
  Isaac C. 2
  Rachel 632
Marton. See Morton.
Martonson. See Morton-
    son.
Martyn, Richard 289
Mary, Q. of Scots 400
Mason, Anne 880
  Betty 488, 489
  Catherine 488
  Charles 488, 489
  Elias 488, 489
  Elizabeth 489
  Jacob 488, 489
  James L. 488
  James W., M. D. 489
  Jo. 879
  John 238
  Joseph 487, 488, 489,
    879, 880
  Joseph H. 488
  Magdalen 489
  Mary 487, 488, 489
  Mary Hewlett 879, 880
  Rachel 488
  Sally 489
  Sarah 488
  Susannah 879
  Thomas 879
  William 879
  William S. 488
Massey, S. 668

Masten, Deborah 488
  Hannah 488
  John 488
  Mary 488
  Sarah 487, 488
  W. M. 488
  William 487, 488
Masters, Alse 562
  John 562
Maston, Edward 177
Masy, Hy. 380
Mather, Richard 74
Mathews, Nannie 267
Matlack, Abigail 899
  Hannah 677
  William 677
Maugridge, John 166
  Mary 166
  Mary Miltin 166
Maul, (?) 880
  Bessie 880
  Bathiah 880
  Helenor 881
  Hellenor 880
  Henry 880
  Isabel 880
  James 880
  Janet 880
  Margaret 880
  Marrion 880
  William 880, 881
Maule, Mary 878
  Susanna 878
Maull, Catherine M. 493
Maury, Mrs. 882
Maviniere, Susanna Horri-
    an 897
Maximilian I, Emperor 274
Maxwell, (?), 499, 506
  Gen. 495, 510
  Christian 394
  John, Lord of 394
  William 502, 510, 811
May, John 602
Mayer, Robt. 98
Mayes, James 808
Mayor, Robert 100
Mayos, Ann 114
  Edward 114
McArthur, Barbara 900
McCall, George 181
McCarty, Ann 858
McCausland, Ro. 808
McClellan, Maj.-Gen.
    George B. 256
McClenachan, Blair 898
  Deborah 898
  Patty 898
McClockey, (?) 405
  Duncan 405
McClosky, William 810
McCluney, William J. 790
McClure, Andrew 811
  Robert 811
McCoombs, Sarah 841
McCoy, Capt. 507
  Mary 811
McCrea, Jane 405
  Janet 405
McCreary, Harriet 634
McCulloch, Annie 879
  Ebenezer 879
  Elizabeth 879
  James 791
  John 879
  Margaret 879
  Mary 879
  Rachel 791
  William 879

McCurdy, Richard 104
McDowell, Anna 829
  Jane 827
  Dr. John 829
  Martha Johnston 829
  Dr. William 827
McFaden, (?) 880
  William 880
McGee, Elizabeth 807
McIlvaine, Andrew 433
  Comfort 322
  Rebecca 680
  Sarah W. 433
  Dr. William 680
McKean, Gov. 698
  Margaret 698
  Sarah 698
McKee, Redick 450
McKenzie, Dr. 679
M'Kim, Rev. John L. 823
McKinney, Abram 502
McLaughlin, Thomas 882
McLean, Daniel 640
  Rebecca 650
McLeen, John 650
McMullin, George O. 796
  John 454
McPeake, John 810
Meade, Gen. 882
  Catherine 881
  Charlotte 881
  Charlotte Hustler 882
  Clara 882
  Elizabeth 881, 882
  Garrett 881
  George 881
  Col. George 882
  Gen. George G. 881, 882
  Henrietta 881, 882
  Henrietta Constantia 881
  John Sergeant 882
  Margaret Butler 882
  Maria 882
  Mariamine 882
  Mary 881
  Adm. R. W. 882
  Richard W. 882
  Richard Worsam 881
  Robert 881, 882
  Salvadora 882
  Sarah Wise 882
  Spencer 882
  William 882
Medary, Samuel 423
Medcalf, Jacob 773, 776
  Rachel 771, 776
  Susanna 773
Medley, Elizabeth 427
  John 428
Mehrkam, Catherine 316
Meigs, Clara F. 882
Mence, Rich'd 569
Merac, Rev. John 884
Mercer, Helen 177
Mercur, James Watts 246, 251
  Ulysses 246
Mereclesdene, Richard 73
Meredith, David 661, 663, 664
  Eliz. 181
  Elizabeth 181
  Hannah 664
  John 241, 664
  Joseph 664
  Rachel 664
  Rebecca 664, 667

Meredith, Reese 181
  Sarah 667
  Susanna 664
  William 520, 664
Merritt, Elizabeth 454
Merton, Jean 405
Mervine, W. M. 903
Messer, (?) 666
  Ann 666
  Elizabeth 661
Metcalf, Esther 822
  Jehu 822
  Mary Wiltbank 822
  Thomas 822
Metcalfe, Lascelles 619
Meuce, Thos. 570
Mewce, Mrs. 742, 751, 758, 759, 760
  Elizabeth 767, 769
  Mrs. Elizabeth 742
  Francis 767
Meyer, Rev. Mr. 824
Meyers, (?) 521
Michell, Alis 607
  Grace 559
  John 224
Michener, (?) 66
  Ezra 16
Michill, Robert 138
Mickle, Samuel 230, 231
Middlemarch, Thomas 389
Middleton, Agnes 577
  Edwin 833
  Elizabeth 569
  Lawrence 569
  Lillian 833
  M. Edward 833
Midlton, Eliz. 100
Mifflin, Gov. 422
  Mary 667, 670
Milax, Mary Hendrey 408
Milbank, Mark 290
Marke 288
Milcombe, Ann 133
Miles, Abigail 520
  Alice 523
  Amanda M. 522
  Ann 517, 523
  Bridget Edwards 522
  Catharine D. 522
  Catherine 521
  Dafydd 523
  David 517, 519, 523
  Edwin 521, 522
  Eliza M. 521
  Emma 521
  Enos 520
  Evan 520
  George Baugh 522
  George K. 517
  George Keiter 522
  Griffith 252, 442, 517, 519, 522, 523
  Hannah 520, 521
  Hannah Jones 521
  Hannah Pugh 520
  Hester 522
  Jacob 521
  James 517, 518, 519, 520, 521, 522, 523
  Jane 519, 520
  Joan 519
  Joanna 520
  John 520, 521, 523
  Joseph 521
  Lewis 522
  Margaret 517, 519, 522, 523
  Martha 252, 522

Miles, Martha Frame 522
  Mary 520, 521
  Mary Frick 521
  Nathaniel 521, 522
  Capt. Nathaniel 521
  Owen Philips 522
  Phebe 518, 519, 523
  Rebekah 521
  Richard 517, 518, 519, 520, 521, 522, 523
  Ruth 518, 519, 520
  Samuel 517, 518, 519, 521, 522, 523
  Sarah 519, 520, 521, 522, 523
  Sarah Elizabeth 522
  Sarah Evans 520
  Sarah Philips 521
  Susan Evans Jones 522
  Tamar 518, 519, 520
  Thamer 518
Mill, Martin 659
Millard, (?) 232, 666
  Elizabeth 666
  Jonathan 666
  Mary 666
  Rachel 666
  Thomas 666
  William 230
Miller, (?) 707
  Abner 882
  Benjamin 882
  Elizabeth 645, 646
  George 893
  Hannah 882
  John 872
  John B. 709
  John William 646
  Joseph 882
  Laura 659
  Louisa 342
  Martha 659
  Martin 659
  Mary 646, 882
  Pamela 882
  Rebecah 882
  Ruth 882
  William 471
Milles, Henry 224
Millner, Anne 226
Mills, Capt. 195
Milnor, Isaac 71
  William 653
Mils, Als 523
Min'r, Robt. Row 881
  Will'm 880
Miner, Asher 423
Mines, Addison 681
  Flavel Scott 681
  Rev. John 681
  Rev. Thomas Joseph Addison 681
Minnemeyer, Elizabeth 628
Minshall, Christopher 562
  Geffrey 566
  Wm. 566
Mires, Joseph 350
Mitchell, John 258
  Rev. John 823
  Matilda 258
Moare, Mary 562
Moltke-Whitfield, Count 454
Mompresson, Judge 150
Monck, Gen. 197
Monk, Gen. 208
  Col. George 191

Monsier, Hance 703
Montgomery, Gen. 868
  Henry 408
  J. 666
  Rev. James 794
  John 666
  John Teakle 794
  William 808
Moode, Elizabeth 860
  William 860
Mooglandt, Belitije 845
Moon, James 60
  Moses 61
  Paul 628
Moor, John 326
Moore, Barbara 806
  Dr. Charles 423
  Edward 272
  James 810, 817
  John 218, 562, 635
  Mary 453, 562
  Milcah Martha Hill 423
  Richard 818
Moray, Andrew de 389
Morcock, Capt. Edward 200
More, Dr. Nicholas 238
Morgan, (?) 667, 778
  Rev. Abel 520
  Ann 473
  Anne W. 790
  Cadwallader 535
  Charles Waln 792
  Hannah 107, 656
  Mary 649
  William 107, 485
Moriarty, G. Andrews 762
Morison, Sir Alex 881
  Bessie 881
  Bethiah 881
  Helenor 881
  Kath'n 881
  Nicholas 881
  Robert 881
  Sr. 881
  Wm. 881
Morress, Steven 871
Morris, (?) 867
  Gov. 326
  Mrs. 503
  Anthony 458, 844, 867
  Benjamin 867
  Catherine 882
  Daniel 458, 540, 789
  Deborah 844, 867
  Elizabeth 448, 867, 882, 883
  Ellin 483
  Ellis 284, 533
  Gulielma Maria 844
  Israel 458, 459, 867
  James 867
  John 458, 459, 483, 844, 867
  Joseph 867
  Lizzie P. 493
  Luke 697
  Margaret 284
  Mrs. Margaret Hill 844
  Mary 844, 867
  Phoebe 867
  Reese 882
  Richard Hill 844
  Robert 644
  Samuel 782, 867
  Sarah 867
  Susanna 867
  Thomas 867
Morris, William 844
Morrison, William 900
Morrons, John 811
Morse, Mary Trumbull 898
Mortemer, Lady Jeanne de 185
Mortimer, Earle 574
Morton/Marton
  (?) 525
  Amy 529
  Andrew 527, 528, 529
  Ann 529
  Ann Robinson 529
  Anna 528
  Anne 527
  Bennet 224
  Christiana 528
  Cornelius 528
  Eamy 529
  Eleanor 529
  Elizabeth 528, 529
  George 528, 529
  Hannah 529
  Helen Kirkbride 42
  John 526, 528
  Jonas 528
  Lawrence 526
  Marton 527
  Mary 529
  Mathias 528
  Morton 525, 528
  Sarah 528
  Susanna 528
Mortonson/Martonson
  Andrew 525, 526, 527, 528
  Bridget 526, 527
  Catherine 527
  Christianna 527
  David 526
  Jacob 526
  John 526, 527, 528
  Lace 525
  Lawrence 527
  Lydia 528
  Margaret 526
  Marton 525, 526, 527, 528
  Mary 527
  Mathias 525, 526, 527, 528
  Morton 525, 527
  Peter 527
  Tobias 527
Mossell, Caroline 831
Moth, Richard 562
Mott, Asher 860
  Gershom 860
  Sarah 860
Moulson, Deborah 803, 804, 805
  Dinah 803
  Edward Williams 803
  Ellen Mary 805
  Ellen Mary Lalanne 803, 804, 805
  Francis Edward 804
  John 803, 804, 805
  Sam'l 803
  Sarah Williams 803, 804, 805
Mount, Jeremy 617
Moxam, Thos. 594
Moyer, Abanton 343
  Emma 343
  F. Rader 343
  Jane 343
  John 343
  Mary 343
Moyer, Oliver 343
  Sarah 343
  Thomas 343
Muffly, Peter 335, 337, 338, 344
Muhlenberg, (?) 461
Muir, (?) 405
  Hannah Glen 405
Mullin, Eli 656
  John 656
  Lydia 656
Munden, Richard 556
Mur, (?) 405
  Hannah Glen 405
Murphy, Dannell 230
Murray, Maj.-Gen. 880
  Bethiah 880
  Humphrey 107
  James 880
  Sir James 880
  John E. 858
  Sir Patrick 880
  Sir Robert 880
Musgrave, Charlotte 787
  Israel 791
  Mrs. Rachel 779
  Rachel McCulloch 791
Musgrove, Thomas 117
Myers, Albert Cook 183, 217, 220, 250, 382 903
Mynne, ffrancys 558
Nannacus, Indian 134
Nansicles, Mary 768
  William 768
Nansiglas, Mary 768
  William 768
Nase, Robert 390
Nash, Anna Maria 422, 425
Nashe, John 601
Nasshe, William 552
Naws, Edward 847
Naylor, Hannah 111
Nealson, John 375
Neelig, John Paul 324
Neeson, John H. 251
Neff, Maria 657, 659
Neidly, John C. 875
Neill, Rev. Edward D. 149
Neip, Agatha 839
  Christine 839
  John 839
Nelson, Henry 59, 117
  Rich. 290
Nenemblahocking, Indian 134
Nesbitt, Alexander 898
  J. M. 898
  John Maxwell 880
Ness, Henry 391
  John de 391
Nevill, Francis 297, 298
Neville, Francis 287
  Sarah 286
Newbery, Capt. 202
Newbie, Bartholomew 374
  Mark 46
Newbold, Caroline 793
  Hannah 855
  James 855
Newbury, Ann 473, 474
Newby, Henry 372
  Katherine 369
  Mark 2
  Miles 371, 372
  Randall 371, 373
  Richard 369, 371, 372
Newcomb, Thomas 490, 655, 656, 895

Newdigate, Isabella 761
  John 760
  Nathaniel 761
Newell, Stephen 414
Newlin, Nich. 142
Newman, David 511
  Richard 573
Nicholas, Wm. 224
Nicholls, Tho. 571
Nichols, Gen. Francis 649
  Harriet 649
Nicholson, Charles 361
  Isabel 381
  John 65
  Mary 361, 364
  Nehemiah 871
Nick, William 767
Niles, Hezekiah 545
Nitschman, Maria 465
Nixon, George 827
  John 901
  Mary 901
  Rebecca 827, 828
Noah, mulatto 51
Noble, Abel 115
  Isaac 716, 717
  John 716, 717
  Katherine 679
  Mary 716, 717
  Temple R. 497
Norman, Anne 883
  Annes 883
  Anthony 564
  Eliza 883
  John 883
  John B. 883
  John Bennett 883
  Joshua L. 883
  Mariam 883
  Mariam B. 883
  Mary 883
  Mills R. 883
  Patience 883
  Purnal 883
  Purnell 883
  Thomas 883
  Thomas L. Judge 883
  Thomas R. 883
Norrell, James 643
  Jane 643
Norris, Elizabeth 857
  Isaac 241, 442, 574, 696
  Susanna 857
North, A. W. 545
Norwood, (?) 664
  John 664
Nugent, Ellen G. 788, 797
Nunes, John 686
  Mary 686
Nunez, Mrs. 847
  Daniel 847
  Mary 847
Nutt, Anna 647
  Samuel 647
Oakham, (?) 445
Oallyver, Wyllym 608
O'Brien, Elizabeth S. 874
  Maria 181
Ocker, John 314
Ogden, Ann 545
  David 545
  Hannah 544, 545, 772
  Hannah Owen 773
  John 542, 544, 773
  Joseph 545
  Marie 545

Ogden, Robert Wharton 545·
  Ruth 843
  Samuel G. 710
  William 544, 545
Ogier, Louisa Perine 790
Ogilvy, Margaret Glen 393
  Walter 394
  Sir Walter 393
Okeford, Tomson 608
Okey, Col. 209
Oldman, Jane 801
  Thomas 801
Olivent, Cathrin 808
Oliver, James 203
  John 304
  Elder Thomas 203
Onderdonck, Bishop H. M. 825
O'Neill, Kathleen 832
Orchard, Sara 560, 600
  Thos. 560, 600
Orecton, Indian 134
Ormsby, Catherine 884
  Edward 884
  Eleanor 884
  George 884
  Henry 884
  John 884
  Margaret 884
  Oliver 796
  Oliveretta 796
  Sarah 796, 884
  William 884
Orr, Mr. 398
  Sir Andrew 398
Orton, Edgar Marshall de 493
  George 883
  George de 493
  George Herbert de 493
  Hannah 883
  William 883
Osborn, Ann 884, 885, 901
  Elizabeth Priscilla 884, 885
  Fraser Mathews 884
  George 884, 885
  George Lucas 884, 885
  George Renaudet 884
  James 884
  Jane 884, 885
  Jane Frances 884
  John A. 885
  John Adrian 885
  Mary Grace 884
  Peter James 884
  Robert 884
  Russel Lillie 885
  Sabella 885
Osborne, Gen. 262
  Ann 62
  Elias 631
  Jane 885
Oswald, Edward 560
O'Syell, Donatus 813
Otto, Dr. Bode 462
Ottor, John 140
Overholt, Jennie C. 522
Owen, Agnes verch 284
  Anne 540
  Aurelius 539
  Edward 531
  Elin 532
  Elizabeth 535, 536, 540, 541

Owen, Esther 539
  Evan 531, 532, 533, 534, 535, 536, 538, 539, 541, 542
  Gainor 532, 535, 536, 539
  Gainor John 531
  George 541
  Griffith 157
  Dr. Griffith 418, 531, 536
  Hannah541, 542, 543, 544
  Sir Hugh 283, 284
  Humphrey 534
  Jane 531, 532, 536, 540, 541
  Jane verch 283, 284
  John 534, 535, 536, 538, 540, 541, 542
  Joshua 247, 248, 534, 535
  Lewis 531, 533
  Lewis ap 283
  Margaret 247, 248, 284
  Martha 247, 248, 539
  Mary 542
  Mary Hoskins 539
  Owen 531, 535, 536, 540, 541, 542
  Rachel 542
  Rebecca 531, 532, 533, 534, 536, 537, 538, 539, 540, 541
  Rebecka 247
  Robert 530, 531, 532, 533, 534, 535, 536, 538, 539, 540, 541, 542, 543, 773
  Robert ap 284
  Rowland 533, 534
  Sarah 540
  Susanna 541, 542, 543
  Susannah 774
  Tacey 540
Owens, Charles Beland 268
  Elizabeth Crispin 268
  Elizabeth Norris 268
  Helen Jean Crispin 268
  Magdalen 489
  Margaret Crispin 268
  Theodoric 268
Oxenden, Lady 622
Oxford, Earl of 574
Padgett, Francis 87
  John 87
  Thomas 379
Padgot, Lydia 100
Page, Jane E. 796
  Josephine O. 796
  Michael 561
Painter, Susanna 853
  Susannah 537
Paisley, John, Abbott of 397
  Robert, Abbott of 395, 396
Palmer, Anthony 477, 845
  Ellen 363
  Emily B. 363
  Jane 845
  John 878
  Gen. John G. 363
  Sarah 342
  Thomasine 477
Pamantur, Nicholas 813
  Thomas 813
Pancoast, Joseph 350

Pancoast, Mary 350
  Sarah 61, 83
  Susannah 83
Pargiter, Frances 742
  Theodore 748
Parker, Mrs. 882
  Alexander 624
  Elizabeth 580
  Emma 834
  John 580
  Lieut. Robert 341
  Sarah 899
Parkinson, Richard 380
Parrish, Dr. Joseph 853
  Susan D. 793
Parrys, (?) 443
Parsley, William 551
Parson, Thomas 224
  William 697
Parsons, Ann 224, 887
  Henry 630
  Thomas 101, 224
  Wm. 326
Partridge, Jeane 623
Paschall, (?) 675
  Benjamin 672
  Margaret 671
  Mary Say 672
  Samuel 671
  Thomas 671, 672
  William 671
Passage, Adelaide C. 788
  Adelaide Charlotte 797
  John 797
  Mary 797
Pastorius, Francis Daniel 878
  Sam'l Dan'l 878
Patchet, Elizabeth 98
Patsching, Alice 224
  Resta 224
  Thomas 224
Pateluna, Indian 134
Paterson, Emily 882
  Nath. 808
Paton, Robert 405
Patrick, Anna Dunklin 647
  Esther 647
  John 647, 648
  Mary 649
  Samuel 647
Patterson, Catherine 343
  Mary 645
Pattison, Mrs. 503
Paul, Josiah 55
  Mary 55
  Sydney 795
Paulin, Willoch 871
Pawley, George 56
  Mary Janney 56
  Sarah 40, 56
Pawling, (?) 797
  Elizabeth Drinker 856
  William 15, 44, 134
Payne, (?) 272
  Sarah 272
Paynter, Albert J. 886
  Alfred Stockley 824
  Eliza 822, 824
  Elizabeth 824
  Jane 886
  John Parker 824
  Mary 824
  Samuel 823, 824
  Samuel Rowland 824
  Sarah 824
  Wm. 886

Peale, Charles Wilson 452
Pearman, Anne 553
  Anthony 553
  Hugh 553
  Jane 553
  John 553
  Mary 553
  Nicholas 553
Pearson, Elizabeth 115
  Margery Smith 902
  Sarah 902
  Thomas 902
Peart, Benjamin 660, 662, 666
  Bryan 662, 663, 666
  Edmond 665
  Elizabeth 663, 666
  Jane 662
  John 665
  Margaret 662
  Mary 660, 661, 663
  Rachel 661, 662, 663, 666
  Ralph 662
  Rebecca 666
  Thomas 663, 665, 666
  William 662, 663, 665
Peasley, Elizabeth 836
  Jonathan 836
Peckham, George 551
  Marie 551
  Mary 551
Peebles, Symon de 389
Peen, Robert 605
  Steeven 605
Peene, Henry 570
  Johane 559
  Thomas 559, 561
  William 561
Peine, Thomas 592
Peirse, Joan Chudleigh 212
  Martin 212
Pelham, Sir Thomas, Bart. 306
Pemberton, John 55
  Phineas 76, 80, 131, 143, 145, 155, 156, 158
  Phinehas 15, 35
Pen. See Penn.
Pene. See Penn.
Penefold, Thos. 224
Penington, Edward 98
Penn/Pen/Pene/Penne.
  (?) 189, 207, 208, 209, 210, 216, 220, 584, 592, 621, 638
  Admiral 190, 199, 200, 202, 207, 215, 593, 608
  Ensign 213
  Gen. 203, 204, 207
  Mr. 214
  Vice Admiral 191
  Widow 586
  Abigall 606
  Adam 553
  Agnes 552, 558, 577, 586, 592, 600
  Agnet 592
  Agnis 585, 607
  Ales 590
  Alice 549, 552, 553, 568, 573, 579, 586, 587, 590, 593, 594
  Alys 589
  Amy 587

Penn, Ann 558, 559, 567, 585, 589, 597, 604, 617
  Anna 588, 590, 591
  Anne 558, 559, 563, 564, 565, 566, 570, 571, 573, 577, 579, 590, 591, 596, 598, 601
  Annys 607
  Anthonie 616
  Anthony 552, 553, 557, 591, 598, 608
  Antony 598
  Arthur 565
  Aubrey 575, 618
  Barbara 553
  Bartholomew 615
  Beate 579
  Bridget 558
  Bridgett 577, 601
  Catherine 559, 574, 586, 597
  Cecylly 598
  Chevall 572
  Christian 557, 560, 561, 563, 585, 600
  Christiana 600
  Christina Gulielma 620
  Cicely 567, 586
  Cisley 552
  Constance 558, 567
  Daniel 584
  Daniell 585
  David 548, 551, 552
  Dennis 618
  Dorathe 616
  Doritey 586
  Dorothie 558
  Dorothy 557, 579, 615
  Dorothye 551
  Edey 586
  Edith 586, 588
  Edmond 592
  Edmund 553, 567, 582
  Edw. 602
  Edward 551, 552, 557, 558, 564, 565, 567, 577, 606, 615
  Edwardus 592
  Eleanor 558, 568, 597
  Elen 551
  Elinor 604, 607
  Eliz. 553, 576, 596
  Eliz'th 577
  Elizabeth 551, 558, 559, 564, 566, 567, 568, 569, 570, 573, 578, 579, 580, 582, 585, 586, 587, 588, 589, 595, 596, 598, 599, 600, 601, 614, 615, 616, 618
  Elizabeth Catherine 583
  Ellen 569
  Ellenor 584, 585
  Ellianor 578
  Ellinora 601
  Elnor 590
  Frances 567
  Francis 547, 553, 557, 558, 564, 567, 568, 578, 582
  Gabriel 569
  George 212, 556, 565, 572, 578, 580, 588, 595, 597, 599, 606, 613, 617

Penn, Georgii 599
  Gervase 566, 578
  Gilbert 552, 553, 558, 568, 582
  Giles 242, 554, 566, 569, 574, 578, 590, 597
  Capt. Giles 189
  Gilles 608
  Grace 559, 579
  Granville 202, 620
  Gregory 584, 585
  Griffyth 557
  Gualteri 591
  Gulielma 604
  Gulielma Maria 223, 224, 573, 575, 603, 604, 621
  Gulielmi 583, 590, 591
  Gulielmus 590, 591
  Gyles 551, 597
  Hanna 618, 619, 628
  Hannae 576
  Hannah 574, 580, 602, 604, 626, 627
  Hannah Margerita 602
  Henrietta 573, 574, 583
  Henry 552, 553, 558, 559, 564, 565, 570, 578, 591, 593, 594, 608
  Hester 585, 605
  Humfrey 579
  Humphrey 553, 567, 612
  Isabell 618
  Isabella 594, 599
  Jacob 561, 586
  James 579, 581, 586, 606, 617
  Jane 585, 596, 608
  Janet 588
  Jean 586
  Joan 605
  Joane 557, 558, 571, 588, 594, 617
  Joanna 599
  Joanne 595
  Johan 557
  Johane 605
  Johanna 552, 598
  Johannis 583
  John 441, 547, 548, 549, 550, 551, 552, 553, 557, 560, 561, 563, 564, 565, 566, 567, 568, 570, 571, 577, 578, 583, 584, 585, 586, 587, 589, 590, 591, 592, 593, 594, 595, 598, 599, 601, 605, 606, 607, 608, 612, 614, 615, 617, 618, 619, 620, 626, 627, 628
  Jonathan 568, 573
  Jone 584, 586, 589, 590, 605, 607, 608
  Joseph 614
  Joyce 597
  Judith 571, 580
  Julian 553, 557, 560, 567
  Juliana 584, 620
  Lady Juliana 620
  Julyan 552
  Katherine 579, 581, 605, 607, 611
  Laetitia 223, 224

Penn, Lawrence 560, 563
  Letitia 621
  Lewce 550
  Lucy 551
  Magdalen 558, 563
  Margaret 549, 553, 554, 555, 557, 558, 559, 563, 564, 567, 580, 587, 588, 602, 603, 608, 612, 613, 615, 618, 626, 627
  Dame Margaret 571, 573, 613
  Margaret Gilbert 572
  Margaret Rastall 593
  Margarete 590
  Margarett 568
  Margerie 558
  Margery 559, 571, 590, 597
  Marg't 577
  Maria 591
  Mariar 587
  Marie 554, 568, 594
  Marke 579
  Martha 553, 557, 573, 583, 603, 606
  Martha Elizabeth 574
  Mary 549, 552, 558, 566, 567, 568, 572, 573, 574, 587, 589, 590, 594, 596, 600, 601, 603, 614, 615, 631
  Marye 550, 604
  Mathew 558, 571, 584, 585
  Mattha 597
  Matthew 578
  Matthias 565
  Mercy 608
  Michael 557, 559, 579, 586, 614, 617
  Nathaniel 565, 590
  Nicholas 607
  Oliver 573
  Oswald 553, 558, 568, 574, 579
  Paul 578
  Peter 565, 599
  Philipe 585
  Phylyp 582
  Rachel 189, 242, 616
  Rachell 272, 597
  Ralph 547, 549, 593, 594, 599
  Raufe 549
  Richard 441, 550, 553, 557, 559, 560, 561, 563, 566, 571, 572, 573, 577, 580, 582, 584, 585, 586, 587, 591, 596, 599, 601, 602, 605, 607, 612, 613, 614, 615, 618, 619, 620
  Richardus 591
  Robert 551, 557, 558, 562, 563, 566, 567, 568, 569, 571, 587, 589, 598, 600, 614, 615
  Roger 550, 553, 574, 583, 593, 606
  Rose 600
  Samuel 571, 578, 590, 600, 616
  Sara 554, 606
  Sarah 564, 568, 571,

(Penn, Sarah)
  572, 573, 574, 585, 589, 605
  Sarra 591
  Sibel Hampden 548
  Sibell 564
  Sibill 578
  Simon 568
  Sophia 620
  Springett 223, 224, 575, 603, 604, 620, 621
  Stephen 580, 608
  Susan 593
  Susanna 554, 578, 616
  Sybyll 590
  Tamson 606
  Thomas 233, 441, 547, 549, 550, 551, 552, 557, 558, 559, 560, 563, 564, 565, 566, 567, 568, 571, 572, 573, 576, 577, 578, 579, 580, 584, 585, 587, 588, 590, 591, 592, 593, 594, 595, 596, 600, 601, 602, 603, 605, 607, 608, 611, 614, 616, 617, 618, 619, 620, 627
  Tompson 608
  Ursula 553, 561, 562, 565
  Walter 569, 604
  Wenifrante 585
  Willia 597
  William 43, 46, 61, 79, 90, 91, 98, 104, 113, 115, 129, 132, 133, 135, 138, 139, 145, 146, 147, 150, 151, 152, 154, 155, 183, 189, 190, 212, 213, 215, 216, 217, 218, 219, 220, 222, 224, 225, 226, 227, 228, 230, 232, 234, 235, 236, 237, 238, 239, 243, 430, 457, 525, 546, 547, 548, 549, 551, 552, 553, 554, 555, 556, 557, 558, 559, 560, 564, 565, 566, 567, 568, 570, 571, 572, 573, 574, 575, 577, 578, 579, 580, 581, 583, 584, 585, 588, 589, 590, 591, 592, 593, 594, 595, 596, 598, 599, 601, 602, 603, 604, 606, 607, 608, 611, 613, 614, 615, 618, 619, 620, 621, 622, 626, 627, 628, 631, 637, 661, 696, 700, 799, 800, 867
  Admiral William 210
  Admiral Sir William 186, 187, 188, 189, 588, 592
  Ensign William 212, 213, 226
  Gov. William 51
  Lady William 190
  Sir William 184, 190, 212, 571, 572, 573, 597, 613
  Willm's 592

Penn, Wyllim 607
  Wyllyam 590, 608
  Wyllym 608
  Zackary 566
Penne. See Penn.
Pennirgton, Ann 163
  Edward 163, 164, 621
  Elizabeth 877
  Isaac 164, 620, 622
  James 622
  John 621, 622
  Martha 877
  Mary 163, 618, 620, 621
  Sara 622
  Sarah 163
  Sarah Jennings 164
  William 621
Penrose, Capt. 195, 198
Peper, Rubin 121
Pepys, Samuel 190, 214, 428
Percival, Sarah 635
Percy, Capt. Hugh 864
Perel, William 390
Perrin, Susanna 618
Perrott, Humfrey 615
  William 615
Perry, Bridgett 629
  Jane 877
Persevell, Jane 631
Peter, Anna 886
  Elizabeth 886
  George 841
  John 886
  John Benedict 886
  Rudolph 886
Peters, (?) 685
  James 627
  Ralph 684
  Rev. Richard 620
Petersilia, Nannie 268
Peterson, Judge 882
  Magdalen 704, 710
  Samuel 527
Pettit, Charles 648
Petty, Elizabeth 128
Peyton, Gerrard 721
Philipp, Rich. 560
Philips, Elizabeth 523
  Sarah 521
Phillip, Rich. 561
Phillips, Elizabeth 888
  Hester 847
  Mercy 438
Phillipse, Charlotte Elizabeth 355
  Frederick 355
Philpott, Thomas 562
Phipp, Gulielmo 576
Physick, Dr. 860
  Emlen 867
  Philip 867
  Philip S. 867
  Philip Syng 860
Pickering, Col. 444
  Thomas 789
Pickett, Anne 859
  Geo. 859
Pierce, Charles 681
  Joan 212
  Martin 232
  Mercy 853
Piersol, Alice 635
  John 635
  Sarah 635
Pierson, Aaron 886
  Benjamin 886
  Charles Edwin 887

Pierson, Clarissa 887
  Daniel 886, 887
  Daniel Waring 887
  Elijah 886
  Elizabeth Ann 887
  Ellen W. 887
  Henry A. 887
  Henry Alexander 887
  John 886
  John Alfred 887
  Keziah 886
  Moses 886
  Patience 886
  Sarah 886
  Susan B. 858
  William Horace 887
Pike, Ebenezer 226, 228
  Ebinezer 226
  John 550
Pill, William 742
Pillerne, Joanne 624
Pine, Joshua 836
  Judith 715
  William 715
Piner, Susannah 224
Pinkerton, Ann 408
Pinnell, Jeoffrey 627
Pinner, Sarah 850
Pinniard, Marie 544
Piper, Mary Ann 831
Pitts, John 813
Platts, Benjamin Keen 633, 634
  David 632, 633, 634
  David R. 633
  David Rittenhouse 634
  Eleanor 632, 634
  Jane 633
  Jesse Keen 632, 633, 634
  Jonas Keen 633, 634
  Jonathan 632, 633
  Jonathan J. 633
  Jonathan Jarman 634
  Letita 632
  Lettitia 633, 634
  Lettitia Gilman 634
  Moses 634
  Rachel 633, 634
  Rebecca 633
  Rebekah 634
  Sarah 633
  Tabitha 633
Playcer, Anne 551
Pleasants, Ann 863
  Israel 863
  Joseph 795
  Mary 795
  Samuel 795, 863
Plumley, Charles 416
Plumly, John 118
Plumsted, Clement 455
  Mary 455
  Rebecca 454, 455
  Thos. 455
Pococke, Marg't 577
Polk, Elizabeth 488
  Ephraim 488
  Mary 488
Pooke, James 624
Poole, Capt. Jonas 200
Pope, Col. 721, 749
  Lieut.-Col. 722
  Ann 718, 721
  Rev. Charles H. 608
  John 628, 631
  Col. Nathaniel 718, 728, 729, 753
  Lieut.-Col. Nathaniel 721

Pope, Thomas 723, 735
  William 631
Popley, Edmund 623, 624
Poree, Chanoine 270
Porter, Diana 306
  George 303, 306
  Hezekiah 635
  James 635
  Gov. James D. 634
  John 634, 635
  Joseph 635
  Mary 635
  Mary Stanley 634
  Nathaniel 634, 635
  Samuel 634
  Samuell 635
  William 634, 635
Potter, Damaris 568
  Francis 568
  Mary 872
Potts, James 667
  Martha 652
  Samuel 667
  Syacy 81
  Thomas 78, 79, 81, 877
  Thomas Maxwell 451, 667, 869
Pounal, Reuben 78
Powel, Sarah 877
Powell, Abigail 867, 887
  Ann 887
  Benjamin 900
  Deborah 887
  Fortune 566
  John 284, 520
  Mary 867
  Samuel 642, 867, 887
  Sarah 867, 887
Power, (?) 548
  Alice 595
  Zacharias 595
Powle, Thos. 594
Powlett, William, Earl 574
Pownall, Eleanor 155
  Hannah 438
  Mary 47
  Reuben 78
Pratt, Experience 513
Pressmall, Robert 243
Preston, (?) 539
  Ann 453
  Henry 453
  Jane 453
  Matt. 614
  Prescilla 453
  Samuel 574
  Thomas 65
  William 453
Prewed, Lady 622
  Sir John 622
Price, Abigail 449, 450, 451
  Ann 450, 635
  Ann Husband 451
  Aves 842
  Bennitt 859
  David 449, 450, 451, 522, 836
  David Elisha 450
  Edward 589
  Eli K. 251
  Eli Kirk 250
  Eliza 847
  Elizabeth 872
  Ellenor 612
  Esther 842
  James 842
  John 449, 451

Price, Joseph 888
  Judith 859
  M. James 842
  Margaret 624
  Margery 450
  Mary 450, 451, 635, 842, 888
  Ruth 842
  Samuel 627
  Sarah 888
  Thomas 635
  William 450, 842
Prichett, Brazilla 888
  Jacob 888
  Josiah 888
  Zachariah 888
Prickett, Ann 889
  John 888
  Josiah 888
Prickitt, Ann 889
  Edmond 889
  Edmund D. 889
  Edward D. 889
  Ellen Virginia 889
  Jacob 889
  Joseph 889
  Josiah 888, 889
  Mary 889
  Mary C. 888, 889
  Rachel 889
  Rachel B. 889
  Rachel L. 889
  Wilkins 889
  William L. 889
  Zachariah 889
Pride, Lieut. 200
Priest, Robert 631
Prince, Robert 231
Prioleau, Mrs. 882
Prior, Edward 224
Prismall, Robert 245
Pritchett, Diana 888
Procter, Thomas 88, 93
Proude, Sir John 622
Prouden, Sir John 593
Provoost, David 716
  Margaret 716
Pryor, Norton 876
  Polly 876
Puckle, Nathaniel 146
Pue, Rebecca Ann 680
Pugh, Catharine 520
  David 520
  Ellis 484
  Evan 486
  Hannah 520
  Jonathan 520
  Mary 521
  Sarah 520
Pulley, Bernarde 379
Pulteney, (?) 689, 690
Pumphrey, Walter 77
Puppen, Mary 885
Purcell, George 613
  John 442, 443
  Wynefred 613
Purchase, Jane 569
Pursell, Jonathan 410
  Lydia 411
Pyle, Mary 787
  Thomas 575, 576
Quare, Daniel 109
Quercy, (?) 377
  Sarah 377
Quicksall, Jonathan 350
Radcliff, Alice
  Jacobo 73
  James 74
Radcliffe, Alan Fenwick 302

Radcliffe, Alice 72, 74, 75, 415
  Edward 33, 40, 68, 71, 76, 77, 116, 415
  Isabel 74
  James 33, 41, 68, 71, 72, 74, 75, 76, 77, 115, 117, 415
  John 68, 72, 77, 115, 117, 415
  Martha 77
  Mary 71, 75
  Mary Rawsthorne 72
  Phebe 39, 40, 71
  Phebe Baker 68, 116
  Rachel 77, 415
  Rebecca 33, 68, 77, 415
  Rebecca West 68
  Richard 72, 73, 74, 76, 77, 415
Radcliffes, (?) 32
Radford, John 614
Radys, Mr. 598
Rae, Robert 805
Robt. M. C. 805
Raffe, Mr. 598
Raguet, Anna 889, 890
  Catherine 890
  Claudine 889, 890
  Claudius Paul 891
  Henry 890
  James 890, 891
  James Condy 890
  James Michael 889
  Mercy Ann 890
  Michael 889
  Nicholas 891
  Susannah 890
  Wm. H. 890
Rakestraw, William 370, 836
Ralfe, George 601
Ralston, Robert 545
Ramsay, Rev. 597
  George, Earl of Dalhousie 402
  Robert 818
  Samuel 818
Randall, Alexander 704
Randolph, Dr. Jacob 867
Ratcliffe, Edward 75
  James 75
  Mary 75
  Rachel 75
  Rebecca 75
  Richard 75
Ratcliff, James 75
Ratcliffe, James 74
Rauellsion, Thomas 173
Rawle, Francis 781
  Margaret 773, 781
  Rebekah 449
  Robert Turner 449
  William 476, 700, 794
  William Hudson 449
Rawsthorne, Widow 74, 75
  Edward 75
  John 74
  Mary 72, 75
  Nicholas 74
Rawthorn, Lawrence 74
Rawthorp, Mary 72
Rawthorpe, Mary 415
Rea, William 298
Read, Rev. Dr. 872
Reading, John 441
  Susanna 575
Reball, John 565

Redd, Christiana 773, 774
Reder, John 335, 336, 337, 344
Redinge, Elizabeth 591
Redstone, Vincent B. 768
Redwood, Hannah 773, 780
  Hannah Holmes 780
  William 780
Reed, Pres. 332
  John 818
  Joseph 474
  Lieut. Timothy 331
Reeder, William C. 250
Rees, (?) 283
  Ed. 799
  Edward 535, 798
  Ellis ap 283, 284
  Evan 533
  Hugh 533
  John 470
  Lewis ap 283
Reich, Christian 841
Reichel, Rev. W. C. 457
Reichert, Johann Frederick 641
Reigart, Catherine S. 658
  John 658
Reily, Doc. 418
  John 818
Reiss, Zachariah 891
Reitzell, Capt. John 317
Renaudet, James 845
  Jane 884
  Mary 845
Rench, M. 667, 669
Reubary, Michael 327
Revell, Thomas 94
Rewell, Jane 561
Reynar, Elizabeth 229
Reynolds, H. E. 422
  Capt. John 346
  William 635
Rhiem, Mary Hilligas 874
Rhoads, James 541
  Mary 863
  Samuel 863
Rhodes, Samuel 697
  William T. 358
Riale, John 107
  Martha 107
Rice, Anna Mariah 891
  Benjamin 891
  Betsy 891
  Catharine 891
  Conrad 891
  Elizabeth 891
  George 891
  Henry 891
  Jacob 891
  John 891
  Margaret 891
  Mary 891
  Peter 891
  Polly 891
  Sallie 891
  Susan 891
  Zachariah 891
Rich, Garrett 230
  Sarah 363
Richard, Lidia 656
  Margaret 656
  Richard ap 638
  Roland 656
  Samuel 656
Richards, (?) 654
  Abigail 649, 655
  Abijah 655
  Anna Maria 650

Richards, Augustus Henry 650
  B. W. 651
  Benjamin Wood 650, 652
  Catherin 655
  Catherine 655, 656
  Charles 650
  Charles Henry 650
  Ebenezer 655, 656
  Edward 642
  Eli 655, 656
  Elizabeth 639, 642, 643, 646, 650, 652, 655
  Frederick 646
  Gainor 656
  George 641
  George Washington 650
  Guenlyon 639
  Hannah 646, 655
  James 639, 640, 641, 642, 643, 644, 645, 874
  Jesse 649, 650, 652
  John 639, 641, 645, 646, 649, 656
  John S. 646
  Joseph 638, 650
  Joseph Ball 650
  Josuah 655
  Lydia 655, 656
  Margaret 643, 645
  Margaret Wood 650
  Mark 641
  Mary 643, 644, 646, 655, 656
  Mary Patrick 649
  Mary Wood 650
  Matthias 641
  Judge Matthias S. 641
  Nathaniel 638
  Owen 637, 639, 640, 641, 642, 643, 644, 646
  Philip 639
  Rebecca 650
  Rowland, 639, 642, 655
  Ruth 643, 644, 645
  Samuel 649, 655
  Sarah 641, 643, 645, 646, 655
  Sarah Ball 649
  Sitnah 656
  Solomon 638
  Stephen 716
  Susannah 642, 655
  Thomas 637, 639, 650
  Thomas Haskins 652
  Thomas S. 649
  Townsend 655
  William 639, 641, 642, 643, 645, 646, 647, 649, 650
Richardson, Elizabeth 77 773, 780
  Francis 31, 106, 697
  Mary 541
  Rebecca 697
  Samuel 541, 772, 773
Riche, Thomas 26
Richeson, Joanna 616
Rickards, Geo. 124
  Patience 124
Rideout, Nicholas 241
Ridgaway, Josiah 892
Ridgway, Ann 795
  Barzillai 892
  Beaula 892
Ridgway, Caleb 892
  Daniell 892
  Elizabeth 844
  Freedom 892
  Hephzibah 892
  Hepzibah 892
  James 844
  Lott 892
  Mary Oldden 844
  Rebecca Ann 844
  Richard 80, 246, 892
  Samuel 892
  Sarah 892
  Susanna 892
  Susannah 892
Rieger, Barbara 864
Riess, Rev. John Jacob 323
Rigg, James 373
Rigge, James 373
Riggs, Caleb S. 341
Rightmeyer, Susan 182
Righton, Elizabeth 617
  Frances 56
Ring, Hannah 482
  Lydia Vernon 482
  Nathaniel 482
Rishton, Jas. 74
Risley, Sarah A. 120
Ritchie, Craig 451
Roach, ffrancis 631
  Mary 879
  Sarah 631
Roades, Amphillis 743, 759
  John 737, 743, 744
  Mary Futcher 358
  Wm. 358, 744, 749
Roads, Jacob 642
Robbens. See Robbins.
Robbins/Robbens
  (?) 158
  David 123
  Eleazer 122
  Elezar 123
  Emily 903
  John 120, 122, 123
  John Bedant 120
  Levi 123
  Lidya 123
  Mary 120, 123, 160
  Molly 123
  Rachel 120
  Richard 123
  Ruth 121
  Samuel 174
  Sarah 123
  Temperance 122, 123
  William 160
Robens, John 121
  Rachel 121
Roberdeau, (?) 700
  Ann Judith 180, 181
  Daniel 700
  Isaac 181, 681
  Robert II, D. of Normandy 184, 185
Robert/Robt
  Elin verch 284
  Griffit 533
  Hugh 534
  Jane 533
  Margaret 533
Robertes, Mrs. 562
  Richard 562
Roberts, Squire 423, 424
  Alban 543
  Algernon 543
  Cessar 612
Roberts, Edward 416, 485, 537
  Eldad 422
  Elizabeth 212, 537, 543
  Ellin 537
  Esther 512
  ffran. 593
  Franklin 543
  Gainor 543
  Hannah 619
  Hugh 470, 485, 531, 532, 535, 536, 537, 697
  James 571
  John 535, 539, 543, 612
  Squire John 422, 424
  Jonathan 543
  Joseph 824
  Katherine 470
  Lewis 437
  Mary 543, 612, 666
  Mary Hillborn 824
  Michael 590
  Owen 485, 537
  Rachel 824
  Richard 612, 613
  Robert 470, 485, 535, 537, 543, 562
  Sarah 645
  Sophia 413
  Tacey 543
  Thomas 512, 612
  William 537
Robertson, Rev. John 814
  Mary 842
  Robert 842
Robeson, Elizabeth 792
  Jonathan 780, 792
  Joseph 792
  Sarah Wharton 792
Robin, Celeste 793
Robinson, Adele Nevins 433
  Alice Ada 433
  Ann 407, 529
  Arcady S. 124
  Charles Austin 431, 433
  Charles Norris 433
  Daniel M. 432, 433
  Edward Louis 433
  Elizabeth Lewden 872
  Emily Hill 433
  Emily Nevins 433
  George Blight 433
  Harriet Lucretia 433
  Horace Percy 433
  J. Armitage 271
  James 407
  John 124
  Miles 373
  Patrick 242
  Robert Coles 433
  Sarah 124
  Thomas 289
  William 215
Robison, Edward 70
  Elizabeth 70
  Hannah 70
  Mary 70
Robt. See Robert.
Rochford, Dennis 134
Rock, Susannah 521
Rockhill, Edward 350
  Solomon 350
Rockingham, Richard 569
Rodenburgh, Lucas 715

Rodger, John 809
Rodman, (?) 47
　Mr. G. H. 549
　Hannah 793
　Dr. John 47
　Samuel 792
　Sarah 792
　Dr. Thomas 47
Roe, Eleanor 633
　Watson 632, 633
Roeder, Maria Margaret 342
Rogers, Elizabeth 301
　Mrs. Harry 407, 896
　John 42
　Magdalen 613
　Mary 290, 291, 301, 775
　Dame Mary 294, 295, 300
　Lady Mary 301
　Lady Mary Marten 300
　Sir Richard 300
　Thomas 31
Roher, Jacob 657
Rohrer, Dr. A. J. 659
　Amos Kaufman 657
　Ann 657, 658
　Ann Eliza 658
　Barbara 657, 658, 659
　Christian 657, 658
　Earl Penn 658, 659
　Elizabeth 657, 658
　Felix Columbus 658
　Helen Eliza 658
　Henry 657, 658
　Henry Neff 657
　Jacob 658
　John 657, 658, 659
　John S. 658, 659
　John Schenck 657
　Magdalena 657, 658, 659
　Magdalena Schenck 658
　Maria 657, 658
　Martin Musser 658
　Mary 658
　Mary Ann 657, 658
　Rebecca S. E. 658, 659
　Reuben S. 659
　Reuben Souder 657
　Samuel Franklin 658, 659
　Susan Ann 657
　Susanna 657
Rollinson, Hannah 864
Rollo, D. of Normandy 269
Roomball, John 768
Rose, Ann 893
　Benjamin 894
　Catherine 894
　Grace 894
　John 893
　Joseph 893, 894
　Matilda 893
　Nathaniel 894
　Samuel 894
　Sarah 893
　Sarah Ann Ursula 893
　Thos. 878, 893
　William 893, 894
Ross, Capt. 787
　George Woods 830
　Henry P. 797
　James 829, 830
　Jane Graham 829
　Joseph 714, 829

Ross, Mary 830
　Mary Jane 830, 831
　Sen. 829
Rothrock, Anna Maria 894, 895
　Benjamin 894
　Catherine 894, 895
　Charity 895
　Daniel 895
　Elizabeth 895
　Eva 894
　Eva Elizabeth 894
　Frederick 894
　George 894, 895
　Jacob 894
　James 895
　John 894, 895
　Joseph 894
　Maria 894
　Peter 894
　Philip 894, 895
　Susanna 894, 895
　Valentine 894
　William 895
Roughhead, Col. 881
Row, Robt. 880
Rowe, Henry 623
　Judith 623
　Col. Valentine 478
Rowland, Ann 533
　Elizabeth 259, 607, 823
　Mrs. James 171
　John 15, 31, 37, 60
　Jonathan 259
　Mary 224
　Mary Francis Risdon 259
　Thomas 224
Roysteron, Alice 74
　Mary 74
Rudd, Dorothy 114
　Jane 113
　Mary 113
Rudderow, Grace 714
Rudman, Andreas 639
Rudolph, John 888
Ruevel, Catharine 886
　Elizabeth 886
　George 886
Ruhl, John E. 875
Rumball, Anne 761
　Edmund 760
　Edward 760, 761
　Mrs. Elizabeth 742
　Elizabeth 758, 760, 768
　John 760
　Mary 761
　Richard 760
　William 760
Rumbaud, Nicholas 750
Rumbold, Elizabeth Washington 750, 752, 759, 767
　John 750
　Mrs. Martha Washington 758
　Col. Richard 750
　Robert 750
　Thomas 751
　William 750
Rumbolde, James 750
Rumboulde, John 768
Rummin, Philip 173
Runckle, Johan Ludwig 309
Runkle, Margaret 264
Runyon, Keziah 513

Runyon, Rune 511
Rush, Abraham 668
　Ann 663, 667
　Aurelia 661, 663
　Benjamin 664, 669
　Dr. Benjamin 660
　Benjamin, M. D. 667
　Catherine 669
　Edward 660
　Elizabeth 660, 661, 662, 663, 664, 665, 666, 667, 668, 669, 670
　Emilia 669
　Esther 664, 669
　Francis 660, 664, 668
　George 669
　Hanna 668
　Harriet 669
　Jacob 660, 667, 669
　James 660, 661, 662, 663, 664, 666, 667, 669, 670
　James Irvine 669
　Jane 660, 662, 665
　John 104, 115, 246, 660, 661, 662, 663, 664, 665, 666, 667, 668, 669, 670
　Capt. John 246
　Joseph 660, 663, 664, 668, 669
　Julia 667
　Louisa 669
　Mary 664, 668, 669
　Rachel 661, 663, 666
　Rebecca 664, 667, 669
　Richard 669
　Samuel 667
　Sarah 661, 663, 664, 668, 669
　Stephenson 667
　Susanna 246, 660, 661, 662, 663, 669
　Thomas 246, 660, 662, 663, 664
　William 660, 661, 663, 664, 666, 667, 668, 669, 670
Rushton, William 631
Russell, Almira DuBois 424
　Martha 710
　Mary 562
　Samuel 424
　Thos. 562
Rutherford, Reuben 515
Rutter, Enoch 646
　Capt. John 341
　John Potts 347
Ryde, Thos. 568
Sadler, Mrs. 762
Saill, Mary 418
St. Eloy, Pet. 557, 611
St. Memin, (?) 649
Saitto, Baroness Orazio Nicola 246
Sale, John 602
Salter, John 789
　Maria 789
　Mary 775
Salway, William 772
Sam, slave 278
Sampson, Irene E. 258
　Martha 621
Sancroft, Dr. William 687
Sandon, Ursula 561
Sands, Mrs. 882
　Jane 62

Sands, Katherin 370
  Lettice Lee 835
  Stephen 61, 62
  Thomas 370
Sandys, Mrs. Alice 742
Sansum, Elizabeth 561
Sargent, John 778
  Robert 595
Sarjant, Cornelius 630
Sasson, (?) 86
  Ann 86
Saunders, Capt. 195
Savage, Jane 564
  Samuel 648
Savig, Robert 567
Sawyer, Arthur 631
Say, Dr. 678
  Ann 676, 677
  Benjamin 674, 676, 677
  Catherine 673
  Constable I. 175
  Elizabeth 671, 673
  Joanna 671, 673
  Johanna 674
  Mary 671, 674
  Paschall 671, 672
  Polly 676, 677
  Rebekah 674, 675, 677
  Rebekah Ann 677
  Susanna 673
  Susanna Catherine 674
  Susannah 674
  Thomas 51, 671, 672, 673, 674, 675, 677
  Thomas, M. D. 53
  William 671, 673
Saymon, Isaac 705
Scanlan, Ed 814
Scarborough, John 439, 442
Scarth, Philip 175
Scattergood, Tho. 247
Schaff, Capt. 716
Schenck, Anna Cumming 717
  Catherine van Burgh 717
  John 659
  Gen. Robert C. 717
  Rev. Wm. 717
Schenk, John 657
  Rev. John 659
  Magdalena 657, 659
Schlatter, (?) 461
Schmale, Henry 646
Schneider, John 313
Scholey, Tho. 247
Schwart, Michael 329
Schwartz, Daniel 329
  George 325
  Magdalena 853
Schwenk, Elizabeth 278, 279
  Matthias 278
Scot, John 815
  Sir Michael 393
Scott, (?) 514
  Isabella 864
  John 27, 601
  Maj. John B. 502
  Lewis A. 796
  Marion 601
  Mary 864
  William 601, 864
Scotten, Jane 412
Scudder, Hanna 895, 896
  Isabella 895
  John Anderson 895
  Joseph 895
  Kenneth Anderson 895

Scudder, Lydia 895
  Nathaniel 895
  Col. Nathaniel 895
Scull, Gideon 872
  Nicholas 276, 441, 697
Searle, (?) 700
  James 700
Seavey, Rev. 597
Seeley, Ephraim 705
  Ruth 843
  Sarah 710
Sefton, Thomas 811
Seiler, Mary 645
Seils, Richard 373
Selby, Margaret 286
  William 286
Selden, (?) 151
  Adelaide Louisa 896
  Elizabeth Ely 896
  George 896
  George Shattuck 896
  Louisa 896
  Louisa S. 896
  Maria 896
  Mary Elizabeth 896
  Olive 896
Sellers, Edwin Jaquette 426
Semple, James 400
  Robert, Lord 397, 400
  Sibilla 400
Senior, William 478
Sergeant, John 841
  Margaretta 882
Sergent, John 841
Sermon, Hannah 437
Seton, Sir Alex 880
  Sir Walter 880
Sevier, John 650
Seward, Mr. 461
Sexten, Richard 551
Seyar, Fran. 303
Seyborne, William 694
Shaeffer, John 845
Shallcross, (?) 82
  Ann 69, 70
  Hannah 70, 793
  John 69, 70, 82
  Joseph 69, 70, 793
  Leonard 29, 30, 68, 69, 70
  Mary 70
  Rachel 69
  Rebecca 69
  Ruth 69, 70
  Sarah 69
  William 69
Sharecross, John 82
Sharp, Sarah 888
Sharpless, Joseph 261
Sharswood, George 873
  James 873
  William 873
Shattuck, Louisa Sophia 896
Shaw, (?) 63
  Ann 229
  Ann M. 887
  Ann Watts 229
  Anthony 380
  Bartholomew 230
  Catherine 230
  John 229, 897
  Marion 396
  Ralph 229
  Robert 396
  Samuel B. 779, 791
  Samuel Wharton 791

Shaw, Sarah Lewis 791
  William 488
Shawe, John 224
Sheehy, Nell 230
Sheepperd, Katherin 370
Sheffer, Theobald 344
Sheikels, (?) 344
  Daniel 336, 337, 344
Shelley, Francis 565
Sheneman, Benjamin 891
Shepard, Andrew 224
  Ann 224
Shepherd, Owen 872
  William 374, 375
Sheppard, Rev. David 122
  Lettitia 633
Shepperd, Mary 370
  William 372, 373, 376
Sherer, Catharine 840
Shinn, James 247
  Mary 247
  Samuel 247
  Susannah 53
  Thomas 242, 247, 547
Shippen, Alice Lee 680
  Ann 686, 687
  Ann Hume 680
  Anne 694, 695, 697
  Charles Carroll 680
  Dorathe 686
  Edward 106, 130, 145, 153, 679, 683, 684, 685, 687, 695, 696, 697, 698, 699, 701
  Edward Shippen 680
  Elizabeth 697
  Emma Manigault 680
  James Parke Farley 680
  Jane G. 791
  Jane Gray 680
  Jenet 686
  John 679, 694, 697
  Joseph 679, 680, 690, 697, 698, 699
  Col. Joseph 682
  Joseph W. 679
  Margaret 685, 699
  Mary 686
  Mary Louisa 680
  Mary Nunes 686
  Rebecca 106
  Richard Henry Lee 680
  Robert 686, 687, 692, 694
  Sarah 699
  Susanna 679
  Thomas Lee 680
  William 679, 680, 684, 686, 687, 688, 689, 690, 691, 695, 697, 700
  Dr. William 679, 697, 699, 700
  Rev. William 687, 694
  William Arthur Lee 680
Shirk, Hannah P. 522
Shirley, Sir Thomas 565
Shockley, Elizabeth 124, 125
  Elizabeth B. 124, 125
  William 124, 125
Shoemaker, Ben 867
  Deborah 775, 790
  Hannah 105
  Isaac 105
  James 105
  Jesse 105

Shoemaker, Jonathan 105
  Mary Ann 775, 791
  Phebe Walton 105
  Susan 680, 775, 790
Shoen, Fran. 812
  Langford 812
Sholl, Peter 335, 336, 344
Shonnan, Ja. 813
Shore, Elizabeth S. 680
  Mary Louise 680
  Thomas 680
Shoulders, Sarah 710
Shourds, Thomas 46
Shugan, Abigail 403
Shuman, H. 340
Shute, Anne 888
  Elizabeth 888
  Hannah 888
  Henry 888
  John 888
  Mary 888
  Samuel 888
  Sarah 888
Siders, George 521
Siegfried, John 343
  Col. John 332, 333
  Maria 343
Silver, Archibald 63
  Sarah 40, 63
Silvers, Elizabeth 646
  Ephraim 646
  Louisa 646
Simcocks, Thomas 565
Simcoke, John 144
Simes, John 521
Simonds, Thomas 112, 618
Simons, Erasmus 565
Simpler, Leah 433
Sims, Dr. John 854
Singnell, Thomas 614
Singould, Thomas 614
Sinkler, Charles 795
Sion, Catherine verch 284
  Howell ap 284
  Margaret verch 284
  Mary 284
  Mary verch 284
Sirket, John 25, 30, 38
Siters, George 521
Sitgreaves, Charlotte 897
  Clement 897
  Harriet 897
  John 897
  Juliana 897
  Kitty 897
  Mary 897
  Samuel 897
  Sarah 897
  Sarah Ann 897
  Susannah 897
  Thomas 897
  William 897
  William Deshon 897
Sketchley, Mary 528
Skinner, Mary 528
Skirm, Abraham 350, 351, 352, 353, 354
  Abram 351
  Alethia 353
  Anna 352
  Anne 354
  Charles C. 353
  Elizabeth 350, 351
  Elizabeth Anderson 353
  Emilia 353
  Hannah 352
  Huldah 352

Skirm, Isaac 351, 354
  John 350, 352
  Joseph 351, 352, 353
  Malenia 353
  Mary 351, 352, 354
  Mary C. 353
  Mary Clark 353
  Mary Elizabeth 353
  Rebeckah 354
  Rebekah 351
  Richard 350, 351, 352, 354
  Sarah 349, 352, 354
  Tacey 352
  Thomas 100
Skirrow, Will'm 98
Skout, Anthony 104
Slayman, Isaac 705
Sloane, Francis Johnston 834
  James Renwick 834
  James Renwick W. 834
  Margaret Milligan 834
  Mary Renwick 834, 835
  Prof. William Milligan 834
Smallwood, Richard 349
  Zebiah 868, 869
Smalwell, John 594
  Sarah 593
Smith, (?) 234, 631
  Dr. 548
  Mr. 783
  Ann 630
  Ann Hunter 646
  Anna Ridgway 795
  Archimedes 896
  Capt. Arthur 233
  Benj. R. 793
  Caroline Ridgway 795
  Charles 215
  Mrs. Cooper 884, 901
  Elias 871
  Elizabeth 55, 646, 874
  Elizabeth Crispin 258, 259
  Emily Sophia 795
  Esther 681, 856
  Dr. George 151, 548
  Hannah 512, 853, 856
  Henry 217, 218
  Mr. J. C. C. 549
  Jacob Ridgway 795
  James 795, 856
  James Charles 795
  Jeremiah 55
  John 25, 26
  John 31, 512, 595, 614, 646, 853, 874
  Joseph 65, 624, 625
  Joseph R. 781
  Joshua 872
  Margaret Wharton 795
  Maria Crispin 258, 259
  Mary 101, 111, 621
  Mary C. 874
  Mary Croasdale 111
  Mary M. 874
  Milton 790
  Capt. Nathan 318
  Ralph 175
  Rebecca 117
  Richard 616, 617, 854
  Col. Richard Penn 831
  Robert 26, 98
  Capt. Robert 616, 617
  Samuel 37, 49

Smith, Sarah Bull 874
  Sarah Logan 853
  Thomas Bull 874
  Timothy 26
  William 109, 111, 621, 630, 649
  William Emerson 258
Snashall, Eliz. 224
  Hen. 224
Snell, (?) 690
Snelson, Nicholas 571
Snowden, John 81
Somerby, Tho. 615
Somerset, Lord 688
Sotcham, Robert 161
Sotheston, Nowell 557
Soudars, Mary 121, 122
Souder, John K. 875
  Maria 657, 659
Southam, Giles 569
  Jane 569
Southcott, Edward 562
Southeby, John 772
Southwell, Robert 213
Spain, Sarah Church 412
Sparling, Capt. 195, 196
Sparrow, Elizabeth 596
  John 596
Speed, Thomas 609, 625
Speer, Ann 808
  Hugh 808
Speke, Thomas 753
Spencer, Isaac 848
  John 848, 850
Spenser, Elizabeth 878
Spotswood, John 881
  Prime 881
  Sir Robert 881
Spratt, Thomas 289
Spreule, Gabriel 401
Spring, Nancy W. 795
Springett, Gulielma Maria 603, 622, 631
  Herbert 76
  John 622
  Sir William 622
Sprogell, Catherine 674
  Susannah Catherine 673
Stackhouse, Benjamin 90
  Ellen 114
  Jennet 114
  John 95, 108, 114, 115
  Margery Hayhurst 114
  Sarah 90
  Thomas 20, 80, 94, 95, 113, 114, 117
Stacy, Elizabeth 78
  John 78
  Mahlon 44, 46, 47, 52, 53, 78, 79, 81, 130
  Mary 78
  Rebecca 53, 78, 79
  Rebecca Ely 52, 78, 81
  Ruth 78, 79, 81
  Sarah 78
Stadler, Mary 858
Stafford, Martha 631
  William 631
Stalcope, John 527
Stambaugh, Mary 659
  Col. S. C. 659
Stamper, Joseph 667
  Susanna 667
  Thomas 667
Standbridge, Susanna 224
Standen, Susanna 224
Standish, Capt. Miles 261

Standley, Valentine 845
Stanford, Thomas 130
Stangboy, John 289
Stanhope, (?) 690
Stanley, William 238
Stanton, Daniel 55
Stapler, Joseph 54
  Martha 76
  Rachel 54, 59, 62, 63
  Stephen 76
  Thomas 41, 59, 60, 63
Stapleton, Nicholas de 387
Staton, Elizabeth 171
  Hester 171
  Margaret M. 171
  Warrington 171
Stayton, Catherine 488
Steather, Anne 662
Steckel, Peter 330, 336
Stedman, Charles 474
Steelman, Andrew 510, 705, 709
  Bridget 703
  Britta 706
  Catherine 703, 706
  Catherine Keen 708
  Catherine Keene 709
  Charles 702, 703, 704, 706, 707, 708, 709, 710
  Daniel 704, 707, 708
  Eleanor 703, 707
  Elizabeth 705, 708, 709, 710
  Eric 703, 704, 706, 707, 708, 709, 710
  Hance 703, 704, 706, 707, 708, 709, 710
  Hannah 851
  Hiram 709, 710
  Isaac 705, 708, 851
  James 703, 704, 705, 706, 707, 708, 709, 710
  James B. 709, 710
  James Boles 709
  Jemima 705, 710
  Jesse 851
  Johannah 706
  John 704, 705, 706, 707, 708, 709, 710
  Judith 851
  Margaret 703
  Mary 703, 706, 707, 851
  Melesent 851
  Millicent 851
  Peter 851
  Phebe 871
  Rebecca 705, 707
  Sarah 705, 707
  Sarah 705, 706, 707, 708, 709, 851
Stenyard, Jo. 290
Stephens, Ellen 614
  James 480
  Samuel 818
Stephenson, Timothy 661
Sterling, Lord 494
  Charles 807
Stern, Abraham 330, 336
Steuart, James 811
Stevenage, Mrs. Margaret 642
Stevens, Erasmus 897
  Hen. 557, 611
  Jane 645
  Persis 897

Stevens, Hon. Thaddeus 659
Stevenson, Ann 163
  Sarah Jennings 164
  Thomas 38, 94, 164
Steward of Scotland, Lord James 390
Steward, Walter the 389
  William 350
Stewart, Adam 898
  Ann 898
  Caroline 898
  Christian Glen 394
  David 394
  Henry 898
  Mary Ann 898
  Robert 394, 898
  Walter 898
  Gen. Walter 898
  Washington 898
  William 898
Stichter, J. L. 875
Stidham, William 319
Stiegel, Anthony 839
  Christine 839
Stirling, Lady 503
  Lord 340
  John 808
Stiteler, George R. 522
Stites, Anna 497, 514
  Benjamin 516
  Charlotte 515
  Emma 515
  Ephraim M. 514
  Henry 516
  Indiana 515
  Isaac 515
  John 514, 515, 516
  Keziah 514
  Squire M. 514
  Margaret 516
  Martin 514
  Mary 514
  Mercy 514
  Richard 515, 516
  Samuel 497, 505, 514, 515
  Sarah 514
  William 515, 516
Stockdale, Amy 116
  Ann 116
  David 118
  Dorothy 117
  Dorothy Iden 118
  Elizabeth 118
  George 118
  Grace 117, 118, 119
  Hannah 118
  Isabel 116
  Jane 119
  John 111, 118
  Mary 118
  Mercy 118
  Phebe 116, 117
  Ralph 115, 116
  Robert 118
  Ruth 119
  Sarah 118
  Thomas 118
  William 71, 99, 100, 101, 103, 104, 108, 109, 115, 116, 118, 119
Stocker, John Clement 796
  Martha R. 787
  Martha Rutter 796
  Mary Katherine 796
Stockton, Abigail 242
  Ann 247, 412

Stockton, Christianna 412
  John 412
  Julia 667, 669
  Mary 242
  Mrs. R. 503
  Richard 242, 412
  William 412
Stodall, Katherine 224
Stokeld, Gerrard 291
Stokes, (?) 716
  Samuel 45
Stoner, Anne 562
  Henry 562
Story, Capt. 202
  John 624, 625
  Capt. Robert 200
  Thomas 685, 696
Storye, John 624
Stote, Francis 688
  Sir Richard 688
Stouffer, George Annie Benners 413
Stout, (?) 788
  Emmeline Davis 796
  Robert 796
  Will'm 98
Stowe, (?) 891
Strade, George 173
Strafford, Earl of. See Wentworth, Sir Thomas.
Strangeways, Arthur 453
Stranguish, Katherine 453
Strangways, Arthur 453
  Katherine 453
Stratford, Mr. 548
Stratton, Abigail 899
  Anna Harris 899
  Benjamin 899
  Benjamin Harris 899
  Gov. Charles C. 899
  Charles Creighton 899
  Daniel Powell 899
  Frances 899
  Harriet 899
  Isabella 899
  James 899
  James Creighton 899
  Dr. John L. 899
  Levi 899
  Maria 899
  Richard 611
  Samuel Creighton 899
  Sarah 899
Strauch, Henry 891
Strawbridge, Welsh 476
Streat, John 594
Stringam, Sara 562
Strong, (?) 635
  John 562
Stroude, Ellner 552
Stuart, David 789
Stubbs, Thomas 74
Studder, Richard 562
Studwy, William 600
Stump, Wyll'm 593
Sturdevant, Mr. 869
Sturgis, Cornelius 241
  Stephen 489
Style, Phill. 571
  W. 571
Suddards, Rev. William 874
Sullivan, Gen. 332
Sumner, Andrew 558
Surer, Anna Eva 870
  John William 870
  Maria Barbara 870

Surer, Ottilia 870
Sutherland, Daniel 705, 706
  William, Earl of 392
Sutton, Mary 844, 867
Suxberry, John 220
Suxbery, John 220
Swan, Henry 224
Sweeney, Jas. 172
  Jane 172
  Mary 172
Sweeten, Mary 710
Swift, John 104, 115, 130, 140, 653, 699
Swince, William 289
Swiney, Jane Armstrong 230
  Robert 230, 231
Swinoe, William 289
Sykes, Elizabeth 376, 781
  Joseph 781
  Robert Wharton 781
  Samuel 781
  William 774, 781
Symcock, John 536
Syme, Ann 893
  Rev. David 893
  Sarah 893
Symmons, Mary 596
Symple, Robert 395
Syng, Elizabeth 54
  Philip 54, 697
Taggert, Joseph 899
  Sarah 899
Talbot, George 769
  Margaret 769
Talbott, George 751
  Margaret Washington 751, 752, 769
Tallman, Benjamin 790
  Dr. Benjamin 775
  Job 779
  Mary 775
  Sarah 773, 779
Tanner, Rachel 800
  Richard Preston 800
  Wm. 595
Tatem, Abraham 668
Tatham, John 94
Tattamy, (?) 462
Tattnall, Commodore Josiah 292
Taylor, A. C. 712
  Achsah 553
  Agnes 553
  Agnes Crain 713
  Ann 453
  Anne 350, 695
  Annie 712
  Anthony 553
  Arthur 631
  Dr. Benjamin C. 713
  C. 31
  Christopher 28, 31, 139
  Clarence Wills 712
  Edmund 453
  Elizabeth 68, 350, 553, 860
  Evelina C. 712, 713
  Evelina Constance 712, 713
  Evelina Constancia Burroughs 713
  Helen Cooper 712
  Helen Elizabeth 712
  Henry Genet 712
  Isabel 100
  James 65

Taylor, Jesse 552
  John 350, 564
  Joice 553
  Jonathan 24
  Julianna 68
  M. B. 712
  Dr. M. W. 386
  Mahlon K. 70
  Margaret 453
  Marmaduke Burroughs 712, 713
  Martha 107
  Mary 107, 350
  Mary Alice 713
  Mary Margaret 553
  Nancy 860
  Nicholas 628
  O. H. 713
  Dr. O. H. 712
  Othniel Gazzam 712, 713
  Othniel Hart 711, 712, 713
  Phebe 106
  Philip 68
  Phoebe 101
  Rebeckah 350
  Richard 106, 630
  Richard Cooper 712
  Samuel 294, 350
  Sarah 350
  Susannah 350
  Thomas 7, 350
  Timothy 100
  W. 842
  William 556, 590, 711, 712, 713
  Wm. Rivers 712, 713
Tempest, Thos. 552
Tempeste, Thos. 551
Tennent, Mrs. 717
  Catherine 715
  Dr. Gilbert 717
  Dr. John 717
  Rev. William 715, 716, 717
Terick, Sam'll 196
Test, Samuel 656
Tetterie, Rebecca 612
Thaine, John 224
Thermor, Alice 556
Thomas, (?) 460
  Ann 518
  Arthur 631
  Cadwalader 485, 531, 538
  Cadwalader ap Hugh 532
  Edward 801
  Eleoner 801
  Ellin Evan 485
  Evan 801
  James 772
  John 437, 470, 532, 533, 534, 538, 543
  Jordeyne, 550
  Joseph 801
  Katherine 470
  Margaret 891
  Micah 772
  Owen 534
  Rachel 771, 772
  Rees 533
  Robert 437
  Samuel 437
  Thomas 519, 520
  Ursula Catherine 861
  William 519, 523
Thompson, Benjamin F. 516
  Elizabeth 791

Thompson, James 886
  Jane C. 886
  John M. 886
  Margaretta 890
  Marsh 502
  Martha 515
  Samuell 890
  Sarah 886
Thomson, Gen. Harry 399
  James 808
Thorn, Elizabeth 351
  John 351
  Joseph 351
  Michael 351
  Thomas 351
Thorne, John 562
  Rev. Lydenham 850
  Mary 561
  William 568
Thornton, Alice 100
  Henry 834
  Margaret 363
  Margaret Washington 770
  Mrs. Penelope 742
  Roger 742
  Samuel 769, 770
  William 379
Thurloe, Secty 209
Thurston, Joseph 793
Tiffin, John 65
Tiler, Ellis 551
Tillney, Mr. 847
Timbrell, William 626
Tingle, Rev. Samuel 849
Tinley, Rev. Samuel 849
Tittere, Rebecca 611
Titus, Edmund 516
  Timothy 26
Todhunter, John 80
Tokey, George 566
Tollye, Joyce 558
Tomlinson, Agnes 98
  Ann 100
  Elizabeth 101
  John 100
  Mary 111
  Tho. 100
Tompkins, Mary 68
Tonkin, (?) 892
  Edward 892
Topham, Christopher 99, 104, 109
Topp, Capt. 873
  Ann 873
  Thomas 873
Torrey, Clarence Almon 632
  Susan Almira Roe 632
Touch, Laird of 880
Tovie, Margery 624
  Nathaniel 624
Towanson, Thomas 381
Tower, Robert 375
Towerman, Edmund 594
Towers, Mary Ann 890
  Richard 375
  Robert 890
Townsend, Mary 871
Townson, John 87
  Thomas 380
Trafford, Lieut. 200
Travers, John 619
  Mathew 622
Trenor, James 817
Trent, William 44
Tresham, Thos. 569
Tribbey, John 896

944

Tripcovich, Commendatore
   Diadato 267
  Oliviero 267
  Pozza, Ctss. Gilda
   267
Troth, Mary 888
Trotter, Hannah 347
  Jonathan 347
  Joseph 697
  Sarah 512
  William 512
Truit, John 850
  Sarah 850
Truitt, Joanna 850
Trusse, Elizabeth 617
Truxton, Elizabeth 886
  Thomas 886
  Wm. 886
Tucke, Chr. 597
Tucker, Gerrard 721
  Stephen 626
Tuckyr, Car. 614
Tudor, Capt. 645
Tugwell, John 224
Tully, John 25, 26, 30
Tunstall, Anne 372
  M. Ann 376
  Ralph 376
Turner, (?) 476
  C. H. B. 172, 883, 886
  Rev. C. H. B. 487,
   850, 855, 865
  George 845
  J. 190
  Jane 561
  Joseph 697
  Robert 240
  William 561
Twells, Edward 792
Twining, Abigail 92
  Ann 127
  Joanna 127
  Margaret Mitchell 92
  Stephen 92, 111
  William 127
Tyson, Elizabeth 877
  Renier 877
Tythe, Peter 319
Tyton, James 300
  Mary 300
Upington, Uslye Bustead
   229
Uppey, Sarah 166
Urian, Benjamin 529
Usher, Rev. Mr. 847
Uz, mulatto 51
Vanaman, Mary 122
Van Buren, Martin 264
van Burgh, Anna 716
  Catharine 716, 717
  Charles 717
  David 716
  Elizabeth 716
  Helena 715
  Johanna 716
  Johannes 716, 717
  Capt. Johannes 716
  Johannes Pieterse 715
  Sir John 717
  Margareta 716
  Maria 716
  Peter 716
  Capt. Peter 716
  Philip 717
van Duren, John 438
Van Dusen, Mr. 869
  Samuel 869
Van Dyck, Lieut.-Col.
   Cornelius 340

Vaneman, Andru 450
  Elizabeth Haines 450
Van Hook, Frances 679
Van Laer, Ann 453
  John 453
Van Reed, Henry 647
van Rensselaer, Hendrick 716
Vansant, Anna Elisabeth
   890
  C. 890
  Claudine 891
  Claudine Raguet 890
  Garret 889
  James Raguet 890
  James Watall 891
  Juliet 890
  Mary W. 890
  Mercy Jane 890
  Silas 890, 891
  Sylas 889
  Wm. Henry 890
Van Sc(h)aick, Col.
   Goose 340
Van Teneyck, Capt. 263
Van Tromp, Admiral 191
Van Vleeck, Bishop
   Jacob 465
  Bishop William Henry
   465
Van Wyck, Mrs. 882
Vaughan, Edward 533
  Mary verch Tudwr 284
  Ro. 573
  Robert 533
  Tudwr 284
Vaux, George 224, 483,
   835
Veal, Enos 632, 633
  Lettitia G. 633
  Rebecca P. 633
Vears, Thomas 112
Venables, Gen. 200, 202,
   203, 204, 207
Verbrugge, Johannes
   Pieterse 715
verch. See under surname.
verch Humphrey. See
   Humphrey.
verch John. See John.
Verney, Sir Edward 743,
   744
  Sir Francis 740,
   743
  John 550
Vernon, Edward 569
  Rich'd 570
  Thomas 569
Vessey, Capt. William
   200
Vichers, Mrs. George E.
   487
Vickus, Richard 631
Vigor, William 619
Villiers, Anne 760
  George, D. of Buckingham 760
  George, Viscount
   Grandison 760
Viney, John 304
Vizar, Ann 596
Vogelson, John A. 250
von Suhm, Margaretta Albertina Conradina
   478
Wabraven, Christianna
   528
Waddington, Nicholas 563

Wade, Major 630
  Anne 561
  John 561
Wadeson, Robert 203, 234
Wadham, Capt. John 886
Wadsworth, James S. 795
Wagner, Esther M. 864
  Esther Maria 864
  John 864
  Margaret 864
  William 864
Waite, John 161
  Joseph 158
Waithman, Mary 98
Wakeman, John 553
Wales, William 380
Walker, (?) 788, 797
  Andrew 810
  Barbara 900
  Benjamin 900
  Elizabeth 878
  Henry 900
  James 850, 899, 900
  James Miers 850
  Jean 900
  John 899, 900
  Joseph 900
  Mary 850
  Robert 604
  Samuel 900
  Sarah 900
  William 601, 900
Walkinwood, Dinah 521
Wall, Ann 894
  James 894
  Jane Gray 680
  Lydia 894
  Mary 79
  Oliver Cromwell 894
  Pierce 894
Wallace, Elizabeth 712
  John 699
  Joshua M., Jr. 680
  Joshua Maddox, M. D.
   680
  Martha 668
  Mary Coxe 680
  Mary Smith 412
  Shippen 680
  Violet Lee 680
  William McIlvaine 680
Wallack, Benjamin 891
Waller, Philip 702
Walling, ffrancis 100
Wallingford, Aldrith 270
  Wigo de 271
Wallis, Alderman 630
  James 617
  Philip 702
  William 897
Walliston, John 557
Walmsley, Elizabeth 113,
   114
  Thomas 113
Waln, Mary 79, 775, 790
  Nicholas 16, 61, 66,
   113, 241, 536
Walpole, (?) 690, 691
  Horace 689
  Sir Horace 688
  Robert 690
  Sir Robert 688
  Thomas 778
Walter, Anna 793
  Eliz. 814
  John 561
  Samuell 562
  Susan 562

Walters, Elizabeth 612
  Oliver 612
Walton, Benjamin 666
  Elizabeth 666, 882, 883
  Hannah 105
  Jacob 438
  John 105
  Phebe 106
  Phebe Atkinson 105
  Rebecca 666
  Samuel 883
  William 103, 104, 105, 106, 107
Ward, Anthony 372, 373
  Elizabeth 853, 860
  Helen 372
  Philip 230
Warde, Anthony 371
  George 370, 374, 375
  Helen 371
  Margaret 375
  Matithia 370
Warder, Rachel 71
  Sarah 27
  Solomon 15, 134
  Willoughby 15, 27, 71
Wardon, Joseph 810
Waren, Michael 642
Waring, Ellen 887
Warmestry, George 303
Warner, Isaac 57
  John 57
  Rebecca 781
  William 57
Warrilow, Thomas 81
Warriner, John 372
Washington, (?) 435, 440, 444, 445, 446, 474, 495, 496, 499, 509, 776
  Col. 723
  Gen. 445, 718, 868, 898
  Lady 742
  Lieut.-Col. 721
  Adam 759
  Alice 742
  Mrs. Amphillis 738, 740, 741, 744, 745, 747, 749, 750, 751, 752, 753, 758, 759, 764, 767
  Ann 720, 724, 725, 726, 727, 733, 735
  Mrs. Ann Brett 719, 724, 725, 726, 727, 729, 731
  Ann Pope 722, 723, 724
  Ann Pope Brodhurst 725, 726, 727, 728, 729, 731, 734, 735, 736
  Lady Dorothy Pargiter 742
  Elizabeth 738, 742, 749, 764, 767
  Frances 742
  Frances Garrard Appleton 736
  George 263, 334, 441
  Gen. George 331, 718
  John 720, 722, 723, 724, 725, 726, 728, 731, 733, 735, 738, 748, 752, 764
  Capt. John 719, 733
  Col. John 718, 724, 725, 726, 727, 729,

Washington, Col. John 730, 731, 732, 733, 734, 735, 736, 737, 738, 744, 745, 746, 747, 748, 749, 751, 752, 753, 755, 756, 757, 758, 759, 761, 763, 764, 766, 767, 770
  Lieut.-Col. John 720
  Maj. John 728
  Sir John 742, 748, 751, 760
  Lawrence 718, 720, 723, 724, 725, 726, 727, 730, 731, 733, 735, 738, 741, 742, 743, 744, 746, 748, 749, 751, 752, 756, 757, 759, 763, 764, 765, 767
  Rev. Lawrence 737, 738, 739, 740, 741, 742, 746, 747, 749, 751, 752, 754, 755, 756, 757, 758, 759, 761, 763, 764, 765, 767, 768, 769
  Margaret 738, 751, 759, 764, 769, 770
  Martha 738, 751, 752, 764, 767
  Mary 749
  Robert 742
  Thomas 743, 744
  William 751, 764
  Sir William 742, 751, 760
Wass, James 130, 163
  Joseph 130
Wastfield, Joane 596
  Walter 596
Waters, Fitz Gilbert 762
Watkins, Hannah 876
Watkis, Thomas 612
Watmough, Capt. P. G. 418
Watson, (?) 63, 452, 453, 476
  Mrs. 845
  Benjamin 869
  James 901
  John 98, 473
  Dr. John 98
  Louisa H. 832
  Mary 614
  Nathan 31
  Peter 869
  Robert 298
  Stephen 381
  Thomas 37, 60, 441, 442
Watts, Edward 229, 230
  John 220, 229, 232
Waven, George 380
Wayne, Anthony 355, 494
Weaver, Ann 272
  Isaac 451
  Peter 641, 642, 643
Webb, Brice 626, 627, 628
  Deborah 56
  John 167
  Ro. 226
Webster, Col. 508
  Clement B. 250
  George 250
  John 661, 663
  Capt. John 508

Webster, Phoebe 663
Weckes, Elizabeth 627, 628
Weedon, George 496
Weeks, Charles 628
  Joseph D. 258
Weidner, Mary 181
  Peter 181
  Susan 182
Weimands, Jacob 648
Weimer, John 891
Weir, Capt. 322
Weiser, Dr. C. Z. 281
Weiss, Rev. George Michael 277
Weitzel, Eugene Lowell 343
  George 343
Welbor, John 846
Welch, Joseph 428
Weld, Elizabeth 427, 428, 429
  Sir Humphrey 430
  John 427, 429, 430
  Mary 430
  Thomas 427, 429, 430
  William 430
Welden, Baron Lui de 659
  Baron Xavier de 659
Welker, George 276
  Veronica 276
Weller, Barbara 894
Wells, Anne 865
  Arthur 54
  Benjamin 865
  Elizabeth 865
  John 441, 443
  Richard 442
Weltner, Lieut.-Col. Lewis 317
Welton, Dr. Richard 477
Wemyess, Isabel de 393
  Sir John de 393
Wentworth, Sir Thomas, 1st E. of Strafford 6
  Sir William 6
Werle, Maria 840
Wescoat, Mary 122
Wessell, Sarah 667
West, And'w 901
  Ann 901
  Benjamin 384, 698, 902
  Benj'n Fuller 901
  Caroline 901
  Eliza Rodney 493
  Elizabeth 68, 384, 901, 902
  Elizabeth Dungan 68
  Francis 901
  Dr. Francis 884
  Fran's 901
  Harry 901
  Helen 901
  James 901
  John 901, 902
  Joseph 541
  Mary 493, 901
  Moses 384
  Nathaniel 68
  Olive 896
  Rebecca 77
  Robert 575
  Samuel 896
  Sarah 575
  Thomas 382, 384, 902
  William 384, 493, 901, 902

West, William Hodge 901
Weste, Nich'as 551
Wester, Amy Crispin 229
Weston, Edith 854
  Dame Grace 567
  Lewis 854
  Sir Richard 567
  Sarah 854
  William 224
Westphal, Harriet 412
Westwood, Mr. 562
  Anne 558
Wetherill, Ann Fearson 248
  Christopher 248
  Mary 248
  Thomas 45, 248
Wetzel, Anna Maria 277
  Barbara 277
  Jacob 276, 277
Wharby, Daniel 224
  Mary 224
Wharmby, Lydia 156
Wharton, (?) 778
  Gouverneur 794
  Alfred 788, 794
  Alfred Clifton 797
  Alida Gouverneur 794
  Amanda Jones 797
  Anna Maria 788
  Anne 793
  Anne H. 771
  Anne Maria 793
  Anthony Morris 788
  Benjamin 773, 774
  Carpenter 773, 781, 795
  Chamless 775, 789
  Charles 774, 780, 781, 782, 792, 793
  Charles Doughty 789
  Charles William 793
  Clementine 789
  Clifton 788, 796
  Clifton Lewis 796
  Clifton Ormsby 796
  Clifton Tucker 797
  Daniel Clark 790
  David Brearley 797
  Deborah 791
  Deborah Claypoole 774
  Deborah Musgrave 790
  Edmund 793
  Edward 680, 791, 794, 797
  Eliza 780
  Elizabeth 793, 796
  Elizabeth Fishbourn 791
  Elizabeth Salter 789
  Elizabeth Shoemaker 790
  Ellen Clifton 788, 797
  Emily 795
  Emmeline Barclay 796
  Esther Fisher 793
  Fishbourne 680, 775, 790, 791
  Francis 795
  Francis Rawle 781, 793, 794
  Franklin 774, 777, 786, 787, 788, 796, 797
  Franklin Nicholas 797
  Frederick Augustus 788
  G. W. 784
  George 774, 789, 797

Wharton, George Mifflin 791
  George Salter 789
  George Washington 788, 796
  Hannah 544, 777, 780, 791, 792, 793
  Hannah Carpenter 791
  Hannah Margaret 781
  Hannah Redwood 781
  Henry 788, 791, 795
  Henry C. 797
  Henry Williams 788
  Hudson 774
  Isaac 773, 781, 793, 794, 795
  Jacob 777
  James 772, 773, 774, 788, 789
  James Salter 789
  Jane 789
  John 772, 773, 774, 775, 781, 788, 789, 790, 791, 795
  John Burgwin 796
  John Halowell 790
  John Salter 789
  Joseph 37, 60, 542, 544, 652, 697, 772, 773, 776, 777, 779, 781, 782, 787, 788, 789, 791, 792, 793, 794, 795, 796, 797
  Joseph Tallman 780
  Josephine 796
  Kearney 775, 789, 790
  Lewis 788
  Lloyd 775, 789
  Louis Duverge 797
  Margaret 794
  Margaret Doughty 789
  Martha 777, 779, 780, 791
  Mary 772, 773, 774, 775, 777, 781, 793
  Mary Ann 788
  Mary Clifton 796
  Mary Craig 795
  Mary Etta 796
  Mary Griffith 795
  Mary Louisa 680
  Mary Moore 790
  Mary Waln 790
  Morris 774
  Nancy 780
  Octavie 797
  Oliver Franklin 796
  Peregrine 788
  Peregrine Hogg 774, 788
  Philip Fishbourn 791
  Rachel 772, 773, 774, 775, 777, 779, 780, 787, 791, 796
  Rebecca 774, 779, 790
  Rebecca Louisa 789
  Rebecca Shoemaker 781, 795
  Redwood 793
  Reynold 774, 788
  Richard 771, 772, 773, 774, 775, 776, 777, 779, 781, 782, 787, 788, 789, 790, 791, 792, 793, 794, 795, 796, 797
  Robert 544, 774, 782, 783, 784, 785, 786, 793

Wharton, Robert Owen 787
  Robert Stout 796
  Robertson 794
  Rodman 793
  Samuel 773, 777, 778, 779, 791
  Samuel Fisher 793
  Samuel Lewis 779, 791
  Sarah 780, 790, 792, 793
  Sarah Norris 775, 790
  Sarah Redwood 781, 792
  Stephen 790, 791
  Susan 790, 791
  Susannah 774, 775, 777
  Thomas 771, 772, 773, 774, 775, 776, 777, 779, 781, 782, 787, 788, 789, 790, 791, 792, 793, 794, 795, 796, 797
  Thomas Carpenter 781, 795
  Thomas Fishbourne 775
  Thomas Isaac 781, 794, 795
  Thomas Lloyd 789
  Thomas Parr 780
  William 774, 781, 788, 791, 792, 793
  William Craig 795
  William Hudson 777
  William Joseph 797
  William Lewis 788, 797
  William Moore 775, 790, 797
Whatlow, John 570
Wheeler, Gilbert 136, 137, 138
Whetman, John 319
Whistler, Dr. 614
Whit, Archibald 809
White, Bishop 787, 792
  Rev. Bishop 885
  Rev. Dr. 898
  Archibald 808, 809
  Barclay 892
  Benjamin 415
  Edmund 761
  Edward 877
  Elizabeth 414, 415, 617
  Elizabeth A. 791
  Francis 415
  George 414
  George H. 795
  Humphrey 414, 415
  James 872
  Joan 414
  John 415, 650, 772
  Capt. John 200
  Joseph 35, 36, 415
  Maggie A. 856
  Maud 414
  Miles 19, 21, 33, 41, 80
  Peter 415
  Roger 414
  Sarah 415
  Simon 414
  Tho. 230
  Thomas 414
  Sir Thomas 414
  Violetta Susan 835
  Wallace W. 856
  William 133, 415, 888

White, Rev. William 791, 885
Whitefield, (?) 460
  Rev. George 461
Whitehead, George 112, 624, 628
Whitton, Richard 106
  Robert 106
Wigglesworth, Alice 113
  Thomas 113
Wight, Jno. 618
Wikoff, Miss 895
  Amanda 896
  Ann 896
  Charlotte 896
  Hanna 896
  Jacob 896
  Lydia Scudder 896
  Matilda 896
  Nathaniel Scudder 896
  Sally 896
  William 895
Wilde, Agnes 98
Wildenfield, Samuel 574
Wildman, John 95, 176
  Joseph 117
  Mary 111
Wilkins, Jacob L. 889
Wilkinson, Lieut. 200
  John 65, 176, 372, 624
  Mary 176
  Robert 372
Wilks, Anna 590
Willard, John 562
Willcox, Abigail 887
  Barnabas 887
Willes, Edward 694
Willet, Dan 136
William I, the Conqueror, K. of England 185, 270
William of Jumieges 269
William, Daniel 801
  Edward 800, 801
  Eleanor 800, 801
  Jane 801
  Joseph 801
  Rebecca 801
  Samuel 802
  Sarah 800, 802
Williams, Daniel 801, 802, 803, 804
  Deborah 802
  Douse 483
  Duffield, 620
  Edward 800, 802
  Ellin 483, 484
  Ellis 483, 484
  Ennion 802, 804
  George 802
  Gwenn 483, 484
  Hannah 800, 802
  Jane 484
  Jane Oldman 801, 802, 803, 804
  Jno. 485
  John Merrick 478
  Joseph 802
  Margaret 483
  Mary 801, 802
  Moses V. 521
  Roger 762
  Sarah 802, 803
  William J. 842
Willing, Chas. 180
  Mary 181
Willings, Charles 697
Willis, Henry 836

Willits, Samuel C. 256
Willson, (?) 819
  Agnes 806, 807
  Andrew 808, 811, 812, 816, 818
  Archibald 809
  Charles 818
  Claud 806
  Daniel 809
  David 808
  Elizabeth 808, 811, 814, 819
  Esther 27, 811
  George 807, 811, 815
  Henry 811
  Hugh 812, 815
  Isaac 811
  Isabell 812
  James 807, 809, 810
  Jean 811
  John 807, 808, 809, 810, 811, 812, 814, 815, 819
  Katherine 807
  Margaret 807, 808, 809, 810, 811, 814
  Mary 807, 814, 815
  Nicholas 819
  Ralph 819
  Sir Ralph 819
  Richard 27
  Robert 811, 819
  Rowland 819
  Samuel 811, 819
  Thomas 101, 808, 809, 811, 816, 818, 819
  Uphamia 818
  William 810, 819
Willsone, James 807
  Margaret 807
Willsonn, James 821
Wilmartin, Catherine 70
  Elizabeth 70
  Hannah 80
  John 70
  Rebecca 70
Wilmarton, Catherine 70
  Paul 70
Wilsford, John 71
Wilson, Mr. 848, 849
  Adam 817
  Agnes Stewart 807
  Alexander 815, 816, 821
  Andrew 810, 812, 821
  Anne 59, 812, 814, 816
  Anthony 59
  Christopher 568
  David 809, 813, 819
  Edith 819
  Edward 65, 567
  Elizabeth 402, 817, 818
  Francis 807
  Gabrael 821
  George 674, 815, 816, 817
  Hannah 814
  Helen 376
  Henry 410, 810
  Hugh 808, 809, 817
  Humphrey 821
  Isaac 410
  Isabel 812
  Isabella 814
  James 674, 675, 676, 809, 813, 815, 818, 820

Wilson, Jannett 807
  John 29, 71, 410, 806, 807, 808, 809, 813, 814, 815, 816, 819, 820, 821
  Mrs. John 357
  Sir John 812, 820
  Jona. 815
  Joseph 410
  Joseph Bonstead 628
  Joshua 808
  Katherine 807
  Lea 349
  Lidia 817
  Mark 816
  Martha 814
  Mary 674, 675, 676, 808, 817, 818
  Mary Paynter 824
  Mary Say 675
  Mathew 815, 816
  Nicholas 814, 819
  Patrick 808, 814
  Sir Ralph 819
  Rebecca 813
  Rebeckah 818
  Rebekah 675
  Richard 439, 813, 821
  Robert 808, 809, 813, 816, 818, 819, 820
  Rowland 819
  Samuel 811, 816, 819
  Capt. Samuel 818
  Samuel I. 824
  Sarah 814, 817
  Sarah Baker 71
  Simon K. 824
  Stephen 71
  Susan 819
  Susannah 674
  Thomas 374, 674, 675, 676, 807, 814, 816, 817, 720, 872
  Tom 818
  William 376, 806, 807, 812, 813, 815, 816, 817, 819, 820
  Sir William 402
Wilsone, James 821
Wilsonn, Robert 821
Wiltbank, Dr. A. S. 825
  Alfred Stockley 823
  Ann 822, 823
  Comly J. 823, 824
  Cornelius 822, 823, 847
  Eliza 823
  Eliza P. 824
  Esther 822
  Frank Comly 823
  Hannah R. 823
  John 822, 823, 824
  Judge John 822
  John Cornelius 823
  John Paynter 823
  Mary 822
  Mary Elizabeth 825
  Rachel Roberts 825
  Robert 822
  Samuel Paynter 823, 825
  Samuel Rowland 823
Wincleoll, Simon 618
Winkworth, John 596
  Richard 596
Winscombe, Sibill 578
Winterborne, Elizabeth 559
Wiperton, Susannah M. 876

948

Wirts, (?) 890
Wirtz, Rev. John Conrad 323
Wise, Mary 598
Wishard, Lord Robert 390
Wishart, Robert 391
Wistar, Dr. 680
  Catherine 521
  Frances 796
  Rachel 796
  Rachel Lewis 796
  Richard 787, 796
  Salome 787, 792
  Sarah 796
  William Lewis 796
Wither, Margaret 98
  Tho. 98
Witherspoon, Dr. 679
  Anna Maria 649
Witney, Civill 565
Woekenweins, Anna Eva 870
  Wendel 870
Wolfe, Hannah Richards 823
Wood, Abraham 893
  Anne 536, 540
  Eleanor 223
  Isaac 649
  John 136
  Joseph 129, 154
  Laber 175
  Margaret 649
  Marguerite Staples Du Puy 347
  Sarah 865
  Mrs. Ursula 893
Woodhull, Margaret Nevins 835
Woodin, (?) 262
  C. R. 263
  Clemuel Ricketts 262
  William Hartman 262, 263
Woodnutt, Mrs. Thomas 656
Woods, Ann 828, 829
  Anna 829, 831
  Florence 831
  George 826, 827, 828
  Henry 828, 829, 830, 831
  Ida 831
  Jane 828
  Jean 826
  John 826, 828, 829
  John George 829, 831
  Lucy P. 831
  Margaretta 829
  Mary 828, 831
  Mary Lythe 829
  Prudence 831
  Rachael 831
  Rebecca 826, 827
  Thomas 826
  William 831
Woodward, Henry 871
  W. W. 872
Wooldridge, Richard 562
Woolley, Ann 353
  Charlotte 353
  Deborah 352
  Edna 353
  Elizabeth 352
  Hannah 352
  Huldah 353
  Huldah Skirm 352
  James 352
  John Tucker 353
  Mary 352
Woolrich, Elizabeth 440

Woolridge, Mary 438
Woolven, Mary 224
Worley, Charity 895
Worrall, Peter 80
Worrell, James C. 795
  Joseph 845
  Peter 854
Worrilow, Elizabeth 81
  John 81
  Walter 81
Worsam, Henrietta Constantia 881
  Hon. Richard 881
Worsfold, Edward 568
Worth, Joseph 176
  Mary 176
Wotton, Margarett 561
Wovs, Mary 490
Wrenn, John 614
Wright, Catherine 903
  Edith 903
  Enoch 903
  Ezekiel 903
  Israel 903
  Jacob 903
  Jemima 903
  John 247, 248
  Joshua 53, 78, 79
  Mary 903
  Rebecca Stacy 54, 81
  Rowland 381
  S. 859
  Susanna 903
  Thomas 224
  William 759
Wrighton, Elizabeth 616
Wylde, An 100
  William 98, 100
Wylie, T. W. J. 408
Wyncoop, Mr. 716
  Mary 717
  Matthew 717
Wyne, Nicholas 613
Wynkoop, (?) 890
  Anna 889
  Henry 889
Wynne, Mary 539
  Dr. Thomas 539
Yardley, Ann 160
  Jane Heath 72
  Thomas 72, 158, 160
  William 72, 140, 141, 155, 156
Yardly, Wm. 142
Yates, Margaret 29
  Susannah 859
Yats, Moise 897
Yeardley, Hannah 164
  Sam'l 164
Yearworth, Peter 814
Yeeles, Mrs. 479
  Arabella 478
  Catherine 478
  Deborah 478
  Elizabeth 478
  Jane 478
  Mrs. Jane 476
  Jane Keith 478
  Mary 478
  Thomas 478
  William 478
Yeoman, Ann 623
  Richard 631
Young, Alexander 811
  Ann 631
  Edward 809
  George 617
  John 809, 848, 850
  Peter 631

Yountz, Helen R. 522
Ysselstein, Rachel Bogart 865
Zane, Abegall 836
  Abigail 837
  Danel 836
  Deborah 837
  Ebenezear 836, 837
  Elizabeth 836, 837
  Elnathan 836
  Es'fer 836, 837
  Grace Rakestraw 836, 837
  Hannah 836, 837
  Hester 836
  Isaac 836, 837
  John 836
  Jonathan 836, 837
  Josep 836
  Joseph 837
  Margratt 836
  Margrett 837
  Mary 837
  Nathan 836
  Nathaniel 836, 837
  Phebe 836
  Rachel 836
  Robert 835, 836
  Rodah 837
  Sarah 836
  William 836, 837
Zinzendorf, (?) 460, 461
Zwingli, (?) 275

Dell, Richard 603
Drew, Roger 217
Ferguson, Rev. Victor 814
Iredell, Rachel 878